SOCIOLOGY

THEMES AND PERSPECTIVES

D1390196

Fourth Edition

SOCIOLOGY
THEMES AND PERSPECTIVES

Michael Haralambos
and Martin Holborn

Collins Educational
An imprint of HarperCollins*Publishers*

Fourth Edition published in 1995 by
Collins Educational
An imprint of HarperCollins *Publishers*
77–85 Fulham Palace Road
Hammersmith
London W6 8JB

First Edition published in 1980 by University Tutorial Press
Second Edition published in 1985 by University Tutorial Press
Third Edition published in 1990 by Unwin Hyman Ltd

British Library Cataloguing in Publication Data is available on
request from the British Library.

ISBN 000 322316 7

Typeset by Create Publishing Services Ltd, Bath

Printed by Martins The Printers Ltd, Berwick upon Tweed

Reprinted 1995

Project management by Emma Dunlop
Copy-edited by Josephine Warrior
Text design by Jacky Wedgwood
Cover design by Moondisks

Preface to the Fourth Edition

The Fourth Edition of *Sociology: Themes and Perspectives* aims to build on the success of the first three editions which sold half a million copies. There is a new chapter on **'Race', Ethnicity and Nationality**, an improved layout and increased use of figures and tables. As in Third Edition, there have been major revisions throughout the book with some older material omitted and newer empirical studies and theoretical developments integrated in the text.

Martin Holborn wrote the new material for the Fourth Edition and Mike Haralambos edited it. The authors would like to thank the many people who contributed in various ways to the Fourth Edition. Nik Jorgensen read and commented on drafts of all the chapters. His comments were always constructive and proved very valuable. Josephine Warrior again edited the book with skill and precision. Pat McNeill initiated the project and Emma Dunlop did a tremendous job in editing, coordinating and seeing the project through to its completion. Their efforts are much appreciated. The help and encouragement of friends and colleagues again contributed a great deal to the project. Many thanks to Jim O'Gorman, Liz Ronayne, Joan Blake, Linda Barton, Alison Robinson and Morag Campbell. James O'Gorman and Liz Ronayne's support was especially appreciated. The new edition could not have been completed without the assistance of the libraries of the University of Central Lancashire, Lancaster University, the Harris Library, Preston, West London Institute of Higher Education and Preston College. Barbara Hothersall's help at Preston College library was invaluable.

The authors would also like to thank the academic experts who commented on chapters and suggested new material for inclusion in the Fourth Edition. These were John Scott (Stratification); Andy Pilkington ('Race', Ethnicity and Nationality); Ken Roberts (Leisure); Keith Grint (Work); Bob Burgess (Education); David Denver (Power, Politics and the State); Jock Young (Crime and Deviance); Alan Walker (Poverty); Michael Reed (Organizations and Bureaucracy); Ray Pawson (Methodology); and P.A. Walters (Sex and Gender).

Martin Holborn would like to thank Emma Holborn for her patience, encouragement and love which made writing the Fourth Edition much more pleasurable than writing the Third. He would also like to thank his parents Denis and the late Sheila Holborn for their support. Sadly Sheila Holborn died before this edition was completed.

Finally, once again thanks to everybody who read or bought the book. We hope it continues to prove useful to students and others with an interest in sociology and that it encourages you to pursue the subject further.

Martin Holborn
Michael Haralambos
February 1995

Preface to the Third Edition

This book aims to provide a systematic introduction to sociology for A level students, undergraduates and the general reader. It attempts to strike a balance between theory and research findings. The major theoretical perspective are introduced in the first chapter and examined in detail in the final chapter. Much of the material in the main body of the book is structured in terms of these perspectives. The emphasis on theory is balanced by detailed consideration of the findings of a range of empirical studies. A separate chapter is devoted to methodology – the study of the methods used to obtain and interpret data and of the general assumptions which underlie the study of society.

First published in 1980, *Sociology: Themes and Perspectives* sold over quarter of a million copies in its first two editions. The Third Edition is a major revision. Existing material has been restructured and updated. In addition there is a large amount of new content which takes account of recent research and new directions and priorities in the subject.

The division of labour for writing the book was as follows: the first two editions were written by Michael Haralambos with Robin Heald as the co-author of Organizations and Bureaucracy. The new material for the Third Edition was written by Martin Holborn.

A book also involves the work of many other people. The original manuscript was typed by Barbara Grimshaw , Pauline Haralambos and Jean Buckley. Their assistance is appreciated. Particular thanks are due to Barbara Grimshaw who did the bulk of the typing, met deadlines often a short notice, yet always produced the highest quality typescript. The help of librarians is essential for a book of this kind. The assistance of the staff at Preston College Library, Lancashire Polytechnic Library, Lancashire County Library, Corporation Street, Preston is gratefully acknowledged. Special thanks are due to William Dickey, Barbara Hothersall and the staff of Preston College Library whose help went well beyond what would normally be expected from the services of a library. Writing a book requires support, interest and constructive criticism from friends and colleagues. In this regard thanks are due to Christine Robinson, Frances Smith, Peter Adamson, Dave Beddow, Maurice Gavan, James O'Gorman, Vincent Farrell, Pauline Cowburn and Terry Richards. James O'Gorman's interest and support was particularly appreciated. We should also like to acknowledge the skilful editorial support of Chris Kington, Simon Boyd and Josephine Warrior.

Michael Haralambos would like to thank Pauline for her unwavering support and encouragement over the four years it took to write the original manuscript. She took over the many responsibilities of running the home and remained cheerful and optimistic when it seemed as though the book would never be completed.

Finally, thank you to everybody who bought the book and for the many kind comments you have made. We hope you enjoy the Third Edition.

Michael Haralambos
Martin Holborn
March 1990

Contents

Contents

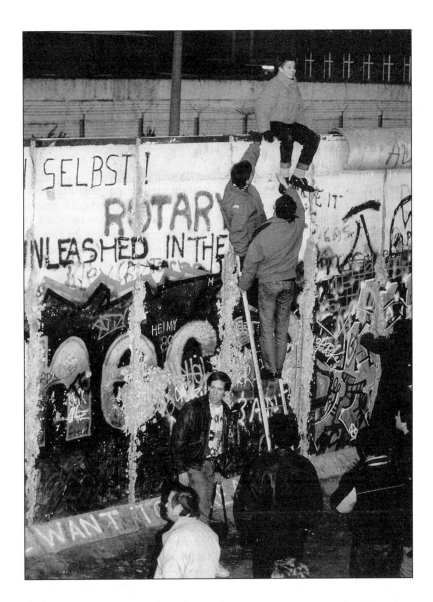

1

The sociological perspective

1

The sociological perspective

■ Introduction

'Human beings learn their behaviour and use their intelligence whereas animals simply act on instinct.' Like most common-sense notions, this idea has an element of truth, but reality is far more complex.

The regimented society of social insects, such as ants and bees, is a lesson in order and organization. Every member has clearly defined tasks in a cooperative enterprise. Thus in a beehive the worker bees, depending on their age, will either feed the young, stand guard and repel strangers, forage for food or ventilate the hive by beating their wings. The behaviour of insects is largely **instinctive**, it is based on programmes contained in the genes which direct their actions. However, we would be mistaken to assume that the behaviour of insects is based *solely* on instinct. Experiments have indicated that at least some have the ability to learn. For example, ants are able to memorize the path through a maze and are capable of applying this learning to other mazes.

If we move from insects to reptiles and on again to mammals, we can see that the importance of learned, as opposed to genetically determined (instinctive), behaviour gradually increases. Studies of macaque monkeys on islands in northern Japan provide some indication of the importance of learned behaviour. On one island the macaques lived in the forested interior. Japanese scientists attempted to discover whether they could change the behaviour patterns of the troupe. They began by dumping potatoes in a clearing in the forest. Gradually the macaques changed their eating habits and became largely dependent on potatoes, a food previously unknown to them, as their staple diet. The scientists slowly moved the food dumps towards the shoreline and the troupe followed. The potatoes were then regularly placed on the beach, which now became the normal habitat for the macaques.

In the months that followed, without any encouragement from the scientists, a number of new behaviour patterns emerged in the troupe. First, some members began washing the potatoes in the sea before eating them. Others started doing the same, until it became standard practice in the group. Then some of the younger macaques began paddling in the sea, and eventually took the plunge and learned how to swim. Their elders imitated them and again, the novel behaviour of the few became the accepted behaviour of the group. Finally, some adventurous youngsters began diving off low rocky outcroppings on the shoreline, a practice which was copied by other members of the troupe.

The Japanese macaques had learned new behaviour patterns and these patterns were shared by members of the group. The simple generalization that animal behaviour is genetically determined whereas the behaviour of humans is learned is clearly incorrect. However, the range and complexity of learned behaviour in humans is far greater than in any other species. This is shown by experiments with humanity's nearest living relative, the chimpanzee. Chimpanzees raised in human households learn as well as human infants of the same age for a few years, but they soon reach the limit of their ability and are rapidly overtaken by human youngsters. Compared to mammals other than humans, chimpanzees have a considerable learning capacity. They can solve simple problems to obtain food, they can learn a basic sign language to communicate with humans and even ape their more intelligent cousins in the famous chimpanzee tea party. Yet despite this capacity to learn, the behavioural repertoire of chimpanzees is rudimentary and limited compared to people.

More than any other species, humans rely for their survival on behaviour patterns that are learned. Humans have no instincts, that is genetically programmed directives to behave in particular ways. An instinct involves not only the impulse to do something, but also specific instructions on how to do it. For example, birds have an instinct to build nests. They have an impulse for nest building and all members of a particular species are programmed to build nests in the same way.

If we look at the range and variety of dwellings constructed by humans we can see the absence of directives based on instinct. The following examples from nineteenth-century North America provide an illustration. In the Arctic, the Eskimo constructed igloos from rectangular blocks cut from closely compacted snow. On the north-west coast of the USA and the west coast of Canada, tribes such as the Nootka built oblong houses with a framework of cedar logs, walled and roofed with planks. On the opposite side of the subcontinent, in the eastern woodlands, the Iroquois also lived in oblong dwellings, known as 'long houses', but they substituted birch bark for planks. On the prairies, the easily transportable conical tipi made from long saplings covered in buffalo hides provided shelter for tribes such as the Sioux and Cheyenne. Further south, the Apache of Arizona and New Mexico lived in domed wickiups made from brushwood and scrub. In the same area, tribes such as the Zuñi and the Hopi built the first apartment houses in the USA. Even today many members of these tribes live in multi-occupation dwellings made from sun-dried mud bricks known as adobe. These examples show clearly that the human genetic code does not contain specific instructions to behave in a particular way.

■ Culture and society

To all intents and purposes a newborn human baby is helpless. Not only is it physically dependent on older members of the species but it also lacks the behaviour patterns necessary for living in human society. It relies primarily on certain biological drives (hunger, thirst, etc.) and on the charity of its elders to satisfy those drives. The infant has a lot to learn. In order to survive, it must learn the skills, knowledge and accepted ways of behaving of the society into which it is born. It must learn a way of life; in sociological terminology, it must learn the **culture** of its society.

Ralph Linton states that 'The culture of a society is the way of life of its members; the collection of ideas and habits which they learn, share and transmit from generation to generation.' In Clyde Kluckhohn's elegant phrase, culture is a 'design for living' held by members of a particular society. Since humans have no instincts to direct their actions, their behaviour must be based on guidelines that are learned. In order for a society to operate effectively, these guidelines must be shared by its members. Without a shared culture, members of society would be unable to communicate and cooperate, and confusion and disorder would result. Culture therefore has two essential qualities: first, it is learned; second, it is shared. Without it there would be no human society.

Culture and behaviour

To a large degree culture determines how members of society think and feel: it directs their actions and defines their outlook on life. Members of society usually take their culture for granted. It has become so much a part of them that they are often unaware of its existence. The following example given by Edward T. Hall provides an illustration. Two individuals, one from North America, the other from South America, are conversing in a hall 40 feet long. They begin at one end of the hall and finish at the other end, the North American steadily retreating, the South American relentlessly advancing. Each is trying to establish the 'accustomed conversation distance' defined by his culture. To the North American, his South American counterpart comes too close for comfort, whereas the South American feels uneasy conversing at the distance his partner demands. Often it takes meetings such as this to reveal the pervasive nature of culturally determined behaviour.

Culture defines accepted ways of behaving for members of a particular society. Such definitions vary from society to society. This can lead to considerable misunderstanding between members of different societies, as the following example provided by Otto Klineberg shows. Among the Sioux Indians of South Dakota, it is regarded as incorrect to answer a question in the presence of others who do not know the answer. Such behaviour would be regarded as boastful and arrogant, and, since it reveals the ignorance of others, it would be interpreted as an attempt to undermine their confidence and shame them. In addition the Sioux regard it as wrong to answer a question unless they are absolutely sure of the correct answer. Faced with a classroom of Sioux children, a white American teacher, who is unaware of their culture, might easily interpret their behaviour as a reflection of ignorance, stupidity or hostility.

Every society has certain common problems to deal with, for example the problem of dependent members such as the very young and the very old. However, solutions to such problems are culturally determined: they vary from society to society. The solutions provided in one society may well be regarded as indefensible by members of other societies.

Under certain circumstances, **infanticide** (the killing of infants) and **geronticide** (the killing of old people) have been practised by certain groups of Australian aborigines, Eskimos and Caribou Indians. Particularly in the more arid parts of Australia, female infanticide was practised to reduce the population in times of famine, and occasionally the baby was eaten. In Tasmania aborigine hunters led a nomadic life that took advantage of the seasonal food supply in different regions. The old and infirm who were too feeble to keep up with the band were left behind to die. The Caribou Indians, who lived to the west of Hudson Bay in Canada, were dependent for their food supply on the caribou herds. Sometimes, in winter, the herds failed to appear. To prevent the starvation of the whole community, priorities were established. First the active male adults were fed because if they were too weak to hunt, nobody would eat. Next, their wives were fed since they could bear more children. Male infants were considered more important than female because they would grow up to become hunters. Old people were the most expendable and in times of famine they committed suicide by walking naked into the snow. If there were no old people left, girl babies would be killed. The practices of infanticide and geronticide are culturally defined behaviour patterns designed to ensure the survival of the group in times of extreme food shortages. Like many of the customs of non-Western societies, they appear strange and even heartless to Westerners, but in the context of the particular society, they are sensible, rational and an accepted part of life.

These examples of culturally defined behaviour have been selected because they demonstrate considerably different behaviour patterns from those of Western society. Examples of behaviours that appear strange to Westerners make it easier to appreciate the idea that human behaviour is largely determined by culture.

■ Socialization

The process by which individuals learn the culture of their society is known as **socialization**. Primary socialization, probably the most important aspect of the socialization process, takes place during infancy, usually within the family. By responding to the approval and disapproval of its parents and copying their example, the child learns the language and many of the basic behaviour patterns of its society. In Western society, other important agencies of socialization include the educational system, the occupational group and the **peer group** (a group whose members share similar circumstances and are often of a similar age). Within its peer group, the young child, by interacting with others and playing childhood games, learns to conform to the accepted ways of a social group and to appreciate the fact that social life is based on rules.

Socialization is not, however, confined to childhood. It is a lifelong process. At the beginning of their working lives, the young bricklayer, teacher and accountant soon learn the rules of the game and the tricks of the trade. Should they change jobs in later life, they will join a different occupational group and may well have to learn new skills and adopt different mannerisms and styles of dress.

Without socialization, an individual would bear little resemblance to any human being defined as normal by the standards of his or her society. The following examples, though they lack the reliability demanded by today's standards of reporting, nevertheless provide some indication of the importance of socialization.

It is reported that Akbar, who was an emperor in India from 1542 to 1602, ordered that a group of children be brought up without any instruction in language, to test the belief that they would eventually speak Hebrew, the language of God. The children were raised by deaf mutes. They developed no spoken language and communicated solely by gestures.

There is also an extensive, though somewhat unreliable, literature on children raised by animals. One of the best documented cases concerns the so-called 'wolf-children of Midnapore'. Two females, aged two and eight, were reportedly found in a wolf den in Bengal in 1920. They walked on all fours, preferred a diet of raw meat, they howled like wolves and lacked any form of speech. It is unclear whether these children had been raised by wolves or whether they had been simply abandoned and left to their own devices in the forest. However, such examples indicate that socialization involving prolonged interaction with adults is essential not only for fitting new members into society but also to the process of actually becoming human.

■ Norms and values

Norms

Every culture contains a large number of guidelines that direct conduct in particular situations. Such guidelines are known as **norms**. A norm is a specific guide to action which defines acceptable and appropriate behaviour in particular situations. For example, in all societies, there are norms governing dress. Members of society generally share norms that define acceptable male and female apparel and that specify appropriate dress for different age groups: in British society, a 70-year-old grandmother dressed as a teenager would contravene the norms for her age group. Norms of dress provide guidelines for what to wear on particular occasions. A formal dance, a funeral, a day out on the beach, a working day in the bank, on the building site or in the hospital – all these situations are governed by norms which specify appropriate attire for the occasion.

Norms of dress vary from society to society. One example concerns a missionary presented with bare-breasted African females in his congregation. Flushed with embarrassment, he ordered a consignment of brassieres. The women could make little sense of these objects in terms of their norms of dress. From their point of view, the most reasonable way to interpret the strange articles was to regard them as headgear. Much to the dismay of the missionary, they placed the two cups on the top of their heads and fastened the straps under their chins.

Norms are enforced by **positive** and **negative sanctions**, that is, rewards and punishments. Sanctions can be informal, such as an approving or disapproving glance, or formal, such as a reward or a fine given by an official body. Continuing the example of norms of dress, an embarrassed

silence, a hoot of derision or a contemptuous stare will make most members of society who have broken norms of dress change into more conventional attire. Usually the threat of negative sanctions is sufficient to enforce normal behaviour. Conversely an admiring glance, a word of praise or an encouraging smile provide rewards for conformity to social norms. Certain norms are formalized by translation into laws which are enforced by official sanctions. In terms of laws governing dress, the nude bather on a public beach, the 'streaker' at a sporting event and the 'flashers' who exposes himself to an unsuspecting individual are subject to official punishments of varying severity. Like informal sanctions, formal sanctions may be positive or negative. In terms of norms associated with dress, awards are made by official bodies such as tailors' organizations to the best-dressed public figures in Britain.

To summarize, norms define appropriate and acceptable behaviour in specific situations. They are enforced by positive and negative sanctions which may be formal or informal. The sanctions which enforce norms are a major part of the mechanisms of social control which are concerned with maintaining order in society.

Values

Unlike norms, which provide specific directives for conduct, **values** provide more general guidelines. A value is a belief that something is good and desirable. It defines what is important, worthwhile and worth striving for. It has often been suggested that individual achievement and materialism are major values in Western industrial society. Thus individuals believe it is important and desirable to come top of the class, to win a race or reach the top of their chosen profession. Individual achievement is often symbolized and measured by the quality and quantity of material possessions that a person can accumulate. In the West, the value of materialism motivates individuals to invest time and energy producing and acquiring material possessions.

Like norms, values vary from society to society. The Sioux Indians placed a high value on generosity. In terms of Sioux values, the acquisitive individual of Western society would at best be regarded as peculiar and more probably would be condemned as grasping, self-seeking and anti-social.

Many norms can be seen as reflections of values. A variety of norms can be seen as expressions of a single value. In Western society the value placed on human life is expressed in terms of the following norms: the norms associated with hygiene in the home and in public places reflect a concern for human life; norms defining acceptable ways for settling an argument or dispute usually exclude physical violence and manslaughter; the array of rules and regulations dealing with transport and behaviour on the highway are concerned with protecting life and limb; the same applies to safety regulations in the workplace, particularly in mining and manufacturing industries. The variety of norms concerned with the health and safety of members of society can be seen as expressions of the value placed on human life.

Many sociologists maintain that shared norms and values are essential for the operation of human society. Since humans have no instincts, their behaviour must be guided and regulated by norms. Unless norms are shared, members of society would be unable to cooperate with or even to comprehend the behaviour of others. Similar arguments apply to values. Without shared values, members of society would be unlikely to cooperate and work together. With differing or conflicting values they would often be pulling in different directions and pursuing incompatible goals. Disorder and disruption may well result. Thus an ordered and stable society requires shared norms and values. This viewpoint will be considered in greater detail in a later section.

▮ Status and role

All members of society occupy a number of social positions known as **statuses**. In Western society, an individual will usually have an 'occupational status' such as bus driver, secretary or solicitor; a 'family status' such as son or daughter, father or mother; and a 'gender status' such as male or female. Statuses are culturally defined, despite the fact that they may be based on biological factors such as sex or race. For example, skin colour assigns an individual to a racial status such as black or white, but this merely reflects the conventions of particular societies. Other biological characteristics such as hair colour have no connection with an individual's status and, in future societies, skin colour may be equally insignificant. Some statuses are relatively fixed and there is

little individuals can do to change their assignment to particular social positions. Examples of such fixed or **ascribed** statuses include gender and aristocratic titles. On rare occasions, however, ascribed statuses can be changed. Edward VIII was forced to abdicate from the throne in 1936 for insisting on marrying an American divorcée. Anthony Wedgewood-Benn renounced his peerage in order to stand for election to the House of Commons. Revolutions in America and Russia abolished the ascribed status of members of the aristocracy. Ascribed statuses are usually fixed at birth. In many societies occupational status has been or still is transmitted from father to son and from mother to daughter. Thus in the traditional Indian caste system, a son automatically entered the occupation of his father.

Statuses that are not fixed by inheritance, biological characteristics, or other factors over which the individual has no control, are known as **achieved** statuses. An achieved status is entered as a result of some degree of purposive action and choice. In Western society an individual's marital status and occupational status are achieved. However, as we will see in the next chapter, the distinction between ascribed and achieved status is less clear-cut than has so far been suggested.

Each status in society is accompanied by a number of norms that define how an individual occupying a particular status is expected to act. This group of norms is known as a **role**. Thus the status of husband is accompanied by the role of husband, the status of solicitor by the role of solicitor, and so on. As an example, solicitors are expected to possess a detailed knowledge of certain aspects of the law, to support their client's interests and respect the confidentiality of their business. Solicitors' attire is expected to be sober, their manner restrained, confident yet understanding, their standing in the community beyond reproach. Playing or performing roles involves social relationships in the sense that an individual plays a role in relation to other roles. Thus the role of doctor is played in relation to the role of patient, the role of husband in relation to the role of wife. Individuals therefore interact in terms of roles.

Social roles regulate and organize behaviour. In particular, they provide means for accomplishing certain tasks. It can be argued, for example, that teaching can be accomplished more effectively if teacher and student adopt their appropriate roles. This involves the exclusion of other areas of their lives in order to concentrate on the matter at hand. Roles provide social life with order and predictability. Interacting in terms of their respective roles, teacher and student know what to do and how to do it. With a knowledge of each other's roles, each is able to predict and comprehend the actions of the other. As an aspect of culture, roles provide an important part of the guidelines and directives necessary for an ordered society.

This section has introduced us to some of the basic concepts used by many sociologists. In doing so, however, we have been presented with a somewhat one-sided view of human society. Individuals have been pictured rather like automatons who simply respond to the dictates of their culture. All members of a particular society appear to be produced from the same mould. They are all efficiently socialized in terms of a common culture. They share the same values, follow the same norms and play a variety of roles, adopting the appropriate behaviour for each. Clearly this picture of conformity has been overstated and the pervasive and constraining influence of culture has been exaggerated. There are two reasons for this. First, overstatement has been deliberately used to make the point. Second, many of the ideas presented so far derive from a particular perspective in sociology which has been subject to the criticisms noted above. We will examine this perspective, known as functionalism, first.

■ Theories of society

In this section we will look at three of the main theories of society. A **theory** is a set of ideas that claims to explain how something works. A sociological theory is, therefore, a set of ideas that claims to explain how society or aspects of society work. The theories in this section represent only a selection from the range of sociological theories. They have been simplified and condensed to provide a basic introduction. Since they are applied to various topics throughout the text, an initial awareness is essential. Criticism of the theories has been omitted from this chapter for the sake of simplicity. We will deal with it throughout the text and in detail in the final chapter.

There are many variations on the basic theories examined in this chapter. Again, for simplicity these variations will not be mentioned at this stage, but will be introduced when they become relevant to particular topics.

■ Functionalism

Functionalism first developed in nineteenth-century Europe. The French sociologist Emile Durkheim was the most influential of the early functionalists. It was developed further by American sociologists such as Talcott Parsons in the twentieth century, and became the dominant theoretical perspective in sociology during the 1940s and 1950s, particularly in the USA. From the mid-1960s onwards, its popularity steadily declined. This was owing partly to damaging criticism, partly to competing perspectives which appeared to provide superior explanations, and partly to changes in fashion. The key points of the functionalist perspective may be summarized by a comparison drawn from biology. If biologists wanted to know how an organism such as the human body worked, they might begin by examining the various parts such as the brain, lungs, heart and liver. However, if they simply analysed the parts in isolation from each other, they would be unable to explain how life was maintained. To do this, they would have to examine the parts in relation to each other, since they work together to maintain the organism. Therefore they would analyse the relationships between the heart, lungs, brain and so on to understand how they operated and appreciate their importance. From this viewpoint, any part of the organism must be seen in terms of the organism as a whole.

Functionalism adopts a similar perspective. The various parts of society are seen to be interrelated and taken together they form a complete system. To understand any part of society, such as the family or religion, that part must be seen in relation to society as a whole. Thus where a biologist will examine a part of the body, such as the heart, in terms of its contribution to the maintenance of the human organism, the functionalist will examine a part of society, such as the family, in terms of its contribution to the maintenance of the social system.

Structure

Functionalism begins with the observation that behaviour in society is structured. This means that relationships between members of society are organized in terms of rules. Social relationships are therefore patterned and recurrent. Values provide general guidelines for behaviour and they are translated into more specific directives in terms of roles and norms. The structure of society can be seen as the sum total of normative behaviour, that is the sum total of social relationships that are governed by norms. The main parts of society, its institutions – such as the family, the economy, the educational and political systems – are major aspects of the social structure. Thus an institution can be seen as a structure made up of interconnected roles or interrelated norms. For example, the family is made up of the interconnected roles of husband, father, wife, mother, son and daughter. Social relationships within the family are structured in terms of a set of related norms.

Function

Having established the existence of a social structure, functionalist analysis turns to a consideration of how that structure functions. This involves an examination of the relationship between the different parts of the structure and their relationship to society as a whole. From this examination, the functions of institutions are discovered. At its simplest, function means effect. Thus the function of the family is the effect it has on other parts of the social structure and on society as a whole. In practice the term function is usually used to indicate the contribution an institution makes to the maintenance and survival of the social system: a major function of the family is the socialization of new members of society. This represents an important contribution to the maintenance of society since order, stability and cooperation largely depend on learned, shared norms and values.

Functional prerequisites

In determining the functions of various parts of the social structure, functionalists are guided by the following ideas. Societies have certain basic needs or requirements which must be met if they are to survive. These requirements are sometimes known as **functional prerequisites**. For example, a means of producing food and shelter may be seen as a functional prerequisite since without them members of society could not survive. A system for socializing new members of society may also be regarded as a functional prerequisite since without culture, social life would not be possible. Having assumed a number of basic requirements for the survival of society, the next step is to look at the parts of the social structure to see how they meet such functional prerequisites. Thus a major function of the economic system is the production of food and shelter. An important function of the family is the socialization of new members of society.

Value consensus

From a functionalist perspective, society is regarded as a system. A system is an entity made up of interconnected and interrelated parts. From this viewpoint, it follows that each part will in some way affect every other part and the system as a whole. It also follows that if the system is to survive, its various parts must have some degree of fit or compatibility. Thus a functional prerequisite of society involves at least a minimal degree of integration between the parts. Many functionalists argue that this integration is based largely on **value consensus**, that is on agreement about values by members of society. Thus if the major values of society are expressed in the various parts of the social structure, those parts will be integrated. For example, it can be argued that the value of materialism integrates many parts of the social structure in Western industrial society. The economic system produces a large range of goods and ever increasing productivity is regarded as an important goal. The educational system is partly concerned with producing the skills and expertise to expand production and increase its efficiency. The family is an important unit of consumption with its steadily rising demand for consumer durables such as washing machines, videos and microwaves. The political system is partly concerned with improving material living standards and raising productivity. To the extent that these parts of the social structure are based on the same values, they may be said to be integrated.

Social order

One of the main concerns of functionalist theory is to explain how social life is possible. The theory assumes that a certain degree of order and stability is essential for the survival of social systems. Functionalism is therefore concerned with explaining the origin and maintenance of order and stability in society. Many functionalists see shared values as the key to this explanation: value consensus integrates the various parts of society. It forms the basis of social unity or social solidarity since individuals will tend to identify and feel kinship with those who share the same values as themselves. Value consensus provides the foundation for cooperation since common values produce common goals. Members of society will tend to cooperate in pursuit of the goals that they share.

Having attributed such importance to value consensus, many functionalists then focus on the question of how this consensus is maintained. Indeed the American sociologist Talcott Parsons has stated that the main task of sociology is to examine 'the institutionalization of patterns of value orientation in the social system'. Emphasis is therefore placed on the process of socialization whereby values are internalized and transmitted from one generation to the next. In this respect, the family is regarded as a vital part of the social structure. Once learned, values must be maintained. In particular those who deviate from society's values must be brought back into line. Thus the mechanisms of social control we discussed earlier in the chapter are seen as essential to the maintenance of social order.

In summary, society, from a functionalist perspective, is a system made up of interrelated parts. The social system has certain basic needs which must be met if it is to survive. These needs are known as functional prerequisites. The function of any part of society is its contribution to the maintenance of society. The major functions of social institutions are those that help to meet the functional prerequisites of society. Since society is a system, there must be some degree of integration between its parts. A minimal degree of integration is therefore a functional prerequisite of society. Many functionalists maintain that the order and stability they see as essential for the maintenance of the social system are largely provided by value consensus. This means that an investigation of the source of value consensus is a major concern of functionalist analysis.

◼ Conflict perspectives

Although functionalists emphasize the importance of value consensus in society, they do recognize that conflict can occur. However, they see conflict as being the result of temporary disturbances in the social system. These disturbances are usually quickly corrected as society evolves. Functionalists accept that social groups can have differences of interest, but these are of minor importance compared to the interests that all social groups share. They believe that all social groups benefit if their society runs smoothly and prospers.

Conflict theories differ from functionalism in that they hold that there are fundamental differences of interest between social groups. These differences result in conflict being a common and persistent feature of society, and not a temporary aberration.

There are a number of different conflict perspectives and their supporters tend to disagree about the precise nature, causes and extent of conflict. For the sake of simplicity, in this introductory chapter we will concentrate upon one conflict theory: Marxism. Other conflict theories will be introduced later in the book. (For example, the influential conflict theory of Max Weber is dealt with in Chapter 2, pp. 36–9.)

◼ Marxism

Marxist theory offers a radical alternative to functionalism. It became increasingly influential in sociology during the 1970s, partly because of the decline of functionalism, partly because of its promise to provide answers that functionalism failed to provide and partly because it was more in keeping with the tenor and mood of the times. Marxism takes its name from its founder, the German-born philosopher, economist and sociologist, Karl Marx (1818–83). The account that follows represents a simplified version of Marxist theory. It must also be seen as one interpretation of that theory: Marx's extensive writings have been variously interpreted, and since his death several schools of Marxism have developed.

Contradiction and conflict

Marxist theory begins with the simple observation that in order to survive, humans must produce food and material objects. In doing so they enter into social relationships with other people. From the simple hunting band to the complex industrial state, production is a social enterprise. Production also involves a technical component known as the 'forces of production', which includes the technology, raw materials and scientific knowledge employed in the process of production. Each major stage in the development of the forces of production will correspond with a particular form of the social relationships of production. This means that the forces of production in a hunting economy will correspond with a particular set of social relationships.

Taken together, the forces of production and the social relationships of production form the economic basis or **infrastructure** of society. The other aspects of society, known as the **superstructure**, are largely shaped by the infrastructure. Thus the political, legal and educational institutions and the belief and value systems are primarily determined by economic factors. A major change in the infrastructure will therefore produce a corresponding change in the superstructure.

Marx maintained that, with the possible exception of the societies of prehistory, all historical societies contain basic contradictions, which means that they cannot survive forever in their existing form. These contradictions involve the exploitation of one social group by another: in feudal society, lords exploit their serfs; in capitalist society, employers exploit their employees. This creates a fundamental conflict of interest between social groups since one gains at the expense of another. This conflict of interest must ultimately be resolved since a social system containing such contradictions cannot survive unchanged.

We will now examine the points raised in this brief summary of Marxist theory in greater detail. The major contradictions in society are between the forces and relations of production. The forces of production include land, raw materials, tools and machinery, the technical and scientific knowledge used in production, the technical organization of the production process and the labour power of the workers. The 'relations of production' are the social relationships people enter into in order to produce goods. Thus in feudal society

they include the relationship between the lord and vassal and the set of rights, duties and obligations that make up that relationship. In capitalist industrial society they include the relationship between employer and employee and the various rights of the two parties. The relations of production also involve the relationship of social groups to the means and forces of production.

The 'means of production' consist of those parts of the forces of production that can be legally owned. They therefore include land, raw materials, machinery, buildings and tools, but not technical knowledge or the organization of the production process. Under capitalism, labour power is not categorized with the means of production since the workers are free to sell their labour. In slave societies, though, labour power is among the means of production since the workforce is actually owned by the social group in power. In feudal society, land, the major means of production, is owned by the lord, whereas the serf has the right to use land in return for services or payment to the lord. In Western industrial society, the means of production are owned by the capitalist, whereas the workers own only their labour, which they hire to the employer in return for wages.

Exploitation and oppression

The idea of contradiction between the forces and relations of production may be illustrated in terms of the infrastructure of capitalist industrial society. Marx maintained that only labour produces wealth. Thus wealth in capitalist society is produced by the labour power of the workers. However, much of this wealth is appropriated in the form of profits by the **capitalists**, the owners of the means of production. The wages of the workers are well below the value of the wealth they produce. There is thus a contradiction between the forces of production, in particular the labour power of the workers, which produces wealth, and the relations of production, which involve the appropriation of much of that wealth by the capitalists.

A related contradiction involves the technical organization of labour and the nature of ownership. In capitalist society, the forces of production include the collective production of goods by large numbers of workers in factories. Yet the means of production are privately owned, and the profits are appropriated by individuals. The contradiction between the forces and relations of production lies in the social and collective nature of production and the private and individual nature of ownership. Marx believed that these and other contradictions would eventually lead to the downfall of the capitalist system. He maintained that by its very nature, capitalism involves the exploitation and oppression of the worker. He believed that the conflict of interest between capital and labour, which involves one group gaining at the expense of the other, could not be resolved within the framework of a capitalist economy.

Contradiction and change

Marx saw history as divided into a number of time periods or epochs, each being characterized by a particular mode of production. Major changes in history are the result of new forces of production. Thus the change from feudal to capitalist society stemmed from the emergence, during the feudal epoch, of the forces of production of industrial society. This resulted in a contradiction between the new forces of production and the old feudal relations of production. Capitalist industrial society required relations of production based on wage labour rather than the traditional ties of lord and vassal. When they reach a certain point in their development, the new forces of production lead to the creation of a new set of relations of production. Then, a new epoch of history is born, one that sweeps away the social relationships of the old order.

However, the final epoch of history, the communist or socialist society that Marx believed would eventually supplant capitalism, will not result from a new force of production. Rather it will develop from a resolution of the contradictions contained within the capitalist system. Collective production will remain but the relations of production will be transformed. Ownership of the means of production will be collective rather than individual and members of society will share the wealth that their labour produces. No longer will one social group exploit and oppress another. This will produce an infrastructure without contradiction and conflict. In Marx's view this would mean the end of history since communist society would no longer contain the contradictions that generate change.

Ideology and false consciousness

In view of the contradictions that beset historical societies, it appears difficult to explain their survival. Despite its internal contradictions, capitalism has continued in the West for over 200 years. This continuity can be explained in large part by the nature of the superstructure. In all societies the superstructure is largely shaped by the infrastructure. In particular, the relations of production are reflected and reproduced in the various institutions, values and beliefs that make up the superstructure. Thus the relationships of domination and subordination found in the infrastructure will also be found in social institutions. In Marx's words, 'The existing relations of production between individuals must necessarily express themselves also as political and legal relations.' The dominant social group or 'ruling class', that is the group that owns and controls the means of production, will largely monopolize political power, and its position will be supported by laws framed to protect and further its interests.

In the same way, beliefs and values will reflect and legitimate the relations of production. Members of the ruling class 'rule also as thinkers, as producers of ideas'. These ideas justify their power and privilege and conceal from all members of society the basis of exploitation and oppression on which their dominance rests. Thus under feudalism honour and loyalty were 'dominant concepts' of the age. Vassals owed loyalty to their lords and were bound by an oath of allegiance which encouraged the acceptance of their status. In terms of the dominant concepts of the age, feudalism appeared as the natural order of things. Under capitalism, exploitation is disguised by the ideas of equality and freedom. The relationship between capitalist and wage labourer is defined as an equal exchange. The capitalist buys the labour power which the worker offers for hire. The worker is defined as a free agent since he or she has the freedom to choose his or her employer. In reality, equality and freedom are illusions: the employer–employee relationship is not equal. It is an exploitative relationship. Workers are not free since they are forced to work for the capitalist in order to survive. All they can do is exchange one form of 'wage slavery' for another.

Marx refers to the dominant ideas of each epoch as 'ruling class ideology'. **Ideology** is a distortion of reality, a false picture of society. It blinds members of society to the contradictions and conflicts of interest that are built into their relationships. As a result they tend to accept their situation as normal and natural, right and proper. In this way a 'false consciousness' of reality is produced which helps to maintain the system. However, Marx believed that ruling class ideology could only slow down the disintegration of the system. The contradictions embedded in the structure of society must eventually find expression.

In summary, the key to understanding society from a Marxist perspective involves an analysis of the infrastructure. In all historical societies there are basic contradictions between the forces and relations of production, and there are fundamental conflicts of interest between the social groups involved in the production process. In particular, the relationship between the major social groups is one of exploitation and oppression. The superstructure derives largely from the infrastructure and therefore reproduces the social relationships of production. It will thus reflect the interests of the dominant group in the relations of production. Ruling class ideology distorts the true nature of society and serves to legitimate and justify the status quo. However, the contradictions in the infrastructure will eventually lead to a disintegration of the system and the creation of a new society in which there is no exploitation and oppression.

■ Interactionism

Although functionalism and Marxism provide very different perspectives on society, they have a number of factors in common. First, they offer a general explanation of society as a whole and as a result are sometimes known as **macro-theories**. Second, they regard society as a system, hence they are sometimes referred to as 'system theories'. Third, they tend to see human behaviour as shaped by the system. In terms of Talcott Parsons's version of functionalism, behaviour is largely directed by the norms and values of the social system. From a Marxist viewpoint, behaviour is ultimately determined by the economic infrastructure.

Interactionism differs from functionalism and Marxism on these three points: it focuses on small-scale interaction rather than society as a whole; it usually rejects the notion of a social

system; and, as a result, it does not regard human action as a response or reaction to the system.

Meaning and interpretation

As its name suggests, interactionism is concerned with **interaction**, which means action between individuals. The interactionist perspective seeks to understand this process. It begins from the assumption that action is meaningful to those involved. It therefore follows that an understanding of action requires an interpretation of the meanings people give to their activities. Picture a man and a woman in a room and the man lighting a candle. This action is open to a number of interpretations. The couple may simply require light because a fuse has blown or a power cut has occurred. Or, they may be involved in some form of ritual in which the lighted candle has a religious significance. Alternatively, the man or woman may be trying to create a more intimate atmosphere as a prelude to a sexual encounter. Finally the couple may be celebrating a birthday, a wedding anniversary or some other red-letter day. In each case a different meaning is attached to the act of lighting a candle. To understand the act it is therefore necessary to discover the meaning held by the actors.

Meanings are not fixed entities. As the above example shows, they depend in part on the context of the interaction. Meanings are also created, developed, modified and changed within the actual process of interaction. A pupil entering a new class may initially define that situation as threatening and even hostile. This definition may be confirmed, modified or changed depending on the pupil's perception of the interaction that takes place in the classroom. The teacher and fellow pupils may come to be perceived as friendly and understanding, and so the pupil's assessment of the situation will change. The way in which actors define situations has important consequences. It represents their reality, in terms of which they structure their actions. For example, if the pupil maintains a definition of the classroom as threatening and hostile, they may say little and speak only when spoken to. Conversely if the definition changed, there would probably be a corresponding change in the pupil's actions in that context.

Self-concepts

The actions of the pupil in the above example will depend in part on that person's interpretation of the way they are perceived. For this reason many interactionists place particular emphasis on the idea of the self. They suggest that individuals develop a 'self-concept', a picture of themselves that has an important influence on their actions. A self-concept develops from interaction processes since it is in large part a reflection of the reactions of others towards the individual: hence the term 'looking glass self' coined by Charles Cooley. Actors tend to act in terms of their self-concept. Thus if they are consistently defined as disreputable or respectable, servile or arrogant, they will tend to see themselves in this light and act accordingly.

The construction of meaning

Since interactionists are concerned with definitions of situation and self, they are also concerned with the process by which those definitions are constructed. For example, how does an individual come to be defined in a certain way? The answer to this question involves an investigation of the construction of meaning in interaction processes. This requires an analysis of the way actors interpret the language, gestures, appearance and manner of others and their interpretation of the context in which the interaction takes place.

One example is the definition of an individual as a delinquent. Research has indicated that police are more likely to perceive an act as delinquent if it occurs in a low-income inner city area. The context will influence the action of the police since they typically define the inner city as a 'bad area'. Once arrested, a male youth, for instance, is more likely to be defined as a juvenile delinquent if his manner is interpreted as aggressive and uncooperative, if his appearance is seen as unconventional or slovenly, if his speech is defined as ungrammatical or slang and if his posture gives the impression of disrespect for authority or arrogance. Thus the black American youth from the inner city ghetto with his cool, arrogant manner and colourful clothes is more likely to be defined as a delinquent than the white 'all-American girl' from the tree-lined suburbs.

Definitions of individuals as certain kinds of persons are not, however, simply based on the preconceptions that actors bring to interaction situations. For example, the police will not automatically define black juveniles involved in a fight as delinquent and white juveniles involved in a

similar activity as non-delinquent. A process of negotiation occurs from which the definition emerges. Often negotiations will reinforce preconceptions, but not necessarily. The young blacks may be able to convince the police officer that the fight was a friendly brawl which did not involve intent to injure or steal. In this way they may successfully promote images of themselves as high-spirited teenagers rather than as malicious delinquents. Definitions and meanings are therefore constructed in interaction situations by a process of negotiation.

Negotiation and roles

The idea of negotiation is also applied to the concept of role. Like functionalists, the interactionists employ the concept of role but they adopt a somewhat different perspective. Functionalists imply that roles are provided by the social system, and that individuals enact their roles as if they were reading from a script that contains explicit directions for their behaviour. Interactionists argue that roles are often unclear, ambiguous and vague. This lack of clarity provides actors with considerable room for negotiation, manoeuvre, improvisation and creative action. At most, roles provide very general guidelines for action. What matters is how they are employed in interaction situations.

For example, two individuals enter marriage with a vague idea about the roles of husband and wife. Their interaction will not be constrained by these roles. Their definition of what constitutes a husband, a wife, and a marital relationship will be negotiated. It will be fluid rather than fixed, changeable rather than static. Thus, from an interactionist perspective, roles, like meanings and definitions of the situation, are negotiated in interaction processes.

In summary, interactionism focuses on the process of interaction in particular contexts. Since all action is meaningful, it can only be understood by discovering the meanings which actors assign to their activities. Meanings both direct action and derive from action. They are not fixed but constructed and negotiated in interaction situations. From their interaction with others, actors develop a self-concept. This has important consequences since individuals tend to act in terms of their definition of self. Understanding the construction of meanings and self-concepts involves an appreciation of the way actors interpret the process of interaction. This requires an investigation of the way in which they perceive the context of the interaction and the manner, appearance and actions of others.

While interactionists admit the existence of roles, they regard them as vague and imprecise and therefore as open to negotiation. From an interactionist perspective, action proceeds from negotiated meanings that are constructed in ongoing interaction situations.

Views of human behaviour

The previous section has briefly examined three theoretical perspectives in sociology. In this section we look at the philosophical views of human behaviour. These views have influenced both the type of data sociologists have collected and the methods they have employed to collect that data.

Views of human behaviour can be divided into those that emphasize external factors and those that stress internal factors. The former approach sees behaviour as being influenced by the structure of society. The latter places more emphasis upon the subjective states of individuals, their feelings, the meanings they attach to events and the motives they have for behaving in particular ways. The use of this 'dichotomy' (sharply defined division) is somewhat artificial. In practice most sociologists make use of the insights provided by both approaches when carrying out research and interpreting the results. There are also a number of variations on each approach. For example, as a later section will show, phenomenologists differ in their approach from other sociologists who emphasize the importance of internal influences upon human behaviour.

Positivism

Many of the founders of sociology believed it would be possible to create a science of society based upon the same principles and procedures as the natural sciences such as chemistry and biology, even though the natural sciences often deal with inanimate matter and so are not concerned with feeling, emotions and other subjective states. The most influential attempt to apply natural science methodology to sociology is known as **positivism**.

Auguste Comte (1798–1857), who is credited with inventing the term sociology and regarded as one of the founders of the discipline, maintained that the application of the methods and assumptions of the natural sciences would produce a 'positive science of society'. He believed that this would reveal that the evolution of society followed 'invariable laws'. It would show that the behaviour of humans was governed by principles of cause and effect that were just as invariable as the behaviour of matter, the subject of the natural sciences.

In terms of sociology, the positivist approach makes the following assumptions: the behaviour of humans, like the behaviour of matter, can be objectively measured; just as the behaviour of matter can be quantified by measures such as weight, temperature and pressure, methods of objective measurement can be devised for human behaviour; such measurement is essential to explain behaviour.

For example, in order to explain the reaction of a particular chemical to heat, it is necessary to provide exact measurements of temperature, weight and so on. With the aid of such measurements it will be possible to observe accurately the behaviour of matter and produce a statement of cause and effect. This statement might read $A \times B = C$ where A is a quantity of matter, B a degree of heat and C a volume of gas. Once it has been shown that the matter in question always reacts in the same way under fixed conditions, a theory can be devised to explain its behaviour.

From a positivist viewpoint such methods and assumptions are applicable to human behaviour. Observations of behaviour based on objective measurement will make it possible to produce statements of cause and effect. Theories may then be devised to explain observed behaviour.

The positivist approach in sociology places particular emphasis on behaviour that can be directly observed. It argues that factors that are not directly observable, such as meanings, feelings and purposes, are not particularly important and can be misleading. For example, if the majority of adult members of society enter into marriage and produce children, these facts can be observed and quantified. Therefore they form reliable data. However, the range of meanings that members of society give to these activities, their purposes for marriage and procreation, are not directly observable. Even if they could be accurately measured, they may well divert attention from the real cause of behaviour. One person may believe they entered marriage because they were lonely, another because they were in love, a third because it was the 'thing to do' and a fourth because they wished to produce offspring. Reliance on this type of data for explanation assumes that individuals know the reasons for marriage. This can obscure the real cause of their behaviour.

The positivists' emphasis on observable 'facts' is due largely to the belief that human behaviour can be explained in much the same way as the behaviour of matter. Natural scientists do not inquire into the meanings and purposes of matter for the obvious reason of their absence. Atoms and molecules do not act in terms of meanings, they simply react to external stimuli. Thus if heat, an external stimulus, is applied to matter, that matter will react. The job of the natural scientist is to observe, measure, and then explain that reaction.

The positivist approach to human behaviour applies a similar logic. People react to external stimuli and their behaviour can be explained in terms of this reaction. They enter into marriage and produce children in response to the demands of society: society requires such behaviour for its survival and its members simply respond to this requirement. The meanings and purposes they attach to this behaviour are largely inconsequential.

It has often been argued that systems theory in sociology adopts a positivist approach. Once behaviour is seen as a response to some external stimulus (such as economic forces or the requirements of the social system) the methods and assumptions of the natural sciences appear appropriate to the study of humans. Marxism has sometimes been regarded as a positivist approach since it can be argued that it sees human behaviour as a reaction to the stimulus of the economic infrastructure. Functionalism has been viewed in a similar light. The behaviour of members of society can be seen as a response to the functional prerequisites of the social system. These views of systems theory represent a considerable oversimplification of complex theories. However, it is probably fair to say that systems theory is closer to a positivist approach than the views which will now be considered.

■ Social action perspectives

Advocates of social action perspectives argue that the subject matter of the social and natural sciences is fundamentally different. As a result the methods and assumptions of the natural sciences are inappropriate to the study of humans. The natural sciences deal with matter. To understand and explain the behaviour of matter it is sufficient to observe it from the outside. Atoms and molecules do not have consciousness: they do not have meanings and purposes that direct their behaviour. Matter simply reacts 'unconsciously' to external stimuli; in scientific language, it 'behaves'. As a result the natural scientist is able to observe, measure and impose an external logic on that behaviour in order to explain it. Scientists have no need to explore the internal logic of the consciousness of matter simply because it does not exist.

Unlike matter, humans have consciousness – thoughts, feelings, meanings, intentions and an awareness of being. Because of this, humans' actions are meaningful: they define situations and give meaning to their actions and those of others. As a result, they do not merely react to external stimuli, i.e. they do not simply behave, they act.

Imagine the response of early humans to fire caused by volcanoes or spontaneous combustion. They did not simply react in a uniform manner to the experience of heat. They attached a range of meanings to it and these meanings directed their actions. They defined fire as a means of warmth and used it to heat their dwellings; as a means of defence and used it to ward off wild animals; and as a means of transforming substances and employed it for cooking and hardening the points of wooden spears. Humans do not just react to fire, they act upon it in terms of the meanings they give to it.

If action stems from subjective meanings, it follows that the sociologist must discover those meanings in order to understand action. Sociologists cannot simply observe action from the outside and impose an external logic upon it.

They must interpret the internal logic which directs the actions of the actor.

Max Weber (1864–1920) was one of the first sociologists to outline this perspective in detail. He argued that sociological explanations of action should begin with 'the observation and theoretical interpretation of the subjective "states of minds" of actors'. As the last section indicated, interactionism adopts a similar approach with particular emphasis on the process of interaction. Where positivists emphasize facts and cause-and-effect relationships, interactionists emphasize insight and understanding. Since it is not possible to get inside the heads of actors, the discovery of meaning must be based on interpretation and intuition. For this reason objective measurement is not possible and the exactitude of the natural sciences cannot be duplicated. Since meanings are constantly negotiated in ongoing interaction processes it is not possible to establish simple cause-and-effect relationships. Thus some sociologists argue that sociology is limited to an interpretation of social action.

Nevertheless, both Weber and the interactionists did think it was possible to produce causal explanations of human behaviour so long as an understanding of meanings formed part of those explanations. Some sociologists, particularly phenomenologists, take the argument further and claim that it is impossible for sociologists to find the causes of human action.

■ Phenomenology

To phenomenologists, it is impossible to measure objectively any aspect of human behaviour. Humans make sense of the world by categorizing it. Through language they distinguish between different types of objects, events, actions and people. For instance, some actions are defined as criminal and others are not; similarly some people are defined as criminals while others are seen as law-abiding. The process of categorization is subjective: it depends upon the opinions of the observer. Statistics are simply the product of the opinions of those who produce them. Thus crime statistics are produced by the police and the courts and they represent no more than the opinions of the individuals involved. If sociologists produce their own statistics these too are the product of subjective opinions, in this case the opinions of sociologists.

Phenomenologists believe that it is impossible to produce factual data and it is therefore impossible to produce and check causal explanations. The most that sociologists can hope to do is to understand the meaning that individuals give to particular phenomena. Phenomenologists do not try to establish what causes crime; instead they try to discover how certain events come to be defined as crimes and certain people defined as criminal. Phenomenologists therefore examine the way that police officers reach decisions about whether to arrest and charge suspects. In doing so, they hope to establish the meaning attached to the words 'crime' and 'criminal' by the police. The end product of phenomenological research is an understanding of the meanings employed by members of society in their everyday life.

Although there are differences between those who support social action and phenomenological views, they agree that the positivist approach has produced a distorted picture of social life.

Peter Berger argues that society has often been viewed as a puppet theatre with its members portrayed as 'little puppets jumping about on the ends of their invisible strings, cheerfully acting out the parts that have been assigned to them'. Society instils values, norms and roles, and humans dutifully respond like marionettes. However, interactionists and phenomenologists believe that humans do not react and respond passively to an external society. They see humans as actively creating their own meanings and their own society in interaction with each other.

■ Sociology and values

The positivist approach assumes that a science of society is possible. It therefore follows that objective observation and analysis of social life are possible. An objective view is free from the values, moral judgements and ideology of the observer: it provides facts and explanatory frameworks which are uncoloured by the observer's feelings and opinions.

An increasing number of sociologists argue that a value-free science of society is not possible.

They maintain that the values of sociologists directly influence every aspect of their research. They argue that the various theories of society are based, at least in part, on value judgements and ideological positions. They suggest that sociological perspectives are shaped more by historical circumstances than by objective views of the reality of social life.

Those who argue that an objective science of society is not possible maintain that sociology can never be free from **ideology**. The term ideology refers to a set of ideas which present only a partial view of reality. An ideological viewpoint also includes values. It involves not only a judgement about the way things are but also the way things ought to be. Thus ideology is a set of beliefs and values that provides a way of seeing and interpreting the world, which results in a partial view of reality. The term ideology is often used to suggest a distortion, a false picture of reality. However there is considerable doubt whether reality and ideology can be separated. As Nigel Harris suggests, 'Our reality is the next man's ideology and vice versa.'

Ideology can be seen as a set of beliefs and values that express the interests of a particular social group. Marxists use the term in this way when they talk about the ideology of the ruling class. In this sense ideology is a viewpoint which distorts reality and justifies and legitimates the position of a social group. Karl Mannheim uses the term in a similar way. He states that ideology consists of the beliefs and values of a ruling group which 'obscures the real condition of society both to itself and others and thereby stabilizes it'. Mannheim distinguishes this form of ideology from what he calls 'utopian ideology'. Rather than supporting the status quo, the way things are, **utopian ideologies** advocate a complete change in the structure of society. Mannheim argues that such ideologies are usually found in oppressed groups whose members want radical change. As their name suggests, utopian ideologies are based on a vision of an ideal society, a perfect social system. Mannheim refers to them as 'wish-images' for a future social order. Like the ideologies of ruling groups, he argues that utopian ideologies are a way of seeing the world that prevents true insight and obscures reality.

Mannheim's ideas will now be applied to two of the major theoretical perspectives in sociology:

Marxism and functionalism. It has often been argued that Marxism is largely based on a utopian ideology, functionalism on a ruling ideology. Marxism contains a vision and a promise of a future ideal society – the communist utopia. In this society the means of production are communally owned and as a result oppression and exploitation disappear. The communist utopia provides a standard of comparison for present and past societies. Since they inevitably fall far short of this ideal, their social arrangements will be condemned. It has been argued that the communist utopia is not a scientific prediction but merely a projection of the 'wish-images' of those who adopt a Marxist position. Utopian ideology has therefore been seen as the basis of Marxist theory.

By comparison, functionalism has often been interpreted as a form of ruling class ideology. Where Marxism is seen to advocate radical change, functionalism is seen to justify and legitimate the status quo. With its emphasis on order and stability, consensus and integration, functionalism appears to adopt a conservative stance. Rapid social change is not recommended since it will disrupt social order. The major institutions of society are justified by the belief that they are meeting the functional prerequisites of the social system. Although functionalists have introduced the concept of **dysfunction** to cover the harmful effects of parts of the system on society as a whole, the concept is rarely employed. In practice, functionalists appear preoccupied with discovering the positive functions, the beneficial effects of social institutions. As a result, the term function is associated with the idea of useful and good. This interpretation of society tends to legitimate the way things are. Ruling class ideology has therefore been seen as the basis of functionalist theory.

It is important to note that the above interpretation of the ideological basis of Marxism and functionalism is debatable. However, a case can be made to support the view that both perspectives are ideologically based.

This section has provided a brief introduction to the question of the relationship between sociology and values. The relationship will be considered in detail throughout the text. Each chapter in the main section of the book will conclude with an interpretation of the values involved in the views that are discussed.

■ The sociological imagination

Although sociologists vary in their perspectives, methods and values, they all share the aim of understanding and explaining the social world. Combining the insights offered by different approaches might be the best way of achieving this goal.

Structural theories of society, such as functionalism and Marxism, emphasize the importance of society in shaping human behaviour. On the other hand, approaches such as interactionism emphasize the importance of human behaviour in shaping society. Many sociologists today believe that good sociology must examine both the structure of society and social interaction. From this viewpoint it is only by combining the study of the major changes in society and individual lives that sociologists can develop their understanding of social life.

This idea is not new. It was supported by the very influential German sociologist Max Weber (1864–1920) and more recently has been examined in depth by the British sociologist Anthony Giddens. However, perhaps the clearest exposition of this view was put forward by the American sociologist C. Wright Mills.

Mills called the ability to study the structure of society at the same time as individual's lives the 'sociological imagination'. Writing in the 1950s

Mills argued that the sociological imagination allowed people to understand their 'private troubles' in terms of 'public issues'. Unemployment, war and marital problems are all experienced by people in terms of the problems they produce in their personal lives. They react to them as individuals, and their reactions have consequences for society as a whole. However, to Mills, they can only be fully understood as issues which are shaped by wider social forces. For example, very specific circumstances might lead to one person becoming unemployed, but when unemployment rates in society as a whole rise, it becomes a public issue that needs to be explained. The sociologist has to consider 'the economic and political institutions of the society, and not merely the personal situation and character of a scatter of individuals'.

According to Mills, then, sociology should be about examining the biography of individuals in the context of the history of societies. The sociological imagination is not just of use to sociologists, it is important to all members of society if they wish to understand, change and improve their lives. Perhaps sociology can be seen as succeeding when it allows people to achieve this imagination, and the theories and studies examined in the rest of the book can be judged in these terms.

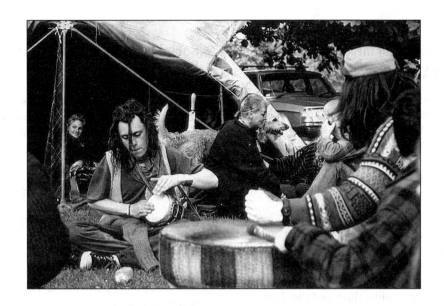

2

Social stratification

2

Social stratification

■ Introduction

Egalitarianism

People have long dreamed of an **egalitarian society**, a society in which all members are equal. In such a society people will no longer be ranked in terms of prestige: no one will experience the satisfaction of occupying a high social status; no one will suffer the indignity of being put in a position which commands little respect. No longer will high status provoke deference and admiration or envy and resentment from those in less 'worthy' positions. Wealth will be distributed equally amongst the population: the rich and poor, haves and have-nots will be a thing of the past. Words such as 'privilege' and 'poverty' will either change their meaning or disappear from the vocabulary. In an egalitarian society, the phrase 'power to the people' will become a reality. There will be an end to some people having power over others: positions of authority and the obedience they command will disappear. Exploitation and oppression will be concepts of history which have no place in the description of contemporary social reality. People will be equal both in the sight of God and in the eyes of their fellow people.

Clearly the egalitarian society remains a dream. All human societies from the simplest to the most complex have some form of **social inequality**. In particular, power and prestige are unequally distributed between individuals and social groups and in many societies there are also marked differences in the distribution of wealth.

1 **Power** refers to the degree to which individuals or groups can impose their will on others, with or without the consent of those others.

2 **Prestige** relates to the amount of esteem or honour associated with social positions, qualities of individuals and styles of life.

3 **Wealth** refers to material possessions defined as valuable in particular societies. It may include land,

livestock, buildings, money and many other forms of property owned by individuals or social groups.

In this chapter we are going to study the unequal distribution of power, prestige and wealth in society.

■ Social inequality and social stratification

It is important at the outset to make a distinction between social inequality and social stratification. The term **social inequality** simply refers to the existence of socially created inequalities. **Social stratification** is a particular form of social inequality. It refers to the presence of distinct social groups which are ranked one above the other in terms of factors such as prestige and wealth. Those who belong to a particular group or stratum will have some awareness of common interests and a common identity. They will share a similar lifestyle which to some degree will distinguish them from members of other social strata. The Indian caste system provides an example of a social stratification system.

Hindu society in traditional India was divided into five main strata: four *varnas* or castes, and a fifth group, the outcaste, whose members were known as untouchables. Each caste was subdivided into *jatis* or subcastes, which in total number many thousands. *Jatis* were occupational groups – there were carpenter *jatis*, goldsmith *jatis*, potter *jatis*, and so on. Castes were ranked in terms of ritual purity.

The Brahmins or priests, members of the highest caste, personified purity, sanctity and holiness. They were the source of learning, wisdom and truth. Only they performed the most important religious ceremonies.

At the other extreme, untouchables were defined as unclean, base and impure, a status which affected all their social relationships. They had to perform unclean and degrading tasks such as the disposal of dead animals. They would be segregated from members of the caste system and lived on the outskirts of villages or in their own communities. Their presence polluted to the extent that even if the shadow of an untouchable fell across the food of a Brahmin it would render it unclean.

In general, the hierarchy of prestige based on notions of ritual purity was mirrored by the hierarchy of power. The Brahmins were custodians of the law, and the legal system they administered was based largely on their pronouncements. Inequalities of wealth were usually linked to those of prestige and power. In a largely rural economy, the Brahmins tended to be the largest landowners and the control of land was monopolized by members of the two highest castes. Although the caste system has been made illegal in modern India, it still exercises an influence, particularly in rural areas.

As shown by the caste system, social stratification involves a **hierarchy of social groups**. Members of a particular stratum have a common identity, like interests and a similar lifestyle. They enjoy or suffer the unequal distribution of rewards in society as members of different social groups.

Social stratification, however, is only one form of social inequality. It is possible for social inequality to exist without social strata. For example, some sociologists have argued that it is no longer correct to regard Western industrial society, particularly the USA, as being stratified in terms of a class system. They suggest that social classes have been replaced by a **continuous hierarchy of unequal positions**. Where there were once classes, whose members had a consciousness of kind, a common way of life and shared interests, there is now an unbroken continuum of occupational statuses which command varying degrees of prestige and economic reward. Thus it is suggested that a hierarchy of social groups has been replaced by a **hierarchy of individuals**.

Although many sociologists use the terms social inequality and social stratification interchangeably, the importance of seeing social stratification as a specific form of social inequality will become apparent as the chapter develops.

Strata subcultures

Before looking at some of the major issues raised in the study of social stratification, it is necessary to examine certain aspects of stratification systems. There is a tendency for members of each stratum to develop their own **subculture**, that is certain norms, attitudes and values which are distinctive to them as a social group. When some members of society experience similar circumstances and problems which are not common to all members, a subculture tends to develop.

For example, it has often been suggested that distinctive working-class and middle-class subcultures exist in Western industrial societies. Similar circumstances and problems often produce similar responses. Members of the lowest stratum in stratification systems which provide little opportunity for improvement of status tend to have a fatalistic attitude towards life. This attitude becomes part of their subculture and is transmitted from generation to generation. It sees circumstances as largely unchangeable; it sees luck and fate rather than individual effort as shaping life and therefore tends to encourage acceptance of the situation. An attitude of fatalism may be seen in typical phrases from traditional low-income black American subculture such as 'I've been down so long that down don't bother me', 'I was born under a bad sign' and 'It's an uphill climb to the bottom.'

Members of a social group who share similar circumstances and a common subculture will be likely to develop a group identity. They tend to have a consciousness of kind, a feeling of kinship with other group members. They will therefore tend to identify with their particular stratum and regard themselves, for example, as middle or working class.

Social mobility

Strata subcultures tend to be particularly distinctive when there is little opportunity to move from one stratum to another. This movement is known as **social mobility**. Social mobility can be upward, for example moving from the working to the middle class, or downward.

Stratification systems which provide little opportunity for social mobility may be described as **closed**; those with a relatively high rate of social mobility as **open**. In closed systems an individual's position is largely **ascribed**: often it is fixed at birth and there is little he or she can do to change status. Caste provides an example of a closed stratification system: individuals automatically belonged to the caste of their parents and, except in rare instances, spent the rest of their life in that status.

By comparison, social class, the system of strati- fication in capitalist industrial society, provides an example of an open system. Some sociologists claim that an individual's class position is largely **achieved**: it results from their personal qualities and abilities and the use they make of them rather than ascribed characteristics such as the status of their parents or the colour of their skin. By com- parison with the caste system, the rate of social mobility in class systems is high.

Life chances

A person's position in a stratification system may have important effects on many areas of life. It may enhance or reduce **life chances**, that is their chances of obtaining those things defined as desirable and avoiding those things defined as undesirable in their society. Referring to Western society Gerth and Mills state that life chances include:

Everything from the chance to stay alive during the first year after birth to the chance to view fine arts, the chance to remain healthy and grow tall, and if sick to get well again quickly, the chance to avoid becoming a juvenile delinquent and very crucially, the chance to complete an intermediary or higher educational grade.

■ Social versus natural inequalities

Biology and inequality

Many stratification systems are accompanied by beliefs which state that social inequalities are bio- logically based. Such beliefs are often found in systems of racial stratification where, for example, whites might claim biological superiority over blacks and see this as the basis for their dominance.

The question of the relationship between bio- logically based and socially created inequality has proved extremely difficult to answer. The eight- eenth-century French philosopher Jean-Jacques Rousseau provided one of the earliest examina- tions of this question. He refers to **biologically based inequality** as: 'natural or physical, because it is established by nature, and consists in a difference of age, health, bodily strength, and the qualities of the mind or the soul'. By comparison, socially

created inequality: 'consists of the different privi- leges which some men enjoy to the prejudice of others, such as that of being more rich, more honoured, more powerful, or even in a position to exact obedience'. (Quoted in Bottomore 1965, pp. 15–16.)

Rousseau believed that biologically based inequalities between people were small and rela- tively unimportant whereas socially created in- equalities provide the major basis for systems of social stratification. Most sociologists would support this view.

However, it could still be argued that biological inequalities, no matter how small, provide the foundation upon which structures of social inequality are built. This position is difficult to defend in the case of certain forms of stratification. In the caste system, an individual's status was fixed by birth. People belonged to their parents' *jati* and automatically followed the occupation of the *jati* into which they were born. Thus no matter what the biologically based aptitudes and capacities of an untouchable, there was no way he or she could become a Brahmin. Unless it is assumed that super- ior genes are permanently located in the Brahmin caste (and there is no evidence that this is the case) then there is probably no relationship between genetically based and socially created inequality in traditional Hindu society.

A similar argument can be advanced in connec- tion with the feudal or estate system of medieval Europe. Stratification in the feudal system was based on landholding. The more land an individual controlled, the greater his or her wealth, power and prestige. The position of the dominant stratum, the feudal nobility, was based on large grants of land from the monarch. Their status was hereditary, land and titles being passed on from parent to child. It is difficult to sustain the argu- ment that feudal lords ultimately owed their posi- tion to biological superiority when children, no matter what their biological make-up, inherited the status of their parents.

Natural and cultural inequality

So far we have not answered the question of what exactly constitutes biological inequality. It can be argued that biological differences become biolo- gical inequalities when people define them as such. Thus André Béteille states that: 'Natural inequality is based on differences in quality, and qualities are not just there, so to say, in nature; they are as human beings have defined them, in different societies, in different historical epochs.'

Biological factors assume importance in many stratification systems because of the meanings assigned to them by different cultures. For example, old age has very different meanings in different societies. In traditional aborigine societies in Australia it brought high prestige and power since the elders directed the affairs of the tribe, but in Western societies, the elderly are usually pensioned off and old age assumes a very different meaning. Even with a change of name to senior citizen, the status of old age pensioner commands little power or prestige.

So-called racial characteristics are evaluated on the basis of similar principles, that is values which are relative to time and place. The physical characteristics of blacks in America were traditionally defined as undesirable and associated with a range of negative qualities. However, with the rise of Black Power during the late 1960s, this evaluation was slowly changed with slogans such as 'Black is beautiful.'

It can therefore be argued that biological differences become biological inequalities only to the extent that they are defined as such. They form a component of some social stratification systems simply because members of those systems select certain characteristics and evaluate them in a particular way. André Béteille argues that the search for a biological basis for social stratification is bound to end in failure since the 'identification as well as the gradation of qualities is a cultural and not a natural process'.

Beliefs which state that systems of social stratification are based on biological inequalities can be seen as **rationalizations** for those systems. Such beliefs serve to explain the system to its members: they make social inequality appear rational and reasonable. They therefore justify and legitimate the system by appeals to nature. In this way a social contrivance appears to be founded on the natural order of things.

Inequalities between men and women and between different 'racial' groups are sometimes seen as being based on biological differences. We will discuss sociologists' views of whether this is justified in later chapters. (See pp. 581–91 on sex and gender and pp. 651–8 on 'race'.)

Having considered social stratification in general terms, we will now look at this subject from the various sociological perspectives.

■ Social stratification – a functionalist perspective

Functionalist theories of stratification must be seen in the context of functionalist theories of society. When functionalists attempt to explain systems of social stratification, they set their explanations in the framework of larger theories which seek to explain the operation of society as a whole. They assume that society has certain basic needs or **functional prerequisites** which must be met if it is to survive. They therefore look to social stratification to see how far it meets these functional prerequisites.

Functionalists assume that the parts of society form an integrated whole and thus examine the ways in which the social stratification system is integrated with other parts of society. They maintain that a certain degree of order and stability is essential for the operation of social systems. They will therefore consider how stratification systems help to maintain order and stability in society. In summary, functionalists are primarily concerned with the function of social stratification: with its contribution to the maintenance and well-being of society.

■ Talcott Parsons – stratification and values

Like many functionalists, Talcott Parsons believes that order, stability and cooperation in society are based on **value consensus**, that is a general agreement by members of society concerning what is good and worthwhile. Parsons argues that stratification systems derive from common values. It follows from the existence of values that individuals will be evaluated and therefore placed in some form of rank order. In Parsons's words, 'Stratification, in its valuational aspect, then, is the ranking of units in a social system in accordance with the common value system.'

In other words, those who perform successfully in terms of society's values will be ranked highly and they will be likely to receive a variety of rewards. At a minimum they will be accorded high prestige since they exemplify and personify common values.

For example, if a society places a high value on bravery and generosity, as is the case of the Sioux Indians, those who excel in terms of these qualities will receive a high rank in the stratification system. The Sioux warrior who successfully raids the Crow and Pawnee, the traditional enemies of his tribe, captures horses and distributes them to others, may receive a variety of rewards. He may be given a seat on the tribal council, a position of power and prestige. His deeds will be recounted in the warrior societies and the squaws will sing of his exploits. Other warriors will follow him in raids against neighbouring tribes and the success of these expeditions may lead to his appointment as a war chief. In this way excellence in terms of Sioux values is rewarded by power and prestige.

Since different societies have different value systems, the ways of attaining a high position will vary from society to society. Parsons argues that American society values individual achievement, efficiency and 'puts primary emphasis on productive activity within the economy'. Thus successful business executives who have achieved their position through their own initiative, ability and ambition, and run efficient and productive businesses, will receive high rewards.

Parsons's argument suggests that stratification is an inevitable part of all human societies. If value consensus is an essential component of all societies, then it follows that some form of stratification will result from the ranking of individuals in terms of common values. It also follows from Parsons's argument that there is a general belief that stratification systems are just, right and proper, since they are basically an expression of shared values. Thus American business executives are seen to deserve their rewards because members of society place a high value on their skills and achievements.

This is not to say there is no conflict between the haves and have-nots, the highly rewarded and those who receive little reward. Parsons recognizes that in Western industrial society 'There will be certain tendencies to arrogance on the part of some winners and to resentment and to a "sour grapes" attitude on the part of some losers.' However, he believes that this conflict is kept in check by the common value system which justifies the unequal distribution of rewards.

Organization and planning

Functionalists tend to see the relationship between social groups in society as one of cooperation and interdependence. Particularly in complex industrial societies, different groups specialize in particular activities. As no one group is self-sufficient it cannot meet the needs of its members. It must, therefore, exchange goods and services with other groups, and so the relationship between social groups is one of **reciprocity** (mutual give and take).

This relationship extends to the strata in a stratification system. To present an oversimplified example, it can be argued that many occupational groups within the middle class in Western society plan, organize and coordinate the activities of the working class. Each class needs and cooperates with the other since any large-scale task requires both organization and execution. In societies with a highly specialized division of labour, such as industrial societies, some members will specialize in organization and planning while others will follow their directives. Talcott Parsons argues that this inevitably leads to inequality in terms of power and prestige. Referring to Western society, he states:

> Organization on an ever increasing scale is a fundamental feature of such a system. Such organization naturally involves centralization and differentiation of leadership and authority; so that those who take responsibility for coordinating the actions of many others must have a different status in important respects from those who are essentially in the role of carrying out specifications laid down by others.

Thus those with the power to organize and coordinate the activities of others will have a higher social status than those they direct.

Power

As with prestige differentials, Parsons argues that inequalities of power are based on shared values. Power is legitimate authority in that it is generally accepted as just and proper by members of society as a whole. It is accepted as such because those in positions of authority use their power to pursue **collective goals** which derive from society's central values. Thus the power of the American business executive is seen as legitimate authority because it is used to further productivity, a goal shared by all members of society. This use of power therefore serves the interests of society as a whole.

Summary and evaluation

Parsons sees social stratification as both inevitable and functional for society.

1 It is inevitable because it derives from shared values which are a necessary part of all social systems.

2 It is functional because it serves to integrate various groups in society.

Power and prestige differentials are essential for the coordination and integration of a specialized division of labour. Without social inequality, Parsons finds it difficult to see how members of society could effectively cooperate and work together. Finally, inequalities of power and prestige benefit all members of society since they serve to further collective goals which are based on shared values.

Parsons has been strongly criticized on all these points. Other sociologists have seen stratification as a divisive rather than an integrating force. They have seen it as an arrangement whereby some gain at the expense of others. They have questioned the view that stratification systems derive ultimately from shared values. We will examine these criticisms in detail in later sections.

▌ Kingsley Davis and Wilbert E. Moore – role allocation and performance

The most famous functionalist theory of stratification was first presented in 1945, in an article by the American sociologists Davis and Moore entitled *Some Principles of Stratification*.

Effective role allocation and performance

Davis and Moore begin with the observation that stratification exists in every known human society.

They attempt to explain 'in functional terms, the universal necessity which calls forth stratification in any social system'. They argue that all social systems share certain functional prerequisites which must be met if the system is to survive and operate efficiently. One such functional prerequisite is **effective role allocation and performance**. This means that:

1 all roles must be filled;
2 they must be filled by those best able to perform them;
3 the necessary training for them must be undertaken;
4 and the roles must be performed conscientiously.

Davis and Moore argue that all societies need some 'mechanism' for insuring effective role allocation and performance. This mechanism is social stratification, which they see as a system which attaches unequal rewards and privileges to the different positions in society.

If the people and positions which make up society did not differ in important respects there would be no need for stratification. However, people differ in terms of their innate ability and talent, and positions differ in terms of their importance for the survival and maintenance of society. Certain positions are more **functionally important** than others. They require special skills for their effective performance and there are a limited number of individuals with the necessary ability to acquire such skills.

A major function of stratification is to match the most able people with the functionally most important positions. It does this by attaching high rewards to those positions. The desire for such rewards motivates people to compete for them and in theory the most talented will win through. Such positions usually require long periods of training which involve certain sacrifices such as loss of income. The promise of high rewards is necessary to provide an incentive to encourage people to undergo this training and to compensate them for the sacrifice involved.

It is essential for the well-being of society that those who hold the functionally most important positions perform their roles diligently and conscientiously. The high rewards built into these positions provide the necessary inducement and generate the required motivation for such performance. Thus Davis and Moore conclude that social stratification is a 'device by which societies insure that the most important positions are conscientiously filled by the most qualified persons'.

Functional importance

Davis and Moore realize that one difficulty with their theory is to show clearly which positions are functionally most important. The fact that a position is highly rewarded does not necessarily mean it is functionally important. They suggest that the importance of a position can be measured in two ways.

1 It can be measured by the 'degree to which a position is functionally unique, there being no other positions that can perform the same function satisfactorily'. Thus it could be argued that doctors are functionally more important than nurses since their position carries with it many of the skills necessary to perform a nurse's role but not vice versa.

2 The second measure of importance is the 'degree to which other positions are dependent on the one in question'. Thus it may be argued that managers are more important than routine office staff since the latter are dependent on direction and organization from management.

To summarize, Davis and Moore regard social stratification as a **functional necessity** for all societies. They see it as a solution to a problem faced by all social systems, that of 'placing and motivating individuals in the social structure'. They offer no other means of solving this problem and imply that social inequality is an inevitable feature of human society. They conclude that differential rewards are functional for society, because they contribute to the maintenance and well-being of social systems.

■ Melvin M. Tumin – a critique of Davis and Moore

Davis and Moore's view provoked a long debate. Tumin, their most famous opponent, has produced a comprehensive criticism of their theory.

Functional importance

He begins by questioning the adequacy of their measurement of the functional importance of positions. Davis and Moore have tended to assume that the most highly rewarded positions are indeed the

most important. However, many occupations which afford little prestige or economic reward can be seen as vital to society. Thus, Tumin argues that 'some labour force of unskilled workmen is as important and as indispensable to the factory as some labour force of engineers'.

In fact a number of sociologists have argued that there is no objective way of measuring the functional importance of positions. Whether lawyers and doctors are considered as more important than farm labourers and refuse collectors is simply a matter of opinion.

Power and rewards

Tumin argues that Davis and Moore have ignored the influence of power on the unequal distribution of rewards. Thus differences in pay and prestige between occupational groups may be due to differences in their power rather than their functional importance. For example, the difference between the wages of farm labourers and coal miners can be interpreted as a result of the bargaining power of the two groups. We will examine this point in detail in later sections.

The pool of talent

Davis and Moore assume that only a limited number of individuals have the talent to acquire the skills necessary for the functionally most important positions. Tumin regards this as a very questionable assumption for three reasons.

1 As the chapter on education indicates, an effective method of measuring talent and ability has yet to be devised.

2 There is no proof that exceptional talents are required for those positions which Davis and Moore consider important.

3 As the chapter on education suggests, the pool of talent in society may be considerably larger than Davis and Moore assume. As a result, unequal rewards may not be necessary to harness it.

Training

Tumin also questions the view that the training required for important positions should be regarded as a sacrifice and therefore in need of compensation. He points to the rewards of being a student – leisure, freedom and the opportunity for self-development. He notes that any loss of earnings can usually be made up during the first ten years of work. Differential rewards during this period may be justified. However, Tumin sees no reason for continuing this compensation for the rest of an individual's working life.

Motivation

According to Davis and Moore, the major function of unequal rewards is to motivate talented individuals and allocate them to the functionally most important positions. Tumin rejects this view. He argues that social stratification can, and often does, act as a barrier to the motivation and recruitment of talent.

This is readily apparent in closed systems such as caste and racial stratification: the ascribed status of untouchables prevented even the most talented from becoming Brahmins. Until recently, the ascribed status of blacks in the USA blocked all but a handful from political office and highly rewarded occupations. Thus closed stratification systems operate in exactly the opposite way to Davis and Moore's theory.

Tumin suggests, however, that even relatively open systems of stratification erect barriers to the motivation and recruitment of talent. As the chapter on education shows, there is considerable evidence to indicate that the class system in Western industrial society limits the possibilities of the discovery and utilization of talent. In general, the lower an individual's class position, the more likely he or she is to leave school at the minimum leaving age and the less likely to aspire and strive for a highly rewarded position. Thus the motivation to succeed is unequally distributed throughout the class system. As a result social class can act as an obstacle to the motivation of talent.

In addition, Tumin argues that Davis and Moore have failed to consider the possibility that those who occupy highly rewarded positions will erect barriers to recruitment. Occupational groups often use their power to restrict access to their positions, so creating a high demand for their services and increasing the rewards they receive. Tumin claims that the American Medical Association has been guilty of this practice. By its control of entry into the profession, it has maintained a shortage of doctors and so ensured high rewards for medical services. In this way the self-interested use of power can restrict the recruitment of talented individuals to highly rewarded positions.

Inequality of opportunity

Tumin concludes that stratification, by its very nature, can never adequately perform the functions which Davis and Moore assign to it. He argues that those born into the lower strata can never have the same opportunities for realizing their talents as those born into the higher strata. Tumin maintains:

> It is only when there is a genuinely equal access to recruitment and training for all potentially talented persons that differential rewards can conceivably be justified as functional. And stratification systems are apparently *inherently antagonistic* to the development of such full equality of opportunity.

Social divisions

Finally, Tumin questions the view that social stratification functions to integrate the social system. He argues that differential rewards can 'encourage hostility, suspicion and distrust among the various segments of a society'. From this viewpoint, stratification is a divisive rather than an integrating force.

Stratification can also weaken social integration by giving members of the lower strata a feeling of being excluded from participation in the larger society. This is particularly apparent in systems of racial stratification. For example, the saying 'On the outside looking in', is a typical phrase from traditional black American subculture. By tending to exclude certain groups from full participation in society, stratification 'serves to distribute loyalty unequally in the population' and therefore reduces the potential for social solidarity.

Tumin concludes that in their enthusiastic search for the positive functions of stratification, the functionalists have tended to ignore or play down its many dysfunctions.

The debate between Davis and Moore and Tumin took place in the 1940s and 1950s. Interest in the issues raised by this debate has recently been revived with the development of 'New Right' perspectives in sociology. In the next section we will analyse the New Right theories of social stratification.

■ Social stratification – a New Right perspective

Introduction

The New Right bases its theories on nineteenth-century Liberalism. This saw the **free market** in capitalist economies as the best basis for organizing society. Market forces encourage competition which stimulates innovation and efficiency. Businesses have to make products which are cheaper or better than those of their competitors in order to survive. Free market economies are based upon the choices made by individuals when spending their money, selling their labour or purchasing other people's labour. They therefore promote individual liberty.

Like their nineteenth-century liberal counterparts, the New Right sociologists believe that excessive state intervention in the economy must be avoided. The state should not act to redistribute resources and interfere with the workings of the free market. If it tries to do so it will undermine economic efficiency. Inefficient concerns will be propped up by the Government needlessly using up resources. State intervention may take away the motivation for people to work hard. If individuals know that the state will help them no matter how little effort they make, there is little incentive to strive for success. Government interference may produce injustice, taking from those who have earned their rewards and giving to those who are undeserving. Furthermore, as the state becomes stronger the freedom of individuals may be suppressed. For all these reasons the New Right is strongly opposed to Marxism and socialism.

The New Right became influential in the 1980s. In politics the British prime minister Margaret Thatcher and the American president Ronald Reagan were closely associated with the New Right. The American economist Milton Friedman and the Austrian academic Friedrich Hayek have contributed much to the development of New Right thinking. In British sociology Peter Saunders and David Marsland have been perhaps the most prominent advocates of using this perspective to analyse society. Marsland's views on poverty will be examined in the next chapter (pp. 147–8) but it is Peter Saunders who has developed a theory of stratification.

■ Peter Saunders – stratification and freedom

An evaluation of the functionalist theory

Saunders is generally sympathetic to Davis and Moore's theory of stratification: he is certainly much less critical than Melvin Tumin. He points out that even critics like Tumin accepted that all societies have been stratified – there has never been a completely egalitarian society. Furthermore, he suggests that systems which reward different positions unequally can be shown to have beneficial effects, such as motivating people to work hard.

However Saunders does not argue that unequal rewards are the only way that a society could get the important positions filled by capable people. He says 'it is possible to imagine a society where all positions are rewarded equally in terms of material resources and formal status'. However, such a society would have serious problems. Some people would not be happy to do the jobs they were allocated and others would not put in the effort needed to do their jobs properly. Saunders believes:

> In the absence of economic rewards and penalties, the only sanctions available would be those involving the threat or use of physical force. Such people, in other words would have to be jailed, or forcibly set to work in supervised colonies, or even executed as an example to others.

This would be necessary because allowing people to get away with doing less than their fair share of work would undermine the whole system by reducing the commitment of others.

Saunders does not therefore accept the functionalist claim that stratification systems based upon economic differences are inevitable. However, he certainly agrees with functionalists that they are desirable. He admits that capitalist societies tend to create more inequality than socialist societies. He says that socialist societies 'are always more repressive' than capitalist ones because they have to be able to get people to carry out their roles. In the absence of adequate economic rewards force must be used. Saunders even predicts that as countries such as China and the former Soviet Union move towards market-based economies 'state coercion may be expected to decline'.

Equality and justice

In developing his own theory of stratification Saunders distinguishes three types of equality.

1 **Formal** or **legal equality** involves all members of society being subject to the same laws or rules. Individuals are judged according to what they do, for example whether they break the law, and not according to who they are. Sanders sees this type of equality as being an integral part of Western capitalist societies, although he admits that 'in practice it is not always as rigorously applied as it might be'. Legal equality does not imply that everybody ends up in the same position.

2 The second type of equality, **equality of opportunity**, means that people have an equal chance to become unequal. Individuals compete for success and those with greater merit achieve more. Merit might involve the ability to work harder or the possession of attributes or characteristics which are valued in a society. A society based on this type of equality is often called a **meritocracy**.

3 **Equality of outcome** goes further than the idea of equality of opportunity. Saunders explains:

If a meritocracy is like a race where everybody lines up together at the start, a fully-fledged egalitarian society would be like a perfectly handicapped race where everyone passes the finishing tape at the same time no matter how hard and fast they have tried to run.

Broadly, Saunders accepts the principles behind the first two conceptions of equality but rejects the third. Following the ideas of Hayek he argues that attempts to create equality of outcome undermine equality of opportunity and legal equality. To get equality of outcome you have to treat people differently. For example 'affirmative action' programmes or 'positive discrimination' designed to equalize the achievements of men and women or

blacks and whites result in discrimination. Whites and males are discriminated against while blacks and females enjoy discrimination in their favour.

Saunders uses an example put forward by another New Right writer, Robert Nozick, to illustrate how pursuing equality of outcome leads to injustice. A group of students could agree before an exam that they should all be given a mark of 50 per cent. All would pass and none would have to fear failure, but it would not be just. Some individuals would feel rightly aggrieved if they were stripped of 30 per cent of the marks they would normally have gained and which they had earned through their own efforts.

Saunders and Nozick therefore adopt a conception of equality based on legal equality and the idea of **entitlement**. Social justice is served when people are allowed to keep those things to which they are entitled. So long as people have earned the resources or money they possess legally through their own work or 'uncoerced exchanges with others' then there should be no question of them being robbed of their possessions. If people pass their wealth on to others then the recipients become entitled to keep it.

Saunders does, however, admit that there is one flaw in this argument. In a society such as Britain, it is not clear that all of the wealthy are actually entitled to what they own. Some of the land in private hands has been passed down to the descendants of Norman warlords who helped William the Conqueror conquer England. Saunders does not want to see the wealth of aristocrats such as the Duke of Westminster or that of the Queen taken from them. To do so would undermine 'the whole basis of modern-day property ownership'. He therefore turns to a second justification for inequality which comes from the work of Hayek.

Both Saunders and Hayek believe that inequality is justified because it promotes economic growth. By allowing and encouraging people to pursue their own self-interest the interests of society as a whole are promoted. Some entrepreneurs who set up businesses fail. When this happens they bear the costs of their own failure. When they succeed they may 'accumulate a fortune, but in doing so they will have added to the productive power and wealth of the society as a whole'. Competition ensures that goods or services increase in quality and fall in price, making them available to a wider section of the population. Not everyone will be able to afford consumer products initially, or indeed in the end, but living standards will constantly increase. The efforts of entrepreneurs makes some of them rich, but at the same time 'the rest of society grows more affluent as it gains by their efforts'. Saunders cites cars, air travel, ballpoint pens, colour televisions, home computers and central heating as examples of things which have become 'within reach of millions of ordinary people'.

Opportunity and inequality

While Saunders clearly believes that competition in capitalist societies benefits the population, he is less clear about whether it is based on equality of opportunity. He makes no claims that Britain or similar societies are perfect meritocracies in which everyone has genuinely equal opportunities to use their talents to achieve success. However, he does refer to arguments and evidence used by other sociologists to suggest that Britain is not meritocratic. As a later section will indicate (see pp. 98–109), studies of social mobility in Britain have reached two central conclusions.

1 People with parents from higher-class backgrounds have more chance of ending up in higher-class jobs themselves than people from lower-class backgrounds.

2 The opportunities to move up the stratification system have increased this century for all social groups because of the decline in lower-class manual jobs and the increase in higher-class non-manual work.

Sociologists who are more critical of capitalism than Saunders tend to stress the first conclusion and use it as evidence that British capitalism is not based on meritocratic lines: it gives greater opportunities to those from higher-class backgrounds. Saunders, though, believes that no such conclusions are justified. He argues that the figures may result from ability being unequally distributed. In other words, the children of lower-class parents are likely to end up in the lower classes themselves because they have less ability. He says:

Different people do have different talents and abilities, and recent discoveries in biochemistry have shown that far more features of personality and character are transmitted genetically from generation to generation than had previously been realised.

Saunders admits that it is not possible to measure innate ability but says, that *if* talent is mainly inherited, it would not be surprising to find most of the offspring of lower-class parents in the lower classes themselves.

If, to Saunders, the first of the above conclusions of social mobility studies does not show there is inequality of opportunity, the second does show the positive benefits of a capitalist economic system. Whatever the **relative** chances of people from different classes getting a higher-class job, the **absolute** chances have increased for everybody. Capitalism creates more well-paid, skilled and white-collar jobs for which people from all backgrounds can compete. Saunders concludes: '*Capitalism is dynamic because it is unequal*, and any attempt to equalise wealth and income will succeed only at the expense of stifling initiative, innovation and social and economic development.'

■ A critique of the New Right perspective

The New Right perspective on stratification is open to a number of criticisms. Some of Tumin's criticisms of Davis and Moore are also relevant to New Right theories. For example, they can be accused of playing down the possible harmful effects of stratification in undermining social cohesion and integration. Saunders's view that socialist societies are inevitably more repressive than free market capitalist ones could be seen as an unjustified, sweeping generalization. For example:

1 Early capitalism was partly based upon the use of slave labour.

2 In South Africa until recently a capitalist-free market economy went hand-in-hand with the apartheid system which separated 'races' and gave black South Africans very few opportunities.

3 In Chile a democratically elected socialist government under the leadership of President Allende was overthrown in the 1970s in a coup led by General Pinochet. Pinochet followed free market economic policies and his seizure of power was partly engineered by the USA. Yet his regime was far more repressive than that of his predecessor. One of Pinochet's

regime's first actions was to round up thousands of potential opponents and take them to the national football stadium. Many were executed.

Examples such as these suggest that the free market and freedom do not inevitably go hand-in-hand.

Gordon Marshall and Adam Swift – social class and social justice

Marshall and Swift have made the most detailed evaluation of Saunders's views on stratification. They criticize him for trying to argue in favour of both equality of opportunity and formal or legal equality. These two principles might coincide but often they do not. For example Marshall and Swift argue:

If a millionaire chooses to bequeath his money to an untalented layabout then justice as entitlement demands that he be permitted to do so, and forbids taxation of the inheritance despite the fact that any normal conception of justice as desert or merit is here clearly violated.

Marshall and Swift then go on to examine the meritocracy thesis. They question the view that market forces necessarily reward merit. Success in business, for example, may depend as much on luck as on the hard work or personal attributes of the entrepreneur.

Furthermore, they advance evidence which they claim shows that capitalist societies are not genuinely meritocratic. They use data from a study conducted by Gordon Marshall, Howard Newby, David Rose and Carolyn Vogler in which a sample of 1,770 British men and women were interviewed. They found that patterns of social mobility were influenced by class even when educational attainment was taken into account. People from working-class backgrounds had less chance than those from higher-class backgrounds of obtaining a position in one of the top classes even when they had the same level of educational qualifications. This undermines Saunders's claim that inequalities between classes could be the result of genetic differences. Working-class people with, for example, the ability to get a degree, were still disadvantaged because of their class background. As Marshall and Swift say:

If people find their place in the occupational order according to meritocratic principles, then the impact of class background should not be apparent in class destinations, except as this is mediated by educational achievements.

As this is not the case Britain cannot be truly meritocratic. The free market does not guarantee that merit is equally rewarded for all social groups. Social justice may therefore be promoted if the state intervenes to 'ensure that the procedures whereby individuals are allocated to occupations are strictly meritocratic'. (For more details of the study by Marshall *et al.* see pp. 68–9.)

■ Social stratification – a Marxist perspective

Marxist perspectives provide a radical alternative to functionalist views of the nature of social stratification. They regard stratification as a divisive rather than an integrative structure. They see it as a mechanism whereby some exploit others, rather than as a means of furthering collective goals. Marxists focus on social strata rather than social inequality in general. Functionalists such as Parsons and Davis and Moore say little about social stratification in the sense of clearly defined social strata whose members have shared interests. However, this view of social stratification is central to Marxist theory.

Marx's views will first be briefly summarized and then examined in more detail.

Classes

1 In all stratified societies, there are two major social groups: a **ruling class** and a **subject class**.

2 The power of the ruling class comes from its ownership and control of the **means of production** (land, capital, labour power, buildings and machinery).

3 The ruling class exploits and oppresses the subject class.

4 As a result, there is a basic **conflict of interest** between the two classes.

5 The various institutions of society, such as the legal and political systems, are **instruments** of ruling-class domination and serve to further its interests.

6 Only when the means of production are **communally owned** will classes disappear, thereby bringing an end to the exploitation and oppression of some by others.

From a Marxist perspective, systems of stratification derive from the relationships of social groups to the means of production. Marx used the term **class** to refer to the main strata in all stratification systems, though most modern sociologists would reserve the term for strata in capitalist society. From a Marxist viewpoint, a class is a social group whose members share the same relationship to the means of production.

For example, in a feudal epoch, there are two main classes distinguished by their relationship to land (the crucial part of the means of production in an agricultural society). They are the **feudal nobility** who own the land, and the **landless serfs** who work the land. Similarly, in the capitalist era, there are two main classes: the **bourgeoisie** or capitalist class which owns the means of production, and the **proletariat** or working class whose members own only their labour which they hire to the bourgeoisie in return for wages.

Classes and historical epochs

Marx believed that Western society had developed through four main epochs:

1 primitive communism;
2 ancient society;
3 feudal society;
4 capitalist society.

Primitive communism is represented by the societies of prehistory and provides the only example of a classless society. From then on, all societies are divided into two major classes: masters and slaves in ancient society, lords and serfs in feudal society and capitalists and wage labourers in capitalist society. During each historical epoch, the labour power required for production was supplied by the subject class, that is by slaves, serfs and wage labourers respectively. The subject class is made up of the majority of the population whereas the ruling or dominant class forms a minority. The relationship between the two major classes will be discussed shortly.

Classes did not exist during the era of primitive communism when societies were based on a socialist mode of production. In a hunting and gathering band, the earliest form of human society, the land and its products were communally owned. The men hunted and the women gathered plant food, and the produce was shared by members of the band. Classes did not exist since all members of society shared the same relationship to the means of production. Every member was both producer and owner, all provided labour power and shared the products of their labour. Hunting and gathering is a subsistence economy which means that production only meets basic survival needs.

Classes emerge when the productive capacity of society expands beyond the level required for subsistence. This occurs when agriculture becomes the dominant mode of production. In an agricultural economy, only a section of society is needed to produce the food requirements of the whole society. Thus many individuals are freed from food production and are able to specialize in other tasks. The rudimentary division of labour of the hunting and gathering band is replaced by an increasingly more complex and specialized division.

For example, in the early agricultural villages, some individuals became full-time producers of pottery, clothing and agricultural implements. As agriculture developed, **surplus wealth**, that is goods above the basic subsistence needs of the community, was produced. This led to an exchange of goods and trading developed rapidly both within and between communities. This was accompanied by the development of a system of private property. Goods were increasingly seen as commodities or articles of trade to which the individual rather than the community had right of ownership.

Private property and the accumulation of surplus wealth form the basis for the development of class societies. In particular, they provide the preconditions for the emergence of a class of producers and a class of non-producers. Some people are able to acquire the means of production and others are therefore obliged to work for them. The result is a class of non-producers which owns the means of production and a class of producers which owns only its labour power.

Dependency and conflict

From a Marxist perspective, the relationship between the major social classes is one of mutual dependence and conflict. Thus in capitalist society, the bourgeoisie and proletariat are dependent upon each other. The wage labourers must sell their labour power in order to survive since they do not own a part of the means of production and lack the means to produce goods independently. They are, therefore, dependent for their livelihood on the capitalists and the wages they offer. The capitalists, as non-producers, are dependent on the labour power of wage labourers, since without it, there would be no production.

However, the mutual dependency of the two classes is not a relationship of equal or symmetrical reciprocity. Instead, it is a relationship of exploiter and exploited, oppressor and oppressed. In particular, the ruling class gains at the expense of the subject class and there is therefore a conflict of interest between them. This may be illustrated by Marx's view of the nature of ownership and production in capitalist society.

The capitalist economy and exploitation

The basic characteristics of a capitalist economy may be summarized as follows.

1 **Capital** may be defined as money used to finance the production of commodities for private gain.

2 In a capitalist economy goods and the labour power, raw materials and machinery used to produce them, are given a monetary value.

3 The capitalists invest their capital in the production of goods.

4 Capital is accumulated by selling those goods at a value greater than their cost of production.

In Raymond Aron's words, 'The essence of capitalist exchange is to proceed from money to money by way of commodity and end up with more money than one had at the outset.' **Capitalism** therefore involves the investment of capital in the production of commodities with the aim of maximizing profit.

Capital is privately owned by a minority, the capitalist class. However, in Marx's view, it is gained from the exploitation of the mass of the population, the working class. Marx argued that capital, as such, produces nothing. Only labour produces wealth. Yet the wages paid to the workers for their labour are well below the value of the goods they produce. The difference between the value of wages and commodities is known as **surplus value**. This surplus value is appropriated in the form of **profit** by the capitalists. Since they are non-producers, the bourgeoisie are therefore exploiting the proletariat, the real producers of wealth.

Marx maintained that in all class societies, the ruling class exploits and oppresses the subject class.

Power and the superstructure

From a Marxist perspective political power comes from economic power. The power of the ruling class therefore stems from its ownership and control of the means of production. Since the **superstructure** of society – the major institutions, values and belief systems – is seen to be largely shaped by the economic infrastructure, the relations of production will be reproduced in the superstructure. Therefore the dominance of the ruling class in the relations of production will be reflected in the superstructure. In particular, the political and legal systems will reflect ruling-class interests since, in Marx's words, 'The existing relations of production between individuals must necessarily express themselves also as political and legal relations.'

For instance, the various ownership rights of the capitalist class will be enshrined in and protected by the laws of the land. Thus the various parts of the superstructure can be seen as instruments of ruling-class domination and as mechanisms for the oppression of the subject class.

In the same way, the position of the dominant class is supported by beliefs and values which are systematically generated by the infrastructure. As noted in the previous chapter, Marx refers to the dominant concepts of class societies as **ruling-class ideology** since they justify and legitimate ruling-class domination and project a distorted picture of reality. For example, the emphasis on freedom in capitalist society, illustrated by phrases such as 'the free market', 'free democratic societies' and 'the free world', is an illusion which disguises the wage slavery of the proletariat.

Ruling-class ideology produces **false class consciousness**, a false picture of the nature of the relationship between social classes. Members of both classes tend to accept the status quo as normal and natural and are largely unaware of the true nature of exploitation and oppression. In this way the conflict of interest between the classes is disguised and a degree of social stability produced, but the basic contradictions and conflicts of class societies remain unresolved.

■ Class and social change

Class struggle

Marx believed that the **class struggle** was the driving force of social change. He stated that 'The history of all societies up to the present is the history of the class struggle.'

A new historical epoch is created by the development of superior forces of production by a new social group. These developments take place within the framework of the previous era. The merchants and industrialists who spearheaded the rise of capitalism emerged during the feudal era. They accumulated capital, laid the foundations for industrial manufacture, factory production and the system of wage labour, all of which were essential components of capitalism. The superiority of the capitalist mode of production led to a rapid transformation of the structure of society. The capitalist class became dominant, and although the feudal aristocracy maintained aspects of its power well into the nineteenth century, it was fighting a losing battle.

The class struggles of history have been between minorities. Capitalism, for instance, developed from the struggle between the feudal aristocracy and the emerging capitalist class, both groups in numerical terms forming a minority of the population. Major changes in history have involved the replacement of one form of private property by another, and of one type of production technique by another: capitalism involved the replacement of privately owned land and an agricultural economy by privately owned capital and an industrial economy.

Marx believed that the class struggle which would transform capitalist society would involve none of these processes. The protagonists would be the bourgeoisie and the proletariat, a minority versus a majority. Private property would be replaced by communally owned property. Industrial manufacture would remain as the basic technique of production in the society which would replace capitalism.

Marx believed that the basic contradictions contained in a capitalist economic system would lead to its eventual destruction. The proletariat would overthrow the bourgeoisie and seize the means of production, the source of power. Property would be communally owned and, since all members of society would now share the same relationship to the means of production, a **classless society** would result. Since history is the history of the class struggle, history would now end. The communist society which replaces capitalism will contain no contradictions, no conflicts of interest, and will therefore be unchanging. However, before the dawning of this utopia, certain changes must occur.

Class consciousness

Marx distinguished between a 'class in itself' and a 'class for itself'. A **class in itself** is simply a social group whose members share the same relationship to the means of production. Marx argues that a social group only fully becomes a class when it becomes a **class for itself**. At this stage its members have class consciousness and class solidarity. **Class consciousness** means that false class consciousness has been replaced by a full awareness of the true situation, by a realization of the nature of exploitation. Then members of a class develop a common identity, recognize their shared interests and unite, so producing **class solidarity**. The final stage of class consciousness and class solidarity is reached when members realize that only by **collective action** can they overthrow the ruling class and take positive steps to do so.

Marx believed that the following aspects of capitalist society would eventually lead to the proletariat developing into a class for itself.

1 Capitalist society is by its very nature unstable. It is based on contradictions and antagonisms which can only be resolved by its transformation. In particular, the conflict of interest between the bourgeoisie and the proletariat cannot be resolved within the framework of

a capitalist economy. The basic conflict of interest involves the exploitation of workers by the capitalists.

2 Marx believed that this first contradiction would be highlighted by a second: the contradiction between **social production** and **individual ownership**. As capitalism developed, the workforce was increasingly concentrated in large factories where production was a social enterprise. Social production juxtaposed with individual ownership illuminates the exploitation of the proletariat. Social production also makes it easier for workers to organize themselves against the capitalists. It facilitates communication and encourages a recognition of common circumstances and interests.

Polarization of the classes

Apart from the basic contradictions of capitalist society, Marx believed that certain factors in the natural development of a capitalist economy will hasten its downfall. These factors will result in the **polarization** of the two main classes: the gap between the proletariat and the bourgeoisie will become greater and the contrast between the two groups will become more stark. Such factors include:

1 First, the increasing use of machinery will result in a **homogeneous working class**. Since 'machinery obliterates the differences in labour' members of the proletariat will become increasingly similar. The differences between skilled, semi-skilled and unskilled workers will tend to disappear as machines remove the skill required in the production of commodities.

2 Second, the difference in wealth between the bourgeoisie and the proletariat will increase as the accumulation of capital proceeds. Even though the real wages and living standards of the proletariat may rise, its members will become poorer in relation to the bourgeoisie. This process is known as **pauperization**.

3 Third, the competitive nature of capitalism means that only the largest and most wealthy companies will survive and prosper. Competition will depress the intermediate strata, those groups lying between the two main classes, into the proletariat. Thus the **petty bourgeoisie**, the owners of small businesses, will 'sink into the proletariat'. At the same time the surviving companies will grow larger and capital will be concentrated into fewer hands.

These three processes – the obliteration of the differences in labour, the pauperization of the working class, and the depression of the intermediate strata into the proletariat – will result in the polarization of the two major classes.

Marx believed he could observe the process of polarization in nineteenth-century Britain when he wrote 'Society as a whole is more and more splitting into two great hostile camps . . . bourgeoisie and proletariat.' Now the battle lines were clearly drawn: Marx hoped that the proletarian revolution would shortly follow and the communist utopia of his dreams would finally become a reality.

Marx's work on class has been examined in detail for the following reasons.

1 Many sociologists claim that his theory still provides the best explanation of the nature of class in capitalist society.

2 Much of the research on class has been inspired by ideas and questions raised by Marx.

3 Many of the concepts of class analysis introduced by Marx have proved useful to Marxists and non-Marxists alike.

4 And, as T.B. Bottomore writing in 1965 noted, 'For the past eighty years Marx's theory has been the object of unrelenting criticism and tenacious defence.' This observation remains true today.

■ Social stratification – a Weberian perspective

The work of the German sociologist Max Weber (1864–1920) represents one of the most important developments in stratification theory since Marx. Weber believed that social stratification results from a struggle for scarce resources in society. Although he saw this struggle as being primarily concerned with economic resources, it can also involve struggles for prestige and for political power.

Market situation

Like Marx, Weber saw class in economic terms. He argued that classes develop in market economies in which individuals compete for economic gain. He defined a class as a group of individuals who share a similar position in a market economy and by virtue of that fact receive similar economic rewards. Thus in Weber's terminology, a person's 'class situation' is basically their 'market situation'. Those who share a similar class situation also share similar life chances. Their economic position will directly affect their chances of obtaining those things defined as desirable in their society, for example access to higher education and good quality housing.

Like Marx, Weber argued that the major class division is between those who own the forces of production and those who do not. Thus those who have substantial property holdings will receive the highest economic rewards and enjoy superior life chances. However, Weber saw important differences in the market situation of the propertyless groups in society. In particular the various skills and services offered by different occupations have differing market values. For instance, in capitalist society, managers, administrators and professionals receive relatively high salaries because of the demand for their services. Weber distinguished the following class groupings in capitalist society:

1 the propertied upper class;
2 the propertyless white-collar workers;
3 the petty bourgeoisie;
4 the manual working class.

In his analysis of class, Weber disagreed with Marx on a number of important issues.

1 Factors other than the ownership or non-ownership of property are significant in the formation of classes. In particular, the market value of the skills of the propertyless varies and the resulting differences in economic return are sufficient to produce different social classes.

2 Weber saw no evidence to support the idea of the polarization of classes. Although he saw some decline in the numbers of the petty bourgeoisie (the small property owners) due to competition from large companies, he argued that they enter white-collar or skilled manual trades rather than being depressed into the ranks of unskilled manual workers. More importantly, Weber argued that the white-collar 'middle class' expands rather than contracts as capitalism develops. He maintained that capitalist enterprises and the modern nation state require a 'rational' bureaucratic administration which involves large numbers of administrators and clerical staff. (We outline Weber's views on bureaucratic administration in Chapter 7, pp. 406–11.) Thus Weber saw a diversification of classes and an expansion of the white-collar middle class, rather than a polarization.

3 Weber rejected the view, held by some Marxists, of the inevitability of the proletarian revolution. He saw no reason why those sharing a similar class situation should necessarily develop a common identity, recognize shared interests and take collective action to further those interests. For example, Weber suggested that individual manual workers who are dissatisfied with their class situation may respond in a variety of ways. They may grumble, work to rule, sabotage industrial machinery, take strike action or attempt to organize other members of their class in an effort to overthrow capitalism. Weber admitted that a common market situation might provide a basis for collective class action but he saw this only as a possibility.

4 Weber rejected the Marxist view that political power necessarily derives from economic power. He argues that class forms only one possible basis for power and that the distribution of power in society is not necessarily linked to the distribution of class inequalities.

Status situation

While class forms one possible basis for group formation, collective action and the acquisition of political power, Weber argued that there are other bases for these activities. In particular, groups form because their members share a similar **status situation**. Whereas class refers to the unequal distribution of economic rewards, status refers to the unequal distribution of 'social honour'.

Occupations, ethnic and religious groups, and most importantly lifestyles, are accorded differing degrees of prestige or esteem by members of society. A status group is made up of individuals who are awarded a similar amount of social honour and therefore share the same status situation. Unlike classes, members of status groups are almost always aware of their common status situation. They share a similar lifestyle, identify with and feel they belong to their status group, and often place restrictions on the ways in which outsiders may interact with them.

Weber argued that status groups reach their most developed form in the caste system of traditional Hindu society in India. Castes and sub-castes were formed and distinguished largely in terms of social honour; lifestyles were sharply differentiated and accorded varying degrees of prestige.

Social closure

Castes also provide a good example of the process described by Weber as **social closure**. Social closure involves the exclusion of some people from membership of a status group. In the caste system social closure is achieved through prohibitions which prevent members of a caste from marrying outside their caste. The caste system is an extreme example of social closure since the exclusion of outsiders from the status group is so complete.

Other status groups erect less formidable barriers to entry. In modern Britain studies of **elite self-recruitment** suggest that certain types of job, such as senior positions in the Civil Service, are usually filled by those who have attended public school. Although individuals who went to state schools have some chance of entering these jobs, public school educated elites largely reserve such positions for themselves and their children's group. (For details of elite self-recruitment see pp. 518-2.)

Class and status groups

In many societies class and status situations are closely linked. Weber noted that 'Property as such is not always recognized as a status qualification, but in the long run it is, and with extraordinary regularity.' However, those who share the same class situation will not necessarily belong to the same status group. For example the *nouveaux riches* (the newly rich) are sometimes excluded from the status groups of the privileged because their tastes, manners and dress are defined as vulgar.

Status groups may create divisions within classes. In a study of Banbury, conducted in the 1950s, Margaret Stacey found that members of the manual working class distinguished three status groups within that class: the 'respectable working class', the 'ordinary working class' and the 'rough working class'. Economic factors influenced the formation of these groups – for example

the 'roughs' were often in the lowest income bracket – but they did not determine status since the income of many 'roughs' was similar to that of members of other status groups.

Status groups can also cut across class divisions. In the USA, blacks, no matter what their class situation, belong to the same status group. This can form the basis for collective political action: in the 1960s and 1970s many middle- and working-class blacks united in various organizations under the banner of the Black Power movement.

Weber's observations on status groups are important since they suggest that in certain situations status rather than class provides the basis for the formation of social groups whose members perceive common interests and a group identity. In addition, the presence of different status groups within a single class and of status groups which cut across class divisions can weaken class solidarity and reduce the potential for class consciousness. These points are illustrated by Weber's analysis of 'parties'.

Parties

Weber defined **parties** as groups which are specifically concerned with influencing policies and making decisions in the interests of their membership. In Weber's words parties are concerned with 'the acquisition of social "power"'.

Parties include a variety of associations from the mass political parties of Western democracies to the whole range of pressure or interest groups which include professional associations, trades unions, the Automobile Association and the RSPCA. Parties often, but not necessarily, represent the interests of classes or status groups. In Weber's words, 'Parties may represent interests determined through "class situation" or "status situation".... In most cases they are partly class parties and partly status parties, but sometimes they are neither.'

The combination of class and status interests can be seen in the various Black Power organizations in the USA. They represent a status group but they also represent class interests. The majority of blacks are working class and many black organizations are directly concerned with improving their class situation.

Weber's view of parties suggests that the relationship between political groups and class and status groups is far from clearcut. Just as status groups can both divide classes and cut across class boundaries, so parties can divide and cut across both classes and status groups. Weber's analysis of classes, status groups and parties suggests that no single theory can pinpoint and explain their relationship. The interplay of class, status and party in the formation of social groups is complex and variable and must be examined in particular societies during particular time periods.

Marx attempted to reduce all forms of inequality to social class and argued that classes formed the only significant social groups in society. Weber argues that the evidence provides a more complex and diversified picture of social stratification.

■ Modern theories of stratification

Most contemporary studies of stratification are based either upon a Marxist or a Weberian perspective.

Some modern sociologists have remained close to the original theories of Marx and Weber. Others have drawn their inspiration from one or other of these classic sociologists, but have made significant alterations to their original theories in an attempt to describe and explain the class structures of capitalist industrial societies. Such sociologists can be referred to as new, or neo-Marxists and neo-Weberians.

There has been a long-standing debate between those who draw their inspiration from Marx, and those who follow Weber, as to which approach is more useful as a way of developing a sociological understanding of class. We will analyse this debate in later sections of this chapter when we deal with the different classes in contemporary capitalism. Contemporary neo-Marxist and neo-Weberian theories of the class structure as a whole will also be examined towards the end of the chapter. In the next section, however, we will consider how the stratification system has changed over time in British society.

■ Changes in the British stratification system

As we discovered in the previous section, most contemporary theories of stratification have been influenced by the pioneering work of Marx or Weber. Despite the differences between these sociologists, both gave primary importance to material inequalities. Marx saw the most important divisions in any system of stratification as stemming from differences in the ownership of wealth, and specifically ownership of the means of production. Weber also saw ownership of wealth as an important criterion for distinguishing classes. Weber, however, placed more emphasis than Marx on divisions within the propertyless class, the class whose members did not own sufficient property to support themselves without working. For this group income levels and other life chances depended largely upon the market situation of the occupational group to which the individuals belonged.

No system of class stratification is fixed and static. The distribution of resources within the class system constantly changes and the size and market situation of occupational groups also alters over time. The next sections will describe some of the broad patterns of change in the composition of the occupational structure and the distribution of income and wealth in Britain in the twentieth century. Later sections will examine the changing position of particular classes in more detail.

■ Changes in the occupational structure

Sociologists from Marx and Weber onwards have debated how best to define social classes. Many, though not all, now base their class categories, at least partly, upon occupational groupings. Official government statistics distinguish between **socio-economic groups**, which, it is claimed, bring together 'people with jobs with similar social and economic status'.

Although there are disagreements about where the boundary between the middle and working classes should be placed, it has often been the case that manual workers are regarded as being working class, and non-manual workers as middle class. In official publications types of **manual job** are usually distinguished according to levels of skill, with separate categories being used for the **unskilled, semi-skilled** and **skilled manual** worker. Non-manual jobs are also usually divided into three categories: **routine non-manual jobs** include clerical and secretarial work; **intermediate non-manual** jobs such as teachers, nurses, librarians and some managers; and the highest class in this scheme, which includes **professionals**, such as doctors and accountants, as well as senior managers.

Although calculated in different ways, Tables 2.1 and 2.2 are both based upon the idea of socio-economic grouping. Table 2.1 shows changes in the occupational structure between 1911 and 1971. Table 2.2 is calculated on a different basis but shows changes between 1975 and 1991. (Table 2.2 includes personal service workers in the same category as semi-skilled manual and so includes a wider range of workers in the lower classes than Table 2.1.)

The shift to non-manual employment

The information contained in the following tables shows that there has been a long-term trend this century for the proportion of non-manual jobs to increase, and of manual jobs to decrease. Less than half of all employees now have manual jobs, whereas in 1911, according to Routh, 79 per cent of jobs were manual. There have been marked increases in professional, managerial, and routine non-manual work.

Over the course of this century various factors have contributed to the shift towards non-manual employment. Manufacturing industry has declined, whilst service industries, which employ a lower proportion of manual workers, have expanded. Between June 1971 and June 1993 the number employed in manufacturing industries fell by over three and a half million, while the number employed in service industries rose by

over three million. In 1986 25 per cent of employees worked in manufacturing; by 1993 this had declined to 20 per cent. Over the same period the proportion employed in services rose from 67 to 71 per cent.

Since the Second World War increasing numbers of people have been employed in jobs connected to the welfare state, particularly in the National Health Service (NHS), education and the welfare services. Employment has also expanded in local and national government. However, government policies since the late 1980s have reduced employment in local government and the civil service as a number of government functions have been privatized. Employment in local government services, for example, fell by about one-third between 1987 and 1993. Most of the recent increases in non-manual work have come from the private sector. Between 1987 and 1993 employment in Great Britain increased by more than 300,000 in banking, finance and insurance, and more than 200,000 in business services.

Gender, full-time and part-time work

Women, particularly married women, have increasingly started taking paid employment this century, but they are not equally distributed throughout the occupational structure. Although women are more likely to have non-manual jobs than men, most female non-manual workers are concentrated in the lowest-paid sectors of non-manual work and have routine non-manual jobs. As Table 2.2 shows, 48 per cent of female employees were in intermediate and junior non-manual jobs in 1991. Most of the remaining female employees (33 per cent) were in semi-skilled or unskilled manual work or personal service jobs.

Table 2.3 shows male and female employment in both part-time and full-time employment. It reveals a number of significant trends.

Between 1984 and 1993 male full-time employment declined (although part-time employment for men increased a little), while female full-time and part-time employment both increased significantly. The traditional male 'breadwinner' with a full-time job is a declining group in the workforce. Women make up a growing proportion of the workforce and are rapidly catching up men. Traditionally studies of class have concentrated on male full-time

Table 2.1 Occupational class and industrial status of the gainfully occupied population in Great Britain, 1911, 1921, 1931, 1951, 1971: numbers in thousands

	All					Males					Females				
	1911	1921	1931	1951	1971	1911	1921	1931	1951	1971	1911	1921	1931	1951	1971
1 Professional															
A Higher															
Employers	—	25	38	34	79	—	25	37	33	75	—	—	—	1	4
Own account	—	36	44	44	59	—	35	41	40	53	—	2	3	4	7
Employees	—	134	158	356	687	—	126	144	326	646	—	8	15	31	40
All	184	195	240	434	824	173	186	222	399	774	11	10	18	36	50
%	1.00	1.01	1.14	1.93	3.29	1.34	1.36	1.50	2.56	4.87	0.20	0.18	0.29	0.52	0.55
B Lower															
Employers	—	18	15	10	25	—	14	8	7	17	—	4	7	3	7
Own account	—	62	70	42	59	—	20	22	22	37	—	42	48	20	22
Employees	—	600	643	1,007	1,863	—	242	270	463	892	—	357	373	544	971
All	560	680	728	1,059	1,946	208	276	300	492	946	352	403	428	567	1,000
%	3.05	3.52	3.46	4.70	7.78	1.61	2.02	2.03	3.16	5.95	6.49	7.07	6.83	8.18	10.95
2 Employers, administrators, managers															
A Employers and proprietors															
Employers	763	692	727	457	621	661	613	646	400	485	102	79	82	56	136
Own account	469	626	682	661	435	339	435	483	494	320	130	191	196	167	115
All	1,232	1,318	1,409	1,118	1,056	1,000	1,048	1,129	894	805	232	270	278	223	251
%	6.71	6.82	6.70	4.97	4.22	7.74	7.69	7.65	5.74	5.07	4.28	4.74	4.44	3.22	2.75
B Managers and administrators															
Own account	21	29	30	31	46	20	27	28	27	35	2	2	2	3	11
Employees	608	675	740	1,215	2,008	486	557	642	1029	1,698	123	118	98	186	310
All	629	704	770	1,246	2,054	506	584	670	1,056	1,733	125	120	100	189	321
%	3.43	3.64	3.66	5.53	8.21	3.91	4.28	4.54	6.78	10.91	2.30	2.11	1.60	2.73	3.51
3 Clerical workers															
Own account	—	1	2	3	22	—	1	2	2	5	—	—	—	1	17
Employees	887	1,299	1,463	2,401	3,457	708	735	815	988	1,008	179	564	648	1,413	2,449
All	887	1,300	1,465	2,404	3,479	708	736	817	990	1,013	179	564	648	1,414	2,466
%	4.84	6.72	6.97	10.68	13.90	5.48	5.40	5.53	6.35	6.38	3.30	9.90	10.34	20.41	27.00
4 Foremen, inspectors, supervisors															
Employees	236	279	323	590	968	227	261	295	511	801	10	18	28	79	168
%	1.29	1.44	1.54	2.62	3.87	1.75	1.91	2.00	3.28	5.04	0.18	0.32	0.45	1.14	1.84
Manual workers															
5 Skilled															
Own account	329	293	268	251	349	170	205	200	214	324	159	88	68	37	25
Employees	5,279	5,280	5,351	5,365	5,045	4,094	4,200	4,223	4,519	4,295	1,185	1,080	1,128	847	750
All	5,608	5,573	5,619	5,616	5,394	4,264	4,405	4,423	4,733	4,619	1,344	1,168	1,196	884	775
%	30.56	28.83	26.72	24.95	21.56	32.99	32.30	29.96	30.36	29.08	24.78	20.50	19.09	12.75	8.48
6 Semi-skilled															
Own account	71	98	96	82	53	41	70	78	73	35	30	28	17	10	18
Employees	7,173	6,446	7,264	7,256	6,258	4,305	3,789	4,181	4,279	3,272	2,868	2,656	3,084	2,978	2,986
All	7,244	6,544	7,360	7,338	6,312	4,346	3,859	4,259	4,352	3,307	2,898	2,684	3,101	2,988	3,005
%	39.48	33.85	35.00	32.60	25.23	33.63	28.30	28.85	27.92	20.82	53.42	47.11	49.51	43.12	32.90
7 Unskilled															
Own account	47	62	78	33	92	38	48	65	29	86	9	14	13	3	6
Employees	1,720	2.678	3,034	2,676	2,895	1,455	2,232	2,580	2,129	1,803	265	446	454	547	1,092
All	1,767	2,740	3,115	2,709	2,987	1,493	2,280	2,645	2,158	1,889	274	460	467	550	1,098
%	9.63	14.17	14.81	12.03	11.94	11.55	16.72	17.92	13.84	11.89	5.05	8.07	7.45	7.94	12.02
All	18,347	19,333	21,029	22,514	25,021	12,925	13,636	14,761	15,584	15,884	5,425	5,697	6,264	6,930	9,138
%	100.00	100.00	100.00	100.00	100.00	100.00	100.00	100.00	100.00	100.00	100.00	100.00	100.00	100.00	100.00

Note: Because numbers are rounded to the nearest thousand, totals may not equal the sum of their parts.

(*Source*: Routh, G (1980). *Occupation and Pay in Great Britain 1906–79*, Macmillan, London and Basingstoke, pp. 6, 7.)

Table 2.2 **Socio-economic group by sex: 1975 to 1991** (All persons aged 16 and over, Great Britain)

Socio economic-group*	1975 %	1977 %	1979 %	1981 %	1983 %	1985 %	1987 %	1989 %	1990 %	1991 %
Men										
Professional	5	5	6	4	5	6	7	7	7	7
Employers and managers	15	15	15	15	17	19	19	20	20	19
Intermediate and junior non-manual	17	17	17	17	15	17	16	16	17	17
Skilled manual and own account non-professional	41	41	40	41	39	37	37	38	37	38
Semi-skilled manual and personal service	17	17	17	18	18	16	15	15	14	14
Unskilled manual	5	5	5	5	5	5	5	5	4	5
Base = 100%	**10,902**	**10,696**	**10,280**	**10,880**	**8,886**	**8,787**	**9,190**	**8,815**	**8,211**	**8,596**
Women										
Professional	1	1	1	1	1	1	1	1	1	1
Employers and managers	4	4	5	5	6	7	8	9	9	9
Intermediate and junior non-manual	46	46	45	46	46	48	47	47	49	48
Skilled manual and own account non-professional	9	9	9	9	9	9	9	9	9	9
Semi-skilled manual and personal service	31	30	30	29	30	27	26	25	25	22
Unskilled manual	9	10	10	10	9	7	9	8	8	11
Base = 100%	**11,799**	**11,514**	**11,102**	**11,743**	**9,754**	**9,439**	**9,976**	**9,600**	**9,061**	**9,254**
Total										
Professional	3	3	3	2	3	3	4	4	4	4
Employers and managers	9	9	10	9	11	13	14	14	14	14
Intermediate and junior non-manual	32	32	32	32	31	33	32	32	34	33
Skilled manual and own account non-professional	24	24	24	24	24	23	23	23	22	23
Semi-skilled manual and personal service	24	23	24	24	24	22	21	20	20	18
Unskilled manual	7	8	8	8	7	6	7	7	6	8
Base = 100%	**22,701**	**22,210**	**21,382**	**22,623**	**18,640**	**18,226**	**19,166**	**18,415**	**17,272**	**17,850**

*The socio-economic group shown is based on the informant's own job (or last job if not in employment).
Excluding those in the Armed Forces and any who have never worked.

(*Source:* Bridgewood, A. and Savage, D. (1993) *General Household Survey 1991*, Office of Population, Censuses and Surveys, London.)

workers. The changes outlined here indicate that this is becoming more and more unjustifiable.

The changing distribution of income

The importance of income

Some sociologists have argued that inequalities in industrial societies are being progressively reduced; others go further and claim that class divisions are disappearing. Income has an important effect upon your life chances: for example the chance of owning your own home and your life expectancy. If income inequalities were gradually disappearing this would be strong evidence that class divisions were weakening.

Some government policies seem designed to achieve greater income equality by redistributing income from more affluent to poorer groups. However, as we will see in the following sections, income can be measured in various ways and

Table 2.3 Full- and part-time[1] employment[2] in the UK: by sex

	Males (thousands)		Females (thousands)	
	Full-time	Part-time	Full-time	Part-time
1984	13,240	570	5,422	4,343
1985	13,336	575	5,503	4,457
1986	13,430	647	5,662	4,566
1987	13,472	750	5,795	4,696
1988	13,881	801	6,069	4,808
1989	14,071	734	6,336	4,907
1990	14,109	789	6,479	4,928
1991	13,686	799	6,350	4,933
1992	13,141	885	6,244	5,081
1993	12,769	886	6,165	5,045

[1] Full/part-time is based on respondents' self-assessment. Excludes those who did not state whether they were full or part-time.

[2] At Spring each year, includes employees, self-employed, those on government training schemes and unpaid family workers.

(*Source:* (1994) *Social Trends*, HMSO, London, 1994, p. 59.)

official statistics should be used with caution. In addition, it should not be assumed that long-term trends in income distribution continue forever: there is evidence that recent years have seen significant changes in these trends in Britain.

The measurement of income distribution

Official statistics measure income in a variety of ways.

1 **Original income** refers to income from sources such as employment, occupational pensions, gifts, alimony payments, and investment. Figures on original income do not include benefits such as state pensions, family credit, and income support, which are paid by the state.

2 **Gross income** is a measure of all sources of income. Most individuals are not, however, free to spend all of their gross income, for some is deducted to pay income tax and national insurance contributions.

3 **Disposable income** is a measure of gross income less the above deductions.

4 Some taxes (indirect taxes) are not paid directly out of income, but are paid by consumers as part of the purchase price of goods. For example, value added tax (VAT), is payable on most categories of goods. Duties

are also payable on products such as petrol, tobacco and alcohol. **Post-tax income** is the measure of income after the above taxes, and taxes such as the Council Tax, are deducted.

5 **Final income** adds on to income after taxes the value of benefits provided by the state which are not given in cash, for example medical care and education.

By examining these different measures it is possible to discover the effects of government policy on the distribution of income. Table 2.4 gives figures for 1991, and is based upon the Family Expenditure Survey.

The effects of taxation and benefits

Table 2.4 demonstrates that even after taxation and benefits are taken into account, considerable income inequalities remain. In 1991 the poorest 20 per cent of households received less than half the average final income, whilst the richest 20 per cent received nearly twice the national average. However, it is clear that benefits help to reduce income inequality. In particular, benefits boost the very low original income of the poorest 20 per cent of households. Overall taxation and benefits also reduce the final income of richer groups in the population, but less than the higher rates of income tax for high earners would suggest. This is partly because poorer groups in the population tend to pay a higher proportion of their income in indirect taxes than richer ones.

The official government figures need to be treated with some caution. Only about 70 per cent of households approached agreed to participate in the Family Expenditure Survey. Furthermore, there is no guarantee that the information obtained is entirely reliable. Individuals may not declare all their income, particularly if they have not been truthful to the Inland Revenue or the DSS. The figures may be particularly prone to underestimating the income of the highest earners, who have more opportunities to hide substantial amounts of income than middle- and lower-income groups.

Trends in income distribution

Despite the limitations of the official figures, they do provide some indication of the overall historical trends in the distribution of income. In 1979 the

Table 2.4   Redistribution of income in the UK through taxes and benefits[1], 1991

	Quntile groups of households ranked by equivalized disposable income[2]					£ per year
	Bottom fifth	Next fifth	Middle fifth	Next fifth	Top fifth	All households
Average per household (£ per year[2])						
Earnings of main earner	1,000	3,870	8,880	13,400	23,990	10,230
Earnings of others in the household	90	610	2,440	5,060	7,640	3,170
Occupational pensions, annuities	200	570	990	1,190	1,550	900
Investment income	180	420	740	1,170	3,630	1,230
Other income	100	180	250	290	400	240
Total original income	1,570	5,650	13,310	21,100	37,220	15,770
plus Benefits in cash						
Contributory	1,920	1,990	1,350	840	560	1,330
Non-contributory	1,970	1,530	970	530	330	1,060
Gross income	5,460	9,170	15,630	22,470	38,110	18,170
less income tax[3] and NIC[4]	200	780	2,140	3,830	7,660	2,920
less Community charge[5] (gross)	540	580	660	680	680	620
Disposable income	4,730	7,820	12,830	17,960	29,790	14,620
less indirect taxes	1,320	1,870	2,920	3,690	4,470	2,860
Post-tax income	3,410	5,940	9,900	14,270	25,320	11,750
plus Benefits in kind						
Education	1,090	900	1,190	890	560	920
National Health Service	1,480	1,410	1,280	1,120	940	1,250
Housing subsidy	140	120	50	30	10	70
Travel subsidies	50	50	50	60	90	60
School meals and welfare milk	70	30	20	10	10	30
Final income	6,230	8,450	12,500	16,380	26,910	14,090

[1] Redistribution of income for definitions of the income measures.

[2] Equivalized disposable income has been used for ranking the households into quintile groups.

[3] After tax relief at source on mortgage interest and life assurance premiums.

[4] Employees' national insurance contributions.

[5] Rates in Northern Ireland.

(*Source:* (1994) *Social Trends,* HMSO, London, 1994, p. 76.)

Royal Commission on the Distribution of Income and Wealth published a report examining the changes in the distribution of income and wealth between 1949 and 1978–9. The results relating to income are summarized in Table 2.5.

Table 2.5 demonstrates that in the period covered there was some income redistribution, but mainly towards middle income groups rather than those on the lowest levels. The top 10 per cent of income earners reduced their share of total income by 3.7 per cent, but the bottom 30 per cent also had their share reduced, in this case by 2.5 per cent. Although there was a slight shift in income distribution – from the top half of income earners to the bottom half – the poorest were not the beneficiaries.

Changes in taxation

The Royal Commission report was published in the same year as Margaret Thatcher's Conservative Government came to power. Successive Conservative governments implemented policies which reversed the slight trend for income redistribution to poorer groups. The policies which had the most direct impact concerned income tax.

Table 2.5   Distribution of income in the UK before and after tax, 1949–1978/79

	Percentage share of total income					
	Before tax			After tax		
	Top 10%	Next 60%	Bottom 30%	Top 10%	Next 60%	Bottom 30%
1949	33.2	54.1	12.7	27.1	58.3	14.6
1954	29.8	59.3	10.9	24.8	63.1	12.1
1959	29.4	60.9	9.7	25.2	63.5	11.2
1964	29.0	61.4	9.6	25.1	64.1	10.8
1967	28.0	61.6	10.4	24.3	63.7	12.0
1973–74	26.8	62.3	10.9	23.6	63.6	12.8
1978–79	26.1	63.5	10.4	23.4	64.5	12.1

(*Source*: A.B. Atkinson, *The Economics of Inequality*, Oxford University Press, 1983, p. 63.)

Income tax is a **progressive tax** because higher earners pay a higher proportion of their income in this tax than lower earners. If overall levels of income tax are cut, and if the higher rates in particular are reduced, the redistributive effects of taxation become smaller. Between 1979 and 1988 the basic rate of this tax was reduced from 33 to 25 per cent, while the highest rate fell from 80 to 40 per cent. In 1992 a lower-rate band of 20 per cent was introduced on the first £2,000 of taxable income; it was widened to £3,000 in April 1994. By the early 1990s the Government was running into problems financing government spending and was forced to raise some taxes. Although most of the extra revenue needed was raised through increases in indirect tax, there was an increase in national insurance contributions of 1 per cent in 1994. National insurance contributions are effectively a form of direct tax.

Since 1979 there has been a distinct shift towards indirect taxation, which tends to take a greater proportion of the income of lower than higher income groups. In 1979 the twin VAT rates of 8 and 12.5 per cent were replaced with a single rate of 15 per cent. In 1991 this was raised again to 17.5 per cent.

In March 1993 it was announced that VAT would be extended to include domestic fuel. Other important types of indirect tax are the duties levied on petrol, alcohol and tobacco. The Institute for Fiscal Studies has calculated that since 1985 with the inclusion of these rises and after allowing for inflation there would be increases in the real level of duty on petrol and tobacco but the duties on alcohol would fall.

There have also been important changes in local taxes used to finance local government. In 1990 the community charge, or 'poll tax', replaced rates. This meant that the taxation system in Britain became more **regressive**, since all those living in particular areas were charged the same, regardless of their ability to pay. Even though there were rebates on the community charge of up to 80 per cent for the poorest, previously the worst-off could claim a full 100 per cent rebate on rates. This tax proved extremely unpopular and in 1993 it was replaced by the rather less regressive council tax. This went back to basing local taxes on the value of property.

Figures from the Central Statistical Office suggest that some of the changes implemented by Conservative governments helped to reverse the trend in redistribution of income from the rich, so that it became redistribution to the rich. Between 1976 and 1986 the top 20 per cent of income earners increased their share of total final income from 37.9 to 41.7 per cent, while the share of the bottom 20 per cent fell from 7.4 to 5.9 per cent. Furthermore, these figures refer to the period before the top rate of income tax was reduced from 60 to 40 per cent, and the poll tax was introduced. Government figures also show that between 1979 and 1991 the net income after housing costs of the poorest 20 per cent in the population fell by 3 per cent between 1979 and 1990–91. Over the same period the richest 20 per cent saw their net income after housing costs rise by over 35 per cent.

Figure 2.1 shows the effects of tax changes on the proportions of their income paid in tax by different groups in the population. The population is

Figure 2.1 Proportions of income taken in personal tax, by decile

Burden of taxes

☐ Tax 1985 ■ Tax 1995
▬ Change in tax burden

(*Source*: Giles, C. and Johnson, P. (1994) *Taxes Down, Taxes Up: The Effects of a Decade of Tax Changes*, The Institute for Fiscal Studies, London, p. 20.)

divided into ten groups ranked according to level of income. Decile 1 represents the 10 per cent of the population with the lowest income; decile 10 the 10 per cent with the highest. The figure shows that between 1985 and 1995 taxation changes continued to favour the better off. The poorest 50 per cent of the population of Britain saw its taxes rise while the richest 50 per cent saw its taxes cut.

Although income inequalities have been reduced in Britain this century, this reduction has not been sufficient to justify the claim that class divisions are disappearing. The figures suggest that the 1980s and the first half of the 1990s saw an increase in income inequality and a strengthening of class divisions.

■ The changing distribution of wealth?

The importance of wealth

Inequalities in the distribution of wealth, like inequalities in the distribution of income, are an important indicator of class divisions and class inequality. A particular form of wealth – the means of production – is especially important to Marxist sociologists. Like income, wealth can affect life chances but to Marxists, ownership of the means of production also gives power. (Today ownership of the means of production usually takes the form of share ownership.)

If it could be shown that over the years there had been a major redistribution of wealth from the rich to the poor, this would indicate a reduction in class inequalities. However, wealth is perhaps even more difficult to measure than income and reliable data prove elusive.

Measuring wealth

The definition and measurement of wealth, like income, is not straightforward. One problem is that the Government does not collect information on wealth for tax purposes. There is no wealth tax on the living, but taxes do have to be paid on the estates of those who have died. Figures on the value of estates left by the deceased are sometimes used to calculate the overall distribution of wealth. However, they may not be a reliable guide to the distribution of wealth among the living: for instance individuals may transfer some of their wealth to other family members before they die. Moreover those who die tend to be older than other members of the population, and wealth is not equally distributed between age groups.

Another method of collecting information on wealth distribution is to use survey research, but this too has its drawbacks. Those who refuse to cooperate with the research may be untypical of the population as a whole, and their failure to take part may distort the findings. Those who do cooperate may not be entirely honest, and the richest members of society may be particularly prone to underestimating their wealth.

Defining wealth

Not only is wealth difficult to measure, defining it is also problematic. Official statistics distinguish between marketable wealth and non-marketable wealth.

1 **Marketable wealth** includes any type of asset that can be sold and its value realized. It therefore includes land, shares, savings in bank, building society or other accounts, homes (minus any outstanding mortgage

Table 2.6 The distribution of private property, from 1911 to 1960

Groups within adult population (aged 25+) owning stated proportions of aggregate personal wealth	Estimated proportion of aggregate personal wealth Period 1911–60 (common basis)				
	1911–13 %	1924–30 %	1936–38 %	1954 %	1960 %
Richest 1% owned	69	62	56	43	42
Richest 5% owned	87	84	79	71	75
Richest 10% owned	92	91	88	79	83
Hence:					
Richest 1% owned	69	62	56	43	42
Next 2–5% owned	18	22	23	28	33
Next 6–10% owned	5	7	9	8	8
95% owned only	13	16	21	29	25
90% owned only	8	9	12	21	17

(*Source:* J. Westergaard and H. Resler, *Class in a Capitalist Society*, 1976, p. 112.)

Table 2.7 The distribution of wealth[1] in the UK 1976 to 1991

	Percentages and £ billion			
	1976	1981	1986	1991
Marketable wealth				
Percentage of wealth owned by[2]				
Most wealthy 1%	21	18	18	18
Most wealthy 5%	38	36	36	37
Most wealthy 10%	50	50	50	50
Most wealthy 25%	71	73	73	71
Most wealthy 50%	92	92	90	92
Total marketable wealth (£ billion)	280	565	955	1694

[1] Estimates for 1976, 1981 and 1986 are based on the estates of persons dying in those years. Estimates for 1991 are based on estates notified for probate in 1991–92. Estimates are not strictly comparable between 1991 and earlier years.
[2] Percentages and total marketable wealth are of population aged 18 and over.

(*Source:* Inland Revenue.)

debts), and personal possessions such as cars, works of art, and household appliances. The figures on marketable wealth exclude the value of occupational pensions which cannot normally be sold. If such pensions are included in the figures, the statistics show wealth as being more equally distributed than is otherwise the case.

2 Non-marketable wealth includes items such as salaries and non-transferable pensions.

From a sociological point of view the official figures on wealth are not ideal. They fail to distinguish between wealth used to finance production and wealth used to finance consumption. Wealth used for production (for example shares) is of particular interest to Marxist sociologists as they believe that power largely derives from ownership of the means of production. The distribution of wealth used for consumption is of less interest to Marxists, though its distribution does give some indication of lifestyle. Such figures are also useful for indicating the distribution of various life chances, for instance the chance that different social groups have of owning their own home.

Trends in wealth distribution

Despite the limitations of the available figures, it is possible to discern overall trends in wealth distribution this century. Table 2.6 shows trends between 1911 and 1960. Table 2.7 shows trends between 1976 and 1991. The figures in the two tables are not strictly comparable since they are calculated on a different basis. The figures in Table 2.6 include an estimate for hidden wealth; those in Table 2.7 do not. The later figures may therefore underestimate the extent to which wealth is concentrated. Furthermore the 1991 figure in Table 2.7 is based on estates notified for probate in 1991–2, whereas the other figures in that table are based on the estates of people dying in those years. Therefore the last figure in Table 2.7 cannot be directly compared with the earlier figures.

Table 2.6 suggests that there has been a considerable reduction in the degree of wealth inequality this century. The changes have clearly been more marked than the changes in the distribution of income. Table 2.7 shows that the trend towards greater equality of wealth distribution continued until the 1980s when it came to a virtual halt. Although the long-term trend is towards greater equality, most wealth still remains concentrated in the hands of a small minority. Thus in 1991 the wealthiest 1 per cent of the population still owned 18 per cent of all marketable wealth and the wealthiest 10 per cent owned 50 per cent, leaving the other 90 per cent of the population to share the other half between them.

A number of factors have contributed to the trends noted above. Westergaard and Resler (who produced the figures for the period up to 1960 in Table 2.6) suggest that the most significant redistribution was within the wealthiest groups, rather than between them and the less well-off. A major reason for this was the transfer of assets from wealthy individuals to friends and other family members in order to avoid death duties.

In recent decades the most important factor has probably been the increasing number of home owners. This is supported by official figures which show that wealth is more unequally distributed when dwellings are excluded. For instance, excluding dwellings in 1991, the richest 1 per cent of the population owned 28 per cent of marketable wealth and the most wealthy 10 per cent owned 63 per cent. Rising living standards for those in work have also enabled many people to buy more consumer goods. Thus most of the redistribution of wealth has probably affected wealth used for consumption rather than for production.

Share ownership

Shares are a particularly important type of wealth used to finance production. In Britain there has certainly been an increase in recent years in the percentage of the population who own shares. Westergaard and Resler estimated that in 1970 only 7 per cent of adults over the age of twenty-five

owned shares. In contrast, a survey conducted in 1988 by the Treasury and the Stock Exchange found that about 21 per cent of the population owned shares. Government figures suggest there was a peak of around eleven million shareholders in 1990. An NOP (National Opinion Polls) survey conducted for the Treasury put the number of shareholders at ten million in 1993.

Much of the increase in share ownership was due to the Government's privatization programme, which encouraged small investors to buy shares in companies such as British Telecom and British Gas. However, most new shareholders have only a small stake in the companies in which they have invested, and in reality they may have little influence upon the way that the companies are run. Most privately owned shares remain in the hands of a small minority of the population.

In addition, as indicated above, since 1990 the numbers of people owning shares has fallen slightly as the privatization programme has slowed down. Furthermore, fewer and fewer shares are owned by private individuals as an increasing proportion come to be owned by institutions. The stockbrokers Phillips & Drew estimated that between 1979 and 1989 the proportion of shares in private hands fell from 33 to 18 per cent.

Wealth taxes

Successive governments in Britain have made much less attempt to tax wealth than income. Before 1974 the main tax on wealth was estate duty, paid on the estate of someone who had died. It was easy to avoid this tax by transferring assets before death. In 1974 the Labour Government introduced capital transfer tax which taxed certain gifts given by people who were alive. In 1981 the Conservative Government abolished capital transfer tax and replaced it with inheritance tax. This raised the limits before which tax on wealth transfers were paid, and abolished taxes on gifts made ten years or more before someone died. In 1986 this period was reduced to seven years and a sliding scale was introduced to determine the amount of tax paid. The longer people survived after giving assets to someone the less tax they paid on the gift. These changes have reduced the burden of taxation on the wealthy considerably.

■ Classes in capitalist societies

Having reviewed changes in the British stratification system, we will now examine the changing position of particular classes within the class structure of capitalist societies, using British and American data. Three main classes – the upper class, the middle class and the working class – will be considered in turn, though as we will show, the location of the boundaries between these classes is disputed. Most of the views dealt with in the following sections have been influenced by Marxist or Weberian theories of stratification.

■ The upper class

■ John Westergaard and Henrietta Resler – a Marxist view of the ruling class

Class divisions

In a 1975 study John Westergaard and Henrietta Resler argue from a Marxist perspective that Britain is dominated by a **ruling class**. They claim that the private ownership of capital provides the key to explaining class divisions.

Westergaard and Resler argue that in detail the class system is complex but in essence it is simple: the major division is still between capital and labour. Sociologists who focus on the details of class, for example, the differences between manual and routine white-collar workers, merely obscure the overall simplicity of the system. Such differences are insignificant compared to the wide gulf which separates the ruling class from the bulk of the wage- and salary-earning population.

Distribution of wealth

To support their argument, Westergaard and Resler point to the concentration of wealth in the hands of a small minority. They say 'The retention of a massive share in all wealth by the top 5 per cent of the population is very striking.' Although there has been some change in the distribution of wealth in Britain this century, this has largely taken place within the richest 10 per cent.

Some members of the ruling class have transferred property to relatives and friends to avoid death duties. The spread of home ownership has spread wealth a little more widely but the ownership of capital in private industry has remained highly concentrated. Thus Westergaard and Resler calculated that in 1970 only about 7 per cent of adults over twenty-five owned any shares and most of them were 'smallholders' with less than £1,000's worth of stock.

Ruling-class power

Westergaard and Resler argue that the maintenance of inequalities of wealth is due to the power of the ruling class. They maintain:

> The favoured enjoy effective power, even when its members take no active steps to exercise power. They do not need to do so – for much of the time at least – simply because things work that way in any case.

It is generally taken for granted (by members of society and governments alike) that investments should bring profit and that the living standards of the propertyless should be based on the demands of the market for their skills. In general, governments have favoured the interests of capital, assuming that the well-being of the nation is largely dependent upon the prosperity of private industry.

Composition of the ruling class

Westergaard and Resler believe that the ruling class is made up of perhaps 5 per cent and at most 10 per cent of the population. It includes the major owners of the means of production, company directors, top managers, higher professionals and senior civil servants, many of whom are large shareholders in private industry. The subordinate classes consist of the bulk of the wage- and salary-earning population.

Westergaard and Resler reject the view that the so-called separation of ownership and control in the joint stock company results in the rise of salaried managers who should properly be placed in a middle class. They argue that 'directors and top executives, in whose hands the major strategic decisions lie, are, in fact, owners of large stock-holdings themselves'. Like the 'absentee owners', their main concern is the maximization of profit. As such, the interests of owners and controllers are largely similar.

Westergaard and Resler put forward a conventional Marxist view of the ruling class. They assume that the ruling class continues to exist. They claim that it is a united group which continues to dominate British society and they argue that social changes have not significantly redistributed wealth and power. These views have been challenged by New Right theorists.

■ Peter Saunders – a New Right view of higher classes

An influential economic elite

Peter Saunders does not deny that there is a small group of people in British society who have considerable wealth and more power than other members of society. He accepts that many directors and top managers own shares in their own and in other companies and he does believe that there is 'an interlocking network at the top of British industry and finance in which the same names and faces keep cropping up with different hats on'. He notes that the hundred biggest companies produce more than half of Britain's manufacturing output and therefore:

a few thousand individuals at most are today responsible for taking the bulk of the key financial and administrative decisions which shape the future development of British industry and banking.

However, Saunders rejects the Marxist view that such people constitute a capitalist ruling class. He sees them as merely 'an influential economic elite'.

Wealth, ownership and the capitalist class

Saunders identifies some groups who might be seen as a capitalist class. These consist of families who continue to own majority shareholdings in established large companies, entrepreneurs who have built up and still own big businesses, and large landowners. However, such people control only a small fraction of the British economy. Most business are run by directors and managers whose income and power derives principally from their jobs and not from their ownership of wealth. He claims that less than 25 per cent of the top 250 British companies are run by managers and directors who own 5 per cent or more of the company's shares. Such people are part of the 'economic elite' but they do not own substantial parts of the means of production, so they cannot be seen as part of the capitalist class.

Furthermore, Saunders argues that 'it is increasingly difficult to identify a specific capitalist class'. Although few people are very rich, many people have a direct stake in owning British enterprises. During the course of this century the proportion of shares owned by individuals has declined. Most shares and a good deal of land is owned by banks, unit trusts, building societies and pension funds. Millions of ordinary people therefore have investments tied up in the capitalist economy by virtue of their pension schemes, endowment mortgages, life insurance policies and savings in banks and building societies. In addition the privatization programme has widened direct share ownership. Saunders therefore claims that the capitalist class 'has fragmented into millions of tiny pieces' and says 'To see these pieces look around you.'

The ruling class

From Saunders's point of view then, directors and managers lack the wealth to be seen as a capitalist class. He further argues that they lack the power to be a ruling class. Although they make many important investment decisions, they do not monopolize power and they frequently fail to get their own way. There are many areas of society which they do not control. These include the Government, the mass media and the education system. Indeed members of the economic elite are 'sometimes dismayed' when politicians, editors and educationalists fail 'to defer to their wishes and interests'.

Saunders believes that the class divisions of previous centuries have been weakened by the development of capitalism. Inequality is essential if a society is to be just and successful but the success of capitalism spreads wealth and power more widely. In doing so it ensures that the most wealthy do not rule society.

■ John Scott – Who Rules Britain?

John Scott has provided the most comprehensive description and analysis of the development of the upper classes in Britain. His analysis suggests that there have been important changes within higher classes in British society, but he does not believe the upper class has disappeared. He discusses many of the trends mentioned by Saunders but he denies that they show the death or fragmentation of the ruling class. Scott uses Weberian concepts and borrows some elements of elite theory. (Elite theory is examined on pp. 515–24.) However, in the end he supports the Marxist view that Britain retains a ruling class.

The historical development of the upper classes

Scott sees classes as consisting of 'clusters of households which stand in a similar position with respect to the distribution of income and wealth and the overall distribution of life chances'. Clusters of households, particularly those in higher classes, may well have groups of inter-marrying and inter-connected families.

The composition of the classes at the top of the British stratification system has changed since pre-industrial times. Before the Industrial Revolution the landed aristocracy and the gentry were the dominant groupings in British society. Family contacts were very important in uniting the upper classes and achieving a high degree of **social closure** (the exclusion of outsiders). The development of British industry in the eighteenth and nineteenth centuries opened up new avenues for achieving success and becoming part of the upper class. Most successful entrepreneurial business people made use of social assets based on kinship, friendship and other social contacts. Most early industrial enterprises were owned and controlled

by groups of individuals united by kinship. It was common for families who were linked through a business partnership to become linked by marriage as well, and vice versa.

Divisions in the upper classes

Scott claims that in the nineteenth century there were three overlapping, but not united, sections of the upper class: landowners, manufacturers and financiers (mainly in the City of London). As the nineteenth century progressed these three groups came closer together. For example, some landowners invested money in manufacturing or industries such as mining, and some manufacturers bought large estates in an attempt to gain the social acceptance enjoyed by the aristocracy.

However, financiers, merchants and bankers, such as the Rothschilds and the Barings, remained the most distinctive group. Scott says that financiers formed a 'tightly integrated group with numerous overlapping business activities'. Most were based in close physical proximity to each other in the City of London; they were often related or united by ties of friendship, and had ample opportunity to meet one another informally in coffee houses or elsewhere. Despite their distinctiveness, they had a good deal in common with the other upper-class groups; and they were an important source of loans for the growing group of entrepreneurs.

The growth of joint stock companies

The development of the industrial and financial bourgeoisie during industrialization ended the dominance of landowners. The potential for conflict between these groups was reduced by kinship and friendship ties, and by involvement together in common enterprises. The opportunities for common involvement in enterprise were, however, limited by the fact that most companies remained family owned. As the nineteenth century gave way to the twentieth, two related changes began to alter the relationship between the upper classes and the ownership of the means of production.

1 First, companies became larger and larger as wealth became concentrated in the hands of a small number of firms.

2 Second, family ownership began to be replaced by the joint stock company in which shares could be bought and sold in the open market.

As late as 1880 the top hundred industrial firms controlled only 10 per cent of the total market for goods. However, legislation in the middle of the nineteenth century had begun to make it easier for partnerships and individually owned firms to issue shares. This allowed them to take advantage of limited liability: the owners of the shares were not liable for repaying the firm's debts. Joint stock companies found it possible to grow larger by issuing new shares to increase their capital, and mergers and takeovers saw the average size of firms grow. According to Scott, by 1909 the top hundred manufacturing companies were producing 15 per cent of total output, and by 1930 26 per cent. He believes that during the inter-war years the three sections of the upper class virtually fused together as they all became increasingly involved in the growing industrial enterprises.

As the twentieth century progressed the family-owned firm became less and less important in British capitalism. From the Second World War onwards the top hundred firms became even more dominant: by 1970 they produced 45 per cent of total output. Many of the major firms became too large to be owned by an individual or single family, and the number of shareholders in each firm increased. At the same time, the proportion of shares held by individuals began to decline. Increasingly, institutions such as pension funds, insurance companies, and unit and investment trusts, held the majority of shares. Table 2.8 shows that by 1988 only twenty-seven of Britain's top 250 companies were controlled by individual entrepreneurs or families. Nevertheless this group included important companies like J. Sainsbury, the supermarket chain, Lonrho, N.M. Rothschild and Barings.

The 'managerial revolution'

Commentators such as Saunders have suggested that a decline in the family ownership of companies has meant that a ruling class based on the ownership of the means of production no longer exists. According to their arguments, shareholdings have become too fragmented for individuals to exercise control over the companies in which they have a stake. A **managerial revolution** has taken place which has resulted in effective control over industry passing from owners to managers. The increasing percentage of shares owned by pension funds, insurance companies, and the like, also implies that the ruling class has lost power. Many of the funds held by such institutions come from investments made by ordinary employees, rather than the most wealthy members of society.

The persistence of the capitalist class

John Scott rejects the view that the changes described above have led to the disappearance of a capitalist class. He says unequivocally that 'There is in Britain today a capitalist class whose members owe their advantaged life chances to the occupancy of capitalist economic locations.' Legal and financial changes have certainly changed this class but according to Scott 'It remains a centrally important feature of contemporary British society.'

During the twentieth century certain types of property have become more widely owned. More people own their own houses and possess consumer goods and cars. However, such possessions are **property for use**. They are important for the lifestyle and life chances of individuals and families, but they do not place individuals in a capitalist

Table 2.8 Control of large companies, 1988

| | Top 250 companies of 1988 (no.) | | |
	Industrial	Financial	Total
Controlled by entrepreneurs	21	6	27
Controlled by institutions	96	17	113
Foreign, state, and other control	83	27	110
Totals	200	50	250

(*Source*: Scott, J. (1991) *Who Rules Britain?*, Polity Press, Cambridge, p. 78.)

Table 2.9   Britain's highest paid directors, 1990

	Company	Annual salary (£)
Lord Hanson	Hanson Trust	1,530,000
Tiny Rowland	Lonrho	1,310,000
Dick Giordano	BOC	937,000
Sir Ralph Halpern	Burton Group	899,000
Sir Kit McMahon	Midland Bank	725,844
Sir Peter Walters	BP	708,722
Geoff Mulcahy	Kingfisher	701,000
Cyril Stein	Ladbroke	603,000
Sir Paul Girolami	Glaxo	598,081
Sir Denys Henderson	ICI	514,000
Allen Sheppard	Grand Metropolitan	506,438

(*Source*: The Guardian, 3 May 1990, p. 9.)

class. Capitalists own **property for power**. This consists of capital invested in land, shares and commercial enterprises in general. True capitalists own considerable amounts of capital and not just, for example, a few hundred shares in one company. Scott notes that the proportion of the population owning any shares increased from 6 per cent in 1984 to 20 per cent in 1988, but most of these shareholdings were very small. It has not resulted in an increase in the numbers of people with large personal shareholdings.

Scott says 'property, and the wealth which it generates, is the primary base of capitalist class privileges' but argues that 'this need not, in every case, be personal property'. Table 2.9 shows the highest-paid company directors in 1990. Clearly, the income of directors like these is such that they can accumulate sufficient wealth to become members of the capitalist class. Scott argues:

Those who hold directorships in large enterprises occupy capitalist locations, and if the income from employment is substantial they may be able to sustain a relatively secure foothold in the capitalist class.

He admits that directors who get their positions late in their careers may not have time to accumulate sufficient wealth to become members of the capitalist class and he says 'the dividing line between the capitalist class and the service class is difficult to draw with any precision'. Nevertheless he rejects the view that there has been a managerial revolution which has undermined the power of a capitalist class. A considerable number of top managers and directors are able to join the capitalist class themselves; the rest are only likely to retain their jobs if their actions favour the interests of the capitalist class.

Scott also attacks the idea that institutional control over many large companies has led to the disappearance of a capitalist class. Even if in theory the assets of pension schemes, banks, insurance companies and similar institutions are owned by a multitude of small investors, in practice they are controlled by a few key members of the capitalist class. The policies of these institutions are largely determined by their directors who are often members of the capitalist class in their own right. These **finance capitalists** make the key investment decisions which affect the lives of millions.

Within this group is an inner core who sit on the boards of more than one company. Scott calculates that in 1988 there were 290 individuals (only five of them women) who held directorships on the boards of two or more of the top 250 companies. This group is in a strong position to coordinate the activities of the capitalist class as a whole because they have connections with a number of capitalist concerns, perhaps involved in different sectors of the economy. Far from leading to the death of the capitalist class, institutional control improves coordination and cooperation within it.

Table 2.10   Britain's richest families, 1990

Family	Estimated wealth (£m)	Main source of wealth
1 The Royal Family	6,700	Land and urban property
2 Grosvenor (Duke of Westminster)	4,200	Land and urban property
3 Rausing	2,040	Food packaging
4 Sainsbury	1,777	Food retailing
5 Weston	1,674	Food production and retailing
6 Moores	1,670	Football pools, retailing
7 Vestey	1,420	Food production
8 Getty	1,350	Oil
9 Maxwell	1,100	Publishing
10 Feeney	1,020	Retailing
11 Hinduja	1,000	Trading
12 Livanos	930	Shipping
13 Goldsmith	750	Retailing and finance
14 Swire	692	Shipping and aviation
15 Ronson	548	Urban property, petrol distribution
16 Barclay*	500	Hotels and urban property
17 Branson	488	Music and aviation
18 Cadogan (Earl Cadogan)	450	Land and urban property
19 Jerwood	400	Trading
20 Portman (Viscount Portman)	400	Land and urban property
21 Thompson	400	Food processing, property

*Not the family associated with Barclays Bank.

(*Source*: Scott, J. (1991) *Who Rules Britain?*, Polity Press, Cambridge, p. 83.)

The composition of the capitalist class

The capitalist class then, includes many of the directors of the largest companies, especially those with multiple directorships, successful entrepreneurs and those who have inherited substantial amounts of wealth. Scott claims that in Britain this means about 0.1 per cent of the adult population, around 43,500 people. Between them members of this group owned about 7 per cent of the nation's wealth in 1986. At that time each was worth a minimum of £740,000. Within this group the richest 200 families all had more than fifty million pounds in assets. Table 2.10 shows the richest families of all in 1990, according to research carried out by the *Sunday Times*.

According to Scott, 104 of the richest 200 families in 1990 owed most of their wealth to inheritance. There are a number of entrepreneurs amongst the most wealthy but the majority of these people started their lives with advantages over much of the population. Scott says:

> Inheriting from their own parents in the entrepreneurial middle class or marrying a woman who had inherited wealth from her parents was the way in which many men secured the funds to invest in the ventures which subsequently made their fortunes.

Some of those who have made recent fortunes have a less secure position than those who possess 'old money' invested in land. Robert Maxwell, whose publishing empire collapsed in debt after his death, is a case in point.

The ruling class

Having claimed to have established that a capitalist class still exists, Scott goes to try to show that it remains a ruling class. He says that a ruling class exists when 'there is both political domination and political rule by a capitalist class'. He goes on to argue:

> This requires that there be a power bloc dominated by a capitalist class, a power elite recruited from this power bloc, in which the capitalist class is disproportionately represented, and there are mechanisms which ensure that the state operates in the interests of the capitalist class and the reproduction of capital.

By a **power bloc** Scott means a group of people who can monopolize political power over a country for some time. The **power elite** are those people from the power bloc who occupy key positions in the state. These positions in Britain include those held by the prime minister, members of the Cabinet, MPs, senior judges and top civil servants.

Scott argues that capitalist interests have dominated state policy over recent decades. Based round the Conservative Party, a power bloc has incorporated many managers and members of the professional middle classes. It has been sustained in office by an even wider **electoral bloc** incorporating some members of the working class, but it remains dominated by capitalists. Many Cabinet members, for example, come from public schools. Only two members of the 1990 Cabinet had not been to a fee-paying school and sixteen had been to Oxford or Cambridge University. Scott also quotes figures showing that top civil servants and others in elite positions continue to be predominantly recruited from public school backgrounds. (Figures on elite self-recruitment are discussed on pp. 518–21.) Elite positions are not completely monopolized by members of the capitalist class, but they are disproportionately represented. Scott concludes 'The evidence on social background and recruitment shows clearly the persistence of a power bloc dominated by the capitalist class.'

Periods of Labour government have not, in Scott's view, made a significant difference. The power bloc has had to give up some of the positions that it usually occupies but its supporters have continued to hold most of the non-elected posts. The Labour Party has therefore '*governed*, but it has not *ruled*'. The state's policies have not only benefited the capitalist class, but the latter's dominance ensures that its interests are never seriously challenged, even by Labour governments. Scott says:

> When the state's activities advantage several classes rather than simply the dominant class, it is still possible to speak of a ruling class, so long as these activities do not undermine the existing relations of production and continue, in the long term, to reinforce them.

The policies of British government's have done just that. According to Scott, British governments have become increasingly constrained in their economic policies. They have to pay close attention to the financial markets if they are going to borrow money, maintain the exchange rate of their currency and attract investment into the country. They cannot afford to ignore the interests of capitalists.

In particular government policy is influenced a great deal by an inner core of finance capitalists in the City of London. The 'city point of view' supported by this group is 'rooted in short-term commercialism' and 'involves a commitment to free international capital flows, stable sterling exchange rates, and tight monetary controls'. It has used informal contacts with the Government, lobbying, contributions to Conservative Party funds and sometimes direct participation in government itself to ensure that its views have prevailed.

Changes in the ruling class

Scott certainly believes that there have been changes in the ruling class. At the start of the century it was based around an 'upper circle of status superiors' many of whom had connections to the aristocracy. Social events like the Henley Regatta, Wimbledon fortnight, the monarch's garden parties and society balls used to be far more important. Nevertheless, public schools, particularly top schools like Eton, continue to be important for developing contacts amongst members of the ruling class. The 'old boy network' is used to fill many jobs in the City of London. Gentlemen's clubs are still used by members of the capitalist class to exchange information and maintain contacts, but the best London restaurants are also becoming important venues for these activities.

While some of the changes that have taken place this century have affected the character of the ruling class, according to Scott its survival and continued domination of British society has never been in question.

Other views on the upper classes

1 Elite theories accept that power is concentrated in the hands of a few, but deny that the power comes from wealth. Instead, they see power deriving from the occupation of top jobs in society (see pp. 515–24 for further details).

2 Pluralists deny that higher social classes monopolize power and believe that in liberal democracies the wishes of the people determine government policy. According to this view, power is dispersed and not concentrated in the hands of the upper classes (see pp. 506–13 for details).

The next chapter will examine quite different views on the 'top' of the stratification system.

The middle classes

Marx and the middle class

The most usual way of defining the **middle class** is to see it as consisting of those individuals who have **non-manual occupations**, that is occupations which involve, in some sense, an intellectual element. If the distinction between manual and non-manual labour is used to distinguish the middle class, then as an earlier section indicated, it is a growing sector of capitalist industrial societies such as Britain.

The attempt to analyse the position of the middle class in the class structure has been a major preoccupation of sociologists of stratification. This has been the case particularly for Marxist and neo-Marxist sociologists, since the growth of the middle class has often been cited as evidence against Marx's theory.

According to many *interpretations* of his work, Marx sees capitalist society as divided into only two classes of any importance: the bourgeoisie and the proletariat. This leaves no room for a middle class. In reality, though, Marx recognized the existence of intermediate classes (for example members of the petty bourgeoisie, such as shop-keepers and small business people). Moreover, the growth of what is usually called the middle class has largely been the result of the increasing amount of white-collar work. In *Capital*, Volume 3, Marx noted this trend when he argued that the increasing size of enterprises made it impossible for them to be run by a single person. In these circumstances it necessitated 'the employment of commercial wage-workers who make up the actual office staff'.

Although he identified the trend towards more non-manual workers, Marx made no detailed attempt to explain how they fitted into his theory of stratification. On the surface at least, as non-owners of the means of production, they could hardly be considered as part of the bourgeoisie. Nor, it is often argued, can they be seen as part of the proletariat. Many commentators have suggested that non-manual workers enjoy considerable advantages in employment over their manual counterparts: they tend to enjoy more job security, work shorter hours, have longer holidays, more fringe benefits, and have greater promotion prospects.

Life chances

A variety of studies have also shown that non-manual workers enjoy advantages over manual workers in terms of their life chances. They are likely to enjoy higher standards of health, and to live longer; they are less likely to be convicted of a criminal offence; they are more likely to own their own house and a variety of consumer goods.

Many of these relative advantages for the middle class may be related to their most obvious material advantage: a higher income. As Table 2.11 shows, there has been a consistent gap between the earnings of the two groups amongst both men and women. The gap in earnings has existed throughout this century. Westergaard and Resler have calculated that in 1913–14 men in full time non-manual employment earned 142 per cent of the average male wage, male manual workers 88 per cent. The situation had changed little by 1960 when the figures were 145 per cent and 82 per cent respectively.

Conflicting perspectives on the middle class

In Weberian terms, the sort of evidence outlined above can be used to suggest that there is a middle

Table 2.11   Gross weekly and hourly earnings of full-time adult employees in Great Britain

	Median gross weekly earnings (£)			
	Manual men	**Non-manual men**	**Manual women**	**Non-manual women**
1986	163.4	219.4	101.1	131.5
1987	173.9	235.7	108.2	142.2
1988	188.0	259.7	115.6	157.1
1989	203.9	285.7	125.9	173.5
1990	221.3	312.1	137.3	191.8
1990*	223.1	305.4	136.2	190.7
1991	235.4	332.2	147.4	211.1
1992	250.7	353.4	156.6	227.6

New Earnings Survey – April of each year

* Two sets of figures are given for 1990 due to a change in the collection of statistical data.
(*Source: (1994) Annual Abstract of Statistics*, HMSO, London, pp. 123 and 124.)

class in Britain, distinguished from the working class through its superior market situation and life chances. From this point of view the middle class is held to consist of non-manual workers. However, this relatively simple and straightforward view has, for a variety of reasons, been rejected by many sociologists.

1 First, the distinction between manual and non-manual work is not seen by some as an adequate way of distinguishing between classes. Often Marxist and neo-Marxist sociologists try to distinguish classes according to their role within the economic system, while Weberians are more likely to analyse class in terms of the market situation of particular occupational groups.

2 Second, on the face of it, the middle class contains an extremely diverse group of workers ranging from secretaries to accountants, shop-assistants to managers, shopkeepers to social workers.

3 Third, the position of particular occupational groups – their wages, conditions of employment and responsibilities – has changed during the course of the century, and these changes may in turn have affected the class structure as a whole.

These complications have led to a whole variety of views as to the composition of the middle class and its place in the social structure. Some have argued that there is a distinctive and relatively homogeneous middle class; others that the middle class as such does not exist. Some of those who accept the existence of a middle class believe that it is divided into many different strata; others that it is divided, but only into two main groupings. The precise location of the boundaries between the middle class and the classes above and below it has also been the subject of dispute. Before we examine the place of the middle class as a whole in the class structure, we will examine the main strata of the middle class in detail.

■ The upper middle class

For the sake of convenience different parts of the middle class will be examined in two main sections. In this first section we will consider the position of the more highly rewarded groups including professionals, senior managers and administrators, and more successful small-business people.

In the early twentieth century small business people (the self-employed and shopkeepers) made up a greater proportion of the working population than they did in 1971. As the size of many businesses grew, the number of employers was reduced. Guy Routh found that the number of employers in Britain declined from 763,000 in 1911 to 621,000 in 1971. The number of self-employed also fell by 24,000 over the same period.

Obviously larger employers might be considered part of the upper class, but the others are often seen as part of the 'old' middle class. Marx predicted that this group, which he referred to as the petty (or *petit*) bourgeoisie, would be progressively squeezed into the proletariat. They would be unable to compete with larger companies which could buy and sell in bulk, and take advantage of advanced technology.

Although the trends up to 1971 provided support for Marx's view on the likely fate of the petty bourgeoisie, data since the 1980s indicate a reversal of previous trends. According to official figures the numbers of self-employed and small proprietors rose from 1,954,000 in December 1971, to 2,902,000 in June 1993, a rise of very nearly one million. Nevertheless, it is the growth of white-collar employment which has accounted for most of the expansion of the upper middle class.

Some sociologists distinguish between different strata of the upper middle class identifying, for example, higher professionals, lower professionals, and managers as separate groups. Others see the upper middle class as being more homogeneous. In the following section we will examine the position of one strata of the upper middle class – the professions – in the class structure.

■ The professions in the class structure

The growth of the professions

This century the **professions** have been one of the fastest growing sectors of the occupational structure. According to Guy Routh the professions rose from 4.05 per cent of the employed population in 1911 to 20.1 per cent in 1985. A similar trend is evident in all Western industrial capitalist societies.

Several reasons have been given for the rapid growth of the professions. The increasing complexity of trade and commerce demands financial and legal experts such as accountants and lawyers. The growth of industry requires more specialized scientific and technical knowledge which results in the development of professions such as science and engineering. The creation of the welfare state and the expansion of local and national government has produced a range of 'welfare professions', and has resulted in the growth of the medical and

teaching professions, as well as the greater employment of professionals in government bureaucracies.

Professionals have been seen both as producers and products of industrialization. Their skills and knowledge are regarded as essential for the development and expansion of industrial economies. In turn, the wealth produced by this development has provided the means to pay for the specialized services which the professionals supply.

Higher and lower professionals

In terms of their market situation, the professionals can be divided into two groups: the higher and lower professionals.

1 The **higher professionals** include judges, barristers, solicitors, architects, planners, doctors, dentists, university lecturers, accountants, scientists and engineers.

2 The **lower professionals** include school teachers, nurses, social workers and librarians.

As Table 2.12 indicates, there have long been significant differences in earnings between the two groups.

Measured in terms of earnings, the market situation of lower professionals is not substantially superior to that of skilled manual workers. However, compared to skilled manual workers, lower professionals have a number of market advantages which include greater security of employment, wider promotion opportunities, annual salary increments, and more valuable fringe benefits.

The functionalist perspective on professions

Various explanations have been advanced to account for the occupational rewards of professionals. These explanations are influenced by the individual sociologist's theoretical perspective and his or her evaluation of the services provided by professionals.

Bernard Barber offers a functionalist view of the role and rewards of higher professionals. He argues that professionalism involves 'four essential attributes'.

1 Professionalism requires a body of systematic and generalized knowledge which can be applied to a

Table 2.12   Relative earnings of main occupational groups from 1913/14 to 1978, male earners only

Occupational group (men only)	Average pay for each man's occupational class expressed as a percentage of the simple average for all men						
	1913–14	1922–24	1935–36	1955–56	1960	1970	1978
Higher professionals	230	206	220	191	195	155	159
Managers and administrators	140	169	153	183	177	180	154
Lower professionals	109	113	107	75	81	100	104
Foremen	69	64	67	65	65	71	71
Clerks	86	95	95	97	97	88	90
Skilled manual workers	74	64	68	77	76	76	83
Semi-skilled manual workers	48	44	46	58	56	68	73
Unskilled manual workers	44	45	45	54	51	61	65
All men	100	100	100	100	100	100	100

(*Source*: Routh, G. (1980) *Occupation and Pay in Great Britain 1906–79*, Macmillan, London and Basingstoke, p. 127.)

variety of problems. For instance, doctors have a body of medical knowledge which they apply to diagnose and treat a range of illnesses.

2 Professionalism involves a concern for the interests of the community rather than self-interest. Thus the primary motivation of professionals is public service rather than personal gain: doctors are concerned primarily with the health of their patients rather than with lining their own pockets.

3 The behaviour of professionals is strictly controlled by a code of ethics which is established and maintained by professional associations and learned as part of the training required to qualify as a professional. Doctors take the Hippocratic Oath which lays down the obligations and proper conduct of their profession. Should they break this code of conduct, their association can strike them from the register and ban them from practising medicine.

4 The high rewards received by professionals, which include the prestige accorded to professional status as well as earnings, are symbols of their achievements. They denote the high regard in which professionals are held and reflect the value of their contribution to society.

Barber argues that the knowledge and skills of professionals provide them with considerable power and it is therefore essential for the well-being of society that this power be used for the benefit of all. He accepts the view that professionals are primarily concerned with service to the community and believes they use their expertise for public benefit. He claims that professionals make important con-

tributions to the functional well-being of society and in addition, their services are highly regarded in terms of society's values. As a result, professionals are highly rewarded.

Criticisms of functionalism

Functionalist explanations of the role and rewards of professionals have been strongly criticized on the grounds that they make the following assumptions, all of which are questionable.

1 First, professionals make important contributions to the well-being of society as a whole.

2 Second, they serve all members of society rather than particular groups.

3 Third, they are concerned with service to the community rather than with self-interest.

In recent years, there has been increasing criticism of the view that professionals provide valuable services to society. Prince Charles has denounced architects for defacing British cities; Margaret Thatcher's governments have challenged the monopolies enjoyed by opticians and the legal profession; planners have been condemned for producing urban chaos; teachers have been attacked for crushing originality and stifling creativity in their pupils; and lawyers have been accused of mystifying the legal system to the point where the layperson finds it largely unintelligible.

In *Medical Nemesis*, a savage attack on the medical profession, Ivan Illich provides an example of this type of criticism. He claims that 'The medical establishment has become a major threat to health.' Contrary to the view promoted by the medical profession, Illich argues that the environment, in particular food, working conditions, housing and hygiene, rather than medical provision, is the main determinant of the health of a population. He notes that the incidence of diseases such as tuberculosis, cholera, dysentery, typhoid and scarlet fever declined rapidly long before medical control. He attributes this decline to changes in the environment rather than to antibiotics and widespread immunization.

In the same way, Illich argues that much of the illness in contemporary society is due to the environment. He claims that industrial society is characterized by boring and monotonous work, lack of freedom for the individual to control his or her own life, and a compulsion to acquire material possessions, inspired by the mistaken belief that they bring happiness and fulfilment. These 'ills' of industrial society are responsible for much of the illness experienced by its members.

In claiming to diagnose and treat this illness doctors can do more harm than good. In Illich's view, such treatment 'is but a device to convince those who are sick and tired of society that it is they who are ill, impotent and in need of repair'. By claiming exclusive rights to the diagnosis of illness, doctors obscure its real source. By treating the individual rather than the environment, doctors not only do little to prevent illness but also direct attention away from measures which could prove more effective.

Space prevents us from giving a full summary of Illich's closely reasoned attack on the medical profession, but his views suggest that the functionalist argument that the higher professions confer positive benefits on society is at least questionable. (See Chapter 12 for Illich's criticisms of the teaching profession, pp. 730–2.)

The Weberian perspective on professions

From a Weberian point of view the professions can be seen as occupational groups which have succeeded in controlling and manipulating the labour market in such a way that they can maximize their rewards. Thus Noel and José Parry define professionalism as 'a strategy for controlling an occupation in which colleagues set up a system of

self-government'. The occupation is controlled primarily in the interests of its members. From this perspective, professionalism involves the following factors.

1 There is restriction of entry into the occupation, which is provided by the profession's control of the training and qualifications required for membership and the numbers deemed necessary to provide an adequate service. By controlling supply, professionals can maintain a high demand for their services and so gain high rewards.

2 Professionalism involves an association which controls the conduct of its members 'in respects which are defined as relevant to the collective interests of the profession'. In particular, professional associations are concerned with promoting the view that professional conduct is above reproach and that professionals are committed to public service. This serves to justify high occupational rewards. By claiming the right to discipline their own members, professional associations largely prevent public scrutiny of their affairs and so maintain the image which they project of themselves.

3 Professionalism involves a successful claim that only members are qualified to provide particular services. This claim is often reinforced by law. Thus in Britain, a series of laws have guaranteed solicitors a monopoly on particular services. These monopolies are jealously guarded: the Law Society has prosecuted unqualified individuals for performing services which are defined as a legal monopoly of the law profession.

In these ways, professions can control rival occupational groups which might threaten their dominance of a section of the market. Parry and Parry conclude that by adopting the strategy of professionalism, certain occupational groups are able to extract high rewards from the market.

Viewing professionalism as a market strategy provides an explanation for the differing rewards of various so-called professions. Some of the occupational groups which claim professional status lack many of the attributes of professionalism. In terms of Parry and Parry's definition, they are professions in name only. They have little control over their market situation and as a result receive lower rewards than occupational groups which are more fully professionalized.

Parry and Parry illustrate this point by a comparison of doctors and teachers. They claim that doctors receive higher rewards than teachers because they are more fully professionalized. This is due largely to the fact that doctors were able to organize themselves into a professional group before the state intervened in medicine and became a major employer of medical practitioners.

The British Medical Association was founded in 1832 and the Medical Registration Act of 1858 granted doctors a monopoly on the practice of medicine and gave them important powers of self-government. Once established as a professional body, doctors had considerable control over their market situation.

Teachers, however, failed to achieve professionalism before state intervention in education. Since the state was largely responsible for initiating and paying for mass education, it was able to establish greater control over teachers. In particular, the state controlled both the supply of teachers and standards for entry into the occupation. Since they lack the market control which professionalism provides, teachers have turned to trade unionism to improve their market situation. Parry and Parry conclude that the differences in occupational reward between doctors and teachers are attributable to the degree of professionalization of the two groups.

Professions as servants of the powerful

The Weberian claim that the professions are able to act primarily in their own interests has been called into question. It has been argued that the higher professionals primarily serve the interests of the wealthy and powerful. Accountants and lawyers are employed in the service of capital, architects build for the wealthy, and doctors and psychiatrists in private practice care for the physical and mental needs of the rich.

The American sociologist C. Wright Mills makes the following observations on the law profession in the USA: rather than being guardians of the law for the benefit of all, lawyers have increasingly become the servants of the large corporation. They are busily employed 'teaching the financiers how to do what they want within the law, advising on the chances they are taking and how to best cover themselves'. Lawyers draw up contracts, minimize taxation, advise on business deals and liaise between banks, commercial and industrial enterprises. In the service of the corporation, the

'leading lawyer is selected for skill in the sure fix and the easy out-of-court settlement'.

The lucrative business open to members of the legal profession means that members of low-income groups are largely unable to afford their services. Mills suggests that the rewards of the professionals are directly related to the demand for their services by the rich and powerful. Since lawyers increasingly serve 'a thin upper crust and financial interests' they are highly rewarded.

C. Wright Mills sees professionals as increasingly becoming the servants of the wealthy and influential, but he does not believe that the individual professionals themselves are losing their power and influence. Although they act more as employees than as members of a profession, they have important positions within the companies for which they work. Indeed, Mills sees some professionals as members of the 'power elite', which dominates American society. For example, he argues that the corporate lawyer acts as a key go-between in the affairs of business, political and military elites. He says 'When you get a lawyer who handles the legal work of investment bankers you get a key member of the power elite.' (For more details of Mills's views on elites see pp. 517–18.)

The deskilling of professions

A number of sociologists have followed Mills in arguing that professionals are increasingly employed in large organizations, and in this situation are less able to pursue the interests of their profession. However, unlike Mills such sociologists see professional groups as losing their power and influence rather than as joining the power elite. This view has been inspired by the work of the American Marxist Harry Braverman.

Braverman claims that **deskilling** has taken place in many white-collar jobs. As the skill content of the work has been reduced, then some white-collar workers have lost the advantages they previously enjoyed over manual employees. They have become **proletarianized**.

Although primarily concerned with routine white-collar work, Braverman does believe that some professional jobs have also become deskilled. The people who do these jobs lose the power they once had, their work is closely regulated, and they are made aware of their subordination. Braverman says 'We may cite here particularly the mass employment of draftsmen and technicians, engineers and accountants, nurses and teachers.' Such groups find that their work becomes more and more routine as it is divided into specialist tasks. Their pay levels are threatened as they become unable to control the supply of labour into their profession: there is always a 'reserve army' of suitably qualified workers ready to step into their jobs.

The declining independence of professions

Braverman's views are rather general but other sociologists have suggested ways in which the position of specific professional groups in the class structure have deteriorated. Geoff Esland points out that since the 1946 National Health Service Act levels of pay and conditions of work in the medical profession, and spending on medical research, have been largely determined by central government. He points to the growth of unionism among junior doctors as evidence of their need to move beyond professionalism as a market strategy for protecting their interests.

Similarly, Martin Oppenheimer claims that many professionals employed in the public sector find that their jobs are 'related to the oppressive functions of government – keeping welfare clients quiet, policing, regulating'. Their jobs become more and more difficult, their independence is eroded, and their wages are threatened by government attempts to cut spending.

Other writers have made similar claims about professionals employed in private companies. Kummar has tried to show how engineers in private industry have had their work increasingly fragmented and broken down into a series of simple individual steps. Computerized systems have reduced the amount of skill required by many engineers and their performance is closely regulated.

Terence Johnson has pointed to the limits that can be placed on some professions by their clients or employers. In the profession of accountancy most practitioners are employed by companies and are not independent advisors. Accountants are expected to be loyal first and foremost to their company, and not to their profession. Some of their skills and knowledge are specific to the company for which they work, and they would be of less value to another company. Consequently accountants are in a highly dependent position

compared to most professions; it is difficult for them to use professionalism as a market strategy.

It is certainly true that during the course of this century professionals have increasingly become employees, rather than being employers or the self-employed. Guy Routh calculated that in 1931, 34 per cent of higher professionals were self-employed or employers; by 1971 this had fallen to 16 per cent. Routh attributes most of this change to the increasing employment of professionals by businesses.

It may also be true that some professional groups have had their independence and autonomy reduced. However, it is certainly an exaggeration to claim that they have been proletarianized. Higher professionals in particular continue to enjoy many advantages over manual workers, and, for that matter, routine non-manual workers.

■ Barbara and John Ehrenreich – the professional–managerial class

Although many sociologists see professionals as a distinctive part of the upper middle class, others have argued that they have much in common with managers. Arguing from a neo-Marxist point of view Barbara and John Ehrenreich claim that there is a distinctive **professional–managerial class**, which consists of:

---

salaried mental workers who do not own the means of production and whose major function in the social division of labor may be described broadly as the reproduction of capitalist culture and capitalist class relations.

The Ehrenreichs estimate that 20–25 per cent of the population are members of the professional–managerial class in the USA. Members of the class include teachers, social workers, psychologists, entertainers, writers of advertising copy, and middle-level administrators, managers and engineers.

In identifying this class the Ehrenreichs diverge from more conventional Marxist accounts of class in capitalist societies. Unlike some other Marxists, the Ehrenreichs believe that there are three main classes in capitalist society rather than two.

Origins and functions

According to their account, the professional–managerial class started to develop towards the end of the nineteenth century as a class which specialized in the 'reproduction of capitalist class relations' became necessary.

1 The first function of the new class was to organize the process of production. Some scientists and engineers are directly involved in developing productive technology for the benefit of the ruling class, while many managers are involved in applying the principle of 'scientific management' to the workforce (see pp. 294–5 for a description and discussion of scientific management).

2 The second function of the professional–managerial class is to exercise social control over the working class. Thus teachers and social workers exercise social control over children and 'problem' members of society.

3 A third function is to propagate ruling-class ideology. This is carried out by groups such as entertainers, teachers and advertising copy writers.

4 The final function that the professional–managerial class perform for the ruling class is helping to develop the consumer goods market, ensuring that the working class consume new products produced by capitalism.

The overall role of the professional–managerial class then is to reproduce the relationship of domination and subordination between the ruling and subject classes.

Evidence of reproduction

Although the Ehrenreichs define the professional–managerial class in terms of the functions it performs for capitalism, they also advance empirical evidence to show that it is a distinct grouping within the stratification system. For example, they claim that children of professional–managerial class parents are more than twice as likely to enter the professional–managerial class themselves, than the children of working-class parents. Entry to the professional–managerial class depends largely upon educational qualifications, and the class helps to reproduce itself by devoting considerable effort to ensuring the educational success of its children. In addition members of the class usually find marriage partners from the same class.

Interests

The Ehrenreichs believe that the professional–managerial class has quite different interests to the working class even though both groups consist of wage labourers. The professional–managerial class is paid out of the surplus produced by the working class. In the course of their work members of the professional–managerial class develop techniques to control the working class. They also encourage the development of false class consciousness. These differences of interest are reflected in the tension, distrust and conflict which is often evident between social workers and clients, managers and workers, and teachers and students.

The professional–managerial class also has different interests from the ruling class. Both groups have an interest in maintaining the capitalist system, but the professional–managerial class has an interest in maximizing its own independence or autonomy; the ruling class, on the other hand, tries to restrict it as far as possible.

Managers and professionals justify or legitimate their position in terms of their technical expertise, objectivity, and rationality. In these circumstances they cannot be seen to be sacrificing their independence for that would undermine their claims to being objective in taking decisions at work. From this point of view members of the professional–managerial class are likely to try to maintain their position by forming themselves into professions. Some groups of workers are more successful than others in achieving this. The Ehrenreichs suggest that between 1880 and 1920 in the USA, medicine, law, social work and teaching established themselves as professions, whilst, for example, engineering did not.

The Ehrenreichs do accept that there is some degree of division within the professional–managerial class. Some members of the class, including some managers, administrators, and engineers, work directly for industry and may aspire to joining the ruling class. Others are not employed directly by the ruling class and work in the liberal arts and service professions. Although there may be some 'suspicion and distrust' between the two sections of the professional–managerial class, the Ehrenreichs stress that the division should not be exaggerated. Professionals in academic institutions often have an administrative and managerial role within the institution; and over 80 per cent of managers have had a college education, half of them studying liberal arts subjects. Such divisions as there are, are no greater than those within the working class.

Class conflict

Having discussed the place of the professional–managerial class in the stratification system, the Ehrenreichs go on to consider the role that it has played in class conflict in the USA over recent decades. They argue that during the 1960s the USA had a growing and increasingly confident professional–managerial class which came into conflict with the ruling class.

Students in particular began to demand greater independence from the ruling class, and claimed the right to run society more in their own interests than those of the ruling class. Organizations such as Students for a Democratic Society contributed to the development of the 'New Left' whose main aim was to ensure that professionals, managers and students were not reduced to being the mere tools of the ruling class.

The Vietnam War was particularly important in stimulating the rise of the New Left. The American capitalist state looked to universities to help it in its war effort, enlisting the help of scientists, engineers, psychologists and sociologists. The Ehrenreichs claim that partly as a reaction against the actions of the Government, 'large numbers of young people pushed professional–managerial class radicalism to its limits and found themselves, ultimately, at odds with their own class'. Students turned against their universities and universities are the most important institutions for the professional–managerial class.

The growing radicalism was partly a consequence of the increasing recruitment of working-class students who were necessary to fill the rising number of professional–managerial class jobs. One section of the New Left allied itself to the black working class who were demanding civil rights, and so acted against the narrow interests of the professional–managerial class.

In the 1970s these developments led to a split within the professional–managerial class. One group distanced itself from the class and adopted a communist ideology, advocating the overthrow of capitalism by the working class. The more moderate group of radicals continued the traditions of the New Left by trying to work within the professions to improve society.

Criticisms of the Ehrenreichs

The Ehrenreichs provide an interesting attempt to analyse the position of one part of the middle class within a neo-Marxist framework. However, they have been criticized by Marxists and non-Marxists alike.

Nicholas Abercrombie and John Urry accuse them of failing to take account of 'proletarianizing tendencies' within the professional–managerial class. After 1971 in the USA there was a reduction in demand for professional and managerial workers. This led to a surplus of qualified workers and made it possible for their work and pay to be devalued. Abercrombie and Urry also claim that the professional–managerial class is 'proportionately and politically stronger' in the USA than in other capitalist countries. They therefore question the degree to which the views of the Ehrenreichs are applicable to Europe.

The American neo-Marxist Erik Olin Wright does not accept that there is a unified professional–managerial class. He argues that capitalist societies remain polarized between two main classes: the ruling class and the working class. He does not deny that there are groups of workers who are intermediate between these two classes, but he argues that they do not constitute a fully developed class. Instead he sees them as occupying a number of strata which are in 'contradictory class locations'. Some of their interests coincide with those of the working class, and some with those of the ruling class, but they do not have a coherent set of interests of their own.

Weberian theories

Weberian and neo-Weberian sociologists generally reject the approach to defining and distinguishing classes adopted by the Ehrenreichs. They deny that classes can be defined in terms of their functions for capitalism and instead stress the importance of the market situation of those in particular occupations.

This has led to one Weberian sociologist, Anthony Giddens, identifying a larger middle class than the professional–managerial class discussed by the Ehrenreichs. From Giddens's point of view the middle class should also include lower-level white-collar workers (for further details see p. 69).

However, the neo-Weberian sociologist John Goldthorpe distinguishes a number of separate white-collar strata. He denies that there is a single professional–managerial class (or as he calls it the **service class**), but instead he sees it as being split in two. He distinguishes between higher-grade managers, administrators and professionals, and those in lower grades but similar jobs. Unlike Marxists and neo-Marxists, Goldthorpe believes that proprietors of businesses should be con-sidered part of the upper and lower strata of the service class, and not part of the ruling class. (See pp. 115–16 for full details of Goldthorpe's class scheme.)

We will consider the implications of these various views for the analysis of the middle class as a whole after we have discussed the lower middle class.

■ The lower middle class

Routine white-collar workers include such groups as clerks, secretaries and shop assistants. The growth in their numbers this century has led to a long-standing debate about their position in the class structure.

1 Some sociologists argue that they have become **proletarianized**, that is they have effectively become members of the working class.

2 Others claim that routine white-collar workers still belong to the middle class.

3 A third viewpoint suggests that they form an intermediate group between the middle and working classes.

■ Proletarianization

The theory of proletarianization suggests that routine white-collar workers have become part of the proletariat and so can no longer be considered middle class. This viewpoint has most usually been associated with Marxist sociologists who have questioned the assumption that the working class is a rapidly declining section of the population in capitalist societies. They see routine non-manual workers as little different from manual workers: they neither own the means of production nor do they perform important social control functions for capitalists. For example, the British Marxists Westergaard and Resler estimated that in 1913–14 male clerks earned 122 per cent of the average manual wage, but by 1971 this had fallen to just 96 per cent. They argued that, at least with respect to earnings, 'male clerks and shopworkers are now firmly among the broad mass of ordinary labour; and indeed often well down towards the bottom of the pile'.

Harry Braverman – the deskilling of clerical work

The American Marxist Harry Braverman supports the proletarianization thesis on the grounds that many routine non-manual jobs have become deskilled. He argues that over the last century or so the number of white-collar jobs has increased rapidly, but at the same time the skill required to do the jobs has been reduced. He calculates that in 1870 0.6 per cent of the population of the USA were engaged in clerical work; by 1970 it had reached 18 per cent. However, at the same time the wages of clerical workers fell in relation to other occupational groups. By 1970 in the USA they earned less on average than any category of manual worker.

According to Braverman, clerical workers in 1870 had many similarities to manual craft workers: both had wide-ranging responsibilities and had plenty of opportunity to use their initi-ative and develop their skills. Each company would employ a small number of clerical workers who would take care of all the dealings an enterprise had with the outside world. Each clerk would have the knowledge and experience to deal with many different tasks, and would be a valued member of the workforce.

As companies grew larger and their clerical workforce expanded, clerical work was reorgan-ized so that each worker specialized in particular tasks. As a result the skills required became minimal. As tasks were broken down the office became like a production line for mental work. Clerical workers lost the opportunity to use their initiative and instead their work became highly regulated. The nature of the work-force changed at the same time as the work. Clerical work was increasingly feminized: by 1970 75 per cent of clerical workers in the USA were women.

Braverman also claims that most 'service workers' have been deskilled. He says:

> the demand for the all-round grocery clerk, fruiterer and vegetable dealer, dairyman, butcher, and so forth, has long ago been replaced by a labor configuration in the supermarkets which calls for truck unloaders, shelf stockers, checkout clerks, meat wrappers, and meat cutters; of these only the last retain any semblance of skill, and none require any general knowledge of retail trade.

Computerization has further reduced the skill required of checkout assistants, and the control of stock and the keeping of accounts have also become largely automated.

Braverman believes that as a consequence of the changes outlined above, the skills required of most routine white-collar workers are now minimal. Basic numeracy and literacy are often all that are required. With mass compulsory education this century the vast majority of the population now have the necessary skills to undertake this type of work. As a result the bargaining position of these workers when they try to find work or gain promotion is little better than that of manual workers.

David Lockwood – a Weberian perspective

According to many Marxists then, the positions in the class structure occupied by most routine non-manual workers have been proletarianized. In an early study of clerks from a neo-Weberian point of view, however, David Lockwood denied that clerks had been proletarianized. Lockwood did not follow Weber in identifying an upper class based on the ownership of property; he did, though, use a Weberian approach to distinguish between different groups of employees. He suggested that there were three aspects of **class situation**. These were market situation, work situation and status situation.

1 By **market situation** he was referring to such factors as wages, job security and promotion prospects.

2 By **work situation** he meant social relationships at work between employers and managers and more junior

staff; this involved consideration of how closely work was supervised.

3 By **status situation** he meant the degree of prestige enjoyed by particular groups of workers in society.

In terms of market situation Lockwood admitted that the wages of clerical workers began to drop below the average for skilled manual workers from the 1930s onwards. However, he claimed that in other respects clerks had retained distinct market advantages over manual workers. They had more job security and were less likely to be laid off or made redundant. They also worked shorter hours, had more chance of being promoted to supervisory and managerial positions, and they were more likely to be given fringe benefits such as membership of a pension scheme. Some manual workers had only overtaken clerical workers in terms of pay because of the overtime they worked.

Lockwood reaches similar conclusions with regard to work situation. He accepts that there have been changes – in particular the modern office has grown in size – but he denies that this has led to clerical workers becoming proletarian. Compared to manual workers clerks still work in relatively small units; they do not work on huge factory floors. Lockwood accepts that clerical work is often divided up into separate departments, but he does not believe that this has led to deskilling. He believes that the division of the clerical workforce into smaller groups with specialized roles leads to closer contacts and greater cooperation between them and management. Furthermore, he claims that attempts to make clerical work more routine have had a limited impact because clerical skills and qualifications have not been standardized. The job of each clerical worker therefore has unique elements. It is not as easy to switch clerical workers around or to replace them as it is with manual workers.

Finally, in terms of status situation Lockwood is more willing to concede a deterioration in the position of the clerical workforce. He attributes this to the rise of the modern office, mass literacy, the recruitment of growing numbers of clerical workers from manual backgrounds, and the increasing employment of female labour in these jobs. Nevertheless, he does not believe that clerical workers have an identical status to the working class. Nor do they have the same status as managers. Lockwood believes that clerks are in a position of **status ambiguity** which falls somewhere between the degree of status enjoyed by the middle and working classes.

John H. Goldthorpe – clerks as an intermediate strata

In a more recent study, John H. Goldthorpe et al. also maintain that clerical workers fall between the working class and the middle class. Like Lockwood they base their analysis on market and work situations, but they do not take account of status situation. They believe that there is an **intermediate strata** sandwiched between what they refer to as the working and service classes. This intermediate strata also includes such groups as personal service workers, the self-employed, and supervisors of manual workers. The intermediate group lacks any strong class identity because of the range of occupations within it, and because many of its members become socially mobile and move into a different class.

A. Stewart, K. Prandy and R.M. Blackburn – clerks and social mobility

Other sociologists have supported Lockwood and Goldthorpe in denying that clerical workers have become proletarian, but they have attacked the proletarianization thesis in a different way. In a study based on a sample of male white-collar workers in firms employing over 500 people, Stewart, Prandy and Blackburn argue that individual workers in the stratification system should be distinguished from the positions that they occupy. To them whether or not routine white-collar work has become deskilled is largely irrelevant in discussing whether the workers in these jobs have become proletarian. This is because most male clerks do not stay as clerks for all their working lives.

Stewart et al.'s figures indicate that only 19 per cent of those who start work as clerks are still employed in clerical work by the time that they are 30. By that age, 51 per cent have been promoted out of clerical work and for them it is merely a stepping-stone to a higher status non-manual job.

The remaining 30 per cent leave clerical work before they are 30. Stewart et al. claim that many of those who are promoted before they are 30 embark upon successful management careers and end up in unambiguously middle-class jobs.

According to this study, clerical work is merely an occupational category through which men pass. Stewart et al. say that 'clerks have diverse relationships to the labour market'. Young men who take clerical work as the first step in a management career can be considered middle class. Older men who change from manual work to non-manual clerical work late in their careers can more reasonably be regarded as proletarian. However as Stewart et al. point out, as the latter have always been proletarian, it is senseless to see them as being proletarianized.

R. Crompton and G. Jones – a defence of the proletarianization thesis

Rosemary Crompton and Gareth Jones have strongly attacked the work of Stewart et al. Crompton and Jones studied 887 white-collar employees in three large bureaucracies: a local authority, a life assurance company, and a major bank. They advance four main arguments to undermine the conclusions of Stewart et al.

1 They point out that the study by Stewart et al. ignored female white-collar workers. In their own sample, a large majority of clerical workers – 70 per cent – were female. Furthermore, they found that female clerical workers were much less likely to achieve promotion than their male counterparts. Crompton and Jones found that 82 per cent of female white-collar workers in their sample were on clerical grades, compared to 30 per cent of men. Only 12 per cent of female workers had reached supervisory and 1 per cent managerial positions, while the equivalent figures for men were 36 per cent and 34 per cent. Thus, the high rates of male upward social mobility out of clerical work were at the expense of the large number of female workers who were left behind. They argue that even if male clerical workers cannot be considered proletarian because of their upward mobility, this is not true of female clerks.

2 Crompton and Jones point out that the high rates of upward mobility for men in the study by Stewart *et al.* depended not only on the immobility of women, but also on the 30 per cent of male clerks who left this type of employment. Crompton and Jones suggest that in the future it will not necessarily be the case that male clerks will be able to enjoy so much upward mobility. If the number of managerial jobs does not continue expanding, more and more men may become trapped in the way that female clerks already are.

3 Crompton and Jones question the view that promotion to managerial and administrative jobs necessarily represents genuine upward mobility. On the basis of their own study they claim that many managerial and administrative jobs have become increasingly routine and require little use of initiative. They claim that employers use the grade structure to encourage loyalty and dedication from employees, but in reality many of the lower-level management and administrative jobs are little different from clerical work. Promotion might not necessarily represent a change in class position for all white-collar workers.

4 Crompton and Jones suggest that Stewart *et al.* ignored one of the central issues in the proletarianization debate, that is, whether clerical work had actually been deskilled. Crompton and Jones disagree that class consists only of people, and has nothing to do with places in the stratification system. They say 'classes can be conceived of as sets of places within the social division of labour'. If the places occupied by clerical workers have lost their advantages over working-class jobs, then clerks can be considered proletarian.

Crompton and Jones carried out detailed investigations of the three institutions they studied and found strong evidence that proletarianization had taken place. Some 91 per cent of their sample of clerical workers did not exercise any control over how they worked: they simply followed a set of routines without using their initiative. As a result their work required very little skill. Deskilling appeared to be closely linked to computerization: least skill was required by the clerks at the most computerized of the institutions, the local authority.

Crompton and Jones concluded that clerical workers were a white-collar proletariat, and that female clerical workers in particular have little chance of promotion to what could be called middle-class or service-class jobs.

G. Marshall, H. Newby, D. Rose and C. Vogler – clerks and personal service workers

In a more recent contribution to the debate Gordon Marshall, Howard Newby, David Rose and Carolyn Vogler have rejected Crompton and Jones's views that clerical work has been deskilled. Marshall *et al.* do accept, though, that personal service workers such as shop assistants, check-out and wrap operators, and receptionists are little different from the working class. Their evidence is based on structured interviews carried out with a sample of 1,770 British men and women.

In one of their questions they asked respondents whether their job required more, less or the same skill as when they had started work. Overall only 4 per cent claimed that their jobs required less skill, and only 4 per cent of women in lower-grade white-collar jobs claimed to have been deskilled. No men in the latter type of job claimed that skill requirements had gone down. Workers were also questioned about such issues as whether they could design and plan important parts of their work, decide on day-to-day tasks, and decide the amount and pace of their work.

From this evidence Marshall *et al.* also conclude that clerical work has not been proletarianized. They support the views of Goldthorpe and Lockwood that clerical workers are in an intermediate class between the working and service classes. However, they did find that personal service workers tended to give different answers to the questions about autonomy at work. For example, 80 per cent of female personal service workers said they could not design and plan important parts of their work; 96 per cent said they could not decide their starting and finishing times; and 63 per cent said they could not initiate new tasks during their work. Marshall *et al.* conclude that personal service workers are 'virtually indistinguishable' from the working class.

The work of Marshall *et al.* draws attention to the position of personal service workers in the stratification system, and they, compared to clerical workers, have been a somewhat neglected part of the workforce in stratification research. Certainly it is hard to see how it is possible to regard, for example, check-out assistants as middle class given their low wages, working conditions, and lack of autonomy at work.

The rejection of the proletarianization theory for clerical workers by Marshall *et al.* must, however, be regarded with some caution. In particular, the significance of the small number who say their work has been deskilled is open to question. The deskilling argument as advanced by Braverman refers to a time-span of a century or more, stretching back far earlier than the experience of those currently employed in such jobs. Indeed, Marshall *et al.* themselves admit that 'a definitive answer to the question of job techniques and job autonomy could be provided only by systematic and direct observation over a prolonged period of time'.

■ Middle class, or middle classes?

As we have seen in the preceding sections, there is no agreement amongst sociologists about the place of the middle class, or classes, in the stratification system. They are divided about which non-manual workers should be placed in the middle class, and disagree about whether the middle class is a united and homogeneous, or divided and heterogeneous group.

Anthony Giddens – the middle class

The simplest position is taken by Anthony Giddens. He argues that there is a single middle class based on the 'possession of educational or technical qualifications'. Unlike the members of the working class who can sell only their manual labour power, members of the middle class can also sell their mental labour power. Giddens distinguishes the middle class from the upper class because the middle class does not own 'property in the means of production' and so has to work for others to earn a living.

John H. Goldthorpe – the service and intermediate classes

Giddens follows Weber's views quite closely, but other neo-Weberians do not agree that there is a single middle class. John Goldthorpe defines class in terms of market and work situation, but he does not follow Weber in distinguishing the propertied from the propertyless. Goldthorpe does not therefore distinguish an upper class, nor does he claim that there is a united middle class. As Figure 2.5 (on p. 116) shows, Goldthorpe sees the highest class as the **service class**, and this includes large proprietors as well as administrators, managers and professionals. This class itself is internally divided between those in upper and lower positions.

Goldthorpe's class in the middle is not called the middle class, but the **intermediate class**. This includes clerical workers, personal service workers, small proprietors and lower-grade technicians. To Goldthorpe these workers have poorer market and work situations than the service class. In his scheme this class is also seen as being internally divided, but nevertheless at the most basic level he sees what is normally regarded as the middle class as being split in two. (For further details of Goldthorpe's views see pp. 115–18.)

K. Roberts, F.G. Cook, S.C. Clark and E. Semeonoff – the fragmented middle class

Some sociologists however, see the middle class as being even more divided than Goldthorpe does.

From a study of images of class, Roberts, Cook, Clark and Semeonoff claim that 'The days when it was realistic to talk about the middle class are gone.' They argue that the middle class is increasingly divided into a number of different strata, each with a distinctive view of its place in the stratification system. Roberts *et al.* base these observations on a survey conducted in 1972, of the class images of a sample of 243 male white-collar workers. They found a number of different images of class, the four most common of which will now be briefly described.

1 Some 27 per cent of the white-collar sample had a **middle mass** image of society. They saw themselves as part of a middle class made up of the bulk of the working population. This middle mass lay between a

small, rich and powerful upper class and a small, relatively impoverished, lower class. No division was drawn between most manual and non-manual workers and within the large central class 'no basic ideological cleavages, divisions of interest or contrasts in life-styles' were recognized. Those who held a middle mass image of society were likely to be in the middle-range income bracket for white-collar workers.

2 The second most common image, held by 19 per cent of the sample, was that of a **compressed middle class**. Those who subscribed to this view saw themselves as members of a narrow stratum which was squeezed between two increasingly powerful classes. Below them, the bulk of the population formed a working class and above them was a small upper class. Small business people typically held this compressed middle-class image. They felt threatened by what they saw as an increasingly powerful and organized working class, and by government and big business which showed little inclination to support them.

3 A third group of white-collar workers saw society in terms of a **finely graded ladder** containing four or more strata. Although this is assumed to be the typical middle-class image of society, it was subscribed to by only 15 per cent of the sample. Those who saw society in these terms tended to be well educated, with professional qualifications, and relatively highly paid. Though they described themselves as middle class, they indicated no apparent class loyalty and often rejected the whole principle of social class.

4 Finally, 14 per cent of the white-collar sample held a **proletarian** image of society. They defined themselves as working class and located themselves in what they saw as the largest class at the base of the stratification system. They saw themselves as having more in common with manual workers than with top management and higher professionals. Those who held a proletarian image were usually employed in routine white-collar occupations with few promotion prospects and relatively low wages.

The wide variation in white-collar class imagery leads Roberts et al. to conclude that 'The trends are towards fragmenting the middle class into a number of distinguishable strata, each with its own view of its place in the social structure.' The diversity of class images, market situations, market strategies and interests within the white-collar group suggests that the middle class is becoming increasingly fragmented. Indeed, the proposition that white-collar groups form a single social class is debatable.

Criticisms of Roberts et al.

The work of Roberts et al. can be criticized for relying on subjective class images. Neo-Weberians such as Goldthorpe prefer to analyse class in terms of market and work situation, while neo-Marxists such as the Ehrenreichs advocate a discussion of the function that different strata perform for capitalism. For most Marxists it is the places in the stratification system (which are produced by the economic system) which are important in defining class, and not the individuals who occupy those places. For some Marxists this leads them to conclude that the middle class is split in two.

Writers such as Crompton and Jones, Braverman and the Ehrenreichs all agree that routine white-collar work has been deskilled and proletarianized. These workers do not have any stake in owning the means of production; they have little autonomy or responsibility at work; and they have lower wages than many members of the working class.

The upper reaches of what is usually referred to as the middle class, are, however, much closer to the bourgeoisie. They are unproductive labourers who do not produce wealth, but carry out important functions for capitalists. For example, managers play a vital role in controlling the workforce. Marxists and neo-Marxists disagree about the extent of their independence from the bourgeoisie. Braverman believes that they have little independence, while the Ehrenreichs claim the professional–managerial class has increasingly come to defend its own interests rather than those of the ruling class.

N. Abercrombie and J. Urry – the polarizing middle class

In a review of debates about the middle class, Nicholas Abercrombie and John Urry argue that both Marxist and Weberian theories of stratification are useful, and that the two approaches can be combined. To Abercrombie and Urry classes consist both of individuals, or people, and the places that they occupy.

They do not agree with Marxists who argue that the capitalist economic system automatically produces certain types of job with particular functions, for they point out that groups of workers can organize to try to protect their work. Thus professional workers have been quite successful in retaining their independence and work responsibilities, while clerical workers have not. The result has been to split the middle class in two.

In terms of the Marxist concept of functions performed, and also in terms of the Weberian concepts of market and work situations, there is a major division between managers and professionals on the one hand, and routine white-collar workers on the other. According to Abercrombie and Urry, whether a Marxist or a Weberian theory of class is used, one section of the middle class has moved closer to the upper class, while the other has more or less become proletarian. In between, the so-called 'middle class' is hard to find.

Mike Savage, James Barlow, Peter Dickens and Tony Fielding – Property, Bureaucracy and Culture

Savage, Barlow, Dickens and Fielding follow many other theories by claiming that the middle class is not a united group. Using data from the Oxford study of social mobility (see pp. 100–3 for details of the Oxford Mobility Study) they argue that the middle class consists of three main groups. These groups are not distinguished from each other according to their seniority in a class hierarchy, but according to the source of the advantages they enjoy over the working class. According to Savage *et al.* the middle classes get their advantaged life chances from three types of assets: property assets, organizational assets and cultural assets. Individuals may have some combination of these three types of asset, but, in Britain at least, distinctive middle classes have developed based on each of these types of asset.

1 The propertied middle class includes those who have substantial **property assets**, and would be regarded by Marxists as part of the bourgeoisie, and small property owners or the '*petit bourgeoisie*'. The self-employed and small employers are included in this category.

2 **Organizational assets** stem from holding positions in large bureaucratic organizations. These assets are held by managers. In the past a considerable number of people gained organizational assets by working their way up a bureaucratic hierarchy in a company without necessarily having high educational qualifications.

3 **Cultural assets** derive mainly from educational attainment and credentials. Professional workers depend most on cultural assets.

According to Savage *et al.* these three sections of the middle class have enjoyed different degrees of success.

The petit bourgeoisie and small property owners were very important in the nineteenth century, but in the twentieth century with the growth of large companies managers gained power at their expense. However, in recent years power deriving from organizational assets has declined in significance. Such assets cannot easily be passed on to children and changes in the organization of work have undermined the position of middle managers. It has become harder for people to work their way up in companies as large bureaucracies have been split up. Savage *et al.* support the view that industry has moved in the direction of becoming **post-Fordist**. This involves getting away from mass production in very large hierarchical firms and instead producing smaller batches of more specialized products in less hierarchical and more flexible firms. (See pp. 214–18 for a discussion of post-Fordism). In the process professional workers with high educational qualifications have gained at the expense of managers whose value to their employers has diminished.

Evaluation

The work of Savage *et al.* does highlight some important divisions within the middle class. However, it can be criticized for failing to distinguish an upper class of the very wealthy from the petit bourgeoisie and small employers. It also concentrates on the higher reaches of the middle class – their theory does not explain the position of routine white-collar workers.

Many writers on the middle class agree that it is divided into distinct groups, but there is much less agreement about what those groups are, or what it is that divides them.

■ The working class

The market situation of manual workers

In official statistics based upon the Registrar General's scale, the working class is usually regarded as consisting of manual workers. As we saw previously (see pp. 56–7), there are important differences between manual and non-manual workers.

1 Non-manual workers, on average, receive higher wages than their manual counterparts.

2 A second market advantage of white-collar workers concerns the differences in income careers between manual and non-manual employees. The wages of manual workers typically rise gradually during their twenties, peak in their early thirties, and then slowly but steadily fall. By comparison, the earnings of many white-collar workers continue to rise during most of their working lives. Manual workers have relatively few opportunities for promotion and their pay structure is unlikely to include incremental increases.

3 A third white-collar market advantage involves security of earnings and employment: compared to non-manual workers, manual workers have a greater risk of redundancy, unemployment, lay-offs, and short-time.

4 Finally, the gross weekly earnings of white- and blue-collar workers do not reveal the economic value of fringe benefits. Such benefits include company pension schemes, paid sick leave, the use of company cars, meals and entertainment which are paid for in part or in total by the employer.

Life chances

The inferior market situation of manual workers is also reflected in their inferior life chances. A variety of studies show that compared to non-manual workers, they die younger and are more likely to suffer from poor health; they are less likely to own their own homes and a variety of consumer goods; they are more likely to be convicted of a criminal offence; and their children are less likely to stay on at school after the age of 16 to achieve educational qualifications, or to go on to higher education. In short, compared to non-manual workers, manual workers have less chance of experiencing those things defined as desirable in Western societies, but more chance of experiencing those things defined as undesirable.

Class and lifestyle

The above evidence suggests that manual workers form at least part of the working class in Britain. As previous sections indicated, some sociologists – particularly those influenced by Marxism – would also include routine non-manual workers in the working class. However, many sociologists would argue that social class involves more than a similar market situation and similar life chances.

In order to become a social class, a collection of similarly placed individuals must to some degree form a social group. This involves at least a minimal awareness of group identity and some appreciation of and commitment to common interests. It also involves some similarity of lifestyle. Members of a social group usually share certain norms, values and attitudes which distinguish them from other members of society. Finally, belonging to a social group usually means that a member will interact primarily with other members of that group. We will now analyse manual workers terms of these criteria for class formation.

Class identity

A number of studies conducted over the past thirty years in Britain indicate that the vast majority of the population believe that society is divided into social classes. These studies show that most manual workers describe themselves as working class, and most white-collar workers see themselves as middle class.

However, there are a number of problems with this type of evidence. As Kenneth Roberts observes, 'because individuals are prepared to label themselves as middle or working class when invited by sociologists, it does not necessarily follow that they ordinarily think in these terms'. Thus class identification may have little significance to those concerned.

In addition, the labels 'middle and working class' may mean different things to different people. In a survey conducted in 1950, F.M. Martin found that 70 per cent of manual workers regarded themselves as working class. The remaining 30 per cent who defined themselves as middle class did so partly because of the meanings they attached to the term working class. They saw the working class as a group bordering on poverty and defined its members as lazy and irresponsible; hence their desire to dissociate themselves from this classification.

However, despite the above problems, the fact that most manual workers define themselves as working class indicates at least a minimal awareness of class identity.

Class subcultures

From his observations of the working class in nineteenth-century England, Engels wrote: 'The workers speak other dialects, have other thoughts and ideals, other customs and moral principles, a different religion and other politics than those of the *bourgeoisie*. Thus they are two radically dissimilar nations . . . ' (Quoted in Parkin 1972, p. 79.)

Few, if any, sociologists would suggest that the gulf between the classes is as great today. Many, though, would argue that the norms, values and attitudes of the working and middle classes differ to some degree. They would therefore feel justified in talking about working-class subculture and middle-class subculture. As a result it has been argued that manual and non-manual workers form social groups distinguished by relatively distinct subcultures.

The proletarian traditionalist and the middle class

Sociologists have long been aware of variations in working-class subcultures. Members of the working class have never had identical lifestyles. Nevertheless, a number of sociologists have identified characteristics which have been seen as typical of the traditional working class. Basing his ideas on classic studies of working-class communities, David Lockwood has described the subculture of one working-class group, the **proletarian traditionalists**. When sociologists try to determine the extent to which the working class might have changed, they tend to make comparisons with the proletarian traditionalist.

The proletarian traditionalist lives in close-knit working-class communities and is employed in long-established industries such as mining, docking and shipbuilding. Such industries tend to concentrate workers together in communities dominated by a single occupational group. These communities are relatively isolated from the wider society. Consequently they tend to produce a strong sense of belonging and solidarity. The workers are very loyal to their workmates and 'a strong sense of shared occupational experiences make for feelings of fraternity and comradeship'.

Friendship with workmates extends into leisure activities. Workmates are often neighbours and relatives as well. They spend much of their leisure time together in pubs and working men's clubs. There is little geographical and social mobility so the sense of belonging to a community is reinforced. The strong social networks 'emphasise mutual aid in everyday life and the obligation to join in the gregarious pattern of leisure'.

The proletarian traditionalist is not an individualist. Lockwood describes 'a public and present-oriented conviviality' which 'eschews individual striving to be different'. Unlike the middle class, proletarian traditionalists do not pursue individual achievement by trying to gain promotion at work or success in running their own businesses. Instead they identify strongly with the pursuit of collective goals. This is often expressed through strong loyalty to a union. This loyalty comes from an emotional attachment to the organization more than from a calculation of the benefits that union membership might bring.

The proletarian traditionalist's attitude to life tends to be fatalistic. From this perspective there is little individuals can do to alter their situation and changes or improvements in their circumstances are largely due to luck or fate. In view of this, life must be accepted as it comes. Since there is little chance of individual effort changing the future, long-term planning is discouraged in favour of **present-time orientation**. There is a tendency to live from day to day and planning is limited to the near future. As a result, there is an emphasis on **immediate gratification**. There is little pressure to sacrifice pleasures of the moment for future rewards; desires are to be gratified in the present rather than at a later date. This attitude to life may be summarized by the following everyday phrases: 'what is to be will be', 'take life as it comes', 'make the best of it', 'live for today because tomorrow may never come'.

By comparison, middle-class subculture is characterized by a **purposive approach** to life;

humanity has control over its destiny and with ability, determination and ambition, can change and improve its situation. Associated with this attitude is an emphasis on **future-time orientation** and **deferred gratification**. Long-term planning and deferring or putting off present pleasures for future rewards are regarded as worthwhile. Thus individuals are encouraged to sacrifice money and/or leisure at certain stages of their lives to improve career prospects.

In addition to particular values and attitudes, members of society usually have a general image or picture of the social structure and the class system. These pictures are known as **images of society** or more particularly, **images of class**.

The proletarian traditionalist tends to perceive the social order as sharply divided into 'us' and 'them'. On one side are the bosses, managers and white-collar workers who have power, and on the other, the relatively powerless manual workers. There is seen to be little opportunity for individual members of the working class to cross the divide separating them from the rest of society.

This view of society is referred to as a **power model** and those who hold it as proletarian traditionalists. Research has indicated that traditional workers may hold other images of society and their perceptions of the social order are not as simple and clearcut as the above description suggests. However, the power model appears to be the nearest thing to a consistent image of society held by a significant number of traditional workers.

By comparison, the middle-class image of society resembles a ladder. There are various strata or levels differentiated in terms of occupational status and lifestyles of varying prestige. Given ability and ambition, opportunities are available for individuals to rise in the social hierarchy. This view of the social order is known as a **status** or **prestige model**.

The above account of proletarian traditionalists is largely based on a description of men. Working-class communities have usually been seen as having strongly segregated gender roles. Husbands have been regarded as the main breadwinners while wives have retained responsibility for childcare and housework. Husbands and wives tend to spend leisure time apart. While the men mix with their work colleagues, women associate more with female relatives. The bond between mother and daughter is particularly strong. (For an example

of a detailed description of gender roles in a traditional working-class community see pp. 340–1.)

Marxism and the working class

Marxist sociologists have tended to support the view that there is a distinctive working class which is distinguished by its non-ownership of the means of production and its role in providing manual labour power for the ruling class. Marxists also tend to see the working class as a social group with a distinctive subculture and at least some degree of class consciousness.

Marx himself predicted that the working class would become increasingly homogeneous: its members would become more and more similar to one another. He assumed that technical developments in industry would remove the need for manual skills. As a result craftspeople and tradespeople would steadily disappear and the bulk of the working class would become unskilled machine minders. The growing similarity of wages and circumstances would increase working-class solidarity. Marx argued:

> The interests and life situations of the proletariat are more and more equalized, since the machinery increasingly obliterates the differences of labour and depresses the wage almost everywhere to an equally low level.

Marx thought that as a consequence members of the working class would be drawn closer together and would eventually form a revolutionary force which would overthrow capitalism and replace it with communism. There have been some revolutionary movements in capitalist industrial societies, but none have come close to success.

Changes in the working class

Some sociologists now believe that during this century the working class has undergone changes which have weakened and divided it, reduced its distinctiveness from the middle class, and removed the potential for the development of class consciousness. One of the most obvious changes is the shrinking size of the working class if it is defined as consisting of manual workers. According to Routh, manual workers declined from 79 per cent of those in employment in 1911, to just under half in 1971.

A somewhat different impression is provided by the *General Household Survey*, a survey carried out regularly by the British Government. This uses slightly different categories from the manual/non-manual division, including personal service workers and self-employed non-professional workers with manual workers. On this basis 48 per cent of the population was found to be in the working class in 1991, compared to 55 per cent in 1975.

In part this decline has been due to de-industrialization as manufacturing industry employs a decreasing percentage of the workforce. Between 1966 and 1993 employment in manufacturing in Great Britain fell from 8.6 to 4.2 million. In 1993 only around 17 per cent of those in employment had jobs in manufacturing. If all jobs in construction and production are combined, they still only represented about 22 per cent of those employed in 1993.

Employment has fallen particularly rapidly in those jobs which are most likely to produce the subculture of the traditional proletarian worker. Heavy industries in which employees tend to live close together in occupational communities have declined, for example, coal mining, dock work and the steel industry. In 1947 there were 74,000 British miners; by 1993 just 36,000 were employed in coal extraction and the numbers were continuing to fall.

Recent declines in manufacturing employment have not just hit the traditional heavy industries though. Huw Beynon says: 'The car workers, it seems have gone the way of miners; as have the shipyard workers, the steel workers and those men . . . who in mechanical engineering factories supplied components for the consumer industries.'

Beynon points out that in 1992 there were more people employed in hotel and catering than in steel, shipyards, cars, mechanical engineering and coal combined.

The new industrial jobs tend to be located in the electronics industries concentrated in such areas as 'silicon glen' in Scotland, East Anglia, the M4 corridor and South Wales. These changes have been accompanied by a major shift in the proportions of men and women employed in manufacturing. Beynon describes the 'rise of industries based upon information technology, in which women play a central part: they manufacture the microchip in factories in the Far East and they assemble the computer boards in the lowlands of Scotland'.

The end of the industrial worker?

Although he accepts that industrial work has changed a great deal and declined significantly, Beynon argues that we are far from witnessing the 'end of the industrial worker' or the demise of the working class. He argues that the decline of industrial work can be exaggerated for a number of reasons.

1 Many manufacturing jobs have not disappeared, they have simply been moved abroad to take advantage of cheaper labour costs. In countries such as Brazil, Mexico, Malaysia, South Korea and Hong Kong, manufacturing employment has been rising rapidly since the war. Manufacturing employment in Britain is also low compared to most other advanced industrial capitalist countries because of 'a competitively weak industrial structure and the economic policies followed in the UK in the 1980s'.

2 Many jobs which are classified as being in the service sector are involved in producing things and the distinction between manufacturing and services is therefore somewhat artificial. For example, workers at McDonald's are mainly involved in 'distinctly manual, repetitive and unpleasant work'. Cooking beefburgers is as much a manual task as assembling motor cars, yet it is not classified as such.

3 Some jobs have been redefined as belonging to the service sector because of changes in who employs the workers rather than changes in the nature of the work. For example, at companies like Nissan, jobs such as cleaning have been subcontracted out to independent companies. As a result they are no longer defined as manufacturing jobs.

Beynon concludes that there are still very substantial numbers of workers involved in manufacturing and it cannot be argued that the industrial worker is disappearing.

Living standards and splits in the working class

Although the number of manual workers declined, average living standards for manual workers in regular employment have improved. According to government figures net income after housing costs for individuals rose by about 35 per cent between 1979 and 1991. The better-paid groups of manual workers were amongst the beneficiaries of this general rise in living standards.

As early as the 1960s some commentators were arguing that rising living standards were creating a new group of affluent members of the working class who have started acting like members of the middle class. **Affluent manual workers** have been seen as developing a privatized home-based lifestyle and as becoming more concerned with purchasing consumer goods than with showing solidarity with their workmates. A recent variation on this theme suggests that home ownership particularly amongst former council house tenants has transformed the attitudes and values of some sections of the working class.

Some sociologists do not accept that affluent manual workers have become middle class, nor that they have developed a more privatized lifestyle, but they do believe that the working class is increasingly split into different groups. Workers with different degrees of skill, and those belonging to particular trades, are more concerned with protecting their own interests than they are in making common cause with the working class as a whole. To some, members of the working class have become interested primarily in the size of their wage packets, and they have little potential for developing class consciousness. We will now examine these views in more detail.

■ Embourgeoisement

Writing in the nineteenth century, Marx predicted that the intermediate strata would be depressed into the proletariat. During the 1950s and early 1960s, a number of sociologists suggested that just the opposite was happening. They claimed that a process of **embourgeoisement** was occurring whereby increasing numbers of manual workers were entering the middle stratum and becoming middle class.

During the 1950s there was a general increase in prosperity in advanced industrial societies and, in particular, amongst a growing number of manual workers whose earnings now fell within the white-collar range. These highly paid **affluent workers** were seen to be increasingly typical of manual workers.

This development, coupled with studies which suggested that poverty was rapidly disappearing, led to the belief that the shape of the stratification system was being transformed. From the triangle or pyramid shape of the nineteenth century (with a large and relatively impoverished working class at the bottom and a small wealthy group at the top), it was argued that the stratification system was changing to a diamond or pentagon shape with an increasing proportion of the population falling into the middle range. In this **middle mass society**, the mass of the population was middle rather than working class.

Economic determinism

The theory used to explain this presumed development was a version of **economic determinism**. It was argued that the demands of modern technology and an advanced industrial economy determined the shape of the stratification system.

For instance, the American sociologist Clark Kerr claimed that advanced industrialism requires an increasingly highly educated, trained and skilled workforce which in turn leads to higher pay and higher status occupations. In particular skilled technicians are rapidly replacing unskilled machine minders.

Jessie Bernard argued that working-class affluence is related to the needs of an industrial economy for a mass market. In order to expand, industry requires a large market for its products. Mass consumption has been made possible by high wages, which in turn have been made possible because large sectors of modern industry have relatively low labour costs and high productivity.

Bernard claimed that there is a rapidly growing **middle market** which reflects the increased purchasing power of affluent manual workers. Home ownership and consumer durables such as washing machines, refrigerators, televisions and motor cars are no longer the preserve of white-collar workers. With reference to the class system, Bernard states:

The 'proletariat' has not absorbed the middle class but rather the other way round . . . In the sense that the class structure here described reflects modern technology, it vindicates the Marxist thesis that social organization is 'determined' by technological forces. (Quoted in Goldthorpe and Lockwood 1969, p. 9.)

Thus Bernard suggests that Marx was correct in emphasizing the importance of economic factors but wrong in his prediction of the direction of social change.

The supporters of embourgeoisement argued that middle-range incomes led to middle-class lifestyles. It was assumed that the affluent worker was adopting middle-class norms, values and attitudes. For example, in Britain, it was believed that affluence eroded traditional political party loyalties and that increasing numbers of manual workers were now supporting the Conservative Party.

The process of embourgeoisement was seen to be accelerated by the demands of modern industry for a mobile labour force. This tended to break up traditional close-knit working-class communities found in the older industrial areas. The geographically mobile, affluent workers moved to newer, suburban areas where they were largely indistinguishable from their white-collar neighbours.

■ J. Goldthorpe, D. Lockwood, F. Bechhofer and J. Platt – *The Affluent Worker in the Class Structure*

Despite the strong support for embourgeoisement, the evidence on which it was based was largely impressionistic. As such, embourgeoisement remained a **hypothesis**, a process that was assumed to be occurring but which had not been adequately tested.

In a famous study entitled *The Affluent Worker in the Class Structure*, conducted in the 1960s, Goldthorpe, Lockwood, Bechhofer and Platt present the results of research designed to test the embourgeoisement hypothesis. They attempted to find as favourable a setting as possible for the confirmation of the hypothesis. Thus if embourgeoisement were not taking place in a context which offered every opportunity, then it would probably not be occurring in less favourable contexts.

Goldthorpe *et al.* chose Luton, a prosperous area in southeast England with expanding industries. A sample of 229 manual workers was selected plus a comparative group of fifty-four white-collar workers drawn from various grades of clerks. The study was conducted from 1963 to 1964 and examined workers from Vauxhall Motors, Skefko Ball Bearing Company and Laporte Chemicals. Nearly half the manual workers in the survey had come from outside the southeast area in search of stable, well-paid jobs. All were married and 57 per cent were home owners or buyers. Relative to other manual workers they were highly paid and their wages compared favourably with those of many white-collar workers.

Although the Luton study was not primarily concerned with economic aspects of class, Goldthorpe and Lockwood argue, like many of the opponents of the embourgeoisement thesis, that similarity of earnings is not the same thing as similarity of market situation. Relative to affluent manual workers, white-collar workers retain many of their market advantages, including 'continuity of employment, fringe benefits, long-term income prospects and promotion chances'. The Luton study tested the embourgeoisement hypothesis in four main areas:

1 attitudes to work;
2 interaction patterns in the community;
3 aspirations and social perspectives;
4 political views.

If affluent workers were becoming middle class they should be largely indistinguishable from white-collar workers in these areas.

Instrumental orientation to work

The affluent workers define their work in **instrumental** terms, as a means to an end rather than an end in itself. Work is simply a means of earning money to raise living standards. Largely because of this **instrumental orientation** they derive little satisfaction from work. They do not compensate for this lack of job satisfaction by building up rewarding social relationships with their workmates. Few have close friends at work or participate in the social clubs provided by their firms. Since they define work as simply a place to make money, they do not see it as a context for making friends.

Most affluent workers accept their position as manual wage earners as more or less permanent. They feel that there is little chance for promotion and that supervisory jobs imply too great a degree of involvement with and commitment to the company. They are concerned with making a 'good living' *from* their firms rather than a 'good career' *within* their firms.

Like the traditional worker, affluent workers see improvements in terms of wages and working conditions resulting from collective action in trade unions rather than individual achievement. However, their attitude to unions differs from traditional working-class collectivism which was based largely on class solidarity, on strong union loyalty and the belief that members of the working class ought to stick together. The affluent workers join with their workmates as self-interested individuals to improve their wages and working conditions. They have no apparent commitment to the ideal of working-class solidarity and regard trade unions in instrumental terms, as a means to personal ends. Thus the **solidaristic collectivism** of the traditional worker has largely been replaced by the **instrumental collectivism** of the affluent worker.

By contrast, white-collar workers do not define work in purely instrumental terms. They expect and experience a higher level of job satisfaction. They make friends at work and the firms' social clubs have a largely white-collar membership. Promotion for the white-collar worker is a desired objective, even a **moral expectation**: they feel an obligation to put their ability into the firm and in return expect long-term security and career opportunities. However, because promotion prospects are increasingly slim for many lower-grade white-collar workers, they are adopting a strategy of instrumental collectivism and joining trade unions in order to improve their market situation.

In general, though, Goldthorpe and Lockwood conclude that in the area of work, there are significant differences between affluent manual workers and white-collar workers. In this respect, the embourgeoisement hypothesis is not confirmed. Affluent workers are not becoming middle class.

Friendship, lifestyle and norms

Supporters of the embourgeoisement thesis argue that once the affluent workers leave the factory gates, they adopt a middle-class lifestyle. Their friendship patterns follow middle-class norms and they associate with their white-collar neighbours as frequently and as freely as with persons of their own occupational status.

Goldthorpe and Lockwood found little support for this view. Affluent workers draw their friends and companions from kin and neighbours and in this respect they follow traditional working-class norms. By comparison, white-collar workers mix more with friends made at work and with persons who are neither kin nor neighbours. Despite the fact that many of their neighbours are white-collar workers, affluent workers nearly always befriend fellow manual workers. They show no desire to mix with members of the middle class and there is no evidence that they either value or seek middle-class status.

In one respect there is a convergence between the lifestyles of the affluent worker and the lower middle class. Both tend to lead a privatized and home-centred existence. The affluent workers' social relationships are centred on and largely restricted to the home. Their time is spent watching television, gardening, doing jobs around the house and socializing with their immediate family. There is no evidence of the communal sociability of the traditional working class. However, apart from the similarity of the privatized and family-centred life of affluent workers and the lower middle class, Goldthorpe and Lockwood argue that the affluent workers have not adopted middle-class **patterns of sociability**. In particular they have not become, nor show any desire to become assimilated into middle-class society.

Images of society

In terms of their general outlook on life, affluent workers differ in important respects from the traditional workers. Many had migrated to Luton in order to improve their living standards rather than simply accepting life in their towns of origin. In this respect, they have a purposive rather than a fatalistic attitude. As we noted previously, however, the means they adopt to realize their goals – instrumental collectivism – are not typical of the middle class as a whole. In addition their goals are distinct from those of the middle class in that they focus simply on material benefits rather than a concern with advancement in the prestige hierarchy.

This emphasis on materialism is reflected in the affluent workers' **images of society**. Few see society in terms of either the **power model** based on the idea of 'us and them' which is characteristic of the traditional workers, or in terms of the **prestige model** which is typical of the middle class. The largest group (56 per cent) sees money as the basis of class divisions. In terms of this money or **pecuniary model**, they see a large central class made up of the majority of the working population. Only a minority made up of the extremes of wealth – that is the very rich and the very poor – fall outside this class. The manual/non-manual distinction is not seen as forming a significant division in the class system.

Although differing from the traditional workers, the affluent workers' outlook on life and image of society do not appear to be developing in a middle-class direction.

Political attitudes

Finally, Goldthorpe and Lockwood found little support for the view that affluence leads manual workers to vote for the Conservative Party. In the 1959 election, 80 per cent of the affluent worker sample voted Labour, a higher proportion than for the manual working class as a whole. Some evidence of an awareness of class interests is indicated – Goldthorpe and Lockwood note:

by far the most common kind of reason given for attachment to the Labour Party was one couched in 'class terms': Labour was typically seen as the party of the working class, as the party for which the manual worker would naturally vote.

However, support for the Labour Party, like support for trade unions, was often of an instrumental kind. There was little indication of the strong loyalty to Labour which is assumed to be typical of the traditional worker.

The 'new working class'

Goldthorpe and Lockwood tested the embourgeoisement hypothesis under conditions favourable to its confirmation, but found it was not confirmed. They conclude that it is therefore unlikely that large numbers of manual workers are becoming middle class. Despite this the Luton workers differ in significant respects from the traditional working class. In view of this, Goldthorpe and Lockwood suggest that they may form the vanguard of an emerging **new working class**. While the new working class is not being assimilated into the middle class, there are two points of **normative convergence** between the classes: privatization and instrumental collectivism.

Finally Goldthorpe and Lockwood argue that the results of their study represent a rejection of economic determinism. The affluent worker has not simply been shaped by economic forces. Instead, 'class and status relationships' have 'an important degree of autonomy, and can thus accommodate considerable change in this infrastructure without themselves changing in any fundamental way'. Thus the lifestyle and outlook of the affluent worker are due in large part to the adaptation of traditional working-class norms to a new situation; they were not simply shaped by that situation.

Embourgeoisement and the privatized worker

David Lockwood believed that the **privatized instrumentalist** revealed by the affluent worker study would gradually replace the proletarian traditionalist. John Goldthorpe went further claiming that working-class instrumentalism was a major factor in causing inflation in the 1970s. As groups of workers pushed for higher wages and tried to keep ahead of other manual workers in the earnings league, industrial costs went up, and with them prices. As prices rose, workers demanded even higher wages.

Stephen Hill – London dockers

A study of London dockers conducted in the 1970s by Stephen Hill provided some support for the view that the privatized instrumental worker was becoming more common. However, the study also raised doubts about the extent to which workers had ever conformed to the image of the proletarian traditionalist.

Stephen Hill suggests that the new working class might not be as new as Goldthorpe and Lockwood believed. The 139 dock labourers in Hill's survey were remarkably similar to the Luton workers. Judging from past studies, the docks are one of the heartlands of proletarian traditionalism. Strong working-class solidarity, long-standing loyalties to unions and the Labour Party, close bonds between workmates, communal leisure activities, an emphasis on mutual aid and a power model of society have been seen as characteristic of dock workers. Either this picture has been exaggerated or there have been important changes in dockland life.

There is probably some truth in both these viewpoints. David Lockwood, writing in 1975, admits that the differences between the traditional and new worker have probably been exaggerated. The system of casual labour in the docks was abolished in 1967 and replaced by permanent employment. The constant threat of underemployment entailed in the casual labour system tended to unite dock workers. The change to permanent employment may have reduced the traditional solidarity of dockland life.

Like the Luton workers, the dockers in Hill's study defined their work primarily in instrumental terms. Their main priority was to increase their living standards. Only a minority made close friends at work, and only 23 per cent reported seeing something of their workmates outside work. Most dockers lived a privatized lifestyle and leisure activities were mainly home and family-centred.

Like the Luton workers, dockers regarded collective action in trade unions as essential for economic improvement. Over 80 per cent of dockers voted Labour, the most common reason for this being an identification with Labour as the party of the working class. Again these findings are very similar to those of the Luton study.

In terms of their views of society, the dockers belied their proletarian traditionalist image. Only 14 per cent saw the class structure in terms of a power model whereas 47 per cent, the largest group subscribing to one particular view, saw society in terms of a money model. In this respect they are again similar to the Luton workers. Hill concludes:

The evidence of dock workers strongly suggests that the working class is more homogeneous than has been allowed for: those who wish to divide it into old and new greatly exaggerate the divisions which actually occur within the ranks of semi-skilled and unskilled workers.

Fiona Devine – *Affluent Workers Revisited*

Fiona Devine has directly tested Lockwood's claim that the privatized instrumentalist would become the typical member of the working class. While Hill had examined a traditional proletarian group and found evidence to support Lockwood, Devine went back to studying 'affluent workers'. Between July 1986 and July 1987 she conducted in-depth interviews with a sample of sixty-two people from Luton. The sample consisted of thirty male manual workers employed on the shop floor at the Vauxhall car plant, their wives, and two further wives of Vauxhall workers whose husbands refused to participate. By returning to Luton Devine was able to make direct comparisons between her own findings in the 1980s and those of Goldthorpe *et al.* in the 1960s.

Geographical mobility

Like the earlier study, Devine's found high levels of geographical mobility. Some 30 per cent of the sample had been brought up away from Luton. However, unlike Goldthorpe *et al.* she did not find that they had moved to Luton in search of higher living standards. With high levels of unemployment in the 1980s many had gone to Luton in search of greater job security. Some of those who had moved from London had done so in order to find more affordable housing.

Orientation to work

Devine found that her sample was interested in using work as a means of improving their living standards. However, they were 'faced with the threat of redundancy and unemployment which hung over their daily lives'. Thus while they wanted to 'better themselves' they were more concerned with attaining greater security. They expected no more than 'small, cumulative gains' in their living standards. Their consumer aspirations were more limited than those of their 1960s counterparts, though they were rather greater than those supposed to be possessed by the 'traditional' working class.

The 1980s sample continued to belong to and support trade unions. Furthermore they saw them as a 'collective means of securing working class interests'. Money was not their only concern and other issues led to feelings of solidarity with fellow workers. Devine says 'Their poor conditions of work, for example, were often shared with fellow workers, and this was recognised to be the case.' They also expressed concern about the distribution of power at work and were interested in securing humane and fair treatment for their colleagues and themselves in their working lives. Many of them were critical of unions, but these criticisms were directed at union tactics and they did not reduce the support for the principle of having unions to defend working-class interests.

Overall, Devine follows Goldthorpe and Lockwood in describing the worker's orientation to work as instrumental collectivism but she found more evidence of collectivism in the 1980s than had appeared to be present in the 1960s. The concern with money and living standards did not prevent them from feeling a sense of solidarity with fellow workers.

Friendship, lifestyle and norms

Like Goldthorpe *et al.* Devine did not find that Vauxhall manual workers were befriending members of the middle class. In some respects they had traditional working-class friendship patterns: men had friends from work and many of their wives retained close contacts with relatives. Men still enjoyed leisure outside the home with other men, particularly playing sports or going to the pub. Traditional gender roles were also in evidence; although many wives had paid employment they still had primary responsibility for domestic

chores. This reduced their freedom to engage in leisure outside the home.

Nevertheless, Devine did find important differences between her sample and the supposed characteristics of traditional workers. She says that they 'were not engaged in extensive sociability in pubs, clubs or whatever' and they did not have a communal existence based on their neighbourhood. Their lifestyles 'did not totally revolve around the immediate family in the home' but at particular stages in the life cycle the home was very important. Families with young children had restricted opportunities for leisure in the community. Men were often working overtime to help provide materially for the family and women had most of the responsibility for childcare. In short their lifestyle was neither as communal as that of the proletarian traditionalist, nor as home-centred and privatized as Goldthorpe *et al.*'s affluent workers.

Images of society

The images of society held by Devine's sample were found to be very similar to those in the earlier study. They had a 'pecuniary model of the class structure' and most saw themselves as belonging to a 'mass working/middle class' in between the very rich and the very poor. This did not though, prevent them from sharing certain values with the traditional working class. Many felt resentment at those who had inherited money and a sense of injustice at the existence of extreme class inequalities. One said 'I disagree with a silver spoon. People should work for their money, not inherit it.' They wanted some redistribution of wealth away from the very rich and with it the creation of a somewhat more egalitarian society.

Political attitudes

Devine did find evidence of declining support for the Labour Party. As Table 2.13 shows, only twenty-four of the sixty-two had voted Labour in the 1979 or 1983 elections. On the surface this would seem to support the view that affluent workers were increasingly voting for individualistic and instrumental reasons. However, Devine did not find that disillusioned Labour Party supporters had abandoned their belief in the values traditionally associated with voting Labour. Instead they had withdrawn their allegiance, perhaps only temporarily, because of the party's political

Table 2.13 Political allegiances of the interviewees in Devine's study

Political allegiance	Number of interviewees
Labour Party supporters	24
Disillusioned Labour Party supporters	24
Non-Labour Party supporters	14
Total	62

(*Source*: Devine, F. (1992) *Affluent Workers Revisited*, Edinburgh University Press, Edinburgh, p. 189.)

failings. They were highly critical of the 'Winter of Discontent' in 1978–9 when a Labour Government had presided over widespread strikes. They were unhappy about the breakdown in relations between the party and the unions. They were also critical of the party's performance in running the economy during the 1970s, and of internal divisions during the 1980s.

A number of the disillusioned voters felt fatalistic about politics. While they still felt that theoretically the Labour Party represented working-class interests, they doubted its ability to deliver economic prosperity or low unemployment. Nine of the disillusioned Labour voters said they intended to vote Conservative at the next election. However, they were hardly embracing the Conservative Party with wholehearted enthusiasm: for them, 'The only positive attraction of the Conservatives was their policy of selling council houses which was seen as "giving people the chance to better themselves".'

Conclusion

Devine's findings are rather different from those of Goldthorpe *et al.* some three decades earlier. She did not find that her sample had become the increasingly instrumental privatized workers predicted. She says:

The interviewees were not singularly instrumental in their motives for mobility or in their orientations to work. Nor did they lead exclusively privatised styles of life. Their aspirations and social perspectives were not entirely individualistic. Lastly, the interviewees were critical of the trades unions and the Labour Party, but not for the reasons identified by the Luton team [i.e. Goldthorpe *et al.*].

Devine rejects the idea of a 'new' working class and denies that the affluent workers have been persuaded to accept capitalist society uncritically. They have aspirations as consumers and their living standards have risen, but they would still like to see a more egalitarian society. They have lost faith in the ability of unions and the Labour Party to deliver this objective, but they have not fundamentally changed their values.

G. Marshall, H. Newby, D. Rose and C. Vogler – continuities in the working class

There is considerable support for Devine's findings in a study of the British stratification system carried out by Gordon Marshall, Howard Newby, David Rose and Carolyn Vogler. Based on a national sample of 1,770 adults, the study found 'sectionalism, instrumentalism, and privatism among the British working class are not characteristics somehow peculiar to the recent years of economic recession'.

Marshall *et al.* claim that historical studies demonstrate the existence of artisans who put primary emphasis on their home life, and who had an instrumental attitude to work, well back into the nineteenth century. Furthermore, their data on contemporary workers suggest that they retain some commitment to their work and do not lead completely privatized lifestyles. For example, 73 per cent of their sample thought that their work was at least as important as any non-work activity, and over half numbered one or more workmates among their friends.

In relation to instrumentalism and privatism Marshall *et al.* claim 'There are no grounds to suppose that these phenomena have been increasing or changing in any significant way.'

▪ Divisions in the working class
Marxism and the homogeneous working class

Marx predicted that members of the working class would become increasingly homogeneous or alike. The American Marxist Harry Braverman agrees with Marx. He claims that the pursuit of profit has led to more and more automation in factories. This in turn has reduced the need for skilled workers and has led to an increasingly undifferentiated and unskilled working class.

Ralf Dahrendorf – the disintegration of the working class

Official employment figures directly contradict this picture, and suggest that during the course of this century the number of skilled manual workers has been increasing, while the number of unskilled manual workers has fallen. Such statistics seem to support the views of the German sociologist Ralf Dahrendorf, rather than those of Marx and Braverman.

Dahrendorf argues that contrary to Marx's prediction, the manual working class has become increasingly heterogeneous or dissimilar. He sees this resulting from changes in technology arguing that 'increasingly complex machines require increasingly qualified designers, builders, maintenance and repair men and even minders.'

Dahrendorf claims that the working class is now divided into three distinct levels: unskilled, semi-skilled and skilled manual workers. Differences in economic and prestige rewards are linked to this hierarchy of skill. Thus skilled craftspeople enjoy higher wages, more valuable fringe benefits, greater job security and higher prestige than semi-skilled and unskilled workers. Dahrendorf argues that in place of a homogeneous proletariat 'we find a plurality of status and skill groups whose interests often diverge'. For example, craftspeople jealously guard their wage differentials against claims for pay increases by the less skilled.

In view of the differences in skill, economic and status rewards and interests within the ranks of manual workers, Dahrendorf claims that 'it has become doubtful whether speaking of the working class still makes much sense'. He believes that during the twentieth century there has been a **decomposition of labour**, a disintegration of the manual working class.

Roger Penn – historical divisions in the working class

Roger Penn agrees with Dahrendorf that the British working class is divided between different levels of skill; however, he does not believe that these divisions are anything new. Penn's views are based upon a study of workers in the cotton and engineering industries in Rochdale between 1856 and 1964.

He found that over the whole of that period the working class was sectionally organized in unions which represented specific groups of workers. The unions of skilled workers used **social closure**: they attempted to limit the recruitment and training of workers in skilled jobs, in order to maintain or improve the bargaining position of their members.

Penn found that unions were fairly successful over long periods of time in maintaining relatively high levels of pay for skilled and semi-skilled workers. Not surprisingly this tended to create competing groups within the working class and to weaken the extent to which members of different segments of the working class could act together. However, if this has been the case for a century or more, it implies that Dahrendorf is wrong to see the working class as being more divided in the twentieth century than it was in the nineteenth.

Ivor Crewe – the 'new working class'

A second argument relating to divisions within the working class originates from studies of voting, and has been used to explain the failure of the Labour Party to retain working-class loyalty in the late 1970s and 1980s in UK elections. On the basis of his studies of British voting patterns, Ivor Crewe claims that the working class is divided, but not according to levels of skill but rather according to more specific factors.

Crewe believes that there is a **new working class** whose members possess one or more of the following characteristics:

1 they live in the South;
2 they are union members;
3 they work in private industry;
4 they own their own homes.

They can be distinguished from the diminishing numbers of **old working class** who live in the North, belong to unions, work directly or indirectly for the Government, and live in council houses. Crewe has used figures such as those in Table 2.14 to suggest that the new working class are deserting the Labour Party in large numbers,

Table 2.14   The two working classes: percentage of three-party vote 1983

| | New working class | | | Old working class | | |
	Owner-occupiers %	Works in private sector %	Lives in South %	Council tenants %	Works in public sector %	Lives in Scotland/ North %
Conservative	47	36	42	19	29	32
Labour	25	37	26	57	46	42
Liberal SDP	28	27	32	24	25	26

(*Source*: Crewe, I. (13 June 1983) 'The disturbing truth behind Labour's rout', *The Guardian*.)

and abandoning the traditional proletarian socialist collectivism.

Crewe accepts that traditional proletarian collectivist views continue to exist, but they are held by an ever decreasing segment of the population. (For further details and evaluation of Crewe's work see pp. 552–4, 559–61 and 568–71.)

G. Marshall, H. Newby, D. Rose and C. Vogler – skill and sectional divisions

Gordon Marshall, Howard Newby, David Rose and Carolyn Vogler have used data from their study of the British stratification system to evaluate the claim that the working class is divided. In general terms they support the view that the working class is divided into strata according to the level of skill involved in their work, but deny that the types of **sectoral** divisions identified by Crewe are significant.

Like Roger Penn, Marshall *et al.* believe that competition between different sections of the working class has created divisions lasting from the nineteenth century until the present day. In the nineteenth century, for example, the 'labour aristocracy' of skilled artisans caused splits in the working class. However, Marshall *et al.* do not claim that such divisions automatically prevent the working class acting as a group. They say:

The 'working class' has always been stratified according to industry, locality, grade and occupation, and was so long before the emergence of Labour as a political force. Yet this prevented neither the emergence of a specifically working

class party on the political stage nor the subsequent structuring of politics along class lines.

According to Marshall *et al.* these class divisions are, nevertheless, much more important than **sectoral cleavages**. They measured the voting intentions of their sample and compared different classes, home owners and tenants, public and private sector workers. Class was most closely connected with voting behaviour while there was no significant difference between the voting intentions of those in public or private sector employment. Council tenants were more likely to vote Labour whatever their social class, but an overwhelming majority of council tenants were working class anyway.

Dennis Warwick and Gary Littlejohn – divisions in mining communities

Warwick and Littlejohn studied four communities in a mining area of West Yorkshire surveying a total of 324 households in 1986 and 1987. They found evidence which appeared to contradict Marshall *et al.*'s views on the insignificance of sectoral cleavages. There was a 'strong element of anti-Thatcherism' amongst owner-occupiers and council tenants alike. For example, a majority in both groups opposed government support for private health and private education and wanted higher taxes for the rich and reduced spending on defence. But there were significant differences in their politics. Some 65 per cent of tenants and 65 per cent of owner-occupiers claimed their parents had voted Labour. However, among males 83 per cent of tenants now supported Labour compared to 57 per cent of those who owned or were buying their own homes.

Warwick and Littlejohn do not follow Crewe in claiming that housing tenure itself is the cause of increased divisions within the working class. Instead they argue that housing tenure reflects a polarization between the relatively economically secure who have regular employment, and the rest. For the less well-off members of the working class insecure employment, low income and poor health and residence in council housing tended to go together. Rising unemployment in the economic recessions combined with the sale of council houses to the better-off had led to a 'cleavage between citizens who still have clear means of participating in democracy, and those who are being pushed into what some call an "underclass"'.

From this point of view then, the major division in the working class is based on economic differences rather than level of skill. While there are sectoral cleavages, these derive from economic inequalities. Warwick and Littlejohn use the concept of an **underclass** very tentatively. This is not surprising since this concept is highly controversial. We will discuss it in detail later in the chapter (see pp. 91–7).

■ Class consciousness

Many Marxist sociologists argue that the contradictions of capitalism will eventually lead to a class-conscious proletariat. **Class consciousness** involves a full awareness by members of the working class of the reality of their exploitation, a recognition of common interests, the identification of an opposing group with whom their interests are in conflict, and a realization that only by collective class action can that opponent be overthrown. When practical steps are taken in pursuit of this goal, the working class becomes a **class for itself**.

Evidence from a variety of studies suggests that the working class is a long way from becoming a class for itself.

The limits to class consciousness

It has often been argued that the image of society held by proletarian traditionalists contains certain elements of class consciousness. The power model with its emphasis on 'us and them' implies some

recognition of common class interests, an indication of class solidarity and at least a vague awareness of an opponent with whom the workers are in conflict.

However the money model, which, judging from the studies of Goldthorpe *et al.*, and Hill, is the dominant image of society held by workers in Britain, suggests that the working class is becoming *less* rather than *more* class conscious.

Further evidence from these studies supports this view. Nearly 70 per cent of the Luton workers believed that the inequalities portrayed in their images of society were a necessary and inevitable feature of industrial society. They were concerned with improving their position in the existing society rather than trying to create a new social order. Given the fact that they had improved their economic position, they had some commitment to the existing order.

Marxists have often argued that the road to revolution involves an alliance between the trade union movement and a radical political party. Workers must see the politics of the workplace and society as one and the same. The Luton workers typically saw the union as an organization limited to advancing their economic interests in the workplace. In fact 54 per cent of the Luton trade unionists expressed clearcut disapproval of the link between trade unions and the Labour Party.

In general the Luton workers saw little opposition between themselves and their employer, 67 per cent agreeing with the statement that at work 'teamwork means success and is to everyone's advantage'. They were largely indifferent to 'exploitation' at work, home and family concerns being their central life interest.

This picture of harmony must not be overdrawn. As Goldthorpe and Lockwood state, the employer–employee relationship is not free from 'basic oppositions of interest'. Workers are concerned with maximizing wages, employers with maximizing profits. The teamwork image of industrial relations held by the majority of workers did not prevent a bitter strike in 1966 at the Luton branch of Vauxhall Motors. Despite the apparent acceptance of the social order by the Luton workers, their responses to a number of questions indicate some resentment about social inequality: 75 per cent agreed with the statement that there is 'one law for the rich and another for the poor' and 60 per cent agreed that big business has 'too much power'.

The dock labourers in Stephen Hill's study expressed similar attitudes to those of the Luton workers. They showed no great hostility to employers or management, the majority being 'fairly indifferent' towards them. Most were opposed to the link between trade unions and the Labour Party. Hill states:

> The dock workers I interviewed were certainly hostile to the traditional alliance between unionism and Labour, refusing to accept the view that these formed the industrial and political wings of an integrated labour movement.

However, despite the lack of radicalism in the workers' views of employers and of the link between trade unions and political parties, Hill did find evidence of left-wing opinions. Over 80 per cent of the dockers agreed with the statements that there is 'one law for the rich and another for the poor' and 'big business has too much power' and nearly 75 per cent agreed that 'the upper classes prevent fair shares'. Thus, like the Luton workers, the dockers appear to hold apparently conflicting radical and conservative views. We will discuss possible reasons for this shortly.

The potential for class consciousness

The studies by Hill, and Goldthorpe and Lockwood may be interpreted as indicating a reduction of the potential for class consciousness. It appears that the proletarian traditionalist has been replaced by the privatized worker who is preoccupied with home and family and largely indifferent to wider political issues. John Westergaard, however, takes a rather different view.

1 First, he argues that the relatively self-contained working-class communities of the proletarian traditionalist encouraged a parochial outlook. Workers tended to have a narrow identification with their occupational group rather than with the working class as a whole. Westergaard argues that the break up of traditional working-class communities may be necessary to provide 'larger conceptions of class identity and wider social vision'.

2 Second, since privatized workers define their work in instrumental terms, their sole attachment to work is the **cash-nexus** or money connection. As such, their attachment to work is single-stranded. It is not strengthened by pride in work, friendships at work or loyalty to the employer. A single-stranded connection is brittle: it can easily snap. If the privatized workers' demands for high wages and rising living standards are not met (for example in times of economic depression) the cash-nexus may well snap and there will be nothing else to hold them to their jobs and make them accept the situation. In such circumstances privatized workers may become increasingly radical and recognize that their interests lie in collective class action.

3 Third, Westergaard argues that the seeds of class consciousness are already present even in the apparently conservative Luton workers. He sees evidence of this from their views on the power of big business and the workings of the legal system, views echoed by the London dockers. Westergaard claims:

> There are patent signs here, as from other evidence, of widespread, indeed routine, popular distrust; of a common sense of grievance, a belief that the dice are loaded against ordinary workers, which involves at the very least a rudimentary diagnosis of power and a practical conception of conflicts of interest between classes.

The persistence of class consciousness

Westergaard's view that the seeds of class consciousness remain within the working class has been supported by Fiona Devine. Her study of affluent workers in Luton during the 1980s (see pp. 80–2 for further details) found considerable evidence of the persistence of class consciousness. The workers wanted to improve their living standards and those of their families, but that did not prevent them from perceiving society as unjust or from desiring change. They shared with other workers a similar living standard and a desire to improve it and gain increased security.

According to Devine, these shared experiences and desires were a basis for class solidarity. The affluent workers' sense of injustice focused on the very rich. Many resented the fact that, unlike ordinary members of society, the very rich did not have to work for a living. This led the affluent workers to hope for:

> a more equitable distribution of resources in so-
> ciety as it stood, and, by implication, a more equal,
> free and democratic society in which people would
> be more justly and fairly rewarded than at present.

Trade unions and the Labour Party were still regarded as 'collective means of securing both individual and collective ends'. However, support for them had declined because some of Devine's sample thought they had failed in delivering improvements for the working class.

While there was a strong awareness of a class division between the very rich and ordinary workers, there was less consciousness of a split between the working class and the middle class. Most of the sample thought that class divisions had declined in significance and saw themselves as belonging to a large class of 'ordinary' working people. Nevertheless, those who were employed at the Vauxhall plant still experienced a strong sense of class division at work. Devine says:

> manual workers at the car plant were aware of a
> sense of superiority and separateness held by the
> foremen and white-collar workers which placed
> them in an inferior position. The status aspects of
> the organisation of the workplace and people's atti-
> tudes of social superiority were a considerable
> source of grievance.

The affluent workers of the 1980s were rather pessimistic about the prospects for changing society but they had not lost desire for change nor their sense of class inequality. According to Devine then, they retained a considerable amount of class consciousness.

Inconsistencies in class consciousness

In many studies of class consciousness there is a tendency to assume that workers do hold a clear, consistent and coherent image of society, and a tendency to mould data into neat, tidy categories. For example, the Luton workers of the 1960s are usually discussed in terms of their money model of society yet only 54 per cent held that model, while 26 per cent had images which fitted neither power, prestige or money models, and 7 per cent had 'no communicable image'. Hill's study revealed that only 47 per cent of dockers held a money model and he was impressed with 'the *range* of different images which people within one group can embrace'. More emphasis might well be given to the variety and diversity of workers' images of society.

In addition, there is evidence which indicates that many workers do not hold clear and consistent views on society. Hill found that the dockers' fairly radical opinions on the power of big business, the workings of the law and the maintenance of inequality by the upper classes were inconsistent with their relatively conservative views on the role of trade unions and the nature of employment. He notes that they 'appeared to have their views fairly well compartmentalized'. As a result the dockers seemed to have no problem with holding apparently contradictory views.

Similar findings were produced from a study of the ideology of 951 unskilled manual workers in Peterborough, conducted in 1970–1 by R.M. Blackburn and Michael Mann. They found that both right- and left-wing views co-existed in the workers' ideology. Blackburn and Mann concluded that the workers did not possess 'consistent and coherent images of society'.

In fact Blackburn and Mann suggest that there is every reason to expect that this should be the case. The workers' experience of subordination and exploitation in the workplace will tend to produce a power model of society and radical attitudes which demand a change in the status quo. However, the workers are also exposed to the ideology of the dominant class broadcast by the mass media and transmitted by the educational system and various other institutions. This ideology is conservative: it supports the existing social arrangements and states that the relationship between capital and labour is right, natural and inevitable. As a result, workers 'remain confused by the clash between conservatism and proletarianism, but touched by both'.

Beliefs and actions

On the basis of questionnaire research into a national sample of British adults, David Marshall, Howard Newby, David Rose and Carolyn Vogler reached somewhat similar conclusions to Black-

burn and Mann. They claimed that class consciousness 'tends not to take the form of a coherent and comprehensive world-view'. Respondents
quite frequently gave inconsistent answers. For
example,

1 Only 30 per cent of those who rejected leaving the
   economy to market forces to produce economic revival
   also supported using government intervention for this
   purpose.

2 Some 19 per cent of those who wanted increased
   taxation to expand the welfare state, were themselves
   unwilling to pay more tax for this purpose.

3 A mere 25 per cent of those who supported the use of
   an incomes policy to reduce wage differentials were
   themselves willing to accept pay restraint to achieve it.

The last two examples suggest that beliefs and
actions will not always coincide so that class consciousness does not necessarily lead to class-based
actions.

The continuing relevance of class

Nevertheless, Marshall *et al.* emphasize the continuing relevance and importance of class for the
British population. Rose and Marshall summarize
some of their findings in the following way:

---

over 90 per cent of our respondents could place
themselves in one of the conventionally defined
class categories; 73 per cent viewed class as an
inevitable feature of British society; and 52 per cent
recognised the existence of class conflicts over
important social issues in Britain.

Furthermore, half of the sample believed there was
a dominant class which possessed economic and
political power, and a lower class which had no
economic and political power.

Marshall *et al.* found a surprisingly widespread
sense of injustice about the distribution of income
and wealth in British society. Table 2.15 shows the
percentage of the population who believed the distribution of income in Britain was unfair, and the
reasons they gave for this belief. The class categories used are based upon John Goldthorpe's
classifications (see pp. 80–1 for further details).
They show that a majority of all social classes
believed that the existing distribution of income

and wealth was unfair, and, although lower
classes were more likely to believe this, the percentage difference between them and higher
classes was not particularly great.

Marshall *et al.* do not claim that there is widespread support for radical changes in the social
structure, but they do believe that there is support
for reforms which would lead to a more equitable
society. They found little optimism, though, that
such reforms were likely, or even possible. Rose
and Marshall claim:

At the risk of oversimplifying, it would appear that
while most people disapprove of social injustice,
they do not think that they can do anything to
change the system. Nor do they think that our
elected leaders will do anything either.

Marshall *et al.* do not believe that class consciousness is automatically produced by the existence of
class divisions. Rose and Marshall say:

---

class consciousness is not simply a matter of individual beliefs, attitudes and values, which can be
explained by reference to social locations and can
be tapped by questions in a survey. To be sure, individuals have beliefs and, experiences which reflect
their social location. But for such beliefs to have
effectiveness, for them to produce class consciousness rather than class awareness, requires that they
be given explanation and direction. That is, they
require organising.

Despite the potential for class consciousness, the
British population has not been mobilized in
support of a programme which would tackle the
sources of their sense of injustice. In this respect,
Rose and Marshall point their fingers at the
Labour Party for having failed to tap the reservoir
of potential support for change.

Many Marxists believe that class consciousness
will eventually be generated by the contradictions
of capitalism. Many non-Marxists would regard
this as a possibility, but an unlikely one: they
would tend to agree with Ken Roberts that 'the
working class remains an unstable and continuing
challenge but not a revolutionary threat'.

Table 2.15 Attitudes to distributional justice by Goldthorpe class

A Is distribution of wealth and income fair?

		Yes	No
	I	31	69
	II	34	66
	III	28	72
Class	IV	44	56
	V	24	76
	VI	25	75
	VII	22	78
	All	29	71
		(368)	(914)

B Why not

	Class						
	I	II	III	IV	V	VI	VII
Distribution favours those at the top							
Gap between have and have-nots is too wide	57	59	63	64	55	63	63
Pay differentials are too wide	21	19	19	19	26	21	19
Too much poverty, wages too low, too many reduced to welfare	13	17	20	16	13	17	18
Some people acquire wealth too easily (unearned income, etc.)	31	16	13	13	20	10	9
The higher paid are not taxed severely enough	9	15	11	9	12	20	16
Welfare benefits are too low	6	5	6	2	8	9	6
The lower paid or working class are taxed too severely	2	3	3	5	3	0	2
Inequalities of opportunity (in education, for jobs, etc.)	2	2	2	0	0	1	2
Unequal regional distribution (of jobs, income, etc.)	4	3	3	0	2	1	2
Distribution favours those at the bottom							
There are too many scroungers around	6	5	12	9	15	8	10
Pay differentials are too narrow	5	4	1	3	4	4	4
The higher paid are taxed too severely	4	2	3	8	3	3	3
Other reasons							
Inequality of wealth and income inevitable	1	4	4	2	7	2	2
Key groups of workers can hold the country to ransom	1	1	0	0	0	0	0
Other reasons							

Note: Percentages in the 'Why not?' columns are based on respondents. Valid cases = 899.

(*Source*: Marshall, G., Newby, H., Rose, D. and Vogler, C. (1988) *Social Class in Modern Britain*, Hutchinson, p. 186.)

■ The lower strata

Although some sociologists see the working class as the lowest stratum in capitalist societies, others argue that there is a group beneath it. The most disadvantaged sections of capitalist society have been described in many ways. Kirk Mann says:

Excluded groups, marginalized groups, underclass, residuum, the poor, reserve army of labour, housing and social security classes, stagnant reserve army, relative surplus population and the lumpen-proletariat are all terms that have been used to describe a layer within, or beneath the working class.

Of these terms **underclass** is the one that has enjoyed the widest currency in recent years. Those sociologists who have identified a group of people at the bottom of the stratification system have seen them as having various distinguishing characteristics. These have included being poor, unemployed or dependent on benefits. In some cases they have been defined as a group whose behaviour contravenes the norms and values of society. Thus some sociologists have emphasized the economic distinctiveness of the lower strata while others have concentrated on their supposed cultural or behavioural differences from the rest of the population.

In the latter case the lower strata have been seen as constituting a social problem which poses a threat to society. They can also, however, be seen as a sociological problem for theories of stratification. Some theories of stratification have been based upon occupations, leaving the unemployed as a group who are difficult to categorize. In this chapter we will focus on the implications of the existence of lower strata for theories of stratification. Later chapters will discuss the relationship between the underclass and poverty (see pp. 154–60) and the underclass and ethnicity (see pp. 717–21).

◼ Marx's view of the lower strata

The lumpenproletariat

Recent years have seen sociologists, journalists and politicians pay considerable attention to the 'problem' of the lower strata, but this interest is nothing new. In the nineteenth century Karl Marx was amongst those who expressed views on these groups. He uses a number of different terms to describe those at the bottom of the stratification system of capitalist societies. He used **lumpenproletariat** to describe the lowest group of all. The picture he paints of them is less than flattering. They are variously seen as:

> This scum of the depraved elements of all classes. . . decayed roués . . . vagabonds, discharged soldiers, discharged jailbirds, escaped galley slaves, swindlers, mountebanks, lazzaroni, pickpockets, tricksters, gamblers . . . brothel keepers . . . tinkers, beggars . . . the dangerous class, the social scum, that passively rotting mass thrown off by the lowest layers of the old society.

It is unclear from Marx's writing whether he regarded this group as a class or not.

Lydia Morris points out that his usage of the term is inconsistent and it may 'variously refer to an historical remnant from an earlier society, a group of individual social degenerates, or a category located outside of the economic system of industrial capitalism'. Although at times Marx does refer to these people as a class, at other times he dismisses the idea that they can form a class because he sees them as having little potential for developing class consciousness or taking collective action.

The reserve army of labour

The term lumpenproletariat has not been widely used by contemporary sociologists but the idea of a **reserve army of labour** has been more influential. It exists because of the way the capitalist economy works. According to Marx, there are inevitably periods of boom, during which more workers are taken on, and periods of slump when many workers lose their jobs. The reserve army of labour consists of those who are employed as substitute workers and who are only needed during the booms. To Marx they perform important functions in capitalist societies. In *Capital* he says: 'The industrial reserve army, during periods of stagnation and average prosperity, weighs down the active army of workers; during the periods of over-production and feverish activity, it puts a curb on their pretensions.' It helps to drive down wage costs for capitalist employers by providing a flexible group of workers who are desperate for jobs and are willing to undercut the wages demanded by other workers. They will take the places of those who are sacked or made redundant. When the profitability of a company falls, threatening its survival, the employer may be forced to recruit cheaper workers from the reserve army of labour. The existence of a reserve army of labour makes it more difficult for the employed workforce to be radical and to resist, for example, the introduction of new machinery or more intensive work practices.

The relative surplus population

Rather confusingly Marx also uses a third term, the **relative surplus population**, to refer to those at the bottom of the stratification system. This includes members of the reserve army of labour but it also embraces groups whom at other times he defines as members of the lumpenproletariat.

The relative surplus population is divided into four.

1 The **floating surplus population** consists of workers who are employed until they reach adulthood but are then dismissed since adults are paid higher wages. (In contemporary Britain those young people on government training programmes who are used as a cheap labour force and are not offered a job on completion of their training could be seen as part of this group.)

2 The **latent surplus population** is made up of agricultural workers who are no longer needed and who are on the point of seeking work in urban areas.

3 The stagnant **surplus population** is part of the active labour force 'but with extremely irregular employment'. It is part of 'an inexhaustible reservoir of disposable labour-power' and it has living standards which are lower than average for the working class. Workers who have been made redundant and whose jobs have been lost as a result of new technology are likely to be in this group. Marx claims that members of the stagnant surplus population tend to have large families – indeed the lower the workers' wages, the more children they have.

4 At the bottom of the relative surplus population 'dwells the sphere of pauperism'. **Pauperism** is itself divided into four groups: first, 'criminals, vagabonds, prostitutes, in short the actual lumpenproletariat'; second, paupers who are capable of working but who simply cannot find jobs; third, 'orphans and pauper children' who are likely to be recruited to the reserve army of labour in prosperous years; and fourth, 'the demoralized, the ragged and those unable to work'. This includes the elderly, victims of industrial accidents, 'the mutilated, the sickly, the widows, etc.'

Evaluation and criticisms of Marx

Some aspects of Marx's work on the lower strata have been quite influential. For example, the concept of a reserve army of labour has been applied by some feminist sociologists to the position of women in modern capitalist societies (see pp. 621–2). However, his views have also been heavily criticized.

Kirk Mann argues that Marx uses a wide range of criteria to distinguish the lower strata from the rest of the working class. He says 'Marx links economic, social and psychological issues to the pathology of individuals and social groups'. He does not stick to using the purely economic definition of class which characterizes his work on other classes. Furthermore, many of Marx's views are so critical of the lower strata they seem to represent little more than personal prejudice. Mann argues:

Even allowing for the late Victorian period, the terms 'stagnant', 'floating', 'latent' and 'lowest sediment' suggest an unsympathetic stance. When he asserts that certain sections of the reserve army of labour breed more rapidly ... and 'succumb to their incapacity for adaptation', while others are part of some criminal class, Marx reproduces the prejudices of the Victorian middle classes.

One reason perhaps why Marx was so critical of the relative surplus population was that he did not see them as having the potential to develop class consciousness. Mann questions this view suggesting, for example that urban riots and the existence of Claimants Unions (organizations for those drawing benefits) show that the 'surplus population' is no more conservative than the working class.

Although Marx's writings on these particular groups seem rather dated, they do reflect problems that more contemporary sociologists have faced in trying to distinguish a group below the working class. Some have emphasized the cultural distinctiveness of such a group while others have looked for a definition based upon economic differences. Both these elements are contained in Marx's work. Unlike Marx, most contemporary sociologists have used the term **underclass** to describe the groups at the bottom of the stratification system.

■ Charles Murray – the underclass in America and Britain

The underclass in America

Although not the first writer in recent times to use the term underclass, the American sociologist Charles Murray has probably done more than anyone else to popularize its usage. In *Losing Ground* published in 1984, Murray argues that the USA has a growing underclass which poses a serious threat to American society. Murray argues that government policies are encouraging increasing numbers of Americans to become dependent on benefits. During the 1960s welfare reforms were introduced which led to an increase in the numbers of never-married black single parents and to many black youths losing interest in getting a job. Increases in the level of benefits and changes in the rules governing them discouraged self-sufficiency. Murray argues that the growing size of the underclass is a threat to the social and economic well-being of the country since its members are responsible for a rising crime rate and the benefits paid to them are costly to taxpayers.

The underclass in Britain

In 1989 Charles Murray visited Britain and wrote an article for the *Sunday Times*. In it he argues that Britain too has a developing underclass although unlike America, it is neither firmly established nor is it mainly composed of ethnic minorities. Murray defines the underclass in terms of behaviour. He says 'the "underclass" does not refer to a degree of poverty, but to a type of poverty'. These types of poor people were known to him in his youth and:

> They were defined by their behaviour. Their homes were littered and unkempt. The men in the family were unable to hold a job for more than a few weeks at a time. Drunkenness was common. The children grew up ill-schooled and ill-behaved and contributed a disproportionate share to the local juvenile delinquents.

Describing himself as 'a visitor from a plague area come to see if the disease is spreading' he finds signs that Britain too is being infected. These signs consist of figures showing rising rates of illegitimacy, a rising crime rate and an alleged unwillingness among many of Britain's youth to take jobs. In certain neighbourhoods traditional values such as beliefs in honesty, family life and hard work have been seriously undermined. As a consequence increasing numbers of children are being raised in a situation where they are likely to take on the underclass values of their parents.

Evaluation of Murray

Murray's views on the underclass add little to theories of stratification. By insisting on using a cultural definition of the underclass he neglects any

economic divisions which contribute to the creation of any such class: in many ways his work is better seen as a theory of poverty than as a theory of stratification. We will therefore evaluate his work in more detail in the next chapter (see pp. 154–7), where we will show that in America much of the evidence suggests that the benefits system does not have the effects he claims. The evidence he uses to make out the case for an underclass in Britain is flimsy and sometimes contradictory.

Murray blames the underclass for its predicament, explaining the situation in terms of its own aberrant behaviour. To quote Kirk Mann, he sees the British underclass as 'criminally violent bastards who refuse to work'. Most sociologists view the so-called underclass rather more sympathetically. Unlike behavioural and cultural accounts of the underclass, structural accounts tend to see the lowest strata in society as the victims of inequality. They therefore tend to make more explicit connections between the underclass and the stratification system of society as a whole.

■ Ralf Dahrendorf – the underclass and the erosion of citizenship

The culture of the underclass

Dahrendorf's characterization of the underclass has some similarities with that of Murray. Dahrendorf also sees it as a type of social illness, calling it 'a cancer which eats away at the texture of societies'. He believes that an underclass exists both in America and Britain and he sees the underclass as having undesirable cultural characteristics. Its culture:

> includes a lifestyle of laid-back sloppiness, association in changing groups of gangs, congregation around discos or the like, hostility to middle class society, peculiar habits of dress, of hairstyle, often drugs or at least alcohol – a style in other words which has little in common with the values of the work society around.

Although this is very similar in tone to Murray's argument, Dahrendorf parts company from him in explaining how the underclass came about.

Changes in work

According to Dahrendorf it is changes in work which have led to the development of an underclass. Technological innovation has made it possible to produce far more with far fewer workers. He says 'we can produce mountains of goods while reducing the number of producers' and claims that current levels of output could be achieved with 20 per cent fewer workers.

Some have argued that jobs in services will replace jobs in manufacturing but Dahrendorf does not think this will eliminate the problem. In much of Europe wage costs are high and this makes many services too expensive for consumers to afford. The consequence is that it generates little extra employment and it does not prevent the growth of an underclass of the unemployed. In the USA, on the other hand, wages are more flexible and it is more common to employ workers at very low wage rates to provide services. The problem is that these wages are so low that those receiving them cannot escape membership of the underclass.

Even those who have relatively well-paid employment are increasingly employed part-time or on short-term contracts. Many worry about their job security and 'such doubts are one of the reasons why they tend to close doors behind them'. The successful majority who have adequate sources of income make sure that their position is protected. Trade unions, companies and educational establishments all tend to exclude the underclass from the institutions which could bring them success. Unions protect their members' wages at the expense of creating unemployment for others. Companies employ the well-qualified and the education system does not give members of the underclass adequate opportunities to gain the qualifications they need. Dahrendorf says 'Those who are in, by and large, stay in, but those who are not, stay outside.'

The underclass and citizenship

Dahrendorf says that a citizen 'has certain entitlements common to all'. Members of the underclass are not full citizens because they do not have an economic stake in society and society provides them with little security. These include many immigrants and young people who have not a chance to become full members of society, while some of the elderly and 'those who have suffered mishaps of one kind or another' have lost their place.

Those who lack a stake in society have no reason to conform to society's norms. They develop their own norms which are sometimes antagonistic to mainstream society and which are passed down from generation to generation. The underclass comes to pose a threat to other members of society. Although it is not a revolutionary force the frustrations of the underclass do lead to rioting and violent crime. It therefore threatens the well-being of those who are full citizens.

Dahrendorf sees no easy solution to the problem of the underclass. He doubts that full employment can ever be achieved again but he does believe that there is something to be gained by a more equitable distribution of work. Job sharing and similar measures will allow more members of society to become full citizens. He also calls for 'a hundred if not a thousand local initiatives' by charismatic individuals who can help the underclass escape from its position by promoting community development schemes.

Evaluation

Dahrendorf provides a rather more convincing explanation of the development of the underclass than Murray, but he too resorts to rather stereotypical descriptions of its behaviour. He includes a wide variety of groups in his underclass: the elderly, those who have suffered 'misfortune', the unemployed, the low-paid and the young and immigrants who have not gained a foothold in society. It is unclear exactly what these groups have in common. While they are all held to lack citizenship rights, Dahrendorf fails to provide a precise definition of those rights.

Furthermore, in his original article he is unclear about whether the underclass should be seen as a class or not. He says 'One may wonder whether the word *class* is as yet appropriate.' The lack of precision in his argument makes it difficult to determine whether the use of the term underclass is appropriate or not. In a later article he says that 'it is precisely not a class' arguing that the underclass is simply a group of people who are not needed by society and who represent a challenge to dominant values.

If Dahrendorf's view that they are not a class is accepted then, as in the case of Murray, his work seems to add little to theories of stratification.

■ Anthony Giddens – the underclass and the dual labour market

The middle class, working class and underclass

Giddens is more confident than Dahrendorf that an underclass exists. He also integrates his theory of the underclass more fully into a theory of stratification and he defines the underclass more precisely. As mentioned earlier in the chapter (see p. 69), Giddens sees the middle class as those who possess educational or technical qualifications. This gives them an advantage in the labour market over the working class who have only their manual labour power to sell. Members of the underclass also have to rely upon selling their manual labour power but compared to the working class they are at a disadvantage when trying to do so. As a result they tend to secure employment in the least desirable and most insecure jobs.

The dual labour market

Giddens argues that contemporary capitalist societies have a **dual labour market**. Jobs in the **primary labour market** have 'high and stable or progressive levels of economic returns, security of employment and some chance of career mobility'. Jobs in the **secondary labour market** have 'a low rate of economic return, poor job security, and low chances of career advancement'. Employers need to plan ahead and to be able to do so they need a reliable and committed group of workers in key positions. High and secure rewards are necessary to ensure the loyalty of these workers. This inevitably raises labour costs. In order to reduce overall costs workers who are in less key positions and who are more easily replaced are paid much lower wages and are offered less job security. It is these secondary sector workers who come to make up the underclass.

The composition of the underclass

Giddens argues that women and ethnic minorities are particularly likely to be found in the underclass. Employers recruit women to underclass jobs partly because of 'social prejudice' but also because they are likely to interrupt their career as a result of marriage and childbirth. Ethnic minorities are also the victims of discrimination and prejudice. In the USA blacks and hispanics form the main members of the underclass. Indeed, at one point Giddens defines the underclass in terms of its ethnicity. He says:

> Where ethnic differences serve as a 'disqualifying' market capacity, such that those in the category are heavily concentrated in the lowest paid occupations, or are chronically unemployed or semi-employed, we may speak of the existence of an *underclass*.

Giddens sees the American underclass as the most developed but also sees West Indians and Asians in Britain, and Algerians in France as constituting underclasses. He notes that migrant workers often become members of the underclass. Many black Americans in the underclass migrated to the cities from rural areas. He claims: 'In many contemporary European societies the lack of an indigenous ethnic minority leads to a "transient underclass" (which turns out not to be so transient after all) being imported from the outside.'

The underclass and class conflict

Giddens argues that there is a basic difference of interest between the underclass and the working class. The underclass are radicalized by their experience of deprivation. On the other hand the working class with relatively secure jobs and comfortable living standards have more conservative attitudes. They are likely to be hostile to calls for radical social change emanating from the underclass.

Evaluation of Giddens

Although Giddens's argument is more coherent than Dahrendorf's, it has also come in for strong criticism.

Kirk Mann has raised serious questions about the concept at the heart of Giddens's theory, that of the dual labour market. He argues that there is no clear dividing line between a primary and secondary labour market. For example, some jobs are well paid but there is little job security; others are poorly paid but relatively secure. It is unclear from the dual labour market theory whether such jobs should be seen as primary or secondary jobs.

Mann also questions the claim that dual labour markets, if they exist, result from the tactics used by employers to recruit suitable workers and keep their labour costs down. He gives an example saying:

The miners in the mid-1970s were able to gain large wage increases and considerable improvements in their pension and other occupational welfare packages, but these were not offered by the National Coal Board (NCB). On the contrary, they were fought for and squeezed from the NCB at a time when the NCB was trying to shed labour.

The labour market is influenced by the actions of workers as well as the wishes of employers.

Perhaps Mann's strongest criticism concerns the theory's attempt to explain why certain groups of workers end up in the dual labour market. According to Mann there is no real explanation of why particular groups are the victims of discrimination. The dual labour market theory fails to provide an account of the 'racist and sexist ideologies' which lead to the exclusion of women and ethnic minorities from many of the better jobs. Furthermore, Giddens and other dual labour market theorists ignore the role of workers and union organizations in excluding women and ethnic minorities.

The relationship between ethnicity and the underclass and between gender and poverty have both been the subject of considerable sociological controversy. We analyse these controversies in later chapters (see pp. 717–19 on ethnicity and the underclass and pp. 145–6 on gender and poverty). Some sociologists have also questioned Giddens's view that the underemployed or semi-employed should be included as part of the underclass. These views will be dealt with later in this section.

■ Duncan Gallie – the heterogeneity of the underclass
Labour market inequalities

Giddens's views on the underclass have also been directly criticized by Duncan Gallie. Like Mann he rejects the idea of a dual labour market suggesting that there is little empirical evidence that it exists. However, he follow Giddens in arguing that there are substantial and increasing numbers of people in a very weak position in the labour market. He says:

A significant sector of the employed population receives pay close to or below the official poverty line and there are marked inequalities of pay by race and gender. There has been a substantial increase in the proportion of part-time rather than full-time work. Perhaps most important of all, there has been a substantial increase in the 1980s of the most severe type of labour market disadvantage, the experience of unemployment.

All of this seems to point to a growing underclass but what Gallie questions is whether the groups involved can be seen as constituting a class.

Divisions in the underclass

To Gallie, an underclass can only be seen as developing where 'labour market disadvantage is associated in an enduring way with specific cultural characteristics'. According to him these characteristics are lacking.

Ethnic minorities are disadvantaged in the labour market, but there is considerable variation in individual situations. Some members of ethnic minorities are very successful. The same applies to women, and in any case women are less likely to be unemployed than men. Although many women leave the labour market when they have young children, most women appear to regard this as 'basically legitimate'. They have little sense of grievance which would lead to these young mothers making common cause with other people who have no paid employment. Women are more likely to be employed in part-time work than men 'but the evidence suggests that women involved in such work have high levels of satisfaction with their employment situation'.

Gallie sees the unemployed as the group most likely to develop some sort of distinctive under-class culture. However, many of the unemployed quickly find work and 'there are huge flows into and out of the stock of the unemployed each month'. That does not disguise the existence of a large and growing group of long-term unem-ployed. Yet even this group is unlikely to develop any sort of underclass consciousness. The long-term unemployed are quite heteroge-neous. Men and women in this group are often in different personal circumstances and individu-als suffering long-term unemployment may be at very different stages in the life cycle. For example, an unemployed female school leaver may feel she has little in common with an unem-ployed man of 55.

Gallie is particularly dismissive of the idea that the unemployed are likely to become a radical, class-conscious force. Unemployment 'is a type of experience that makes effective collective action extremely difficult'. The unemployed lack mater-ial resources and depression and a sense of power-lessness which often follow from sustained periods of unemployment can lead to them losing the motivation and self-confidence necessary to take collective action.

The underclass and the working class

Gallie also finds little evidence of a political split between the working class and the underclass. Members of the working class who have kept their jobs have not tended to blame unemployment on the laziness or personal inadequacy of those without jobs. There is no evidence of a 'conserva-tive backlash' against them.

Despite all his arguments Gallie does not dismiss the idea of an underclass out of hand. He does say:

The one case where the concept of an underclass would appear to have some relevance is that of

the long-term unemployed. Their deprivations are distinctive from those generated directly by the employment relationship and they have the type of stability over time that is assumed by underclass theory.

Even this tentative use of the term is qualified. Gallie points out that the long-term unemployed have close connections with the working class: most were formerly manual workers or came from working-class backgrounds.

■ W.G. Runciman – the underclass as claimants

The underclass and the class structure

Runciman has devised a seven class model of the British class structure based upon differences in **control, ownership** and **marketability**. We examine this model in detail later in this chapter (see pp. 118–20). At the bottom of the class struc-ture he identifies an underclass. He explicitly rejects Giddens's view that it should be defined as 'a category of workers systematically disadvan-taged in the labour market'. Runciman mentions Gallie's work in suggesting that a different defini-tion of the underclass is needed.

Runciman defines the underclass as: 'those members of British society whose roles place them more or less permanently at the economic level where benefits are paid by the state to those unable to participate in the labour market at all'.

Many are from ethnic minority backgrounds, and many are women, particularly single mothers, but it is their reliance upon state benefits that places them in the underclass, not their gender or ethnicity. (A similar view which also sees the underclass as consisting of claimants has been put forward by Frank Field. It is discussed in the next chapter, see pp. 157–60.)

Criticisms of Runciman

Runciman appears to offer a straightforward and plausible definition of the underclass. However, Hartley Dean and Peter Taylor-Gooby have attacked his views. They point out that Runciman stresses the importance of 'career' in class analysis: that is, the future prospects and past history of individuals in the class system must be examined before allocating them to a class. Yet Runciman fails to take this into account when considering the underclass.

For example, figures suggest that on average lone parents stay as lone parents for a mere 35 months. Similarly most of the long-term unemployed have had jobs in the past. They are unstable members of the working class rather than members of a stable underclass. To Dean and Taylor-Gooby the so-called underclass is simply too unstable and impermanent to be seen as a class.

They also attack Runciman for basing his definition of the underclass on quite different criteria to his definition of other classes. The underclass are not defined in terms of their relationship to the market but in 'purely institutional terms'. They exist in a relationship with the state, not the economic system. In terms of Runciman's definition, their existence depends upon the existence of state benefits. Nevertheless, in comparing his class scheme with classes in Britain in 1910, Runciman equates the underclass with a 'loafer class' described by an Edwardian commentator called D'Aeth. Dean and Taylor-Gooby say

> The implication would seem to do Runciman's argument no good at all, because without an institutional relationship to the post-war welfare state, the roles assigned to the underclass are defined in terms of behaviour – the intermittence of their labour and their drinking habits.

■ Conclusion

Dean and Gooby-Taylor's latter criticism is not particularly strong. However Runciman defines the Edwardian underclass, it is clear that the contemporary underclass is defined in terms of its dependence on benefits and not in terms of behaviour. This dependence can be seen as a consequence of the lack of control, power and particularly marketability possessed by the underclass.

However, Dean and Gooby-Taylor do have a point when they suggest that there is a constant danger of the term underclass being misused. They say that 'Underclass is a symbolic term with no single meaning, but a great many applications . . . It represents, not a useful concept, but a potent symbol.' It has become a symbol of 'socially constituted definitions of failure'. However it is used by sociologists, in society in general it is used to lay the blame on the disadvantaged for the social problems of which they are victims.

Dean suggests that the term underclass should be abandoned. Not only is it misused – in his view no underclass as such exists. He says that it 'does not usefully define a real or tangible phenomenon.' The debate about the underclass *has* touched on important issues though. He therefore concludes:

> Recent structural and cultural changes have intersected, not to produce an 'underclass', but to shift the boundaries between core workers, peripheral workers and non-workers; between the individual and the family; and between the citizen and the welfare state. Such changes have also exacerbated regional inequalities and inner-city decay and, some would argue, may have contributed to rising levels of crime. We should not go in search of the underclass, but strive for a better understanding of structural and cultural changes and their complex interrelationships and effects.

A leading American sociologist, William Julius Wilson, agrees with sociologists such as Dean and Gooby-Taylor that it has become dangerous to use the term underclass. He says 'it has become hopelessly polluted in meaning, ideological overtones and implications, and should be dropped'. However, he does not deny that there is a distinctive group at the bottom of the American stratification system. He therefore adopts a new term 'ghetto poor' to replace underclass. (More details of Wilson's work are to be found on pp. 717–18.)

Whatever they are called and however they are defined, members of the lowest strata in capitalist societies are significantly worse off than manual workers in regular employment. Whether they can be seen as the lowest stratum of the working class or as a separate class remains a moot point. (The next chapter, Poverty, also focuses on those at the bottom of the stratification system.)

■ Social mobility in capitalist society

Having looked at the different classes, we will now consider the amount of movement from one class to another within capitalist society.

Ascription and achievement

This section examines the nature of social mobility in capitalist society. It is generally agreed that the rate of **social mobility** – the amount of movement from one stratum to another – is significantly higher in industrial as compared to pre-industrial societies. Industrial societies are therefore some-times described as **open**, as having a relatively low degree of **closure**.

In particular, it is argued that status in pre-industrial societies is largely **ascribed**, whereas in industrial societies it is increasingly **achieved**. As a result ascribed characteristics such as class of origin, sex, race and kinship relationships have less and less influence on an individual's social status. Status is seen to be increasingly achieved on the basis of merit: talent, ability, ambition and hard work are steadily replacing ascribed charac-teristics as the criteria for determining a person's position in the class system. Indeed, a number of sociologists have suggested that this mechanism of social selection is built into the values of industrial society. Thus Talcott Parsons argues that achieve-ment is one of the major values of American society. Individuals are judged and accorded pres-tige in terms of their occupational status which is seen to be largely achieved by their own effort and ability.

The importance of social mobility

Sociologists are interested in social mobility for a number of reasons.

1 The rate of social mobility may have an important effect on class formation. For example, Anthony Giddens suggests that if the rate of social mobility is low, class solidarity and cohesion will be high. Most individuals will remain in their class of origin and this will 'provide for the reproduction of common life experiences over generations'. As a result distinctive class subcultures and strong class identifications will tend to develop.

2 A study of social mobility can provide an indication of the life chances of members of society. For example, it can show the degree to which a person's class of origin influences his or her chances of obtaining a high status occupation.

3 It is important to know how people respond to the experience of social mobility. For example, do the downwardly mobile resent their misfortune and form a pool of dissatisfaction which might threaten the stability of society?

Before considering these issues, it is necessary to examine the nature and extent of social mobility in capitalist society.

Types of social mobility

Sociologists have identified two main types of social mobility.

1 The first, *intra*generational mobility, refers to social mobility within a single generation. It is measured by comparing the occupational status of an individual at two or more points in time. Thus, if a person begins her or his working life as an unskilled manual worker and ten years later is employed as an accountant, she or he is socially mobile in terms of intragenerational mobility.

2 The second type, *inter*generational mobility, refers to social mobility between generations. It is measured by comparing the occupational status of sons with that of their fathers (and only rarely the occupational status of fathers or mothers with that of their daughters). Thus, if the son of an unskilled manual worker becomes an accountant, he is socially mobile in terms of intergenerational mobility.

This section will focus mainly on intergenerational mobility, the type of social mobility most fre-quently studied by sociologists.

Problems of measurement

There are many problems associated with the study of social mobility.

1 Occupation is used as an indicator of social class and researchers use different criteria for ranking occupations. Many researchers classify occupations in terms of the prestige associated with them; others

place more emphasis on the economic rewards attached to them. As a result, occupational classifications differ and the results of various studies are not strictly comparable.

2 A further problem arises from the fact that it is not possible to identify many members of the bourgeoisie on the basis of their occupations: a person's occupation does not necessarily say anything about the extent of their investments in private industry.

3 Furthermore, many studies of social mobility have not included data on women's mobility, and patterns of female mobility tend to be rather different from men's. This is largely because women tend to be concentrated in particular parts of the occupational structure.

In view of these and other problems, the findings of social mobility studies must be regarded with caution.

◼ David Glass – social mobility before 1949

The first major study of intergenerational mobility in England and Wales was conducted by David Glass and his associates in 1949. The main findings of this study are summarized in Table 2.16.

The percentages in the horizontal rows (in the top right-hand corner of each cell) compares the status of sons with the status of their fathers. Thus, taking all the sons whose fathers were in the status category 1, 38.8 per cent of these sons are themselves in category 1, 14.6 per cent are in category 2 and so on through to category 7 in which only 1.5 per cent of sons born into category 1 are located. The figures in bold print, going diagonally across the table, indicate the extent to which sons share the same status as their fathers. For example, 27.4 per cent of all sons whose fathers were in category 7 are themselves in that same category in 1949.

The percentages in the vertical columns (in the bottom left-hand corner of each cell) refer to the parental status of the men found in each category in 1949. For example, of all the men in status category 1 in 1949, 48.5 per cent have fathers who were in that category, 15.5 per cent have fathers who were in category 2 and so on. The bold figures show the percentage of men in each category who have the same status as their fathers. For example, 25 per cent of all the men in category

7 are the sons of fathers from that category.

Overall, the table indicates a fairly high level of intergenerational mobility. Nearly two-thirds of the men interviewed in 1949 were in a different status category from that of their fathers. Roughly one-third moved upward and one-third downward. However, for the most part, the change in status is not very great. Most mobility is short range: sons generally moving to a category either adjacent or close to that of their fathers. There is little long-range mobility either from top to bottom or vice versa.

In the higher status categories there is a considerable degree of **self-recruitment** – a process by which members of a stratum are recruited from the sons of those who already belong to that stratum. The way the figures are presented tends to disguise the degree of self-recruitment. From the table it appears that the highest level of self-recruitment is in category 5: in 1949, 50 per cent of the members of category 5 are the sons of fathers who were in that same category. However since category 5 is by far the largest group, a relatively high degree of self-recruitment is to be expected. By comparison, category 1 is a very small group made up of just over 3.5 per cent of the sample. Yet in 1949, 48.5 per cent of the members of category 1 are the sons of fathers who were in that same category. This is over 13 times greater than would be expected by chance. If parental occupation had no influence on a person's status, only some 3.5 per cent of the sons in category 1 would have fathers in that category.

Family background appears to have an important influence on life chances. The higher the occupational status of the father, the more likely the son is to obtain a high status position. Most men are likely to stay at roughly the same level as their fathers and this is particularly true at the top end of the scale. Glass's study therefore reveals a significant degree of inequality of opportunity.

Criticisms of Glass

Any conclusions drawn from this study must, however, be tentative. The research methodology has been the subject of lengthy criticism. In particular, it has been argued that Glass's findings do not reflect changes in the occupational structure before 1949. For example, a comparison of the actual numbers of sons born into the first four status categories (shown in the right-hand vertical

Table 2.16   Social mobility in England and Wales before 1949

		Sons' status category in 1949							
		1	2	3	4	5	6	7	Total
Fathers' status category	1	**38.8**	14.6	20.2	6.2	14.0	4.7	1.5	100.0
		48.5	11.9	7.9	1.7	1.3	1.0	0.5	(129)
	2	10.7	**26.7**	22.7	12.0	20.6	5.3	2.0	100.0
		15.5	**25.2**	10.3	3.9	2.2	1.4	0.7	(150)
	3	3.5	10.1	**18.8**	19.1	35.7	6.7	6.1	100.0
		11.7	22.0	**19.7**	14.4	8.6	3.9	5.0	(345)
	4	2.1	3.9	11.2	**21.2**	43.0	12.4	6.2	100.0
		10.7	12.6	17.6	**24.0**	15.6	10.8	7.5	(518)
	5	0.9	2.4	7.5	12.3	**47.3**	17.1	12.5	100.0
		13.6	22.6	34.5	40.3	**50.0**	43.5	44.6	(1510)
	6	0.0	1.3	4.1	8.8	39.1	**31.2**	15.5	100.0
		0.0	3.8	5.8	8.7	12.5	**24.1**	16.7	(458)
	7	0.0	0.8	3.6	8.3	36.4	23.5	**27.4**	100.0
		0.0	1.9	4.2	7.0	9.8	15.3	**25.0**	(387)
Total		100.0	100.0	100.0	100.0	100.0	100.0	100.0	
		(103)	(159)	(330)	(459)	(1429)	(593)	(424)	(3497)

Status categories

No.   Description
1   Professional and high administrative
2   Managerial and executive
3   Inspectional, supervisory and other non-manual (higher grade)
4   Inspectional, supervisory and other non-manual (lower grade)
5   Skilled manual and routine grades of non-manual
6   Semi-skilled manual
7   Unskilled manual

(*Source*: Glass, D.V. (1954) *Social Mobility in Britain*, Routledge & Kegan Paul, p. 183.)

column of the table) with the number found in those categories in 1949 (shown in the horizontal row across the bottom) suggests a contraction of white-collar occupations. However, as Payne, Ford and Robertson note, there was a 16 per cent expansion of these occupations during the thirty years preceding 1949. This throws doubt on the validity of Glass's sample. It suggests that his findings may seriously underestimate the rate of social mobility and in particular the degree of long-range upward mobility. (For a detailed criticism of Glass's methodology see Payne, Ford and Robertson 1977.)

■ The Oxford Mobility Study

After 1949, the next major study of social mobility in England and Wales was conducted in 1972. Known as the Oxford Mobility Study, it was undertaken by a group of sociologists at Nuffield College, Oxford. The results cannot be compared in detail with those of the 1949 study since different criteria were used as a basis for constructing the various strata. Where Glass used a classification based on occupational prestige, the Oxford study categorized occupations largely in terms of their market rewards. These categories are based

Table 2.17 The Oxford study of mobility

		\multicolumn{8}{c}{Sons' class in 1972}
		1	2	3	4	5	6	7	Total
Fathers' class	1	**45.7** 25.3	19.1 12.4	11.6 9.6	6.8 6.7	4.9 3.2	5.4 2.0	6.5 2.4	100.0 (680)
	2	29.4 13.1	**23.3** **12.2**	12.1 8.0	6.0 4.8	9.7 5.2	10.8 3.1	8.6 2.5	100.0 (547)
	3	18.6 10.4	15.9 10.4	**13.0** **10.8**	7.4 7.4	13.0 8.7	15.7 5.7	16.4 6.0	100.0 (687)
	4	14.0 10.1	14.4 12.2	9.1 9.8	**21.1** **27.2**	9.9 8.6	15.1 7.1	16.3 7.7	100.0 (886)
	5	14.4 12.5	13.7 14.0	10.2 13.2	7.7 12.1	**15.9** **16.6**	21.4 12.2	16.8 9.6	100.0 (1072)
	6	7.8 16.4	8.8 21.7	8.4 26.1	6.4 24.0	12.4 31.0	**30.6** **41.8**	25.6 35.2	100.0 (2577)
	7	7.1 12.1	8.5 17.1	8.8 22.6	5.7 17.8	12.9 26.7	24.8 28.0	**32.2** **36.6**	100.0 (2126)
Total		100.0 (1230)	100.0 (1050)	100.0 (827)	100.0 (687)	100.0 (1026)	100.0 (1883)	100.0 (1872)	(8575)

Classes

No. Description

1 Higher professionals, higher grade administrators, managers in large industrial concerns and large proprietors

2 Lower professionals, higher grade technicians, lower grade administrators, managers in small businesses and supervisors of non-manual employers

3 Routine non-manual – mainly clerical and sales personnel

4 Small proprietors and self-employed artisans

5 Lower grade technicians and supervisors of manual workers

6 Skilled manual workers

7 Semi-skilled and unskilled manual workers

(*Source*: Goldthorpe, J. (1980) *Social Mobility and Class Structure in Modern Britain*, Clarendon Press, pp. 44 and 48.)

on John Goldthorpe's original seven class scheme which was introduced earlier in the chapter and will be discussed later (see pp. 115–17).

Table 2.17 summarizes the main findings on intergenerational mobility from the Oxford survey.

Absolute mobility

The 1972 study revealed higher rates of long-range mobility than the 1949 study. For example,

Table 2.17 shows that 7.1 per cent of sons of class 7 fathers were in class 1 in 1972. In addition, the table suggests that there are high rates of **absolute mobility** (the total amount of social mobility); in no social class did more than 50 per cent of the sample originate from the same social class. The Oxford Mobility Study found high rates of social mobility, and more was upward than downward. It also found that the chances of those from working-class backgrounds reaching a higher social class had improved during the course of the century.

Table 2.18   Relative mobility chances of different generations

Your chance of ending up in the service class	Jobs as a proportion of male employment

Then if your father was:

Working   14%

Intermediate   25%

Service   55%

Now if your father is:

Working   18%

Intermediate   30%

Service   62%

Then: 13% Service, 33% Intermediate, 54% Working

Now: 25% Service, 30% Intermediate, 45% Working

(*Source*: Kellner, P. and Wilby, P. (13 January 1980) *Sunday Times*, p. 13.)

Relative mobility

On the surface, these findings seem to support the claim that British society is becoming more open. However, the study found that relative mobility chances varied greatly between the classes, and the relative chances had changed little during the course of the century.

The concept of **relative mobility** refers not to the *total* amount of social mobility, but to the *comparative chances* of those from various class backgrounds of reaching particular positions in the social structure. Thus 45.7 per cent of sons with class 1 fathers – but just 7.1 per cent of those with class 7 fathers – ended up in class 1.

By comparing the relative mobility chances of different generations it is possible to determine whether the class structure has become more open. In Table 2.18 those born in 1908–17 are compared with those born in 1938–47. The seven class scheme usually used by Goldthorpe is simplified by amalgamating classes to reduce the number of classes to three. (The service class consists of classes 1 and 2, the intermediate class of classes 3, 4 and 5, and the working class of classes 6 and 7.)

Table 2.18 shows that the chances of members of all social classes attaining service-class jobs increased over the period studied. However, this was largely the result of changes in the occupational structure: service-class jobs as a proportion of male employment rose from 13 to 25 per cent, while intermediate jobs declined from 33 to 30 per cent, and working-class jobs from 54 to 45 per cent. The relative chances of the sons of those from different classes taking advantage of the increasing room at the top of the stratification system changed little.

This has been neatly summarized by Kellner and Wilby as the **1:2:4 rule of relative hope**. This rule suggests that over the period covered, as a rough estimate, whatever the chances of a working-class boy reaching the service class, they were twice as great for intermediate-class boys, and four times as great for service-class boys. In other words, there has been no significant increase in the openness of the British stratification system.

Trends since the Oxford Mobility Study

In a follow-up study John H. Goldthorpe brought figures on social mobility more up-to-date by examining data from the 1983 *British Election Survey*. He wanted to discover whether in the period 1972–83 economic recession had produced different patterns of mobility to those found in the Oxford study of a period characterized by a period of economic expansion.

Overall he found few differences between the results of the two studies. Service-class jobs continued to expand as a proportion of all male jobs; absolute mobility continued to increase, but relative mobility stayed about the same.

However, he did find that unemployment had affected the position of all classes, and the working class in particular. There were still opportunities for upward mobility from the working class, but members of the working class were more likely to become unemployed than members of the higher classes.

■ Elite self-recruitment

The Oxford Mobility Study and Goldthorpe's later work suggest that there is not a high degree of social closure at the top of the British stratification system, but Goldthorpe can be criticized for ignoring the existence of small **elites**, or in Marxist terms a ruling class. Goldthorpe's class 1 is a relatively large grouping containing 10–15 per cent of the male working population. Studies which concentrate on small elite groups within class 1 reveal a much higher degree of closure.

The process by which members of wealthy and powerful groups are drawn from the children of those who already belong to such groups is known as **elite self-recruitment**. The following studies indicate the degree of elite self-recruitment in Britain.

1 A study by Willmott and Young conducted in 1970 in the London area included a sample of 174 managing directors. It revealed that 83 per cent were the sons of professionals and managers.

2 A survey by Stanworth and Giddens designed to investigate the social origins of company chairmen revealed a high degree of elite self-recruitment. Out of 460 company chairmen in 1971, only 1 per cent had manual working-class origins, 10 per cent had middle-class backgrounds, and 66 per cent came from the upper class which was defined as 'industrialists, landowners, (and) others who possess substantial property and wealth'. (There were insufficient data to classify the remaining 23 per cent.)

Thus the Oxford study, while showing a relatively high rate of mobility into class 1, does not indicate the degree of elite self-recruitment. Though class 1 as a whole appears fairly open, elite groups within that class are relatively closed.

■ Gender and mobility

J.H. Goldthorpe and C. Payne's views on gender and social mobility

A second major problem with the Oxford Mobility Study is the fact that it ignores women. Goldthorpe believes that the unit of stratification in industrial societies is the family. The class position of the family is given by the occupation of the main breadwinner, which is usually a man. However, other sociologists hotly dispute these claims . (For details of the debate on gender and stratification see pp. 629–31.)

With specific reference to gender and social mobility, Goldthorpe and Payne have examined data from the 1983 British *Election Survey* to determine what difference it makes to the results of studies of social mobility if three different approaches are adopted to including women in the data.

1 In the first approach women are included but their class is determined by their husband's occupation. Goldthorpe and Payne found this made little difference to either the absolute or relative rates of intergenerational social mobility found in studies using an all-male sample.

2 In the second approach the occupation of the partner in full-time employment with the highest class position is used to determine the class of both partners. Single women are included on the basis of their own job. This approach also made little difference to relative mobility rates although Goldthorpe and Payne conceded that it does at least allow information on women who are unattached, or who are household heads, to be included.

3 In the third approach individuals are allocated to classes on the basis of their own jobs. This did show that absolute mobility rates for women and men were very different. This was largely due to the fact that women are distributed differently from men in the occupational structure (see later sections). However, once again this method of including women in the data made little difference to the intergenerational, relative mobility rates of different classes. In other words the mobility chances of women compared to other women from different classes were as unequal as the social mobility chances of men compared to men from other classes.

Table 2.19   Gross mobility rates by gender in the Scottish Mobility Study in 1974–75

| Gender | Mobility (%) | | | % Upwardly mobile found in | |
	Upward	Static	Downward	Classes I or III	Classes II or IV
Men	42.5	27.4	30.4	44	29
Women	32.2	19.9	48.8	6	67

(*Source*: Abbott, P. and Payne, G. 'Women's social mobility reconsidered' in Payne, G. and Abbott, P. (eds) (1990) *The Social Mobility of Women*, Falmer Press, Basingstoke, p. 18.)

Goldthorpe and Payne therefore felt they could conclude that the non-inclusion of women in earlier studies of social mobility was not important since it made little difference to the overall results, at least in terms of determining the openness of the stratification system.

Alternative views

Michelle Stanworth is highly critical of Goldthorpe for insisting on categorizing women in social mobility studies according to the class of their husband. She prefers an approach based upon individuals being allocated to a class according to their own job.

Some research seems to support Stanworth's view in that it shows important differences in the social mobility of men and women. Anthony Heath has used data from the 1972 and 1975 *General Household Surveys* to examine the intergenerational mobility of women. He compared women's social class with their father's class (though not their mother's), and reached the following conclusions.

1 Women of class 1 and 2 origins were much more likely to be downwardly mobile than men of the same class origin. This was largely because of the preponderance of females in class 3 (routine non-manual jobs).

2 Women from higher social classes were less likely to follow in their father's footsteps than men from the same classes.

3 On the other hand, women of class 5, 6 or 7 origins were far more likely to be upwardly mobile to class 3 than their male counterparts, although Heath points out that whether this movement can be considered 'upward mobility' is a moot point. As indicated earlier, some

sociologists do not believe that routine non-manual workers have any significant advantages over most manual workers (see pp. 75–6, 78–9).

Heath argues 'The "losses" experienced by the daughters of high status fathers are not balanced by the "gains" accruing to those from low-status origins.' If Heath is to be believed, then the British stratification system is less open than studies based on males would suggest.

Rather similar conclusions have been reached by Pamela Abbott and Geoff Payne. They used data from a study of social mobility in Scotland to compare men and women. This study was carried out by Geoff Payne in 1974–5 and used a sample of 5,000 men born between 1909 and 1955 and 3,500 wives of these men. Table 2.19 shows the gross mobility rates of the men and women in the sample.

The data demonstrate that many more women than men were downwardly mobile, fewer women were upwardly mobile, and very few of the women who did manage to be upwardly mobile ended up in the top two classes. Once again they suggest that the omission of women from data can give a misleading impression of absolute mobility rates.

■ The Essex study of mobility

As part of their study of social class in Britain Gordon Marshall, David Rose, Howard Newby and Carolyn Vogler collected data on social mobility (details of the study can be found on pp. 68–9). Since the study collected data on male and female mobility rates it allows some evaluation of the controversies about female mobility. It is also provides more recent data than the Oxford Mobility Study as it was carried out in

Table 2.20 Class distribution of respondents by sex and class of chief childhood supporter at same age as respondent—Goldthorpe class categories

				Males					
				Class of respondent					
(n = 632)		I	II	III	IV	V	VI	VII	Total
	I	27.7	31.9	12.8	· 6.4	4.3	10.6	6.4	100.0 (47)
	II	20.8	39.6	3.8	11.3	1.9	13.2	9.4	100.0 (53)
Class of	III	25.0	21.9	0.0	6.3	9.4	31.3	6.3	100.0 (32)
chief childhood	IV	14.4	15.6	5.6	28.9	10.0	11.1	14.4	100.0 (90)
supporter	V	14.4	18.9	4.5	7.2	13.5	13.5	27.9	100.0 (111)
	VI	8.0	12.4	9.5	6.6	14.6	23.4	25.5	100.0 (139)
	VII	11.9	8.1	4.4	11.9	10.0	18.8	35.0	100.0 (160)

				Females					
				Class of respondent					
(n = 425)		I	II	III	IV	V	VI	VII	Total
	I	13.8	27.6	48.3	3.4	0.0	0.0	6.9	100.0 (29)
	II	14.3	42.9	32.1	0.0	0.0	0.0	10.7	100.0 (28)
Class of	III	4.2	37.5	37.5	4.2	0.0	4.2	12.5	100.0 (24)
chief childhood	IV	9.1	25.5	30.9	9.1	3.6	1.8	20.0	100.0 (55)
supporter	V	0.0	27.5	42.5	6.3	1.3	6.3	16.3	100.0 (80)
	VI	3.6	15.3	44.1	2.7	5.4	8.1	20.7	100.0 (111)
	VII	2.0	8.2	30.6	8.2	6.1	5.1	39.8	100.0 (98)

(*Source*: Marshall, G., Rose, D., Newby, H. and Vogler, C. (1988) *Social Class in Modern Britain,* Unwin Hyman, London, p. 77.)

1984. The study collected information on both intergenerational and intragenerational mobility.

Table 2.20 shows Marshall *et al.*'s results on intergenerational mobility. These are based on a comparison between the respondent and the person who was their 'chief childhood supporter' at the same age as the respondent. It uses Goldthorpe's original seven class model (see pp. 115–16 for details of this model).

Like earlier studies the Essex study found there had been an expansion of white-collar jobs and consequently there were high absolute rates of upward mobility. The results for men are fairly similar to those in the Oxford study, but the results for women show different patterns of social mobility. They confirm the findings of Heath, and Abbott and Payne that women's mobility patterns are affected a great deal by the concentration of women in routine non-manual jobs. Large numbers of women were both upwardly and downwardly mobile into class III.

Odds ratios

The Essex study also expressed the data collected in terms of **odds ratio tables** measuring relative mobility chances. In other words Marshall *et al.* compared the chances of people from different classes of getting into particular classes in society.

1 Table 2.21 compares the class of a person's chief childhood supporter's class with that person's first job.

2 Table 2.22 compares the class of a person's chief childhood supporter with that person's current job.

3 Table 2.23 compares a person's class in their first job with their current class.

The tables are based upon a simplified three class version of Goldthorpe's scheme (i.e. service class, intermediate class and working class). For example Table 2.21 shows that when men from service- and working-class backgrounds compete

Table 2.21 Relative mobility chances in terms of odds ratios, by Goldthorpe class and sex. Transition from class of origin to class position on entry into employment

Pairs of origin classes 'in competition'	Pairs of destination classes 'competed for'					
	Men			Women		
	S vs I	S vs W	I vs W	S vs I	S vs W	I vs W
S vs I	2.02	4.13	2.05	2.43	4.63	1.90
S vs W	1.95	7.76	4.09	3.84	14.07	3.63
I vs W	0.96	1.88	2.00	1.58	3.04	1.91

Key S = Service (classes I and II);
 I = Intermediate (classes III,IV, and V);
 W = Working (classes VI and VII).

(*Source*: Marshall, G., Rose, D., Newby, H. and Vogler, C. (1988) *Social Class in Modern Britain*, Unwin Hyman, London, p. 105.)

Table 2.22 Relative mobility chances in terms of odds ratios, by Goldthorpe class and sex. Transition from class of origin to present class position

Pairs of origin classes 'in competition'	Pairs of destination classes 'competed for'					
	Men			Women		
	S vs I	S vs W	I vs W	S vs I	S vs W	I vs W
S vs I	2.75	3.09	1.12	1.67	3.75	2.23
S vs W	4.00	7.35	1.82	3.77	12.95	3.43
I vs W	1.47	2.37	1.62	2.23	3.45	1.54

Key S = Service (classes I and II);
 I = Intermediate (classes III,IV, and V);
 W = Working (classes VI and VII).

(*Source*: Marshall, G., Rose, D., Newby, H. and Vogler, C. (1988) *Social Class in Modern Britain*, Unwin Hyman, London, p. 105.)

Table 2.23 Relative mobility chances in terms of odds ratios, by Goldthorpe class and sex. Transition from class on entry into employment to present class position

Pairs of origin classes 'in competition'	Pairs of destination classes 'competed for'					
	Men			Women		
	S vs I	S vs W	I vs W	S vs I	S vs W	I vs W
S vs I	2.39	8.71	3.64	4.31	10.96	2.51
S vs W	6.08	41.68	7.01	6.04	50.00	8.15
I vs W	2.54	4.79	1.93	1.40	4.56	3.25

Key S = Service (classes I and II);
 I = Intermediate (classes III, IV, and V);
 W = Working (classes VI and VII).

(*Source*: Marshall, G., Rose, D., Newby, H. and Vogler, C. (1988) *Social Class in Modern Britain*, Unwin Hyman, London, p. 105.)

Figure 2.2   Relationship between class of origin, class destination and sex

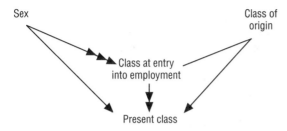

(*Source*: Marshall, G., Rose, D., Newby, H. and Vogler, C. (1988) *Social Class in Modern Britain*, Unwin Hyman, London, p. 110.)

for service-class rather than working-class destinations, those from service-class backgrounds are 7.76 times as successful. For women the equivalent figure is 14.07.

According to the authors, the tables support Goldthorpe's contention that relative intergenerational mobility rates for women are influenced by class in a similar way and to a similar extent as those of men. Marshall *et al.* say 'Overall patterns among women and men are not dissimilar although there are differences in the relative odds pertaining to particular transitions.' According to this view, class background influences women's mobility as much as it does men's, although the absolute patterns of mobility are different for the sexes because women are more highly concentrated in certain parts of the stratification system than men.

Sex, class, intergenerational and intragenerational mobility

The Essex study also examined the relationship between sex, class of origin and class at entry into employment and present class. Figure 2.2 illustrates its findings. The number of heads in the arrow indicates the strength of the effects involved. Thus the data suggests that sex has a particularly strong influence on first jobs but a rather weaker effect upon current class. Class of origin has a strong effect upon present class and the first job also affects the class people end up in.

The data include some interesting findings on intragenerational mobility. Some 84 per cent of men who started their careers in service-class jobs

and who came from service-class backgrounds were still in the service class when they were interviewed. However only 64 per cent of men who started work in the service class but came from working-class backgrounds were still in it. (For women the corresponding figures were 77 per cent and 43 per cent.) Thus even when individuals start their careers in the upper part of the stratification system, class background still exercises a strong influence on their chances in life, dragging down a considerable proportion of those from working-class backgrounds.

■ **Explanations of mobility rates**

The following reasons have been given to account for the rate of social mobility in industrial society.

1 There is considerable change in the occupational structure. For example, in Britain, the proportion of manual workers in the male labour force has declined from 70 per cent in 1921 to 55 per cent in 1971 so for each succeeding generation, there are more white-collar and fewer blue-collar jobs available. This helps account for the finding of the Oxford study that upward mobility considerably exceeds downward mobility.

2 Manual and non-manual fertility rates differ. In particular, working-class fathers have generally had more children than middle-class fathers. This differential fertility can also be seen as a reason for the relatively high rate of upward mobility. As the Oxford study indicated, class 1 fathers did not produce sufficient sons to fill the rapidly growing numbers of class 1 occupations. As a result, recruitment from lower strata was essential to fill those positions.

3 Many sociologists have argued that occupational status in industrial society is increasingly achieved on the basis of merit. Jobs are allocated in terms of talent and ability, rather than through family and friendship connections. Education is seen to play a key part in this process. The educational system grades people in terms of ability, and educational qualifications have a growing influence on occupational status and reward. Since educational opportunities are increasingly available to all young people, no matter what their social background, the result is a more open society and a higher rate of social mobility. This view, however, has been strongly criticized. The arguments involved are complex and will be discussed in detail in Chapter 5.

■ Class formation and class conflict

The nature and extent of social mobility in Western industrial societies pose a number of questions concerning class formation and class conflict.

Marx believed that a high rate of social mobility would tend to weaken class solidarity: classes would become increasingly heterogeneous as their members ceased to share similar backgrounds. Distinctive class subcultures would tend to disintegrate since norms, attitudes and values would no longer be passed from generation to generation within a single stratum. Class identification and loyalty would weaken since it would be difficult for mobile individuals to feel a strong consciousness of kind with other members of the class in which they found themselves. As a result, the intensity of class conflict and the potential for class consciousness would be reduced.

Ralf Dahrendorf believes that this situation has arrived in modern Western societies. He argues that as a result of the high rate of social mobility, the nature of conflict has changed. In an open society, there are considerable opportunities for individual advancement. There is therefore less need for people to join together as members of a social class in order to improve their situation. In Dahrendorf's words 'Instead of advancing their claims as members of homogeneous groups, people are more likely to compete with each other as individuals for a place in the sun.' As a result class solidarity and the intensity of specifically class conflict will be reduced. Dahrendorf then goes a step further and questions whether the rather loose strata of mobile individuals can still be called social classes. However, he stops short of rejecting the concept of class, arguing that 'although mobility diminishes the coherence of groups as well as the intensity of class conflict, it does not eliminate either'.

In an article based on the Oxford Mobility Study, John H. Goldthorpe and Catriona Llewellyn make the following observations on the relationship between social mobility and class formation.

1 The findings of the Oxford study indicate that the highest degree of homogeneity in terms of social background is found in the manual working class: in 1972 around 70 per cent of its members are the sons of manual workers.

2 If present trends continue, this level of self-recruitment will increase.

Goldthorpe and Llewellyn claim that this 'offers a very favourable basis for strategies of solidarity'. In other words, the similarity of origins and experience of the majority of manual workers provides a basis for collective action in pursuit of common interests.

The Oxford study indicates a high rate of mobility out of the working class. As Dahrendorf suggests, this might encourage individual rather than collective strategies. However, since upward mobility is substantially greater than downward mobility, relatively few people move down into the working class. Goldthorpe and Llewellyn argue that collective strategies may well be encouraged by:

> decreasing mobility into the working class, which must make for a steadily greater homogeneity of origins among its members and thus, one might suppose, for a greater potential for solidarity.

By comparison, the middle class is increasingly heterogeneous in terms of the social background of its members: in Goldthorpe's words, it is 'a class of low classness' (quoted in Bourne 1979, p. 291). It lacks coherence and class solidarity, an observation which matches Kenneth Roberts's picture of a 'fragmentary' middle class.

Mobility and social order

A number of sociologists have attempted to assess the effects of mobility on social order. Frank Parkin has seen the relatively high rate of upward mobility as a 'political safety-valve'. It provides opportunities for many able and ambitious members of the working class to improve their situation. As a result, the frustration which might result (if opportunities for upward mobility were absent) is prevented from developing.

To some degree this will weaken the working class. The upwardly mobile have found individual solutions to the problems of low status and low pay; if they remained within the working class, they might well join with other members in collectivist strategies which might benefit the class as a whole.

In addition those who move out of the working class show little desire to improve the lot of their class of origin. Research from a number of Western societies indicates that upwardly mobile individuals tend to take on the social and political outlooks of the class into which they move. American studies in particular suggest that those who move upward into the middle class often become more conservative than those born into it. Thus the upwardly mobile pose no threat to social stability: indeed, they can be seen to reinforce it.

Similar conclusions have been drawn from studies of downward mobility. American sociologists Harold Wilensky and Hugh Edwards examined the response of **skidders** – persons moving down into the working class – to the experience of social demotion. They found that the downwardly mobile tend to be more politically conservative than those born into and remaining within the working class. The experience of downward mobility did not lead them to reject the social order and so threaten the stability of society. Instead they clung to middle-class values, anticipating upward mobility and a restoration of their former status. Their presence in the working class tends to weaken that class since they are not really a part of it. Wilensky and Edwards state:

Skidders, along with other workers who escape from working-class culture psychologically or actually, function to reduce working-class solidarity and social criticism from below – and therefore slow down the pusch towards equality.

Thus both upward and downward mobility tend to reinforce the status quo: both introduce conservative elements into social strata; both appear to weaken working-class solidarity and therefore reduce the intensity of class conflict.

■ Gender and social class

The issue of social mobility illustrates how gender was neglected in many early studies. When men were the main breadwinners in most families and comparatively few married women worked, to the predominantly male sociologists carrying out research women seemed of little importance in theories of class. However, as women have increasingly combined paid work with domestic tasks and have become as numerous as men in the labour force, it has become impossible to construct theories of stratification without considering the position of women. However, since women are more likely to work part-time than men, some women are housewives, and male and female partners may have jobs in different classes, the inclusion of women poses a number of theoretical problems for theories of stratification.

On the one hand women might be seen as a part of the class structure without in any way forming a distinctive group within it. In other words individual men and women are first and foremost members of a class rather than members of the gender groups 'male' and 'female'. This suggests that a working-class woman has more in common with a working-class man than with a middle-class woman.

Alternatively gender groupings might be seen to cut across social class, and perhaps even be more important than class. This view implies that a working-class woman would have more in common with a middle-class woman than with a working-class man.

There are numerous variations on these points of view. In the following sections we demonstrate different ways in which sociologists have struggled to resolve the problem of the relationship between class and gender.

The household as the unit of class analysis

The first and simplest way to deal with the relationship between gender and class is to more or less ignore it. In official statistics in Great Britain a person's class is determined by the occupation of the 'head' of their household.

Before the 1981 census males were always considered to be the head of households in which women also lived. Thus all the women in such a household were deemed to have the same class as the male 'head'. In the 1981 census the possibility of having a female 'head' of the household was first accepted, but in practice the class of the household was still very likely to be determined by the occupation of the husband. Single women and those in all-female households make up the vast majority of women whose class is measured in terms of their own occupation.

Ann Oakley points out that many sociological studies have followed this procedure. The family has been taken as the unit of stratification, and the family's class has been derived from the occupation of the family's head.

One supporter of this approach is Frank Parkin. He argues that the social and economic rewards of women are largely determined by their marital and family relationships and, in particular, by the status of the male breadwinner. Parkin states:

If the wives and daughters of unskilled labourers have some things in common with the wives and daughters of wealthy landowners, there can be no doubt that the differences in their overall situation are far more striking and significant.

In other words, the inequalities of sexual status are insignificant compared to the inequalities of class status.

However, Nicky Britten and Anthony Heath point to an obvious problem with this approach. In some families, which they term **cross-class families**, it is the woman who has the higher class occupation on the Registrar General's Scale, for example a male manual worker married to a female non-manual worker. From an analysis of the data from *The Child Health and Education Study* of 1980 they found significant differences between these families and those in which both husband and wife had a manual job. For example over 79 per cent of cross-class families had an income of over £99 per week, compared to 67 per cent of families with two manual workers. This might indicate that in cross-class families the wife's occupation is the best indicator of the family's class position.

Nevertheless, some sociologists maintain, with only slight reservations, that a woman's social class should still usually be determined with reference to her husband's occupation. For example, Westergaard and Resler assert 'it is still men's occupational circumstances far more than women's that set the essential circumstances of life for most households, however much one may

deplore this'. In other words, Westergaard and Resler would claim that they are not being sexist, they are simply taking account of the 'facts': the class position and life chances of a family – indeed the type of employment done by the wife – are all largely dependent on the husband's job.

John Goldthorpe – husbands, wives and class positions

John Goldthorpe further defends this position. He agrees with Parkin, and Westergaard and Resler that the family is the unit of stratification. Furthermore he relates class to a family's position in the labour market. He does not believe though, that a male, where present, should automatically be considered head of a household. The head should be defined as 'the family member who has the greatest commitent to, and continuity in, the labour market'.

In theory this position might pose problems for existing ways of measuring class. If it were found that many wives had a greater involvement in, and commitment to, the labour market than their husbands, then the class position of many families might have been mistakenly defined in the past.

Furthermore, if there were many families in which it was unclear whether the husband or the wife had the greater involvement in the labour market, and their jobs placed them in different classes, it would be difficult to determine in which class to place many families. According to Goldthorpe these problems do not arise for the following reasons.

1 First, by using data from the Oxford Mobility Study, (for further details of this study see pp. 104–5), Goldthorpe claims that the vast majority of working wives withdraw from work once or more during their working life. Thus it is their husbands who have a greater commitment to paid work and therefore it is on the basis of the husband's work that the class of the family should be calculated.

2 Second, Goldthorpe denies that there are a large number of cross-class families in which the wife has a higher social class than the husband. He argues that many families only *appear* to be cross-class families because the class of the wife has been determined in an inappropriate manner. Most female non-manual workers have routine or unskilled white-collar jobs. Goldthorpe claims that these women have a much less favourable market situation than their male counterparts in lower-

level non-manual jobs. The female workers tend to get lower pay, less fringe benefits and enjoy less job security. In these circumstances it makes little sense to attribute such families to the middle class: the woman's job does not provide the family with middle-class life chances, and the husband's job is still the best measure of the family's class.

Criticisms of Goldthorpe

In a reply to Goldthorpe, Anthony Heath and Nicky Britten insist that 'women's jobs do make a difference', although they accept some of Goldthorpe's criticisms of the concept of cross-class families.

They admit that some non-manual jobs for women offer little significant advantage over male manual jobs. They accept that women working in sales (for example, shop assistants), and in personal services (for example, hairdressing), do not have what could reasonably be called middle-class jobs. However, those in professional, supervisory and managerial occupations clearly have a superior market situation to husbands in manual jobs. Furthermore, female junior office workers also have advantages over male manual workers.

Heath and Britten therefore conclude that most families with female non-manual workers must still be regarded as cross-class families.

Stronger criticisms of Goldthorpe are advanced by Michelle Stanworth. She argues quite simply that husbands and wives should be allocated to classes as individuals rather than as part of a family unit. Using data from the *General Household Survey* of 1979 she found that only 19 per cent of working men were the sole providers of financial support for their wives. Furthermore, she also suggests that the material situation of husband and wife are not necessarily the same.

There may be inequalities within the family, for example if the husband has more money to spend on personal consumption than the wife.

Individuals and families as units of stratification

David Rose and Gordon Marshall agree to some extent with both Goldthorpe and Stanworth. Their research into social class in Britain conducted in 1984 (see pp. 79–80, 98–100 for further details) found that some **class actions** taken by women seemed to be affected more by the class of their family than their own class. For example, the voting intentions of wives were better predicted by the class of their husbands than their own class.

On the other hand, Rose and Marshall found that **class fates** were affected more by the class of individuals than the class of their families. Women had less chance of upward social mobility than men, regardless of their husband's occupation.

Rose and Marshall concluded:

---

an approach to class analysis which takes the individual as the unit of analysis is as legitimate as one which takes families as the basic unit. Indeed, we believe that both approaches are important because social classes are made up of neither individuals nor families but of individuals in families.

None of the approaches that we have discussed so far considers the possibility that women and men should be seen as constituting distinctive strata in the stratification system. This possibility is discussed on pp. 629–31.

■ Contemporary theories of stratification

As we indicated earlier in the chapter, most contemporary approaches to stratification take their inspiration from either Marx's or Weber's writings on class. In this section we will examine the work of a leading neo-Marxist theorist Erik Olin Wright, and a leading neo-Weberian, John Goldthorpe. Their work represents perhaps the best-known attempts to update the work of Marx and Weber on class by applying it to con-

temporary societies. We have already mentioned Wright and particularly Goldthorpe in earlier parts of this chapter. Here their models of the class structure as a whole will be compared and evaluated. We end this section with an analysis of the work of W.G. Runciman, who draws on the work of Marxists and Weberians in producing an alternative view of class in contemporary Britain.

■ Erik Olin Wright – a neo-Marxist theory of class

The American neo-Marxist Erik Olin Wright has been developing theoretical approaches to class since the 1970s. His work has undergone a number of changes and his early work will be examined first.

One of the biggest problems for Marxist theories of class in the twentieth century has been the growth of a middle class of salaried employees. Unlike the bourgeoisie they are not owners of the means of production yet compared to the proletariat they can command relatively high wages and they enjoy a fair amount of job security. In developing a neo-Marxist approach to class, Wright was concerned to develop a framework which could explain the position of this group without resorting to Weberian concepts.

Marxist approaches emphasize that classes are antagonistic groups with different interests and they are differentiated by their role in production. Weberians emphasize relationships in the market, for example in buying and selling labour power, rather than relationships in production.

Wright's first solution to this problem was to use the concept of **contradictory class locations**.

The early theory – basic classes

In his early theory, Wright starts off by distinguishing three classes. Within the capitalist mode of production the **bourgeoisie** is distinguished from the **proletariat**. The former group has control over the means of production, control over labour power and control over investments and accumulation. The proletariat have none of these types of control.

The third class, the **petty bourgeoisie**, is involved in a different mode of production, **simple commodity production**. Wright comments that 'real capitalist societies always contain subordinate modes of production other than the capitalist mode of production itself'. Simple commodity production is not based upon the exploitation of wage labour by employers but is 'production organized for the market by independent self-employed producers who employ no workers'. The petty bourgeoisie has control over the means of production and some control over investments and the accumulation process, but no control over labour power as its members employ no workers.

Contradictory class locations

This leaves some workers who are in 'contradictory locations within class relations' because they have some characteristics in common with two classes, rather than being pure members of one. Managers, supervisors, technocrats and 'foremen' are in a contradictory location between the bourgeoisie and the proletariat. They have some degree of control but not as much as the bourgeoisie or as little as the proletariat. For example, top managers have control over the means of the means of production and the labour power of others, but only partial control over investments. 'Foremen' do not have control over the means of production or over investment, but they do have minimal control over the labour power of others.

Between the petty bourgeoisie and the bourgeoisie are **small employers**. Wright defines this group as consisting of those who employ other workers but more than half the profit their business makes comes from their own labour or that of other family members.

Semi-autonomous wage-earners are situated between the proletariat and the petty bourgeoisie. They have some control over how they work and what they produce and therefore have minimal control over the means of production. Wright cites laboratory researchers, professors in elite universities and 'certain highly skilled craftsmen' as examples.

Wright estimated that in the USA in 1969 the bourgeoisie made up 1–2 per cent of the population, the petty bourgeoisie 4–5 per cent, the proletariat 41–54 per cent, small employers 6–7 per cent, semi-autonomous employees 5–11 per cent, and managers and supervisors 30–35 per cent. His illustration of the class system is reproduced in Figure 2.3

Revising the theory

In the 1980s Wright became concerned with some aspects of his original theory. He was particularly troubled by the category 'semi-autonomous employees' as it had proved 'impossible to operationalize in a rigorous manner'. Furthermore, his whole scheme was based on degrees of control or domination of one class by another. He decided that *exploitation* rather than *domination* should be central to any Marxist theory of class. After trying unsuccessfully to resolve these and other

Figure 2.3   The relationship of contradictory class positions to class forces in capitalist society

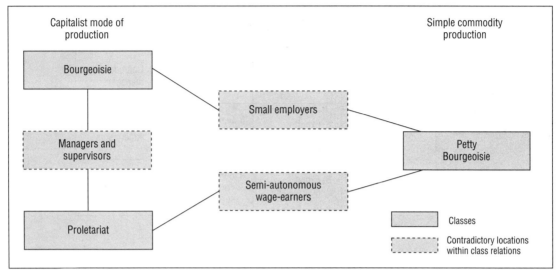

(*Source*: Wright, E.O. (1983) *Class, Crisis and the State*, Verso Books, London, p. 63.)

problems by modifying the original theory, he chose to abandon it in favour of a new one.

Exploitation

In line with his thinking Wright set about producing a new Marxist set of class categories based on exploitation. After considering various alternatives he decided that exploitation involves 'the appropriation of the fruits of labour' of one class by another. It always involves a situation where the class doing the exploiting would be harmed if the exploited class stopped working.

Exploitation results from the unequal distribution of a particular asset, but in different economic systems the crucial asset which is unequally distributed varies.

1 In **feudalism** it is labour power which is unequally distributed when the feudal aristocracy coercively extracts the surplus labour of the serfs.

2 In **capitalism** the means of production are unequally distributed as capitalists exploit workers through buying and selling labour power and commodities.

3 In **statism** (by which Wright means communist societies with a strong central state such as the former USSR) organizational assets are unequally distributed. With private ownership of the means of production

virtually abolished, those who hold senior positions in the organizations which control production use their position to exploit others. Wright describes this exploitation by bureaucrats, managers and party officials as 'planned appropriation and distribution of surplus based on hierarchy'.

4 Finally Wright distinguishes exploitation based on skills. This would be characteristic of a future socialist society when democratization had taken place and in which society was no longer organized on hierarchical principles. Despite the considerable equality in such a society, those with particular skills might be able to use them to procure 'negotiated redistribution of surplus from workers to experts'.

A new typology of class locations

Wright goes on to observe, as he did in his earlier work, that societies are rarely characterized by a single mode of production. This enables him to develop a typology of classes in capitalist society based upon the ownership or non-ownership of different assets which can form the basis for exploitation.

First he divides the class structure into the owners and non-owners of the means of production. Amongst the owners he distinguishes those who own enough to hire workers and do not have

Figure 2.4   Wright's second class map

Production assets Owners of means of production		Non-owners (wage labourers)			
Own sufficient capital to hire workers and not work	1 Bourgeoisie	4 Expert managers	7 Semi-credentialled managers	10 Uncredentialled managers	+
Own sufficient capital to hire workers but must work	2 Small employers	5 Expert supervisors	8 Semi-credentialled workers	11 Uncredentialled supervisors	0
Own sufficient capital to work for self but not to hire workers	3 Petty Bourgeoisie	6 Expert non-managers	9 Semi credentialled supervisors	12 Proletariat	–
	+	0	–		

Skill/credential assets

(right vertical axis label) Organization assets

(*Source*: Wright, E.O. (1985) *Classes*, London, p. 88.)

to work themselves, those who hire workers but also have to work themselves, and the petty bourgeoisie who work for themselves and don't employ other workers.

Wage labourers are then distinguished according to whether they have above average, about average or below average skill/credential (or qualification) assets and organizational assets. This leads to nine categories of wage labourers ranging from the skilled, well-qualified expert managers with powerful positions in organizations to the proletarians who lack skill, qualifications or positions of power. His typology is illustrated in Figure 2.4.

Wright concludes from his new typology that class conflict and class struggle is considerably more complex than it seems in the traditional Marxist theory with its emphasis on the division between just two classes: the bourgeoisie and the proletariat. He goes as far as to suggest there might be alternatives to the proletariat ushering in changes in capitalism. Bureaucratic managers are seen as 'having the potential to pose an alternative to capitalism along state socialist lines'.

Criticisms of Wright

Wright's theory of class has come in for extensive criticism. Stephen Edgell points to some of the most damaging. He argues that Wright has abandoned the distinctive features of a Marxist approach to class. For example, Marxists see class in relational terms. That is, classes are distinct entities which have particular roles in the economic system (such as employer and employees, slave and slave owner). They are not distinguished in gradational terms, that is by placing individuals on a continuum according to say how much they earn or how much money they have. Yet Wright's theory ends up being gradational by categorizing people according to their level of organizational and skill/credential assets.

Edgell also argues that it is not clear why the possession of skill or the lack of it should lead to the exploitation of one group by another. It might lead to different wage levels but that in itself does not constitute exploitation.

Edgell concludes that the inclusion of organizational and skill/credential assets means that Wright's position has become almost identical to Weber's. In effect Wright is doing no more than distinguishing different market and work situations which can be better understood from a Weberian perspective.

In the Essex study of class in Britain Gordon Marshall *et al.* set out to test Wright's theory and compare it with Goldthorpe's (which will be discussed next). They came down firmly against Wright. Like Edgell they believe that Wright's new scheme 'closely resembles' Weberian conceptions of class. Their strongest attack, though, is based upon putting Wright's class categories into operation.

The Essex study tried using both Wright's earlier and later class schemes. Using the earlier scheme they found, as Wright himself had suspected, that the category 'semi-autonomous employee' caused confusion. Using Wright's own criteria for allocating occupations to categories, this class included some teachers, computer programmers, social workers, coal miners, motor mechanics and process workers. This unlikely combination of people was put together simply because they were not capitalists or managers and they all claimed they had autonomy at work. When Marshall *et al.* tried using Wright's new class scheme they also found many apparent discrepancies. For example, the 'proletarians' included a buying and purchasing supervisor, an investment broker, a secretarial supervisor and a hospital matron. On the other hand, a skilled machinist is among those seen as belonging to a higher class on the grounds that he has an apprentice working under him.

Wright himself has tried to defend himself from this type of criticism. He accepts that there are such anomalies but argues that they stem simply from **operational choices** involved in applying the scheme. Although the procedures for allocating people to classes might need to be altered, in his view this does not undermine the overall conceptual framework.

■ John Goldthorpe – a neo-Weberian theory of class

Goldthorpe's approach to class has been highly influential and widely used in British sociology. While Wright has concentrated on the theoretical development of a Marxist approach, Goldthorpe has been more concerned with the practical application of Weberian ideas. Goldthorpe's class scheme was originally developed for the particular purpose of studying social mobility, and was the basis for the Oxford Mobility Study (see pp. 100–2).

The basis of Goldthorpe's scheme

Goldthorpe's class scheme is based on Lockwood's distinction between market and work situations which was originally used in his study of clerical work (see pp. 66–7). However, the procedure Goldthorpe adopted for determining market and work situations was much simpler than that used by Lockwood. Instead of using questionnaire or interview data to determine, for example, autonomy at work, he uses just two types of information: a job title and information about whether the person was self-employed, an employer or an employee. Each individual is then given an employment status (e.g. large proprietor or self-employed without employees) and is placed in an occupational group according to the type of work he or she does. The former information is held to be a measure of work situation; the latter of market situation. Individuals are then allocated to pre-determined class categories according to a combination of their work and market situations.

This procedure led to Goldthorpe identifying seven classes as illustrated in Figure 2.5. Each class was said to combine:

> occupational categories whose members would appear . . . to be typically comparable, on the one hand, in terms of their sources and levels of income, their degree of economic security and chances of advancement . . . ; and, on the other, in their location within systems of authority and control governing the process of production in which they are engaged, and hence their degree of autonomy in performing their work-tasks and roles.

The seven classes are sometimes collapsed into three. The **service class** contains only white-collar occupations and includes both employers and employees. The **intermediate class** is made up of a mixture of white- and blue-collar workers and it includes small proprietors and the self-employed as well as employees. The **working class** is made up of employed blue-collar workers.

As we discussed in a previous section (see pp. 103–4), Goldthorpe allocates individuals to a class according to the position of the male head of household where there is one. This scheme was originally devised to study male mobility patterns but Goldthorpe insists that class position stems from the position of the family not the individual, and in practice the position of the family is determined by the position of the male breadwinner.

Figure 2.5   Goldthorpe's class scheme

Classes	No.	Description
Service class	1	Higher professionals, higher grade administrators, managers in large industrial concerns and large proprietors
	2	Lower professionals, higher grade technicians, lower grade administrators, managers in small businesses and supervisors of non-manual employees
Intermediate class	3	Routine non-manual—mainly clerical and sales personnel
	4	Small proprietors and self-employed artisans
	5	Lower-grade technicans and supervisors of manual workers
Working class	6	Skilled manual workers
	7	Semi-skilled and unskilled manual workers

(Source: Goldthorpe, J.H. (1980) *Social Mobility and Class Structure in Modern Britain*, Clarendon Press, Oxford, pp. 44 and 48.)

Modifications to the scheme

Goldthorpe has undertaken one major revision to his class scheme. This is illustrated in Figure 2.6. The modification was carried out for use in an international study of male mobility. The following changes were made.

1   The top two classes were merged since, Goldthorpe claimed, it would be difficult to distinguish clearly between them in all countries in a cross-national study.

2   Classes 5 and 6 were merged for the same reason to form an enlarged working class. Lower-grade technicians and supervisors of manual workers were effectively demoted from the intermediate class to the working class. Goldthorpe has described this group as a 'marginal case' but has not fully explained the reason for the change.

3   Separate classes of farmers and agricultural workers were added to the scheme to take account of the importance of agriculture in some societies.

Criticisms of Goldthorpe

Not surprisingly Goldthorpe has been criticized by supporters of Wright's neo-Marxist class scheme. Goran Ahrne, a Swedish sociologist who has applied Wright's class scheme in his own country, is a case in point. Ahrne notes that Goldthorpe makes very little attempt to explain the theoretical thinking behind the scheme. He says: 'The theoretical basis of

the model is not clearly elaborated and, moreover, it is neither very logical nor theoretically consistent. At best it may be regarded as a well-made commonsensical classification of occupations.'

According to Ahrne, Goldthorpe's criteria for distinguishing different market and work situations are inadequate. The approach adopted to market situation contains no discussion of supply and demand for labour power, and the approach to work situations contains no way of measuring autonomy and control at work. Ahrne also argues that the ranking of classes is arbitrary: Goldthorpe does not explain why the petty bourgeoisie are allocated to class 4 (in the original scheme) while routine non-manual workers are in class 3. Nor does Goldthorpe explain why particular types of worker who seem to have much in common are placed in different classes. For example, a self-employed electrician is placed in the intermediate class while a self-employed engineer is placed in the service class.

The muddled theoretical thinking continues in the descriptions of the classes. Ahrne notes that 'two additional grounds for classification are introduced which are neither explained nor discussed'. These are the distinctions between higher-grade and lower-grade and between manual and non-manual work. Ahrne concludes:

the class model as a whole does not contain any rigorous theoretical logic. It seems to be a mixture

Figure 2.6 Goldthorpe's class scheme (revised version)

1	Classes I and II	All professionals, administrators and managers (including large proprietors), higher-grade technicans and supervisors of non-manual workers
2	Class III	Routine non-manual employees in administration and commerce, sales personnel, other rank-and-file service workers
3	Class IVab	Small proprietors, self-employed artisans and other 'own-account' workers with and without employees (other than in primary production)
4	Class IVc	Farmers and smallholders and other self-employed workers in primary production
5	Class V and VI	Lower-grade technicians; supervisors of manual workers and skilled manual workers
6	Class VIIa	Semi- and unskilled manual workers (other than in primary production)
7	Class VIIb	Agricultural and other workers in primary production

(*Source*: Goldthorpe, J.H. (revised edition 1987) *Social Mobility and Class Structure in Modern Britain*, Clarendon Press, Oxford, p. 305.)

of practical and commonsensical considerations that may work for certain mobility studies, but whose application gives very little theoretical insight into the relationship between structurally derived power relations and everyday class realities.

In an early critique Roger Penn raised what he saw as problems with Goldthorpe's concepts of the service and intermediate classes. By merging large proprietors and managerial and professional workers into a service class, Goldthorpe seemed to be denying the existence of a separate ruling or upper class. Penn also argued that the intermediate class included a diverse range of groups. Some small proprietors, for example, are in a highly advantageous position compared to most workers in the intermediate class.

Goldthorpe has been strongly attacked by feminist sociologists. As we discovered earlier in the chapter, such sociologists argue that using the work of the male head of household to determine the position of women in the class structure is inappropriate. Others go further and argue that the whole class scheme is based on the characteristics of men's jobs and therefore gives a misleading impression of the social structure. For example, S. Arber, A. Dale and N. Gilbert have constructed an alternative class scheme which includes some classes which are made up largely of female

workers. Sometimes known as the **Surrey occupational class scale** it adopts a nine class model and includes secretarial and clerical workers as class 4, and shop and personal service workers as class 6.

A defence of Goldthorpe

In the Essex study of class carried out by Gordon Marshall *et al.* Goldthorpe's class scale was tested and was generally supported by the data. According to those authors, his class categories work much better than Wright's when used to collect data. People placed together in a particular class were found to have more in common with each other than was the case when Wright's categories were used.

Marshall *et al.* argue that Goldthorpe is justified in putting employers and top managers together in the service class. There are so few members of the bourgeoisie that they are unlikely to crop up in significant numbers in a mobility study. In any case the distinction between the two groups has become blurred as family or individual ownership of firms has declined. Marshall *et al.* cite the example of one individual in their study, an engineer who has bought a partnership in his firm with his savings after working his way up from the shop floor. They argue that his situation is little different from that of top managers who earn enough money to put some aside to invest.

Marshall *et al.* do, however, criticize Goldthorpe's approach to gender and stratification. They point out, for example, that men's social mobility cannot be understood or explained adequately if women are allocated to the same class as their husbands. Men and women have to compete with each other for jobs, and, as women form an increasing proportion of the labour force, the mobility chances of men are heavily influenced by the jobs held by women. Mobility patterns cannot be understood while ignoring half the workers.

◼ W.G. Runciman – the class structure, roles and power

In an attempt to determine the number of classes in British society, W.G. Runciman has developed a new approach to analysing the stratification system. This approach uses both Marxist concepts, such as 'the means of production', and Weberian ones, such as 'marketability'.

Roles and classes

Runciman starts by arguing that the class structure consists of sets of roles. A **role** is defined as a position 'embodying consistently recurring patterns of institutional behaviour informed by mutually shared beliefs about their incumbents' capacity directly or indirectly to influence the behaviour of each other'. **Occupational roles** are the most important, but not everyone has an occupational role. Those without jobs should also be assigned roles according to the 'economic power attaching to whatever different roles they occupy'. A person married to someone with a job should be seen as having the same role as their spouse, assuming they share the economic power of their spouse. Where partners have different jobs then both should be given the class of the one with the highest ranking role, again assuming that they share their economic power. Whether power is shared cannot be determined theoretically but needs to be determined from the evidence in each case.

For those with jobs, classes should be determined using the concept of a **career**. In other words it is necessary to take account of promotion prospects as well as current position. Some male white-collar workers, for example, might be seen as being in a higher class than some female white-collar workers who have similar jobs but much less chance of moving into management. Where individuals have more than one role (for example if they have two jobs), the highest ranking role should again be used to determine a person's class.

Classes and power

Runciman then goes on to explain how roles should be allocated to classes. He defines classes as: 'sets of roles whose common location in social space is a function of the nature and degree of economic power (or lack of it) attaching to them through their relation to the institutional processes of production, distribution and exchange'.

Economic power can come from three sources.

1 **Ownership** or 'legal title to some part of the means of production'.

2 **Control** or 'a contractual right to direct the application to the process of production of some part of the means of production, whether fixed or financial assets or labour'. Managers and supervisors are examples of people who possess control by virtue of their jobs.

3 **Marketability**, or the possession of an 'attribute or capacity' which can be sold to employers. In other words this refers to the skills, qualifications and the ability to carry out physical labour possessed by individual workers.

The class an individual belongs to is determined by examining a combination of these three types of economic power. People can end up in a higher class by having ownership control or marketability, or indeed any combination of the three.

Runciman illustrates this approach with the example of three engineers. Engineer A is an employee who earns £40,000 per year and has a good pension scheme. Engineer B owns a small engineering business which he has been able to buy through mortgaging his house. After paying interest, he makes £10,000 per year profit. Engineer C is a self-employed freelance engineer who employs his wife as his secretary and earns between £10,000 and £40,000 depending on how successful the year was.

All three of these people should be placed in the same class according to Runciman. They have different sorts of power. The first derives most of his power from control, the second from ownership and the third from marketability, but each has about the same amount of power.

Those towards the bottom of the stratification system have little or no control over production, have very little wealth, and little or nothing in the way of marketable skills or capacities.

The seven classes

Runciman identifies seven classes based upon the possession of different amounts of ownership, control and marketability. These are detailed in Table 2.24 with Runciman's estimate of the percentage of the British population in each class.

The highest class, which he calls the upper class, contains between a fifth and a tenth of 1 per cent of the population. It is made up of the owners of the means of production, the most senior managers and those with absolutely exceptional marketability. He cites examples of each of these three types: the Duke of Northumberland who qualifies in terms of ownership; the chief executive of Shell who has control; and 'the senior partners of the biggest firms of City accountants' who have marketability. Runciman specifically excludes very highly paid entertainers because their role is 'irrelevant' to 'the institutional processes of production, distribution and exchange'.

Runciman chooses to divide the middle class into three groups. The higher-grade professionals, senior civil servants and managers are placed in the highest of these three classes and routine white-collar workers in 'more or less "deskilled"' jobs are placed in the lowest of them. He argues that there is sufficient gap between the economic

Table 2.24 The Runciman classes

Class	Size in 1990
Upper class	0.2–0.1%
Upper middle class	<10%
Middle middle class	15%
Lower middle class	20%
Skilled working class	20%
Unskilled working class	30%
Underclass	5%

(*Source*: Runciman, W.G. (1990) 'How many classes are there in contemporary British society?' *Sociology*, vol. 24, no. 3, pp. 377–96.)

power of these two extremes in the middle class to justify the inclusion of a third group in between. This **middle middle class** includes lower professions and middle managers. Proprietors who are not in the upper class are allocated to one of the middle classes according to what 'the scale and kind of their property makes appropriate'. Runciman argues that workers such as shop assistants, checkout operators and copy- and audio-typists have insufficient economic power in terms of the marketability of their skills to be placed in the middle class. Instead they are seen as part of the working class.

The working class itself is divided in two: an **upper** or **skilled working class**, and a **lower** or **unskilled working class**. Semi-skilled workers are seen as belonging to the lower working class since, according to Runciman, it has become common for workers with minimal skills to be defined as semi-skilled. When he uses the terms skilled, semi-skilled and unskilled, Runciman is not referring to some abstract measure of technical knowledge which is required to carry out jobs. Instead he is thinking of the different degrees of marketability, control and ownership which individual workers possess. Thus a worker might be placed in the upper working class on the grounds of ownership if they own their own tools, on the grounds of control if they have control over the operation of machinery, or on the grounds of marketability if their skills are in demand.

Unlike Wright or Goldthorpe, Runciman distinguishes an underclass at the bottom of the stratification system. It consists of those: 'whose roles place them more or less permanently at the economic level where benefits are paid by the state to those unable to participate in the labour market at all'.

In effect members of the underclass have no control, ownership or marketability. (We described and evaluated Runciman's views on the underclass in more detail earlier in the chapter, see pp. 96–7.)

Operationalizing the class scheme

Runciman made no attempt to use his class scheme for research, but he did suggest how that might be done. It would be necessary to determine individuals' jobs, the amount and source of their income, their 'actual and prospective capital resources', and their economic position within the household. These different types of information could then be combined to determine a person's class.

Evaluation of Runciman

There are a number of problems with Runciman's class scheme. It would be extremely difficult to use in research since it means gathering a wide range of data on individuals and the households in which they live. In survey research many respondents might be unwilling or unable to give precise details of, for example, their wealth.

Runciman also offers no clear dividing lines between the classes: it is unclear how much marketability, power or control a person needs to be placed in a particular class. His view that groups such as the self-employed or small proprietors should not be seen as constituting separate classes is somewhat controversial. Runciman himself admits that such groups might be distinctive in terms of 'inter-generational mobility rates' and 'socio-political attitudes' but he is still unwilling to allocate them to a separate class because they do not necessarily have similar amounts of economic power as one another.

In addition because Runciman uses a gradational approach to class, where the differences between classes are a matter of degree rather than

kind, his decision to settle on seven classes seems rather arbitrary. He could just as easily have settled on a six- or an eight-class model.

Rosemary Crompton, however, argues that Runciman's scheme is one of the approaches to the class structure which has had some success in coming to terms with the social changes which have taken place since the Second World War. She argues that these changes include:

---

a move away from the conventionally established 'class' boundary between manual and non-manual work following the expansion of the service sector and the routinization and feminization of much lower-level white-collar employment; an emphasis on the diversity of middle class locations, and the identification of the poorest and most deprived as an 'underclass' – this identification being linked, to varying degrees, with the condition of state dependency. A major element of continuity, however, lies in the persisting concentration of economic, organizational and political power within an 'upper' class which comprises only a small minority of the population.

Her description of changes in the class structure provides a succinct summary of some of the main social trends discussed in this chapter.

■ Sociology, values and social stratification

It is evident from this chapter that sociologists are not neutral, dispassionate observers of the social scene. Like everybody else, they see the world in terms of their values and attitudes. To some degree this will affect their analysis of society. Their commitment to a particular set of values will influence what they see, what they look for, what they consider important, what they find and how they interpret their findings. Some sociologists have carried this argument a stage further and claimed that not only are the views of particular sociologists value-based, but also the major theoretical perspectives within the discipline. Thus, as the

previous chapter indicated, functionalism and Marxism have been seen as ideologically based. It has been argued that functionalism is founded on a conservative ideology, Marxism on a radical ideology. This argument can be illustrated from theories of social stratification.

At first sight, functionalist views on stratification appear value-free. The language of the functionalists is sober and restrained and their analyses have a scientific ring to them. However, functionalist theories of stratification have been strongly attacked for what many see as their right-wing, conservative bias.

On this basis, Alvin Gouldner criticizes Davis and Moore's assertion that social stratification is inevitable in all human societies. Gouldner claims that this statement is little more than an article of faith. He sees it as based ultimately on the conservative doctrine that 'the social world is for all time divided into rulers and ruled'. This implies that attempts to fundamentally change or eradicate systems of social stratification will be harmful to society. As a result, it can be argued that functionalist views provide support and justification for social inequality.

Gouldner claims that the logical conclusion of functionalist theories is that 'equality is a dream'. By suggesting that an egalitarian society is an illusion, the functionalists direct research away from alternatives to social stratification. This again encourages acceptance of the status quo rather than demands for radical change.

Finally, Gouldner argues that the basic assumptions of functionalist theory are essentially conservative. Functionalism is concerned with explaining the basis of social order. In pursuit of this aim, it focuses on the contributions of the various parts of society to the maintenance of order. Since stratified societies often provide evidence of order and stability, functionalism leads sociologists to assume that social stratification contributes to this situation. Since order and stability are assumed to be 'good' for society, any attempts to dismantle systems of social stratification will be seen as harmful to society. In Gouldner's words, the functionalist position implies that 'only "evil" – social disorder, tension or conflict – can come from efforts to remove the domination of man by man or to make fundamental changes in the character of authority'. In this way Gouldner claims that functionalism advocates the maintenance of the status quo.

By comparison, Marxist theories are openly radical. They advocate fundamental social change in many contemporary societies. They begin from the value judgement that some form of communist system is the only just and fair social arrangement. From this standpoint they evaluate various forms of social stratification. This often results in a passionate condemnation of social inequality, particularly of class systems in capitalist society.

The ideological basis of Marxist theory is clearly revealed in the use of value-laden terms such as 'exploitation' and 'oppression'. Indeed Marxists usually make no secret of their political views. For example, the British sociologist John Westergaard openly condemns the concentration of power and wealth in capitalist society. Writing with Henrietta Resler in the early 1970s, he argued that private property is increasingly threatened in Britain and added 'We ourselves hope that this threat will become a reality.'

It has often been argued that Marxist views of the contours of the class system are ideologically based. Starting from the judgement that capitalist society is divided into exploiters and exploited leads to the idea of a two-class system. Many non-Marxists argue that this view ignores other important divisions in society.

Thus David Lockwood attacks those Marxists who dismiss the clerks' middle-class identification as false class consciousness. Lockwood argues that this identification is based on real differences between the position of clerks and manual workers. He claims that Marxists who dismiss these differences as insignificant are allowing their political views to influence their judgement.

Marxists often respond in the same vein. They accuse sociologists who focus on divisions within and between the so-called middle and manual working classes of a conservative bias. They claim that this directs attention away from the concentration of wealth and power at the top and, in doing so, protects privilege.

Marxists have levelled similar accusations against studies of social mobility. For example, the Soviet sociologist Alexandrov accuses American 'bourgeois sociologists' of using the concept of social mobility to disguise the real nature of class exploitation under capitalism. The results of social mobility studies give the impression of an open society with considerable opportunity for upward mobility, but Alexandrov maintains that nearly all mobility occurs within the proletariat, not across 'real' class boundaries. In particular, there are minimal opportunities for workers to enter the bourgeoisie. The picture of a relatively open society presented by mobility studies disguises this situation and so conceals the extent to which the bourgeoisie maintains its wealth and power.

In this section we have shown that it is possible to argue that theories of stratification are based ultimately on ideology. Indeed many sociologists accept this view and make no secret of their commitment to particular values. For example, Dahrendorf's position is clear when he approvingly quotes Kant to the effect that social inequality is 'a rich source of much that is evil, but also of everything that is good'. From the authors' viewpoint, however, there is much more to applaud in Melvin Tumin's statement that:

The evidence regarding the mixed outcomes of stratification strongly suggests the examination of alternatives. The evidence regarding the possibilities of social growth under conditions of more equal rewarding are such that the exploration of alternatives seems eminently worthwhile.

It may be that only a commitment to a more egalitarian society will lead to the kind of research that Tumin advocates.

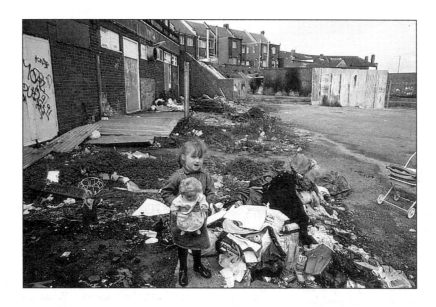

3

Poverty

3

Poverty

◼ Introduction

The word **poverty** implies an undesirable state. It suggests that individuals or groups who are in poverty need to be helped so that their situation is changed. Poverty, in other words, is a social problem. However, as we shall see later, for some groups in society poverty can be useful. Generally speaking, though, poverty is generally considered to be an undesirable social problem for which a solution should be found.

1 The first step in the solution of a problem is to identify it and this requires a **definition**.

2 The second step is to assess the size of a problem which involves the **construction of ways to measure it**.

3 Once the problem has been identified, defined and measured, the next step is to discover what **causes** it.

Therefore, only after answers have been obtained to the questions 'What is poverty?', 'What is the extent of poverty?', and 'What are the causes of poverty?' can the question 'What are the solutions to poverty?' be asked.

In this chapter we are going to examine some of the answers that social scientists have given to these four questions.

◼ The definition and measurement of poverty

Since the nineteenth century when rigorous studies of poverty first began, researchers have tried to establish a fixed yardstick against which to measure poverty. There have been three main areas of controversy over the basic principles on which such a yardstick can be based.

Absolute and relative poverty

First, researchers have disputed whether poverty should be measured in **absolute** or **relative** terms. Some writers have argued that there is a minimum standard that can be applied to all societies below which individuals can be said to be 'in poverty'. Measures of **absolute poverty** are usually based upon the idea of **subsistence**. In other words, people are in poverty if they do not have the resources to physically maintain human life.

Supporters of the concept of **relative poverty**, however, tend to dismiss this view. They argue that a definition must be related to the standards of a particular society at a particular time. According to this view, the point at which the dividing line which separates the poor from other members of society is drawn will vary according to how affluent that society is.

Material and multiple deprivation

The second area of controversy concerns whether poverty can be defined purely in **material terms**, or whether the definition should be wider. Some sociologists assume that poverty consists of a lack of material resources – in British society, for instance, a shortage of the money required to buy those commodities judged to be acceptable for maintaining an acceptable standard of living.

Other commentators, though, believe that poverty involves more than **material deprivation**. They see poverty as a form of **multiple deprivation** that can have many facets. For example, some have argued that inadequate educational opportunities, unpleasant working conditions, or powerlessness can be regarded as aspects of poverty.

None of these conditions is necessarily directly related to the income of the individual. Each implies that broader changes other than simply increasing the income of the worst-off members of society are necessary if poverty is to be eliminated.

Inequality and poverty

The third area of controversy concerns the relationship between **inequality** and poverty. From one point of view any society in which there is inequality is bound to have poverty. In other words, if all those individuals with below average incomes were defined as poor, then the only way that poverty could be eradicated would be to abolish all inequality in income. This is because if some people have higher than average incomes, inevitably others must fall below the average.

Most sociologists who adopt a relative definition of poverty accept that some reduction in inequality is necessary if poverty is to be reduced, but they do not believe it is necessary to abolish inequality altogether to solve this social problem. They argue that it is possible to establish a minimum standard, a **poverty line**, which might be below the average income. The **poor** can then be defined as those whose income or resources fall so far short of the average within a society that they do not have an acceptable standard of living. Thus it would be possible to have a society with some inequality where poverty no longer exists.

We will now look at these competing definitions and methods of measuring poverty, paying particular attention to the way that these definitions have been used, and the figures they produce. The next section will therefore consider the questions, 'What is poverty?', and 'What is the extent of poverty?'

■ Absolute poverty

The concept of **absolute poverty** usually involves a judgement of basic human needs and is measured in terms of the resources required to maintain health and physical efficiency. Most measures of absolute poverty are concerned with establishing the quality and amount of food, clothing and shelter deemed necessary for a healthy life.

Absolute poverty is often known as **subsistence poverty** since it is based on assessments of minimum subsistence requirements. This means that those who use absolute measurements usually limit poverty to material deprivation.

Absolute poverty is generally measured by pricing the basic necessities of life, drawing a poverty line in terms of this price, and defining as poor those whose income falls below that figure.

There have been many attempts to define and **operationalize** (put into a form which can be measured) the concept of absolute poverty. For example, in their 'Level of Living Index' Drewnowski and Scott define and operationalize basic physical needs in the following way:

1 **nutrition**, measured by factors such as intake of calories and protein;

2 **shelter**, measured by quality of dwelling and degree of overcrowding;

3 and **health**, measured by factors such as the rate of infant mortality and the quality of available medical facilities.

Some concepts of absolute poverty go beyond the notion of subsistence and material poverty by introducing the idea of **basic cultural needs**. This broadens the idea of basic human needs beyond the level of physical survival. Drewnowski and Scott include education, security, leisure and recreation in their category of basic cultural needs. The proportion of children enrolled at school is one indication of the level of educational provision; the number of violent deaths relative to the size of the population is one indication of security; and the amount of leisure relative to work time is one measure of the standard of leisure and recreation.

Criticisms of the concept of absolute poverty

The concept of absolute poverty has been widely criticized. It is based on the assumption that there are minimum basic needs for all people, in all societies. This is a difficult argument to defend even in regard to subsistence poverty measured in terms of food, clothing and shelter. Such needs vary both between and within societies.

Thus Peter Townsend argues 'It would be difficult to define nutritional needs without taking account of the kinds and demands of occupations and of leisure time pursuits in a society.' For instance, the nutritional needs of the nomadic hunters and gatherers of the Kalahari Desert in

Africa may well be very different from those of members of Western society. Within the same society, nutritional needs may vary widely, between, for example, the bank clerk sitting at his desk all day and the labourer on a building site.

A similar criticism can be made of attempts to define absolute standards of shelter. Jack and Janet Roach give the following illustration:

City living, for example, requires that 'adequate' shelter not only protects one from the elements, but that it does not present a fire hazard to others and that attention be paid to water supplies, sewage, and garbage disposal. These problems are simply met in rural situations.

Thus flush toilets, which may well be considered a necessary part of adequate shelter in the city, could hardly be considered essential fixtures in the dwellings of traditional hunting and gathering and agricultural societies.

The concept of absolute poverty is even more difficult to defend when it is broadened to include the idea of **basic cultural needs**. Such 'needs' vary from time to time and place to place and any attempt to establish absolute, fixed standards is bound to fail.

Drewnowski and Scott's basic cultural need for security is a case in point. Financial security for aged members of the working class in nineteenth-century England involved younger relatives providing for them, whereas today it is largely met by state old age pensions and private insurance schemes. Increasing longevity, reduction in the size of families, and earlier retirement have altered the circumstances of the aged. Definitions of adequate provision for old age have changed since the last century. Thus, in terms of security, both the situation and expectations of the aged in England have changed and are not strictly comparable over time.

A similar criticism can be applied to attempts to apply absolute standards to two or more societies. For instance, recreational and leisure provision in the West may be measured in terms of the number of televisions, cinemas, parks and playing fields per head of the population. However, the concept of leisure on which this is based and the items in terms of which it is measured may be largely irrelevant for other societies: the Hopi and Zuñi Indians of the southwestern USA have a rich ceremonial

life and this forms the central theme of their leisure activities. Recreational needs are therefore largely determined by the culture of the particular society.

Any absolute standard of cultural needs is based in part on the values of the researchers which to some degree reflect their particular cultures. Peter Townsend notes that when societies are compared in terms of recreational facilities 'Cinema attendance and ownership of radios take precedence over measures of direct participation in cultural events', such as religious rituals and other ceremonies. This is a clear illustration of Western bias.

■ Budget standards and poverty

One common approach to measuring poverty is to use what has been called the **budget standards** approach. This involves calculating the cost of purchases which are considered necessary to raise an individual or a family out of poverty. It has been used in some classic and contemporary studies of poverty in Britain. The British Government used it in calculating the level at which to set the means-tested benefit national assistance (now called income support) when it was introduced in 1948. It has also been used by the US Government in setting benefit levels.

One of the earliest and most famous studies of poverty was conducted by Seebohm Rowntree. In his early work the budget standards approach was originally based upon something very close to an absolute definition of poverty. (In Rowntree's later work and in contemporary sociology, budget standards have been based upon more relative definitions of poverty.)

Seebohm Rowntree – trends in poverty in Britain

Rowntree's original method of defining or measuring poverty comes closest to the use of an absolute and material or subsistence definition in Britain.

Rowntree conducted a study in York in 1899 and drew a poverty line in terms of a minimum weekly sum of money which was 'necessary to enable families to secure the necessaries of a healthy life'. The money needed for this subsistence level existence covered fuel and light, rent, food, clothing, household and personal sundries and was adjusted to family size. According to this measure, 33 per cent of the survey population lived in poverty.

Rowntree conducted two further studies of poverty in York, in 1936 and 1950, based largely on a similar methodology. However, in the later studies he included allowances for some items which were not strictly necessary for survival. Amongst these items were: newspapers, books, radios, beer, tobacco, holidays and presents. Despite the inclusion of the extra items he found that the percentage of his sample population in poverty had dropped to 18 per cent in 1936 and 1.5 per cent in 1950.

He also found that the causes of poverty changed considerably over half a century. For example, inadequate wages, major factors in 1899 and 1936, were relatively insignificant by 1950. Table 3.1 summarizes the results of Rowntree's surveys.

By the 1950s it appeared that poverty was a minor problem. 'Pockets' remained (for example among the aged) but it was believed that increased welfare benefits would soon eradicate this lingering poverty. The conquest of poverty was put down to an expanding economy – the 1950s were the years of the 'affluent society' – to government policies of full employment and to the success of the welfare state. It was widely believed that the operation of the welfare state had redistributed wealth from rich to poor and significantly raised working-class living standards.

Throughout the 1950s and 1960s researchers became increasingly dubious about the 'conquest of poverty'. Rowntree's concept of subsistence poverty, and the indicators he used to measure poverty, were strongly criticized. His measurement of adequate nutrition is a case in point. With the help of experts, Rowntree drew up a diet sheet which would provide the minimum adequate nutritional intake and, in terms of this, decided upon the minimum monies required for food. However, it is very unlikely that this minimum budget would meet the needs of the poor. As Martin Rein argues, it is based on:

an unrealistic assumption of a no-waste budget, and extensive knowledge in marketing and cooking. An economical budget must be based on knowledge and skill which is least likely to be present in the low-income groups we are concerned with.

Rowntree's estimates further ignore the fact that the majority of the working class spends a smaller percentage of its income on food than his budget allows. He does not allow for the fact that choice of food is based on the conventions of a person's social class and region, not upon a diet sheet drawn up by experts. Thus Peter Townsend argues that 'in relation to the budgets and customs of life of ordinary people the make-up of the subsistence budget was unbalanced'.

Rowntree's selection of the 'necessaries of a healthy life' was based on the opinions of himself

Table 3.1 Rowntree's studies of York

Causes of poverty	Percentage of those in poverty		
	1899	1936	1950
Unemployment of chief wage earner	2.31	28.6	Nil
Inadequate wages of earners in regular employment	51.96	42.3	1.0
Old age	5.11	14.7	68.1
Sickness		4.1	21.3
Death of chief wage earner	15.63	7.8	6.4
Miscellaneous (including large family)	24.99	2.5	3.2
Totals	100	100	100
Percentage of survey population in poverty	33	18	1.5

(*Source*: Adapted from Coates and Silburn, *Poverty: The Forgotten Englishmen*, Penguin Books, London, 1973, p. 46.)

and the experts he consulted. In his original 1899 study these necessities were very limited and genuinely included only the basic items necessary for living in an industrial society. However, as we saw earlier, in his later research he extended what he considered necessities quite considerably. In the 1936 survey he expanded the idea of 'human needs' to include personal items such as a wireless, a holiday, books and travelling. Five shillings (25 pence) was estimated to be the cost of such items in 1936. In his later work then, Rowntree used a measure of poverty significantly above subsistence level.

Furthermore, the inclusion of such items as holidays anticipated the views of some of the supporters of relative poverty. Despite these alterations, Rowntree's studies revealed a dramatic decline in the amount of poverty. Rising living standards and improvements in the state benefits available to those on low incomes seemed to have reduced the poor to a very small fraction of the British population. In the 1960s, though, poverty was 'rediscovered' as researchers developed and applied the concept of relative poverty.

Jonathan Bradshaw, Deborah Mitchell and Jane Morgan – the usefulness of budget standards

Bradshaw *et al.* admit that the budget standards approach which prices the necessities needed to avoid poverty has its limitations. For example, they accept that it 'inevitably involves judgements – judgements about what *items* should be included, about the *quantity* of items that are required and about the *price* that should be fixed to the items'.

Nevertheless, they feel that budget standards approaches are useful because they focus attention on the amount paid in benefits to recipients of welfare. They offer sociologists the chance to assess whether benefit levels can provide adequately for people's needs.

Bradshaw *et al.* accept the criticism of Rowntree's work which points out that it is unrealistic to expect people to have a no-waste budget. To overcome this problem they base their research on how people actually spend their money rather than how experts feel they ought to spend it. Bradshaw *et al.* used data from the *Family Finances Survey* to estimate how families spent their money. They then calculated what the families could afford to buy if they were receiving 110 per cent of basic supplementary benefit levels in 1986. (Supplementary benefit was the main means-tested benefit in Britain in 1986.) They based their research on 110 per cent of benefit levels rather than 100 per cent, to allow for extra sources of income such as gifts, borrowing and part-time work. In 1986 110 per cent of supplementary benefit for a family with two children under 11 gave the family a weekly income of £74.88.

At this level of income the family was found to have a very low standard of living. They could not afford a holiday and could have just a one-day outing once a year. They could not afford to go to the cinema, nor to buy books, magazines or bicycles. Running a car was too expensive for them and they could afford only one haircut per year.

The researchers examined the weekly menu of a family with two children. They went to Tesco's supermarket in Barrow and bought the shopping found to be typical of families on benefit. Despite buying the cheapest lines and assuming no food would be wasted, they still found the diet to be 6,500 calories short of what a family needed for the week. The children's diets had too little iron and calcium in them and all family members were eating too little fibre and too much fat.

Bradshaw *et al.* argue that studies such as theirs illustrate how deprived people living on benefits are compared to other members of society. They claim:

It is possible that the resurrection of budget standards methodology in the analysis of living standards in the UK could lead to a more considered review of the way we treat the seven million people in the UK dependent on Supplementary Benefit.

Paul Spicker argues that Bradshaw *et al.*'s approach has its limitations. He points out that people's quality of life is not entirely determined by how they spend money. For example, living standards can be improved by the unpaid labour of family members. Furthermore, the budget standards approach always involves some judgement about what are necessities and in Bradshaw's work no clear poverty line is identified. However, Spicker supports the collection of data on what people actually spend rather than what experts say they should spend. He concludes 'If there is a way to identify patterns of deprivation as a matter of fact with levels of income, this seems to be it.'

▊ Relative poverty and deprivation

In view of the problems associated with absolute and subsistence standards of poverty, many researchers have abandoned them. Instead they have defined and measured poverty in terms of the standards specific to a particular place at a particular time. In this section we will consider those definitions.

In a rapidly changing world, definitions of poverty based on relative standards will be constantly changing. Thus Samuel Mencher writes:

The argument for relative standards rests on the assumption that for practical purposes standards become so fluid that no definition of need, no matter how broad, satisfies the ever changing expectations of modern life.

The argument is put in a nutshell by I.M. Rubinow: 'Luxuries become comforts, comforts become necessaries.' In Western society, products and services such as hot and cold running water, refrigerators and washing machines, medical and dental care, full-time education and motor cars either have or are travelling the road from luxuries, to comforts, to necessaries. Thus in Peter Townsend's words, any definition of poverty must be 'related to the needs and demands of a changing society'.

Moreover it has been argued that it is necessary to discuss poverty in terms of lifestyles. It is not sufficient to see poverty simply as lack of material possessions and the facilities necessary for material well-being. Rather these sociologists believe poverty also exists where members of society are excluded from the lifestyle of the community to which they belong.

▊ Peter Townsend – poverty as relative deprivation

Peter Townsend has carried out a number of studies of poverty including one of the most detailed that has been undertaken in Britain. In the 1960s and 1970s he played a major part in highlighting the continuing existence of poverty, and in forcing the issue back on to the political agenda. He has also been the leading supporter of defining poverty in terms of **relative deprivation**: he stresses that poverty should be defined in relation to the standards of a particular society at a particular time. Furthermore he believes that poverty extends beyond a simple lack of material resources. Townsend identifies three ways of defining poverty.

The state's standard

The first is the **state's standard of poverty**, on which the official statistics used to be based. Townsend calculates these figures on the basic rate of supplementary benefits (now income support) with the addition of housing costs for different types of household. All those who fall below this level are held to be in poverty, while those receiving income between 100 per cent and 139 per cent of benefit levels are held to be in the margins of poverty. However, Townsend dismisses this standard as 'neither social nor scientific'. He sees it as being arbitrarily determined by the government of the day, and points out that from year to year it varies in relation to the average income of the population.

The relative income standard of poverty

The second definition of poverty Townsend calls the **relative income standard of poverty**. This is based upon identifying those households whose income falls well below the average for households with the same composition (the same numbers of adults and children). He defines those who get 50 per cent or less of the average as poor, and those receiving 80 per cent or less as being in the margins of poverty. (The British Government has now adopted a relative income standard of poverty.) This definition has the benefit of being truly relative. As average income changes, then clearly the poverty line will change as well.

However, Townsend does not accept this definition either.

1 Again he points out that the point at which such a poverty line is drawn is arbitrary: 60 per cent, 70 per cent or 90 per cent could be taken as the dividing lines with no less and no more justification.

2 Nor does he believe that inequality and poverty are the same thing. For example, he argues that you cannot simply define, say, the poorest 20 per cent of the population as poor, for how badly off they are will depend on, among other factors, how developed the welfare system is. They might be considerably better off in a society like Sweden, which has a highly developed welfare system, than a country such as the USA.

3 Furthermore, he wishes to extend the concept of poverty beyond material disadvantage. To Townsend poverty involves the lifestyles associated with material shortage, and not the material shortage itself.

Relative deprivation

Townsend asserts that 'Poverty can be defined objectively and applied consistently only in terms of the concept of relative deprivation.' He justifies this claim on the grounds that society determines people's needs: for example, it determines and conditions even the need for food. It affects the amount of energy that 'different sections of the population habitually expend not only at work but in community and family pursuits'. Their obligations as parents, wives or husbands, friends or neighbours, as well as the work they have to do if they are employed, influence how many calories individuals will have to consume each day. Society also determines what types of foodstuff are available and influences patterns of food consumption through its culture. For instance, tea is closely tied up with British culture and lifestyles: members of British society are expected to be able to offer visitors to their homes a cup of tea, and many workers would be outraged if management threatened to remove their right to a mid-morning tea break. Tea, Townsend reminds us, is 'nutritionally worthless' but 'psychologically and socially essential' in Britain.

In developing this **concept of relative deprivation** Townsend argues that it should be thought of in terms of the resources available to individuals and households, and the styles of living which govern how those resources are used. He believes that concentrating exclusively on income to assess a household's material situation ignores other types of resources that might be available. It neglects capital assets (those who own their home may be better off than those renting), and ignores occupational fringe benefits, gifts, and the value of public social services such as education and healthcare.

He also feels that in the study of poverty it is necessary to move beyond consumption (the purchase of goods) to an examination of how resources affect participation in the lifestyle of the community. Townsend argues that poverty involves an inability to participate in approved social activities which are considered normal, such as visiting friends or relatives, having birthday parties for children, and going on holiday. The cost of such activities can vary greatly – a month on a Mediterranean cruise is considerably more expensive than a weekend's camping close to home – but to Townsend individuals suffer deprivation if they cannot afford even the cheapest form of such activities.

On the basis of these arguments Townsend defines poverty in the following way:

> Individuals, families and groups in the population can be said to be in poverty when they lack the resources to obtain the types of diet, participate in the activities and have the living conditions and amenities which are customary, or at least widely encouraged or approved, in the societies to which they belong. Their resources are so seriously below those commanded by the average individual or family that they are, in effect, excluded from the ordinary living patterns, customs and activities.

Poverty in the United Kingdom

In *Poverty in the United Kingdom* Townsend used his definition to measure the extent of poverty in the UK. (He also collected figures on the basis of the other two definitions he had identified so that he could compare them with his own.) His research was based upon a social survey using questionnaires. In 1968–9 his researchers collected information on 2,052 households containing 6,098 individuals in fifty-one parliamentary constituencies in Britain.

The deprivation index

In order to put his definition of poverty into operation Townsend devised a **deprivation index**. This index covered a total of sixty specific types of deprivation relating to households, diets, fuel and lighting, clothing, household facilities, housing conditions and amenities, working conditions, health, education, the environment, family life, recreation and social activities. From this original list he selected twelve items which he believed would be relevant to the whole of the population (and not just to certain sections of it) and calculated the percentage of the population deprived of them (Table 3.2)

Each household was given a score on a deprivation index. The more respects in which a household was found to suffer deprivation, the higher its score. Townsend then calculated the average score for households with different levels of income expressed as a percentage of basic supplementary benefit levels. He claimed to find a threshold for levels of income below which the amount of deprivation suddenly increased rapidly. This threshold was found to be at about 150 per cent of basic supplementary benefit levels. He therefore decided to classify all households who did not have this level of resources as suffering from poverty.

Townsend adjusted the income deemed necessary for each family according to the numbers in it, whether adults were working, the age of any children, and whether any members were disabled. Because of the procedures he had followed he felt able to claim that his figures and definition were 'scientific' and 'objective'.

On the basis of these calculations Townsend found that 22.9 per cent of the population (or 12.46 million people) were in poverty in 1968–9. This compared with 6.1 per cent in poverty according to the state standard, or 9.2 per cent in poverty according to the relative income standard. Townsend found that poverty was much more widespread than other research had suggested.

He also went on to identify the groups that were most at risk of suffering poverty in modern Britain. He found:

Middle-aged professional and managerial workers employed throughout the year living alone, in married couples or with small families, were least likely to be poor. Elderly people who had been unskilled manual workers and children in the families of young unskilled manual workers, especially those with substantial experience of unemployment, sickness or disablement, or in one-parent families, were most likely to be poor.

Criticisms of Townsend's early research

Despite the enormous impact Townsend's early work has had on British poverty research, some writers have criticized it. David Piachaud argues that the index on which Townsend's statistics are based is inadequate. In commenting on the items included in the index Piachaud writes 'It is not clear what they have to do with poverty, nor how they were selected.' In particular he questions the view that going without a Sunday joint and not eating fresh meat or cooked meals are necessarily associated with deprivation: they might reflect social and cultural differences. He claims 'It is no indicator of deprivation if someone chooses to stay at home, eating salads and uncooked breakfasts.'

Dorothy Wedderburn also criticizes Townsend's index. She describes the decision to include certain items and exclude others as arbitrary. She would have preferred Townsend to actually carry out research into what was customary behaviour in society. As a result she sees the index as reflecting Townsend's personal opinions: it is subjective and not an 'objective' basis for measuring deprivation.

A problem that faces all poverty researchers is that of finding a point at which it is possible to draw a poverty line. Townsend claimed to have found such a point below which deprivation starts to increase rapidly. Piachaud believes that the selection of this point (at 150 per cent of basic supplementary benefit levels) is as arbitrary as any other. From a close examination of Townsend's data Piachaud disputes the view that deprivation starts to increase rapidly below this level of income. Other researchers, such as M. Desai, have reanalysed Townsend's data, and have supported his claim that there is a poverty threshold.

Table 3.2 The deprivation index

Characteristic	Percentage of population
1 Has not had a week's holiday away from home in last 12 months	53.6
2 *Adults only.* Has not had a relative or friend to the home for a meal or snack in the last 4 weeks	33.4
3 *Adults only.* Has not been out in the last 4 weeks to a relative or friend for a meal or snack	45.1
4 *Children only* (under 15). Has not had a friend to play or to tea in the last 4 weeks	36.3
5 *Children only.* Did not have party on last birthday	56.6
6 Has not had an afternoon or evening out for entertainment in the last two weeks	47.0
7 Does not have fresh meat (including meals out) as many as four days a week	19.3
8 Has gone through one or more days in the past fortnight without a cooked meal	7.0
9 Has not had a cooked breakfast most days of the week	67.3
10 Household does not have a refrigerator	45.1
11 Household does not usually have a Sunday joint (3 in 4 times)	25.9
12 Household does not have sole use of four amenities indoors (flush WC; sink or washbasin and cold-water tap; fixed bath or shower; and gas or electric cooker)	21.4

(*Source*: Townsend 1979, p. 250.)

Perhaps the most damaging criticism of Townsend advanced by Piachaud concerns the implications of his definition of poverty for measures designed to eradicate it. Using Townsend's deprivation index as a measure of poverty, all inequality of wealth and income could be removed from society, but 'poverty' might still remain if people chose to become vegetarian or not to go on holiday. As Piachaud puts it, 'Taken to its logical conclusion, only when everyone behaved identically would no one be defined as deprived.' To tackle what Townsend calls poverty would involve creating uniformity in people's behaviour, because Townsend did not attempt to discover whether it was choice or shortage of money which led to people in his survey scoring points on the deprivation index.

Amartya Sen argues that there is 'much to be said' for Townsend's concept of relative deprivation. However, Sen believes that 'relative deprivation even including all its variants – cannot really be the *only* basis for the concept of poverty'. He suggests that there is an:

irreducible core of *absolute* deprivation in our idea of poverty, which translates reports of starvation, malnutrition and visible hardship into a diagnosis of poverty without having to ascertain first the relative position.

Thus if famine was very widespread in a society, it would make little sense to argue that there was no poverty on the grounds that there was little inequality since everybody was short of food.

Sen accepts that resources needed to avoid absolute deprivation vary from society to society. The diet and shelter required in different circumstances will vary, but to him that does not prevent poverty researchers from determining when people have too little for their most basic needs. To Sen then, 'the approach of relative deprivation supplements rather than supplants the analysis of poverty in terms of absolute dispossession'.

Townsend has defended himself against Sen. He has argued that Sen's concentration on absolute deprivation is politically dangerous. Potentially at least it gives governments in affluent societies an excuse to cut back their welfare states to an absolute bare minimum. Furthermore, Townsend claims that Sen offers no clear definition of absolute deprivation. Sen uses a variety of terms such as 'starvation', 'malnutrition' and 'hunger' to describe the situation where people's basic food needs are not being met. Yet 'starvation' and 'hunger' mean rather different things and Sen offers no clear criteria for determining when people's diets are inadequate and they are therefore in poverty.

Despite Townsend's defence, Sen may have a point in arguing that different types of poverty should be distinguished. Most of Sen's research has been conducted in the Third World where absolute deprivation, however defined, remains a real problem. At least in terms of international comparisons, the idea of absolute deprivation as poverty may still be useful.

The London study

In his more recent work Townsend has used slightly different research methods. He has continued to define poverty in terms of relative deprivation, but he has amended the way the concept is operationalized.

In 1985–6 Townsend, Corrigan and Kowarzik used this new approach in a study of a sample of 2,703 Londoners. In this study Townsend *et al.* distinguished between material deprivation and social deprivation.

Material deprivation covered dietary deprivation, clothing deprivation, housing deprivation, deprivation of home facilities, deprivation of environment, deprivation of location and deprivation at work.

Social deprivation covered lack of employment rights, deprivation of family activity, lack of integration into the community, lack of participation in social institutions, recreational deprivation and educational deprivation.

Initially seventy-seven items were included in the index to measure these different types of deprivation but seven were excluded because the deprivation was found to affect more than 50 per cent of the population. In this way Townsend *et al.* hoped to establish which activities in their index

represented 'standard or majority norms, conventions and customs'.

Townsend *et al.* made more allowance for variations in taste than was the case in Townsend's earlier study. For example, in measuring dietary deprivation different questions were used for meat-eaters and vegetarians. Scores from the material and social deprivation indexes were aggregated to produce an overall deprivation score for each household.

In the London research Townsend *et al.* distinguished between objective and subjective deprivation. **Objective deprivation** was measured using the deprivation index. **Subjective deprivation** was measured by asking respondents the level of income their household required to escape poverty. Detailed information was also collected on the income received by each household.

The London findings

Townsend *et al.* followed Townsend's earlier study in trying to establish a threshold at which multiple deprivations began to increase. Table 3.3 shows the level of income needed to prevent multiple deprivation in comparison to the basic level of means-tested benefit excluding housing costs. It proved to be rather greater than in the earlier study, ranging from 203 per cent of benefit levels for a single person under sixty to 150 per cent for a couple with three children.

Self-assessments of how much money households needed to escape poverty proved to be very similar to the estimates made by the researchers. For example, the respondents estimated that £110 per week was needed by a couple with two children, while the researchers estimated £109 per week. For single parents the equivalent figures were £80 and £81, and for a single person under sixty, £60 and £64. However, there was a more substantial difference for a couple under sixty. Respondents estimated that their needs were much higher (£104) than the researchers did (£75).

Nevertheless Townsend *et al.* concluded that their estimate of the poverty threshold was broadly similar to that of the population in their sample. Both methods of determining a poverty threshold showed that benefit levels were inadequate, with Londoners themselves suggesting that an average 61 per cent more than basic benefit levels was needed to escape poverty in 1985–6.

Table 3.3   Weekly income required to surmount deprivation as a percentage of basic means-tested assistance scales

Household type	Weekly income required, after deduction of housing costs, as a percentage of basic means-tested assistance scales
Single person >60	203
Couple >60	157
Couple with two children	151
Couple with three children	150
Single parent with one child	168

Note: Assumptions have had to be made about the ages of children so that basic rates could be estimated.

(*Source*: Townsend, P. (1993) *The International Analysis of Poverty*, Harvester Wheatsheaf, London, p. 61.)

Joanna Mack and Stewart Lansley – *Poor Britain*

In between Townsend's earlier and later research London Weekend Television financed a study of poverty which built on Townsend's methods. It was conducted by Joanna Mack and Stewart Lansley and took account of many of the methodological criticisms of Townsend made by sociologists such as Piachaud. Although Townsend's later study in London did modify the methods to some extent, it still used a deprivation index consisting of items chosen by the researchers and it still made no attempt to measure why people were not participating in some activities.

Mack and Lansley followed Townsend in defining poverty in relative terms and in attempting to directly measure the extent of deprivation. However, unlike Townsend, they tried to distinguish between styles of living which people could not afford, and those which they did not choose.

Furthermore, Mack and Lansley devised a new way of determining what were the 'necessities' of life in modern Britain. These researchers accepted the point made by Piachaud that taste might influence whether some people went without items on a deprivation index. In order to overcome this problem they decided to include in their research a question relating to each item respondents said they lacked, asking them whether it was by choice, or forced upon them by financial shortage. Those

who said it was a matter of choice were not defined as being deprived of that item.

Furthermore Mack and Lansley excluded some items from the index which groups with high income were as likely, or nearly as likely, to say they lacked by choice as groups on low incomes. They suggested that where these particular items were concerned, the cost of them depended to a significant extent on where people lived. (For example, the costs of a garden would be much greater for a resident in a fashionable and prosperous area of London than for a person living in an economically depressed northern town.) Lack of a television set was also ignored because the number who did not have this item was so small that no conclusions could be drawn from the data.

After the exclusion of such items and individual scores on their index, Mack and Lansley argued that their figures would accurately reflect the extent of involuntary deprivation.

Public perception of necessities

The second area in which this study tried to improve on Townsend's work was in the selection of items for inclusion in the index. Mack and Lansley wanted to avoid the accusation that their choice of items was purely arbitrary. They rejected Rowntree's use of experts to determine basic needs and went beyond Townsend's subjective choices of what he thought was customary. They argued that it was possible to measure the standards of a society in order to provide a more objective basis for defining relative deprivation.

In their research Mack and Lansley asked respondents what they considered necessities in contemporary Britain. Although these answers could represent no more than the subjective opinions of members of society, they did at least give some indication of what the population considered to be customary, socially approved and of vital importance to social life. Furthermore, Mack and Lansley claimed to have discovered a large degree of consensus about what were seen as

necessities. Their findings are summarized in Table 3.4.

They decided to take the cut-off point as 50 per cent, that is, when an item became a necessity because a majority of the population classified it as one. The lack of a television, the lack of self-contained accommodation, the lack of a garden and the lack of money for public transport were excluded for reasons which have already been explained. This left them with a deprivation index of twenty-two items. On the basis of this index Mack and Lansley went on to measure the extent of poverty which they defined as 'an enforced lack

Table 3.4   The public's perception of necessities

Standard-of-living items in rank order	Percentage classing items as necessity	Standard-of-living items in rank order	Percentage classing items as necessity
1 Heating to warm living areas of the home if it's cold	97	18 New, not secondhand clothes	64
2 Indoor toilet (not shared with another household)	96	19 A hobby or leisure activity	64
3 Damp-free home	96	20 Two hot meals a day (for adults)	64
4 Bath (not shared with another household)	94	21 Meat or fish every other day	63
5 Beds for everyone in the household	94	22 Presents for friends or family once a year	63
6 Public transport for one's needs	88	23 A holiday away from home for one week a year, not with relatives	64
7 A warm waterproof coat	87	24 Leisure equipment for children, e.g. sports equipment or a bicycle*	57
8 Three meals a day for children*	82	25 A garden	55
9 Self-contained accommodation	79	26 A television	51
10 Two pairs of all-weather shoes	78	27 A 'best outfit' for special occasions	48
11 Enough bedrooms for every child over 10 of different sex to have his/her own*	77	28 A telephone	43
		29 An outing for children once a week*	40
12 Refrigerator	77	30 A dressing gown	38
13 Toys for children*	71	31 Children's friends round for tea/ a snack once a fortnight*	37
14 Carpets in living rooms and bedrooms	70	32 A night out once a fortnight (adults)	36
15 Celebrations on special occasions such as Christmas	69	33 Friends family round for a meal once a month	32
16 A roast meat joint or its equivalent once a week	67	34 A car	22
17 A washing machine	67	35 A packet of cigarettes every other day	14
Average of all 35 items = 64.1		* For families with children only	

(*Source*: Mack and Lansley, 1985, p. 54.)

of socially perceived necessities'. Only those people who lacked three or more items were considered to be poor.

Using a sample of 1,174 people who were questioned in February 1983, Mack and Lansley produced the following results. According to their calculations there were 7.5 million people in poverty in Britain – 5 million adults and 2.5 million children – in all 13.8 per cent of the population. Although this figure is substantially less than that reached by Townsend in 1968–9, it still shows that poverty remains an important problem in contemporary Britain.

Because the figures were calculated on a different basis from those of Townsend, they were not strictly comparable, and did not therefore demonstrate that the amount of poverty had decreased. Indeed, Mack and Lansley thought that the amount of poverty had probably increased in the years preceding their study. They found that the share of national earnings from employment received by the poorest 40 per cent of the population had fallen from 15.6 per cent in 1965 to 10.2 per cent in 1976.

Mack and Lansley also pointed to a number of government decisions which had made the recipients of welfare payments worse off. In particular they claimed that some policies of the Thatcher Government would probably have increased the amount of poverty. Unemployment had risen, but the earnings-related supplement for the short-term unemployed had been abolished. Old age pensions had risen more slowly than average wages, and there had been dramatic cuts in housing benefits after the autumn of 1983.

The follow-up study

In 1990 the same researchers carried out a follow-up study using a sample of 1,800 people. Once again they conducted a survey to determine public perceptions of necessities. They found that public perceptions of necessities had changed. A weekly outing for children, children's friends round once a fortnight, a telephone and a best outfit for special occasions were now seen as necessities by more than half the population. They were therefore added to the index. Televisions were included.

Some new items were added which were also seen as necessities by the majority. These were:

1 a decent standard of decoration in the home;

2 savings of at least £10 per week;

3 home contents insurance;

4 participation in out-of-school activities for children;

5 fresh fruit and vegetables every day.

This produced an index of thirty-two items.

Changes between 1983 and 1990

The 1990 study found there had been a big increase in poverty. The numbers lacking three or more of the necessities, and therefore in poverty according to Mack and Lansley's definition, had risen from 7.5 million in 1983 to 11 million in 1990. The number in severe poverty, defined as lacking seven or more items, had gone up from 2.5 million in 1983 to 3.5 million in 1990.

Two-thirds of the poor in 1990 were found to be dependent on state benefits. Mack and Lansley argued that much of the increase in the numbers of poor resulted from changes in the benefits system.

1 Pensions were indexed to prices rather than wages as in 1979, so that as wage earners became better off pensioners became relatively poorer. Pensioners made up one-tenth of the poor in 1983 but one-fifth of the poor in 1990.

2 Invalidity benefit and income support (previously supplementary benefit) had also fallen well behind average earnings.

3 Two-thirds of single parents were found to be poor compared to just under 50 per cent in 1983.

4 Many of the poor had been hit by the replacement of single payments with the social fund in 1988.

(We discuss these changes in benefits in more detail on p. 170.)

Criticisms of Mack and Lansley

The inclusion of entirely new items in the 1990 index raises questions about the comparability of the data from the two studies. Obviously, the more items which are included as necessities, the greater the number of people who will be found to be lacking three or more necessities. Thus at least part of the increase in poverty found in comparing the two studies may have resulted from the changes in the surveys rather than from changes in society.

Using a public opinion poll to determine what

are considered necessities is an advance over Townsend's approach which relies largely on the judgements of the researcher. However, even Mack and Lansley's method is heavily influenced by the choices made by the researchers. They have to chose what items to question the public about before they can determine what is considered deprivation. Many other items apart from those chosen could have been included.

The researchers also shaped the findings by defining poverty as lacking three or more items. If they had settled on two or four items as the dividing line they would have produced a different estimate of the total numbers in poverty. As David Piachaud points out, Mack and Lansley's approach 'still requires expert involvement in defining questions and determining answers'.

Piachaud also points out that there is a problem with individuals who spend their money on items which are not considered necessities. For example, some people could not afford to pay for an adequate diet or adequate housing because they spent large amounts of money on cigarettes or leisure pursuits. To Piachaud there needs to be 'some judgement about what margin, if any, needs to be allowed for non-necessities'. Again this involves the use of the opinion of 'experts' and further undermines the claim that the results of such studies are based upon definitions of poverty supported by the general public.

Robert Walker tries to overcome the problem of expert judgement by trying to 'democratize' the process of determining what necessities are. He argues that Mack and Lansley's approach fails to do justice to the complexity of the problem. The survey data they use gives respondents no chance to determine what *quality* of goods and services people need. For example, is a threadbare carpet adequate, or should it be in better condition? Moreover, Mack and Lansley gave the respondents no opportunity to include items they were not asked about nor any chance to discuss the issues involved and reflect in depth on the necessities of contemporary living.

Walker therefore proposes that basic needs should be determined not by groups of experts, nor by survey methods, but by panels of ordinary people who are given the opportunity to have in-depth discussions. These members of the public could then produce costed descriptions of the minimum acceptable basket of goods and services needed by different family types.

In this way a definition of poverty could be based upon a genuine consensus amongst a sample of the population rather than being based upon the majority voting system used in Mack and Lansley's survey research. So-called experts would no longer define poverty in their own terms, yet an informed and carefully considered definition of poverty could be produced.

An obvious problem with Walker's suggestion is the assumption that a consensus would be reached. It is quite likely that the members of the public on the panel would disagree about a minimum acceptable living standard. Furthermore, there would be no guarantee that the same living standard would be agreed by a different panel. Once again an objective or 'democratic' definition of poverty would prove elusive.

Having looked at various attempts to define and measure poverty, we will now consider the 'official' approach to this subject.

■ Official statistics on poverty

Some countries employ an **official poverty line** and produce regular statistics on poverty. The USA is an example. Other countries, such as Britain, do not have an official poverty line but do produce some statistics on low incomes.

Statistics on official poverty, or low incomes, are not necessarily based upon sophisticated sociological definitions of poverty. What is more, statistics from different countries are calculated in a variety of ways and therefore cannot always be compared. Nevertheless, official statistics do provide valuable information about the extent of poverty, or at least low incomes. They also give some indication of how poverty is distributed between different social groups.

■ British statistics
Low Income Family statistics

Although Britain has never had an official poverty line it has published statistics on low incomes. Figures on **Low Income Families** were first produced by the then Department of Health and Social Security in the early 1970s. This set of figures was dropped by the Department of Social Security in 1988. However, the Institute for Fiscal Studies, an independent research institute, has continued to produce figures on Low Income Families since 1988 by extrapolating from official statistics.

Low Income Family statistics measure the numbers of families who are receiving different levels of income in relation to the main means-tested state benefit. They are calculated using figures from an annual government survey, the *Family Expenditure Survey*, and figures published by the Department of Social Security on benefits claimants. The basic state means-tested benefit was originally called national assistance, later supplementary benefit and now income support.

National assistance was first introduced in 1948 with the implementation of the *Beveridge Report* which laid the foundations of the welfare state. The level at which national assistance was first set was based upon the work of Seebohm Rowntree. Beveridge thought that Rowntree's 1899 poverty index was insufficiently generous and claimed to have based the initial benefit levels upon the 1936 index. However, Frank Field argues that the benefits were set at a lower level than that which Rowntree's research indicated was necessary to raise people out of poverty. According to Field, for single men and women they were set at 55 and 66 per cent of Rowntree's level respectively. Pensioners also received less than was necessary to raise them up to Rowntree's 1936 poverty line, but children were treated more generously.

National assistance and its later equivalents have been paid to those who can demonstrate that they have a low income. They have been intended to provide a basic minimum income for those suffering material hardship. Figures have been produced by a number of different researchers on those receiving income at or below the level of these benefits and those who receive 140 per cent or less of the basic benefit level.

As we saw earlier in this chapter, poverty researchers like Townsend and Mack and Lansley argue that families need well above basic benefit levels to escape from poverty. The figures on those receiving the same or less than basic benefit levels, and those receiving less than 140 per cent of basic levels, have both been used by some commentators as a measure of poverty.

The advantages and disadvantages of Low Income Family statistics

When the Department of Social Security decided to discontinue publishing Low Income Family statistics it gave a number of reasons.

1 It argued that benefit levels were being used both to measure the extent of poverty and to alleviate poverty. This led to a paradox: if the Government put benefit levels up, more people fell into the category Low Income Family, yet the poor were receiving more money. In other words, attempts to help the poor created more poverty.

2 It claimed that the use of the family as the unit of analysis overstated the extent of low income. Many households had more than one family living in them (for example parents and married children), and the pooling of resources between family units could help to compensate for the low income of one unit.

3 A 140 per cent of benefit levels might be considered too generous as a measure of low income.

Christopher Giles and Steven Webb of the Institute for Fiscal Studies do not regard such criticisms as a justification for abandoning statistics on Low Income Families.

1 They point out that it is possible to adjust the figures to take account of the changes in the real value of benefit. They have produced such figures based on the 1979 benefit levels adjusted for inflation in later years (see p. 139).

2 Giles and Webb see the second criticism as more serious, but any poverty figures are bound to run into the problem of the distribution of resources within households. Calculating the income of individuals, households or families as the basis for poverty statistics are all problematic.

3 The third criticism is dismissed as unimportant. A 140 per cent of benefit levels does not have to be taken as the cut-off point between the poor and non-poor; 100, 110 or 120 per cent can be used as alternatives.

Some critics of the Government have suggested that these figures were discontinued in 1988 for political reasons. If the Institute for Fiscal Studies had not carried on producing them, it would have been impossible to calculate changes in the numbers of 'poor' using official sources. Abandoning the figures could therefore be seen as a cynical attempt to hide an increase in poverty which had resulted from government policies.

Figures on Low Income Families do not correspond exactly to any sociological definition of poverty, but they do provide a rough guide to trends in poverty. Giles and Webb praise this measure for its simplicity and for the ease with which household size can be taken into account since households with different compositions receive different levels of benefit. They also note that it is useful for determining the numbers of people who are slipping through the 'safety-net' of the welfare state, and receiving less than basic benefit levels.

Trends in Low Income Families

Figure 3.1 shows the numbers and percentages of the population with different levels of income in relation to benefit levels. There was a marked rise between 1979 and 1989 (the last available figure) with the percentage living at or below benefit

Figure 3.1 Numbers of people living in or on the margins of poverty in 1979 and 1989 (defined as 140 per cent of supplementary benefit and below)

(*Source*: Oppenheim, C. (1993) *Poverty the Facts,* Child Poverty Action Group, London, p. 33.)

levels rising from 14 to 20 per cent of the population. The percentage receiving less than 140 per cent of benefit levels rose from 24 to 29 per cent.

Between 1979 and 1989 the numbers of pensioners on supplementary benefit/income support fell, but the numbers of lone parents, couples with children, the unemployed and the long-term sick on benefits all rose. Most of the increase in the numbers of people living below supplementary benefit levels resulted from a rise in the numbers of single people without children on very low incomes.

As mentioned above, the Institute for Fiscal Studies has also calculated trends in Low Income Families using 1979 benefit levels as a base and allowing for inflation. Over the period 1979–89 supplementary benefit/income support levels have increased by about 15 per cent above the rate of inflation. Using the 1979 base there would have been scarcely any change in the numbers of people living below benefit levels: the number would have declined very slightly from 3,170,000 in 1979 to 3,140,000 in 1989.

Homelessness

The figure opposite suggests that using a fixed poverty line there may have been some reduction in poverty during the decade in question. However, this may be somewhat misleading. People living in institutions such as nursing homes, residential homes, hospitals and prisons, and the homeless are excluded from the statistics. Many of those excluded have low incomes and the homeless have some of the lowest incomes of all.

While there has probably been a reduction in the numbers in institutions, there has been a big increase in homelessness. The housing pressure group, Shelter, has estimated that homelessness nearly tripled between 1978 and 1992. In 1991 about 420,000 people were accepted as homeless by local authorities in England and Shelter estimated there were a further 1.7 million 'unofficial homeless'. These consisted of about 8,000 people sleeping rough, approximately 50,000 unauthorized tenants and squatters, 137,000 single people in hostels or lodgings, 77,000 insecure private tenants and about 1,200,000 people living with friends or relatives who needed a home of their own.

Not all these groups would be excluded from the statistics on Low Income Families but nevertheless the rise in all types of homelessness would make a significant difference to the figures if the homeless were included. Indeed it can be argued that some of the homeless are suffering from absolute poverty since they do not even have adequate shelter.

Households Below Average Income

When the Government discontinued its statistics on Low Income Families in 1988 it replaced them with figures on Households Below Average Income. So far it has produced figures for the period 1979–89.

These figures are based on household incomes both before and after housing costs, adjusted to take account of household size.

This method allows figures to be produced which show the number of households falling below different levels in relation to average income. For example, the number of households receiving 50 per cent or less of the average household income is sometimes taken as a measure of the numbers in poverty. It also allows trends in the income of richer and poorer sections of the population to be compared. The population is divided into ten groups of 10 per cent (or deciles) according to income, and the living standards of each decile can be tracked over time.

Households Below Average Income statistics provide a useful measure of income inequality and can be used as one way of measuring relative poverty. Giles and Webb argue that the figures are useful because they are comprehensive and they are not tied to benefit levels which are affected by political decisions. Figures such as those on the proportion of households receiving less than half the average income allow clear comparisons over time and between countries.

However, Giles and Webb note that the figures were never intended to be a measure of poverty and what they actually measure is simply income distribution. Peter Townsend has also attacked what he calls the 'relative income standard of poverty' (see pp. 129–30). Nevertheless such statistics do provide useful information on inequality, and inequality is an important aspect of relative definitions of poverty.

Trends in income distribution

Figure 3.2 shows trends in the proportions of children, and of the population as a whole, living in households which receive less than 50 per cent of the average income. It is based on research by Alissa Goodman and Steven Webb which used data from the *Family Expenditure Survey* for 1961–91. It includes figures calculated Before Housing Costs (BHC) and After Housing Costs (AHC).

The figures show a very big increase. For example, in 1961 11 per cent of the population had an income of less than 50 per cent of the mean but this had more than doubled to 24 per cent in 1991.

This increase has been caused by significant shifts in income distribution. Figure 3.3 shows the changes in the real income of decile groups between 1979 and 1988–9 both before and after housing costs. It is based on research by Christopher Giles and Steven Webb for the Institute for Fiscal Studies. It shows that on average real income rose by some 30 per cent over this period but all the poorer-than-average decile groups had a below average increase in income. The poorest 10 per cent had a very small increase before housing costs but they were actually 10 per cent worse off in 1988–9 than they were in 1979 after housing costs were taken into account.

Over the decade the composition of the bottom decile changed. According to Giles and Webb the unemployed increased from 16 to 30 per cent of the poorest decile, and the 'other' category (which includes the long-term sick and disabled and students) went up from 18 to 23 per cent.

Another increasingly numerous group in the bottom decile were mortgage payers who had a reasonably high income (so they did not receive income support) but their housing costs were so high they had little disposable income left after paying their mortgage. This group made up 10 per cent of the bottom decile after housing costs in 1979, but 20 per cent in 1988–9.

Official statistics and trends in British poverty – conclusion

Nearly all the official figures suggest there has been a rise in poverty. There are more people living at or below the level of the basic means-tested benefit, more living below 140 per cent of that level, more earning less than 50 per cent of average income, and after housing costs the poorest 10 per cent of the population have become

Figure 3.2 Proportion of the total population below half mean income

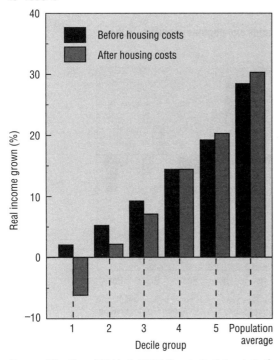

(*Source*: Goodman, A. and Webb, S. (1994) *For Richer for Poorer,* Institute for Fiscal Studies, p. 23.)

Figure 3.3 Real income growth by decile group 1979 to 1988–9

(*Source*: Giles, C. and Webb, S. (1993) *Poverty Statistics: A Guide for the Perplexed*, Institute for Fiscal Studies, London, p. 40.)

worse off in real terms. The proportion of the population living at or below the 1979 benefit level in real terms has changed very little, but the amount of homelessness has certainly increased,

suggesting that absolute poverty has returned as a serious problem in Britain.

We examined some of the reasons for the changes in income distribution in an earlier chapter (see pp. 42–6), and we will explore more reasons for some of the other changes later in this chapter when theories of poverty are discussed (see particularly pp. 160–3).

■ Poverty – international comparisons

Poverty in the European Community

European Community figures on poverty take two main forms. Some use the average income of the EC as a whole as a way of measuring poverty. In terms of the percentages of the population with income below 40 per cent of the EC average, Britain has relatively little poverty. In 1985 Britain had a lower poverty rate than Eire, Spain, Greece, Portugal, France and Germany, and a higher rate than Belgium, The Netherlands and Denmark.

However, a rather different picture emerges when poverty is calculated in terms of households with below average income and expenditure in each country. Figure 3.4 shows that in 1987–9 Britain had a higher proportion of households

Figure 3.4 European poverty–rates 1987–9: income and expenditure data compared

(*Source*: Eurostat, *Patterns of Poverty in Europe*, Aldi Hagenaas, Klaas de Vos and Asghar Zaidi, Rotterdam: Erasmus University, 1991.)

Figure 3.5 Percentage change of households and persons in poverty in the 1980s

(*Source*: Cross, M. '*Generating the "new poverty": a European comparison*' in Simpson, R. and Walker, R. (eds) (1993) *Europe: For Richer or Poorer?*, Child Poverty Action Group, London, p. 7.)

with an income less than 50 per cent of the national average than the nine other European countries included in the figure.

In addition, during the 1980s European figures show a big increase in poverty in Britain whereas in most countries it was declining. Figure 3.5 shows Britain experienced an increase of over 30 per cent in households in poverty during the 1980s, whereas in most countries poverty fell. One reason for this might be the declining proportion of government spending going on welfare in the 1980s and the low level of welfare spending in Britain compared to most countries in Europe.

The poverty index in the USA

The **poverty index** used by the Social Security Administration in the USA is based on the minimum cost of an adequate diet multiplied by three since it is estimated that a typical poor family spends one-third of its income on food. The poverty line is drawn in terms of the minimum income required to buy 'a subsistence level of goods and services'.

Unlike Rowntree's definition, though, some account is taken of cultural variations in the consumption of food. Instead of estimating the cost of an ideal diet, the US Government has carried out surveys into the actual dietary habits of the population and has based estimates of the cost of food on this information.

The US Government began to keep figures on poverty in 1959 when the poverty rate stood at 22.4 per cent. It dropped considerably during the 1960s, and levelled out at 11–12 per cent throughout much of the 1970s. Towards the end of the 1970s the numbers officially estimated to be in poverty began to rise, and stood at 14 per cent in 1987. This represented some 33 million people. At the end of 1990 there were slightly fewer in poverty, 32.5 million. In that year a family of four was seen as needing an income in excess of $12,675.

The figures from the USA give some cause for optimism: they indicate that poverty in the long-term is falling. Like many official statistics though, they need to be used cautiously. There have been numerous criticisms of the way that the American statistics are calculated.

The President's Commission on Income Maintenance Programs, a commission set up in 1968 to investigate poverty in the USA, makes several criticisms of the poverty index.

1 It does not reflect contemporary conventions of reasonable living standards. The minimum income assessed for a family to remain above the poverty line does not allow for many of the goods and services considered necessities by the population as a whole. According to the Commission, such 'necessities might include a car, an occasional dessert after meals, rugs, a bed for each family member, school supplies, or an occasional movie'.

2 No provision is made in the 'subsistence level goods and services' budget for medical care or insurance or for the purchase of household furnishings.

3 The Commission states that the monies deemed necessary for transportation 'would not cover even daily transportation for a worker'.

4 The Commission is particularly critical of the monies allocated for food, many of its criticisms echoing those made of Rowntree's food budget. It concludes that 'only about one-fourth of the families who spend that much for food actually have a nutritionally adequate diet'.

Fixed standards of poverty, such as those of the Social Security Administration, will ultimately result in the virtual disappearance of poverty. Although the poverty index is adjusted annually to reflect price changes, it does not reflect changing expectations and living standards. Writing in the mid-1960s, Herman P. Miller, Chief of the Population Division of the US Bureau of the Census stated:

We have been measuring poverty by an absolute standard based on relationships that existed in 1955. If we continue to use this definition long enough, we will, in time, eliminate poverty statistically, but few people will believe it – certainly not those who continue to have housing, education, medical care and other goods and services which are far below standards deemed acceptable for this society. (Quoted in Miller and Roby 1970, p. 42.)

One indication of the changing extent of poverty is provided by comparing the relative share of national income received over a period of time by low-income groups. This gives a very different picture from the optimistic trend indicated by official statistics. The President's Commission on Income Maintenance Programs states 'Despite all of our income and welfare programs we have not altered appreciably the structure of this Nation's income distribution.' This means that those at the bottom did not receive a larger share of national income.

More recent figures suggest that in relative terms poverty in the USA has been increasing. For example, between 1978 and 1987 the poorest 20 per cent of the population experienced a 8 per cent reduction in their share of the total national income, while the share of the richest 20 per cent went up by 13 per cent. As in Britain, the rich have been getting richer and the poor relatively poorer in recent years.

Figure 3.6   The risk of poverty by economic status in 1988/9

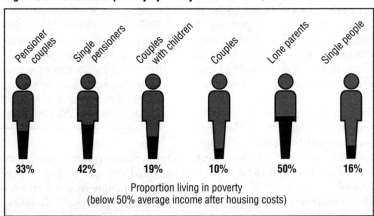

(*Source*: Oppenheim, C. (1993) *Poverty: the Facts*, Child Poverty Action Group, London, p. 43.)

Figure 3.7   The risk of poverty by family status in 1988/9

(*Source*: Oppenheim, C. (1993) *Poverty: the Facts*, Child Poverty Action Group, London, p. 43.)

■ The social distribution of poverty

The chances of being in poverty are not equally distributed. Some groups are much more prone to ending up in poverty than others, while the chances relating to particular groups change over time.

In this section we will briefly outline some of the variations in poverty rates.

Economic and family status

1 Figures 3.6 and 3.7 show the risk of poverty according to economic and family status in Britain in 1988–9.

They are based on the numbers of individuals in households receiving below 50 per cent of average household income after housing costs.

2 Figure 3.6 shows that participation in the labour market, at least on a full-time basis, greatly reduces the risk of poverty. Retirement and unemployment are both strongly associated with poverty.

3 Figure 3.7 shows that lone parenthood leads to a high risk of poverty: one in two lone parents is poor. About a third of pensioner couples are poor but the evidence suggests that the elderly are making up a declining proportion of those in poverty. Some 31 per cent of the

Table 3.5 Personal weekly incomes of adults, analysed by sex and family status in 1990/1

	Pensioners		Non-pensioners		
	Single	Married	Single	Married no children	Married with children
Men					
Number	0.9m	2.6m	5.1m	5.5m	5.8m
Average income	£97	£109	£123	£208	£223
Less than £25	nil	nil	5%	2%	1%
Women					
Number	3.5m	2.6m	4.5m	5.5m	5.8m
Average income	£81	£40	£106	£87	£60
Less than £25	nil	24%	6%	31%	35%

(*Source*: Oppenheim, C. (1993) *Poverty: the Facts*, Child Poverty Action Group, London, p. 94.)

poorest 10 per cent of the population were pensioners in 1979, but this had declined to just 14 per cent in 1988–9. This was partly the result of a big rise (from 9 to 22 per cent) in the proportion of single childless people in this group.

Gender and poverty

Most figures on poverty are not broken down in terms of sex but are based on households. However, it is possible to produce estimates of the numbers of men and women in poverty by using data on the proportions of men and women in households with particular economic and family statuses. There are more female than male pensioners, for example, and the vast majority of lone parents are female. On this basis the Child Poverty Action Group estimates there were about 5.1 million women but only 3.4 million men in poverty in 1989.

Within households income may not be distributed equally. Women tend to have smaller independent incomes than men and there is no guarantee that they will share fully the income of their husbands or partners. Research by P. Esam and R. Berthoud for the Policy Studies Institute estimated that in 1990–1 more than 4.6 million women had an independent income of less than £25 per week. This compared to just 0.4 million men (quoted in C. Oppenheim, 1993, p. 94). Table 3.5 shows the weekly incomes of men and women by family status according to Esam and Berthoud's research. Some of the reasons that

account for the greater number of women in poverty include the following features.

1 Women are less likely than men to have occupational pensions and income from investments.

2 Married women are less likely than married men to be working.

3 More women than men rely upon benefits as their main source of income.

4 Lone parents are vulnerable to poverty, and a large majority are women. The majority of pensioners are also women.

Caroline Glendinning and Jane Millar give the following reasons for women having higher rates of poverty than men.

1 Women are disadvantaged in the labour market. They are seen as **secondary workers** because their primary role is seen as domestic (as housewives and mothers) and so they spend more time away from the labour market than men, and are more likely to have part-time jobs. They are also seen as secondary workers in that the employment of married women is seen as less important than that of their husbands so they are not expected to earn a **family wage**, that is, enough to support their spouse and children.

2 Women are 'disadvantaged in access to social security benefits'. Only 60 per cent of women are entitled to maternity leave and many women care for sick and

elderly relatives, yet they receive very small state allowances for doing so. The intermittent and often part-time employment of women leaves many ineligible for unemployment benefit and redundancy pay.

3 Within the household men usually 'command more of the family resources (of money, of food, of space and so on) and this is legitimated by their status as breadwinners'.

Glendinning and Millar summarize their argument by saying:

The causes of poverty among women are thus a result of complex but mutually reinforcing threads, which have their origins in the limitations placed upon women by the current gendered division of labour and by the assumptions of female financial dependency upon men.

Ethnicity and poverty

National figures on ethnicity and poverty are not available. However, there have been local studies which give some indication of the incidence of poverty in different ethnic groups. Kaushika Amin and Carey Oppenheim quote a study carried out by Islington Council which found that in 1987 40 per cent of ethnic minorities but only 30 per cent of whites were living in poverty (defined as having an income less than 140 per cent of supplementary benefit levels).

This study also tried to measure material deprivation directly using indicators such as diet, working conditions, home facilities, clothing, housing and local facilities. It found that 37 per cent of the Afro-Caribbeans in Islington, 35 per cent of Asians and 47 per cent of Irish suffered material deprivation. This compared to 33 per cent of whites. (We examine inequality between ethnic groups in detail in Chapter 7.)

■ Individualistic and cultural theories of poverty

In the previous sections we have considered the questions 'What is poverty?' and 'What is the extent of poverty?' We are now going to look at some of the responses to the third question, 'What are the causes of poverty?'

■ Individualistic theories

The earliest theories of poverty were also perhaps the simplest. They placed the blame for poverty with the poor themselves. Those who suffered from very low incomes did so because they were unable or unwilling to provide adequately for their own well-being. From this point of view neither society nor the social groups to which individuals belonged were accountable, and society should not therefore be responsible for providing for the needs of the poor. Such **individualistic theories** of poverty were particularly popular in the nineteenth century.

Herbert Spencer – 'dissolute living'

The nineteenth-century English sociologist Herbert Spencer was a severe critic of the poor. He dismissed the views of those who showed sympathy with the 'poor fellow' who was living in poverty. Why, he asked, did they not realize that he was usually a 'bad fellow', one of the 'good-for-nothings . . . vagrants and sots, criminals . . . men who share the gains of prostitutes; and less visible and less numerous there is a corresponding class of women'.

According to Spencer it was unnatural to help those engaged in 'dissolute living' to avoid the consequences of their actions. Those who were too lazy to work should not be allowed to eat. The key to explaining why particular individuals became poor lay in an examination of their moral character.

Spencer thought that the state should interfere as little as possible in the lives of individuals. If the poor law or welfare system gave the poor more than an absolutely minimum amount, laziness and moral decline would spread through the population. Individuals would be attracted to the easy life on offer to those not prepared to work for their own living. As a result society would suffer. Its economy would not be successful.

Spencer believed strongly in the evolutionary ideas which were so popular in Victorian Britain. It was Spencer, not, as is often thought, the biologist Charles Darwin, who coined the phrase 'survival of the fittest'. If society was to evolve and become more successful the most able and the hardest-working would have to be allowed to keep the rewards of their efforts. The weak, the incompetent and the lazy should be condemned to a life of poverty since it was no more than they deserved. Poverty was a necessity for society for without it incentives for work would be missing.

'Scroungers'

Such explanations of poverty remain influential in modern Britain. According to Peter Golding and Sue Middleton, most newspaper reporting of welfare claimants portrays them as 'scroungers'. According to their research there are numerous stories in the press about how those living on social security are enjoying comfortable, even extravagant lifestyles at the taxpayer's expense.

Individualistic explanations continue to be accepted by a considerable proportion of the public in Britain. However, their popularity has been declining. The European Commission conducted surveys of attitudes to poverty in Europe in 1976 and 1989. In the earlier survey 43 per cent of respondents in Britain thought poverty was due to laziness. In the later survey this figure had fallen to 18 per cent. In all EC countries, apart from Denmark, the proportion blaming poverty on laziness had declined but Britain remained the country where people were most likely to explain poverty in this way.

Few sociologists today accept individualistic explanations of poverty. At the very least, sociologists see poverty as a characteristic of a social group such as a family or a community, and not as a characteristic of individuals. Most sociologists would go further and argue that it is not the generosity but the inadequacy of the welfare state, or the structure of society itself which is responsible for the existence of poverty in the midst of affluence. For some, individualistic explanations of poverty are no more than an 'ideological smoke screen' to hide the injustices suffered by the poor. To the American writer William Ryan it is an example of 'blaming the victims' for what they suffer at the hands of others.

■ The New Right – the culture of dependency

The politics of the Conservative Governments of Margaret Thatcher are associated with the ideas of the 'New Right'. Carey Oppenheim argues that since John Major replaced Margaret Thatcher in 1990 'the debate has shifted and the language changed' but the change may be more apparent than real. There have not, for example, been significant changes in social security policy.

Hartley Dean and Peter Taylor-Gooby, who are critics of the idea of a **culture of dependency**, have identified its key characteristics.

1 First, it assumes that people often act in ways that are motivated by rational calculations about the effort needed to secure rewards. If, for example, too much effort is required to secure a small rise in income, people will not bother to work.

2 Second, and to some extent contradicting the first point, people are strongly influenced by people around them, particularly those in the same neighbourhood. The choices made by individuals are affected by the choices made by those around them. If there are few people going out to work in an area, then others living there may not bother to work themselves.

3 Third, the culture of dependency theory has a moral dimension. It extols the virtues of self-reliance and hard work, and denigrates dependence on others and laziness. For example in 1987 John Moore, the then Secretary of State for Health and Social Security, said 'dependence in the long run decreases human happiness and reduces human freedom . . . the well-being of individuals is best protected and promoted when they are helped to be independent' (quoted in H. Dean and P. Taylor Gooby, 1992, p. 3).

A few contemporary sociologists, such as David Marsland, have adopted the philosophy of the

New Right and have used some of the thinking behind the concept of dependency culture to explain poverty.

David Marsland – poverty and the generosity of the welfare state

Marsland argues that low income results from the generosity of the welfare state rather than from personal inadequacy. He is particularly critical of **universal welfare provision**: the provision of welfare for all members of society regardless of whether they are on low or high incomes. Examples of universal provision in Britain include education, healthcare, and child benefits.

Marsland believes that such benefits have created a culture of dependency. He says 'The expectation that society, the state, the government, "they", will look after our problems tricks us into abdicating from self-reliance and social responsibility.' He argues that welfare 'hand-outs' create incentives for staying unemployed; they ridicule competition and discourage self-improvement through education. Furthermore, by increasing public expenditure they take money away from investment in industry and thus hinder the production of wealth.

Marsland does not believe that all benefits should be withdrawn, but he does argue that they should be restricted to those in genuine need and who are unable to help themselves. Benefits should be targeted on groups such as the sick and disabled, and should not be given to those who are capable of supporting themselves. According to Marsland, reliance upon the huge, centralized bureaucracy of the welfare state 'weakens the vitality of the family, the local community, and voluntary associations, which are the natural arenas of genuine mutual help'. He concludes:

Critics of universal welfare provision are not blaming the poor, as welfarist ideologues allege. On the contrary, these are the foremost victims of erroneous ideas and destructive policies imposed on them by paternalists, socialists, and privileged members of the professional New Class.

We will examine government policies which have

been influenced by the New Right in a later section (see pp. 170–1).

Bill Jordan – the advantages of universal benefits

Bill Jordan argues that Marsland is wrong to attribute the culture of dependency to universal welfare provision. If such a culture exists, it is created by 'targeted', means-tested benefits received by only the very poor. He says 'Selective systems trap people in poverty and passivity, and exclude them from the opportunities and incentives enjoyed by their fellow-citizens.' If, for example, those in work have to pay for education and healthcare, and the unemployed do not, then, 'many unskilled and partially disabled people will not be able to afford to work'.

Jordan claims that societies such as the USA which rely upon means-tested benefits tend to develop a large underclass which has little chance of escaping from poverty. If members of the underclass take low-paid jobs, they lose benefits and the right to free services, and they may end up worse off. In such societies the only way to persuade some people to work is to impose heavy penalties on them if they do not.

To Jordan, poverty does not result from an over-generous welfare system, but instead is caused by a system which is too mean. He says that the only way to tackle poverty is to have 'universal provision, which brings everyone up to an acceptable level. Far from creating dependence it frees people from dependence.'

Hartley Dean and Peter Taylor-Gooby – The Explosion of a Myth

Dean and Taylor-Gooby have attempted to explode the 'myth' of dependency culture. They argue that it is 'based upon socially constituted definitions of failure' and does not really identify a difference between the independent and the dependent. Nobody is truly independent in contemporary Britain or in similar societies. They say:

When we speak of individual autonomy, or the sovereignty of the worker, the consumer or the citizen, we must remember that the human individual remains dependent upon other human individuals and social structures.

For example, workers are dependent upon employers, consumers on those who supply the goods, and the citizen is responsible upon the state for 'physical security and the regulation of other human individuals and social structures'. The benefit claimant is not in a qualitatively different position to other members of society who are also dependent in various ways.

Dean and Taylor-Gooby's objections to dependency theory though, are not simply philosophical. In 1990 they carried out eighty-five in-depth interviews with social security claimants of working age in south London and Kent.

This research did not find that many benefit claimants had lost interest in working. Only fourteen of those interviewed showed little interest in working. Four of this group nevertheless hoped to come off benefits eventually, eight had health problems or caring responsibilities which prevented them working, one had taken early retirement and only one had rejected the idea of working. He was a man in his fifties who described himself an anarchist, and who had rejected the work ethic after a career working as a technician in the oil industry.

Dean and Taylor-Gooby did find evidence that the benefits system discouraged some people from taking low-paid work. Over half of those interviewed made some reference to the problems associated with losing means-tested benefits if they went out to work. This seems to support Jordan's claim that it is means-tested benefits (like income support and family credit) rather than universal benefits which can create disincentives to work. But there was no evidence that the disincentives had led to a dependency culture. For example, only twenty-one people said that their circle of friends and relatives contained many claimants. As Dean and Taylor-Gooby observe, 'Clearly most respondents could not be said to be enmeshed in a claiming culture.'

According to this study the ambitions, attitudes and social networks of most benefits claimants are little different from those of other members of society. They want to earn their own living and would prefer not to have to turn to the state for a basic income. For them the state is a last resort, and one they would rather avoid. Dean and

Taylor-Gooby conclude 'The social security system does not foster a dependency culture, but it constructs, isolates and supervises a heterogeneous population of reluctant dependants.'

■ The culture of poverty

Many researchers have noted that the lifestyle of the poor differs in certain respects from that of other members of society. They have also noted that poverty lifestyles in different societies share common characteristics. The circumstances of poverty are similar, in many respects, in different societies. Similar circumstances and problems tend to produce similar responses, and these responses can develop into a culture, that is the learned, shared, and socially transmitted behaviour of a social group.

This line of reasoning has led to the concept of a **culture of poverty** (or, more correctly, a **subculture of poverty**), a relatively distinct subculture of the poor with its own norms and values. The idea of a culture of poverty was introduced in the late 1950s by the American anthropologist, Oscar Lewis. He developed the concept from his fieldwork among the urban poor in Mexico and Puerto Rico. Lewis argues that the culture of poverty is a 'design for living' which is transmitted from one generation to the next.

A design for living

As a design for living which directs behaviour, the culture of poverty has the following elements.

1 On the **individual level**, in Lewis's words:
    the major characteristics are a strong feeling of marginality, of helplessness, of dependence and inferiority, a strong present-time orientation with relatively little ability to defer gratification, a sense of resignation and fatalism.

2 On the **family level**, life is characterized by:
    free union or consensual marriages, a relatively high incidence in the abandonment of mothers and children, a trend towards mother-centred families and a much greater knowledge of maternal relatives. There are high rates of divorce and desertion by the male family head resulting in matrifocal families headed by women.

3 On the **community level**, 'The lack of effective participation and integration in the major institutions of

the larger society is one of the crucial characteristics of the culture of poverty.' The urban poor in Lewis's research do not usually belong to trade unions or other associations, they are not members of political parties, and 'generally do not participate in the national welfare agencies, and make very little use of banks, hospitals, department stores, museums or art galleries'. For most, the family is the only institution in which they directly participate.

Perpetuating poverty

The culture of poverty, then, is seen as a response by the poor to their place in society. According to Lewis it is a 'reaction of the poor to their marginal position in a class-stratified and highly individualistic society.'

However, the culture of poverty goes beyond a mere reaction to a situation. It takes on the force of culture since its characteristics are guides to action which are internalized by the poor and passed on from one generation to the next. As such the culture of poverty tends to **perpetuate poverty** since its characteristics can be seen as mechanisms which maintain poverty: attitudes of fatalism and resignation lead to acceptance of the situation, whilst the failure to join trades unions and other organizations weakens the potential power of the poor.

Lewis argues that once established, the culture of poverty:

---

tends to perpetuate itself from generation to generation because of its effect on children. By the time slum children are age six or seven, they have usually absorbed the basic values and attitudes of their subculture and are not psychologically geared to take full advantage of changing conditions or increased opportunities which may occur in their lifetime.

Lewis argues that the culture of poverty best describes and explains the situation of the poor in colonial societies or in the early stages of capitalism as in many Third World countries. However, although it is common in such societies not everyone adopts the culture of poverty. In advanced capitalist societies and (the then) socialist societies, the culture of poverty is non-existent, weakly developed or affects a fairly small minority. In the USA, for example, Lewis estimates that only some 20 per cent of the poor adopt the lifestyle of the culture of poverty.

Other sociologists, however, have argued that the idea of a culture of poverty can be applied to most of the poor in advanced industrial societies. For example, in *The Other America* Michael Harrington writes of the American poor:

There is, in short, a language of the poor, a psychology of the poor, a world view of the poor. To be impoverished is to be an internal alien, to grow up in a culture that is radically different from the one that dominates the society.

Lower-class subculture

The American anthropologist Walter B. Miller has developed his thinking along lines similar to Lewis. Although not directly concerned with poverty, Miller's ideas have been linked to the culture of poverty.

Miller argues that the American lower class – the lowest stratum of the working class – has a distinctive subculture with its own set of **focal concerns**. These include an emphasis on toughness and masculinity, a search for thrills and excitement, present-time orientation, and a commitment to luck and fate rather than achievement and effort as a means of realizing goals.

Miller emphasizes the idea of value to a greater degree than Lewis, arguing that members of the lower class are committed to their focal concerns. Miller's picture is more of a self-contained viable cultural system, without the disorganization and breakdown implied by Lewis.

Like Lewis's culture of poverty, Miller's lower-class subculture is self-perpetuating, being transmitted from one generation to the next. Miller argues that 'lower class culture is a distinctive tradition, many centuries old with an integrity of its own'.

Miller's catalogue of lower-class traits, like that of Lewis, offers no handholds to escape from poverty. From one perspective this may be functional. Miller suggests that lower-class subculture is functional in providing the necessary adaptation for a 'low-skilled labouring force'. Aspects of this adaptation include 'high boredom tolerance' and the 'capacity to find life gratification outside the world of work'. Faced with boring, low-paid jobs and high rates of unemployment, members of the lower class have responded by developing their own focal concerns which provide a measure of satisfaction.

The concepts of the culture of poverty and lower-class subculture have two important factors in common.

1 They see the poor as different from the rest of society, as a group with a distinctive subculture.

2 They see this subculture as maintaining the poor in their present circumstances.

Criticisms

Since its introduction, the culture of poverty theory has met with sustained criticism. The actual existence of a culture of poverty has been questioned. Research in low-income areas in Latin American and African countries which are in the early stages of capitalist development and should therefore provide evidence of a thriving culture of poverty, has cast some doubt on Lewis's claims.

Kenneth Little's study of West African urbanization reports a proliferation of voluntary associations for mutual aid and recreation organized by poor rural migrants to the cities.

William Mangin's research in the *barriadas* of Peru, shanty towns surrounding major cities, reveals a high level of community action and political involvement. Members of the *barriadas* often organize their own schools, clinics and bus co-operatives, have a high level of participation in community politics and show little of the family break-up described by Lewis. Mangin is impressed with 'the capacity for and evidence of popular initiative, self-help and local community organization'. He does concede, however, that some squatter communities and city slums in Latin America can be characterized by the culture of poverty.

Audrey J. Schwartz's research in the slum areas or *barrios* of Caracas in Venezuela reveals little evidence of apathy and resignation, present-time orientation or broken families, and he concludes that the subculture of the *barrios* does not perpetuate and maintain poverty.

Evidence from advanced industrial societies casts further doubt on the culture of poverty thesis, and, in particular, its application to Western society. From their research in Blackston (a pseudonym for a low-income Black American community), Charles and Betty Lou Valentine state 'It is proving difficult to find community patterns that correspond to many of the subcultural traits often associated with poverty in learned writings about the poor.' They found a great deal of participation in local government, constant use of welfare institutions and 'a veritable plethora of organizations' from block associations to an area-wide community council. The Valentines conclude that 'Apathetic resignation does exist, but it is by no means the dominant theme of the community.'

The research of the Valentines suggests that the lifestyle of the poor is more variable than had been previously thought. Similar conclusions about poverty in Britain are reached by Nicola Madge and Muriel Brown. In their book *Despite the welfare state* they review the findings of a major research project into deprivation conducted by the Social Science Research Council. Madge and Brown state:

> All the evidence suggests that cultural values are not important for the development and transmission of deprivation. Generally speaking people do not necessarily bring up their children as they were brought up . . . Further there is nothing to indicate that the deprivations of the poor, racial minorities or delinquents, to cite but three examples, are due to constraints imposed by culture.

◼ Situational constraints – an alternative to a culture of poverty

The second and major criticism of the culture of poverty has centred round the notion of culture. Despite the research referred to above, there is evidence from both advanced and developing industrial societies to support Lewis and Miller's characterization of the behaviour of the poor.

The use of the term 'culture' implies that the behaviour of the poor is internalized via the socialization process and once internalized is to some degree resistant to change. It also implies, particularly with respect to Miller's focal concerns, that aspects of the behaviour of the poor derive from values. Again there is the suggestion of resistance to change. Indeed, Miller argues that members of the lower class have a preference for, and a commitment to their subculture.

Thus both Lewis and Miller suggest, with their notion of culture, that despite the fact it was initially caused by circumstances such as unemployment, low income and lack of opportunity, that once established, the subculture of low-income groups has a life of its own. This implies that if the circumstances which produced poverty were to disappear, the culture of poverty might well continue. This is made even more likely by Lewis's and particularly Miller's view that the culture of poverty and lower-class subculture respectively are largely self-contained and insulated from the norms and values of the mainstream culture of society. The poor, to a large degree, therefore live in a world of their own.

Culture versus situational constraints

These arguments have been strongly contested. Rather than seeing the behaviour of the poor as a response to established and internalized cultural patterns, many researchers view it as a reaction to **situational constraints**. In other words, the poor are constrained by the facts of their situation: by low income, unemployment and the like, to act the way they do, rather than being directed by a culture of poverty.

The situational constraints argument suggests that the poor would readily change their behaviour in response to a new set of circumstances once the constraints of poverty were removed. Thus Hylan Lewis, an American sociologist who had conducted considerable research on the behaviour of the poor, argues:

> It is probably more fruitful to think of lower class families reacting in various ways to the facts of their position and to relative isolation rather than the imperatives of a lower class culture.

The situational constraints thesis also attacks the view that the poor are largely insulated from mainstream norms and values. It argues that the poor share the values of society as a whole, the only difference being that they are unable to translate many of those values into reality. Again, the situational constraints argument suggests that once the constraints of poverty are removed, the poor will have no difficulty adopting mainstream behaviour patterns and seizing available opportunities.

Mainstream values

Tally's Corner by Elliot Liebow is a major piece of research which strongly supports the situational constraints thesis. The study is based on participant observation of black 'streetcorner men' in a low-income area of Washington DC.

The men are either unemployed, underemployed (working part-time) or employed in low-paid, unskilled, dead-end jobs as manual labourers, elevator operators, janitors, bus boys and dishwashers. Their view of work is directed by mainstream values. The men want jobs with higher pay and status but they lack the necessary skills, qualifications and work experience. They regard their occupations from the same viewpoint as any other member of society. In Liebow's words 'Both employee and employer are contemptuous of the job.'

When streetcorner men blow a week's wages on a 'weekend drunk' or pack in a job on an apparent whim, the middle-class observer tends to interpret this behaviour as evidence of present-time orientation and inability to defer gratification. However, Liebow argues that it is not the time orientation that differentiates the streetcorner man from members of the middle class, but his future. Whereas middle-class individuals have a reasonable future to look forward to, the streetcorner man has none. His behaviour is directed by the fact that 'he is aware of the future and the hopelessness of it all'.

In the same way Liebow argues that it is not inability to defer gratification that differentiates the streetcorner man from members of the middle class, but simply the fact that he has no resources to defer. Middle-class individuals are able to invest in the future, to save, to commit time and effort to their jobs and families both because they have the resources to invest and because of the likelihood their investment will pay off in the form of promotion at work and home ownership and home improvement. The streetcorner man lacks the resources or the promise of a payoff if he invests what little he has. With a dead-end job or no job at all, and insufficient income to support his wife and family he is 'obliged to expend all his resources on maintaining himself from moment to moment'.

Liebow argues that what appears to be a cultural pattern of immediate gratification and present-time orientation is merely a situational response, a direct and indeed a rational reaction to situational constraints. Rather than being directed by a distinctive subculture, the behaviour of the streetcorner man is more readily understandable as a result of his inability to translate the values of mainstream culture – values which he shares – into reality.

Family life and situational constraints

Liebow applies similar reasoning to the streetcorner man's relationship with his wife and family. The men share the values of mainstream culture. They regard a conventional family life as the ideal and strive to play the mainstream roles of father and breadwinner. However their income is insufficient to support a wife and family. Faced daily with a situation of failure men often desert their families. Liebow writes:

> To stay married is to live with your failure, to be confronted with it day in and day out. It is to live in a world whose standards of manliness are forever beyond one's reach.

Increasingly the men turn to the companionship of those in similar circumstances, to life on the streetcorner. Their conversation often revolves around the subject of marriage and its failure which is explained in terms of what Liebow calls the **theory of manly flaws**. The failure of marriage is attributed to manliness which is characterized by a need for sexual variety and adventure, gambling, drinking, swearing and aggressive behaviour. Men often boast about their 'manly flaws' illustrating their prowess with a variety of anecdotes, many of which have little relation to the truth. The theory of manly flaws cushions failure and in a sense translates it into success, for at least on the streetcorner, manly flaws can bring prestige and respect. In Liebow's words, 'weaknesses are somehow turned upside down and almost magically transformed into strengths'.

On closer examination, however, Liebow found little support for the streetcorner man's rationale for marital failure. Marriages failed largely because the men had insufficient income

to maintain them. The matrifocal families that resulted were not due to a culture of poverty, but simply to low income. The emphasis on manliness, which coincides with Miller's focal concern of masculinity, was not a valued aspect of lower-class culture, but simply a device to veil failure.

Liebow concludes:

> The streetcorner man does not appear as a carrier of an independent cultural tradition. His behaviour appears not so much as a way of realizing the distinctive goals and values of his own subculture, or of conforming to its models, but rather as his way of trying to achieve many of the goals and values of the larger society, of failing to do this, and of concealing his failure from others and himself as best he can.

Liebow therefore rejects the idea of a culture of poverty or lower-class subculture and sees the behaviour of the poor as a product of situational constraints, not of distinctive cultural patterns.

Situational constraints and culture

A compromise between the extremes of Liebow on the one hand and Lewis and Miller on the other is provided by Ulf Hannerz. He sees some virtue in both the situational constraints and cultural arguments.

Hannerz, a Swedish anthropologist, conducted research in a Black low-income area of Washington DC. In his book *Soulside* he argues that if a solution to a problem such as the theory of manly flaws, becomes accepted by a social group, it is learned, shared and socially transmitted, and is therefore cultural. To some degree it is based on values since the theory of manly flaws provides a male role model to which to aspire. This model is therefore not simply a cushion for failure, a thinly veiled excuse. To some degree it provides an alternative to the mainstream male role model.

Like Liebow, Hannerz sees the theory of manly flaws as a response to situational constraints but unlike Liebow, he argues that if these constraints were removed, this 'model of masculinity could constitute a barrier to change'. However, Hannerz concludes that situational constraints are more powerful in directing the behaviour of the poor than cultural patterns. Unlike Miller, he argues that the cultural patterns that distinguish the poor exist alongside and are subsidiary to a widespread commitment to mainstream values. He does not see 'the ghetto variety of the culture of poverty as a

lasting obstacle to change'. Since the behaviour of the poor contains a cultural component, it may hinder change once the situational constraints are removed. There may be a **cultural lag**, a hangover from the previous situation, but Hannerz believes that this would only be temporary.

■ The underclass and poverty

In recent years the concept of an **underclass** has become widely used and increasingly controversial. We discussed the underclass debate in Chapter 2 in terms of its relevance to theories of stratification. However, some theories based on the concept are also highly relevant to poverty. For example, some theories, based on similar ideas to those employed in individualistic and cultural theories of poverty, have been used to explain the existence of an underclass.

■ Charles Murray – the underclass in Britain

As we outlined in Chapter 2 (pp. 91–2) Charles Murray is an American sociologist who first developed ideas on the underclass in his home country. He visited Britain in 1989 and claimed that Britain too was developing an underclass.

Members of the underclass were not simply the poorest members of society – they were those whose lifestyles involved a 'type of poverty'. According to Murray, this involves particular forms of behaviour. He says:

> When I use the term 'underclass' I am indeed focusing on a certain type of poor person defined not by his condition, e.g. long-term unemployed, but by his deplorable behaviour in response to that condition, e.g. unwilling to take the jobs that are available to him.

Other types of 'deplorable behaviour' which are typical of the underclass are committing crimes and having illegitimate children. Murray does not claim that all poor people, nor all those who are unemployed or reliant upon benefit, engage in

deplorable behaviour. It is a minority who act in this way, but ultimately their behaviour will influence others. He claims:

> Britain has a growing population of working-aged, healthy people who live in a different world from other Britons, who are raising their children to live in it, and whose values are contaminating the life of entire neighbourhoods . . . for neighbours who don't share those values cannot isolate themselves.

Murray puts forward evidence in three areas to support his claims.

Illegitimacy

First, he looks at **illegitimacy**. He points out that in 1979 Britain had an illegitimacy rate of 10.6 per cent of births which was low compared to most Western industrial societies. By 1988, though, it had risen to 25.6 per cent, higher than many comparable countries and not far behind the USA.

Murray cites figures to show that most illegitimate children are born to women from lower social classes and not to middle-class career women, and he suggests that in some areas the absence of a father has become the norm. For example, he relates a story about a girl in Birkenhead who was embarrassed when her father went to watch her in a school play because he was the only father there.

Murray notes that many births are jointly registered to a mother and father (69 per cent in 1987), and of these 70 per cent give the same address, suggesting they live together. Even so, Murray does not believe that this undermines his argument. He questions whether relationships between cohabiting parents are as stable as those between married ones, although he admits that he has no evidence to show the former are less stable. To Murray, the rising illegitimacy rate is important because illegitimate children will tend to 'run wild' and the lack of fathers results in 'a level of physical unruliness which makes life difficult'.

Crime

Second, Murray associates the development of an underclass with **rising crime**. Writing in 1989 he claimed that Britain had a rate of property crime that was at least as high and probably higher than that of the USA. In 1988, for example, England had a burglary rate of 1,623 per 100,000 compared to a US rate of 1,309 per 100,000. Violent crime was lower in Britain but Murray pointed out that it was rising rapidly, even though the proportion of young males in the population was falling.

Murray argues that crime is so damaging because communities become fragmented if rates of victimization are high. People become defensive and suspicious of one another and retreat into their homes. As crime becomes more common and more widely accepted, young boys start to imitate the older males and take up criminal activities themselves. As the crime rate rises further the community becomes ever more fragmented and informal social controls which encourage conformity are weakened even further.

Unemployment

Murray does not see **unemployment** itself as a problem; instead, it is the unwillingness of young men to take jobs that creates difficulties. He says there is an 'unknown but probably considerable number of people who manage to qualify for benefit even if in reality very few job opportunities would tempt them to work'. Like illegitimacy and crime rates, unemployment is much higher in the lowest social class of unskilled manual workers, some of whom are becoming members of the underclass.

According to Murray attitudes to work were changing in Britain at the end of the 1980s. Those in their thirties and forties who found themselves unemployed were generally much more committed to work than younger groups. The older generations of working-class males saw it as

humiliating to rely on benefits, while the younger generations were happy to live off the state. Murray argues:

> Talking to the boys in their late teens and early twenties about jobs, I heard nothing about the importance of work as a source of self-respect and no talk of just wanting enough income to be free of the benefit system.

In Murray's view such attitudes are disastrous. He claims that 'when large numbers of young men don't work the communities around them break down'. Young men without jobs are unable to keep a family, so they are unlikely to get married when they father children and the illegitimacy rate rises. Supporting a family is one way for young men to prove their manhood. In the absence of family responsibilities they find other, damaging ways to prove themselves, for example through violent crime.

Causes and solution

Murray sees the increase in illegitimacy as a consequence of changes in the benefits system. He calculates that at 1987 prices an unemployed single mother with a young child received just £22 in benefits in 1955. Furthermore she had no special privileges on housing lists. The stigma of illegitimacy was also much greater. However, the value of benefits grew, the 1977 Homeless Person's Act made pregnant women and mothers a priority in the allocation of housing and the stigma of illegitimacy decreased. By the 1980s therefore, having an illegitimate child as a single mother and raising it alone had gone from ' "extremely punishing" to "not so bad" '. There has always been a potential for rising illegitimacy because 'sex is fun and babies are endearing' but in earlier decades it had been held in check by the prohibitive financial and social costs of single motherhood. This was no longer true.

Crime, too, according to Murray has become less severely punished. Official statistics show that compared to earlier decades criminals in the 1980s were less likely to be caught; if caught less likely to be convicted; and if convicted less likely to receive a severe penalty.

Murray offers no clear explanation as to why commitment to work should have declined amongst young men but he does assert that providing more jobs will not solve the problem. He claims that some American cities in the second half of the 1980s had plenty of well-paid low-skilled jobs but members of the underclass were simply unwilling to take them.

Murray's solution to the problems is perhaps surprising given the causes that he identifies. He does not, for example, suggest radical cuts in benefits or simply imposing stiffer sentences in the courts. He implies that such solutions are too drastic to be implemented or are impractical. For example, no political party in Britain supports the drastic cuts in benefits which would be needed to deal with illegitimacy and the prison population might have to triple to deal effectively with crime.

What Murray suggests instead is that local communities should be given 'a massive dose of self-government'. They should take over responsibility for education, housing and criminal justice. With this power the local community would ensure that the problems were tackled. He says:

My premise is that it is unnatural for a neighbourhood to tolerate high levels of crime or illegitimacy or voluntary idleness among its youth: that, given the chance, poor communities as well as rich ones will run their affairs so that such things happen infrequently.

■ Critics of Murray

Murray's analysis of the underclass owes much to some of the theories of poverty we have already examined. Like New Right theories, it sees benefits as producing groups who are unable or unwilling to earn their own living. Like the culture of poverty theory it sees the lifestyle of certain groups at the bottom of society as contributing to their own plight. However, it is unlike any single theory of poverty and it has become sufficiently influential to generate fierce criticism.

Alan Walker – blaming the victims

Alan Walker argues that Murray puts forward totally inadequate evidence to support his case by

relying upon 'innuendos, assertions and anecdotes'. Furthermore, Walker suggests that the best evidence there is does not point to the existence of an underclass.

For example, research by Madge and Brown commissioned to investigate Sir Keith Joseph's claim that there was a 'cycle of disadvantage' found that at least 50 per cent of those born in a disadvantaged home did not end up disadvantaged themselves. This contradicts Murray's claims that supposed underclass attitudes and values would inevitably rub off on younger generations.

Walker also refers to official figures to attack Murray's views on illegitimacy. About 60 per cent of illegitimate births to women younger than twenty are registered by both parents. Lone parenthood is often short-lived. Research by John Ermisch found that the median length of lone parenthood for a never-married woman in the early 1980s was less than three years. Most found a partner in a relatively short time. Most children born to such mothers do not spend the whole of their childhood with a single parent.

Walker argues that most of the so-called underclass have conventional attitudes. They want stable relationships and paid employment. It is not their values that prevent them from achieving their aims but a lack of opportunities. Walker criticizes government policy for the plight of the underclass. He says that Murray's theory 'diverts attention . . . from the real problems: pauperization and social segregation as acts of government policy'.

In other words, Walker believes the poor are the victims of social policy rather than the cause of society's social problems.

Joan C. Brown – single motherhood

Brown is critical of Murray's ideas on single motherhood. She quotes figures which show that divorced single mothers on average spend longer claiming benefits than never-married single mothers although Murray blames the latter group for the ills of the underclass.

She questions Murray's arguments about single motherhood becoming accepted as the norm in some neighbourhoods. Where there is a concentration of single mothers it is usually due to council housing policy which allocates them to houses in particular areas, and nothing to do with neighbourhoods becoming tainted by values which undermine family life.

Furthermore divorce has become very common in all strata of society and is not confined to lower classes. The 1983 *British Social Attitudes Survey* found that 90 per cent of those aged 18–34 did not believe pre-marital sex to be wrong. Again she concludes that it is not possible to argue that there are distinctive underclass attitudes which are confined to poor women.

Nicholas Deakin – Murray's tripod

Deakin notes that Murray's argument rests upon a three-legged argument based on illegitimacy, crime and unemployment. Deakin believes that at least two of those legs are very shaky.

Murray describes illegitimacy as 'the purest form of being without parents' yet himself admits that many 'illegitimate children do indeed share a household with cohabiting but unmarried parents'. Like Walker and Brown, Deakin points out that single-parenthood 'is not a static condition, still less an immoral one' but simply 'a stage in the life which may lead in a variety of different directions'.

The second part of the tripod rests upon the use of official statistics. However, these are well-known for being highly unreliable so the data Murray uses are unconvincing. Deakin does not deny that there has been a big rise in unemployment but neither that nor a few anecdotes demonstrates that attitudes to work have changed amongst a supposed underclass.

Anthony Heath – the attitudes of the underclass

The critics of Murray discussed so far raise serious doubts about Murray's evidence but Anthony Heath has actually collected data to test the claim that the attitudes of the underclass are different. He used information from the *British Election Survey* of 1987 and the *British Social Attitudes Survey* of 1989. He confined his study to people of working age. He identified those in the surveys who did not have paid employment and who claimed income support and compared them to the rest of the sample.

Heath found that 86 per cent of the underclass said they would like to have a paid job compared to 57 per cent of those in families where at least one person was working. This suggests that Murray is wrong to argue that those reliant on benefits are less willing to work than others.

Heath also found that in most respects members of the underclass had similar attitudes towards marriage as other members of society. Some 22 per cent agreed that 'married people are generally happier than unmarried people' compared to 25 per cent of those from employed family units. Members of the underclass were more likely to agree that 'It is better to have a bad marriage than no marriage at all'(10 per cent compared to 2 per cent), and that 'Couples don't take marriage seriously enough when divorce is easily available' (61 per cent compared to 54 per cent). However they were less likely to agree that 'People who want children ought to get married' (47 per cent against 64 per cent).

Most of the evidence uncovered by Heath then, suggests that the majority of the underclass (if they can be said to exist) have conventional aspirations. They want jobs and happy marriages but they are slightly less likely than other members of society to believe that people should get married before having children.

■ Frank Field – *Losing Out*
The underclass and citizenship

Frank Field is a British Labour MP and campaigner against poverty. Like Charles Murray in 1989 he argued that Britain had a growing underclass amongst the poor. However, there the similarity with Murray ends. Field does not see the underclass as having a distinctive culture and he does not see them as a pathological group undermining the well-being of society. Instead he regards the underclass as the victims of social change and government policies.

Field links the growth of an underclass to the reduction of citizenship rights. In 1949 T.H. Marshall had argued that civil rights were largely established in the eighteenth century, political rights (such as the right to vote) in the nineteenth century, and social and economic citizenship rights were the main concern of the twentieth century. For example, the development of a welfare state was providing citizens with the right to a basic living standard. Field regards this description of citizenship as an oversimplification but he accepts the general thrust of the argument.

However, he goes on to claim that since 1979 'the 300-year-old evolution of citizenship as an incorporating force in British society has been thrown into reverse'. This in turn has resulted in the growth of an underclass who are denied the economic and social citizenship rights enjoyed by others.

The composition of the underclass

According to Field the underclass consists of three main groups.

1 The first group is the **long-term unemployed.** There is a continual flow of people into and out of unemployment and those who are unemployed for a short time do not form part of the underclass. The two main groups among the long-term unemployed are school leavers who have never had a job and older workers who have been unemployed for long periods. With rising unemployment in the 1970s and 1980s the unemployed have swelled the ranks of the underclass considerably.

2 A second group which has been growing rapidly is **single-parent families**. Between 1979 and 1987 there was an increase of more than 200 per cent in the number of single mothers claiming welfare benefits. Some in this situation are only briefly dependent on benefits: it is those who are 'dependent on welfare for very long periods of time' who are part of the underclass.

3 The third group consists of **elderly pensioners** who depend on state benefits because they do not have an occupational pension. Field says that 'many of them live in the worst housing conditions, and their income does not adequately compensate for the extra expense arising from the disabilities that accompany extreme old age'. Unlike the first two groups the elderly make up a declining proportion of the very poor.

What members of Field's underclass have in common is that they are all reliant upon state benefits which are too low to give them an acceptable living standard, and they have little chance of escaping from reliance upon benefits. Furthermore their chances of escape have been declining as the

forces which have created an underclass have also made the predicament of its members more difficult.

The causes of the underclass

Field attributes the development of the underclass to four main causes.

1 Rising levels of unemployment have made more people of working age reliant upon benefits and have led to a big increase in the numbers of long-term unemployed.

2 Social changes and government policy have widened the gap between higher and lower classes. Field specifically claims that Margaret Thatcher's Government had a 'determination to widen class differences' in the 1980s.

3 Living standards in society as a whole have risen but the poorest members of society have been excluded from the benefits enjoyed by the increasingly affluent.

4 There has been a change in public attitude towards those who have failed to be economically successful. The public has become less sympathetic and more inclined to blame the poor for their plight. According to Field 'This has led to a psychological and political separation of the very poorest from the rest of the community.' A 'drawbridge' mentality has developed: successful members of the working class have cut themselves off from those who have had less success. The underclass has therefore become increasingly distinct from the working class.

Field devotes most of his attention to discussing the first three causes of the underclass and these will now be examined in more detail.

Unemployment and employment

Field points out that unemployment is more likely to affect members of the working class, particularly those with unskilled or semi-skilled jobs. Changes in the economy, particularly the decline of manufacturing, have led to a reduction in the number of unskilled and semi-skilled jobs available. Young workers and members of ethnic minorities are also more likely to become unemployed. These groups also have an above average risk of suffering from long-term unemployment.

The long-term unemployed have found their living standards undermined by changes in government policy. In 1982 the unemployed lost the right to earnings-related supplements to unemployment benefit, sick pay and industrial injury benefit. Furthermore unemployment benefit was restricted to the first twelve months after becoming unemployed and it is far from generous. For example, in 1989 benefit for a married couple was valued at 54 per cent of the state pension for an equivalent couple.

Another problem is the rise of part-time work and the decline of full-time work. Privatization and the contracting out of jobs have contributed to the growth of part-time work, as has the growth of the service sector. Part-time workers have very limited employment rights. Many are not in an occupational pension scheme and they have little job security. Their jobs are usually low paid. Such workers are in a vulnerable position and are 'struggling to keep themselves from dropping into the abyss of the underclass'.

Inequality and living standards

Field points to many measures which have increased inequality and reduced the living standards of those on benefits. While taxes for the better-off were cut, benefits were made less generous. For example, before Margaret Thatcher took office, old age pensions and invalidity benefit were increased in line with inflation, or with average wage rises, whichever was the higher. In 1980 though, the link to average wages was removed. Although the benefits maintained their real value, those receiving them no longer shared in the rising prosperity of the employed.

Child supplements for those receiving unemployment and sick pay also started being phased out in 1980. From 1985 child benefit was increased less than other benefits and in 1987 and 1988 it was frozen. A number of changes were made to housing benefit in the 1980s which reduced the amount of benefits received by many of those entitled to it. Some benefits, for example unemployment benefit in 1982, became taxable.

According to Field there was a fundamental contradiction in the social security policies of the 1980s (policies which largely continued under John Major in the 1990s). The Government wanted to discourage reliance upon benefits but also to target benefits on the most needy. The problem with this is that targeting via means-tested benefits increases dependency and creates a poverty trap from which it is difficult to escape. If the poor increase their earnings so that they no longer need to claim income support, they lose their entitlement to other benefits such as housing benefit. This means that they are not much better off. Single parents may have the additional problem of paying for childcare if they take up paid employment, which may leave them worse off than if they were drawing benefits. Field believes that such policies have created a large and growing underclass 'immobilized at the bottom of our society'.

Overall the policies of the 1980s massively increased inequalities between the rich and poor. Privatization and the spread of share ownership and home ownership led to more people enjoying some economic security. Rising wages for those in employment combined with tax cuts made many people better off. Members of the working class with secure jobs could buy their council houses; however the poorest could not and as benefits were changed they became worse off. (We discussed trends in income inequality in Chapter 2, see pp. 42–6.)

Solutions

Field sees government policy as the main factor creating an underclass and he sees changes in government policy as the main way of solving the problem. His proposals include a wide range of measures intended to get rid of large-scale unemployment, to improve the living standards of those on benefits, to give claimants incentives to get off benefits and to reduce inequality.

Field proposes moving civil service jobs to areas of high unemployment, targeting government purchases on such areas and improving training. The unemployed should be guaranteed employment training so they develop the skills necessary to work in a way which will allow their employers to compete internationally. Temporary work schemes should be set up for those who cannot find work even after retraining.

Pensions and child benefits should both be increased. This would mean that many people would no longer need to claim means-tested benefits. Unemployment benefit should continue indefinitely for those who are willing to accept suitable jobs.

Income support should no longer take a spouse's earnings into account since this discourages many married people from finding work. Single parents should be allowed to earn more before their benefits are cut. Their benefit reductions should be based on a sliding scale, allowing them to keep more of their earnings and giving them a greater incentive to work. It should be possible to offset the costs of childcare against tax to ensure that paid employment is worthwhile for single parents.

Inequality should be reduced through a minimum wage of 55 per cent of the average earnings in a particular industry. Tax allowances for the better-off, such as tax relief on mortgages, should be cut or phased out. National insurance should be changed so that there is no upper limit and high earners would therefore pay more.

Conclusion

Field's views on the underclass are very similar to many conflict theorists' views on poverty which we will discuss in the next section. Many sociologists accept that there is a group of the poor at the bottom of the stratification system but would not accept that it is appropriate to call them an underclass. Others believe that there is an underclass but do not define it as consisting of long-term benefit claimants. These views were discussed in Chapter 2 (see pp. 91–6), while the relationship between the underclass and ethnicity is examined on pp. 717–21.

■ Conflict theories of poverty

The sociology of poverty has increasingly come to be studied within a conflict perspective. Those working within this perspective argue that it is the failure of society to allocate its resources fairly that explains the continued existence of poverty. Poverty is not held to be the responsibility of those who suffer from it. Instead they are seen as the 'victims'.

To some extent conflict theorists disagree about the reasons why society has failed to eradicate poverty.

1 Some see poverty to be primarily the consequence of the failings of the welfare state.

2 Others place more emphasis on the lack of power and weak bargaining position of the poor which places them at a disadvantage in the labour market. They are either unable to sell their labour, or are prevented from receiving sufficient rewards from it to lift themselves out of poverty.

3 Many conflict theorists relate the existence of poverty to wider structural forces in society, in particular the existence of a stratification system.

4 Marxists tend to believe poverty is an inherent and inevitable consequence of capitalism. They cannot envisage the defeat of poverty without the total transformation of society.

Thus although there are broad similarities between the sociologists we will look at in the following sections, there are also some areas of disagreement.

■ Poverty and the welfare state

Recent studies of poverty have found that those who rely upon state benefits for their income are among the largest groups of the poor. If poverty is defined in relative terms, and the definition advanced means that benefit levels do not raise the recipient above the poverty line, then a great deal of poverty can simply be attributed to inadequate benefits.

Nevertheless, it might be argued that the welfare state still makes a major contribution to reducing poverty, or at least to improving the relative position of those who are poor. It is widely assumed that one effect of the welfare state is to redistribute resources from the rich to the poor as at first sight it appears that both taxation and welfare payments do this.

Taxation

This view has been challenged by some conflict sociologists. Some taxes are certainly **progressive**, that is, they lead to the better-off paying a greater proportion of their income to the Government than the lower income groups. **Direct taxes** such as income tax are levied at different levels according to income, and those on very low pay may not even reach the threshold where they start paying tax.

However, **indirect taxation** (taxes levied on the purchase of goods) tends to be **regressive**. Taxes such as VAT (Value Added Tax) and duties on

Table 3.6 Impact of tax changes 1985–95, by decile group

Decile	Percentage losing	Percentage gaining	Average gain/loss (£ per week)	Average gain/loss (percentage of net income)
1	66	7	–3.0	–2.9
2	44	13	–1.4	–1.4
3	47	23	–1.8	–1.5
4	43	40	–1.1	–0.8
5	37	50	0.7	0.4
6	33	57	1.6	0.7
7	29	64	3.1	1.2
8	25	69	4.4	1.5
9	23	72	6.3	1.8
10	20	76	31.3	5.8
All	37	47	4.10	1.70

(*Source*: Giles, C. and Johnson, P. (1994) *Taxes Down, Taxes Up: The Effects of a Decade of Tax Changes*, the Institute for Fiscal Studies, London, p. 11.)

alcohol and tobacco tend to take up a greater proportion of the income of poorer sections of the community than richer ones.

Since 1978–9 the tax burden on the low paid has increased while the burden on the high paid has been reduced. Direct taxation has become less progressive, indirect taxation has increased and the relative position of those on low incomes has worsened. Official statistics showed that between 1979 and 1987 the share of national income going to the poorest 10 per cent of the population fell from 9.5 to 7.6 per cent whereas the share going to the richest 10 per cent went up from 35 to 41 per cent. Christopher Giles and Paul Johnson have examined the effects of tax changes between 1985 and 1995 in a study for the Institute for Fiscal Studies. Table 3.6 shows the results. It divides the population into tenths or deciles, decile 1 being the poorest and decile 10 the richest. It shows that as a result of tax changes the poorest decile has lost an average of £3 per week or 2.9 per cent of their income, while the richest decile has gained £31.30 or 5.5 per cent of their income.

The figures quoted above do not take into account resources received by members of the population which do not count as income and do not incur tax. Frank Field has shown that those on higher incomes tend to receive a greater proportion of their income in kind from their employer than those on low incomes. For example, they are more likely to be provided with life assurance and health insurance policies, interest-free loans, assistance with housing costs and company cars. Share schemes for employees are also increasingly used as a way of avoiding tax and limiting the redistributive effects of the taxation system.

Who benefits?

Undoubtedly some welfare benefits primarily benefit those on the lowest incomes: income support, unemployment benefit and family credit are all directed at the poorest members of society. However, while they may prevent absolute poverty, some sociologists argue that welfare benefits do little to eradicate relative poverty.

Julian Le Grand suggests that the *Strategy of Equality* through the provision of social services has failed. From an examination of education, healthcare, housing and transport subsidies he argues that the better-off members of British society have benefited considerably more than the poor. In education the children of top income groups are more likely to stay on in education after the age of 16, and more likely to go to university. He calculates that the families in the top 20 per cent of income groups received nearly three times as much expenditure on their children's education as those in the bottom fifth.

In the field of healthcare Le Grand claims that those on higher incomes again benefit more from the services provided. The actual amounts spent on different income groups do not vary a great deal; however, lower socio-economic groups are more likely to suffer from illness, and therefore need more medical care than the higher groups. It is this extra care that they do not receive. Le Grand found 'The evidence suggests that the top socio-economic group receives 40% more NHS expenditure per person reporting illness than the bottom one.'

The DHSS *Inequalities in Health Working Group Report*, better known as the *'Black Report'*, published in 1981, reached similar conclusions. It confirmed the **inverse care law**: those whose need is less get more resources, while those with a greater need tend to get less. For example, it found that doctors tend to spend more time with middle-class patients, and middle-class areas tend to have more doctors per head of the population than working-class ones.

Le Grand finds a similar picture in relation to housing expenditure.

1 Poorer households do receive substantially greater benefits than richer ones from various forms of direct expenditure on housing. General subsidies on the supervision and maintenance of council housing and rent rebates and allowances (now replaced by housing benefits) do favour lower-income groups.

2 However, higher-income groups benefit considerably more from indirect expenditure. In particular tax relief on mortgage interest payments provides a major saving for those homeowners who have mortgages.

3 Furthermore, capital gains tax is not charged on homes which increase in value and are sold at a profit.

4 Improvement grants for houses are one form of direct expenditure which favours the better-off.

Le Grand concludes that from housing policy, 'the richest group receives nearly twice as much as public subsidy per household as the poorest group'.

Perhaps even more surprisingly, Le Grand finds transport policy favours the better-off. This is partly because richer members of society, particularly affluent commuters in the southeast of Britain, make a great deal more use of British Rail, whose running costs are heavily subsidized. The effects of subsidization of bus and coach travel are less clear, but on balance he finds that it benefits higher-income groups marginally more than lower ones.

Many of Le Grand's figures date from the 1970s. However, writing in 1987, he argues that

changes since the 1970s had done little to alter the overall picture.

1 Some changes resulted in improvements and services benefiting higher-income groups even more than they had done in the past: subsidies to council housing had been cut while mortgage tax relief had been expanded.

2 On the other hand, the replacement of rent rebates and allowances with housing benefits (which are means-tested) was likely to have benefited the poor.

3 The expansion of private education might also have cut state expenditure on the education of higher-income groups.

These changes more or less balanced each other out.

Le Grand reaches a startling conclusion on the effects of expenditure on the social services, which is quite contrary to widely held assumptions. He says:

> It has failed to achieve full equality of whatever kind for most of the services reviewed. In those areas where data are available it has failed to achieve greater equality over time; and, in some cases, it is likely that there would be greater equality if there was no public expenditure on the services concerned.

Michael Mann has reviewed some of the more recent changes in state policy and their effects. He quotes a 1987 report on health which suggested that the gap between expenditure on richer and poorer groups had increased since the *Black Report* was published. Mann notes that expenditure on council housing fell sharply in the 1980s and points to the massive expenditure on road transport as 'skewed in favour of the better off'. Certainly some of the benefits enjoyed by the more wealthy have been removed or reduced. For example, privatization has limited the amount of subsidy paid by Government and local authorities for public transport. Tax relief on mortgage interest payments has been limited to the first £30,000 and restricted to the lowest rate of tax. Taxation of company cars has been tightened up.

At the same time, though, there are new ways for the affluent to limit their tax bills. They can invest a limited amount in a TESSA (Tax Exempt Special Savings Account) and they can put money into a PEP (Personal Equity Plan), both of which are exempt from taxation. There is little reason to suppose then, that overall state policies favour the poor any more than they did when Le Grand first analysed them.

■ Poverty, the labour market and power

Not all of those who experience poverty in countries such as Britain and the USA rely on state benefits for their income. Nor can their poverty be primarily attributed to the failure of the social services to redistribute resources. A considerable proportion of the poor are employed, but receive wages that are so low that they are insufficient to meet their needs. In this section we examine the explanations that have been provided for some workers getting paid significantly less than even the average for manual work.

Market situation and poverty

In part the low wages of some groups can be explained in Weberian terms. Weber argues that a person's **class position** is dependent upon his or her **market situation**. It depends upon the ability of individuals and groups to influence the labour market in their own favour so as to maximize the rewards they receive.

The following explanations have been put forward to account for the market situation of the low paid.

1 In advanced industrial societies, with increasing demand for specialized skills and training, the unemployed and underemployed tend to be unskilled with low educational qualifications. Liebow's streetcorner men, with few skills or qualifications, can command little reward on the labour market.

2 With increasing mechanization and automation, the demand for unskilled labour is steadily contracting.

3 Many, though by no means all, low-paid workers are employed either in declining and contracting industries or labour-intensive industries such as catering. It has been argued that the narrow profit margins of many such industries maintain low wage levels.

It is important to note that pay may be defined as low in relation to the circumstances of the individual. Thus a wage which may provide a family of four with a reasonable living standard may reduce a family of eight to poverty. The circumstances of the poor may therefore be due to family size rather than low wages as such. However, from their study of St Ann's, a low-income district in Nottingham, Coates and Silburn state:

We found very clear evidence that it was not the legendary fertility of the poor which explained their condition. For most families living on the borderline of poverty, it was the second or third child, rather than the fifth or sixth, who plunged them below it.

The poverty of the low paid is not primarily due to family size, but simply to low pay.

The dual labour market

Some sociologists and economists now argue that there are two labour markets. The **dual labour market theory** sees jobs in the **primary labour market** offering job security, promotion prospects, training opportunities and relatively high wages. By comparison, the **secondary labour market** offers little job security, few possibilities for promotion or training, and low wages.

The primary labour market tends to be found in large and prosperous corporations which to some extent can protect themselves against competition from smaller firms. The smaller companies may depend heavily on the corporations for business. They are in a weaker position and so cannot offer their employees the same advantages. Women and members of ethnic minorities may be particularly concentrated in the secondary labour market and as a consequence are over represented in low-paid jobs. (For further details and evaluation of the dual labour market theory see pp. 620 and 718–19.)

Changes in the labour market

Hartley Dean and Peter Taylor-Gooby argue that the 1980s and early 1990s saw a number of changes in the labour market which made more people in Britain vulnerable to poverty.

1 Manufacturing industry declined. The proportion of GDP (Gross Domestic Product – the total value of goods and services) produced by the manufacturing sector fell from 28 per cent in 1979 to 22 per cent in 1989. There was a corresponding increase in the service sector.

2 A considerable number of the new service sector jobs do not provide economic security. Many of the jobs are part-time and have low pay and little job security. Dean and Taylor-Gooby suggest that about one-third of the labour force was employed in 'peripheral' jobs in the mid-1980s. The idea of peripheral jobs is similar to the idea of jobs in the secondary labour market.

3 Economic change has hit particular parts of the country at different times leading to regional unemployment and poverty. Unemployment hit the North, Scotland, Wales, the Midlands and Northern Ireland in the early 1980s, but the South East experienced particular problems at the end of that decade and at the start of the 1990s.

4 The decline of unionism has reduced the ability of workers to defend their rights and thereby ensure that their employment prevents them falling into poverty. Union membership has declined, partly as a consequence of the increased employment of part-time workers who are less likely to be in unions. High unemployment and government legislation have reduced union power. This is reflected in a fall in the number of days lost in strikes. (See pp. 224–36 for a detailed discussion of unions in Britain.)

Dean and Taylor-Gooby sum up by saying that these changes have 'created a pattern of employment that increases the vulnerability to dependency on last-resort social welfare of those unable to gain access to secure and well-paid jobs'.

Poverty and power

The question of the power of the poor is examined by Ralph Miliband in an article entitled 'Politics and Poverty'. He argues that in terms of power, the poor are the weakest group competing for the scarce and valued resources in society. Miliband states that 'The poor are part of the working class but they are largely excluded from the organizations which have developed to defend the interests of the working class.' There are no organizations with the power of trade unions to represent the interests of the unemployed, the aged, the chronically sick or single-parent families. Because of their lack of income the poor do not have the resources to form powerful groups and sustain pressure.

Even if they were able to finance well-organized interest groups, the poor lack the economic sanctions to bring pressure to bear. Apart from low-paid workers, the main groups in poverty cannot take strike action and so threaten the interests of the powerful.

Their bargaining position is weakened still further by their inability to mobilize widespread working-class support, since non-poor members of the working class tend not to see their interests and those of the poor as similar. In fact there is a tendency for members of the working class to see certain groups in poverty, such as the unemployed, as 'scroungers' and 'layabouts'. Efforts by the poor to promote their interests and secure public support are weakened by the 'shame of poverty', a stigma which remains alive and well.

Compared to other interests in society which are represented by pressure groups such as employers' federations, trade unions, ratepayers' associations and motoring organizations, the poor are largely unseen and unheard. More often than not they have to rely on others championing their cause, for example, organizations such as Shelter and the Child Poverty Action Group, and former trade union leaders such as Jack Jones who has campaigned on behalf of the pensioners and low paid.

Ralph Miliband concludes that the key to the weak bargaining position of the poor is simply their poverty. He states that 'economic deprivation is a source of political deprivation; and political deprivation in turn helps to maintain and confirm economic deprivation'.

■ Poverty and stratification

Most conflict theorists move beyond explaining why particular individuals and groups are poor in an attempt to relate poverty to the organization of society as a whole. They claim that poverty is rooted in the very structure of society. The key concept used in this explanation is that of class, but some conflict theorists see class and poverty as less closely connected than others.

Peter Townsend – poverty, class and status

In the conclusion to *Poverty in the United Kingdom* Peter Townsend states 'The theoretical approach developed in this book is one rooted in class relations.' In particular he sees class as a major factor determining 'the production, distribution and redistribution of resources', or, in other words, who gets what. However, according to his definition, poverty is also related to the cultural patterns of a society, the lifestyles which govern 'the expectations attaching to membership of society'. The relationship between different classes is not a sufficient explanation of poverty because it does not entirely explain how lifestyles develop and certain types of social behaviour become expected.

Townsend's use of the word 'class' is closer to that of Weber than of Marx. He argues that the distribution of resources is not always directly related to the interests of capital and capitalists. Some agencies of the state, he claims, act in their own interests, or act as checks on the operations of capitalists, and not simply as committees for handling the affairs of the bourgeoisie. For example, the Civil Service might be more concerned with preserving its own status and power than with maximizing profits for capitalists. Agencies such as the Health and Safety Executive, which is concerned with implementing the legislation governing health and safety at work and elsewhere, may limit the behaviour that is allowed in the pursuit of profit. The labour market, Townsend points out, is not just influenced by individuals and groups competing for higher pay, but also by institutions such as the Equal Opportunities Commission. They therefore also have an effect on the extent of poverty.

Townsend uses the Weberian concept of **status** to explain the poverty of those reliant on state benefits. The poor are a group who, in addition to lacking wealth, lack prestige. To Townsend the low-status groups include retired elderly people, the disabled, the chronically sick, one-parent families and the long-term unemployed. As a consequence of their low status, their opportunities for access to paid employment are severely restricted. (These views are similar to Frank Field's arguments about the underclass, which we discussed on pp. 157–60.)

The internationalization of poverty

In more recent writing Townsend has stressed that poverty has an international dimension. International institutions such as the World Bank and the International Monetary Fund influence the distribution of resources in the world. The International Monetary Fund can impose conditions on governments which borrow money from it, which affect the poor. For example, they can ask governments to cut public expenditure by reducing the welfare programmes on which the poor rely.

Although these institutions mainly affect the poor in the Third World, others, such as the EC, have an important impact on the poor in the First World. For example, European employment legislation affects the rights of low-paid and part-time workers in member countries.

Furthermore the **internationalization of industry** affects poverty in the First and Third Worlds alike. Cheap labour in Third World countries may be paid poverty wages. This can also create poverty in the First World as jobs are transferred from the high-wage economies of Europe, North America and Japan to low-wage economies, and as a result, unemployment rises in the First World. Alternatively First World workers may be forced to take pay cuts as a consequence of competition from low-wage economies in Africa, Asia and South America. These pay cuts may push them into poverty.

Townsend argues, therefore, that poverty can no longer be explained or understood by examining any one country in isolation.

Marxism, class and poverty

Marxist sociologists place less emphasis than most theories of poverty on differentiating the poor from other members of the working class. Rather than seeing them as a separate group, Ralph Miliband believes they are simply the most disadvantaged section of the working class. Westergaard and Resler go further, claiming that concentrating on the special disadvantages of the poor 'diverts attention from the larger structure of inequality in which poverty is embedded'. Marxists would see Townsend as failing to emphasize these wider structures sufficiently. Miliband concludes:

The basic fact is that the poor are an integral part of the working class – its poorest and most disadvantaged stratum. They need to be seen as such, as part of a continuum, the more so as many workers who are not 'deprived' in the official sense live in permanent danger of entering the ranks of the deprived; and that they share in any case many of the disadvantages which afflict the deprived. Poverty is a class thing, closely linked to a general situation of class inequality.

Poverty and the capitalist system

To many Marxists, poverty can be explained in terms of how it benefits the ruling class. Poverty exists because it serves the interests of those who own the forces of production. It allows them to maintain the capitalist system and to maximize their profits.

Poverty and the labour market

Members of the subject class own only their labour which they must sell in return for wages on the open market. Capitalism requires a highly motivated workforce. Since the motivation to work is based primarily on monetary return, those whose services are not required by the economy, such as the aged and the unemployed, must receive a lower income than wage earners. If this were not the case, there would be little incentive to work.

The motivation of the workforce is also maintained by unequal rewards for work. Workers compete as individuals and groups with each other for income in a highly competitive society. In this respect, the low-wage sector forms the base of a competitive wage structure. Low wages help to reduce the wage demands of the workforce as a whole, since workers tend to assess their incomes in terms of the baseline provided by the low paid. J.C. Kincaid argues that 'standards of pay and conditions of work at the bottom of the heap influence the pattern of wages farther up the scale'. He maintains that low wages are essential to a capitalist economy since:

from the point of view of capitalism the low-wage sector helps to underpin and stabilize the whole structure of wages and the conditions of employment of the working class. The employers can tolerate no serious threat to the disciplines of the labour market and the competitive values which support the very existence of capitalism.

If the low-wage sector were abolished by an increase in the real value of the wages of the low paid, several of the possible consequences would be harmful to the capitalist class.

1 The delicate balance of pay differentials would be shattered. Other groups of workers might well demand, and possibly receive, real increases in their wages. This would reduce profit margins.

2 Wages within the working class might become increasingly similar. This might tend to unite a working class, which is now fragmented and divided by groups of workers competing against each other for higher wages. A move towards unity within the working class might well pose a threat to the capitalist class.

3 If the real value of the wages of the low paid were increased, the pool of cheap labour, on which many labour-intensive capitalist industries depend for profit, might disappear.

Containment and the working class

Since, from a Marxist perspective, the state in capitalist society reflects the interests of the ruling class, government measures can be expected to do little except reduce the harsher effects of poverty. Thus Kincaid argues:

It is not to be expected that any Government whose main concern is with the efficiency of a capitalist economy is going to take effective steps to abolish the low-wage sector.

Despite claims to the contrary, there is little evidence that the welfare state has led to a major redistribution of wealth from the rich to the poor. Westergaard and Resler dismiss the theory that the welfare state, by using the power of the state to modify the workings of market forces, has created a more equal distribution of wealth. They argue:

The state's social services are financed largely from the wages of those for whose security they are primarily designed. They make for little redistribution from capital and top salaries ... they reshuffle resources far more within classes – between earners and dependants, healthy people and the sick, households of different composition, from one point in the individual's life cycle to another – than they do between classes.

Thus the bulk of monies received by members of the working class have been paid or will be paid in the form of taxes by themselves or other members of that class.

Westergaard and Resler argue that the ruling class has responded to the demands of the labour movement by allowing the creation of the welfare state, but the system operates 'within a framework of institutions and assumptions that remain capitalist'. In their view, 'the keyword is "containment"': the demands of the labour movement have been contained within the existing system. Westergaard and Resler argue that poverty exists because of the operation of a capitalist economic system which prevents the poor from obtaining the financial resources to become non-poor.

Kincaid summarizes the situation in the following way: 'It is not simply that there are rich and poor. It is rather that some are rich *because* some are poor.' Thus poverty can only be understood in terms of the operation of the class system as a whole since the question 'Why poverty?' is basically the same question as 'Why wealth?' Therefore from a Marxist perspective, poverty like wealth, is an inevitable consequence of a capitalist system.

The Marxist view appears to show why poverty exists, but is less successful than other conflict approaches in explaining why particular groups and individuals become poor. It is not particularly sensitive to variations in income within the working class. It fails to differentiate clearly the poor from other members of the working class, and to provide an explanation of their poverty.

■ The 'functions' of poverty

In *More Equality*, Herbert J. Gans argues that 'poverty survives in part because it is useful to a number of groups in society'. Poverty benefits the non-poor in general and the rich and powerful in particular. They therefore have a vested interest in maintaining poverty. For them poverty is not a social problem. From this perspective, Gans outlines the following **functions of poverty** for the non-poor.

1 Every economy has a number of temporary, dead-end, dirty, dangerous and menial jobs. The existence of poverty ensures that such work is done. Gans argues that 'poverty functions to provide a low-wage labour pool that is willing – or rather, unable to be unwilling – to perform dirty work at low cost'. Without the low paid, many industries would be unable to continue in their present form. Gans claims that hospitals, the catering trade, large sections of agriculture and parts of the garment industry are dependent on low-wage labour. Raising wages would increase costs with 'obvious dysfunctional consequences for more affluent people'. Thus at one and the same time, poverty ensures that 'dirty jobs' are done and, by getting them done cheaply, subsidizes the non-poor sections of the population.

2 Poverty directly provides employment and financial security for a fast-growing section of the labour force. In Gans's words 'Poverty creates jobs for a number of occupations and professions that serve the poor, or shield the rest of the population from them.' These include the police, probation officers, social workers, psychiatrists, doctors and the administrators who oversee the 'poverty industry'. In Britain, the social security system employed some 80,000 staff in 1976 and the cost of administration amounted to £649 million. However altruistic their motives, Gans suggests that those employed to deal with the poor have a vested interest in poverty.

3 Gans argues that the presence of the poor provides reassurance and support for the rest of society. They provide a baseline of failure which reassures the non-poor of their worth. Gans claims that 'poverty helps to guarantee the status of those who are not poor'. It does this by providing 'a reliable and relatively permanent measuring rod for status comparison'. Since they are relatively powerless, the poor also provide an effective scapegoat for the non-poor. Gans maintains that 'The defenders of the desirability of hard work, thrift, honesty and monogamy need people who can be accused of being lazy, spendthrift, dishonest and promiscuous to justify these norms.' Gans argues that the poor function to reinforce mainstream norms since norms 'are best legitimated by discovering violations'.

From a somewhat different perspective, therefore, Gans has reached a similar conclusion to those who argue that poverty must be analysed in terms of class inequality. From both viewpoints poverty exists because it benefits the rich and because the poor are powerless to change their situation. Gans concludes that poverty persists 'because many of the functional alternatives to poverty would be quite dysfunctional for the more affluent members of society'.

We have now outlined various responses to the first three questions posed at the beginning of this chapter. In the final section we will turn our attention to the fourth question: 'What are the solutions to poverty?'

■ Poverty – solutions and values

Initially we will consider government measures to deal with poverty and proposals to solve poverty, together with the ideologies which underlie them. First, the ideological aspects of the culture of poverty thesis will be examined, since it formed the basis for government policy in the fight against poverty in the USA.

Like all members of society, sociologists see the world in terms of their own values and political beliefs, despite their attempts to be objective. This is particularly apparent in the area of poverty research. Gans has suggested that 'perhaps the most significant fact about poverty research is that it is being carried out entirely by middle-class researchers who differ – in class, culture, and political power – from the people they are studying'.

Some observers argue that the picture of the poor presented by many social scientists is largely a reflection of middle-class value judgements. In particular, the idea of a culture of poverty has been strongly criticized as a product of middle-class prejudice. Charles A. Valentine in *Culture and Poverty*, a forceful attack on bias in poverty research, states:

Scarcely a description can be found that does not dwell on the noxiousness, pathology, distortion, disorganization, instability or incompleteness of poverty culture as compared to the life of the middle classes.

From the viewpoint of the culture of poverty, the poor themselves are a major obstacle to the removal of poverty. It therefore follows that at least a part of the solution to poverty is to change the poor, since, by implication, they are partly to blame for their situation. The direction in which the poor must be changed is also influenced by

middle-class values: they must adopt middle-class norms and values. In short, as Valentine puts it, 'the poor must become "middle class"'.

The war on poverty

Many observers argue that this line of reasoning formed the basis of USA's government policy towards poverty. In 1964, President Lyndon B. Johnson declared a '**war on poverty**' with the passing of the Economic Opportunity Act and the formation of the Office of Economic Opportunity to coordinate measures to fight poverty. The comments of the American anthropologist Thomas Gladwin represent the views of many social scientists on this campaign:

The whole conception of the War on Poverty rests upon a definition of poverty as a way of life. The intellectual climate in which it was nurtured was created by studies of the culture of poverty, notably those of Oscar Lewis . . . (which) provide the basis for programs at the national level designed very explicitly to correct the social, occupational and psychological deficits of people born and raised to a life of poverty.

The Office of Economic Opportunity created a series of programmes designed to re-socialize the poor and remove their presumed deficiencies.

1 The Job Corps set up residential camps in wilderness areas for unemployed, inner-city youth with the aim of 'building character' and fostering initiative and determination.

2 Many 'work experience' programmes were developed to instil 'work habits'.

3 The Neighbourhood Youth Corps created part-time and holiday jobs for young people.

4 A multitude of job training schemes were started to encourage 'work incentive' and provide the skills required for employment.

The aim of many of these schemes was to undo the presumed effect of the culture of poverty by fostering ambition, motivation and initiative.

To counter the culture of poverty at an earlier age, government money was pumped into schools in low-income districts with the aim of raising educational standards. Operation Head Start, begun in January 1965, was intended to nip the culture of poverty in the bud. It was an extensive programme of pre-school education for the children of low-income families. According to Charles Valentine:

> Head Start is one of the many current programs designed to inculcate a middle-class 'culture' among the poor with the hope that so equipped they may eventually rise from their poverty.

Much of the effort of the Office of Economic Opportunity was directed towards **community action,** the idea of local community self-help. The Office encouraged and financed self-help organizations run by the poor which covered a range of projects from job training and community business ventures to legal services and youth clubs. The idea was for the poor, with help, to pull themselves up by their own bootstraps, to throw aside the culture of poverty and become enterprising and full of initiative like their middle-class mentors.

Compared to the above programmes, direct aid in the form of cash payments to the poor received low priority. Edward James in *America Against Poverty*, a study of the 1960s war on poverty, states that direct aid was the 'least popular antipoverty strategy in America'.

Why the war on poverty was lost

The war on poverty was not designed to eradicate poverty by providing the poor with sufficient income to raise them above the poverty line. Lee Rainwater argues:

> The goal of the war was not to directly provide resources that would cancel out poverty, but to provide opportunities so that people could achieve their own escape from poverty.

By changing the poor it was hoped to provide them with the opportunity to become upwardly mobile. S.M. Miller and Pamela Roby state 'The programs aimed at the young, like Head Start, obviously aim for intergenerational social mobility while those designed for older people seek intragenerational mobility.'

The war on poverty is a typically American solution reflecting the values of American culture with its emphasis on individual achievement in the land of opportunity. As Walter B. Miller neatly puts it, 'Nothing could be more impeccably American than the concept of opportunity.' The poor must make their own way: they must achieve the status of being non-poor, they must seize the opportunities that are available like every other respectable American. Commenting on the war on poverty, Elinor Graham states:

> Above all, it is 'the American way' to approach social-welfare issues, for it places the burden of responsibility upon the individual and not on the socio-economic system. Social services are preferred to income payments in an ideological atmosphere which abhors 'handouts'.

By the late 1960s many social scientists felt that the war on poverty had failed, as did the poor if the following comment by a welfare recipient is typical: 'It's great stuff this War on Poverty! Where do I surrender?' (quoted in James 1970, p. 61). The poor remained stubbornly poor despite the energy and resolve of the Office of Economic Opportunity. Increasingly sociologists argued that solutions to poverty must be developed from stratification theory rather than the culture of poverty theory.

From this perspective, Miller and Roby argue that 'poverty programs should be recognized as efforts to engineer changes in the stratification profiles of the United States'. They and others argue that the very concept of poverty and the way in which it spotlights and isolates the poor has disguised the true nature of inequality, and proved to be counterproductive in providing solutions.

Once poverty is recognized as an aspect of inequality, and not merely a problem of the poor, solutions involve restructuring society as a whole. It can now be argued that the main obstacle to the eradication of poverty is not the behaviour of the poor but the self-interest of the rich. Thus Gans maintains that 'the prime obstacles to the elimination of poverty lie in an economic system which is dedicated to the maintenance and increase of wealth among the already affluent'.

Stratification and solutions to poverty

From the perspective of stratification theory, the solution to poverty involves a change in the stratification system. This war on poverty would be far harder to wage than the previous one since it would require considerable sacrifice by the rich and powerful.

The degree of change required is debatable and proposals reflect to some degree the values and political bias of the researchers. The suggestions put forward by Miller and Roby are rather vague. They advocate 'A re-allocation of American wealth to meet a reasonable set of priorities, a redistribution of goods and power to benefit the bottom half of the population.' However they hasten to add 'we are not implicitly arguing the case for complete equality'.

Lee Rainwater's proposals are more specific. He advocates a redistribution of income so that 'no family has an income that is below the average for all families'. He proposes the money be raised by redistributing only increases in national income rather than reducing the current income of the more wealthy. This he believes 'avoids the problems of direct confrontation involved in the older model of "soaking the rich to give to the poor"'.

But neither Rainwater nor Miller and Roby propose an alternative to the capitalist economic system. They assume that the changes they propose can take place within the context of American capitalism.

The war on poverty has its basis in traditional American liberalism.

1 It is **American** because of its insistence on individual initiative, its emphasis on opportunity and its distaste for direct provision of cash payments to the poor.

2 It is **liberal** because the reforms it attempted did not seek to alter the basic structure of society: American capitalism was taken for granted and any change in the situation of the poor must take place within its framework.

While the solutions to poverty proposed by American sociologists such as Rainwater, Miller and Roby are more radical and would involve modifications to the structure of society, they remain basically liberal. They would take place within the framework of capitalism and would not involve a fundamental change in the structure of society.

Even so, they had little influence on the policies followed by Presidents Reagan and Bush in the 1980s and 1990s. According to Richard H. Ropers, these involved drastic cuts in programmes for those on low incomes, increases in taxation for the low paid and reductions for the wealthiest. Reagan and Bush's policies were based on 'New Right' theories which were also influential in Britain. They are discussed in the next section.

Poverty and the expansion of welfare in Britain

In Britain governments have not declared war on poverty. Between 1945 and 1979 successive governments were less averse than their American counterparts to providing cash payments to the poor, and to providing universal services (such as education and healthcare) to everyone regardless of ability to pay. Governments added to the provisions of the welfare state partly with the aim of alleviating poverty.

Critics argued that these developments were inadequate. According to Kincaid benefits to the poor were 'pitifully low' and 'left millions in poverty'. The harsher edges of poverty may have been blunted by the welfare state, but poverty, at least in relative terms, remained. Welfare professionals may have cushioned some of the misery produced by poverty, but they had not solved the problem.

New Right solutions

Margaret Thatcher's and John Major's Conservative Governments after 1979 followed rather different policies. Inspired by the ideas of the New Right, they decided to try to reduce welfare expenditure, move away from universal benefits and services, and target resources on the poor.

The intention was to free economic resources to create a more dynamic economy. As the economy grew, and living standards rose, economic success would 'trickle down' to those on low incomes so that their living standards would rise along with everyone else's. Reducing or replacing universal benefits would destroy the dependency culture which made people rely too heavily on state hand-outs. Means-tested benefits like income support would go only to those who were not in a position to help themselves and who were in genuine need.

In line with these policies the welfare system was reformed in April 1987. Supplementary benefit was replaced by income support. Before 1987 the single-payments system allowed those on a low income to claim money for necessities such as household equipment, furniture, clothing and bedding, which they could not otherwise afford. This system was replaced by the social fund, under which loans rather than grants for such necessities became the norm. These loans had to be paid back out of benefit received. Only those who could afford to pay back the loans were offered them: some individuals were too poor to be given loans. The Government argued that this system would make claimants more responsible and encourage them to plan ahead in managing household budgets. The Government also cut the amount spent on housing benefits. Much of the money saved by the latter measure was spent on replacing family income supplement with family credit. Both were means-tested benefits designed to boost the incomes of those with low incomes, but family credit was more generous.

In September 1988 the Government raised the age at which people became entitled to income support from 16 to 18. In theory all 16 and 17 year olds were guaranteed a place on a Youth Training Scheme which would provide them with an income. The intention was to prevent the young becoming victims of the dependency culture.

Criticisms of New Right policies

Critics argued that far from reducing poverty these measures increased it. Many of those reliant on welfare had their income cut. With the replacement of single payments by the social fund some people were unable to buy necessities. The Child Poverty Action Group claimed that there were insufficient YTS places for all 16 and 17 year olds. Those who were not supported by their families and who could not find employment or a place on a training scheme could end up destitute and homeless.

The Conservative Government claimed, however, that its policies benefited those on low incomes. According to government figures, the average income of the poorest 20 per cent of the population rose by 5.5 per cent in real terms between 1979 and 1985. This, the Government claimed, supported its view that the benefits of economic growth would trickle down to those on low incomes.

However, the economist John Hills points out that the government's figures did not take account of changes in indirect taxes such as VAT and duties on petrol, alcohol and tobacco. Hills claims that when these are taken into account the real income of the poorest 20 per cent of households actually fell by 6 per cent between 1979 and 1986. Over the same period the richest 20 per cent of households saw their real income rise by 26 per cent. If his figures are correct, they seem to undermine the New Right's claim that prosperity will automatically solve the problem of poverty.

Most of the evidence contained in earlier sections of this chapter suggests that poverty increased in the late 1980s and early 1990s, again indicating that New Right policies may have added to the problem rather than solving it.

Welfare and redistribution as solutions to poverty

Some feel the answer to poverty is to be found in improving welfare provisions. Mack and Lansley claimed that raising benefit levels can have a significant impact. To 'solve' the problem they estimated that supplementary benefit (now income support) would need to rise to 150 per cent of its then level, but the problem could be reduced by lower rises. On the basis of their opinion poll evidence they concluded 'People do accept that the problems of the poor should be tackled, and that the state has a responsibility to tackle them.'

Furthermore, the majority of the public declared themselves willing to make sacrifices to achieve this objective. Some 74 per cent said they would accept a 1 pence in the pound increase in income tax in order to help the poor. However, only 34 per cent were prepared to support a 5 pence in the pound increase for the same purpose, which would, according to Mack and Lansley lift between one-third and one-half of the poor out of poverty. Mack and Lansley admit that poverty could not be eradicated in the lifetime of one parliament, but despite this they believe it is possible to make major inroads into the problem. There is enough public support for a policy to help the poor for a government at least to make a start without losing popularity.

Peter Townsend sees the solution to poverty resting on a wider range of measures including the alteration of welfare provisions and action to redistribute wealth, income and power.

1 He proposes higher levels of benefit in relation to average wages and measures to eradicate unemployment.

2 In addition he suggests that the state should abolish excessive wealth and income by imposing legally enforced maximums.

3 Furthermore, public ownership and industrial democracy should be expanded so that power becomes more widely dispersed and the other changes become politically possible.

Despite the radical nature of the changes he proposes, he stops short of suggesting revolutionary change. He adds:

It would be wrong to suggest that any of this is easy or even likely. The citadels of wealth and privilege are deeply entrenched and have shown a tenacious capacity to withstand assaults.

Carol Walker and Alan Walker also argue for a wide range of measures to tackle poverty.

1 They criticize recent government emphasis in Britain on using means-tested benefit. They claim that such benefits are difficult and costly to administer, tend to create disincentives to work and remain unclaimed by a sizeable minority of those who are entitled to them. For example, in 1989 £470 million in housing benefit and £1,020 million in income support went unclaimed.

2 Walker and Walker would prefer a greater emphasis on universal benefits which, although expensive, are more effective at reducing poverty and encouraging people to escape from dependence on welfare.

3 To them it is 'incomprehensible' that some people being paid benefits also have to pay tax. An integration of the tax and benefits systems could remove such anomalies and help ensure that everybody has the means to avoid poverty.

4 They would also like to see more policies aimed at preventing people from falling into poverty. In particular they would like governments to have an 'active employment strategy' which would provide work for the unemployed and help to give the disabled and lone parents the opportunity to earn their own living.

Frank Field's suggestions for changes in government policy to help the underclass can also be seen as possible solutions to poverty. (See pp. 159–60.)

■ Marxist solutions

Given the sort of difficulties that Townsend mentions, some Marxist sociologists do not accept that such changes are possible within a capitalist system. While capitalism remains, significant changes in the provisions of the welfare state are impossible. The 'walls of the citadels of wealth and privilege' will not be breached without a full-scale assault which seeks not merely to breach them, but to destroy them altogether. Because Marxists see poverty as simply one aspect of inequality, the solution to poverty does not involve reforms in the social security system, in the provision of additional payments or services to those defined as poor. Instead it requires a radical change in the structure of society. Thus, Ralph Miliband argues that poverty will only be eradicated with the removal of inequality in general which 'requires the transformation of the economic structures in which it is embedded'.

Westergaard and Resler take a similar view, maintaining that no substantial redistribution of wealth can occur until capitalism is replaced by a socialist society in which the forces of production are communally owned. As long as the free market system of capitalism determines the allocation of reward, they argue that inequality will remain largely unchanged. Kincaid concludes that, since capitalism is based on the maximization of profit rather than the satisfaction of human need, 'poverty cannot be abolished within capitalist society, but only in a socialist society under workers' control, in which human needs, and not profits, determine the allocation of resources'.

Clearly Marxist views are ideologically based. Sociologists who adopt them are committed to the principles of socialism and equality. They regard capitalism as an exploitive system and condemn the inequality it generates. However, there seems little immediate prospect that the changes they propose will take place in Britain, the USA or other capitalist countries. A communist revolution does not seem imminent and, furthermore, even the more moderate policies suggested by Peter Townsend do not appear to enjoy either widespread public support or the support of any of the major political parties.

Mack and Lansley's research offers some hope for the poor in Britain. It indicates that members of the public would be prepared to accept some improvements in benefits provided by the state for the poor even if it hit their own pockets. If this minimal action is not taken, then many would agree with the conclusion of these researchers that the outlook is bleak for people like the 59-year-old benefit claimant they interviewed. He said 'I'm wondering whether it's worthwhile going on living, quite honestly. It's not living, it's existing.'

4

Work, unemployment and leisure

4

Work, unemployment and leisure

The nature of work

Defining work and non-work

The concept of **work** appears easy to define, but in reality it is not. Keith Grint claims that 'no unambiguous or objective definition of work is possible'. He examines a number of definitions to illustrate his point.

1 First, he considers whether work can be seen as 'that which ensures individual and societal survival by engaging with nature'. One problem with this definition is that many activities commonly regarded as work – for example writing sociology books! – may not be seen as essential or necessary for a society's survival.

2 Second, he argues that work cannot defined simply as employment. Many activities in which people are employed are also done by people who are not employed. Examples include washing up, ironing, childminding and even breastfeeding.

3 Third, Grint denies that work can be defined as 'something we have to do' whether we like it or not. Eating and drinking come into this category but are not usually seen as work.

4 Fourth, work cannot be seen as non-leisure activities. Activities which are leisure for some may be work for others, such as playing football. In any case work and leisure can take place simultaneously and be hard to separate. A round of golf for a manager with an important customer may combine work and leisure. In some societies work and leisure run together in nearly all activities. Grint refers to the anthropologist Malinowski's study of the Trobriand Islands where it was found that there 'is no separation between the work of gardening and the associated rituals – they are one and the same process'.

Grint concludes that work is socially defined: any definition has to be specific to a particular society at a particular time. He says 'Work, then, in its physical features and its linguistic descriptions is socially constructed . . . there are aspects of social activities which we construe as work and this embodies social organization.'

In modern Western societies Grint sees employment as a type of work, but not the only type. Whether other activities are seen as work depends upon 'whose interpretation of the activity carries the most weight'. Grint himself, for example, clearly defines housework as work, but he recognizes that some people do not and he says:

> the subordinate and gendered status of domestic labour and its popular classification as non-work is a valuable reminder of the significance of patriarchal ideology in the evaluation of work.

In other words it is men's definitions of work which have usually carried the most weight with the result that much of the effort expended by women has not been seen as work.

Attitudes to work in pre-industrial societies

Attitudes towards work have varied historically and from society to society. Furthermore, they vary within society and may be the focus for considerable conflict. These varying attitudes reflect the values and sometimes the interests of those who hold them.

According to Keith Grint, the ancient Greeks regarded work as part of 'the sphere of necessity' as opposed to 'the sphere of freedom'. It was looked down on and a good deal of the work was performed by slaves. He says:

anyone who *had* to work at an occupation all the time was ignoble, and. . . the essence of ennoblement lay in the realm of politics, a realm based on but untarnished by, the labour of other, lesser mortals.

In hunter–gatherer societies the situation is somewhat different. Grint claims that productive activity is kept to the minimum necessary. There is no work ethic and as soon as there is enough food, hunting and gathering stops. In fact such societies often have no concept of work as such and 'Work and non-work are not so much merged as irrelevant terms to describe the activity.'

In pre-industrial Britain before the advent of factories most work took place in or close to the home. Agriculture and domestic textile production were the two most common types of work for lower classes. A number of historians and sociologists have argued that pre-industrial workers did only as much work as they felt they had to. Shoshana Zuboff says:

Work patterns were irregular, alternating between intense effort and idleness. Most work activities emanated from the home, and the distractions of the family, the taverns, and the social web of the community limited any undivided attention to work.

Domestic textile workers retained considerable control over their work and they frequently resisted efforts to get them to work harder. There was a widespread practice of 'St Monday'. People would work extra hard for part of the week to enable them to have Monday off. This custom often followed on from weekend drinking sessions and early industrial entrepreneurs such as James Watt found their workers would be drunk if they tried to force them to work on Monday

Higher classes too, had little enthusiasm for physical labour. Zuboff argues that three influences produced a contempt for labour which went back as far as the Middle Ages.

1 First, the Greek and Roman tradition which saw labour as associated with slavery.

2 Second, 'the barbarian heritage that disdained those who worked the land and extolled the warrior who gained his livelihood in bloody booty'.

3 Third, a Jewish and Christian tradition which 'admired contemplation over action'. It is notable that the Bible sees work as punishment for sin. Since Adam and Eve were expelled from the Garden of Eden, humans have had to earn their living by the sweat of their brow.

Until a few centuries ago, then, work has generally been an irrelevant concept or has been seen as something to be avoided altogether or at least minimized. Until relatively recently working hours for individuals were not regular. Yet many contemporary studies of the unemployed have shown that many of them miss work a great deal, and not just because their income drops (see pp. 247–50). Modern Western attitudes towards work are therefore very different from those in ancient, hunter–gatherer or pre-industrial societies. This raises the question of where have these contemporary attitudes come from.

■ The origin of contemporary attitudes to work

Following the ideas of Weber, some sociologists have argued that protestantism had an important role in producing a contemporary work ethic. Weber argued that certain forms of Protestantism, particularly those based on Calvinism, encouraged a distinctive attitude to work. Calvinists saw their work as a calling from God and they worked with dedication and commitment to convince themselves that God had chosen them to go to heaven. (Weber's ideas are examined in detail on pp. 459–62.)

The **Protestant work ethic**, as it is sometimes known, encouraged a much more positive attitude towards work than had been the case before. The elevation of work to a moral duty was encouraged by Victorian Englishmen such as Samuel Smiles. Keith Grint quotes Smiles's doctrine that 'Heaven helps those who help themselves.' The belief of such Victorians in saving money and not wasting it, working hard and living sober lifestyles, closely resembles the beliefs of early Calvinists.

The Industrial Revolution itself was the second major source of modern attitudes to work. The historian E.P. Thompson argues that large-scale, machine-powered industry necessitated the introduction of new working patterns and with them new attitudes. According to Thompson pre-industrial work was regulated by **task orientation**: the necessities of the job determined when and how hard people worked. For example, the changing seasons regulated agricultural work while domestic textile workers determined how hard they worked and when they completed their tasks. Work and leisure werc intermingled so there was 'no great sense of conflict between labour and passing the time of day'.

With industrialization the expensive machinery had to be kept in use to repay the capital costs and employers therefore sought to, and eventually succeeded in, imposing regular work patterns on employees.

These patterns of work were based round time rather than tasks. Thompson says 'Time is now currency: it is not passed but spent.' Workers who were used to a considerable amount of control over their work patterns experienced the new working day in the factory, with its emphasis on punctuality, as oppressive. They resented having to work to the clock. The early factory owners had considerable problems trying to persuade people to take jobs in the factories. When they had recruited workers they often regarded their reluctant employees as work-shy and lazy. They therefore sought to change their attitudes and get them to accept new working patterns. According to David Lee and Howard Newby:

---

workers brought up under the assumptions of 'task orientation', were subject to massive indoctrination on the folly of 'wasting' time by their employers, a moral critique of idleness which stemmed from the Puritan work ethic.

Many contemporary attitudes to work can be traced back to such Victorian ideas. These include the unemployed demanding the right to work, students and young adults working hard to progress in their career, and employers penalizing workers who are persistently late. However, both during the Industrial Revolution and since, some individuals and groups have questioned the virtue of devoting themselves to work or the wisdom of feeling guilty if they are 'wasting time'. For example, Keith Grint quotes the Russian anarchist Kropoptkin who attacked the Victorian work ethic saying:

---

let us begin by satisfying our needs of life, joy and freedom. And once all will have experienced this well-being we will set to work to demolish the last vestiges of the bourgeois regime, its morality derived from the account book.

Clearly, Kropotkin's views are emotive and value-laden, but the same can be said of those who have glorified hard work.

Different sociological views on work, leisure and unemployment have also been strongly influenced by the values of their authors. Indeed, sociologists who are strongly committed to an ideal of work and leisure often produce the most interesting and influential views on the subject. Karl Marx (whose ideas are similar to those of Kropotkin) is a case in point, and we will examine his views in the next section.

■ Work and leisure – conflict perspectives

■ Karl Marx – alienated labour

To Marx, work – the production of goods and services – held the key to human happiness and fulfilment. Work is the most important, the primary human activity. As such it can provide the means either to fulfil people's potential or to distort and pervert their nature and their relationships with others.

In his early writings Marx developed the idea of **alienated labour**. At its simplest **alienation** means

that people are unable to find satisfaction and fulfilment in performing their labour or in the products of their labour. Unable to express their true nature in their work, they are estranged from themselves: they are strangers to their real selves. Since work is a social activity, alienation from work also involves alienation from others. Individuals are cut off from their fellow workers.

Marx believed that work provided the most important and vital means for people to fulfil their basic needs, their individuality and their humanity. By expressing their personality in the creation of a product, workers can experience a deep satisfaction. In seeing their product used and appreciated by others, they satisfy their needs and thereby express their care and humanity for others. In a community in which everyone works to satisfy both their individual needs and the needs of others, work is a completely fulfilling activity. In Marx's words 'each of us would in his production have doubly affirmed himself and his fellow men'.

Apart from possibly the dawn of human history, Marx argued that this ideal has yet to be realized. Throughout history humanity's relationship to its work has been destructive both to the human spirit and to human relationships.

The origins of alienation

Marx speculated that the origin of alienation is to be found in an economic system involving the exchange of goods by a method of barter. Within such a system the products of labour become **commodities**, articles of trade. With the introduction of money as a medium of exchange, they become commodities for buying and selling, articles of commerce. The products of labour are mere 'objects' in the market, no longer a means of fulfilling the needs of the individual and the community. From an end in themselves, they become a means to an end: a means for acquiring the goods and services necessary for survival. Goods are no longer a part of the individual who produces them. In this way 'the worker is related to the *product of his labour* as to an *alien* object'.

Alienation springs initially from the exchange of goods in some form of market system. From this develops the idea and practice of private property, the individual ownership of the means of production. Marx argues that 'although private property appears to be the basis and the cause of alienated labour, it is rather a consequence of the latter.' Once the products of labour are regarded as commodity objects, it is only a short step to the idea of private ownership. A system of private property then feeds back on to the forces which produced it and heightens the level of alienation. This can be illustrated by capitalist economies in which the ownership of the means of production is concentrated in the hands of a small minority. Alienation is increased by the fact that workers do

not own the goods they produce.

From the idea that workers are alienated from the product of their labour stems a number of consequences. Workers become alienated from the act of production, their actual work. Since work is the primary human activity, they become alienated from themselves. As a result, the worker:

---

does not fulfil himself in his work but denies himself, has a feeling of misery rather than well-being, does not develop freely his mental and physical energies but is physically exhausted and mentally debased. The worker therefore feels himself at home only during his leisure time, whereas at work he feels homeless.

Work ceases to become an end in itself, a satisfaction and fulfilment of human needs. It simply becomes a means for survival. As a means to an end work cannot produce real fulfilment.

Alienated from the product of their work, the performance of their labour and from themselves, workers are also alienated from their fellows. They work to maintain the existence of themselves and their families, not for the benefit of the community. Self-interest becomes more important than concern for the social group.

Marx regarded the economic system, the **infrastructure**, as the foundation of society which ultimately shaped all other aspects of social life. He divided the infrastructure into two parts: the 'means of production' and the 'relations of production'.

The means of production are the more important since, according to Marx, 'The social relations within which individuals produce, *the social relations of production, are altered, transformed, with the change and development of the material means of production*.' The **means of production** are the means used for producing goods. Thus, under feudalism, an agrarian economy, land is the most important part of the means of production. Under capitalism, the raw materials and machinery used to manufacture the products of industry are major aspects of the means of production.

The **relations of production** are the social relationships associated with the means of production. In a capitalist economy, the relationship of the two main groups in society to the means of production is that of ownership and non-ownership. The capitalists own the means of production;

the workers simply own their labour which, as wage earners, they offer for hire to the capitalists.

Alienation and capitalism

Marx argued that the nature of work in society can only be understood by examining it in terms of the infrastructure. He believed that a capitalist infrastructure inevitably produced a high level of alienation.

In a capitalist economy, a small minority own the means of production. Workers neither own nor have any control over the goods they produce. Like their products, workers are reduced to the level of a commodity. A monetary value is placed on their work and the costs of labour are assessed in the same way as the costs of machinery and raw materials. Like the commodities they manufacture, workers are at the mercy of market forces, of the law of supply and demand. During an economic recession many workers will find themselves jobless with few means of support. However, the unemployed are not alienated in the conventional Marxist sense of the word. Alienation is a consequence of wage labour.

Wage labour is a system of slavery involving the exploitation of workers. Only labour produces wealth yet workers receive, in the form of wages, only a part of the wealth they create. The remainder is **appropriated** (taken) in the form of profits by the capitalists. Thus, the majority of society's members, the **proletariat**, usually work for and are exploited by a minority, the **bourgeoisie**.

Capitalism is based on self-interest, avarice and greed. It is a system of cut-throat competition concerned with the maximization of profit rather than the satisfaction of real human need. Trapped within this system, both capitalists and workers are alienated from their true selves. Members of both groups are preoccupied with self-interest in a system which sets individual against individual in a struggle for survival and personal gain.

Marx saw two important characteristics of industrial society – the mechanization of production and a further specialization of the division of labour – as contributing to the alienation of the workforce. However, he stressed that the capitalist economic system, rather than industrialization as such, is the primary source of alienation.

Marx argued that the **mechanization of production** reduces the physical effort involved in work but 'The lightening of the labour even

becomes a sort of torture, since the machine does not free the labourer from work, but deprives it of all interest.' Mechanization and associated mass production reduces the need for skill and intelligence and removes from work:

> all individual character and consequently all charm for the workman. He becomes an appendage of the machine, and it is only the most simple, most monotonous, and most easily acquired knack, that is required of him.

Industrial society also involves a **further specialization of the division of labour**. People are trapped in their occupational roles since they must specialize in a particular activity in order to earn their living. In Marx's words 'each man has a particular exclusive sphere of activity, which is forced upon him from which he cannot escape.' Freedom and fulfilment are not possible when people are imprisoned in a specialized occupation since only a limited part of themselves can be expressed in one job. As we shall see, this is very different from Durkheim's assessment (see pp. 184–6.)

Communism and the end of alienation

Marx's solution to the problem of alienated labour is a communist or socialist society in which the means of production are communally owned and the specialized division of labour is abolished. He believed that capitalism contained the seeds of its own destruction: the concentration of alienated workers in large-scale industrial enterprises would encourage an awareness of exploitation, of common interest and facilitate organization to overthrow the ruling capitalist class. In a communist society workers would at one and the same time produce goods for themselves and the community, and so satisfy both individual and collective needs.

Evaluation

Marx's theory of alienation has been criticized in a number of ways. His views on alienation under communism have been regarded as simplistic and

naive by many critics. In his analysis of East European Communism, Milovan Djilas argues that
though the means of production were communally
owned, they were controlled by and for the benefit
of a ruling elite. He claims that 'Labour cannot be
free in a society where all material goods are
monopolized by one group.'

Marx also gives little indication of how the
specialized division of labour can be abolished in
socialist society. He simply states that:

---

in a communist society, where nobody has one
exclusive sphere of activity but each can become
accomplished in any branch he wishes, society regulates the general production and thus makes it
possible for me to do one thing today and another
thing tomorrow, to hunt in the morning, fish in the
afternoon, rear cattle in the evening, criticize after
dinner, just as I have a mind, without ever becoming hunter, fisherman, shepherd or critic.

Marx thus pictures a society in which members are
able to train for those jobs which interest them
and move from one task to another as the mood
takes them.

Many critics have questioned the practical possibility of such a system. The collapse of communism in the former USSR and Eastern Europe
during the late 1980s and early 1990s suggests
that the abolition of the specialized division of
labour is unlikely to take place.

Marx has also been attacked for his work on
alienation by some Marxists. Some have argued
that this early part of his work is too abstract and
philosophical. As defined by Marx, alienation is
impossible to measure. Workers cannot be asked if
they are alienated since their alienation would
prevent them realizing that they were. It is therefore also impossible to support or disprove his
theory. Marxists such as Louis Althusser have
therefore dismissed this part of Marx's writings as
unscientific. They argue that only Marx's later
writings focusing on economics and exploitation
provide a proper basis for a scientific Marxist
understanding of society.

We will deal with further criticisms of Marx's
views as the chapter progresses, but for an examination of the concept of alienation within the
general framework of Marxist theory, see Chapter
14, pp. 880–2.

■ Herbert Marcuse –
alienation from work and
leisure

Marcuse is a neo-Marxist who has tried to develop
Marx's original theory of alienation. Although he
accepts much of Marx's work, Marcuse places less
emphasis than Marx himself on the centrality of
work to people's lives. He puts more stress on the
consumption of products.

When Marx first outlined his views on alienated labour – in 1844 – workers in industry
worked between twelve and sixteen hours a day.
Alienated in the factory, workers had few opportunities for fulfilment in leisure. They had time for
little else save what Marx described as 'animal
functions' – eating, sleeping and procreating.
Existing on subsistence wages, often in appalling
living conditions, workers had few means for self-
fulfilment in leisure even if they did have the time.
Marx regarded non-work time as simply a means
for the workforce, the fodder of capitalism, to
recover and recuperate from its labour – and
reproduce itself.

Advanced industrial society has seen a significant reduction in working hours – in Western
Europe and America industrial employees work
on average between forty and forty-six hours a
week – and a steady rise in the living standards of
the population as a whole. It would appear that
the opportunity for self-fulfilment in leisure has
greatly increased but many neo-Marxists argue
that this opportunity has not been realized.

Leisure and 'false needs'

In *One Dimensional Man*, Marcuse discusses both
capitalist societies and the former communist societies of Eastern Europe. He argues that all
advanced industrial societies crush the potential
for personal development. Work is 'exhausting,
stupefying, inhuman slavery'. Leisure simply
involves 'modes of relaxation which soothe and
prolong this stupefaction'. It is based on and
directed by **false needs** which are largely imposed
by a mass media controlled by the establishment.
Needs are false if they do not result in true self-fulfilment and real satisfaction. If the individual feels
gratified by the satisfaction of false needs, the
result is merely 'euphoria in unhappiness', a
feeling of elation on a foundation of misery.
Marcuse claims that:

Most of the prevailing needs to relax, to have fun, to behave and consume in accordance with the advertisements, to love and hate what others love and hate belong to this category of false needs.

Members of society no longer seek fulfilment in themselves and in their relationships with others. Instead, 'The people recognise themselves in their commodities; they find their soul in their automobile, hi-fi set, split-level home, kitchen equipment.' The circle is now complete: industrial man or woman is alienated from every sphere of his or her life.

Marcuse presents a very pessimistic view of the nature of leisure in industrial society. He pictures a mindless 'happy robot' compulsively chasing false needs. He suggests that the term **happy consciousness** which describes the false belief that 'the system delivers the goods', is more appropriate today than Marx's phrase **false class consciousness**. Relative affluence and the extension of leisure have simply changed chains of iron into chains of gold. Ruling classes and ruling elites have strengthened their hold over the workforce by making its exploitation more bearable.

False needs serve to divert attention from the real source of alienation. Their satisfaction simply coats the bitter pill with sugar. At one and the same time false needs provide a highly motivated labour force which works for the money to consume, and a ready market for the products of industry.

■ C. Wright Mills – white-collar alienation

C. Wright Mills rejects some aspects of the Marxist perspective on society. He believes that society is dominated by a **ruling elite** rather than a ruling class which owns the means of production. Nevertheless he accepts that there is a conflict of interest between the main groups in society: the ruling elite and the mass of the population. Furthermore in a study of the American middle classes entitled *White Collar*, he applies Marx's concept of alienation to non-manual workers.

Mills states that the expansion of the **tertiary sector** (the service sector) of the economy in advanced capitalist societies has led to a 'shift from skills with things to skills with persons'. Just as manual workers become like commodities by

selling their 'skills with things', a similar process occurs when non-manual workers sell their 'skills with persons' on the open market.

Mills refers to this sector of the economy as the **personality market**. A market value is attached to personality characteristics and as a result people sell pieces of their personality. Therefore managers and executives are employed not simply because of their academic qualifications and experience, but for their ability to get on with people. The salesperson is given a job for his or her apparent warmth, friendliness and sincerity.

However, because aspects of personality are bought and sold like any other commodity, individuals are alienated from their true selves. Their expression of personality at work is false and insincere. Mills gives the example of a girl working in a department store, smiling, concerned and attentive to the whims of the customer. He states 'In the course of her work, because her personality becomes the instrument of an alien purpose, the salesgirl becomes self-alienated.' At work she is not herself.

In the salesroom, in the boardroom, in the staffroom, in the conference room, men and women are prostituting their personalities in pursuit of personal gain. Mills regards American society as a 'great salesroom' filled with hypocrisy, deceit and insincerity. Rather than expressing their true personalities and feelings, people assume masks of friendliness, concern and interest in order to manipulate others to earn a living.

Mills's pessimistic view of the sale of personality in American capitalist society is summarized in the following quotation:

The personality market, the most decisive effect and symptom of the great salesroom, underlies the all-pervasive distrust and self-alienation so characteristic of metropolitan people... People are required by the salesman ethic and convention to pretend interest in others in order to manipulate them... Men are estranged from one another as each secretly tries to make an instrument of the other, and in time a full circle is made – one makes an instrument of himself and is estranged from It also.

In this way people are alienated from themselves and from each other.

▌ Criticisms of conflict perspectives

Conflict perspectives on the nature of work and leisure are open to a number of criticisms.

1 First, they are based partly on a rather vague picture of what people could and ought to be. It can be argued that this view says more about the values of particular sociologists than it does about people's essential being. Many of the arguments are grounded in assumptions about human nature which are impossible to prove.

2 Second, they tend to ignore the meanings held by members of society. If people claim fulfilment in work and/or leisure, there is a tendency to dismiss their views as a product of false class consciousness. This particularly applies to Marxist views.

3 Third, conflict perspectives are very general. As Alasdair Clayre notes, they tend to lump together diverse occupations and leisure activities and create a simple model of 'man in industrial society'.

Possible correctives to these shortcomings will be dealt with in later sections, but we will now look at work from a functionalist perspective.

▌ Emile Durkheim – *The Division of Labour in Society* – a functionalist view

Where Marx was pessimistic about the division of labour in society, Emile Durkheim was cautiously optimistic. Marx saw the specialized division of labour trapping workers in their occupational role and dividing society into antagonistic social classes. Durkheim saw a number of problems arising from specialization in industrial society, but believed the promise of the division of labour outweighed the problems. He outlined his views in *The Division of Labour in Society*, first published in 1893.

Pre-industrial society – mechanical solidarity

Durkheim saw a fundamental difference between pre-industrial and industrial societies. In the former there is relatively little social differentiation: the division of labour is comparatively unspecialized. Most people are involved in hunting and gathering. **Social solidarity** in pre-industrial societies is based on similarities between individual members. They share the same beliefs and values and, to a large degree, the same roles. This uniformity binds members of society together in a close-knit communal life.

Durkheim refers to unity based on resemblance as **mechanical solidarity**. Durkheim describes the extreme of mechanical solidarity in the following way:

> Solidarity which comes from likeness is at its maximum when the collective conscience completely envelops our whole conscience and coincides with all points in it. But at that moment our individuality is nil. It can be borne only if the community takes a small toll of us.

In a society based on mechanical solidarity, members are, as it were, produced from the same mould.

Industrial society – organic solidarity

Solidarity in industrial society is based not on uniformity but on difference. Durkheim referred to this form of unity as **organic solidarity**. Just as in a physical organism, the various parts are different yet work together to maintain the organism (for example the heart, liver, brain in the human body), so in industrial society occupational roles are specialized yet function together to maintain the social unit.

Where Marx saw the division of labour as divisive, Durkheim believed it could increase the interdependence of members of society and so reinforce social solidarity. In order to produce goods and services more efficiently, members of industrial society specialize in particular roles.

Specialization requires cooperation. For example, a large range of specialists are required to design, manufacture and market a particular product. Members of society are dependent on each other's specialized skills and this interdependence forms the basis of organic solidarity.

However, the interdependence of skills and the exchange of goods and services are, in themselves, insufficient as a basis for social solidarity. The specialized division of labour requires rules and regulations, a set of moral codes which restrain the individual and provide a framework for cooperation. The exchange of goods and services cannot be based solely on self-interest, 'for where interest is the only ruling force each individual finds himself at war with every other.'

Durkheim saw the development of **contract** as a beginning of the moral regulation of exchange. Two parties enter into a legal agreement based on a contract for the exchange of goods and services. Contracts are governed by a general legal framework and grounded in shared beliefs about what is just, reasonable, fair and legitimate, but Durkheim saw the growth of contract as only a beginning. It was insufficient as a moral foundation for industrial society.

Anomie

Durkheim believed that the specialized division of labour and the rapid expansion of industrial society contained threats to social solidarity. They tended to produce a situation of **anomie** which, literally translated, means normlessness.

Anomie is present when social controls are weak, when the moral obligations which constrain individuals and regulate their behaviour are not strong enough to function effectively. Durkheim saw a number of indications of anomie in late nineteenth-century industrial society, in particular high rates of suicide, marital break-up and industrial conflict. Such behaviour indicates a breakdown of normative control.

Industrial society tends to produce anomie for the following reasons. It is characterized by rapid social change which disrupts the norms governing behaviour. In Durkheim's elegant phrasing, 'The scale is upset; but a new scale cannot be immediately improvised. Time is required for the public conscience to reclassify men and things.'

In particular Durkheim argued that the customary limits to what people want and expect from life are disrupted in times of rapid change. Only when desires and expectations are limited by general agreement can people be happy, since unlimited desires can never be satisfied.

In industrial society people become restless and dissatisfied since the traditional ceiling on their desires has largely disintegrated. Increasing prosperity resulting from economic expansion makes the situation more acute. Durkheim states:

> With increased prosperity desires increase. At the very moment when traditional rules have lost their authority, the richer prize offered these appetites stimulates them and makes them more exigent and impatient of control.

A new moral consensus about what people can reasonably expect from life is required. This will involve the regulation of competition in the exchange of goods and services. Exchange must be governed by norms regulating prices and wages which involves a general agreement on issues such as a fair and reasonable return for services. This agreement will set limits on people's desires and expectations.

Not only rapid social change but the specialized division of labour itself tends to produce anomie. It encourages individualism and self-interest since it is based on individual differences rather than similarities. There is a tendency for the individual to direct his or her own behaviour rather than be guided and disciplined by shared norms.

Although Durkheim welcomed this emphasis on individual freedom, he saw it as a threat to social unity: it tends to erode a sense of duty and responsibility towards others, factors which Durkheim saw as essential for social solidarity. He maintains:

> If we follow no rule except that of a clear self-interest in the occupations that take up nearly the whole of our time, how should we acquire a taste for any disinterestedness, or selflessness or sacrifice?

Occupational associations and anomie

Whereas Marx's solution to the problem of alienation was radical – the abolition of capitalism and its replacement by socialism – Durkheim believed that the solution to anomie can be provided within the existing framework of industrial society. The self-interest which dominates business and commerce should be replaced by a code of ethics which emphasizes the needs of society as a whole. In Durkheim's words 'economic activity should be permeated by ideas and needs other than individual ideas and needs.'

Durkheim sees occupational associations as the means to subject economic activity to moral regulation. Various industries should be governed by freely elected administrative bodies on which all occupations in the industry are represented. These bodies would have the power 'to regulate whatever concerns the business: relations of employers and employed – conditions of labour – wages and salaries – relations of competitors one to the other and so on'.

Such associations would solve the problem of anomie in two ways.

1 They would counter individualism by reintegrating individuals into a social group which would re-establish social controls.

2 By establishing a consensus about the rewards various members of society could reasonably and justifiably expect, normative limits would be placed on individual desire. This consensus would form the basis for rules to regulate economic activity.

In particular, Durkheim believed that inheritance as a mechanism for distributing property would gradually die out because of its 'fundamental injustice'. Property would be owned by occupational associations and exchanged by means of contracts. Economic rewards would be based on the contribution of the services of various occupations to the well-being of the community. Then, 'the sole economic inequalities dividing men are those resulting from the inequality of their services'.

Durkheim envisaged a delicate balance between the state and occupational associations. In the absence of occupational associations, the state might assume despotic powers and, conversely, without some form of state regulation, each association might assume despotic control over its members. In addition the state would coordinate and regulate economic activity on a national level and enforce a **common morality**, a moral consensus which is essential for social solidarity.

This vision of an efficiently functioning organic solidarity was influenced by Durkheim's view of professional associations – the voluntary associations which administer the practice of professionals such as doctors and lawyers. In professional associations, he saw many of the features that were lacking in industry and commerce. These included a clearly established code of conduct which is binding on all members, and a sense of duty, responsibility and obligation to the community as a whole. Durkheim saw such **professional ethics** as the key to a future moral order in industrial society.

■ The professions – a prototype for a future moral order?

As outlined in Chapter 2, (pp. 58–9), the functionalist view of the professions largely mirrors Durkheim's optimism. The **professional association** integrates individual members into an occupational group. Through its control of training and education, the association establishes both professional competence and professional ethics. Control of occupational behaviour in terms of these ethics is established by the power of the association to bar particular members from practising if they break the established code of conduct. For example, doctors can be struck off the register and barred from practice for professional misconduct.

Professional ethics emphasize altruism: a regard for others rather than a narrow self-interest. Professionals are supposed to be concerned with serving the community in general and their clients in particular, rather than supporting sectional interests or furthering their own interests. Thus lawyers are the guardians of the law in the interests of society as a whole; doctors, directed by their Hippocratic oath, are concerned first and foremost with the health of the community. The relatively high rewards (in terms of income and prestige) received by professionals reflect their important contribution to the well-being of society. This functionalist view of professionals thus provides a model for Durkheim's future moral order.

The personal service ethic

Writing in 1970, the British sociologist, Paul Halmos, saw indications that some of Durkheim's hopes were being translated into reality. In a study entitled *The Personal Service Society* he argues that the 'personal service professions' which include psychiatry, social work, nursing, teaching and medicine, are having a profound influence on the moral values of Western societies. The ideology of the personal service professions 'advocates concern, sympathy, and even affection for those who are to be helped. . . it admits the central significance of concern and personal involvement'.

Halmos believes that this emphasis on concern for others is permeating all areas of social life including the world of business and commerce. Industry is increasingly employing personnel managers and industrial relations experts who have been exposed in their training to the personal service ethic. Although management still puts profit first, it is more concerned with the well-being of the workforce and responsibility to the community as a whole. Halmos claims that 'No matter how hypocritical and mercenary we judge the motives behind these measures and tactics, the new habits of tact and consideration substantially reform the standards of human relationships.' He admits that the personal service ethic is only beginning to filter through into industry, but maintains that 'the ethos of the personal service professional becomes increasingly the ethos of the industrial society in which its constant growth has been made possible'.

This optimism must be tempered with the 'anti-professional' perspectives examined in Chapter 2 (pp. 60–2), and the negative views of the professions outlined in the following sections.

Self-interest

The first view sees professionalism as a **self-interested strategy** to improve the market situation of an occupational group.

1 A profession obtains a monopoly on a particular service which it jealously guards.

2 In the absence of competition it can obtain a high return for its services.

3 By controlling entry into the profession, it can limit the number of practitioners and maintain a high demand and therefore a high reward for its services.

4 It creates a demand for these services by fostering the myth that they are necessary and valuable to the client.

The success of this strategy may be seen from the ever increasing demand for medical treatment and legal services. Professional ethics, and in particular the emphasis on altruism, care and community service, are simply a smokescreen which serves to disguise professional self-interest.

Servants of the powerful

The second view sees professionals, in Baritz's phrase, as 'the **servants of power**'. From a Marxist perspective it involves the proletarianization of the professional which entails the loss of independence by professional groups.

Increasingly professionals are directly employed by the state and private industry. Industry employs lawyers specializing in business, commercial and corporation law, and accountants dealing with the growing complexity of company finance. Similarly, scientists, civil, mechanical and electrical engineers are salaried employees rather than independent practitioners charging fees for their services. As such, members of these professions can be seen as the servants of capital.

A similar argument applies to the personal service professions. Employed mainly in the service of the state, they serve the interests of ruling classes or ruling elites rather than the community as a whole. Doctors, psychiatrists and social workers undermine opposition to capitalist exploitation or elite domination by defining individuals as medical, psychiatric or social problems, and treating them as such. In this way attention is diverted from the real cause of 'social problems'. As we will see, the teaching profession can be seen in a similar light. Whatever their professed ideals, teachers maintain establishment power with their role in reproducing a society and culture which favours the interests of powerful groups.

The critical views of the professions we have just outlined suggest that Durkheim's moral reintegration of a society based on organic solidarity will require more fundamental changes than occupational associations. Durkheim sees differences in reward based on a consensus of the occupation's value to the community. However, he underestimates the possibility that once some are more equal than others, they have the power to define their services as more worthy and valuable than others, and in doing so further their own interests.

■ Technology and work experience

In this section we return to issues raised by Marxist approaches to work. We will look at the meaning and experience of work but examine these factors largely in terms of specific occupations, rather than in terms of society as a whole. In particular we will consider with the influence of production technology on the organization of work, and on the behaviour and attitudes of workers.

■ Robert Blauner – alienation and technology

In a famous study published in the 1960s entitled *Alienation and Freedom*, the American sociologist Robert Blauner examines the behaviour and attitudes of manual workers in the printing, textile, automobile and chemical industries. He sees production technology as the major factor influencing the degree of alienation that workers experience.

Blauner defines alienation as 'a general syndrome made up of different objective conditions and subjective feelings and states which emerge from certain relationships between workers and socio-technical settings of employment'.

Objective conditions refer mainly to the technology employed in particular industries. Blauner argues that technology largely determines the amount of judgement and initiative required from workers and the degree of control they have over their work. From an analysis of various forms of technology, he assesses the degree of alienation they produce.

Subjective feelings and states refer to the attitudes and feelings that workers have towards their work. This information is obtained from questionnaires. Blauner considers workers' attitudes as a valid measure of their level of alienation. Thus if workers express satisfaction with their work, they are not alienated. He thus rejects Marxist views which argue that workers in capitalist society are automatically alienated because of their objective position in the relations of production. (From a Marxist perspective, if workers express satisfaction with their jobs, this is an indication of false consciousness.)

Blauner claims to account for attitudes towards work in terms of production technology. Thus different forms of technology produce different attitudes towards work and therefore varying degrees of alienation. Blauner divides the concept of alienation into four dimensions:

1 the degree of control workers have over their work;

2 the degree of meaning and sense of purpose they find in their work;

3 the degree to which they are socially integrated into their work;

4 the degree to which they are involved in their work.

In terms of these four dimensions, the alienated worker has a sense of **powerlessness, meaninglessness, isolation** and **self-estrangement.**

Craft technology

Blauner first examines the printing industry arguing that it typifies pre-industrial craft technology. (His study was conducted at a time when neither mechanical nor computerized typesetting were widespread.) Questionnaire data from workers in the four industries show that printers have the highest level of job satisfaction. For example, only 4 per cent of printing workers found their work dull and monotonous compared to 18 per cent in textiles, 34 per cent in the automobile industry and 11 per cent in the chemical industry.

Blauner argues that in terms of his four dimensions of alienation, printers are **non-alienated workers**: they have control over their work and therefore do not experience a sense of powerlessness. Work is done by hand rather than machine. The compositor selects the type, sets it into blocks and arranges the blocks on the page, all by hand. Printing technology demands skill, judgement and initiative. Blauner states that 'because each job is somewhat different from previous jobs, problems continually arise which require a craftsman to make decisions'.

The nature of print technology means that the worker is largely free from external supervision. Self-discipline, rather than control from supervisors or managers, largely determines the quality of the product, the speed of work and the quantity of output. Work which is based on a craft worker's knowledge, skills and decisions does not lend itself to external supervision. Blauner concludes that the 'printer's freedom and control is largely due to the nature of craft technology'.

Compared to many industries, printing does not involve a highly specialized division of labour or a standardized product. These factors contribute to the relatively high degree of meaning and purpose printers find in their jobs. By working on a large segment of the product, they can see and appreciate their contribution to the finished article – the newspaper, book or magazine. Because each product is in some way different, they can recognize their distinctive contribution. For these reasons, Blauner describes printing as 'work with meaning and purpose'.

Largely because of the nature of print technology, the printer identifies with the craft and other craft workers. Print technology encourages printers to develop their skills and take a pride in their work. They are not tied to a machine and this allows them to move round the shop floor and talk to others. In terms of the third dimension of alienation – the degree of social integration – printers are not socially isolated. They are integrated into an occupational community, make friends at work and continue those friendships outside the factory gates. Printers are active in various craft clubs and associations and have a high level of trades union membership and involvement. (The points raised in this paragraph are developed with reference to print unions in Chapter 5, pp. 291–4.)

Due to their control over their work, the meaning they find in work and their integration into an occupational community, printers do not experience self-estrangement from work. Blauner argues that 'Work for craft printers is a source of involvement and commitment. It is not chiefly a means to life, but an expression of their selfhood and identity.'

Mechanization – machine minding'

If the craft industry represents pre-industrial production, the textile industry is typical of the early stages of industrialization. Most textile workers are machine minders. They tend a dozen or so machines, feeding them with yarn and mending breaks in the yarn. The traditional craft skills of weaving are, in Blauner's words 'built into the machine'.

In terms of the first dimension of alienation – degree of control – textile workers experience a sense of powerlessness. They are tied to their machines with little freedom of movement. Their tasks are routine and repetitive, requiring little judgement or initiative and offering few opportunities to take decisions. The pace and rhythm of their work is largely controlled by machines. The more machines a single worker can tend, the lower production costs. As a result, textile workers are subject to relatively strict supervision by supervisors who are mainly concerned with 'driving workers'. Blauner concludes that dominated by machines and policed by supervisory staff, textile workers do experience a sense of powerlessness.

Production technology in textiles provides little opportunity for meaning and purpose in work. The product is standardized and the worker performs only a few routine operations. The work involves little skill and variety and the individual worker's contribution to the finished product is small. These factors largely prevent workers from taking a pride in and deriving a sense of purpose from their work.

Blauner argues that the objectively alienating factors of textile technology should result in subjective alienation in terms of the last two dimensions of alienation. Thus the textile worker should feel isolated and self-estranged. However, this is not the case. Blauner explains this in terms of the community setting of the industry. The workers in his survey lived in small, close-knit communities, united by ties of kinship and religion. The majority of the adults worked in the textile mills. They felt a part of the industry because they were a part of the community.

In the USA the industry is set in the 'Deep South'. Small southern towns tend to be traditional in outlook, their inhabitants having lower aspirations and levels of education than the general population. Blauner argues that this accounts for the surprisingly low level of self-estrangement felt by the workers. He states that 'Because of their traditional backgrounds, they do not expect variety in work or inherent interest in millwork and therefore do not define repetitive, non-involving jobs as monotonous.' Thus, some of the alienating tendencies of textile technology are countered by influences from outside the factory.

Mechanization – assembly line production

Blauner argues that alienation is found in its most extreme form in assembly line production in the automobile industry. His data indicate that 34 per cent of manual workers in the industry find their jobs dull and monotonous, but this figure rises to 61 per cent for those working directly on the assembly line.

Workers on the line have little control over their work. The line determines the speed of work and affords little freedom of movement. The particular job, tools and techniques used are 'predetermined by engineers, time-study technicians and supervisors'. Decisions are taken out of the worker's hands and there is little call for skill, judgement or initiative. Supervision involves policing the workforce since output depends largely on physical effort. Assembly line technology gives workers little control over their work and as a result they experience a sense of powerlessness.

Mass production on assembly lines affords little opportunity for experiencing meaning and purpose in work. The product is standardized, the work is routine and repetitious and tasks are highly fragmented – broken down into their simplest components with each worker specializing in a small number of operations. For example, workers may spend their entire working day attaching wing mirrors or hub caps. As a result they find it difficult to identify with the product. Their particular contribution to and responsibility for the final product is minimal.

Workers on assembly lines are socially isolated. They do not feel a part of the company for which they work nor are they integrated into an occupational community of workmates. They are tied to the line, working as individuals rather than in groups, and have little opportunity to socialize with their fellow workers. Unable to identify with the product or with a particular skill, they do not form occupational communities like the craft printers. The nature of their work does not involve them in close cooperation and consultation with management. As a result there tends to be a clear distinction between management and workers.

Assembly line technology produces a high level of self-estrangement. In fact many workers felt hostility towards their work. The only aspects of the job which those in the survey liked were levels of pay and security of employment. The high degree of alienation produced an **instrumental** attitude to work – work was simply a means to an end. Hostility towards work and an instrumental approach to work accounts in part for the rela-

tively high level of strikes and unrest in the automobile industry.

Automation

Finally, Blauner examines work in the chemical industry which involves the most recent developments in production technology. The oil and chemical industries employ automated continuous process technology whereby the raw materials enter the production process, the various stages of manufacture are automatically controlled and conducted by machinery, and the finished product emerges 'untouched by human hand'.

Blauner believes that automation reverses the 'historic trend' towards increasing alienation in manufacturing industry. It restores control, meaning, integration and involvement to the worker. Although the product is manufactured automatically, the worker has considerable control over and responsibility for production. Work in chemical plants involves monitoring and checking control dials which measure factors such as temperature and pressure. Readings indicate whether or not adjustments must be made to the process. Blauner states that these decisions require 'considerable discretion and initiative'. Work also involves the maintenance and repair of expensive and complicated machinery. Skilled technicians range freely over the factory floor; there is considerable variety in their work compared to routine machine minding and assembly line production. In direct contrast to assembly line workers, none of the process workers felt they were controlled or dominated by their technology.

Compared to craft work, Blauner argues that in continuous process technology, 'the dominant job requirement is no longer manual skill but responsibility.' This emphasis on responsibility restores meaning and purpose to work, it is an 'important source of satisfaction and accomplishment'.

Process technology halts the increasingly specialized division of labour. It integrates the entire production process and since workers are responsible for the overall process, they can see and appreciate their contribution to the finished product. Their sense of purpose is increased by the fact that process workers operate in teams with collective responsibility for the smooth running of the machinery. Again, this encourages the individual worker to feel a part of the overall production process.

Unlike the assembly line worker, the process worker does not experience social isolation. The integration of maintenance and repair workers into a team and its movement round the factory floor furthers the integration of the workforce. Since physical effort is no longer involved in actual production, management no longer needs to police the workforce to drive it to greater effort. The line between management and workers tends to become blurred since their relationship is based on consultation rather than coercion. Both management and workforce are concerned with the trouble-free operation of production machinery. To further this shared goal the consultation of workers 'with supervisors, engineers, chemists and other technical specialists becomes a regular, natural part of the job duties'.

Blauner argues that the technology of automated production integrates the workforce as a whole. This has important consequences for industrial relations. Blauner claims that the process worker will be 'generally lukewarm to unions and loyal to his employer'. Unlike craft workers, process workers do not identify with a craft as such and form strong unions on the basis of this identification; unlike assembly line workers, they do not simply work for money and consequently strongly support unions as a means to increase their wage packets.

Because the process workers are non-alienated in terms of the first three dimensions of alienation, they are involved in their work. Blauner claims that process work provides 'an opportunity for growth and development'. He concludes that 'Since work in continuous process industries involves control, meaning and social integration, it tends to be self-actualizing instead of self-estranging.'

The importance of technology

Blauner admits that technology does not completely shape the nature of work. He states:

> Whereas technology sets limits on the organization of work, it does not fully determine it, since a number of different organizations of the work process may be possible in the same technological system.

However, he does see technology as the major factor influencing the behaviour and attitudes of workers. It therefore follows that a reduction in levels of alienation, as Blauner defines it, will largely involve changes in production technology.

He suggests that variation of work organization within a given technology would go some way to solving the problem. For example, **job rotation**, 'a policy that permits the worker to move from one subdivided job to another' would have the effect of 'adding variety to his work and expanding his knowledge of the technical process.' Similarly, **job enlargement**, which reverses the trend towards task fragmentation and increases the worker's area of responsibility, would have some beneficial results. For instance, Blauner points to a job enlargement scheme at IBM where machine operators were given the added responsibility of setting up and inspecting their machines. He claims that this 'not only introduced interest, variety and responsibility and increased the importance of the product to the worker, it also improved the quality of the product and reduced costs'.

Blauner argues, though, that such variations on existing technology are insufficient to solve the problem of alienation. What is needed is a new technology, designed not only to produce goods at minimum economic cost, but also at minimum personal cost to the worker.

Criticisms of Blauner

Blauner's study can be criticized on a number of points.

1 From a Marxist perspective, Blauner has ignored the basic cause of alienation – the objective position of the worker in the relations of production in a capitalist economic system. From this perspective, the printer and the process worker are just as alienated as the assembly line worker. All are exploited wage labourers. Blauner's solutions to alienation will therefore leave the basic cause untouched. At best they will produce a 'happy robot', who may feel satisfied at work, but will still be alienated from it.

2 The second major criticism of Blauner's study involves his use of questionnaire data. He relies heavily on this information for measuring the degree of alienation experienced by workers. It is extremely difficult to interpret the results of questionnaires. For example, if workers state that they like a job, this may mean that

they are satisfied with one or more of the following factors: wages, occupational status, social relationships at work, the amount of interest and involvement the job provides, the present job in comparison with past jobs, and so on. It may be possible to design a sophisticated questionnaire which separates out the various factors involved, but problems still remain.

As Blauner admits, the way a question is worded 'may favor one response rather than another' and 'the meaning of the question may not always be the same to the worker as it is to the interviewer.' In addition, there is a tendency for all workers to express satisfaction with their jobs. Since a person's self-image is partly determined by occupation, an admission of dissatisfaction with work might well undermine his or her self-respect.

3 A third criticism is advanced by Keith Grint. Grint suggests that Blauner greatly exaggerates the influence of a particular type of work within each industry. For example, Blauner emphasizes that alienation is common among all workers in car plants. However, he himself points out that only 18 per cent actually work on the assembly lines which are deemed responsible for causing the alienation.

4 Grint also claims that Blauner's own arguments undermine his claims about the impact of technology at work. In discussing women's work and alienation, Blauner said that 'women have, on the average, less physical stamina than men' but he also argues that since 'working women often double as housewives and mothers, it is to be expected that they would be fatigued by their work.' Grint says 'His assumption is conventionally patriarchal and simultaneously self-contradictory.' Not only does he make a totally unsupported claim about women's stamina, he also proceeds to argue against his own view that the fatigue of women workers is down to their sex. In the process he shows that factors other than technology, such as outside domestic responsibilities, have a strong influence on attitudes to work.

Theo Nichols and Huw Beynon – the chemical industry

Nichols and Beynon agree that Blauner exaggerates the extent to which technology shapes work. They do so by directly contradicting Blauner's claims about the chemical industry. In a study of seven chemical plants in Britain they found little evidence that alienation had decreased and the amount of skilled and rewarding work had increased. In six of the seven plants, control room operatives were a minority of the workforce.

Nichols and Beynon claim that about 50 per cent of the work in the chemical industry in Britain involves virtually no skill. A manager at one of the plants they studied, a fertilizer factory, distinguished between 'scientific work' and 'donkey work'. Of the 180 workers at that factory only forty did scientific work. The rest were largely unskilled labourers who spent their working day loading, packing, sealing and then humping round the factory heavy bags of fertilizer. The company had introduced job rotation for these workers but Nichols and Beynon found little evidence that this had reduced alienation. One worker commented:

You move from one boring, dirty, monotonous job. And then to another boring, dirty, monotonous job. And somehow you're supposed to come out of it all 'enriched'. But I never feel 'enriched' – I just feel knackered.

Nichols and Beynon also deny that monitoring and checking control dials is fulfilling work. In many plants control room operatives worked alone and felt isolated. Many expressed boredom with their work: much of the time they had nothing to do but stare at the dials. Most found it difficult to concentrate and sometimes this led to stress. The operatives were responsible for very expensive machinery – and there was the constant danger of a major accident. During an incident at an ammonia plant the control room operatives had been given just a few seconds' warning before a major explosion. Ten men were injured, one was permanently disabled and another suffered from nervous tension because of the accident. Nichols and Beynon conclude that work in control rooms 'is noisy and it can be stressful and lonely', though they concede that it 'is not as arduous as packing bags.'

Nichols and Beynon provide a very different picture of the chemical industry to that provided by Blauner. Consequently they do not accept that automated continuous process technology increases the skills required of workers, produces more job satisfaction and reduces alienation. They believe that, if anything, the reverse is true.

Goldthorpe and Lockwood *et al.* – work orientation

From their study of 'affluent workers' in Luton, Goldthorpe and Lockwood *et al.* question the importance given by Blauner to technology in shaping workers' attitudes and behaviour. They reject Blauner's **deterministic** approach which tends to see workers' behaviour as a predictable reaction to production technology. Instead they adopt a **social action perspective**. This approach emphasizes the 'actors' own definitions of the situations': Goldthorpe and Lockwood *et al.* maintain that a large part of the behaviour of the Luton workers cannot be explained as a reaction to production technology. Instead, they maintain that the way workers define and give meaning to their work largely accounts for their attitudes and behaviour.

Production technology and work orientation

Goldthorpe and Lockwood *et al.* studied workers in three firms which employed a range of production technology. The study was carried out in the 1960s. Their sample of 250 men included assembly line workers at the Vauxhall car company, machine operators, machine setters and skilled maintenance workers at the Skefko Ball Bearing Company, and process workers and skilled maintenance workers at Laporte Chemicals. In terms of **intrinsic job satisfaction** (that is the satisfaction people derived directly from the performance of their work) the pattern was similar to that described by Blauner. For example, the skilled maintenance workers had a higher level of intrinsic job satisfaction than the machinists and assemblers. However, there was little relationship between technology and 'the range of attitudes and behaviour which they more generally displayed as industrial employees'.

Goldthorpe and Lockwood *et al.* argue that their most significant finding is the similarity in the affluent workers' attitudes and behaviour, despite the variation in production technology. In particular, all workers had a strongly **instrumental orientation** towards their work: they defined work primarily as a means to an end, in particular as a means for obtaining money to raise their living standards. This instrumental orientation cannot be explained in terms of production technology since workers experienced differing technologies. Goldthorpe and Lockwood *et al.* argue that it can only be explained in terms of 'the wants and expectations which men bring to their work'.

Instrumental orientation

An instrumental orientation directs much of the affluent workers' behaviour. All workers were strongly attached to their firms and generally regarded employers in a positive light. This is understandable in terms of their instrumental orientation since the firms paid above average wages for manual work and provided fairly secure employment. If anything, process workers were more likely 'to reveal critical or hostile attitudes towards their firm', a finding in direct contrast to those of Blauner. Again, this can be explained in terms of the affluent workers' instrumental orientation. The wage levels of process workers were below those of the assemblers, machine operators and setters. Since money is the prime consideration, process workers tended to be less satisfied with their employers.

In general, the affluent workers formed few close ties with their workmates either on the shop floor or beyond the factory gates. Again, in direct contrast to Blauner's findings, process workers were less likely than other workers to form close relationships with their workmates. Goldthorpe and Lockwood *et al.* argue that the general lack of close attachments results from the workers' instrumental orientation. They define work simply as a means for making money, not as a place for making friends.

This definition also shapes their attitude to trades unions. Four-fifths of all workers believed that unions should limit their concerns to obtaining higher wages and better working conditions. Goldthorpe and Lockwood *et al.* refer to the affluent workers' relationship to their unions as **instrumental collectivism**. The affluent worker joins a union with fellow workers for instrumental reasons, the union being regarded as a means to personal ends. Most workers do not see union solidarity as a worthwhile end in itself, nor do they think unions should promote radical change in society as a whole.

Goldthorpe and Lockwood *et al.* conclude that the attitudes and behaviour of affluent workers are little influenced by technology. They stem primarily from their instrumental orientation, from the meanings and expectations they bring to work. They find little support for Blauner's comparison of the isolated alienated assembly line worker and the integrated non-alienated process worker. They argue that what happens outside the factory is more important in shaping workers' behaviour and attitudes than what happens inside.

In particular, Goldthorpe and Lockwood assign priority to 'ongoing changes in working-class life outside work and most notably in this respect changes within the family'. They argue that manual workers are increasingly home and family centred. Largely because of higher living standards, family life is 'more inherently rewarding' which means that workers can satisfy 'their expressive and affective needs through family relationships'. They are therefore less likely to look to work for these satisfactions. The more family life becomes a central life interest, the more workers will see their work in instrumental terms. It will increasingly become a means to raise family living standards.

Instrumental orientation and consumption

Goldthorpe and Lockwood *et al.* admit that on the surface, affluent workers appear very similar to Marx's alienated worker: they simply sell their labour to the highest bidder and see work in instrumental terms. However, Goldthorpe and Lockwood do not see the affluent workers' instrumental orientation and concern with consumption as a reaction to alienation at work. Instead, they argue:

Rather than an overriding concern with consumption standards reflecting alienation in work, it could be claimed that precisely such a concern constituted the motivation for these men to take, and to retain, work of a particularly unrewarding and stressful kind which offered high pay in compensation for its inherent deprivations.

Many affluent workers selected highly paid 'alienating' work *because of* their instrumental orientation. Goldthorpe and Lockwood conclude that the emphasis on consumption and instrumentality stems not from alienation at work but from 'whatever social-structural or cultural conditions generate "consumption-mindedness"'.

Goldthorpe and Lockwood *et al.* also reject the views of neo-Marxists such as Herbert Marcuse who see the emphasis on consumption as the result of false needs imposed by a capitalist mass media. They see no reason why the affluent worker's concern 'for decent, comfortable houses, for labour-saving devices, and even such leisure goods as television sets and cars' should be seen as a reflection of false needs. Goldthorpe and Lockwood *et al.* conclude:

It would be equally possible to consider the amenities and possessions for which the couples in our sample were striving as representing something like the minimum basis on which they and their children might be able to develop a more individuated style of life, with a wider range of choices, than has hitherto been possible for the mass of the manual labour force.

Methodological considerations

Before drawing any general conclusions from Goldthorpe and Lockwood's study, it is important to consider their sample.

1 The men were married, aged between 21 and 46, and 86 per cent had one or more dependent children. As Goldthorpe and Lockwood admit, men in this situation are more likely than unmarried, younger or older men to see work in instrumental terms.

2 The men had moved to Luton from various parts of Britain, specifically for high wages and regular employment. They may well be more instrumentally orientated than manual workers in general.

3 Luton, as 'a town of migrants', would encourage home and family-centred life since workers had left many of their relatives and friends in their towns of origin.

4 The sample contained a higher proportion of downwardly mobile individuals than the national average. Since there is a tendency for downwardly mobile workers to retain a white-collar reference group in terms of which they judge themselves, they may be more likely than manual workers in general to aspire to higher living standards. However, as the following section indicates, an instrumental orientation may well be typical of manual workers in general.

5 The sample consisted entirely of men and it therefore tells us nothing about women's attitudes to work. (Further aspects of the Luton study and a more recent

study of 'affluent workers' are examined in Chapter 2, pp. 77–82.)

Wedderburn and Crompton – technology and work orientation

From research in northeast England, Dorothy Wedderburn and Rosemary Crompton found some support for the views of both Blauner, and Goldthorpe and Lockwood. They studied a large chemical complex which they called 'Seagrass' and concentrated on two works on the same site. The first employed continuous process technology; the second used machines to produce chemically based yarn. In the yarn factory much of the work involved machine minding and the pace of work was largely determined by machines.

Wedderburn and Crompton's sample contrasts in several ways with the affluent worker sample.

1 Only a 'tiny minority' of the workforce had lived outside the area.

2 The sample was random – 30 per cent of the sample was made up of workers over 46, 10 per cent were unmarried.

3 Nearly half the men earned wages which were below the national average.

Despite these differences, Wedderburn and Crompton found that the men's orientation to work was very similar to that of the Luton workers. In assessing their jobs, the Seagrass workers listed four main considerations – the level of pay, the security of the job, the good welfare benefits and good working conditions. In fact, 'job interest', as a reason for staying in their present employment, was mentioned by fewer members of the Seagrass than the Luton sample. Wedderburn and Crompton conclude that the manual workers at Seagrass were no less instrumental than those of Luton.

Although this general orientation towards work bore no relationship to technology, Wedderburn and Crompton found that, 'different attitudes and behaviour within the work situation could be manifested by different groups of workers largely in response to the differences in the prevailing technologies and control systems.' Process workers in the largely automated plant found their jobs interesting, felt they had sufficient freedom to try out their own ideas and adequate discretion in the organization of their work tasks. In contrast workers in the machine shop found their work boring and felt they had little freedom or discretion in the organization of their work.

Attitudes produced by technology tended to be transferred to the supervisory system. Workers who found their jobs interesting tended to regard supervisors in a favourable light; those who found work boring tended to resent supervision. In part, these attitudes were shaped by differences in the nature of supervision in the two works, differences which reflected the demands of technology. In the process works, supervisors were 'troubleshooters' who used their technical expertise to assist workers to solve problems. As a result, their relationship with the workers tended to be cooperative. In the machine shop, supervisors were more concerned with quality control and tended to police the workforce.

Wedderburn and Crompton found that compared to the continuous process plant, workers in the machine shop had a higher rate of absenteeism and a higher strike level. They argue that these factors are strongly influenced by the technologies employed in the two works.

Wedderburn and Crompton's study strikes a balance between those of Blauner, and Goldthorpe and Lockwood. They had the benefit of both pieces of research before conducting their study and so were able to frame their questionnaire in terms of both viewpoints. They conclude that the general orientation of the Seagrass workers towards their work cannot be accounted for by technology. However, they maintain that important aspects of work-related attitudes and behaviour are influenced by production technology.

◼ Automation, class and society

As the most recent form of production technology, automation has attracted the interest of a number of sociologists. Several have argued that automation has important consequences which extend well beyond the workplace. In particular, it has been suggested that automation may produce important changes both within the working class and in the relationship of the working class to the rest of society. In this section we will examine three studies which explore the wider implications of automation.

◼ Robert Blauner – automation and class integration

Blauner saw alienation reaching its height with mass production industry based on mechanized assembly line technology. This posed problems for the integration of industrial society since it tended to produce division rather than unity.

The alienation produced by mechanized mass production led to hostility between workers and management, to divisions in the workplace expressed in terms of 'us and them'. The ending of craft production resulted in a shift of power from workers to management. Production was now organized and directed by management and control of the workforce tended to be repressive.

The high level of alienation encouraged an instrumental approach to work. The relative weakness of the workforce led to the formation of powerful unions to represent workers' interests. In line with the instrumental orientation of their members, unions exerted strong pressure on employers for higher pay. The result was conflict between employers and managers on the one side, and workers and unions on the other.

Blauner sees automation as reversing this trend towards instability and division. Automation produces the non-alienated worker; it replaces **dissent** (disagreement) between workers and management with **consensus** (agreement). Repressive and coercive control is succeeded by consultation and cooperation. Militant trades union activity is transformed into loyalty to the firm. The hostility produced by alienation is dissipated by 'meaningful work in a more cohesive, integrated industrial climate'.

These factors combine to transform the worker. His or her **social personality** is increasingly like that of 'the new middle class, the white-collar employee in bureaucratic industry'. Blauner concludes that automation has led to a:

---

decline in the worker's class consciousness and militancy, a development that reflects the growing consensus between employers and employees and the increase in the worker's feeling that he has a stake in industry.

In this way, automation has halted the tendency towards disintegration and division and is increasingly integrating the working class into the structure of capitalist society.

◼ Serge Mallet – automation and class conflict

The French Marxist sociologist Serge Mallet's view of the promise of automation differs radically from Blauner's interpretation. Where Blauner sees automation reducing the possibility of class conflict, Mallet sees just the opposite.

Although he largely agrees with Blauner that automation leads to a greater integration of workers in the factory, Mallet argues that this will not lead to a more general integration of workers into capitalist society. He maintains that automation will highlight the major contradiction of capitalism: the collective nature of production and the private ownership of the means of production. Since workers in automated industry have greater control over and responsibility for production, they will tend to see themselves as the real controllers of industry. The consultation and cooperation between process workers, technicians and operating managers will tend to unite them and encourage a recognition of common interests. The conflict between their interests and those of the higher-level managers and owners of the company will therefore be brought sharply into focus.

Workers will increasingly question the basis of ownership and control and demand worker control of the enterprise. This will revitalize the trades union movement which will no longer be represented by centralized, bureaucratic organizations distanced from the shop floor. Instead, union power will be decentralized and based on **syndicalist** principles, that is worker control at the level of the company.

Mallet sees workers in automated production forming the vanguard of the class struggle. He believes that they will provide an example which the working class as a whole will tend to follow. Mallet's work was published in 1975. Developments in work and trades unionism since then do not seem to have supported his claims.

■ Duncan Gallie – automation reconsidered

While admiring the boldness and breadth of Blauner and Mallet's interpretations, the British sociologist Duncan Gallie questions the soundness of the data on which they are based.

Blauner's data on process workers were taken from a survey conducted in 1947 which included only seventy-eight workers in the chemical industry. To this he added twenty-one interviews with process workers in a Californian company which he conducted in 1961. Apart from the small size of the 1947 sample, it gives no indication of the number of workers directly working with automated technology. This information is necessary since there are other technologies employed in chemical works.

From a close examination of Mallet's writings, Gallie states 'It is difficult to form any impression at all of how he carried out his study.' Gallie concludes his assessment of Blauner and Mallet's methodology with the comment 'It is difficult to avoid the feeling that the data bases on which these theories rest are perilously frail.'

Automation and workers' attitudes in Britain and France

In a study entitled *In Search of the New Working Class*, Duncan Gallie attempts to test the theories of Blauner and Mallet. If either Blauner or Mallet are correct, automated technology should have important consequences, whatever its national or regional setting. Gallie selected four oil refineries for investigation: two in France and two in Britain. By designing his research in this way, he hoped to assess the impact of technology which was independent of the influence of national or regional variations. In Britain, for example, he selected

refineries in very different areas: one was in Kent, a prosperous area in southeast England, the other in Grangemouth in Scotland, an area with a history of high unemployment.

Gallie's findings provided little support for either Blauner or Mallet. He discovered significant differences between the British and French workers, differences which could only be accounted for by the distinctive histories of the two societies and by the nature of British and French working-class subculture and national culture. Gallie states:

> The emergence of new forms of technology occurs, not in some form of social vacuum, but in societies with well-established institutional arrangements, and with distinctive patterns of social conflict.

Wage rates and differentials

Gallie's findings may be summarized as follows. Both British and French workers were paid high wages compared with other manual workers. Blauner and Mallet had argued that pay was no longer a central concern for workers in automated industry, but while over 90 per cent of the British workers were satisfied with their pay and living standards, over 66 per cent of the French workers were dissatisfied. The latter expressed their feelings in the form of strikes. From 1963 to 1972, twenty-four strikes brought production to a halt in the two French refineries, pay being the major issue in most of the stoppages. Only one strike closed down production in the British refineries over the same time period.

The difference in levels of satisfaction over pay can partly be explained by the methods of establishing wage rates. In France part of the workers' wages was made up of a 'merit bonus' which was based on length of service and 'good behaviour'. This system produced mistrust and ill-feeling since workers saw it as a means of management coercion and control.

French workers also differed from the British in their view of pay differentials between management and workers. Whereas only 2–3 per cent of British workers objected to the difference in salaries, the figure for the French workers was around 33 per cent.

Gallie maintains that differences in attitudes over pay between the two groups of workers 'can only be understood in terms of the broader context of the workers' perceptions of their societies, and of their reference groups and aspirations'.

Attitudes to work

Gallie found little support for Blauner's picture of non-alienated workers who were involved in their work. In both Britain and France 'The commonest attitude towards work in all our refineries was one of indifference.'

Though many of the hardships of mechanized mass production had been removed, others had taken their place. Continuous process industry involves round-the-clock production which requires shift work. Workers believed that this disrupted their family and social life, and produced ill-health.

A second problem in all refineries involved staffing levels, since it is difficult to determine adequate levels for automated technology. Such problems threaten the stability and harmony which Blauner sees as typical of automated industry. In general, these problems were settled peacefully in British refineries whereas in France they were a source of conflict between workers and management.

Management and workers

Where Blauner saw increasing cooperation and consensus between management and workers, Mallet saw increasing conflict between workers and junior-level management on one side and higher-level management on the other. Blauner's picture is closest to the situation in British refineries. There, workers largely identified with management objectives such as increasing the efficiency of the firm. They felt that management was concerned with their interests and welfare and not simply with profits for the benefit of shareholders. By comparison, the French workers believed that management was largely concerned with shareholders' interests and cared little for the welfare of workers. Their attitude towards management tended to be antagonistic, based on a view of 'us and them'.

Gallie found little evidence to support Mallet's claims about the demand for worker control. Only a very small minority of French workers and an even smaller minority of British actually wanted worker control. However, the French workers did want more participation in decision making than their British counterparts. For example, they were more likely to want a say in high-level financial decisions whereas the British defined such issues as management's job. Gallie's data reveal a sharp difference between British and French workers over their view of decision making. In Britain, some 80 per cent of workers believed that decisions about issues such as staffing levels and salaries were made by agreement between management and workers. Over 66 per cent of their French counterparts believed that decisions were made either by management alone or by management after consultation with workers. The French workers tended to see the negotiation machinery as a charade whereas the British did not. As a result, Gallie states that for the French workers, 'The predominant feeling was one of powerlessness.'

Explanations of differences between British and French workers

Gallie argues that a number of factors explains the variation in attitudes between British and French workers.

1 Working-class subcultures in the two countries differ. In particular 'French workers were more committed to egalitarian values than their British equivalents.'

2 Management 'styles' and philosophy differ. French management retains a tighter, more autocratic control over decision making and tends to be paternalistic. (**Paternalism** refers to a style of authority whereby those in control act like a father, distributing rewards and punishments at their discretion, based on the belief that they know what's best for those subject to their authority.) French management had considerable discretion in deciding the size of the worker's 'merit bonus' which formed an important part of his or her income. By comparison, British management operated on a 'semi-constitutional' basis. Wages were formally negotiated and there were no discretionary payments by management.

3 There were important differences in the negotiating machinery and union representation in the two countries. In France, wages were negotiated at national level; in Britain the important negotiations were at plant level. As a result British workers were more directly involved in the decision-making process. Gallie argues that in general:

The less participative the decision-making system, the less will workers regard it as legitimate. A lower degree of legitimacy will in turn be associated with a higher degree of generalized distrust of management's motives.

4 The major unions in Britain and France had very different conceptions of their role. Gallie describes the French unions as **unions of ideological mobilization**: they were committed to the overthrow of capitalism and saw their main role as raising the consciousness of workers. In Britain, unions saw their major role as directly representing the wishes of their members, and as such they were mainly concerned with negotiating for better pay and conditions. Gallie argues that as a result of the above factors, 'The British workers had an image of the firm that was essentially "co-operative" while the French workers had an image that was essentially "exploitive".'

Automation and class – conclusions

A number of important conclusions stem from Gallie's study. The British refineries are closer to Blauner's picture; the French closer to that drawn by Mallet. This leads to a rejection of the theories of both authors. Automated production, in and of itself, does not necessarily lead to a closer integration of the workforce into capitalist society, as Blauner suggested, nor does it necessarily herald the emergence of class consciousness and class conflict as Mallet predicted. In fact automated technology itself appears to have little effect on wider social issues. Management style, the nature of decision making, trades union philosophy and organization and working-class subculture appear far more important.

Gallie concludes that if the changes predicted by either Blauner or Mallet do occur, it will not be for the reasons that either suggests. He states:

Rather, it will depend on changing cultural expectations within the working class, on changes in management attitudes, and on changes in trade union objectives. Similarly, it will follow from our argument that if these developments do occur, the automated sector will not be particularly distinctive. Rather, it will be participating in a very much broader movement occurring within industry in the particular society.

The last phrase in this quotation is particularly important. Though both France and Britain share a capitalist mode of production, the response of workers to that fact will be modified by the factors which Gallie describes, factors which differ considerably between the two countries.

This finding has important implications for the study of work. It suggests that studies which concentrate simply on an analysis of work in capitalist systems are inadequate. They require in addition, an analysis of the peculiarities of the particular society in which capitalist economies are set.

▮ Computers, technology and changes in work

Technological determinism

Many recent studies of work and technology have paid particular attention to the impact of computers on patterns of work. However, they have not confined themselves to looking at this specific type of technology, but have also examined the nature of the relationship between work and technology in general. In doing so they have considered questions raised in the work of sociologists such as Blauner, Goldthorpe and Lockwood *et al.*, and Gallie.

The key issue in these debates is the question of technological determinism. Keith Grint says that 'technological determinism considers technology to be an exogenous and autonomous development which coerces and determines social and economic organisations and relationships.' In other words particular technology forces work to be organized in a particular way. It therefore has a direct impact on such things as the extent to which workers are alienated, and class relationships in society as a whole.

Blauner's theories are often taken as a good example of technological determinism. Although

Blauner describes technology as simply 'the most important single factor' shaping an industry, much of his book does give technology a determining role.

Social determinism

At the opposite extreme is **social determinism**. Grint describes this as assuming that 'technological changes are themselves socially engineered and/or that work relationships are, in any case, derived from, and ultimately determined by, cultural and/or social aspects'. In other words outside social factors determine how technology is developed, used and what it means for relationships at work. Grint cites Goldthorpe and Lockwood *et al.* as leading exponents of this position. In their approach, the orientations that people bring to work largely shape the way they react to particular technology. Duncan Gallie's work is another good example of social determinism. For him, technology in itself has 'very little importance for the social integration of the workforce'.

Contemporary commentators on computer technology and changes at work tend not to adopt such extreme positions. Most argue for something in between technological and social determinism. In the discussion that follows, we will start with those theories which are closer to a position of technological determinism and move towards those which come closer to social determinism.

▉ Shoshana Zuboff – *In the Age of the Smart Machine*

The power of technology

Shoshana Zuboff is an American sociologist who has studied the impact of computers on patterns of work in the USA. She attaches very great importance to information technology and argues that it has enormous potential to transform work. Indeed she believes that technology has always shaped social life to a considerable degree. She sees medieval castles, telephones and light bulbs as examples of technologies which have altered social life in fundamental ways. For example, the telephone allows intimate conversation without physical presence and the electric light 'rescues the night from darkness'. In her view the widespread adoption of computers in the workplace will have no less of an impact.

However, Zuboff is not simply a technological determinist. She does not believe that computers in themselves will determine the nature of work. The choices made by humans have had and will continue to have an important role. We will discuss the precise relationship she sees between technology and human choice later in this section. First however, we will review the research on which her conclusions are based.

Zuboff's research

Zuboff decided to conduct research in places of work that were introducing new information technology. She was interested in examining the impact of computer technology as workers were experiencing its introduction. Between 1981 and 1986 she studied eight organizations which were either introducing information technology or extending its role. These were: two pulp mills and one pulp and paper mill (Piney Wood, Tiger Creek and Cedar Bluff); part of a telecommunications company (Metro Tel); the dental claims operation of Consolidated Underwriter's Insurance; the Brazilian office of Global Bank; the pharmaceuticals company DrugCorp; and an office dealing with stock and bond transfer at Universal Technology. This range of institutions allowed Zuboff to study the impact of new technology amongst blue-collar workers, clerical workers and managers. She used a mixture of small-group discussions, interviews and participant observation.

Computers and manual work

For manual workers information technology was affecting the whole experience of working. Physical effort was becoming less important and manual skills were declining in significance. According to Zuboff, skilled manual workers had traditionally used skills based on the physical experience of manipulating things and they developed 'experience-based knowledge'. They used their bodies in '*acting-on* equipment and materials'. At paper mills such as Tiger Creek computers completely changed the skills required. Workers now controlled the production process through manipulating abstract symbols on computer screens. One said:

With computerization I am further away from my job than I have ever been before. I used to listen to the sounds the boiler makes and know just how it was running. I could look at the fire in the furnace and tell by its color how it was burning... I feel uncomfortable being away from these sights and smells. Now I only have numbers to go by.

now required their bodily presence in the service of routine interaction with a machine. Jobs that had once required their voices now insisted that they be mute.

Information technology was challenging the assumptions of manual workers about the nature of their work. **Intellective skills** were replacing manual ones so that although some old skills became redundant, new ones were replacing them. According to Zuboff one of the main effects of computer technology is to 'informate' the workplace. That is, it greatly increases the quantity of information available to workers and managers. How managers choose to use that information determines whether the increase in new skills outweighs the loss of old skills.

White-collar work

While blue-collar workers act on materials, white-collar workers 'act with' other people. They are important for coordinating the activities of a company. Although their work is much less physical than that of blue-collar workers, it has not always been entirely abstract. For example, taking a file out of a filing cabinet does contain a physical element to it.

In Consolidated Underwriting and the stock and bond transfer department of Universal Technology, computerization had similar effects for clerical workers. Paper files were replaced by computer screens. The workers lost personal contacts with customers and other workers and increasingly worked on their own at a screen processing data. In both offices the possibility of using initiative was taken away from the workers and many felt they were overqualified for the work they were now doing. A number of the clerks complained of 'eye strain, nervous exhaustion, physical strain, irritability, enervation, sedentariness, back pain, short tempers and intolerance'. Zuboff explains this in the following way:

Automation meant that jobs which had once allowed them to use their bodily presence in the service of interpersonal exchange and collaboration

Some of the clerical workers were asked to draw pictures illustrating the experience of work before and after computerization. Two of these pairs of drawing are reproduced on the next page. They graphically illustrate how the workers felt they were affected by the technological changes.

The effects of information technology were rather different at Global Bank Brazil. At the insurance company and the stock and bond office it was used to increase the volume of work through automation. At the bank the computers were used to informate. They made more information available to workers and this was used to improve the quality of the service they provided. Bankers had easier access to details of customers' accounts on a database and this allowed them to take a more active role in helping to manage their finances. Interpersonal contacts with customers remained important, but they were now supported by more objective data about their financial affairs. Much of the routine work was carried out by the computers, meaning there was less need for routine clerical workers.

Authority and the 'information panopticon'

Just as information technology was sometimes used to automate and sometimes to informate, it could also be used to make work more or less hierarchical.

Some of the companies studied by Zuboff used computers to introduce what she calls the **information panopticon**. The **panopticon** was an architectural design devised by the British philosopher Jeremy Bentham. It consisted of a central tower from which activities in all wings of the building could be centrally monitored. The design was used in some prisons and factories because it facilitated control over the workers or inmates. Information technology can be used for a corresponding purpose.

Zuboff argues that the principles of centralized monitoring have now become a feature of the way

Figure 4.1 A transfer assistant, before and after computerization

'Before I was able to get up and hand things to people without having someone say, what are you doing? Now, I feel like I am with my head down, doing my work.'

(*Source*: Zuboff, S. (1988) *In the Age of the Smart Machine,* Basic Books, New York, p. 146.)

some companies have used information technology. Indeed, according to her analysis, information technology makes the behaviour of workers much more transparent than it has ever been before. At Metro Tel, in the telecommunications company, computers were used to allocate tasks to workers, calculate the time they should take and monitor workers' efficiency. At Cedar Bluff the 'Overview System' allowed management to monitor all the decisions made by workers operating the plant's equipment and to determine who was at fault when something went wrong.

When they were used to create an information panopticon, computers were reinforcing the authority of managers and strengthening hierarchies. For example, at Metro Tel craft workers were closely monitored by supervisors, supervisors by lower-level management, lower-level management by the next level of managers up, and so on.

Figure 4.2 A benefits analyst, before and after computerization

'My supervisor is frowning because we shouldn't be talking. I have on the stripes of a convict. It's all true. It feels like a prison in here.'

(*Source*: Zuboff, S. (1988) *In the Age of the Smart Machine,* Basic Books, New York, p. 147.)

Computers undermining hierarchy

In some of the companies studied by Zuboff computers were having a very different effect. Information technology was breaking down traditional hierarchies.

At DrugCorp a computer-conferencing system called DIALOG was introduced in 1978. Workers throughout the company used computer communications to contribute ideas and raise issues about particular areas of the company's work. Workers from different levels in the hierarchy could subscribe to each of the conferences. Having subscribed they could contribute ideas to the conference or take ideas from it at will. The system was mainly designed to help research and development and to encourage innovation in the development of new products. According to Zuboff DIALOG 'helped create a new culture of information sharing and discussion'. It helped to break down barriers between different levels in the hierarchy. Lower and higher levels began to share knowledge and information rather than simply giving and receiving instructions. As at Global Bank Brazil, knowledge became a collective resource being used to its maximum potential to help the company.

In fact towards the end of her research, senior managers at DrugCorp replaced DIALOG with a less flexible system of computer-based communications which mainly involved sending routine electronic mail. It was, Zuboff believed, a retrograde step, a case of how 'the old world tries to suffocate the new'.

Technology and choice

Zuboff concludes from her study that managers can chose to use the new technology to go in either of two opposite directions. They can use it to informate, spread information more widely, undermine traditional hierarchies and make an organization more creative; or they can use it to automate, monitor employees more closely, reinforce traditional hierarchies and make the organization more rigid. Zuboff argues that there is an 'interplay between essence and choice in the computerized workplace'. The technology has an essence, it has particular capabilities, but how it is put to use is chosen by managers. She compares this to a kaleidoscope. A change in an organiza-

tion's technology 'wields the power of the hand at the turning rim'. It 'lays open new choices' and challenges the old orthodoxies. However, whereas the fragments in the kaleidoscope fall into place at random, in an organization the final shape of things is determined by managerial decisions.

In this context Zuboff does not sound particularly like a technological determinist. However, at other points in her book she clearly indicates what sort of choices she thinks will have to be made in the future. At Piney Woods one of the managers had asked '"Are we all going to be working for a smart machine, or will we have smart people around the machine?"' Zuboff believes more smart people will be needed. According to her, the traditional, rigid and hierarchical organization is unlikely to prosper and may be forced to adapt. She says:

---

it is unlikely that a traditional organization will achieve the efficiencies, standards of quality, or levels of innovation that have become mandatory in an environment marked by the competitive challenges of global markets and deregulation.

Firms will be forced to use the information that computers can provide constructively. While they can choose not to in the short-term, in the long-term they will need to use smart people rather than trying to replace them with the machine.

◼ Jon Clark, Ian McLoughlin, Howard Rose and Robin King – *The Process of Technological Change*

Determinism and choice

Jon Clark, Ian McLoughlin, Howard Rose and Robin King have examined the impact of new technology through a study of telephone exchanges in Britain. Like Zuboff they are opposed to simple technological determinism, insisting that human choices are a crucial part of technological innovation. However, they also argue that the technology itself has a strong influence on work.

Unlike Zuboff they see the choices that humans have as being limited once the technology has been introduced and established. During the process of introducing it though, they do believe there is considerable scope for influencing the way the technology will ultimately affect work. While Zuboff tends to assume that managers determine how technology is used, Clark *et al.* note that non-managerial workers can also exert considerable influence.

Engineering systems

The theory developed by these sociologists is based upon the concept of an engineering system. An engineering system does not just consist of the technology (the hardware and the software) but also of the way it is set up or 'functionally arranged (configured) in certain specific ways' within an organization. The systems and working practices which surround the technology exert a strong influence on how it is used. Thus Clark *et al.* say:

while agreeing that outcomes cannot be explained in terms of the capabilities of 'the technology', we suggested that it was equally erroneous to reject the notion that it can have an independent influence.

The technology does influence work, but it is not the only influence.

Technology in telephone exchanges

The study used to support this position examined the replacement of electro-mechanical Strowger telephone exchange systems with the semi-electronic TXE4 system. The researchers used self-report diaries, semi-structured interviews and observation in eight British Telecom exchanges which were making the change.

The old Strowger systems connected callers in a step-by-step mechanical process. The machinery required a considerable amount of routine maintenance. Some of the maintenance required was predictable and could be organized in advance by supervisors. Apart from the routine work the engineers also corrected faults which cropped up. The process of connecting calls could be seen and heard by engineers looking for faults. Physical familiarity with the machinery was vital in correcting them, so experience was essential for repairing the equipment. Maintenance engineers could expect to progress to a senior grade as they became more experienced. Supervisors usually rose from the shopfloor so like senior engineers they had considerable experience of the technology.

TXE4 systems are rather different. They are quiet when operating and it is not possible to physically observe switches being made to connect calls. Calls are connected through a matrix and a fault tends to affect a greater number of calls than a fault in a Strowger exchange.

Technology and skills

Clark *et al.* argue that the technical features of these two systems had a strong influence on the skills required to accomplish work tasks. (They call these skills **skill in the task**.) For example, TXE4 exchanges required 'mental diagnostic skills' as opposed to the 'refined manual skills' necessitated by the Strowger exchanges. The new exchanges produced a more 'abstract working relationship with the equipment'. The new skills were more easily developed through formal training programmes than through experience. TXE4 exchanges were more suited to teamwork since faults could not be isolated from the rest of the system while one person worked to correct them.

However, the technology had a much less direct impact on **skills in the person** – the way skills are distributed to individuals with particular occupational positions. Managers, unions and the work groups of supervisors and maintenance workers had a good deal of influence over how skills came to be distributed. Conflict and negotiation determined how the overall 'engineering system' incorporated the new technology.

For example, in two of the British Telecom areas studied the maintenance workers' union, the POEU, was influential in determining which staff were retrained to carry out the sophisticated maintenance work on the new equipment. In the event it was the senior technicians who received the training. This left the junior technicians with little chance of promotion. Experience alone was no longer sufficient to develop the skills required at senior levels. The position of supervisors was also weakened. Many were unfamiliar with the technical details of TXE4 exchanges so they found it hard to monitor and exercise detailed control over the work of the senior technicians. In the third British Telecom area the POEU branch was much less powerful or well organized. Here, senior technicians had less success in defending their position.

Conclusion

Once the technology had been set up and was in routine operation, it became very hard for the different groups of workers to change their relationship to the technology. Clark *et al.* conclude therefore that there are **critical junctures** at which groups can intervene to try to influence the way technology is used. Although the nature of the work tasks is largely determined by the nature of the technology, who does the tasks is not, and can be altered at these critical junctures. After this point 'social chances become frozen within a given technology.'

Keith Grint is amongst those who have attacked this view of the relationship between work and technology. He denies that the nature of work ever becomes 'frozen'. Grint says 'inasmuch as technology embodies social aspects it is not a stable and determinate object. . . but an unstable and indeterminate artefact whose precise significance is negotiated but never settled'.

We will discuss Grint's own views at the end of this section. First, however, we will examine the theory of Rob Kling. Like Grint he does not believe that theories such as that of Clark *et al.* have distanced themselves sufficiently from technological determinism.

▊ Rob Kling – the consumption of technology

The varied effects of computers

The American sociologist Rob Kling is critical of the types of theory we have examined so far in this section. He disagrees with Zuboff that computer technology is necessarily going to transform society in a particular direction, or indeed at all. He also accuses Zuboff, amongst others, of using evidence which is 'carefully selected to fit. . . her logic of social change'.

Nor does he agree with Clark *et al.* that technological innovation has predictable effects once it has been set up and is operating routinely. Instead Kling argues that technology can have very many different effects and these depend partly upon how it is used or 'consumed'. In other words, even after being designed, purchased and operated routinely, computers can be used in different ways. Sometimes computers transform social relationships at work and in the wider society, but they can also reinforce existing relationships or have a negligible impact. Sometimes computers deskill work; at other times they make work more skilled. He is therefore opposed to deterministic theories of the relationship between computers and social change.

Studies of computerization

Kling cites a number of his studies to illustrate the diverse effects of computerization. In a study of the introduction of an 'Urban Management Information System' to local government in an American city there was little evidence it achieved any of its stated aims. These aims were: improving efficiency by providing easier access to data; improving management; and reducing paperwork. Instead Kling found 'UMIS's primary value was in *enhancing the welfare agency's image* when it dealt with federal funders and auditors.'

In another study of computerization Rob Kling and Tom Jewett examined computerization in a mortgage bank (Western Mortgage) and the sales department of a big pharmaceuticals company (Coast Pharmaceuticals). In both companies the introduction of new computer systems during 1987 led to an expansion of the range of jobs done by clerical workers. At Coast Pharmaceuticals the workers changed from 'order entry clerks' to 'customer service representatives'. In their new role they had more responsibility and greater contact with customers. At Western Mortgage clerical workers' jobs changed from manually entering information on ledgers to entering it directly on computers. Although they learned some new computer skills, the change restricted their movement round the office and gave them less opportunity for casual social contacts. Unlike Coast Pharmaceuticals they remained fairly routine clerical workers and the new technology had relatively little impact.

With Suzanne Iacano Rob Kling studied a high technology manufacturing (PRINTCO) firm in the early 1980s. Many of the staff they talked to claimed that their new computerized inventory control system saved money and increased efficiency. However, nobody had actually estimated any savings involved and nor could they give any evidence that these savings were real. Kling and Iacano claimed that this system was really used so that material managers could 'gain control over the purchasing staff and. . . help production line managers battle with projections made by marketing staff'. Workplace discipline was tightened and material control managers increased their influence in the firm.

Conclusion

Rob Kling believes that computers can have very diverse effects on work. They can have a larger or smaller impact, and they can increase or decrease skills in particular jobs. He denies that there has been a 'computer revolution' changing work in very fundamental ways. The effects vary from job to job. There have been 'some major structural transformations in banking' and major changes in the work of copy typists, but most white-collar work has been altered in 'interesting procedural ways without radically restructuring the organization of work'. In other areas such as schooling there have been 'negligible changes'. Many of the benefits claimed for new computer systems are exaggerated and some may not be real at all.

The effects of computerization are strongly influenced by what Kling calls the 'social organization of access to information systems', or how in effect the technology is used or consumed. He gives the example of university students using computers. If the 'chemistry lab' model is used so that students have to use computers at fixed times, it will tend to regiment their lives. Technology will have a very different effect if a 'library model' is used so the students can complete their computer work at their own convenience. The technology might be identical, but the effects are different.

On the other hand, Kling does at times claim that the precise nature of the technology can have a significant impact. In particular, different software packages can require different types of worker to use them. For example:

---

some data base management systems require that each new capability be programmed by a skilled programmer (e.g., Revelation). Others, which have powerful commands on menu systems (such as Paradox), allow the moderately skilled to navigate through data bases in complex ways.

Thus systems such as Revelation will employ a small number of very skilled programmers and deskilled operatives while Paradox requires routine white-collar workers to increase their skills. So although Kling argues that the same technology can be consumed in different ways leading to different results, he also believes that the technology itself has an independent effect on the outcome.

(We will examine the question of whether work has been deskilled in detail in later sections. See pp. 208–14.)

■ Keith Grint and Steve Woolgar – discourse and computers

Technology and discourse

Grint and Woolgar have perhaps gone further than other sociologists in attacking technological determinist accounts of the effects of computers. In a debate with Kling they have argued that he attributes too little importance to the interpretation of the meaning of technology by human actors. They point out that although Kling says that particular technology can be consumed in different ways, he nevertheless identifies a technical core which has at least an influence on the uses to which new technology can be put. For example, they quote Kling's argument about one type of database encouraging deskilling when another does not.

To Grint and Woolgar, a technology cannot be separated from the interpretation put on it by actors. They argue that the **discourse** surrounding a technology – the way people talk about it and determine what it is – is what in the end decides the effects it has. They say 'Discourse is foundational to social action not, as Kling would have it, some impoverished effort to look at mere talk.' By looking at the way people talk about technology, sociologists can study who has the power to get their version of what the technology means accepted. Those who succeed in getting their version accepted exercise power and are likely to be able to use the technology to favour their own interests.

According to this view the 'nature and capacity' of a technology never becomes completely fixed but is 'essentially indeterminate, both during conception, design, and development and beyond the point of sale and use'.

The capacity of technology

Keith Grint gives the following example to illustrate these views. If a new technology is introduced capitalists may argue that the essential capacity of the technology is that it can increase production while reducing costs. On the other hand an anti-capitalist may claim that it inherently has the capacity to reduce the effort required of workers. To both sides their analysis is objective, and used in any other way the technology is being misused and its inherent capacity distorted.

From Grint's point of view the technology has no inherent capacity: it simply has different meanings which depend on the audience looking at it. The disagreement between the two sides in the example above is not just about how the technology is deployed, it is also about what it can do; what its capacity is. Grint says:

> We do not have contrary interpretations of the same machine; what the machine is and what it will do are social constructions such that we actually construct different machines.

Grint goes on to acknowledge that which interpretation is accepted is not a matter of chance. The power to define what technology is, is not equally distributed. He argues:

> What tends to happen is that so called 'experts' are endowed with sufficient status to persuade the majority of lay people that they are right and the rest of us are wrong. After all, if an expert tells us. . . that you cannot get leukaemia by working in a nuclear power station (despite the rumours), or that there is no link between ill health and unemployment (despite the rumours). . . – who are we to believe?

Evaluation

Grint and Woolgar raise important questions about how technology is used and show that there are always choices involved in deploying it. Some people have argued that they go too far in appearing to suggest that technological capacity is entirely a matter of interpretation.

In a defence of his own work Rob Kling pointed out that guns have certain capacities which, for example flowers, do not. It is harder to kill people with flowers than guns. Grint and Woolgar replied to this criticism that even in the case of a gunshot wound there are social processes involved in interpreting what has happened. They say 'John F. Kennedy's assassination is a classic example of the difficulty of providing an irrefutable, "objective" account of the damage caused by "the bullet".' They conclude 'we do not argue that the bullet (technology) is irrelevant but that the process by which it achieves relevance is irredeemably social.'

Their discourse analysis of technology has some similarity with the perspective of ethnomethodology. Like ethnomethodology, it is not always clear about how certain groups get their definitions of social reality, or the capacity of a technology, accepted and why. Thus although Grint says that 'experts' tend to have more chance to get their own way in this respect, he also seems to argue that all social groups have a good chance of their definitions being accepted. He claims:

> power can be regarded as a consequence of action rather than a cause. Thus, control over work organisations and their technologies is grounded in the actions of subordinates not the commands of superordinates: if subordinates refuse to act, or refuse to accept superordinate definitions of technological capacity, then superordinate power rapidly dissolves.

It is doubtful whether the experience of most workers would match this view. Certainly Harry Braverman, whose views we will examine next, would be likely to dismiss it as fantasy.

■ The labour process and the degradation of work

Between the mid 1970s and the mid 1980s much of the research in the sociology of work was devoted to an analysis of the **labour process**. Paul Thompson defines the labour process as 'the means by which raw materials are transformed by human labour, acting on the objects with tools and machinery'. The preceding discussions of technology, work orientation, automation and computerization clearly touch upon the labour process, but they do not directly address the issues raised by the most influential figure in labour process theory, Harry Braverman. Braverman published his book: *Labour and Monopoly Capitalism, The Degradation of Work in the Twentieth Century* in 1974 and since then a vast amount of literature has been produced which discusses his views.

Within this literature the emphasis has been, in Paul Thompson's words, on 'Who owns, controls and designs work' and the 'consequences of these social relations on forms of technology and the divisions of labour'. We will examine Braverman's theory first, before considering the critical responses to it.

■ Harry Braverman – a Marxist view of the labour process

Braverman follows Marx in arguing that work within capitalist society is alienating. However, Braverman does not believe that work has been equally degraded during all periods of capitalism: he claims that the twentieth century has seen a particularly rapid **degradation** of work. Braverman discusses automation and class, but he does not see changes in the labour process as being a direct consequence of automation; instead he sees automation as a consequence of attempts to change the labour process. In particular Braverman believes that the level of skill required in work has been progressively reduced under capitalism mainly because employers have used deskilling as a method of controlling the workforce.

Braverman bases his argument upon the observation that usually under capitalism, 'what the worker sells, and what the capitalist buys, is not

an agreed amount of labor, but the power to labor over an agreed period of time'. In other words, an employee is not normally paid to expend a certain amount of effort, or to produce a certain number of goods, but rather to give up a certain number of hours to work for the employer. In early periods of capitalism capitalists made workers labour for very long hours in order to get them to produce more and increase profits or surplus value, but this was not the most effective way to increase productivity.

Braverman claims that human labour power is 'infinite in potential': the amount that people can produce is almost unlimited. However, in simply buying the workers' time the employer is not guaranteeing that that potential is realized. What is actually produced is:

> limited by the subjective states of the workers, by their previous history, by the general social conditions under which they work as well as the particular conditions of the enterprise, and by the technical setting of their labor.

Braverman argues that the development of the labour process under capitalism has been shaped by employers' attempts to overcome these limitations.

Deskilling and the reduction of labour costs

Braverman accepts that all societies have had social divisions of labour in which some individuals carry out separate and specialized roles. However, he claims that only modern capitalism has produced the **manufacturing divisions of labor** or the 'breakdown of the processes involved in the making of the product into manifold operations performed by different workers'. By breaking the work involved in production down into its constituent parts, the capitalists can reduce labour costs. They no longer need to employ skilled craft workers at high rates of pay to make a whole product: unskilled workers can carry out the simplest parts of production. The more the work is divided up and broken down the smaller the proportion of work requiring skilled labour. Thus, for example, in modern factories complex consumer products can largely be produced by unskilled workers because each worker need understand only part of the production process. As a consequence work is deskilled.

Braverman sees deskilling as the product of management decisions rather than technology. In particular he believes that the **scientific management** of Frederick W. Taylor has had a profound impact upon the organization of work in capitalism. (We describe scientific management in more detail on pp. 294–5.)

Scientific management and control over production

Taylor first published his views in the early part of the twentieth century in the USA, and Braverman has analysed the consequences of the principles upon which scientific management was based.

1 Taylor's first principle was that management should gather together all the traditional knowledge of working people in a particular industry and reduce this knowledge to 'rules, laws, and formulae'. To Braverman this greatly diminished the power of workers and their control over production because managers took from them the knowledge necessary to make production possible.

2 Taylor's second principle was that 'brain work' should be taken away from the factory floor and carried out in a planning department. Braverman calls this the 'separation of conception from execution' and he argues that it makes the detailed control of the labour process by management easier.

3 The third principle was that management should plan out and give written instructions to every worker specifying exactly what they should do.

To Braverman, when all three steps were followed the management achieved control over the workforce. Although the workers as human beings retained their critical faculties, they had lost their skills and overall knowledge of the production process so there was little they could do to resist the employers. Braverman believes that under modern capitalism:

labor power has become a commodity. Its uses are no longer organized according to the needs and

desires of those who sell it, but rather according to the needs of its purchasers, who are, primarily, employers seeking to expand the values of their capital.

Management 'concessions'

Management does make some attempt to respond to the problems created for employees by deskilled and degrading work. It does so not out of charity, but out of self-interest. It needs to prevent resistance from workers.

One way of doing this is to use industrial psychology and the human relations school of management to **habituate** workers to oppressive working conditions. Braverman does not therefore regard human relations management as an alternative to scientific management but as a way of making the tight control of scientific management slightly more tolerable. (For a description of the human relations school see pp. 295–7.)

Braverman accepts that a second way of making workers accept new management techniques is the concession of higher wages to some employees. However, as these higher wages are paid to a shrinking proportion of the workforce, and to workers who are increasingly productive, they do not threaten the profitability of the capitalist enterprise.

Braverman is extremely pessimistic about the position of workers. He sees them as increasingly trapped without the possibility of challenging management control. He says:

the working class is progressively subjected to the capitalist mode of production, and to the successive forms which it takes, *only as the capitalist mode of production conquers and destroys all other forms of organization of labor, and with them the alternatives for the working population.*

Evidence for deskilling

As well as discussing the general processes through which skill is destroyed, Braverman also provides some more specific evidence to support his case. Official census statistics in the USA appear to show an increase in the number of semi-skilled or skilled manual workers, but Braverman questions the validity of these statistics. He points out that in the 1930s the basis on which the statistics were calculated was changed so that any operatives who tended or minded machines became classified as semi-skilled, despite the fact that the training needed to carry out their job might be minimal. Many such workers learn to do their job in two to twelve weeks which hardly compares with the apprenticeship of traditional craft workers which would last several years. As the number of such craft workers has declined rapidly, so the overall level of skill within the working class has been dramatically reduced.

Braverman also believes that the falling number of rural labourers has led to a deskilling of the workforce. In 1900 17.7 per cent of the working population of the USA were in the category 'farm laborers and foremen'. By 1970 this had declined in 1.7 per cent. Farm labourers have always been classified as unskilled so as their numbers fell as a proportion of the working population, the skills of American workers might appear to be rising. In reality, Braverman claims, farm labourers are far more skilled than the operatives in industry who are classified as semi-skilled. He says of the farm labourer:

> he was the product of years of farm life and had a mastery of a great many skills involving a knowledge of land, fertilizer, animals, tools, farm machinery, construction skills, etc.

Braverman is aware that official figures in the USA, and indeed in other capitalist countries, show that an increasing proportion of the workforce is employed in non-manual occupations. Again, on the surface, this might seem to contradict the deskilling thesis. However, he believes that many non-manual jobs have themselves been deskilled. For example, he claims that professional workers such as draftspeople, technicians, engineers, nurses and teachers have lost some of their skills (see pp. 61–2 for further details of this argument). He goes further in arguing that routine white-collar workers such as clerks, secretaries and retail sales workers have been so deskilled that they have now become members of the proletariat. (For a full discussion of the proletarianization thesis see pp. 65–9). Overall, Braverman estimates that some 70 per cent of the labour force in the USA are now members of the proletariat whose work has undergone a process of degradation involving the removal of skill, responsibility and control.

Between the proletariat and bourgeoisie is an intermediate group of lower-level managers, marketing and finance specialists, engineers and technicians who exercise authority and control over the workforce. They are themselves, though, subject to the overall control of top management and the bourgeoisie. Braverman believes that control and skill have become polarized. There has been an increase in control and skill for some of the intermediate group, but as Braverman puts it, 'the mass of workers gain nothing.'

■ Responses to Braverman

Reactions to Braverman's provocative theory have been both numerous and varied. Some sociologists have been highly supportive of Braverman and have presented evidence which seems to bear out his claims. Others have argued that Braverman paints an oversimplified picture of changes, although they accept that there have been some areas of work which have been deskilled. Some sociologists have been much more critical and have suggested that in recent years work has been **reskilled** not deskilled.

We will examine the evidence to support Braverman before considering the main areas of critical debate arising from his work.

Labour and Monopoly Capital has prompted some Marxist sociologists to carry out case studies of changes in the labour process to provide support for Braverman. For example, in the book *Case Studies on the Labour Process*, edited by Andrew Zimbalist, a number of American writers tried to show how work had been degraded in occupations as diverse as carpentry, coal mining, car assembly, jewellery making and clerical work in insurance.

Deskilling in the printing and typesetting industries

Andrew Zimbalist himself carried out a case study on the printing industry. Zimbalist describes how in the nineteenth century printing remained the preserve of craft workers. Before the 1880s type-setting was carried out entirely by hand and was a highly skilled job which required both manual and mental skill. However, employers progressively introduced new technology such as semi-automatic typesetting machines which cut out some of the manual skills required by typesetters. In the 1950s photo-typesetting machines were introduced, and gradually these machines were developed and the skills necessary to operate them were reduced. The third generation of these machines introduced word processing and according to Zimbalist this destroyed the traditional craft of typesetting. At the *Washington Post* and the *New York Times* the new technology was used to break the power of print workers' unions: it removed most of the skill from their work and reduced their independence so that they could be controlled more closely by management.

Similar processes have taken place in Britain. Rupert Murdoch successfully challenged the power of the printing unions by moving the production of his newspapers (*The Times*, *Sunday Times*, *Sun* and *News of the World*) to a new printing works at Wapping which used advanced computer-based printing technology. This allowed journalists and advertising copymakers to type material directly into computers without print union members being involved. It enabled Murdoch to dismiss print union workers and replace them with members of the Electricians Union, the EETPU, who agreed to a no-strike deal.

As we indicated in an earlier section of this chapter indicated (see pp. 188–91) Blauner used printing and typesetting as an example of a traditional craft–occupation. Zimbalist's work and the British example show how even one of the last strongholds of craft work has been deskilled and the power of the workers and their control over the labour process have been drastically reduced.

However, this example could also be used to challenge some of Braverman's assumptions. The deskilling of printing and typesetting took place long after the development of scientific management, suggesting that he may have exaggerated its influence. Furthermore in neither Britain nor the USA did print workers accept their deskilling passively. Although they were eventually unable to protect the craft skills of their jobs they did fight and delay new working practices. These and other criticisms of Braverman will now be examined.

The craft worker and deskilling

Some critics of Braverman argue that his theory simply does not fit the facts: Braverman may have greatly exaggerated the importance of craft work in the nineteenth century. As Paul Thompson points out:

A large proportion of the industrial population was, and is, in non-factory manual occupations like transport and mining. Although they had a specific type of skill and control of their own, it could not be compared with factory work concerned with discrete operations on separate machines.

Craig Littler notes that industries such as food processing and tobacco were set up using semi-skilled and unskilled labour from the start and never used craft workers. Braverman has also been accused of having a romantic image of a 'golden age' of work and of making invalid claims about the amount of skill and autonomy that were necessary for workers in the past. Thompson suggests that craft workers' 'skills could frequently be exaggerated compared to non-craft workers'.

Scientific management and managerial control

A second area of criticism concerns the importance of Taylorism and scientific management as methods used to control the workforce. All Braverman's examples are taken from the USA and on this basis he assumes that scientific management was the main method of control used in all capitalist countries.

Craig Littler has pointed out that Taylorism had much less influence in Britain than it had in the USA. Although scientific management was influential in Britain it was only in the 1930s that it began to be used by a considerable number of employers. Littler also believes that Braverman attributes too much importance to Taylorism in some industries where there was a move away from craft skills. He says:

Even within a traditional metal working firm. . . with all the signs of craft deskilling, the transition to non-craft working had largely occurred before Taylor's disciples set foot on the factory floor.

Conflict and methods of control

Many sociologists who are sympathetic to Marxism do not disagree with Braverman that capitalists try to control the labour process, but they do deny that scientific management is the predominant method of control, and that control is necessarily complete.

For example, Richard Edwards describes the workplace as a **contested terrain** in which both the degree of control achieved by the management, and the type of control used will vary. Edwards points out that unions and informal methods of control are also used by employers as they seek to get their own definitions of 'a fair day's work' accepted. Although Edwards portrays management as ultimately being quite successful in controlling the labour process, the type of control used has had to be adapted to take account of worker resistance and changed circumstances.

According to Edwards, nineteenth-century capitalism was characterized by small firms with relatively few resources. They relied upon **simple control** exercised by the entrepreneurial owners of the businesses, and perhaps a small number of supervisors and managers. Edwards argues 'These bosses exercised power, personally intervening in the labor process often to exhort workers, bully and threaten them, reward good performance, hire and fire on the spot.'

As production became concentrated in the hands of a smaller number of larger firms towards the end of the nineteenth century, simple control became less effective. Furthermore, in the early decades of the twentieth century the American labour movement became better organized and more able to resist simple control. Employers turned to more sophisticated **structural control** methods.

The first type of structural control to be used was **technical control**. Under this method machinery directed the labour process. For example, on production lines the pace of work and nature of the tasks performed is largely determined by the machinery of the production line itself.

Edwards believes that since the Second World War the second type of structural control, **bureaucratic control**, has gradually replaced technical control. It developed first as a way of controlling the increasing number of non-manual workers who could not readily be controlled by technical means. This type of control 'rests on the principle of embedding control in the social structure or social relations of the workplace'. Workers are controlled through the creation of complex hierarchies in which there are clear lines of authority and the behaviour of different workers within the hierarchy is constrained by written rules. Competition for promotion is used to divide the labour force. Within the hierarchy workers are encouraged to be in conflict with each other rather than uniting to challenge management control.

Unlike Braverman, Edwards sees the use of technology and bureaucratic hierarchies as more important than scientific management as control strategies. He also sees techniques of control as passing through different stages rather than a single method being dominant throughout the history of capitalism. Edwards does accept, though, that simple and technical control continues to exist today in some capitalist enterprises.

Andy Friedmann – control and worker resistance

A rather more critical view of Braverman is taken by Andy Friedmann. Although he sees control over the labour process as a vital influence upon managerial strategies, he accepts that other factors are also important. Furthermore he argues that worker resistance to management can do more than change the type of control used over them; it can also reduce the amount of control that managers have over some sections of the workforce.

Friedmann's work is based upon a distinction between 'direct control' and 'responsible autonomy'. Under **direct control** every aspect of a worker's labour is tightly controlled and directed by management (as was the aim of scientific management). However, there is no guarantee that management will be able, as Braverman assumes, to maintain direct control. It may be forced to concede some degree of responsible autonomy.

Friedmann defines **responsible autonomy** as 'the maintenance of managerial authority by getting workers to identify with the competitive aims of the enterprise so that they will act "responsibly" with a minimum of supervision'. In other words some workers can be left to monitor their own work and use their initiative so long as they are willing to accept the need to work for the profitability of the company. Workers may be able to force management to accept responsible autonomy if they are well organized, and particularly if they are **central workers**. The skills and capacities of central workers are essential to the long-term profitability of the company. Skilled workers are the most likely to be central workers, while unskilled workers are more likely to be **peripheral**. (This is because the latter are less essential to the company's profits since they can easily be replaced.)

Although workers' resistance is the most important factor determining the amount of autonomy that workers have, other factors such as market forces can have an impact. For example, where companies operate in an uncertain market – where what is produced needs to be changed frequently to meet consumer demand – a flexible workforce with responsible autonomy may be needed.

Friedmann believes that responsible autonomy and direct control have existed side by side during all stages of capitalism, and indeed both may be present within a single enterprise at a particular time. However, he does believe that overall capitalism has moved towards granting more workers responsible autonomy, and he does not agree with Braverman that deskilling is an inevitable consequence of the development of capitalism. For instance, in a study of Coventry car workers, Friedmann found considerable autonomy under the gang system. Employers worked in groups with their own elected gang leader, who was free to negotiate directly with management on behalf of the gang.

Friedmann's work raises the question of whether changes in work in recent years contradict Braverman's claim that capitalism would progressively degrade work. We will deal with this issue in a later section (see pp. 214–18). However, Friedmann does share with Braverman the assumption that at least some degree of control is maintained over the workforce, and like Braverman he sees the attempt to control the workforce as central to the way work is organized.

Braverman, Edwards and Friedmann may all exaggerate the importance of control over the workforce for management. New technology might be introduced for the straightforward reason that products can be produced more cheaply because fewer workers are required. It may have little to do with how easy it will be to control the workforce using the new technology.

Furthermore it cannot be assumed that attempts to control the workforce will be successful. As we will discover in the next section, some workers may be able to defend the definition of their work as skilled even when it goes against the interests of their company.

Skill, worker resistance and power

Braverman's theories prompted a sociological interest in the concept of **skill**. Although Braverman questioned the definitions of skill used in the US census, he did not produce a clear definition of skill himself. He appeared to assume that it could be objectively measured, but later writers have suggested that the definition of skill is, at least in part, a social construction. Groups of workers, and indeed management, may try to impose definitions of skill in their own interests. Some workers may be able to retain the definition of their work as skilled even when the skills required for it are reduced; others may never gain recognition for the skills required in their jobs.

A number of feminist critics of Braverman have argued that he failed to recognize the amount of skill required in some work done predominantly by women. Veronica Beechey points out that 'There are, for instance, forms of labour which involve complex competencies and control over the labour process, such as cooking, which are not conventionally defined as "skilled".' Beechey suggests that in some areas where women have been brought into the labour force they might be doing highly skilled work which is not recognized as such by employers. This raises questions about the extent to which deskilling has taken place. Furthermore, Braverman assumes that deskilling, when it does occur, is a consequence of managerial strategies. Some feminist writers argue that male-dominated trades unions can have as much impact. Sylvia Walby has described how men have been far more successful than women in protecting their skills, and the definition of their jobs as skilled, in engineering, textiles and clerical work.

In a study of the engineering and textile industries in Rochdale, Roger Penn describes how some groups of skilled manual workers were able to protect the skills of their work, not just from female workers but also from management. Penn argues that these workers successfully used techniques of social exclusion even when management had the technical means to deskill their jobs. **Social exclusion** involves the prevention of management from controlling the labour process. It also involves the prevention of other workers (particularly less skilled workers) from taking over parts of their job.

Penn believes that workers in occupations in which factory production preceded automation were able to develop techniques of social exclusion within the factory and were able to defend their skills. Engineers and mule spinners came into this category and they successfully resisted deskilling for many decades. In particular areas of the country such as Rochdale, local conditions (particularly a shortage of skilled labour) allowed the engineers to protect their skills as late as the 1960s. In other parts of the country engineering was deskilled decades earlier. For other occupations which were originally skilled, automation and factory production occurred simultaneously. Groups such as weavers and cardroom workers were not well enough organized to resist deskilling.

Penn's work shows that management is not always free to impose the labour process it desires upon workers. Workers can do more than force management to change its control strategy: they can successfully resist deskilling for many decades. Penn accuses Braverman of a type of determinism for seeing deskilling as the inevitable result of the capitalists' need to control the labour force. Like some feminist critics he claims that Braverman pays too little attention to the power of male trades unions.

▮ Flexibility and post-Fordism

A number of writers have argued that since the 1970s there have been important changes in industry and work in general. They put forward a quite different perspective upon work to that supported by Braverman: they believe that changes in work in recent years have *increased* the amount of skill required by many workers. What is more, they see a number of factors other than the need to control the workforce as shaping the organization of work by employers. From this point of view there has been a trend away from the techniques of production associated with 'Fordism'.

Fordism

Fordism is named after Henry Ford, the American car manufacturer who pioneered mass production. It involves the use of a moving assembly line which controls the pace of work. Under this system workers perform repetitive assembly tasks which require little training or skill. The parts used are designed so that they can be assembled easily. Machines are used to produce standardized parts for products which are mass produced. Products made using this system tend to be relatively cheap. Labour costs are held down because there is little need to employ skilled labour. Because of the large number of products produced, overheads and capital costs, such as the cost of machinery, are relatively low.

From Braverman's point of view such production methods, when combined with scientific management, do indeed deskill work and make it easier for management to control the labour process. However, Braverman's views are called into question if, as some now believe, Fordism is outdated and is being replaced.

Post-Fordism and flexible specialization

Michael J. Piore is amongst those who believe that capitalist countries have entered a **post-Fordist era**. He claims that much work is now organized according to the principles of **flexible specialization**. Many of these principles originated in Japan but have been adopted by employers in other capitalist countries partly as a response to the success of Japanese business.

According to Piore, manufacturers have used new technology, particularly computers, to make manufacturing more flexible. For example, computer numerical controlled machine tools can be frequently reprogrammed to perform different tasks. This enables manufacturers to make goods in small batches economically: it no longer costs vast amounts to shift from the production of one product to the production of another.

According to Piore, new technology helps

industry to meet changing demands. Consumers are increasingly demanding more specialized products, and the demand for mass produced articles is decreasing.

Piore believes that these developments have resulted in changes in patterns of work and management. As companies become more flexible, they require more flexible and skilled workers. He says:

These developments seem to be producing an employment structure in which low-skilled repetitive tasks are reduced (eliminating semi-skilled jobs), but the highly skilled work involved in designing products or in shifting from one product to another remains, albeit often in a new form more closely linked to the computer.

More flexible working requires a more flexible organizational structure. Firms are organized less hierarchically with more communication between departments. Managerial practices also change. Many companies have adopted the Japanese *kanban* or **just-in-time system** whereby large stocks of parts are no longer held in reserve. Instead they are delivered just before they are needed to the appropriate workers. Apart from cutting costs, this also allows the product to be changed almost instantaneously.

Workers in companies which are changing along these lines need to be more broadly trained as their work becomes increasingly varied. Because of their long training and the importance of their skills to their companies, they enjoy more job security, and management makes greater attempts to enlist their cooperation.

Some firms have adopted another Japanese technique, **quality circles**. In quality circles groups of workers and managers meet together periodically to discuss how the production or performance of the company can be improved.

Other initiatives may include workers' representatives sitting on company boards, and profit-sharing schemes which enable workers to benefit from any success the company enjoys.

Flexible specialization then, increases the skills needed by the workforce, and unlike industries where scientific management techniques are used, workers may cooperate with management in organizing the labour process. By implication, job satisfaction increases and industrial conflict decreases.

The theory of flexible specialization also implies a move away from the concentration of capital in giant corporations and an increase in the number and importance of small businesses. Another supporter of the flexible specialization theory, C. Sabel, points to the Third Italy region as an example of how industry is likely to develop in the future. This region in the north of Italy enjoyed considerable economic success in the 1970s. It is based upon networks of small- and medium-sized firms which cooperate together making use of each others' specialist skills. The Italian clothing firm Benetton is used by Sabel as an example of flexible specialization. It changes its products frequently and uses a wide range of suppliers in order to respond to the rapidly changing demands of the fashion market.

The flexible firm – core and peripheral workers

Similar views have been developed by the British economist John Atkinson in his theory of the **flexible firm**. Atkinson believes that a variety of factors have encouraged managers to make their firms more flexible. Economic recession in the 1970s and 1980s, and the consequent reduction in trades union power, technological changes and a reduction in the working week, have all made flexibility more desirable and easier to achieve.

According to Atkinson flexibility takes two main forms.

1 **Functional flexibility** refers to the ability of managers to redeploy workers between different tasks. Functional flexibility requires the employment of multi-skilled employees who are capable of working in different areas within a firm. Such flexible workers form the **core** of a company's workforce. They are employed full-time and have considerable job security. The core is usually made up of 'managers, designers, technical sales staff, quality control staff, technicians and craftsmen'. These are shown as A in Figure 4.3.

2 **Numerical flexibility** is provided by peripheral groups. Numerical flexibility refers to the ability of firms to reduce or increase the size of their labour force. The first peripheral group have full-time jobs but enjoy less job security than core workers. These workers might be 'clerical, supervisory, component assembly and testing', and they are easier to recruit than core workers because their skills are common to employment in many different firms. These are shown as B in Figure 4.3. The

Figure 4.3   The flexible firm

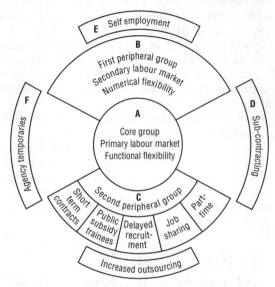

(*Source*: Atkinson, J. (1985) 'The changing corporation', p. 19 in D. Clutherback (ed.) *New Patterns of Work*, Gower, Aldershot.)

second peripheral group of workers are even more flexible. They are not full-time permanent employees. They may work part-time, on short-term contracts, under temporary contracts or under a government training scheme. (These are shown as C in Figure 4.3.) Atkinson believes that flexible firms are making increasing use of external sources of labour. More work is subcontracted (D) and the self-employed (E) and agency temporaries (F) are also used.

Figure 4.3 shows how Atkinson sees the flexible firm and the wide range of labour sources that are available to increase functional and numerical flexibility.

Atkinson does not go as far as Piore in believing that the trend towards flexibility increases the skills and autonomy of the workforce. He certainly believes that core workers benefit from the changes. They learn a greater variety of skills and increase their functional flexibility. Management also allows participation by core workers in the decision-making processes of the firm.

On the other hand the further away workers are from the core group, the less likely they are to enjoy such benefits. Peripheral workers may not be required to broaden their skills, and employers may give them little opportunity to participate in decision making.

Like Piore, Atkinson offers no support for the view of Braverman that work has been deskilled.

Unlike Piore, Atkinson does not imply that most workers have their skills increased or broadened in flexible companies. Peripheral workers usually require less skill, and have their work more closely controlled than core workers.

■ Criticism and evaluation of theories of flexibility

Theories about the increasing flexibility of work have been controversial because they contradict the widely held belief among sociologists that work is becoming less satisfying and less skilled. Anna Pollert is one of the strongest critics, indeed she has tried to 'dismantle' the **theory of flexibility**. Pollert argues that the theory of flexibility 'conflates and obscures contradictory processes within the organisation of work'. She believes that the theory is certainly oversimplified and at times inaccurate.

Production methods

In the first place, Pollert does not believe that Fordist production methods have ever been as dominant as flexibility and post-Fordist theories imply. Small batch production has been important throughout the twentieth century and companies with the flexibility to produce specialized products are nothing new. Pollert does not believe either that there has been any marked reduction in the importance of mass production. She says:

> one can look at a whole range of industries which are based upon mass and large batch production and continue to sell well to large markets: food, drinks, flat-pack furniture, DIY goods, toiletries, records, toys – the list covers most consumer goods.

She also points out that the success of Japanese business is largely the result of producing cheap, well-designed and reliable products rather than specialist products in small numbers. The spread of more flexibility in industry is in any case limited by the cost of new technology. Computer-controlled machinery is very expensive and often only big firms can afford it. For example, in the clothing industry only the large manufacturers have the resources to adopt computer-aided design and computer-controlled cutting systems.

Flexibility and skill levels

Second, Pollert questions the views that flexibility, where it has been introduced, has led to the workforce requiring more skills. Basing her argument upon a number of empirical studies she claims that flexibility can have a wide variety of effects upon work. She says that more flexible production may lead to 'continuing dependence on traditional skills, deskilling, skill increases and skill polarisation'. Management and workers may well come into conflict as a result of the introduction of new technology or management proposals for new working practices. Pollert points out that either side 'can wrest gains and suffer costs in the negotiation of change'. Once again Pollert finds the theory of flexibility oversimplified.

The peripheral workforce

Third, Pollert attacks Atkinson's claim that companies are making increasing use of a peripheral workforce. On the basis of a number of statistical studies Pollert argues that the amount of temporary work has fluctuated, but has not increased dramatically: part-time workers declined as a proportion of the manufacturing workforce between 1979 and 1986, and there is little evidence that subcontracting increased in the first half of the 1980s. Peripheral workers of these types have always been an important part of the labour force, and clear-cut increases in these types of employment would be expected if Atkinson was correct about the move towards numerical flexibility.

Skill levels and new technology

Stephen Wood also criticizes Piore and Atkinson. Like Anna Pollert he questions the view that the changes associated with flexibility have led to workers needing greater skills. His own study of two British steel-rolling mills found that new technology did help to increase the range of products produced, but it did not increase significantly the skills needed by workers. He suggests that many of the workers who do highly skilled jobs with the new technology were skilled workers to start with and have not had their skills increased. In other

cases flexibility for workers means little more than having to move between semi-skilled jobs which require very little training.

Wood accuses supporters of theories of flexibility of greatly exaggerating their case. He questions the degree to which there has been a move towards specialized production by asking 'What proportion of the cars of even the British royal family or president of the USA are custom-built?' He attacks Piore and Sabel for ignoring the negative consequences of changes in work for the British workforce in the 1980s. These include 'job losses, unemployment, tightening of performance standards, labour intensification, changing employment contracts and reduction of the power of trade unions and workers' representatives'.

Multi-tasking and the intensification of labour

Paul Thompson is perhaps slightly less critical of theories of flexibility than Wood. He accepts that 'The modern worker does frequently have to be more flexible.' He suggests that teamworking could be here to stay and he does detect a move away from Taylorism and scientific management. Nevertheless he thinks that the 'extent and novelty of flexibility has been grossly exaggerated'.

Thompson argues that many jobs have not been reskilled but have simply been expanded to include a greater range of tasks each of which requires little skill. He found evidence of this **multi-skilling** or **multi-tasking** in his own research at Leyland Volvo bus plant. He also claims that it is typical of fast food outlets such as McDonald's. Workers are expected to be able perform a variety of tasks involved in preparing and selling the food, but there is little skill involved and virtually no opportunity for workers to use their initiative. They have to follow very detailed sets of rules telling them how to do their jobs.

Thompson acknowledges that some of the old methods of controlling and monitoring workers have been relaxed, but new methods of control have been put in their place. Some companies use new technology to monitor the performance of workers; others award daily or weekly scores to encourage poor staff to work harder. Nissan UK uses a 'Neighbour Watch' system which involves workers monitoring each other. Companies also use more intensive recruitment processes, such as detailed psychological tests, and workers are expected to conform more closely to 'corporate culture and norms'.

Japanese companies and those using similar management methods have also succeeded in making workers work harder. As Thompson points out, policies such as just-in-time are intended to get rid of the slack in the production process. Production targets are regularly increased as the pace of the work gets faster and faster.

Overall, Thompson believes that important changes are taking place in work, but they are not as the supporters of flexibility describe them. The changes are more limited than they first appear; they do not always lead to reskilling; and they frequently result in an intensification of work. To Thompson ideas such as post-Fordism are unwarranted generalizations. The claims about changes in work are far too sweeping. In different countries, companies and sectors of the economy, the extent and nature of changes can be very different.

Flexibility and control

Braverman claimed that in the twentieth century management tightened its control over the labour process, but theories of flexibility imply that management increasingly shares control with core workers. Maryellen R. Kelley has tried to evaluate these competing claims in a study of management and new technology. She studied industries in the USA which used programmable automation involving computer-controlled machinery. Her study was based upon responses to questionnaires from production managers in 1,015 plants of which 43 per cent had adopted programmable automation. The data were collected in 1986–7.

Kelley distinguished between three types of control.

1 In factories using **'strict Taylorist' control**, machines were programmed by engineers or management. If Braverman was correct this would be the predominant type of control.

2 **Worker-centred** control existed where blue-collar or manual workers programmed the machines. If theories of increasing flexibility were correct this type of control would be predominant.

3 In factories where manual and non-manual workers both played a part in programming **shared control** existed.

Table 4.1 Types of control in US manufacturing plants

	Plants %	Total employment %
Strict Taylorist	24.0	47.1
Shared control	44.8	41.1
Worker centred	31.2	11.8

(*Source*: Kelley, M. R. 'Alternative forms of work automation under programmable automation', in S. Wood (ed.) (1989) *The Transformation of Work?*, Unwin Hyman, London, p. 239.)

As Table 4.1 shows, no one pattern of control was dominant and Kelley concluded that neither Braverman nor flexibility theories were supported by her research. Worker-centred control was found to be more common in relatively small plants, and 70 per cent of the plants with worker-centred control did concentrate on producing small batches. This might seem to support theories of flexibility; however, over 50 per cent of factories using strict Taylorist control also specialized in small batches. Furthermore because worker-centred control was more common in small plants, only 11.8 per cent of the workforce benefitted from this type of control.

The future of work

Braverman's theory of the degradation of work, and Piore and Atkinson's theory of flexible specialization reach very different conclusions about the direction that work is moving in. Braverman adopted a Marxist approach and was very pessimistic. Piore and Atkinson used more conventional economic theories and reached predominantly optimistic conclusions. Nevertheless, criticisms of the theories suggest that they share a common fault: all three writers claim that work is developing in one particular direction. They ignore evidence which shows that work may develop in different ways in different industries and types of employment: while much work is becoming less skilled and more tightly controlled, other work is retaining or increasing its skill content and becoming more flexible.

Conflict and cooperation at work

Having looked at various theories concerning the changing nature of work in society, we will now consider a different aspect of this subject: conflict and cooperation.

Forms of conflict

Conflict at work can take many different forms.

1 Conflict may occur between managers and non-managerial workers or between different groups of non-managerial workers. The former type of conflict has usually been the focus of sociological study because it has often been assumed that those in positions of authority at work have different interests to their subordinates, but conflict is also common between groups of workers. For example, semi-skilled and skilled workers may clash over such issues as wage differentials and job demarcation.

2 Conflictual behaviour by workers can take a variety of forms. These include sit-ins, working to rule, refusal to work overtime, absenteeism, leaving the job, working with less than normal effort, and striking.

3 As Richard Hyman points out, many of the actions taken by workers may be a response to management behaviour. Employers and their managers may initiate conflict. Hyman says 'conflict with the *employee* can take the form of plant closure, sacking, victimization, blacklisting, speed-up, safety hazards, arbitrary discipline and so on'.

In one form or another conflict is a common feature of work. It is not, though, by any means universal. In many places of work employees routinely obey instructions and carry out their work tasks without perceiving a conflict of interests between themselves and their employers, and without engaging in conflictual behaviour. In some places of work managers enlist the assistance of other workers in increasing the efficiency and success of the company, and consult workers' representatives on proposed changes.

Some sociologists emphasize the extent to which there is cooperation based upon common interests at work; others the extent of conflict based upon different interests. These different perspectives will now be examined with particular reference to the role of trades unions in society.

Consensus and cooperation in work

From a functionalist perspective society is characterized by **shared interests**. As we saw in Chapter 2, functionalists such as Talcott Parsons and Kingsley Davis and Wilbert E. Moore do not believe that there should be any conflict of interests between employers, managers, and other workers (see pp. 26–7 for details).

Talcott Parsons claims that 'the whole occupational sphere is dominated by a single fundamental goal. That of "success".' He believes there is a value consensus in industrial societies based upon individual achievement and economic efficiency. Workers at all levels in a company will recognize that it is necessary for individuals to carry out specialized tasks according to their ability, and that it is necessary for the activities of a company to be coordinated by workers who hold positions of authority. If a company is successful, everyone benefits: shareholders receive larger dividends as the company becomes more profitable; workers can enjoy higher wages and job security.

From this point of view conflict damages everyone's interests since it prevents the success of the company. If there is conflict it is due to minor malfunctions in the system, and the removal of conflict can be achieved with reform of industrial relations rather than a radical change in the structure of industrial society. Summarizing this point of view V.L. Allen states 'Given the assumption of consensus of the existence of a common purpose then it must be possible to envisage a completely strike-free economy as a permanent state.'

Pluralism, trades unions and the institutionalization of industrial conflict

From the pluralist perspective, differences of interest do exist in industrial societies. For example, employees have an interest in increasing their wages, whilst employers have an interest in keeping wages low so that profits can remain high. However, employees also want to keep their jobs and it is therefore against their interests to press for wages that will make their industry bankrupt.

Moreover as consumers, workers may realize that excessive wage demands will lead to inflation which in turn will devalue their wage packets. In this situation it is possible for different interest groups such as employees and employers to resolve their differences through negotiation.

Pluralists believe that power in industrial societies is dispersed between many different interest groups, all of which have some power. **Trades unions** form the major groups representing the interests of employees. A number of sociologists who support the pluralist position have argued that largely through trade unionism the working class has been integrated into capitalist society. Conflict between employers and employees exists, but it has been **institutionalized** in terms of an agreed set of rules and procedures. The net result is increasing stability in industrialized society. No longer is the working class seen as a threat to social order; there is less and less chance of the type of conflict which Marx predicted. (See pp. 506–13 for an outline of pluralist views.)

Ralf Dahrendorf – industrial democracy

The German-born sociologist Ralf Dahrendorf argues that pluralism 'provides an opportunity for success for every interest that is voiced'. He believes that the voice of the working class is growing louder through its formal associations. He sees a trend towards a more equal balance of power between employers and employees and the development of what he terms **industrial democracy**. Dahrendorf makes the following case.

Democracy in industry begins with the formation of workers' interest groups. In particular, interest groups are necessary to represent workers since employers cannot negotiate with a disorganized collection of employees.

For workers' interest groups to be effective, they must be recognized as legitimate by employers and the state. This has been an uphill struggle in capitalist societies. In nineteenth-century Britain employers strongly resisted the formation of trades unions, often insisting that their workers sign a document declaring that they were not union members. In America, particularly during the 1930s, organized crime syndicates were sometimes employed by companies to prevent their workforce forming trades unions. However, by the latter half of this century unions were generally accepted as legitimate by employers and the state. Dahrendorf regards this as the major step towards industrial democracy and the institutionalization of industrial conflict.

With the formation of workers' interest groups a number of processes occurred which furthered the integration of the working class into the structure of capitalist society.

1 Negotiating bodies were set up for formal negotiation between representatives of employers and workers. Such negotiations take place within a framework of agreed-upon rules and procedures. Conflict is largely contained and resolved within this framework.

2 Should negotiations break down, a machinery of arbitration has been institutionalized in terms of which outside bodies mediate between the parties in dispute.

3 Within each company workers are formally represented, for example by shop stewards, who represent their interests on a day-to-day basis.

4 There is a tendency 'towards an institutionalization of workers' participation in industrial management'. Dahrendorf gives the example of workers appointed to the board of directors in certain European countries.

In the above ways, the voice of labour is heard in capitalist enterprises and there is a trend towards **joint regulation** of industry by workers and employers.

Trades unions and the integration of the working class

The American sociologist Seymour M. Lipset has argued that trades unions 'serve to integrate their members in the larger body politic and give them a basis for loyalty to the system'.

His views may be illustrated by the role of unions in British society of the 1970s. Not only were unions involved in decision-making processes at the shop-floor level, they were regularly consulted by the central Government. Union officials sat frequently on government advisory committees, and cabinets had regular meetings with members of the TUC to discuss important national and international issues. Although there were sometimes confrontations between the Government and unions, there was also a good deal of cooperation.

Some sociologists have referred to this as an era of **corporatism**. Although there is no one agreed definition of corporatism, it involves the Government consulting and cooperating with employers and trades unions in the formulation of economic policy. From 1962 one of the main forums in which these groups worked together was the National Economic Development Council. In 1975 the National Enterprise Board was established through which employers, unions and Government developed policies jointly for firms receiving state aid.

The Labour Government of 1974–9 cooperated with the TUC during most of its term in office through the 'Social Contract'. Under the Social Contract the TUC agreed to moderate wage demands and to try to avoid strike action in return for being able to influence government economic policies.

The picture which emerges from this section is of fully fledged interest groups – trades unions – effectively representing workers' interests. Industrial conflict has been institutionalized and the working class has been integrated into both the capitalist enterprise and society as a whole. However, as we will show in a later section (see pp. 359–61), this picture does not square easily with the large number of strikes that took place in the 1970s. Furthermore, the Labour Government's attempts to control wage rises led to the 'Winter of Discontent' of 1978–9 in which employees such as lorry drivers, health service workers and local authority workers took strike action.

This was followed by the electoral success in 1979 of the Conservatives under Mrs Thatcher. Successive Conservative Governments made little attempt to incorporate unions in decision-making processes. This suggests that the era of corporatism was no more than a temporary phase: industrial capitalist societies may not be able to institutionalize conflict between employers and employees permanently.

Marxist writers believe there are fundamental differences of interest between the owners of the means of production and the proletariat. We will now look at their views.

■ Conflict and consent at work – Marxist perspectives

Marxist sociologists agree that employers and the working class have fundamentally different interests. They believe that workers are exploited by the bourgeoisie because they are not paid the full value of their labour. The bourgeoisie exploits workers by extracting **surplus value** (the difference between the value of the work done and the wages paid).

Thus to Marx, capitalism entailed the need for companies to be profitable. If they were not, capital would not be invested in them and they would not survive. To be profitable they had to be based upon the extraction of surplus value and the exploitation of workers.

This conflict of interests provides the basis upon which conflict can develop within work.

Profit, conflict and control

This point of view has been developed by Craig R. Littler and Graeme Salaman. In order to achieve the maximum amount of profit employers need to control their labour force to make them as productive as possible. They therefore tend to make labour 'as unskilled as is feasible, cheapen it and regulate it so that workers are constrained to act according to the specifications of the employer.' By doing these things, though, employers create the conditions which can lead to conflict. Littler and Salaman say 'Such tendencies create an increasingly serious disadvantage: the loss of employee good will, the emergence of worker resistance, and high levels of labour turnover and absenteeism.'

Many Marxists who have studied the labour process argue that employers cannot afford to allow worker resistance and conflict to reach excessive levels. They require at least some degree of consent and cooperation from the workforce. Littler and Salaman say 'the enterprise, quite obviously, reveals at one and the same time relations of co-operation and integration, and relations of conflict and exploitation.' Cooperation is needed so that workers expend enough effort to be productive and so that management can coordinate those efforts.

The manufacture of consent

In a study based on participant observation in a machine shop in the USA which was published in 1979, Michael Burawoy argues that employers have been able to **manufacture consent** by abandoning very strict control over the labour process. In this way they have been able to disguise exploitation at work, persuade workers that they enjoy rights and benefits at work, and have given workers the chance to adapt to the control exercised over them.

1 Workers are unable to see that they are being exploited at work because employers can blame low wages or job losses on the market and not on themselves. For example, they can claim that the workers cannot expect excessive wage rises or the preservation of all jobs if the company is to compete successfully with others.

2 Burawoy suggests the state's legal regulation of industry limits the actions that management can take and protects it from trying to control work too closely. In doing so the state protects management from itself and prevents excessive conflict. Although writing about the USA, Burawoy's point can be applied to Britain. Such laws as the Employment Protection Act and the Sex Discrimination Act encourage workers to believe that their rights are being protected. They can see themselves as what Burawoy calls **industrial citizens**, protected from exploitation by the law.

3 According to Burawoy, management increasingly allows workers to engage in 'making out'. It does not control the workforce too closely and give them the chance to relieve boredom and avoid fatigue while still meeting or exceeding management production targets. Rules are not enforced too severely and work is not monitored too closely so that workers do not feel oppressed. The workers themselves – through 'making out' activities – create the conditions under which they are willing to cooperate with management and cope with their jobs. As such they contribute to the creation of their own acceptance of exploitation.

Coercion and control

Other Marxist sociologists, though, do not agree that workers are so willingly persuaded to consent to their own exploitation. From this point of view cooperation within work is not chosen by workers but is forced upon them by **coercion**.

For example, Richard Hyman points out that strikes were much more common in Britain in the 1970s than they were in the 1980s. He attributes this to the **coercive pacification** of the workforce under Mrs Thatcher's Conservative Governments. Changes in trades union law and increasing unemployment weakened the bargaining power of workers so that they had little choice but to cooperate with management: workers have no hope of forcing management to accept their demands if they can be replaced easily and have little chance

of finding a new job if sacked. (For further details of Hyman's views in relation to strikes see pp. 226–8.)

Variations in conflict and consent

A more complex view of consent and conflict at work is advanced by P.K. Edwards and Hugh Scullion in a study published in 1982. In a comparison of seven factories in Britain they try to show that the amount of conflict and consent varies depending upon a range of factors. In two clothing factories there was little conflict. Management rigidly controlled the workforce yet for the most part this control was accepted by the workers. In a large metals factory management control was less severe, yet conflict between management and workers was much more evident.

According to Edwards and Scullion the degree to which workers consent to management direction or come into conflict with it depends upon the precise techniques of managerial control used, and the circumstances of particular groups of workers. For example, in the clothing factories workers tended to accept the tight controls as natural and inevitable. Many of them had come straight from school, and had no experience of other work. Dissatisfied workers tended to leave the companies. The workforces had not organized themselves to challenge management, and individual workers were too isolated to try to change the status quo.

In the large metals factory the management was in a much weaker position. The company that owned the factory was not very profitable and the wages they paid were comparatively low. Management could not try to control the skilled workers, upon whom it relied, too closely because they were difficult to replace. The skilled workers were well organized. They saw the management as incompetent and often came into conflict with it. They resented the low wages and on a number of occasions successfully challenged management attempts to increase control over the labour process.

To Edwards and Scullion then, neither conflict nor consent are typical of the workplace. Both are possible depending on particular circumstances. Where management does achieve a high degree of control it can be the result of coercion or achieving consent, or a combination of both tactics. Like the other Marxists examined in this section, Edwards and Scullion believe that differences of interest between management and workers mean that the potential for conflict is always present at work. Unlike writers such as Burawoy, they do not believe that managers have been successful in manufacturing consent and controlling the workforce at all places of work.

Trades unions and the power of labour

Marxist perspectives

In terms of his hopes for the future of the working class, Marx saw both danger and promise in the formation of trades unions. He feared that they might be 'too exclusively bent upon the local and immediate struggles with capitalism'. In other words, trades unions could become preoccupied with furthering the interests of their particular members. In doing so they could lose sight of the overall struggle between capital and labour.

In spite of this Marx believed that unions contained the potential to become 'organized agencies for superseding the very system of wage labour and capital rule'. By uniting workers in a struggle against employers, unions could provide help to create class consciousness. Cooperation between unions against employers on a local level could lead to class solidarity on a national level. In this way unionism could eventually lead to the formation of revolutionary political parties which would seize power.

Trade union consciousness

Marx's optimism was shared by few of his successors. For example, Lenin (who was the first leader of the USSR) argued that unions were limited to developing **trade union consciousness**, that is a recognition of shared interests by members of a particular union rather than an awareness of the common interests of the working class as a whole. This would tend to limit union demands to improvements in wages, hours and working conditions within specific industries. Lenin feared that unions were becoming increasingly self-interested, furthering the interests of their particular members at the expense of other workers.

However, he did believe that 'the trade unions were a tremendous step forward for the working class'. He saw them as an important part of the class struggle, but argued that trade union consciousness could only be widened by linking unions to a political party representing the interests of the working class as a whole.

Modern Marxists are generally pessimistic about the role of unions in the class struggle. Ralph Miliband claims that compared to employers, unions have little power. He states:

> What a firm produces; whether it exports or does not export; whether it invests, in what and for what, and for what purpose; whether it absorbs or is absorbed by other firms – these and many other decisions are matters over which labour has at best an indirect degree of influence and more generally no influence at all.

Not only do unions lack an effective voice in these issues, they show little sign of demanding one. Richard Hyman argues that 'Management still commands; workers are still obliged to obey. Trade unionism permits debate around the terms of workers' obedience; it does not challenge the fact of their subordination.'

Competition between trades unions

The limits of trades union power are apparent from V.L. Allen's analysis of their failure to achieve their basic aim: the economic protection of workers. In pursuit of this aim, unions jealously protect their right to **free collective bargaining**, the right to bargain freely with individual employers on behalf of their members.

Allen argues that unions cannot properly represent workers by this procedure. He maintains that workers' economic interests can only be furthered by a significant redistribution of wealth. This would require considerable government interference in the mechanisms of the **free market economy**. As a result the unions would lose their right to free collective bargaining.

As it is, unions operate within the free price mechanism and for this reason are unable to properly represent their members' interests. For example, if they win higher wages, the employer can pass on the increased costs by raising the price of the product. The worker therefore suffers as a consumer: the wage rise is wiped out by higher prices.

Free collective bargaining means that unions compete with each other in the open market and consequently the more powerful unions gain greater rewards than the less powerful. They also compete with employers, but since they have little control over investment, prices and profit and its distribution, the competition is far from equal. As Richard Hyman notes, despite their vigorous efforts, unions have largely failed to improve the economic position of their members. Writing in 1972, Hyman states:

> throughout this century the share of wages and salaries in the national income has barely deviated from the figure of 60 per cent. Trade unions have not succeeded in winning for their members any part of the percentage of production accruing to profits; they have merely held on to the same relative share of a growing economy.

Given this situation, V.L. Allen argues that trades unions cannot realize even 'their moderate aims of protection satisfactorily without revolutionary

change', a change that will involve a massive redistribution of wealth. In practice however:

> Instead of being directly concerned about the redistribution of income and devising a means to achieve this, they show satisfaction with fractional changes in money wage rates. In doing this they accept the expectations which the employers have deemed suitable for them.

By operating within the framework of a capitalist economic system, unions accept it and make it legitimate. By negotiating with employers, they recognize and accept the system of employment and wage labour. Allen concludes:

> Trade unions then, have acquired aims which are legitimate within the context of capitalist society. They are limited aims, concerning wages, hours of work and working conditions, which can be achieved without unduly disturbing the fabric of capitalism.

Having considered the various perspectives' views on the role of trades union in society, we will now look at what might occur when cooperation between employers and employees breaks down.

Types of industrial conflict

As we noted earlier, there are a number of different types of industrial conflict. In the following sections we will concentrate on two specific types of conflict: strikes and industrial sabotage.

Strikes

Strikes are an obvious expression of industrial conflict. Richard Hyman isolates five elements in the definition of a strike.

1 It is an actual **stoppage** of work which distinguishes the strike from activities such as overtime bans and go-slows.

2 It is a **temporary** stoppage of work – employees expect to return to work for the same employer after the strike is over.

3 It is a **collective act** involving a group of employees and as such it requires a certain amount of worker solidarity and organization.

4 It is the action of **employees**, and this distinguishes the strike from so-called 'rent strikes' and refusals by students to attend lectures.

5 It is nearly always a **calculative act**, an act which is specifically designed to express grievances, to seek a solution to problems, to apply pressure to enforce demands.

Strikes may be official or unofficial. **Official strikes** have the recognition and backing of the union; **unofficial strikes**, sometimes known as **wildcat strikes**, do not.

Striking can be an effective bargaining strategy. Ralph Miliband makes the following observation:

On innumerable occasions demands which, the unions and workers were told, could not conceivably be granted since they must inevitably mean ruin for a firm or industry or inflict irreparable damage on the national economy, have somehow become acceptable when organized labour has shown in practice that it would not desist.

Strikes bring results. In a study of strikes, Richard Hyman concludes that they 'regularly prove highly effective in speeding negotiations towards an acceptable conclusion.'

Strike statistics

Strikes make news. From the 1950s to the mid 1980s the impression often given by the mass media in Britain was that of a strike-prone workforce ready to stop work at the drop of a hat. However, even when the Donovan Commission, a government-sponsored investigation into industrial relations, reported in 1968, it found that in terms of working days lost through strikes 'the United Kingdom's recent record has been about average compared with other countries' (quoted in Hyman 1972, p. 31). The UK had some years with a high strike rate in the 1970s, but strikes declined in the 1980s. In 1992 out of eighteen industrialized countries only Switzerland, Austria, the Netherlands and Sweden had a lower strike rate than the UK (quoted in *Employment Gazette* December 1993, p. 546).

Statistics on strike activity require careful interpretation.

1 First, Hyman points out that British statistics are based on reports provided by employers. Some employers may be more conscientious in recording stoppages than others. Some may leave certain disputes unrecorded to give the impression of good industrial relations. Others may include every single stoppage in the hope of providing evidence for legal restrictions on strikes.

2 Second, different countries use different definitions when compiling strike statistics. In the UK a strike is only included in the statistics if at least ten workers have been involved and the strike has lasted at least one day, or 100 or more working days have been lost. Political strikes are not included. By contrast in Austria, the Netherlands and Japan there are no restrictions on the size of strike before it is included in the statistics. Germany uses a similar definition to Britain's but includes political strikes and excludes strikes by civil servants. In the USA only strikes involving more than 1,000 workers for at least a day or a complete shift feature in the statistics. Clearly international comparisons should take account of these differences.

3 Third, whether a strike qualifies for inclusion is often a matter of interpretation. Keith Grint notes that a 1974 strike by dockers in favour of May Day being a public holiday was defined as an industrial dispute, while an engineering strike against the sequestration of union funds was not. The annual figures are determined by such interpretations.

4 Finally, there are a number of ways of measuring the significance of strikes. These include the actual number of stoppages, the number of workers involved in strikes and the number of working days 'lost' through strike action. Table 4.2 gives statistics for these three measures for Britain from 1900 to 1993.

The figures show that there can be wide fluctuations from year to year. A single major strike can affect the figures a great deal. For example, in 1984 the miners' strike accounted for 22.4 million working days lost, 83 per cent of the total for the year.

However, despite the fluctuations some trends can be detected. Figure 4.4 shows strike trends between 1895 and 1989 by averaging figures over five-year periods. The 1980s saw a substantial reduction in striking, however measured. Furthermore, as Table 4.2 shows, the figures have fallen further since 1989. Since records began in 1891, 1992 saw the smallest number of days lost through strikes in the UK. Although the number of working days lost due to strikes increased in 1993, strikes were still at a historically very low level.

Changes in patterns of striking

Some sociologists have tried to make sense of strike statistics by dividing recent British industrial relations history into periods. J. Durcan, W.E.J. McCarthy and G.P. Redman have identified four district phases of strike activity between 1945 and 1973.

1 They describe 1945–52 as the period of **post-war peace**. Unions tried to cooperate with the Labour Government in the attempt to reconstruct British industry. There were relatively few strikes.

Table 4.2 British strike statistics: annual averages from 1900 to 1993

	Number of strikes	Workers involved ('000)	Striker-days ('000)
1900–10	529	240	4,576
1911–13	1,074	1,034	20,908
1914–18	844	632	5,292
1919–21	1,241	2,108	49,053
1922–5	629	503	11,968
1926	323	2,734	162,233
1927–32	379	344	4,740
1933–9	735	295	1,694
1940–44	1,491	499	1,816
1945–54	1,791	545	2,073
1955–64	2,521	1,116	3,889
1965–9	2,380	1,208	3,951
1970–74	2,885	1,564	14,077
1975–9	2,310	1,640	11,663
1980	1,330	842	11,964
1981	1,338	1,499	4,266
1982	1,528	2,103	5,313
1983	1,364	574	3,754
1984	1,221	1,464	27,135
1985	903	791	6,402
1986	1,074	720	1,920
1987	1,016	887	3,546
1988	781	790	3,702
1989	701	727	4,128
1990	630	298	1,903
1991	369	176	761
1992	253	148	528
1993	211	385	649

(*Source:* Hyman, R. (1977) from the *Department of Employment Gazette*, and *Department of Employment Gazette*, September 1994, p. 27.)

2 The second phase, 1953–9, which Durcan *et al.* call **the return of the strike**. The Labour Government lost office and unions were less willing to cooperate with the Conservatives. There was a feeling among workers that the era of post-war austerity was over and they began to demand regular wage rises. Wage demands were also fuelled by rising prices.

3 The period 1960–8 is termed the **shop-floor revolt**. There were few large-scale strikes but a rising number of small-scale strikes in nearly every industry. There was increasing confidence among shop stewards who organized strikes in individual plants.

4 The fourth phase, 1969–73, is described as the **formal challenge**. Large-scale official disputes became more common and the number of striker-days lost reached record levels.

Hyman argues that Durcan *et al.* identify some of the main trends, but tend to oversimplify the developments. He says:

> Rather than distinct phases, it may be more accurate to speak of overlapping and at times contradictory tendencies, each dominant to a greater or lesser degree at particular points of time.

Nevertheless, Hyman himself claims to be able to identify three phases since 1973.

1 The years 1974–6 were those of the **Social Contract**. In summer 1975 the TUC agreed to cooperate with the Labour Government in trying to curb pay claims. In return the Government formulated economic policy in consultation with the TUC.

2 During 1977–9 there was a **revival of struggle**. Inflation caused a decline in the real value of wages and public sector employees in particular went on strike to protect their wages.

3 Hyman describes the third of his phases as the era of **coercive pacification** in which the actions of Mrs Thatcher's Conservative Governments pushed unions onto the defensive. Force was used to pacify the unions and reduce their willingness and ability to strike. This period, and the period since Mrs Thatcher's replacement as prime minister will now be considered in more detail.

Richard Hyman – Thatcherism and the attack on unions in the 1980s

Hyman claims:

> All post-war British Governments regardless of party (with the partial exception of Heath's first two years) had shared a commitment to the consensual management of a 'mixed economy'. Thatcherite conservatism broke with the commitments of previous Governments.

Figure 4.4   UK strikes 1895–1989: number of strikers (millions), strikes (thousands), days lost (ten millions)

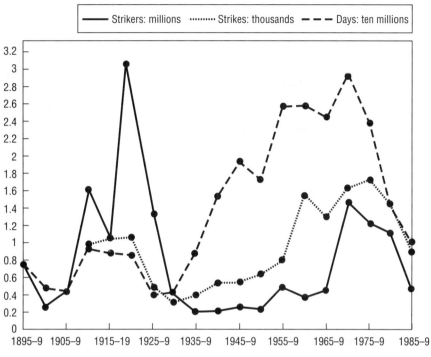

(*Source*: Grint, K. (1991) *The Sociology of Work: An Introduction*, Polity Press, Cambridge, p. 171.)

According to Hyman the Conservatives blamed union extremists for British economic problems and tried to reduce the power of the unions. They believed that policies designed to create full employment left unions with too much bargaining power. The Conservatives were determined that the Government should intervene less in the economy. Instead, market forces should be allowed to control economic developments. Hyman says:

> The succession of anti-union laws, the attacks on public welfare, the 'privatization' of state industries and services, the deliberate creation of mass unemployment, are all logical reflections of a passionate faith in the virtues of competitive capitalism.

The Government developed what Hyman calls a **multi-pronged offensive**. The first part of this involved changes in trades union laws.

1 The **1980 Employment Act** outlawed **secondary picketing** by strikers: it became illegal for them to picket anywhere other than their own place of work. Secondary action, taken in sympathy with another group who were in dispute, became liable for claims for damages, except in special circumstances. Secondary action was only immune from claims for damages where it involved employees of a customer or supplier of the company where industrial action was being taken.

2 The **1982 Employment Act** narrowed the definition of a trades dispute to one which was 'wholly or mainly' about terms and conditions of employment. Disputes which were not covered by immunities became liable to claims for damages. Furthermore, it became possible for courts to grant injunctions telling unions not to engage in unlawful strikes or other types of industrial dispute. If they failed to comply unions were subject to large fines and their funds could be **sequestrated** (temporarily confiscated). The Act also enabled companies to selectively fire striking workers without it being regarded as unfair dismissal.

3 The **Trade Union Act of 1984** made it necessary for secret ballots to be held before industrial action if the action was to be legal. Social security laws were also

amended so that the benefits strikers' families received were calculated on the assumption that strikers were receiving strike pay, whether or not they were.

4 More recent legislation has further tightened restrictions on unions. The **1990 Employment Act** specified that actions involving more than one employer had to be preceded by a separate ballot for each employer involved. Under this Act unions were made responsible for unofficial strike action taken by their members and therefore became liable for claims for damages in such disputes. The **pre-entry closed shop** was also made illegal: it was no longer possible to make membership (or non-membership) of a union a precondition of a job offer.

5 The **Trade Union Reform and Employment Rights Act of 1993** gave union members the right not to have union subscriptions taken from their pay without their written consent. It required strike ballots to be conducted postally and independently scrutinized. It also established a new **Citizen's Right** to take legal action to restrain illegal industrial action.

These changes made it much more difficult for unions and their members to take strike action and sustain it. They placed severe limits upon the legality of strikes and meant that unions and strikers could face prohibitive costs. Not surprisingly they led to a more cautious approach to industrial action by some unions, and so contributed to a fall in the number of strikes, although the legislation itself caused some industrial unrest.

According to Hyman the Government's second line of attack involved the removal of legal protections for employees. For example, fair wages clauses in government contracts were removed. The power of Wages Councils to set minimum wages in some industries was first of all reduced and then in 1993 the Wages Councils were abolished altogether.

The third part of the offensive was to reduce the amount of consultation between Government and unions. Hyman felt that the disdain shown by the Government for trades unions forced the TUC to withdraw from the National Economic Development Council in 1982. The removal of union membership rights at GCHQ in Cheltenham in 1984 led to unions cutting more links with the Government.

Fourth, according to Hyman, the Conservative Government attacked public sector employees. Budgetary controls on local authorities and nationalized industries forced them to offer low wage

increases and stricter conditions of employment. Hyman points to examples such as British Leyland, where he considers there was 'a systematic attack on shop steward organisation', British Steel, where the number employed was halved, and British Rail where 'a succession of disputes has been provoked over pay and working conditions'.

Hyman recognizes that some of these policies led in the short term to serious disputes such as the steel strike in 1980, and the miners' strike in 1984–5. Nevertheless, he believes that in the long term they weakened unions and reduced the number of strikes. In both the disputes mentioned above, unions failed to get significant concessions from the Government.

Finally, Hyman argues that the rapid rises in unemployment in the early 1980s led to a weakening of union power and a reduction in the effectiveness of strikers. Unionists became more concerned about keeping their jobs, and less willing to risk losing them by striking.

Summing up his argument Hyman says:

> each defeat discourages others from the risk of a strike. This negative demonstration effect is part of a process which may be termed 'coercive pacification'; sustained mass unemployment and a governmental offensive have systematically undermined most workers' collective strength and confidence.

Evaluation of Hyman

Keith Grint questions the view that Conservatism under Thatcher and Major has been the principal cause of a reduction in union power. He points out that the fall in official strike figures started before 1979 when the Conservatives returned to power.

Furthermore, declines in strike activity have not been confined to Britain but have occurred in all large Western societies with the exception of Denmark, Finland and New Zealand. These international trends clearly cannot be attributed to British politics. Grint also argues strikes do not necessarily show that unions are strong, and lack of strikes that they are weak. He describes some strikes as 'last-ditch defences' by workers faced with the prospect of unemployment, while in the period 1979–91 wages for British workers kept substantially ahead of inflation and productivity. This hardly seems to indicate union weakness.

Grint does not claim that government policies have had no impact on the union movement, but he sees other factors as having a stronger influence. In particular he believes that the overall economic situation has the biggest effect on strikes and union power.

Paul Smith and Gary Morton – union exclusion in the 1980s and 1990s

Like Hyman, Smith and Morton have also examined the effects of government policies on union power and have noted how employment legislation has been used to weaken unions. However, they have also considered in detail how employers have used the legislation and how changes in work have affected unions. They use John Goldthorpe's concepts of union inclusion and exclusion. **Inclusion** involves allowing unions to participate in decision making; **exclusion** involves isolating and marginalizing unions. For much of the 1970s British Governments tried inclusion, for example, negotiating the 'social contract' with union leaders. According to Smith and Morton the 1980s and 1990s have seen a move towards the exclusion of unions. This has not just been a direct effect of government legislation but has also resulted from employers using the increased freedom of manoeuvre which changed circumstances have offered them.

Smith and Morton note that union membership fell from 13.2 million in 1979 to 10.04 million in 1990. At the same time the number of strikes was falling and union power was apparently on the wane. Some employers have excluded unions by **derecognition**: refusing to recognize unions as the legitimate representatives of workers and refusing to negotiate with them. This is particularly common in shipping and provincial and national newspapers. Half the larger ships owned by UK companies are sailed under flags of convenience and are not therefore subject to union agreements. Companies such as Cunard and Sealink have withdrawn from national collective agreements with shipping unions. Similarly News International and Associated Newspapers are amongst the major newspaper groups which no longer negotiate with the National Union of Journalists.

Other employers have not gone so far but have employed partial exclusion policies. They have recognized the right of unions to exist but have tried to minimize their influence. This has been achieved in a number of ways.

1 Some companies have introduced **performance-related pay**. Under this system workers are paid according to their individual work performance. **Collective agreements** negotiated with unions become less important or completely redundant. A similar method of reducing union influence is to issue **individual contracts** to employees. Since their conditions are different it becomes very difficult for unions to negotiate on behalf of large groups of workers. Many privatized companies have used these techniques. British Telecom, for example, has introduced both performance-related pay and individual contracts for managerial staff and is extending the latter to sales staff.

2 A second way in which union influence has been reduced is through the use of subcontracting. When work is subcontracted non-unionized labour taking over the work may replaced unionized labour. The theories of Post-Fordism and the flexible firm (discussed on pp. 214–18) both suggest that firms are making more use of subcontracting. Increased subcontracting has also resulted from government policy. A number of areas of government and local authority employment have become subject to compulsory competitive tendering: private companies are given the opportunity to bid to take over the work. Smith and Morton comment that in local authorities this has led to 'widespread wage cuts and worsened conditions accomplished with relatively little union resistance'.

3 The unions' collective bargaining power has been further undermined as large organizations have been split into smaller units. Many large companies have handed over bargaining power to subsidiaries. Examples include Cadbury, Courtaulds, Pilkington, Prudential and United Biscuits. These changes make it easier for employers to pick off more troublesome groups of workers without risking a dispute throughout the whole company or organization. For example, in the public sector London Transport was divided into thirteen subsidiaries in 1989. When one of them, London Forest Travel, succeeded in opposing wage cuts and worsened conditions, much of its operation was closed down.

4 Another technique which has been used is the replacement of full-time permanent employees with workers on fixed-term contracts. British Coal and the BBC are among the organizations to have done this. In

British Telecom catering, transport, cleaning, catering and security are all now provided by contract and often non-unionized labour.

Smith and Morton argue then that such union exclusion policies are an important part of the current restructuring of work, 'the object of which is to consolidate the *de facto* redistribution of power to employers'. By implication it therefore makes it more difficult for unions to take industrial action, including going on strike. However, Smith and Morton do qualify their claims saying that 'To date, employers' exclusion policies have been tentative and exploratory.' They also say that 'The result of union exclusion policies cannot be predetermined' and unions' own responses to them will partly determine the extent to which they will undermine union power.

The causes of strikes

In the previous section we examined changes in the number of strikes in Britain as a whole. In this section we will analyse both the reasons for some groups of employees being more **strike-prone** than others, and the factors that contribute to individual strikes.

Strikes are not spread evenly throughout the labour force. In Britain from 1966 to 1970, the number of days lost through strikes, relative to the size of the workforce in particular industries, was greatest in the dock industry followed by the car industry, shipbuilding and coal mining. Table 6.3 gives the figures for 1991 and 1992 and the average for 1983–92. It shows that coal mining and motor vehicle manufacture both remained more likely to experience strikes than other areas of industry. 'Other transport equipment' and sea transport were also liable to strikes over the 1983–92 period.

Strikes and community integration

A number of explanations have been put forward to account for why some industries are more strike-prone than others. In a study of strikes in eleven countries Clark Kerr and Abraham Siegel found that miners, dockers and seamen had the

highest strike records. They argue that **community integration** is the key to explaining strike activity in these occupations.

Miners, dockers and seamen tend to live in occupational communities which are relatively isolated from the wider society. In such communities, a **consciousness of kind** develops which involves a strong awareness of shared grievances, a close emotional commitment to trade unionism, and a high level of working-class solidarity. Shared grievances and worker solidarity, set in the context of a close-knit community, tend to make strike action (a collective act requiring some degree of solidarity) more likely.

Some doubt is thrown on Kerr and Siegel's theory by Stephen Hill's study of London dockers. Hill found little evidence of the community integration which is supposed to be typical of dockland life. The London dockers were remarkably like the affluent workers studied by Goldthorpe and Lockwood. Their life style was largely privatized and their orientation to work and trades unions primarily instrumental. Whatever the merits of Kerr and Siegel's explanation, it is not supported by Hill's particular case study. (For further details of Hill's research see Chapter 2, p. 80.)

Strikes and technology

A second explanation for variation in strike activity emphasizes the role of technology. This explanation has been used to explain the high frequency of strikes in the car industry. It is based on the type of arguments developed by Robert Blauner: assembly line technology produces a high level of alienation which leads to hostile relationships between workers and management. Strikes, as an expression of industrial conflict, will therefore be more likely in industries employing this kind of production technology.

This explanation is unable, however, to account for variation in strike activity within the same industries in different countries. As Richard Hyman notes 'Why does the strike record for the British motor industry contrast so markedly with the comparative harmony in Germany or Japan, when the technology of car assembly is internationally uniform?' The weakness of the technological argument has already

Table 4.3 Working days lost per 1,000 employees (UK)

Industry group (SIC 1980)	1992[a]	1991[a]	Average 1983–92
All industries and services	24	34	
Energy and water	83	76	
Manufacturing	20	46	
Services	25	31	
Agriculture, forestry and fishing	2	1	1
Coal extraction	120	349	12,361
Extraction and processing of coke, mineral oil and natural gas	—	—	247
Electricity, gas, other energy and water	94	15	28
Extraction of metal ore and minerals	–	3	
Metal manufacture and processing	68	21	316 }
Non-metallic mineral products	5	27	
Chemicals and synthetic fibres	—	—	4
Metal goods	16	62	91
Mechanical engineering	45	91	171
Electrical engineering and equipment	31	77	98
Instrument engineering	—	30	75
Motor vehicles	38	19	1,120
Other transport equipment	39	182	1,084
Food, drink and tobacco	1	48	114
Textiles	1	1	70
Footwear and clothing	4	5	61
Timber and wooden furniture	—	—	33
Paper, printing and publishing	10	4	86
Other manufacturing industries	32	22	72
Construction	12	15	69
Distribution, hotels and catering, repairs	—	2	3
Railways	7	10	283
Other inland transport	18	99	163
Sea transport	—	2	928
Other transport and communication	7	35	672
Supporting and miscellaneous transport services	5	1	286
Banking, finance, insurance, business services and leasing	—	3	3
Public administration, sanitary services and education	85	93	174
Medical and health services	1	1	43
Other services	29	32	42

[a] **Based on the latest available mid-year (June) estimates of employees.**

(*Source*: *Department of Employment Gazette*, May 1993.)

been seen from Duncan Gallie's account of British and French oil refineries. Despite working with similar technologies, the French workers had a far higher strike record than their British counterparts.

W.W. Daniel and Neil Millward conducted a study of industrial relations in Britain based upon structured interviews with management and workers at 2,041 places of employment. The study was undertaken for the Department of Employment, the Policy Studies Institute and the Social Science Research Council. Their data did not support the view that technology influenced the number of strikes. Manual workers in single-product factories were no more prone to striking than those employed elsewhere.

Strikes and negotiating procedures

A third explanation for variation in strike activity deals with the effectiveness of the negotiating machinery available for settling disputes. A.M. Ross and P.T. Hartman compared strike levels in fifteen countries between 1900 and 1956. They concluded that strikes are least likely to occur when there are well-established procedures for consultation and negotiation. If procedures exist whereby grievances can be speedily formulated and efficiently channelled into negotiating machinery, strikes will be unlikely.

This view was supported by the *Devlin Report*, a government-sponsored investigation into the dock industry. The *Report* argued that a major reason for the high level of strikes in the industry was the ineffectiveness of the machinery for resolving disputes.

Daniel and Millward examined a number of aspects of negotiating procedures. Contrary to the arguments advanced above they found that establishments with an agreed negotiating procedure were more likely to experience industrial action than those with no agreed procedures.

Daniel and Millward found that strikes were more common in establishments with a large number of manual workers; small establishments had fewer strikes. They also found that the greater the percentage of the workforce who were members of unions, the more likely they were to go on strike. The sex of the workforce made little difference in establishments with few union members, but in highly unionized places of work those with a predominantly male workforce were most likely to go on strike. Share ownership schemes for employees appeared to make strikes among manual workers less likely.

Although Daniel and Millward's findings are interesting, they made no attempt to explain the reasons for the statistical patterns they discovered.

Strikers' definition of the situation

The explanations for variations in strike levels between different industries that we have just outlined have been criticized by Richard Hyman. He argues that they largely ignore the strikers' defi-nition of the situation. For example, workers in one industry may define strikes as a last resort, while those in another may see strikes as a routine and even natural part of industrial life.

Hyman argues that workers do not simply react to production technology or negotiating machinery and predictably strike or not strike as the case might be. They define their work situation and the act of striking in a particular way. Hyman does not deny that factors such as production technology can influence behaviour, but maintains that they are translated into action via the meanings given to them. Thus an explanation of the strike-prone British car industry and the relatively strike-free situation in the same industry in Japan and Germany requires a knowledge of the meanings and definitions that workers give to industrial life.

Disputes over wages and redundancies

So far the discussion of strikes has concentrated on the question of why some industries are more strike-prone than others. In the remainder of this section we consider the reasons for strikes in general.

The biggest single cause of strikes has traditionally been disputes over wages. The statistics in Table 4.4, produced by the Department of Employment, show that disputes over pay remain a very important cause of strikes. However, disputes over redundancies have become increasingly important and in 1992–3 involved more than four times as many workers as disputes over pay. Clearly this was related to the recession. Workers may have become more defensive, trying to protect their jobs rather than trying to improve their living standards by increasing their wages. High unemployment may have made workers reluctant to strike over pay. Low inflation may have made industrial action over pay seem less necessary.

Given the importance of pay as a cause of disputes in earlier years, sociologists devoted considerable attention to explaining why pay seemed to have preoccupied workers. From one point of view the emphasis on pay was not surprising because of the widespread instrumental orientation of the labour force. From their analysis of a strike at the Pilkington glass factory in St Helens in 1970, Tony Lane and Kenneth Roberts argued that the promise of a quick financial reward was a

Table 4.4 UK stoppages in progress: cause

	Twelve months to July 1994		
	Stoppages	Workers involved	Working days lost
Pay: wage-rates and earnings levels	53	32,000	105,000
extra wage and fringe benefits	20	3,300	3,000
Duration and pattern of hours worked	13	4,900	10,000
Redundancy questions	37	172,100	177,000
Trades union matters	6	700	1,000
Working conditions and supervision	4	600	—
Manning and work allocation	27	22,500	46,000
Dismissal and other disciplinary measures	21	5,000	13,000
All causes	**181**	**241,000**	**356,000**

(*Source: Department of Employment Gazette*, October 1994.)

major factor accounting for the rapid spread of the strike around the factory. They claim:

This instrumental approach towards work may have several repercussions for industrial relations. Workers with such a disposition may well use whatever tactics appear most effective to maximize their earning power. They may bargain through union officials or shop stewards, they may work-to-rule, go slow, bar overtime or strike.

However, even when a strike is mainly concerned with money, it inevitably involves questions of power. A strike itself is a power struggle and it may well reflect discontent with the nature of authority and control in the day-to-day running of industry. As Lane and Roberts argue, workers sell more than their labour. 'He' also 'undertakes to abide by a set of rules, he submits to a system of authority.' This involves a sacrifice of certain areas of freedom, a sacrifice which will not be lost on the worker even if he or she does define work in primarily instrumental terms. Lane and Roberts state that 'If he treats his *labour* as a commodity it does not follow that he expects himself, as a person, to be treated as a commodity.'

Disputes over authority and control

It can be argued that, to some degree, discontent about the nature of authority and control in industry underlies all strikes. In some disputes, it is clearly a central issue. From his analysis of the Ford strike of 1969, Huw Beynon states 'It was, as the Halewood stewards never tired of saying, not a money strike but a strike of principle.' The principle concerned control.

Ford had offered the workers a package which, in financial terms, was very acceptable. It involved a wage rise, holiday benefits and lay-off payments. In Beynon's words 'This would have suited the lads. A pay increase, a holiday bonus and a bit of security. That sounded great.'

However, the package also placed important restrictions on the power of the workforce. It included a 'good behaviour clause', which stated that many of the benefits would be cancelled for a six-month period for any 'unconstitutional action' by a group of workers. This covered activities such as unofficial strikes, overtime bans and restriction of output in general. In addition, workers were required to give twenty-one days' notice of an official strike. As one shop steward told Beynon, 'If they get away with this one it will be all up. We'll be back to Victorian times. The ball and chain won't be in it.' In the case of the Ford strike, economic considerations took second place to the principle of control.

A somewhat different approach to the explanation of strikes involves an analysis of events immediately preceding a strike. This approach was used by Alvin Gouldner in his study entitled *Wildcat Strike*. The strike he observed was preceded by a growing sense of grievance and by mounting tension which finally exploded into an outright stoppage of work. New machinery and new management had been introduced into the company and this altered the relationship between management and workers. New rules were enforced and supervision was tightened up. What had been seen as an easy-going relationship with management was now seen by the workers as rigid and coercive. Dissatisfaction with the new regime mounted until it was finally expressed in strike action.

Interestingly, the strikers' demands were for higher wages. They did not regard it as legitimate to challenge management's authority to manage. They expressed their discontent in terms of a wage demand which they felt was legitimate according to the rules of the game. In the end the workers accepted a wage rise as compensation for the new authority structure.

Strikes as normal

The view of the outbreak of a strike as an emotional outburst in response to accumulated grievances and growing tension in the workplace does not explain the origins of all strikes. Lane and Roberts's analysis of the Pilkington strike indicates that it was not preceded by a build up of discontent. Morale was not particularly low, labour turnover not particularly high, there was no change in the number of disputes in the factory, things were 'normal'. Lane and Roberts state:

This means of course that workers can be drawn into a strike without being conscious of an exceptionally wide range of grievances, and without being subject to unusual stress on the shop floor. A strike, in other words, can gather momentum under 'normal' working conditions.

This leads Lane and Roberts to regard strikes as a normal feature of industrial life. The Pilkington workers were dissatisfied with wage levels and relationships with management but these were facts of working life. And it is the facts of working life that Lane and Roberts see as the basis for strikes. They conclude that 'The nature of work, the terms of the employer–employee relationship, the integration of the trade unions into the power structure, all make strikes inevitable.'

■ Industrial sabotage

Laurie Taylor and Paul Walton define **industrial sabotage** as:

---

that rule-breaking which takes the form of conscious action or inaction directed towards the mutilation or destruction of the work environment (this includes the machinery of production and the commodity itself).

Drawing on a wide range of data from the writings of journalists, historians and sociologists, Taylor and Walton classify acts of industrial sabotage in terms of the meanings and motives which direct them. They identify three main motives: 'attempts to reduce tension and frustration'; 'attempts at easing the work process'; and 'attempts to assert control'.

They argue that each type of sabotage indicates the prevalence of distinctive strains or problems within the workplace'.

Attempts to reduce tension and frustration

Taylor and Walton provide the following example to illustrate the first type of sabotage. Two seamen were cleaning out sludge from the tanks of a ship. They had been working for a week and only had two buckets for the purpose. With more buckets the job could have been considerably shortened but the foreman told them he lacked the authority to issue any from the ship's stores. Tired and frustrated, the seamen picked up their buckets and smashed them to smithereens against the bulkhead. This action provided a release for tension and frustration.

Saboteurs in similar situations explain their actions in the following way. They have reached the end of their tether, and often an incident occurs which they feel is the last straw. Sabotage makes them feel better: it gets things off their chest. Such actions are usually spontaneous and unplanned. In the above example, the seamen didn't say a word, they just looked at each other and with a single thought, smashed their buckets.

Taylor and Walton argue that such forms of sabotage 'are the signs of a powerless individual or group'. They tend to occur in industries where unions are absent or ineffective, and where there is little or no history of collective industrial action. In this situation there are few opportunities to remove the source of grievances. Sabotage provides a means of temporarily releasing frustration when workers lack the power to remove its source.

Attempts at easing the work process

The motive directing the second type of sabotage is simply to make work easier. Taylor and Walton give the example of workers in an aircraft factory whose job was to bolt the wing to the fuselage of the plane. When the bolt did not align with the socket some workers used a 'tap' to recut the thread of the socket. This provided the extra thousandth or so of an inch to enable the bolt to be screwed into the socket. The plane was seriously weakened by this procedure, and with sufficient vibration, the bolt could fall out. Despite the fact that taps were officially banned and regular inspections were held to stamp out their use, workers continued to use them.

Taylor and Walton argue that this type of sabotage is typical of industries in which workers have to 'take on the machine', where they work against the clock and wages are dependent on output. By cutting corners, workers can increase output and from their point of view, cut through red tape and get on with the job.

Attempts to assert control

The third type of sabotage directly challenges authority and is used by workers in an attempt to gain greater control. Usually it is planned and coordinated. Taylor and Walton give the example of car workers in Turin. A series of strikes had failed to bring production to a halt so the strikers turned to vandalism and violence to secure their objectives. They smashed production lines and intimidated strike breakers.

Taylor and Walton suggest that this form of sabotage was most common during the early stages of industrialization before trades unions were fully established. For example, machine smashing by groups such as the Luddites in England during the

1820s and 1830s was used as a strategy for raising wages. Taylor and Walton argue that 'In functional terms we could describe trade-union negotiation as taking over from sabotage and other forms of direct action and institutionalizing conflict through collective bargaining.' However, judging from investigations into a number of industries, sabotage (as an attempt to assert control) still regularly occurs.

In *Working for Ford*, a study of Ford's Halewood plant on Merseyside, Huw Beynon notes a number of examples of sabotage directed by a desire for greater control. During Beynon's research, management refused to accept joint consultation with the unions about the organization of work on the shop floor. Management decided issues such as the speed of particular jobs and manning levels. In their demand for greater control, workers would sometimes pull out the safety wire to stop the assembly line. Action such as this forced management to allow workers some control over the speed of the line.

A similar strategy was used by workers in the paint shop who sanded down the cars after an early coat of paint. If they believed they were having to work too quickly or there were insufficient people to do the job, they would sand paint off the style lines, the angles on the body that give the car its distinctive shape. Usually they won the point and got what they wanted.

Taylor and Walton argue that sabotage directed by a desire to assert control tends to occur in the following situations:

1 where there is a history of militancy;

2 a general recognition of who is to blame for grievances;

3 and few opportunities for effective protest through official channels.

Motives for sabotage can and often do overlap. The examples from Halewood may be seen as attempts both to reduce frustration and assert control. Taylor and Walton expected sabotage motivated by a desire for control to increase in Britain. Writing in 1971, they stated:

There appears to be a systematic government and official trade-union campaign not only to reduce strike activity but at the same time to implement productivity agreements which tend to reduce the workers' area of autonomy within the factory.

If the weapons in the workers' armoury are blunted in this way, the desire for control may be increasingly channelled into industrial sabotage.

P.K. Edwards and Hugh Scullion – the social organization of industrial conflict

Most studies of industrial conflict concentrate on one particular type of conflict, for instance, strikes or industrial sabotage. Edwards and Scullion argue that each type of industrial conflict cannot be examined in isolation: companies which have low levels of one type of conflict may have high levels of another. They believe that both the level and the type of industrial conflict experienced in different companies are closely related to the strategies used by management to control the labour process.

Edwards and Scullion examined industrial conflict in seven British factories using unstructured interviews, observation and content analysis of company records. They studied many types of behaviour which could be seen as involving conflict between management and workers: labour turnover, absenteeism, breaches of factory discipline, industrial sabotage, the withdrawal of co-operation and effort by workers, and strikes. All the factories had some conflict but the type of conflict varied.

Labour turnover and absenteeism

In two clothing factories industrial conflict mainly took the form of **labour turnover** and **absenteeism**. Both were small firms and the workforce was strictly controlled. At an underwear factory workers resented the use of disciplinary measures by management. At a hosiery factory the tedium of the work caused discontent among workers, yet management was able to control most aspects of workforce behaviour.

There was little collective organization in the workforces. Both factories paid workers according to piecework, so there was little point in industrial sabotage or withdrawing effort. Many of the

workers were young women and the easiest way to escape from the frustrations of their work was simply to leave. A high rate of labour turnover was tolerated by the management because it was quite easy to replace workers who left. Absenteeism was not a major problem because workers could easily be moved from one part of a factory to another and payment by piecework meant that wage costs were not affected.

Control of the shop floor

The situation was very different in a large metals factory. Labour turnover was lower than in the clothing factories and absenteeism was rare. In most other respects there was a good deal of industrial conflict.

The company that owned the factory was doing badly and the wages of the skilled craft workers were declining compared to those paid by other employers. The company, though, relied upon their skilled workers to maintain continuous production. They could not afford a high rate of labour turnover amongst workers who were difficult to replace at the wage levels they were able to pay. The workers on the shop floor were well organized and with this combination of circumstances managers had difficulty in maintaining control over some aspects of the labour process.

Absenteeism in the large metals factory was rare. Work was carried out under a gang system whereby a group of workers agreed to fulfil a quota for production. Shop stewards were responsible for organizing each gang of workers in order to meet this quota; with the considerable bargaining power of the workers they were able to ensure that the quotas were not very demanding. It was therefore often possible for a gang to finish work early and leave the factory, or even to organize rotas so that workers took unofficial days off. In these circumstances absenteeism was unnecessary.

Similarly there was little point in industrial sabotage when workers already enjoyed so much control. Conflict tended to arise when management tried to reassert control over the labour process by, for example, trying to prevent early leaving or trying to reduce manning levels. Workers responded to these measures by withdrawing cooperation or staging short strikes, steps which usually succeeded in getting management to back down.

Sophisticated control

In a factory that Edwards and Scullion refer to as the 'process factory' there was relatively little industrial conflict. Managers operated a system of **sophisticated control**. Workers had to work shifts and the shift system was potentially a source of conflict. However, employees were selected carefully and the requirements of the shift system were explained to them before they were taken on. Managers regularly consulted workers; they did not require workers to clock in or out and allowed work groups some independence. Employees also received a guaranteed annual salary. Nevertheless, the behaviour of workers was closely monitored and quiet warnings would be issued if they stepped too far out of line. In general this system of sophisticated control succeeded in producing a loyal workforce who were reluctant to take action against management.

One cause of conflict which did remain was the rigidity of the shift system. Management was unwilling to grant time off for personal reasons and this led to some absenteeism. Even this form of conflict was kept within strict limits since absences were carefully recorded and action was taken if an individual's absence record came to be regarded as unsatisfactory. There were shop stewards in the process factory but they usually worked harmoniously with management. They rarely became a focus for organized resistance to management control.

Management strategies and other influences on conflict

Edwards and Scullion's study shows that the presence or absence of industrial conflict is closely related to the strategies used by management to control the workforce. Particular strategies produce particular types of conflict. For example, strong control tends to produce absenteeism and rapid labour turnover. Where workers enjoy considerable control over the labour process withdrawal of cooperation and the occasional strikes are more likely to result. Sophisticated control techniques, if used carefully, can minimize the amount of conflict.

Edwards and Scullion do not claim, though, that management control strategies are the only factor determining the level and type of industrial conflict. The profitability of a company, the local labour market, the strength of workers' organizations and the characteristics of the workforce all play a part in patterns of industrial conflict. Workers may compromise more if their company faces bankruptcy or if alternative employment is hard to find. They may take action more frequently if they are represented by powerful unions or shop stewards. Young and unskilled workers may be less assertive than older and skilled workers. Thus to Edwards and Scullion patterns of industrial conflict cannot be fully understood without reference to the complex set of circumstances at each place of work.

■ Unemployment

In the first part of this chapter we have looked at the issue of work; in the second part we will consider the issue of 'no work' – that is, unemployment.

■ Unemployment statistics

Since the 1970s unemployment has become an important political issue. Government statistics showed that in the 1980s and 1990s unemployment reached higher levels than at any time since the Second World War. Between 1948 and 1966 the official unemployment rate in the UK averaged less than 2 per cent of the workforce. It increased slightly in the 1960s, and in the 1975–8 period rose above 6 per cent. After a drop it rose again to 4.8 per cent in 1980, and then nearly doubled in two years to 9.5 per cent in 1982. Unemployment statistics reached a peak in 1985 and 1986: in both years 11.8 per cent of the workforce was out of work. Unemployment figures then began to fall steadily reaching 5.8 per cent in 1990. They reached another peak of 10.8 per cent in January 1992 before falling slowly to 9.2 per cent in June 1994.

Figure 4.5 Unemployment trends 1980–93

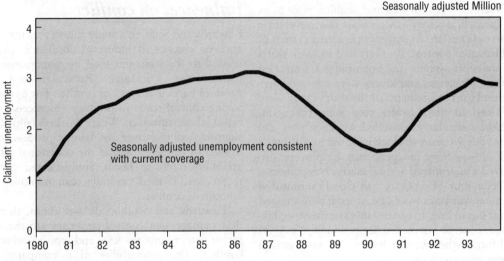

(*Source: Employment Gazette*, January 1994.)

In the period 1948–66 the number of people out of work averaged about 350,000. By 1979 the figure was 1,200,000 and it then rose rapidly to reach an average of 3,289,000 in 1986. By March 1989 unemployment statistics had fallen below 2 million but they rose again to exceed 3 million in 1993. Figure 4.5 shows trends in unemployment between 1980 and 1993. The figures on which it is based are **seasonally adjusted**, that is they take account of variations in the labour market in particular months to reveal the **underlying trend**.

Official statistics as an overestimation

Although most commentators would accept that official unemployment figures provide a general indication of trends in unemployment, they need to be treated with great caution. Some critics of the statistics have argued that they exaggerate the amount of unemployment. For example, in October 1985 Sir Michael Edwardes, the former chair of British Leyland, Lord Young, the then Employment Secretary, and Jeffrey Archer, the novelist and former vice-chair of the Conservative Party, all claimed publicly that up to one million people were included in the unemployment statistics who should not be. This was because they were working and claiming benefit illegally or were not genuinely looking for work.

However, such claims might themselves be exaggerated. In a survey of 1,000 unemployed people in 1982 the Economics Intelligence Unit found that only 8 per cent said they had done any paid work (quoted in Watts 1983, p. 159). In a study of the Isle of Sheppey R.E. Pahl found that the unemployed were no more likely to engage in officially unrecorded 'informal work' than those with paid employment.

It is difficult to measure the number of people claiming to be unemployed who are not seriously looking for work. However, in a review of the evidence Kevin Hawkins claims 'there is no evidence to suggest that any more than a small minority of the unemployed are unconcerned about getting another job'.

Official statistics as an underestimation

Sociologists usually argue that official unemployment statistics underestimate the amount of unemployment rather than exaggerate it. Certainly government figures can be misleading because the basis on which they are calculated has been changed.

Between 1979 and 1987 Mrs Thatcher's Conservative Governments changed the method of calculating unemployment statistics nineteen times, and nearly all of these changes removed substantial numbers from the unemployment register. For example:

1 after November 1982, those who were not eligible for benefits were excluded from unemployment figures;

2 in March 1983 men over 60 who were claiming long-term supplementary benefit (now called income support) were no longer required to sign on and so were no longer recorded as unemployed;

3 in September 1988 benefit regulations were changed so that most people under 18 became ineligible for income support resulting in some 90,000 being taken off the unemployment register.

As a consequence of these and other changes the underestimation of unemployment through the exclusion of those who cannot claim benefits may be very considerable.

Furthermore, there is strong evidence that many people who are unemployed and would like to obtain a job do not bother to register because they are not entitled to claim any benefits. This applies particularly to many married women.

Unemployment figures have been further reduced by various training schemes which remove young people in particular from the unemployment register. According to the *Employment Gazette* there were 270,000 people on youth training schemes in May 1994 and a further 138,000 receiving Training for Work.

In view of the changes outlined above it is clear that officially recorded trends in unemployment cannot be taken at face value. They may have underestimated the extent to which unemployment grew up to 1986 and exaggerated the amount it has fallen since then. Thus while the Department of Employment claimed 3,276,861 people were unemployed in October 1985, a TUC estimate put the figure at around 4,500,000.

The Department of Employment's own *Labour Force Survey* uses a social survey to collect information on unemployment using the International Labour Office's (ILO) definition of unemployment. This defines the unemployed as those who were without work in a particular week, who were available to start work in the next fortnight and who were waiting to start a job or had looked for work in the previous month. Although this excludes some people without a job who would like one but have not recently been seeking work (including people on training schemes), it is a broader definition than that based on benefit claimants used for the standard government statistics.

According to figures based on the ILO definition there were 2,300,000 unemployed in spring 1991, 220,000 more than the official figure of 2,080,000, (quoted in *Department of Employment Gazette* July 1992, p. 347). There were actually 890,000 non-claimants who were unemployed in terms of the ILO definition, but the official definitions includes some claimants who are not defined by the ILO as seeking or available to start work.

■ The social distribution of unemployment

Unemployment is not equally distributed among groups in the population. Despite the limitations of official figures it is possible to discern overall patterns.

Class

Table 4.5 (based upon the Labour Force Survey and the ILO definition of unemployment) shows that lower social classes are generally more likely to experience unemployment. The figures are based upon those unemployed in the survey who had left their last job within the previous eight years. Of these people over two-thirds were manual workers in spring 1993. Only 4.5 per cent of the unemployed were from professional occupations in 1993 whereas 14.1 per cent were from craft and related jobs, and 13.3 per cent were plant or machine operatives.

Gender

The official figures show considerably higher rates of unemployment for men than women. In July 1994 there were 1,998,000 men registered as unemployed compared to 645,100 women. According to these statistics women make up just over 24 per cent of the unemployed. However, these statistics for women are likely to be an underestimate given that married women are usually ineligible for the benefits which would lead to them being registered.

The ILO statistics in Table 4.5 give a somewhat different picture. According to this measure

Table 4.5   The unemployed in Great Britain: by sex and previous occupation group

	Spring 1992			Spring 1993		
	All %	Men %	Women %	All %	Men %	Woman %
All ILO unemployed (thousands)	2,649	1,785	863	2,804	1,904	900
(rate)	9.6	11.4	7.2	10.2	12.3	7.4
All unemployed with previous occupation stateda (thousands)	2,241	1,556	685	2,355	1,646	710
SOC major groups						
1 Managers and administrators	4.6	5.0	3.6	4.9	5.2	4.4
2 Professional occupations	2.7	3.0	2.1	3.5	4.1	2.7
3 Associate professional and technical	5.0	6.9	2.9	5.0	6.5	3.4
4 Clerical and secretarial occupations	6.9	10.3	5.4	7.2	12.2	5.5
5 Crafts and related occupations	12.9	13.2	10.8	14.1	14.6	10.3
6 Personal and protective service occupations	7.7	10.3	6.3	7.8	11.3	5.9
7 Sales occupations	7.8	9.0	7.0	9.0	11.3	7.7
8 Plant and machine operatives	13.2	12.9	14.2	13.3	13.2	13.5
9 Other occupations	13.7	20.1	6.8	14.1	20.1	7.6
All non-manual previous occupationsb	5.1	5.6	4.7	5.6	6.2	5.0
All manual previous occupationsb	12.5	14.4	8.3	13.0	15.3	8.3
Economically active people aged 16 and over						

a Excludes those who left job more than eight years ago.
b The manual/non-manual classification is based on an individual occupation and cannot be deduced from SOC major groups.

(*Source*: *Employment Gazette*, July 1994, p. 255.)

women made up just over 33 per cent of the unemployed in spring 1994. ILO figures probably also underestimate the number of unemployed women since considerable numbers of married women may wish to work without actively seeking employment.

Although unemployment is still probably higher for men, it should be noted that women are more likely than men to do part-time jobs, and full-time employment may be elusive for women.

Age

Table 4.6 gives unemployment rates as a percentage of the economically active males and females in each age group. It is based on the ILO definition of unemployment. The figures show high rates of unemployment for the young, particularly for men under 29, and below average rates for both men and women over 40.

It has been generally accepted that youth unemployment was one of the most serious unemployment problems of the 1980s and 1990s. However, there is evidence to suggest that unemployment is more likely to be a long-term problem for older members of the workforce.

Ethnicity

The evidence concerning ethnicity and unemployment is more straightforward. Figure 4.6 is based on data from the *Labour Force Survey* for spring 1993. It shows that ethnic minorities suffer from higher rates of unemployment. The survey found that less than 10 per cent of whites were unemployed, compared to over 25 per cent of blacks and around 30 per cent of Pakistanis/ Bangladeshis. The unemployment rate for Indians and other ethnic minorities also exceeds the national average. Unemployment is particularly common among younger members of ethnic minorities.

Table 4.6 UK unemployment rates¹: by sex and age

	1986 percentage	1991 percentage	1992 percentage	1993 percentage
Makes				
16–19	21.8	16.5	18.7	22.0
20–29	15.7	12.3	15.3	16.4
30–39	9.4	7.8	10.4	10.3
40–49	7.8	5.8	7.8	8.8
50–64	9.3	8.4	10.4	11.9
65 and over	9.3	5.9	4.9	4.6
All males aged 16 and over	11.7	9.2	11.5	12.4
Females				
16–19	19.8	13.2	13.8	16.0
20–29	14.4	9.4	9.4	10.2
30–39	10.1	6.9	7.2	7.0
40–49	6.7	4.9	5.0	4.7
50–59	6.1	5.1	5.0	5.6
60 and over	5.1	4.4	3.1	3.9
All females aged 16 and over	10.7	7.2	7.2	7.5

¹ Unemployment based on the ILO definition as a percentage of all economically active. At Spring each year.

Region

Finally, there are considerable variations in the regional distribution of unemployment. Unemployment tends to be highest in regions which have traditionally relied upon the heavy industries; these were badly hit in the recessions of the late 1970s and early 1980s.

The recession at the start of the 1990s hit the usually more prosperous areas in the south of England and service sector jobs harder, but it was still the north of England, Northern Ireland and Wales which bore the brunt of unemployment. This is reflected in the official figures for 1992 which showed that Northern Ireland had the highest rate of unemployment at 14.2 per cent, while the lowest rate was in East Anglia at 7.8 per cent. The North, North West, Wales and Yorkshire and Humberside all had rates of 10 per cent or over, while the South East, South West and East Midlands all had recorded rates of below 10 per cent. Nevertheless, the gap between unemployment rates in different regions of the UK narrowed in the early 1990s and there were some surprising figures for 1992. For example, Scotland had a comparatively low unemployment rate at 9.5 per cent, while Greater London had a higher rate of 10.4 per cent.

Statistically then, you are most likely to suffer from unemployment if you are a young unskilled male worker living in Northern Ireland, Wales or the northern parts of England. White, middle-aged, professional workers living in the South East are much less likely to be unemployed.

■ The causes of unemployment

Economists distinguish between a number of types of unemployment.

Frictional unemployment

Frictional unemployment occurs when workers change jobs but do not move immediately to their new job. They are unemployed for a short time as they search for work or wait to take up a new position. Economists regard frictional unemployment as inevitable in a changing economy and it is not usually seen as a serious problem.

Structural unemployment

Structural unemployment occurs when jobs are available and there are workers seeking employ-

Figure 4.6 Unemployment rates: by ethnic origin.

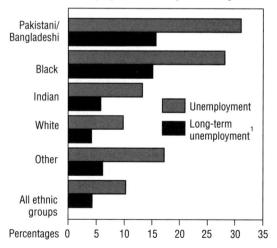

¹ Unemployed based on the ILO definition as a percentage of all economically active.

(*Source: Social Trends*, 1994, p. 63.)

ment, but the workers do not match the jobs. There are two main types of structural unemployment: regional and sectoral.

1 **Regional unemployment** exists where unemployed workers do not live in the areas where suitable vacancies are available. In the second half of the 1980s as unemployment fell it became difficult to fill some vacancies in South East England because of labour shortages in that region despite high unemployment in other parts of Britain.

2 **Sectoral unemployment** exists when the unemployed lack the appropriate skills or qualifications to fill vacancies. As old industries decline and new ones develop, some workers are left with obsolete skills. In Britain, workers in such industries as textiles, coal mining, shipbuilding and iron and steel who have been made redundant have found it difficult to find work which matches their skills.

Cyclical unemployment

Both frictional and structural unemployment occur when vacancies are available for the unemployed. Although these types of unemployment accounted for some of the unemployment during recent decades in Britain, clearly they could not account for it all. The number of unemployed far exceeded the number of vacancies: the supply of labour exceeded the demand for workers by employers. Such a situation is sometimes called **cyclical unemployment**.

All western economies experience fluctuations with periods of depression and boom following one another. These economic cycles may be short-term, with minor fluctuations over four to six year periods, or they may be long-term. For example, the British economy experienced a major depression in the 1930s, which was followed by a post-war economic boom in the 1950s and 1960s, which in turn was followed by recession in the 1970s and 1980s.

This raises the question of why Britain experienced such a severe depression which led to such rapid rises in unemployment in those decades. We will consider different explanations for this depression later in this section.

The concept of cyclical unemployment does imply that unemployment will fall to comparatively low levels in the future. However, some writers claim that capitalist, industrial economies have changed in such a way that full unemploy-

ment will never occur again. In particular it has been suggested that new technology has permanently reduced the demand for labour.

Technological change and deindustrialization

Recent decades have seen a continuing decline in the importance of manufacturing industry. In June 1975 there were 7.35 million workers in manufacturing industry; by March 1993 there were just 4.175 million. Over the same period employment in coal, oil and natural gas extraction and processing fell more by more than 230,000 and by 108,000 in energy supply jobs. At the same time employment in service industries rose by more than 2,500,000. Some have seen these changes as representing a deindustrialization of Britain with serious implications for future levels of unemployment.

In 1979 Clive Jenkins and Barrie Sherman predicted the **collapse of work**. They estimated that over twenty-five years there would be a job reduction of five million, or some 23 per cent of the labour force. They acknowledged that service sector jobs would increase, but new technology would lead to a large reduction in manufacturing employment.

Jenkins and Sherman attached particular importance to microprocessors. Products incorporating microchips would require fewer parts. Machines using the new technology would be easier to maintain and test. Computers would result in more efficient stock control thereby decreasing the amount of stock held in warehouses. Fewer clerical staff would be required because microcomputers and computer-controlled machines would drastically reduce the numbers involved in the direct production of goods. As a result of such changes a typical company could cut its workforce by 50 per cent.

Jenkins and Sherman give the example of television production. When Thorn Electrical Industries decided to copy Japanese television manufacturers by changing to new technology this resulted in the workforce at assembly plants being cut by half while maintaining the same level of output.

Colin Gill has suggested that new technology threatens to reduce the workforce in numerous occupations. Amongst the groups threatened are printers, welders, draughtspeople, laboratory technicians, engineers, sales staff, warehouse workers, postal staff, supervisors and mineworkers.

Not only did Gill anticipate a decline in manufacturing industry, but he also said 'the prospects for continued employment growth in the existing service industries looks bleak.' He suggested that the concentration of retailing in large supermarkets and other shops would tend to reduce employment. He believed that employment in banking, insurance and professional services would be hit by new information technology, which would allow routine aspects of these jobs to be automated. In other areas there was no guarantee of increased employment. The level of government employment largely depends upon government policies, and in the 1980s the British Government was reluctant to expand the workforce in areas such as education and health.

The recession of the early 1990s seemed in line with some of Gill's pessimism. Redundancies in areas such as financial services, hotels and distribution increased considerably and white-collar workers added significantly to the ranks of the unemployed.

Despite the strong arguments advanced to support the view that technological change has led to rising unemployment, other commentators attach more importance to weaknesses in the British economy. For example, Kevin Hawkins points out that many industrial jobs have moved to other countries rather than disappearing altogether. Britain has lost manufacturing jobs at the same time as consumers have bought increasing amounts of imported goods. British industry has found it difficult to compete successfully with overseas competition. Jobs have been created in Japan, other European Community countries, and newly industrialized countries of the Third World, such as Taiwan and Hong Kong, but not in Britain.

From this point of view high unemployment levels are not inevitable. They could be reduced if Britain's economy and industry could become more efficient and competitive.

■ Theories of unemployment – market liberal theory

During much of the period since 1945 it was accepted by Labour and Conservative Governments alike that the Government could and should maintain low levels of unemployment. Much of this thinking stemmed from the work of the British economist J.M. Keynes.

Keynes argued that unemployment in the 1930s was caused by a lack of demand in the economy. If too few goods were purchased then production would be cut back and jobs would be lost. If the demand for goods were increased then the process would be reversed and unemployment would fall. It was therefore the duty of the Government to manage demand in the economy; an increase in government spending could cut unemployment.

Successive Governments were committed to a mixed economy. Government control over key industries would allow the Government to manipulate the economy so that mass unemployment could be avoided.

In the 1970s the consensus about broad economic policy was eroded. Governments faced the problem of rising inflation as well as rising unemployment. Measures designed to reduce unemployment could lead to increased inflation. The Conservative party under Mrs Thatcher turned to **market liberal economic theories** which challenged Keynes's view that the Government could solve economic problems by increasing demand in the economy.

Monetarism

The most influential economist advocating market liberal policies was the American Milton Friedman. He advocated **monetarist** policies to control inflation. He believed that inflation was caused by too much money chasing too few goods. The Government could reduce or even eliminate the problem by reducing the money supply, that is, allowing less money to circulate in the economy. This necessitated cutting back on government spending and not expanding it, as Keynes advocated.

To Friedman there was a **natural rate** of unemployment in any economy. The Government could not reduce unemployment below the natural rate without causing excessive inflation unless there were other fundamental economic changes. The natural rate of unemployment was affected by such factors as the level of unemployment benefit and the flexibility of wage rates.

Classical free market economists such as Adam Smith had argued that unemployment could not exist in the long-term. The unemployed would be prepared to work for lower wages in order to get a job, and at lower wage rates it would be profitable for employers to take workers on. The demand for and supply of labour would come into balance and unemployment would disappear.

Friedman pointed out that there was not, in reality, a totally free market in labour. Unions could use their power to drive up wages artificially high, and unemployment benefits would discourage people from working for low wages. Other important factors would be the mobility of the labour force, and the availability and cost of information about job vacancies.

Government economic policy

These views were reflected in the policies of the Conservative Governments of Margaret Thatcher and John Major from 1979. They tried to cut public expenditure, reduce the power of unions by changes in the law, and make benefits for the unemployed less generous. The overall policy was intended to reduce the role of the state in economic affairs and leave **market forces** to determine the way the economy developed.

It was hoped that these policies would make British industry more competitive, allowing efficient industry to prosper. The burden of taxation on successful industries would be reduced if the Government ceased to subsidize inefficient industries. Nationalized industries were to be privatized and public subsidies to inefficient 'lame duck' industries would be withdrawn.

Criticisms of government policies

Critics of those policies have argued that far from reducing unemployment, they actually caused it to increase. John MacInnes points out that the short-term effects hardly supported the claim that the measures would produce lower unemployment levels:

employment in manufacturing fell by 21 per cent shedding 1.5 million jobs between December 1979 and December 1982. Total employment fell by 2 million (9 per cent) in the same period.

MacInnes accepts that a world recession would have led to rising unemployment whatever policies the Government followed, but he claims the slump in Britain was deeper than in other advanced industrial countries, and he attributes this to government policies. He argues that the Government simply lowered demand in the economy, and this 'dampened economic activity sufficiently to reduce inflationary pressures, but at the cost of a large drop in output, slower growth and much higher unemployment.'

MacInnes acknowledges that after 1983 unemployment figures fell, but he questions the claim that this demonstrates the long-term success of Mrs Thatcher's free market policies. He puts forward the following arguments.

1 Compared to other countries, Britain's employment record was poor. Between 1980 and 1986 total UK employment fell by 3 per cent, but by rather less (2 per cent) in the European Community as a whole. In the USA employment rose by 10 per cent over the same period.

2 Some of the decline in unemployment was due to changes in the definition in unemployment, and increased numbers on government programmes such as the Youth Training Scheme.

3 All of the increased employment between March 1983 and September 1986 was due to a rise of some 388,000 in the number of part-time jobs. MacInnes calculates that over this period the number of full-time jobs actually fell by over 50,000.

He therefore concludes that the recovery after 1983 'did little to reverse the rise in unemployment', which he believes the Government's policies had encouraged.

After MacInnes made the above comments unemployment rose again, suggesting that he was right to question the claim that free market policies would solve the problem. The number of full-time employees fell by more than a million between March 1991 and March 1993, during the recession of the early 1990s. Furthermore a number of commentators, such as Frank Field, have argued that the Government had abandoned any attempt at pursuing full employment. Indeed, Norman Lamont, the first chancellor in John Major's Government, described unemployment as 'a price well worth paying' to achieve other economic goals such as reducing inflation.

▉ Marxist theories of unemployment

Unlike Keynes and supporters of market liberal theories, Marx saw unemployment as resulting from the capitalist system itself. He did not believe that in the long-term capitalist economies could be managed to eliminate unemployment, nor did he think that market forces would reduce unemployment of their own accord. Marx saw unemployment as an endemic problem of capitalism, and one which could get progressively worse.

However, he did not believe that capitalist economies always had and would have high levels of unemployment. He believed that such economies went through cycles. Periods of expansion in which there was full employment were followed by periods of crisis during which unemployment rose. Recoveries from crises were only temporary. Each successive crisis would be worse than the previous one until eventually the capitalist system was destroyed.

Marx believed that capitalist economies worked in the following way. The bourgeoisie are primarily interested in maximizing the amount of surplus value produced. (**Surplus value** is the difference between the costs of producing commodities and the price they are able to sell them for.) In order to be successful, members of the bourgeoisie must compete with each other. To succeed they must invest some of their profits in new machinery which can produce goods more efficiently. In this process they accumulate **capital** in the form of machinery used in production.

During **booms**, the over-accumulation of capital takes place. The bourgeoisie install new machinery, but as their businesses expand they find there are not enough workers to operate it. Because workers are scarce, competition between firms for workers forces them to raise wages. Increased wage levels inevitably mean that the rate of profit falls, since the higher the wages the smaller the proportion of the total costs of production that becomes surplus value. As the rate of profit falls the confidence of the bourgeoisie is reduced, and they are less willing to invest in new technology. Furthermore, at the new and higher rates of pay much of the old machinery that is being used is no longer profitable and has to be scrapped.

The boom is followed by a **slump**. With the lack of new investment, and old machinery being taken out of production, unemployment inevitably rises. Eventually unemployment forces down wage rates, profitability, business confidence and investment increase, and the economy starts to expand again.

Capitalists require workers who can be hired during booms, and fired during slumps. Marx refers to the part of the workforce who are used in this way as the **reserve army of labour**. The unemployed are the victims of the cyclical way in which the capitalist economy works.

The processes described above explain why Marx thought capitalism went through periods of crisis in which unemployment rose. However, they do not explain why he thought these crises would get progressively worse.

According to Marx's **labour theory of value**, it is only labour power, or work, which actually creates wealth or surplus value. As production becomes increasingly mechanized the bourgeoisie invest a greater proportion of their capital in machinery. Labour costs decline as a proportion of the bourgeoisie's expenditure on production. Rises in productivity can increase the surplus value produced by each worker, but as the price of investment in new machinery rises it becomes increasingly difficult for profits to remain high. To maintain profits each worker has to be exploited at a higher rate.

To Marx, this situation cannot continue indefinitely. Workers will eventually realize they are being exploited, develop class consciousness, and overthrow the capitalist system.

Clearly, Marx's predictions that capitalism would collapse have not come true. Indeed the economic system of some former communist countries has come closer to collapse than that of most advanced capitalist countries. Nevertheless capitalist economies have not proved as manageable as economists like Keynes believed. Governments have not been able to manipulate economies in such a way that mass unemployment has become a thing of the past.

Britain's economic decline

Marx's general theory of capitalism claims to explain why mass unemployment occurs periodically in capitalist economies, but it does not explain why Britain should have suffered particularly severe economic problems.

The British Marxist historian E.J. Hobsbawm argues that Britain's economic decline can be traced back to the nineteenth century. He claims that Britain suffered from being the first country to industrialize. British industry invested heavily in machinery in the earliest stages of industrialization and failed to modernize in response to competition. The costs of scrapping obsolete equipment discouraged new investment. This lack of investment prevented Britain competing effectively with developing competitors such as West Germany and the USA.

The British bourgeoisie were able to prevent the rate of profit falling too low in the nineteenth and early twentieth centuries because the British Empire provided a market for British goods, even if they were not produced competitively. Furthermore, the British economy tended to move increasingly into trade and finance where profits were more predictable than in manufacturing. Much British capital went abroad and was used to improve the efficiency of overseas competitors. Hobsbawm concludes 'Britain, we may say, was becoming a parasitic rather than a competitive economy, living off the remains of world monopoly, the underdeveloped world, and her past accumulations of wealth.'

In *The British Economic Disaster* Andrew Glyn and John Harrison note that some of the economic trends noted by Hobsbawm continued in Britain after 1945. Investment in new machinery was low, investment abroad was high. Although the sun set on the British Empire after the war, Britain contin-

ued to trade with ex-colonies with whom it had preferential tariffs. This continued to protect British industry from overseas competition but discouraged capitalists from investing in Britain. Adequate profits could be made without taking too many risks.

Glyn and Harrison, though, attach more importance to the labour market and trades unions than Hobsbawm. They argue that Britain suffered from greater labour shortages than competitors. Japan and the rest of Europe had reserves of underemployed agricultural labour on which it could draw, whereas Britain did not. When combined with strong union organization this led to real wages rising faster than in competitor countries. Wages rose faster than productivity which squeezed profits, discouraged investment in Britain, encouraged investment abroad and ultimately led to 'Britain's economic disaster' and mass unemployment.

■ The effects of unemployment

■ The effects on society

Numerous claims have been made about the effects of mass unemployment on society. Usually the effects have been seen as detrimental to society. Adrian Sinfield argues than unemployment 'devalues or debases the standard or quality of life in society'. He believes it does so in the following ways.

1 Those remaining in work feel less secure and may have their standard of living threatened. This is partly because of short-time working and reductions in the amount of overtime, and partly due to the reduced bargaining power of workers which leads to downward pressure on wages.

2 The workforce becomes less willing to leave an unsatisfactory or unsatisfying job because of the fear

that they will be unable to find new employment. It becomes less mobile and the number of frustrated and alienated workers increases.

3 Divisions within society are likely to grow. The unemployed and those in unsatisfying work may blame weak groups in society for their problems. Male workers accustomed to full-time work, for example, may attribute their unemployment to married women entering the labour market. Immigrants and ethnic minorities may be used as scapegoats with the result that racial tensions increase.

4 Sinfield believes that high unemployment reduces the chance of equality of opportunity being achieved. With a surplus of labour, employers need no longer make an effort to recruit women, ethnic minorities, the young, the old, the disabled and handicapped, or former inmates of prisons or mental hospitals. For example,

writing in 1981 Sinfield claimed that the proportion of firms which had more than 3 per cent registered disabled in their workforce had fallen from two-thirds to one-third with the rise of mass unemployment.

John Lea and Jock Young argue that unemployment among the young leads to the marginalization of some members of society. Those who have never worked feel they have no stake in society. Since they are not members of unions they lack the institutional means to express their discontent. According to Lea and Young this helped to create a **subculture of despair** in some inner city areas of Britain and contributed to the urban riots of the 1980s. (See pp. 640–3 for further details of Lea and Young's views.)

Many social problems have been linked to unemployment. Sheila Allen and Alan Watson say:

Links between unemployment and a wide range of social problems have been made by academics, politicians and journalists. Ill-health, premature death, attempted and actual suicide, marriage breakdown, child battering, racial conflicts and football hooliganism are a few of the examples that have been cited.

Many of these can be seen as the effects of unemployment on the individual rather than on society, and some will be examined in the next section. However, clearly they also have implications for society. If unemployment does cause or contribute to these problems then it may threaten the stability of society by undermining the family, and causing racial tension and crime.

Solving these problems also has economic costs. For instance, greater expenditure may be required on the NHS to finance the treatment of those who become ill due to unemployment. Unemployment has direct economic costs as well. John MacInnes points out that government expenditure on benefits rises with increased unemployment. Between 1979 and 1985, £33 billion was spent on unemployment benefits. The Government also loses the taxation it would have received if the unemployed had been in work.

Despite the strength of many of these claims about the negative effects of unemployment, they should be treated with some caution. Allen and Watson suggest that each problem linked with unemployment may be caused by 'a complex of interacting factors which belie any simple cause effect relationship promulgated in popular debate'. As we will see in the next section, it can be difficult to isolate the effects of unemployment from other variables.

■ The personal effects of unemployment

Financial effects

Perhaps the most obvious effects of unemployment are financial. Melanie White quotes a study by the Office of Population, Censuses and Surveys which found that over two-thirds of families with parents under 35 were in debt after three months' unemployment.

The severity of the financial impact of unemployment has been due to two main factors.

1 There has been an increase in the number of **long-term unemployed**, those who had been out of work for a year or more. At the start of the 1990s claimants lost their right to claim unemployment benefit after twelve months. They then had to rely upon means-tested income support which is paid at a lower rate. Then in the 1993 budget it was announced that unemployment benefit was to be changed to a 'jobseeker's allowance'. This allowance would cease after just six months. The longer a person is out of work, the greater the financial hardship is likely to be as savings are eaten up and financial problems mount.

2 Relative to wages, unemployment benefits have been declining. According to Kay, in 1982 they fell to their lowest level in comparison to wages for thirty years. Even if the actual living standards of the unemployed are higher than they were in the 1930s, the amount of relative poverty caused by unemployment in the 1980s has been considerable. (See pp. 129–37 for a discussion of relative poverty.)

Social effects of unemployment

Many of the effects of unemployment are less easily measured than the financial ones. Leonard Fagin and Martin Little argue that the unemployed lose more than money when they lose their job.

1 They claim that work gives people a **sense of identity** of who they are and what their role in society is. It is a source of relationships outside the family. Unemployment tends to reduce social contacts.

2 Work also provides **obligatory activity**. In a study of unemployed men in London Fagin and Little claimed 'most of the men we saw found immense difficulties in creating a framework which would impose on them a regular, purposeful activity.' They found it hard to occupy themselves.

3 A closely related aspect of work which is lost with unemployment is its ability to **structure psychological time**. Work divides the day and week into time periods and Fagin and Little found the unemployed had difficulty organizing their time without this framework. The men they studied spent more of their time in bed but their sleep was restless and they felt more tired than they did when they were working.

4 Fagin and Little also point out that work provides opportunities to develop skills and creativity and it provides a **sense of purpose**. This sense of purpose tended to be lost with unemployment and was reflected in men making statements such as 'I'm surplus to requirement', 'I'm marginal, a nobody, and nobody gives a bugger', and 'I'm on the scrap heap at fifty-five.'

5 Finally, Fagin and Little suggest that income from work provides **freedom and control outside work**. In particular it creates the possibility of engaging in leisure activities which cost money.

Leisure and unemployment

One possible gain from being unemployed is the increase in leisure time. However P. Kelvin, C. Dewberry and N. Morley Burber found that only certain types of leisure activities increased with unemployment (quoted in Tess Kay 1989, p. 38). The unemployed spend more time watching television, doing housework, reading, engaging in practical activities and hobbies. Kelvin *et al.* found no change in games playing, religious activities, creative activities and general outdoor leisure. Social life and 'going out' both decreased, as did active participation in sport and spectating at sports events. Predictably the unemployed spent more time watching sport on television.

Overall Kelvin *et al.* found that leisure was not an adequate substitute for work because most of the leisure was solitary and passive and failed to compensate for the loss of social contacts at work. They concluded that 'the "leisure" activities of the unemployed are at best palliatives for boredom, and mostly, for most of the unemployed, they are inadequate as that'.

It is difficult to tell, though, how far these changes in leisure are the direct result of unemployment and how far they are simply due to financial hardship. Low-paid workers may be as restricted by money in their leisure pursuits as the unemployed.

Psychological reactions to unemployment

Many commentators from the 1930s onwards have claimed that the unemployed react to the loss of work in a series of stages. The psychological reactions are often quite different amongst the newly unemployed compared to those who have been out of work for some time. Fagin and Little claim to have identified four main stages.

1 The first, which they call the **phase of shock**, was experienced by only a small number of their sample. It consisted of a sense of disbelief and disorientation.

2 The second stage, that of **denial and optimism**, was more common. In this stage, the unemployed are positive and optimistic. They see unemployment as a temporary situation and resolve to take advantage of it. They tend to seek work enthusiastically during this stage, but there is also a sense of being on holiday. If financial problems are not immediate, the unemployed tend to use some of their free time constructively in leisure pursuits. This stage is particularly common amongst workers who felt little attachment to their jobs and they may even feel relieved to have escaped from them.

3 Fagin and Little found that nearly all those who remained unemployed went through the third stage, **anxiety and distress**. The unemployed became more concerned about finding work and anxious about their futures.

4 They found the final stage was **resignation and adjustment**. The long-term unemployed eventually came to terms with their situation. They accepted that their prospects of finding work were slim, lowered their expectations for the future, and became apathetic.

Although many researchers have identified similar sequences of psychological reaction amongst the unemployed, Peter Kelvin and Joana Jarrett warn that such descriptions may oversimplify the effects of unemployment. They stress that reactions to unemployment vary with individual circumstances. Furthermore, some of the reactions may be caused by poverty rather than unemployment as such. They refer to research carried out in the 1930s which showed that not all the long-term unemployed became apathetic. Those whose incomes remained high often remained 'unbroken' (quoted in P. Kelvin and J.E. Jarrett 1985, p. 19).

Similarly, Adrian Sinfield argues that unemployment affects different groups in different ways depending upon their previous experiences, expectations, and the social groups they belong to. For example, a young person with no experience of full-time work might experience unemployment differently from an older worker made redundant after decades of working life. We will discuss some of the differences in the experience of unemployment between social groups later.

Health and unemployment

Perhaps the most dramatic claims about the effects of unemployment relate to health. In a review of research on this subject Jeremy Laurance refers to studies which have reached the following conclusions.

1 Unemployed school leavers in Leeds were found to experience poorer mental health than those who get jobs.

2 A study based upon the 1971 census in Britain found a 20 per cent higher mortality rate amongst unemployed men compared to the employed, even when social class and age were controlled.

3 Researchers in Edinburgh in 1982 found that the suicide and attempted suicide rate was eleven times higher for unemployed men than employed men.

4 National studies of child development in Britain have found that the children of the unemployed are on average shorter than other children of the same age.

Laurance refers in some detail to a study by a GP in Calne, a small country town in Wiltshire. Employment in the town was dominated by a large sausage factory. After it closed, and unemployment rose, consultation rates increased by 20 per cent, and outpatient referrals to hospital went up by 60 per cent.

Laurance is aware that none of the studies actually prove that unemployment causes health problems. Many variables can affect health, and not all of them can be controlled in research. Furthermore the studies do not explain how and why unemployment might lead to ill-health. Neverthe-

less he concludes that there is at least strong circumstantial evidence that the effects of unemployment can go beyond the financial and psychological.

Youth and the effects of unemployment

Many of the resources that the British Government has allocated to dealing with unemployment have been directed at young people. Most, though not all, training schemes have been set up for school-leavers. This implies that unemployment is a particularly serious problem for the young.

This view is supported by Paul Willis. On the basis of a study conducted in Wolverhampton in 1984, he argues that a 'new social condition' has been created for youth in areas of high unemployment. Unemployment disrupts the normal transition to adulthood. The young unemployed are denied the opportunity to become independent from parents and often experience long periods of poverty. They are denied the opportunity to take on family responsibilities and planning for marriage is postponed.

Willis believes that financial hardship prevents them from enjoying a normal social life. Without work, leisure activities have less meaning and increasing amounts of time are spent at home. Young people are left in limbo, in a state of 'suspended animation', unable either to look forward to or make the transition to adult status. They become bored, frustrated and demoralized. This often leads to stress and conflict within the family.

Not all researchers agree with Willis that unemployment hits the young hardest. Ken Roberts accepts that young people do not enjoy unemployment, but he believes they are better equipped to deal with it than older unemployed workers. He says 'as newcomers to the workforce young people have no established occupational identities to shatter.' Since they have not experienced work, they do not lose the sense of identity that work provides for older unemployed people. Very often many of the peers of the young unemployed will also be out of work so the sense of deprivation they experience will be muted. Indeed, financially they may be better off on training schemes or claiming benefits than they were at school. Many can also rely upon generous support from their families. Roberts claims that research evidence suggests that young people suffer less psychological and physical harm from unemployment than older people.

In research involving interviews with 551 16–20 year olds in Liverpool, Manchester, Wolverhampton and London in 1979–81, Kenneth Roberts, Maria Noble and Jill Duggan found many of the young were not committed to finding full-time permanent work. Over half the periods of unemployment experienced by those they studied were caused by youths leaving work voluntarily. Some of them preferred intermittent employment and were less than keen to stay forever in what were often unskilled, low-paid and tedious jobs.

Despite these findings Roberts *et al.* do not claim that youth unemployment does not cause problems. None of their sample actually enjoyed being out of work. Even if unemployment did not cause much psychological damage, it did lead to boredom. The young unemployed had the 'daily dilemma of what to do and where to go'.

There is evidence to suggest that even with these qualifications Roberts *et al.* underestimate the impact of unemployment on the young. For example, in a study of 1,150 unemployed 17 year olds carried out in 1982, Peter Warr, Michael Banks and Philip Ullah produced strong evidence that unemployment was affecting their health. They found the unemployed youths to be suffering from significantly higher levels of psychological distress than their employed counterparts examined in other studies. Some 82 per cent of the symptoms described by the unemployed youths were said to have started at or after the time when they became unemployed.

Gender and the effects of unemployment

Most of the research on the effects of unemployment has been carried out into male unemployment. Official figures tend to disguise the extent of female unemployment and it tends to be assumed that unemployment is a particular problem for men.

Sinfield suggests that female *employment* rather than unemployment is often seen as the problem. Women are expected to be primarily committed to being housewives and mothers rather than workers. The increasing employment of married women outside the home has some-

times been held responsible for rises in male unemployment. Work is often seen as a central source of identity for men, but as less important for women. Women might be expected to suffer less from unemployment because domestic life offers them a sense of identity and purpose.

In the 1980s new research started to challenge such assumptions. Using data from questionnaires and interviews carried out in Brighton in 1983, Felicity Henwood and Ian Miles compared the situation of unemployed men and women. They collected data on access to certain types of experience. These were:

1 meeting a broad range of people;

2 keeping busy most of the day;

3 feeling they were contributing to society;

4 believing they received respect from society;

5 and having things to do at regular times during the day.

Henwood and Miles found that unemployed men and women had less access to these experiences than the employed. Amongst the unemployed in their sample they detected no significant sex differences; women were as deprived of these experiences by unemployment as men.

A lack of these experiences also affected housewives who were not seeking work outside the home. Although their lives were more structured and they had more sense of purpose than unemployed women, they were as deprived of social contacts and things to keep them busy during the day. This research suggests that unemployment is at least potentially as damaging for women as it is for men, and that housewives suffer some of the problems associated with unemployment.

It is sometimes assumed that working women suffer few financial hardships from unemployment. In a study of women made redundant from a clothing factory in Castleford and another in Harrogate, Angela Coyle challenged this assumption. She found that even in families where the husband had the highest wage the wife's wage was usually 'a crucial component of family household income'. Furthermore Coyle points out that many women are divorced, widowed, separated or unmarried, and they rely upon their own wage.

In terms of psychological effects she did find that some women turned their attention to domestic work after being made redundant. For a short time this helped them, but after a while they began to feel isolated. They missed the social contacts and sense of purpose provided by employment outside the home.

Married women often resented returning to a state of financial dependence on men. She also noted that many women took work in the first place to escape from the restrictive limitations of their domestic roles. She says 'the family may soften the blow of job loss, but in the end the family appears to be the trap.'

There is also evidence that young women find unemployment just as traumatic as men. In Warr, Banks and Ullah's study (described above) of 1,150 unemployed 17 year olds the 'Females consistently reported more distress, depression and anxiety, and among the white subsample were considerably more concerned than males about the stigma of being unemployed.' The females were also found to be more committed to finding work than the males.

■ The effects on communities

The social and personal effects of unemployment can perhaps best be illustrated by examining how they interact when unemployment impinges upon a whole community. This is likely to happen when a community relies heavily upon a single source of employment which is abruptly closed down. With the closure of many pits in the UK in recent years, a number of mining communities have been hit in this way.

Studying mining communities

In the early 1990s Chas Critcher, Bella Dicks and Dave Waddington studied two pit villages in Yorkshire. In one village the pit had been shut for six months; in the other for two years. In these villages they conducted unstructured interviews. In spring 1992 they conducted a survey in these and two other pit villages, one of which was 'safe' from closure and another where closure was threatened. They used a twenty-one item questionnaire to measure the level of stress in the four communities. The questionnaire contained questions on psychological symptoms such as anxiety, physical symptoms such as high blood pressure, and behavioural symptoms such as sleeplessness.

Table 4.7 Levels of personal stress in four mining communities (based on a 10 per cent sample)

	Medium stress	High stress	Medium/High combined
Closed six months	28	13	41
Closed two years	21	13	34
'Threatened'	15	13	28
'Safe'	16	5	21

(*Source*: Critcher, C., Dicks, B. and Waddington, D. (1992) 'Portrait of Despair' *New Statesmen and Society*, 23 October, p. 17.)

Stress and personal problems

The results of their survey of stress levels are presented in Table 4.7. They suggest that job security in the 'safe' village helped to keep stress down, while pit closure and even threatened pit closure raised stress considerably. The stress resulting from the loss or threatened loss of a job was made worse because others in the community were also suffering from stress and so would find it more difficult to give support. Critcher, Dicks and Waddington say:

> A woman who worked in the pit canteen described to us how miners had sustained her through her husband's serious illness and the death of her father. She feared the loss of such moral support as much as her loss of earnings.

However, that is not to say that loss of earnings did not have a major impact. In the pit village where the closure had taken place six months earlier, 46.2 per cent of the ex-miners remained unemployed. In the village where closure had taken place two years earlier the picture was scarcely better: 45.7 per cent were still unemployed. Many of those who had found work had been forced to accept 'low pay and job insecurity in the building trade or driving'.

The search for work contributed to high stress levels. One man described how he became anxious after numerous unsuccessful job applications. Although he eventually found work cleaning public buildings it was not before he had started suffering from palpitations and had been put on beta blockers by his doctor. As financial pressures built up 'Cars were sold, and holidays abroad became a distant memory.' With no local employment there was little demand for the houses. They became impossible to sell, preventing people moving in search of job opportunities elsewhere.

Although most of those made redundant in the pits were men, women in the community suffered just as much. The wives of the miners had 'to bear the brunt of family poverty and male despair'. They were faced by 'the hourly presence of an often demoralised partner'. When the women found work to help the family budget their male partner sometimes resented their own loss of status as a breadwinner. Women were also particularly anxious about the prospects for their children. The end result was that:

> many of these women were isolated in a spiral of anxiety and financial hardship, unable to salvage much hope at all for the future, other than a natural optimism and a belief that somehow they would come through.

Social and economic problems

Not surprisingly the widespread personal problems in the two villages caused social and economic problems for the communities as a whole.

The local economy suffered. Some local shops, pubs and services closed down or shed staff as the spending power of local consumers fell. The appearance of the villages began to deteriorate and community facilities started to decay. Informal mechanisms of social control began to break down. A crime prevention officer in one of the villages reported a 27 per cent increase in crime in one year and thought the following year's increase would be more than 35 per cent. Burglary, car theft, joy-riding and petty theft were increasing in both the villages, and there was evidence that drug-taking was also rising. Marriages and family life were coming under increasing stress.

The overall picture presented by Critcher, Dicks and Waddington of the village six months after closure was of 'a community struggling to come to terms with a total disorientation of its established patterns of work, family and communal life'. In both villages the impact of pit closure was enormous. They conclude:

> When we talk of the devastation of mining communities, there is only slight exaggeration. Some do manage to adjust to radically changed circumstances. Others just get by. Some are driven to despair.

Leisure

The sociology of leisure is a comparatively new area of sociology. Although sociologists had made passing references to leisure, it was only in the 1970s that it started to be studied as a distinctive topic. Early contributions to this debate tended to concentrate on the relationship between leisure and other areas of social life, particularly work and the family. We will look at these first.

Stanley Parker – the influence of work on leisure

Stanley Parker defines **leisure** as a residual category of time: it is the time left over after other

obligations have been attended to. He distinguishes five aspects of people's lives.

1 **Work** is the time spent in paid employment.

2 **Work obligations** refers to time which is taken up as a consequence of employment, but is not actually spent working. Travel to and from work is an example of a work obligation.

3 **Non-work obligations** involve such activities as housework and childcare.

4 Time is also occupied by **physiological needs**. People have to spend time engaged in activities such as eating, sleeping, washing and defecating.

5 The time left over is defined as **leisure**.

Although work only takes up part of people's lives, Parker argues that leisure activities are 'conditioned by various factors associated with the way people work'. In particular, he suggests that the amount of autonomy people have at work (the amount of freedom to take decisions and organize their work) the degree of involvement they find in work, and their level of intrinsic job satisfaction, are directly related to their leisure activities.

Parker bases his findings on a series of interviews he conducted with bank clerks, childcare officers and youth employment officers, plus published material on a range of occupations studied by sociologists. He sees the relationship between work and leisure falling into three main patterns: the extension pattern, the neutrality pattern and the opposition pattern.

The extension pattern

In the **extension pattern** work extends into leisure: there is no clear dividing line between the two. Activities in both spheres are similar, and work is a central life interest rather than family and leisure. Time for activities which can be defined exclusively as leisure is short and is used mainly for the 'development of personality', for example, reading 'good' literature or going to the theatre.

This pattern is associated with occupations providing a high level of autonomy, intrinsic job satisfaction and involvement in work. Jobs which typify this pattern include business, medicine, teaching, social work and some skilled manual trades. For example, outside statutory office hours, businesspeople often entertain clients and colleagues at the dinner table or on the golf course, contexts in which business and pleasure are combined. Parker found that the social workers in his survey spent much of their free time in activities connected with their work. Some helped to run youth clubs; others met to discuss clients' problems.

The neutrality pattern

In the **neutrality pattern** a fairly clear distinction is made between work and leisure. Activities in the two spheres differ and family life and leisure, rather than work, form the central life interest.

This pattern is associated with occupations providing a medium to low degree of autonomy, which require the use of only some of the individual's abilities, and where satisfaction is with pay

and conditions rather than work itself. Hours of leisure are long compared to the extension pattern and are used mainly for relaxation. Leisure is often family centred, involving activities such as the family outing. Occupations typically associated with the neutrality pattern include clerical workers and semi-skilled manual workers.

The opposition pattern

In the **opposition pattern** work is sharply distinguished from leisure. Activities in the two areas are very different and leisure forms the central life interest.

This pattern is associated with jobs providing a low degree of autonomy, which require the use of only a limited range of abilities and which often produce a feeling of hostility towards work. Hours of leisure are long and used mainly to recuperate from and compensate for work. The opposition pattern is typical of unskilled manual work, mining and distant water fishing.

The data for Parker's opposition pattern is drawn mainly from two studies: *Coal is Our Life* by Dennis, Henriques and Slaughter, a study of coal miners in Featherstone, Yorkshire, and *The Fishermen* by Jeremy Tunstall, a study of distant water fishermen in Hull. Both occupations have a high death and injury rate, and involve work in extreme and demanding conditions, all of which produces high levels of stress. The leisure activities of the miners and fishermen revolve around drinking in pubs and working men's clubs in the company of their workmates. The authors of both studies see this form of leisure as a means of relief and escape from the demands and dangers of work. Tunstall states 'Fishermen say "Of course fishermen get drunk. Anybody who does what we do has to get drunk to stay sane".' Dennis *et al.* describe the miners' leisure as 'vigorous' and 'predominantly frivolous' in the sense of 'giving no thought to the morrow'. They argue that the insecurity produced by the high rate of death and injury encourages an attitude of living for the moment which is expressed in having a good time down at the working men's club.

Parker's theory of work and leisure was first published in 1972, and since then he has moderated his position to accept that other factors exert an influence on leisure patterns. Nevertheless he has remained convinced that work is the most important factor shaping leisure. This assumption and other features of his work can be challenged on a number of grounds.

Criticisms of Parker

First, Parker tends to ignore factors other than work which shape leisure patterns. As we will see in the following section, Rhona and Robert Rapoport believe that family lifestyle is the most important influence on leisure. Parker also ignores the influence of class on leisure patterns. His opposition pattern may represent a traditional working-class lifestyle, expressed in an extreme form by miners and distant water fishermen, rather than a response to particular occupations. In any case, the lifestyles of miners and fishermen may have changed considerably since the research on which Parker's views are based. With rising living standards and the decline of traditional industries, close-knit occupational communities of groups such as miners and fishermen may be rapidly disappearing.

National culture is another factor which can affect leisure patterns. Research on the leisure of managers illustrates this point. American managers fit squarely into the extension pattern: the manager's life is portrayed as all work and no play with a working week of over sixty hours. Even when leisure was used purely for relaxation, nearly three-quarters of the managers in one survey stated that they saw 'leisure time as a refresher to enable you to do better work'.

This subordination of leisure to work is not reflected in Britain. A survey by John Child and Brenda Macmillan of 964 British managers revealed that only 2.3 per cent mentioned that leisure time was used 'to improve their careers and performance in their jobs'. Nearly a quarter specifically stated that leisure was a means to escape from and forget about work.

British managers come closest to Parker's neutrality pattern. They worked some twenty hours a week less than their American counterparts. They used their relatively long hours of leisure for relaxation and enjoyment. Playing and watching sport, home improvements and hobbies such as photography, were major leisure-time activities. Child and Macmillan conclude that 'British managers prefer to compartmentalize their lives so that the job is forgotten during their leisure time.'

Child and Macmillan argue that a large part of the differences can be explained in terms of the cultures of the two societies. American culture

places a greater emphasis on the work ethic, on the importance of individual achievement and self-improvement, and upon work as a means to these ends.

A second line of criticism suggests that Parker's analysis is rather **deterministic**: it does not allow for individual choice in leisure activities and the wide variety of leisure pursuits engaged in by people who have the same jobs. John Clarke and Chas Critcher say of Parker's theory:

> it fails to allow adequately for human agency and tends to reduce social behaviour to the level of a cultural reflex, in this case to the influence of work.

Clarke and Critcher also advance a third criticism of Parker, that his work does not deal successfully with the leisure patterns of women. They believe that housework should be seen as a form of work, and not as a non-work obligation. Parker does not explain the influence of housework on leisure and he does not take account of the open-ended nature of domestic obligations for many women. Clarke and Critcher suggest that in some cases women may not feel able to lay claim to any leisure 'once they have accepted the overwhelming responsibilities of motherhood'. Gender differences as well as work influence patterns of leisure.

■ Rhona Rapoport and Robert N. Rapoport – leisure and the family life cycle

Rhona Rapoport and Robert Rapoport argue that family life is as important as work in shaping leisure. They see work, leisure and the family as being closely connected and the effects of them on each other can be related to the life cycle. At different stages of the life cycle individuals exhibit varying attitudes to work, family and leisure. The life cycle relates to 'relatively constant preoccupations arising from psycho-biological maturational processes'. The Rapoports identify four main stages in the life cycle.

1 The first phase, **adolescence**, refers to those aged roughly between 15 and 19. The major preoccupation in this phase is a quest for personal identity. The Rapoports say:

young people explore their environments, look for new ones, sample new experiences – all in an attempt to crystallise their personal identities which will underpin a transition to independence.

Some of the activities typical of this phase are arts and crafts, dancing, making music, participating in pop festivals, travelling and sports.

2 The second phase is that of **young adulthood**. The Rapoports see it as lasting for about ten years after a person leaves school. For young adults the preoccupation is with establishing a social identity rather than a personal one. This is partly achieved through becoming associated with particular institutions and through an attempt to establish intimacy with and commitment to other people. The main concerns are with occupations, relationships with members of the opposite sex, parental and family relationships, and friendship interests. To some extent leisure interests narrow during this phase. Much leisure is focused on places where heterosexual contacts can be made. Nightclubs, discos, pubs and sport centres are frequented by young adults.

3 The third phase is called the **establishment phase** and occurs roughly between the ages of 25 and 55. During it people are no longer rehearsing future roles but are trying to establish a satisfying lifestyle. Work, family, friends and community activities are all important. Physical activities become less important for men and for both men and women home-centred leisure activities become more central. Children, homes and gardens, and watching television become more significant than in previous phases.

4 The Rapoports refer to the final phase simply as the **later years** and it starts roughly at the age of 55 or with retirement. The preoccupation at this phase is 'a sense of social and personal integration. . . of personal meaning and harmony with the world around one.' Patterns of leisure vary a great deal in this phase and in part depend upon such factors as health and income. Poor health or low income restrict the opportunities for leisure for some. Despite the variety of leisure patterns, the Rapoports do note a tendency for it to become more home-centred and grandchildren are sometimes a focus for leisure.

Throughout their book, *Leisure and the Family Life Cycle*, the Rapoports stress that many factors other than the life cycle influence leisure patterns (for instance, gender and class) and they acknowledge that there is a great deal of variation between individuals going through a particular stage. Nevertheless, they believe that leisure can only be understood with reference to preoccupations which are typical of the different phases.

Criticisms of the Rapoports

The Rapoports have been criticized for having both an inadequate theory and inadequate evidence. Clarke and Critcher claim that despite the many qualifications made by the Rapoports, they put too much emphasis on the life cycle. According to Clarke and Critcher this is because the life cycle has a biological basis and therefore the Rapoports see it as more fundamental than other factors.

Clarke and Critcher argue that the meaning of different phases of the life cycle are socially constructed and not biologically based. They say 'The possibility that society *constructs* age, through its organisation of education, housing, retirement and its images of young and maturity, has been lost.'

Ken Roberts argues that the Rapoports' study lacks systematic evidence. It uses case study material to illustrate the points being made but no attempt is made to analyse the data to see how typical the case studies are. Furthermore, the Rapoports do not even specify how the material was collected.

We will now examine Ken Roberts's own views on leisure.

■ Ken Roberts – a pluralist perspective on leisure

Ken Roberts takes a rather broader view of leisure than Stanley Parker or the Rapoports. He does not deny that work and the life cycle influence leisure, but he sees other factors as important as well. He stresses the variety of leisure patterns that are available to individuals, and he sees leisure as involving freedom to choose. Indeed, Roberts defines leisure in terms of choice. He says 'Leisure is not the whole of non-work but, within this area, includes only those activities (and inactivities) that are relatively self-determined.' In other words individuals are only engaging in leisure when they feel they are choosing what to do themselves.

Things which people have to do, or feel they have to do, cannot be leisure. Some activities such as paid employment and physical necessities like eating or sleeping clearly do not count as leisure according to this definition. To Roberts, activities such as tending the garden and paying a visit to ageing relatives only count as leisure if they are done freely and not out of a sense of obligation.

Roberts accepts the claim of pluralists that Britain and other advanced industrial societies are essentially democratic. (For a full discussion of pluralism see pp. 124–35.) There are many different groups in society and an enormous variety of leisure interests. The latter are affected by class, age, sex, marital status, education and many other factors. All groups in society have the opportunity to pursue their interests within the limits laid down by the law. The public simply take part in the leisure activities they enjoy.

Leisure and choice

Roberts argues against theories which claim that the public have their leisure interests manipulated by others. He denies that the state and commercial enterprises impose patterns of leisure on people. He says 'The providers have no captive audience.' The state provides some facilities but this does not guarantee that it can shape patterns of leisure. Roberts points out:

---

members of the public can pick and choose. They do not have to use country parks, Forestry Commission nature trails, art centres or sports halls. People only use the facilities that they find useful, and if the public sector does not satisfy their tastes, individuals can turn to commercial provision or self-help.

They can also join pressure groups to encourage the Government to subsidize the types of leisure pursuits that they most enjoy.

According to Roberts, commercial providers of leisure have to respond as much as the Government does to public tastes. However much they try to manipulate the public through advertising or other means, people are free to choose the goods and services they buy. The declining public demand for bowling-alleys has forced many to close down, while the commercial sector has had to respond to new leisure interests. For example, travel firms have responded to the increasing demand for cheap package holidays abroad.

If neither the state nor private companies provide the leisure opportunities the public wants then individuals can provide their own: there are 'participant-run dart and domino leagues, golf clubs and photography societies, while kids play street football and arrange their own informal games'.

Social factors and leisure

Although he stresses the freedom of choice in leisure activities, Roberts does not deny that social factors influence patterns of leisure. People choose to engage in leisure pursuits which fit in with their personal circumstances, lifestyle and the social groups to which they belong.

Roberts uses data from a survey he conducted in 1972 to examine the factors influencing leisure. The sample used consisted of 474 economically active males in Liverpool. On the basis of his evidence Roberts claims that work has relatively little influence on people's leisure pursuits. He also points out that even excluding the unemployed, about half the population do not have paid work. The young, retired and full-time housewives do not have their leisure influenced by work simply because they are not 'working'. He disagrees with Stanley Parker that work is the central factor shaping leisure amongst those who do have a job. In all occupational groups television takes up the largest single block of leisure time, and alcohol, tobacco, gambling and sex are popular throughout the occupational structure.

Roberts accepts that class affects leisure, but rejects the view that it is the dominant influence. Activities such as going to the theatre are predominantly middle class, but they take up only a minute amount of leisure time. Low income limits the leisure activities of some groups, but he claims nearly everyone has enough money to participate in a sport and have a holiday of some sort.

Family life cycle and leisure

Roberts attributes far more importance to the family life cycle than he does to work. His findings are broadly in line with those of the Rapoports. For example, he found that unmarried people under 30 spent less time watching television and more time socializing than their married counterparts.

Roberts differs from the Rapoports in placing more emphasis on the influence of factors other than the life cycle.

1 He recognizes gender as being important and suggests that women have less leisure time than men.

2 He found education also had a strong influence. Those who had stayed on longer in education watched less television and spent more time outside their homes with friends.

3 Finally he argues that styles of marriage are important. Married couples who have joint conjugal roles tend to engage in home-centred leisure, while those with segregated conjugal roles tend to go out more. (For a definition of joint and segregated conjugal roles see p. 359.)

Roberts's views differ from those we examined earlier in the emphasis he places on the variety of factors influencing leisure. To Roberts, leisure is defined as a matter of choice and is characterized by diversity. There are social influences on leisure, but compared to work it is an area of life in which individuals enjoy great freedom.

John Clarke and Chas Critcher – leisure in capitalist Britain

John Clarke and Chas Critcher have developed a neo-Marxist approach to the sociology of leisure. Their work has been influenced by the Italian Antonio Gramsci who himself developed Marx's theories. (For a discussion of Gramsci's work see pp. 530–2.)

Clarke and Critcher argue that writers such as Roberts greatly exaggerate the degree of freedom and choice involved in leisure. They accept that individuals do have some freedom in their leisure activities, but they are limited and constrained by capitalism. Leisure is an arena of struggle between different social groups (in particular classes) but it is not an equal struggle. The bourgeoisie are in a stronger position to shape leisure than subordinate classes.

Capitalism and leisure

Clarke and Critcher claim that the very existence of capitalism shapes the nature of work and leisure. Before the Industrial Revolution there was no clear dividing line between these two spheres of life. Those working in agriculture and domestic textile production could to a large extent determine when and how hard they worked. For example, there was the widespread practice of taking Monday off, which was known as 'St Monday'. Leisure and work could sometimes be combined: people often drank alcohol whilst working.

The Industrial Revolution and the development of capitalism initially had two main effects: it removed many of the opportunities for leisure, and led to a clear demarcation between work and leisure.

Investment in industrial machinery required people to work increasingly long hours and any flexibility was lost. The machinery had to be used to the full to get the maximum return from the investment and the workforce had to be present at the same time. With the excessive working hours working-class leisure became largely confined to the tavern.

By the 1880s leisure began to grow: working hours were reduced and living standards rose. However, the freedom and flexibility of leisure in pre-industrial times did not return.

According to Clarke and Critcher, the two most important influences on leisure became the state and capitalist enterprise. Both began to play a crucial role in defining leisure and determining the leisure opportunities available.

The state plays an important role in licensing certain leisure activities such as pubs, wine bars, casinos and betting shops, and 'undesirables' are excluded from holding licenses. Films and videos are censored or cleared for release. Health and safety legislation regulates the conditions under which leisure goods and services can be consumed. Through these measures the state is empowered to ensure that leisure is safe and orderly but at the same time limits are placed upon the ways that leisure time can be spent.

Another important area of state involvement in leisure is its regulation of public space. There is inequality of access to private space, particularly housing, for leisure purposes, and the disadvantaged tend to use public spaces such as the street and parks for leisure. In these circumstances the young, ethnic minorities and the working class in general have part of their recreation controlled by the police who might deem some of their activities on the street as inappropriate. Clarke and Critcher suggest that conflict over the use of public space was one factor contributing to the urban riots of the early 1980s in Britain.

They also claim that the state is concerned to prevent disorderly leisure which might be a threat to social stability. Working-class leisure patterns are discouraged. Middle-class tastes and culture are promoted and subsidized by the state. Leisure centres have had some success in increasing working-class involvement in sport, but in general there is a middle class and male bias in the sports which are promoted. The Sports Council's most funded sports are squash, swimming, athletics, sailing, rowing, tennis and golf. Summing up Clarke and Critcher say:

> in relation to both body and mind, the state has pushed policies aimed at drawing subordinate social groups into 'rational recreation' in order to curb the potential dangers of free time.

If people are engaged in officially sanctioned leisure pursuits they cannot be engaged in violence, riots or political agitation.

The commercialization of leisure

Perhaps the most important aspect of leisure under capitalism, according to Clarke and Critcher, is its commercialization. Leisure has become big business and an important source of profit for the bourgeoisie. Clarke and Critcher quote figures which indicate that in 1978–9 leisure accounted for over 25 per cent of consumer spending in Britain.

The commercial provision of leisure is dominated by large companies which have a wide variety of leisure interests. For example, the Rank Organization is involved in the film industry, the manufacture of hi-fi and videos through subsidiaries like Bush and Wharfedale, has interests in dancing, bowling and bingo, and owns hotels, marinas and Butlins.

Clarke and Critcher claim that such large corporations have the power to persuade consumers of leisure needs. The leisure industry creates new products and services and then tries to convince consumers that they should purchase them.

In some areas of leisure provision a few large companies dominate the market and restrict consumer choice. In the brewing industry the 'big six'

– Watney Mann, Bass Charrington, Allied, Scottish and Newcastle, Whitbread and Courage – have taken over many smaller breweries and closed them down. They have reduced the number of beers available, closed pubs and tightened their control over the remaining pubs by replacing tenants with salaried managers. At the same time they have tried to change the character of pubs, altering the layouts and replacing traditional pub games with more profitable juke boxes and fruit machines.

Although Clarke and Critcher believe that the state and private enterprise have restricted choice and manipulated tastes, they do not believe that they have completely dominated leisure. They claim that leisure, like other areas of social life, has been affected by class struggle. The state and private enterprise have tried to establish their **hegemony** or domination of leisure, but they have not been entirely successful. In some areas they have met with effective resistance.

For instance the Campaign for Real Ale resisted the large brewers' attempts to replace natural with keg beers and to some extent reversed the trend towards reducing the range of beers available. Similarly, the state has not always been successful in persuading the working class and other subordinate groups to accept participation in the leisure pursuits which it has promoted.

Criticisms of 'class domination' theories

Despite the qualifications to the argument of Clarke and Critcher, they clearly see leisure as being a far more restricted area of social life than pluralists such as Roberts. However, Roberts himself dismisses what he calls **class domination theories** of leisure.

To Roberts leisure choices are as free as can be expected in any society. Companies try to make a profit out of leisure, but they can only succeed if they provide what consumers want. The state may intervene in leisure, but in doing so it tends to increase choice rather than restrict it. Roberts argues:

> if recreational opportunities are to be made available to economically disadvantaged groups, public provision is a logical if not the only method. If the state did not subsidize sport and other forms of

recreation that involve the use of land, the majority of children would be unable to participate.

The pluralist and neo-Marxist perspectives on leisure offer quite different interpretations of this area of social life. Perhaps both tend to generalize and pay too little attention to evidence which contradicts their respective theories.

▌Gender and leisure

All the theories of leisure examined so far have been accused of neglecting or dealing inadequately with the question of gender. As Sheila Scraton puts it 'Until the 1980s women were largely absent as focuses of leisure analyses except as appendages to men or unproblematically defined as part of the nuclear family.' Since the start of the 1980s feminist sociologists have begun to examine women's leisure in its own right and have devoted increasing attention to the question of the relationship between gender and leisure patterns.

A number of feminists have criticized earlier work which made reference to this issue, but failed to explore it in great depth. Eileen Green, Sandra Hebron and Diana Woodward say that Parker's early work was based almost entirely around the leisure of male workers. They note that Ken Roberts suggests gender is important and accepts that women have less leisure than men, but his work contains only short discussions of the issue. Sheila Scraton argues that the Rapoports paid more attention to gender than Parker and Roberts, but their theory lacked any analysis of power or structural inequalities which led to women having less access to leisure than men. Clarke and Critcher's work has been rather better received by feminist writers, but Green *et al.* nevertheless say that it shows a 'surprising lack of engagement with well-known feminist work in the area'.

Gender and patterns of leisure

All feminist writers on gender and leisure agree that there are important differences between men's and women's leisure. They argue that not only do men and women tend to take part in different types of leisure, but women also have less access to

leisure opportunities than men.

The following table and figure present the findings of structured interview research from the *General Household Survey* of 1990. Table 4.8 shows that the only sports games and physical activities that women take more part in than men are indoor swimming, keep fit/yoga and netball. Some 59 per cent of men but only 38 per cent of women had participated in one activity other than walking in the previous four weeks.

Figure 4.7 shows less variation in home-based leisure patterns between women and men. Both had very high rates of participation in watching television, visiting or entertaining friends or relatives, and listening to the radio, records and tapes. However, there was a marked difference between participation in DIY, predominantly done by men, and dressmaking, needlework or knitting, overwhelmingly done by women. This seems to reflect traditional conjugal roles.

Furthermore the table and figure do not reveal differences in the amount of time available to men and women for leisure nor differences in the circumstances in which women and men can engage in leisure. Feminist research, which is discussed below, suggests that in both these respects women are severely disadvantaged.

Liberal and radical feminist perspectives on leisure

While all feminist perspectives see women as disadvantaged in relation to leisure, different feminist approaches disagree about the extent of the problem, the causes of it and solutions to it. Sheila Scraton, though not herself a liberal feminist, has described how liberal feminists see the problem. (The liberal feminist perspective on society is discussed on p. 593.)

Scraton claims that liberal feminists focus on unequal opportunities to participate in leisure and particularly unequal access to leisure facilities. They believe that these inequalities result from the process of socialization through which women and men learn distinctive gender roles. Thus 'discriminatory practices based on stereotypical assumptions about gender' prevent women from enjoying the same opportunities as men.

Liberal feminists seek to change this situation by highlighting these discriminatory practices and getting them changed. Scraton cites initiatives by

Table 4.8 Participation in sports, games and physical activities: participation rates in the four weeks before interview, by gender. Persons aged 16 or over, Great Britain

Active sports games and physical activities	Men 1990	Women 1990
	Percentage participating in the four weeks before interview	
Walking	44	38
Swimming: indoor	11	13
Swimming: outdoor	4	4
Snooker/pool/billiards	24	5
Keep fit/yoga	6	16
Cycling	12	7
Darts	11	4
Golf	9	2
Running (jogging, etc.)	8	2
Weight lifting/training	8	2
Soccer	10	0
Tenpin bowls/skittles	5	3
Badminton	4	3
Squash	4	1
Lawn/carpet bowls	3	1
Tennis	2	2
Fishing	4	0
Table tennis	3	0
Water sports (excluding sailing)	2	1
Cricket	2	0
Horse riding	1	1
Sailing	1	1
Self defence	1	0
Ice skating	1	1
Basketbal	1	0
Athletics—track & field	1	0
Hockey	1	1
Climbing	1	0
Rugby	1	0
Motorsports	1	0
Skiing	1	1
Netball	0	1
At least one activity (excluding walking)	58	39
At least one	73	57
Base = 100%		

(*Source*: (1990) *General Household Survey*, HMSO, London, p. 180)

the Sports Council as an example. The Sports Council has identified women as one 'target group' who are not taking advantage of the opportunities available, and has initiated campaigns to encourage more women to participate in sports.

Liberal feminism is a **reformist** perspective: it claims that gender inequalities can be successfully tackled through gradual piecemeal reform without requiring fundamental changes in society. Amongst the reforms advocated, and sometimes achieved, by liberal feminists are the provision of childcare facilities, special transport arrangements and women-only sessions at leisure centres.

More radical feminists tend to welcome these sorts of initiatives but argue that they cannot lead to fundamental changes. As Scraton puts it:

Critical feminist theory argues, however, that women's access to existing structures and institutions will not challenge the deep rooted gender inequalities that have become institutionalised and fundamental to social practices.

Radical feminists believe that the structure of society prevents equality between men and women and only changes in the social structure can end them. One such approach will now be examined.

■ Eileen Green, Sandra Hebron and Diana Woodward – a socialist feminist perspective

Green *et al.* describe themselves as **socialist feminists**, but their work perhaps is based more on feminist ideas than socialist ones. They say that 'the concept of patriarchy is central to our theoretical analysis' and much of their work is concerned with showing how men restrict the leisure opportunities of women. Their work is based partly upon a review of other studies and partly on their own research. They studied a total of 707 women in Sheffield using questionnaires, interviews and discussion groups. The interviews and discussion groups were also conducted with the male partners of the women being studied.

Figure 4.7 Participation in selected leisure activities in the four weeks before interview, by gender. Persons aged 16 or over, Great Britain

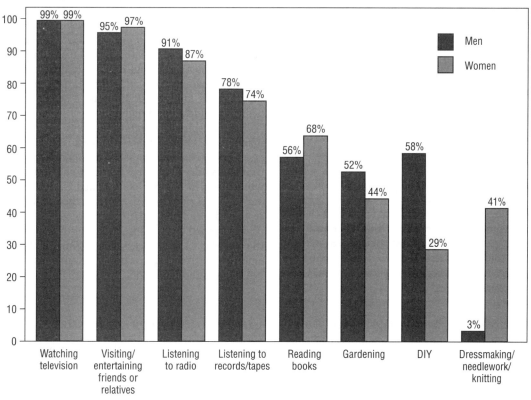

(*Source:* (1990)*General Household Survey*, HMSO, London, p. 159.)

The definition of leisure

Green *et al.* start by arguing that the definitions of work and leisure used by male sociologists are inappropriate. Such definitions tend to be based on men with full-time jobs and fail to take account of the situation of women. To many of the women interviewed leisure was a 'vague and amorphous concept'. They found it hard to separate leisure from other aspects of their lives but often saw it as a state of mind. Many women regarded it as doing things which they enjoyed or as the chance to please themselves. They did not see leisure in terms of particular periods of time or as specific activities.

Green *et al.* claim that it is much harder for women to forget about work and put aside specific time periods for their leisure. Women tend to have open-ended domestic responsibilities, particularly when they have young children. Whether they have paid employment or not, they are invariably

'on call' to tend to the needs of other family members. Some women with part-time jobs actually saw those jobs as a form of leisure. For example, working in a bar on a Saturday night could be seen as an opportunity to socialize and escape from domestic chores.

Thus Green *et al.* claim that studies of women show that leisure can only be defined subjectively: there is no objective way of separating work and leisure independently of the opinions of those being studied.

Patterns of work and leisure

From their own research Green *et al.* reached a number of conclusions about patterns of work and leisure for men and women.

1 Overall men have more time for leisure than women. Women found it harder to plan their leisure because their domestic responsibilities were open-ended.

2 Women had less money than men, and many wives were still financially dependent on their husbands. This restricted the types of leisure they could engage in.

3 Furthermore, the attitudes of men further restricted the options open to women. Green *et al.* say 'many groups of women are expected to choose their leisure time activities mainly from within the limited range of home and family-oriented activities which are socially defined as acceptable, womanly pursuits.'

Thus the emphasis in Green *et al.*'s theory is on the constraints imposed on women's leisure.

Leisure and social control

According to Green *et al.*, the constraints which limit women's leisure stem from structural features of patriarchal capitalist societies. Systems of social control prevent women from having the same freedom with regard to leisure as men. Green *et al.* argue:

---

social control operates at a number of levels across what may be seen as a continuum ranging from non-coercive forms to actual physical violence. In addition such forms of control are closely related to ideologies of gender and gender-appropriate behaviour.

Physical violence and sexual attacks outside the home make women afraid to venture out, particularly if they are on their own and it is dark. This makes it difficult for women to engage regularly in leisure outside their home, especially in winter. Husbands or partners may use anything from physical violence to mild disapproval to persuade women to limit their leisure to respectable activities. In the Sheffield study men seemed much more willing to allow their wives, partners or daughters to go to activities such as yoga, keep fit and night school classes, than to pubs and clubs.

Many venues for leisure activities outside the home are dominated by males and women may feel uncomfortable in them. Green *et al.* claim that men use joking, ridicule and sexual innuendo to put women down in leisure venues where they are unwelcome. In their study 80 per cent of the women said they felt uncomfortable in a pub on their own; 90 per cent in wine bars.

Along with financial constraints and hostility from men, ideology also controls women's behav-

iour and limits their activities. Women themselves often accept patriarchal ideology and monitor their own and each other's behaviour to make sure it does not exceed the boundaries of feminine respectability. For example, mothers feel guilty about leaving their children and so tend to give up previous leisure pursuits once their first child is born. One woman in Sheffield remarked 'As soon as I had my baby I felt different, I didn't feel as though I could go to a nightclub.'

Relationships between mothers and their married daughters enable women to support one another but can encourage the maintenance of traditional gender roles across generations. If married women's leisure is not constrained by any of the above systems of social control, then it will be restricted simply by lack of time. Some 97 per cent of the married women interviewed in Sheffield did the majority of the housework. Women with paid employment tended to do a 'double shift' of housework and paid work.

Other influences on leisure

Green *et al.* do not claim that gender is the only influence on leisure, nor do they think that all women are in the same position. Their study of Sheffield found that class and income level, age, ethnic group, and 'work and domestic situation' all had an effect.

Women from higher classes and higher-income levels tend to have more opportunity to engage in expensive leisure pursuits. Higher-class women participate more in sport, yoga and keep fit than women from lower classes.

Single, young employed women have perhaps the most freedom. Although their employment limits the time they have for leisure, they have more financial independence than married women and usually less responsibility for housework and childcare. Single women have weaker ideological restrictions on their leisure outside the home, and they have no husbands to frown on their behaviour.

The Sheffield research suggested that getting married depressed participation rates in sport even more than having children. Having children does have a big impact though. Women's recreation often becomes family recreation and not something for them to enjoy purely on their own account. For example, mothers tend to go swimming with their children rather than on their own.

Gender, ethnicity and leisure

Ethnic minority women have their leisure limited not just by virtue of their gender but also as a result of their ethnicity. As well as sexual harassment they are 'subjected to racial oppression in the form of institutionalised discrimination as well as random interpersonal acts of harassment and racial attack.' As a consequence they may be even more unwilling than other women to go out to leisure activities. Green *et al.* quote a study conducted for the Greater London Council (GLC) which found that 54 per cent of all London women but only one-third of Afro-Caribbean women travelled for pleasure each week.

Although women of Asian and Afro-Caribbean ethnic minorities share common problems which result from racism, they have different cultural traditions which affect their leisure. In traditional Asian rural kinship systems 'Personal preferences and autonomy are rigorously subordinated to the interests of the household unit, which is hierarchically ordered under the authority of the eldest male.' Although the situation of Asian women in Britain is very varied 'there are clear cultural and religious barriers to their attainment of autonomy and sexual equality, above and beyond those faced by most white and Afro-Caribbean women.'

For example, Green *et al.* claim that Asian men are reluctant to encourage women to be mobile and this is reflected in figures from the GLC's study which showed that two-thirds of Asian women felt unsafe walking in public places and 95 per cent would not go out alone after dark.

Afro-Caribbean women are rather less restricted in their leisure. Green *et al.* say that they have more power in their families than Asian women and this encourages independence. They say that black women 'are able to draw on the historical tradition of the powerful matriarch, mainstay of the family, as a source of confidence and inspiration.' Leisure is less home-based than for Asian women but is still limited. As well as fear of racially motivated attacks, financial hardship, inadequate state facilities for childcare (especially for single mothers), and the demands of factory employment all create problems for many Afro-Caribbean women. In addition 'Isolation from an extended network of female kin removes a source both of childcare and of leisure companions.'

Conclusion

The work of Green *et al.* suggests that a number of factors work alongside gender to shape women's opportunities, or lack of opportunities to enjoy leisure. Although the emphasis is very much on the constraints on women, Green *et al.* are not entirely pessimistic. They found that women do have some success in making opportunities for leisure. This partly stems from 'women's informal sociability', that is, their ability to:

---

develop and maintain friendships at school, in the workplace, outside the school gates, at the shops and bus stop, and in any number of other unpromising leisure venues where women meet regularly.

Women are also slightly more active than men in voluntary organizations and are more likely to attend night classes. Although these are relatively 'safe' and acceptable forms of leisure activity which do not challenge gender stereotypes, they do offer women some opportunities to increase their independence from men. Furthermore, some women are being more ambitious and are trying to challenge male domination of leisure. Green *et al.* say:

---

we did talk to women who are making real inroads into the male bastions of leisure, and to many others who are managing to claim some time and pleasure for themselves in the face of very limited resources.

■ The retreat from work to leisure

Writing in 1960, the American sociologist Harold Wilensky stated 'Already there are indications that the withdrawal from work as a central life interest, long noted for the working class, is spreading to the vast majority of the population.' As we have discovered in previous sections, manual workers tend to define their work in instrumental terms. Work is largely a means to an end: a means to provide the income for non-work concerns. Like Parker, Wilensky argues that leisure is influenced by work, but he is concerned with work in general rather than specific occupations. His argument may be summarized as follows.

In modern industrial society, elites will increasingly plan and organize the work activities of the labour force. The centralization of planning and innovation will mean that even at the level of middle management, work will become more and more routine, and autonomy will diminish. The specialized division of labour in large-scale bureaucracies and organizations results in the work situation of the mass of white-collar workers becoming increasingly similar to that of factory workers. As a result, work for the majority of the population offers few opportunities for fulfilment.

Leisure as a central life interest

In response to this situation, leisure replaces work to a greater extent as a central life interest. Wilensky states 'Where ties to occupation and workplace become weak, the quest for alternative ties is intensified.' He sees a trend developing whereby the typical wage or salary earner will 'segregate his work from life and retire into the heartwarming circle of kin and friend'.

Wilensky believes that this trend holds both promise and danger but he feels the threat of leisure is greater than the promise. The average worker may retreat into a contented apathy, unconcerned about work or the wider community, snug in the warmth and security of family and friends. In this situation the worker is open to manipulation by ruling classes and ruling elites.

Marxist views of the dangers of a leisure-orientated society have already been examined. The ruling elite version presented by C. Wright Mills, with its picture of a manipulated mass society, is similar.

C. Wright Mills believes that there is a clear division between work and leisure for the mass of the population, a division he calls **the big split**. Mills argues that the work ethic has been replaced by the leisure ethic. When the two compete, 'leisure wins hands down.' His view of the relationship between work and leisure is summed up in the following pessimistic statement: 'Each day men sell little pieces of themselves in order to try to buy them back each night and weekend with the coin of "fun".'

Yet leisure does not provide the fulfilment which work denies. The techniques of mass production employed in manufacturing industry have been applied to the leisure industry. Organized spectator sport, bingo, movies, radio and television provide mass-produced leisure which affords escape rather than fulfilment.

Mass leisure activities 'astonish, excite and distract but they do not enlarge reason or feeling, or allow spontaneous dispositions to unfold creatively'. They create a fantasy world into which the masses escape in non-work hours, a world in which 'the amusement of hollow people rests on their own hollowness and does not fill it up'.

Leisure as freedom

Mills's views echo Wilensky's fears about the danger of a leisure-orientated society. Wilensky, however, also foresaw the possibility of a positive outcome of the trend towards leisure. It may provide 'new leisure commitments more personally satisfying and socially integrating'.

The British sociologist Tom Burns develops this view. Burns argues that leisure provides considerable freedom for the individual to exercise choice and design and to create and find meaning in life. Burns uses Goffman's idea of **styling of activities** which refers to the creative process whereby individuals present themselves in particular ways and so portray a desired self-image. The various styles of young people ranging from punks and teddy boys to hippies and Hell's Angels provide obvious examples. **Styling** occurs throughout society and is expressed in the choice of household decoration and furniture, the design of gardens, hairstyles, clothes and lifestyles in general.

Burns argues that the styling of activities is not simply shaped by the nature of work as Parker implies. He finds support for his argument from Michael Crozier's study of French office workers. Crozier found a wide range of variation in the form and content of the office workers' leisure activities despite the similarity of their work.

Burns claims that styling also overrides 'the organized apparatus of leisure and consumption'. Individuals do not merely passively consume the products of industry and the provisions of mass entertainment. Instead they actively manipulate and exploit them, accepting some, rejecting some and modifying others. For example, in designing the interior of their houses, they select, modify and arrange various products to suit their particular style. In this way they actively create their own identity: they design a setting which reflects their desired self-image. Burns concludes that styling gives 'meaning and significance' to life.

Leisure influencing work

The priority which the mass of the labour force appears to give to non-work concerns has led some sociologists to suggest that rather than work influencing leisure, the reverse is increasingly the case. The affluent workers studied by Goldthorpe and Lockwood selected and defined their work in terms of non-work concerns. Many gave up jobs which they found more interesting to move to Luton. They defined a relatively high living standard and a family-centred life as their main priority. These concerns shaped their choice of occupation, their definition of work, their attitude towards their firms, and their view of the role of unions.

From his studies in France, Joffre Dumazedier argues that leisure values are increasingly influencing work in a number of ways. He notes that many people, particularly the young, choose jobs with reference to the types of leisure they want. They look at the leisure facilities available in the area when selecting a job. They consider the hours they will have to work in terms of their leisure requirements. Dumazedier argues that industry must adapt to accommodate leisure values by the provision of recreational facilities, flexi-hours and similar amenities and concessions.

The limits to the growth of leisure

Although he acknowledges that leisure is increasingly important in industrial societies, Roberts does not believe that it is becoming as important as some writers assume. He says 'the containment of work is a slow and long-term rather than a cataclysmic impending change.'

According to Roberts, the most rapid decline in working hours took place between 1850 and 1918 when the typical working week in industry fell from over seventy to fifty-four hours. Between the 1940s and the end of the 1970s the typical working week in factories fell by only three hours.

Roberts points out that not all groups in society have increasing amounts of leisure. Some professional jobs have become more demanding and consume more of the workers' time than in the past. Furthermore, married women increasingly have employment as well as domestic responsibilities, leaving little time for leisure.

Roberts accepts that overall leisure has increased, but it has had little impact on some areas of social life. People have not used their leisure to participate more in politics, and he says 'work remains work rather than an interest pursued for its intrinsic satisfaction.' Roberts concludes:

> There are limits to how widely the influence of leisure is spreading throughout the social structure. Work and politics are two areas of life where its impact is slight and, while this remains so, talk of a leisure society is ill-advised.

Inequality, consumerism and leisure

Sheila Scraton agrees with Roberts that there has been some increase in leisure, but argues that it has not affected everyone in the same way. She says 'The 1980s were a time of leisure expansion' and gives the increasing number of bowling alleys, leisure centres, fitness studios and theme parks as examples of this expansion. However, these changes were closely related to the development of **consumer culture**: buying things is as important as doing things for contemporary leisure. For example, Scraton suggests that 'the acquisition of particular trade names on training shoes or leisure garments' has become 'a leisure pursuit in itself'. Many people do not bother actually playing sport in their designer sports gear.

In Britain Thatcherism and compulsory competitive tendering led to local authorities losing control of many facilities as private companies took them over. As a consequence 'the divisions in opportunity for participation in leisure have become more pronounced.'

As leisure becomes increasingly dominated by market forces some people enjoy better provision, but those with fewer resources become worse off. The latter group include the unemployed, the poor, the elderly and the disabled. Scraton also believe that sexism and racism reduce the leisure opportunities of women and men.

From this viewpoint advanced industrial capitalist societies are only becoming leisure societies for some of the population; for the disadvantaged leisure is contracting. Furthermore any increase in leisure in such societies may be at the expense of leisure opportunities in other parts of the world. Scraton points out that many consumer leisure products are produced in the 'sweat shops' of South America and Asia where the workers have very little chance to enjoy leisure.

■ Sociology, values and work and leisure

As with every topic in sociology, it is not possible to be objective and neutral about subjects such as work, unemployment and leisure. Throughout this chapter it is apparent that the range of views presented owes much to the values and ideology of particular sociologists. At times this is obvious with Marx's passionate condemnation of work in capitalist society; at others it is less apparent with Blauner's relatively restrained analysis of work in the USA.

As with Marxist perspectives in general, Marxist views of work and leisure are based on a **radical utopian ideology**.

1 It is **radical** because it looks forward to a fundamental change in the structure of society.

2 It is **utopian** because it looks forward to an ideal society.

3 It is **ideological** because in the last analysis, it is based on a set of values about what people ought to be, about the nature of human fulfilment and how best it can be realized.

In evaluating and analysing work and leisure in industrial society, Marxists use their picture of the communist utopia as a point of reference, as a standard of comparison. Since work and leisure in industrial society fall far short of this ideal, Marxist views are openly critical.

However, their ideological content should not lead to the outright dismissal of such views. Marx's concept of alienation has been one of the most stimulating and productive ideas in sociol-ogy. Ideology can produce important insights. Richard Hyman's interpretation of industrial conflict in capitalist society is strongly influenced by a commitment to an egalitarian society organized on lines similar to those outlined by Marx. It provides an important balance to the more orthodox functionalist view.

It can be argued that ideology intrudes too far into analysis. The picture of leisure presented by Marcuse is clearly based on value judgements. Edward Shils has criticized Marcuse and sociologists who take similar views, claiming that their analysis of society stems from a 'frustrated attachment to an impossible ideal of human perfection and a distaste for one's own society and human beings as they were' (quoted in Swingewood 1977, p. 18).

Marcuse's views can be seen as a reflection of his frustration about the lack of interest shown by the American public in issues he considered vital. Since they apparently enjoyed activities he regarded as superficial, and worse, activities which distracted their attention from important matters, Marcuse saw them as satisfying false needs. It can be argued that Marcuse's *One Dimensional Man* is ideology and little else.

In *Alienation and Freedom*, Robert Blauner states that he studied work 'from the viewpoint of the intellectual observer with his own values and conceptions of freedom and self-realization'. His viewpoint can be seen as an expression of American liberalism. He is largely uncritical of the structure of capitalist society and by implication, accepts it as just and fundamentally sound. His proposals for change are based on liberal ideology in that they involve reform rather than radical change. The changes in production technology which he advocates to improve the quality of work can take place within the existing framework of industrial society. Blauner's liberal views tend to focus his attention on the workplace rather than the wider society.

Whether their views are radical or liberal, many sociologists regard work in industrial society as largely unfulfilling. In particular, they have tended to contrast the independent, creative, presumably fulfilled craft workers of pre-industrial days with the factory worker in industrial society. The 'alienated' factory worker suffers by comparison.

Robert Blauner argues that this comparison is based on a romanticized picture of craft work and an idealization of pre-industrial society in general. He notes that less than 10 per cent of the medieval labour force was made up of craft workers whereas the vast majority of workers were peasants engaged in monotonous drudgery. Blauner argues that an idealized view of the past is partly responsible for the concept of the alienated worker in modern industrial society.

Like everybody else, sociologists look at the present in terms of a picture of the past.

5

Organizations and bureaucracy

5

Organizations and bureaucracy

▌ Introduction

'Our society is an organizational society' argued the American sociologist Amitai Etzioni. We are born in hospitals, educated in schools, employed by business firms and government agencies, join trade unions and professional associations and are laid to rest in churches. In sickness and in health, at work and at play, life in modern industrial society is increasingly conducted in organizational settings.

In this chapter we look at **organizations**, which Etzioni defines as 'social units that are predominantly oriented to the attainment of specific goals'. Organizations therefore differ from **social units**, such as the family, friendship groups and the community, because they are designed to realize clearly defined goals: schools are designed to transmit knowledge, hospitals to treat the sick, industrial firms to manufacture goods, and so on.

Organizations are not a new invention. They were created to pursue specific goals in many pre-industrial societies. In Ancient Egypt a permanent workforce of several thousand skilled workers was formed to build the pyramids. In addition, a large-scale organization was developed to construct and maintain a complex series of dykes, canals and ditches that controlled the flood waters of the Nile and irrigated the fields. Modern industrial societies, however, are distinguished from their pre-industrial counterparts by the number, size and scope of organizations. In the view of many sociologists, organizations have become the dominant institutions of contemporary society.

Organizations and the division of labour

The spread of organizations is closely related to the increasingly specialized division of labour in society. In the earliest form of human society (the hunting and gathering band) the division of labour was rudimentary: usually the men hunted and the women gathered nuts, fruit, roots and berries. In order to survive, all adult members of the band had to be involved in subsistence activities. This tended to prevent the development of social units specializing in activities other than the acquisition of food. The invention of agriculture some 10,000 years ago provided the basis for a specialized division of labour and the development of organizations. Agriculture frees a part of the population from subsistence activities and allows some individuals to specialize in particular tasks. Thus in the early farming communities, full-time craftsmen such as potters, weavers and toolmakers emerged.

The growing efficiency of agriculture and technological innovation result in a smaller proportion of the population being able to meet the community's subsistence requirements. This allows more and more members of society to specialize in tasks not directly related to subsistence.

As the division of labour becomes more specialized, it requires direction and coordination. For example, in Ancient Egypt a range of specialists was employed to construct the pyramids. They included quarrymen, masons, toolmakers, engineers, surveyors, artists, scribes and overseers. Their specialist tasks required direction and co-ordination if they were to be combined to produce an end product.

Similarly, in modern industry, the organization of a complex series of tasks is essential: the manufacture of cars, for instance, requires the coordination of a range of specialized operations. Some people must therefore have the authority to direct and organize the activities of others: if explicit rules did not govern the dimensions of the various components that make up a car, they simply would not fit together. Thus a highly specialized division of labour tends to generate a hierarchy of authority and a system of rules. When these factors are combined in the pursuit of a specific goal, an organization is formed.

The work of Max Weber is usually taken as the starting point in the sociology of organizations.

Weber believed that a particular form of organization – 'bureaucracy' – was becoming the defining characteristic of modern industrial society. His work is mainly concerned with a comparison of bureaucracy and the forms of organization found in pre-industrial societies.

■ Max Weber – bureaucracy and rationalization

Max Weber (1864–1920) believed that bureaucratic organizations were the dominant institutions of industrial society. We will examine Weber's definition of **bureaucracy** in detail shortly but briefly, he saw it as an organization with a hierarchy of paid, full-time officials who formed a chain of command. A bureaucracy is concerned with the business of administration: with controlling, managing and coordinating a complex series of tasks. Bureaucratic organizations are increasingly dominating the institutional landscape: departments of state, political parties, business enterprises, the military, education and churches are all organized on bureaucratic lines.

To appreciate the nature of modern society, Weber maintained that an understanding of the process of bureaucratization is essential. Marxists see fundamental differences between capitalist and socialist industrial societies. To Weber their differences are minimal compared to the essential similarity of bureaucratic organization. This is the defining characteristic of modern industrial society.

■ Bureaucracy and rational action

Weber's view of bureaucracy must be seen in the context of his general theory of social action. He argued that all human action is directed by meanings. Thus, in order to understand and explain an action, the meanings and motives which lie behind it must be appreciated. Weber identified various types of action that are distinguished by the meanings on which they are based. These include 'affective' or 'emotional action', 'traditional action' and 'rational action'.

1 **Affective or emotional action** stems from an individual's emotional state at a particular time. A loss of temper which results in verbal abuse or physical violence is an example of affective action.

2 **Traditional action** is based on established custom. Individuals act in a certain way because of ingrained habit: because things have always been done that way. They have no real awareness of why they do something; their actions are simply second nature.

3 By comparison, **rational action** involves a clear awareness of a goal: it is the action of a manager who wishes to increase productivity or of a builder contracted to erect a block of flats. In both cases the goal is clearly defined. Rational action also involves a systematic assessment of the various means of attaining a goal and the selection of the most appropriate means to do so. Thus if a capitalist in the building trade aimed to maximize profit, she or he would carefully evaluate factors such as alternative sites, raw materials, building techniques, labour costs and the potential market, in order to realize her or his goal. This would entail a precise calculation of costs and the careful weighing up of the advantages and disadvantages of the various factors involved. The action is rational since, in Weber's words, rational action is 'the methodical attainment of a definitely given and practical end by means of an increasingly precise calculation of means'.

Weber believed that rational action had become the dominant mode of action in modern industrial society. He saw it expressed in a wide variety of areas: in state administration, business, education, science and even in Western classical music. He referred to the increasing dominance of rational action as the '**process of rationalization**'.

Bureaucratization is the prime example of this process. A bureaucratic organization has a clearly defined goal. It involves the precise calculation of the means to attain this goal and systematically eliminates those factors which stand in the way of the achievement of its objectives. Bureaucracy is therefore rational action in an institutional form.

■ Bureaucracy and control

Bureaucracy is also a system of control. It involves a hierarchical organization in which superiors strictly control and discipline the activities of subordinates. Weber argued that in any large-scale task, some people must coordinate and control the activities of others. He stated that 'the imperative coordination of the action of a considerable number of men requires control of a staff of persons.' In order for this control to be effective, it must be regarded as **legitimate**. There must be a 'minimum of voluntary submission' to higher authority.

Legitimacy can be based on various types of meanings. For example, it can result from traditional or rational meanings and therefore can take the form of traditional authority or rational authority. The *form* of the organizational structure derives from the *type* of legitimacy on which it is based. In Weber's words:

> According to the kind of legitimacy which is claimed, the type of obedience, the kind of administrative staff developed to guarantee it and the mode of exercising authority, will all differ fundamentally.

To understand bureaucracy, it is therefore necessary for us to appreciate the type of legitimacy on which bureaucratic control is based. These models are outlined in Chapter 9 (pp. 501–2).

Weber identified three forms of legitimacy which derive from the three types of social action discussed previously. Affective, traditional and rational actions each provide a particular motive for obedience, a motive based respectively on emotion, custom and rationality. These types of legitimate control are 'charismatic authority', 'traditional authority' and 'rational–legal authority'. Each results in a particular form of organizational structure. Weber constructed models to represent each type of authority.

1 Charismatic authority and organizational structure

Organizational structures that derive from **charismatic authority** are fluid and ill-defined. Those who occupy positions of authority either share the charisma of the leader or possess a charisma of

their own. They are not selected on the basis of family ties to the leader or on the basis of technical qualifications. There is no fixed hierarchy of officials and no legal rules govern the organization of leaders and followers. Jesus's disciples provide an example of leadership positions in a charismatic movement. There is no systematically organized economic support for the movement: its members typically rely on charity or plunder. Since charismatic authority depends for its control on the person of the leader, it is necessarily short-lived. After the leader's death, the movement must become 'routinized' in terms of either traditional or rational–legal authority if it is to survive. Thus the organizational control of the Christian church is no longer directly based on the charisma of its founder. Instead it has been routinized in terms of both traditional and rational–legal authorities.

2 Traditional authority and organizational structure

The organizational structure which derives from the second type of authority, **traditional authority**, takes two main forms: the first is a household of personal retainers that includes relatives, favourites and servants who are dependent for support on the head of the household; the second is a system of vassals such as feudal lords who swear an oath of loyalty to the king or queen and hold land on this basis. The duties of both the household retainers and vassals are defined by custom but may be changed according to the inclination of the particular ruler.

3 Rational–legal authority and organizational structure

Like other forms of authority, **rational–legal authority** produces a particular kind of organizational structure. This is **bureaucracy** which Weber defined as 'A hierarchical organization designed rationally to coordinate the work of many individuals in the pursuit of large-scale administrative tasks and organizational goals.' Weber constructed an ideal type of the rational–legal bureaucratic organization. He argued that bureaucracies in modern industrial society are steadily moving towards this 'pure' type. The ideal type of bureaucracy contains the following elements:

1 'The regular activities required for the purposes of the organization are distributed in a fixed way as official duties.' Each administrative official has a clearly defined area of responsibility. Complex tasks are broken down into manageable parts with each official specializing in a particular area. For example, state administration is divided into various departments such as education, defence and the environment. Within each department, every official has a clearly defined sphere of competence and responsibility.

2 'The organization of offices follows the principle of hierarchy; that is every lower office is under the control and supervision of a higher one.' A chain of command and responsibility is established whereby officials are accountable to their immediate superior both for the conduct of their own official duties and those of everybody below them.

3 The operations of the bureaucracy are governed by 'a consistent system of abstract rules' and the 'application of these rules to particular cases'. These rules clearly define the limits of the authority held by various officials in the hierarchy. Obedience to superiors stems from a belief in the correctness of the rules. The rules also lay down fixed procedures for the performance of each task. They impose strict discipline and control, leaving little room for personal initiative or discretion.

4 The 'ideal official' performs his or her duties in 'a spirit of formalistic impersonality...without hatred or passion'. The activities of the bureaucrat are governed by the rules, not by personal considerations such as feelings towards colleagues or clients. The actions are therefore rational rather than affective. Business is conducted 'according to *calculable rules* and "without regard for persons"'.

5 Officials are appointed on the basis of technical knowledge and expertise. Weber stated that 'Bureaucratic administration means fundamentally the exercise of control on the basis of knowledge. This is the feature of it which makes it specifically rational.' Thus officials are selected in terms of the contribution their particular knowledge and skills can make to the realization of organizational goals. Once appointed, the official is a full-time paid employee and his or her occupation constitutes a career. Promotion is based on seniority or achievement or a combination of both.

6 Bureaucratic administration involves a strict separation of private and official income. Officials do not own any part of the organization for which they work nor can they use their position for private gain. In Weber's words 'Bureaucracy segregates official activity as something distinct from the sphere of private life.'

The 'technical superiority' of bureaucracy

The ideal type bureaucracy is never completely achieved in reality. Several of its characteristics are found in the state administrations of Ancient Egypt, China and the later stages of the Roman Empire. The ideal type is most closely approximated in capitalist industrial society where it has become the major form of organizational control.

The development of bureaucracy is due to its 'technical superiority' compared to organizations based on charismatic and traditional authority. Weber argued that 'The decisive reason for the advance of bureaucratic organization has always been its purely technical superiority over any other form of organization.' This superiority stems from the combination of specialist skills subordinated to the goals of the organization. Personal emotions and interests which might detract from the attainment of those goals are excluded, while a set of rational rules is designed specifically to further the objectives of the organization. Compared to other forms of organization, tasks in a bureaucracy are performed with greater precision and speed, and with less friction and lower costs.

Bureaucracy and freedom

Although Weber appreciated the technical advantages of bureaucratic organization, he was also aware of its disadvantages. He saw the strict control of officials restricted to very specialized tasks as a limitation of human freedom. The uniform and rational procedures of bureaucratic practice largely prevent spontaneity, creativity and individual initiative. The impersonality of official conduct tends to produce 'specialists without spirit'.

Weber foresaw the possibility of people trapped in their specialized routines with little awareness of the relationship between their jobs and the organization as a whole. He wrote 'It is horrible to think that the world would one day be filled with little cogs, little men clinging to little jobs and striving towards the bigger ones.'

Weber also saw the danger of bureaucrats becoming preoccupied with uniformity and order, of losing sight of all else and becoming dependent on the security provided by their highly structured niche in the bureaucratic machine. He believed it is as if:

> we were deliberately to become men who need 'order' and nothing but order, become nervous and cowardly if for one moment this order wavers, and helpless if they are torn away from their total incorporation in it.

To Weber, the process of rationalization, of which bureaucracy is the prime expression, is basically irrational. It is ultimately aimless since it tends to destroy the traditional values that give meaning and purpose to life. For him, the 'great question' is:

> what can we oppose to this machinery in order to keep a portion of mankind free from this parcelling-out of the soul, from this supreme mastery of the bureaucratic way of life? (Quoted in Nisbet 1967, p. 299)

Despite his forebodings, Weber thought that bureaucracy was essential to the operation of large-scale industrial societies. In particular, he believed that the state and economic enterprises could not function effectively without bureaucratic control. It therefore made little sense to try and dispense with bureaucracies. However, Weber was fearful of the ends to which bureaucratic organization could be directed. They represented the most complete and effective institutionalization of power so far created. In Weber's eyes, 'bureaucracy has been and is a power instrument of the first order – for the one who controls the bureaucratic apparatus'.

Weber was particularly concerned about the control of state bureaucratic administration. He saw two main dangers if this control was left in the hands of bureaucrats themselves.

1 Particularly in times of crisis, bureaucratic leadership would be ineffective. Bureaucrats are trained to follow orders and conduct routine operations rather than to make policy decisions and take initiatives in response to crises.

2 In capitalist society, top bureaucrats may be swayed by the pressure of capitalist interests and tailor their administrative practices to fit the demands of capital.

Weber argued that these dangers could only be avoided by strong parliamentary control of the state bureaucracy. In particular, professional politicians must hold the top positions in the various departments of state. This will encourage strong and effective leadership since politicians are trained to take decisions. In addition it will help to open the bureaucracy to public view and reveal any behind-the-scenes wheeling and dealing between bureaucrats and powerful interests. Politicians are public figures, open to public scrutiny and the criticism of opposition parties. They are therefore accountable for their actions.

■ Bureaucrats and politicians

Even with politicians at the head of state bureaucracies, problems remain. Weber observed that 'The political master always finds himself *vis-à-vis* the trained official, in the position of a dilettante facing the expert.' Professional politicians lack the technical knowledge controlled by the bureaucracy and may have little awareness of its inner workings and procedures. They are largely dependent on the information supplied by bureaucrats and upon their advice as to the feasibility of the measures the politician wishes to take. The politician may well end up being directed by the bureaucrat. Tony Benn commented that important details of the nuclear power programme in Britain were kept from him by civil servants when he was the minister in charge of energy.

Seymour M. Lipset shows that it is possible for government bureaucracy to exercise considerable control over its 'political masters' in his study of a socialist government in the Canadian province of Saskatchewan. The Cooperative Commonwealth Federation (CCF) came to power in 1944 with a programme of socialist reform. In order to implement this programme the CCF had to operate through the local government bureaucracy. Many top civil servants were opposed to its reforms and succeeded in either modifying or preventing them. They persuaded the new government that parts of its programme 'were not administratively feasible'. At times the bureaucrats actually reversed the directives of the politicians. A cabinet minister decided that government work should be done by government employees rather than by private concerns; despite this the civil servants continued to give contracts to private industry. The CCF was particularly concerned to grant government aid to less wealthy farmers and provide leases for landless veterans, yet the bureaucrats continued the policy of the previous administration and supported the wealthy farmers. Although they didn't have it all their own way, some top civil servants boasted of '"running my department completely" and of "stopping hare-brained radical schemes"'.

Lipset's study illustrates Weber's fears of the power of bureaucrats to act independently from their 'political masters'. Weber believed that only strong parliamentary government could control state bureaucracy. He suggested that state bureaucrats should be made directly and regularly accountable to parliament for their actions. The procedure for doing this was the parliamentary committee which would systematically cross-examine top civil servants. In Weber's view, 'This alone guarantees public supervision and a thorough inquiry.'

Weber's view of bureaucracy is ambivalent. He recognized its 'technical superiority' over all other forms of organization. He believed that it was essential for the effective operation of large-scale industrial society. While he saw it as a threat to responsible government, he believed that this threat could be countered by strong political control. However, he remained pessimistic about the consequences of bureaucracy for human freedom and happiness.

The debate with Weber

Bureaucracy and efficiency

Although Weber died in 1920 much of the research on organizations since then can be seen as a debate with Weber. Students of organizations have refined, elaborated and criticized his views. One part of his theory that has been questioned is the proposition that a bureaucracy organized on the lines of Weber's ideal type is the most efficient way of realizing organizational goals. It has often been argued that certain aspects of the ideal type of bureaucracy may, in practice, reduce organizational efficiency. Whether such a criticism is justified depends on how Weber's ideal type is interpreted.

Weber used the ideal type as a model to compare three forms of authority and the organizational structures which develop from them. Compared to organizations based on traditional and charismatic authority, Weber was clear that the rational 'legal bureaucracy is technically superior'. But whether or not Weber believed that an organization structured on the lines of his ideal type bureaucracy would, in practice, maximize efficiency is not entirely clear. Certainly he would regard it as the most rational form of organization but does this mean he saw it as the most efficient way of realizing organizational goals?

Many sociologists maintain that Weber argued that rationality equals efficiency. Thus, the more closely an actual organization approximates the ideal type, the more efficient it would be. Peter Blau adopts this interpretation, claiming that Weber saw bureaucracy as 'an organization that maximizes efficiency in administration'.

However, some sociologists have argued that Weber did not mean that the ideal type bureaucracy, if translated into reality, would be the most efficient form of administration. For example, Martin Albrow argues that Weber saw rational bureaucratic procedures as the most effective means of *measuring* efficiency, not necessarily of *ensuring* it. Thus strict bureaucratic procedures allow the amount of money, time and energy expended in achieving organizational goals to be calculated. They therefore provide a means of measuring the efficiency of an organization and this is what makes them rational. In and of themselves they do not guarantee efficiency.

Whether or not the criticisms of Weber that follow are justified depends in part on the way his work is interpreted. Certainly there are grounds for arguing that Weber equated rational bureaucratic procedures with efficiency. As Dennis Warwick notes, 'The language which Weber uses in his discussion of bureaucracy fairly glows with notions of the high achievement of this form of administration.'

Robert K. Merton – the dysfunctions of bureaucracy

In an article entitled 'Bureaucratic structure and personality' Robert K. Merton argues that certain aspects of bureaucratic procedure may be dysfunctional to the organization. In particular, they may encourage behaviour which inhibits the realization of organizational goals.

1 Bureaucrats are trained to comply strictly with the rules, but when situations arise which are not covered by the rules this training may lead to inflexibility and timidity. Bureaucrats have not been taught to improvise and innovate and in addition they may well be afraid to do so. Their career incentives such as promotion are designed to reward 'disciplined action and conformity to official regulations'. Thus it may not be in their interests to bend the rules even when such action might further the realization of organizational goals.

2 The devotion to the rules encouraged in bureaucratic organizations, may lead to a changing of goals. There is a tendency for conformity to official regulations to become an end in itself, rather than a means to an end. The bureaucrat may lose sight of the goals of the organization and therefore reduce its effectiveness. In this way, so-called bureaucratic 'red-tape' may stand in the way of providing an efficient service for the clients of the organization.

3 The emphasis on impersonality in bureaucratic procedures may lead to friction between officials and the public. For example, clients in a job centre or a maternity clinic may expect concern and sympathy for their particular problems. The businesslike and impartial treatment they might receive can lead to bureaucrats being seen as cold, unsympathetic, abrupt and even arrogant. As a result, clients sometimes feel that they have been badly served by bureaucracies.

While agreeing that the various elements of bureaucracy outlined in Weber's ideal type serve to further organizational efficiency, Merton maintains that they inevitably produce dysfunctional consequences. He suggests that 'the very elements which conduce towards efficiency in general produce inefficiency in specific instances'.

■ Peter Blau – formal and informal structure

Weber has often been criticized for focusing exclusively on the **formal structure** of bureaucracy, that is the official rules and procedures, the authorized hierarchy of offices and the official duties attached to them. His critics have argued that unofficial practices are an established part of the structure of all organizations. They must therefore be included in an explanation of the functioning of organizations.

Peter Blau claims that Weber's approach 'implies that any deviation from the formal structure is detrimental to administrative efficiency'. However, on the basis of the results of his own work and other research, Blau maintains that there is 'considerable evidence that suggests the opposite conclusion'. This view can be illustrated from Blau's study of a federal law enforcement agency.

This study was based on observation of the behaviour of agents working in one of nine district agencies of a federal bureau based in Washington DC. The agents were employed to inspect businesses to determine whether laws dealing with standards of employment had been broken. Roughly half their time was spent 'in the field', auditing company books and interviewing employers and employees. The rest of their time was spent at the agency office processing the various cases. The laws involved were extremely detailed and it was often difficult to determine exactly how they applied to particular cases. The official rules stated that any difficulties which arose must be taken to the supervisor. Agents were not allowed to discuss cases with their colleagues since the records of the firms were strictly confidential, but they were often reluctant to consult the supervisor since their promotion prospects were largely dependent on the latter's evaluation of their work. Frequent consultation might well indicate incompetence. Agents therefore sought advice and guidance from each other. They discussed cases with their colleagues in direct violation of the official rules.

Unofficial practices and efficiency

Blau claims that this unofficial practice served to increase the agents' efficiency. Information and experience were pooled and problem-solving facilitated. Knowledge of the complex regulations was widened and the various ways in which the law could be interpreted were shared. Considerable time was saved since, rather than searching through a 1,000-page manual of regulations and two shelves of books on court cases, agents simply asked each other about a regulation or a reference.

Blau argues that assistance and consultation transformed the agents from a collection of individuals into a cohesive working group. As a result anxiety over decision making, for example whether or not to prosecute a company, was reduced since agents knew they could rely on their colleagues' advice and experience. The case of the federal agents provides an example to illustrate Blau's argument that 'Paradoxically, unofficial practices that are explicitly prohibited by official regulations sometimes further the achievement of organizational objectives.'

In all organizations, groups of workers form and establish their own norms of work practice. These **informal groups** and the norms they develop are an integral part of the structure of organizations. One interpretation of Weber's model of bureaucracy argues that the most efficient form of administration involves explicit procedures for the performance of every task. If these procedures are strictly followed, and supervised and coordinated by management, then efficiency will be maximized. However, Blau argues that no system of official rules and supervision can anticipate all the problems which may arise in an organization. Efficiency can only be maximized by the development of **informal work norms** by groups of workers, and such norms can also have the effect of reducing organizational efficiency.

The informal structure – a case study

These points are illustrated by Blau's study of interviewers working in an American employment agency. The goal of the agency was to place applicants in suitable jobs. The performance of the interviewers was evaluated on the basis of the number of interviews they conducted. After the Second World War, jobs became increasingly scarce and the interviewers tended to dismiss clients for whom jobs could not be quickly found.

In order to increase the efficiency of the agency, a new procedure was introduced. Interviewers were now evaluated in terms of the number of applicants they actually placed in jobs. This change had unanticipated consequences. Interviewers competed for the 'job slips' on which details of job openings were recorded, and even hid them from one another. This tended to result in clients being placed in jobs that were not suited to their training and experience. If interviewers had been aware of the full range of available jobs, they would have been better able to match jobs and applicants.

Within the employment agency there were two groups of interviewers, Section A and Section B. Interviewers in Section A hoarded job slips and competed with each other. Those in Section B developed cooperative rather than competitive work norms and shared their job slips. Their productivity was higher than that of Section A – they filled a larger proportion of the job openings they received.

Blau explains these differences in work practices and productivity in the following way.

Most of the interviewers in Section A were appointed on a temporary basis and this produced insecurity. In order to gain a permanent position, they were anxious to impress their superiors. In addition, their supervisor laid great stress on performance records. Those in Section B had permanent appointments and their supervisor did not base their evaluation primarily on productivity. In addition, members of Section B had shared a similar training programme that emphasized concern for the client and intensive counselling. From this they developed a 'common professional code' in terms of which competition for job slips was rejected on moral grounds. Members of Section A had not shared a similar training programme and this tended to prevent a common code from developing.

Because of the above factors, Section B established cooperative norms, and a cohesive group developed whereas Section A remained competitive and fragmented. With reference to the goals of the organization, Section B was more efficient.

Blau's study of interviewers in an employment agency indicates that official rules and procedures cannot, by themselves, maximize efficiency. No set of rules can anticipate all the problems which arise in a bureaucracy. To some degree such problems will be handled in terms of the informal norms of groups of workers. Variations in these norms will result in differing levels of efficiency.

Blau's study of federal agents indicates that, in certain circumstances, contrary to the implications of Weber's argument, breaking official rules can increase organizational efficiency.

In general, Blau's research shows the importance of studying the informal structure of organizations. It supports his view that 'A bureaucracy in operation appears quite different from the abstract portrayal of its formal structure.' Although formal and informal structures can be separated for purposes of analysis, in practice they form a single structure. We will return to the subject of informal groups and norms later in the chapter.

■ Alvin W. Gouldner – degrees of bureaucratization

Weber presented an ideal type of bureaucracy and argued that organizations in modern industrial society were increasingly moving towards that model. However, he had little to say about why actual organizations varied in terms of their approximation to the ideal type, apart from suggesting that bureaucracy was particularly suited to the administration of routine tasks. Alvin W. Gouldner's study of a gypsum plant in the USA seeks to explore this problem. Its concern is to 'clarify some of the social processes leading to different degrees of bureaucratization'.

Degrees of bureaucratization – a case study

The plant consisted of two parts: a gypsum mine and a factory making wallboards, for which gypsum was a major ingredient. There was a significant difference in the **degree of bureaucratization** between the mine and the factory. In the mine the hierarchy of authority was less developed and the division of labour and spheres of competence were less explicit: there was less emphasis on official rules and procedures and less impersonality both in relationships between workers and between them and the supervisors. Since, in Gouldner's view, these elements are 'the stuff of which bureaucracy is made', then 'bureaucratic organization was more fully developed on the surface than in the mine'.

The following examples illustrate this point. In the mine, supervisors usually issued only general instructions, leaving it to the miners to decide who was to do the job and how it was to be done. If miners wanted assistance, they rarely went through the 'proper channels' to obtain orders to direct others to assist them. They simply asked their workmates for help. Official duties were not clearly defined. Miners rotated jobs amongst themselves and often repaired machinery, a job which in the factory was the clear prerogative of the maintenance engineer. Lunch hours were irregular, varying in length and the time at which they were taken.

Supervisors accepted and worked within this informal organization. They were 'one of the lads' and placed little emphasis on their officially superior status. One miner summarized the situation as follows: 'Down here we have no rules. We are our own bosses.'

By comparison, the factory was considerably more bureaucratic. The hierarchy of authority, the division of labour, official rules and procedures and impersonality were more widespread and developed.

Factors influencing bureaucratization

Gouldner gives the following reasons for the difference in degrees of bureaucratization between the mine and the surface. Work in the mine was less predictable: the miners had no control over the amount of gypsum available and could not predict various dangers such as cave-ins. No amount of official procedures could control such factors. Miners often had to make their own decisions on matters which could not be strictly governed by official rules, for example, strategies for digging out the gypsum and propping up the roof. Since the problems they encountered did not follow a standard pattern, a predetermined set of rules was not suitable for their solution.

By comparison, the machine production of wallboard in the factory followed a standard routine and could therefore be 'rationalized' in terms of a bureaucratic system. Fixed rules and a clearly defined division of labour are more suited to predictable operations.

The ever-present danger in the mine produced strong work group solidarity which in turn encouraged informal organization. Miners depended on their workmates to warn them of loose rocks and to dig them out in the event of a cave-in. In the words of one old miner, 'Friends or no friends, you got all to be friends.' A cohesive work group will tend to resist control from above and to institute its own informal work norms.

Bureaucracy and worker resistance

Part of Gouldner's study is concerned with the arrival of a new manager at the gypsum plant. He came with instructions from head office to cut costs and raise productivity. From the start he attempted to abolish unofficial practices, insisted on the rigorous application of formal rules and instituted a new set of rules which severely limited the workers' autonomy – for example they were not allowed to move round the factory at will. Rule breaking was to be reported to the appropriate authorities, official reports of the details were to be passed up the administrative hierarchy, and punishments were to be strictly imposed in accordance with the rules. The new manager thus attempted to increase the degree of bureaucratization in the plant.

Gouldner argues that management will tend to do this when it believes that workers are not fulfilling their work roles. The degree to which it achieves this will depend on the 'degree of bureaucratic striving on management's part' and the 'degree of resistance to bureaucratic administration among the workers'.

Despite the forceful attempts of the new manager to impose a strongly bureaucratic system, it was effectively opposed by the miners. Gouldner attributes their success to strong work group solidarity: they were able to present a united front to management and frustrate many of its demands. In addition, the miners' immediate supervisors, who worked with them underground, were also opposed to the new system. They believed that the miners should be exempt from certain rules and that this privilege was justified by the dangers of the job.

A number of tentative conclusions may be drawn from Gouldner's study.

1 Bureaucratic administration is more suited to some tasks than others. In particular, it is not well suited to non-routine, unpredictable operations.

2 The advance of bureaucracy is not inevitable. As the case of the gypsum miners indicates, it can be successfully resisted.

3 Gouldner suggests that sociologists who are concerned with a utopian vision which involves the abolition of bureaucracy would be more fruitfully employed in identifying 'those social processes creating variations in the amount and types of bureaucracy. For these variations do make a vital difference in the lives of men.' By directing their research to this area, sociologists may be able to give direction to those who wish to create organizations with greater democracy and freedom.

Tom Burns and G.M. Stalker – mechanistic and organic systems

Gouldner's conclusions are supported by the findings of research by Burns and Stalker. From a study of 20 Scottish and English firms, mainly in the electronics industry, Burns and Stalker argue that bureaucratic organizations are best suited to dealing with predictable, familiar and routine situations. They are not well suited to the rapidly changing technical and commercial situation of many sectors of modern industry such as the electronics industry.

Mechanistic and organic systems–definitions

Burns and Stalker construct two ideal types of organization which they term **mechanistic** and **organic**. The firms range between these extremes in their research.

The **mechanistic organization** is very similar to Weber's model of bureaucracy. It includes a specialized division of labour with the rights and duties of each employee being precisely defined. Specialized tasks are coordinated by a management hierarchy that directs operations and takes major decisions. Communication is mainly vertical: instructions flow downward through a chain of command; information flows upwards and is processed by various levels in the hierarchy before it reaches the top. Individuals in the organization are responsible for discharging their particular responsibility and no more. He or she 'pursues his task as something distinct from the real tasks of the concern as a whole, as if it were the subject of a sub-contract. "Somebody at the top" is responsible for seeing to its relevance.'

By comparison, areas of responsibility are not clearly defined in **organic organizations**. The rigid hierarchies and specialized divisions of labour of the mechanistic systems tend to disappear. The individual's job is to employ his or her skills to further the goals of the organization rather than simply carry out a predetermined operation. When a problem arises, all those who have knowledge and expertise to contribute to its solution meet and discuss. Tasks are shaped by the nature of the problem rather than being predefined. Communication consists of consultation rather than command, of 'information and advice rather than instructions and decisions'. Although a hierarchy exists, it tends to become blurred as communication travels in all directions and top management no longer has the sole prerogative over important decisions, nor is it seen to monopolize the knowledge necessary to make them.

Stability and change

Burns and Stalker argue that mechanistic systems are best suited to stable conditions, organic systems to changing conditions. In the manufacturing industry, stable conditions exist when demand for a product is relatively constant, when the product is standardized and when there is a low level of innovation in its manufacture and development. In such a situation, tasks are fairly routine and therefore suited to the fixed procedures, specialized division of labour and hierarchical structure of mechanistic systems.

Unstable conditions exist when there are rapid changes in the market (for example, the loss of old customers and a demand for new and different products); when there are changes in knowledge and technology (for example, new scientific discoveries which affect the product and innovations in manufacturing processes); and when the product is not standardized (for example, customers demanding an order to fit their specific requirements). Burns and Stalker claim that organic systems are best suited to this type of situation. They are flexible and fluid and can therefore adapt more readily to changing conditions. They allow the pooling of information and knowledge and the formation of various combinations of skills and expertise. As a result 'the limits of feasible action are set more widely'. When novel and unfamiliar problems arise, an organic system can rapidly mobilize its resources to solve them. In the absence of a clear-cut division of labour and a rigid system of vertical communication, everybody with something to contribute joins in the task at hand. With each individual concerned primarily with furthering organizational goals rather than with a limited area of responsibility, there is an emphasis on cooperating to see the job through. Thus operatives, supervisors, graphic designers, design engineers, product engineers, scientists in the laboratory and works managers discuss policy, share information and technical knowledge and generally contribute to the solution of problems.

Despite the fact that the electronics firms in Burns and Stalker's study were faced with unstable conditions, only some of them had adopted an organic system. Several clung tenaciously to the mechanistic system making only minor changes to meet new and unfamiliar situations. This was in spite of the fact that the existing system was 'clearly inefficient and ineffective' in terms of the stated goals of the organization.

However, Burns and Stalker note that the mechanistic system can effectively serve other ends and this, they suggest, is the reason for its retention. They argue that within any organization, individuals and groups have their own goals which are often in conflict with those of others, and which may diverge from the stated goals of the organization.

From this perspective, Burns and Stalker suggest the following reasons for resistance to an organic system. The organic system demands a greater commitment by members of the organization. Individuals must become involved in many areas, learn new skills and deal with matters beyond their specialized knowledge. They lose the security of a clearly defined area of competence and responsibility. Burns and Stalker suggest that some individuals resist the change to organic systems because they refuse to make further 'commitments in their occupational existence at the expense of the rest of their lives'. Thus several top managers clung to mechanistic systems because they 'provided protection against the involvements the new order demanded of them'.

Status and power in organizations

Organizations are institutions in which members compete for status and power. They compete for the resources of the organization (for example, finance to expand their own departments), for career advancement and for power to control the activities of others. In pursuit of these aims, groups are formed and sectional interests emerge. As a result, policy decisions may serve 'the ends of the political and career systems rather than those of the concern'. In this way the goals of the organization may be displaced in favour of sectional interests and individual ambitions.

Burns and Stalker suggest that these preoccupations sometimes prevent the emergence of organic systems. Many of the electronics firms in their study had recently created research and development departments employing highly qualified and well-paid scientists and technicians. Their high pay and expert knowledge were sometimes seen as a threat to the established order of rank, power and privilege. Many senior managers had little knowledge of the technicalities and possibilities of new developments in electronics. Some felt that close cooperation with the experts in an organic system would reveal their ignorance and show that their experience was now redundant. They feared that they would lose authority, and their autonomy in decision making would be reduced. Some even reacted by separating the new departments as far as possible physically and administratively from the existing organization.

As a result, the research teams were concerned only with the earliest stages of development. This impaired efficiency since close cooperation between the various departments was essential to further the overall goals of the organization. For example, the research department might develop a product which, for technical reasons, was impossible to manufacture; cooperation with the production department could well have prevented this. In the same way, ongoing communication with the marketing department would be more likely to produce a commodity which would be successful in the marketplace. An organic system would meet these requirements but was often prevented from developing by the internal politics of the organization.

Several important points emerge from Burns and Stalker's research.

1 There is no one ideal form of organization which will maximize efficiency in every situation. Mechanistic systems are more suited to stable conditions, organic systems to changing conditions.

2 It is difficult to define organizations in terms of their goals since within an organization there are individuals and groups pursuing goals which may diverge from those of the organization. In certain instances, the organization may serve individual and group interests rather than its stated goals.

3 Organizations do not 'naturally' evolve into forms which can most effectively realize organizational goals. The form they take is also subject to the internal politics of the organization, to private goals and sectional interests.

■ The decline of bureaucracy

Burns and Stalker's work was published in 1961 but in a number of ways it anticipated future developments in the sociology of organizations. In recent years some writers have begun to argue that contemporary societies have begun to move away from organizations run on bureaucratic lines towards ones which use more organic systems. From this point of view the ideal type bureaucracy as described by Weber was well suited to earlier periods of industrial society but it is rapidly becoming outdated. This type of argument goes beyond Burns and Stalker's view that mechanistic systems were inefficient in some areas of social life, by claiming that they may be in decline in society as a whole.

■ Henry Mintzberg – from bureaucracy to adhocracy

Mintzberg is a contemporary management theorist who has distinguished different types of orga-
nizational structure. Like Gouldner and Burns and Stalker he believes that different structures are suited to different sets of circumstances or, as he puts it, different 'contingencies'. Mintzberg develops a more complex typology of organizations than these other writers arguing that there are five main types of organization. In each type a different group in the organization assumes most importance.

The five parts of an organization

According to Mintzberg the following are the basic groups found in organizations.

1 The **operating core** consists of the workers who actually produce the goods or provide the services which the organization supplies. Members of the operating core might, for example, be involved in 'writing consulting reports, educating students, cutting hair, or curing illness'.

2 The **strategic apex** has overall responsibility for controlling the organization, coordinating its activities and developing strategy. It consists of top-level managers and their assistants.

3 The **middle line** acts as intermediary between the strategic apex and the operating core. It includes middle managers and supervisors.

4 The **technostructure** is not directly involved in producing goods and supplying services; instead it designs and plans work and products or trains workers. Its main role is to standardize the work done by others. The responsibilities of the technostructure can include 'scheduling production, carrying out time-and-method studies of the operators' work, and instituting systems of quality control'.

5 The **support staff** is a more diverse group and is made up of specialist units which support the organization's work from 'outside its operating work flow'. In a university, people in the university press, payroll department and those who manage student residences are support staff. In a manufacturing company examples include lawyers, mailroom staff and cafeteria workers. Figure 5.1 illustrates how Mintzberg's model could be applied to a manufacturing company.

Five types of organization

1 The **simple structure**, as its name suggests, produces the least complex type of organization. Usually it has 'little or no technostructure' and few support staff. The strategic apex is the most important part of this structure and often a single 'chief executive' directs and supervises the operating core. This structure is typical of new organizations and of small ones. It is most suited to operating in simple environments which can be understood by a single person. The most typical example of a simple structure is a small entrepreneurial firm which operates in a specialist market.

2 The **machine bureaucracy** is closest to Weber's ideal type bureaucracy. It tends to carry out routine and standardized tasks and to have well-defined hierarchies. The technostructure is the key part of this type of organization because it is here that tasks are standardized. Mintzberg cites national post offices, giant car manufacturing companies, prisons and airlines as the sort of organizations which tend to adopt this structure. It is most appropriate in large organizations working in stable and simple environments.

3 The **professional bureaucracy** also tends to work in a stable environment and to carry out standardized and

repetitive tasks. However, in this case the standardization is not imposed by technocrats within the organization but derives from the training of its professional workers. Teachers, doctors, accountants and social workers all undergo training which gives them standardized skills and knowledge. Within an organization such workers are allowed considerable autonomy to apply their skills and knowledge to the needs of clients. In the professional bureaucracy the operating core is the most important part of the organization.

4 The **divisionalized form** is typical of large organizations which operate in a number of different markets. The organization is split into divisions with each part responsible for activities related to one of these markets. These markets might be different types of product or different geographical areas. For example, multinational corporations usually establish divisions dealing with different countries or areas of the world. In many cases each division is run as a machine bureaucracy. This type of organization works best in diverse but stable markets. Coordination is achieved by imposing standards of performance on each division and then measuring their success. The middle line managers play a vital role in this process.

5 The **adhocracy** is the last of Mintzberg's organizational structures and the one which poses a threat to the dominance of bureaucracy. It will therefore be examined in more detail than the others.

The adhocracy

Although the professional bureaucracy and the divisionalized form are different from Weber's ideal type bureaucracy, they are still types of bureaucracy, variations on a theme. The **adhocracy** is very different because it does not attempt to standardize the activities of an organization. Instead it is based upon teams which frequently change their shape, personnel and relationship to each other. These teams may well contain highly trained professional staff but they are not employed to carry out standardized procedures. The purpose of an adhocracy is to innovate, to come up with new ideas and solve novel problems. This often involves bringing together experts from different spheres and getting them to work together and combine their skills in multi-disciplinary teams. Operating experts, middle line managers and support staff will all be found together in a single team. In Mintzberg's words

Figure 5.1   Members and units of a manufacturing firm

STRATEGIC APEX

Board of Directors

President

Executive Committee   President's Staff

TECHNOSTRUCTURE

Strategic Planning

Controller

Personnel Training

Operations Research

Production Scheduling

Work Study

Technocratic Clerical Staff

MIDDLE LINE

VP Operations   VP Marketing

Plant Managers   Regional Sales Managers

Foremen   District Sales Manager

SUPPORT STAFF

Legal Counsel

Public Relations

Industrial Relations

Research and Development

Pricing

Payroll

Reception

Mailroom

Cafeteria

OPERATING CORE

Purchasing Agents   Machine Operators   Assemblers   Salespersons   Shippers

(*Source*: Mintzberg, H. (1983) *Structure in Fives: Designing Effective Organizations*, Prentice-Hall, adapted from pp. 11 and 18.)

they form 'an organic mass . . . working together in ever-shifting relationships on ad hoc projects'. Support staff usually play a crucial role in adhocracies with managers trying to coordinate activities in each team.

Mintzberg uses a number of examples to illustrate this type of structure. One is the Manned Space Flight Center of NASA (the US space agency) which changed its structure no less than 17 times during its first eight years. He also discusses the National Film Board of Canada, an agency of the Government which is involved in making short, often documentary films. A large number of support units, with expertise in areas such as budgeting, purchasing, animation and sound, back up the teams involved in producing a particular film. In this organization top and middle managers, workers in the operating core and specialists from the support staff all get involved in deciding on which films should be made and what the overall strategy of the organization should be. Other types of organization where adhocracies are common include consul-

tancy and advertising firms, and engineering companies producing prototypes.

Adhocracies and the future

Clearly adhocracies are very different from Weber's ideal type bureaucracy. They are not very hierarchical and they do not govern the activities of their members through a system of formal rules. The jobs carried out by individuals are not rigidly tied to their position in the organization and people are not necessarily employed by the organization on a permanent basis. If adhocracies were becoming more widespread then this would pose a serious challenge to Weber's belief that modern societies would become increasingly bureaucratic.

Mintzberg believes there has long been a variety of organizational structures and different types of structure will always be suited to different sets of circumstances. However, he also believes there is a trend towards adhocracy. He says 'If Simple Structure and Machine Bureaucracy were yesterday's structures, and Professional Bureaucracy and the Divisionalized Form are today's, then Adhocracy is clearly tomorrow's.'

This, he argues, is because adhocracy is suited to rapidly changing and unpredictable environments in which constant innovation is necessary as customers or clients demand new products or services. Most new industries operate in such an environment. He gives the examples of 'aerospace, electronics, think-tank consulting, research, advertising, film-making, petrochemicals, virtually all the industries that grew up since World War 2'. Adhocracies are also suited to areas of manufacturing which have automated, removing the need to monitor closely the activities of operators. As computer technology advances, more manufacturing companies become potential adhocracies.

Mintzberg does believe that adhocracies have limitations. They are not efficient at carrying out ordinary, routine tasks, and communications between individuals and groups in the organization are time-consuming and expensive. There is considerable potential for conflict in adhocracies and not everyone working in them appreciates their uncertainty, confusion and ambiguity. Nevertheless he sees them as 'the only configuration for those who believe in more freedom with less bureaucracy' and as the 'structure for a population growing ever better educated'.

■ Stewart R. Clegg – modern and postmodern organizations

Like Mintzberg, Stewart Clegg has raised the possibility that organizations may be moving away from the bureaucratic model. He sees bureaucracy as typical of 'modern' societies but he suggests we may be moving into a 'postmodern' era in which traditional bureaucracies may be dated. Like Gouldner, Burns and Stalker and Mintzberg, he also examines the reasons why organizations take on different forms. We will discuss this aspect of his work first.

French bread

Clegg argues that 'Weber's pessimism concerning the necessary rationalization and bureaucratization of the modern world was misplaced'. While

he accepts that modernity produces tendencies in this direction, he believes that it is by no means inevitable that organizations develop in the way that Weber envisaged.

Clegg uses the example of French bread to illustrate his point. In countries such as Britain and the USA most bread is manufactured in large bureaucratic companies such as Rank Hovis. They produce standardized products that remain saleable for several days and can be widely distributed. In France the situation is very different. Some 50,000 bakeries, about one for every 1,000 of the population, produce non-standardized bread products which rapidly go stale and which are supplied almost exclusively to a localized population. Only 3 per cent of bakeries employ more than five people.

In many ways French bread production is highly inefficient and it seems irrational that people should choose to go into the business. Bakers typically start work at 3 or 4 a.m. and work a nine or ten hour day for six days a week. Usually the baker's wife runs a shop selling the bread. It probably opens at 7 or 8 a.m. and closes at around 8 p.m., although usually with a three-hour break in the early afternoon. The wives work hard for no salary and the job gives them little social status. Customers have to shop every day to get their bread. A weekly supermarket shop will not suffice as the bread soon goes off.

To those involved in buying and selling bread though, it does make sense. Customers are willing to tolerate the inconvenience because the bread tastes better. In French culture this is important. The bakeries continue because there is a supply of people ready to take over when the baker and his wife are ready to retire. They are usually workers from rural areas who welcome the chance to run their own business and their background prepares them for the long hours and arduous work. Bakers usually lend money to the peasants who take over their business so that it can be handed on. In other predominantly industrial countries an independent peasantry has hardly survived. This is one factor which has contributed to the retention of the small bakery in France.

There have been attempts to rationalize French bread production. In 1966 the largest flour-milling company in France refused to supply flour in small quantities to bakers in Paris. For a week the bakers found it difficult to carry on but they soon found that a number of small flour mills near the city had survived. Many were on the verge of closing down and were using only around 20 per cent of their capacity. As a result the small Paris bakers were able to obtain flour supplies and to thwart the attempts of big business to put an end to their bakeries.

Thus, to Clegg, organizations are not just shaped by impersonal market forces. The lifestyle or culture of the society in which they are based and of the people who work in them can also be important. As Clegg puts it 'the cultural resources which people have available to them' may enable them to resist the seemingly inevitable march of big, rationally organized business.

Variations in business organizations

The cultural resources of the people who create organizations can also lead to large companies taking on very different forms. Each form may not appear rational in terms of Weber's model but, according to Clegg, it is rational in terms of the culture of the society within which the organization developed.

Clegg uses the Italian firm Benneton as an example and also discusses variations in business organizations in three East Asian countries: Taiwan, South Korea and Japan.

Benneton is unlike most big capitalist enterprises in that it only directly employs small numbers of people. The 2,500 Benneton shops are not run or owned by the parent company but are franchises. The shopkeepers have to sell Benneton products but they own their own shops. Furthermore, much of the actual production of Benneton garments is not carried out by Benneton itself. Assembling, ironing and finishing the garments is largely done by subcontractors. Benneton uses sophisticated technology to respond rapidly to changes in the fashion market. For instance, information on sales is fed directly from the tills in the shops to the company. Benneton itself is responsible for designing new garments and for advertising, but for much of its activity it relies upon its network of contacts with shop owners and subcontracting firms.

According to Clegg this successful formula developed out of the culture of the Veneto region of northeast Italy. It was here that Benneton began in 1965. He says 'In this area the extensive use of subcontracting had never been wholly superseded by the factory organization of production.'

Japan is well known for having developed its own distinctive and successful business organizations, but South Korea and Taiwan have also enjoyed increasing business success despite the fact that they are very different from Japan. South Korea has become dominated by very large business organizations, often responsible for producing the whole of a product. In contrast the manufacture of bicycles, televisions and other products in Taiwan is carried out by networks of smaller firms which subcontract to each other.

Clegg argues that these differences are due to variations in government policy and culture. In South Korea the Government has taken a very active role in promoting and investing in a few big companies. In Taiwan this has not happened. There organizations have been shaped by patterns of inheritance. Family businesses are not left to the eldest son but are usually divided equally between brothers. Because of this businesses are split up. However, family contacts are used to maintain networks of companies cooperating together to provide benefits for all those involved. Japan is different again and will be discussed on pp. 286–7.

Clegg concludes by stating that he is opposed both to **under-socialized** and **over-socialized** views of organizations. The former view suggests that the values, beliefs and lifestyles of those who work in organizations have little influence. Instead organizations are seen as being driven by external factors such as technology or world markets. The latter view suggests that organizations are entirely the product of the values, beliefs and lifestyles of the people who produce and work in them.

To Clegg neither position is correct. Culture affects the way people approach the problem of designing organizations, but decisions are made within the context of international markets, the available technology, the policies of a particular government, and so on. Weber's views on bureaucracy suggested organizations would become increasingly alike as they moved towards increasing rationality. Clegg finds no evidence of this. This is because what seems rational and efficient in one context may not seem to be so in another.

Modern organizations and postmodernity

In recent years a number of sociologists have begun to argue that advanced capitalist nations are entering a new period of history called **post-**

modernity. The modern era is coming to an end and as it does so fundamental changes may be taking place in many parts of society. The theory of postmodernism is examined in detail in the final chapter (see pp. 907–14). Stewart Clegg has tried to apply this theory to the study of organizations.

In Clegg's opinion, Weber's ideal type of bureaucracy describes the typical modern organization. He describes it as 'composed of a number of tendencies, such as an increasing specialisation and hierarchy, stratification, formalisation, standardisation and centralisation of organisational action'. As we saw earlier, Clegg does not believe that these tendencies have led to all organizations becoming bureaucratic. Nevertheless, he does argue that there has been pressure pushing them in this direction. He sees Fordist methods of mass production using assembly lines with a very highly specialized division of labour as 'the foundations on which this bureaucratic superstructure' was based (Fordism is discussed on p. 214).

Clegg argues that a new set of postmodern tendencies may have started to shape organizations. Of these the crucial tendency is 'de-differentiation'. Modern organizations were characterized by **differentiation**. On assembly lines and in bureaucratic offices jobs were broken down into individual tasks so that people's work became more and more specialized. **De-differentiation** involves the opposite process: jobs are put back together again so that people's work and role within an organization become more diverse and less specialized. The steadily increasing division of labour goes into reverse.

The causes of postmodern organizations

According to Clegg, by the 1970s the modernist model of organizations 'had begun to run out of steam'. There was a world economic crisis as big companies found it increasingly difficult to maintain or increase their profits. There were few areas of work left to rationalize so that efficiency could be increased. Decades of full employment had strengthened workers' organizations and the costs of controlling work through strict surveillance were increasing. As advanced economies 'deindustrialized', many of the old heavy manufacturing plants which were run along bureaucratic lines were closed down. In these circumstances, organizations began to seek a new model.

This model was to be found in Japan. Clegg says that many commentators believe that 'Japan represents the "vanguard" of postmodern management and organisations' while 'modernist organisational forms are increasingly being confined to less developed industries, tending to be located within less developed areas of the world economy'.

The features of postmodern organizations

Clegg distinguishes between modern and postmodern organizations in the following ways.

1 Modern companies have often developed as conglomerates with distinct parts of the organization dealing with different aspects of the company's activities. Japanese companies tend to concentrate on a particular area of expertise. For example Sony has special expertise in miniaturizations and NEC in digital technology. The strategy for the company does not come from a central source coordinating the activities of the diverse parts of the conglomerate. Instead strategy originates from members of the organization with 'core competencies', that is a particular expertise in the area on which the organization concentrates.

2 Japanese companies are not based upon the rigid hierarchy typical of bureaucracies. Instead employees tend to work more in teams. A team might have responsibility not just for production but also for maintaining machines, reducing wastage, ensuring quality control and suggesting 'technological and process improvements'. Individual workers are expected to have multiple skills. **Quality circles**, discussion groups involving members of a work team, are used to stimulate innovation.

3 In bureaucracies coordination and control tends to be based upon close monitoring of workers. In Japanese companies there is greater emphasis on encouraging loyalty to the enterprise. Some companies use 'spiritual training', which Clegg describes as 'akin to techniques of religious conversion'. Most encourage workers to feel involved in the decisions that the company takes, making it more difficult to protest or resist once they have been made. For example, the *ringi* system for making decisions involves circulating documents with

new proposals so that all workers get a chance to comment and point out possible problems. As a result 'opposition will have been "cooled-out" before decisions have been made'. Loyalty among core workers in Japanese companies is encouraged through the provision of considerable job security, or even jobs for life.

4 Japanese companies place a greater emphasis on long-term planning based on careful research than typical modernist organizations. The Japanese Government plays a major role by supplying information through the Ministry of International Trade and Industry.

5 In Japanese companies rewards are not usually based purely upon an individual's performance. Seniority based on length of service is important for determining wages for the core workers. These workers are usually men. When performance is taken into account, it is often based on the performance of a work team rather than an individual. Japanese companies make considerable use of symbolic rewards. One example is awarding shields to the best performing teams. Again these are designed to encourage loyalty to the company.

Winners and losers in postmodern organizations

The main beneficiaries of the type of organization described by Clegg are men who have permanent jobs in one of the large Japanese corporations. This is particularly true of those who have worked in one company for many years and who are seen as having 'core competencies', or special skills, which the company needs. There are few women in this position and employment is considerably less well rewarded outside the big companies. There is a great deal of subcontracting so that much of the work needed by the major corporations is not carried out by their own employees. Workers in subcontracting firms have much less job security and less access to training.

Conclusion

According to Clegg the modern era produced a trend towards bureaucratic organizations, but they did not triumph everywhere. Similarly, the competitive success of Japanese companies encourages other countries to adopt similar

arrangements, but not every organization will become postmodern. Furthermore, Japan does not offer the only model of successful postmodern organizations. In Sweden too there has been a movement away from the use of rigid organizational hierarchies. There, however, a much greater emphasis has been placed on industrial democracy, giving workers more real control over the owners of industry. Clegg sees this as preferable to the Japanese system which gives special privileges to only a few workers. However, on the whole he believes that the model adopted by the Japanese is likely to be adopted more widely.

■ **Paul Thompson – the end of bureaucracy?**

Neither Mintzberg nor Clegg believe that bureaucracy, as described by Weber is about to disappear. However, both do see it as in long-term decline. Paul Thompson has reviewed the evidence about the alleged decline of bureaucracy and has reached rather different conclusions.

Centralization, power and control

Thompson accepts that there has been some decentralization of decision making in organizations. However, this relates largely to 'increased operational autonomy' for lower management and it often occurs 'within a more tightly controlled framework'. For example, individual parts of a company may have more chance to determine how they spend money, but their budgets are rigidly controlled from above. Many individual workers also appear to have more independence from bureaucratic control, but computer technology can be used to monitor and direct their activities.

Thompson quotes the examples of General Motors where computers generate data on the productivity of individuals and an Italian engineering company which uses computer screens to issue instructions to workers. In companies like Benneton, decentralization of production and retailing of products is accompanied by the 'centralisation of marketing and complete managerial control over the design, cutting and finishing of garments'.

Thompson describes Mintzberg's claim that there is little emphasis on planning and control in advanced organizations (or adhocracies) as 'well off the mark'. He also questions the view that Japanese organizations have replaced status hierarchies with teamwork. He says 'Japanese management is obsessed with differences, even to the point of desk size and position and the depth of bow according to position in the hierarchy.'

Rules

Thompson accepts that some modern organizations expect greater flexibility from their members. Often, however, this simply involves adding extra responsibilities to their jobs and does not necessarily mean any reduction in the extent to which workers are subject to rules. In Japan 'visiting production managers have found extensive use of work study in which the supervisor has a central role in setting standards and targets'. Another good example is McDonald's. Their workers are required to work in flexible teams (or 'crews' as they are called) but they must nevertheless follow incredibly detailed rules laid down in a 385-page book. For example, cooks are told they must turn (but not flip) hamburgers one at a time and cashiers are required to smile at every customer and to make eye contact with them.

Thompson suggests that far from increasing the freedom of workers some Japanese organizations are simply finding new ways of ensuring conformity. He quotes a report on Matsushita which requires workers to recite a business code and sing the company song daily, and to contribute at least three suggestions to a quality circle each month. On Japanese railways workers have been required to vow to increase productivity.

Conclusion – the future of bureaucracy

Thompson is, then, highly critical of those who have implied the possible end of bureaucracy. He suggests that advocates of such a view tend to take examples of highly untypical organizations and overestimate their importance. Consequently 'the impression is given that all new forms of business activity are dynamic and in constant flux'. He goes on to say 'This reaches its logical absurdity in descriptions of "adhocracies", which can apparently operate without **any** standardisation of activities and change shape with such frequency as to "make your head swim".'

Thompson argues that bureaucratization is a 'universal **tendency** in modern organization (and the state) that requires the performance of complex tasks and management of competing interests according to observable rules and norms'. This does not mean that it is inevitable that all large organizations are bureaucratic. Nor does it mean that bureaucracy cannot change. It can change but it will still retain certain core characteristics.

Thompson then compares contemporary organizations with Weber's ideal type. Bureaucracies continue to be run according to rules, but the nature of the rules has been changing. Instead of specifying what tasks should be carried out they put greater emphasis on the type of behaviour required. Hierarchies continue to exist, but they no longer specify that each person has a very specific area of competence. More flexibility and multiple skills are expected. Employees at the bottom of the hierarchy may have more opportunity to use their initiative, but their performance is still closely monitored. Individual parts of organizations may have been given more autonomy but this has not led to a real decentralization of power. There is now 'more sophisticated coordination and strengthened control of strategic resources and decisions'. Those at the top of the hierarchy retain control over all the important decisions. Finally Thompson suggests there has been a move away from requiring bureaucrats to be impersonal and rationalistic in the performance of their duties. A new emphasis on 'corporate culture', encourages employees to get emotionally involved in their work and to 'love their company'. (Corporate culture is discussed later, see pp. 298–9.)

If Thompson is correct then Weber's analysis of the ideal type of bureaucracy remains a useful analytical tool. Bureaucracy is not inevitable and it can be substantially modified, but rumours of its death have been greatly exaggerated.

Bureaucracy and democracy

Marxist perspectives

To Weber, bureaucracy is not necessarily incompatible with democracy. Rather, it is a response to the administrative requirements of all industrial societies, whether capitalist or communist. The nature of ownership of the means of production makes relatively little difference to the need for bureaucratic control but from a Marxist perspective, bureaucracy can only be understood in relation to the forces of production.

Thus in capitalist society, where the means of production are owned by a minority – the ruling class – state bureaucracy will inevitably represent the interests of that class. Many Marxists have seen the bureaucratic state apparatus as a specific creation of capitalist society. Its role and the reasons for its development have been outlined in Chapter 9 (pp. 503–5). Weber believed that responsible government could be achieved by strong parliamentary control of the state bureaucracy. This would prevent the interests of capital from predominating. Lenin, the first communist leader of the USSR disagreed. He maintained that Western parliaments were 'mere talking-shops' while the 'real work of government was conducted behind closed doors by the state bureaucracy'. In his view 'The state is an organ of class rule, an organ for the oppression of one class by another.'

Lenin and the democratization of bureaucracy

Since state bureaucracy is ultimately shaped by a capitalist infrastructure, its control can only be eliminated by a radical change in that infrastructure. In terms of Marxist theory, this requires the communal ownership of the means of production. Since state bureaucracy is basically a repressive means of control, it must be smashed and replaced by new, truly democratic institutions.

Lenin believed that after the dictatorship of the proletariat was established in the USSR in 1917, there would be a steady decline in state bureaucracy. He recognized that some form of administration was necessary but looked forward to the proposals outlined by Marx and Engels. Administrators would be directly appointed and subject to recall at any time. Their wages would not exceed those of any worker. Administrative tasks would be simplified to the point where basic literacy and numeracy were sufficient for their performance. In this way, everybody would have the skills necessary to participate in the administrative process. As outlined in the previous chapter, members of a truly communist society would no longer be imprisoned in a specialized occupational role.

Lenin looked forward to a future in which 'all may become "bureaucrats" for a time and that, therefore, nobody may be able to become a "bureaucrat"'. He envisaged mass participation in administration which would involve 'control and supervision by all'. In this way the repressive state bureaucracies of the West would be replaced by a truly democratic system.

Bureaucracy in the USSR

Lenin offered little more than a vague and general blueprint for the future. He gave few specific details of how the 'democratization' of state bureaucracy was to be accomplished and of how the new institutions would actually work. In practice, the 1917 revolution was not followed by the dismantling of state bureaucracy but by its expansion. Lenin put this down to the 'immaturity of socialism', but there is no evidence that the USSR reversed the trend towards bureaucratization during its later years. In fact many observers have seen bureaucracy as the organizing principle of Soviet Communism.

For example, writing in 1965, Alfred Meyer argued that 'the USSR is best understood as a large, complex bureaucracy comparable in its structure and functioning to giant corporations, armies, government agencies and similar institutions in the West'.

As outlined in Chapter 2 Milovan Djilas painted a similar picture with particular emphasis on what he saw as the exploitive nature of bureaucratic control. According to Djilas, political bureaucrats in the USSR directed the economy for their own benefit. The mass of the population was seen to have little opportunity to participate in or control the state administration.

■ Robert Michels – bureaucracy and democracy

Marxist hopes for truly democratic organizations in a communist society were dismissed as mere illusions by the Italian sociologist Robert Michels (1876–1936). *Political Parties*, first published in 1911, is a study of European socialist parties and trade unions with particular emphasis on the German Socialist Party. These organizations were committed to the overthrow of the capitalist state and the creation of a socialist society. They claimed to be organized on democratic principles, directly representing the interests and wishes of their members. Michels claimed that these ideals bore little resemblance to what actually happened.

Democracy and bureaucracy

Michels began his analysis with the observation that 'Democracy is inconceivable without organization.' In a large complex society, the only way individuals can effectively voice their wishes and press their interests is by joining together and forming an organization. This is particularly true of the relatively powerless working-class masses for whom combination and cooperation are essential.

However, organization sounds the death knell of democracy. Direct participation by large numbers of people in the running of an organization is, in practice, impossible. Apart from the practical difficulties of assembling thousands of people, direct involvement in decision making would be so cumbersome and time consuming that nothing would get done. Since 'direct' democracy is impracticable, it can only be replaced by some form of representative system whereby 'delegates represent the mass and carry out its will'. Yet Michels maintained that even this truncated form of democracy founders in practice.

The 'iron law of oligarchy'

Once a system of representative democracy is established in trade unions and political parties, it results in the appointment of full-time officials and professional politicians. The administrative tasks involved inevitably lead to the creation of a bureaucracy which by its very nature is undemocratic. The effective operation of the organization requires a specialized division of labour that necessitates control and coordination from the top. The result is a 'rigorously defined and hierarchical bureaucracy'.

As the organization grows and administrative duties proliferate, 'it is no longer possible to take them in at a glance'. They become increasingly incomprehensible to those without specialist knowledge and training. Faced with this complexity, rank and file members of trades unions and political parties tend to leave matters to their leaders. Decisions are increasingly taken by executive committees within the bureaucracy, rather than by assemblies of the rank and file. Thus the very organization which was created to represent its members ends up by largely excluding them from participation and decision making. In Michels's words 'The oligarchical structure of the building suffocates the basic democratic principle.' He maintained that organizations inevitably produce **oligarchy**, that is rule by a small group or elite. This is the **iron law of oligarchy**.

Once established, bureaucracy brings with it all the deficiencies which Michels believes are an integral part of such organizations. Dependent on the orders and direction of superiors, the initiative of subordinates is crushed. Individuality is suppressed as bureaucrats slavishly follow official procedures and regulations. There is a 'mania for promotion'. With advancement dependent on the judgement of higher authority, subordinates bow and scrape to their superiors while adopting an arrogant stance to those beneath them in the hierarchy. In Michels's eyes 'Bureaucracy is the sworn enemy of individual liberty, and of all bold initiative in matters of internal policy.' It is 'petty, narrow, rigid and illiberal'.

The 'displacement of goals'

Even if these deficiencies and the oligarchical nature of bureaucratic structures are accepted, is it not still possible for the interests of the rank and file to be represented?

Again Michels was pessimistic. He argued that once the leadership is established at the top of the bureaucratic pyramid, its primary concern is the maintenance of its own power. Leaders wish to retain the privileges and status which their position brings, a concern which takes priority over the stated goals of the organization. This involves a **displacement of goals** whereby preservation of the organization becomes an end in itself rather than a means to an end. The organization will become increasingly conservative as leaders refrain from taking any action that might endanger their position.

This was particularly apparent in the case of the German Socialist Party. Its commitment to the overthrow of the capitalist state was steadily pushed into the background. Its leaders joined the existing ruling elite, forming a part of the political power structure. Forceful pursuit of the party's original goals might have resulted in its destruction and with it the leadership's loss of power.

Leaders are able to maintain power for a variety of reasons. They learn the skills of the political game which they play to their own advantage. Such skills include 'the art of controlling meetings, of applying and interpreting rules, of proposing motions at opportune moments'. Entrenched at the top of a bureaucratic hierarchy, they have the power to control communication to the rank and file. Their control over the publications of the party or union, for instance, enables them to put across their own viewpoint. Leaders have considerable say in the appointment of officials in the organization and can therefore select those who support their policies.

Like the early elite theorists, with whom he is usually bracketed, Michels believed that the masses have a psychological need to be led. This is accompanied by a veneration of leaders, who often become cult figures. The experience of power tends to make leaders see themselves in a similar light. They come to believe in their own greatness to the point where some take the view that *'Le parti c'est Moi'*. Thus leaders see their own interests and the maintenance of the organization as indistinguishable.

A ruling elite

The failure of democracy on the organizational level means that it cannot hope to succeed on the societal level. Society is ruled by an elite that consists of the leaders of various organizations and parties. The overriding concern of this ruling élite is the maintenance of its own power.

This applies both to capitalist and communist societies. Michels predicted that a proletarian revolution and the establishment of a socialist society would result in 'a dictatorship in the hands of those leaders who have been sufficiently astute and sufficiently powerful to grasp the sceptre of dominion in the name of socialism'. (Michels belongs within the tradition of classical elite theory. For details of this theory see Chapter 9, pp. 515–17.)

Michels believed that organization was essential to democracy. However, as a matter of 'technical and practical necessity', organizations adopt a bureaucratic structure. This inevitably produces oligarchical control which brings an end to democracy. Michels concluded that:

> It is organization which gives birth to the dominion of the elected over the electors, of the mandatories over the mandators, of the delegates over the delegators. Who says organization, says oligarchy.

◼ Union democracy – Lipset, Trow and Coleman

Organizational democracy – a case study

Michels made sweeping generalizations based on an examination of particular cases. He asserted that organizations inevitably result in the exclusion of the majority from participation in decision making and in domination by a self-interested oligarchy. In a famous study entitled *Union Democracy*, Lipset, Trow and Coleman examine the organizational structure of the International Typographical Union (ITU), which they claim provides an exception to the iron law of oligarchy.

The ITU, a craft printers' union, is unique among American unions in that it contains two parties. This system provides a constant check on the party in power and serves to generate alternative policies to those of the existing leadership. National and local officials are elected twice a year by the membership. A change in leadership often results in a real change of policy. For example, one administration supported arbitration with employers, but was replaced by more militant opposition which argued that union demands should be reinforced by strike action. Frequent elections and a two-party system mean that the rank and file can actually determine union policy. In addition, many decisions such as basic changes in union regulations and increases in officials' salaries are put to a referendum. More often than not, the proposals of the leadership are defeated. Decisions on whether or not to hold a referendum are not monopolized by the leadership: a method exists whereby referenda can be initiated by the rank and file.

For these reasons, Lipset *et al.* claim that the ITU is a democratic organization. There is a high degree of participation by the rank and file who have the power to effect real changes in union policy and to control the activities of their leaders. However, the ITU is a unique case. Only a combination of exceptional factors has produced its particular organizational structure. Those factors include the following.

1 Printers have a strong identification with their craft which encourages direct participation in union affairs. They tend to form occupational communities and organize a variety of social clubs for members of the craft. From the experience of organizing and running such clubs, many printers learn the political skills necessary for participation in union politics. In addition, social clubs provide union activists with the opportunity to encourage the more apathetic to become involved in union activities.

2 The ITU was formed in 1850 by an amalgamation of local unions. A history of local autonomy led to a resistance to centralized control. Even before the formation of the ITU, something akin to a two-party system existed in the local unions.

3 The borderline position of printers between the middle and working class tended to produce moderate and radical factions and therefore a basis for the two-party system.

4 Demand for control of union leadership was due partly to the history of secret societies in the printing trade. These societies attempted to control appointments to union offices and foremen's jobs and were distrusted and opposed by non-members.

5 The incomes of the rank and file and union leaders were fairly similar and therefore a return to the shop floor did not mean a sharp drop in income for union officials. As a result they would not be motivated to cling to power 'at any cost'.

Lipset *et al.* argue that the combination of the above factors has led to democracy in the ITU. However, they are pessimistic about the potential for democracy in organizations in general. They argue that large-scale organization requires a bureaucratic structure. This makes democracy unlikely since those at the top have 'control over financial resources and internal communications, a large permanently organized political machine, a claim to legitimacy, and a near monopoly over political skills'. They therefore admit that the implications of their analysis 'for democratic organizational politics are almost as pessimistic as those postulated by Robert Michels'.

■ Philip Selznick – the Tennessee Valley Authority

A somewhat different perspective on the question of democracy and organization is provided by Philip Selznick's famous study of the Tennessee Valley Authority (TVA). Like Michels, he studied an organization which claimed to be democratic and showed how this claim was frustrated in practice. Selznick adopts a functionalist approach, arguing that organizations have basic needs, the most fundamental of which is the need for survival. Such needs place severe constraints on the behaviour of members of the organization. In particular, if the goal of democracy threatens the existence of the organization, that goal is likely to be displaced in order to ensure the organization's survival. In Selznick's words, 'ideals go quickly by the board when the compelling realities of organizational life are permitted to run their natural course.'

The TVA was a government agency created in 1933 to plan and direct the development of the Tennessee River Valley area which covered seven southern states in the USA. It formed part of President Roosevelt's 'New Deal' policy which aimed to combat poverty and lift America out of the Depression. Roosevelt stated that the TVA:

---

should be charged with the broadest duty of planning for the proper use, conservation, and development of the natural resources of the Tennessee River drainage basin and its adjoining territory for the general social and economic welfare of the nation.

In particular, it was concerned with the construction of dams, flood control, the generation of hydroelectricity, the production and distribution of chemical fertilizer, forestry, and improvements in farming and land use in general. The TVA was to develop the region with the aim of directly benefiting all the people living there, and ultimately the nation as a whole.

Popular welfare was coupled with the idea of popular participation. The TVA's 'grass roots' policy stated that local people should enter into a partnership with the organization for the development of their region. In pursuit of this end the authority would administer its programme through existing institutions in the area. Local interests would be represented on the policy-making bodies of the TVA and in this way people in the Tennessee Valley would participate in decisions affecting their future. The TVA looked forward to 'a democratic partnership with the people's institutions'.

Administration

Selznick argues that the reality of the TVA's administration was very different from its democratic ideals. Most of his research is concerned with the authority's agricultural programme directed by its Agricultural Relations Department. In line with the grass roots policy, the TVA operated through local institutions. It linked up with the land-grant colleges – agricultural colleges established in the previous century by grants of land from the Government. Representatives of the colleges were appointed to the Agricultural Relations Department which decided on matters of policy. The agricultural programme was administered through the colleges' extension services run by agents in each of the counties in the states.

However, the land-grant colleges were closely tied to the interests of the wealthier farmers. The county agents had little or nothing to do with the impoverished, mainly black, tenant farmers. The services they offered – advice on new agricultural developments and marketing – were monopolized by the wealthier white farmers. In addition, the land-grant colleges had strong links with the American Farm Bureau Federation, a national association which represented the wealthier farming interests. The county agents recruited members for the Federation, and in return the Federation lobbied at national level in support of the land-grant colleges.

By appointing representatives of the land-grant colleges to its policy-making body and administer-

ing its agricultural programme through the county agents, the TVA supported the dominant farming interests in the area. This can be seen from the following examples.

Part of the agricultural programme was concerned with testing fertilizers and demonstrating their uses to local farmers. The farmers paid the freight charges on the fertilizer and used it as directed. Since freight charges amounted to only a fraction of the fertilizer's value, there was no shortage of volunteers for the programme. Participants were selected by the county agents. Following their usual procedures, they chose only the wealthier farmers who thus obtained large supplies of cheap fertilizers and the benefit of TVA expertise regarding its use.

As part of its power programme, the TVA built a series of dams along the Tennessee River and its tributaries. This created reservoirs, and the authority originally planned to develop the land surrounding them for public recreation. However, the Agricultural Relations Department, 'speaking for the local landowners', strongly opposed this policy. The building of reservoirs enriched the surrounding land and local landowners were therefore anxious to retain control over it. Under pressure from the Agricultural Relations Department, the TVA changed its policy and allowed the land to remain under private ownership. Thus the public, whose funds had paid for the reservoirs, failed to benefit either from the projected recreational areas or the increases in land values.

Organizational survival

With these and other examples, Selznick argues that the TVA, far from representing the interests of the public, ended up serving 'the established farm leadership'. By working through the larger and more powerful local interest groups and institutions, it merely reinforced the existing power structure. Selznick argues that the democratic ideals of the TVA failed to materialize for the following reasons. The primary need of any organization is to survive. Much of the behaviour of members of an organization can be understood in terms of this requirement. In order to maintain itself, the TVA had to adapt to its environment. In practice, this meant it was forced to compromise its democratic ideals in order to secure the cooperation of the local power structure without which it could not operate.

In Selznick's view, the TVA had to adapt itself 'not so much to the people in general as to the actually existing institutions which have the power to smooth or block its way'. By appointing representatives of the dominant farming interests to its policy-making body and by delegating the administration of its agricultural programme to those same interests, the TVA averted a major threat to its survival. In doing so, however, it lost all claims to be democratic.

The pessimism of Michels, Selznick and to a lesser extent Lipset, Trow and Coleman is not shared by all commentators on bureaucracy. For example, B. Guy Peters believes that it may be possible to have effective popular control over state bureaucracies (see pp. 311–12).

■ The managerial tradition

Many of the studies of behaviour in organizations have been influenced by the priorities of management. They have been concerned with how to make organizations more efficient and in particular, how to improve the productivity of workers. Mouzelis has referred to research directed by these concerns as 'the managerial tradition'. We will now consider four major schools of thought within this tradition – 'scientific management', 'human relations', 'neo-human relations' and 'corporate culture'.

■ Scientific management

The theory of **scientific management** was first spelt out in detail by Frederick W. Taylor whose book, *The Principles of Scientific Management*, was published in America in 1911. The turn of the century in the USA was a time of rapid industrial expansion. Compared to today, the organization of work on the shop floor was left much more in the hands of workers and supervisors. Workers often brought their own tools to suit their individual preferences, and decisions about the speed of machines were often left to the particular operator. There were few systematic training programmes to teach workers their jobs and often skills were acquired simply by watching more experienced colleagues. Decisions about the selection of personnel, rest periods and lay-offs were frequently left to individual supervisors.

Scientific principles and the design of work

Taylor argued that such arrangements were haphazard and inefficient. In their place he suggested the following scheme of scientific management which he claimed would maximize productivity.

According to Taylor, there is 'one best way' of performing any work task. It is the job of management to discover this way by applying scientific principles to the design of work procedures. For example, various tools should be tested to find the most efficient for the job; rest periods of differing length and frequency should be tried to discover the relationship between rest and productivity; and the various movements involved in the task should be assessed in order to find those that are least time consuming and produce the lowest level of fatigue. Experimenting with different task designs will result in the discovery of the most efficient way of doing a particular job.

With this approach, Taylor laid the foundations for what has come to be known as **time and motion studies**. Once management has developed 'a science for each element of a man's work', it must then select and train workers in the new methods. Workers and tasks must be closely matched. For example, workers with low intelligence are best suited to simple, repetitive tasks. Once suitable personnel have been selected, they must then be trained to perform tasks according to the directives laid down by management. Instructions are to be followed to the letter. In Taylor's words, 'Each man receives in most cases written instructions, describing in detail the task he is to accomplish, as well as the means to be used in doing the work.'

Finally, the cooperation of the workforce is obtained by monetary incentives. Taylor assumed that people's primary motivation for work was financial. Thus in order to maximize productivity and obtain work of the highest quality, the manager must give, 'some special incentive to his men beyond that which is given to the average in the trade'. In practice this usually involved a wage incentive scheme based on piece-work – payment according to the amount of work done. Taylor believed that the scientific planning of work tasks, the selection and systematic training of suitable workers for the performance of those tasks plus a carrot-and-stick system of financial incentives would maximize productivity.

Taylor saw scientific management as the solution to many of industry's problems.

1 It would increase both the quantity and quality of the product.

2 It promised to end conflict between employers and employees. Since the employer is concerned with higher profits and the worker with higher wages, they share an interest in raising productivity. Increased productivity reduces labour costs and results in higher profits which in turn allow for higher wages.

A fair day's work and a just system of payment can be established in accordance with the principles of scientific management. This will end conflict between management and labour since nobody can argue about 'scientific facts'.

Criticisms of scientific management

Taylor's ideas have been strongly criticized despite the fact that many of his critics admit that their application has generally resulted in increased productivity and his ideas probably still dominate the thinking of many managers today.

Two of the assumptions that underlie Taylor's principles have been singled out for particular criticism.

1 Taylor assumed that people's primary motivation for work is economic and they will therefore respond positively to financial incentives. This view of motivation, based on a concept of 'economic man', has been rejected as overly simplistic.

2 Taylor viewed workers as individuals rather than members of social groups. His plan to increase productivity involved the provision of financial incentives for individual workers. He failed to consider the influence of informal work groups on the behaviour of the individual worker.

We will examine these points in the next section.

■ Human relations

Many of the central ideas of the human relations school grew out of an investigation at the Hawthorne plant of the Western Electric Company in Chicago. From 1927 to 1932, a team headed by Elton Mayo, a professor at the Harvard Business School, conducted a series of experiments designed to investigate the relationship between working conditions and productivity.

Mayo began with the assumptions of scientific management, believing that the physical conditions of the work environment, the aptitude of the worker and financial incentives were the main determinants of productivity. He therefore examined the relationship between productivity and variables such as levels of lighting and heating, the length and frequency of rest periods, and the value of monetary incentives. The results were inconclusive; there appeared to be no consistent relationship between productivity and the various factors examined.

Productivity and workers' attitudes

Mayo then changed the direction of his research. Instead of focusing on the factors deemed important by scientific management, he examined workers' attitudes towards their work and their behaviour as members of informal work groups.

The two sides of Mayo's research can be seen from the following study. Fourteen men were placed in an observational setting known as the Bank Wiring Observation Room. There were nine wiremen who connected wires to banks of terminals, three soldermen who each soldered the work of three wiremen, and two inspectors who tested the completed job. The quality and the quantity of each man's output were carefully measured. In addition, the men were given tests to measure their manual dexterity and intelligence.

Contrary to expectations, the researchers found no relationship between the results of these tests and the individual worker's output. The men's pay was based in part on a group incentive scheme. The more the group produced above a certain level, the more money each worker received. In theory every worker would maximize his output in terms of his capabilities. In practice this did not happen. Each individual restricted his output so as to maintain a uniform weekly rate of production for the group. The researchers discovered that the workers had established a norm which defined a fair day's work, and that this norm, rather than standards set by management, determined their output.

Even so there were marked differences between the output levels of individual wiremen, differences which bore no relationship to dexterity and intelligence. The researchers claimed that these differences could only be explained in terms of the interpersonal relationships within the work group. Most of the workers belonged to one or other of two informal groups. Differences in output were most closely related to informal group membership. One group emphasized that the worker should not produce too much with phrases such as 'Don't be a ratebuster'; the other that he should not produce too little with phrases such as 'Don't be a chiseler'. Largely as a result of these standards, the output of the wiremen in the two groups differed.

The Hawthorne studies moved the emphasis from the individual worker to the worker as a member of a social group. They saw behaviour as a response to group norms rather than simply being directed by economic incentives and management-designed work schemes. According to Roethlisberger and Dickson (who produced a detailed report on the Hawthorne studies) the behaviour of the wiremen 'could not be understood without considering the informal organization of the group'. They argue that informal work groups develop their own norms and values that are enforced by the application of group sanctions. For example, wiremen who exceeded their group's output norm became the butt of sarcasm and ridicule, they suffered mild forms of physical violence and risked being cold-shouldered by the group. Roethlisberger and Dickson argue that the power of such sanctions derives from the dependence of the individual upon the group. Individuals have a basic need to belong, to feel part of a social group. They need approval, recognition and status, needs which cannot be satisfied if they fail to conform to group norms. Thus when the wiremen stopped work early because they had filled their quota as defined by the group, 'they were yielding to a pressure far stronger than financial incentive', that is, the pressure of group norms.

Workers' needs and productivity

From the Hawthorne studies, and research which they largely stimulated, the human relations school developed. It stated that scientific management provided too narrow a view of people and that financial incentives alone were insufficient to motivate workers and ensure their cooperation. In addition management must attend to a series of needs which are common to all workers.

Organizational psychologists have catalogued a range of needs for which workers are assumed to require satisfaction in their employment. These include **social needs** such as friendship, group support, acceptance, approval, recognition and status, and the need for **self-actualization** which involves the development of the individual's talents, creativity and personality to the full. If these needs are not met, workers suffer psychologically and the efficiency of the organization is impaired.

Thus Roethlisberger and Dickson argue that in order to maximize productivity, managers must make sure that the 'personal satisfactions' of workers are met and only then will they be 'willing to cooperate'. Management must accept and cooperate with informal work groups since they provide a context in which many of the workers' needs are satisfied. Through the use of supervisory staff trained in human relations skills, managers must ensure that the norms of informal groups are in line with the goals of the organization.

One way of accomplishing this objective is to invite groups of workers to participate in decision making. This is based on the idea that workers will be more committed to their tasks if they have a voice in determining how those tasks are to be performed. By discovering ways of involving informal work groups within the organization, these groups can become a major driving force for the realization of organizational goals.

Evaluation of the human relations school

Research into the application of human relations techniques has produced inconsistent findings which do not allow any no firm conclusions to be reached. For example, a study by Coch and French examined methods of introducing changes in production methods and piece rates among women workers in a pyjama factory. Four groups of workers were involved. The first group was simply informed about the changes. The second group met with management who explained the need for changes and discussed them with the group. Representatives of the group later discussed the new piece rate scheme in detail with management and were trained in the new production methods that they then taught to the other members of the group. A third and fourth group participated more directly in the changes. Every member went through the same procedures as the representatives of the second group.

Within the first 40 days of the changeover, the first group had a 17 per cent rate of labour turnover whereas no member of the other groups resigned. Even when the first group gained experience of the new production methods, its output was consistently lower than that of the other groups. In addition it had a markedly lower level of reported job satisfaction. The third and fourth groups achieved the highest rate of production, which suggests that productivity is related to the degree of participation by workers in matters that affect their work. However, an attempt to replicate this study in another factory failed to produce similar results (discussed in Tausky 1970).

■ The 'neo-human relations' perspective

Paul Thompson and David McHugh argue that after the Second World War a new version of the human relations school began to influence managers in organizations. Like the original one it aimed to make workers more productive by ensuring that the organization helped to satisfy human needs. However, rather than concentrating on groups within the workplace, the **neo-human relations** school paid more attention to the nature of the work itself. It tried to find ways of making the work more intrinsically satisfying.

One of the most influential management theorists proposing these ideas was F. Herzberg. He believed that workers became more productive when they were given greater responsibility for carrying out a complete task. He therefore thought that workers should have greater control over planning their own work and for inspecting it when complete. Herzberg was strongly opposed to Taylorist work practices and in 1973 he predicted

that they would disappear within a decade. To Herzberg and other similar management theorists, the traditional production line was highly inefficient since the boredom induced by repeatedly carrying out one task greatly reduced workers' motivation.

A number of companies followed this line of thinking by introducing 'work humanization' programmes. At the Volvo truck plant, for example, the conventional production line was abandoned. Instead people worked in semi-autonomous teams carrying out a number of tasks. Each team was responsible for manufacturing a major section of the car. Workers largely controlled the pace of production. This innovation led to impressive gains in productivity. A wide range of measures was taken in other companies to make work more satisfying. Paul Thompson says that at Philips, for example, the measures ranged from 'simple job rotation, to improving the physical environment and sophisticated job enrichment exercises'.

Evaluation of the neo-human relations perspective

Thompson and McHugh argue that these developments were related to:

---

tight labour markets and high levels of employment which gave firms problems in recruiting and retaining workers and an upsurge in industrial unrest through strike waves and less formally through absenteeism, high labour turnover and sabotage.

Work humanization appeared to increase productivity and reduce industrial unrest in some of the companies which tried it but Thompson and McHugh describe the effects as 'uneven'. They argue that the greatest benefits were found in white-collar work and craft jobs that had least need for job enrichment schemes. In any case, most of these initiatives disappeared once unemployment began to rise and organizations found it less difficult to recruit and retain suitable workers. Companies like Volkswagen and General Motors abandoned their schemes during the 1970s' recession.

Thompson and McHugh claim that the schemes were bound to be limited. If they were too radical and allowed too much worker participation they would undermine the authority of managers. Polaroid's Training Director ended worker participation when it threatened to make supervisors and managers superfluous.

▮ Corporate cultures

In the 1980s management theory turned away from job enrichment schemes and looked elsewhere for ways of improving organizational efficiency. As discussed earlier in this chapter Mintzberg argued that organizations should be less bureaucratic, and others turned to Japanese corporations for inspiration. However, some American writers argued that their own country had examples of organizations that were very successful in motivating workers. The motivation came from the culture of the organization.

Terence Deal and Allen Kennedy claim that every organization has its own **corporate culture**: its own set of values and ways of doing things. The culture has 'a powerful influence throughout an organization; it affects practically everything – from who gets promoted and what decisions are made, to how employees dress and what sports they play'. Because it has such an influence, organizations are more likely to be successful if they have a strong and appropriate culture.

Deal and Kennedy use a number of illustrative examples of what they see as good practice. They start their book by citing a story about National Cash Register Corporation. The retired chairman of the company claimed that when visiting an NCR site in Germany at the end of the Second World War, he found two former NCR employees clearing the rubble where a factory had once stood. On the chairman's arrival they said 'We knew you'd come.' NCR's 'hard driving sales-orientated culture' had withstood the devastation of a world war.

Tandem Corporation, a computer company based in Silicon Valley, is also used as an example of a corporation with a strong culture. According to Deal and Kennedy this company has a philosophy that is shared by most employees. This is based round slogans such as 'Get the job done no matter what it takes' and 'Tandemize it – means make it work'. Noticeboards and T-shirts are used to promote the slogans. Tandem lacks a traditional organizational hierarchy but members of the corporation are able to work together because of the presence of unwritten rules stressing the importance of people. There is an 'open door' policy allowing anyone in the company to talk to

anyone else. Corporate cultures are often maintained through stories about heroes. At Tandem the charismatic chief executive, Jim Treybig, is one hero; the other main one is the product, a mainframe computer system based upon two separate computers linked together. This product 'provides the metaphor for the "working together" philosophy'.

Rituals and ceremonies are also used to communicate a culture and give it extra strength. Tandem has a Friday afternoon 'beer-bust' where all employees get together and have a kind of company party.

Deal and Kennedy believe that a strong corporate culture integrates employees into the company. It makes them identify with their company – they feel a sense of belonging and pride. A culture can provide values and norms that provide a sense of direction and regulate behaviour without the need for heavy-handed authoritarian management. Above all it can have an 'amazing' impact on productivity. Deal and Kennedy say 'In the extreme, we estimate that a company can gain as much as one or two hours of productive work per employee per day.' It is not surprising, therefore, that they claim that a strong culture has led to the success of many American companies. They mention the computer giant IBM, General Motors, Polaroid, Kellogg's, General Electric, McDonald's and Xerox amongst many others.

Evaluation of corporate culture

Paul Thompson and David McHugh argue that there is little evidence for the claims that 'strong cultures exist' and that they are the main reason for the success of some companies. They point out that much of the evidence is anecdotal, as in Deal and Kennedy's story about the National Cash Register Corporation. Like most other proponents of the theory, Deal and Kennedy made no attempt to ask non-managerial workers about the culture of companies. The 'consequence is that what executives and managers say in words or on paper is taken as proof'. Even if the companies quoted as having a strong culture are successful, this does not demonstrate that the culture is the cause of the success. The advocates of corporate culture have failed to measure the other factors that could lead to success. For example, Thompson and McHugh quote research which suggested that IBM's success was the result of undercutting competitors in some areas, while overcharging customers in areas of the computer industry where they had a virtual monopoly. The success of McDonald's might have more to do with the use of cheap, non-unionized, part-time teenage employees doing work which is very closely regulated by the company, than it has to do with a corporate culture. Thompson and McHugh describe much of the evidence as 'resting on bland management statements, unattributed

quotes and plain assertion'. They see the whole approach as mistaking 'style as substance'. They do not deny that some companies do have distinctive cultures but they believe that writers such as Deal and Kennedy greatly exaggerate their importance. Furthermore they ignore the existence of divisions, conflicts and differences of interest within organizations. We will look at these issues in the next section of this chapter.

▋Power and conflict in organizations

Whatever their differences, all the management theories examined above assume that members of organizations share common interests. From this perspective managers, professionals, unskilled workers, and male and female employees all benefit if the organization prospers. A successful organization is better able to achieve its goals and all its members can be more highly rewarded.

Many sociologists of organizations have challenged this viewpoint. They have identified differences of interest between groups in organizations and studied the way power is exercised and conflicts develop. We begin by examining Marxist perspectives on power and conflict in organizations and go on to examine power and conflict in relation to one group of workers – professionals.

▋Marxist perspectives on organizational power and conflict

Organizations and the control of labour

Harry Braverman is an influential Marxist sociologist who has examined conflicts of interest between groups of workers. He denies that the interests of capital and labour can be compatible. He examines the ways that management theories have been used in organizations and he is particularly critical of scientific management. He sees it as a means of strengthening the dominance of capital over labour. He claims that in capitalist society the fundamental teachings of scientific management 'have become the bedrock of all work design'. Scientific management has been adopted as a means

of controlling alienated labour and is part of the process whereby the worker is increasingly transformed into an 'instrument of capital'.

The detailed planning and design of work tasks by management drastically reduces worker control over the labour process. Work becomes dehumanized as workers, constrained by management directives, simply 'function as cogs and levers'. The reduction of worker control over the labour process is essential for the continuing accumulation of capital. If workers directed their own work, it would not be possible 'to enforce upon them either the methodological efficiency or the working pace desired by capital'. Thus, far from welcoming scientific management, Braverman denounces it as a means for increasing the efficiency of the exploitation of labour in capitalist society. Braverman's work is examined in greater detail in Chapter 4 (see pp. 208–14).

Stuart Clegg and David Dunkerley agree with Braverman that the basic function of work organizations is to control alienated and exploited labour. However, they disagree with Braverman about the importance of scientific management. They argue that a variety of strategies are used for controlling the labour force depending upon the role of particular groups within the capitalist system.

Unskilled workers

The most exploited members of society tend to be unskilled workers who are not owners of the means of production. Often they make up part of the 'reserve army of labour' who drift in and out of employment. To a large extent these workers are disciplined by factors outside the organizations in which they work. It is the ever-present risk of unemployment and life on welfare payments that gives them little choice but to conform to pursuing the goals that organizations lay down for them.

Skilled workers

The more skilled manual workers, like their less skilled counterparts, do not own the means of production. However, their technical knowledge does imply that they could gain control over the means of production. Their knowledge of how products are produced potentially gives them considerable power. They are hard to replace, and in some circumstances they might even begin to threaten the dominance of employers within the organization. It is this group that is controlled by scientific management.

Like Braverman, Clegg and Dunkerley see scientific management as a way of overcoming opposition from workers. Ideologically, it legitimates the idea of a fair day's pay for a fair day's work. Furthermore, technological innovations make it easier to control and regulate the skilled worker, and the increasing division of labour makes it difficult for even the most skilled workers to understand the whole production process. In these ways any threat from skilled workers is minimized.

The intermediate group

Clegg and Dunkerley identify an intermediate group between manual workers and the ruling class. This group consists of supervisory, professional and managerial workers. Like manual workers they do not own the means of production, but unlike them they do have considerable control over the methods of production. Clegg and Dunkerley regard them as 'non-producers' and 'exploiters'. Their job is essentially to act in the interests of capital by overseeing and directing work within organizations. They are not subject to the rigid discipline of scientific management in carrying out their work tasks: they require, and are given, greater freedom and flexibility in their jobs.

Often their commitment to the organization to which they belong is encouraged by the application of the ideas of the human relations school to their work. Many managers are trained in management schools to apply the techniques of scientific management to the organization of the work of their subordinates. Business education serves as training in the techniques and ideologies that help

to maximize and justify the production of surplus value.

Owners and controllers of the means of production

Owners and controllers of the means of production include the owners of family businesses, shareholders in larger concerns and state employees directed with the task of running state-owned industries. In the private sector market forces limit the way in which organizations and their owners can operate. Clegg and Dunkerley believe that state-owned industries act in much the same way: their policies are also constrained by the market since they provide goods and services which are sold in it. In non-capitalist state activities (such as education) the organizations are not directly governed by market conditions. Nevertheless they tend to be hierarchical, and the state may use them in the overall interests of capitalism. Some parts of the state, such as education, largely function to produce false class consciousness in the population, while others, such as the police and the army, intervene when there is a threat to the overall stability of society.

The limits to control

Clegg and Dunkerley are aware that the control of organizations in the interests of capitalism can be challenged by workers. They accept that workers are not entirely taken in by ruling-class ideology. Nevertheless they believe that workers have had very limited success in establishing control over their own organizations. For example, most attempts to establish workers' cooperatives in Britain have been in industries that have been experiencing severe difficulties, such as the Norton Villiers Triumph motorcycle cooperative at Meriden. As a result most cooperatives have struggled to survive, let alone expand. They have therefore posed little threat to the overall dominance of capitalist-orientated control over organizations.

Summary and evaluation

The work of Clegg and Dunkerley demonstrates that the way organizations operate and the behaviour of their members are at least partly controlled by factors external to the organizations themselves. In particular they are constrained by the overall operation of the economic system of a society.

Clegg and Dunkerley also introduce a historical element into the analysis of organizations. They try to show that methods of controlling the workforce change as capitalism changes. For example, they claim that in work organizations under capitalism there has been a general trend away from coercive methods of control towards the use of more ideological methods.

However, their work is more applicable to private or state-run industries than to other types of organization. They are more able to account for how businesses operate than charities or hospitals. Furthermore, they may tend to underestimate the extent to which groups with a lowly position within organizational hierarchies can wrest concessions from those in more elevated positions, and retain some control over their own work.

Some Marxist sociologists of work organizations have paid greater attention to the existence of conflict within organizations. Graham Salaman argues that 'organizational employees actively strive to avoid and divert control; they seek to maximize their own interests.' Salaman refers to 'the various ways in which members seek to circumvent the official rules and regulations, to interrupt the organised flow of work, or avoid obtrusive procedures and systems'. Some of these methods of resistance (for example, strikes and industrial sabotage) are examined in more detail in Chapter 4 (see pp. 224–36).

■ Professionals and organizations

Marxists tend to focus on economic conflict in organizations. A rather different type of conflict has been identified by many sociologists who have studied the position of professionals in organizations. They argue that there can be a fundamental role conflict for professionals. Their role as members of an organization may conflict with their role as professionals. Such sociologists have often taken Weber as their starting point and criticized his view of bureaucratic authority and expert knowledge.

Weber argued that 'Bureaucratic administration means fundamentally the exercise of control on the basis of knowledge.' He saw the combination of authority and expertise as the feature of

bureaucracies which made them specifically rational. His model implies that there is a match between individuals' positions in the hierarchy and their level of technical expertise. Weber saw this aspect of bureaucratic authority as increasingly important arguing that 'The role of technical qualifications in bureaucratic organizations is continually increasing'. Trends in the employment of professionals lend support to this observation: growing numbers of professionals – scientists, engineers, accountants, lawyers, doctors – are working in organizational settings.

Bureaucratic and professional authority

However, Weber has been criticized for failing to distinguish between bureaucratic and professional authority. **Bureaucratic authority** is based on tenure of an office in a bureaucratic hierarchy. The official is obeyed, first and foremost, because of the position he or she holds. **Professional authority** is based on knowledge and expertise. The professional commands obedience because of this specialist knowledge rather than his or her position in a bureaucratic hierarchy. There is, therefore, a basic difference between these two forms of authority. Hospitals are a good illustration of these points as conflicts may occur between the medical professionals and the senior administrative staff.

In many organizations the most highly qualified members are found in the middle rather than the highest levels of the hierarchy. Burns and Stalker's research indicated that the ranking of experts below non-experts can lead to conflict.

The increasing pace of technical innovation in electronics means that experts have a growing part to play in the industry. However, this can undermine the legitimacy of senior management whose authority is based ultimately on the position they occupy in the hierarchy rather than technical expertise. Often they lack the specialist knowledge to understand and appreciate the significance of new developments in the industry. Burns and Stalker claim that 'the legitimacy of the hierarchical pyramid of management bureaucracy has been threatened by the sheer volume of novel tasks and problems confronting industrial concerns.' If senior managers recognize the professional authority of their subordinates, their own authority might be called into question.

As Burns and Stalker show, managers in some firms were prepared to take this risk and adopt an organic system. This meant that on occasions they deferred to expert knowledge and therefore devolved some of their power to the specialists. This tended to produce insecurity as the chain of command was no longer clearly defined.

In other firms senior management clung to the traditional bureaucratic system to ward off the 'threat' of the experts. As noted in the previous section, senior management remained secure but, since they failed to fully harness the expertise of the professionals, the efficiency of the organization suffered. Burns and Stalker's research indicates some of the problems that can develop when both bureaucratic and professional authorities are present in the same organization.

Professional versus administrative action

A number of researchers have argued that, at least in theory, there is a basic incompatibility between professional and administrative action.

Professional action stems from an individual judgement based on specialist knowledge. Professionals have the freedom to make decisions on the basis of their expertise. They may consult with colleagues but the final decision is theirs. Thus Amitai Etzioni argues that 'the ultimate justification for a professional act is that it is, to the best of the professional's knowledge, the right act'.

Administrative action has a different basis. In Etzioni's words, 'The ultimate justification for an administrative act is that it is in line with the organization's rules and regulations, and that it has been approved – directly or by implication – by a superior ranking official.'

Etzioni argues that professional and administrative action are, in principle, fundamentally opposed. The autonomy, self-regulation and individual decision making required by the professional conflicts with the hierarchical control and official rules of bureaucratic administration. As a result, the employment of professionals in organizations may produce role conflict. Professionals may experience conflict between their role as an employee and their role as a professional: as employees, professionals must follow the rules and obey superiors; as professionals they must follow their professional judgement which might result in

disregarding official regulations and disobeying higher authority.

The avoidance of role conflict

A number of studies have suggested that this role conflict need not arise. A study by Mary Goss examines supervisory relationships among a group of doctors in an outpatient clinic of a large American teaching hospital. Senior physicians organized the schedule of patients and performed various other administrative tasks. In addition they advised junior doctors about diagnosis and treatment. Potential conflict between an administrative hierarchy and professional autonomy was prevented from materializing for the following reasons. Doctors had the right to accept or reject the advice of their superiors. They made the final decisions and in this way professional autonomy was preserved. The administrative duties of the senior physicians were seen as separate from the professional area of work. As such, they did not erode the professional freedom of other doctors since, in Goss's words, 'administrative decisions covered only activities they viewed as non-professional or ancillary to their work'. In this way the individual doctor's authority in terms of patient care remained intact. The professional role requires only that the doctor 'be free to make his own decisions in professional matters as opposed to administrative concerns'.

Goss's study therefore shows that an administrative hierarchy and professional authority do not necessarily conflict in practice. However, it deals with the administration of professionals by professionals. It is therefore likely that the senior members of the hierarchy would be particularly sensitive to the requirements of the professional role.

Other research has indicated that in organizations where non-professionals administer the work of professionals, accommodations are made which reduce the possibility of role conflict. In a large-scale study of 154 public personnel agencies and 254 government finance departments in the USA, Peter Blau examines the relationship between the authority structure of the organizations and the qualifications of their employees. He found that the higher the qualifications of the employees, the higher the ratio of management personnel.

At first sight this appears strange since the greater the expertise of the staff, the less guidance and supervision they should require. In addition, a highly qualified staff will be likely to have professional status and to demand the autonomy associated with it.

On further investigation, however, Blau found that a high ratio of managers was compatible with a low level of supervision and a high degree of autonomy. He discovered that the higher the level of qualifications of the staff, the more authority and decision making was decentralized. When responsibility is delegated, a high ratio of managers is required, not for supervision and direction but for communication and consultation. Since an expert staff can make greater contributions to operating procedures, there is a greater need to ensure that information flows upwards from the lower ranks. Thus a relatively large number of managers is needed to 'facilitate the flow of upward communication' and so take full advantage of the contributions of the experts.

Blau argues that 'What is inappropriate for an organization staffed by experts is a hierarchy in which official authority is centralized in the hands of a few managers.' Blau concludes that authority structures in organizations are modified in relation to the degree of expertise of the staff. The greater the expertise, the more decision making and responsibility is delegated. In this way the requirement of professionals for autonomy and freedom from supervision is at least partially met.

Professional autonomy and organizational control

In many organizations it appears that organizational goals are effectively served by granting a relatively high degree of autonomy to professional employees. While those who support individual freedom might welcome this development, others, who fear what they see as the largely unrestricted power of organizations, view it with concern. Blau and Schoenherr regard the methods used to harness professional expertise to the service of organizations as a far more effective means of control than commands issued by an authoritarian hierarchy, than detailed rules and close supervision, or the incentives provided by financial reward. They argue that:

> The efforts of men can be controlled still far more efficiently than through wages alone by mobilizing

their professional commitments to the work they can do best and like to do most and by putting these highly motivated energies and skills at the disposal of organizations.

Thus people can be controlled by giving them the freedom to exercise their skill and expertise in accordance with the high standards of their profession and by channelling the high motivation associated with the professional role into the service of the organization.

This type of control is particularly effective since, because it is compatible with 'our values of human freedom and integrity', and it reduces resistance. Yet despite the autonomy given to highly qualified employees, management is still in control because they decide which professionals to recruit and which departments to expand or contract. Blau and Schoenherr claim that in organizations employing a high proportion of professionals 'That type of power suffices to govern the organization, though there is virtually no domination of individuals within it.' They regard this form of control as 'insidious' because it is deceptive and hidden. It does not involve:

> the experience of being oppressed by the arbitrary will of a despot and sometimes not even the need to comply with directives of superiors, but merely the internalized obligation to perform tasks in accordance with standards of workmanship.

Insidious control means that people are far less aware of being controlled.

Blau and Schoenherr argue that the increasing employment of professionals in organizations has two main results.

1 It increases the control of the organization over its members.

2 It increases the power of the organization in society since professional skills and expertise are mobilized in the service of organizational goals.

Blau and Schoenherr claim that:

> The professionalization of organizations, by which is meant that decisions are made by technical experts both interested and qualified in specialized fields of competence, enhances the internal efficiency and the external power of organizations.

Marxist views

Similar conclusions have been reached by Marxist sociologists. Graham Salaman argues that the autonomy allowed for professionals within organizations does not usually conflict with the achievement of organizational goals. Professionals may be free to make technical decisions relating to their own areas of expertise, but this does not allow them to control the overall objectives towards which they are working. Thus accountants help companies to reduce their tax bills, and psychologists and sociologists use their expertise to assist management in their effort to extract the maximum possible surplus value from their workers. Salaman is scornful of the professional employee of organizations, describing him or her as 'the palace eunuch, well rewarded for important services, but unable and unwilling to question the real nature of his contribution or the real power behind his spurious freedom'.

Peter Armstrong agrees that professionals within capitalist organizations act in the interests of the capitalist class. However, he sees them as having a more important role than that implied by Salaman and he also believes that professionals can benefit themselves as well as serving their capitalist masters.

Armstrong argues that there can be rivalry between different groups of professionals as they strive for dominance within an organization. For example, he claims that engineering professionals have gradually lost power in companies while accountants have gained it. In the early decades of the century engineers served the interests of capitalists by specializing in the function of controlling the labour force. Scientific management was based on the principles of mechanical engineering. It was not therefore surprising that engineers often got the job of applying the theory of scientific management in particular organizations. However, more recently accountants have gained ground and managers in British and American companies are now far more likely to be accountants than engineers. According to Armstrong this is because they have succeeded in establishing auditing techniques as an alternative basis for controlling labour. Instead of strict controls over the details of work, large corporations with many different divisions tend to use budget allocation and measures of efficiency and profitability as methods 'used to discipline and control department managers'.

Thus groups of professionals can try to make themselves indispensable to capitalists by adapting their particular skills so that they perform a key role in the organization. Any conflict is more likely to be between professional groups rather than between professionals and the capitalist organization. Armstrong concludes 'demands for autonomy may express not so much a desire for independence, but an ambition to be numbered amongst the controllers rather than amongst the controlled'.

■ Organizations – an interactionist perspective

In an earlier section organizations were viewed as systems, and the behaviour of their members as a response to the systems' needs. Thus Selznick argued that members of the TVA acted as they did in response to the needs of the system, in particular its need to survive in a potentially hostile environment. From this perspective, members of an organization are constrained to act in particular ways and have little say about how they act. This is an essentially determinist view since it sees human behaviour as determined by external stimuli. The behaviour is shaped by the constraints imposed by the needs of the system. The organization rather than its members is seen to control organizational behaviour.

From an interactionist perspective, action is not entirely determined by external forces. Instead it is largely directed by the meanings which actors give to objects, events and the activities of themselves and others. In David Silverman's words, 'Action arises out of meanings which define social reality.' For example, a range of meanings may be attached to an order issued by a member of a bureaucracy. It may be defined by subordinates as reasonable or unreasonable; they may regard obedience as demeaning or involving no loss of self-respect. As a result of the meaning given to the order it may be obeyed willingly or unwillingly, it may be ignored or flatly refused.

In order to understand the action of subordinates, it is therefore necessary to discover the meanings that direct it. From an interactionist perspective, meanings are not determined by forces external to the actor. They are created, modified and changed by actors in interaction situations. Thus in order to understand action, the sociologist must examine the process of interaction and interpret the meanings that develop within it and which guide and direct it.

■ Erving Goffman – total institutions

The first major study of an institution from an interactionist perspective was conducted by Erving Goffman in the late 1950s. He spent a year observing interaction in a mental hospital in Washington DC with the aim of understanding the social world of the inmate 'as this world is subjectively experienced by him'. In particular, he was concerned with how the patients' self-concept – their view of self – was modified or changed by their experience within the institution. Goffman claims that this can only be understood by interpreting the meanings given to that experience by the patient.

The study was widened to include organizations which share certain characteristics with mental hospitals. They include prisons, concentration camps, orphanages, monasteries and army barracks – organizations Goffman refers to as 'total institutions'. A **total institution** is defined as:

> a place of residence and work where a large number of like-situated individuals, cut off from the wider society for an appreciable period of time, together lead an enforced, formally administered round of life.

Goffman draws on a range of published material – novels, autobiographies and social science research – to suggest that there are basic similarities between many of the social processes which occur in such institutions.

Total institutions and the self

Goffman claims that total institutions are 'the forcing houses for changing persons; each is a natural experiment on what can be done to the self'. In order to understand this process, it is necessary to examine the interactions which take place from the viewpoint of the inmates.

Within a total institution people are usually cut off from the outside world and from long-standing relationships with family, friends and work groups. It is in these wider social contexts that individuals' self-concepts are sustained. Their picture of themselves as, for example, breadwinners, friends and workmates, is mirrored and reflected in their interaction with others who respond to them in terms of these identities. These reflections of self are largely absent in total institutions.

Individuals' self-concepts are also embedded in their name, their appearance, their clothes and personal possessions. Admission procedures to total institutions involve the removal of many items from this identity kit. Individuals may lose their name, being referred to by a number as in some military and penal institutions, or adopt a new name as in the French Foreign Legion and some religious orders. Their clothes may be replaced by those issued by the institution, such as army and prison uniforms and monks' habits. Their appearance may be changed, for instance by prison and military haircuts, and shaven heads in certain religious orders. Some or all of their personal possessions may be removed, as happens in prisons, mental hospitals and many religious institutions. Since a part of the individual's self-concept is invested in his or her name, appearance and possessions, Goffman argues that changes in these aspects are 'saying' something to the new inmate. Specifically they state that they are no longer the person they were.

The mortification of self

Many of the admission procedures and future interactions within total institutions not only tend to change but also to **mortify the self**. In Goffman's words, the inmate 'begins a series of abasements, degradations, humiliations, and profanations of self. His self is systematically, if often unintentionally, mortified.' They may be searched, undressed, bathed, disinfected and fingerprinted. They may be forced to humble themselves before superiors: in a monastery the novice may have to prostrate himself before the abbot; in the army the raw recruit may have to snap to attention in the presence of an officer and accept a string of abuse from non-commissioned officers. In some total institutions, the inmate requires permission to perform even the most basic of human functions and in certain cases their humiliation is increased by an absence of privacy.

Such experiences tend to break down the inmates' former self-concept. The self is then slowly rebuilt, partly by means of rewards and punishments administered by those in authority. In prisons and mental hospitals especially, 'a small number of clearly defined rewards or privileges are held out in exchange for obedience to staff in action and spirit'. Thus a cigarette ration, an additional cup of coffee or an extra hour's recreation are awarded to those whose behaviour is deemed appropriate by the staff. Failure to humble the self and act in accordance with official directives results in punishments which continue the mortification process. Many such punishments are known 'in the inmate's home world as something applied to children or animals'. They may include solitary confinement, a diet of bread and water, and the withdrawal of privileges such as cigarettes and recreation.

Goffman argues that many of the actions of inmates can only be understood with reference to the strict supervision and mortification of self that occurs in many total institutions. Smuggling food from the kitchen, fiddling the cigarette ration, and conning the staff in various ways may assume great importance to the inmate. According to Goffman such actions tell 'him' that 'he is still his own man, with some control over the environment'. Were they to submit completely to those in authority they would lose all sense of self-determination and personal efficacy.

Modes of adaptation

Not all inmates respond in the same way to life in total institutions. Goffman identifies five modes of adaptation which inmates may employ at different stages in their career in the institution, or alternate between during different points.

1 The first is **situational withdrawal**. Inmates withdraw attention from everything except events immediately surrounding their bodies and minimize their interaction with others. In mental hospitals this is known as 'regression'; in penal institutions as 'prison psychosis'.

2 A second response is the **intransigent line**. Inmates flatly refuse to cooperate with the staff and show continued hostility towards the institution. The staff often makes fierce efforts to break this line of resistance. In military barracks inmates may be locked in the stockade; in prisons they may be placed in solitary confinement; and in mental hospitals they may be isolated from other patients, given electric shock treatment or even a lobotomy. The strong reprisals against the intransigent line often mean that it is a short-lived adaptation.

3 A third response is **colonization**. Inmates become 'institutionalized': they find a home from home and define life in the institution as more desirable than life on the outside. Such inmates often make concerted efforts to remain inside as their day of release approaches.

4 A fourth response is **conversion**. Here the individual adopts the staff's definition of the model inmate and acts out the part. This adaptation reaches its most extreme form in Chinese prisoner of war camps where some Americans enthusiastically embraced communist doctrine.

5 Finally, in most total institutions the majority of inmates adopt a strategy which some of them call **playing it cool**. The aim is to stay out of trouble and involves alternating between the other modes of adaptation depending on the situation. By playing it cool, the inmate will have 'a maximum chance, in the particular circumstances, of eventually getting out physically and psychologically undamaged'.

Despite the sustained assault on the self in total institutions, Goffman claims that for most inmates a radical and permanent change of self does not occur. This is partly because they are able to defend themselves from the mortification process by playing it cool. Goffman is scornful of the official goals of organizations such as prisons and mental hospitals that present themselves as institutions that treat, cure and rehabilitate their clients. He concludes that 'Many total institutions, most of the time, seem to function merely as storage dumps for inmates.'

Goffman's analysis of total institutions differs from previous approaches to organizations because of its emphasis on understanding action in terms of meanings. From an interactionist perspective, an answer to the question, 'What happens in organizations?' involves an investigation and interpretation of the meanings which actors assign to objects, events and activities. Goffman argues that an individual's name, clothes and possessions are symbols, and are impregnated with meaning. By interpreting this meaning, she or he is able to assess the significance of the removal of these symbols. Clearly this form of analysis relies heavily on the sensitivity and interpretive skills of the observer. Since it is not possible to enter the consciousness of others, there is no certainty that the meanings identified by the observer are those employed by the actors.

Pre-institutional experience and adaptations

The interactionist perspective has often been criticized for what many see as its narrow focus. It tends to concentrate on small-scale interaction contexts and ignores the wider society. Thus Goffman gives little consideration to the inmates' experiences in the outside world before they entered total institutions.

The possible significance of this omission can be seen from John Irwin's study of prison life in California. Irwin argues that an understanding of particular inmates' responses to imprisonment requires a knowledge of their pre-prison experience. He distinguishes a number of 'criminal identities' which inmates bring with them to prison. These include 'the thief' and 'the dope fiend'.

Thieves see themselves as professional criminals and are committed to this identity and its associated lifestyle. They regard society in general as corrupt and see nothing immoral about their criminal activities. **Dope fiends** are, or have been, addicted to an opiate – morphine or more usually heroin. They see themselves as junkies and view their addiction as a way of escaping from a dull, routine and monotonous world. However, their commitment to a criminal identity is less strong than that of the thief.

Irwin identifies a number of adaptations to prison life. The first is **doing time** which involves maximizing the comforts of prison life, avoiding trouble and getting out as soon as possible. This strategy is typically selected by thieves who maintain their commitment to a criminal career and are anxious to resume it.

A second adaptation, **gleaning**, is chosen by the individual who, 'sets out to "better himself" or "improve himself" and takes advantage of the resources that exist in prison to do this'. Thus the gleaner often enrols for educational courses and is frequently found in the prison library. Thieves rarely adopt this strategy whereas dope fiends, who are less strongly committed to a criminal identity, are more likely to turn to gleaning. Despite the fact that gleaning involves a desire to change one's identity, dope fiends are still influenced by their former view of life. In line with their previous concern to escape dullness and routine, they tend to 'avoid practical fields and choose styles which promise glamor, excitement or color'. They sometimes find what they're looking for in creative arts, social sciences or philosophy.

Irwin's study suggests that pre-institutional experience may have important influences on modes of adaptation within total institutions. Analysis which is limited to the confines of the institution may therefore prove inadequate for an understanding of organizational behaviour.

■ Resistance to total institutions

In a study of the maximum security unit of Durham prison Stanley Cohen and Laurie Taylor found, like Irwin, that the inmates' experiences before prison had an important effect on how they behaved once inside it. Like Goffman they tried to understand how inmates experienced the total institution, but they found that some of Goffman's theory was not applicable to Durham. Their research suggested that not all total institutions produced the modes of adaptation described by Goffman. In particular Cohen and Taylor found much greater resistance to authority.

The only adaptation mentioned by Goffman that involved resistance was intransigence, and he believed that even this stance was likely to be short-lived. Goffman saw modes of adaptation as ways in which the individual tried to retain their sense of self. Cohen and Taylor found that many types of behaviour in prison were collective reactions to shared problems. Furthermore in Durham, some types of resistance went well beyond trying to protect a sense of self. Some were ways of fighting back and attempting to actually change the prison.

Types of resistance

Cohen and Taylor identify five types of resistance.

1 The first, **self-protecting**, involves the inmates rejecting the labels that have been applied to them. Since the maximum security wing tends to house some of Britain's most notorious criminals (for example, the Great Train Robbers) the prison is often the subject of media attention. Cohen and Young argue, however, that even in these circumstances the inmates do not look upon themselves primarily as criminals. Many retain contacts with the outside world, and they see themselves partly in terms of more conventional social roles. They do not necessarily have a low opinion of themselves. For instance, the prisoners as a group tend to look down on prison officers, most of whom they regard as dull-witted and ignorant. Self-protecting is the least public and dramatic form of resistance employed by the prisoners.

2 The second type of resistance involves **campaigning**. Letters or petitions are sent to politicians and pressure groups and stories are leaked to the press. These activities are designed either to establish the innocence of an inmate, or to complain about prison conditions.

3 The third and least frequent type of resistance is the **escape attempt**; most prisoners see this as impractical.

4 The fourth, and a fairly common way of resisting, is the **hunger strike**. This is usually a successful way of gaining media attention and making the public aware of grievances. For example, hunger strikes were used to complain about the restrictions placed on the number of visitors.

5 The final method of resisting, **confronting**, provides the most direct way of challenging the authorities. This is a form of collective protest in which property is destroyed and the inmates take over parts of the prison. On one occasion a prison warder was briefly held hostage.

Cohen and Taylor conclude from their study that it is dangerous to generalize about total institutions. There are specific factors that lead the inmates of Durham Prison to behave differently from those of Goffman's Washington mental hospital.

1 The prisoners are not seriously affected by degrading admission procedures. Most have had some previous experience of prison and the process of entering prison poses little threat to their sense of self.

2 Their sentences are so long that there is little incentive for them to cooperate with the authorities. Any prospects of release are so remote that the threat of losing parole is not an effective method of social control.

3 Finally, Cohen and Taylor suggest that particular circumstances can influence the behaviour of those in institutions. In this respect Durham Prison has a history of successful protest that encourages new inmates to engage in active resistance. An early hunger strike at the prison, for example, achieved its objective of securing a more varied diet at the prison.

■ Organizations as negotiated order

Goffman's work on total institutions suggests how patients in mental hospitals alter their behaviour in order to adapt to the institution. Anslem Strauss, D. Erlich, R. Bucher, M. Sabschin and L. Schatzman provide a more complete interactionist account of how organizations work. Although they note the existence of both rules and a hierarchy of social roles within organizations they claim that neither are fixed and inflexible. From this perspective, organizational structures are constantly changing and they result from continual negotiation among organizational members, and between them and their clients.

Rules versus negotiated order

From a study of a psychiatric hospital they discovered that many of the organization's rules were 'stretched, negotiated, argued, as well as ignored or applied at convenient moments'. There were a number of reasons why the hospital operated in a quite different way to Weber's ideal type of a bureaucracy.

1 There were so many rules than nobody actually knew them all.

2 The senior administrators rarely tried to apply the rules strictly.

3 The overall aim of the organization – to return patients to the community in better health – was extremely vague and open to different interpretations. Different groups of staff in the hospital tended to support the use of different types of method to achieve this aim. Some psychiatrists supported the use of drugs and electric

shock treatment; others put more faith in talking through patients' problems with them. Often staff could not even agree about the basic question of whether a patient had been cured and should be released. The nurses generally thought that the patients' mental state could be judged by their day-to-day behaviour. Psychiatrists were more concerned with evaluating deeper and less obvious personality changes in their patients. In these circumstances there was plenty of room for disagreement about whether the treatment was being successful or unsuccessful, whether it should be continued, changed or discontinued.

4 Finally, it was generally agreed in the hospital that no two patients had identical problems: each was a unique case. The staff therefore believed that it was almost impossible to adhere to strict and formal rules and at the same time provide adequate treatment for all their patients.

According to Strauss et al. then, the rules themselves had comparatively little impact on how the hospital was run. These writers go beyond critics of Weber who argue that rules are sometimes bent, or who believe that breaking rules can at times help an organization to achieve its aims. The rules in the hospital were 'much less like commands, and more like general understandings'. Interaction and negotiation between organizational members and their clients determined how the hospital worked as an organization. The rules themselves were of secondary importance.

Power and negotiation

Another aspect of this study examined the distribution of power within the hospital. Most perspectives on organizations assume that those in senior positions can largely determine how their subordinates act. Most perspectives also assume that clients are simply the passive recipients of the goods or services that the organization provides for them.

Strauss *et al.*, however, claim that all the groups involved in the organization had some power.

1 Patients could be uncooperative, and sometimes succeeded in negotiating changes in their treatment or placement in the hospital.

2 The aides who were responsible for most of the manual work spent more time with the patients than anybody else. They often knew the patients well and their

conversations with them could influence the extent to which the patients progressed.

3 Nurses were responsible for implementing the instructions of doctors. Sometimes they ignored the instructions or modified them in line with their own beliefs about how the hospital could be most efficiently run. At other times they questioned the doctors' decisions or referred them to administrators over the doctors' heads.

4 Although in theory the administrators had overall control over the running of the hospital and the actions of the psychiatrists, the doctors guarded their professional independence strongly. The administrators lacked both the time and knowledge to check closely and regulate what happened on the wards from day to day.

Strauss et al. painted a picture of an organization in which all the groups had to negotiate constantly with other staff or patients in order to get their own way. Nobody monopolized power and the way the hospital was run was constantly changing. Although their findings are based on a single case study, Strauss et al. claim that their findings could be applied to any organizations in which there were different occupational groups or where professionals were employed. Thus they believe their findings would be equally applicable to universities, corporations or government agencies.

Criticisms of Strauss et al.

As John Hughes argues, however, psychiatric hospitals may be far from typical of bureaucratic organizations. He doubts that Strauss *et al.*'s theory would be as widely applicable as the authors claim. Special features of mental hospitals (such as the ambiguous nature of the service they provide) might make their activities more open to negotiation than those of other organizations. In addition interactionist approaches such as that adopted by Strauss *et al.* can be criticized for concentrating on interaction and negotiation within the organization. The meanings that govern interaction might be generated by the wider society.

For example, definitions of criminality or psychological disorder may have their origins in the structure of society: the actions of psychologists and other employees in mental hospitals might be limited by definitions of deviance which are imposed by powerful members of society. (For further details of this view see pp. 414–19.)

▮ Organizations – a dialectical view

In an interesting attempt to overcome the limitations of existing theories of organizations, J. Kenneth Benson has advocated a dialectical approach to analysing them. (The concept of dialectics was first used by the German philosopher Hegel, and later developed by Karl Marx. **Dialectics** refers to processes whereby changes result from tensions and conflicts between incompatible forces – for further details see p. 879.) From this point of view organizations are not fixed and permanent structures but are constantly created, recreated or changed by clashes between the different groups within or outside them.

Benson believes that many sociologists of organizations have exaggerated the extent to which they are stable and unchanging. He accepts that people create organizations that then limit their own behaviour. He says 'people produce a social world which stands over them constraining their actions'. Nevertheless, the constraints are far from absolute: there remains considerable scope for individuals and groups to shape and change the organizations with which they come into contact.

Contradiction and change

One reason for this is that organizations never function completely smoothly without tension or conflict. There are always likely to be contradictions within organizations and these create the potential for change.

1 Different departments in a bureaucracy may compete for resources and control over particular parts of the organization.

2 Administrators and professionals may disagree about how the organization should be run, and they might compete to have their views put into practice.

3 Participants in organizations may have fundamentally different interests, for example management and workers often have quite different viewpoints about wage levels.

According to Benson, such basic contradictions always threaten the stability of the organization in the long term.

Other groups may also come together to resist attempts to control them within the organization. Benson points to how some of the many blacks in American prisons see these organizations as institutions of racial oppression and have tried to challenge the authority of those who run them.

Benson notes that contradictions may also develop as the organization tries to deal with a variety of external groups. Labour organizations often face problems in securing the cooperation of both management and unions in implementing their training programmes.

In some respects Benson paints a picture of organizations which is not too dissimilar from that provided by interactionists such as Strauss. Both agree that organizations can constantly change, they are unstable and all their members have some opportunity to influence the direction of the changes that take place. However, unlike Strauss, Benson acknowledges that there are limits to the extent to which organizations are a 'negotiated order'. Some issues are non-negotiable and all organizations are subject to interventions by groups external to the organization. For example, student protests in US universities in the 1960s were repressed with the aid of the police and military forces. Some organizational members are in a stronger position than others to use legal or military power to determine the final outcome of conflicts within the organization.

Benson's dialectical approach to organizations draws upon some of the insights produced by interactionism, but sets them within the framework of an overall Marxist perspective. As such he tries to combine an analysis of factors internal to the organization with an analysis of external factors. He attributes more importance to the conscious actions of the groups and individuals involved than some Marxists who adopt a more deterministic approach. Benson does not believe, for example, that the 'needs' of the capitalist system completely shape organizations. However, he provides only a very vague outline of how organizations should be studied. He does not explain how his approach can be applied in detail to the sociology of organizations, nor does he provide any case studies to illustrate the benefits of his approach.

■ The problem of organizations

Organizations in modern society have been pictured as threatening individual liberty and undermining democracy, yet, paradoxically, they have also been seen as essential requirements for a democratic society and as a means for the protection of individual freedoms. This ambivalent view of organizations is contained in the writings of Peter Blau. He claims that 'Democratic objectives would be impossible to attain in modern society without bureaucratic organizations to implement them.'

Thus 'equal justice under the law', a basic democratic principle, requires a bureaucratic organization to put it into practice. Those who enforce the law must be subject to uniform standards and strict rules in order to ensure equity and fairness and to prevent personal considerations from influencing their conduct. In Blau's words, 'This is another way of saying that bureaucratically organized enforcement agencies are necessary for all members of society to be equal under the law.'

Organizations as a threat to democracy

Yet Blau, like many other writers, fears that organizations are moving beyond popular control and undermining democracy. He sees this process as the major problem of Western industrial society. Power and resources are increasingly concentrated in organizational settings. They are employed in the first instance for the benefit of the organization rather than for society as a whole. Thus when a corporation decides to invest in a particular area, its major concern is not the welfare of the local people but its priorities as a corporation. (For further views on the power of organizations see Chapter 9, pp. 532–3 and p. 541.) In addition, the vast majority of the population is excluded from any participation in its decisions.

Blau claims that 'The concentration of organizational power in the hands of a few men shielded from public surveillance and control poses a serious threat to democracy.' Life in modern societies is shaped more and more by organizations over which people have little or no control. Blau argues that 'what is required is a readjustment of our democratic institutions to make them capable of controlling the power of organizations'. But having diagnosed the problem, Blau gives no specific suggestions for its solution.

Organizations and accountability

In a study of state bureaucracy, B. Guy Peters examines the question of popular control. He sees the major problem not so much in terms of the mechanisms that exist to control and influence bureaucracies – parliamentary committees, the judiciary and interest groups – but in terms of the motivation of the public to make use of these mechanisms. Peters argues that 'In practice, most methods of accountability depend upon individual or group actions to press demands before the mechanisms go into operation.' He regards public apathy as the greatest danger to bureaucratic accountability and a democratic state.

However, Peters is cautiously optimistic for the following reasons.

1 The development of public education and the mass media serves to increase information about bureaucratic activity.

2 In some Western democracies, there are signs that state bureaucracy is becoming more open. In the USA, Watergate (which uncovered corruption in President Nixon's administration) was followed by President Carter's policy of 'open government' and the so-called 'sunshine laws' which allow public access to the meetings and records of many administrative bodies. In Sweden state bureaucrats make written records of both their decisions and the reasons for them. This information is available to citizens on request.

Peters argues that such measures are a necessary first step towards popular control of bureaucracy. Without information, members of the public will have great difficulty fighting bureaucratic decisions. In the light of these trends, Peters concludes that:

We may expect greater public concern and involvement in public affairs. How effective this will be will ultimately depend upon the willingness of the population to persist in pressing their demands and using the mechanisms available to them.

The cautious optimism of this conclusion must, however, be tempered with the more pessimistic views we discussed in earlier sections and the various perspectives on power and politics outlined in Chapter 9.

Sociology, values and organizations

Alvin Gouldner has written that:

> A commitment to a theory may be made because the theory is congruent with the mood or deep-lying sentiments of its adherents, rather than merely because it has been cerebrally inspected and found valid.

Thus support for a particular theory may owe more to the values of the sociologist than the explanatory power of the theory. Gouldner goes on to suggest that a part of organization theory is to some degree a product of the sentiments of either unrealistic dreamers or dyed-in-the-wool pessimists. Gouldner's ideas may be illustrated by a comparison of Marxist theory and the views of élite theorists such as Michels.

Marxist predictions of the disappearance of bureaucracy in a classless society owe much to a commitment to a utopian vision. Even when faced with the proliferation of bureaucracy in the former communist states of Eastern Europe, many Marxists argued that the situation merely represented a stage of transition to an egalitarian society. They hoped and even believed that the days of the dictatorship of the proletariat were numbered. This can be seen as a product of wishful thinking rather than a scientific prediction. According to Nicos Mouzelis:

> This kind of optimism, as well as the conception of history as a succession of well-defined stages leading towards freedom and human happiness, is a part of the eighteenth and nineteenth-century humanist faith in the future of man and in the idea of progress.

This faith and the radical change it advocates finds no support in the conservative views of Michels. His dictum that organization equals oligarchy suggests that Marxists should stop dreaming the impossible dream, that they should accept the inevitable and learn to live with it. Like the early élite theorists such as Pareto and Mosca, with whom he is often bracketed, Michels was Italian and his ideas may well owe something to his cultural background. As C.J. Friedrich observes, the elite theorists were 'offspring of a society containing as yet many feudal remnants'. The authoritarian nature of feudalism contained in these survivals may well have encouraged a belief in the inevitability of rule by a minority. In addition, as Lukács suggests, elite theory found its strongest support in European societies such as Italy in which democratic institutions were least well developed. Contrary to these observations, Michels was committed to socialist principles in his younger days. However, he later transferred his allegiance to the fascist dictator Benito Mussolini who personified the 'iron law of oligarchy'.

Mouzelis sees the pessimism and conservative bias of élite theory as a reaction to the over-optimistic predictions which preceded it. He claims that:

> The increasing stress on the pessimistic side reflects a general disillusionment and loss of faith which partly came as a reaction to the earlier overconfidence in the human reason and the inevitable march of history towards progress.

Gouldner chides both those he considers unrealistic optimists and those he sees as confirmed pessimists, a description he applies to both Michels and Selznick. He claims that the former look forward to 'a utopian and hence unattainable vision of democracy' whereas the latter picture 'an attainable but bureaucratically undermined, hence imperfect democracy'. Gouldner argues that the choice does not lie with one or other of these alternatives, with either perfection or flawed reality. Limiting the choice to these alternatives closes other options. Gouldner suggests a cautiously optimistic – and in his view a more realistic – approach which would explore ways in which organizations could be made more democratic. The results of such research might well fall far short of the utopian ideals of many Marxists, but they may give direction to those who wish to develop more democratic organizations. And, in Gouldner's view, such developments might well make 'a vital difference to the lives of man'.

It is difficult, if not impossible, for sociologists to avoid being influenced by the attitudes which they bring with them to their research and the way they select and interpret their data. From his work on total institutions and other studies, it is clear that Erving Goffman's sympathies lie with the underdog. He admits that in his study of psychiatric patients, he adopted a 'partisan view', a bias which is strengthened by his admission that he came to the mental hospital 'with no great respect for the discipline of psychiatry'. In addition, Goffman suggests that his former experience may have led him to overemphasize the effect of the degradations suffered by the inmates. He states 'I want to warn that my view is probably too much that of a middle-class male; perhaps I suffered vicariously about conditions that lower class patients handled with little pain.'

This chapter has focused on the sociology of organizations and has dealt only briefly with a large body of research that derives from the managerial tradition. This tradition, which includes scientific management, the human relations school, the neo-human relations school and corporate culture, has been strongly attacked for what many see as its pro-management bias. Its critics have argued that its priorities are those of management, that the problems it seeks to solve are those for which managers require solutions.

Therefore the managerial tradition has been concerned with increasing organizational efficiency and raising productivity: its critics have argued that when workers' needs have been considered, it has been in terms of these priorities. They claim that the concern for workers' needs is based on the assumption that fulfilled workers produce more.

In Labour and Monopoly Capitalism, the American Marxist Harry Braverman launches a blistering attack on Frederick Taylor. Braverman claims that scientific management:

---

starts, despite occasional protestations to the contrary, not from the human point of view but from the capitalist point of view, from the point of view of the management of a refractory work force in a setting of antagonistic social relations. It does not attempt to discover and confront the cause of this condition, but accepts it as an inexorable given, a 'natural' condition. It investigates not labor in general, but the adaptation of labor to the needs of capital. It enters the workplace not as the representative of science, but as the representative of management masquerading in the trappings of science.

Thus Braverman argues that Taylor begins from an acceptance of the capitalist system and therefore fails to see the exploitive nature of capitalist relations of production. Braverman sees scientific management as simply a further weapon in the armoury of oppression.

Similar charges have been levelled at other management theories. However, discussing one such theory Mouzelis argues, 'the fact that human relations findings might help the employer to manipulate his employees in a more effective way, does not destroy their scientific validity'.

Many sociologists may be too ready to dismiss the findings of their colleagues because they disagree with the ideological assumptions which they see underlying those findings.

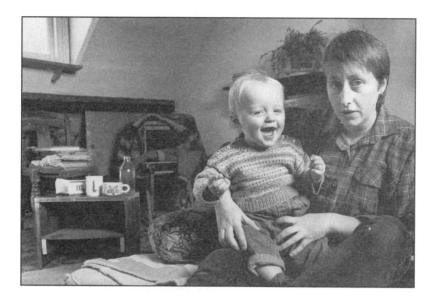

6
Families and households

Families and households

Introduction

Many sociologists have regarded the family as the cornerstone of society. It forms the basic unit of social organization and it is difficult to imagine how human society could function without it. Although the composition of the family varies – for example in many societies two or more wives are regarded as the ideal arrangement – such differences can be seen as variations on a basic theme. In general, therefore, the family has been seen as a universal social institution, an inevitable part of human society. On balance it has been regarded as a good thing, both for the individual and society as a whole.

For some time it has been thought natural and normal for households to be based around families.

This view has tended to divert attention from interesting and important questions. For example, it has discouraged serious and detailed consideration of alternatives to the family. Recently, new perspectives on the family have questioned many of the assumptions of the more traditional view. These approaches have not assumed that the family is inevitable – in fact they have often been openly critical of the institution of the family. During the late 1960s, for instance, the Women's Liberation Movement began attacking the oppression of women within the family. This attack was developed by some feminist writers into a condemnation of the family as an institution.

In this chapter we begin by examining the assumption of the 'universality' of the family.

Is the family universal?

George Peter Murdock: the family – a universal social institution

In a study entitled *Social Structure*, George Peter Murdock examined the institution of the family in a wide range of societies. Murdock took a sample of 250 societies ranging from small hunting and gathering bands to large-scale industrial societies. He claimed that some form of family existed in every society and concluded, on the evidence of his sample, that the family is universal.

Murdock defines the family as follows:

> The family is a social group characterized by common residence, economic co-operation and reproduction. It includes adults of both sexes, at least two of whom maintain a socially approved sexual relationship, and one or more children, own or adopted, of the sexually cohabiting adults.

Thus the family lives together, pools its resources and works together, and produces offspring. At least two of the adult members conduct a sexual relationship according to the norms of their particular society.

Such norms vary from society to society. For example, among the Banaro of New Guinea, the husband does not have sexual relations with his wife until she has borne a child by a friend of his father. The parent–child relationship, therefore, is not necessarily a biological one. Its importance is primarily social, children being recognized as members of a particular family whether or not the adult spouses have biologically produced them.

Variations in family structure

The structure of the family varies from society to society. The smallest family unit is known as the **nuclear family** and consists of a husband and wife and their immature offspring. Units larger than the nuclear family are usually known as **extended**

families. Such families can be seen as extensions of the basic nuclear unit, either **vertical extensions** – for example, the addition of members of a third generation such as the spouses' parents – and/or **horizontal extensions** – for example, the addition of members of the same generation as the spouses such as the husband's brother or an additional wife. Thus the functionalist sociologists Bell and Vogel define the extended family as 'any grouping broader than the nuclear family which is related by descent, marriage or adoption'.

Either on its own or as the basic unit within an extended family, Murdock found that the nuclear family was present in every society in his sample. This led him to conclude that:

> The nuclear family is a universal human social grouping. Either as the sole prevailing form of the family or as the basic unit from which more complex forms are compounded, it exists as a distinct and strongly functional group in every known society.

However, as we will discover in the following sections, Murdock's conclusions might not be well founded.

■ Kathleen Gough – the Nayar

Some societies have sets of relationships between kin which are quite different from those which are common in Britain. One such society was that of the Nayar of Kerala in Southern India prior to British rule being established in 1792. Sociologists disagree about whether this society had a family system or not, and thus whether or not it disproves Murdock's claim that the family is universal.

Kathleen Gough has provided a detailed description of Nayar society. Before puberty all Nayar girls were ritually married to a suitable Nayar man in the *tali*-rite. After the ritual marriage had taken place, however, the *tali* husband did not live with his wife, and was under no obligation to have any contact with her whatsoever. The wife owed only one duty to her *tali* husband: she had to attend his funeral to mourn his death.

Once a Nayar girl reached or neared puberty she began to take a number of visiting husbands, or '*sandbanham*' husbands. The Nayar men were usually professional warriors who spent long periods of time away from their villages acting as mercenaries. During their time in the villages they were allowed to visit any number of Nayar women who had undergone the *tali*-rite and who were members of the same or lower caste as themselves. With the agreement of the woman involved, the *sandbanham* husband arrived at the home of one of his wives after supper, had sexual intercourse with her, and left before breakfast the next morning. During his stay he placed his weapons outside the building to show the other *sandbanham* husbands that he was there. If they arrived too late then they were free to sleep on the veranda, but could not stay the night with their wife. Men could have unlimited numbers of *sandbanham* wives, though women seem to have been limited to no more than 12 visiting husbands.

An exception to the family?

Sandbanham relationships were unlike marriages in most societies in a number of ways.

1. They were not a lifelong union: either party could terminate the relationship at any time.

2. *Sandbanham* husbands had no duty towards the offspring of their wives. When a woman became pregnant it was essential according to Nayar custom that a man of appropriate caste declared himself to be the father of the child by paying a fee of cloth and vegetables to the midwife who attended the birth. However, it mattered little whether he was the biological parent or not, so long as someone claimed to be the father, because he did not help to maintain or socialize the child.

3. Husbands and wives did not form an economic unit. Although husbands might give wives token gifts, they were not expected to maintain them – indeed it was frowned upon if they attempted to. Instead the economic unit consisted of a number of brothers and sisters, sisters' children, and their daughters' children. The eldest male was the leader of each group of kin.

Nayar society then was a **matrilineal** society. Kinship groupings were based on female biological relatives and marriage played no significant part in the formation of households, the socializing of children, or in the way that the economic needs of the members of society were met.

In terms of Murdock's definition, no family existed in Nayar society since those who maintained 'a sexually approved adult relationship' did not live together and cooperate economically. Only the women lived with the children. Either, then, Murdock's definition of the family is too narrow, or the family is not universal. Gough claims that marriage, and by implication the family, existed in Nayar society. In order to make this claim though, she had to broaden her definition of marriage beyond that implied in Murdock's definition of the family. She defines marriage as a relationship between a woman and one or more persons in which a child born to the woman 'is given full birth-status rights' common to normal members of the society.

■ The New World black family – an exception to the rule?

Murdock's definition of the family includes at least one adult of each sex. A significant proportion of black families in the islands of the West Indies, parts of Central America such as Guyana, and the USA do not include adult males. The 'family unit' often consists of a woman and her dependent children, sometimes with the addition of her mother. This may indicate that the family is not universal as Murdock suggests, or that it is necessary to redefine the family and state that the minimal family unit consists of a woman and her dependent children, own or adopted, and that all other family types are additions to this unit.

Female-headed families are sometimes known as **matriarchal** families and sometimes as **matrifocal** families, though both these terms have been used in a number of senses. We will use the term matrifocal family here to refer to female-headed families.

The causes of matrifocal families

Matrifocal families are common in low-income black communities in the New World. In the USA in 1985 51 per cent of all black children lived with their mothers but not their fathers. The percentage is also high in other New World societies. For example, Nancie González in her study of Livingston, Honduras, in 1956, found that 45 per cent of black Carib families had female heads. (See pp. 353–4 for comments on lone parenthood and ethnicity in Britain.)

The high level of matrifocal families has been

seen as a result of one or more of the following factors.

1 Melville J. Herskovits argues that the West African origin of New World blacks influenced their family structure. In traditional West Africa, a system of **polygyny** (a form of extended family with one husband and two or more wives) and considerable female economic independence meant that the husband played a relatively marginal role in family life. Herskovits maintains that this pattern continues to influence black family life.

2 A second argument sees the system of plantation slavery as a major factor accounting for matrifocal families. M.G. Smith (one of the main supporters of this view) notes that under slavery, the mother and children formed the basic family unit. Families were often split with the sale of one or more of their members, but mothers and dependent children were usually kept together. The authority of the male as head of the family was eroded because he was subject to the authority of the plantation owner who, with his white employees, had the right of sexual access to all female slaves. Formed under slavery, the model of the matrifocal family is seen to have persisted.

3 A third argument sees the economic position of blacks in the New World as the basic cause of the matrifocal family. Elliot Liebow, whose views are outlined in Chapter 3 (pp. 152–3), sees female-headed families resulting from desertion by the husband because he has insufficient funds to play the role of father and breadwinner.

4 A final argument accepts that poverty is the basic cause of matrifocal families but states also that matrifocality has become a part of the subculture of the poor. This view is contained in Oscar Lewis's concept of the culture of poverty. From his research in a low-income black area of Washington DC, Ulf Hannerz argues that female-headed families are so common that to some degree they have become an expected and accepted alternative to the standard nuclear family. From this argument matrifocal families are not simply a product of poverty but also of culture. (See Chapter 3, pp. 149–54, for a general discussion of the relationship between poverty, culture and family structure.)

Can we then see the matrifocal family as an exception to Murdock's claim that the family is universal, or, if it is accepted as a family, to his claim that the nuclear family is a universal social group? In order to decide this, we will first consider the arguments which support Murdock, and then the arguments against him.

Support for Murdock

1 Statistically, the female-headed family is not the norm either within black communities or in the societies in which they are set.

2 The matrifocal family is often a nuclear family that has been broken. Particularly in the USA, it is usually a product of separation or divorce. It did not begin life as a matrifocal family.

3 The mainstream model of the nuclear family is valued by blacks and regarded as the ideal.

4 Many sociologists view the female-headed family as a family 'gone wrong', as a product of social disorganization and not, therefore, a viable alternative to the nuclear family. It has been accused of producing maladjusted children, juvenile delinquents and high school dropouts. Since it does not appear to perform the functions of a 'proper family', it is regarded as a broken family and not as a viable unit in its own right.

Arguments against Murdock

The following arguments support the view that the matrifocal family should be recognized as an alternative to the nuclear family.

1 Simply because in statistical terms the matrifocal family is not the norm, does not mean it cannot be recognized as an alternative family structure. In many societies which practise polygyny, polygynous marriages are in the minority yet sociologists accept them as a form of extended family.

2 As Hannerz argues, in low-income black communities matrifocal families are to some extent expected and accepted.

3 Members of matrifocal families regard the unit as a family.

4 The matrifocal family should not be seen simply as a broken nuclear family. From her West Indian data, González argues that the female-headed family is a well-organized social group which represents a positive adaptation to the circumstances of poverty. By not tying herself to a husband, the mother is able to

maintain casual relationships with a number of men who can provide her with financial support. She retains strong links with her relatives who give her both economic and emotional support. González states 'By dispersing her loyalties and by clinging especially to the unbreakable sibling ties with her brothers, a woman increases her chances of maintaining her children and household.' In a situation of poverty, 'the chances that any one man may fail are high'.

5 The supposed harmful effects of the matrifocal family on the children are far from proven. From an analysis of data from the USA, Herbert J. Gans states that 'the matriarchal family structure and the absence of a father has not yet proven pathological, even for the boys who grow up in it'.

The above arguments suggest that the matrifocal family can be regarded as a form of family structure in its own right. If these arguments are accepted, it is possible to see the matrifocal family as the basic, minimum family unit and all other family structures as additions to this unit.

Matrifocal families, and one-parent families in general, are becoming more common in Britain. We will consider the significance of this development later in this chapter (see pp. 349–50).

■ The universality of the family – conclusion

Whether the family is regarded as universal ultimately depends on how the family is defined. Clearly though, a wide variety of domestic arrangements have been devised by human beings which are quite distinctive from the 'conventional' families of modern industrial societies. As Diana Gittins puts it:

While it can be argued that all societies have beliefs and rules on mating, sexuality, gender and age relations, the content of rules is culturally and historically specific and variable, and is in no way universal.

Having considered these questions, we will now examine the various sociological perspectives on the family.

▌ The family – a functionalist perspective

The analysis of the family from a functionalist perspective involves three main questions.

1 First, 'What are the functions of the family?' Answers to this question deal with the contributions made by the family to the maintenance of the social system. It is assumed that society has certain **functional prerequisites** or basic needs that must be met if it is to survive and operate efficiently. The family is examined in terms of the degree to which it meets these functional prerequisites.

2 A second and related question asks 'What are the functional relationships between the family and other parts of the social system?'

It is assumed that there must be a certain degree of fit, integration and harmony between the parts of the social system if society is going to function efficiently. For example, the family must be integrated to some extent with the economic system. We will examine this question in detail in a later section when the relationships between the family and industrialization are considered.

3 The third question deals with the functions performed by an institution or a part of society for the individual. In the case of the family, this question considers the functions of the family for its individual members.

▌ George Peter Murdock – the universal functions of the family

Functions for society

From his analysis of 250 societies, Murdock argues that the family performs four basic functions in all societies which he terms the **sexual, reproductive, economic** and **educational**. They are essential for social life since without the sexual and reproductive functions there would be no members of society, without the economic function (for example the provision and preparation of food) life would cease, and without education (a term Murdock uses for socialization) there would

be no culture. Human society without culture could not function.

Clearly, the family does not perform these functions exclusively. However, it makes important contributions to them all and no other institution has yet been devised to match its efficiency in this respect. Once this is realized, Murdock claims, 'The immense utility of the nuclear family and the basic reason for its universality thus begin to emerge in strong relief.'

Functions for individuals and society

The family's functions for society are inseparable from its functions for its individual members. It serves both at one and the same time and in much the same way. The sexual function provides a good example of this. Husband and wife have the right of sexual access to each other and in most societies there are rules forbidding or limiting sexual activity outside marriage. This provides sexual gratification for the spouses. It also strengthens the family since the powerful and often binding emotions which accompany sexual activities unite husband and wife. The sexual function also helps to stabilize society. The rules which largely contain sexual activity within the family prevent the probable disruptive effects on the social order that would result if the sex drive were allowed 'free play'. The family thus provides both 'control and expression' of sexual drives and in doing so performs important functions not only for its individual members, but also for the family as an institution and for society as a whole.

Murdock applies a similar logic to the economic function. He argues that, like sex, it is 'most readily and satisfactorily achieved by persons living together'. He refers in glowing terms to the division of labour within the family whereby the husband specializes in certain activities, the wife in others. For example in hunting societies men kill game animals which provide meat for their wives to cook and skins for them to make into clothing. This economic cooperation within the family not only goes a long way to fulfilling the economic function for society as a whole, but also provides 'rewarding experiences' for the spouses working together which 'cement their union'.

Murdock argues that his analysis provides a 'conception of the family's many-sided utility and thus of its inevitability'. He concludes that:

> No society has succeeded in finding an adequate substitute for the nuclear family, to which it might transfer these functions. It is highly doubtful whether any society will ever succeed in such an attempt.

Criticisms of Murdock

Murdock's picture of the family is rather like the multi-faceted, indispensable boy-scout knife. The family is seen as a multi-functional institution which is indispensable to society. Its 'many-sided utility' accounts for its universality and its inevitability.

In his enthusiasm for the family, however, Murdock does not seriously consider whether its functions could be performed by other social institutions and he does not examine alternatives to the family. As D.H.J. Morgan notes in his criticism, Murdock does not answer 'to what extent these basic functions are inevitably linked with the institution of the nuclear family'.

In addition, Murdock's description of the family is almost too good to be true. As Morgan states, 'Murdock's nuclear family is a remarkably harmonious institution. Husband and wife have an integrated division of labour and have a good time in bed.' As we will see in later sections, some other researchers do not share Murdock's emphasis on harmony and integration.

◼ Talcott Parsons – the 'basic and irreducible' functions of the family

Parsons concentrates his analysis on the family in modern American society. Despite this, his ideas have a more general application since he argues that the American family retains two 'basic and irreducible functions' which are common to the family in all societies. These are the 'primary socialization of children' and the 'stabilization of the adult personalities of the population of the society'.

Primary socialization

Primary socialization refers to socialization during the early years of childhood which takes place mainly within the family. **Secondary socialization** occurs during the later years when the family is less involved and other agencies (such as the peer group and the school) exert increasing influence.

There are two basic processes involved in primary socialization: the **internalization of society's culture** and the **structuring of the personality**.

Unless culture is internalized, that is absorbed and accepted, society would cease to exist since without shared norms and values social life would not be possible. However, culture is not simply learned, it is 'internalized as part of the personality structure'. The child's personality is moulded in terms of the central values of the culture to the point where they become a part of him or her. In the case of American society, personality is shaped in terms of independence and achievement motivation, which are two of the central values of American culture.

Parsons argues that families 'are "factories" which produce human personalities'. He believes they are essential for this purpose since primary socialization requires a context which provides warmth, security and mutual support. He can conceive of no institution other than the family which could provide this context.

Stabilization of adult personalities

Once produced, the personality must be kept stable. This is the second basic function of the family, the **stabilization of adult personalities**. The emphasis here is on the marriage relationship and the emotional security the couple provide for each other. This acts as a counterweight to the stresses and strains of everyday life which tend to make the personality unstable.

This function is particularly important in Western industrial society since the nuclear family is largely isolated from kin. It does not have the security once provided by the close-knit extended family. Thus the married couple increasingly look to each other for emotional support.

Adult personalities are also stabilized by the parents' role in the socialization process. This allows them to act out 'childish' elements of their own personalities which they have retained from childhood but which cannot be indulged in adult society. For example, father is 'kept on the rails' by playing with his son's train set.

According to Parsons, therefore, the family therefore provides a context in which husband and wife can express their childish whims, give and receive emotional support, recharge their batteries and so stabilize their personalities.

Criticisms of Parsons

This brief summary of Parsons's views on the family is far from complete. Other aspects will be discussed later in this chapter (pp. 335–7) and in Chapter 10 (p. 587), but here we will consider some of the arguments which attack his perspective.

1 As with Murdock, Parsons has been accused of idealizing the family with his picture of well-adjusted children and sympathetic spouses caring for each other's every need.

2 His picture is based largely on the American middle-class family which he treats as representative of American families in general. As D.H.J. Morgan states, 'there are no classes, no regions, no religious, ethnic or status groups, no communities' in Parsons's analysis of the family. For example, Parsons fails to explore possible differences between middle- and working-class families, or different family structures in ethnic minority communities.

3 Like Murdock, Parsons largely fails to explore functional alternatives to the family. He does recognize that some functions are not necessarily tied to the family. For instance, he notes that the family's economic function has largely been taken over by other agencies in modern industrial society. However, his belief that its remaining functions are 'basic and irreducible' prevents him from examining alternatives to the family.

4 Finally, Parsons's view of the socialization process can be criticized. He sees it as a one-way process with the

children being pumped full of culture and their personalities being moulded by powerful parents. He tends to ignore the two-way interaction process between parents and children. There is no place in his scheme for the children who twist their parents round their little finger.

■ Brigitte and Peter Berger – a defence of the bourgeois family

In *The War Over the Family* Brigitte and Peter Berger discuss the views put forward by both defenders and critics of the contemporary family. They claim that their aim is to 'capture the middle ground' in the debate over the family. However, they end up siding with those (such as functionalists) who stress the beneficial rather than the harmful aspects of family life.

The Bergers accept that the family is not perfect, but they argue that there is no 'viable alternative' to the 'bourgeois family' which can effectively meet the needs both of individuals and of society in the modern world.

The origins of the bourgeois family

According to the Bergers the bourgeois family originated amongst the middle class in nineteenth-century Europe, particularly in Germany and Victorian Britain, and it is now dominant throughout the Western world. Its main characteristics were that it was child-centred (the welfare of children was of primary importance); it had strict moral values; emphasized economic success; and was highly religious.

The child-centred family developed as child mortality rates fell. Parents had more incentive to invest resources and emotional energy in their children's upbringing once the children had a strong likelihood of surviving to adulthood.

The family and individualism

The Bergers argue that the bourgeois family combines strong discipline with individualism. Children learn the importance of moral values in the bourgeois family and they also learn to respect their parents. At the same time they develop as autonomous, independent individuals. The bourgeois family is founded upon bonds between individuals and teaches children to respect the individuality of others, just as their parents respect their individuality. The family is a private realm in which individuality can blossom because people can partially escape the demand for conformity imposed by the wider society.

The bourgeois family is based upon the existence of private property. According to the Bergers, private property is the precondition for individuals developing a sense of a private self, independent of others. Without private property, it is difficult for the child to develop a sense of responsibility to others. The Bergers say:

> Only if the child has a sense of what is properly his can he share that property with others; in the absence of private property of any sort, there can be no deliberate acts of sharing.

Problems with collective child-rearing

Berger and Berger argue that collective child-rearing in kibbutzim and communes compares unfavourably with child-rearing in the bourgeois family. They claim that the evidence shows that collective child-rearing creates conformist,

dependent personalities: people who are dominated as individuals by the social groups to which they belong. Collective child-rearing is based upon shallow relationships between individual adults and particular children and consequently the child develops less respect for others as individuals.

On the other hand, the bourgeois family is based on stronger personal bonds: it balances freedom and restraint, individual self-realization and social responsibility. Unlike kibbutzim and communes, the bourgeois family produces people capable, when necessary, of standing up against the community; people who can act and think independently even though they respect the basic values of society.

Criticisms

Although the Bergers show an awareness of critical views of the family they take little account of them. They stress the beneficial aspects of the family almost as much as functionalists. In doing so, they neglect the possible psychological problems that family life can produce. They also attach little importance to the extent to which the family has restricted the role of women in modern societies.

Having looked at various positive perspectives on the family, in the next section we will turn to some more critical views of the family.

Critical views of the family

Even the analysis of the Bergers suggests that, all things considered, the family is functional both for its members and society as a whole. Increasingly, this picture of the family is coming under strong criticism. Some observers are suggesting that, on balance, the family may well be dysfunctional both for society and its individual members. This criticism has mainly been directed at the family in Western industrial society.

Edmund Leach – A Runaway World?

In a study entitled *A Runaway World?* Edmund Leach presents a pessimistic view of the family in

industrial society. Leach, an anthropologist, has spent many years studying small-scale pre-industrial societies. In such societies the family often forms a part of a wider kinship unit. An extensive network of social relationships between a large number of kin provides practical and psychological support for the individual. This support is reinforced by the closely knit texture of relationships in the small-scale community as a whole.

By comparison, in modern industrial society, the nuclear family is largely isolated from kin and the wider community. Leach summarizes this situation and its consequences as follows:

> In the past kinsfolk and neighbours gave the individual continuous moral support throughout his

life. Today the domestic household is isolated. The family looks inward upon itself; there is an intensification of emotional stress between husband and wife and parents and children. The strain is greater than most of us can bear.

Thrown back almost entirely on its own resources, the nuclear family becomes like an overloaded electrical circuit. The demands made upon it are too great and fuses blow. In their isolation, family members expect and demand too much from each other. The result is conflict. In Leach's words, 'The parents and children huddled together in their loneliness take too much out of each other. The parents fight; the children rebel.'

The family and society

Problems are not confined to the family. The tension and hostility produced within the family find expression throughout society. Leach argues that the 'isolation and the close-knit nature of contemporary family life incubates hate which finds expression in conflict in the wider community'. The families in which people huddle together create barriers between them and the wider society. The privatized family breeds suspicion and fear of the outside world. Leach argues that:

Privacy is the source of fear and violence. The violence in the world comes about because we human beings are forever creating barriers between men who are like us and men who are not like us.

Only when individuals can break out of the prison of the nuclear family, rejoin their fellows and give and receive support will the ills of society begin to diminish. Leach's conclusion is diametrically opposed to the functionalist view of the family. He states 'Far from being the basis of the good society, the family, with its narrow privacy and tawdry secrets, is the source of all our discontents.'

■ R.D. Laing – *The Politics of the Family*

In *The Politics of the Family* and a number of other publications, R.D. Laing presents a radical

alternative to the functionalist picture of the 'happy family'. Laing is a **phenomenological psychiatrist**: he is concerned with interaction within the family and the meanings which develop in that context. His work is largely based on the study of families in which one member has been defined as schizophrenic.

Laing argues that the behaviour of so-called schizophrenics can only be understood in terms of relationships within the family. Far from viewing schizophrenia as madness, he argues that it makes sense in terms of the meanings and interactions which develop within the family. As such it can be seen as reasonable behaviour.

Laing maintains that the difference between so-called 'normal' and 'abnormal' families is small. It therefore follows that a lot can be learned about families in general by studying those labelled as abnormal.

Exploitation in the family

Laing views the family in terms of sets of interactions. Individuals form alliances, adopt various strategies and play one or more individuals off against others in a complex tactical game. Laing is preoccupied with interaction situations which he regards as harmful and destructive. Throughout his work he concentrates on the exploitive aspects of family relationships. The following example illustrates his approach.

Jane is defined as schizophrenic. She is in a perpetual reverie, her own little dream world, which consists of a game of tennis. It is a mixed doubles match; she is the ball. Jane sits motionless and silent and eats only when fed. The adults in the family are in a state of conflict, her father and his mother being ranged against her mother and her mother's father. The two halves of the family communicate only through Jane; she is the go-between. The strain eventually becomes too much for her and she escapes into her dream world. However, as her 'dream' shows, even in this world she cannot escape from the clutches of the family. The game of tennis symbolizes the interaction patterns in the family.

With examples such as this, Laing shows how the family can be a destructive and exploitive institution.

Laing refers to the family group as a **nexus**. He argues that 'the highest concern of the nexus is reciprocal concern. Each partner is concerned about what the other thinks, feels, does.' Within the nexus there is a constant, unremitting demand for mutual concern and attention. As a result there is considerable potential for harm: family members are in an extremely vulnerable position.

Thus if a father is ashamed of his son, given the nature of the nexus, his son is deeply affected. As he is emotionally locked into the nexus, he is concerned about his father's opinion and cannot brush it off lightly. In self-defence he may run to his mother who offers protection. In this way Laing argues that 'A family can act as gangsters, offering each other mutual protection against each other's violence.'

Reciprocal interiorization

From interaction within the nexus, **reciprocal interiorization** develops: family members become a part of each other and the family as a whole. They **interiorize** or **internalize** the family. Laing argues that 'To be in the same family is to feel the same "family" inside.' The example of Jane illustrates this process – her little world is an interiorization of family interaction patterns.

Laing regards the process of interiorization as psychologically damaging since it restricts the development of the self. Individuals carry the blueprint of their family with them for the rest of their life. This prevents any real autonomy or freedom of self; it prevents the development of the individual in his or her own right. Self-awareness is smothered under the blanket of the family. As a result of family interiorization, Laing states 'I consider most adults (including myself) are or have been more or less in a hypnotic trance induced in early infancy.'

The family 'ghetto'

Like Leach, Laing argues that problems in the family create problems in society. Due to the nature of the nexus and the process of interiorization, a boundary or even a defensive barrier is drawn between the family and the world outside. This can reach the point where 'Some families live in perpetual anxiety of what, to them, is an external persecuting world. The members of the family live in a family ghetto as it were.' Laing argues that this is one reason for so-called maternal overprotection. However, 'It is not "over" protection from the mother's point of view, nor, indeed, often from the point of view of other members of the family.'

This perception of the external threat of a menacing society tends to unite and strengthen the nexus. The barrier erected between the family and the world outside may have important consequences. According to Laing it leads family members, particularly children, to see the world in terms of 'us and them'. From this basic division stem the harmful and dangerous distinctions between Gentile and Jew, black and white and the separation of others into 'people like us' and 'people like them'.

Within the family children learn to obey their parents. Laing regards this as the primary link in a dangerous chain. Patterns of obedience laid down in early childhood form the basis for obedience to authority in later life. They lead to soldiers and officials blindly and unquestioningly following orders. Laing implies that without family obedience training, people would question orders, follow their own judgement and make their own decisions. If this were so, American soldiers might not have marched off to fight what Laing regards as a senseless war in Vietnam in the 1960s and we might no longer live in a society which Laing believes is largely insane.

Despite Laing's preoccupation with the dark side of family life, he stated in an interview in 1977:

I enjoy living in a family. I think the family is still the best thing that still exists biologically as a natural thing. My attack on the family is aimed at the way I felt many children are subjected to gross forms of violence and violation of their rights, to humiliation at the hands of adults who don't know what they're doing.

■ Criticisms of Leach and Laing

Leach and Laing in their different ways have presented a radical alternative to the functionalist perspective on the family but their work is open to a number of criticisms.

1 Neither has conducted detailed fieldwork on the family in contemporary industrial society and in fact Laing's

research is limited to investigations of families in which one member has been defined as schizophrenic.

2 Both talk about 'the family' with little reference to its position in the social structure. For example, there is no reference to social class in Laing's work and therefore no indication of the relationship between class and family life.

3 Leach examines the family over time but the work of Laing lacks any historical perspective.

4 Both authors examine the Western family from their particular specialized knowledge: Leach from his work on family and kinship in small-scale non-Western societies, and Laing from his study of schizophrenia and family life. This inevitably colours their views. In itself, this is not a criticism, but it is important to be aware of the source of their perspectives.

5 To some degree Leach and Laing begin with a picture of a society out of control or even gone mad. Leach in *A Runaway World?* implies that society has got out of

hand; Laing goes even further by suggesting that many aspects of contemporary society are insane. Such views of society will produce what many consider to be an extreme and unbalanced picture of the family. However, it is possible to accuse the functionalists of the opposite bias. For example, Parsons gives the impression of an immensely reasonable society ticking over like clockwork. In this context a well-adjusted, contented family is to be expected.

Leach and Laing have provided a balance to the functionalist view which has dominated sociological thinking on the family for many years. Laing, in particular, has given important insights into interaction patterns within the family. In doing so he may, as D.H.J. Morgan suggests, have come 'closer to family life as it is actually experienced than do many of the more orthodox presentations'.

In the next section we will consider the Marxist view of the family.

▌Marxist perspectives on the family

▌Friedrich Engels – the origin of the family

The earliest view of the family developed from a Marxist perspective is contained in Friedrich Engels's *The Origin of the Family, Private Property and the State*, published in 1884.

Like many nineteenth-century scholars, Engels took an evolutionary view of the family, attempting to trace its origin and evolution through time. He combined an evolutionary approach with Marxist theory, arguing that as the mode of production changed, so did the family.

During the early stages of human evolution, Engels believed that the means of production were communally owned and the family as such did not exist. This era of **primitive communism** was characterized by promiscuity. There were no rules limiting sexual relationships and society was, in effect, the family.

Although Engels has been criticized for this type of speculation, the anthropologist Kathleen Gough argues that his picture may not be that far from the truth. She notes that the nearest relatives to human beings, the chimpanzees, live in

'promiscuous hordes' and this may have been the pattern for early humans.

The evolution of the family

Engels argued that, throughout human history, more and more restrictions were placed on sexual relationships and the production of children. He speculated that from the promiscuous horde, marriage and the family evolved through a series of stages which included polygyny to its present stage, the monogamous nuclear family. Each successive stage placed greater restrictions on the number of mates available to the individual.

The monogamous nuclear family developed with the emergence of private property, in particular the private ownership of the means of production, and the advent of the state. The state instituted laws to protect the system of private property and to enforce the rules of monogamous marriage. This form of marriage and the family developed to solve the problem of the inheritance of private property. Property was owned by males and, in order for them to pass it on to their heirs, they had to be certain of the legitimacy of those heirs. They therefore needed greater control over women so that there would be no doubt about the paternity of the offspring. The monogamous family provided the most efficient device for this purpose. In Engels's words:

> It is based on the supremacy of the man, the express purpose being to produce children of undisputed paternity; such paternity is demanded because these children are later to come into their father's property as his natural heirs.

Evidence for Engels's views

Engels's scheme of the evolution of the family is much more elaborate than the brief outline described above. It was largely based on *Ancient Society*, an erroneous interpretation of the evolution of the family by the nineteenth-century American anthropologist, Lewis Henry Morgan. Modern research has suggested that many of its details are incorrect. For example monogamous marriage and the nuclear family are often found in hunting and gathering bands. Since humanity has lived in hunting and gathering bands for the vast majority of its existence, the various forms of group marriage postulated by Engels (such as the promiscuous horde) may well be figments of his imagination.

However, Gough argues that 'the general trend of Engels's argument still appears sound'. Although nuclear families and monogamous marriage exist in small-scale societies, they form a part of a larger kinship group. When individuals marry they take on a series of duties and obligations to their spouse's kin. Communities are united by kinship ties and the result is like a large extended family. Gough argues that:

> It is true that although it is not a group marriage in Engels's sense, marriage has a group character in many hunting bands and in most of the more complex tribal societies that have developed with the domestication of plants and animals. With the development of privately owned, heritable property, and especially with the rise of the state, this group character gradually disappears.

(Further aspects of Engels's views on the family are examined in Chapter 10, pp. 598–9).

■ Eli Zaretsky – personal life and capitalism

Eli Zaretsky has analysed more recent developments in the family from a Marxist perspective. He argues that the family in modern capitalist society creates the illusion that the 'private life' of the family is quite separate from the economy. Before the early nineteenth century the family was the basic unit of production. For example, in the early capitalist textile industry production of cloth took place in the home and involved all family members. Only with the development of factory-based production were work and family life separated.

In a society in which work was alienating Zaretsky claims the family was put on a pedestal because it apparently 'stood in opposition to the terrible anonymous world of commerce and industry'. The private life of the family provided opportunities for satisfactions which were unavailable outside the walls of the home.

Zaretsky welcomes the increased possibilities for a personal life for the proletariat offered by the reduction in working hours since the nineteenth century. However, he believes that the family is unable to provide for the psychological and personal needs of individuals. He says 'it simply cannot meet the pressures of being the only refuge in a brutal society'. The family artificially separates and isolates personal life from other aspects of life. It might cushion the effects of capitalism but it perpetuates the system and cannot compensate for the general alienation produced by such a society.

Furthermore, Zaretsky sees the family as a major prop to the capitalist economy. The capitalist system is based upon the domestic labour of housewives who reproduce future generations of workers. He also believes the family has become a vital unit of consumption. The family consumes the products of capitalism and this allows the bourgeoisie to continue producing surplus value. To Zaretsky only socialism will end the artificial separation of family private life and public life, and produce the possibility of personal fulfilment.

Next we will examine the family from a feminist viewpoint.

■ Feminist perspectives on the family

The influence of feminism

In recent decades feminism has probably had more influence on the study of the family than any other approach to understanding society. Like Laing, Leach and Marxists, feminists have been highly critical of the family. However, unlike other critics they have tended to emphasize the harmful effects of family life upon women. In doing so they have developed new perspectives and highlighted new issues.

Feminists have, for example, introduced the study of areas of family life such as housework and domestic violence into sociology. They have challenged some widely held views about the inevitability of male dominance in families and have questioned the view that family life is

becoming more egalitarian. Feminists have also highlighted the economic contribution to society made by women's domestic labour within the family. Above all, feminist theory has encouraged sociologists to see the family as an institution involving power relationships. It has challenged the image of family life as being based upon cooperation, shared interests and love, and has tried to show that some family members, in particular men, obtain greater benefits from families than others.

In later sections of this chapter we will consider the impact of feminism on the study of conjugal roles, domestic labour, social policy and marriage. In the next section, however, we will examine some of the feminist theoretical approaches to understanding the family.

■ Marxist/feminist perspectives on the family

Marxists such as Engels and Zaretsky have acknowledged that women are exploited in marriage and family life but they have emphasized the relationship between capitalism and the family, rather than the family's effects on women. Marxist feminists use Marxist concepts but see the exploitation of women as a key feature of family life. The next few sections will examine how these theories have been applied to the family. (More details of the Marxist feminist approach can be found in Chapter 10, pp. 606–9.)

The production of labour power

Margaret Benston states that:

The amount of unpaid labor performed by women is very large and very profitable to those who own the means of production. To pay women for their work, even at minimum wage scales, would involve a massive redistribution of wealth. At present, the support of the family is a hidden tax on the wage earner – his wage buys the labor power of two people.

The fact that the husband must pay for the production and upkeep of future labour acts as a strong discipline on his behaviour at work. He cannot easily withdraw his labour with a wife and children to support. These responsibilities weaken his bargaining power and commit him to wage labour. Benston argues:

As an economic unit, the nuclear family is a valuable stabilizing force in capitalist society. Since the production which is done in the home is paid for by the husband–father's earnings, his ability to withhold labour from the market is much reduced.

Not only does the family produce and rear cheap labour, it also maintains it at no cost to the employer. In her role as housewife, the woman attends to her husband's needs thus keeping him in good running order to perform his role as a wage labourer.

Fran Ansley translates Parsons's view, that the family functions to stabilize adult personalities, into a Marxist framework. She sees the emotional support provided by the wife as a safety-valve for the frustration produced in the husband by working in a capitalist system. Rather than being turned against the system which produced it, this frustration is absorbed by the comforting wife. In this way the system is not threatened. In Ansley's words:

> When wives play their traditional role as takers of shit, they often absorb their husbands' legitimate anger and frustration at their own powerlessness and oppression. With every worker provided with a sponge to soak up his possibly revolutionary ire, the bosses rest more secure. (Quoted in Bernard 1976, p. 233.)

Kathy McAfee and Myrna Wood make a similar point in their discussion of male dominance in the family. They claim:

> The petty dictatorship which most men exercise over their wives and families enables them to vent their anger and frustration in a way which poses no challenge to the system. (Quoted in Rowbotham 1973, p. 58.)

Ideological conditioning

The social reproduction of labour power does not simply involve producing children and maintaining them in good health. It also involves the reproduction of the attitudes essential for an efficient workforce under capitalism. Thus David Cooper argues that the family is 'an ideological conditioning device in an exploitive society'. Within the family, children learn to conform and to submit to authority. The foundation is therefore laid for the obedient and submissive workforce required by capitalism.

A similar point is made by Diane Feeley who argues that the structure of family relationships socializes the young to accept their place in a class-stratified society. She sees the family as an authoritarian unit dominated by the husband in particular and adults in general. Feeley claims that the family with its 'authoritarian ideology is designed to teach passivity, not rebellion'. Thus children learn to submit to parental authority and emerge from the family preconditioned to accept their place in the

hierarchy of power and control in capitalist society.

(Marxist views on the role of the family in capitalist society mirror Marxist analysis of the role of education; see Chapter 12, pp. 135–40.)

Criticisms

Some of the criticisms of previous views of the family also apply to Marxist approaches. There is a tendency to talk about 'the family' in capitalist society without regard to possible variations in family life between social classes and over time. As D.H.J. Morgan notes in his criticism of both functionalist and Marxist approaches, both 'presuppose a traditional model of the nuclear family where there is a married couple with children, where the husband is the breadwinner and where the wife stays at home to deal with the housework'.

More recent Marxist/feminist work on the family has taken greater account of variations in family life. Michèlle Barrett and Mary McIntosh believe the idea of 'the family' is misleading given the wide variations that exist in life within families and the varieties of household types in which people live. (We discuss family and household diversity on pp. 346–57.) If there is no one normal or typical family type, then it may be impossible to claim that the family always performs particular functions either for men or for capitalism.

The 'anti-social' family

Barrett and McIntosh do believe that there is a very strong ideology supporting family life. To them 'the family' is 'anti-social' not just because it exploits women, and benefits capitalists, but also because the ideology of the family destroys life outside the family. They say 'the family ideal makes everything else seem pale and unsatisfactory'. People outside families suffer as a consequence. Family members are so wrapped up in family life that they neglect social contact with others. 'Couples mix with other couples, finding it difficult to fit single people in.'

Life in other institutions (such as children's homes, old people's homes and students' residences) comes to be seen as shallow and lacking in meaning. They argue that homes for the handicapped could be far more stimulating for, say, Down's syndrome sufferers, if it were not for life in institutions being devalued by the ideology of the family.

Like other feminists, they point out that the image of the family as involving love and mutual care tends to ignore the amount of violent and sexual crimes that take place within a family context. They note that 25 per cent of reported violent crimes consists of assaults by husbands on their wives, and many rapes take place within marriage.

They do not deny that there can be caring relationships within families, but equally they do not think that families are the only places in which such relationships can develop. They say the ideology that idealizes family life:

> has made the outside world cold and friendless, and made it harder to maintain relationships of security and trust except with kin. Caring, sharing and loving would all be more widespread if the family did not claim them for its own.

■ Radical feminist perspectives on the family

There are many varieties of radical feminism. As Valerie Bryson says, 'the radical feminist label has been applied in recent years to a confusingly diverse range of theories'. She says 'it is the site for far ranging disagreements at all levels of theory and practice'. However, Bryson does identify some key characteristics which distinguish **radical feminists** from other feminists.

1 'It is essentially a theory of, by and for women' and therefore 'sees no need to compromise with existing perspectives and agendas'. Radical feminist ideas tend to be novel rather than adaptations of other theories such as Marxism.

2 'It sees the oppression of women as the most fundamental and universal form of domination'. Society is seen as **patriarchal**, or male dominated, rather than capitalist, and women are held to have different interests from those of men.

Radical feminists do not agree on the source of male domination but most do see the family as important in maintaining male power. We will now analyse one major radical feminist theory of the family.

■ Christine Delphy and Diana Leonard – *Familiar Exploitation*

Types of feminism

Delphy and Leonard are unlike most radical feminists in that they attach considerable importance to material factors in causing women's oppression. In this respect they have some similarity with Marxist feminist theories. In particular Delphy and Leonard attach special importance to work and say that their approach 'uses Marxist methodology'. Nevertheless they see themselves as radical feminists for they believe that it is men, rather than capitalists or capitalism, who are the primary beneficiaries of the exploitation of women's labour. To them the family has a central role in maintaining patriarchy. They say:

> We see the familial basis of domestic groups as an important element in continuing the patriarchal nature of our society: that is, in the continuance of men's dominance over women and children.

The family as an economic system

Delphy and Leonard see the family as an economic system. It involves a particular set of '*labour relations* in which men benefit from, and exploit, the work of women – and sometimes that of their children and other male relatives'. The key to this exploitation is that family members work not for themselves but for the head of household. Women in particular are oppressed not because they are socialized into being passive, nor because they are ideologically conditioned into subservience, but because their work is appropriated within the family. Delphy and Leonard argue 'It is primarily the *work* women do, the uses to which our bodies can be put, which constitutes the reason for our oppression.'

Delphy and Leonard identify the following features as the main characteristics of the family as an economic system.

1 Every family-based household has a social structure which involves two types of role. These are head of household and their dependents or helpers. Family households have members who are connected by kinship or marriage. Female heads of household are uncommon. Figures indicate that only about one in ten adult women in Britain aged 16 to 60 heads a household. Most of these women are single or widows and there are no other adults present. Only one in 25 women of 16 to 60 heads a household which contains other adults. Where a male adult relative is present it is usually he who takes over as head of household. In the case of married women, even if she has the main income and owns the house, 'she is at least semi-subordinate, owing her husband respect and obedience and having responsibility for domestic (and sexual and emotional) labour'.

2 The male head of household is different from other members because he 'decides what needs doing in a given situation' and assigns tasks to other members or delegates to them. Other family members may change his mind about decisions, but it is his mind to change. He makes the final decision.

3 The head of household provides maintenance for other family members, and they receive a share of family property on his death. However, they have to work for him unpaid.

4 The type and amount of work family members have to do is related to sex and marital status. Female relatives have to do unpaid domestic work; wives in addition have to carry out 'sexual and reproductive work'. Although the precise allocation of tasks varies from household to household, domestic work remains a female responsibility.

5 Money and resources for maintenance and money inherited by dependents is not related to the amount of work done. A man must provide for his dependents' basic needs, and may be very generous, but unlike an employer he does not purchase labour power by the hour, week or amount produced. The amounts inherited by family members are more related to position, with, for example, sons inheriting more than daughters, than to work.

6 The relations of production within the family often

therefore involve payment in kind (such as a new coat or a holiday) rather than payment in money.

7 The economic relationships rarely involve formal contracts or bargaining. This means that family members must use informal methods of negotiation. For example, 'Wives and children have to study their husbands and fathers closely and handle them carefully so as to keep them sweet.' The male heads have to find informal ways of motivating their workers and if possible, 'foster their subordinates' feelings of affection for them'.

8 'The head of the family may have a near monopoly over, and he always has greater access to and control of, the family's property and external relations.'

9 When dependents, particularly wives, have paid employment outside the home they still have to carry out household tasks, or pay others out of their wages to do housework or care for children for them.

Domestic labour

Having outlined how the family works as an economic system, Delphy and Leonard go on to examine in more detail who contributes to and who benefits from family life. They admit that most men do some housework but such tasks are usually done by women. They claim that 'time-budget studies show . . . that the amount of time women spend on domestic work has not declined this century and they still do twice as much each day as men in all western and eastern bloc countries even when they have paid employment'. Furthermore there is 'a clear order of responsibility to care for children, the sick and elderly'. This responsibility always falls on female relatives where they are available except in special circumstances (for example, if the wife is disabled).

On the other hand, when men marry they end up doing only half the housework they did as bachelors. However much they may decide to 'help' their wives, husbands do not assume responsibility for housework.

Supporting husbands

As well as carrying out housework and caring for children, the sick and older people, women also contribute a great deal to their husbands' work and leisure by providing 'for their emotional and sexual well-being'. Drawing on the work of a British sociologist, Janet Finch, Delphy and

Leonard describe some of the types of help provided by wives. Sometimes they provide direct help, doing office work for a self-employed husband, proofreading books if their husband is an author, doing constituency work if he is an MP. They may stay at home to answer the phone or arrange dinner parties for colleagues of their husband.

Wives also give moral support, 'observing and moderating his emotions, arranging entertainment and relaxation, and supplying personal needs'. Wives are there to listen when their husbands unburden themselves of their work problems. They provide 'trouble-free sex' which is important since 'men frequently unwind best post-coitally'. Wives also make the house into a home so that it is 'comfortable warm and undemanding'. Women even control their own emotions so that they can provide emotional care for husbands. They 'flatter, excuse, boost, sympathize and pay attention to men', all to give them a sense of well-being.

In contrast men make little contribution to their wife's work. They find it 'psychologically, socially or legally impossible' to work under their wives' direction. They might give some assistance to working wives, but the husband's career remains the central one.

Consumption

Delphy and Leonard believe then, that wives contribute much more work to family life than their husbands. Despite this they get fewer of the material benefits of family life than men. Men retain ultimate responsibility for family finances, and women consume less than male family members. The (usually) male head of household has the 'decision-making power' to determine what goods are produced or bought for the family and who uses them. For instance, 'the food bought is the sort *he* likes, and he gets more of it and the best bits'. Husbands get more leisure time, more access to the family car, or to the best car if there is more than one, sons get more spent on their education than daughters. In every area of family consumption it is the status of different family members which shapes who gets what.

Empirical evidence

Delphy and Leonard use four main sources to try to back up their claims. Three of these are studies of British factory workers and their families. They use Goldthorpe and Lockwood's 1962 study of affluent workers in Luton (see pp. 77–9 for further details), a 1970s study of 500 workers and their wives in a Bristol company which made cardboard packing cases, and a 1980s study of redundant steel workers in Port Talbot, Wales. They also use data from Christine Delphy's own studies of French farming families.

Although the studies did not always contain the data needed to test their theories, they found support for their arguments in a number of areas. The following are a few examples.

1 In Bristol the researchers found that husbands did not want their wives to take paid employment and often discouraged them from doing so. Wives had little influence on their husbands' patterns of work.

2 In Port Talbot most men strongly resisted doing housework, even though they were unemployed. They saw redundancy as a threat to their masculinity and didn't want it further undermined by doing 'women's' jobs in the house. Only 25 per cent of the sample gave more than occasional help with housework and in no case did the husband take the main burden of housework. The Port Talbot study also found that the husband usually retained control of the family finances.

3 Delphy's research revealed that wives' labour was vital to the success of French farms. Farms owned by bachelors enjoyed considerably less success than those owned by married men. Nevertheless wives had little autonomy and were given the 'arduous, least-valued tasks'. Wives had very little say in how the farm was run and farms were usually handed down to sons.

Conclusion and summary

Delphy and Leonard believe that the family is a patriarchal and hierarchical institution through which men dominate and exploit women. Men are usually the head of household, and it is the head who benefits from the work that gets done. Women provide '57 varieties of unpaid service' for men including providing them with a 'pliant sexual partner and children if he wants them'. Wives do sometimes resist their husband's dominance – they are not always passive victims – but 'economic and social constraints' make it difficult for women to escape from the patriarchal family.

Delphy and Leonard do not think there are simple solutions to the problems created by the family. Individual men may love their wives, but that does not stop them exploiting them. Single mothers cannot escape from patriarchy 'because they are often poor and their situation is always difficult'. Lesbians 'may be downright ostracized and physically attacked'. In the end they admit that they do not know what strategy feminists should use to change the family, but they believe that women should continue to struggle to improve their lives, both inside and outside family life.

Evaluation

Delphy and Leonard provide a comprehensive analysis of the family from a radical feminist perspective. They highlight many ways in which the family can produce or reinforce inequalities between women and men. However, their work can be criticized both theoretically and empirically.

1 Theoretically, Delphy and Leonard do not succeed in demonstrating that inequality is built into the structure of the family. Their argument is based upon the assumption that all families have a head, usually a man, and it is the head who ultimately benefits from family life. However, they do not show theoretically or empirically that *all* families have a head who has more power than other family members. They fail to acknowledge that there may be some families in which power is shared. It may well be possible to find

inequalities in every household, but that does not necessarily mean that one person is dominant.

2 Empirically, their work is based upon unrepresentative data. The three British studies used are all of manual workers, and two of them are rather dated. Most researchers have found less gender inequality in middle-class than working-class families, so these studies may have an in-built bias towards supporting their theory. Furthermore they were not specifically directed at testing Delphy and Leonard's theory. The relevant data are often therefore absent from the research.

3 Delphy's study of French farming families was specifically directed at testing their theories, but farming families are hardly typical of other families. Family members tend to work in the family business, the farm, and few wives have an independent source of income which could reduce marital inequality.

Delphy and Leonard tend to make rather sweeping statements about inequality which may not apply equally to all families. In doing so they perhaps overstate their case by denying the possibility of exceptions.

In this section we have studied the family from a variety of perspectives. We will now turn our attention to various themes which are significant to our understanding of the family as a unit of social organization. The first theme that we will consider is the effect of industrialization on the family.

■ The family and industrialization

■ The pre-industrial family

A major theme in sociological studies of the family is the relationship between the structure of the family and the process of industrialization. (**Industrialization** refers to the mass production of goods in a factory system which involves some degree of mechanized production technology.) There are a number of problems which arise from relating the family to industrialization.

1 First, the process of industrialization does not follow the same course in every society.

2 Second, industrialization is not a fixed thing but a developing process. Thus the industrial system in

nineteenth-century Britain is different in important respects to that of today.

3 Further difficulties arise from the fact that there is not one form of pre-industrial family but many.

Much of the research on the family and industrialization has led to considerable confusion because it is not always clear what the family in industrial society is being compared to. In addition, within industrial society there are variations in family structure. As a starting point therefore, it is necessary for us to examine the family in pre-industrial societies in order to establish a standard for comparison.

The family in non-literate societies

In many small-scale, non-literate societies, the family and kinship relationships in general are the basic organizing principles of social life. Societies are often divided into a number of kinship groups such as **lineages**, which are groups descended from a common ancestor. The family is embedded in a web of kinship relationships. Kinship groups are responsible for the production of important goods and services. For example, a lineage may own agricultural land which is worked, and its produce shared, by members of the lineage.

Members of kinship groups are united by a network of mutual rights and obligations. In some cases, if individuals are insulted or injured by someone from outside the group, they have the right to call on the support of members of the group to seek reparation or revenge. Many areas of an individual's behaviour are shaped by his or her status as kin. An uncle, for example, may have binding obligations to be involved with aspects of his nephew's socialization and be responsible for the welfare of his nieces and nephews should their father die.

Something of the importance of family and kinship relationships in many small-scale societies is illustrated by the following statement by a Pomo Indian of northern California.

What is a man? A man is nothing. Without his family he is of less importance than that bug crossing the trail. In the white ways of doing things the family is not so important. The police and soldiers take care of protecting you, the courts give you justice, the post office carries messages for you, the school teaches you. Everything is taken care of, even your children, if you die; but with us the family must do all of that. (From Aginsky 1968)

In this brief description of the family in small-scale, pre-industrial society we have glossed over the wide variation in family and kinship patterns which are found in such societies. Even so, it does serve to highlight some of the more important differences between the family in kinship-based society and the family in industrial society.

The 'classic' extended family

A second form of pre-industrial family, sometimes known as the **classic extended family**, is found in some traditional peasant societies. This family type has been made famous by C.M. Arensberg and S.T. Kimball's study of Irish farmers entitled *Family and Community in Ireland*.

As in kinship-based societies, kinship ties dominate life, but in this case the basic unit is the extended family rather than the wider kinship grouping. The traditional Irish farming family is a **patriarchal extended family**, so-called because of the considerable authority of the male head. It is also **patrilineal** because property is passed down the male line. Within the family, social and economic roles are welded together, status being ascribed by family membership.

On the farm the father–son relationship is also that of owner–employee. The father–owner makes all important decisions (such as whether to sell cattle) and directs the activities of all the other members of the extended family. He is head of the family and 'director of the firm'.

Typically, the classic extended family consists of the male head, his wife and children, his ageing parents who have passed on the farm to him, and any unmarried brothers and sisters. Together they work as a 'production unit', producing the goods necessary for the family's survival.

Some people have argued that as industrialization proceeds, kinship-based society and the classic extended family tend to break up and the nuclear family – or some form of modified extended family – emerge as the predominant family form.

■ Talcott Parsons – the 'isolated nuclear family'

Structural isolation

Talcott Parsons argues that the **isolated nuclear family** is the typical family form in modern industrial society. It is 'structurally isolated' because it does not form an integral part of a wider system of kinship relationships. Obviously there are social relationships between members of nuclear families and their kin but these relationships are more a matter of choice than binding obligations.

Parsons sees the emergence of the isolated nuclear family in terms of his theory of social evolution. (This theory is outlined in Chapter 14, pp. 871–4.) The evolution of society involves a process of **structural differentiation**. This simply means that institutions evolve which specialize in fewer functions. In this sense, no longer do the family and kinship groups perform a wide range of functions. Instead specialist institutions such as business firms, schools, hospitals, police forces and churches take over many of their functions.

This process of differentiation and specialization involves the 'transfer of a variety of functions from the nuclear family to other structures of the society'. Thus in industrial society, with the transfer of the production of goods to factories, specialized economic institutions became differentiated from the family. The family ceases to be an economic unit of production.

The family and the economy

Functionalist analysis emphasizes the importance of integration and harmony between the various parts of society. An efficient social system requires the parts to fit smoothly rather than abrade. The parts of society are **functionally related** when they contribute to the integration and harmony of the social system.

Parsons argues that there is a functional relationship between the isolated nuclear family and the economic system in industrial society. In particular the isolated nuclear family is shaped to meet the requirements of the economic system. A modern industrial system with a specialized division of labour demands considerable geographical mobility from its labour force. Individuals with specialized skills are required to move to places where those skills are in demand. The isolated nuclear family is suited to this need for geographical mobility. It is not tied down by binding obligations to a wide range of kin and, compared to the pre-industrial families described above, it is a small, streamlined unit.

Status in the family

Status in industrial society is **achieved** rather than **ascribed**. Individuals' occupational status is not automatically fixed by their ascribed status in the family or kinship group. Parsons argues that the isolated nuclear family is the best form of family structure for a society based on achieved status.

In industrial society, individuals are judged in terms of the status they achieve. Such judgements are based on what Parsons terms **universalistic values**, that is values that are universally applied to all members of society. However, within the family, status is ascribed and, as such, based on **particularistic values**, that is values that are applied only to particular individuals. Thus a son's relationship with his father is conducted primarily in terms of their ascribed statuses of father and son. The father's achieved status as a bricklayer, schoolteacher or lawyer has relatively little influence on their relationship since his son does not judge him primarily in terms of universalistic values.

Parsons argues that in a society based on achieved status, conflict would tend to arise in a family unit larger than the isolated nuclear family. In a three-generation extended family, in which the children remained as part of the family unit, the following situation could produce conflict. If the son became a doctor and the father was a labourer, the particularistic values of family life would give the father a higher status than his son. Yet the universalistic values of society as a whole would award his son higher social status. Conflict could result from this situation which might undermine the authority of the father and threaten the solidarity of the family.

The same conflict of values could occur if the nuclear family were extended horizontally. Relationships between a woman and her sister may be problematic if they held jobs of widely differing prestige.

The isolated nuclear family largely prevents these problems from arising. There is one main breadwinner, the husband–father. His wife is mainly responsible for raising the children and the latter have yet to achieve their status in the world of work. No member of the family is in a position to threaten the ascribed authority structure by achieving a status outside the family which is higher than the achieved status of the family head.

These problems do not occur in pre-industrial society. There, occupational status is largely ascribed since an individual's position in the family and kinship group usually determines his or her job. Parsons concludes that given the universalistic, achievement-orientated values of industrial society, the isolated nuclear family is the most suitable family structure. Any extension of this basic unit may well create conflict which would threaten the solidarity of the family.

As a consequence of the structural isolation of the nuclear family, the conjugal bond – the relationship between husband and wife – is strengthened. Without the support of kin beyond the nuclear family, spouses are increasingly dependent on each other, particularly for emotional support. As we outlined previously, Parsons argues that the stabilization of adult personalities is a major function of the family in industrial society. This is largely accomplished in terms of the husband–wife relationship.

▎William J. Goode

In *World Revolution and the Family* William J. Goode surveys the relationship between family structure and industrialization in various parts of the world. Like Parsons, he argues that industrialization tends to undermine the extended family and larger kinship groupings. Goode offers the following explanations for this process.

1 The high rate of geographical mobility in industrial society decreases 'the frequency and intimacy of contact among members of the kin network'.

2 The relatively high level of social mobility also tends to weaken kinship ties. If members of a working-class family become upwardly mobile, for example, they may adopt the lifestyle, attitudes and values of their new social class. This would tend to cut them off from their working-class kin.

3 Many of the functions once performed by the family have been taken over by outside agencies such as schools, business and welfare organizations. This reduces the dependency of individuals on their family and kin.

4 The importance of achieved status in industrial society means that the family and kinship group have less to offer their members. The family cannot guarantee its members a job or directly provide the necessary education and training to obtain one. The highly specialized division of labour in industrial society makes it even more difficult for an individual to obtain a job for a relative. As Goode states, 'He may not be in a suitable sector of the occupational sphere, or at a level where his influence is useful.'

Ideology and the nuclear family

However, Goode does not regard the pressures of industrialization as the only reason for the break-down of extended family ties. He argues that the move to nuclear families has been 'far more rapid than could be supposed or predicted from the degree of industrialization alone'.

Goode believes that the ideology of the nuclear family has encouraged its growth, particularly in non-Western societies. This is due partly to the prestige of Western ideas and lifestyles. Since the nuclear family is found 'in many areas where the rate of industrialization is slight' Goode recognizes 'the independent power of *ideological* variables'. He also argues that the spread of the nuclear family is due in part to the freedom it affords its members.

Kenneth Little supports this point in his study of migration from rural kinship-based societies to urban industrial centres in West Africa. In the towns, many migrants welcomed the freedom from obligations to their kinsmen.

Role bargaining

Goode applies the concept of **role bargaining** to his study of the family. This means that individuals attempt to obtain the best possible 'bargain' in their relationships with others. They will attempt to maximize their gains. In terms of family relationships, this means they will maintain relationships with kin and submit to their control if they feel they are getting a good return on their investment of time, energy and emotion.

With respect to the extended family and industrialization, Goode argues that 'It is not so much that the new system is incompatible, as it offers an alternative pattern of payments.' In other words, extended family patterns can operate in industrial society. Although it costs time and money, the rapid transport system in modern society means that 'the individual can maintain an extended kin network if he wishes to do so'. However, the 'alternative pattern of payments' offered by industrial society provides a better bargain for many people. They gain more by rejecting close and frequent contacts with kin beyond the nuclear family, than by retaining them.

Goode uses the concept of role bargaining to explain social class differences in family structure. From his world survey, Goode finds that extended family patterns are most likely to occur in the upper classes. Since members of ruling classes and elites have an important influence on appointments to top jobs, the retention of family ties makes economic sense. In Goode's terms it is an effective role bargain. Lupton and Wilson's study of the kinship connections of 'top decision makers' gives some indication of the importance of family connections in the British upper class. (See Chapter 9, pp. 518–21, for details of this study and related research.) By comparison, members of the lower strata 'have little to offer the younger generation to counteract their normal tendency to independence'.

Goode concludes that extended kinship ties are retained if individuals feel they have more to gain than to lose by maintaining them.

■ Peter Laslett – the family in pre-industrial societies

The family in kinship-based society and the classic extended family represent only two possible forms of family structure in pre-industrial society. Historical research in Britain and America suggests that neither was typical of those countries in the pre-industrial era.

Peter Laslett, a Cambridge historian, has studied family size and composition in pre-industrial England. From 1564 to 1821 he found that only about 10 per cent of households contained kin beyond the nuclear family. This percentage is the same as for England in 1966. Evidence from America presents a similar picture.

This surprisingly low figure may be due in part to the fact that people in pre-industrial England and America married relatively late in life and life expectancy was short. On average, there were only a few years between the marriage of a couple and the death of their parents. However, Laslett found no evidence to support the formerly accepted view that the classic extended family was widespread in pre-industrial England. He states that 'There is no sign of the large, extended co-residential family group of the traditional peasant world giving way to the small, nuclear conjugal household of modern industrial society.'

The 'Western family'

Following on from his research in England, Laslett began to draw together the results of research into pre-industrial family size in other countries. He reached the conclusion that the nuclear family was not just typical of Britain. He uncovered evidence that there was a distinctive 'Western family' found also in northern France, The Netherlands, Belgium,

Scandinavia and parts of Italy and Germany. This type of family was typically nuclear in structure: children were born relatively late, there was little age gap between spouses and a large number of families contained servants. This family type contrasted with Eastern Europe and other parts of the world (such as Russia and Japan) where the extended family was more common.

According to Laslett it was at least possible that the predominance of the nuclear family was a factor which helped Western Europe to be the first area of the world to industrialize. He reversed the more common argument that industrialization led to the nuclear family, claiming that the nuclear family had social, political and economic consequences which in part led to industrialization.

Brigitte and Peter Berger have suggested how this type of family encouraged industrialization. They believe the nuclear family helped to produce **modernity**: it led to ways of thinking conducive to industrial development. In particular nuclear families encouraged individuals to have a greater sense of self-reliance and independence: qualities often thought to be amongst those required by early entrepreneurs.

Family diversity in pre-industrial societies

Although Laslett has successfully exploded the myth that the extended family was typical of pre-industrial Britain, his conclusions should be viewed with some caution.

Michael Anderson points out some contradictory evidence in Laslett's own research. Laslett's research might have shown average household size to be under five, but it also revealed that a majority of the population in pre-industrial Britain (53 per cent) lived in households consisting of six or more people. Anderson also referred to other research which suggests a much greater variety of household types than Laslett's theory of the Western family implies. For instance, research has shown that in Sweden extended families were very common. Furthermore, there is evidence of considerable variation within Britain: the gentry and yeoman farmers, for example, tended to have much larger households than the average.

For these reasons Anderson is critical of the idea of the 'Western family'. He believes pre-industrial Europe was characterized by family diversity without any one type of family being predominant.

■ Michael Anderson – household structure and the Industrial Revolution

Michael Anderson's own research into the effects of industrialization on families does not, however, support the view that during industrialization extended families began to disappear.

Using data from the 1851 census of Preston, Michael Anderson found that some 23 per cent of households contained kin other than the nuclear family, a large increase over Laslett's figures and those for today. The bulk of this 'co-residence' occurred among the poor. Anderson argues that co-residence occurs when the parties involved receive net gains from the arrangement. He states:

If we are to understand variations and changes in patterns of kinship relationships, the only worth-while approach is consciously and explicitly to investigate the manifold advantages and disadvantages that any actor can obtain from maintaining one relational pattern rather than another.

Extended families and mutual aid

Preston in 1851 was largely dependent on the cotton industry. Life for many working-class families was characterized by severe hardship resulting from low wages, periods of high unemployment, large families, a high death rate and overcrowded housing. In these circumstances, the maintenance of a large kinship network could be advantageous to all concerned.

1 In the absence of a welfare state, individuals were largely dependent on kin in times of hardship and need. Ageing parents often lived with their married children, a situation which benefited both parties. It provided support for the aged and allowed both the parents to work in the factory since grandparents could care for the dependent children.

2 The high death rate led to a large number of orphans, many of whom found a home with relatives. Again the situation benefited both parties. It provided support for the children who would soon, in an age of child labour, make an important contribution to household income.

3 A high rate of sickness and unemployment encouraged a wide network of kin as a means of mutual support:

with no sickness and unemployment benefits, individuals were forced to rely on their kin in times of hardship.

4 Co-residence also provided direct economic advantages to those concerned. Additional members of the household would lower the share of the rent paid by each individual.

5 Finally, the practice of recruiting for jobs through kin encouraged the establishment of a wide kinship network. Anderson notes that the system of '"Asking for" a job for kin was normal in the factory towns and the employers used the kinship system to recruit labour from the country.'

Anderson's study of Preston indicates that, in the mid-nineteenth century, the working-class family functioned as a mutual aid organization. It provided an insurance policy against hardship and crisis. This function encouraged the extension of kinship bonds beyond the nuclear family. Such links would be retained as long as they provided net gains to those involved. Anderson concludes that the early stages of industrialization increased rather than decreased the extension of the working-class family.

■ Elizabeth Roberts – family life and duty

Like Anderson, Elizabeth Roberts has studied family life in Lancashire. She conducted a study of working-class women in three Lancashire towns: Preston, Barrow and Lancaster. The study used oral history techniques, interviewing people about their past lives, in order to examine family life between 1890 and 1940.

Like Anderson, Roberts found that extended kinship links remained very strong in working-class families with family members helping each other out in many different ways. However, her findings differ from Anderson's in two important respects.

1 Roberts found evidence of a great deal of support being given by working-class women to family members in other households as well as to the family members with whom they lived.

2 She denies Anderson's claim that family relationships are largely based upon self-interest. Roberts found that women often gave practical, emotional and even financial support to other family members without

getting or expecting much in return. Indeed, providing this help often cost the giver a good deal in time, effort and sometimes money. Roberts therefore argues that family relationships were based rather more on emotions and values than calculating self-interest. People helped their relatives because they felt affection or a sense of duty towards them, and not only because they had something to gain.

Evaluation

Janet Finch suggests a number of possible explanations for the differences in the findings of Roberts and Anderson.

1 First, their studies refer to different time periods. Finch advances the possibility that family life had become less harsh and had stabilized by the end of the nineteenth century, giving people more opportunity to give unselfish support to their kin.

2 Second, the differences could relate to gender. Roberts's study was based upon studies of women and it could be that women are more likely than men to have a strong sense of duty towards relatives.

3 Third, the differences could be a result of using different research methods. Anderson largely used quantitative data from census returns; Roberts used qualitative data from in-depth interviews. Interviews would be more likely to reveal a sense of duty towards relatives than statistical data.

Finch concludes that the two studies do not necessarily have to be seen as contradictory. It may be that they highlight different aspects of family life in which:

Feelings of affection and concepts of duty are taken into calculations about mutual advantage based on material considerations. The result is patterns of support whose basis is probably far more complex than it appears to an outsider and which also perhaps includes the expectation that love and affection themselves will be reciprocated.

Whatever the basis of support between kin, Roberts and Anderson are in agreement that nineteenth-century industrialization did not destroy extended family relationships. This conclusion is also supported by the next research that we will consider, that of Young and Willmott.

■ Michael Young and Peter Willmott – four stages of family life

Michael Young and Peter Willmott conducted studies of family life in London from the 1950s to the 1970s. In their book, *The Symmetrical Family*, they attempt to trace the development of the family from pre-industrial England to the 1970s. Using a combination of historical research and social surveys, they suggest that the family has gone through four main stages. In this section we will concentrate on their analysis of the working-class family.

Stage 1 – the pre-industrial family

Stage 1 is represented by the pre-industrial family. The family is a unit of production: the husband, wife and unmarried children work as a team, typically in agriculture or textiles. This type of family was gradually supplanted as a result of the Industrial Revolution. However, it continued well into the nineteenth century and is still represented in a small minority of families today, the best examples being some farming families.

Stage 2 – the early industrial family

The Stage 2 family began with the Industrial Revolution, developed throughout the nineteenth century and reached its peak in the early years of the twentieth century. The family ceased to be a unit of production since individual members were employed as wage earners. Throughout the nineteenth century working-class poverty was widespread, wages were low and unemployment high. Like Anderson, Young and Willmott argue that the family responded to this situation by extending its network to include relatives beyond the nuclear family. This provided an insurance policy against the insecurity and hardship of poverty.

The extension of the nuclear family was largely conducted by women who 'eventually built up an organization in their own defence and in defence of their children'. The basic tie was between a mother and her married daughter, and in comparison the **conjugal bond** (the husband–wife relationship) was weak. Women created an 'informal trade union' which largely excluded men. Young and Willmott claim that 'Husbands were often squeezed out of the warmth of the female circle and took to the pub as their defence.'

Compared to later stages, the Stage 2 family was often headed by a female. Unlike the situation of New World black families, however, this resulted more from the high male death rate than from desertion by the husband.

The Stage 2 family began to decline in the early years of the twentieth century but it is still found in many low-income, long established working-class areas. Its survival is documented in Young and Willmott's famous study entitled *Family and Kinship in East London*. The study was conducted in the mid-1950s in Bethnal Green, a low-income borough in London's East End. Bethnal Green is a long settled, traditional working-class area. Children usually remain in the same locality on marriage. At the time of the research, two out of three married people had parents living within two or three miles of their residence.

There was a close tie between female relatives. Over 50 per cent of the married women in the sample had seen their mothers during the previous day, over 80 per cent within the previous week. There was a constant exchange of services such as washing, shopping and babysitting, between female relatives. Young and Willmott argued that in many families the households of mother and married daughter are 'to some extent merged'. As such they can be termed extended families which Young and Willmott define as 'a combination of families who to some degree form one domestic unit'.

Although many aspects of the Stage 2 family were present in Bethnal Green, there were also indications of a transition to Stage 3. For example, fathers were increasingly involved in the rearing of their children.

Stage 3 – the symmetrical family

In the early 1970s, Young and Willmott conducted a large-scale social survey in which 1,928 people were interviewed in Greater London and the outer Metropolitan area. The results formed the basis of their book, *The Symmetrical Family*.

Young and Willmott argue that the Stage 2 family has largely disappeared. For all social classes, but particularly the working class, the Stage 3 family predominates. This family is characterized by 'the separation of the immediate, or nuclear family from the extended family'. The trade union of women is disbanded and the husband returns to the family circle.

Life for the Stage 3 nuclear family is largely home-centred, particularly when the children are young. Free time is spent doing chores and odd jobs around the house and leisure is mainly 'home-based', for example watching television. The conjugal bond is strong and relationships between husband and wife are increasingly 'companionate'. In the home 'They shared their work; they shared their time'. The nuclear family has become a largely self-contained, self-reliant unit.

Young and Willmott use the term **symmetrical family** to describe the nuclear family of Stage 3. 'Symmetry' refers to an arrangement in which the opposite parts are similar in shape and size. With respect to the symmetrical family, conjugal roles, although not the same – wives still have the main responsibility for raising the children although husbands help – are similar in terms of the contribution made by each spouse to the running of the household. They share many of the chores, they share decisions, they work together, yet there is still men's work and women's work. Conjugal roles are not interchangeable but they are symmetrical in important respects.

Reasons for the rise of the symmetrical family

Young and Willmott give the following reasons for the transition from Stage 2 to Stage 3 families.

1 A number of factors have reduced the need for kinship-based mutual aid groups. They include an increase in the real wages of the male breadwinner, a decrease in unemployment and the male mortality rate, and increased employment opportunities for women. Various provisions of the welfare state such as family allowances, sickness and unemployment benefits, and old age pensions have also reduced the need for dependence on the kinship network.

2 Increasing geographical mobility has tended to sever kinship ties. In their study of Bethnal Green, Young and Willmott showed how the extended kinship network largely ceased to operate when young couples with children moved some 20 miles away to a new council housing estate.

3 The reduction in the number of children, from an average of five or six per family in the nineteenth century to just over two in 1970, provides greater opportunities for wives to work. This in turn leads to greater symmetry within the family since both spouses are more likely to be wage earners and to share financial responsibility for the household.

4 As living standards rose, the husband was drawn more closely into the family circle since the home was a more attractive place. It became more comfortable with better amenities and a greater range of home entertainments.

Class and family life

Young and Willmott found that the home-centred symmetrical family was more typical of the working class than the middle class. They argue that members of the working class are 'more fully home-centred because they are less fully work-centred'. Partly as compensation for boring and uninvolving work, and partly because relatively little interest and energy are expended at work, manual workers tend to focus their attention on family life. Young and Willmott therefore see the nature of work as a major influence on family life.

The 'Principle of Stratified Diffusion'

In *The Symmetrical Family* Young and Willmott devise a general theory which they term the **Principle of Stratified Diffusion**. They claim that this theory explains much of the change in family life in industrial society. Put simply, the theory states that what the top of the stratification system does today, the bottom will do tomorrow. Lifestyles, patterns of consumption, attitudes and expectations will diffuse from the top of the stratification system downwards.

They argue that industrialization is the 'source of momentum', it provides the opportunities for higher living standards and so on. However, industrialization alone cannot account for the changes in family life: it cannot fully explain, for example, why the mass of the population has chosen to adopt the lifestyle of Stage 3 families. To complete the explanation, Young and Willmott maintain that the Principle of Stratified Diffusion is required.

Industrialization provides the opportunity for a certain degree of choice for the mass of the population. This choice will be largely determined by the behaviour of those at the top of the stratification system. Values, attitudes and expectations permeate down the class system; those at the bottom copy those at the top.

A Stage 4 family?

Applying the Principle of Stratified Diffusion to the future, Young and Willmott postulate a possible Stage 4 family. They examine in detail the family life of managing directors, which, in terms of their theory, should diffuse downwards in years to come. Managing directors are work-centred rather than home-centred, 'my business is my life' being a typical quote from those in the sample. Their leisure activities are less home-centred and less likely to involve their wives than those of Stage 3 families. Sport was an important area of recreation, particularly swimming and golf. The wife's role was to look after the children and the home. As such the managing director's family was more asymmetrical than the Stage 3 family.

Young and Willmott suggest that changes in production technology may provide the opportunity for the Stage 4 family to diffuse throughout the stratification system. As technology reduces routine work, a larger number of people may have more interesting and involving jobs and become increasingly work-centred. Young and Willmott admit that 'We cannot claim that our 190 managing directors were representative of managing directors generally'. However, given the evidence available, they predict that the asymmetrical Stage 4 family represents the next major development.

Evaluation

A number of features of Willmott and Young's work are open to criticism. Many feminists have attacked the concept of the 'symmetrical family' arguing that there has been little progress towards equality between husband and wife (see pp. 361–6 for details). There is also little evidence that the 'Principle of Stratified Diffusion' has led to the 'Stage 4 family' becoming typical of all strata. Married women have continued to take paid employment and few working-class families can afford to adopt the lifestyle and family arrangements of managing directors. Later research by Peter Willmott has not used or supported the concept of the 'Stage 4 family' as we will see on p. 346.

▄ The middle-class family

Contacts with kin

Many of the arguments examined in preceding sections suggest that the middle-class family should be less attached to kin beyond the nuclear unit than its working-class counterpart. The middle-class job market is more geographically mobile and more financially secure. There is therefore less opportunity and less need to maintain a wide kinship network. However, a number of studies have shown that middle-class families maintain close contacts with kin beyond the family.

Research conducted in the late 1950s by Willmott and Young in Woodford, a largely middle-class London suburb, showed that, despite the fact that kin were more geographically dispersed compared to Bethnal Green, fairly regular contacts were maintained. In Bethnal Green, 43 per cent of husbands and wives had seen their mothers in the previous 24 hours, compared to 30 per cent in Woodford. Although in Woodford there was less frequent contact with parents while the latter were employed, the frequency of contact was much the same as Bethnal Green when parents retired. On retirement, middle-class parents often moved to Woodford to live near their married children.

In their study of Swansea, South Wales, conducted in the early 1960s, Rosser and Harris found that levels of contact between parents and married children were similar to those in Bethnal Green. This applied both to middle- and working-class families. Despite the wider dispersal of kin in Swansea, improved transportation facilities (particularly the family car) made frequent contact possible. Rosser and Harris state that 'The picture that emerges, then, is of a vigorous kinship grouping wider than the elementary (nuclear) family, similar to that described in the Bethnal Green studies.' As in Bethnal Green, the Swansea families exchanged services with kin beyond the nuclear family and provided each other with support in times of need. Rosser and Harris conclude:

In Swansea, a high level of industrialization, social mobility and a wider dispersal of the family has not prevented the maintenance of high levels of contact

---

and the interchange of services between related households.

Quantity and quality of contacts

A major problem in studies of the family is the difficulty of measuring the importance of kin beyond the nuclear family. In a study of middle-class family life also carried out in Swansea, Colin Bell questions whether the frequency of actual face-to-face contacts between kin provides an accurate assessment. Bell points to the importance of contact by telephone and mail. He also distinguishes between the quantity and quality of contacts. For example, bumping into mum on a street corner in Bethnal Green may have far less significance than a formal visit to mother by her middle-class daughter. Bell found a lower level of direct face-to-face contact with kin beyond the nuclear family than in either the Woodford sample or Rosser and Harris's middle-class sample. Despite this relatively low level of contact, he argues that compared to the working class, 'Middle-class kin networks may have fewer day-to-day demands but I think that there is little evidence to suggest that they necessarily show any different affective quality.' Thus direct contact may be less frequent but the emotional bonds are the same.

Bell makes a similar point about the provision of services for kin beyond the nuclear family. They may not be as numerous as those provided in the working class, but they may be just as significant. He found that aid from parents, especially the son's father, was particularly important during the early years of marriage. It often took the form of loans or gifts to help with the deposit on a house or the expenses of the first baby. Bell concludes that kin beyond the nuclear family still play an important part in the lives of many middle-class families.

Similar conclusions were reached by Graham Allan in research conducted in a commuter village in East Anglia in the early 1970s. Although he found some evidence that the relationship between working-class wives and their mothers was particularly close, in general there was little difference between the middle- and working-class kinship networks. In both cases relationships were characterized by a 'positive concern' for the welfare of the kin regardless of the frequency of face-to-face contacts.

■ Contemporary family networks

In more recent research conducted during the 1980s in a north London suburb Peter Willmott found that contacts with kin remained important in both the middle and working class. In the area he studied about a third of the couples had moved to the district in the previous five years. Only a third of the total couples had parents or parents-in-law living within ten minutes' travelling distance. However, despite the distance between their homes, two-thirds of the couples saw relatives at least weekly. Working-class couples saw relatives more frequently than middle-class couples, but the differences were not great.

Maintaining contact was relatively easy for most families because so many had access to cars. Most also had homes that were sufficiently spacious for relatives to come and stay. Some 90 per cent had telephones which enabled them to keep in touch with relatives even if they did not meet face-to-face.

Willmott also found that 'relatives continue to be the main source of informal support and care, and that again the class differences are not marked'. For example, nearly 75 per cent had relatives who sometimes helped with babysitting and 80 per cent looked to relatives to help them when they needed to borrow money.

Evidence from America provides a similar picture. Studies from a number of cities in the USA show that, for both middle and working classes, the degree of contact and exchange of services with kin beyond the nuclear family is similar to the British pattern.

■ Janet Finch – family obligations and social change

Janet Finch has studied changes in family life using a slightly different viewpoint from the studies discussed above. In a review of research conducted by many different sociologists she has discussed the changing nature of family obligations. Her work is particularly concerned with the extent to which members of a family feel obliged to offer assistance to their kin and feel a sense of duty towards

them. This obviously also involves considering what help is given as well as the reasons behind the decision to give help. She says:

My focus is upon assistance and support which is exchanged within kin groups in adult life: Who does what, for whom and in what circumstances? In particular I am concerned to understand how far this is underscored by duty, obligation or responsibility.

Finch examines the extent to which relatives feel an obligation to provide accommodation by sharing households, to give economic, emotional or moral support, practical help, financial assistance and personal care, for example by nursing a sick relative. She considers the possibility that there was a 'Golden Age' before the Industrial Revolution in which family obligations were much stronger and family members helped each other far more.

The myth of a 'Golden Age'

Overall Finch argues that the idea of a 'Golden Age' of the family which was undermined by the Industrial Revolution is a myth. For example, she says that there is no evidence that relatives automatically assumed responsibility for elderly relatives in pre-industrial times and 'most elderly people who are married have always lived only with their spouse'. When **primogeniture** (inheritance by the first-born son) was the main principle governing inheritance, parents made little or no financial provision for children other than the eldest son in their wills. Some changes have certainly taken place: far fewer children are permanently looked after by relatives other than their own parents, and in the last 50 years a smaller proportion of the single elderly has been living with relatives. However, such changes are largely a result of demographic trends. Because life expectancy has risen there are fewer orphans and more elderly people in the population. Because average family size has gone down since the last century there are fewer children with whom the rising numbers of elderly might live.

In any case, according to Finch, much of the assistance given in the past was based upon mutual self-interest rather than a selfless sense of obligation to family members. People who took relatives' children into their households often employed them as servants. When kin outside the immediate nuclear family have lived with each other in the past this has often been for the purpose of sharing housing costs. Before, during and since the Industrial Revolution most kin relationships have not been characterized by unconditional giving by some relatives to others, but have been based upon 'reciprocal exchange on the basis of mutual advantage'.

One exception to this general rule has been the relationship between parents and children. It has been and remains common for parents to help their children without expecting equivalent support in exchange.

Factors influencing family obligations

Finch stresses that the extent and nature of family obligations felt by people varies enormously from one family to another and is shaped partly by interpersonal relationships between the individuals involved. Nevertheless family obligations are influenced by social factors such as region, gender, ethnicity, generation and the economic situation of the family and its members. Kin relationships remain special to people and people generally feel more of a sense of duty to members of their family than to anybody else. However, having independence is also important to members of families and reliance upon kin is usually seen as a last resort rather than the first. The family can offer a safety net in times of need and it can offer mutual benefits but people try to avoid relying upon it too much.

These characteristics of family relationships are not new according to Finch. Although the circumstances in which family relationships are made have changed enormously since pre-industrial times, there is no evidence that in general there is less sense of obligation to kin than there was in the past.

■ The isolated nuclear family?

The evidence we have presented so far under the heading of 'The family and industrialization' provides a somewhat confusing picture. On the one

hand there is Talcott Parsons's isolated nuclear family, and on the other a large body of evidence suggesting that kin beyond the nuclear family play an important part in family life and the importance of that role may not have been diminishing.

In America a number of researchers have rejected Parsons's concept of the isolated nuclear family. Sussman and Burchinal, for example, argue that the weight of evidence from a large body of research indicates that the modern American family is far from isolated. They maintain that the family can only be properly understood 'by rejection of the isolated nuclear family concept'.

Parsons replied to his critics in an article entitled 'The normal American family'. He argues that close relationships with kin outside the nuclear family are in no way inconsistent with the concept of the isolated nuclear family. Parsons states that 'the very psychological importance for the individual of the nuclear family in which he was born and brought up would make any such conception impossible'.

However, he maintains that the nuclear family is structurally isolated. It is isolated from other parts of the social structure such as the economic system. For example, it does not form an integral part of the economic system as in the case of the peasant farming family in traditional Ireland.

In addition, the so-called 'extended families' of modern industrial society 'do not form firmly structured units of the social system'. Relationships with kin beyond the nuclear family are not obligatory; they are a matter of individual choice. In this sense, 'extended kin constitute a resource which may be selectively taken advantage of within considerable limits'. Thus extended families do not form 'firmly structured units' as in the case of the classic extended family or the family in kinship-based societies.

Evidence from Rosser and Harris's Swansea research supports Parsons's arguments. Rosser and Harris maintain that the nuclear family is 'a basic structural unit of the society' and though kinship relationships beyond the nuclear family are important to individuals, in terms of the social structure as a whole they are 'not of major and critical importance'.

The Swansea study revealed a 'vast variation' in kinship relationships. Members of some families were in daily contact with kin beyond the nuclear family; members of other families rarely saw their relatives. Janet Finch's review of recent family research also found a great variety of relationships within families. This is the expected finding in view of Parsons's emphasis upon individual choice. It supports his claim that extended families are not 'firmly structured units of the social system'.

■ The 'modified extended family'

In order to clear up the confusion surrounding the term 'isolated nuclear family', Eugene Litwak argues that a new term, the **modified extended family** should be introduced to describe the typical family in modern industrial society. Litwak defines the modified extended family as:

> a coalition of nuclear families in a state of partial dependence. Such partial dependence means that nuclear family members exchange significant services with each other, thus differing from the isolated nuclear family, as well as retain considerable autonomy (that is not bound economically or geographically) therefore differing from the classical extended family. (Quoted in Morgan 1975, p. 65.)

The 'modified elementary family'

Graham Allan accepts Litwak's view that kin outside the nuclear family continue to be important in industrial society. On the basis of his own research in a commuter village in East Anglia, he argues that in normal circumstances non-nuclear kin do not rely on each other. In many families there may be little exchange of significant services most of the time. However, in most families the members do feel an obligation to keep in touch. For example, very few married children break off relationships with their parents altogether, and brothers and sisters usually maintain contact. Although significant services are not usually exchanged as a matter of course, kin frequently recognize an obligation to help each other in times of difficulty or crisis.

Unlike Litwak, Allan believes that these kinds of relationships are confined to an inner or 'elementary' family consisting of wives and husbands, their parents, children, brothers and sisters. The obligations do not extend to uncles, aunts, nephews, nieces, cousins or more distant kin. Allan therefore prefers the term **modified elementary family** to modified extended family, since to him it more accurately describes the range of kin who are important to an individual.

The 'dispersed extended family'

On the basis of research carried out in London in the 1980s, Peter Willmott has reached broadly similar conclusions to Litwak and Allan. He claims that the **dispersed extended family** is becoming dominant in Britain. It consists of two or more related families who cooperate with each other even though they live some distance apart. Contacts are fairly frequent, taking place on average perhaps once a week, but less frequent than they were amongst extended families who lived close together. Cars, public transport and telephones make it possible for dispersed extended families to keep in touch. Members of dispersed extended families do not rely on each other on a day-to-day basis.

Like Litwak, Willmott sees each nuclear family unit as only partially dependent upon extended kin. Much of the time the nuclear family is fairly self-sufficient but in times of emergency the existence of extended kin might prove invaluable. Thus Willmott argues that in modern Britain 'although kinship is largely chosen, it not only survives but most of the time flourishes'.

In this section we have focused on the changes in household composition and kinship networks that have accompanied industrialization in Britain. We will now examine the extent to which the idea of a 'typical family' is accurate.

■ Family diversity

Although some historians such as Michael Anderson have pointed to a variety of household types in pre-industrial times and during industrialization, it has generally been assumed that a single type of family is the dominant one in any particular era. Whether the modern family is regarded as nuclear, modified extended, modified elementary or dispersed extended, the assumption has been that this type of family is central to people's experiences in modern industrial societies. However, recent research has suggested that such societies are characterized by a plurality of household and family types, and the idea of a typical family is misleading.

The 'cereal packet image' of the family

Ann Oakley has described the image of the typical or 'conventional' family. She says 'conventional families are nuclear families composed of legally married couples, voluntarily choosing the parenthood of one or more (but not too many) children'.

Leach has called this the 'cereal packet image of the family'. The image of the happily married couple with two children is prominent in advertising and the 'family-sized' packets of cereals and other types of product are aimed at just this type of grouping. It tends also to be taken for granted that this type of family has its material needs met by the male breadwinner, while the wife has a predominantly domestic role.

Households in Britain

The view that this image equals reality has been attacked by Robert and Rhona Rapoport. They drew attention to the fact that in 1978, for example, just 20 per cent of families consisted of married couples with children in which there was a single breadwinner. There has been a steady decline in the number of households consisting of married couples with dependent children from 38 per cent in 1961 to 24 per cent in 1992. There has been a corresponding increase in single person households in the same period with the proportion of people living in single-parent families more than quadrupling from 2.5 per cent to 10.1 per cent. We will discuss single-parent families in more detail on pp. 349–51.

A global trend

According to Rhona Rapoport the decline of conventional family forms and the increasing diversity is not confined to Britain. She sees it as part of a global trend. She quotes figures showing a movement towards diverse family structures in very different European countries. In Finland the percentage of households consisting of a nuclear family declined from 63.8 per cent in 1950 to 60 per cent in 1980. In Sweden the decline was from 52.4 per cent in 1960 to 42.6 per cent in 1980 and in East Germany from 56.7 per cent in 1957 to 48.7 per cent in 1977. She also points to an enormous increase throughout Europe in the proportion of married women who have paid employment which suggests there are changing roles for men and women within marriage and consequently new family forms are developing.

Types of diversity

The fact that the 'conventional family' no longer makes up a majority of households or families is only one aspect of diversity identified by the Rapoports. They identify five distinctive elements of family diversity in Britain.

1 First, there is what they term **organizational diversity**. By this they mean there are variations in family structure, household type, patterns of kinship network, and differences in the division of labour within the home. For example, there are the differences between conventional families, one-parent families, and **dual-worker families**, in which husband and wife both work.

There are also increasing numbers of **reconstituted families**. The reconstituted family is the second 'emerging form' identified by the Rapoports. These families are formed after divorce and remarriage. This situation can lead to a variety of family forms. The children from the marriages of the new spouses may live together in the newly reconstituted family, or may live with the original spouses of the new couple. Although it might be seen to reflect a failure to create a happy family life, some adults in a reconstituted family may find positive aspects of reconstitution.

On the basis of a study conducted in Sheffield, Jacqueline Burgoyne and David Clark claim that some individuals in this situation see themselves as 'pioneers of an alternative lifestyle'. They may choose to remain unmarried to their new partner, and may find advantages in having more than two parental figures in their children's lives. Sometimes they believe that step-siblings gain from living together.

Some couples in Sheffield felt a considerable sense of achievement from the successful reconstitution of a family. (For further details on divorce, see pp. 371–7.)

2 The second type of diversity is **cultural diversity**. There are differences in the lifestyles of families of different ethnic origins and different religious beliefs. There are differences between families of Asian, West Indian and Cypriot origin, not to mention other ethnic minority groups. (We discuss ethnic family diversity in more detail on pp. 351–4.) Differences in lifestyle between Catholic and Protestant families may also be an important element of diversity.

3 There are differences between middle- and working-class families in terms of relationships between adults and the way children are socialized.

4 There are differences that result from the stage in the lifecycle of the family. Newly married couples without children may have a different family life to those with dependent children and those whose children have achieved adult status.

5 The fifth factor identified by the Rapoports as producing family diversity is **cohort**. This refers to the periods at which the family has passed through different stages of the family lifecycle. Cohort affects the life experiences of the family. For example, those families whose children were due to enter the labour market in the 1980s may be different from others: the high rates of unemployment during that period may have increased the length of time for which those children were dependent on their parents.

Regional diversity

In addition to these five aspects of diversity identified by the Rapoports, David Eversley and Lucy Bonnerjea point to **regional diversity**. They argue that there tend to be distinctive patterns of family life in different areas of Great Britain.

1 In what they term 'the sun belt' (the affluent southern parts of England) two-parent upwardly mobile families are typical. Eversley and Bonnerjea claim that this area attracts **family builders**.

2 They describe a number of coastal regions as the 'geriatric wards'. Much of the south coast (from Cornwall to Sussex, for example) has a

disproportionate number of retired couples without dependent children, and widows and widowers.

3 Older industrial areas suffering from long-term decline tend to have fairly conventional and traditional family structures.

4 Inner-city areas tend to have greater concentrations of both one-parent and ethnic minority families.

5 What they describe as 'newly declining industrial areas' (particularly likely to be found in the Midlands) have more diverse family patterns.

6 The final type of region identified by Eversley and Bonnerjea is the truly rural area. Here, the family-based farm tends to produce strong kinship networks.

The significance of family diversity

According to the Rapoports, a fundamental change is taking place in British family life. Although there has always been some degree of family diversity they believe that both the amount and its importance have increased. The Rapoports claim that diversity is no longer simply the result of economic misfortune and the failure to achieve what was traditionally regarded as a happy family life. They argue that more people are now choosing to have different types of family life. Furthermore they claim that it is increasingly socially acceptable to avoid basing your life around the 'conventional' family. They say:

Families in Britain today are in a transition from coping in a society in which there was a single over-riding norm of what family life should be like to a society in which a plurality of norms are recognised as legitimate, indeed, desirable.

The Rapoports welcome these changes, seeing the tolerance of family diversity as an important element of human rights.

Before evaluating the Rapoports' claim that there is no longer a consensus on what type of family life is desirable, two particularly important sources of diversity – single parenthood and ethnicity – will be examined in more detail.

The increase in single parenthood

As we mentioned earlier, single-parent families have became increasingly common in Britain. According to government statistics, in 1961 2.5 per cent of the population lived in households consisting of a lone parent with dependent children but by 1992 this had more than quadrupled to 10.1 per cent. Between 1972 and 1991 the percentage of children living in single-parent families increased from 8 per cent to 18 per cent. The Joseph Rowntree Foundation has quoted figures showing that in 1989 lone-parent families made up 14 per cent of all British families. Of the main Western European countries only Denmark had such a high proportion. In Spain, Ireland, Italy and Portugal the figure was 10 per cent or less while in Greece it was under 5 per cent. Throughout Europe and in advanced industrial countries such as Japan and the USA, the proportions have been increasing.

Although useful, such figures on single parenthood need to be interpreted with caution. They provide only a snapshot picture of the situation at one point in time and do not represent the changing family life for many individuals. Many more children than the above figures seem to suggest spend part of their childhood in a single-parent family, but many fewer spend all their childhood in one. Single parenthood is often a transitional state before, between or after periods where a family has two parents. Greg Duncan and Willard Rodgers have estimated from survey data on children born between 1967 and 1969 in the USA that less than a third of children born into a single-parent family stayed in one throughout their childhood.

It should also be borne in mind that many children who live in a single-parent household do see and spend time with their other parent. Furthermore even in two-parent families one parent (usually the mother) might be responsible for the vast majority of the childcare. In terms of children's experience then, the distinction between single-parent and two-parent households is not clear cut.

The causes of single parenthood

Single-parent families can result from the death of one spouse, divorce, and separation (desertion by one partner or from a deliberate choice). The *General Household Survey* of 1990 found that the vast majority of single parents were women. It showed that 18 per cent of families were headed by a lone mother, but only 2 per cent by lone fathers. Some 7 per cent of families were headed by a lone mother who was divorced, 4 per cent by one who was separated, 6 per cent by a single lone mother, and just 1 per cent by a widow.

The proportion of lone-parent families resulting from these different circumstances has been changing. Between 1971 and 1991 the proportion of single lone mothers who were divorced rose from 21 per cent to 43 per cent. There was also a substantial rise in the percentage of single lone mothers, in this case from 16 per cent to 34 per cent. On the other hand the proportion of lone mothers who were widowed fell from 21 per cent to 6 per cent. Clearly then, the rise in single parenthood is closely related both to increases in the divorce rate and to an increase in births outside marriage. We discuss the causes of the rise in divorces later in this chapter on pp. 373–5.

Some writers see the rise of single parenthood as a symptom of increased tolerance of diverse family forms. For example, the Rapoports claim that the single-parent family is an important 'emerging form' of the family which is becoming accepted as a legitimate alternative to other family structures.

However, there is little evidence that a large number of single parents see their situation as ideal and actively choose it as an alternative to dual parenthood. A number of Conservative politicians have argued that the increase in single parenthood is a consequence of the welfare state. John Selwyn Gummer has claimed that there are 'perverse incentives' for young women to become pregnant so that it increases their chance of being allocated council housing. In July 1993 two other Conservative ministers, Peter Lilley and John Redwood, expressed concern about the cost of welfare payments to single-parent families and the possibility that the availability of such payments encouraged single parenthood.

On the other hand, there are a number of reasons for supposing that the welfare state is not responsible for the increases.

1 First, some commentators do not believe that lone parenthood gives advantages to those seeking local authority housing. In 1993 John Perry, policy director of the Institute of Housing, said:

> I've not been able to find a single housing authority which discriminates in favour of single parents over

couples with children. The homeless get priority, but there is no suggestion that a homeless single parent gets priority over a homeless couple. (Quoted in *The Independent on Sunday* 11 July 1993.)

2 Second, as the next section indicates, single parents who are reliant upon benefit tend to live in poor housing conditions and to have low standards of living. There is little material incentive to become a single parent.

3 Third, there is evidence that a large majority of single parents do not wish to be reliant on state benefits. They would prefer to work for a living but find it impractical to do so. A 1991 DSS survey found that 90 per cent of single parents would like to work at some point in the future and 55 per cent would start work immediately if they could obtain suitable help with childcare. (Quoted in *The Observer* 11 July 1993.)

David Morgan suggests that the rise in lone parenthood could partly be due to changing relationships between men and women. He says important factors causing the rise could include 'the expectations that women and men have of marriage and the growing opportunities for women to develop a life for themselves outside marriage or long-term cohabitations'.

A longer term trend that helps to account for the increase could be a decline in the stigma attached to single parenthood. This is reflected in the decreasing use of terms such as 'illegitimate children' and 'unmarried mothers' which seem to imply some deviation from the norms of family life, and their replacement by concepts such as 'single-parent families' which do not carry such negative connotations. The reduction in the stigma of single parenthood could relate to 'the weakening of religious or community controls over women'.

The consequences of single parenthood

Single parenthood has increasingly become a contentious issue with some arguing that it has become a serious problem for society. For example, in a letter to *The Times* in 1985 Lady Scott said:

A vast majority of the population would still agree, I think, that the normal family is an influence for good in society and that one-parent families are bad news. Since not many single parents can both earn a living and give children the love and care they need, society has to support them; the children suffer through lacking one parent. (Quoted in Fletcher 1985, p. 151.)

Similar sentiments have been expressed by British Conservative politicians and have begun to influence social policies (see pp. 378–80). Sociologists such as Charles Murray have even gone so far as to claim that single parenthood has contributed to creating a whole new strata of society, the **underclass**, a claim we consider in detail on pp. 91–7. However, while most commentators agree that single parenthood can create problems for individual parents, many sociologists do not see it as a social problem and some believe that it is a sign of social progress. As Sarah McLanahan and Karen Booth have said:

Some view the mother-only family as an indicator of social disorganization, signalling the 'demise of the family'. Others regard it as an alternative family form consistent with the emerging economic independence of women.

Single parenthood and living standards

However single parenthood is viewed, there is little doubt that it tends to be associated with low living standards. The *General Household Survey* of 1990 found that single-parent families were disadvantaged in comparison to other British families in numerous ways. They were less likely to own their own homes and more likely to live in council accommodation and/or flats. For example only 37 per cent of lone parents but 76 per cent of other families were owner–occupiers. Lone mothers had less chance of being in work than mothers living with partners, and were likely to have lower educational qualifications. Lone-parent families also had much lower average incomes. Some 70 per cent of lone-mother families had an income below £150 per week in 1990 compared to 10 per cent of families consisting of married couples and dependent children.

Many of these differences stem from the likelihood of lone-parent families relying upon benefit.

British government figures show that in 1961 one in six lone parents received government benefits but by 1993 over three-quarters did so. According to DSS figures from 1993, the average single parent with one child received just £67.55 per week in income support although they might in addition receive extra child allowance and housing benefit to cover rent or mortgage payments.

Other effects

More controversial than the low average living standards of lone parents is the question of the psychological and social effects on children raised in such families. Sara McLanahan and Karen Booth have listed the findings of a number of American studies which seem to indicate that children are harmed by single parenthood. These studies have claimed that such children have lower earnings and experience more poverty as adults; children of mother-only families are more likely to become lone parents themselves, and they are more likely to become delinquent and engage in drug abuse.

The findings of such studies must be treated with much caution. As McLanahan and Booth themselves point out, the differences outlined above stem partly from the low income of lone-parent families and not directly from the absence of the second parent from the household.

E.E. Cashmore has questioned the assumption that children brought up by one parent are worse off than those brought up by two. Cashmore argues that it is often preferable for a child to live with one caring parent than with one caring and one uncaring parent, particularly if the parents are constantly quarrelling and the marriage has all but broken down.

Cashmore also suggests that single parenthood can have attractions for the parent, particularly for mothers since conventional family life may benefit men more than women. He says:

Given the 'darker side of family life' and the unseen ways in which the nuclear unit serves 'male power' rather than the interests of women, the idea of parents breaking free of marriage and raising children single-handed has its appeals.

It can give women greater independence than other family situations. However, Cashmore does acknowledge that many lone mothers who are freed from dependence on a male partner end up becoming dependent on the state and facing financial hardship. He concludes that 'Lone parents do not need a partner so much as a partner's income.'

David Morgan does believe that the evidence suggests that the children of single parents fare less well than those from two-parent households. He qualifies this by saying that 'we still do not know enough about what causes these differences'. As with the effects of financial hardships, the children could be affected by the stigma attached to coming from a single-parent family. Morgan argues that 'It is possible, for example, that school teachers may be more likely to label a child as difficult if they have the knowledge that a particular child comes from a single-parent household.'

For Morgan, it is very difficult to disentangle the direct and indirect effects on children of being brought up in a single-parent household and therefore dangerous to make generalizations about such effects.

▮ Ethnicity and family diversity

Ethnicity can be seen as one of the most important sources of family diversity in Britain. Immigrant groups, and their descendants, from different cultural backgrounds may introduce family forms which differ significantly from those in the country to which they emigrate.

British sociologists have paid increasing attention to the family patterns of ethnic minority groups. They have been particularly concerned to establish the extent to which the family relationships typical of the societies of origin of the ethnic minorities have been modified within the British context. Thus sociologists have compared ethnic minority families in Britain with families both in the country of their origin and with other British families.

Although some changes in the traditional family life of these groups might be expected, the degree to which they change could provide important evidence about the theory of increasing family diversity. If it is true that cultural diversity is becoming increasingly accepted in Britain, then these families could be expected to change little. If, however, the families of ethnic minorities are

Figure 6.1   Households: by type of household and ethnic group

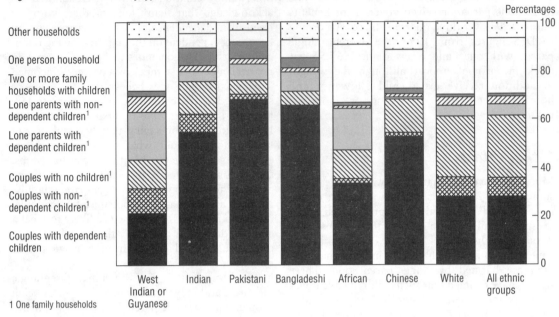

Other households

One person household

Two or more family
households with children

Lone parents with non-
dependent children[1]

Lone parents with
dependent children[1]

Couples with no children[1]

Couples with non-
dependent children[1]

Couples with dependent
children

1 One family households

West Indian or Guyanese   Indian   Pakistani   Bangladeshi   African   Chinese   White   All ethnic groups

(*Source: Social Trends 22,* 1992, HMSO, London, 1992, p. 42.)

becoming more similar to those of other members of British society, family diversity resulting from ethnic differences might be only temporary.

Statistical evidence

Statistical evidence from government sources does suggest that these are some differences in the prevalence of different household types in different ethnic groups. Figure 6.1 shows that Asian ethnic minority households are significantly more likely than the average to include a couple with dependent children or two or more families, but they are less likely to include a single person. West Indian/Guyanese households include a relatively high proportion of lone parents and a relatively low proportion of couples without children or couples with dependent children. In 1989–91 51 per cent of West Indian mothers were lone mothers compared to just over 10 per cent of Pakistani/Bangladeshi mothers.

We will now examine the significance of variations in family life by ethnic group.

South Asian families

Roger Ballard has examined South Asian families in Britain and compared them to families in South Asia itself. Migration from this area began in the 1950s and was mainly from the Punjab, Gujerat and Bengal. Although there are important differences in family life within these groups which stem from area of origin, religion and caste, Ballard identifies some features generally held in common.

Families in South Asia are based traditionally around a man, his sons and grandsons, and their respective wives and unmarried daughters. These family groups ideally live and work together in large multigenerational households sharing both domestic and production tasks. In practice in the past many households were not as large as might be expected. A high death rate limited the number of generations living together, and sons might establish different households after their father's death when the family land was divided up.

Changes in South Asian families

Ballard found that some changes had taken place in Asian families in Britain. Women were increasingly working outside the home, and production was less frequently family based because wage labour provided the most common source of income. Ballard claims that married couples in Britain expect more independence from their kin. In some families extended kinship networks are less important than they traditionally are because some of the kin remain in South Asia or live in distant parts of Britain. Families were also split into smaller domestic units, partly because British housing was rarely suited to the needs of large groupings.

The strengthening of South Asian families

Despite these changes, Ballard says:

> It should not be assumed that such upheavals have either undermined or stood in contradiction to family unity. On the contrary migration has taken place within the context of familial obligations and has if anything strengthened rather than weakened them.

Many migrants found British culture seemed to attach little value to family honour and placed relatively little emphasis on maintaining kinship ties. As a result many first-generation immigrants became conservative and cautious in their attitudes to family life. They were vigilant in ensuring that standards of behaviour in the family did not slip and kept a close check on their children.

Ballard found that many children had the experience of two cultures. They behaved in ways that conformed to the culture of the wider society for part of the time, but at home conformed to their ethnic subculture. Although children increasingly expected to have some say in their marriage partners, they generally did not reject the principle of arranged marriages.

The majority of families relied on wage labour but some of the more successful began to establish family businesses (such as buying a shop) which

provided a new focus for the family's economic activities.

Ballard found that despite the distances involved, most families retained links with their village of origin in Asia. Extended kinship links could stretch over thousands of miles. He found that money was sometimes sent to help to support family members who remained in Asia.

In Britain, despite the housing problems, close family ties remained. By living close together, or buying adjoining houses and knocking through a connecting door, people were able to retain strong family links.

Ballard concluded that South Asians had suffered comparatively little disruption to family life as a result of settling in Great Britain.

Cypriot families in Britain

Similar conclusions were reached by Robin Oakley in his study of Cypriot families in Britain. This group numbers around 140,000, and in some areas, particularly London, the Cypriot community has been established since just after the First World War. Most of the immigration took place in the 20 years following the Second World War.

According to Oakley, Cypriots traditionally have very strong extended family ties, and parents retain strong connections with married children. There are taboos against seeking outside help to solve family problems, and families are not child-centred – children are expected to pull their weight like other family members. Oakley found little evidence that these patterns had changed significantly among British Cypriot families despite the length of time some of them had been in Britain. There were relatively few elderly Cypriots in Britain and for this reason extended kinship links were somewhat weaker than in Cyprus itself.

Families in the West Indies

Research into the family life of West Indians in Britain and in the Caribbean has found greater diversity in their cultural patterns. Jocelyn Barrow argues there are three main West Indian family types in the Caribbean.

1 The **conventional nuclear family,** or 'Christian marriage', which is often little different from nuclear families in Britain. Families of this type tend to be

typical of the more religious or economically successful groups in the population.

2 The second main type found in the West Indies, the **common-law family**, is more frequently found among the less economically successful. An unmarried couple lives together and looks after children who may or may not be their biological offspring.

3 The third type Barrow calls the **mother household**, in which the mother or grandmother of children is head of the household and for most of the time at least the household contains no adult males. This type of household often relies a good deal on the help and support of female kin living nearby to enable the head of the household to fulfil her family responsibilities.

West Indian families in Britain

To a large extent research has shown that a similar mixture of family types exists in Britain amongst West Indian groups. Geoffrey Driver, however, has found that in some cases what appears to be a nuclear family is rather different beneath the surface. He uses the example of a family called the Campbells. In this family the wife took on primary responsibility both for running the household and for being the breadwinner after her husband lost his job. In reality then, this was a mother-centred family, even though it contained an adult male.

Barrow found that mother-centred families in Britain, whether or not they contained an adult male, could rely less on the support of female kin than they could in the West Indies. They were much less likely to live close to the relevant kin, and in some cases appropriate kin were still in the West Indies, and could not therefore be called on to provide assistance.

However, she discovered that equivalent networks tended to build up in areas with high concentrations of West Indians. Informal help with childcare and other domestic tasks is common among neighbours, and self-help projects such as pre-school playgroups are frequent features of West Indian communities.

Ethnicity and family diversity – conclusion

The general picture provided by these studies, then, suggests that immigrants and their descendants have adapted their family life to fit British circumstances, but have not fundamentally altered the relationships on which their traditional family life was based. This would suggest that the existence of a variety of ethnic groups has indeed contributed to the diversity of family types to be found in Britain. These ethnic minorities have succeeded in retaining many of the culturally distinctive features of their family life.

Nevertheless, there is also evidence of changes taking place in the families of ethnic minorities, and British culture may have more effect on future generations. The Cypriot example, though, demonstrates the considerable resilience of the culture of an ethnic group, some of whom have been settled in Britain for well over half a century.

■ Robert Chester – the British neo-conventional family

In a strong attack upon the idea that fundamental changes are taking place in British family life, Robert Chester argues that the changes have been only minor. He claims that the evidence advanced by writers such as the Rapoports is misleading, and the basic features of family life have remained largely unchanged for the vast majority of the British population since the Second World War. He argues:

> Most adults still marry and have children. Most children are reared by their natural parents. Most people live in a household headed by a married couple. Most marriages continue until parted by death. No great change seems currently in prospect.

Percentage of people versus percentage of households

Chester believes that a snapshot of household types at a particular time does not provide a valid picture of the British family.

The first point that Chester makes is that a very different picture is produced if the percentage of people in various types of household is calculated, instead of the percentage of households of various types. Households containing parents and children contain a greater percentage of the population than the percentage of households they make up. This is because family households tend to have more members than other types of household.

Chester's arguments were based upon figures

Table 6.1   Households and people in households in Great Britain 1981 and 1992

Type of household	% of households 1981	% of people 1981	% of people 1992
One person	22	8	11.1
Married couple	26	20	23.4
Married couple with dependent children	32	49	39.9
Married couple with independent children	8	10	10.9
Lone parent with dependent children	4	5	10.1
Other	9	8	4.6

(*Source*: Modified from *Social Trends* 13 and 24.)

from 1981. As Table 8.1 shows, the way the figures are calculated does make a difference. In 1981 40 per cent of households were made up of parents and children but over 57 per cent of people lived in such households.

The nuclear family and the life cycle

The second point made by Chester is that life cycles make it inevitable that at any one time some people will not be a member of a nuclear family household. Many of those who live in other types of household will either have experienced living in a nuclear family in the past, or will do so in the future. He says 'The 8 per cent living alone are mostly the elderly widowed, or else younger people who are likely to marry.' He describes the parents–children household as 'one which is normal and is still experienced by the vast majority'.

The 'neo-conventional family'

According to Chester there is little evidence that people are choosing to live on a long-term basis in alternatives to the nuclear family. However, he does accept that some changes are taking place in family life. In particular many families are no longer 'conventional' in the sense that the husband is the sole breadwinner. He accepts that women are increasingly making a contribution to household finances by taking paid employment outside the home.

However, he argues that although 58 per cent of wives, according to his figures, work, often they only do so for part of their married lives, and frequently on a part-time basis. Many give up work for the period when their children are young; a minority of married mothers (49 per cent) are employed, and only 14 per cent of working married mothers have full-time jobs. Because of such figures he argues that 'The pattern is of married women withdrawing from the labour force to become mothers, and some of them taking (mostly part-time) work as their children mature.'

Although he recognizes this as an important change in family life compared to the past, he does not see it as a fundamental alteration in the family. He calls this new family form – in which wives have some involvement in the labour market – the **neo-conventional family**. It is little different from the conventional family apart from the increasing numbers of wives working for at least part of their married lives.

Conclusion – family diversity in Britain

While Chester makes an important point in stressing that nuclear families remain very common and feature in most people's lives, he perhaps overstates his case. As Table 6.1 shows, there has been a continuing reduction in the proportion of people living in parents-and-children households, from 57.7 per cent in 1981 to 50.8 per cent in 1992. The percentages of people living alone or in lone-parent households have increased. Thus since

Chester was writing there has been a slow but steady drift away from living in nuclear families in Britain.

The position has perhaps best been summed up by Kathleen Kiernan and Malcolm Wicks in saying 'Although still the most prominent form, the nuclear family is for increasing numbers of individuals only one of several possible family types that they experience during their lives.'

Diversity and European family life

At the end of the 1980s the European Co-ordination Centre for Research and Documentation in Social Sciences organized a cross-cultural study of family life in 14 European nations. These were Belgium, Finland, France, the German Democratic Republic and Federal Republic of Germany (the study was carried out before re-unification), Great Britain, Hungary, Italy, The Netherlands, Norway, Poland, Sweden, and the then Soviet Union and Yugoslavia.

The findings of individual national studies were analysed and compared by Katja Boh. She tried to 'trace the tendencies in changes of family patterns' in order to:

answer the crucial question whether these tendencies converge, which would mean that family patterns in European family life are becoming more similar, or the recent political and economic developments have produced differences contributing to a greater diversity in family life patterns.

Evidence of diversity

In most aspects of family life Boh found a wide range of patterns in different countries.

1 The likelihood of married women working varied greatly, with well over 80 per cent in work in the Soviet Union but less than one third in Belgium and The Netherlands.

2 Marriage rates appeared to be diverging. In 1932

Poland had the highest rate at 8.3 marriages per thousand of the population; Norway had the lowest at 6.2. By 1984 the gap between the highest rate (10.3 in the USSR) and the lowest (4 in Sweden) was much greater.

3 Boh noted that cohabitation as an alternative to marriage was becoming common in Sweden and Finland but remained comparatively rare in Belgium and Italy.

4 She also discovered that the number of children born per woman was greatest in the Soviet Union and Poland and lowest in the Federal Republic of Germany and The Netherlands.

5 As we discussed previously, single parents are much more common in some European countries than others. Boh found the highest rates in 1981 were in Finland whilst the lowest were in the Soviet Union.

Common trends

Although most of the evidence showed that family life was very different in different European countries, some evidence did point to certain trends being extremely widespread. All European countries had experienced rising divorce rates and many had made it easier to get divorced. Cohabitation appeared to have become more common in most countries and the birth rate had declined everywhere.

Convergence in diversity

The existence of diverse patterns of family life but some common trends in Europe seems at first sight to be contradictory. However, Katja Boh argues that together they produce a consistent pattern of **convergence in diversity**. While family life retains considerable variations from country to country, throughout Europe a greater range of family types is being accepted as legitimate and normal. This has been caused by:

Increasing gender symmetry in work patterns, more freedom in conjugal choice and a more hedonistic view of marriage and love, premarital and experimental sexuality, higher marriage instability and alternative forms of 'living together', decreasing fertility and change in forms of parenting.

Boh concludes:

Whatever the existing patterns are, they are characterised by the acceptance of diversity that has given men and women the possibility to choose inside the

boundaries of available options the life pattern that is best adapted to their own needs and aspirations.

Having surveyed the ways in which the structure of the family may have changed over the years, we will now investigate whether the functions of the family have also changed.

The changing functions of the family

The loss of functions

Many sociologists argue that the family has lost a number of its functions in modern industrial society. Institutions such as businesses, political parties, schools, and welfare organizations now specialize in functions formerly performed by the family. Talcott Parsons argues that the family has become:

on the 'macroscopic' levels, almost completely functionless. It does not itself, except here and there, engage in much economic production; it is not a significant unit in the political power system; it is not a major direct agency of integration of the larger society. Its individual members participate in all these functions, but they do so as individuals, not in their roles as family members.

However, this does not mean that the family is declining in importance – it has simply become more specialized. Parsons maintains that its role is still vital. By structuring the personalities of the young and stabilizing the personalities of adults, the family provides its members with the psychological training and support necessary to meet the requirements of the social system. Parsons concludes that:

the family is more specialized than before, but not in any general sense less important, because society is dependent *more* exclusively on it for the performance of *certain* of its vital functions.

Thus the loss of certain functions by the family has made its remaining functions more important.

This view is supported by N. Dennis who

argues that impersonal bureaucratic agencies have taken over many of the family's functions. As a result, the warmth and close supportive relationships which existed when the family performed a large range of functions have largely disappeared.

Dennis argues that in the impersonal setting of modern industrial society, the family provides the only opportunity 'to participate in a relationship where people are perceived and valued as whole persons'. Outside the family, individuals must often interact with strangers in terms of a number of roles. Adopting roles such as employee, customer, teacher and student, they are unable to express many aspects of themselves or develop deep and supportive relationships. Dennis argues:

marriage has become the only institution in which the individual can expect esteem and love. Adults have no-one on whom they have the right to lean for this sort of support at all comparable with their right to lean on their spouse.

Young and Willmott make a similar point, arguing that the emotional support provided by family relationships grows in importance as the family loses many of its functions. They claim that the family:

can provide some sense of wholeness and permanence to set against the more restricted and transitory roles imposed by the specialized institutions which have flourished outside the home. The upshot is that, as the disadvantages of the new industrial and impersonal society have become more pronounced, so the family has become more prized for its power to counteract them.

The maintenance and improvement of functions

Not all sociologists would agree, however, that the family has lost many of its functions in modern industrial society. Ronald Fletcher, a British sociologist and a staunch supporter of the family, maintains that just the opposite has happened. In *The Family and Marriage in Britain* Fletcher argues that not only has the family retained its functions but those functions have 'increased in detail and importance'. Specialized institutions such as schools and hospitals have added to and improved the family's functions, rather than superseded them.

1 Fletcher maintains that the family's responsibility for socializing the young is as important as it ever was. State education has added to, rather than removed, this responsibility since 'Parents are expected to do their best to guide, encourage and support their children in their educational and occupational choices and careers.'

2 In the same way, the state has not removed the family's responsibility for the physical welfare of its members. Fletcher argues that:
   The family is still centrally concerned with maintaining the health of its members, but it is now aided by wider provisions which have been *added* to the family's situation since pre-industrial times.
   Rather than removing this function from the family, the state provision of health services has served to expand and improve it. Compared to the past, parents are preoccupied with their children's health. State health and welfare provision has provided additional support for the family and made its members more aware of the importance of health and hygiene in the home.

3 Even though Fletcher admits that the family has largely lost its function as a unit of production, he argues that it still maintains a vital economic function as a unit of consumption. Particularly in the case of the modern home-centred family, money is spent on and in the name of the family rather than the individual. Thus the modern family demands fitted carpets, three-piece suites, washing machines, television sets and 'family' cars.

Young and Willmott make a similar point with respect to their symmetrical Stage 3 family. They argue that 'In its capacity as a consumer the family has also made a crucial alliance with technology.' Industry needs both a market for its goods and a motivated workforce. The symmetrical family provides both. Workers are motivated to work by their desire for consumer durables. This desire stems from the high value they place on the family and a privatized lifestyle in the family home. This provides a ready market for the products of industry.

In this way the family performs an important economic function and is functionally related to the economic system. In Young and Willmott's words, 'The family and technology have achieved a mutual adaptation.'

Neo-Marxist views

As we have seen in previous chapters, this economic function looks rather different from a neo-Marxist perspective. Writers such as Marcuse and Gorz argue that alienation at work leads to a search for fulfilment outside work. However, the capitalist-controlled mass media, with its advertisements that proclaim the virtues of family life and associate the products of industry with those virtues, simply creates 'false needs'. With pictures of the 'Persil mum' and the happy family in the midst of its consumer durables, the myth that material possessions bring happiness and fulfilment is promoted. This myth produces the obedient, motivated worker and the receptive consumer that capitalism requires. The family man or woman is therefore ideal material for exploitation. (We analysed Marcuse's views in more detail in Chapter 4, pp. 182–3.)

Feminism and economic functions

Feminist writers have tended to disagree with the view shared by many sociologists of the family that the family has lost its economic role as a unit of production and has become simply a unit of consumption. They tend to argue that much of the work that takes place in the family is productive but it is not recognized as such because it is unpaid and it usually done by women. The contribution to economic life made by women is frequently underestimated.

The radical feminists Christine Delphy and

Diana Leonard accept that industrialization created new units of production such as factories, but deny that it removed the productive function from the family. Some productive functions have been lost, but others are performed to a much higher standard than in the past. They cite as examples 'warm and tidy rooms with attention to decor, and more complex meals with a variety of forms of cooking'. The family has taken on some new productive functions, such as giving pre-school reading tuition to children, and functions such as washing laundry and freezing food have been reintroduced to the household with the advent of new consumer products. They also point out that there are still a fair number of families which continue to act as an economic unit producing goods for the market. French farming families, which have been studied by Christine Delphy, are a case in point. (We discussed Delphy and Leonard's work in more detail earlier, see pp. 331–4. The function of housework in the economy is discussed in more detail on pp. 367–9.)

Summary

In summary, most sociologists who adopt a functionalist perspective argue that the family has lost several of its functions in modern industrial society but they maintain that the importance of the family has not declined. Rather, the family has adapted and is adapting to a developing industrial society. It remains a vital and basic institution in society.

Others dispute the claim that some of these functions have been lost, or argue that new functions have replaced the old ones. From all these viewpoints the family remains a key institution.

In this section we have discussed the various functional roles that the family performs; in the next we focus on the various roles within the family.

■ Conjugal roles

A major characteristic of Young and Willmott's symmetrical family is the degree to which spouses share domestic work and leisure activities. Relationships of this type are known as **joint conjugal roles**, as opposed to **segregated conjugal roles**.

In the Stage 2 family, conjugal roles, the marital roles of husband and wife, were largely segregated. There was a clear cut division of labour between the spouses in the household, and the husband was relatively uninvolved with domestic chores and raising the children. This segregation of conjugal roles extended to leisure. The wife associated mainly with her female kin and neighbours; the husband with his male workmates, kin and neighbours. This pattern was typical of the traditional working-class community of Bethnal Green.

In the Stage 3 symmetrical family, conjugal roles become more joint. Although the wife still has primary responsibility for housework and child-rearing, husbands become more involved, often washing clothes, ironing and sharing other domestic duties. Husband and wife increasingly share responsibility for decisions which affect the family. They discuss matters such as household finances and their children's education to a greater degree than the Stage 2 family.

Young and Willmott argue that the change from segregated to joint conjugal roles results mainly from the withdrawal of the wife from her relationships with female kin and the drawing of the husband into the family circle. We looked at the reasons they give for this in a previous section (pp. 340–2).

■ Conjugal roles and social networks

Close-knit and loose-knit networks

In a famous study entitled *Family and Social Network* Elizabeth Bott presents an interesting and original interpretation of the nature of conjugal roles. She based her study on in-depth interviews with 20 families in Greater London.

Bott found a relationship between conjugal

roles and social class, with the most extreme segregation occurring in working-class families. However, since joint conjugal roles were also found in working-class families, class alone could not explain the nature of husband–wife relationships.

Bott claims that the explanation for the variation in conjugal roles lies in social relationships which the husband and wife bring with them to the marriage. Each spouse before marriage has a social network – a number of people with whom he or she interacts on a fairly regular basis. If most or all of the members of a social network know each other and meet regularly, Bott terms the network **close-knit**: it has a high degree of **connectedness**. If, on the other hand, members of the network are linked only or mainly through one individual (that is they are either strangers or meet infrequently) Bott terms the network **loose-knit**: it has a low degree of connectedness.

Bott found that close-knit networks are associated with segregated conjugal roles; loose-knit networks with joint conjugal roles. In her words:

The degree of segregation in the role-relationship of husband and wife varies directly with the connectedness of the family's social network. The more connected the network, the greater the degree of segregation between the roles of husband and wife. The less connected the network, the smaller the degree of segregation between the roles of husband and wife.

Bott explains the relationship between social network and conjugal roles in the following way. If the husband and wife each bring a close-knit network with them to the marriage, they will be less dependent on each other for companionship and emotional support. Each will have a close-knit group of friends and relatives to fall back on. Also, with most or all members of the network knowing each other, there will tend to be more pressure on the member who gets married to keep in touch and maintain his or her obligations to the group.

By comparison, there is likely to be less emotional support from a loose-knit network and less pressure on a married member to retain contact. Spouses who bring loose-knit networks to their marriage will tend to be thrown together. They will be more dependent on each other for companionship and support; they will be more likely

to join together in domestic work and leisure activities.

Bott's study has been criticized for its methodology. Her sample consists of only 20 couples. Her measurements of network connectedness and degree of conjugal role segregation have been criticized as imprecise. However, her work remains influential and has stimulated considerable research.

Degree of domesticity

Rosser and Harris examined Bott's arguments in their study of family life in Swansea. They accept her point that there is a relationship between conjugal roles and social networks but they place greater emphasis on what happens during married life, rather than the social relationships which precede it. In particular, they argue that the 'critical factor' is the 'degree of *domesticity* of the woman involved'.

If the wife, as in the past, is tied to the house with frequent pregnancies and has to spend a large part of her life involved in child-rearing, she will tend to build up a close-knit network of female kin and neighbours who are similarly involved with domestic matters. Associated with this pattern of family life are traditional attitudes concerning the domesticity of women contained in such phrases as 'a woman's place is in the home'.

With a greater number of women in paid employment and a change in attitudes towards the female role, women are losing their former **compulsive domesticity**. Now they have less time to retain or build up a separate network of female relatives and friends. They also have less in common with them. As a result their social networks are becoming increasingly loose-knit, while their conjugal roles are becoming increasingly joint.

■ Inequality within marriage

Much of the recent research on conjugal roles has been concerned with determining the degree of inequality between husband and wife within marriage. However, different researchers have measured different aspects of inequality. Some have concentrated on the division of labour in the home: they have examined the allocation of responsibility for domestic work between husband and wife and the amount of time spent by spouses on particular tasks. Others have tried to measure the distribution of power within marriage.

Young and Willmott are amongst those who have argued that conjugal roles are increasingly becoming joint. However, most sociologists who have carried out research in this area have found little evidence that inequality within marriage has been significantly reduced.

Conjugal roles, housework and childcare

The symmetrical family

Young and Willmott argued that the change from the Stage 2 to the Stage 3 family led to a change from segregated to joint conjugal roles in the symmetrical family. Although the wife still had primary responsibility for housework and child-rearing, husbands became more involved. In fact, from their research Young and Willmott found that 72 per cent of husbands did housework other than washing up during the course of a week. They also argued that husbands and wives increasingly shared both leisure activities and decision making. As the wife withdrew from relationships with female kin, men were increasingly drawn into the family circle. (There are more details of Young and Willmott's work on pp. 340–3.)

Young and Willmott's views have been heavily criticized. Ann Oakley argues that their claim of increasing symmetry within marriage is based on inadequate methodology. Although the figure of 72 per cent sounds impressive, she points out that it is based on only one question in Young and Willmott's interview schedule: 'Do you/does your husband help at least once a week with any household jobs like washing up, making beds (helping with the children), ironing, cooking or cleaning?' Oakley notes that men who make only a very small contribution to housework would be included in the 72 per cent. She says:

A man who helps with the children once a week would be included in this percentage, so would

(presumably) a man who ironed his own trousers on a Saturday afternoon.

Ann Oakley – housework and childcare

A rather different picture of conjugal roles emerged in Oakley's own research. She collected information on 40 married women who had one child or more under the age of five, who were British or Irish born, and aged between 20 and 30. Half of her sample were working class, half were middle class and all lived in the London area.

Like Elizabeth Bott she found greater equality in terms of the allocation of domestic tasks between spouses in the middle class than the working class. However, in both classes few men had a high level of participation in housework and childcare: few marriages could be defined as egalitarian. Only 15 per cent had a high level of participation in housework by men, and 25 per cent in childcare as shown in Table 6.2.

Middle-class couples

In a more recent study S. Edgell tested Young and Willmott's theory of the symmetrical family by examining conjugal roles in a sample of 38 middle-class couples.

The symmetrical family was thought by Young and Willmott to be particularly typical of the middle class, but Edgell found little evidence to support this view. None of the couples in his sample was classified as having joint conjugal roles in relation to housework, although 44.6 per cent did have joint conjugal roles in relation to childcare. In these cases most childcare tasks were shared, although women might still spend more time on them.

Survey data

The studies of both Oakley and Edgell are based on small samples which are not representative of the population as a whole. However, studies with much larger samples have been undertaken as part

Table 6.2 Husband's participation in domestic tasks

	High	Medium	Low
Husband's participation in housework			
Working class	10%	5%	85%
Middle class	20%	45%	35%
Husband's participation in childcare			
Working class	10%	40%	50%
Middle class	40%	20%	40%

(*Source*: adapted from Ann Oakley, *The Sociology of Housework,* Basil Blackwell, Oxford, second edition, 1985, p. 137.)

Table 6.3 Household division of labour by marital status in Great Britain, 1984

Percentages	Married people Actual allocation of tasks					
	Mainly man		Mainly woman		Shared equally	
	1984	1991	1984	1991	1984	1991
Household tasks						
(percentage allocation)						
Washing and ironing	1	3	88	84	9	12
Preparation of evening meal	5	9	77	70	16	20
Household cleaning	3	4	72	68	23	27
Household shopping	6	8	54	45	39	47
Evening dishes	18	28	37	33	41	37
Organization of household money and bills	32	31	38	40	28	28
Repairs of household equipment	83	82	6	6	8	10
Childrearing						
(percentage allocation)						
Looks after the children when they are sick	1	1	63	60	35	39
Teaches the children discipline	10	9	12	17	77	73

(*Source*: *Social Trends*, 1986, p. 36 and *British Social Attitudes Survey*, 1992, 7, 102 and 103.)

of *The British Social Attitudes Survey*. Using a sample of over 1,000 married respondents it asked who usually carried out household tasks. Table 6.3 shows the results from the 1984 and 1991 surveys. Like Edgell's study it found more sharing of child-rearing than household tasks. It also showed some movement towards a more egalitarian household division of labour over time. In terms of the household tasks there was more sharing of responsibilities and there were more households in which men did most of the washing and ironing, cooking, cleaning, shopping and washing up.

However, the number of households in which men were mainly responsible for these tasks remained small minorities in 1991 and repairing household equipment was the only type of task which was more likely to be carried out by men.

Divisions of labour in the Northwest

Lancaster Regionalism Group also used survey data collected in 1988 to investigate the household division of labour. The study, carried out by a group based at Lancaster University, was confined to northwest England and the sample of 323 households was predominantly middle class and contained disproportionate numbers of couples aged 36–59. This was because the questionnaires were administered by 'A' Level Sociology students to their parents. The sample cannot therefore be considered representative, but in some other respects the methods used were an improvement on previous studies.

The Lancaster Group decided to include questions on who *last* carried out household tasks as well as who *usually* did them. They argued that when people stated that tasks were usually shared, this might disguise the fact that in many cases the task would still be carried out by women more often than men. In fact, the main effect of using this type of question was to reveal that children made a greater contribution to housework than is usually found.

The questionnaire covered a wide range of tasks, 45 in all, and yielded predictable results. The researchers found 'Husbands tend to do a very much larger proportion of tasks concerned with home maintenance, home improvement and car maintenance.' On the other hand 'Women do the vast proportion of routine housework, domestic production and childcare.' Women cooked the last meal in 79 per cent of households, last washed the clothes in 87 per cent, tidied up in 72 per cent and bathed the children in 71 per cent.

The Lancaster researchers also decided to examine the popularity of different household tasks. Clearly some tasks are less pleasant and less interesting than others, and they wanted to see whether the male or female partner was likely to get the unpopular jobs. From a list of 20 tasks, ironing, washing clothes and washing dishes were most frequently chosen as things which were never enjoyed. Although men had last washed the dishes in 23 per cent of households, in only 5 per cent had they last done the ironing and in only 3 per cent had they last washed the clothes. Respondents were not asked whether they enjoyed cleaning the toilet but as Alan Warde, one of the researchers puts it, 'cleaning lavatories is the bottom line – the

least pleasant and least prestigious of all tasks'. It was also overwhelmingly women's work: the woman had last done this in 81 per cent of households.

As well as finding out who did what, and how popular tasks were, these researchers also decided to ask whether people thought their household's division of labour was fair. They found a considerable proportion of men, 42 per cent, who thought they were doing less than their fair share. Thus there was some evidence that attitudes had changed but 'the actual pattern of behaviour remains much as it was in an earlier generation'.

Mary Boulton – women and childcare

All the above studies have focused simply upon the allocation of tasks in the home. Mary Boulton argues that they exaggerate the extent of men's involvement in childcare and she denies that questions about who does what give a true picture of conjugal roles. To her childcare:

---
is essentially about exercising responsibility for another person who is not fully responsible for herself and it entails seeing to all aspects of the child's security and well-being, her growth and development at any and all times.

Boulton claims that although men might help with particular tasks, it is their wives who retain primary responsibility for children. It is the wives who relegate non-domestic aspects of their lives to a low priority. From her own study of 50 young married mothers in London who did not have full-time jobs, only 18 per cent of husbands gave extensive help with childcare, while 36 per cent gave moderate help and 46 per cent minimal help. Husbands therefore had a major share of the responsibility for childcare in less than 20 per cent of the families she studied.

■ Conjugal roles and hours worked

Examining who does what within the home has been the most common method employed by sociologists studying conjugal roles. However, it can be argued that this may give a misleading picture, for it does not indicate how time-consuming different tasks are. It may be that the tasks carried out by women take up less time than those carried out by men.

Young and Willmott

In *The Symmetrical Family* Young and Willmott collected information on how husbands and wives spent their time. They asked members of their sample to keep a record of time spent on different tasks, including paid employment and domestic work. The results, shown in Table 6.4, draw a rather different picture to that of other studies of the way tasks are allocated.

In this study it seemed to be 'women not in paid work' (i.e. housewives without a job) who did least work, although women with part- and full-time jobs did rather more work than men. Overall the differences between men's and women's work time were not that great.

Criticisms of Young and Willmott

Graham Allan has suggested that Young and Willmott's study might underestimate the hours spent on work by women. He points out that the study involved married couples aged between 30 and 49. It therefore excluded younger married women who would be more likely to have young children, and who might therefore spend more time on domestic tasks.

Allan's criticism of Young and Willmott's work seems to be supported by Ann Oakley's estimates of the amount of time spent on housework by the women in her study. Oakley's sample were all aged between 20 and 30 and had young children. None of the sample spent less than 48 hours each week on housework. The woman who spent least time on these tasks was the only one in the sample who had a full-time job. The average number of hours spent on housework each week was 77, and this figure included five women who had part-time paid jobs.

Hours worked and social change

None of the above studies made any attempt to measure directly changes in hours worked by husbands and wives over time. Jonathan Gershuny has examined how social changes have affected the burden of work for British husbands and wives. Perhaps the most important change affecting this area of social life has been the rise in the proportion of wives taking paid employment outside the home. Sociologists such as Oakley have argued that women have increasingly been taking on a **dual burden**: they have retained primary responsibility for household tasks whilst also being expected to have paid employment. As Gershuny points out, this could lead to increased inequality between husbands and wives as a rising proportion of women suffer from this dual burden.

Gershuny examined 1974 and 1975 data from the BBC Audience Research Department and 1987 data from an Economic and Social Research Council project to discover how the share of work had changed. As Figure 6.2 shows, in 1987 the husbands of working women continued to do less than half the total paid and unpaid work done by their spouses. However, in other household types

Table 6.4 Average hous of paid and unpaid work (diary sample: married men and women aged 30 to 49)

	Men	Women working full-time	Women working part-time	Women not in paid work
Total for week				
Paid work, travel to work and household tasks	59.4	63.3	61.1	45.5

(*Source*: M. Young and P. Willmott, *The Symmetrical Family*, p. 111.)

Figure 6.2 Husband's proportion of the total (paid and unpaid) work of the spouse pair in 1974/5 and 1987. The dual burden pattern continues, but men's proportion of the total household work has risen

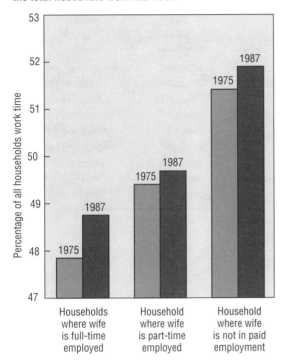

(*Source:* J. Gershuny 1992, in Abercrombie and Warde (eds) *Social Change in Contemporary Britain*, Polity Press, Cambridge, 1992, p. 86.)

husbands did more than half the total work, and in all categories the husbands' share of work had risen.

Gershuny looked particularly closely at the possibility that the dual burden of working women was increasing inequality in hours worked. Although the dual burden remained, men did seem to be making more effort to do housework when their wives were in paid work. Husbands of wives with full-time employment increased the average time spent daily on cooking and cleaning from around 20 minutes in the mid-1970s to more than 40 minutes in 1987.

Types of work

Although Gershuny found that total working hours for husbands and wives were 'about the same' he noted that 'there is still differential specialization'. Simple figures on the amount of work done by husbands and wives do not give an accu-

rate picture of the nature of their respective responsibilities. Graham Allan suggests that the work that women carry out in the home may be tedious and less satisfying than the more creative tasks that are frequently done by men. He says 'much female domestic work is monotonous and mundane, providing few intrinsic satisfactions'.

However, it can, of course, be argued that much paid work outside the home carried out by men is also alienating, although it is not usually as socially isolating as looking after young children. Gershuny's evidence shows that men were starting to take on more of the mundane household tasks, but they continued to be a primarily female responsibility.

■ Conjugal roles and power

Decision making

Another approach to studying conjugal roles is to examine power within marriage. This has usually been attempted through an examination of who makes the decisions. In terms of a common sexist phrase, it is a question of who 'wears the trousers' in the family. Edgell, in his study *Middle-Class Couples*, interviewed both husbands and wives about who made the decisions, and also asked them which decisions they thought were the most important. Wives dominated in those areas of decision making concerning interior decorations, domestic spending and children's clothes. All of these areas, though, were considered unimportant. Men dominated three areas of decision making – those relating to moving house, finance and the car – all of which were regarded as important. These findings are shown in Table 6.5.

Decisions relating to money closely reflected the overall pattern that Edgell discovered. He found that, typically, the husband decided the overall allocation of financial resources and had most say in the case of decisions involving large sums of money, whereas the wife, in every family in the sample, tended to make the minor decisions.

Agenda setting and ideological power

As we discover in Chapter 9, power is a complex concept and may be measured in a number of

Table 6.5   The importance, frequency and pattern of decision making in different areas of family life

Decision area	Perceived importance	Frequency	Decision maker (majority pattern)
Moving	Very important	Infrequent	Husband
Finance	Very important	Infrequent	Husband
Car	Important	Infrequent	Husband
House	Very important	Infrequent	Husband and wife
Children's education	Very important	Infrequent	Husband and wife
Holidays	Important	Infrequent	Husband and wife
Weekends	Not important	Frequent	Husband and wife
Other leisure activities	Not important	Frequent	Husband and wife
Furniture	Not important	Infrequent	Husband and wife
Interior decorations	Not important	Infrequent	Wife
Food and other domestic spending	Not important	Frequent	Wife
Children's clothes	Not important	Frequent	Wife

(*Source*: Stephen Edgell, *Middle-class Couples*, p. 58.)

ways. Power can be exercised through **agenda setting**, that is deciding what questions and issues are discussed (Steven Lukes's second face of power), as well as through actually making decisions. Nothing in Edgell's research indicated that wives enjoyed more of this type of power to compensate for their lack of influence over important decisions. Husbands usually set the agenda for marital debate. The possibility of moving to another area, for example, was only raised when it became desirable in order to improve the husband's career prospects.

Nor did wives seem to possess more **ideological power**, the ability to persuade people to do things that are against their interests (Lukes's third face of power). Many, though not all, wives in the study accepted that traditional gender roles should be maintained, and the husband should be the dominant 'partner'. When asked about her attitude to sexual equality, an industrial scientist's wife replied that 'women generally like to be dominated by men, this is instinctive', while a dentist's wife said 'most women would become too hard and lose sight of the fact that they were female'. Edgell found that about half of the husbands, but surprisingly even more of the wives – about two-thirds – regarded sexual equality as a bad thing.

Graham Allan neatly summarizes the way that ideological factors limit women's power in many marriages when he describes 'the taken-for-granted-assumptions which emphasize the predominance of the male over the female in almost every sphere of domestic life'. In any struggle for power within the family he claims, 'the female is chronically disadvantaged from the start by the socially constructed framework of values and norms which constrain her options'.

Inequality within marriage

Most of the evidence suggests that women are still a long way from achieving equality within marriage in contemporary Britain. They are still primarily responsible for domestic tasks and they have less power than their husbands within marriage. In terms of the amount of hours spent 'working' though, the general picture of inequality seems to be less clear cut. Husbands of wives with full-time jobs do seem to be taking over some of the burden of housework although the change is slow and considerable inequality remains. (For more details on the effects of marriage on husbands and wives see pp. 633–4).

The domestic labour debate

As we have seen in the previous section, research suggests that women continue to take primary responsibility for work in the home, or 'domestic labour'. On its own this information tells us little about the significance of this division of labour but over a number of years Marxist and feminist sociologists have been debating what role domestic labour plays in society. Starting from a Marxist analysis of the economy, they have discussed whether domestic labour can be seen as directly or indirectly productive, and whether or not it produces surplus value for the ruling class.

Those involved in this debate agree that we live in a **patriarchal capitalist** society: one dominated by men and the owners of the means of production. They are all sympathetic to calls for women's liberation, but disagree about the importance that should be attached to changing domestic labour in order to achieve this objective.

Capitalism and domestic labour

Wage labour and domestic labour

Susan Himmelweit points out that there are a number of clear differences between wage labour and domestic labour.

1 Wage labour is paid and usually takes place over specified periods of time. Domestic labour is unpaid and the time periods when work or non-work takes place are not clearly separated.

2 For the waged worker, work and leisure, production and consumption, are separate, and wages and conditions of work are negotiable. By contrast domestic labourers work in the home, which is also a centre of leisure and consumption: they cannot directly negotiate wages and conditions and have no contract of employment.

3 Furthermore, paid work, on the surface, appears to be a far more central part of the economic system. Paid workers are often involved in producing commodities which are sold in the market. It is this process which directly creates surplus value for the bourgeoisie, and the commodities produced are counted as part of the

Gross National Product. The woman (or man) engaged in domestic labour does not appear to have an economic role. He or she provides services for their spouse and/or children rather than commodities. The work is tied up with emotional bonds between spouses, not with impersonal economic relationships.

Domestic labour and the production of labour power

Despite these apparent differences, some of the feminists who first examined this issue argued that in reality domestic labour was as integral a part of the capitalist mode of production as any other form of labour. In *The Power of Women and the Subversion of the Community* Maria Dalla Costa and Selma James argue that women domestic labourers are as productive as men who earn wages outside the home. They do not just produce **use-values** – goods and services which are useful – but also the surplus value that allows the bourgeoisie to exploit the proletariat.

Although she does not produce goods to sell, the housewife does produce another type of commodity: labour power. The family is a 'social factory'. It produces humans who have the ability to sell their labour power to the employer, and it is labour power that produces value.

Selma James outlines what is necessary before a human can labour:

First it must be nine months in the womb, must be fed, clothed and trained; then when it works its bed must be made, its floors swept, its lunch box prepared, its sexuality not satisfied but quietened, its dinner ready when it gets home, even if this is eight in the morning from the nightshift . . . to describe its basic production and reproduction is to describe women's work.

In this way the family creates and maintains labour power and is therefore vital to capitalism.

Capitalism exploits men who work, but the family ensures women are doubly exploited. Dalla Costa and James claim that 'women are the slaves of wage slaves'. These writers argue that the interests of both women and the proletariat can be met by the abolition of capitalism and the family: they see the family as part of the economic base rather than the superstructure.

Dalla Costa and James believe there is no basic contradiction between Marxism and feminism. They advocate the introduction of wages for housework for at least that would ensure that women were no longer the 'slaves to wage slaves'. This would lead to the redistribution of wealth from the ruling class who would then be required to pay the full costs of producing and reproducing the labour power that they hire.

Domestic labour as 'unproductive labour'

Similar, though not identical, conclusions were reached by Wally Secombe. Secombe accepts that there are important differences between wage labour and domestic labour. He sees domestic labour as what Marx called **unproductive labour**: it does not directly produce surplus value for the capitalist (that is, producing commodities that the capitalist can sell at a higher price than the costs of producing them). Domestic labour produces labour power, which the capitalist does not sell, but hires.

Secombe does not, therefore, go as far as Dalla Costa and James in seeing domestic labour as being virtually the same as wage labour. However, he agrees that it plays a vital part in the economic system, because without it capitalism would have no labour force from which to extract surplus value.

At first sight the work of the housewife appears to have nothing to do with the economic system, but to Secombe this is an illusion. He sees the whole economic system as resting upon the necessity for labour power to be produced and reproduced by those who labour in the home. He compares the situation to a play. The audience watching from their seats see only the actors and actresses; they forget that behind the scenes the stagehands have been necessary for the play to be performed at all. The stagehands are 'as indispensable to the entire production' as the work of housewives is to the capitalist system.

Secombe is less optimistic than Dalla Costa and James about the potential for housewives acting on their own to transform capitalism. He argues that their physical isolation in the home and the indirect way in which they are exploited, mean

that they have less power to change society than working women. He sees demands for wages for housework as less important than the forging of an alliance between housewives and male and female workers in a struggle against capitalism.

■ Men and domestic labour

Domestic labour – a separate mode of production

So far the sociologists we have examined in this section have emphasized that housework in its present form is created by capitalism, and capitalism benefits from it. However, some sociologists deny that it is primarily capitalism that benefits from the current division of labour within the family. Instead they see men as the main beneficiaries. Christine Delphy agrees with Dalla Costa and James, and Secombe that housewives perform an important economic function; she argues, however that it is not for capitalists, but for their husbands.

To Delphy housework is quite separate from capitalism; it forms a separate **mode of production**. The exploitation of the oppressed is the exploitation of women by men. Women are exploited not by selling their labour to an employer who extracts surplus value, but by working only for the subsistence provided by their husbands. The relations of productions are not based upon a work contract, but on the marriage contract. Through marriage the wife's labour is stolen by her husband.

Even if the wife takes paid labour outside the home, she usually continues to perform domestic labour free of charge. Where it proves impossible for the wife to both take up paid employment and carry out the domestic tasks, then her wages are often used to pay for services such as childcare and laundry. In this case, Delphy argues, the working woman is in effect paid nothing. She simply pays for her own subsistence and the family services she used to perform herself.

Delphy concludes that women's oppression cannot be tackled in alliance with the proletariat, for it is a part of the proletariat – their husbands – who are exploiting them. She believes that women should organize independently to overthrow patriarchy: they should challenge the existing family relationships which produce their exploitation by men.

Evaluation

Despite the differences between the points of view examined so far, all the sociologists we have considered agree that domestic labour functions to benefit one or both of men and capitalists. They are all highly critical of the family and believe it produces the exploitation of women.

All these approaches are very theoretical and tend to ignore historical evidence about the changing role of the family, the diversity of family forms, and the variety of relationships that exist within marriage.

Moreover it is questionable how vital some aspects of domestic labour are for the reproduction of labour power. Ray Pahl points out that some tasks which today are taken for granted may not have been done at all in the past. He claims that in much of the pre-industrial period there are no records of domestic cleaning taking place in households other than those of the landed gentry. Furthermore, washing and cleaning clothes was done very infrequently in the past. If this is the case, it appears that labour power can be successfully reproduced without some of the tasks which writers such as Dalla Costa and James, and Secombe regard as essential.

As we have seen in the previous section, although women retain the primary responsibility for domestic tasks in contemporary Britain, domestic labour is not exclusively carried out by women. In a small minority of households men may actually do the majority of the work. Generalizations that domestic labour is carried out by women for the benefit of men are therefore over-simplifications.

Domestic labour, the 'family wage' and 'use values'

Humpheries argues that domestic labour can benefit all family members, even though she is opposed to the existing sexist division of labour in the household. She argues that during the nineteenth century when women increasingly withdrew from the labour force, the bargaining position of male workers improved. With less individuals seeking work there was the possibility that in times of relatively full employment employers would have to increase wages even if it reduced the surplus value created.

More importantly, the principle of the **family wage** became established. The male breadwinners had to be paid enough to support their wives and children, who in previous centuries would themselves have been contributing to the family income. Humpheries points out that if several members of the household are employed, each can be given a lower rate of pay if the employer is only paying sufficient to cover the subsistence needs of the household.

As well as reducing the extent to which workers were being exploited, the family wage also freed the wife to improve the living standards of the family as a whole, including herself as an individual, by the **use values** she created with her domestic labour.

Humpheries does not suggest that domestic labour should be confined to women, nor that all its consequences are beneficial for working-class families. Nevertheless, she does throw some doubt on the claim that it benefits only men and capitalists. (For more details on women in the labour market and the relationship between wages and domestic labour, see pp. 614–29.)

As we have seen in these sections, some sociologists believe important changes are taking place in family life in Britain, changes that are challenging the dominance of the 'conventional family' in society. Some commentators also see marriage itself as an institution that is under threat. In the next section we will focus on this viewpoint as we consider marital breakdown.

■ Marriage and marital breakdown

Two main types of evidence are usually advanced to support the claim that the institution of marriage is in danger.

■ 'Threats' to marriage

1 First, it is argued that marriage is becoming less popular – decreasing numbers of people are getting married. More people are developing alternatives to conventional married life.

2 Second, there are increasing numbers of marital breakdowns reflected in rises in the divorce rate.

Although, on the surface, there seems an element of truth in both these claims, they must be regarded with considerable suspicion. The view that the family is breaking up in modern society, may, at the very least, be an exaggeration.

Marriage rates

Writing in the early 1980s, Robert Chester was amongst those who noted that marriage rates among young adults had declined in many Western countries. First Sweden and Denmark began to have falling marriage rates among the under thirties. The trend continued in Britain, the USA and West Germany in the early 1970s, and later spread to France. In 1971 in Britain one in 11 teenage women got married; by 1981 this had fallen to one in 24. Between 1981 and 1990 the marriage rate in Britain for all age groups fell from 7.1 per year per thousand of the eligible population to 6.8. In the European Community it also fell over the same period in France, Greece, Eire, Italy and Portugal.

However, Chester did not see the figures as conclusive evidence of a decline in the popularity of marriage. He said 'Mainly we seem to be witnessing a delay in the timing of marriage, rather than a fall-off in getting married at all.' He thought that future generations might marry less frequently, but he believed there would be only a small (if any) reduction in marriage rates.

Statistical evidence since Chester advanced these arguments seems to support his case. Marriage rates in the European Community as a whole were unchanged between 1981 and 1990 and actually increased in Denmark, West Germany,

Luxembourg, The Netherlands and Spain.

Cohabitation

An alternative to marriage is cohabitation by couples who are not legally married. According to the *General Household Survey* the percentage of non-married women who were cohabiting more than doubled between 1979 and 1991 from 11 per cent to 23 per cent.

However, Chester argued that in most cases cohabitation is only a temporary phase: most of those who cohabit get married eventually. In some cases one or both of the partners is separated but not divorced from a previous spouse, and so is not free to get married. Others see the period of cohabitation simply as a trial marriage, and intend to get married if it proves satisfactory. Most cohabiting couples intend to and do get married if they have children. Chester concluded that 'In practice, only about 2 per cent of single women aged between 18 and 49 are living and bearing children in "consensual unions" which may be permanent.'

Evidence which can be used to support Chester's view can be found in a 1981 study of a representative sample of the people of Sheffield and Aberdeen. Jacqueline Burgoyne and David Clark asked their sample whether they thought cohabitation outside marriage was a good idea. Some 38 per cent thought it was if cohabitation was a prelude to marriage, but this figure was reduced to only 15 per cent if it was a permanent alternative to marriage. In a later study of 29 cohabiting couples in Sheffield, Burgoyne found that the majority saw cohabitation 'as a way of testing out their relationship before they committed themselves more fully' while a minority expressed 'opposition to the whole institution of marriage'.

A rather different view has been taken by Joan Chandler. She sees the increase in cohabitation as rather more significant and says, 'The time couples spend cohabiting is lengthening and increasingly they appear to be choosing cohabitation as a long-term alternative to marriage.' Chandler suggests that this is reflected in the increasing proportions of children born out of marriage – partners no longer feel as much pressure to marry to legitimize a pregnancy. She argues:

Many of today's parents have detached childbearing and rearing from traditional marriage and 28 per cent of children are now born to unmarried mothers. However, many fewer are born to residentially lone parents, as 70 per cent of these children are jointly registered by parents who usually share the same address.

Although Chandler sees cohabitation as increasingly popular, she does point out that it is nothing new. Unofficial self-marriage, in some parts of the country, called 'living over the brush', was very common in past centuries. She quotes research which estimates that as many as a quarter to a third of couples lived in consensual unions in Britain in the eighteenth century.

Communes

Two other alternatives to the marriage-based household which exist in Western societies are single-parent families (see pp. 349–51), and communes. Andrew McCulloch defines **communes** as 'experimental household groups which practise an ideology of sharing'. In the USA communes are relatively commonplace: (McCulloch quotes a 1975 study by J. Jerome that put the number at 25,000) but they are much less numerous in Britain. McCulloch's own research over a five-year period uncovered 67 communes, but only six of them survived over the full five years, and he believed that by the end of the research there were only 50 left.

The values of members of communes pose a significant challenge to marriage and the family. As McCulloch puts it, those who form or join communes are often looking for somewhere where they can 'be themselves' and live collectively rather than in small, isolated, nuclear family units. However, in numerical terms communes represent very little threat to traditional familial and marital values.

One reason why communes tend to be short-lived is the problem of new generations and how they fit into the communal group. Many communes encourage the free development of sexual relationships between their members, and this raises the question, 'at what age does the child become a sexual participant in the group and what are the consequences of this?'

One solution to this type of problem is the formation of **collective** rather than **communal** households. Collective households consist of a number of nuclear family units, and although there may be a considerable amount of sharing between the units, there are limits on what is shared. McCulloch claims that this type of household is becoming increasing popular, and is often a successful solution to the problems of urban living. Ideologically, however, it seems less of a radical departure from traditional marriage than the communal household.

■ Marital breakdown

The second type of evidence which suggests a threat to contemporary marriage concerns the apparent rise in marital breakdowns. The usual way of estimating the number of such breakdowns is through an examination of the divorce statistics, but these statistics do not, on their own, provide a valid measure of marital breakdown.

Marital breakdown can be divided into three main categories:

1 **divorce**, which refers to the legal termination of a marriage;

2 **separation**, which refers to the physical separation of the spouses: they no longer share the same dwelling;

3 and so-called **empty-shell marriages**, where the spouses live together, remain legally married, but their marriage exists in name only.

These three forms must be considered in any assessment of the rate of marital breakdown.

Divorce statistics

Despite minor fluctuations, there has been a steady rise in divorce rates in industrial societies throughout this century. In 1911 859 petitions for divorce were filed in England and Wales of which some three-quarters were granted a decree absolute. Table 6.6 presents statistics on divorce for England and Wales from 1961 to 1990.

The dramatic increase in petitions in 1971 was due in part to new divorce legislation. This increase did not simply represent a backlog of couples waiting to legally end an unsatisfactory marriage, since the number of petitions continued to rise during the following years.

Some indication of the significance of the above figures is provided by the following comparisons.

Table 6.6 Divorce in England and Wales

	1961	1971	1976	1981	1986	1987	1988	1989	1990
Petitions filed (thousands) England and Wales	32	111	145	170	180	183	183	185	192
Decrees nisi granted (thousands) England and Wales	27	89	132	148	153	150	155	152	158
Decrees absolute granted (thousands) England and Wales	25	74	127	146	154	151	153	151	153
Persons divorcing per thousand married people England and Wales	2.1	6.0	10.1	11.9	12.9	12.7	12.8	12.7	12.9

(*Source: Social Trends* 23, 1993.)

In 1991 there were 350,000 marriages but 171,000 divorces meaning that there were nearly half as many divorces as marriages. According to Joan Chandler, 'If trends continue, approximately 40 per cent of marriages presently being formed will end in divorce.' The proportion of marriages which are remarriages has also been rising. For example, 15 per cent of all marriages in 1961 were remarriages for one or both partners; by 1991 this figure had risen to 36 per cent. Whichever way the figures are presented, the increase in divorce is dramatic, although in Britain the rapid rise in the divorce rate stabilized in the late 1980s, albeit at a historically very high level.

Britain's divorce rate is also very high in comparison with most other industrial societies: in the European Community only Denmark had a higher rate in 1990; elsewhere, the USA also has a higher rate than Britain. However, an increase in the divorce rate has been experienced in nearly all industrial societies over the past few decades and is by no means unique to Britain.

Separation statistics

Reliable figures for separation are unobtainable. In Britain, some indication is provided by applications to a magistrates' court for a legal separation order but many spouses separate without going to court, and for these there are no figures available. Chester suggests that:

It might be expected that modern couples would be more ready than others in the past to regularize unsatisfactory marital situations, and that the number of unrecorded breakdowns has been falling.

Chester estimates that the number of recorded separations increased during the 1960s by about 65 per cent. This does not necessarily mean an increase in separations since the number of unrecorded separations is unknown. Although the numbers are small compared with divorce, there was a marked increase in judicial separations in the 1970s and early 1980s. In 1972 133 were granted; in 1984, 4,445. However, from this high point numbers fell and there were only 1,747 judicial separations in 1991.

Empty-shell marriages

Estimates of the extent of empty-shell marriages can only be based on guesswork. Even where data exist, the concept is difficult to **operationalize** (that is put into a measurable form). For example, if a couple express a high level of dissatisfaction with their relationship, should this be termed an empty-shell marriage?

Historical evidence gives the impression that empty-shell marriages are more likely to end in separation and divorce today than in the past. William J. Goode argues that in nineteenth-century America:

People took for granted that spouses who no longer loved one another and who found life together distasteful should at least live together in public amity for the sake of their children and of their standing in the community.

Even though an increasing number of empty-shell marriages may end in separation and divorce today, this does not necessarily mean that the proportion of such marriages, in relation to the total number of marriages, is decreasing.

In view of the problems involved in measuring marital breakdown, Robert Chester reaches the following conclusion: 'Contemporary marriages certainly have higher recorded breakdown rates, and they very probably have higher total breakdown rates, although the latter conclusion should be regarded as tentative'.

■ Explanations for marital breakdowns

In *When Marriage Ends*, Nicky Hart argues that any explanation of marital breakdown must consider the following factors:

1 those which affect the value attached to marriage;

2 those which affect the degree of conflict between the spouses;

3 and those which affect the opportunities for individuals to escape from marriage.

We will first consider these factors from a functionalist perspective. From this viewpoint, behaviour is largely a response to shared norms and values. It therefore follows that a change in the rate of marital breakdown is to some degree a reflection of changing norms and values in general, and, in particular, those associated with marriage and divorce.

The value of marriage

Functionalists such as Talcott Parsons and Ronald Fletcher argue that the rise in marital breakdown stems largely from the fact that marriage is increasingly valued. People expect and demand more from marriage and consequently are more likely to end a relationship which may have been acceptable in the past. Thus Ronald Fletcher argues that 'a relatively high divorce rate may be indicative not of *lower* but of *higher* standards of marriage in society'.

This view finds some support from the increasing priority given to marriage and the family by the spouses in Young and Willmott's **symmetrical family** and Goldthorpe and Lockwood's **privatized family**. The high rate of remarriage also lends support to Parsons and Fletcher's arguments. Thus, paradoxically, the higher value placed on marriage may result in increased marital breakdown.

Conflict between spouses

Hart argues that the second set of factors which must be considered in an explanation of marital breakdown are those which affect the degree of conflict between the spouses. From a functionalist perspective it can be argued that the adaptation of the family to the requirements of the economic system has placed a strain on the marital relationship. It has led to the relative isolation of the nuclear family from the wider kinship network. William J. Goode argues that, as a result, the family 'carries a heavier emotional burden when it exists independently than when it is a small unit within a larger kin fabric. As a consequence, this unit is relatively fragile'. Edmund Leach makes a similar point. He suggests that the nuclear family suffers from an emotional overload which increases the level of conflict between its members.

In industrial society, the family specializes in fewer functions. It can be argued that, as a result, there are fewer bonds to unite its members. The economic bond, for example, is considerably weakened when the family ceases to be a unit of production. N. Dennis suggests that the specialization of function which characterizes the modern family will lead to increased marital breakdown. Dennis argues:

In so far as companionship, a close, durable, intimate and unique relationship with one member of the opposite sex becomes the prime necessity in marriage, a failure in this respect becomes sufficient to lead to its abandonment.

Put simply, when love goes, there's nothing much left to hold the couple together.

The ease of divorce

So far we have considered the factors which affect the value attached to marriage and those which affect the degree of conflict between spouses. The third set of factors which Hart considers essential to an explanation of marital breakdown are those which affect the opportunities for individuals to escape from marriage.

If, as the <u>functionalists argue, behaviour is directed by norms and values,</u> a change in the norms and values associated with divorce would be expected. It is generally agreed that the stigma attached to divorce has been considerably reduced. This, in itself, will make divorce easier.

Goode argues that the change in attitudes towards divorce is part of the more general process of secularization in Western societies. (**Secularization** refers to the declining influence of the church and of religious belief in general – we discuss secularization, in more detail in Chapter 11, pp. 479–97.) During the nineteenth century, the church strongly denounced divorce, insisting that the phrase 'till death do us part' be taken literally. During this century, despite a strong rearguard action, the church has had to accommodate the rising divorce rate by taking a less rigid view.

However, the official church position is probably less important than the declining influence of religious beliefs and values in general in industrial society. Many sociologists argue that **secular** (that is non-religious) beliefs and values increasingly direct behaviour. In terms of divorce, Goode argues this means that 'Instead of asking, "Is this moral?" the individual is more likely to ask, "Is this a more useful or better procedure for my needs?"'.

Divorce legislation

The changing attitudes towards divorce have been institutionalized by various changes in the law which have made it much easier to obtain. In Britain, before 1857, a private act of parliament was required to obtain a divorce. This was an expensive procedure beyond the means of all but the most wealthy.

Since 1857, the costs of obtaining a divorce have been reduced and the grounds for divorce have been widened. Divorce legislation was influenced by the idea of **matrimonial offence**, the notion that one or both spouses had wronged the other. This was the idea behind the Matrimonial

Causes Act of 1857 which largely limited grounds for divorce to adultery. Though divorce legislation in 1950 widened the grounds to include cruelty and desertion, it was still based on the same principle.

The Divorce Reform Act, which came into force in 1971, no longer emphasized the idea of matrimonial offence and so avoided the need for 'guilty parties'. It defined the grounds for divorce as 'the irretrievable breakdown of the marriage'. This made divorce considerably easier and accounts in part for the dramatic rise in the number of divorces in 1971.

New legislation relating to divorce was introduced at the end of 1984. This reduced the period a couple needed to be married before they could petition for divorce from three years to one. It also altered the basis on which financial settlements were determined by the courts. From 1984 the conduct of the partners became something the courts could take into account. If the misbehaviour of one partner was responsible for the divorce they could be awarded less than would otherwise have been expected. The intention behind this seemed to be to counteract what some saw as the anti-male bias in maintenance payments from men to their ex-wives.

Despite a reduction in costs, divorce was still an expensive process during the first half of this century. It was beyond the means of many of the less wealthy. This was partly changed by the Legal Aid and Advice Act of 1949 which provided free legal advice and paid solicitors' fees for those who could not afford them. The economics of divorce were further eased by the extension of welfare provisions, particularly for single parents with dependent children. Although many consider these provisions far from generous, they do provide single-parent families with the means to exist without the support of the second partner.

Women, paid employment and marital conflict

So far, the analysis of marital breakdown has proceeded mainly from a functionalist perspective. Hart presents a Marxist alternative though it does not form the theoretical basis of her work. She argues that the increasing divorce rate can be seen as a 'product of conflict between the changing economic system and its social and ideological superstructure (notably the family)'.

In advanced capitalist industrial societies, there is an increasing demand for cheap female wage labour. Wives are encouraged to take up paid employment not only because of the demand for their services, but also because the capitalist-controlled media has raised **material aspirations** – the demand for goods that families desire. These material aspirations can only be satisfied by both spouses working as wage earners. However, conflict results from the contradiction between female wage labour and the normative expectations which surround married life. 'Working wives' are still expected to be primarily responsible for housework and raising children. In addition, they are still expected, to some degree, to play a subservient role to the male head of the household. These **normative expectations** contradict the wife's role as a wage earner since she is now sharing the economic burden with her husband. Conflict between the spouses can result from this contradiction, and this conflict can lead to marital breakdown.

Official statistics seem to support the view that it is largely wives' dissatisfaction with marriage that accounts for the rising divorce rate. In 1989 73 per cent of divorce petitions were filed by wives, and just 27 per cent by husbands. This was a dramatic change in comparison with 1946 when wives accounted for 37 per cent of petitions and husbands for 63 per cent.

■ The social distribution of marital breakdown

Income and class

We will conclude this section with an examination of the variation in divorce rates between different social groups within society.

Marital breakdown is not spread evenly across the population: the changes which have influenced the rate of marital breakdown do not affect all members of society in the same way but are mediated by the social structure. For example, changes in society are filtered through the class system and to some degree affect members of different classes in different ways. As a result there are class variations in rates of marital breakdown.

In the USA, there is an inverse relationship between income and marital breakdown: the lower the family income, the higher the rate of

Table 6.7 Divorce and social class in England and Wales

Social class of husband		Standardized divorce rate
I	Professional	47
II	Intermediate	83
IIIN	Skilled, non-manual	108
IIIM	Skilled, manual	97
IV	Partly skilled	111
V	Unskilled	220
	Armed forces	270
	Unemployed	225
	All social classes	100

(*Source:* Quoted in J. Burgoyne, R. Ormrod and M. Richards *Divorce Matters,* Penguin Books, Harmondsworth, 1987, p. 34.)

separation and divorce. Low income can place a strain on the marital relationship. It has been argued that, in poverty areas, expectations of marital success are lower, as is the stigma attached to marital breakdown. It has been suggested that marital breakdown has become self-perpetuating in many low-income groups.

In Britain, the situation is similar. Table 6.7 shows the results of a study by Haskey of the social class of a sample of 2,164 divorcing couples in England and Wales in 1979. It shows that in general non-manual workers have considerably lower divorce rates than manual workers, although skilled manual workers do have a lower rate than routine white collar workers. The divorce rate is particularly high amongst the unskilled and the unemployed, suggesting that material hardship may be an important factor shaping British divorce rates. However, Haskey notes that the divorce rate is also very high amongst families where the husband is in the armed forces and therefore in secure and reasonably well-paid employment. This suggests that specific occupations might encourage divorce.

Age

Apart from social class, a number of other factors are associated with the variations in divorce rates. There is an inverse relationship between age at marriage and divorce: the lower the age at marriage, the higher the rate of divorce. In Britain, from 1985 to 1989 the divorce rate for teenage marriages was roughly double the overall rate, while for those who married when over 45, it was less than half.

A number of reasons have been given for this. There may be greater economic pressure on the teenage marriage since the spouses are only beginning their working lives and their wages are likely to be low. Compared to all marriages, a higher proportion of teenage marriages are undertaken to legitimize a pregnancy. In addition, teenagers are more likely to change their outlook and so 'grow apart'. They are less likely to have the experience to select a compatible partner and less likely to be aware of the responsibilities that marriage entails.

Another part of the reason may be related to social class. Working-class couples are more likely than the middle class to marry as teenagers and their class rather than age at marriage may be the main factor influencing their divorce rate.

The marital status of parents

There is an association between individuals' likelihood to get divorced and the marital status of their parents. If one or both spouses have parents who are or have been divorced, there is a greater possibility that their marriage will end in divorce.

The usual explanation is that marital conflict produces psychological instability in the children who express this instability in their own marriage. However, Hart argues that the experience of having divorced parents may reduce the individual's aversion to divorce. In addition, divorced parents may be more likely, if not to encourage the divorce, at least not to oppose it as strongly as non-divorced parents.

Background and role expectations

Statistics indicate that the chances of marital breakdown are increased if the spouses have different social backgrounds, for example if they come from different class or ethnic groups. Conflict may result from partners having different marital role expectations which stem from the subculture of their particular social group. When spouses share similar backgrounds, there is a greater likelihood that their friends will be similar and this will tend to reinforce the marriage. In Goode's words, it is probable 'that those who are alike in many respects will share a similar and approving circle'.

In advanced industrial society, the increasing rate of social and geographical mobility results in greater opportunities for marriage between individuals of differing social backgrounds and therefore a greater potential for marital conflict.

Occupations

Finally, various studies have indicated a relationship between particular occupations and high rates of divorce. Nicky Hart finds that long-distance lorry drivers, sales representatives and some engineers and technicians, whose jobs require frequent separation from their spouses, have higher than average divorce rates. Apart from the possibility of lessening the dependence of the spouses upon each other, such jobs provide the husband in particular with a greater opportunity to meet members of the opposite sex away from the company of his spouse.

T. Noble finds a similar relationship between particular occupations and high rates of divorce. Actors, authors, artists, company directors and hotel-keepers have high divorce rates, which Noble argues result from their high degree of involvement in their work and low involvement in their marriage.

We have examined only some of the many factors associated with the variation in divorce rates. The researcher is faced with a multitude of factors and it is difficult to establish which are more important than others. With reference to the particularly rapid rise in the overall rate of marital breakdown in recent years, Hart assigns priority to the changing role of women in society. We consider this in detail in Chapter 10.

■ Conclusion

A decline in the rate of marriage, increasing cohabitation outside marriage, the development of communes, the rising number of single-parent families and the apparent increase in marital breakdown, all seem to suggest the decline of marriage as an institution in modern Britain. Yet all these changes are open to different interpretations, and none – at least on its own – seems likely to make marriage obsolete in the near future.

It is easy to exaggerate the extent to which there has been a retreat from marriage. Robert Chester says 'On the evidence, most people will continue not only to spend most of their lives in a family environment, but also to place a high value on it'.

The socialist feminist sociologists Pamela Abbott and Claire Wallace are also rather sceptical of the belief that the family and marriage are in danger of falling apart. They suggest that this view has been encouraged by the 'New Right', right-wing politicians and thinkers whose views and policies are discussed on pp. 378–80. To Abbott and Wallace, such people have succeeded in setting the agenda of public debate about the family by trying to portray it as under serious threat from moral decay in society as a whole, and they have carefully interpreted the evidence to support their case. Abbot and Wallace say:

We are told how many marriages end in divorce, how many children live in single-parent families and so on. Yet we can also look at these statistics another way – to show the stability of the family. Six out of ten couples who get married in the 1990s,

---

according to present trends, will stay together until one of them dies. Seven out of eight children are born to parents living together, three-quarters of whom are legally married. Only one in five children will experience parental divorce by the time he or she is 16; that is, four out of five children born to a married couple will be brought up by them in an intact family. In 1985, 78 per cent of British children under 16 were living with both natural parents who were legally married.

These sociologists recognize the increasing diversity of family forms but see the alleged decline of the family and marriage as having been exaggerated for political ends.

C.C. Harris draws a cautious conclusion based upon the ambiguous evidence. He says 'the case that marriage and the family in Britain are at present in a process of "deinstitutionalization" is simply not proven'. Instead he recognizes that there has been an increase in the number of people living outside of households based on married couples. He believes it is possible to detect, particularly from the delaying of marriage, 'the emergence of a period of extra-familial independence among young adults' and argues that the recognition of 'dysfunctional' aspects of married life has led a small minority of the population to begin to explore alternatives, at least for a temporary phase of their lives.

▉ The family, politics and social policy

International comparisons

Until recently sociologists have paid little attention to the relationship between social policy and the family. As Graham Allan points out, Britain does not have a government ministry responsible for family affairs, and traditionally it has not had a specific package of government policies aimed at the family. Most European countries have both of these.

Adrian Wilson has given examples from a variety of societies and historical periods of how the state has tried to directly shape family life.

1 In the USSR the post-revolutionary communist government of the 1920s took measures intended to weaken and ultimately destroy the family. Divorce and abortion were made much easier to obtain.

2 In Romania under Ceausescu family life was encouraged. Those who remained unmarried after the age of 25 had to pay extra income tax, a measure intended to increase the birth rate.

3 In China, on the other hand, couples had to apply for permission to have more than one child, and there were penalties for those who did not make their contribution to solving the problem of overpopulation.

4 In Britain, though, the family has usually been regarded as an area where it is inappropriate for the state to interfere too much, since, as Allan puts it 'the state is concerned with regulation, control and coercion; the family is thought of as an area for love, intimacy and personal fulfilment'. In short, the family belongs to the private sphere, and should therefore, for the most part, be left alone.

Bias towards conventional families

Despite the traditional British belief that politicians should not interfere in the family, state policies have always had an impact on family life. Taxation, welfare, housing and education policies all influence the way people organize their domestic life. The policies adopted can encourage people to live in certain types of household and discourage them from living in other types. Furthermore, in recent decades the family has come to be seen as a legitimate and important subject of public debate.

Feminists and other radical critics of government policies see them as biased. They have argued that they tend to favour the traditional nuclear family in which there are two parents – a male breadwinner and a wife who stays at home when there are young children. Allan argues 'Much state provision . . . is based upon an implicit ideology of the "normal" family which through its incorporation into standard practice discourages alternative forms of domestic organization from developing.' To Allan these policies encourage 'the standard form of gender and generational relations within families'. In other words, they assume that one family member will put primary emphasis during their life on childcare rather than work; that families will usually take care of their elderly and sick; and that wives are economically dependent on their husbands.

Daphne Johnson argues that schools are organized in such a way that it is difficult for single-parent families and dual-worker families to combine work with domestic responsibilities. School hours and holidays mean that families with children find it difficult for the adult members to combine the requirements of employers with their domestic responsibilities.

Roy Parker claims that state assistance (of a practical rather than financial nature) tends not to be given to the elderly and sick if they live with relatives. It is assumed that the family will care for them. In both the care of the elderly and infirm and the care of children, this generally means that wives will be expected to take up these domestic responsibilities, or at least to work only part-time.

The traditional conjugal roles of wives in the 'conventional' family are further reinforced by some parts of the taxation and benefits systems. For example, married women can only receive invalidity pensions if they can show that their physical condition prevents them from doing housework, a rule that does not apply to men and single women. Until recently married women also could not claim the Invalid Care Allowance; it was taken for granted that they should carry out 'caring' family roles, and were not therefore given financial compensation for doing so.

In 1993 the Child Support Agency was established. It oversees the payment of maintenance by 'absent' parents to the parents responsible for looking after children. Its work therefore covers divorced, separated and never-married couples who live apart. The agency was set up to make sure that fathers in particular would find it more difficult to escape financial responsibility for their children. In this respect it can be seen as supporting the traditional family by imposing financial costs on those who do not live in one.

The Child Support Agency has been highly controversial and highly criticized. For example, many argue that its main aim is not to help children but rather to save the Treasury money since maintenance payments usually reduce the benefits paid to single mothers. Indeed, in its first year the agency was set a target of saving £530 million of taxpayers' money. However, it is clear that Conservative ministers have supported the agency not just to save money but also because they see it as helping to uphold moral values relating to parental responsibility.

■ Pamela Abbott and Claire Wallace – the family and the New Right

Pamela Abbott and Claire Wallace have examined a very different view of the family and social policy which was put forward by the New Right in Britain and the USA in the 1980s. Instead of arguing that government policy was biased in favour of the conventional family, the New Right argued that government policy was undermining it and policies had to be changed.

In Britain New Right thinking was promoted by individual journalists and academics, for example Paul Johnson and Roger Scruton, and by 'think tanks' such as the Centre for Policy Studies and the Adam Smith Institute. In the USA a variety of pressure groups has campaigned to reassert traditional morality and family relationships. Abbott and Wallace describe them as a 'Pro-Family' movement and say that it 'developed out of an alliance of political, religious, anti-feminist and pro-life anti-abortion groups'. In Britain the 'Pro-Family' movement has not been as strong but an anti-abortion movement, individuals like Victoria Gillick (who campaigned to stop doctors prescribing contraceptives to girls under 16 without parental consent), and organizations like Families Need Fathers (which is opposed to divorce) have supported similar causes to their American counterparts.

Abbott and Wallace argue that the New Right advocates 'liberal economic policies with support for conservative social moral values'. Members of the New Right see the family as being under threat from permissiveness, social changes and government policies and this in turn threatens the stability of society. To them the family operates properly when it remains stable and the wife is responsible for socializing children so that they conform to society's norms and values. The husband, as principal breadwinner, is disciplined by the need to provide for his family. The New Right sees many signs of the family becoming unable to carry out its proper role. These include 'working mothers (who by taking paid work fail to put the needs of their children first), increased divorce rates, higher numbers of single-parent families and open homosexuality'. It argues that such changes have played a major role in causing social problems such as crime, delinquency and drug abuse.

The New Right and politics

In trying to influence political debate and the actions of governments, the New Right has tried to change what it sees as harmful social policies. Abbot and Wallace argue that in both Britain and the USA the New Right has attacked the welfare systems for encouraging deviant lifestyles and family forms. For example, welfare payments have allowed mothers to bring up their children in single-parent families, taxation policies have discriminated against married couples, divorce laws have made it easier to end marriage, and abortion laws and the relaxation of laws against homosexuality have undermined traditional morality.

Indeed, from this point of view, government policy has further undermined the family by taking from conventional families and giving to deviant households. Welfare payments to single-mothers have driven up taxation to the point

where wives with young children are forced to take paid employment to make ends meet. As a result, even those who wish to live in conventional nuclear families which include a housewife are unable to do so, and more children are socialized in unsatisfactory ways.

The New Right has been in a position to influence social policy because of the election of political leaders sympathetic to its views. These include Ronald Reagan, president of the USA from 1980 to 1988, and Margaret Thatcher who was prime minister of Britain throughout the 1980s. Abbott and Wallace say of Reagan:

> He put himself firmly on the side of the 'pro-family' movement in supporting both the patriarchal nuclear family as necessary and inevitable and in seeing welfare reforms as at least partly responsible for the decline of the American family.

In Britain Margaret Thatcher also supported many aspects of New Right thinking on the family. She agreed that the family was a vital institution for maintaining social stability. In a speech in May 1988, Thatcher said:

> The family is the building block of society. It's a nursery, a school, a hospital, a leisure place, a place of refuge and a place of rest. It encompasses the whole of society. It fashions beliefs. It's the preparation for the rest of our life and women run it.

Soon after coming to office Thatcher set up a Family Policy Group consisting of Ferdinand Mount, a prominent New Right academic, and senior cabinet ministers. Abbott and Wallace describe the group's recommendations in the following way:

> They thought that mothers with young children should be encouraged to stay at home, that financial disincentives against motherhood should be removed to facilitate this, that the tax/benefits system should be orientated more towards the family. . . they also suggested that the family, in the

widest sense, should be encouraged to take on responsibility for the disabled, the elderly and unemployed 16-year-olds.

After Thatcher left office Conservative politicians continued to call for policies to support the nuclear family. In 1993 the Welsh minister, John Redwood, expressed his concern about single parenthood and said 'The natural state should be the two-adult family caring for their children.'

The New Right and policies

On the surface it would appear that the New Right had a major impact on government policy on both sides of the Atlantic. Abbott and Wallace do identify some policies which were influenced by its ideas. In America, for example, in 1984 new legislation required states to ensure that biological fathers contributed to supporting their offspring when they did not live with the mother.

In Britain from April 1988 benefits were withdrawn from 16–18 year olds who did not take up a place on a training scheme. This was partly to try to force families to take responsibility for maintaining unemployed teenagers. Conservative governments have also followed policies supporting 'community care' for the elderly and disabled rather than care in state institutions. In practice this has meant care by family members, and usually women. The 1988 budget changed taxation so that cohabiting couples could no longer claim more in tax allowances than a married couple. It also prevented cohabiting couples from claiming two lots of income tax relief on a shared mortgage when a married couple could only claim one.

However, in many other ways the New Right failed to achieve the changes it wanted. Abbott and Wallace say that in the USA, 'few of the policies of the pro-family movement were implemented. Nor did the traditional two-parent patriarchal family consistently benefit from economic policies'.

In Britain the New Right also had limited success. In terms of moral policies divorce was actually made easier in 1984 and legislation was enacted which gave 'illegitimate' children the same rights as those born within marriage. In terms of economic policies, some changes seem to have given a relative advantage to single parents. From 1987 to 1988 the extra benefit payable to single parents was increased, while the Child Benefit payable to all mothers was frozen. Family Credit, introduced to replace Family Income Supplement in 1988, allowed single parents claiming it to earn more before benefit starts to be reduced.

Conservative governments have not introduced any tax or benefits policies to encourage mothers to stay at home with young children and to Abbot and Wallace many Thatcherite policies actually undermined family life. Such policies include the freezing of Child Benefit, economic policies which have forced up unemployment, the emphasis on home ownership and opposition to the provision of council housing, cuts in education spending and the real levels of student grants. All these policies have hit the finances of many families with the result that far from encouraging self-reliance, 'Many families and individuals have had their ability to care for themselves *reduced*, not increased.'

To Abbott and Wallace the main purpose of government policies under Thatcher was to reduce public spending; maintaining the traditional family was very much a secondary consideration. For example, the 1988 Immigration Act abolished the rights of British and long-settled Commonwealth citizens to be joined by their wives and children unless it could be shown that they could be maintained without relying upon welfare payments. In practice, Abbott and Wallace claim, the policies ended up making more families dependent on welfare and 'the main outcome was the polarisation between the poor and the better off'. They conclude:

the welfare and economic policies advocated by the New Right – insofar as they have been implemented by the Thatcher and Reagan administrations – have been more concerned with reasserting the rights of middle-class men and maintaining capitalism than they have been with a genuine concern for men, women and children and the quality of their lives.

■ Sociology, values and the family

Writing about the values which surround the American family, Sussman and Burchinal state:

> Most Americans reject the notion that receiving aid from their kin is a good thing. The proper ideological stance is that the individual and his family should fend for themselves. The family in this instance is nuclear in structure and consists of husband and wife and children.

Like those they write about, sociologists are members of society and members of families. They too have been exposed to family ideology. Their views of the family are unlikely to be free from their beliefs about what the family ought to be. In fact Talcott Parsons's picture of the isolated nuclear family is essentially no different from Sussman and Burchinal's description of family ideology in American society. It can be argued that the concept of the isolated nuclear family owes more than a little to his values.

As in all areas of sociology, functionalist perspectives on the family have been accused of having a conservative bias. With their emphasis on the universality and inevitability of the family, they justify its existence. With their preoccupation with the positive aspects of the family they provide it with legitimation. As Barrington Moore argues, these views may say more about the hopes and ideals of sociologists than the reality of their subject matter. He states:

> Among social scientists today it is almost axiomatic that the family is a universally necessary social institution and will remain such through any foreseeable future ... I have the uncomfortable feeling that the authors, despite all their elaborate theories and technical research devices, are doing little more than projecting certain middle-class hopes and ideals onto a refractory reality. (Quoted in Morgan 1975, p. 3.)

In other words, the view that the family is here to stay through time immemorial may be primarily a reflection of middle-class values.

D.H.J. Morgan argues that functionalist perspectives on the family 'give emphasis to the limits of human activity rather than the potentialities'. In doing so they adopt a conservative stance. By emphasizing the universal necessity for the family and the vital functions it performs for the social system, they imply that individuals must accept the inevitable. Members of society must form families and act accordingly within the limits set by the requirements of the social system.

Although functionalist views on the family are no longer particularly influential in sociology, similar views are still influential in society. New Right perspectives on the family have a remarkable similarity to those of functionalists. Both approaches see the nuclear family as the ideal, neither believes there are viable alternatives to living in families, neither examines the ways in which families can harm individuals, and both see families as vital to producing social stability.

However, they do differ in the extent to which they see the family as under threat. For example, Parsons and Fletcher see the rising divorce rate as an indication that people value family life, and happy families split up only to be reformed as even happier families. Members of the New Right, on the other hand, see divorce as just one symptom of a serious moral decline. As the family breaks down and single parenthood becomes more common, they see a danger of the young being inadequately socialized and becoming an ever greater problem for society.

Functionalists and the New Right can both be accused of having a very idealized picture of life in nuclear families. For the most part they have made little attempt to actually investigate family life, simply assuming that all is sweetness and light. This cosy image has been shattered by sociologists and psychiatrists who have studied some of the less savoury aspects of life in families. In R.D. Laing's studies of schizophrenia, feminist studies of domestic violence, and Marxist and feminist research on labour and power within households, an alternative image of the family has been presented. From this point of view the family is, or at least can be, exploitive, violent and psychologically damaging.

Unlike functionalists, feminists, Marxists and other radical critics cannot be accused of seeing the family through rose-tinted spectacles. However they can be accused of letting their value judgements direct their theories and research. Marxists start with the assumption that capitalism is evil; feminists with the assumption that society is patriarchal and women are exploited by men. From these starting points their sociology follows a predictable path. Evidence is gathered to confirm their theories and they usually display little self-doubt in their dedication to their particular perspective.

A rather different and arguably less judgemental view is advocated by some sociologists who have written about family diversity. They neither want to preserve the traditional family, nor to dismiss it as a harmful institution. Instead they believe that all domestic living arrangements should be accepted and respected whether they are nuclear families, communes, extended families, gay and lesbian couples, single person or single-parent households. Rhona Rapoport describes this as the **secular pluralist orientation.** She sees it as 'characterised by tolerance towards the diversity of family forms' and argues that it will 'be followed by people advocating human rights'.

However, even this view is influenced by a particular set of values, in this case libertarian values. Furthermore, as Rapoport admits:

Problems may arise as regards limits. The norm of free choice may be applicable to adults, but where children are involved the main issue is to serve their best interests in some form of domestic arrangement.

What is in the best interests of children, or for that matter adults, will always to some extent be a value judgement.

Crime and deviance

Crime and deviance

▮ Introduction

In everyday language to **deviate** means to stray from an accepted path and many sociological definitions of deviance simply elaborate upon this idea. In other words, we often find that deviance consists of those acts which do not follow the norms and expectations of a particular social group. Deviance may be **positively sanctioned** (rewarded), **negatively sanctioned** (punished), or simply accepted without reward or punishment.

In terms of the above definition of deviance, soldiers on the battlefield who risk their lives above and beyond the normal call of duty may be termed deviant, as may physicists who break the rules of their discipline and develop a new theory. Their deviance may be positively sanctioned: a soldier may be rewarded with a medal and a physicist with a Nobel Prize. In one sense, though, neither is deviant since both conform to the values of society: the soldier to the value of courage, and the physicist to the value of academic progress.

By comparison, murderers not only deviate from society's norms and expectations but also from its values, in particular the value placed on human life. Their deviance generally results in widespread disapproval and punishment.

A third form of deviance consists of acts that depart from the norms and expectations of a particular society but are generally tolerated and accepted. The little old lady with a house full of cats or the old gentleman with an obsession for collecting clocks would fall into this category. Usually their eccentricities are neither rewarded nor punished by others. Such people are simply defined as a 'bit odd' but harmless, and therefore tolerated.

The sociological study of deviance

In practice, the field of study covered by the sociology of deviance is usually limited to deviance that

results in negative sanctions. The American sociologist Marshall B. Clinard suggested that the term 'deviance' should be reserved for 'those situations in which behaviour is in a disapproved direction, and of a sufficient degree to exceed the tolerance limit of the community'. Although not all sociologists would accept this definition, it does describe the area usually covered by studies of deviance.

In terms of Clinard's definition, crime and delinquency are the most obvious forms of deviance. **Crime** refers to those activities that break the law of the land and are subject to official punishment; **delinquency** refers to acts that are criminal, or are considered antisocial, which are committed by young people.

However, many disapproved deviant acts are not defined as criminal. For example, alcoholism and attempted suicide are not illegal in Britain today.

In practice sociologists have tended to focus their attention on the following types of deviance that generally fall within Clinard's definition: crime and delinquency, illegal drug use, prostitution, mental illness, suicide, alcoholism and homosexuality.

The definition of deviance

Deviance is relative: there is no absolute way of defining a deviant act. Deviance can only be defined in relation to a particular standard and no standards are fixed or absolute. As such, what is regarded as deviant varies from time to time and place to place. In a particular society an act that is considered deviant today may be defined as normal in the future. An act defined as deviant in one society may be seen as perfectly normal in another. Put another way, deviance is **culturally determined** and cultures change over time and vary from society to society.

For instance, at certain times in Western society it has been considered deviant for women to smoke, use make-up and consume alcoholic drinks in public. Today this is no longer the case. In the same way definitions of crime change over time. Homosexuality used to be a criminal offence in Britain. In 1969, however, homosexual acts conducted between consenting male adults over 21 in private were made legal, and in 1994 the age of consent was reduced to 18.

If we compare modern Western culture with the traditional cultures of the Teton Sioux Indians of the USA we will see how deviance varies from society to society.

As part of their religious rituals during the annual Sun Dance ceremony, Sioux warriors mutilated their bodies: leather thongs were inserted through strips of flesh on their chests and attached to a central pole. Warriors had to break free by tearing their flesh and in return were granted favours by the supernatural powers. Similar actions by members of Western society might well be viewed as masochism or madness.

Conversely behaviour accepted as normal in Western society may be defined as deviant in Sioux society. In the West the private ownership of property is an established norm: members of society strive to accumulate wealth and substantial property holding brings power and prestige. Such behaviour would have incurred strong disapproval amongst the Sioux and those who acted in terms of the above norms would be regarded as deviant. Their own norms prevented the accumulation of wealth. The Sioux had no conception of the individual ownership of land: the produce of the hunt was automatically shared by all members of the group. Generosity was a major value of Sioux culture and the distribution rather than the accumulation of wealth was the route to power and prestige. Chiefs were expected to distribute gifts of horses, beadwork and weapons to their followers.

So far, the concept of deviance suggested is fairly simple: deviance refers to those activities that do not conform to the norms and expectations of members of a particular society. As studied by sociologists, it usually refers to those activities which bring general disapproval from members of society. Deviance is a relative concept: actions are only deviant with regard to the standards of a particular society at a particular time in its history.

However, we will discover that this view of deviance will become more complex as this chapter develops. First, however, we will consider some non-sociological explanations of deviance. These explanations pose straightforward questions such as 'Why do some individuals steal?' Often the answers are similarly straightforward, being based on the following lines of reasoning:

1 Deviant behaviour is different from normal behaviour. Therefore deviants are different from normal people.

2 Deviant behaviour is a social problem since it harms individuals and can have a disruptive effect on social life. Therefore deviants are a social problem.

3 Since they are abnormal, and their behaviour is undesirable, they must have some kind of pathology: they must be sick.

4 The answer to the question 'Why deviance?' therefore lies in diagnosing the illness from which the deviant is presumed to be suffering.

Much of this reasoning has strong moral overtones since it is assumed that no normal person would have any desire to stray from the straight and narrow. The two main non-sociological diagnoses of the deviant are 'physiological' and 'psychological'. Both claim to have discovered scientifically the causes of deviance, just as doctors attempt to explain physical illness scientifically. **Physiological theories** claim that deviants have some organic defect or pathology: in other words they are born with some defect, or they develop one during their lives. (They might, for example, be affected by having a poor diet.) **Psychological theories** claim that it is the deviants' minds rather than their bodies that are ill: some emotional disturbance in their past left them mentally unbalanced. This mental imbalance causes or influences their deviance.

In the next section we will look at these rival theories about what causes deviance in more detail.

Physiological and psychological theories of deviance

Physiological theories

Most physiological or biological explanations of deviance argue that particular individuals are more prone to deviance than others because of their genetic make-up. Genetically inherited characteristics either directly cause or predispose them towards deviance. Such theories are similar to the 'common-sense' notions that people whose eyes are close together, or whose eyebrows meet cannot be trusted.

In the nineteenth century 'scientific' explanations of human behaviour became increasingly popular. Cesare Lombroso, an Italian army doctor, was one of the first writers to link crime to human biology. In his book, *L'Uomo Delinquente*, published in 1876, Lombroso argued that criminals were throwbacks to an earlier and more primitive form of human being. He claimed to have identified a number of genetically determined characteristics which were often found in criminals. These included large jaws, high cheek bones, large ears, extra nipples, toes and fingers, and an insensitivity to pain. According to Lombroso, these were some of the outward signs of an inborn criminal nature. Later research found no support for Lombroso's picture of the criminal as a primitive biological freak.

Despite these crude beginnings, there is still some support for physiological theories of deviance. Sheldon and Eleanor Glueck claim to have found a causal relationship between physical build and delinquent activity. They argue that stocky, rounded individuals (a body type known as **mesomorph**), tend to be more active and aggressive than those with other builds, and that they are therefore more prone to committing crimes.

In the 1960s British criminologists believed they had made an important breakthrough in the search for a scientific theory of crime. They claimed they had found a precise genetic cause of criminality, **chromosome abnormalities**. Chromosomes transmit inherited characteristics from parents to children. Normally females have two X chromosomes, while males have one X and one Y. Occasionally though, males have an extra Y chromosome. A number of researchers found that there was an unusually high proportion of men with this abnormality in high security prisons for the mentally ill.

Today biochemical theories of crime are supported by some criminologists. Henry E. Kelly believes that chemical imbalances in the body can cause crime. **Hypoglycaemia**, a condition in which there is too much sugar in the blood, may lead sufferers to commit crimes. Vitamin deficiencies may, according to Kelly, have the same effect. Chemical imbalances are partly the result of inherited characteristics, but they may also be caused by environmental factors such as a poor diet.

The modern supporters of biological theories of deviance are more cautious than their predecessors. They do not suggest that individuals are total prisoners of their genes. Instead they argue that biological factors predispose an individual to deviant behaviour.

Criticisms of physiological theories

Other sociologists tend to dismiss biological theories of deviance, arguing that any association between physical characteristics and deviant behaviour can be explained in other ways. For example, Taylor, Walton and Young provide an alternative explanation for the link between mesomorphism and delinquency. They suggest that:

It may well be that lower working-class children, who are more likely to be found in the criminal statistics, are also by virtue of diet, continual manual labour, physical fitness and strength, more likely to be mesomorphic.

Similarly they claim that males with chromosome abnormalities have a bizarre appearance and behave in ways that others find odd. These differences may exclude them from 'normal' social life, which in turn may lead them to crime.

A further problem for biological theories is that behaviour attributed to biological causes may not necessarily lead to criminal acts. The biochemistry of the body may indeed affect behaviour, but as Kelly, Holborn and Makin point out, 'A diabetic at work without a recent insulin injection approaching the lunch break may become tense, erratic, short tempered, but that behaviour does not constitute a criminal act.' None of these theories has been able to demonstrate convincingly that there is a causal relationship between biology and crime.

Psychological theories

Psychological theories share certain similarities with biological theories.

1 They see the deviant as different from the population as a whole.

2 He or she is abnormal in a normal population.

3 The abnormality predisposes him or her to deviance.

However, psychological theories differ in that they see the deviant's sickness and abnormality as lying in the mind rather than the body. The British psychologist Hans Eysenck includes a physiological element in his theory but he places primary emphasis on the mind. He argues that there is a link between genetically based personality characteristics and criminal behaviour. He maintains that individuals inherit different personality traits which predispose them towards crime. In particular the extrovert is likely to break the law because 'he craves excitement, takes chances, often sticks his neck out, acts on the spur of the moment, and is generally an impulsive individual'. Furthermore, extroverts are harder to condition than introverts. It is more difficult for parents to socialize them to act in accordance with society's laws, norms and values.

John Bowlby took psychological theories a stage further. He did not believe deviance was inherited; rather he explained it in terms of a child's early socialization. In his book *Forty-four Juvenile Thieves* he maintained that children needed emotional security during the first seven years of their lives. This could be provided most effectively by a close, intimate and loving relationship with their natural mother. If the child was deprived of motherly love, particularly during the early years, a psychopathic personality could develop. Psychopaths tend to act impulsively with little regard for the consequences of their actions. They rarely feel guilt, and show little response to

punishment or treatment. Bowlby claimed that delinquents who were **chronic recidivists** (that is they constantly broke the law with little regard for the possible consequences) had suffered from maternal deprivation during their early years. Often they had been raised in orphanages, where they had been deprived of an intimate relationship with a mother figure. (You can read further details and criticisms of Bowlby's views in Chapter 10, pp. 588–9.)

Criticisms of psychological theories

As with biological theories, many sociologists tend to dismiss psychological explanations of deviance.

1 They argue such theories neglect social and cultural factors in the explanation of deviance. For example, Eysenck may have mistaken differences in values for personality types. His description of extrovert characteristics is very similar to the **subterranean values**, which, according to Matza, direct delinquent behaviour. Values are learned rather than being genetically determined. (We discuss Matza's views on pp. 601–3.)

2 Some sociologists argue that the methodology of many of the studies is suspect. There is little agreement amongst psychologists about what constitutes mental health and how to measure personality characteristics.

3 Many sociologists reject the priority given to childhood experience. They dismiss the view that the individual is the captive of his or her early experience, or conditioning, which is simply acted out in later life as this approach ignores a vast number of social factors which influence behaviour during a person's life.

4 Marshall B. Clinard rather scornfully likens psychological theories of deviance to the older notion of 'possession by devils'. The devil has been replaced by the character defect; exorcism by the priest has been replaced by treatment by the psychiatrist.

Despite their rejection by many sociologists, biological and particularly psychological theories are still widespread and accepted as valid by the various agents of social control. Both types of theory have serious implications for the treatment of deviance. Put simply, if deviants are 'sick', they must be treated and cured. This view has resulted in the use of 'cures' ranging from drugs, electric shock treatment, various forms of psychotherapy, to lobotomy (the removal of part of the brain), and castration for sex offenders. Carried to its extremes, the implications of such treatments are frightening, particularly in the hands of powerful rulers.

One Flew Over the Cuckoo's Nest (a book by Ken Kesey subsequently made into a film) illustrates how such theories can be used to justify drastic 'treatments' for troublesome individuals. The hero is a patient in a mental hospital who appears quite sane but he causes problems for the authorities and he is eventually forced to have a lobotomy to make him more placid.

Similarly Aldous Huxley's *Brave New World* would no longer be a work of fiction if one New York psychiatrist had his way. In 1970 he proposed that psychological tests should be given to 6 year olds to uncover any criminal tendencies. He advocated psychiatric treatment for those who revealed such tendencies. Apparently this scheme was seriously considered by the American government, but was not put into practice (discussed in Cohen 1971, pp. 11–12).

Having introduced some of the basic ideas about deviance, in the rest of this chapter we are going to examine sociological theories of deviance. You will find that the criticisms of the above theories from a sociological perspective will become clearer as the chapter develops.

Deviance – a functionalist perspective

The functions of deviance

Rather than starting with the individual, a functionalist analysis of deviance begins with society as a whole. It looks for the source of deviance in the nature of society rather than in the biological or psychological nature of the individual.

At first sight it seems strange that some functionalists should argue that deviance is a necessary part of all societies, and that it performs positive functions for social systems. After all, deviance breaks social norms and values. With the functionalist emphasis on the importance of shared norms and values as the basis of social order, it would appear that deviance is a threat to order and should therefore be seen as a threat to society. All functionalists agree that **social control mechanisms** such as the police and the courts, are necessary to keep deviance in check and so protect social order. However, many argue that a certain amount of deviance has positive functions: that it even contributes to the maintenance and wellbeing of society.

Crime as inevitable

Emile Durkheim developed this argument with his discussion of crime in *The Rules of Sociological Method*. He argued that crime is an inevitable and normal aspect of social life. Crime is present in all types of society, indeed the crime rate is higher in the more advanced, industrialized countries. According to Durkheim, crime is 'an integral part

of all healthy societies'. It is inevitable because not every member of society can be equally committed to the **collective sentiments** (the shared values and moral beliefs of society). Since individuals are exposed to different influences and circumstances, it is 'impossible for all to be alike'. Therefore not everyone is equally reluctant to break the law.

Durkheim imagines a 'society of saints' populated by perfect individuals. In such a society there might be no murder or robbery, but there would still be deviance. The general standards of behaviour would be so high that the slightest slip would be regarded as a serious offence. Thus the individual who simply showed bad taste, or was merely impolite, would attract strong disapproval from other members of that society.

Crime as functional

Crime is not only inevitable, it can also be functional. Durkheim argued that it only becomes **dysfunctional** (harmful to society) when its rate is unusually high or low. He argues that all social change begins with some form of deviance. In order for change to occur, yesterday's deviance must become today's normality. Since a certain amount of change is healthy for society (so it can progress rather than stagnate), so is deviance. If the collective sentiments are too strong there will be little deviance, but neither will there be any change, nor any progress. The collective sentiments must have, therefore, only 'moderate energy' so they do not crush originality: both the originality of the criminal, and the originality of the genius. In Durkheim's words:

> to make progress individual originality must be able to express itself. In order that the originality of the idealist whose dreams transcend this century may find expression it is necessary that the originality of the criminal, who is below the level of his time, shall also be possible. One does not occur without the other.

Thus the collective sentiments must not be too powerful to block the expression of people like Jesus, William Wilberforce, Martin Luther King, Mother Theresa, or Bob Geldof.

Durkheim regarded some crime as 'an anticipation of the morality of the future'. In this way terrorists or freedom fighters may represent a future established order – consider the example of Robert Mugabe, a freedom fighter who later became prime minister of Zimbabwe.

If crime is inevitable, what is the function of **punishment**? Durkheim argues that its function is not to remove crime in society but to maintain the collective sentiments at their necessary level of strength. In Durkheim's words, punishment 'serves to heal the wounds done to the collective sentiments'. Without punishment the collective sentiments would lose their force to control behaviour and the crime rate would reach the point where it became dysfunctional. Thus in Durkheim's view a healthy society requires both crime and punishment; both are inevitable, both are functional.

The positive functions of deviance

Durkheim's views have been developed by a number of sociologists. Albert K. Cohen analyses two possible functions of deviance.

1 Deviance can be a **safety valve**, providing a relatively harmless expression of discontent. In this way social order is protected. For example, Cohen suggests that 'prostitution performs such a safety valve function without threatening the institution of the family'. It can provide a release from the stress and pressure of family life without undermining family stability, since relationships between prostitutes and their clients usually avoid strong emotional attachments.

2 Cohen also suggests that certain deviant acts are a useful **warning device** to indicate that an aspect of society is malfunctioning. This may draw attention to the problem and lead to measures to solve it. Thus truants from school, deserters from the army or runaways from Borstal institutions may 'reveal unsuspected causes of discontent, and lead to changes that enhance efficiency and morale'.

Durkheim and Cohen have moved away from the picture of the deviant as psychologically or biologically abnormal. Durkheim suggests that society itself generates deviance for its own well-being. Cohen argues that certain forms of deviance are a natural and normal response to particular circumstances. Yet apart from his work on suicide (examined in Chapter 13, pp. 817–20) Durkheim does not explain why particular individuals or groups seem more prone to deviance than others. Nor does he explain why certain forms of deviance appear to be associated with particular groups in the population. It was not until Robert K. Merton's famous work in the 1930s that answers to these questions were provided within a functionalist framework.

■ Robert K. Merton – social structure and anomie

Merton argues that deviance results not from 'pathological personalities' but from the culture and structure of society itself. He begins from the standard functionalist position of **value consensus**, that is, all members of society share the same values. However, since members of society are placed in different positions in the social structure (for example they differ in terms of class position) they do not have the same opportunity of realizing the shared values. This situation can generate deviance. In Merton's words, 'the social and cultural structure generates pressure for socially deviant behaviour upon people variously located in that structure'.

Cultural goals and institutionalized means

Using the USA as an example, Merton outlines his theory as follows. Members of American society share the major values of American culture. In particular they share the goal of success, for which they all strive and which is largely measured in terms of wealth and material possessions. The 'American Dream' states that all members of society have an equal opportunity of achieving success, of owning a Cadillac, a Beverley Hills mansion and a substantial bank balance. In all societies there are institutionalized means of reaching culturally defined goals. In America, the accepted ways of achieving success are through educational qualifications, talent, hard work, drive, determination and ambition.

In a balanced society an equal emphasis is placed upon both cultural goals and institutional-ized means, and members are satisfied with both. But in America great importance is attached to success and relatively less importance is given to the accepted ways of achieving success. As such, American society is unstable and unbalanced. There is a tendency to reject the 'rules of the game' and to strive for success by any available means. The situation becomes like a game of cards in which winning becomes so important that the rules are abandoned by some of the players. When rules cease to operate a situation of normlessness or **anomie** results. In this situation of 'anything goes', norms no longer direct behaviour and deviance is encouraged. However, individuals will respond to a situation of anomie in different ways. In particular, their reaction will be shaped by their position in the social structure.

Responses to cultural goals

Merton outlines five possible ways in which members of American society can respond to success goals.

1 The first and most common response is **conformity**. Members of society conform both to success goals and the normative means of reaching them. They strive for success by means of accepted channels.

2 A second response is **innovation**. This response rejects normative means of achieving success and turns to deviant means, in particular, crime. Merton argues that members of the lower social strata are most likely to select this route to success. They are least likely to succeed via conventional channels, and so there is greater pressure upon them to deviate. Their educational qualifications are usually low and their jobs provide little opportunity for advancement. In Merton's words, they have 'little access to conventional and

legitimate means for becoming successful'. Since their way is blocked, they innovate, turning to crime which promises greater rewards than legitimate means.

Merton stresses that membership of the lower strata is not, in itself, sufficient to produce deviance. In some more traditional European societies those at the bottom of the social structure are more likely to accept their position since they have not internalized mainstream success goals. Instead they have developed distinctive subcultures which define success in terms which differ from those of the wider society. (In Chapter 2, pp. 73–4 and Chapter 3, pp. 149–51, we discuss traditional working-class subculture and the 'culture of poverty'.) Only in societies such as the USA, where all members share the same success goals, does the pressure to innovate operate forcefully on the lower classes.

Finally Merton argues that those who innovate have been 'imperfectly socialized so that they abandon institutional means while retaining success-aspirations'.

3 Merton uses the term **ritualism** to describe the third possible response. Those who select this alternative are deviant because they have largely abandoned the commonly held success goals. The pressure to adopt this alternative is greatest for members of the lower middle class. Their occupations provide less opportunity for success than those of other members of the middle class. (We analyse the market situation of the lower middle class in Chapter 2, pp. 65–9.) However, compared with members of the working class, they have been strongly socialized to conform to social norms. This prevents them from turning to crime. Unable to innovate and with jobs that offer little opportunity for advancement, their only solution is to scale down or abandon their success goals. Merton paints the following picture of typical lower middle-class 'ritualists'. They are low-grade bureaucrats, ultra-respectable but stuck in a rut. They are sticklers for the rules, follow the book to the letter, cling to red tape, conform to all the outward standards of middle-class respectability, but have given up striving for success. Ritualists are deviant because they have rejected the success goals held by most members of society.

4 Merton terms the fourth, and least common response, **retreatism**. It applies to 'psychotics, autists, pariahs, outcasts, vagrants, vagabonds, tramps, chronic drunkards and drug addicts'. They have strongly internalized both the cultural goals and the institutionalized means, yet are unable to achieve success. They resolve the conflict of their situation by abandoning both the goals and the means of reaching

them. They are unable to cope and 'drop out' of society, defeated and resigned to their failure. They are deviant in two ways: they have rejected both the cultural goals and the institutionalized means. Merton does not relate retreatism to social class position.

5 **Rebellion** forms the fifth and final response. It is a rejection of both the success goals and the institutionalized means and their replacement by different goals and means. Those who adopt this alternative wish to create a new society. Thus urban guerrillas in Western European capitalist societies adopt deviant means – terrorism – to reach deviant goals such as a communist society. Merton argues that 'it is typically members of a rising class rather than the most depressed strata who organize the resentful and rebellious into a revolutionary group'.

To summarize, Merton claims that his analysis shows how the culture and structure of society generates deviance. The overemphasis upon cultural goals in American society at the expense of institutionalized means creates a tendency towards anomie. This tendency exerts pressure for deviance, a pressure which varies depending on a person's position in the class structure.

Criticisms of Merton

Critics have attacked Merton's work for neglecting the power relationships in society as a whole within which deviance and conformity occur. Laurie Taylor argues:

It is as though individuals in society are playing a gigantic fruit machine, but the machine is rigged and only some players are consistently rewarded. The deprived ones either resort to using foreign coins or magnets to increase their chances of winning (innovation), or play on mindlessly (ritualism), give up the game (retreatism), or propose a new game altogether (rebellion). But in the analysis nobody appeared to ask who put the game there in the first place and who takes the profits.

Thus Taylor criticizes Merton for not carrying his analysis far enough: for failing to consider who makes the laws and who benefits from the laws. To continue Taylor's analogy, the whole game may have been rigged by the powerful with rules which guarantee their success. These rules may be the laws of society.

Since Merton's original work, other sociologists have modified his theory in order to try to develop more satisfactory explanations for crime and delinquency. We will now examine the ideas of some of these sociologists.

■ Structural and subcultural theories of deviance

Structural theories of deviance are similar to Merton's theory. They explain the origins of deviance in terms of the position of individuals or groups in the social structure.

Subcultural theories explain deviance in terms of the subculture of a social group. They argue that certain groups develop norms and values which are to some extent different from those held by other members of society. For example, some groups of criminals or delinquents might develop norms which encourage and reward criminal activity. Other members of society may regard such activities as immoral, and strongly disapprove of them. Subcultural theories claim that deviance is the result of individuals conforming to the values and norms of the social group to which they belong. Members of subcultures are not completely different from other members of society: they may speak the same language, wear similar clothes, and attach the same value to family life. However, their subculture is sufficiently different from the culture of society as a whole to lead to them committing acts which are generally regarded as deviant.

Often structural and subcultural theories are combined as in Albert Cohen's analysis of delinquency. The development of subcultures is explained in terms of the position of groups or individuals in the social structure.

■ Albert K. Cohen – the delinquent subculture

Cohen's work is a modification and development of Merton's position. From his studies of delinquency, he makes two major criticisms of Merton's views on working-class deviance.

1 First, he argues that delinquency is a collective rather than an individual response. Whereas Merton sees individuals responding to their position in the class structure, Cohen sees individuals joining together in a collective response.

2 Second, Cohen argues that Merton fails to account for **non-utilitarian crime** such as vandalism and joy-riding which do not produce monetary reward. Cohen questions whether such forms of delinquency are directly motivated by the success goals of the mainstream culture. He agrees, however, that Merton's theory is 'highly plausible as an explanation for adult professional crime and for the property delinquency of some older and semi-professional thieves'.

Cohen begins his argument in a similar way to Merton. Lower working-class boys hold the success goals of the mainstream culture, but due largely to educational failure and the dead-end jobs which result from this, they have little opportunity to attain them. This failure can be explained by their position in the social structure. Cohen supports the view that **cultural deprivation** accounts for the lack of educational success of members of the lower working class. (We outline the theory of cultural deprivation in Chapter 12, pp. 748–50.)

Stuck at the bottom of the stratification system with avenues to success blocked, many lower working-class boys suffer from **status frustration**, that is they are frustrated and dissatisfied with their low status in society. They resolve their frustration not by turning to criminal paths to success, as Merton suggested, but by rejecting the success goals of the mainstream culture. They replace them with an alternative set of norms and values in terms of which they can achieve success and gain prestige. The result is a **delinquent subculture**. It can be seen as a collective solution to the common problems of lower working-class adolescents.

The delinquent subculture not only rejects the mainstream culture, it reverses it. In Cohen's words, 'the delinquent subculture takes its norms from the larger culture but turns them upside down'. Thus a high value is placed on activities such as stealing, vandalism and truancy which are condemned in the wider society. Cohen describes the delinquent subculture in the following way: 'Throughout there is a kind of *malice* apparent, an enjoyment of the discomfiture of others, a delight in the defiance of taboos.' He illustrates this theme with the example of defecating on the teacher's desk.

But the delinquent subculture is more than an act of defiance, a negative reaction to a society which has denied opportunity to some of its members. It also offers positive rewards. Those who perform successfully in terms of the values of the subculture gain recognition and prestige in the eyes of their peers. Thus stealing becomes, according to Cohen, not so much a means of achieving success in terms of mainstream goals, but 'a valued activity to which attaches glory, prowess and profound satisfaction'. Cohen argues that in this way lower working-class boys solve the problem of status frustration. They reject mainstream values which offer them little chance of success and substitute deviant values in terms of which they can be successful. Cohen thus provides an explanation for delinquent acts which do not appear to be motivated by monetary reward.

Like Merton, Cohen begins from a structural perspective: because there is unequal access to opportunity, there is greater pressure on certain groups within the social structure to deviate. However, he parts company from Merton when he sees some delinquency as being a collective response directed by subcultural values. In this way he shows how pressure from the social structure to deviate is reinforced by pressure from the deviant subculture.

Criticisms of Cohen

Steven Box believes that Cohen's theory is only plausible for a small minority of delinquents. He questions Cohen's view that most delinquent youths originally accepted the mainstream standards of success. Rather than experiencing shame and guilt at their own failure, Box argues, they feel resentment at being regarded as failures by teachers and middle-class youths whose values they do not share and cannot accept. They turn against those who look down on them; they will not tolerate the way they are insulted.

Cohen has also been criticized for his selective use of the idea of lower-class subculture. David

Bordua argues that he uses it to explain the educational failure of lower working-class youngsters, with the notion of cultural deprivation, but he does not use it to explain delinquency. Thus whereas cultural deprivation is passed on from one generation to the next, this does not seem to happen with the delinquent subculture. It appears to be created anew by each generation reacting to its position in the social structure.

Richard A. Cloward and Lloyd E. Ohlin – *Delinquency and Opportunity*

In *Delinquency and Opportunity* the American sociologists Cloward and Ohlin combine and develop many of the insights of Merton and Cohen. While largely accepting Merton's view of working-class criminal deviance, they argue that he has failed to explain the different forms that deviance takes. For example why do some delinquent gangs concentrate on theft while others appear preoccupied with vandalism and violence?

Cloward and Ohlin argue that Merton has only dealt with half the picture. He has explained deviance in terms of the **legitimate opportunity structure** but failed to consider the **illegitimate opportunity structure**. In other words, just as the opportunity to be successful by legitimate means varies, so does the opportunity for success by illegitimate means. For example, in one area there may be a thriving adult criminal subculture which may provide access for adolescents; in another area this subculture may not exist. Thus, in the first area, the adolescent has more opportunity to become a successful criminal.

By examining access and opportunity for entry into illegitimate opportunity structures, Cloward and Ohlin provide an explanation for different forms of deviance.

They begin their explanation of working-class delinquency from the same point as Merton: that is, there is greater pressure on members of the working class to deviate because they have less opportunity to succeed by legitimate means. Cloward and Ohlin then distinguish three possible responses to this situation: the 'criminal subculture', the 'conflict subculture' and the 'retreatist subculture'. The development of one or other of these responses by young people depends upon

their access to and performance in terms of the illegitimate opportunity structure.

Structure and subculture

1 **Criminal subcultures** tend to emerge in areas where there is an established pattern of organized adult crime. In such areas a 'learning environment' is provided for the young: they are exposed to criminal skills, deviant values and presented with criminal role models. Those who perform successfully in terms of these deviant values have the opportunity to rise in the professional criminal hierarchy. They have access to the illegitimate opportunity structure. Criminal subcultures are mainly concerned with **utilitarian crime** – crime which produces financial reward.

2 **Conflict subcultures** tend to develop in areas where adolescents have little opportunity for access to illegitimate opportunity structures. There is little organized adult crime to provide an 'apprenticeship' for the young criminals and opportunities for them to climb the illegitimate ladder to success. Such areas usually have a high turnover of population and lack unity and cohesiveness. This situation tends to prevent a stable criminal subculture from developing. Thus access to both legitimate and illegitimate opportunity structures is blocked. The response to this situation is often gang violence. This serves as a release for anger and frustration and a means of obtaining prestige in terms of the values of the subculture.

3 Finally Cloward and Ohlin analyse Merton's retreatist response in terms of legitimate and illegitimate opportunity structures. They suggest that some lower-class adolescents form **retreatist subcultures** organized mainly around illegal drug use because they have failed to succeed in both the legitimate and illegitimate structures. In this sense they are double failures: they have failed to become successful by legitimate means and they have failed in terms of either criminal or conflict subcultures. As failed criminals or failed gang members they retreat, tails between their legs, into retreatist subcultures.

Criticisms of Cloward and Ohlin

Cloward and Ohlin have produced the most sophisticated version of structural and subcultural theory. By combining the work of Merton and Cohen, and adding the notion of the illegitimate opportunity structure, they attempt to explain the variety of forms that deviance might take. Nevertheless they may not have provided a convincing explanation for every type of deviant subculture.

Taylor, Walton and Young comment 'It would be amusing, for instance, to conjecture what Cloward and Ohlin would have made of the Black Panthers or the hippies.' They argue that Merton, Cohen, and Cloward and Ohlin share one major fault in common: they all assume that everybody in America starts off by being committed to the success goal of achieving wealth. Taylor, Walton and Young believe there is a much greater variety of goals which individuals pursue. A man or a woman, for example, may refuse to take a new job or accept a promotion which offers higher pay, because it would disrupt their family life, reduce the amount of leisure time they enjoyed, or result in greater stress. Furthermore, they claim that some groups, such as hippies, made a conscious choice to reject the goal of financial success; they did not simply react to their own failure.

Walter B. Miller – lower-class subculture

The final view that we will examine in this section of the chapter is that of Walter B. Miller. It differs from those of Cohen, and Cloward and Ohlin.

Miller does not see a deviant subculture arising from the inability of the members of lower social strata to achieve success. Instead he explains crime in terms of the existence of a distinctive lower-class subculture.

Miller believes that for centuries members of the American lower class have had their own cultural traditions which differ significantly to those of higher strata. He claims that their values and way of life, which are passed on from generation to generation, actively encourage lower-class men to break the law.

Focal concerns

This **distinctive cultural system** which may be termed 'lower class', includes a number of **focal concerns**, that is major areas of interest and involvement. Included in these focal concerns are 'toughness', 'smartness' and 'excitement'.

1 **Toughness** involves a concern for masculinity and finds expression in courage in the face of physical threat and a rejection of timidity and weakness. In

practice this can lead to assault and battery in order to maintain a reputation for toughness.

2 **Smartness** involves the 'capacity to outsmart, outfox, outwit, dupe, "take", "con" another'. It is expressed in the repertoire of the hustler, the conman, the cardsharp, the pimp, the pickpocket and the petty thief.

3 **Excitement** involves the search for thrills, for emotional stimulus. In practice it is sought in gambling, sexual adventures and alcohol, all of which can be combined in a night out on the town.

This 'heady mixture' can result in damage to limb, life and property.

Two factors tend to emphasize and exaggerate the focal concerns of lower-class subculture in the lives of adolescents: first, their tendency to belong to a peer group which demands close conformity to group norms; and second, the concern of young people with status which is largely achieved in terms of peer group norms. Thus the status of a lower working-class youth can depend on his reputation for toughness and smartness in the eyes of his friends.

Delinquency and focal concerns

Miller concludes that delinquency is simply the acting out, albeit in a somewhat exaggerated manner, of the focal concerns of lower-class subculture. It results from socialization into a subculture with 'a distinctive tradition, many centuries old with an integrity of its own'.

Although this subculture has a life of its own, Miller does give reasons for its origin and maintenance. It stems from and is partly sustained by the necessity for a pool of low-skilled labour. Low-skilled workers require the ability to endure routine, repetitive and boring activity and to tolerate recurrent unemployment. Lower-class subculture provides the means to live with this situation. Its focal concerns provide satisfactions outside work and help to deal with the dissatisfaction produced by work: the emphasis on excitement in the subculture compensates for the boredom of work.

Miller presents a picture of members of the lower class living in a world of their own, totally insulated from the rest of society. They appear to pursue their focal concerns with no reference to the mainstream culture. Many sociologists would disagree with this view. In his criticism of Miller, David Bordua states:

Miller seems to be saying that the involvements in lower-class culture are so deep and exclusive that contacts with agents of middle-class dominated institutions, especially the schools, have no impact.

(We analyse the concept of lower-class subculture in more detail in Chapter 3, pp. 150–1 and Chapter 12, pp. 748–52.) Unlike Miller, most sociologists who use the concept of subculture to

explain deviance, see it as secondary to a structural explanation.

In this section we have considered subcultural and structural theories which tend to see deviant behaviour as produced by forces beyond an individual's control. Pressurized by their position in the social structure, by their membership of a deviant subculture, or their presence in an area of social disorganization, individuals stray from the path of convention. In the following section we will look at a very different theory of delinquency.

David Matza – delinquency and drift

The American sociologist David Matza has attacked some of the assumptions on which subcultural and structural theories are based, and produced his own distinctive explanation of delinquency. His work suggests that many sociological theories of delinquency are misleading in two ways.

1 They make deviants appear more distinctive than they really are.

2 They present an **over-deterministic view** of the origins of deviance. (**Determinism** is the doctrine that states that people have little or no freedom to direct their own actions since they are controlled by external forces.) 'Trapped by circumstances', the individual is automatically propelled down the path of deviance. Matza believes that this view ignores the choices and alternatives which are always available for human action.

In contrast to subculture theories Matza argues that male delinquents are not in opposition to society's norms and values. In fact, to a considerable extent they are committed to the same norms and values as other members of society. Society has a strong moral hold over them and prevents them from engaging in delinquent activities for most of the time. Matza backs up this claim by noting that delinquents often express regret and remorse when faced with what they have done. Furthermore, his own research suggests that most delinquents in training school express disapproval of crimes such as mugging, armed robbery, fighting with weapons, and auto theft. Far from being committed to crime, delinquents are only

occasional, part-time law-breakers; they are 'casually, intermittently, and transiently immersed in a pattern of illegal activity'.

Techniques of neutralization

If delinquents then are generally committed to conventional norms and values, how is it possible for them to contemplate illegal acts? Matza claims that in certain circumstances they are able to 'neutralize' the **moral bind of society**: they are able to convince themselves that the law does not apply to them on this particular occasion. Deviance becomes possible when they use **techniques of neutralization** which temporarily release them from the hold that society has over them.

Techniques of neutralization include:

1 **Denial of responsibility** for a deviant act – the delinquents may remove responsibility from themselves by blaming their parents or the area in which they live.

2 **Denial of injury** resulting from the act – the delinquents may argue that joyriding does not harm anyone, it is just a bit of mischief and that they were borrowing rather than stealing the car.

3 **Denial that the act was basically wrong** – an assault on a homosexual or a robbery from an extortionate store owner can be presented as a form of 'rough justice'.

4 **Condemnation of those who enforce the rules** – the

police may be seen as corrupt, teachers as unjust and hypocritical.

5 And finally **appeal to higher loyalties** – the delinquents may argue that they broke the law not out of self-interest but to help their family or friends.

Matza argues that the use of techniques of neutralization throws serious doubts on the idea of deviant subcultures.

1 They are evidence of guilt and shame which indicates at least a partial acceptance of mainstream norms and values. If there really were a delinquent subculture, there would be no need to resort to techniques of neutralization, since there would be no guilt to neutralize.

2 Techniques of neutralization often employ one set of mainstream norms to justify breaking others. Thus assaulting homosexuals is justified as it supports mainstream norms of sexual behaviour. Again, this shows some degree of commitment to mainstream culture.

Subterranean values

Once potential delinquents have freed themselves from the normal constraints society exercises over them delinquency becomes a possibility. They are in a state of **drift** and may or may not break the law. Whilst the state of drift explains why people can break the law, it does not explain why they should wish to.

Matza explains the attraction to deviance in terms of **subterranean values**. This set of values encourages enjoying yourself, acting on the spur of the moment, self expression, being aggressive and seeking excitement. These values, according to Matza, exist throughout society alongside **formal values** which encourage hard work and planning for the future. The 'respectable' member of society will only act in accordance with subterranean values during leisure activities, such as drinking in a bar, visiting the bowling alley, or playing football. Delinquents do not hold different values to other members of society; they simply express subterranean values at the wrong place and time. For example, they may seek excitement at school, or they could be aggressive while at work. Again Matza stresses that delinquents share more in common with other members of society than earlier theories would suggest.

The mood of fatalism and the mood of humanism

So far Matza has explained why delinquency is possible, and is attractive to some adolescents. This is not sufficient, however, to explain why they embark on delinquency. Before this is likely some 'preparation' may be necessary: they may have to learn some of the skills they will require (such as those needed to break into a car) from more experienced delinquents. They also need a strong push to step over the dividing line between deviance and conformity for the first time. As they drift they may be pushed towards or away from deviance according to the circumstances.

The final decision to step over the line comes when adolescents experience the **mood of fatalism**. They feel powerless: other people are pushing them around, telling them what to do. To overcome this feeling they need to take some action which will make things happen, and 'restore their **mood of humanism**'. They wish to stop feeling like a victim of circumstances, and to prove to themselves that they too are human beings who can influence events around them. Committing a delinquent act assures them of at least some response, even if it is a negative one. At the very least they can expect their action to be noticed, and to lead to a police investigation. Once they have taken this step it becomes easier to contemplate other delinquent acts, but Matza emphasizes that delinquency never becomes more than an occasional activity.

The subculture of delinquency

Matza uses the term 'subculture of delinquency', rather than delinquent subculture. Although he has done no more than reverse the order of the words, the concept he uses is quite different from the traditional view of a subculture.

1 The norms and values of the subculture of delinquency allow delinquent acts, but do not demand them of members of the group.

2 The conventional values of society have a considerable influence on the behaviour of the delinquent.

3 The subculture of delinquency is a loose-knit group of adolescents. Individuals frequently drift into and out of the group; they are not committed, full-time members.

Criticisms of Matza

Matza's work is radically different from previous explanations of delinquency. He rejects the view that delinquents are pathological, that they are different from other members of society, and are sick. He denies that deterministic theories can explain human behaviour. Instead he stresses the choices that are available to all human beings, including delinquents. His work is important in challenging the assumptions on which earlier theories were based. Nevertheless Matza himself has been criticized.

Taylor, Walton, and Young raise doubts about the view that those who use the techniques of neutralization are never challenging the dominant values in society. They point out that denying your behaviour is wrong is quite different from explaining it away as the result of sickness or an accident. It may indeed represent a complete rejection of society's norms and values; 'A homosexual who says he cannot help being a homosexual because he is sick is very different from the homosexual who denies the fact of harm to the victim, who declares that "gay is 'good'".'

Steven Box questions the evidence that Matza uses in support of his theory. Box suggests that it may not be possible to take the statements of delinquents at face value: when they express regret and remorse for their offences they may not be sincere; when they explain the reasons for their acts they may be attempting to justify themselves, rather than to provide an accurate account of their motives.

Despite these drawbacks, Matza's work has raised some important questions about deviance. In particular it has questioned the view that deviants hold quite untypical values. Now we will consider the relationship between deviance and official statistics.

■ Deviance and official statistics

Many theories of deviance are based in part on official statistics provided by the police, the courts, and other government agencies involved in law enforcement. In countries such as Britain and the USA, these statistics consistently show that some groups are more involved in crime than others. The working class, the young, males and members of some ethnic minorities are all more likely to commit crimes than the middle class, the elderly, females and whites – according to official data. Some sociologists have taken these figures at face value and have then proceeded to explain why such groups should be so criminal. Merton, Cohen, Cloward and Ohlin, and Miller all assume that working-class men are the main offenders, though they differ in their explanations as to why this should be so. If it could be shown that the reliability of the figures is open to question, it would raise serious doubts about their theories.

In Britain official statistics on crime are published annually. They provide criminologists, the police, the courts, the media and anyone else who is interested with two main types of datum.

1 They provide information on the total number of crimes 'known to the police'. This information is often taken as an accurate measure of the total amount of crime. The data allow comparisons to be made between crimes, and with previous years. Often the figures receive widespread publicity through the media. The statistics often show increases in crime over previous years, and they may lead to concern that the country is being engulfed in a crime wave. Figure 7.1 shows that the crime rate appears to have increased rapidly since 1951 in England, Wales, Northern Ireland and Scotland.

2 The official statistics provide information on the social characteristics of those who have been convicted of offences. It is these figures on which a number of theories of crime have been based.

Each of these sets of figures will now be examined in detail.

Unrecorded crime

It is quite obvious that not all crimes which take place are recorded by the police. There is much evidence of a substantial 'dark figure' of unrecorded crimes.

Figure 7.1   Notifiable offences recorded by the police

1 Indictable offences up to and including 1978. Excludes criminal damage of £20 or under in England and Wales and £200 or under in Northern Ireland.

2 Scottish figures are for crimes and are not comparable with those for England and Wales and Northern Ireland.

(*Source: Social Trends*, HMSO, London, 1994, p. 151.)

Before a crime is recorded at least three things must happen.

1 It must come to someone's attention that a crime has taken place.

2 It must be reported to the relevant agency.

3 That agency must be willing to accept that the law has been broken.

Not all crimes, though, have a specific victim who is aware that they have been wronged. If you return home to find a broken window and valuable items missing from your house, it will not take you long to work out that you have been burgled. Crimes such as tax evasion, however, do not have a single victim to report the offence. In this case the victim is the community as a whole which has been deprived of tax revenue. The extent of this type of crime is difficult to measure for it can only be uncovered by investigation. Nevertheless, it is possible to estimate the amount of crime of which victims are aware, but which is not reported to the police, or recorded as crime by them.

Victimization studies

In 1983, 1985, 1988 and 1993 the Home Office Research and Planning Unit published the first four *British Crime Surveys*. These studies contain data on crime in Britain in 1981, 1983, 1987 and 1991 (see Table 7.1). They attempt to overcome some of the limitations of the annual criminal statistics. Instead of relying on police records the Home Office carried out **victimization studies**. These involved asking individuals if they had been the victim of crime in the previous year. They were also asked whether they had reported the crimes, and whether the police had recorded them. The 1988 survey used a sample of 5,000 adults aged 16 or over in Scotland, and 10,392 in England and Wales. The studies confirmed that the criminal statistics are highly unreliable.

Information was collected on vandalism, burglary, theft in dwellings, theft from motor vehicles, theft of motor vehicles, bicycle theft, wounding, robbery and theft from the person, and sexual offences during 1987. The survey found that only 37 per cent of these crimes were reported to the police. Nearly half of those who did not report the

Table 7.1   A comparison of British Crime Survey and notifiable offences listed by the police

Figures in 000s	1991 Police	1991 BCS	% reported	% recorded of number reported	% recorded of all BCS crimes	% change 87–91		% change 81–91	
						Police	BCS	Police	BCS
Comparable with recorded offences									
Acquisitive crime	2,264	6,174	60	62	37	40	28	95	96
Vandalism	410	2,730	27	56	15	35	–7	105	1
Violence	198	809	48	51	24	34	9	93	21
Total	2,872	9,713	50	60	30	39	14	96	49
Vandalism	410	2,730	27	56	15	35	–7	105	1
Burglary: attempts and no loss	145	660	53	42	22	35	–1	96	76
Burglary: with loss	480	705	92	74	68	28	36	74	88
Theft from motor vehicles	769	2,400	53	61	32	36	14	128	86
Theft of motor vehicles	481	517	99	94	93	46	34	68	81
Attempted thefts of and from vehicles	13	890	41	33	14	88	107	336	395
Bicycle theft	225	564	69	58	40	70	45	78	161
Wounding	157	626	48	52	25	33	11	86	23
Robbery and theft from person	82	622	40	33	13	19	26	55	4
Other BCS offences									
Other household theft	—	1,838	29	—	—	—	21	—	21
Common assault	—	1,757	26	—	—	—	18	—	25
Other personal theft	—	1,744	38	—	—	—	–3	—	10
All BCS offences	—	15,052	43	—	—	—	13	—	36

Notes

1   **Acquisitive crimes**: burglary, thefts of and from vehicles (including attempts), bicycle thefts, theft from the person. **Vandalism**: household property and vehicles. **Violence**: wounding and robbery.

2   Police figures have been adjusted to improve comparability with the BCS. The main adjustments needed are: to exclude offences against victims aged under 16, and vandalism against public property; and to add offences recorded only by the British Transport Police (which are excluded from police figures). Police figures for 'burglary' comprise burglary in a dwelling only. Police figures of thefts of and from motor vehicles exclude 'nil value' incidents; these are shown as 'attempted thefts of and from vehicles'. Some adjustment is also made to exclude incidents involving commercial vehicles.

3   Totals do not sum to sub-totals because of rounding. Percentage changes based on unrounded numbers.

(*Source*: Home Office Research on Statistics Department, *Research Findings*, October 1992, p. 6.)

crime did not do so because they thought the offence was too trivial; 32 per cent said the police would 'not have bothered or been interested'; 2 per cent mentioned the inconvenience of reporting, 1 per cent a dislike of the police, and 1 per cent fear of reprisals.

Once an offence had been reported the police did not always accept that an offence had taken place. For example, about a third of all crimes against property reported were not recorded by the police. The survey found that the official figures on the numbers of different types of crime

taking place were very misleading. Rates of reporting varied from 10 per cent for vandalism to 86 per cent for the theft of motor vehicles. Clearly it would not be sensible to rely on the official figures given these variations in non-reporting.

The Home Office research also raised doubts about the trends in crime revealed by official statistics. According to police figures, reported offences rose by no less than 96 per cent between 1981 and 1991. In part this rise was accounted for by an increase in the likelihood of offences being reported. In 1981 the *British Crime Survey* found that 31 per cent of offences were reported; by 1991 this had risen to 43 per cent.

From these findings it appears that Official Crime Statistics have exaggerated the growth of crime, but a substantial increase does seem to have taken place for some types of crime. As Table 7.1 shows, the British Crime Survey found increases in all categories of crime studied in the survey. The amount of increase varied greatly, however, from a 395 per cent increase in attempted thefts of and from vehicles, and a 161 per cent increase in bicycle theft, to just a 1 per cent increase in vandalism. The surveys found a significant rise in crimes of violence (21 per cent), but a much smaller increase than that indicated by police figures (93 per cent).

Although victimization studies provide an indication of trends in crime and an estimate of how many crimes remain unrecorded, the data from them are not entirely reliable. Jock Young points out three main problems with victimization studies.

1 In most victimization studies a substantial minority, usually 20–25 per cent, refuse to cooperate with researchers. Those who do not take part are likely to be untypical of the population as a whole and their absence from the data is likely to distort the figures.

2 Victims may be more likely to conceal certain types of crime because of embarrassment or a misplaced sense of guilt. Crimes such as domestic violence and sexual crimes might be particularly prone to under-recording.

3 Changing public perceptions might affect the willingness of the public to regard acts as criminal. For example, people may have become less tolerant of crimes of violence or acts of vandalism and they would therefore be more likely to report less serious acts to researchers. On the other hand the opposite might have taken place so that the figures underestimate any increase in crime.

Given these problems the trends revealed in victimization studies should be treated with caution, although they are probably more reliable than those shown in official statistics.

The characteristics of offenders

It is clear then that there are many offences which are not known to the police, or are not recorded by them. An even smaller proportion of offenders are

successfully prosecuted and find their way into official statistics, for only 30–40 per cent of serious offences are cleared up. It is possible, at least in theory, that the people caught, tried and convicted are a representative cross-section of all those who commit offences. On the other hand, it could be that some sections of society are much more likely to be convicted than others, irrespective of whether they have committed more crimes.

A number of sociologists have devised an alternative to official statistics for discovering the characteristics of criminals. **Self-report studies** use questionnaires or interviews to collect information about individuals, and to ask them to admit to the number of crimes they have committed. The data collected can then be compared with official conviction rates to discover which offenders are most likely to be convicted.

Steven Box has reviewed forty such studies on delinquency conducted in a number of different countries. On the basis of this evidence Box rejects the view presented in the official statistics that working-class youths are much more likely to engage in delinquency than middle-class youths. He says 'we should be very sceptical of those who continue to argue that delinquency is located at the bottom of the stratification system'.

Of course it is possible that those replying to questionnaires or interviews might not be truthful about the amount of crime they commit. Various tests have been carried out to check on the results of these studies. These tests range from the use of lie detectors, to questioning adolescents' friends about crimes they claim to have taken part in. Generally it has been found that about 80 per cent of those who reply tell the truth. Self-report studies are not, therefore, entirely reliable. However, they do locate many more offenders than those who are convicted and appear in official statistics. As such they are probably considerably more reliable than the latter.

Bias in official statistics

Self-report studies suggest that there may be consistent police bias against working-class delinquents and in favour of middle-class delinquents. Some indication of why this might be so is provided by William Chambliss's study of two American delinquent gangs from the same city.

The 'roughnecks' were a group of working-class delinquents. They often got involved in fights, they siphoned petrol from parked cars, and frequently went shoplifting. Both the police and the community regarded them as a 'bad bunch of boys'. The police looked on them with suspicion, and all of them were arrested at least once.

The 'saints', in contrast, came from respectable, middle-class homes. None of them ever received so much as a ticket for a motoring offence from the police, though they were stopped and questioned on a number of occasions. Chambliss claimed that the 'saints' actually carried out more delinquent acts than the 'roughnecks', and some of their actions were of a very serious nature. They often drove when drunk, stealing was not uncommon, and they even placed barricades across roads just after sharp bends to catch out unsuspecting motorists.

On the basis of this study Chambliss claims that the police frequently do not take middle-class delinquency seriously. The 'saints' did not conform to the police's image of typical delinquents. With the help of their middle-class parents when necessary, they were able to persuade the authorities that their activities were harmless pranks rather than serious delinquent acts.

White-collar crime

So far it has been suggested that official statistics do not give an accurate picture of the extent of delinquency among middle- and working-class adolescents. Unfortunately few self-report studies have been conducted on adults so it is not possible to compare official statistics and the findings of self-report studies on adult crime. Even so, there is evidence that offences committed by adults of high social status are less likely to lead to arrests and convictions than those committed by adults of low social status.

Edwin Sutherland was the first sociologist to study what has come to be known as 'white-collar crime'. Sutherland defines **white-collar crime** as 'crimes committed by persons of high social status and respectability in the course of their occupations'. Such crimes include bribery and corruption in business and politics, misconduct by professionals such as doctors and lawyers, the breaking of trade regulations, food and drug laws and safety regulations in industry, the misuse of patents and trademarks, and misrepresentation in advertising.

There is evidence to suggest that such offences are widespread. In business in the UK, for example, the Guinness affair involved senior executives making illegal deals on the Stock Exchange to inflate artificially the value of Guinness shares which were to be exchanged for shares in Distillers in a takeover. Ernest Saunders, the chairman of Guinness at the time of the offences, received a prison sentence. Ian Taylor argues that in Britain there has been:

---

an enormous explosion of fraud and corruption that has accompanied the construction of a free market economy since 1979, and which has escalated since the Big Bang of 27 October 1986, when the London Stock Exchange was significantly opened up to a largely unregulated system for the marketing of financial securities.

One common type of fraud is **insider dealing**, in which shares in a company are bought by individuals who know that the company is about to be the subject of a takeover bid. These individuals illegally use their knowledge to make a killing on the stock market.

A number of prominent businessmen have been accused of fraud when their businesses got into debt and collapsed. Peter Clowes was one such businessman who was convicted of fraud in 1992: some of the £113 million invested in his businesses was spent on personal luxuries such as a yacht. In 1993 Asil Nadir fled Britain and went to Cyprus to escape prosecution on fraud charges involving £25 million arising from the collapse of his company Polly Peck.

Perhaps the best-known businessman accused of fraud was Robert Maxwell. He was the owner of Mirror Group newspapers and numerous other businesses before his mysterious drowning near the Canary Islands in 1991. Maxwell had used money from the pension fund of Mirror Group employees to stave off the collapse of his business empire. When it finally collapsed it left debts of some £2 billion.

The inadequacy of the City regulation of business and banking was also illustrated with the bankruptcy of BCCI (the Bank of Credit and Commerce International) in 1991. The bank lost more than $10 billion in trading that was not recorded in its accounts, and by making fictitious loans. A report into the collapse headed by Lord Justice Bingham denounced the Bank of England's failure to predict the collapse as 'a tragedy of errors, misunderstandings and failures of communication'.

Corruption on a massive scale took place during the 1970s when enormous amounts of money were lent by banks to governments in less developed countries such as the Philippines (where President Marcos invested vast sums in bank accounts abroad) and Mexico (where it has been estimated $40 billion went missing). The end result of such loans and the corruption that they encouraged was a worldwide debt crisis in which many poorer nations ended up heavily indebted to richer countries.

Offences committed by businesses do not just involve loss of money; some also result in injury, disability or loss of life. In 1984 an escape of poisonous gas from a chemical plant at Bhopal in India killed more than 3,000 people and caused permanent injury to a further 20,000. The escape of gas was caused by inadequate safety procedures at the plant which was owned by a subsidiary of the US multinational corporation Union Carbide. No criminal charges were brought against the company when it agreed to pay $470 million in compensation to victims and their families.

Another tragic example of the consequences of negligence was the *Herald of Free Enterprise* disaster: 188 people died when the P & O car ferry sank after setting sail from Zeebrugge harbour with its bow doors open.

John Braithwaite has studied corporate crimes committed by pharmaceutical companies and discovered that they are alarmingly common.

The US Securities and Exchange Commission encouraged drug companies to reveal 'questionable payments' (or in plainer language bribery) in return for a promise that they would not be prosecuted. All the major companies had spent substantial amounts on such payments. American Hospital Supply had apparently spent $5,800,000 on bribery. For example, it had bribed Mexican health inspectors not to enforce the Mexican Health Code at its plant in that country. Braithwaite found extensive negligence and fraud in the testing of drugs: test results were sometimes falsified, or results for tests which had never taken place were simply made up. There was a great deal of evidence of unsafe manufacturing practices being used which could lead to faulty heart pacemakers or non-sterile medical products being distributed.

The most dramatic example of the possible effects of crimes like these is the 'thalidomide affair'. This drug was manufactured by Chemie Grunethal of Germany; it was used as a sleeping pill or tranquillizer. However, the use of the drug by pregnant women led to over 8,000 seriously deformed babies being born throughout the world. Despite numerous examples of adverse reactions from clinical tests, the drug was marketed with little delay, the advertising proclaiming that it was 'completely safe'. The company was slow to withdraw the product even when the drug's disastrous effects were known.

White-collar crimes involving politicians and state officials come to light from time to time. The 'Watergate' affair is one of the best-known examples. The US President Nixon was forced to leave office as a result of his involvement in the break-in and attempted bugging of the offices of political opponents, and in using illegal sources of money to fund political campaigns. In another US political scandal, 'Irangate' government officials were found to have been involved in the illegal exchange of arms for hostages with the Government of Iran.

In Britain accusations have been made that members of the Thatcher Government knowingly allowed companies to export products for military use, including parts for a 'supergun' to the Government of Iraq. This contravened the Government's own ban on such exports during the Iran–Iraq war.

Michael Woodiwiss claims that the US Government has a history of promoting drug trafficking. During the Vietnam war 'opponents charged that the CIA was knowingly financing its operations from opium money'. This was confirmed in a book written by Orrin DeForest, a senior investigations officer with the CIA. To raise more money army officers allowed heroin to be smuggled back to America in the corpses of American soldiers. The bodies were cut open and had up to 50 lb of heroin concealed inside.

British intelligence organizations have also been accused of engaging in illegal activities. For example, in his book *Spycatcher* (which the British Government tried to suppress) Peter Wright claimed that during the period when Harold Wilson was prime minister the security services were involved in numerous unauthorized buggings and burglaries.

A number of factors combine to reduce the apparent extent and seriousness of white-collar crime.

1 It is difficult to detect: many white-collar crimes are 'crimes without victims'.

2 In cases of bribery and corruption, both parties

involved may see themselves as gaining from the arrangement, both are liable to prosecution, and therefore neither is likely to report the offence.

3 In cases where the victim is the public at large (such as misrepresentation in advertising) few members of the public have the expertise to realize that they are being misled or a knowledge of the legal procedure to redress the wrong. In such cases detection and prosecution is often left to a government agency who rarely have the personnel or finance to bring more than a few cases to court in the hope of deterring the practice.

Many white-collar crimes if detected, are rarely prosecuted. In the thalidomide affair no individual was ever found guilty of a criminal offence. Only one court case, in Canada, for compensation for one deformed baby, was ever completed. With their massive resources and skilled lawyers, the companies involved used delaying tactics to such an effect that every other case was settled out of court.

Often white-collar crimes are dealt with administratively by the various boards, and commissions and inspectorates are appointed to deal with them. 'Official warnings' rather than prosecutions are frequently the rule. In the case of professionals, their own associations usually deal with misconduct, and again prosecution is rare. In extreme cases doctors and lawyers may lose their licence to practice, but more often their professional associations simply hand down a reprimand.

The sociological study of white-collar crime provides some support for the view that there is one law for the rich and another for the poor. Edwin Sutherland argues that there is a consistent bias 'involved in the administration of criminal justice under laws which apply to business and the professions and which therefore involve only the upper socio-economic group'. The matter is neatly summarized by Willy Sutton, a professional bank robber, who stated:

Others accused of defrauding the government of hundreds of thousands of dollars merely get a letter from a committee in Washington asking them to come in and talk it over. Maybe it's justice but it's puzzling to a guy like me. (Quoted in Clinard 1974, p. 266.)

Official statistics probably underestimate the extent of white-collar and corporate crime to a far greater degree than they underestimate the extent of crime in general. As a result, official statistics portray crime as predominantly working-class behaviour. Many sociological theories have seen social class as the key to explaining criminal deviance. This conclusion may not be justified in view of the nature of criminal statistics which may give a misleading impression about the relationship between class and crime. Different classes may commit different types of crime, but it is not possible to be certain that lower classes are significantly more prone to crime than higher ones.

Statistics and theories of crime

All the theories of crime and deviance examined so far assume that criminals and deviants are a small minority of the population and attempts have been made to explain crime in terms of the differences between the criminals and the remainder of the population. Thus criminals and deviants have particular biological characteristics, a defective upbringing, a particular place in the social structure, and so on.

However, studies of crimes which do not appear in the official statistics suggest that crime is very widespread in all social strata. In America the President's Commission on Law Enforcement and the Administration of Justice found 91 per cent of those questioned in a survey admitted having committed crimes for which they could have been imprisoned. Studies of a wide range of occupations and industries suggest that crime is a normal feature of working life, from managing directors to shop-floor workers.

If most members of society are deviant, at least occasionally, then new ways of looking at deviance, new questions about deviance, and perspectives which differ radically from those so far considered are needed. Accordingly we will now analyse an alternative perspective on crime and deviance.

■ Deviance – an interactionist perspective

The interactionist perspective differs from previous approaches in two ways.

1 First, it views deviance from a different theoretical perspective.

2 Second, it examines aspects of deviance which have been largely ignored by previous approaches. It directs attention away from deviants as such and the motivations, pressures and social forces which are supposed to direct their behaviour. Instead it focuses upon the interaction between deviants and those who define them as deviant. The interactionist perspective examines how and why particular individuals and groups are defined as deviant and the effects of such a definition upon their future actions. For example, the interaction between the deviant and various agents of social control such as parents, teachers, doctors, police, judges and probation officers may be analysed. The effects upon the individual of being defined as a criminal or delinquent, as mentally ill, as an alcoholic, prostitute or homosexual may be examined.

The interactionist approach emphasizes the importance of the **meanings** the various actors bring to and develop within the interaction situation. Thus it may examine the picture of the 'typical delinquent' held by the police and note how this results in a tendency to define lower-class rather than middle-class lawbreakers as delinquents.

Meanings are not, however, fixed and clearcut. They are modified and developed in the interaction process. Thus, from an interactionist perspective, the definition of deviance is negotiated in the interaction situation by the actors involved. For example, whether or not a person is defined as mentally ill will depend on a series of negotiations between him or her and a psychiatrist.

The approaches so far considered with their emphasis on deviants simply reacting to external forces largely beyond their control, are close to a **positivist** position. Interactionists reject the positivist approach. They stress the importance of factors internal to the individual. Individuals do not react passively to external forces: they attach meanings to events before deciding how to respond.

■ Howard S. Becker – labelling theory

The definition of deviance

One of the most influential statements on deviance is contained in the following quotation from Howard S. Becker, one of the early exponents of the interactionist approach. Becker argues:

> *social groups create deviance by making the rules whose infraction constitutes deviance*, and by applying those rules to particular people and labelling them as outsiders. From this point of view, deviance is *not* a quality of the act the person commits, but rather a consequence of the application by others of the rules and sanctions to an 'offender'. The deviant is one to whom the label has successfully been applied; deviant behavior is behavior that people so label.

Becker is suggesting that in one sense there is no such thing as a deviant act. An act only becomes deviant when others perceive and define it as such.

The act of nudity in Western society provides an illustration. Nudity in the bedroom, where the actors involved are husband and wife, is generally interpreted as normal behaviour. Should a stranger enter, however, nudity in his or her presence would usually be considered deviant. Yet, in particular contexts, such as nudist camps or certain holiday beaches, nudity in the presence of strangers would be seen as perfectly normal by the participants. A male spectator at a cricket match who 'streaked' across the pitch may be viewed as 'a bit of a lad' but if he stood and exposed himself to the crowd, he might be regarded as 'some kind of a pervert'. Thus there is nothing intrinsically normal or deviant about the act of nudity. It only becomes deviant when others label it as such.

Whether or not the label is applied will depend on how the act is interpreted by the audience. This in turn will depend on who commits the act, when and where it is committed, who observes the act, and the negotiations between the various actors involved in the interaction situation.

Becker illustrates his views with the example of a brawl involving young people. In a low-income neighbourhood, it may be defined by the police as evidence of delinquency; in a wealthy neighbourhood as evidence of youthful high spirits. The acts are the same but the meanings given to them by the audience differ.

In the same way those who commit the act may view it in one way; those who observe it may define it in another. The brawl in the low-income area may involve a gang fighting to defend its 'turf' (territory). In Becker's words, they are only doing what they consider 'necessary and right, but teachers, social workers and police see it differently'. If the agents of social control define the youngsters as delinquents and they are convicted for breaking the law, those youngsters then become deviant. They have been **labelled** as such by those who have the power to make the labels stick.

Thus Becker argues 'Deviance is not a quality that lies in behavior itself, but in the interaction between the person who commits an act and those who respond to it.' From this point of view deviance is produced by a process of interaction between the potential deviant and the agents of social control.

Possible effects of labelling

Becker then examines the possible effects upon an individual of being publicly labelled as deviant. A label defines an individual as a particular kind of person. A label is not neutral: it contains an evaluation of the person to whom it is applied. It is a **master status** in the sense that it colours all the other statuses possessed by an individual. If individuals are labelled as criminal, mentally ill or homosexual, such labels largely override their status as parent, worker, neighbour and friend. Others see them and respond to them in terms of the label and tend to assume they have the negative characteristics normally associated with such labels.

Since individuals' self-concepts are largely derived from the responses of others, they will tend to see themselves in terms of the label. This may produce a **self-fulfilling prophecy** whereby 'the deviant identification becomes the controlling one'. (We examine the self-fulfilling prophecy theory in more detail in Chapter 12, pp. 762–4.)

Becker outlines a number of possible stages in this process.

1 Initially the individual is publicly labelled as deviant. This may lead to rejection from many social groups. Regarded as a 'junkie', a 'queer', a 'nutter', a 'wino' or a

'tearaway', he or she may be rejected by family and friends, lose his or her job and be forced out of the neighbourhood.

2 This may encourage further deviance. For example, drug addicts may turn to crime to support their habit since 'respectable employers' refuse to give them a job.

3 The official treatment of deviance may have similar effects. Ex-convicts may have difficulty finding employment and be forced to return to crime for their livelihood. Becker argues:

> the treatment of deviants denies them the ordinary means of carrying on the routines of everyday life open to most people. Because of this denial, the deviant must of necessity develop illegitimate routines.

4 The **deviant career** is completed when individuals join an **organized deviant group**. In this context they confirm and accept their deviant identity. They are surrounded by others in a similar situation who provide them with support and understanding.

5 Within the group a **deviant subculture** develops. The subculture often includes beliefs and values which rationalize, justify and support deviant identities and activities. For example, Becker states that organized male homosexual groups provide the individual with a rationale for his deviance:

> explaining to him why he is the way he is, that other people have also been that way, and why it is all right for him to be that way.

The subculture also provides ways of avoiding trouble with conventional society. The young thief, socialized into a criminal subculture, can learn various ways of avoiding arrest from older and more experienced members of the group. Becker argues that once individuals join an organized deviant group, they are more likely than before to see themselves as deviants and to act in terms of this self-concept. In this context the deviant identification tends to become 'the controlling one'.

Jock Young – labelling and marijuana users

The value of Becker's approach to the labelling of deviance can be seen from its application by Jock Young in his study of 'hippie' marijuana users in

Notting Hill in London. Young examines the meanings which colour the police view of the hippies, how their reaction to the hippies is directed by these meanings, and the effects upon the hippies of this reaction. The police tend to see hippies as dirty, scruffy, idle, scrounging, promiscuous, depraved, unstable, immature, good-for-nothing drug addicts. Young argues that police reaction to the hippies in terms of these meanings can 'fundamentally alter and transform the social world of the marijuana smoker'. In particular, drug taking which begins as 'essentially a peripheral activity of hippie groups' becomes a central concern.

Police action against marijuana users tends to unite the latter and make them feel different. As such, they rationalize and accept their difference. In self-defence they retreat into a small, closed group. They exclude 'straights' not only for reasons of security (secrecy about marijuana use is important to avoid arrest) but also because they develop a deviant self-concept which makes it more difficult to include members of conventional society.

In this context deviant norms and values develop. Having been defined and treated as outsiders, the hippies tend to express and accentuate this difference. Hair is grown longer, clothes become more and more unconventional. Drug use becomes transformed from a peripheral to a central activity, especially as police react more strongly against the deviance they have helped to create.

Young argues that because of increased police activity, 'drug taking in itself becomes of greater value to the group as a symbol of their difference, and of their defiance of perceived social injustices'. In this situation a deviant subculture evolves and deviant self-concepts are reinforced, all of which makes it increasingly difficult for the hippies to re-enter conventional society.

Howard Becker – the origins of 'deviant' activity

Howard Becker's approach stresses the importance of the public identification of a deviant. It suggests that a **deviant label** can lead to further deviance, and can even change individuals' self-concepts so that they come to regard themselves as deviant for the first time.

However, Becker argues that this process is by no means inevitable. Ex-convicts do get jobs and go 'straight'; drug addicts do sometimes give up their habit and re-enter conventional society.

Furthermore, Becker does try to explain how individuals get involved in deviant activities in the first place. He conducted his own study of marijuana smoking in order to explain how the habit could start and noted that various conditions had to be met if the first experimentation with the drug was to lead to regular use.

As an interactionist, Becker emphasizes the importance of the **subjective meanings** given to experiences. Thus the physical experiences that result from taking drugs are interpreted by the individual as he or she interacts with others. With regard to marijuana Becker says, 'The user feels dizzy, thirsty; his scalp tingles, he misjudges time and distance.' These effects will not necessarily be defined as pleasurable: other experienced smokers will need to reassure the new user that the effects are indeed desirable, and should be sought again.

Unlike the other theories of crime and deviance we have looked at in this chapter, Becker examines becoming deviant as a process. Merton identified a single cause of deviance (anomie) to explain deviance throughout a person's life; Becker stresses that the reasons for deviance might change as time passes and circumstances alter. Thus the reason why someone tries marijuana for the first time could be quite different from the reasons for continuing after being caught and labelled. Becker uses what he calls a 'sequential' approach to the explanation of deviance, and at any stage in the sequence it is possible that the deviant will return to conformity.

■ Edwin M. Lemert – societal reaction – the 'cause' of deviance

Like Becker, Edwin M. Lemert emphasizes the importance of **societal reaction** – the reaction of others to the deviant – in the explanation of deviance. Lemert distinguishes between 'primary' and 'secondary' deviation.

Primary deviation

Primary deviation consists of deviant acts before they are publicly labelled. There are probably any number of causes of primary deviation and it is largely a fruitless exercise to inquire into them for the following reasons.

1 First, samples of deviants are based upon those who

have been labelled and are therefore unrepresentative. For example, it makes little sense to delve into the background of convicted criminals to find the cause of their deviance without examining criminals who have not been caught.

2 Second, many so-called deviant acts may be so widespread as to be normal in statistical terms. Thus most males may at some time commit a homosexual act, engage in delinquent activities and so on.

In fact, Lemert suggests that the only thing 'known' deviants probably have in common is the fact that they have been publicly labelled as such.

Not only is the search for the causes of primary deviation largely fruitless, primary deviation itself is relatively unimportant. Lemert argues that it 'has only marginal implications for the status and the psychic structure of the person concerned'. Thus Lemert suggests that the odd deviant act has little effect on individuals' self-concepts and status in the community, and does not prevent them from continuing a normal and conventional life.

Secondary deviation

The important factor in 'producing' deviance is societal reaction, the public identification of the deviant and the consequences of this for the individual concerned. **Secondary deviation** is the response of the individual or the group to societal reaction.

Lemert argues that studies of deviance should focus on secondary deviation which has major consequences for the individual's self-concept, status in the community and future actions. In comparison, primary deviation has little significance. Lemert argues that 'In effect the original "causes" of the deviation recede and give way to the central importance of the disapproving, degradational, and isolating reactions of society.'

Thus, Lemert claims that societal reaction can be seen as the major 'cause' of deviance. This view, he argues, 'gives a proper place to social control as a dynamic factor or "cause" of deviance'. In this way Lemert neatly reverses traditional views of deviance: the blame for deviance lies with the agents of social control rather than with the deviant.

Stuttering and societal reaction

Lemert is particularly convincing in his paper entitled *Stuttering among the North Pacific Coastal*

Indians which examines the relationship between societal reaction and deviance. Previous research had indicated a virtual absence of stuttering among North American Indians: indeed most tribes did not even have a word for this speech irregularity. However, Lemert's investigation of deviance in various tribes living in the North Pacific coastal area of British Columbia revealed evidence of stuttering both before and after contact with whites. In addition the languages of these tribes contained clearly defined concepts of stutterers and stuttering. It is particularly significant that their inland neighbours, the Bannock and Shoshone, had no words for stuttering and research, using a large-scale sample of members of these tribes, found no evidence of actual stuttering.

The North Pacific coastal Indians have a rich ceremonial life, involving singing, dancing and speech-making. Their legends and stories are filled with references to famous orators and outstanding speeches. From an early age, children are initiated into ceremonial life, and parents stress the importance of a faultless performance. There are rigorous and exacting standards to be met; rituals must be performed exactly as they should be. If they do not meet these standards, children shame their parents and suffer the ridicule of their peers. In particular there is a highly developed sensitivity to any speech defect. Children and parents alike are anxious about any speech irregularity and respond to it with guilt and shame. Lemert concludes that stuttering is actually produced by societal reaction. The concern about and the reaction to speech irregularities actually creates them. He argues that the culture, both past and present:

seems favorable to the development of stuttering, that stutterers were and still are socially penalized, that parents tended to be specifically concerned or anxious about the speech development of their children, that children were anxious about ritual performances involving solo verbal behavior.

In other American Indian societies, where such concerns were largely absent, stuttering was unknown. Thus Lemert argues that societal reaction, prompted by a concern about particular forms of deviance, can actually produce those forms of deviance.

■ Erving Goffman – deviance and the institution

In general, interactionists view the various institutions for the treatment of deviance – the prisons, mental hospitals and reform schools – as a further set of links in a long chain of interactions which confirm the label of deviance both for the individual so labelled and for society as a whole. In a series of trendsetting essays, Erving Goffman examined the treatment of mental patients in institutions. He argues that although the stated aim of such institutions is to cure and rehabilitate, a close examination of interaction patterns within the institution reveals a very different picture.

Mortification

Goffman is particularly concerned with how, via a series of interactions, pressure is placed upon inmates to accept the institution's definition of themselves. Upon entry, 'he begins a series of abasements, degradations, humiliations, and profanities of self. His self is systematically, if often unintentionally, mortified.'

This **mortification process** strips inmates of the various supports which helped to maintain their former self-concepts. Often their clothes (an important symbol of identity) are removed. Their possessions (a further symbol of identity) may be taken away and stored for the duration of their stay. They may be washed, disinfected and their hair cut. They may then be issued with a new 'identity kit' such as regulation clothes and toilet articles. Such standardized items tend to remove individuality and define the inmate simply as a member of a uniform mass.

Once the entry phase is over, the inmate settles down to an endless round of **mortifying experiences**. Each day is strictly timetabled into a set of compulsory activities controlled by the staff. Patients are allowed little freedom of movement, few opportunities to show initiative or take decisions. Throughout their stay, their actions are scrutinized and assessed by the staff in terms of the rules and standards which they have set. Many of these regulations can be degrading. For example, in some mental hospitals, a spoon is the only utensil provided for the patients to eat with.

Goffman summarizes what mental hospitals in particular and treatment institutions in general 'say' to the inmates about themselves:

> In the mental hospital, the setting and the house rules press home to the patient that he is, after all, a mental case who has suffered from some kind of social collapse on the outside, having failed in some over-all way, and that here he is of little social weight, being hardly capable of acting like a fully-fledged person at all.

The effects

Not surprisingly, inmates in treatment institutions become anxious as their day of release approaches. At best they have not been prepared for life on the outside; at worst they have accepted the institution's definition of themselves as hopeless, hapless deviants. A small minority become **institutionalized**: they believe themselves unable to function in the outside world, cling to the security of the institution and go to great lengths to remain inside.

Despite this Goffman argues that the effects of the institution upon the majority of inmates are not usually lasting. There is a period of temporary **disculturation**, which means that the former inmate must re-learn some of the basic 'recipes' for living in the outside world. However, the most lasting and important consequence is the label 'ex-mental patient' or 'ex-convict'. This, rather than the experience of being inside, makes re-entry into conventional society difficult.

Goffman reaches the rather pessimistic conclusion that many treatment institutions, 'seem to function merely as storage dumps for inmates'. Like societal reaction in general, treatment institutions serve to reinforce rather than reduce deviance. He does, however, stress that some ex-patients are able to successfully fight against the label. They do not see themselves as mentally ill, and can convince others that they have returned to normality. They survive despite the handicap of their stay in the institution. (We study Goffman's research in more detail in Chapter 5, pp. 305–7.)

■ Deviance and the interactionist perspective – criticisms and evaluation

In the 1960s the interactionist view of deviance enjoyed wide popularity. For many sociologists the work of writers such as Becker, Lemert and

Goffman became the accepted, orthodox perspective on deviance. Nevertheless in the 1970s it began to provoke strong criticism. Interactionists rallied to the defence of their work and attempted to show that the criticisms were unjustified.

The definition of deviance

The first line of criticism attacks the interactionist definition of deviance. Becker and Lemert argue that deviance was created by the social groups who defined acts as deviant. Taylor, Walton and Young, however, claim that this view is mistaken. To them most deviance can be defined in terms of the actions of those who break social rules, rather than in terms of the reaction of a social audience.

For example, it is true that in some circumstances deliberately killing another person may be regarded as justified: you may be acting in self-defence, or carrying out your duties as a soldier. But whoever makes up the social audience, a 'premeditated killing for personal gain' will always be regarded as deviant in our society. As Taylor, Walton and Young put it, 'we do not live in a world of free social meanings': in many circumstances there will be little or no freedom of choice in determining whether an act is regarded as deviant or not.

The origins of deviance

A second, related criticism of interactionism is that it fails to explain why individuals commit deviant acts in the first place. Lemert claims it is not necessary to explain primary deviance, since it is very common and it has no impact on a person's self-concept. Many sociologists do not accept this claim.

Although most people do commit deviant acts from time to time, different individuals tend to commit different types of deviance. One person might steal, another might break health and safety legislation, and a third might smoke marijuana. Clearly it is important to explain why individuals should choose to turn to one form of deviance rather than another.

Furthermore, it is clear that many deviants realize they are breaking the norms of society, whether or not they are caught and labelled. As Taylor, Walton and Young argue:

> while marijuana smokers might regard their smoking as acceptable, normal behaviour in the company they move in, they are fully aware that this behaviour is regarded as deviant in the wider society.

Taylor, Walton and Young therefore suggest that it is necessary to explain why the marijuana smokers decide to take the drug despite their knowledge that it would be condemned by most other members of society.

It can also be argued that it is wrong to assume that primary deviance will have no effect on someone's self-concept. Even if people keep their deviance secret, they know that they are capable of breaking the law and this could well affect both their opinion of themselves and their later actions.

Labelling as deterministic

The third major criticism of the interactionist perspective is that it is too **deterministic**. It assumes that once a person has been labelled their deviance will inevitably become worse. The labelled person has no option but to get more and more involved in deviant activities. Thus Ronald Ackers states:

> One sometimes gets the impression from reading the literature that people go about minding their own business, and then – 'wham' – bad society comes along and slaps them with a stigmatized label. Forced into the role of deviant the individual has little choice but to be deviant. (Quoted in Gibbons and Jones 1975, p. 131.)

Critics like Ackers are suggesting that individuals might simply choose to be deviant regardless of whether they have been labelled. Thus labelling does not cause most terrorists to turn to crime: they are motivated by their political beliefs to break the law.

As Alvin W. Gouldner notes in his critique of Becker, the interactionists tend to portray the deviant as someone who is passive and controlled by a 'man-on-his-back', rather than as an active 'man-fighting-back'. If individuals can choose to take part in deviance, they may also decide to ignore a label and to give up deviance 'despite' it.

The Swedish sociologist Johannes Knutssen argues that interactionists have not produced sufficient evidence to show that labelling will amplify deviance. Knutssen feels that labelling theorists have taken the effects of labels to be 'self-evident-truths', without producing the research findings necessary to support their case.

Labelling, laws and law enforcement

The final major criticism is that interactionists fail to explain why some people should be labelled rather than others, and why some activities are against the law and others are not. Why, to use Becker's example, should the police regard a brawl in a low-income neighbourhood as delinquency, and in a wealthy neighbourhood as no more than youthful high spirits? Why should laws against robbery be enforced strictly, when factory legislation is not? Why should it be illegal to smoke marijuana but not cigarettes? The critics of labelling theory claim that they do not provide satisfactory answers to these types of question.

A defence of interactionism

Interactionists have not taken this barrage of criticism lying down. In an article entitled 'Labelling Theory Reconsidered' Becker attempted to defend himself from these attacks. More recently Ken Plummer has advanced the claim that labelling theory has been 'misunderstood' and unfairly criticized.

Ken Plummer accepts the first criticism while insisting that the reaction of a social audience to a deviant act is still important. He acknowledges that rule-breaking behaviour can be regarded as deviant whether or not it is discovered and labelled. He calls this form of deviance **societal deviance**. Plummer defines this as behaviour which breaks the laws of society, or which is commonly sensed by most of society's members to be deviant. For example, homosexuality is commonly regarded as deviant, and so by this definition a secret homosexual would be a deviant. Nevertheless Plummer suggests it is never certain whether a particular act or individual will be regarded as deviant by a social audience.

Situational deviance consists of those acts which others judge to be deviant given the context in which they take place. A member of a rugby team who drinks heavily might be regarded as 'one of the lads', while in different situations others who actually drink less might be seen as alcoholics. Plummer therefore accepts that deviance depends partly on what you do but, he reminds the critics, it also depends on the social reaction.

The second criticism – that interactionists ignore the initial causes of deviance – is dismissed by Plummer. He points out that in practice interactionists have devoted considerable attention to explaining primary deviance. For example, Becker tries to explain how it is possible to get involved in marijuana smoking. Some versions of labelling theory start their account of deviance at the point when labelling first occurs, but many interactionists deal with the earlier stages of becoming deviant. Becker himself claimed that he regretted calling his approach 'labelling theory'; he preferred it to be seen as an interactionist approach which did not concentrate exclusively on labels.

Plummer finds it even more difficult to accept that interactionist theories of deviance are deterministic. He points out that the whole interactionist perspective places great stress on the choices open to individuals as they interpret what happens around them and decide how to respond. It is quite different from a positivist approach which sees people's behaviour as directed by external forces beyond their control. As Plummer puts it:

To take a theory that is sensitive to self, consciousness and intentionality and render it as a new determinism of societal reaction could only be possible if the theory were totally misunderstood in the first place.

He notes that Goffman's mental patients provide an excellent example of labelled deviants who fight against and often overcome the labels that are thrust on them against their will (see p. 306 for further details). Becker saw the deviant as passing through a series of stages in his or her deviant career. At no stage does he say that it is inevitable that a person will continue to be a deviant – indeed Becker stresses that a deviant career could be abandoned at any stage.

The final major criticism of labelling theory is also rejected by Plummer. He believes that the labelling perspective opened up the whole question of who had the power to make society's rules, and apply them to particular individuals. It raised for the first time the very issues that critics claimed it ignored. Nevertheless it can be argued that interactionists do not satisfactorily answer these questions. Because of their emphasis on social action, they are not particularly concerned with the distribution of power in society as a whole.

Whatever the limitations of the interactionist perspective on deviance it has made an important contribution to this area of sociology. It has shown that the definition of deviance is not a simple process. It challenges the view of the deviant as an abnormal, pathological individual. It questions positivistic and deterministic theories of crime. Finally it raises the issue of who has the power to label acts and individuals as deviant. As such it has had a considerable influence even on those sociologists in the 1970s and 1980s who rejected the interactionist approach to deviance.

Having considered the interactionist perspective on deviance and criticisms of it, we will now look at deviance from the phenomenological perspective.

Deviance – a phenomenological perspective

Aaron V. Cicourel – the negotiation of justice

The phenomenological approach to deviance has some similarities to the interactionist perspective. Both phenomenology and interactionism:

1 emphasize the importance of the way that the law is enforced;

2 are concerned with the process of labelling individuals as deviant;

3 and concentrate on studying the subjective states of individuals rather than the structure of society as a whole.

However, interactionists and phenomenologists approach the study of deviance in different ways. **Phenomenologists** do not claim to produce causal explanations; they seek to understand what a phenomenon is. Thus phenomenologists attempt to discover what deviance is by examining the way that some acts and individuals come to be defined or labelled as deviant. Unlike interactionists they stop short of claiming that labelling causes people to commit more deviant acts.

Ethnomethodology is an American sociological perspective which attempts to apply the principles of phenomenology to the study of society. The work of the American ethnomethodologist Aaron V. Cicourel on the treatment of delinquency in two Californian cities provides a good example of how this perspective has been applied to the study of deviance.

Defining delinquency

The process of defining a young person as a delinquent is not simple, clearcut and unproblematic. It is complex, involving a series of interactions based on sets of meanings held by the participants. These meanings can be modified during the interaction so that each stage in the process is negotiable.

The first stage is the decision by the police to stop and interrogate an individual. This decision is based on meanings held by the police of what is 'suspicious', 'strange', 'unusual' and 'wrong'. Such meanings are related to particular geographical areas. Inner city, low-income areas are seen as 'bad areas' with a high crime rate; consequently behaviour in such areas is more likely to be viewed as suspicious. Interrogation need not lead to arrest. The process is negotiable but depends largely on the picture held by the police of the 'typical delinquent'. If the appearance, language and demeanour of the young person fits this picture, she or he is more likely to be arrested.

Once arrested, the young person is handed over to a juvenile officer (probation officer) who also has a picture of the 'typical delinquent'. If the suspect's background corresponds to this picture, she or he is more likely to be charged with an offence. Factors assumed to be associated with delinquency include 'coming from broken homes, exhibiting "bad attitudes" toward authority, poor school performance, ethnic group membership, low-income families and the like'.

It is not therefore surprising that Cicourel found a close relationship between social class and delinquency. Most young people convicted of offences had fathers who were manual workers. On a seven-class occupational scale, Cicourel found that one third come from class 7.

Cicourel explains the preponderance of working-class delinquents by reference to the meanings held by the police and juvenile officers and the interactions between them and the juveniles. When middle-class juveniles were arrested, there was less likelihood of them being charged with an offence: their background did not fit the standard picture of the delinquent. Their parents were better able to negotiate successfully on their behalf. Middle-class parents can present themselves as respectable and reasonable people from a nice neighbourhood, who look forward to a rosy future for their child. They promise cooperation with the juvenile officers, assuring them that their offspring is suitably remorseful.

As a result, the middle-class juvenile is often defined as ill rather than criminal, as accidentally straying from the path of righteousness rather than committed to wrongdoing, as cooperative rather than recalcitrant, as having a real chance of reforming rather than being a 'born loser'. He or she is typically 'counselled, warned and released'. Thus in Cicourel's words, 'what ends up being called justice is negotiable'.

Cicourel based his research on two Californian cities, each with a population of around 100,000. The socio-economic characteristics of the two populations were similar. In terms of structural theories, the numbers of delinquents produced by the pressures of the social structure should be similar in each city. However, Cicourel found a significant difference in the numbers of delinquents arrested and charged. He argues that this difference can only be accounted for by the size, organization, policies and practices of the juvenile and police bureaus.

For example, the city with the highest rate of delinquency employed more juvenile officers and kept more detailed records on offenders. In the second city, the delinquency rate fluctuated sharply. Cicourel argues that in this city the response of the police to delinquency 'tends to be quite variable depending on publicity given to the case by the local paper, or the pressure generated by the mayor or chief or Captain of Detectives'. Thus societal reaction can be seen to directly affect the rate of delinquency.

Cicourel argues that delinquents are produced by the agencies of social control. Certain individuals are selected, processed and labelled as deviant. Justice is the result of negotiation in the interaction process. The production of delinquents is also dependent on the ways in which police and juvenile bureaus are organized, their policies, and the pressures from local media and politicians that are brought to bear on them.

In view of these observations Cicourel questions structural and subcultural theories of deviance which see deviance as a product of pressure from the social structure. He concludes:

The study challenges the conventional view which assumes 'delinquents' are 'natural' social types distributed in some ordered fashion and produced by a set of abstract 'pressures' from the 'social structures'.

Criticisms of Cicourel

Cicourel's study provides some useful insights into juvenile justice in the USA. He attempts to show how the meanings held by the various officials lead to some individuals being defined as delinquent.

However, critics such as Taylor, Walton and Young argue that he fails to explain how these meanings originate. He fails to show why, for instance, the police see the 'typical delinquent' as coming from a low-income family. In common with other phenomenologists and ethnomethodologists he does not explain who has power in society, and how the possession of power might influence the definition of crime and deviance.

The same cannot be said of Marxists, whose theories on deviance we will now examine.

■ Traditional Marxist perspectives on deviance

Sociologists such as William Chambliss, Milton Mankoff, Frank Pearce and Laureen Snider have used Marxist concepts to provide a framework for understanding deviance in capitalist societies.

Such sociologists see power as largely being held by those who own and control the means of production. The superstructure reflects the relationship between the powerful and the relatively powerless: the ruling and subject classes. As part of the superstructure, the state, the agencies of social control, the law and definitions of deviance in general, reflect and serve ruling-class interests.

As an instrument of the ruling class, the state passes laws which support ruling-class interests, maintain its power and coerce and control the subject class. (We look at Marxist views on the role of the state in Chapter 9, pp. 524–30.) Laws are not an expression of value consensus but a reflection of ruling-class ideology. Thus, a general commitment to laws by members of society as a whole is an aspect of false class consciousness since, in practice, laws benefit only the ruling minority.

In the next few sections we will consider these views and their implications in detail. Neo-Marxist and other conflict perspectives on deviance will be examined later in this chapter.

■ Who makes the law? Who benefits?

From a Marxist perspective laws are made by the state which represents the interests of the ruling class.

Many sociologists have noted the large number of laws dealing with property in capitalist society. For example, Hermann Mannheim writes 'the history of criminal legislation in England and many other countries, shows that excessive prominence was given by the law to the protection of property'. According to William Chambliss such laws were largely unnecessary in feudal society where land, unmovable property, was the main source of wealth and landowners were 'the undisputed masters of the economic resources of the country'.

However, the increasing importance of trade and commerce (which involves movable property) and the eventual replacement of feudalism by capitalism resulted in a vast number of laws protecting the property interests of the emerging capitalist class. Chambliss argues:

> The heart of a capitalist economic system is the protection of private property, which is, by definition, the cornerstone upon which capitalist economies function. It is not surprising, then, to find that criminal laws reflect this basic concern.

Laureen Snider notes that the capitalist state is often reluctant to pass laws which regulate large capitalist concerns and which might threaten their profitability. She points out that capitalist states often use vast sums of money trying to attract investment from corporations. They offer new investors tax concessions, cheap loans and grants, and build expensive infrastructures to help companies operate successfully. Having tried so hard to attract inward investment, the state is unwilling to risk alienating large corporations. Snider says:

> the state is reluctant to pass – or enforce – stringent laws against pollution, worker health and safety; or monopolies. Such measures frighten off the much sought-after investment and engender the equally dreaded loss of confidence.

The national interest and the powerful

However, laws are sometimes passed which appear to be designed to protect the consumer against private enterprise. In all advanced capitalist societies there are laws, apparently framed in the national interest, which provide the state with powers to control industry and commerce. Examples include laws on pollution and the protection of the environment. Yet it can be argued that many such laws not only serve ruling-class interests, but are often shaped and promoted by the very groups whose power they are supposed to curb.

One example of ruling-class control of legislation is provided by James Graham's study of the Drug Abuse Prevention and Control Act passed by the Nixon administration in 1970. Attempts were made to place greater controls on the manufacture and supply of amphetamine, known in illegal drug circles as 'speed'. Amphetamine is a stimulant which if taken in large quantities can do considerable harm. Over 90 per cent of amphetamine on the illicit market was legally manufactured by the large drug corporations. Graham claims that due to pressure placed on politicians by the drug corporations, attempts to place stricter controls on amphetamine manufacture and distribution failed. Graham concludes 'The end result is a national policy which declares an all out war on drugs which are not a source of corporate income.'

His conclusion is echoed by Senator Eagleton who maintains that public welfare takes second place to corporation profits. Eagleton states 'When the chips were down, the power of the drug companies was simply more compelling' (quoted in Graham 1976, p. 121).

Law and the subject class

In this section we have followed the argument that the law is an instrument of the ruling class, used to maximize its profits, control its workforce, and further its interests in general. Can all laws be seen in this light?

Frank Pearce argues that many laws which appear to benefit only the subject class in reality benefit the ruling class as well. Factory legislation protecting the health and safety of workers provides an example. Pearce writes:

> The majority of laws in Britain and America work in favour of the capitalists, yet many laws do also benefit the other social classes, not only because the system needs a healthy, safe population of producers and consumers but also because it needs their loyalty.

This section has also given the impression that laws are directly instituted and promoted by the ruling class. There is, though, considerable evidence against this view. Government bureaucracies and interest groups are important sources of

law but from a Marxist perspective, the law will generally support ruling-class interests no matter what its source. As Poulantzas has argued, the state can most effectively represent the ruling class when members of that class do not directly govern (see Chapter 9, pp. 527–8).

From this viewpoint government bureaucracies can be expected to act independently from direct ruling-class control and to take initiatives. They may make decisions which are not necessarily supported by all members of the ruling class at the time, but in the long term these help to maintain the stability of the capitalist system. They may make concessions to pressure groups in order to prevent more serious and widespread protests.

For example, the Southern Christian Leadership Conference led by Martin Luther King can be seen as partly responsible for the civil rights laws of the mid 1960s. This legislation guaranteed black Americans equal rights under the law in areas such as voting, education and employment. However, Michael Haralambos argues that such laws can also be seen as serving ruling-class interests. In the Deep South mechanical cotton pickers and chemical weedkillers had removed the need for black fieldhands. Racial prejudice and discrimination were no longer needed to provide a large, passive, low-paid workforce. Movements such as the Southern Christian Leadership Conference which mobilized hundreds of thousands of blacks in the southern states, may well have threatened capitalist interests. In the late 1960s some Black Power groups in the urban ghettos were openly anti-capitalist. Concessions such as the civil rights legislation effectively defused the massive, organized black protest movements in the South.

Non-decision making

Just as important as laws that are passed are laws that are not passed. **Non-decision making** is as important as decision making. In Chapter 9 it is argued that the ruling class had the power to ensure that only 'safe decisions' were taken and to prevent many issues from ever reaching the point of decision. William Chambliss applies this argument to the law.

Chambliss suggests that much of what takes place in the creation of rules is 'non-decision making'. He gives examples of situations which may well be legally defined as criminal if the ruling class did not control beliefs about what should and should not be. Thus a movie magnate hires a nightclub and spends $20,000 on a lavish birthday party for his daughter, while people are starving a few blocks away. The wife of the US Attorney General has 200 pairs of shoes while in the Appalachian Mountains, parents cannot afford to buy their children a single pair. Such behaviour is justified by ruling class ideology with statements such as 'They've earned their money; they have a right to spend it as they see fit.'

Few break through the barriers of false class consciousness. Angela Davis, a former leader of the Black Panthers, a militant Black American organization, is the exception rather than the rule when she claims:

> The real criminals in this society are not all the people who populate the prisons across the state, but those people who have stolen the wealth of the world from the people. (Quoted in Taylor, Walton and Young 1973, p. 27.)

In her eyes the real criminals are members of the capitalist class. Ruling-class control of the superstructure prevents such views from becoming widespread, from developing into major issues, and from being translated into law.

Who breaks the law? Who gets caught?

Corporate crime

Sociologists who have been strongly influenced by Marxism tend to argue that crime is widespread in all social strata. As we discovered in an earlier section (see pp. 402–4), there are many examples of illegal behaviour by white-collar criminals and corporations. Laureen Snider argues 'Many of the most serious antisocial and predatory acts committed in modern industrial countries are corporate crimes.' Snider claims that corporate crime does more harm than the 'street crimes', such as burglary, robbery and murder, which are usually seen as the most serious types of crime. Writing in 1993 she pointed out that figures suggest that corporate crime costs more, in terms of both money and lives, than street crime.

For example, in a typical year in the USA about 20,000 people are murdered, and in Britain about 600. This compares in the USA with an annual death toll of 14,000 from industrial accidents (many resulting from breaking safety regulations), 30,000 from 'unsafe and usually illegal' consumer products, 100,000 from occupationally induced diseases and 'hundreds of thousands of cancer deaths are caused by legal and illegal environmental pollution'. In Britain workplace accidents account for 600 deaths and 12,000 injuries annually.

According to Snider street crime involves losses of around $4 billion each year in the USA. However, losses from corporate crime are more than twenty times greater. In recent years 312 US savings and loan companies have been unable to pay their debts due to fraudulent activities such as insider dealing, failing to disclose accurate information in accounts, and racketeering. The General Accounting Agency has estimated the total costs of bailing out these companies as a minimum of $325 billion and more probably around $500 billion. This means it is likely to cost every household in the USA $5,000.

Despite the enormous costs of corporate crime, both the penalties and the chances of prosecution for those involved in it are usually small. Snider argues that enforcement agencies are expected to balance the costs of enforcing regulations (for example in lost profits or jobs) with the benefits. Prosecutions are normally used as a last resort and it is more likely to be small businesses which are taken to court rather than the big corporations who do most harm.

Quoting from a variety of studies Snider notes that under US anti-trust legislation there were 1,551 prosecutions from 1890 to 1969 but only 4.9 per cent of offenders received a prison sentence. In fact, for the first 71 years of the laws no business leaders were imprisoned – the only people sent to jail were labour leaders. Some 80 per cent of the fines imposed were under $5,000.

In Britain a study by W.G. Carson examined the enforcement of factory legislation. A sample of 200 firms in southeast England were found by the Factory Inspectorate to have committed 3,800 offences over a four-and-a-half year period from 1961 to 1966. All the companies had committed at least one offence, yet there were only ten prosecutions.

Frank Pearce claims that if violations of laws such as anti-trust legislation are widespread yet the numbers of prosecutions are small, then prosecutions must serve a purpose other than the regulation of business. This purpose, he claims, is to maintain the myth that the law applies equally to rich and poor, that the state is a neutral body, above sectional interests, guarding the welfare of society as a whole.

A second reason for the small number of prosecutions is to create the impression that corporate crime is minimal. Revelation of the widespread nature of corporation crime could well threaten capitalist power.

Organized crime

Pearce also considers the relationship between the ruling-class and organized crime in America. He argues that organized crime 'has been encouraged, ignored or repressed in direct relationship to its utility to the American ruling class'. Pearce claims that particularly during the 1920s and 1930s, gangsters were often employed by large companies for a variety of purposes. They were used to break strikes by intimidating workers, to infiltrate and control unions, and to put competitors out of business.

During the 1930s, the Detroit automobile companies fought a long battle against attempts by their workers to form unions. Fords and General Motors hired gangsters in an effort to terrorize workers into submission. They lost the battle but continued the war, using gangsters to intimidate militant left-wing trade union leaders. During the 1950s these leaders were replaced by more moderate men: the need for gangsters was over and they were dropped from the payroll. In Pearce's words, 'they are a poor substitute for compliant right-wing trade unionists'.

Using examples such as this, Pearce sees organized crime as the servant of the ruling class, to be used when and where it suits its purposes.

Crime and the ruling class in Seattle

In an important study of crime in Seattle, Washington, William Chambliss argues that organized crime is not merely the servant of the ruling class but rather an integral part of it. His research covered nearly ten years, from 1962 to 1972, and was based on interviews with a variety of informants including police officers, government officials, professional thieves, racketeers and prostitutes. Chambliss argues that crime occurs throughout all social strata. The major differences between strata are the types of crimes committed and the nature of law enforcement.

Chambliss claims that power, in the form of money and influence, is the key factor which determines who gets arrested and who does not. During the time of his study over 70 per cent of the arrests in Seattle were for public drunkenness. Skid row rather than upper-class suburbia preoccupied the police. The courts and the jails were filled with the poor and the powerless.

Chambliss claims that the major crime syndicate in Seattle was made up of leading businessmen, political leaders and law enforcement officers. The syndicate organized illegal gambling, bookmaking, prostitution, pornography and the sale and distribution of drugs. Its tentacles spread throughout the ruling class. The vice president of a local bank helped the syndicate to conceal its large tax-free profits and sat on the board of a syndicate-owned 'shark' loan company. Those who threatened to 'blow the whistle' on the syndicate's activities were murdered. Drowning was a favourite method since it could be conveniently glossed over as suicide by the coroner, a brother-in-law of a member of the syndicate. Payoffs and bribes to local politicians and government officials were standard practice with the result that local government bureaucracy turned a blind eye to the syndicate's activities. Complaints from residents in low-income areas about the presence of brothels and gambling casinos in their neighbourhoods were ignored by the powers that be. From this type of evidence, Chambliss reaches the following conclusions.

1 Those who operate organized crime in American cities are not members of some 'criminal class' – they belong to the economic and political elite.

2 It is not only the small minority of active syndicate members within the ruling class who profit from crime. The class as a whole benefits, since monies gained from illegal activities are used to finance legal business operations.

3 Corruption of local political and law enforcement agencies is essential for organized crime to flourish.

4 Criminal acts which favour ruling-class interests will

not be penalized; those that do not will be subject to legal sanctions.

▌Why break the law? Why enforce the law?

Capitalism and crime

Many Marxists see crime as a natural 'outgrowth' of capitalist society. They argue that a capitalist economic system generates crime for the following reasons.

1 The economic infrastructure is the major influence upon social relationships, beliefs and values. The capitalist mode of production emphasizes the maximization of profits and the accumulation of wealth.

2 Economic self-interest rather than public duty motivates behaviour.

3 Capitalism is based on the private ownership of property. Personal gain rather than collective well-being is encouraged.

4 Capitalism is a competitive system. Mutual aid and cooperation for the betterment of all are discouraged in favour of individual achievement at the expense of others. Competition breeds aggression, hostility, and – particularly for the losers – frustration.

William Chambliss argues that the greed, self-interest and hostility generated by the capitalist system motivates many crimes on all levels of society. Members of each stratum use whatever means and opportunities their class position provides to commit crime. Thus in low-income areas the mugger, the petty thief, the pusher, the pimp and the prostitute use what they've got to get what they can. In higher-income brackets, business people, lawyers and politicians have more effective means at their disposal to grab a larger share of the cake.

Given the nature of capitalist society, and particularly American society, David Gordon argues that crime is rational, it makes sense. In a 'dog eat dog' society where competition is the order of the day, individuals must fend for themselves in order to survive. This is particularly true for the American poor, since the USA has minimal welfare services compared to other advanced industrial societies. Gordon concludes that 'Most crimes in this country share a single important similarity – they represent rational responses to the competitiveness and inequality of life in capitalist societies.'

Selective law enforcement

From a Marxist viewpoint, the selective enforcement of the law has a number of important consequences. As noted above, the occasional prosecution of ruling-class crime perpetuates the fiction that the law operates for the benefit of society as a whole, that the state represents the public interest and that the extent of ruling-class crime is small. Conversely, frequent prosecution of members of the subject class has equally important consequences.

David Gordon argues that the practice of law enforcement in the USA supports the capitalist system in three ways.

1 By selecting members of the subject class and punishing them as individuals, it protects the system which is primarily responsible for their criminal deviance. Individuals are defined as 'social failures' and as such they are responsible for their criminal activities. In this way blame and condemnation are directed at the individual rather than the institutions of capitalism. Gordon argues that the practice of law enforcement serves to 'reinforce a prevalent ideology in this society that individuals, rather than institutions, are to blame for social problems'.

2 The imprisonment of selected members of the subject class 'legitimately' neutralizes opposition to the system. American blacks are heavily over-represented amongst those arrested for 'street crimes' such as robbery and aggravated assault. A New York chief of police neatly summarized the situation when he compared the role of the police in Harlem (the main black ghetto in New York City) to that of an army of occupation. Few have the insight of one black ex-convict who sums up Gordon's view of imprisonment when he states:

> It didn't take me any time to decide I wasn't going back to commit crimes. Because it's stupid, it's a trap, it only makes it easier for them to neutralize you. (Quoted in Gordon 1976, p. 208.)

3 Gordon argues that defining criminals as 'animals and misfits, as enemies of the state', provides a justification for incarcerating them in prisons. This keeps them hidden from view. In this way the most embarrassing

extremes produced by the capitalist system are neatly swept under the carpet. If something were really done to help those who broke the law, if their problems were made public, the whole system might be questioned. But, Gordon concludes:

> By keeping its victims so thoroughly hidden and rendering them so apparently inhuman, our system of crime and punishment allows us to forget how sweeping a 'transformation' of our social ideology we would require in order to begin solving the problem of crime.

Gordon argues that the selective enforcement of the law serves to maintain ruling-class power and to reinforce ruling-class ideology. Further arguments in support of this view can be added to those he outlines.

1 The selective application of the law gives the impression that criminals are mainly located in the working class. This serves to divert attention from ruling-class crime.

2 It can also serve to divert the attention of members of the subject class from their exploitation and oppression.

3 It directs a part of the subject class's frustration and hostility (produced by this situation of exploitation) onto the criminals within their own class. The muggers, murderers and thieves can provide a scapegoat for the frustrations of the alienated masses.

4 This provides a safety valve, releasing aggression which might otherwise be directed against the ruling class.

5 It also serves to divide the subject class, particularly in low-income areas, where there is a tendency for people to see their enemies as the criminals within their own class.

Finally, what effect does selective law enforcement have upon crime itself? From his study of Seattle, William Chambliss reaches the following conclusion. Law enforcement agencies are:

> *not* organized to *reduce crime* or to enforce public morality. They are organized rather to *manage* crime by cooperating with the most criminal groups and enforcing laws against those whose crimes are minimal. By cooperating with criminal groups law enforcement essentially produces more crime.

Criticisms of conventional Marxism

Marxist theories have come in for heavy criticism from 'left realists'. They tend to see such theories as putting undue emphasis on corporate crime at the expense of neglecting street crime. Left realists argue that crimes such as burglary, robbery and other violent crimes cause greater harm than Marxist theories seem to imply. The victims of such crimes are usually working class and the consequences can be devastating for the victims. To them, Marxism offers a rather one-sided view of crime and in doing so offers no way of dealing with the types of crimes which are of most concern to most members of the population. We will discuss these views in more detail on pp. 426–33.

■ Deviance – neo-Marxist perspectives

Neo-Marxist sociologists of crime and deviance share many similarities with their Marxist counterparts but they diverge from one or more aspects of conventional Marxist theory. Like Marxists, these sociologists accept that society is characterized by competing groups with conflicting interests. Furthermore, they are all critical of existing capitalist societies, and they share a concern about the unequal distribution of power and wealth within such societies. However, none accept that there is a simple and straightforward relationship between the infrastructure of society and deviance. Although most of these sociologists (including Taylor, Walton and Young, Paul Gilroy, and Stuart Hall) have been strongly influenced by Marxism, their work differs in important respects from that of the Marxists we have examined so far. They can therefore be termed **neo-Marxist** approaches to deviance.

■ Ian Taylor, Paul Walton and Jock Young – *The New Criminology*

In 1973 Taylor, Walton and Young published *The New Criminology*. It was intended to provide a radical alternative to existing theories of crime and deviance. In some respects Taylor, Walton and Young's views are similar to those of the Marxist writers who have just been examined.

1 They accept that the key to understanding crime lies in the 'material basis of society'. Like Marx, they see the economy as the most important part of any society.

2 They believe capitalist societies are characterized by inequalities in wealth and power between individuals and that these inequalities lie at the root of crime.

3 They support a radical transformation of society: indeed, they suggest that sociological theories of crime are of little use unless they contribute in a practical way to the 'liberation of individuals from living under capitalism'.

However, in important respects they differ from more conventional Marxist approaches. As such we can see *The New Criminology* as a neo-Marxist perspective on crime.

Crime, freedom and political action

Much of the work by Taylor, Walton and Young is concerned with criticizing existing theories of crime. Marx himself is judged by them to have produced inadequate explanations of crime. He is criticized for coming close to providing an economically deterministic theory. Although they believe economic determinism is untypical of Marx's work in general, when he tried to explain crime they claim that he saw the criminal as driven to crime by the poverty into which capitalism forced some sections of the population.

Taylor, Walton and Young insist that criminals choose to break the law. They reject all theories which see human behaviour as directed by external forces. They see the individual turning to crime 'as the meaningful attempt by the actor to construct and develop his own self-conception'.

The New Criminology denies that crime is caused by biology, anomie, by being a member of a subculture, by living in areas of social disorganization, by labelling or by poverty. It stresses that crimes are often deliberate and conscious acts with political motives. Thus the Women's Liberation Movement, the Black Power Movement and the Gay Liberation Front are all examples of 'people-fighting-back' against the injustices of capitalism.

Furthermore, many crimes against property involve the redistribution of wealth: if a poor resident of an inner-city area steals from a rich person, the former is helping to change society. Deviants are not just the passive victims of capitalism: they are actively struggling to alter capitalism.

Like conventional Marxists Taylor, Walton and Young wish to see the overthrow of capitalism and its replacement with a different type of society. Unlike conventional Marxists they refer to the type of society they wish to see as 'socialist' rather than 'communist'. They place greater emphasis than many Marxists on freedom in any future society. They wish to see a society in which groups which are now seen as deviant are tolerated. They believe that hippies, ethnic minorities, homosexuals and perhaps even drug users should simply be accepted in an ideal society, and not turned into criminals by persecution. In capitalist society people have severe restrictions placed upon their behaviour. Taylor, Walton and Young urge support and sympathy for groups who struggle to escape from the chains with which capitalism limits their freedom.

A 'fully social theory of deviance'

In the final chapter of *The New Criminology* Taylor, Walton and Young attempt to outline what they believe would be a **fully social theory of deviance**. From their critical examination of earlier theories they conclude that deviance needs to be explained from a number of angles simultaneously. They claim that other writers, including Marxists, have tended to give incomplete, or one-sided explanations of crime. They identify seven aspects of crime and deviance which they believe should be studied.

To them, a complete theory examines both the way society as a whole is organized, and the way that individuals decide to carry out criminal acts.

1 The criminologist first needs to understand the way wealth and power are distributed in society.

2 He or she must consider the particular circumstances surrounding the decision of an individual to commit an act of deviance.

3 It is necessary to consider the deviant act itself, in order to discover its meaning for the person concerned. Was the individual, for example, showing contempt for the material values of capitalism by taking drugs? Was he or she 'kicking back' at society through an act of vandalism?

4 Taylor, Walton and Young propose that the criminologist should consider in what ways, and for what reasons other members of society react to the deviance. How do the police or members of the deviant's family respond to the discovery of the deviance?

5 The reaction then needs to be explained in terms of the social structure. This means that the researcher should attempt to discover who has the power in society to make the rules, and to explain why some deviant acts are treated much more severely than others.

6 Taylor, Walton and Young then turn to labelling theory. They accept that it is necessary to study the effects of deviant labels. However, they emphasize that labelling may have a variety of effects. The amplification of deviance is only one possible outcome. Deviants may not even accept that the labels are justified: they might see their actions as morally correct and ignore the label as far as possible.

7 Finally Taylor, Walton and Young say that the relationship between these different aspects of deviance should be studied, so that they fuse together into a complete theory.

The New Criminology has had a considerable impact on the sociology of deviance. Many sociologists were attracted to this approach: it seemed to combine some of the insights provided by both interactionist and Marxist perspectives and offer a highly sophisticated approach to studying deviance which could finally overcome the limited and partial picture provided by the previous theories. However it should be remembered that Taylor, Walton and Young had only sketched an outline of how they believed crime should be studied, and that this could be developed further.

■ Paul Gilroy – the myth of black criminality

In a series of articles, Paul Gilroy has used a similar approach to that of Taylor, Walton and Young in analysing the relationship between race and crime in Britain. In keeping with *The New Criminology* Gilroy claims that crimes committed by ethnic minorities are frequently conscious and deliberate political acts. He believes that they can only be understood once the existence of racism in British society is acknowledged. Furthermore, he suggests that many of the widely held beliefs about black criminality are 'myths'.

Gilroy examines British society as a whole and finds that this capitalist society in the 1970s and 1980s created both the political revolt of blacks and Asians, and the racist policies of the police towards these groups.

Crime as political struggle

Gilroy rejects the view that black criminals are pathological. He denies that belonging to an 'alien culture' or the poor socialization of ethnic minorities is responsible for some of them becoming criminal. Instead he sees these groups as defending themselves and hitting back at a society which treats them unjustly.

He believes that immigrants to Great Britain brought with them 'legacies of their political, ideological, and economic struggles in Africa, the Caribbean and the Indian subcontinent, as well as the scars of imperialist violence'. In anti-colonial struggles the populations of these countries learned how to organize themselves to resist their exploitation. Once they arrived in Britain these ethnic minorities used the marches, demonstrations and riots which had first developed in their native lands. In areas such as Southall, Toxteth, Brixton, Handsworth and the St Paul's area of Bristol, they hit back against police harassment, racially motivated attacks and discrimination.

According to Gilroy the Rastafarian movement has provided a focus for West Indians to organize themselves politically. Rastafarianism is more than a religion: it also involves political beliefs. 'Rastas' believe that white society is corrupt and oppressive, and they aim to overthrow it to create their own heaven on earth.

Although Gilroy sees ethnic minority crime as part of a political struggle, he denies that ethnic minorities are more prone to being criminal than other sections of the population. He claims that 'black criminality' is a myth. He argues that the police have negative stereotypes of West Indians and Asians. West Indians are often seen as 'wild and lawless', or more specifically as 'muggers'. Asians are frequently regarded with suspicion by the police. In particular they are suspected of being illegal immigrants.

Gilroy provides some support for the view that such stereotypes exist by quoting the statements of various policemen. For example, he refers to a police officer in Brixton saying to a reporter 'We are here to give our coloured brethren all the help we can – all they need to go somewhere else' (quoted in the Centre for Contemporary Cultural Studies *The Empire Strikes Back*, p. 150).

Furthermore, he points out that the Police Federation magazine has carried stories claiming that Jamaica deliberately shipped convicts to Britain during periods of high immigration. Gilroy believes that official statistics which show heavy West Indian involvement in street crime cannot be trusted. Since the police are largely responsible for enforcing the law, their racialist stereotypes will lead to them arresting members of the West Indian and Asian communities almost regardless of whether they have committed any offence.

In some respects Gilroy's views are similar to interactionist and labelling perspectives on deviance. However, he goes further than them in attempting to explain why racial prejudice and stereotypes exist in the first place.

Gilroy argues that British capitalism is undergoing an economic 'crisis', which has led to high levels of unemployment. Ethnic minorities are a 'surplus population' over and above that which is needed for a labour force by the British bourgeoisie. In this situation blacks and Asians are blamed for the problems which are in reality the creation of the capitalist system. Furthermore, their alleged responsibility for crime helps to justify calls for their 'repatriation' to their countries of origin.

Like Taylor, Walton and Young, Gilroy tries to explain crime in terms of the social structure of society as a whole, and particularly its relationship to the workings of the capitalist economic system.

Gilroy's views have attracted strong criticism from John Lea and Jock Young and we will consider these criticisms later in the chapter. In the next section, however, we will examine a more

detailed attempt to explain one particular crime – 'mugging' – from a neo-Marxist perspective.

■ *Policing the crisis – mugging, the state, and law and order*

Stuart Hall, Chas Critcher, Tony Jefferson, John Clarke and Brian Roberts have attempted to provide a detailed explanation of the crime of 'mugging' in Britain. Like Taylor, Walton and Young and Paul Gilroy their work is influenced by a Marxist perspective, yet differs from traditional Marxist views. *Policing the Crisis* comes close to providing what Taylor, Walton and Young called a 'fully social theory of deviance'. The wide-ranging argument presented in the book deals with the origins and nature of mugging, the social reaction to the crime, and the distribution of power in society as a whole. The sole aspect of crime which is dealt with only in passing is the effect of labelling on the deviants themselves.

Hall differs from Paul Gilroy and Taylor, Walton and Young in two important ways.

1 He does not share their belief that most crimes are political acts, especially since most of the victims of street crime are 'people whose class position is hardly distinguishable from that of the criminals'. 'Muggers' rarely choose the rich as victims – rather they tend to rob from individuals who share their own disadvantaged position in society.

2 He is perhaps more heavily influenced by the work of the Italian Marxist Antonio Gramsci than directly by the work of Marx himself. The influence of Gramsci will become increasingly apparent as this section develops.

'Mugging', the media and moral panic

In the thirteen months between August 1972 and August 1973, sixty events were reported as 'muggings' in the national daily papers. Dramatic individual cases of such crimes were highlighted in the media. On 15 August 1972 Arthur Hills was stabbed to death near Waterloo Station in London. For the first time a specific crime in Britain was labelled a 'mugging' in the press. On 5

November 1972 Robert Keenan was attacked by three youths in Birmingham. He was knocked to the ground and had some keys, five cigarettes and 30p stolen. Two hours later the youths returned to where he still lay, and they viciously kicked him and hit him with a brick.

It was stories such as these which highlighted an apparently new and frightening type of crime in Britain. Judges, politicians and the police lined up with the media in stressing the threat that this crime posed to society. Many commentators believed that the streets of Britain would soon become as dangerous as those of New York or Chicago. The Home Secretary in the House of Commons quoted an alarming figure that there had been a 129 per cent increase in muggings in London in the previous four years.

Hall *et al.* argue that there was a 'moral panic' about crime. They try to explain why there should be such a strong reaction to, and widespread fear of mugging. They reject the view that the panic was an inevitable and understandable reaction to a new and rapidly increasing form of violence. As far back as the nineteenth century footpads and garrotters (who half strangled their victims before robbing them) had committed violent street crimes similar to those of the modern mugger. Violent robberies were not therefore a new crime at all – indeed as recently as 1968 an MP had been kicked and robbed in the street without the crime being labelled a 'mugging'.

Hall and his colleagues note that there is no legal crime called 'mugging'. Since legally there is no such crime it was not possible for the Home Secretary to accurately measure its extent. They could find no basis in the criminal statistics for his figure of a 129 per cent rise over four years. From their own examination of the statistics there was no evidence that violent street crime was rising particularly fast in the period leading up to the panic. Using the nearest legal category to 'mugging' – robbery or assault with intent to rob – the official statistics showed an annual rise of an average of 33.4 per cent between 1955 and 1965, but only a 14 per cent average annual increase from 1965 to 1972. This type of crime was growing more slowly when the panic took place than it had done in the previous decade.

For these reasons Hall *et al.* could not accept that the supposed novelty or rate of increase of the crime explained the moral panic over it. They argued that both mugging and the moral panic could only be explained in the context of the problems that were faced by British capitalism at the start of the 1970s.

Capitalism, crisis and crime

Economic problems produced part of the 'crisis'. Many Marxists believe that capitalism faces deeper and deeper crises as time passes. Marx believed that only labour power produced wealth. In capitalist societies labour was exploited because the bourgeoisie kept a proportion of the wealth created by the workforce in the form of profit or **surplus value**. In order to compete with other manufacturers, capitalists needed to invest in new and more efficient machinery. However, as this mechanization took place, less and less labour power would be necessary to manufacture the same quantity of goods. Since surplus value was only created through labour power, the dwindling workforce needed to be increasingly exploited if profits were to be maintained. Eventually this problem would lead to a declining rate of profit, rising unemployment and falling wages. According to Hall *et al.*, such a crisis hit Britain at the time of the mugging panic.

The crisis of British society, however, went beyond economic problems. It was also a crisis of 'hegemony', a term first used by Antonio Gramsci. **Hegemony** is the political leadership and ideological domination of society. (We discuss Gramsci and hegemony in more detail on pp. 530–2.) According to Gramsci, the state tends to be dominated by parts of the ruling class. They attempt to win support for their policies and ideas from other groups in society. They try to persuade the working class that the authority of the state is being exercised fairly and justly in the interests of all. A crisis in hegemony takes place when the authority of the state and the ruling class is challenged.

In 1970–72 the British state faced both an economic crisis and a crisis of hegemony. From 1945 until about 1978 there had been what Hall *et al.* call an **inter-class truce**: there was little conflict between the ruling and subject class. Full employment, rising living standards, and the expansion of the Welfare State secured support for the state, and acceptance of its authority by the working class. As unemployment rose and living standards ceased to rise rapidly, the basis of the inter-class truce was undermined. It became more difficult for the ruling class to govern by consent.

Hall *et al.* provide a number of examples of the

challenge to the authority – to the hegemony – of the state.

1 Northern Ireland degenerated into open warfare.

2 There was a growth in student militancy and increased activity from the Black Power movement.

3 The unions posed perhaps the biggest single threat: in 1972 there were more workdays lost because of strikes than in any year since 1919. The miners were able to win a large payrise by using **flying pickets** which prevented coal reaching key industries and power stations.

Since the Government was no longer able to govern by consent, it turned to the use of force to control the crisis. It was in this context that street crime became an issue. Mugging was presented as a key element in a breakdown of law and order. Violence was portrayed as a threat to the stability of society, and it was the black mugger who was to symbolize the threat of violence.

In this way the public could be persuaded that society's problems were caused by immigrants rather than the faults of the capitalist system. The working class was effectively divided on racial grounds, since the white working class was encouraged to direct its frustrations towards the black working class.

Crisis and the control of crime

The Government was also able to resort to the use of the law and direct force to suppress the groups that were challenging them. Force could be justified because of the general threat of violence. Special sections of the police began to take action against the 'mugger'. The British Transport Police was particularly concerned with this crime. In February 1972, six months before the 'mugging' panic began, it set up a special squad to deal with violent crime on the London Underground. Hall *et al.* claim that the police in general, and this special squad in particular, created much of the 'mugging' which was later to appear in the official statistics. Following the argument of interactionists, they suggest that the police amplified, or made worse, the deviance they were supposed to be controlling.

They give examples of police pouncing unannounced on black youths of whom they were suspicious. Often this would provoke a violent reaction in self-defence by the youths, who would

then be arrested and tried for crimes of violence. Many of the 'muggers' who were convicted following incidents like these had only police evidence used against them at trial. 'Victims' of their crimes were not produced because, Hall *et al.* imply, there were no victims in some cases. The societal reaction to the threat of violence led to the labelling of large numbers of young blacks as deviants. Labelling helped to produce the figures which appeared to show rising levels of black crime, which in turn justified stronger police measures.

Hall *et al.* do not claim that the reactions to crime, 'mugging', and other 'violence' was the result of a conspiracy by the ruling class. The police, the Government, the courts and the media did not consciously plan to create a moral panic about street crime; the panic developed as they reacted to changing circumstances.

Neither were the media directly manipulated by the ruling class or the Government: different newspapers included different stories, and reported 'mugging' in different ways. Nevertheless, there was a limited range of approaches in the press to the issue. Most stories were based on police statements, court cases or were concerned with the general problem of the 'war' against crime. Statements by the police, judges and politicians were therefore important sources of material for the press. Consequently the newspapers tended to define the problem of 'mugging' in similar ways to their sources: criminal violence was seen as senseless and meaningless by most of the press. It was linked to other threats to society, such as strikes, and was seen as a crime which needed to be stamped out as quickly as possible. A number of judges who stressed the need for deterrent sentences to turn back the tide of crime were quoted directly. Assistant Commissioner Woods of the Police Federation was widely quoted when he said 'mugging' was a 'reflection of the present violent society' and he declared that 'we are not going to let the thugs win'.

However, if the crisis in Britain produced the conditions in which a moral panic was likely, the media was largely responsible for 'orchestrating public opinion', and directing its attention and anger against the black mugger.

Black crime

Although *Policing the Crisis* concentrates on the moral panic about crime, Hall *et al.* also make some attempt to explain black criminality. Many immigrants to Britain from the Commonwealth arrived in the 1950s and early 1960s. They were actively encouraged to come to the country during a period of full employment and labour shortage. London Transport, for example, recruited large numbers of West Indians to fill low-paid jobs which might otherwise have remained vacant.

The recession in the early 1970s hit immigrant groups hard. They became a 'surplus labour force' many of whom were not required for employment. Thus Hall *et al.* estimate that at the time in question, black unemployment was twice the national average, and for school leavers it was four times higher than normal. Those who remained in employment often had to do menial and low-paid jobs, which some referred to as 'white man's shit work'. Some opted out of the employment market altogether. They turned to 'hustling' for money, using petty street crime, casual drugs dealing, and prostitution to earn a living. Hall *et al.* do not find it surprising that some of this surplus labour force became criminals. They claim:

---

a fraction of the black labouring class is engaged in the traditional activity of the wageless and the workless: doing nothing, filling out time, trying to survive. Against this background is it not too much to say that the question 'Why do they turn to crime?' is a practical obscenity?

From this point of view street crime is seen as a survival strategy by an unwanted reserve army of labour.

Policing the Crisis – *an evaluation*

Policing the Crisis provides a sophisticated analysis of the crime of 'mugging' from a neo-Marxist perspective.

1 It suggests that the moral panic about mugging was not a rational response to a new and rapidly growing crime, but to the economic crisis and the crisis of hegemony for the British state.

2 The societal reaction to this crime can only be understood as part of the shift by the dominant class from ruling the country by consent, towards ruling it by force.

3 One result of the increasingly repressive policies and the greater use of the law, was the labelling of black 'muggers', and the amplification of the crime.

4 The media focused public concern about violence on black immigrants, and in doing so disguised the real reasons for the crisis.

5 The rise in black criminality was largely the result of police labelling, but some West Indians were forced into crime in order to survive as unemployment left them little alternative.

Given the range of issues that this study deals with, it is not surprising that other sociologists have raised criticisms. David Downes and Paul Rock have identified two major weaknesses.

1 First, they argue that the book contradicts itself. It appears to claim simultaneously that black street crime was not rising quickly, that it was being amplified by police labelling, and that it was bound to rise as a result of unemployment. According to this criticism Hall *et al.* are trying to have their cake and eat it. They change their view on whether these crimes were rising or not according to how it fits their argument.

2 Second, Downes and Rock believe that *Policing the Crisis* fails to show that the moral panic over 'mugging' was caused by a crisis of British capitalism. They point out that there have been numerous moral panics, for example, about the violence of teddy boys, and mods and rockers, and in 1979–80 about widespread strikes in the 'winter of discontent'. Downes and Rock do not believe that each of these moral panics could be explained by a corresponding crisis in the British economy and society.

Jock Young has also been critical of *Policing the Crisis*. Young argues that the study provided no evidence that the public, as opposed to the media, were panicking about 'mugging', nor did it show that the public identified this crime with blacks. However, he also argues that it would have been quite rational if the public were concerned about 'mugging' and other types of street crime. As a new left realist, he claims that such crimes have been increasing and are a serious problem.

Having reviewed various Marxist and Neo-Marxist perspectives on crime and deviance, we will now look at a perspective that developed more recently – that of left realism.

Left realism

Since the early 1980s a number of sociologists have developed a perspective on crime and deviance usually referred to as **left realism**. Amongst the most prominent supporters of this perspective are Jock Young, John Lea, Roger Matthews and Richard Kinsey. Left realism originated in Britain but has begun to influence criminologists in other parts of the world including Canada and Australia. Left realist criminologists are critical of perspectives which see longer sentences and more prisons as the solution to crime, but they also oppose the views of what they term 'left idealists'. In their view this includes a variety of Marxists, neo-Marxists and radical feminists.

Politically left realists tend to see their approach as being close to the position of the British Labour Party. Jock Young and John Lea describe themselves as 'socialists' and support the reform of society rather than the revolutionary change advocated by some Marxists. They argue that right-wing politicians in industrial capitalist societies have been particularly successful in presenting themselves as the parties representing the forces of law and order. Left idealists have not provided alternative policies on law and order since they have suggested that social justice cannot be achieved without a radical transformation of society. Left realists have tried to counter the popularity of right-wing law-and-order policies by presenting what they see as realistic proposals for change within the framework of existing societies which address the concerns of ordinary people.

The problem of crime

One of the basic tenets of left realism is that crimes other than white-collar crimes are a serious problem and they need to be explained and tackled. Left realists counter a number of arguments which criminologists have advanced to suggest that such crimes are not serious.

1 Jock Young argues that there has been a real and significant increase in street crime since the Second World War. According to this view criminology has undergone an **aetiological crisis** (or crisis of explanation) resulting from the rapid increase in officially recorded street crimes in most democratic industrial societies. In Britain, the USA and most

Western European countries, crime rates recorded by the police have risen alarmingly.

Some sociologists have tried to deny that the apparent increase is real by pointing to the unreliable nature of criminal statistics. From this point of view increased reporting of crime and changes in police recording of crime might account for the figures. However, Young believes that the rises have been so great that changes in reporting and recording cannot account for all of the increase. He points to evidence from the *British Crime Survey* (see pp. 399–401 for details) which shows that at least part of the rising tide of crime is real. There is more reporting of crimes, but there are also more victims.

2 Some sociologists have advanced the view that the chances of being the victim of street crime are minimal. Lea and Young point out that while the average chances of being a victim are small, particular groups might face high risks. It is not the rich who are the usual targets of muggers or thieves, but the poor, the deprived, ethnic minorities or inner-city residents. For example, Lea and Young calculate that unskilled workers are twice as likely to be burgled as other workers. In some of the poorer areas of London the chances of being mugged might be four times the average for the city as a whole. In the USA figures indicate that black men and women are more likely to be murdered than to die in a road accident. It is the deprived groups in society who are most likely to be harmed by these crimes; it is also they who suffer most if they are the victims of these offences. Those with low incomes suffer more if they are robbed or burgled: crime adds to and compounds the other problems that they face.

3 Crime is widely perceived as a serious problem in urban areas and this perception has important consequences. Left realists have carried out a considerable number of victimization studies examining such issues as the extent of crime and attitudes towards crime. These studies have been conducted in, amongst other places, Merseyside, Islington, Hammersmith and Fulham. In the *Second Islington Crime Survey* no less than 80.5 per cent of those surveyed saw crime as a problem affecting their lives. Fear of crime was widespread. Some 35 per cent sometimes felt unsafe in their own homes. Many people altered their behaviour to avoid becoming victims of crime. This was particularly true of women. The authors said, 'women are not only less likely to go

out after dark, but also stay in more than men because of fear of crime. When women do go out they are more careful than men.'

4 Lea and Young attack the idea that offenders can sometimes be seen as promoting justice. For example, they attack the image of the criminal presented in *The New Criminology* as a type of modern-day Robin Hood. They deny that muggers can be seen as stealing from the rich and redistributing income to the poor. As we saw earlier, most of the victims of crimes such as burglary and robbery are themselves poor.

5 Left realists do not deny the importance of white-collar and corporate crime. Recent victimization studies carried out by left realists have started including questions on such crimes and they accept that they are commonplace and serious. However, they do argue that left idealist criminologists have concentrated on these types of crime too much and to the exclusion of other crimes.

6 Left realists also acknowledge the importance of other crimes which tend to be emphasized by left-wing and feminist criminologists, and perhaps neglected by the police. Thus they have also included questions in victim studies on crimes such as sexual assaults and sexual harassment, racially motivated attacks and domestic violence. They do, though, accuse left idealists of 'schizophrenia' over crime. Lea and Young say:

There is the story of a seminar in North London where one week the students, reeling from the impact of a description of the deplorable results of imprisonment on inmates decide to abolish prisons. But then next week, after being, quite correctly, informed by a speaker from the Women's Movement of the viciousness of many anti-female offences, decided to rebuild them.

Left realists claim to have redressed the balance by taking all types of crime equally seriously.

Ethnicity and crime

As well as attacking left idealists for denying the importance of street crimes, they also attack them for denying that certain types of crime are more common amongst ethnic minorities. Just as they believe the official statistics on the rise in crime reflect a real change, they also believe that statistics on the ethnic background of offenders are not entirely fabricated.

Paul Gilroy is a particular target of Lea and Young. They seriously question his view that police racism accounts entirely for the official statistics which suggest that ethnic minorities are more prone to crime. They quote the figure that 92 per cent of crimes known to the police are brought to their attention by the public, and only 8 per cent are uncovered by the police themselves. In such circumstances, they argue, it is difficult to believe that the preponderance of blacks in the official figures is entirely a consequence of discrimination by the police.

Lea and Young also make use of the work of the Home Office researchers Stevens and Willis. They calculate that to explain the differences between whites and blacks convicted of offences in 1975 it would have been necessary for the police to have arrested 66 per cent of all black offenders, but only 21 per cent of all white offenders. They argue that it is more likely that blacks do commit some crimes more often than whites.

They also point to a number of aspects of criminal statistics which cannot be explained by police racism alone. The recorded rate for crimes committed by whites is consistently slightly higher than that recorded for Asians. They maintain that 'police racism would have to manifest itself very strangely indeed to be entirely responsible for such rates'.

Furthermore, in the 1960s the recorded rates for first-generation West Indian immigrants were lower than the national average. Even today the official statistics for offences such as burglary show the rate for West Indians to be lower than that for whites. If these statistics were produced by police racism, then they must have exercised positive discrimination in favour of some ethnic minority groups at times.

Lea and Young accept that policing policies and police racism exaggerate the black crime rate. Nevertheless, they do believe that there has been a real increase in the number of certain crimes (particularly robbery) committed by blacks. They find it hard to understand why left idealists such as Gilroy cannot bring themselves to believe that unemployment and racial discrimination might result in ethnic minorities committing more street crime than others.

Lea and Young are even more critical of Gilroy's claim that such black crime as there is results from a continuation of the 'anti-colonial struggle' conducted in the native lands of immigrants. They point out that most young West Indians are second-generation immigrants who have lived since birth in

Britain. Most of their parents in the 1950s and 1960s appear from the statistics to have been highly law abiding. It is hard to see then how they could have passed down the tradition of the 'anti-colonial struggle' to their children.

In any case, most of the victims of crimes committed by blacks are also black. How, Lea and Young enquire, can crimes committed against members of their own community be seen as a political attack on the white racist state? To them it is far more plausible that street crime is a reaction to the oppression that West Indians have experienced in Britain.

The explanation of crime

In *What is to be Done about Law and Order* John Lea and Jock Young began to develop an approach to explaining criminality. They see crime as rooted in social conditions and argue that crime is closely connected to deprivation. However, they reject those views which suggest that factors such as poverty and unemployment can be seen as directly responsible for crime. A considerable amount of crime, (for example white-collar offences) can only take place if people are working. Groups such as old age pensioners often have low incomes, but despite this they have exceptionally low crime rates. In the 1930s unemployment was very high, yet the crime rate was low compared to the 1980s. In recent writing Jock Young has stressed how rising living standards and the development of welfare provisions have gone hand in hand with a rising crime rate since the Second World War. Lea and Young also note that first-generation West Indian immigrants also had low rates of crime although most of them had low-paid jobs. They conclude that a more sophisticated analysis is required. They base their attempt to explain crime around three key concepts: relative deprivation, subculture and marginalization.

Relative deprivation

Lea and Young believe that deprivation will only lead to crime where it is experienced as **relative deprivation**. A group experiences relative deprivation when it feels deprived in comparison to other similar groups, or when its expectations are not met. It is not the *fact* of being deprived as such, but the *feeling* of deprivation which is important. Thus in modern societies the media (and particularly

advertisers) stress the importance of economic success and the consumption of consumer goods. All individuals are exposed to the values which suggest people should aspire to middle-class lifestyles and patterns of consumption.

Ethnic minorities today feel more deprived than they did in the past when the media and advertising were less highly developed. Lea and Young claim that part of the difference in Asian and West Indian crime rates can be explained by West Indians having internalized materialist values to a greater extent than Asians whose traditional cultural and religious beliefs have remained stronger. Rather like Merton, they argue that rising crime is partly the result of rising expectations for high standards of living, combined with restricted opportunities to achieve this success because of unemployment.

In *Ten Points of Realism* Jock Young stresses that relative deprivation is experienced in all social strata. Anybody can feel deprived and 'crime can, therefore, occur anywhere in the social structure and at any period, affluent or otherwise'. It can explain the theft of luxuries as well as necessities and crimes committed by white-collar criminals who crave the lifestyles of those better off than themselves. To Young, relative deprivation can also help explain violent crime: relative deprivation can cause frustration which in turn can cause violence.

Subculture

The second key concept Lea and Young use is that of **subculture**. They see subcultures as the collective solution to a group's problems. Thus if a group of individuals share a sense of relative deprivation they will develop lifestyles which allow them to cope with this problem. However, a particular subculture is not an automatic, inevitable response to a situation. Human creativity will allow a variety of solutions to be produced. For example, second-generation West Indian immigrants' subcultural solutions to their problems include the Rastafarian and Pentecostalist religions, as well as 'hustling' for money and street crime. (For more details on West Indian religions see pp. 469–70).

Lea and Young stress that crime is only 'one aspect, though generally a small one, of the process of cultural adaptation to oppression'. Unlike Gilroy, they see West Indian crime as a response to conditions in Britain rather than as a continuation of traditions from the West Indies.

Marginalization

The third and final key concept is that of **marginalization**. Marginal groups are those who lack organizations to represent their interests in political life, and who also lack clearly defined goals. Lea and Young argue that marginal groups in society are particularly prone to the use of violence and riots as forms of political action.

Lea and Young believe that 'participation in the process of production' is the key to a group avoiding marginality. Workers have clearly defined objectives such as higher wages and improved working conditions. Furthermore, their membership of unions provides them with involvement in pressure group politics. Thus they have no need to resort to violence.

In contrast, young unemployed West Indians do not have clearly defined aims, or pressure groups to represent them. Rather than precise grievances they feel a general sense of resentment that the future does not seem to offer an interesting, worthwhile and rewarding life. Since they have no pressure groups to express these frustrations they are more likely to take to the streets and resort to rioting.

More recent writing by left realists has made little use of the concept of marginalization, but the concepts of relative deprivation and subculture have remained central to their work.

■ Dealing with crime

Policing problems

Left realist criminologists pay considerable attention to practical ways in which the problem of crime might be reduced. In *Losing the Fight Against Crime* Richard Kinsey, John Lea and Jock Young put forward a variety of suggestions about ways of changing policing. They argue that there are a number of flaws in current policing practice.

1 As crime has risen the police have failed to improve the clear-up rate. The Metropolitan Police, for example, hardly increased their clear-up rate at all between 1976 and 1981 despite a 12 per cent increase in personnel. In the 1973–83 period police efficiency in terms of crimes cleared up per officer fell by 18 per cent meaning that on average each Metropolitan police officer only cleared up four crimes a year. As a result the clear-up rate has become extremely low for most offences, and as low as 8 per cent for burglaries in the Metropolitan Police District in 1983. In such circumstances the police become unable to deter crime.

2 The police actually spend little of their time involved in investigating crime. Using evidence from Home Office research, Kinsey, Lea and Young estimate that the average officer probably spends less than an hour a day on investigation and follow-up work.

3 Evidence from victimization studies and other sources shows over 90 per cent of crimes known to the police are notified to them by the public. Most crimes which are cleared-up are also solved as a result of information received from the public. However, research suggests that public confidence in the police has declined, particularly in inner-city areas and amongst members of ethnic minorities. For example, the Policy Studies Institute found that in 1983 75 per cent of West Indians aged 15–24 in London thought that the police fabricated evidence, 82 per cent thought they used violence on suspects and 66 per cent thought they made false records of interviews (quoted in Kinsey, Lea and Young 1986, p. 66). As trust breaks down between the police and some sections of the public, the flow of information from the victims of crime dries up.

4 Lacking the information which is necessary to solve crime the police resort to new policing methods. They drift towards what Kinsey, Lea and Young call **military policing**. Without the support of the community the police have to resort to tactics such as stopping and searching large numbers of people in an area or using surveillance technology to find suspects. This leads to the **mobilization of bystanders**. Even those who are not directly involved with the police come to see police officers as part of an alien force intent upon criminalizing local residents almost regardless of their guilt. As a result, a vicious circle is initiated: declining information leads to more military-style policing and information provided by the public is reduced further. This process is illustrated in Figure 7.2.

A good example of this process occurred in 1981. The Brixton riots were sparked by a police operation, *Swamp 81*, in which the streets of Brixton were flooded by police stopping and searching people suspected of offences.

Improving policing

How then can the police improve their performance and begin to clear up more crime? Kinsey, Lea and Young argue that the key to police success

Figure 7.2 The vicious circle of the collapse of consensus policing

(*Source:* Kinsey, Lea and Young, *Losing the Fight Against Crime*, Oxford: Blackwell, 1986, p. 42.)

lies in improving relationships with the community so that the flow of information on which the police rely increases. To achieve this they propose that **minimal policing** should be used. This is:

---

a style of policing under a system of democratic accountability in which information is freely given by the public and where the police are sufficiently trusted to do the job they are paid for – the full and proper investigation of crime.

This approach involves maximizing the role of the public in shaping police policy. Kinsey, Lea and Young believe that the public should have much more power to shape policing through democratically elected police authorities. These should be able to issue guidelines and direct the police towards dealing with the crimes that are of most public concern. The public should play a major role in determining which incidents the police become involved in. Unless directed to take action by police authorities, the police should only respond to public requests for help.

Kinsey, Lea and Young see little role for stopping and searching suspects and little point in

having police on the beat. Such police practices either antagonize the public on whom the police rely or are ineffective. It is only very rarely that police on the beat actually discover crimes.

The police should spend as much of their time as possible actually investigating crime. Kinsey, Lea and Young believe that if the police act in these ways, they can regain the trust of the public and become more effective in clearing up the crimes which are of most public concern.

Over-policing and under-policing

Although he has argued that the public should establish priorities for the police, Jock Young has also identified areas which he believes are over-policed and under-policed. In other words he thinks the police and the state devote too much of their time and energy to dealing with certain types of crime, and not enough to others. In the former category are minor drug offences and juvenile 'status' crimes such as under-age drinking; in the latter there are a wide range of offences where he believes tighter control by the state is necessary. These include racially motivated attacks, corporate crime, pollution, and domestic crimes of physical and sexual abuse.

Tackling the social causes of crime

Jock Young does not believe that crime can be dealt with simply by improving the efficiency of the police. As we saw in earlier sections, he and other left realists see the problem of crime as rooted in social inequalities. Only if those inequalities are significantly reduced will the problem of crime be reduced.

Young and Matthews argue 'objectives within the criminal justice system are linked to wider social and political objectives of greater equality, opportunity and freedom of choice'. Young suggests that improving leisure facilities for the young, reducing income inequalities, raising the living standards of poorer families, reducing unemployment and creating jobs with prospects, improving housing estates and providing 'community facilities which enhance a sense of cohesion and belonging' all help to cut crime. He does not believe that the criminal justice system is the main source of crime control. He says 'It is not the "thin Blue Line", but the social bricks and mortar of civil society which are the major bulwark against crime.' Young insists that 'social causation is given the highest priority'.

The multi-agency approach

Left realists have not tended to say a great deal about how the wider social causes of crime such as excessive income inequality can be tackled. They have concentrated on suggesting shorter-term and more readily achievable ways of reforming institutions. However, such proposals are not limited to the police.

Young advocates a 'multi-agency' approach. For example, councils can improve leisure facilities and housing estates, while the family, the mass media and religion have a role in improving the 'moral context' which permits so much crime. Social services, victim support schemes and improved security can help alleviate the problems of actual or potential victims. In Young's view the public also have a vital role to play in dealing with crime.

■ The square of crime

As we have seen in the above discussion, left realists have examined many facets of crime. These include the causes of crime, the nature of crime statistics, policing, public attitudes towards crime and the police, the chances of being a victim of crime, and so on. In recent years these elements have been brought together into one theoretical approach to the understanding of crime. This has been called the **square of crime.**

As Figure 7.3 shows, the square of crime involves four elements:

1 the state and its agencies;

2 the offender and their actions;

3 informal methods of social control (sometimes called 'society' or 'the public');

4 the victim.

Left realists believe that crime can only be understood in terms of the inter-relationships between these four elements. Roger Matthews states:

Figure 7.3   The square of crime

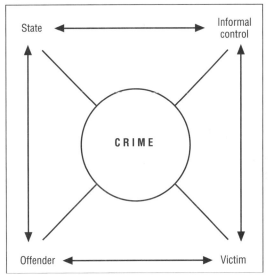

(*Source*: *Sociology Review*, February 1993, p. 28.)

---

crime is, in an important sense, a socially-constructed phenomena. Its meaning is profoundly influenced by considerations of time and space. Its construction is based upon the interaction of four key elements – victims, offenders, the state and the public.

The idea that crime is socially constructed, that social factors determine who and what is considered criminal, is nothing new. Labelling theorists, phenomenologists and Marxists all agree that this is the case. The idea that crime needs to be examined from different angles is not new either. For example, *The New Criminology* proposed just such an approach.

However, left realism claims to go beyond these approaches in a number of ways. Left realists pay far more attention to victims and public opinion than the approaches mentioned above. The New Criminology pays little or no attention to victims in examining crime. Matthews and Young claim that many other theories concentrate on just one part of the square of crime: labelling theory on the state, control theory on the public, positivism on the offender and victimology on the victim. Left realists do not accept that one element of the square of crime is always of prime importance. The importance of different elements varies from crime to crime. Matthews says:

432 SOCIOLOGY: THEMES AND PERSPECTIVES

> Each particular form of crime will have a different set of determinants within this framework and will involve a different combination of the key elements within the square. Thus corporate crime and street crime involve different types of victim–offender relation and are regulated by a different combination of formal and informal controls.

Multiple aetiology

Whatever the type of crime though, left realists believe that each of these four elements is crucial, and together they determine what crime is, as well as what causes it and how it might be dealt with. Jock Young calls this the **principle of multiple aetiology**. Crime by its very nature is a product of formal and informal rules, of actions by offenders, of reactions by victims and the state and its agencies. It is therefore important to try to understand why people offend, what makes the victims vulnerable, the factors that affect public attitudes and responses to crime, and the social forces which influence the police.

For example, when examining changes in violent behaviour in a country both alterations in the amount of violence and in public and police attitudes about what constitutes serious violence have to be examined. Young says:

> Deviance and control cannot be studied independently of each other. You cannot study changes in policing without changes in patterns of crime ... Systems of social control profoundly affect deviance and changes in deviance patterns of control.

The idea of the square of crime can be illustrated by considering the different elements that go to make up crime. For crime to exist there must be laws prohibiting behaviour. The existence or otherwise of those laws is influenced by the public. For an infraction to take place there must be an offender (or someone perceived as an offender) and, usually, a victim.

A variety of social factors influence the behaviour of the victim. For many offences it is the victim who decides whether the offence is reported. Victims will be influenced by prevailing social values in deciding whether they think an offence is immoral, illegal and worth reporting.

The relationship between victim and offender might affect both the victim's willingness to report the crime and the impact that the crime has on him or her. For example, wives might be unwilling to report the domestic violence of their husbands, or they might see the behaviour as 'normal'. The crimes of a spouse will have a different impact to those of a stranger.

The response of the police or other authorities then determines whether the offender is defined as criminal or not. Public opinion can have an impact on the behaviour of authorities. As labelling theorists point out, the decisions and actions of the criminal justice system can influence the future behaviour of those convicted of crime. Changes in any of these areas can affect the crime rate and the problems which criminality poses for society.

■ Evaluations of left realism

Since left realism is highly critical of many existing theories of crime and deviance it is not surprising that it has itself been the subject of criticism.

Failure to explain the causes of crime

Gordon Hughes attacks left realism on a number of counts but argues that its major failing is in its attempts to explain the causes of street crime. On one level left realists have simply failed to carry out the necessary research. Hughes says 'The empirical investigation of offenders' motives remains the yawning gap in the NLR research on crime.' The concentration on victimization studies has prevented left realists from gathering their own data on the motives of offenders. The data they have collected are largely quantitative and statistical and cannot reveal the subjective states of offenders. Thus according to Hughes 'NLR offers no empirical account of the subjective worlds of the street criminal but, instead, appears to rely for the most part on speculation.'

The reliance upon subculture theory

Hughes also criticizes left realism for its reliance upon subculture theory. He says 'NLR uses subcultural analysis without any fundamental or radical revision.' By doing so it falls into the trap of repeating some of the errors of the original subculture theories. For example, it assumes that there are shared values throughout society and it is only when these break down that crime becomes likely. It is equally possible to argue that crime stems from the existence of many different sets of values, some of which tolerate certain types of crime. To Hughes, left realism tends to concentrate on the criminal subculture in terms of Cloward and Ohlin's categories, (see pp. 394–5), or the adaptation of innovation in terms of Merton's approach (see pp. 390–2). In doing so it neglects other responses to relative deprivation such as retreatism or ritualism. Hughes also claims that concentrating upon the criminal subculture in relation to ethnic minorities might lead to 'a further fanning of the stereotype, "black = criminal"'.

He concludes that the work of left realists tends to oversimplify the causes of crime, it 'reduces law-breaking to the effects of deprivation and selfishness' while giving less sophisticated explanations of the various responses to deprivation than those offered by Albert Cohen, Merton or Cloward and Ohlin.

Corporate and organized crime

Left realists are certainly aware of corporate crime and see it as a major problem. However, Vincenzo Ruggiero argues that they have neglected its investigation and that this type of crime cannot be readily understood within the framework of their theory. He says that they do not consider how crime can be integrated into work carried out for corporations. Nor do they examine the way that offenders can themselves be the victims of criminal organizations (for example the drug taker being exploited by the pusher or the prostitute by the pimp). Victims tend to be seen as the victims of

aberrant individuals within the square of crime, not as the victims of corporations or 'central and local authorities'. Lip service is paid to issues such as corporate crime but they are not integrated into the theory.

The strengths of left realism

Most of the critics acknowledge that left realist criminology has made some contribution to the development of sociological theories of crime and deviance. Gordon Hughes sees it as having the following strengths.

1 It has revived some useful sociological concepts such as relative deprivation.

2 It has promoted debate and theoretical development within the subject.

3 It has highlighted the problems that street crime can cause for weak members of society.

4 It has explored the position of victims much more than most previous theories and it 'avoids the worst excesses of both "the right" and "the left" in neither glorifying nor pathologizing the police and other state agencies'. Overall though, Hughes concludes:

In its efforts to expunge itself of its own past sins of romanticism, NLR has jettisoned many of the valuable gains made by radical theory over the past two decades.

In the preceding sections we have covered the main perspectives on crime and deviance. We will now look at the subject from a different angle – that is, the relationship between gender and crime.

■ Gender and crime

■ Gender and patterns of crime

Writing in 1977 Carol Smart stated:

Our knowledge is still in its infancy. In comparison with the massive documentation on all aspects of male delinquency and criminality, the amount of work carried out on the area of women and crime is extremely limited.

She put forward a number of reasons for this neglect.

1 Women tend to commit fewer crimes than men so female offenders are seen as less of a problem for society.

2 Most crimes committed by women seem to be of a comparatively trivial nature and may therefore be considered unworthy of research.

3 Sociology and criminology have both tended to be dominated by males. In the main they have been studied by men and the studies have been about men.

4 Traditional criminology is motivated by a desire to control, behaviour that is regarded as problematic. Since women's criminality has been seen as much less problematic than men's, it has received correspondingly less attention.

Although the years since Smart's study have seen much more interest in the study of female crime and deviance, many general theories in this area of sociology continue to neglect gender as a factor influencing criminality. This is despite the fact that official figures suggest that gender is perhaps the most significant single factor in whether an individual is convicted of crime. Sociological theories which fail to explain this relationship could therefore be seen as inadequate.

In 1990 according to official criminal statistics there were 423,000 male offenders convicted or cautioned for indictable offences compared to 86,100 females. Some 298,000 males and 44,000 females were found guilty of indictable offences in the same year. In 1990 males were more than seven times as likely as females to be cautioned for or convicted of violence against the person, seventeen times more likely to be convicted or cautioned

in cases of robbery, more than twenty times as likely in cases of burglary, and females were held responsible for only 1 per cent of sexual offences by the authorities.

Official figures have raised three main questions about gender and crime.

1 Do women really commit fewer crimes than men, or are the figures misleading? Some sociologists have suggested that women's offences are consistently under-recorded by the authorities.

2 Although women continue to commit comparatively few crimes, some people have suggested that the proportion of crimes committed by women has been increasing. According to a number of commentators this alleged increase has resulted from 'women's liberation'. Is this so?

3 Why do those women who do break the law commit crimes?

In the following sections we examine the answers that sociologists have given to these questions.

■ Official statistics, criminality and gender

Pollak – the 'masked' female offender

Writing in 1950, Otto Pollak argued that official statistics on gender and crime were highly misleading. He claimed that the statistics seriously underestimated the extent of female criminality. From an examination of official figures in a number of different countries he claimed to have identified certain crimes that are usually committed by women but are particularly likely to be unreported.

1 He assumed that nearly all offences of shoplifting and all criminal abortions were carried out by women, and then asserted that such crimes were unlikely to come to the attention of the authorities.

2 He also argued that many unreported crimes were committed by female domestic servants.

3 Pollak accepted official definitions of crime when he pointed out all the offences of prostitution that were not reported. Male clients of prostitutes were assumed to have engaged in no illegal activities.

4 He even went so far as to suggest that women's domestic roles gave them the opportunity to hide crimes such as poisoning relatives and sexually abusing their children.

Pollak then went on to give reasons as to why there should be an under-recording of female crime.

1 He argues that the police, magistrates and other law enforcement officials tend to be men. Brought up to be chivalrous, they are usually lenient with female offenders so that fewer women appear in the statistics. However, he regards this as only a minor factor.

2 Second, and to Pollak more important, women are particularly adept at hiding their crimes. He attributes this to female biology. Women have become accustomed to deceiving men because traditional taboos prevent women from revealing pain and discomfort resulting from menstruation. Furthermore, women also learn to mislead men during sex. Men cannot disguise sexual arousal when they get an erection whereas women can take part in sexual intercourse whilst faking interest and pleasure.

Criticisms of Pollak

Not surprisingly, Pollak's totally inadequate analysis has been subject to fierce criticism. Frances Heidensohn points out just a few of the numerous flaws in his argument.

1 She notes that later research indicates that much shoplifting is committed by men.

2 Changes in the law have reduced the number of illegal abortions.

3 Even at the time that Pollak was writing there had been a very large reduction in the number of female domestic servants.

4 Heidensohn draws attention to the number of crimes committed against prostitutes by male customers, and the frequency of male crimes in domestic life. All the evidence indicates that men are considerably more likely than women to commit violent and sexual offences in the privacy of their home.

5 Pollak's statistical analysis is based upon little evidence and many unsupported assumptions. The same can be said of his attempt to explain the supposed 'masking' of female crime. For example, Heidensohn comments that the 'concealment of menstruation is by no means universal and changed sexual mores have long since

made nonsense of his view of passive, receptive females brooding vengeance'.

Heidensohn regards Pollak's work as being based upon an unsubstantiated stereotypical image of women and notes his unwillingness to attribute male crime to a biological predisposition to aggression and violence.

Although the claim that women are naturally more likely to conceal crimes can be readily dismissed, the possibility that women are treated more leniently by the legal authorities warrants closer examination.

Criminality, sex and the law

In theory at least, the vast majority of laws are sex-blind: the possibility of being charged or the type of offence for which you are charged does not depend upon your sex. However, there are a few laws that only apply to members of one sex. For example, only men can be convicted of rape or offences of homosexuality in Britain. On the other hand only women can be convicted of infanticide or soliciting as prostitutes. In reality, only a very small proportion of crimes come into one of these categories and legal definitions therefore make little difference to the overall statistics for male and female crime.

Leniency towards female offenders

Since Pollak's work there have been numerous **self-report studies** in which individuals are asked about what crimes they have committed. (For further comments on this type of study see p. 401.) Although such studies have their methodological limitations, they do give some indication of the extent of unreported crime and the chances that different groups have of escaping the discovery and prosecution of their offences.

Some self-report studies have supported Pollak's claim that female offenders are more likely to escape conviction than males. Writing in 1981, Anne Campbell pointed out that female suspects were more likely than male suspects to be cautioned rather than prosecuted. Official statistics show that this remains true. In 1990 of males recorded as offending, 29 per cent were cautioned and 71 per cent convicted. In the case of women 49 per cent were cautioned and 51 per cent were convicted.

A study by Hilary Allen based upon an examination of 1987 criminal statistics showed apparent leniency towards female offenders. For example 73 per cent of women but only 54 per cent of males found guilty of indictable motoring offences were given fines. This difference very largely resulted from more men being given prison sentences. In 1976 Campbell compared a self-report study on her own sample of 66 urban schoolgirls aged 16 with similar data on a sample of 397 16-year-old males collected by West and Farrington. These sources of data showed that 1.33 offences were committed by males for every 1.0 committed by females. This contrasted with 1976 official figures on convictions which showed 8.95 male convictions for every female conviction.

On the surface these data provide support for the '**chivalry**' thesis which claims that police and courts are lenient towards female offenders.

Evidence against the 'chivalry' thesis

In contrast, most other researchers have not found support for the chivalry thesis. Steven Box has reviewed the data from self-report studies in Britain and the USA. Although a few of these studies indicate some leniency towards females, the majority do not. He is able to conclude:

---

the weight of evidence on women committing serious offences does not give clear support to the view that they receive differential and more favourable treatment from members of the public, police or judges.

He goes on to say 'it would not be unreasonable to conclude that the relative contribution females make to serious crime is fairly accurately reflected in official statistics'.

All self-report studies rely upon the respondent's ability and willingness to tell the truth. Some researchers have tried to measure crime more directly using observation. Abigail Buckle and David P. Farrington carried out a small-scale observational study of shoplifting in a British department store in southeast England in 1981. Shoplifting is one crime where female offenders nearly match male offenders in the official statistics. This study found that 2.8 per cent of the 142 males observed shoplifted but only 1.4 per cent of

the 361 females did so. Obviously this study uses far too small a sample to draw firm conclusions, but as one of the few attempts to measure crime directly it does provide some evidence against the chivalry thesis.

Sentencing policy

Another approach to evaluating the 'chivalry' thesis is to examine sentencing policy. In 1983 David P. Farrington and Allison Morris conducted a study of sentencing in Magistrates Courts. They started out by noting that some official figures did imply more leniency towards women. For example, in 1979 6.6 per cent of men but only 2 per cent of women found guilty of indictable crimes were imprisoned. Farrington and Morris examined data on sentencing for 408 offences of theft in Cambridge in the same year. Some 110 of these offences were committed by women.

Although men received more severe sentences than women, the research found that the differences disappeared when the severity of offences was taken into account. Farrington and Morris concluded 'There was no independent effect of sex on sentence severity.'

However, these findings were not replicated in a more recent study carried out by Roger Hood in the West Midlands in 1989 that used a sample of 2,884 male and 433 female defendants in Crown Courts. Hood compared the sentencing of men and women, controlling for variables which he had found affected the sentencing of men. He found that white women were given custodial sentences 34 per cent less often than men in similar cases, and black women 37 per cent less often.

As we will discover in later sections though, this does not necessarily mean that women are always treated sympathetically by the legal system.

Criminal justice as biased against women

A rather different point of view is put forward by those who argue that women are treated more harshly by the criminal justice system than men.

This view can be supported by evidence which suggests that male offenders are sometimes treated more sympathetically than their female victims. This is particularly the case with rape trials. Carol Smart argues that such trials 'celebrate notions of male sexual need and female sexual capriciousness'. She quotes the following statements by trial judges in rape cases in support of this claim:

> It is well known that women in particular and small boys are likely to be untruthful and invent stories (Judge Sutcliffe 1976) . . . Women who say no do not always mean no. It is not just a question of how she says it, how she shows and makes it clear. If she doesn't want it she only has to keep her legs shut (Judge Wild 1982) . . . It is the height of imprudence for any girl to hitch-hike at night. That is plain, it isn't really worth stating. She is in the true sense asking for it (Judge Bertrand Richards 1982).

Many researchers have claimed that men are treated leniently in cases of domestic violence. In a pioneering study of domestic violence by Dobash and Dobash it was found that police officers were 'very unlikely to make an arrest when the offender has used violence against his wife'.

Double standards in criminal justice

A number of empirical studies and commentaries on gender and crime have reached the conclusion that males and females are treated differently and inequitably by the justice system but not always to the detriment of women. Basing her arguments on a review of available evidence, Heidensohn suggests that women are treated more harshly when they deviate from societal norms of female sexuality. Sexually promiscuous girls are more likely to be taken into care than similar boys. On the other hand courts may be reluctant to imprison mothers with young children.

To Heidensohn the justice system is influenced by attitudes to gender in society as a whole. These are based upon 'dual' and 'confused' assumptions about women which see women as 'virgin and whore, witch and wife, Madonna and Magdalene'.

As we noted earlier, Hilary Allen's study of sentencing found that women were treated quite leniently in the case of motoring offences. She found that women were more likely to escape with low-tariff punishments across a range of offences and were certainly less likely to get sent to prison. However, she also found that women were more likely to be put on probation than men for some offences.

Like Heidensohn, Allen argues that the policies are tied up with conventional definitions of femininity and masculinity. Men's offences are often put down to aggression or greed. Men are more likely to be fined and imprisoned partly because they are seen as being less central to family life than women. The loss of money from a fine or the loss of a parent through imprisonment is regarded as less problematic for a family if the offender is a man than a woman. Women are seen as being less inherently deviant than men and courts find it harder to understand their criminal activity. Consequently courts are more likely to order reports on female offenders in the search for 'underlying psychological meanings'. Probation may be used instead of a fine with the intention of helping the female offender. In this case though, what could be seen as 'chivalry' by the courts could also be seen as disadvantaging women and reinforcing sexist ideologies about masculinity and femininity.

■ The causes of female crime and deviance

Physiological causes

Not surprisingly some of the earliest attempts to explain female criminality were based upon physiological or biological theories. Indeed, one of the pioneers of biological theories of male crime, Caesare Lombroso, also attempted to explain female crime. (We provide more details of Lombroso's theories on p. 387.) Writing with William Ferrero in *The Female Offender* Lombroso devoted considerable attention to comparing anatomical features of female criminals and noncriminals. For example he reported data comparing brains and skulls, the width of cheek bones, size of jaws and even the size of the thighs of prostitutes and 'normal women'! Nevertheless, his overall argument is that rather that being the cause of female criminality, biology tends to prevent women becoming criminal.

Writing about male crime, Lombroso had suggested that criminals could be identified through the presence of 'stigmata' or physical abnormalities such as having an extra toe or nipple. Lombroso and Ferrero found few examples of such abnormalities amongst female criminals. To them this suggested that most female offenders were not true, biological, criminals. They broke the law only occasionally and their crimes were not serious. They claimed that women had a deficient moral sense, and were inclined to be vengeful and jealous but 'In ordinary cases these defects were neutralised by piety, maternity, want of passion, sexual coldness, by weakness and an underdeveloped intelligence.'

Nevertheless they did believe that a few women were born criminals. These women were so exceptional and started life with such 'enormous' 'wickedness' that each was 'consequently a monster'. They tended to be more masculine than other women.

Lombroso's work has long been discredited. For example, Heidensohn comments:

> his work was fanciful rather than scientific. His detailed measurements were not subject to any tests of significance and his 'analysis' of photographs of 'fallen women' is as objective as an adjudication in a beauty contest.

Such criticisms have not prevented some later sociologists seeking biological explanations both for women's conformity, and, when it occurs, their deviance. Most sociologists, however, have rightly focused on possible social causes of female crime.

Female crime and women's liberation

Freda Adler – the 'new female criminal'

In 1975 the American writer Freda Adler claimed that women's liberation had led to a new type of female criminal and an increase in women's contribution to crime.

Adler starts by rejecting biological theories. For example, she denies a direct link between hormones, aggression and criminality. She points out that there are *many* passive men with normal androgen levels who are less aggressive than women'. (We discuss sex and gender differences and hormones on pp. 582–3.) She argues that differences in the behaviour of males and females are socially determined, and changes in society have led to changes in that behaviour.

Adler quotes numerous statistics which appear to show increasing female involvement in crime, particularly in some crimes which have traditionally been committed mainly by men. She says that in the USA between 1960 and 1972 robberies by women went up 277 per cent, men's by only 169 per cent. Embezzlement by women rose by 280 per cent in the same period, whereas for men the figure rose by a mere 50 per cent. Overall arrest rates for females were rising three times as fast as those for males and particularly quickly among female delinquents.

To Adler this suggested that future generations of adult criminals would show a narrowing gap in the crime rates of males and females. She also claimed that similar trends of rising female crime could be discerned in Western Europe, New Zealand and India.

Why then were women becoming so much more involved in crime? Adler believed that the main reason was that women were taking on male social roles in both legitimate and illegitimate areas of activities. She stressed the pace and extent of change saying:

> There is a tide in the affairs of women as well as men, and in the last decade it has been sweeping over the barriers which have protected male prerogatives and eroding the traditional differences which once nicely defined the gender roles.

As women entered the labour force in increasing numbers, they wanted increased representation in jobs previously reserved for men. The same applied in criminal careers. 'The female criminal knows too much to pretend, or return to her former role as a second-rate criminal confined to "feminine" crimes such as shoplifting and prostitution.' Instead women were getting involved in robbing banks, mugging, loan sharking and even murder.

Adler's views proved to be very controversial, particularly as they could be used to imply that women's liberation was a bad thing. They stimulated considerable research into the question of whether women's crime was increasing.

Carol Smart – a critique of Adler

Carol Smart is amongst those who have responded

to Adler's argument. She advances the following criticisms.

1 Adler incorrectly assumes that rates of delinquency are an accurate guide to future patterns of adult crime. This is a mistake since 'It is well known that juvenile delinquency and adult crime are quite different phenomena, involving largely different personnel, different motivations and different purposes.'

2 Extending the argument to include changes in female crime rates in countries as diverse as New Zealand and India ignores 'cultural variations, different criminal codes and legal systems, different methods of collating statistics and different degrees of "emancipation" for women'.

3 Smart points out that Adler's views are largely based upon official statistics which are notoriously unreliable.

However, Smart then goes on to claim that official figures for England and Wales do not in any case support Adler's theory about crime and emancipation. Although women's crime did increase in proportion to men's from 1965 to 1975, it had increased more rapidly from 1935 to 1946 and from 1955 to 1965 before the women's liberation movement had made significant progress.

Criticisms of Smart

Smart's own views have themselves been the subject of criticism by Roy Austin. He looked more closely at the official figures used by Smart. He agreed with her observations about indictable crime in general, but found that they did not apply to Class 1 offences (violence against the person and sexual offences), nor to Class 2 offences (burglary and robbery). In both these categories 1965–75 had shown the most rapid increase in female crime compared to men's. Since these were just the sort of crimes that Adler had claimed would increase with female liberation, the figures undermined Smart's case.

Steven Box and Chris Hale – liberation versus marginalization

Box and Hale are rather dismissive of Smart's and Austin's attempts to determine whether female liberation leads to rising crime. They say 'the

Smart–Austin disagreement is based on analyses too weak to sustain either position'. Both of them made a number of mistakes.

1 They included sexual crimes in their figures. Some of these are sex specific or include consensual sexual acts between adults (such as homosexuality) and are not therefore relevant to the debate.

2 Neither Austin nor Smart controlled for the changing proportions of males and females in the population.

3 Neither made any attempt actually to measure female liberation.

Methods

Box and Hale set out to avoid such mistakes in their own research. They allowed for changing proportions of males and females in the population, excluded sexual crimes and used four measures of female liberation. They took declines in the birth rate and increases in the numbers of single women as indicators of liberation since these suggested freedom from the patriarchal family. Increasing rates of participation in the labour force and rises in the number of female graduates and undergraduates were also taken as indicators of liberation.

Box and Hale were concerned that changes in police procedures might have affected the way that female crime was dealt with so that women's offences had become more likely to be recorded. They therefore examined changes in the number of women police officers as a possible indicator of changing police routine.

They also noted the argument that most female offenders who committed serious crimes tend to come from lower-class backgrounds. Such women were the least likely to be touched by emancipation. It was possible therefore that recession and increased economic marginalization could account for any increase in female crime. Rates of female unemployment were used as a way of indicating the amount of economic marginalization amongst women.

Findings

Official figures showed a large absolute increase in female indictable crime in 1951–79 in England and Wales. However, male crimes were increasing at the same time and the proportion of violent crimes against the person committed by women had scarcely increased. On the other hand property crime by women had increased from 13 per cent to 22 per cent of the total.

When Box and Hale came to examine the relationship between various measures of liberation and female crime, they found little evidence that liberation was causing crime. None of the variables measuring liberation was found to be statistically significant.

However, they did detect a statistical relationship between male crime rates and those of women. This suggested that social forces which had nothing to do with female liberation were acting to push up crime rates for both sexes.

Box and Hale also found a relationship between the increasing employment of women police officers and the recording of violent crime by women. They suggested that perhaps the theory that female liberation had increased women's crime had 'sensitised' the authorities to the 'problem' and resulted in female crimes of violence becoming more likely to be recorded.

Changes in the way acts were labelled could perhaps explain such changes as there had been in the figures. They also found a relationship between unemployment rates and crime rates amongst women. This was particularly strong for property crimes.

Reviewing the debate about female crime and women's liberation Box concluded:

The major factor accounting for most of the increase in property offences seems to be economic marginalization. In other words, as women become economically worse off, largely through unemployment and inadequate compensatory levels of welfare benefits, so they are less able and willing to resist the temptations to engage in property offences as a way of helping to solve their financial difficulties.

Evaluation

Like all the other studies discussed in this section Box and Hale's work relies upon official statistics and as such the findings can only be tentative. Nevertheless it is more sophisticated than other studies and Box is fairly convincing when he says 'Female liberation does not appear to have been

the demonic phenomenon described by criminologists and accepted by the media, police and criminal justice officials.'

Official figures do not suggest this statement has become any less true. In 1980 women made up 17.18 per cent of those convicted or cautioned for indictable offences. The figure had declined marginally to 17.01 per cent by 1990. In 1990 women made up only 8.38 per cent of those found guilty of crimes of violence against the person, a figure which is very similar to that for 1951.

■ Pat Carlen – women, crime and poverty

Sample and methods

In 1985 Pat Carlen conducted a study of 39 women aged 15–46 who had been convicted of one or more crimes. She carried out lengthy and in-depth unstructured taped interviews with each of the women. Most were from the London area and twenty were in a prison and youth custody centre at the time of interviewing. Most of the women were working class (as are most women with criminal convictions) and they had committed a range of offences. Twenty-six had convictions for theft or handling stolen goods, sixteen for fraud or similar offences, fifteen for burglary, fourteen for violence, eight for arson, six for drugs offences and four for prostitution-related crime.

Like Box, Carlen does not believe that liberation has resulted in an increase in crimes by women. Most of her sample had been touched little by any gains that women had experienced in, for example, access to a wider range of jobs. Instead most had experienced their opportunities becoming increasingly restricted. Carlen argues that the working-class background of most of her sample is fairly typical of female offenders convicted of more serious crimes, although she is aware that 'white-collar' female criminals might be escaping conviction for their offences. She says 'when women do break the law those from lower socio-economic groups are more liable to criminalization than are their middle-class sisters'.

By reconstructing the lives of such women from in-depth interviewing, Carlen hoped to identify the sets of circumstances that led to their involvement in crime.

Control theory

Carlen adopts **control theory** as her theoretical approach. Control theory has influenced a considerable number of criminologists and was first explicitly outlined by an American sociologist, T. Hirschi, in 1969. It starts with the assumption that humans are neither naturally wicked and prone to crime, nor are they naturally virtuous and prone to conformity. Instead humans are essentially rational and they will turn to crime when the advantages seem to outweigh the disadvantages and are more appealing than the likely rewards of conformity.

According to Carlen, working-class women have been controlled through the promise of rewards stemming from the workplace and the family. Such women are encouraged to make what she calls the 'class deal' and the 'gender deal'. The **class deal** offers material rewards such as consumer goods for those respectable working-class women who work dutifully for a wage. The **gender deal** offers 'psychological and material rewards . . . emanating from either the labours or the "love" of a male breadwinner'. When these rewards are not available or women have not been persuaded that these rewards are real or worth sacrifices, the deals break down and criminality becomes a possibility.

Factors encouraging deviance

Carlen found that the women attributed their criminality to four main factors. These were drug addiction (including alcohol), the quest for excitement, being brought up in care, and poverty. She places particular emphasis on the last two factors: very often the abuse of drugs and the desire for excitement were the consequence of being brought up in care or of being poor.

In all, thirty-two of the women had always been poor, four of the remaining seven were unemployed at the time of being interviewed, and only two had good jobs. A majority of the women (twenty-two) had spent at least part of their lives in care.

Rejection of the class deal

Poverty and being brought up in care led to the women rejecting the class and gender deals. Few of

the women had experience of the possible benefits of the class deal. They had never had the access to the consumer goods and leisure facilities which society portrays as representing the 'good life'.

Attempts to find a legitimate way of earning a decent living had been frustrated. For example, six of the women had been through the Youth Training Scheme but returned to being unemployed at the end of their training. A number had gained qualifications in prison but had found them to be of no use in finding a job. Many had experience of day-to-day 'humiliations, delays and frustrations' in trying to claim benefits. They had 'a strong sense of injustice oppression and powerlessness'. Crime was a way of resisting the injustices and trying to solve the problems of poverty. The women had little to lose by turning to crime, and potentially a good deal to gain.

Rejection of the gender deal

According to Carlen, women generally are deterred from committing crime because they are brought up to see themselves as the 'guardians of domestic morality'. They also have less opportunity to commit crimes because they are more closely supervised than males, first by parents and later by husbands. Patriarchal ideology promises women happiness and fulfilment from family life. For most of the women in the study, though, the gender deal had not been made, or had been rejected. They had been freed from family life or so closely supervised that they felt oppressed by the family. Carlen says:

---

when young girls have been brought up in situations where absolutely no rewards (and many severe disabilities) have been seen to emanate from familiness, when, too the technologies of gender discipline have been unusually harsh or oppressive, women's adult consciousness has been constituted within an immediate experience of the fundamental oppression inherent in the gender deal; . . . they have resisted it.

Some of the women had been sexually or physically abused by their fathers. Eight of them had been physically attacked by male partners. For the twenty-two women who had been in care there had been little opportunity to 'acquire the psychological commitment to male-related domesticity'. Spending time in care broke attachments to friends and family and reduced some of the potential social costs of isolation which could result from crime. Running away from care, usually with no money, or leaving care, sometimes homeless and unemployed, could easily lead on to crime. Carlen describes the situation of women leaving care in the following way:

> Ill-equipped (both materially and by their previous experiences) for living on their own, many of the women had soon begun to think that crime was the only route to a decent standard of living. They had nothing to lose and everything to gain.

Convictions and prison sentences merely served to restrict the women's legal opportunities even further and make the attractions of crime greater.

Conclusion

Carlen's study was based upon a small sample of mainly working-class women involved in fairly serious crimes. It is therefore dangerous to generalize from her findings. Nevertheless it does provide strong support for the view that criminal behaviour becomes more likely when society's mechanisms of social control break down. Other sociologists have examined social control mechanisms to explain why women seem so much more likely to conform than men.

■ Female conformity

Frances Heidensohn – women and social control

As earlier sections have indicated, however inaccurate official statistics may be, it seems clear that women do commit fewer serious crimes than men. Frances Heidensohn has tried to explain why this should be so. Like Pat Carlen she uses control theory as the basis of her explanation. Building on the work of other sociologists she argues that male-dominated patriarchal societies control women more effectively than they do men, making it more difficult for women to break the law. Control operates at home, in public and at work.

Control of women at home

Being a housewife directly restricts women limiting opportunities for criminality. Heidensohn describes domesticity as 'a form of detention'. The endless hours spent on housework and the constant monitoring of young children leave little time for illegal activities. A 'very pervasive value system' persuades women that they must carry out their domestic responsibilities dutifully or they will have failed as mothers and wives. Women who challenge the traditional roles of women within the family run the risk of having them reimposed by force. Heidensohn says 'many observers confirm that wife-battering is in fact an assertion of patriarchal authority'.

Men may also use their financial power if they are the main or only wage earner to control women's behaviour. Daughters as well as wives are more closely controlled by the family. They are usually given less freedom than boys to come and go as they please or stay out late at night and are expected to spend more time doing housework.

Control of women in public

In public women are controlled by the male use of force and violence, by the idea of holding on to a 'good' reputation, and by the 'ideology of separate spheres'.

Women often choose not to go out into public places because of the fear of being attacked or raped. Heidensohn quotes the 1986 *Islington Crime Survey* which found that 54 per cent of women but only 14 per cent of men often or always avoided going out after dark because of fear of crime. She quotes Susan Brownmiller's claim that rape and fear of rape 'is nothing more or less than a conscious process of intimidation by which all men keep all women in a state of fear' (quoted in Heidensohn 1985, p. 182). Heidensohn stops short of endorsing this view but does argue that the sensational reporting of rapes and the unsympathetic attitude of some police and judges to rape victims act as forces controlling women.

Women also tend to limit their behaviour in public places because of the risk of being labelled unrespectable, of being seen as a 'slag, slut or bitch'. The wrong sort of 'dress, demeanour, make-up and even speech' can damage a girl's reputation in the eyes of men.

The **ideology of separate spheres** which sees a woman's place as being in the home 'has become part of the system that subtly and sometimes brutally confines women'. Women are not expected to raise their concerns in public and place them on the political agenda. If they try, they may be ridiculed and told to return to where they belong – in the home. Such a fate befell the Greenham Common women who protested about the siting of American nuclear weapons in Britain.

Control of women at work

At work women are usually controlled by male superiors in the hierarchy, and workers' own organizations, trade unions, are also dominated by men. Women may also be intimidated by various forms of sexual harassment that discourage female employees from asserting themselves or from feeling at home at work. Sexual harassment 'ranges from whistles and catcalls and the fixing of pinups and soft porn pictures, to physical approaches and attacks which could be defined as possibly indecent and criminal'. Heidensohn quotes surveys which find that up to 60 per cent of women have suffered some form of sexual harassment at work.

Conclusion – conformity and deviance

Heidensohn's argument about causes of conformity by women fits in well with Carlen's views on the causes of deviance. Both are based on control theory and both agree that crime and deviance by women take place when controls break down and women lose the real or imagined incentives to conform. Heidensohn suggests that some female criminals may be those who have 'perceived the bias of the system and decided to push against it'. For other women it is the restrictions themselves that force them into reliance upon crime. She says 'women are particularly vulnerable because they are so economically exploited'. If they lose the 'protection' of a man they may turn to crimes such as prostitution as the only way to earn a reasonable living.

Many of Heidensohn's arguments are based upon generalizations, some of which do not apply to all women. She does not always support her claims with strong empirical evidence. However, she does present a plausible explanation of why such a gap remains between men's and women's crime rates. In doing so she highlights some of the inequalities between men and women that remain.

Sociology, values and deviance

It is clear from this chapter that the sympathies of many sociologists tend to lie with the deviant. This will inevitably influence their research. In a paper entitled *Who's Side are We On*, Howard Becker argues that it is impossible to conduct research 'uncontaminated by personal and political sympathies.' Like many sociologists he believes that a value-free sociology is not possible. Becker claims that his sympathies are with the 'underdog', the deviant who is labelled by the agencies of social control. These sympathies tend to colour the views of the entire interactionist school. The villains of the piece are the agents of social control: the police, the judges, the probation and prison officers, the doctors and the psychiatrists, those who process the deviants and slap on the labels. In terms of their critical view of control agencies, Becker claims that politically, 'interactionist theories look (and are) rather Left'.

Alvin Gouldner takes a rather different view.

He accuses the interactionists of adopting a 'bland liberal position' which advocates cosmetic reform rather than radical change. In criticizing the agencies of social control they fail to attack the real causes of deviance which lie in society itself. Gouldner argues that this failure is due to the interactionists' ideological stance. Their liberal views lead them to regard the basic foundations of society as sound. More radical commitments would demand fundamental changes in the structure of society rather than the less repressive measures of social control which the interactionists advocate.

Gouldner claims that many members of the interactionist school have a romantic identification with the more colourful and exotic deviants. He suggests that they 'get their kicks' from a 'titillated attraction to the underdog's exotic difference'. He claims that 'theirs is a school of thought that finds itself at home in the world of hip, drug addicts, jazz musicians, cab drivers, prostitutes, night people, drifters, grifters and skidders: "the cool world"'. Gouldner argues that this identification by largely middle-class sociologists with the 'cool underworld' colours their choice of research subjects, their perspectives and conclusions. It leads at best to rather bland sympathies with the underdog and a relatively mild reproach to the agencies of social control to lay off and leave the deviants alone. Gouldner regards this as a poor substitute for a radical critique of society as a whole.

Functionalists such as Merton have also been accused of 'bland liberalism' by their more radical critics. Merton's view of society is critical but the changes indicated by his conclusions suggest reform rather than radical change. He sees inequality of opportunity as the major cause of crime and delinquency and implies that measures to increase equal opportunity will solve many of society's problems. With a basic commitment to US society in the first place and a belief that its foundations are fundamentally sound, Merton is directed towards criticism and reform rather than condemnation and radical change. This may well have prevented him from questioning the system itself, and, as Laurie Taylor suggested, asking basic questions such as, 'Who made the rules in the first place?'

If the interactionists and functionalists can be accused of liberal bias, the same can hardly be said of some of the Marxists. Commitment to radical change reverberates through their writings. Starting from the value judgement that private property is theft, Marxist sociologists reject the basic structure of class society. Their political views result in a condemnation of ruling-class crime and a sympathetic treatment of the crimes of the subject class. When Marxists such as Frank Pearce refer to the 'naked barbarity' of capitalism it is clear that commitments other than scientific objectivity direct and influence their choice of subject matter, their methods of analysis and their conclusions.

The 'New Criminology' of Taylor, Walton and Young is, if anything, even more idealistic than conventional Marxist theories. These writers wish to 'create a society in which the facts of human diversity, whether personal, organic or social, are not subject to the power to criminalize'. However, they do not make it clear which laws could be abolished and which, if any needed to be retained.

New left realists (including Jock Young, one of the authors of the *New Criminology*) label such approaches as left idealism and attack them as hopelessly romantic. Left realists advocate a more sober analysis and are less sympathetic to the criminal. Their research suggests that criminals are not Robin Hood figures redistributing wealth and thereby helping the working class, but as further damaging the already difficult lives of inner-city residents. Kevin Stevenson and Nigel Brearly summarize Young's change of heart well in discussing his changing views on drug use. They say 'Young's view of illegal drug use has shifted from a libertarian concern with the rights to self-determination of young drug users to the concerns of an anxious parental generation.' Left realists still describe themselves as socialist, and still seek a more egalitarian society, but they opt for limited reform rather than radical or even revolutionary changes.

Feminist criminologists such as Carol Smart start by attacking previous criminology as having an in-built male bias. They see it as having been written by men, about men and for men. Since the 1970s research by women has begun to redress the imbalance. However, in doing so some feminist sociologists have in turn been influenced by their values and have made questionable generalizations about the attitudes and behaviour of men. For example, when Brownmiller claimed that rape was 'nothing more or less than a conscious process of intimidation by which all men keep all women in a state of fear' she certainly allowed the strength of her feelings to influence her analysis.

Since the issues of crime, deviance and conformity are essentially about what humans consider to be right and wrong, it is hardly surprising that values impinge on this area of study to a very great extent.

8

Religion

8

Religion

■ Introduction

1 'In the beginning was the Word, and the Word was with God, and the Word was God.' The God of Christianity is a supreme being, his word is the ultimate truth, his power is omnipotent. His followers worship him and praise him and live by his commandments.

2 The Dugum Dani live in the Highlands of New Guinea. They have no god, but their world is inhabited by a host of supernatural beings known as *mogat*. The *mogat* are the ghosts of the dead. They cause illness and death and control the wind and the rain. The Dugum Dani are not pious – they do not pray. Their rituals are not to honour or worship the *mogat* but to placate and appease them.

3 The Teton Sioux lived on the northern prairies of the USA. The worlds of nature, on which they were dependent, were controlled by the *Wakan* powers. The powers were stronger and more mysterious than those of people. They caused the seasons to change, the rains to fall, the plants to grow and the animals to multiply. In this way they cared for the Sioux. The Sioux did not worship the *Wakan* powers but invoked their aid: they appealed to the powers for assistance or protection.

Supernatural beliefs are present in every known society and their variety seems to be endless. Any definition of religion must encompass this variety. At its simplest, **religion** is the belief in the supernatural. This definition, however, fails to incorporate the idea that supernatural forces have some influence or control upon the world, a notion that always accompanies belief in the supernatural. Thus Roland Robertson states that religion 'refers to the existence of supernatural beings that have a governing effect on life'. Melford E. Spiro adopts a similar definition when he states that religion is based on 'beliefs in superhuman beings and in their power to assist or harm man'.

All definitions emphasize certain aspects of religion and exclude others. Those of Robertson and Spiro focus on the nature of religious belief. We will look at other definitions that place greater emphasis on other aspects of religion (for example religious practice) throughout this chapter.

■ Religion – a functionalist perspective

The functionalist perspective examines religion in terms of society's needs. Functionalist analysis is primarily concerned with the contribution religion makes to meeting these needs. From this perspective, society requires a certain degree of social solidarity, value consensus, and harmony and integration between its parts. The function of religion is the contribution it makes to meeting such functional prerequisites, for example, its contribution to social solidarity.

■ Emile Durkheim
The sacred and the profane

In *The Elementary Forms of the Religious Life*, first published in 1912, Emile Durkheim presented what is probably the most influential interpretation of religion from a functionalist perspective. Durkheim argued that all societies divide the world into two categories: the **sacred** and the profane, or more simply, the sacred and the non-sacred. Religion is based upon this division. It is 'a unified system of beliefs and practices related to sacred things, that is to say things set apart and forbidden'.

It is important to realize that:

By sacred things one must not understand simply those personal things which are called gods or spirits; a rock, a tree, a spring, a pebble, a piece of wood, a house, in a word anything can be sacred.

There is nothing about the particular qualities of a pebble or a tree that makes them sacred. Therefore sacred things must be symbols, they must represent something. To understand the role of religion in society, the relationship between sacred symbols and what they represent must be established.

Totemism

Durkheim used the religion of various groups of Australian aborigines to develop his argument. He saw their religion, which he called **totemism**, as the simplest and most basic form of religion.

Aborigine society is divided into several clans. A clan is like a large extended family with its members sharing certain duties and obligations. For example, clans have a rule of **exogamy**, that is members are not allowed to marry within the clan. Clan members have a duty to aid and assist each other: they join together to mourn the death of one of their number and to revenge a member who has been wronged by someone from another clan.

Each clan has a totem, usually an animal or a plant. The totem is a symbol. It is the emblem of the clan, 'It is its flag; it is the sign by which each clan distinguishes itself from all others.' However, the totem is more than this, it is a sacred symbol. It is carved on the bullroarer, the most sacred object in aborigine ritual. The totem is 'The outward and visible form of the totemic principle or god.'

Durkheim argued that if the totem 'Is at once the symbol of god and of the society, is that not because the god and the society are only one?' Thus he suggested that in worshipping god, people are in fact worshipping society. Society is the real object of religious veneration.

How does humanity come to worship society? Sacred things are 'considered superior in dignity and power to profane things and particularly to man'. In relation to the sacred, humans are inferior and dependent. This relationship between humanity and sacred things is exactly the relationship between humanity and society. Society is more important and powerful than the individual. Durkheim argued that 'Primitive man comes to view society as something sacred because he is utterly dependent on it.'

But why does humanity not simply worship society itself? Why does it invent a sacred symbol like a totem? Because, Durkheim argued, it is easier for a person to 'visualize and direct his feelings of awe toward a symbol than towards so complex a thing as a clan'.

Religion and the 'collective conscience'

Durkheim believed that social life is impossible without the shared values and moral beliefs which form the **collective conscience**. In their absence, there would be no social order, social control, social solidarity or cooperation. In short, there would be no society. Religion reinforces the collective conscience. The worship of society strengthens the values and moral beliefs that form the basis of social life. By defining them as sacred, religion provides them with greater power to direct human action.

This attitude of respect towards the sacred is the same attitude applied to social duties and obligations. In worshipping society, people are, in effect, recognizing the importance of the social group and their dependence upon it. In this way religion strengthens the unity of the group: it promotes social solidarity.

Durkheim emphasized the importance of **collective worship**. The social group comes together in religious rituals full of drama and reverence. Together, its members express their faith in common values and beliefs. In this highly charged atmosphere of collective worship, the integration of society is strengthened. Members of society express, communicate and understand the moral bonds which unite them.

Criticisms of Durkheim

Durkheim's ideas are still influential today, although they have been criticized. Some anthropologists have argued that he is not justified in seeing totemism as a religion and most sociologists believe that Durkheim has overstated his case. Whilst agreeing that religion is important for promoting social solidarity and reinforcing social values, they would not support his view that religion is the worship of society. Durkheim's views on religion are more relevant to small, non-literate societies, where there is a close integration of culture and social institutions, where work, leisure, education and family life tend to merge, and where members share a common belief and value system. They are less relevant to modern societies, which have many subcultures, social and ethnic groups, specialized organizations and a range of religious beliefs, practices and institutions.

◼ Bronislaw Malinowski

Like Durkheim, Malinowski uses data from small-scale non-literate societies to develop his thesis on religion. Many of his examples are drawn from his fieldwork in the Trobriand Islands off the coast of New Guinea. Like Durkheim, Malinowski sees religion as reinforcing social norms and values and promoting social solidarity. Unlike Durkheim, however, he does not see religion as reflecting society as a whole, nor does he see religious ritual as the worship of society itself. Malinowski identifies specific areas of social life with which religion is concerned, and to which it is addressed. These are situations of emotional stress that threaten social solidarity.

Religion and life crises

Anxiety and tension tend to disrupt social life. Situations that produce these emotions include **crises of life** such as birth, puberty, marriage and death. Malinowski notes that in all societies these life crises are surrounded with religious ritual. He sees death as the most disruptive of these events and argues that:

> The existence of strong personal attachments and the fact of death, which of all human events is the most upsetting and disorganizing to man's calculations, are perhaps the main sources of religious beliefs.

Religion deals with the problem of death in the following manner. A funeral ceremony expresses the belief in immortality, which denies the fact of death, and so comforts the bereaved. Other mourners support the bereaved by their presence at the ceremony. This comfort and support checks the emotions which death produces, and controls the stress and anxiety that might disrupt society. Death is **socially destructive** since it removes a member from society. At a funeral ceremony the social group unites to support the bereaved. This expression of social solidarity reintegrates society.

Religion, prediction and control

A second category of events – undertakings that cannot be fully controlled or predicted by practical means – also produces tension and anxiety. From his observations in the Trobriand Islands, Malinowski noted that such events were surrounded by **ritual**.

Fishing is an important subsistence practice in the Trobriands. Malinowski observed that in the calm waters of the lagoon 'fishing is done in an easy and absolutely reliable manner by the method of poisoning, yielding abundant results without danger and uncertainty'. However, beyond the barrier reef in the open sea there is danger and uncertainty: a storm may result in loss of life and the catch is dependent on the presence of a shoal of fish which cannot be predicted. In the lagoon, 'where man can rely completely on his knowledge and skill', there are no rituals associated with fishing whereas fishing in the open sea is preceded by rituals to ensure a good catch and protect the fishermen. Although Malinowski refers to these rituals as magic, others argue it is reasonable to regard them as religious practices.

Again we see ritual used for specific situations that produce anxiety. Rituals reduce anxiety by providing confidence and a feeling of control. As with funeral ceremonies, fishing rituals are social events. The group unites to deal with situations of stress, and so the unity of the group is strengthened.

Therefore we can summarize by saying that Malinowski's distinctive contribution to the sociology of religion is his argument that religion promotes social solidarity by dealing with situations of emotional stress that threaten the stability of society.

▌ Talcott Parsons

Religion and value consensus

Talcott Parsons argues that human action is directed and controlled by norms provided by the social system. The cultural system provides more general guidelines for action in the form of beliefs, values and systems of meaning. The norms which direct action are not merely isolated standards for behaviour: they are integrated and patterned by the values and beliefs provided by the cultural system. For example, many norms in Western society are expressions of the value of materialism. Religion is part of the cultural system. As such, religious beliefs provide guidelines for human action and standards against which people's conduct can be evaluated.

In a Christian society the Ten Commandments operate in this way. They demonstrate how many of the norms of the social system can be integrated by religious beliefs. For example, the commandment 'Thou shalt not kill' integrates such diverse norms as the ways to drive a car, to settle an argument and to deal with the suffering of the aged. The norms that direct these areas of behaviour prohibit manslaughter, murder and euthanasia but they are all based on the same religious commandment.

In this way religion provides general guidelines for conduct which are expressed in a variety of norms. By establishing general principles and moral beliefs, religion helps to provide the consensus which Parsons believes is necessary for order and stability in society.

Religion and social order

Parsons, like Malinowski, sees religion addressed to particular problems that occur in all societies. He argues that in everyday life, people 'go about their business without particular strain'. If life were always like this, 'religion would certainly not have the significance that it does'. However, life does not always follow this smooth pattern. The problems that disrupt it fall into two categories.

1 The first 'consists in the fact that individuals are "hit" by events which they cannot foresee and prepare for, or control, or both'. One such event is death, particularly premature death. Like Malinowski, and for similar reasons, Parsons sees religion as a mechanism for adjustment to such events and as a means of restoring the normal pattern of life.

2 The second problem area is that of 'uncertainty'. This refers to endeavours in which a great deal of effort and skill have been invested, but where unknown or uncontrollable factors can threaten a successful outcome. One example is humanity's inability to predict or control the effect of weather upon agriculture. Again, following Malinowski, Parsons argues that religion provides a means of adjusting and coming to terms with such situations through rituals which act as 'a tonic to self-confidence'.

In this way religion maintains social stability by relieving the tension and frustration that could disrupt social order.

Religion and meaning

As a part of the cultural system, religious beliefs give meaning to life; they answer 'man's questions about himself and the world he lives in'. This function of religion is particularly important in relation to the frustrations we discussed in the last sections, which threaten to shatter beliefs about the meaning of life and so make human existence meaningless. Why should a premature death occur? It is not something people expect to happen or feel ought to happen. Social life is full of contradictions that threaten the meanings people place on life. Parsons argues that one of the major functions of religion is to 'make sense' of all experiences, no matter how meaningless or contradictory they appear.

A good example of this is the question of suffering: 'Why must men endure deprivation and pain and so unequally and haphazardly, if indeed at all?' Religion provides a range of answers: suffering is imposed by God to test a person's faith; it is a punishment for sins; and suffering with fortitude will bring its reward in Heaven. Suffering thus becomes meaningful.

Similarly, the problem of evil is common to all societies. It is particularly disconcerting when people profit through evil actions. Religion solves this contradiction by stating that evil will receive its just deserts in the afterlife.

Parsons therefore sees a major function of religion as the provision of meaning to events that people do not expect, or feel ought not, to happen; events that are frustrating and contradictory. Religion 'makes sense' of these events in terms of an integrated and consistent pattern of meaning. This allows intellectual and emotional adjustment. On a more general level, this adjustment promotes order and stability in society.

Criticisms of the functionalist approach

The functionalist perspective emphasizes the positive contributions of religion to society and tends to ignore its dysfunctional aspects. With its preoccupation with harmony, integration and solidarity, functionalism neglects the many instances where religion can be seen as a divisive and disruptive force. It bypasses the frequent examples of internal divisions within a community over questions of religious dogma and worship; divisions that can lead to open conflict. It gives little consideration to hostility between different religious groups within the same society, such as Catholics

and Protestants in Northern Ireland or Hindus and Muslims in India. In such cases religion can be seen as a direct threat to social order. As Charles Glock and Rodney Stark state in their criticism of functionalist views on religion:

> We find it difficult to reconcile the general theory with considerable evidence of religious conflict. On every side it would seem that religion threatens social integration as readily as it contributes to it. The history of Christianity, with its many schisms, manifests the great power of religion not merely to bind but to divide.

The Marxist perspective on religion, which we are going to consider next, provides an interesting contrast to functionalist views.

Religion – a Marxist perspective

In Marx's vision of the ideal society, exploitation and alienation are things of the past. The means of production are communally owned, which results in the disappearance of social classes. Members of society are fulfilled as human beings: they control their own destinies and work together for the common good. Religion does not exist in this communist utopia because the social conditions that produce it have disappeared.

To Marx, religion is an illusion which eases the pain produced by exploitation and oppression. It is a series of myths that justify and legitimate the subordination of the subject class and the domination and privilege of the ruling class. It is a distortion of reality that provides many of the deceptions which form the basis of ruling-class ideology and false class consciousness.

Religion as 'the opium of the people'

In Marx's words, 'Religion is the sigh of the oppressed creature, the sentiment of a heartless world and the soul of soulless conditions. It is the opium of the people.' Religion acts as an opiate to dull the pain produced by oppression. It does nothing to solve the problem: it is simply a misguided attempt to make life more bearable. As

such, religion merely stupefies its adherents rather than bringing them true happiness and fulfilment. Lenin argued 'Religion is a kind of spiritual gin in which the slaves of capital drown their human shape and their claims to any decent life.'

From a Marxist perspective, most religious movements originate in oppressed classes. Their social conditions provide the most fertile ground for the growth of new religions. Thus Engels states that:

> Christianity was originally a movement of oppressed people; it first appeared as the religion of slaves and emancipated slaves, of poor people deprived of all rights, or peoples subjugated or dispersed by Rome.

Religion can dull the pain of oppression in the following ways.

1 It promises a paradise of eternal bliss in life after death. Engels argued that the appeal of Christianity to oppressed classes lies in its promise of 'salvation from bondage and misery' in the afterlife. The Christian vision of heaven can make life on earth more bearable by giving people something to look forward to.

2 Some religions make a virtue of the suffering produced by oppression. In particular, those who bear the deprivations of poverty with dignity and humility will be

rewarded for their virtue. This view is contained in the well-known biblical quotation 'It is easier for a camel to pass through the eye of a needle, than for a rich man to enter the Kingdom of Heaven.' Religion thus makes poverty more tolerable by offering a reward for suffering and promising compensation for injustice in the afterlife.

3 Religion can offer the hope of supernatural intervention to solve the problems on earth. Members of religious groups such as the Jehovah's Witnesses live in anticipation of the day when the supernatural powers will descend from on high and create heaven on earth. Anticipation of this future can make the present more acceptable.

4 Religion often justifies the social order and a person's position within it. God can be seen as creating and ordaining the social structure as in the following verse from the Victorian hymn 'All things bright and beautiful':

> The rich man in his castle,
> The poor man at his gate,
> God made them high and lowly,
> And ordered their estate.

In this way, social agreements appear inevitable. This can help those at the bottom of the stratification system to accept and come to terms with their situation. In the same way, poverty and misfortune in general have often been seen as divinely ordained as a punishment for sin. Again the situation is defined as immutable and unchangeable. This can make life more bearable by encouraging people to accept their situation philosophically.

Religion and social control

From a Marxist viewpoint, religion does not simply cushion the effects of oppression, it is also an instrument of that oppression. It acts as a **mechanism of social control**, maintaining the existing system of exploitation and reinforcing class relationships. Put simply, it keeps people in their place. By making unsatisfactory lives bearable, religion tends to discourage people from attempting to change their situation. By offering an illusion of hope in a hopeless situation, it prevents thoughts of overthrowing the system. By providing explanations and justifications for social situations, religion distorts reality. It helps to produce a **false class consciousness** that blinds

members of the subject class to their true situation and their real interests. In this way it diverts people's attention from the real source of their oppression and so helps to maintain ruling-class power.

Religion is not, however, solely the province of oppressed groups. From a Marxist perspective, ruling classes adopt religious beliefs to justify their position both to themselves and to others. The lines 'God made them high and lowly and ordered their estate' show clearly how religion can be used to justify social inequality not simply to the poor, but also to the rich. Religion is often directly supported by the ruling classes to further their interests. In the words of Marx and Engels, 'the parson has ever gone hand in hand with the landlord'. In feudal England the lord of the manor's power was frequently legitimated by pronouncements from the pulpit. In return for this support, landlords would often richly endow the established church.

Evidence to support Marxism

There is considerable evidence to support the Marxist view of the role of religion in society.

The caste system of traditional India was justified by Hindu religious beliefs. In Medieval Europe, kings and queens ruled by divine right. The Egyptian Pharaohs went one step further by combining both god and king in the same person. Slave owners in the southern states of America often approved of the conversion of slaves to Christianity, believing it to be a controlling and gentling influence. Susan Budd notes that in the early days of the industrial revolution in England, employers 'explicitly supported religion as a means of subjugating the masses and keeping them sober and working'. Whether or not religion had the desired effect is difficult to say but even in our time in the shanty towns around large Brazilian cities, Pentecostalism is growing rapidly in popularity. Ministers tell their poverty-stricken followers that their poverty results from their sins.

In addition Steve Bruce has pointed out that in the USA today conservative Protestants, the 'New Christian Right', consistently support right-wing political candidates in the Republican Party, and attack more liberal candidates in the Democratic Party. In 1980 they 'targeted' 27 liberal candidates for attack; 23 of them lost. The New Christian Right supported Ronald Reagan in his successful campaign for the presidency in 1984. In the 1988 presidential campaign, however, Reagan was unsuccessfully challenged for the Republican nomination for president by one of the New Christian Right, Pat Robertson. Robertson is one of a number of television evangelists who have tried to gain new converts to their brand of Christianity and spread their political and moral messages through preaching on television.

According to Bruce the New Christian Right have supported 'a more aggressive anti-communist foreign policy, more military spending, less central government interference, less welfare spending, and fewer restraints on free enterprise'. Although Bruce emphasizes that they have had a limited influence on American politics it is clear that they have tended to defend the interests of the rich and powerful at the expense of other groups in the population.

However, conflicting evidence suggests that religion does not always legitimate power; it is not simply a justification of alienation or a justification of privilege, and it can sometimes provide an impetus for change. Although this is not reflected in Marx's own writing, nor in much of Engels's earlier work, it is reflected in Engels's later work and in the perspectives on religion advanced by more recent neo-Marxists. We will examine these views after the next section, which considers the relationship between religion and communism.

Religion and communism

Marx stated that 'Religion is only the illusory sun which revolves round man as long as he does not revolve round himself.' In a truly socialist society individuals revolve round themselves and religion, along with all other illusions and distortions of reality, disappears.

Whatever the merits of this prophecy, it certainly does not reflect the situation in the socialist Israeli kibbutzim. Many kibbutzim are fervently religious and their members appear to experience no contradiction between religion and socialism.

In the USSR under communism the strength of religion was harder to gauge. After the revolution of 1917 the communist state placed limits on religious activity and at times persecuted religious people. Soviet law restricted religious worship to designated churches and other places of prayer. Religious instruction to children was banned. Geoffrey Hosking estimated that there were more

than 50,000 Russian Orthodox churches before the 1917 revolution, but by 1939 only about 4,000 remained. Writing in the 1970s, David Lane claimed that there were about 20,000 Russian Orthodox churches in 1960, but nearly half of these had been closed by 1965 due to the policies of Khrushchev.

On the surface such figures suggest that religion had declined, but this may have been due to the activities of the ruling elite rather than to a loss of faith by the population. Lane claimed that religion probably had little hold over the population, but it had, nevertheless, shown a certain resilience to communism. This resilience was reflected in one estimate which placed the number of baptized Orthodox Christians in the period 1947–57 at 90 million, which is roughly the same as in 1914. In 1988 Geoffrey Hosking argued 'The Soviet Union is already a much more "religious" country than Britain or most of Western Europe.'

When President Gorbachov instituted a policy of *glasnost* or openness, restrictions on religion were relaxed. In April 1988 Gorbachov said 'Believers are Soviet working people and patriots, and they have every right to express their convictions in a fitting manner.' In 1989 and 1990 unrest in a number of Soviet republics suggested the continued strength of religious belief. The Roman Catholic Church in Lithuania was one source of demands for independence. In 1990 conflict between Soviet Muslims in Azerbaijan and Soviet Christians in Armenia led to troops being deployed to restore order.

When the USSR began to divide and Communist Party rule was abandoned, religious convictions became even more evident. In 1991, David Martin described how church bells were used to summon millions of people to link arms around the Baltic states of Latvia, Lithuania and Estonia. In other former communist countries there were 'enormous gatherings in Poland to celebrate the feast of the Assumption and the passionate pilgrimages of the Serbs to monastic shrines at Kosova'.

It is doubtful whether Marx would regard either kibbutzim, set in the context of a capitalist Israel, or the former USSR with its marked inequality, as truly socialist societies. Even so, these examples suggest that there is more to religion than a set of beliefs and practices which develop in societies based on the private ownership of the means of production. (See Chapter 14, pp. 880–2, for an analysis of religion within the general framework of Marxist theory.)

■ Engels and neo-Marxists – religion as a radical force

Engels – Christianity and social change

Roger O'Toole, commenting on the Marxist sociology of religion, argues that 'Beginning with the work of Engels, Marxists have undoubtedly recognized the active role that may be played by religion in effecting revolutionary social change.' Thus in *On the History of Early Christianity* Engels compares some of the early Christian sects that opposed Roman rule to communist and socialist political movements. He said 'Christianity got hold of the masses exactly as modern socialism does, under the shape of a variety of sects.' While Christianity originated as a way of coping with exploitation among oppressed groups, it could become a source of resistance to the oppressors and thus a force for change.

Otto Maduro – the relative autonomy of religion

Maduro is a contemporary neo-Marxist. While accepting many aspects of Marx's analysis of religion, he places greater emphasis on the idea that religion has some independence, or 'relative autonomy', from the economic system of the bourgeoisie. He denies that religion is always a conservative force and, indeed claims that it can be revolutionary. He says:

> Religion is not necessarily a functional, reproductive or conservative factor in society; it often is one of the main (and sometimes the only) available channel to bring about a social revolution.

Maduro claims that up until recently Catholicism in Latin America has tended to support the bourgeoisie and right-wing military dictatorships which have represented its interests. The Catholic Church has tended to deny the existence of social conflicts between oppressive and oppressed classes. It has recognized some injustices, such as poverty and illiteracy, but has suggested that the solution lies with those who already have power. The Catholic Church has also supported members of the clergy who have assisted private enterprise and government projects, it has celebrated military

victories but failed to support unions, strikes, and opposition political parties.

On the other hand, more recently Catholic priests have increasingly demonstrated their autonomy from the bourgeoisie by criticizing them and acting against their interests. Maduro believes that members of the clergy can develop revolutionary potential where oppressed members of the population have no outlet for their grievances. They pressurize priests to take up their cause and theological disagreements within a church provide interpretations of a religion which are critical of the rich and powerful.

All these conditions have been met in Latin America and have led to the development of **liberation theology** (for further details of liberation theology see p. 462).

■ Bryan S. Turner – a materialist theory of religion

Bryan Turner follows Marx in arguing that religion rises from a material base: that is, he agrees that religion relates to the physical and economic aspects of social life. Unlike Marx, however, Turner does not believe that religion has a universal role in society, nor does he believe that religion is always an important part of ruling-class ideological control. He questions the belief that religion has always been a powerful force, persuading subject classes to accept the status quo.

Religion and feudalism

Marxists have tended to assume that in the feudal period religion (in particular Roman Catholicism in Europe) was a belief system that played a fundamental part in integrating society. Turner rejects the view that religion was as important for serfs and peasants as it was for feudal lords. On the basis of historical evidence he claims the peasantry was largely indifferent to religion: their main concern was simply survival.

By comparison, religion played an important part in the lives of the ruling class, the feudal lords. In feudalism wealth consisted of, and power derived from, the ownership of land by private individuals. For the ruling class to maintain its dominance it had to pass on property to an heir. Usually a system of **primogeniture** was used: the eldest son of a landowner inherited all his father's land. This prevented the splitting up of estates which would have reduced the concentration of power in the hands of particular individuals. It was therefore vital to the workings of feudalism and the maintenance of a dominant class that there was a legitimate male heir for each landowner. Premarital promiscuity and adultery both jeopardized the production of such an heir. Marriage and the legitimacy of children were propped up and defended by the church. Thus in Turner's words, 'religion has the function of controlling the sexuality of the body in order to secure regular transmission of property via the family.' Without religion it would have been difficult to ensure there were recognized legitimate heirs who could retain concentrated landholdings in their family's possession.

A secondary function of religion under feudalism also stemmed from primogeniture. There was a surplus of younger sons who did not inherit land. In military feudalism sons might meet an early death, so it was necessary to have a number of heirs in case one or more were killed. But those who did not receive an inheritance had to have some means of support. Monasteries provided one solution to the problem of the surplus males.

Religion and capitalism

Turner believes that in modern capitalism, religion has lost the one vital function that it had for the ruling class. Today, he claims, individual and family property are much less important for the maintenance of ruling-class power. Property has become **depersonalized** – most wealth is concentrated in the hands of organizations (such as banks, pension funds and multinational corporations) rather than in the hands of individuals. In these circumstances religion is no more than an optional extra for modern capitalist societies. Since the transmission of property via the family is no longer vital to the system, society can tolerate, and the church accept, divorce and illegitimacy.

Turner's views on religion are similar to the more general views on the **dominant ideology thesis** advanced by Abercrombie, Hill and Turner. They believe modern capitalist societies do not possess a widely accepted ruling-class ideology, and that such an ideology is not necessary for the continuance of capitalist domination: the ruling class use coercion and naked economic power to maintain their position. Turner *et al.* therefore question Marx's beliefs about the importance of religion in producing false class consciousness in capitalist societies. (For more details on the dominant ideology thesis see pp. 534–5.)

Having discussed the Marxist views on religion, we will now turn to a completely different analysis of the role of religion in society.

■ Rodney Stark and William Sims Bainbridge – religion and compensators

Unlike Durkheim, the American sociologists Stark and Bainbridge see religion as meeting the needs of individuals rather than those of society as a whole. Unlike Marx, they see religion as meeting universal human needs rather than those which stem from class inequality and exploitation. Furthermore they reject the view, shared by the classic sociologists of religion, that the development of industrial capitalist societies would, one way or another, ultimately undermine religion. Stark and Bainbridge claim that religion helps to meet universal human needs. As such, changes in society cannot diminish its appeal.

Human desires

They start with the basic premise that 'Humans seek what they perceive to be rewards and try to avoid what they perceive to be costs.' In short, people do what they believe will be good for them. This provides quite a straightforward basis for human decision making but individuals may still face problems.

1 Many of the things which people desire, for example wealth and status, are scarce and cannot be attained by everyone.

2 Some things which people strongly desire may not be available at all. One such desire, and one that is crucial for their theory, is a desire for life after death. Even without convincing evidence that eternal life is possible, people continue to want it and it is here that the roots of religion lie.

Compensators

Stark and Bainbridge recognize that religion might not actually provide people with eternal life, but what it does offer is a 'compensator'. A **compensator** is 'the belief that a reward will be obtained in the distant future or in some other context which cannot be verified'. They are a type of IOU – if individuals act in a particular way they will eventually be rewarded. In the absence of immediate rewards people are liable to turn to compensators.

Some political activists would like society to be transformed. If there is little evidence that the transformation is likely, they may develop the belief in a future revolution as a compensator. Similarly a compensator is exchanged for a reward when a parent persuades a child that working hard now will eventually lead to fame and riches. Some compensators are quite specific, for example the promise of a cured wart; others are more general. The promise of eternal life is an example of a general compensator.

Compensators and the supernatural

Sometimes individuals want rewards that are so great and so remote from everyday experience that the possibility of gaining them can only be contemplated alongside a belief in the supernatural. Stark and Bainbridge say:

> Since time immemorial humans have desired to know the meaning of existence. Why are we here? What is the purpose of life? Where will it all end? Moreover, people have not just wanted answers to these questions; they have desired particular kinds of answers – that life has meaning. But for life to have a great design, for there to be intention behind history, one must posit the existence of a designer or intender of such power, duration, and scale as to be outside the natural world of our senses.

Only belief in a god allows us to have answers to our most fundamental questions. According to this viewpoint religion consists of organizations which offer 'general compensators based on supernatural assumptions'.

Religious pluralism and secularization

Since religion answers universal questions, and it offers compensators that meet universal human needs, religion can neither disappear nor seriously decline. If churches compromise their beliefs in the supernatural they become less appealing as a source of compensators. Thus 'for religious organizations to move markedly in the direction of non-supernaturalism is to pursue the path to ruin'. If this happens people turn to different religious organizations, and particularly to new sects and cults that has a greater emphasis on the supernatural. (We will discuss sects and cults on pages 571–3.)

According to Stark and Bainbridge American society has become characterized by religious pluralism as people have sought new sources of compensators. They quote J. George Melton's 1978 *Encyclopedia of American* religions that listed no less than 1,200 different religious groups. They deny that there are many people who lack beliefs and they do not believe that secularization (for a definition of secularization see p. 479) has taken place or will take place in the future. They claim that 'the majority of people who say they have no religious affiliation express considerable belief in the mystical and supernatural'. In other words, they have not lost their need for supernatural compensators. Furthermore, Stark and Bainbridge quote survey evidence which suggests that 60 per cent of those whose parents had no religious affiliation claim a religious affiliation for themselves. Where agnosticism or atheism existed, they were not passed on to succeeding generations.

■ Stark and Bainbridge – an evaluation

Stark and Bainbridge have provided the most recent comprehensive attempt to develop a sociological perspective on religion. Their work has provided a number of insights into religious organizations and religious change. However, it has not been without its critics.

Roy Wallis and Steve Bruce argue that the available evidence contradicts their theory. New religious movements have not gained sufficient recruits to replace those lost from more established religions. (The evidence for and against the theory of secularization is examined in detail on page 479.)

Wallis and Bruce also criticize Stark and Bainbridge for ignoring social and cultural influences on the questions that individuals ask and the rewards they seek. It is by no means inevitable that people seek the kinds of reward for which religion offers compensators. Society, culture and socialization might create the need for religion rather than universal human desires. Wallis and Bruce say:

---

since most people are born into a social world in which religious beliefs already exist, belief in another world with supernatural characteristics opens up the possibility of wanting things there as well as rather than instead of here.

By reducing their explanation of religion to supposedly universal needs Stark and Bainbridge neglect the social factors which help to create and sustain religion. We will consider some of these factors in the next section which looks at religion from a phenomenological perspective.

■ Religion – a phenomenological perspective

■ Peter Berger and Thomas Luckmann

The work of Peter Berger and Thomas Luckmann is an important development in the sociology of religion. They have put forward a phenomenological view of religion: religion is produced by members of society subjectively interpreting and giving meaning to the world around them. To Berger and Luckmann, religion is one of the most important devices used by humans to categorize and give meaning to the physical and social world. They see the sociology of religion as part of a larger field – the sociology of knowledge – which is concerned with the meanings and definitions of reality held by members of a society.

Every society has its own body of knowledge: for example, traditional Eskimo society has a shared knowledge of life and the world that differs from other societies. This **universe of meaning**, as Berger and Luckmann term it, is socially derived; it is a product of society and in turn feeds back and helps produce society.

A universe of meaning includes not only high-level philosophical ideas about the meaning of life, but also everyday knowledge that is taken for granted. A universe of meaning requires constant **legitimation**: it needs repeated reinforcement and justification. Members of society must be told and re-told that their universe of meaning is real, true, correct, 'legitimate'. Without this support, a universe of meaning would tend to crumble, life would become meaningless, and the stability of society would be threatened.

Religion helps to build, maintain and legitimate universes of meaning. Berger and Luckmann write 'Throughout human history religion has played a decisive part in the construction and maintenance of universes.' According to Berger, religion performs this function in the following way: 'Religion is the audacious attempt to conceive the entire universe as being humanly significant.' Thus humanity constructs knowledge and meaning about the whole universe and its place within it.

One example of this is the Christian view of the creation of the world and humanity given in the *Book of Genesis*. Berger continues 'Religion legitimates so effectively because it relates the precarious reality of empirical societies with ultimate reality': that is, knowledge learned from observation and experience is supported and 'made real'.

Religion provides ultimate answers that cannot

be questioned by those who believe. For instance, people observe that the sun rises every morning and, in some societies, this is confirmed and explained by the idea that the sun is controlled by supernatural powers. Religion also legitimates social institutions 'by locating them within a sacred and cosmic frame of reference'. In this sense law is located in religion when a legal offence becomes a sin against God; authority is located in religion when kings speak for gods or become gods as in the case of the Pharaohs of ancient Egypt. In other words religion legitimates, and so supports, social institutions.

Each universe of meaning is grounded in a social base. This social base – the social structure of society – is called its **plausibility structure**. If this plausibility structure is destroyed, so is the universe of meaning. Neither can exist without the other. When the Inca Empire was destroyed by the Spaniards, the social base of Inca religion was shattered. Without its plausibility structure, Inca religion died.

Berger and Luckmann argued that all certainty is basically uncertain; it has a very precarious foundation. Things are real because people believe they are real. Life is meaningful because of the meaning people give to it. Things make sense because they are defined in terms of common sense.

However, this reality, these meanings, this sense are arbitrary. There is no universal standard or yardstick against which they can be measured and shown to be true. The universe of meaning is a social construction of reality. One society's reality is another's pretence; things defined as meaningful in one society are meaningless in another; common sense in one society is nonsense in another. Because of the arbitrary nature of the universe of meaning, it is precarious, insecure and easily shattered. It therefore requires constant legitimation. Berger and Luckmann argue that religion is probably the most effective mechanism for the legitimation of universes of meaning. Unlike other sources of legitimation, only religion links meaning with ultimate reality.

Criticisms of Berger and Luckmann

Berger and Luckmann's views on religion are open to a number of criticisms. Rather like functionalists, they tend to assume that religion unites society and they neglect examples of societies where religion is divisive or causes conflict. Furthermore, they tend to think that religious beliefs are widely held, and they fail to account for the continued existence of societies where many members are indifferent to religion.

As Glover and Strawbridge put it, 'it is far from clear that human beings either require or actually achieve social order to the extent that Berger and Luckmann claim'.

We have now looked at religion from each of the main perspectives. In the next section we are going to consider the involved nature of the various relationships between religion and social change.

■ Religion and social change

There are a number of possible relationships between religion and social change. Religion may be a factor that impedes social change, or it may help to produce it. Another possibility is that religion itself has no influence on changes in society, but there is nevertheless a causal relationship between the two. From this point of view it is social change in society as a whole that leads to changes in religion.

■ Religion as a conservative force

Functionalists and Marxists have generally dismissed the possibility that religion can cause changes in society. They believe that religion acts as a conservative force and that it is changes in society that shape religion, not vice versa.

Religion can be seen as a 'conservative force' in

two senses, depending on the meaning attached to the word 'conservative'. The phrase **conservative force** is most usually used to refer to religion preventing change and maintaining the status quo. Functionalists have claimed it acts in this way because it promotes integration and social solidarity. As we discovered in previous sections, from a functionalist perspective religion provides shared beliefs, norms and values, and helps individuals to cope with stresses that might disrupt social life. In these ways it facilitates the continued existence of society in its present form. Marx had similar views, although he saw religion as maintaining the status quo in the interests of the ruling class rather than those of society as a whole.

'Conservative' may, however, be used in another way: it can refer to traditional beliefs and customs. Usually if religion helps to maintain the status quo it will also maintain traditional customs and beliefs. For example, the stance of successive popes against the use of contraception has restricted the growth of artificial methods of birth control in Roman Catholic countries. But in some circumstances religion can support social change while at the same time promoting traditional values. This often occurs when there is a revival in fundamentalist religious beliefs.

Conservatism, fundamentalism and social change

Recent years have seen the rise of fundamentalist religious beliefs in different parts of the world. Donald Taylor defines **fundamentalism** as involving the following.

1 A group of people perceive a challenge to an ultimate authority, usually a God, in which they believe.

2 These people decide that the challenge cannot be tolerated.

3 They reaffirm their belief in the authority that is being challenged.

4 They oppose those who have challenged the established beliefs, and often they use political means to further their cause.

According to this view fundamentalism involves the reassertion of traditional moral and religious values against changes that have taken place and those who support the changes. If fundamentalists are successful they succeed in defending traditional vales but at the same time changing society by reversing innovations that have taken place.

In a book of articles edited by Lionel Caplan, fundamentalism was identified among a wide variety of religious groups throughout the globe. These included Sikh fundamentalists in the Punjab, Hindu fundamentalism amongst Sri Lankans in Britain, and Islamic fundamentalism in Turkey. Steve Bruce has analysed fundamentalism amongst Protestant groups in Northern Ireland, Scotland and the USA.

However, perhaps the most dramatic example of fundamentalism causing social change through the imposition of a return to traditional values has been in Iran. Under the last Shah, Iranian society underwent a process of change. One aspect of this change was the liberalization of traditional Islamic attitudes to women. In 1979 the Iranian revolution, which was partly inspired by Islamic fundamentalism, took place and these changes were reversed. In this case, it can be argued, religious beliefs contributed to producing revolutionary change. Religion did not therefore act as a conservative force in one sense of the word. Nevertheless, in terms of supporting traditional values it did act as a conservative force. The two meanings of the word conservative should therefore be distinguished.

■ Changes in society and religion

Most sociologists agree that changes in society lead to changes in religion.

1 Talcott Parsons, for example, believes that as society developed, religion lost some of its functions (for further details, see p. 491).

2 Marx believed that a change in the infrastructure of society would lead to changes in the superstructure, including religion. Thus Marx anticipated that when a classless society was established, religion would disappear.

3 Bryan Turner claims religion lost its function of facilitating the smooth transfer of property from generation to generation when feudalism gave way to capitalism.

4 Berger and Luckmann argue that the destruction of a society and its 'plausibility structure' leads to the disappearance of the religion associated with it.

5 As later sections of this chapter will show, supporters of the secularization theory think that industrialization has led to profound changes that have progressively reduced the importance of religion in society (see pp. 479–97).

So far then, it appears to be generally agreed that first, religion helps to maintain the status quo and that second, changes in religion result from changes in the wider society. Some sociologists, however, have argued that religion can cause social change and we will now investigate this third possibility.

■ Max Weber – *The Protestant Ethic and the Spirit of Capitalism*

Both functionalists and Marxists emphasize the role of religion in promoting social integration and impeding social change. In contrast, Weber argued that in some circumstances religion can lead to social change: although shared religious beliefs might integrate a social group, those same beliefs may have repercussions which in the long term can produce changes in society.

Marx is generally regarded as a **materialist**. He believed that the material world (and particularly people's involvement with nature as they worked to secure their own survival) shaped their beliefs. Thus to Marx the economic system largely determined the beliefs that were held by individuals. In Marxist terms the mode of production determined the type of religion that would be dominant in any society.

Unlike Marx, Weber rejected the view that religion is always shaped by economic factors. He did not deny that at certain times and in certain places, religion may be largely shaped by economic forces, but he denied that this is always the case. Under certain conditions the reverse can occur, that is, religious beliefs can be a major influence on economic behaviour.

Weber's **social action theory** argues that human action is directed by meanings and motives. (See Chapter 14, pp. 889–91, for a discussion of Weber's general theory.) From this perspective, action can only be understood by appreciating the

world view, the image or picture of the world held by members of society. From their world view, individuals obtain meanings, purposes and motives that direct their actions. Religion is often an important component of a world view. In certain places and times, religious meaning and purposes can direct action in a wide range of contexts. In particular, religious beliefs can direct economic action.

Capitalism and ascetic Protestantism

In his most famous book, *The Protestant Ethic and the Spirit of Capitalism*, Weber examines the relationship between the rise of certain forms of Protestantism and the development of Western industrial capitalism. In the first part of his argument Weber tries to demonstrate that a particular form of Protestantism, ascetic Calvinist Protestantism, preceded the development of capitalism. He also tries to show that capitalism developed initially in areas where this religion was influential. Other areas of the world possessed many of the necessary prerequisites yet they were not amongst the first areas to develop capitalism. For example, India and China had technological knowledge, labour to be hired and individuals engaged in making money. What they lacked, according to Weber, was a religion that encouraged and facilitated the development of capitalism. The first capitalist nations emerged among the nations of Western Europe and North America that had Calvinist religious groups. Furthermore, most of the earliest capitalist entrepreneurs in these areas came from the ranks of Calvinists.

Having established a relationship – a **correlation** between Calvinism and capitalism by comparing religion and economic development in different parts of the world – Weber goes on to explain how and why this type of religion was linked to capitalism.

Calvinist Protestantism originated in the beliefs of John Calvin in the seventeenth century. Calvin thought that there was a distinct group of the **elect** – those chosen to go to heaven – and they had been chosen by God even before they were born; and those who were not among the elect could never gain a place in heaven however well they behaved on earth.

Other versions of Christianity derived from the beliefs of Martin Luther. Luther believed that individual Christians could affect their chances of reaching heaven by the way that they behaved on earth. It was very important for Christians to develop faith in God, and to act out God's will on earth. In order to do this they had to be dedicated to their calling in life. Whatever position in society God had given them, they must conscientiously carry out the appropriate duties.

At first sight, Lutheranism seems the doctrine more likely to produce capitalism. However, it encouraged people to produce or earn no more than was necessary for their material needs. It attached more importance to piety and faith than to the accumulation of great wealth.

The doctrine of predestination advocated by Calvin seems less likely to produce capitalism. If certain individuals are destined for heaven regardless of their earthly behaviour – and the rest were equally unable to overcome their damnation – there would be little point in hard work on earth.

Weber points out, though, that Calvinists had a psychological problem: they did not know whether they were amongst the elect. They suffered from a type of inner-loneliness or uncertainty about their status and their behaviour was not an attempt to earn a place in heaven, but rather to convince themselves that they had been chosen to go there. They reasoned that only the chosen people of God would be able to live a good life on earth. If their behaviour was exemplary they could feel confident that they would go to heaven after death.

The interpretation the Calvinists put on the doctrine of predestination contributed to them becoming the first capitalists.

The Protestant Ethic

The **Protestant Ethic** which Weber describes (and which enabled Calvinists to convince themselves that they were amongst the elect) developed first in seventeenth-century Western Europe. The ethic was **ascetic,** encouraging abstinence from life's pleasures, an austere lifestyle and rigorous self-discipline. It produced individuals who worked hard in their careers or **callings,** in a single-minded manner. Making money was a concrete indication of success in one's calling while success in one's calling meant the individual had not lost grace in God's sight.

John Wesley, a leader of the great Methodist revival that preceded the expansion of English

industry at the close of the eighteenth century, wrote:

> For religion must necessarily produce industry and frugality, and these cannot but produce riches. We must exhort all Christians to gain what they can and to save all they can; that is, in effect to grow rich. (Quoted in Weber 1958, p. 175.)

These riches could not be spent on luxuries, fine clothes, lavish houses and frivolous entertainment, but in the glory of God. In effect this meant being even more successful in terms of one's calling, which in practice meant reinvesting profits in the business.

The Protestants attacked time wasting, laziness, idle gossip and more sleep than was necessary – six to eight hours a day at the most. They frowned on sexual pleasures; sexual intercourse should remain within marriage and then only for the procreation of children (a vegetable diet and cold baths were sometimes recommended to remove temptation). Sport and recreation were accepted only for improving fitness and health, and condemned if pursued for entertainment. The impulsive fun and enjoyment of the pub, dance hall, theatre and gaming house were prohibited to ascetic Protestants. In fact anything that might divert or distract people from their calling was condemned. Living life in terms of these guidelines was an indication that the individual had not lost grace and favour in the sight of God.

The spirit of capitalism

Weber claimed that the origins of the spirit of capitalism were to be found in the ethic of ascetic Protestantism. There had been no shortage throughout history of those who sought money and profit: pirates, prostitutes and money lenders in every corner of the world had always pursued wealth. However, according to Weber, both the manner and purpose of their pursuit of money were at odds with the spirit of capitalism.

Traditionally money seekers engaged in speculative projects: they gambled in order to gain rewards. If successful they tended to spend money frivolously on personal consumption. Furthermore, they were not dedicated to making money for its own sake. Weber argued that labourers who had earned enough for their family to live comfortably, and merchants who had secured the luxuries they desired, would feel no need to press themselves harder to make more money. Instead, they sought free time for leisure.

The ascetic Protestant had a quite different attitude to wealth and Weber believed that this attitude was characteristic of capitalism. He argued that the essence of capitalism is 'the pursuit of profit and forever renewed profit'.

Capitalist enterprises are organized on rational bureaucratic lines. Business transactions are conducted in a systematic and rational manner with costs and projected profits being carefully assessed. (We examine Weber's views on rational action in detail in Chapter 5, pp. 271–3, and in this chapter, p. 479.)

Underlying the practice of capitalism is the **spirit of capitalism**, a set of ideas, ethics and values. Weber illustrates the spirit of capitalism with quotes from two books by Benjamin Franklin, *Necessary Hints to Those that would be Rich* (1736) and *Advice to a Young Tradesman* (1748). Franklin writes 'Remember that time is money.' Time wasting, idleness and diversion lose money. 'Remember that credit is money.' A reputation for 'prudence and honesty' will bring credit as will paying debts on time. Business people should behave with 'industry and frugality', and 'punctuality and justice' in all their dealings.

Weber argued that this spirit of capitalism is not simply a way of making money, but a way of life that has ethics, duties and obligations. He claimed that ascetic Protestantism was a vital influence in the creation and development of the spirit and practice of capitalism: a methodical and single-minded pursuit of a calling encourages rational capitalism. Weber wrote 'restless, continuous, systematic work in a worldly calling must have been the most powerful conceivable lever for the expansion of the spirit of capitalism'. Making money became both a religious and business ethic. The Protestant 'interpretation of profit-making justified the activities of the businessman'.

Weber claimed that two major features of capitalist industry (the standardization of production and the specialized division of labour) were encouraged by Protestantism. The Protestant 'uniformity of life immensely aids the capitalist in the standardization of production'. The emphasis on the 'importance of a fixed calling provided an ethical justification for this modern specialized division of labour'.

Finally, Weber noted the importance of the creation of wealth and the restrictions on spending it, which encouraged saving and reinvestment:

> When the limitation of consumption is combined with this release of acquisitive activity, the inevitable result is obvious: accumulation of capital through an ascetic compulsion to save. The restraints that were imposed on the consumption of wealth naturally served to increase it, by making possible the productive investment of capital.

The ascetic Protestant way of life led to the accumulation of capital, investment and reinvestment. It produced the early businesses that expanded to create capitalist society.

Materialism and Weber's theory

Weber then, believed he had discovered and demonstrated that religious beliefs could cause economic change. He claimed that he had found a weakness in Marx's materialism which implied that the economic system always shaped ideas.

However, it should be stressed that Weber did not discount the importance of the economy and material factors. He said 'It is, of course, not my aim to substitute for a one-sided materialistic an equally one-sided spiritualistic causal interpretation of culture and of history.' Capitalism was made possible not just by Calvinist Protestantism, but also by the technology and economic system of the countries in which it developed. Material factors were as important as ideas in its development; neither could be ignored in any explanation.

Weber – an evaluation

Since its publication Weber's work has received both criticism and support from researchers.

1 Sombart, an early critic, argued that Weber was mistaken about the beliefs held by Calvinists. According to Sombart, Calvinism was against greed and the pursuit of money for its own sake.

Weber himself countered this argument. He pointed out that it was not the beliefs of Calvinists that were important in themselves. The doctrine of predestination was not intended to produce the rational pursuit of profit, but nevertheless that was one of its unintentional consequences and the evidence was the way that ascetic Protestants actually behaved.

2 A second criticism points to parts of the world where Calvinism was strong, but capitalism did not develop until much later. For example, Switzerland, Scotland, Hungary and parts of The Netherlands all contained large Calvinist populations but were not among the first capitalist countries.

Gordon Marshall dismisses this criticism. He argues that the critics demonstrate a lack of understanding of Weber's theory. Weber did not claim that Calvinism was the only factor necessary for the development of capitalism. His theory cannot therefore be disproved simply by finding Calvinist countries that failed to become capitalist comparatively early. In his own study of Scotland Marshall found that the Scottish had a capitalist mentality but were held back by a lack of skilled labour and capital for investment, and by government policies that did not stimulate the development of industry.

3 A potentially more damaging criticism of Weber's theory originates from Marxist critics such as Kautsky. Kautsky argues that early capitalism preceded and largely determined Protestantism. He sees Calvinism developing in cities where commerce and early forms of industrialization were already established. In his view Protestantism became the ideology capitalists used to legitimate their position.

This is a chicken and egg question – which came first: Calvinism or capitalism? The answer depends upon how capitalism is defined. To Weber pre-capitalist money-making ventures were not organized rationally to ensure continued profit.

Marshall disputes this. He suggests that the medieval merchant classes behaved quite rationally considering the conditions of the time. It was not their psychological attitude that encouraged them to make what Weber saw as risky investments, but the situation they faced. In England the risks involved in trading were balanced by investments in land. Buying landed estates was not an example of conspicuous consumption, but of the prudent spreading of investments. In The Netherlands too, the business classes spread their risks but more money went into merchant trading because of the price of land. Even so, defenders of Weber insist that a distinctive rational capitalist entrepreneur did not emerge until after Calvinism.

4 A fourth criticism of Weber does not deny that Calvinism was an important factor which helped lead to capitalism, but questions the view that it was the

religious beliefs of Calvinists that led to them becoming business people. According to this view, nonconformist Calvinists devoted themselves to business because they were excluded from holding public office and joining certain professions by law. Like the Jews in Eastern and Central Europe, they tried to become economically successful in order to overcome their political persecution.

In reply to this criticism, supporters of the Protestant ethic thesis argue that only Calvinist minorities developed the distinctive patterns of capitalist behaviour which involved rational planning for slow but sure capital growth; only they could develop capitalist businesses before capitalism was established.

Despite the considerable effort devoted to discussing Weber's theory by historians and sociologists alike, no agreement has been reached about its accuracy. Nevertheless, whatever the merits of this particular study, Weber does successfully highlight the theoretical point that ideas – in this case religious ideas – can conceivably lead to economic change.

Religion and social change – conclusion

Many sociologists do now accept that religion can be a force for change. Despite the examples that can be used to support the functionalist and Marxist view that religion promotes stability, other examples contradict their claims.

G.K. Nelson points to a number of cases where religion has undermined stability or promoted change.

1 In Northern Ireland Roman Catholicism has long been associated with Irish Republicanism.

2 In the USA in the 1960s the Reverend Martin Luther King and the Southern Christian Leadership Council played a leading role in establishing civil rights and securing legislation intended to reduce racial discrimination.

3 Also in the 1960s a number of radical and revolutionary groups emerged within the Roman Catholic Church in Latin America. They preached **liberation theology**, arguing that it was the duty of church members to fight against unjust and oppressive right-wing dictatorships. Thus in 1979 Catholic revolutionaries supported the Sandinistas when they seized control in Nicaragua.

4 In Iran Islamic fundamentalism played a part in another 1979 revolution, in this case led by the Ayatollah Khomeini.

5 Poland provides another example of religion stimulating change. The Roman Catholic Church opposed the communist state in Poland, and it supported the attempts of the free trade union Solidarity to achieve changes in Polish society. In 1989 the communist monopoly on power was broken when Solidarity was allowed to contest and win many seats in the Polish Parliament.

6 In South Africa Archbishop Tutu was a prominent opponent of apartheid.

Examples such as these lead Nelson to conclude that 'far from encouraging people to accept their place, religion can spearhead resistance and revolution'. In many cases when religion has been a force for change in society, the society that results may be strongly influenced by that religion.

Engels, unlike Marx, did realize that in some circumstances religion could be a force for change. He argued that groups which turned to religion as a way of coping with oppression could develop into political movements which sought change on earth rather than salvation in heaven. Some contemporary neo-Marxists have followed Engels and developed this view (see p. 453 for further details).

Religion and revolutionary movements

Leland W. Robinson argues that in some circumstances revolutionary movements deliberately try to use religion in their attempts to change society. He claims that three things are necessary if this is to happen.

1 The classes with the potential to become revolutionary need to have a predominantly religious world view. In the Third World this is often the case, particularly in Latin America, the Near East and South Asia. Europe is less religious and revolutionary movements have not usually tried to use religion. There are however exceptions, such as the role of the Roman Catholic Church in undermining the communist state in Poland.

2 The main religion needs to have a theology that can be interpreted in such a way that it can be used against those in power. Buddhism tends to stress the separation of religion and society into different spheres. Christianity and Hinduism have more revolutionary potential. For example, Gandhi used the Hindu concept of ***Sarvodaya*** (the welfare of all) to attack British colonial rule and to inspire rural peasants and the urban poor to turn against the British.

3 It is also necessary for the clergy and the revolutionary classes to have close contacts. Robinson argues that in countries such as Paraguay the clergy usually come from and remain in close contact with local communities. Here they have opposed the repressive regime of Stroessner. In Cuba the Catholic Church was so remote from ordinary people that it did not support Castro's communist revolution of 1956–9. A 1957 survey of 4,000 agricultural workers in Cuba found that only 7.8 per cent said they had had any dealings with the Catholic clergy.

Where the above three factors are present it is sufficient for revolutionaries to be able to make use of religion. It becomes even more likely when the revolutionary classes all share the same religion, where this is different to the religion of those in power, and where there are no alternative organizations available through which to organize. In many countries in South America, such as Guatemala, Chile and El Salvador where the police and military have been used to crush other organizations such as trade unions, religion is the only remaining outlet for dissent.

Conservative or radical religion?

Merideth B. McGuire also examines the factors which influence the type of role that religion plays in society commenting 'The question is no longer "Does religion promote social change?" but rather, "In what way and under what conditions does it promote rather than inhibit change?".' Unlike Leland, McGuire does not concentrate exclusively on the revolutionary potential of religion. She identifies five main factors that determine the potential of religion to change society.

1 The first factor is the **beliefs** of the particular religion. Religions that emphasize adherence to strong moral codes are more likely to produce members who are critical of society and who seek to change it. If a religion stresses concern with this world, it is more likely to result in actions by its members which produce change than a religion which confines itself to a concern with sacred and spiritual matters. Thus Protestantism can have more impact on social change than Buddhism.

2 The second factor is the **culture** of the society in which a religion exists. In societies where religious beliefs are central to the culture (such as in Latin America), anyone wishing to produce change tends to use a religious legitimation for their actions. In Britain, however, religion plays a less central role in societal culture, so it tends to play a less important role in justifying changes in society.

3 What McGuire describes as the **social location** of religion is the third important factor. This concerns the part that religion plays in the social structure. Again the greater the importance of religion the greater its potential to play a part in producing change. Where an established church or other religious organization plays a major role in political and economic life, then there is considerable scope for religion having an impact on processes of change.

4 The final factor is the **internal organization** of religious institutions. According to McGuire, religions with a strong, centralized source of authority, have more

chance of affecting events. On the other hand, the central authority might try to restrain the actions of parts of the organization. For example, in 1978 at the Puebla Conference in Mexico the Pope clashed with Latin American Roman Catholic bishops who were advocating liberation theology.

McGuire provides only a sketchy outline of the factors determining whether religion acts as a conservative force maintaining the status quo or as a force for change. Nevertheless she does provide a starting point for analysing the relationship between religion and social change.

In the next section we will examine different types of religious organization and the wide variety of ideologies that have been supported by different organizations. We will also discover that conservative and radical ideologies tend to be associated with different types of religious organization.

■ Religious organizations

Individuals may have their own religious beliefs without belonging to any particular organization: they may form their own personal and unique relationship with a god or some source of spiritual power. However, many members of society express their religious beliefs through organizations, and the organizations tend to shape those beliefs. Social factors influence the types of organization that are created, who joins them and how they develop. At the same time religious organizations may themselves influence society.

Before we examine these issues, it is necessary for us to distinguish between the different types of religious organization. There have been a number of attempts to categorize them, but no system fits perfectly the infinite variety of such organizations that have existed throughout the world. Nevertheless, it is possible broadly to distinguish three main types of religious organization.

■ The church

Ernst Troeltsch in 1931 was one of the first writers to try to distinguish different types of religious organization. Troeltsch used the term **church** to

refer to a large religious organization. Individuals do not have to demonstrate their faith to become members of a church, indeed often they are born into it. In some churches the practice of baptism ensures that all the children of members are automatically recruited before they are old enough to understand the faith.

In principle a church might try to be **universal** – to embrace all members of society – but in practice there might be substantial minorities who do not belong. Because of its size, members of a church are drawn from all classes in society, but the upper classes are particularly likely to join. This is because, in Troeltsch's words, a church usually 'stabilizes and determines the political order'.

Churches are sometimes closely related to the state. For example, the Roman Catholic Church in the Middle Ages had important political, educational and social functions. Even in contemporary Britain the Queen is both head of the Church of England and head of state. Churches are likely to be ideologically conservative and support the status quo: an opinion poll in 1988 found that 63 per cent of active lay members of the Church of England supported the Conservative Party, which received only 43 per cent of the total votes in the 1987 election. (Quoted in Davie 1989, p. 87.)

This type of organization accepts and affirms life in this world: members can play a full part in social life and are not expected to withdraw from society. In many circumstances a church will jealously guard its monopoly on religious truth, and will not tolerate challenges to its religious authority. For example, the Roman Catholic Church at one time used the Inquisition to stamp out heresy. Churches are formal organizations with a hierarchy of professional, paid officials.

Today, churches in many countries do not conform to some of these characteristics.

1 The percentage of the population who are members of a church can vary widely. For example, according to the UK *Christian Handbook*, in Britain in 1990 just 1,838,659 people were members of the established Anglican Church out of a total population of over 59,000,000.

2 Many churches today do not claim a monopoly of the religious truth – other religions are tolerated. In Britain there is a growing diversity of religious groupings that are tolerated by the Church of England.

3 Furthermore, the **ecumenical movement**, which seeks unity between varying Christian religious groups, demonstrates the extent to which churches are now willing to compromise their beliefs.

4 Churches are not always ideologically conservative and they do not always support the dominant groups in a society: the General Synod of the Church of England clashed with the British Conservative Government in the l980s and l990s over issues such as poverty and conditions in Britain's inner cities. Davie claims there is a growing gap within the Church of England between lay members, who tend to be conservative, and senior officials such as bishops, who tend to be more radical.

5 In some circumstances the churches are not connected to the state, and may even act as a focus of opposition to it. Before the overthrow of communism in Poland the Roman Catholic Church opposed the communist government, and in many parts of Latin America liberation theology has also led to conflict between the Catholic Church and the state. Roland Robertson argues that throughout the world there has been an increase in church–state tensions. Far from identifying closely with the state, churches are increasingly distancing themselves from it. Robertson notes tensions between the state and Shiite fundamentalists in the Middle East, Coptic Christians in Egypt, Maronite Christians in Lebanon, Sikhs in India and Islamic fundamentalists in Pakistan, Indonesia and the

Philippines. He points out that many churches are **transnational** organizations, their activities are not confined to a single country. He argues that in the modern 'world system', nation states interact with each other by pursuing non-religious, secular national interests. In international trade and diplomacy there is little room for the consideration of theological issues. Consequently national governments tend to come into conflict with the moral concerns of domestic churches and transnational religious organizations.

Churches in industrial societies tend to be larger and more conservative than other religious groups. Some industrialized societies have retained fairly strong churches that continue to conform to most of the characteristics outlined by Troeltsch. Roy Wallis and Steve Bruce claim of the Roman Catholic Church, 'In those places where it is dominant, e.g. Spain, Portugal and the Republic of Ireland, it acts as a universal church, claiming authority over the society as a whole.' In the Republic of Ireland the bishops continue to receive state support for the moral teachings of Catholicism, and as recently as 1983 they were able to denounce a well-established Pentecostal Protestant religious group as a dangerous cult which should not be tolerated.

In other countries though, the Catholic Church is not in a position to act in such ways and has to co-exist peacefully with a plurality of other religions making no special claims on the state. Similarly, in Iran there is close identification between Islam and the state, but in countries such as Turkey the Muslim religion has much less influence on the state and politics.

■ Denominations

Troeltsch's original categorization of religious organizations did not include 'denominations'. As Troeltsch based his work on an analysis of religion in sixteenth-century Europe, his classification was therefore not capable of describing the variety of religions in the USA, or for that matter in modern Britain. According to Stark and Bainbridge the term **denomination** is usually used to refer to an organization that shares several but not all of the supposed features of a church. It is often seen as a kind of watered-down church which has some similarities to a sect (which we will discuss in the next section). In a study of religion in the USA, H.R. Neibuhr was the first sociologist to differentiate clearly the denomination from the church.

1 Unlike a church, a denomination does not have a universal appeal in society. For example, in Britain in 1990 Methodists could claim 483,387 members, and there were 241,832 Baptists. Like churches, denominations draw members from all strata in society, but unlike churches they are not usually so closely identified with the upper classes. Often a considerable number of denominations exist within a particular society. In the USA there is no established church, but a large range of denominations.

2 Unlike a church, a denomination does not identify with the state and approves the separation of church and state.

3 Denominations do not claim a monopoly of the religious truth. According to Bryan Wilson this type of organization is 'Prepared to take its place along with other organizations and often to cooperate with them in affairs of common interest.'

4 Denominations are usually conservative: members generally accept the norms and values of society, although they may have marginally different values from those of the wider society. Some denominations place minor restrictions on their members. For instance, Methodists are discouraged from drinking and gambling, but drinking in moderation is tolerated, and drinkers are not excluded from the denomination.

5 In other respects denominations have the same characteristics as churches: new members are freely admitted and they have a hierarchy of paid officials.

A slightly different view is taken by Wade Roof and William McKinney. According to them the main difference between denominations and other types of religious organizations is that in denominations 'primary emphasis is upon the free, unco-erced consent of the individual and a type of religiosity emphasizing practical, everyday faith'. The children of members are not automatically recruited and individuals have more control over their own faith than in churches. Congregations have greater power and 'religion is more a personal and inward phenomenon than something that comes from an objective institution'. Rather than restricting the behaviour of members, denominations free them to make their own choices. In a denomination faith is more 'this-worldly than other-worldly' – more concerned with living a moral life than with strict adherence to a theological doctrine.

The concept of denomination is no less problematic than the concept of church. It covers a wide range of organizations from Jehovah's Witnesses to Methodists, from Pentecostalists to Baptists. Some organizations are classified as sects by some sociologists but as denominations by others.

Stark and Bainbridge are highly critical of the concept of a denomination. They argue that the addition of denominations to the distinction between church and sect only 'renders fluid and uncertain an intellectual scheme that was supposed to be a solid basis for analysis'. Indeed, they claim that the division of religious organizations into discrete types obscures rather than clarifies the differences between them (see pp. 471–3 for further details of their argument).

Sects

According to Troeltsch **sects** have characteristics that are almost diametrically opposed to those of churches.

1 They are both smaller and more strongly integrated than other religious organizations.

2 Rather than drawing members from all sections of society and being closely connected to the state, Troeltsch claimed sects are 'connected with the lower classes, or at least with those elements in Society which are opposed to the State and Society'.

3 Far from being conservative and accepting the norms and values of society sects are 'in opposition to the world'. They reject the values of the world that surrounds them, and their detachment from it may be 'expressed in the refusal to use the law, to swear in a court of justice, to own property, to exercise dominion over others, or to take part in war'.

4 Sect members may be expected to withdraw from life outside the sect, but at the same time they may wish ultimately to see changes take place in the wider society.

5 Members of a sect are expected to be deeply committed to its beliefs. They may be excluded from the sect if they fail to demonstrate such a commitment.

6 Young children cannot usually enter the sect by being baptized if they are not old enough to understand the significance of the ceremony. They must join voluntarily as adults, and willingly adopt the lifestyle and beliefs of the sect. In particular they must sacrifice 'worldly pleasures' in order to devote themselves to their religious life. In this sense, sects exercise a

stronger control over individuals' lives than, for example, the modern Church of England. Sects share this characteristic with religions such as Islam, in countries where religious beliefs still have a strong hold over social life.

7 Like the Roman Catholic Church in Europe in the Middle Ages, sects tend to believe that they possess a monopoly of the religious truth.

8 Unlike churches though, they are not organized through a hierarchy of paid officials. If central authority exists within a sect, it usually rests with a single **charismatic leader**, whose personality and perceived special qualities persuade the followers to adhere to his or her teachings.

A number of sects conform closely to the preceding description, for example the People's Temple, an American sect of the 1970s. When this sect came to an end it had just 900 members. It was founded in California by the Reverend Jim Jones and although it recruited a considerable number of relatively affluent whites, it had a particular appeal to black ghetto dwellers of northern California.

The sect had a radical ideology: it claimed to be based upon a Marxist philosophy and it strongly opposed prejudice and discrimination. Many members withdrew from participation in the outside world in the early stages of the sect's development, giving over their homes and property to Reverend Jones. Some continued to work outside, but eventually the sect became completely isolated as its members moved to set up a commune at 'Jonestown' in the rainforests of Guyana.

The degree of integration within the group was tragically illustrated when in 1978 the entire membership died after taking cyanide. Some committed suicide on the orders of their leader; others were murdered by being tricked into taking the poison.

In common with many other sects, members were expected to demonstrate their faith, in this case by such acts as signing confessions to crimes they had not committed, suffering public humiliations if Jones believed they had done something wrong, and by drinking unidentified liquids of an unpleasant colour. Jones exercised strict control over his followers. His charismatic leadership was strengthened by fraudulent attempts to demonstrate his religious powers. 'Miracle healings' would take place where followers would pretend to have been instantly cured of cancer by spitting out pieces of chicken liver they had concealed in

their mouth. Careful scrutiny of members' dustbins allowed Jones to claim divine fortune-telling powers.

Although the People's Temple is an extreme example of a sect, many other religious organizations display similar characteristics. But there are also numerous exceptions. It is possible to find sects of vastly different sizes, with a wide variety of ideologies, contrasting attitudes to the outside world, varying degrees of control over their membership and with or without a professional clergy and a charismatic leader. Bryan Wilson accepts that Troeltsch's description of sects may have been accurate in terms of European countries until quite recently. However, it does not account for or adequately describe the proliferation of sectarian groups in Europe and the USA in recent decades. Nor does it take account of the development of **new religious movements** and **cults**, some of which fail to conform to at least some of the usual characteristics of religions. We will now consider these.

■ Types of sect, cult and new religious movements

There have been numerous attempts to classify the wide variety of small religious, spiritual or mystical groups which have sprung up. Eileen Barker suggests that they could be classified according to the religious tradition from which they originate. For example, Hari Krishna and the disciples of Bhagwan Rajneesh take their inspiration from the Hindu religion, Zen groups from Buddhism, and the Children of God from Christianity. The Unification Church (better known as the Moonies) combines elements from Taoism, Confucianism, Spiritualism and Buddhism, although it is based primarily around the *Bible*. Other groups have an occult, pagan or witchcraft source. Some groups have little connection with previous religions but are part of what Barker calls the **Human Potential Movement**, which attempts to liberate human potential through some technique – Primal Therapy, for example, uses screaming.

However, Barker also points out that some groups 'are so idiosyncratic that they would appear to defy any classification'. She cites a Japanese group who regarded Thomas Edison (the American inventor) as a minor god, and the Kennedy Worshippers who numbered around

2,000 and saw the assassinated president of the USA John F. Kennedy as a god.

Barker suggests that another way of classifying new religious movements is according to the degree of commitment shown by their members. The People's Temple (see p. 467) is at one extreme while some other movements such as Transcendental Meditation (see p. 470) require little more of their members than to attend a short course. Eileen Barker puts forward the above classification schemes as no more than tentative suggestions. Other sociologists, such as Roy Wallis, have developed much more detailed systems of classification.

▪ Roy Wallis – *The Elementary forms of the New Religious Life*

Wallis's views are illustrated in Figure 8.1. He divides new religious movements into three main groups. Like Troeltsch the principal criterion he uses to categorize religious organizations is their relationship to the outside world. He therefore distinguishes between them according to whether the movement and its members **reject, accommodate** or **affirm** the world. He represents his typology with a triangle, and notes the existence of some groups (those in the central box) which do not fit neatly into any single category.

World-rejecting new religious movements (sects)

The **world-rejecting new religious movements** have most of the characteristics of a sect described by Troeltsch.

1 They are usually a clearly religious organization with a definite conception of God. For example, the Unification Church, better known as the 'Moonies' – after their leader Reverend Sun Myung Moon – pray in a conventional way to a 'Heavenly Father'.

2 In other respects though, such groups are far from conventional. Their ideology is invariably highly critical of the outside world, and the movement expects or actively seeks change.

3 Some groups are **millenarian**: they expect God's intervention to change the world. The Black Muslims in the USA are a case in point. They prophesy that in the year 2,000 Allah will destroy the whites and their religion.

4 In order to achieve salvation members are expected to have a sharp break from their conventional life when they join the movement. Organizations of this type act as **total institutions**, controlling every aspect of their

Figure 8.1   Types of new religious movement

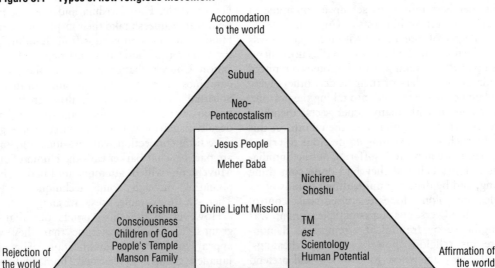

(*Source*: R. Wallis, *The Elementary Forms of the New Religious Life*, Routledge & Kegan Paul, London, 1984.)

members' lives. (For more details on total institutions see pp. 305–8). As a result they often develop a reputation for 'brainwashing' their members, since families and friends find it hard to understand the change that has taken place in the organization's member.

5 Limited contact with the outside world might be allowed to facilitate fund-raising. Moonies in San Francisco help to support the group by selling flowers, and members of other movements distribute literature or sell records for the same purpose. Sometimes they simply beg for money claiming to be collecting for charity.

6 The leadership of the groups may be quite prepared to have contacts with the outside world in an attempt to try to change society without waiting for divine intervention. Jim Jones, leader of the ill-fated People's Temple, had close contacts with Californian politicians. Louis Farrakhan, leader of the 'Nation of Islam', a faction of the Black Muslims, became heavily involved in US politics. In particular Farrakhan supported the black Democratic Party presidential candidate, the Reverend Jesse Jackson, in his attempts to promote policies designed to benefit disadvantaged minorities. Farrakhan himself though was strongly criticized for making apparently anti-Semitic comments.

7 Although they are usually radical, there can be conservative elements in the beliefs and actions of such organizations. The Unification Church is strongly anti-communist, and has supported South Korean military dictatorships. Many of the movements are morally puritanical, perhaps forbidding sex outside marriage for example.

8 World-rejecting new religious movements vary enormously in size: the 'Moonies' have an international following while other groups are small and locally based.

9 Nearly all of them tend to be based around some form of communal lifestyle, and as such develop unconventional ways of living.

Thus, despite the variations within these groups, none of them are content with the world as it is.

Wallis sees most world-rejecting new religious movements as sects. He defines sects as groups that claim to be uniquely legitimate and which advocate religious doctrines which are widely regarded as deviant. They have 'an authoritative locus for the attribution of heresy' and are hostile to the state and non-members.

World-accommodating new religious movements (denominations)

The **world-accommodating new religious movements** are usually offshoots of an existing major church or denomination. For example, neo-Pentecostalist groups are variants of Protestant or Roman Catholic religions, while Subud is a world-accommodating Muslim group.

Typically these groups neither accept nor reject the world as it is: they are primarily concerned with religious rather than worldly questions. As Wallis puts it:

> The world-accommodating new religion draws a distinction between the spiritual and the worldly in a way quite uncharacteristic of the other two types. Religion is not constructed as a primarily social matter; rather it provides solace or stimulation to personal interior life.

The religious beliefs of followers might help them to cope with their non-religious social roles, but the aim of the religion is not to create a new society nor to improve the believers' chances of success in their lives. Instead, world-accommodating sects seek to restore the spiritual purity to a religion that it believes has been lost in more conventional churches and denominations. Many of the members of these organizations were, before joining, members of churches or denominations with which they had become disillusioned. Pentecostalists hold that the belief in the Holy Spirit has been lost in other Christian religions. The Holy Spirit speaks through Pentecostalists, giving them the gift of 'speaking in tongues'.

It is the spiritual and religious aspects of world-accommodating groups which differentiate them from other religious organizations, but they can still be seen as denominations. According to Wallis denominations have a 'respectable' set of religious beliefs and are tolerant of the existence of other religions. Most of the members of world-accommodating groups live conventional and conforming lives outside their religious activities.

This is demonstrated by Ken Pryce's study of West Indians in the St Paul's district of Bristol. He found that Pentecostalists lived respectable lives. They usually had, or wished to have, normal jobs. Unlike some members of the local community, they did not earn their living from prostitution or by selling drugs, and they did not belong to radical political movements.

World-affirming new religious movements (cults)

The **world-affirming new religious movements** are very different from all other religious groups, and may indeed lack some of the features normally thought to be central to a religion. Wallis says that such a group 'may have no "church", no collective ritual of worship, it may lack any developed theology or ethics'. However, these groups do claim to be able to provide access to spiritual or supernatural powers, and in that sense can be regarded as religions.

Rather than rejecting existing society or existing religions, world-affirming groups accept the world as it is and they are not particularly critical of other religions. What they offer the follower is the potential to be successful in terms of the dominant values of society by unlocking spiritual powers present in the individual. Salvation is seen as a personal achievement and as a solution to personal problems such as unhappiness, suffering or disability. Individuals usually overcome such problems by adopting some technique that heightens their awareness or abilities.

World-affirming movements are not exclusive groups: they seek as wide a membership as possible. Rather than trying to convert people as such, they try to sell them a service commercially. Followers carry on their normal lives except when undergoing training; often courses are held at weekends or at other convenient times so as not to cause disruption. There is little social control over the members, or customers, and they are not normally excluded from the group if they fail to act in accordance with its beliefs.

An example of a world-affirming new religious movement is provided by Transcendental Meditation or TM. TM is based upon the Hindu religion, but during at least some periods of its development the religious elements have been played down. First introduced to the West in the late 1950s, it achieved prominence in 1968 when the Beatles met its leading proponent, the Maharishi Mahesh Yogi. TM involves a meditational technique whereby a follower is given a personal *mantra* on which to concentrate for 20 minutes in the morning and evening. It is claimed that this technique can provide 'unbounded awareness' which can have beneficial effects for individuals and for society. Some followers of TM claim that in areas where as little as 1 per cent of the population have been initiated, crime, accidents and sickness are all reduced. Initiation is a simple matter and can take place in just a couple of hours with further follow-up sessions lasting just a few hours more. An advanced course in the powers of TM, the *Siddi* programme, claims to provide occult powers such as the ability to levitate. This course was on sale in the USA in 1980 for $3,000.

As with some other new religious movements there have been attempts to make deliberate use of TM's teachings to solve social problems. Teachers have been dispatched to areas of civil unrest in the hope of converting local leaders who, it was hoped, would in turn use their new powers to overcome the area's problems. In the 1992 British general election hundreds of followers of TM stood for parliament as representatives of the Natural Law Party, offering the voters harmonious rule in line with the natural laws of the universe as discovered by the Maharishi.

There are some groups which do not conform perfectly to the above description of world-affirming new religious movements. Over a period they develop an inner-core of followers who attach great significance to the teachings and start to live more as members of a world-rejecting movement. TM, for instance, has developed an exclusive inner-group of members trained in advanced techniques who have characteristics a little closer to those of world-rejecting sects.

In addition, other world-affirming groups may think that their beliefs have a potential beyond helping individuals achieve success. They may believe that their training, if sufficiently widespread, could contribute to solving problems such as racial conflict, or even world hunger. Such political aims are not, however, the main concern of world-affirming new religious movements – they are merely a possible by-product of their teachings.

To Wallis, most world-affirming new religious movements are **cults**. Cults are like sects in that they have religious beliefs that are widely regarded as deviant, but unlike sects cults tolerate the existence of other religions. Cults are 'loosely structured, tolerant, and non-exclusive'. They have a rapid turnover in membership and are relatively undemanding on their followers.

The 'middle ground'

Wallis realizes that no religious group will conform exactly to the categories he outlines. He says 'all actual new religious movements are likely to combine elements of each type to some extent'. Indeed, he points to a number of groups that occupy an intermediate position, such as the Healthy Happy Holy Organization (3HO), and the Divine Light Mission. Comparing them to the three main types he says 'They combine in various degrees all three types, and more particularly elements of the conventional society and the counterculture.'

3HO, for example, is similar to world-accommodating new religious movements in that it is an offshoot of an established religion, in this case Sikhism.

As in world-affirming movements, it employs techniques that it is claimed will bring personal benefits such as happiness and good health. In common with TM, 3HO hopes its teaching will have spin-offs for the outside world: in fact, nothing less than world unity. 3HO is not exclusive. Classes are provided for those who are not full members so they can receive benefits from the teachings. Even fully committed members are expected to have conventional marriages and to hold down conventional jobs.

On the other hand 3HO does have some characteristics in common with world-rejecting movements. The organization has a clear concept of God. Members dress unconventionally in white clothing and turbans. They live in communes or *ashrams*, but the *ashrams* do not involve total sharing: individuals pay for their own room and board. Some restrictions are placed on behaviour: members of 3HO are vegetarians and abstain from alcohol, tobacco and mind-altering drugs.

Occupying as it does the **middle ground**, 3HO allows its followers to combine elements of an alternative life style with conventional marriage and employment.

Roy Wallis – an evaluation

James A. Beckford commends Wallis' scheme for recognizing that new religious movements do not always fit neatly into one category or another and for outlining the differences in the types of individuals recruited by different types of movement (we outline Wallis's views on recruitment on pp. 474–5). However, Beckford also offers some criticisms of Wallis.

1 He argues that Wallis's categories are difficult to apply. It is not made clear whether the teachings of the movement or the beliefs and outlooks of the individual members distinguish the different orientations to the world.

2 Beckford feels that Wallis pays insufficient attention to the diversity of views that often exists within a sect or cult.

3 Beckford also questions the worth of defining some groups as 'world rejecting'. In his view no group can afford to reject the world altogether since they rely upon contacts with the wider economic system for their very survival.

Nevertheless Beckford does not deny that a **typology**, or list of types, of new religious movements, is useful. In contrast, Stark and Bainbridge, whose views we examine next, reject the idea of using a typology to distinguish new religions.

■ Rodney Stark and William Sims Bainbridge – un-ideal types

Typologies, correlates and attributes

According to Stark and Bainbridge, none of the typologies of new religious movements, sects, churches and denominations developed by other sociologists is a sound basis for categorization. All of them consist of lists of characteristics which each type is likely to have. However, these characteristics are not found in every religious organization placed in each category. Not all churches try to convert all members of society and not all sects are exclusive.

Such characteristics used to distinguish organizations are **correlates,** sets of characteristics that tend to be found together in the same organizations. They are not however **attributes**, characteristics that an organization must have if it is to be defined as a church, denomination, sect or cult. Defining types of organization in terms of correlates tends to lead to confusion since most organizations are in some ways exceptions to the rule.

Stark and Bainbridge therefore argue that typologies of religious organization should be abandoned altogether. Instead they adopt the ideas of Benton Johnson, an earlier sociologist of religion. Johnson argued that religious organizations could be compared in terms of a single attribute and could be placed at any point on a continuum in terms of this attribute. Johnson said:

A church is a religious group that accepts the social environment in which it exists. A sect is a religious organisation that rejects the social environment in which it exists. (Quoted in R. Stark and W.S. Bainbridge 1985, p. 23.)

Thus they claim that religious groups can be compared in terms of the degree of conflict that exists between them and the wider society. The use of such a definition allows clear comparisons. For example, the Catholic Church in the USA is nearer to the sect end of the continuum than the Catholic Church in the Republic of Ireland. It also allows changes over time to be clearly described: organizations might change to become in greater or lesser tension with the environment.

Sects and cults

Stark and Bainbridge then go on to argue that there are different kinds (they are careful to avoid using the word types) of religious movement in a high degree of tension with their social environment.

1 **Sects** are groups which are formed as an offshoot of an existing religion as a result of division or schism within that religion.

2 **Cults**, on the other hand, are new religions, or at least they are new in a particular society. Some result from cultural **importation** where a religion from other societies is introduced into one in which it had not previously been practised. Thus Eastern religions introduced into the USA are examples of imported cults. Some cults, though, are entirely new. These result from cultural **innovation**, they are unconnected to existing religions.

Stark and Bainbridge go on to suggest that cults exhibit different degrees of organization and can be divided into three types.

1 **Audience cults** are the least organized and involve little face-to-face interaction. Contacts are often maintained through the mass media and the occasional conference. Many of the members of the audience for such cults may not know each other. Astrology is an example of an audience cult, as is the belief in UFOs.

2 **Client cults** are more organized and usually offer services to their followers. In the past they tended to offer 'medical miracles, forecasts of the future, or contact with the dead', though more recently they have 'specialised in personal adjustment'. Scientology, for example, offers its clients the opportunity to clear 'engrams' (repressed memories of painful experiences) from the brain, while the Reich Foundation offers the promise of the 'monumental orgasm'.

3 **Cult movements** involve followers much more. They try to satisfy all the religious needs of their members and, unlike client and audience cults, membership of other faiths is not permitted. They do however vary considerably in their strength. Some require little more than occasional attendance at meetings and acceptance of the cult's beliefs, but others shape the whole of a person's life. The Reverend Sun Myung Moon's Unification Church is an example of a cult movement. Many client cults become cult movements for their most dedicated followers, for example practitioners of TM who take the *Siddi* programme (see p. 470 for a short description of TM).

Cults and compensators

Stark and Bainbridge argue that different types of cult offer different types of rewards and compensators for their followers. In line with their general theory of religion (discussed on pp. 454–6) they believe that religious organizations exist to meet the needs of individuals.

Audience cults offer very weak compensators which may provide 'no more than a mild vicarious thrill or social entertainment'. Watching Uri Geller allegedly bend a spoon through psychic power does not promise the audience any great improvement in their lives.

Client cults on the other hand, offer more valuable specific compensators. Stark and Bainbridge say 'If astrologers really could improve our life chances by telling us the right day to make investments, get married, or stay away from the office, those would indeed be valuable rewards.'

On the other hand these cults do not offer general compensators such as an explanation of the meaning of life or the promise of life after death. General compensators are provided by cult movements.

Conclusion

Stark and Bainbridge offer a different, and they would claim superior, method of distinguishing religious organizations to that of Wallis. They make some useful distinctions between different types of cult; however, in doing so, they contradict themselves. They develop their own typology and fail to notice that some groups will not conform to all the characteristics they attribute to audience cults, client cults or cult movements

■ Reasons for the growth of sects and cults

Religious sects and cults are not a new phenomenon: they have existed for centuries. Despite this, most existing sects and cults originated in the twentieth century and the 1960s saw the appearance of many new organizations. Table 8.1 shows the date of origin of the 417 native-born sects and 501 cults uncovered in the early 1980s in the USA by Stark and Bainbridge.

Although it is widely believed that these types of religious movement are more common in the USA than in Europe, Stark and Bainbridge uncovered evidence that there were proportionately more in some European countries. For example, they claimed that in the late 1970s in the USA there were 2.3 cult movements per million inhabitants, compared to 3.2 per million in England and Wales. In England and Wales they found no less than 153 different cult movements.

The growth of sects and cults can be explained either in terms of why particular individuals choose to join, or in terms of wider social changes. In reality these reasons are closely linked, for social changes affect the number of people available as potential recruits.

Marginality

Max Weber provided one of the earliest explanations for the growth of sects. He argued that they were likely to arise within groups that were **marginal** in society: members of groups outside the mainstream of social life often feel they are not receiving the prestige and/or the economic rewards they deserve. One solution to this problem is a sect

based on what Weber called 'a theodicy of disprivilege' (a **theodicy** is a religious explanation and justification). Such sects contain an explanation for the disprivilege of their members and promise them a 'sense of honour' either in the afterlife or in a future 'new world' on earth.

Bryan Wilson has pointed out that a variety of situations could lead to the marginalization of groups in society, which in turn could provide fertile ground for the development of sects. These situations include defeat in war, natural disaster or economic collapse. Radical and undesirable changes such as these are not the only circumstances that can encourage sect development.

In part, the growth of sects in the USA in the 1960s was accomplished through the recruitment of marginal and disadvantaged groups. The Black Muslims, for example, aimed to recruit 'the negro in the mud', and the sect seemed to offer hope for some of the most desperate blacks. However, for the most part, in the 1960s and 1970s the membership of the world-rejecting new religious movements was drawn from amongst the ranks of young, white, middle-class Americans and Europeans. Wallis does not believe that this contradicts the theory that marginal members of society join world-rejecting sects. He argues that many of the recruits had already become marginal to society. Despite their middle-class backgrounds, they were usually 'hippies, drop-outs, surfers, LSD and marijuana users'. Their marginality may have been further increased by arrests for drug use or activities involved with radical politics. They were attracted to the communal lifestyle which the sect offered.

Relative deprivation

However, this does not explain why quite affluent middle-class youth should become marginal members of society in the first place. The concept of 'relative deprivation' can be used to explain their actions. **Relative deprivation** refers to subjectively perceived deprivation: that which people actually feel. In objective terms the poor are more deprived than the middle class, but in subjective terms certain members of the middle class may feel more deprived than the poor. They do not lack material wealth, but feel spiritually deprived in a world they see as too materialistic, lonely and impersonal. According to Wallis, they therefore seek salvation in the sense of community offered by the sect.

Table 8.1 When American sects and cults formed. Percent formed in the indicated period

Historical period	Sects (405)[a]	Cults (484)[a]
1899 and before	19	7
1900–1929	22	8
1930–1949	23	10
1950–1959	16	14
1960–1969	14	38
1970–1977	3	23
	100	100

[a]No date of founding known for 12 sects and for 17 cults.

(*Source*: Stark, R. and Bainbridge, W.S. (1985) *The Future of Religion*, University of California Press, p. 131.)

Stark and Bainbridge also employ the concept of relative deprivation in explaining the origin of sects. They define sects as organizations which break away from an established church and they believe that it is the relatively deprived who are likely to break away. Splits take place when churches begin to compromise their beliefs. When the more successful members of a religion try to reduce the amount of tension between that religion and the outside world, the less successful resent it and break away.

Social change

A number of sociologists, such as Bryan Wilson, argue that sects arise during periods of rapid social change when traditional norms are disrupted, social relationships come to lack consistent and coherent meaning, and the traditional universe of meaning is undermined.

Wilson uses the example of the early Methodist movement which had the characteristics of a sect. He sees the rise of Methodism as the response of the urban working class to the 'chaos and uncertainty of life in the newly settled industrial areas'. He claims that they had to evolve 'new patterns of religious belief to accommodate themselves to their new situation'. In a situation of change and uncertainty, the sect offers the support of a close-knit community organization, well-defined and strongly sanctioned norms and values, and a promise of salvation. It

provides a new and stable universe of meaning which is legitimated by its religious beliefs.

The growth of new religious movements

Wallis has pointed to a number of social changes which he believes accounted for the growth of new religious movements in the 1960s. Some of these had important effects on youth in particular.

1 The growth of higher education and the gradual lengthening of time spent in education created an extended period of transition between childhood and adulthood. Youth culture developed because there was an increasing number of young people who had considerable freedom but little in the way of family or work responsibilities.

2 At the same time there was a belief that developing technology would herald the end of poverty and economic scarcity.

3 Radical political movements were also growing in the 1960s providing an alternative to dominant social norms and values.

Wallis claims that in these circumstances world-rejecting new religious movements were attractive because of the potential they seemed to offer for 'A more idealistic, spiritual and caring way of life, in the context of more personal and loving social relationships.' It has also been suggested that the growth of such movements is related to secularization. In general terms **secularization** means a decline in the importance of religion in society. (For details of the relationship between sects and secularization see pp. 487–8.)

Wallis provides only a very sketchy explanation of recruitment to world-accommodating religious movements. He claims that those with a substantial stake in society but who nevertheless have reasons for being dissatisfied with existing religions tend to join them.

World-affirming new religions, as we saw in an earlier section, are very different from the other types. They do not involve a radical break with a conventional lifestyle, they do not strongly restrict the behaviour of members, and they offer material and practical advantages to their followers. For all these reasons they might be expected to appeal to different groups in society than other religious movements, and to develop in different circumstances.

World-affirming new religious movements usually develop after world-rejecting ones, and more of them have survived longer. Research suggests that members of groups such as Erhard's Seminar Training have members with above average incomes and education who are somewhat older than those of world-rejecting groups. To Wallis what they offer is a 'means of coping with a sense of inadequacy among social groups which are, by the more obvious indicators, among the world's more successful and highly rewarded individuals'. It is primarily the emphasis placed upon individual success in terms of status, income and social mobility, that stimulates these 'religions' to develop.

Actually achieving success may in another sense motivate individuals to join these groups. Individuals may feel that in the successful performance of their social roles (such as their jobs) they lose sight of their real selves. A world-affirming religious movement might allow the rediscovery of this real 'self'.

Bryan Wilson has argued that these religions offer immediate gratification for those who take part. Wallis suggests that those who are socialized into being dedicated to their work and who have internalized the Protestant work ethic, find it hard to enjoy their leisure activities while feeling free from guilt. In an increasingly leisure and consumer-orientated society, Wallis believes world-affirming organizations offer a path to guilt-free spontaneously enjoyed leisure.

The explanations provided above offer some general reasons why world-affirming movements should be popular in advanced industrial societies, but do not explain why particular individuals should join, nor why they are popular at particular periods of time. More specific theories have been devised to account for what Wallis calls movements of the middle ground.

Several sociologists studying these movements have claimed that they help to reintegrate people into society, while allowing them to retain some elements of an alternative lifestyle. These movements appeal to those members of the counterculture or world-rejecting religious movements who have become disillusioned, or feel they need to earn a living in a conventional way. They offer a stepping-stone back towards respectability. Thus Mauss and Peterson describe the members of one such group, the Jesus Freaks, as 'penitent young prodigals'. (Quoted in Wallis, p. 75.) These middle-ground groups were particularly successful from the mid–1970s onwards, when economic recession and the decline in the numbers of people willing to live alternative lifestyles provided a large pool from which recruitment might take place.

■ The development of sects
Sects as short-lived organizations

In 1929 H.R. Neibuhr made a number of observations about the way that religious sects changed over time. He argued that sects could not survive as sects beyond a single generation. Either they would change their characteristics, compromise and become denominations, or they would disappear altogether. He advanced the following arguments to support this view.

1 Sect membership was based upon voluntary adult commitment: members chose to dedicate themselves to the organization and its religion. Once the first generation started to have children though, the latter would be admitted as new members when they were too young to understand the teachings of the religion. These new members would not be able to sustain the fervour of the first generation. Consequently the sect might become a denomination.

2 Sects which relied upon a charismatic leader would tend to disappear if the leader died. Alternatively the nature of the leadership would change: no longer would the charisma of an individual hold the sect together. This would allow the bureaucratic structure of a denomination with its hierarchy of paid officials to emerge.

3 Neibuhr argued that the ideology of many sects contained the seeds of their own destruction. Sects with an ascetic creed would encourage their members to work hard and save their money. As a result the membership would be upwardly socially mobile, and would no longer wish to belong to a religious group which catered for marginal members of society. Once again the sect would have to change or die: either becoming like a denomination or losing its membership.

According to Neibuhr then, there was no possibility of a sect surviving for long periods of time without losing its extreme teachings and rejection of society. One example that illustrates this well is that of the Methodists before they became a denomination: as the Methodist membership rose in status in the nineteenth century, the strict disciplines of the sect and its rejection of society were dropped, and it gradually came to be recognized as a denomination.

The life cycle of sects

However, Bryan Wilson rejects Neibuhr's view that sects are inevitably short lived. He points out that some sects do survive for a long time without becoming denominations. To Wilson the crucial factor is the way the sect answers the question 'What shall we do to be saved?' Sects can be classified in terms of how they answer this question. Only one type, the **conversionist sect**, is likely to develop into a denomination. This is the **evangelical sect**, typical of the USA, whose aim is to convert as many people as possible by means of revivalist preaching. Becoming a denomination does not necessarily compromise its position: It can still save souls.

The other types of sect cannot maintain their basic position in a denominational form. **Adventist sects**, such as the Seventh Day Adventists and Jehovah's Witnesses, provide an example of the reason why. Adventist sects await the Second Coming of Christ, who will judge humanity and establish a new world order. Only sect membership will guarantee a place in the new order. The rich and powerful and those who follow conventional religions will be excluded from Christ's kingdom on earth. Adventists sects are founded on the principle of separation from the world in the expectation of the Second Coming. To become a denomination they would have to change this basic premise. Separation from the world and denominationalism are not compatible.

Thus Wilson concludes that a sect's prescription for salvation is a major factor in determining whether or not it becomes a denomination.

Internal ideology and the wider society

Roy Wallis takes a more complex view of the paths followed by sects: he feels the chances of sects surviving, changing or disappearing are affected both by the internal ideology of the sect and by external social circumstances.

Since Wallis distinguishes a variety of different types of sect he argues that they are likely to follow different paths. According to him, the development of sects may involve them changing from one type of sect to another, rather than becoming denominations. Wallis does not believe that there is any single or inevitable path that any type of sect will follow, and the changes that do take place may be specific to a particular historical period.

World-rejecting sects do often change their stance as time passes. Like Neibuhr, Wallis sees the possibility that such groups may soften their opposition to society and become more world-accommodating. This seems to have been particularly common in the 1970s when economic recession discouraged some members from dropping-out and rejecting society altogether. The Children of God, for example, weakened their opposition to other religions and no longer thought of non-members as servants of Satan.

Wallis accepts that charismatic leaders have difficulty in retaining personal control over a religious movement indefinitely, and this may also result in changes. If the organization grows, a process which Weber described as the **routinization of charisma** can take place. A more bureaucratic organization develops so that some of the leader's personal authority becomes vested in his (or untypically her) officials or representatives. Nevertheless the changes may stop well short of denominalization.

Wallis also recognizes that sects can disappear. World-rejecting sects may actually be destroyed by the charismatic leader, as in the case of Jim Jones's People's Temple. Social changes may lead to the members becoming less marginal in society, so threatening the base on which the sect was founded. However, as new groups in society become marginal, new sects will arise.

According to Wallis then, world-rejecting sects do tend to be unstable, but new ones emerge, and those that do survive may become more world-accommodating while continuing to exist as sects.

World-affirming movements are less likely than world-rejecting ones to be based on a charismatic leader or to have members who are marginal or deprived. They also require less sacrifice and commitment from members, and for this reason are not so likely to disappear. Instead, since their services are often sold as a commodity, they are vulnerable to a loss of support from their consumers. To the extent that they sell themselves in the market place, they are subject to the same problems as a retailer. If the public no longer needs, or gains benefits from their services, they will lose customers. To Wallis though, world-affirming movements are more likely to change to attract a new clientele than to cease to exist.

Transcendental Meditation (TM), for example, initially emphasized its spiritual elements and in the second half of the 1960s it succeeded by identifying closely with the counter-culture. In the 1970s the counter-culture declined and TM tried to broaden its appeal by emphasizing the practical benefits – the worldly success – that the meditation claimed to offer.

Wallis points out that consumers might tire of a product that fails to deliver its promises. One response is to try to gain an inner-core of committed followers. TM did just this through the *Siddi* programme and perhaps in this way helped to guarantee a permanent following.

Wallis believes that world-affirming movements are flexible and they can change relatively easily as they seek to survive and prosper. In some circumstances they can also become more religious and spiritual (like world-rejecting movements) for at least an inner-core of followers.

The position of the movements of the middle ground is by its very nature more precarious. Since they are in an intermediate position they are likely to shift between being world-rejecting and world-affirming, depending upon circumstances and the needs and wishes of the membership. This can lead to splits within the movements of the establishment of rival organizations. One British movement of this type, the Process, was founded in 1963 and split into two separate groups in 1973. If these splits do not take place it is likely that such movements fluctuate between the two extremes, continuing in one form or another, but not establishing a clear and permanent ideology and identity.

Wallis says little about how world-accommodating movements develop, but these seem the most stable of the new religious movements. Indeed some are not particularly new: Pentecostalism has survived little changed since the early years of the twentieth century. As Wallis points out, this type of 'new' religious movement has most in common with denominations.

Thus although Wallis does not agree with Neibuhr that sects inevitably disappear or become denominations, his work does suggest that there may be tendencies in these directions. Religious movements most similar to denominations are the

likeliest to remain stable. World-rejecting movements, which have most in common with the type of sects Neibuhr described, are the least likely to survive for long periods in their original form.

■ Millenarian movements

So far the discussion of religious organizations has been confined to industrial societies. New religious movements have also developed in other parts of the world at various times. Many such movements, known as **millenarian movements**, are similar to adventist sects in that they promise that the world will be transformed suddenly and soon. Peter Worsley defines them as movements:

---

in which the imminence of a radical and supernatural change in the social order is prophesied or expected, so as to lead to organization and activity, carried out in preparation for this event, on the part of the movement's adherents.

Millenarian movements prophesy a merger of the world of the supernatural and the world of people in a new order, free from pain, death, sin and all human imperfections. Often millenarian movements develop in societies that have undergone, or are undergoing, colonization or settlement by non-natives.

The Ghost Dance

The Ghost Dance religion of the Teton Sioux illustrates the development of a millenarian movement. From 1860 to 1877 the Teton fought numerous battles with white settlers and the US army to protect their territory and maintain their way of life. After their final defeat in 1877, they lost most of their land and were confined to relatively small reservations.

With the virtual extermination of the buffalo herds, the economic base of Teton society was destroyed, and with it their traditional way of life. Reservation authorities instructed the Teton to take up farming. This largely failed because the land was unsuitable, and the few crops that did grow were often destroyed by drought or plagues of grasshoppers. By 1890 the Teton were largely dependent on government beef rations. From 1889 to 1890 the hardship of the Teton became acute. Crop failures and disease among their cattle were coupled with a drastic reduction in government beef rations and outbreaks of measles, influenza and whooping cough to which the Teton had a low natural resistance. On one reservation, the death rate rose to 45 a month in a population of 5,500. Apathy and despair were widespread.

From these circumstances the Ghost Dance religion developed. It prophesied that the world would be renewed, the whites would be buried under a new layer of earth and the buffalo would be restored in abundance. Dead Indians would return to earth and the Teton would live according to their traditional culture, forever free from death, disease and misery. To fulfil this prophecy, the Teton had merely to believe and perform the Ghost Dance.

Excitement and anticipation swept through the reservations. Fearing trouble, reservation authorities called in the army. An encampment of dancers at Wounded Knee was surrounded by troops and a chance shot led to a massacre of 300 Teton. Many were wearing 'ghost shirts' which were supposed to make them invulnerable to bullets. The failure of the ghost shirts ended the Ghost Dance religion.

The social origins of millenarian movements

Millenarian movements have occurred in many areas of the world and in all levels of society. However, they are found primarily in deprived groups: oppressed peasants, the urban poor, and peoples under colonial rule. They are often a response to disasters such as plague, famine and drought and to severe economic depression, although they can occur without acute economic and physical deprivation, as in the case of the **cargo cults** of the Melanesian Islands of the South Pacific.

The concept of relative deprivation can be applied to this situation: the islanders feel deprived when they compare their position with that of their European rulers. The cargo cults promise a new world in which the islanders will enjoy the wealth of the Europeans.

Millenarian movements are usually found in situations of rapid social change, involving the disruption of traditional social norms. They are often a response by native peoples to the impact of Western culture. In a study of millenarian movements in Europe between the eleventh and sixteenth centuries, Cohn finds that they tended to develop in expanding urban areas where traditional norms have been undermined.

Millenarian movements are usually preceded by a crisis which brings discontent to a head and a feeling that the normal ways of solving problems are inadequate. In David Aberle's words, 'A sense of blockage, of the insufficiency of ordinary action is the source of the more supernaturally based millenarian movements.'

Millenarian movements do not inevitably occur in response to the above conditions; they are only one possible response to them. The history of the Teton Sioux shows a number of alternative responses:

1 armed aggression;

2 a new way of life – farming;

3 a religion based on passive acceptance and resignation – the Ghost Dance was followed by the Peyote Way, an inward-looking religion based on an Indian version of Christianity and mystical experiences produced by the drug peyote;

4 political agitation – the rise of 'Red Power' in the late 1960s and early 1970s.

The Marxist view of religion as a response to exploitation and oppression helps to explain many millenarian movements. Engels argues that millenarian movements are an awakening of 'proletarian self-consciousness'. He sees them as an attempt by oppressed groups to change the world and remove their oppression here and now, rather than in the afterlife. Peter Worsley takes a similar view in his study of cargo cults. He sees them as a forerunner of political awareness and organization.

Some millenarian movements, particularly in Africa and Melanesia, do develop into political movements. However, this is generally not the case in Medieval Europe and North America.

The next major area we are going to investigate in the sociology of religion is the complex one of secularization – what it is, and whether it is actually taking place in society today.

■ Secularization

Support for the secularization thesis

Although sociologists have disputed whether religion encourages or inhibits social change, most agree that changes in society will lead to changes in religion. Furthermore, many have claimed that social change would lead to the weakening or even disappearance of religion.

In the nineteenth century it was widely believed that industrialization and the growth of scientific knowledge would lead to **secularization**. August Comte, the French functionalist sociologist, believed human history passed through three stages. Each stage was characterized by a different set of intellectual beliefs.

1 In the first, **theological stage**, religious and superstitious beliefs would be dominant.

2 These would be weakened as society passed into the second, **metaphysical stage**, during which philosophy would become more important.

3 Religious belief would disappear altogether in the final, **positive stage**, in which science alone would dominate human thinking and direct human behaviour.

Durkheim did not agree that religion was doomed to total obsolescence. He once commented that there was 'something eternal in religion'. Nevertheless he did anticipate that religion would be of declining social significance. In an industrial society in which there was a highly specialized division of labour, religion would lose some of its importance as a force for integrating society. Social solidarity would increasingly be provided by the education system rather than the sort of religious rituals associated with the more simple societies.

Weber too anticipated a progressive reduction in the importance of religion. He thought that in general people would act less in terms of emotions and in line with tradition, and more in terms of the rational pursuit of goals. **Rationalization** would gradually erode religious influence (for further details see pp. 459–61).

Marx did not believe that industrialization as such would herald the decline of religion, but he did believe that it would set in motion a chain of events that would eventually lead to its disappearance. Religion, according to Marx, was needed to

legitimate inequality in class societies, but capitalism would eventually be replaced by classless communism, and religion would cease to have any social purpose.

Some contemporary sociologists have followed in the footsteps of many of the founders of the subject, believing that industrialization has indeed led to religion losing some of its importance. Bryan Wilson, for example, argues that secularization has taken place. He defines secularization as 'the process whereby religious thinking, practice and institutions lose social significance'.

Problems with the secularization thesis

Despite widespread support for the theory of secularization, a number of issues have raised doubts about it.

1 Some sociologists have questioned the belief that religion was as important in the past as has been widely assumed. If pre-industrial societies were not truly religious, then religion may have declined little, if at all.

2 The role of religion in different industrial societies varies considerably. It is possible that secularization is a feature of the development of some industrial societies, but not of others.

3 The concepts of religiosity and secularization are not given the same meanings by different sociologists. Problems arise in evaluating the theory of secularization because of the absence of a generally agreed definition. Glock and Stark argue that 'Perhaps the most important attribute of those who perceive secularization to be going on is their commitment to a particular view of what religion means.' Thus one researcher might see the essential characteristic of religion as worship in a religious institution. As a result she or he may see a decline in church attendance as evidence of secularization. Another might emphasize religious belief which is seen as having nothing necessarily to do with attending a religious institution.

In an attempt to clarify the issue, the following studies of secularization will be classified in terms of some of the many ways in which the process has been conceptualized and measured.

Institutional religion – participation

Statistical evidence

Some researchers have seen religious institutions and the activity associated with them as the key element in religious behaviour. From this viewpoint they have measured the importance of religion in society in terms of factors such as church attendance, church membership and participation in ceremonies such as marriages which are performed in church.

In these respects, a good deal of the statistical evidence does seem to point towards secularization. However, the evidence needs to be examined carefully: some does not appear to support the secularization thesis; the evidence varies between countries; and the reliability and validity of many of the statistics are open to question. (For an explanation of the terms **validity** and **reliability** see p. 829.)

We will now examine the statistics relating to different types of participation in institutional religion.

Church attendance in Britain

Some of the strongest evidence for the secularization thesis as applied to Britain seems to come from church attendance statistics. The earliest available survey statistics on church attendance originate from the 1851 'Census of Religion'. This found just under 40 per cent of the adult population attending church. In England and Wales the figures dropped to 35 per cent by the turn of the century and 20 per cent in 1950.

In 1979 and 1989 two new Church Censuses were carried out. In both of these clergy were asked to make comparisons with five years earlier and estimate changes in the size of their congregations. The 1979 census was based on average attendance during the month of November. The 1989 census was based upon an attempt to collect information from every Christian church in England on Sunday 15 October of that year. A church was defined as 'a body of people meeting on a Sunday in the same premises primarily for the purposes of public worship at regular intervals'. 'Church' was used in a very wide sense – the study included figures on Anglicans, Roman Catholics, Orthodox Religions, Christian denominations and

Table 8.2 Total adult churchgoers 1975–1989

Year	Adult churchgoers	Percentage change	Percentage of adult population
		%	%
1975	4,093,000		11.3
		–2	
1979	4,025,000		11.0
		–7	
1985	3,755,000		9.9
		–1	
1989	3,706,900		9.5

(*Source*: Brierley, Peter (1991) *'Christian' England*, MARC Europe, p. 30.)

the House Church Movement (in which small groups get together to pray in each others' homes or in other buildings which are not normally used for religious purposes). Altogether 390,000 'churches' were discovered, 70 per cent of which returned the questionnaires on which the statistics were based. The overall results are given in Table 8.2.

These figures show a continuing drop in church attendance which appears to indicate a sustained process of secularization. Attendance at special Christian ceremonies such as baptisms and marriages has also declined. There were 554 baptisms per thousand live births in 1960 compared to 428 per thousand in 1976. The basis on which baptism figures were calculated changed after 1976 but the decline has continued. There has also been a noticeable drop in the number of marriages conducted in church. In 1929 56 per cent of marriages in England and Wales were conducted in the Church of England compared with 37 per cent in 1973.

Church membership in Britain

Table 8.3 shows the number of church members and the number of separate congregations or churches in the UK in 1990. It also shows the percentage change since 1985. In the UK as a whole only 14.6 per cent were members of churches (including the major denominations), a fall of 4 per cent compared with five years earlier. In 1970 20.4 per cent of adults were members. The figure for 1990 falls even lower for England on its own with just 12.1 per cent belonging to a church. In contrast membership of religious organizations remains much stronger in Northern Ireland where

Table 8.3 Total church members and churches and by country within UK 1990

	Members					Churches or congregations				
	UK	**England**	**Wales**	**Scotland**	**N Ireland**	**UK**	**England**	**Wales**	**Scotland**	**N Ireland**
Methodist	483,387	414,028	15,932	6,853	46,574	7,500	6,734	435	57	274
Independent	408,999	278,858	67,177	44,364	18,600	7,402	5,514	920	608	360
Baptist	241,842	171,892	41,088	20,292	8,570	3,439	2,356	761	219	103
Pentecostal	165,321	139,814	10,125	5,913	9,469	2,251	1,920	154	97	80
of which										
Pentecostal/										
Holiness	95,663	70,911	9,755	5,528	9,469	1,286	970	147	89	80
Afro-Caribbean	69,658	68,903	370	385	–	965	950	7	8	–
Others	123,677	108,275	5,131	7,658	2,613	1,889	1,562	86	181	60
Total free church	1,423,226	1,112,867	139,453	85,080	85,826	22,481	18,086	2,356	1,162	877
Roman Catholic[1]	1,945,626	1,281,520	60,596	277,500	326,010	4,457	3,333	215	485	424
Anglican	1,838,659	1,544,228	108,431	36,000	150,000	18,278	16,315	1,178	310	475
Presbyterian	1,291,672	113,188	70,738	832,120	275,626	5,503	1,649	1,186	2,093	575
Orthodox	265,258	241,803	10,157	13,165	133	205	190	6	7	2
Total 1990	6,764,441	4,293,606	389,375	1,243,865	837,595	50,924	39,573	4,941	4,057	2,353
Total 1985	7,046,453	4,391,396	399,978	1,355,726	899,353	49,830	38,269	5,339	3,994	2,228
Percentage change	–4%	–2%	–3%	–8%	–7%	+2%	+3%	–7%	+2%	+6%
Percentage of adult population 1990	14.6%	11.1%	16.5%	30.1%	67.7%					

[1] Based mostly on Mass attendance

(*Source*: Brierley, Peter and Longley, David (eds) (1991) *UK Christian Handbook, 1992/93 edition*, MARC Europe, London. p. 210.)

just over 66 per cent of adults continue to belong to a church.

The above figures refer only to Christian churches. Membership of some non-Christian churches and other religious organizations has been increasing. Table 8.4 shows members and congregations of non-Trinitarian religions, while Table 8.5 shows active members and groups of other religions. The tables include a number of sects (such as the Moonies and the International Society for Krishna Consciousness), and some religious groups of Asian origin (such as Hindus, Buddhists, Sikhs and Muslims) that have developed primarily because of immigration to Britain.

Both tables show an increase in membership or active membership of around 16 per cent between 1985 and 1990. All the main religions of Asian origin have steadily increased their membership, and Scientology, Jehovah's Witnesses and Krishna Consciousness are amongst the sects that have been growing. Of the groups listed, only the Jewish religion, the Church of Christ the Scientist, the New Church and the Theosophists have seen

their numbers decline. Overall these changes represent an increase in membership of just over 320,000 over this five-year period. This compares with a decline in membership of some 282,000 in Table 8.4, and suggests that the total membership of religious organizations has increased.

Interpreting the evidence on participation and membership

Most of the long-term evidence on membership and attendance seems to support the secularization theory. Although recent years have seen a growth in smaller religious organizations, compared to the nineteenth century and early decades of the twentieth century there is little doubt that fewer people attend a place of worship or belong to a religious organization. However, this evidence offers far from conclusive support for the secularization thesis. As Grace Davie says, 'Religious statistics are notoriously hard to handle.'

Table 8.4 Non-Trinitarian Churches, members and congregations, 1985 and 1990

	Members						Congregations					
	1985	1990					1985	1990				
	UK	UK	England	Wales	Scotland	N Ireland	UK	UK	England	Wales	Scotland	N Ireland
Children of God[1][15]	500	500	500	–	–	–	20	20	20	–	–	–
Christadelphians[2]	20,000[1]	20,000[1]	17,800	1,150	900	70	330	320[1]	278	23	18	1
Christian Community	1,000	1,000[1]	1,000[1]	–	–	–	9	9[1]	9	–	–	–
Church of Christ, Scientist	13,500[1]	11,000	10,1000	200	500	200	238	225[1]	207	5	10	3
Jehovah's Witnesses[2]	97,945[1]	116,612	99,812	6,800	7,400	2,600	1,167	1,318	1,128	77	84	29
Church of Jesus Christ of Latter-Day Saints (Mormons)	132,810	149,000[1]	115,000	7,500	19,000	7,500	353[6]	400[1]	310	20	50	20
New Church	1,805	1,712	1,597	15	100	–	40	36	34	1	1	–
Church of Scientology[16]	50,000[1]	75,000	68,000	1,000	5,000	1,000	10[4]	13	11	0	1	1
Spiritualists[7][8]	48,837[3]	55,000[3]	34,800	9,000	9,700	1,500	563[1]	550[1]	505	24	16	5
Theosophists[10]	4,923[1]	4,700	4,650[11]	–	–	50[1]	58[4]	56	55	–	–	1
Unification Church (Moonies)[2][14]	350[13]	350[1][13]	300	20	30	–	30	30[1]	26[1]	1[1]	3[1]	–
Unitarian and Free Christian Churches	10,000	10,000	7,300[1]	1,100[1]	200[1]	1,400[1]	248	250	182[1]	30[1]	4[1]	34[1]
The Way	500	600[1]	480	40	55	25	35	45	36	3	4	2
Worldwide Church of God	2,460	3,440	2,750	120	280	290	41	41	31	2	5	3
Others[1]	10,000	10,000	7,500	1,000	1,000	500	100	100	75	10	10	5
Total 1990	–	458,914	371,669	27,945	44,165	15,135	–	3,413	2,907	196	206	104
Total 1985	394,630	–	317,099	25,223	40,485	11,823	3,242	–	2,771	184	196	91
Percentage Change	–	+16%	+17%	+11%	+9%	+28%	–	+5%	+5%	+7%	+5%	+14%

1 Estimate
2 Country estimates pro rata to number of congregations in 1985
3 Practitioners
4 Revised figure
5 Full-time
6 Of which 243 are actual church buildings
7 A summation of figures of three different groups
8 Country estimates pro rata to Greater World Christian Spiritualist Association
9 Including 910 direct members of the Greater World Christian Spiritualist Association, but with congregations of 12,000 for the Association alone
10 A summation of figures of four different groups
11 Including 1,600 members of the Theosophical Society in England
12 Non-ordained national leaders
13 Full-time "core" members; excludes an estaimed 8,000 associate members and 100 "Practising" members
14 Membership numbers from *New Religious Movements*, by Dr Eileen Barker, HMSO 1989
15 Also called "Family of Love"
16 Handles the science of dianetics

(*Source*: Brierley, Peter and Longley, David (eds) (1991) *UK Christian Handbook, 1992/93 edition*, MARC Europe, London, p. 238.)

Both the reliability and validity of the statistics are open to question. Nineteenth-century church attendance figures pose special problems because the methods of data collection used do not meet today's standards of reliability. More recent figures may be hard to trust as well. Some commentators argue that attendance and membership figures may be distorted by the ulterior motives of those who produce them. Some churches, for example the Roman Catholic Church, may underestimate the numbers in their congregation in order to reduce the capitation fees they have to pay to central church authorities. Others, particularly Anglican churches, may overestimate the figures to produce impressive totals, particularly where there may be a risk of a church with a small congregation being closed down.

Membership figures can be calculated in different ways, and various churches, denominations and other religious groups use different criteria.

1 Members of the Roman Catholic Church and the Church of England are normally taken to be those who have been both baptized and confirmed. The numbers may therefore include people who, although officially members, have taken no part in church life since their confirmation.

Table 8.5   Other Religions, active members and groups, 1985 and 1990

	Active members						Buildings/Groups					
	1985	1990					1985	1990				
	UK	UK	England	Wales	Scotland	N Ireland	UK	UK	England	Wales	Scotland	N Ireland
Ahmadiyya Movement	7,500[6]	7,700	7,000	300	300	100	37[6]	38	30	3	3	2
Buddhists[2, 7, 12]	23,000	27,500	24,000	2,500	1,000	—	86	105	85	12	8	—
Hindus[1, 7]	130,000	140,000	118,000	6,000	10,000	6,000	130	140	135	1	3	1
International Society for Krishna Consciousness[11]	40,000	50,000	46,000	500	2,000	1,500	3[6]	15	11	1	1	2
Jews[3, 4, 7]	109,150[1]	108,400[1]	103,000	800	4,200	400	330[1]	330[1]	314	2	13	1
Muslims[5]	852,900	990,000	930,000	16,500	42,000	1,500	926[6]	1,020	970	30	16	4
Satanists[1]	150[6,13]	180[13]	160[1]	5[1]	10[1]	5[1]	33	35[1]	30[1]	2[1]	2[1]	1[1]
School of Meditation	6,000	7,000	6,650	100[8]	200[8]	50[8]	2	2	2	—	—	—
Sikhs	320,000[8]	390,000[9]	300,000	20,000	60,000	10,000	125[6]	149	142	2	5	0
Others[10]	112,250	137,250	110,400	10,550	11,000	5,300	139	169	144	10[1]	10[1]	5[1]
Total 1990	—	1,858,030	1,645,210	57,255	130,710	24,855	—	2,003	1,863	63	61	16
Total 1985	1,600,950	—	1,436,668	46,936	101,389	15,956	1,811	—	1,681	60	54	16
Percentage Change	—	+16%	+15%	+22%	+29%	+56%	—	+12%	+11%	+5%	+13%	0%

1 Estimate
2 Figures based on surveys of all Buddhist groups in 1975, 1980 and 1985
3 Heads of households, male and female, affiliated to synagogues
4 These figures are about one-third of the Jewish Community
5 Including non-South Asians
6 Revised figure
7 Country estimates pro rata to 1985 figures
8 Estimates pro rata to national population
9 Total community is about half a million people
10 These include the Aetherius Society, Ananda Marga, Elan Vital, Emissaries of Divine Light, Insight, Neo-Pagans, TOPY and Yoga (Raja, Sahaja and Eckankar) which are mentioned along with others in Dr Eileen Barker's *New Religious Movements*, HMSO 1989
11 The "Hare Krishna" movement
12 Including Western Buddhist Order and Nichiren Shoshu (Soka Gakkai) Buddhists
13 Active members taken as one per cent of community

(*Source*: Brierley, Peter and Longley, David (eds) (1991) *UK Christian Handbook, 1992/93 edition*, MARC Europe, London, p. 239.)

2 The Church of Wales, on the other hand, bases its figures on those attending Easter Communion.

3 Figures giving the numbers who are held to be members of the Jewish religion simply document the number of Jewish heads of household, regardless of how often or whether they attend a synagogue.

Because of these variations figures on church membership are highly unreliable, and the trends indicated by the figures may be misleading.

Statistics on participation in religious institutions provide only one type of indicator of the religious commitment of individuals and may be only tenuously linked to the strength of religious beliefs. Those, like Bryan Wilson, who see such figures as a measure of secularization are influenced by the traditional view that a religious person is one who goes to church. As Peter Glasner argues, 'These studies have in common the identification of religion with "church-orientated" religion.'

The decline in church attendance can be interpreted in a number of ways.

1 David Martin claims that the relatively high attendances in Victorian Britain may have been influenced by non-religious factors. He believes that in the nineteenth century church-going was a sign of middle-class respectability to a greater extent than it is today. Many Victorians may have attended church to be seen, rather than to express deep religious convictions.

2 Robert N. Bellah argues that a decline in institutional religion cannot be taken as indicating a decline in religious belief and commitment. Religion today may be expressed in different ways. Bellah suggests that there has been a move from collective worship to privatized worship, and from clerical to individual interpretations of doctrine. He claims that 'the assumption in most of the major Protestant denominations is that the church member can be responsible for himself.'

3 It is also possible that many individuals who hold religious beliefs, and whose behaviour is also partly directed by such beliefs, are not formally registered as church members.

We will now examine some evidence relating to religious belief and activity outside the context of religious organizations.

Belief, churchgoing and atheism

Opinion poll evidence is perhaps the simplest type of data relating to religious beliefs. However, there are a variety of questions that can and have been asked about religious beliefs, and the questions asked determine the impression given by the data.

For example, in the early 1980s the European Values Systems Study Group found that 76 per cent of the British population believed in God, 58 per cent defined themselves as a religious person, 50 per cent said God was important in their life, 45 per cent believed in life after death, and only 19 per cent had had a spiritual experience. These sorts of data suggest that the majority of the population retain religious beliefs, even if only a minority attend religious ceremonies with any regularity, and the continuing strength of religious belief could be used as evidence against secularization.

However, the data can also be used to support the secularization theory. Grace Davie notes that opinion poll data indicates that younger generations are less religious than older ones. She says 'Not only have young people left our churches, they are, it seems, rejecting even nominal belief.' If they continue to reject religion as they get older, this could be seen as offering strong support for the secularization thesis.

Peter Brierley has used data from the 1989 English Church Census and elsewhere to estimate the percentages of the population who are Christian and non-Christian. He has also divided Christians up into **churchgoers**, **nominal Christians** (church members who do not attend regularly), and **notional Christians** (those who say they are Christian but who are neither church members nor attenders). Non-Christians are divided into the secular and those who hold non-Christian religious beliefs. Figure 8.2 shows Brierley's estimates with the figures for 1980 shown in brackets.

As Brierley says 'The diagram shows that change in the British religious scene is relatively slow – a percentage point or two over a decade.' There is some evidence that the population is

moving away from participation in institutional Christian religion but retaining religious beliefs. There is some evidence of an increase in atheism and agnosticism, but the change is slight. (We will examine the data relating to religion in the USA later, see p. 486.)

■ Institutional religion – disengagement and differentiation

Disengagement

Some researchers, as we have just noted, have seen the truly religious society in terms of full churches. They have therefore seen empty churches as evidence of secularization. Others have seen the truly religious society as one in which the church as an institution is directly involved in every important area of social life. In terms of this emphasis, a **disengagement** or withdrawing of the church from the wider society is seen as secularization. David Martin states that this view is concerned with 'the ecclesiastical institution, and specifically with any decline in its power, wealth, influence, range of control and prestige'.

Compared to its role in Medieval Europe, the church in contemporary Western society has undergone a process of disengagement. In the Middle Ages, there was a union of church and state. Today, apart from the right of bishops to sit in the British House of Lords, the church is hardly represented in government. Bryan Wilson, writing in 1977, believed there had been a sharp decline in the political role of the church in Britain. He said:

A Prime Minister's correspondence 80 years ago dealt seriously with archiepiscopal opinion; 40 years ago the Bishops had a significant voice in the abdication crisis; today we have even seen the occasion when the Prime Minister was 'too busy' to see the Archbishop of Canterbury.

Ecclesiastical control of education and social welfare has been superseded by secular organizations under state control. Church patronage of the arts was reflected by the fact that most art in the

Figure 8.2   Religious structure of population in Great Britain 1990 (figures in brackets give 1980 percentages)

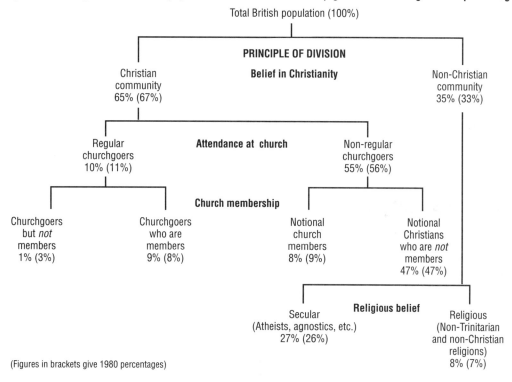

(Figures in brackets give 1980 percentages)

(*Source*: Brierley, Peter (1991) *'Christian' England*, MARC Europe, p. 203.)

Middle Ages was based on religious themes. Today secular themes predominate.

Bryan Wilson argues that the Church of England today provides little more than traditional ritual to dramatize important turning points in the life cycle: namely, birth, marriage and death. He sees its disengagement from the wider society as evidence of secularization.

However, the power of the church in the Middle Ages need not necessarily be seen as a golden age of religion. As David Martin suggests, 'the height of ecclesiastical power can be seen either as the triumph of the religious or its more blasphemous secularization.' Thus today, the church's specialization in specifically religious matters may indicate a purer form of religion, untainted by involvement with secular concerns such as politics. Martin also suggests that there has been a shift in the focus of religion away from 'the institutions of the state and the economy' towards 'the needs and sentiments of people'.

Structural differentiation

An alternative to the view that disengagement equals secularization is provided by Talcott Parsons. Parsons agrees that the church as an institution has lost many of its former functions. He argues that the evolution of society involves a process of **structural differentiation**: various parts of the social system become more specialized and so perform fewer functions. (This idea forms part of Parsons's theory of social evolution, outlined in Chapter 14, pp. 871–4.)

However, the differentiation of the units of the social system does not necessarily lessen their importance. As we saw in a previous section, Parsons argues that religious beliefs still give meaning and significance to life. Churches are still the fount of religious ethics and values.

As religious institutions become increasingly specialized, Parsons maintains that their ethics and values become increasingly generalized. In American society, for instance, they have become the basis for more general social values. Thus many of the values of American society are at once Christian and American. This has resulted in the 'endowment of secular life with a new order of religious legitimation'. From this perspective, disengagement, or in Parsons's terminology, structural differentiation, does not equal secularization.

To some degree this interpretation rests on Parsons's belief that Christian values direct behaviour in American society. Many critics of the American way of life would disagree with this view.

■ Institutional religion – religious pluralism

Some researchers imply that the truly religious society has one faith and one church. This picture is influenced by the situation in some small-scale, non-literate societies, such as the Australian aborigines, where the community is a religious community. Members share a common faith and at certain times of the year the entire community gathers to express this faith in religious rituals. In terms of Durkheim's view of religion, the community is the church. Medieval European societies provided a similar picture: there the established church ministered to the whole society.

Steve Bruce argues that religious pluralism results from a variety of sources all of which have 'undermined the communal base to religious orthodoxy'. England expanded to incorporate Scotland and Ireland which had different religious traditions while migration has led to a plurality of religious groups in both North America and Europe. Industrialization reduced the contact between social classes and helped create new, predominantly working-class versions of Christianity such as Methodism. Modernization and industrialization bring with them the **social fragmentation** of society into a plurality of cultural and religious groups. The consequence is that the state can no longer support a single religion without causing conflict. The **plurality of religions** reminds individuals that their beliefs are a personal preference, a matter of choice, and no longer part and parcel of their membership of society.

Wade Roof and William McKinney have reached broadly similar conclusions about the development of religion in the USA. They quote figures, shown in Table 8.6, which show Protes-

Table 8.6　Trends in Religious Preference in the USA, 1952–1985

	1985	1952	Percentage change
Protestant	57	67	− 15
Catholic	28	25	+ 12
Jewish	2	4	− 50
Other	4	1	+ 300
None	9	2	+ 350

(*Source*: Princeton Religion Research Center (February 1986), *Emerging Trends*, vol. 8, no. 2 quoted in Roof, W.C. and McKinney, W. (1987) *American Mainline Religion*, Rutgers University Press, New Brunswick, p. 16.)

tantism declining and an increase in the percentage of the population with no religious preference or who believe in religions other than Protestantism, Catholicism or Judaism. Roof and McKinney quote a 1976 Gallup Survey which showed 4 per cent of the American population said they had been involved in TM, 3 per cent in yoga, 2 per cent in mysticism and 1 per cent claimed involvement in Eastern religions. Like Wilson they argue that religious pluralism has meant that religion 'has lost force as an integrative influence'. Similarly to Bruce, they believe that religious pluralism has created a 'new voluntarism', where religious beliefs become a matter of choice for the individual. They also refer to a 1978 Gallup Poll in the USA in which 81 per cent of those questioned agreed with the statement 'An individual should arrive at his or her own religious beliefs independent of any churches or synagogues.'

Pluralism and social solidarity

Bryan Wilson argues that if there are a number of denominations in society, each with its own version of the 'truth', they can at best only reflect and legitimate the beliefs of a section of the population. In this way, 'religious values cease now to be community values.' Religion no longer expresses and reinforces the values of society as a whole and so ceases to perform its traditional function of promoting social solidarity.

Berger and Luckmann make a similar point. Instead of one religious institution with a single, unchallenged view of the supernatural, there are now many with divergent views. Berger and Luckmann argue that the emergence of denominations weakens the influence of religion. No longer is a single universe of meaning provided for all members of society.

The ecumenical movement

During the past 30 years, there has been a movement towards the unity of Christian churches and denominations known as the **ecumenical movement**. This may reverse the trend towards religious pluralism. Wilson however, interprets the ecumenical movement as further evidence of secularization. He argues that 'Organizations amalgamate when they are weak rather than when they are strong, since alliance means compromise and amendments of commitment.' He believes that ecumenism represents a declining Christianity grasping at straws. Though it has caught the imagination of some churchpeople, Wilson argues that the ecumenical movement has aroused little general interest and produced few positive results.

Sects, cults and secularization

The continuing proliferation of sects has been interpreted by some researchers in much the same way as the spread of denominations. It has been seen as a further fragmentation of institutional religion and therefore as evidence of the weakening hold of religion over society.

Accurate measurements of the numbers of sects and the size of their memberships are not available. Although Roy Wallis believes there has been a decline in new religious movements since the late 1970s, some of the older established sects in Britain have grown. Jehovah's Witnesses's membership rose from 62,000 in 1970 to 116,000 in 1990. There are certainly more sects today, though, than there were before the Second World War.

Stark and Bainbridge have shown that the 1960s had the highest rate of cult formation in the USA. Some 23 per cent of the cults they uncovered were formed between 1970 and 1977, 38 per cent in the 1960s, 14 per cent in the 1950s, and the remaining 25 per cent before 1950.

Despite contradictions in the evidence, the apparent vitality of sects seems to provide evidence against the secularization theory. World-

rejecting sects are perhaps the most religious type of organization, since they demand greater commitment to the religion than other organizations. If they are stronger than in the past, it suggests that religion retains a considerable appeal for the populations of advanced industrial societies. Andrew Greeley believes that the growth of new religious movements represents a process of **resacrilization**: interest in, and belief in, the sacred is being revived. Societies such as Britain and the USA are, if anything, becoming less secular.

Rodney Stark and William S. Bainbridge also deny that secularization has taken place. They believe that some established churches may have lost part of their emphasis on the supernatural, but secularization never proceeds far because new religious groups with more emphasis on the supernatural constantly emerge. They put forward statistical evidence to support this claim. According to their figures on religious activity in different states of the USA, cults thrive where conventional religions are weak. For example, in California relatively few people are churchgoers but many believe in supernatural phenomena. (For further details of Stark and Bainbridge's theory of religion see pp. 454–6 and pp. 471–3.)

Nevertheless other sociologists see the growth of sects as evidence of secularization. Peter Berger argues that belief in the supernatural can only survive in a sectarian form in a secular society. In order to maintain a strong religious belief and commitment, individuals must cut themselves off from the secularizing influences of the wider society, and seek out the support of others of like mind. The sect, with its close-knit community organization, provides a context where this is possible. From this viewpoint, the sect is the last refuge of the supernatural in a secular society. Sects are therefore evidence of secularization.

Bryan Wilson takes a similar view maintaining that sects are 'a feature of societies experiencing secularization, and they may be seen as a response to a situation in which religious values have lost social pre-eminence'. In other words, sects are the last outpost of religion in societies where religious beliefs and values have little consequence.

Bryan Wilson is particularly scathing in his dismissal of the religious movements of the young in the West, such as Krishna Consciousness which emerged during the 1960s in the USA. He regards them as 'almost irrelevant' to society as a whole claiming that 'They add nothing to any prospective reintegration of society, and contribute nothing towards the culture by which a society might live.' By comparison, Methodism, in its early days as a sect, provided standards and values for the new urban working class, which helped to integrate its members within the wider society. In addition, its beliefs 'steadily diffused through a much wider body of the population'.

In contrast he feels that the new religious movements show no such promise. Their members live in their own enclosed, encapsulated little worlds. There they emphasize 'hedonism, the validity of present pleasure, the abandonment of restraint and the ethic of "do your own thing"'. Wilson is scornful of their 'exotic novelty' which he believes offers little more than self-indulgence, titillation and short-lived thrills. He believes that movements which seek for truth in Asian religions and emphasize the exploration of the inner self, for example Krishna Consciousness, can give little to Western society. They simply 'offer another way of life for the self-selected few rather than an alternative culture for mankind'. Rather than contributing to a new moral reintegration of society, they simply provide a religious setting for 'dropouts'. They do not halt the continuing process of secularization and are 'likely to be no more than transient and volatile gestures of defiance' in the face of a secular society.

Similar conclusions are reached by Roy Wallis. According to Wallis, 'new religious movements involve only a very small proportion of the population . . . and even then often for only very brief periods during the transition to adulthood.' For those who join world-affirming movements the motives for joining are largely secular anyway: they wish to get on in the world rather than pursue other-worldly concerns. Wallis claims that for most of the population new religious movements are 'a matter of profound indifference'.

■ Institutional religion – the secularization of religious institutions in the USA

Will Herberg – denominations and internal secularization

We can therefore return to the quotation from Charles Glock and Rodney Stark which we considered earlier, 'Perhaps the most important

attribute of those who perceive secularization to be going on is their commitment to a particular view of what religion means.' The relevance of this remark will already be apparent. It is particularly true of Will Herberg, a long-time observer of religion in the USA. To Herberg, **authentic religion** means:

1 an emphasis on the supernatural;

2 a deep inner conviction of the reality of supernatural power;

3 a serious commitment to religious teachings;

4 a strong element of theological doctrine;

5 a refusal to compromise religious beliefs and values with those of the wider society.

This is just what Herberg does not find in the established denominations in America. He claims that 'Denominational pluralism, on the American plan, means thorough-going secularization.' The major denominations have increasingly emphasized this world as opposed to the other world; they have moved away from traditional doctrine and concern with the supernatural; they have compromised their religious beliefs to fit in with the wider society. Because of this, they have become more like the secular society in which they are set.

Compared to Western Europe, membership and attendance of religious institutions in the USA is high. The *Yearbook of American Churches* states that from 1940 to 1957, their membership rose from 49 per cent of the population to 61 per cent, while average weekly attendance rose from 37 per cent to 40 per cent. Though there was a slight decline in attendance during the 1960s and early 1970s, average weekly attendance still involves 40 per cent of the population or more. According to survey data published in 1987 by Wade Roof and William McKinney, 46 per cent of the American population attended church nearly every week or more often, and a further 21 per cent were occasional attenders. Their data also showed that only 6.9 per cent of Americans claimed no religious preference.

Such figures seem to suggest that even if secularization has affected Europe, it has not taken place in the USA. However, writing in 1960 Herberg interpreted the evidence differently. Despite this relatively high level of participation in religious institutions, Herberg argues that it is directed by secular rather than religious concerns. In *Protestant – Catholic – Jew: An Essay in American*

Religious Sociology, he presents the following arguments.

1 Herberg sees a need for Americans to identify with a social group. This is particularly apparent with the third generation of the major wave of immigrants to the USA. Rather than identifying with their ethnic groups, members of this generation now 'identify and locate themselves socially in terms of one of the three great subcommunities – Protestant, Catholic, Jewish – defined in religious terms'. This generation regards itself as American first and foremost (rather than Irish, Polish, German, Swedish, etc.) and church membership and attendance is a symbol and expression of this identification. It is a way of announcing that a person is a complete American. In Herberg's words, 'Not to be – that is not to identify oneself and be identified as – either a Protestant, a Catholic, or a Jew is somehow not to be an American.'

2 Herberg believes that American society is becoming increasingly 'other-directed'. The **other-directed** person is concerned with fitting in, conforming, being popular and sociable, whereas the **inner-directed** person is concerned with achievement and is less influenced and directed by the opinions that others may have of him or her. The other-directed person wants, above all, to be accepted by, and feel he or she belongs to, a social group. Herberg sees church membership as a means to this sense of belonging. He writes 'Being religious and joining a church is, under contemporary American conditions, a fundamental way of "adjusting" and "belonging".' The church provides the sociable, secure and conforming environment that 'other-directedness' requires. Religion has become 'a way of sociability or "belonging" rather than a way of reorienting life to God. It is thus frequently a religiousness without serious commitment, without real inner conviction.'

3 Herberg argues that religion in America is subordinated to the **American Way of Life**, to the central values and beliefs of American culture. The American Way of Life 'embraces such seemingly incongruous elements as sanitary plumbing and freedom of opportunity, Coca Cola and an intense faith in education'. It includes a commitment to democracy and free-enterprise.

Christianity and Judaism have been shaped by the American Way of Life, they have become 'Americanized'. The late President Eisenhower once said 'Our government makes no sense unless it is founded on a deeply held religious faith – and I don't care what it is.' The particular denomination is not important because they all support and sanctify the American Way of Life. There is relatively little emphasis on theology and doctrine, rather 'ethical behaviour and a good life' are stressed. The 'good life' is based on the central values of American society rather than the word of God. Sermons in American churches often echo the vast American literature on success and motivation, which reflects the high value placed on achievement in American society. Thus the Revd. Irving E. Howard writes in the magazine *Christian Economics*, 'Jesus recommends faith as a technique for getting results.'

4 Herberg claims that the major denominations in America have undergone a process of secularization. They increasingly reflect the American Way of Life rather than the word of God. For the typical churchgoer, religion is 'something that reassures him about the essential rightness of everything American, his nature, his culture and himself'. But from Herberg's viewpoint, this has little to do with the real meaning of religion.

Changes in American religion

Herberg's views on religion in the USA have been challenged on a number of grounds. Roof and McKinney accepted that Herberg's analysis had much merit when it was written in the 1950s but they argued that 'it failed to ring true in the America of the 1980s'.

1 The belief in the American Way of Life has been increasingly challenged since the 1960s. Events such as the assassination of President Kennedy, the war in Vietnam (which was unpopular with many Americans), and the struggle for civil rights which exposed injustice in American society, led in some quarters to increasing criticism of American culture. In these circumstances it became more difficult for religion to act in the way suggested by Herberg as the consensus on moral values in the USA no longer existed.

2 Individuals no longer felt such a strong need to identify with one of the major religious groupings of Protestant, Catholic and Jew. As we saw earlier (see p. 486) Clark and McKinney argue that the American religious scene is increasingly characterized by pluralism.

3 Not all religious groupings seem to have turned their back on what Herberg would see as authentic religion. Like other commentators, Clark and McKinney have noted the growth of conservative Protestant religions (sometimes called the **New Christian Right**) which seem to combine a serious commitment to religious teachings, a strong element of theological doctrine and a refusal to compromise religious beliefs. As such, they seem to directly contradict Herberg's claims about secularization within religious institutions.

Institutional religion – the New Christian Right

Wade and McKinney categorize the following religious groups in America as being Conservative Christians: Southern Baptists, Churches of Christ, Evangelicals/ Fundamentalists, Nazarenes, Pentecostalists/Holiness, Assemblies of God, Churches of God and Adventists. Using survey data they estimated that conservative Protestants made up 15.8 per cent of the American population in 1984. Their evidence suggests that these groups have been growing since the 1920s. In 1967 the Southern Baptist Convention overtook Methodists as the largest Protestant denomination. Roof and McKinney quote a 1976 Gallup Poll which found that 34 per cent of the population said they had been 'born again'.

Roof and McKinney's data also show that conservative Protestants are more likely than any other religious group in the USA to attend church and believe in God. They have rejected any move towards liberal values and instead have strongly supported traditional morality. Conservative Protestants have been strong opponents of abortion, extramarital or premarital sex, homosexuality and the relaxation of divorce laws. They have supported literal interpretations of the *Bible*, campaigning against the teaching of evolutionary biology on the grounds that it contradicted the biblical account of God's creation of the earth.

A number of sociologists have noted the many ways in which conservative Protestants have succeeded in publicizing and promoting their views in the USA. According to James Davison Hunter, by the early 1980s they had set up 450 colleges and 18,000 schools, established 275 periodicals, 70 evangelical publishing houses and 3,300 Christian bookshops. They had also started 65 television stations and intervened in numerous political campaigns.

Hunter does not claim that the growth of conservative Protestantism disproves the secularization thesis, but he does believe that it challenges it. He says:

Secularization may yet prove to be the ultimate design for contemporary society, but that is unlikely. Minimally, one can say that it is not a straight-line occurrence, as is often assumed; cycles of secularity and religious upsurge are evident.

The limited impact of conservative Protestantism

A different view is taken by Steve Bruce who argues that the New Christian Right has had very little impact. Very few of its members who stood for national office won their elections. No more than five senators supported the New Christian Right and they failed to get any new Federal legislation passed. Opinion polls showed no shift towards their views on moral issues. In Bruce's view they achieved no more than to 'remind cosmopolitan American that fundamentalists were not extinct and still had some rights'.

If Bruce is to be believed, the New Christian Right may have slowed down the process of secularization within its own religious institutions, but it has failed to do any more than that. Indeed he believes that the only reason the New Christian Right gets so much attention is that its members are unusual for holding strong religious convictions in a largely secular world.

Internal secularization in Britain

Less attention has been devoted to the possibility that British churches and denominations have undergone secularization. However, Steve Bruce does believe that British mainstream churches have abandoned, or at least watered down, a number of their religious convictions. These include beliefs in the virgin birth, Christ's bodily resurrection (the former Bishop of Durham, David Jenkins, called it a 'conjuring trick with a bag of bones'), heaven and hell, and the expectation that Christ would return to earth. Bruce also points out that most British Christian churches have ceased to claim a monopoly of the religious truth.

In the previous sections we have examined approaches to secularization largely in terms of institutional religion. Our focus now changes to a more general view of the role of religion in Western society and is concerned with the influence of religious beliefs and values on social norms and values, social action and consciousness. As in previous sections, assessments of the importance of religion depend largely on the observer's interpretation of what constitutes a 'religious society' and religiously motivated action. We will consider four main views of the changing role of religion in Western industrial society. They can be classified under the headings of 'generalization', 'individuation', 'transformation' and 'desacrilization'.

Religion and society – generalization

As we noted in a previous section, Talcott Parsons argues that as religious institutions become more specialized, religious values become increasingly **generalized**. He begins from the judgement that American society is a highly moral society and this morality is based ultimately on Christian values. Although social values are no longer recognized as distinctly religious values, they are grounded on Christian principles. Religious beliefs no longer specifically direct particular actions. However, since they are incorporated within society's value system, they provide general guidelines for conduct. In this sense, they have become generalized.

The practice of medicine provides an example. In many small-scale, non-literate societies religion and medicine went hand in hand in the person of the *shaman*. As both a religious leader and a curer, the *shaman* combined 'practical' medicine with religious ritual to cure the sick. Today the curing of illness is no longer surrounded by religious ritual: hospitals are secular institutions, yet the practice of medicine is based on the Christian value that the community has a duty to care for and cure the sick. This general directive has replaced the specific religious rituals which surrounded the cure of illness.

In this way Parsons argues that religious beliefs and values have become generalized. They form the basis of social values and so provide general guidelines for action.

David Martin applies a similar argument to British society. He maintains that Christian values are an integral part of social values. For example, they provide 'a check in terms of divine limits set to any form of power whatsoever; they are absolutely fundamental in British society in a manner scarcely paralleled elsewhere'. Unfortunately, Martin does not develop this statement and

his analysis remains at a rather vague and abstract level.

As with Martin's statement, the main problem with the generalization thesis is its vagueness. Neither Parsons nor Martin provide much evidence to support their views. Beginning with the assumption that the USA and Britain are basically Christian societies, it is possible to see Christian values directing many aspects of social life. However, it is just as possible to argue that social values have a secular foundation.

Religion and society – individuation

Robert N. Bellah states that 'The analysis of modern man as secular, materialistic, dehumanized and in the deepest sense areligious seems to me fundamentally misguided.' Bellah argues that sociologists who judge the significance of religion in terms of religious institutions are mistaken. He maintains that 'Now less than ever can man's search for meaning be confined to the church.' Religion is increasingly an individual quest for meaning rather than a collective act of worship.

In this way religion has undergone a process of **individuation** whereby individuals work out their own salvation and follow their own path to 'ultimate meaning'. The importance of religion has not declined – rather its form of expression has changed.

Bellah claims that in contemporary Western society, there is an:

> increasing acceptance of the notion that the individual must work out his own ultimate solutions and that the most the church can do is provide him with a favourable environment for doing so, without imposing on him a prefabricated set of answers.

No longer is religious doctrine imposed. People today have greater freedom than ever before to search for and construct their own ultimate meanings.

Bellah's arguments are based in part on his view of religion which he defines as 'a set of symbolic forms and acts which relate man to the ultimate conditions of his existence'. This definition contains no mention of the supernatural. It simply suggests that any search for ultimate meaning, for answers to questions concerning the meaning and purpose of life, is basically a religious quest.

Many researchers would argue that Bellah has stretched the concept of religion too far. In addition, Bellah fails to provide detailed evidence to show that the search for ultimate meaning is widespread in contemporary Western society.

◼ Religion and society – transformation

Rather than seeing religious beliefs as either generalized or individuated, a number of sociologists argue that they have become **transformed** into 'secular guides to action' in Western society. Though many of society's values have religious origins, their connection with religion has been severed.

The most famous statement of this position is made by Max Weber. He sees the origin of the spirit of capitalism in ascetic Protestantism. However, even by the eighteenth century, particularly in the USA, the 'pursuit of wealth' had been 'stripped of its religious and ethical meaning'.

Weber believed that ascetic Protestantism contained the seeds of its own destruction. It encouraged involvement and success in this world and its strict disciplines provided a rational outlook on life yet once its teachings were incorporated into a rational capitalist system, religious direction and validation were rapidly eroded.

Two factors were instrumental in transforming ascetic Protestantism into secular guides to action.

1 The first is the 'secularizing influence of wealth'. Wealth provides its own rewards and satisfactions and gradually they alone provided sufficient motivation for the continued accumulation of wealth. As a result, Weber believed that 'material goods have gained an increasing and finally an inexorable power over the lives of men as at no previous period of history'.

2 The second factor involves the mechanization of production in industrial society. Religious motivation provided the initial drive to work hard and accumulate wealth. Mechanized production technology, rather than people, provides the basic driving force of industrial society and technology does not require religious motivation. The 'spirit of religious asceticism' is no longer necessary because 'victorious capitalism, since it rests on mechanical foundations, needs its support no longer'. Industrial society has developed its own driving force, its own impetus.

As outlined earlier in the chapter, there is considerable controversy over Weber's interpretation of the relationship between ascetic Protestantism and capitalism. It is debatable whether or not the guides to action in modern society had their origin in religious beliefs.

Even if Weber's interpretation is accepted, it is still not clear whether the beliefs of ascetic Protestantism have been transformed or generalized. It could be argued that the Protestant Ethic which sees hard work as a virtue and a moral duty still survives as a general guide to action. Although evidence presented in Chapter 4 suggests that this is not the case, it does not disprove the possibility of generalization. (See pp. 193–4 for evidence which suggests that work in Western society is increasingly seen in instrumental terms and pp. 264–5 for evidence which suggests that leisure values are replacing the work ethic.)

◼ Religion and society – desacrilization

A number of sociologists have argued that the sacred has little or no place in contemporary Western society, that society has undergone a process of **desacrilization**. This means that supernatural forces are no longer seen as controlling the world, action is no longer directed by religious belief and human consciousness has become secularized.

Disenchantment

Weber's interpretation of industrial society provides one of the earliest statements of the desacrilization thesis. He claimed that industrial society is 'characterized by rationalization and intellectualization and, above all, by the "**disenchantment** of the world"'. The world is no longer charged with mystery and magic; the supernatural has been banished from society. The meanings and motives which direct action are now rational.

Weber's concept of rational action and his view that industrial society is undergoing a process of rationalization have been examined in detail in Chapter 5 (pp. 271–3). Briefly, **rational action** involves a deliberate and precise calculation of the importance of alternative goals and the effectiveness of the various means for attaining chosen goals.

For example, if an individual's goal is to make money, he or she will coldly and carefully calculate the necessary initial investment and the costs involved in producing and marketing a commodity in the most economical way possible. His or her measurements will be **objective**: they will be based on factors which can be quantified and accurately measured. He or she will reject the means to reach that goal which cannot be proven to be effective.

Rational action rejects the guidelines provided by emotion, by tradition or by religion. It is based on the cold, deliberate reason of the intellect which demands that the rationale for action can only be based on the proven results.

Science and reason

A number of sociologists have accepted Weber's interpretation of the basis for action in industrial society. In *Religion in a Secular Society*, Bryan Wilson states that:

Religious *thinking* is perhaps the area which evidences most conspicuous change. Men act less and less in response to religious motivation: they assess the world in empirical and rational terms.

Wilson argues that the following factors encouraged the development of rational thinking and a rational world view.

1 Ascetic Protestantism, which 'created an ethic which was pragmatic, rational, controlled and anti-emotional'.

2 The rational organization of society which results in people's 'sustained involvement in rational organizations – firms, public service, educational institutions, government, the state – which impose rational behaviour upon them'.

3 A greater knowledge of the social and physical world which results from the development of the physical, biological and social sciences. Wilson maintains that this knowledge is based on reason rather than faith. He claims that:

Science not only explained many facets of life and the material environment in a way more satisfactory (than religion), but it also provided confirmation of its explanation in practical results.

4 The development of rational ideologies and organizations to solve social problems. Ideologies such

as communism and organizations such as trade unions offer practical solutions to problems. By comparison, religious solutions such as the promise of justice and reward in the afterlife, do not produce practical and observable results.

Wilson argues that a rational world view is the enemy of religion. It is based on the testing of arguments and beliefs by rational procedures, on assessing truth by means of factors which can be quantified and objectively measured. Religion is based on faith and as such is non-rational. Its claim to truth cannot be tested by rational procedures.

Peter Berger develops some of Weber's and Wilson's ideas within the framework of the sociology of knowledge. He maintains that people in Western society increasingly 'look upon the world and their own lives without the benefit of religious interpretations'. As a result there is a **secularization of consciousness**. Berger argues that the 'decisive variable for secularization' is 'the process of rationalization that is the prerequisite for any industrial society of the modern type'. A rational world view rejects faith which is the basis of religion. It removes the 'mystery, magic and authority' of religion.

Steve Bruce places more stress on the specific role of scientific beliefs themselves in undermining religion. He argues that technological advances reduce the number of things that need to be explained in religious terms. It has given individuals a greater sense of control over the natural world and less need to resort to supernatural explanations or remedies. He says:

We may still go to church to celebrate the successful conclusion of the harvest but we use chemical fertilisers and weed-killers rather than prayer to ensure a good crop. When all the conventional medical solutions have been exhausted, we may pray for the health of a loved one but only a very few small sects reject conventional medicine and trust instead to the Lord.

In this section we have considered the **desacrilization thesis**, that is the view that religion and the sacred have largely been removed from the meanings which guide action and interpret the world, and from the consciousness of humanity. This view is difficult to evaluate since it is largely based on the impressions of particular researchers rather than 'hard' data. In addition, it compares industrial society with often unspecified pre-industrial societies in which, presumably, religion provided a guide to action and a basis for meaning. We will deal with the problems involved in this approach in the following section.

Religion in pre-industrial societies

As we saw in the previous sections, the term 'secularization' has been used in many different ways. Whichever way it has been used though, the supporters of the theory of secularization have tended to take for granted that pre-industrial societies were highly religious. Some researchers have challenged this view.

Larry Shiner notes those who argue that the social significance of religion has declined have 'the problem of determining when and where we are to find the supposedly "religious" age from which decline has commenced'.

The anthropologist Mary Douglas argues that the use of supposedly 'religious', small-scale non-literate societies as a basis for comparison with modern 'secular' societies is unjustified. She states that:

The contrast of secular with religious has nothing whatever to do with the contrast of modern with traditional or primitive . . .The truth is that all varieties of scepticism, materialism and spiritual fervour are to be found in the range of tribal societies.

It is simply an illusion concocted by Westerners that 'all primitives are pious, credulous and subject to the teaching of priests or magicians'.

In the same way, the search for the golden age of religion in the European past may provide an equally shaky standard for comparison. From his study of religion in sixteenth- and seventeenth-century England, K.V. Thomas states:

We do not know enough about the religious beliefs and practices of our remote ancestors to be certain of the extent to which religious faith and practice have actually declined. (Quoted in Glasner 1977, p. 71.)

W.M. William's study of Gosforth, a village in Cumbria, indicates one of the traps into which some sociologists may have fallen. The parish records indicated a low level of church attendance for some 400 years, but each new Anglican vicar believed this to be a recent trend. The theory of secularization cannot therefore be adequately tested unless there is careful analysis of the importance of religion in the past.

Secularization – international comparisons

Most sociologists studying secularization have concentrated on making observations about, and researching into, particular modern industrial societies. They have, nevertheless, often assumed that secularization is a universal and perhaps inevitable process. Bryan Wilson claims, for example, 'Secularization, then, is a long term process occurring in human society.' However, even Wilson, a leading advocate of secularization, admits 'The actual patterns in which it is manifested are culturally and historically specific to each context.' The nature and extent of the changes in the role of religion in society may vary so much in different parts of the world that it is misleading to see secularization as a single process.

By concentrating on Britain and the USA, sociologists have had a rather narrow view of social change and religion. For instance, they have not accounted for the revival over recent years of Islamic fundamentalism in Iran and other countries. David Martin has taken a wider view than most sociologists by looking at the changing role of religion in a range of societies. Martin's research shows very different patterns of religious practice in various advanced industrial countries. In some cases it shows marked differences within single societies. Martin argues that the role and strength of religion in modern societies is determined by a number of factors.

1 The first important factors are the degree of religious pluralism and the dominant religion. Societies where the Roman Catholic Church claims a monopoly of the religious truth are usually very different to those where Protestantism and Catholicism both have a major foothold, or where there is a greater variety of denominations and churches.

2 The political system of a society and the relationship between church and state both have a significant impact on the importance of religion within that society.

3 The third major factor is the extent to which religion helps to provide a sense of national, regional or ethnic identity.

We will now study a number of examples which illustrate Martin's **general theory of secularization**.

Variations in religious participation

The level of participation in religion varies widely in Protestant societies. In the USA 40 per cent or more of the adult population attend church each Sunday, in England the figure is just over 10 per cent, while in Sweden it falls as low as 5 per cent. Martin explains these variations in the following way.

1 In the USA there is a high degree of religious pluralism and no official connection between church and state. There is also a plurality of immigrant groups of different ethnic origin. Religious participation is therefore not confined to higher status groups who can support a religion closely identified with the state. A plurality of religions flourish as ethnic minorities try to maintain their separate identities. While participation in religion is very high, religion does not play a vital role in the functioning of society. Social solidarity is cemented more by patriotism and by a belief in the American way of life than by shared religious beliefs.

2 In Britain there is an association between the Church of England and the state. However, there is also considerable religious pluralism. Protestant-dissenting denominations draw membership and support from lower social classes who may not be attracted to the established church. Attendance is quite low because of the association of church and state, but not as low as in Sweden where the church is virtually a department of state. In some parts of Britain, such as Wales and Scotland, attendances are higher than the average because of an association between religion and nationalism.

3 Sweden has the lowest attendance figures because of the dominance of a single church and its association with the state. As a result of this close association, and the lack of alternative religious organizations, church attendance is largely confined to higher social classes.

In all these societies then, religion retains some influence. Where a church retains important functions religious participation tends to be low, but it is much higher in societies where religion appears to have lost many of its functions.

In Roman Catholic countries such as France, Spain, Italy and Portugal, the church still has an important role in society. It influences government policy in areas such as education and laws relating to marriage, divorce, contraception and abortion. Attendances at church are high and, according to Martin, Catholic societies are generally less secular than Protestant ones. There is little religious pluralism and what divisions there are tend to be within the Roman Catholic Church rather than between different religious organizations.

However, such societies frequently have deep social divisions: often there is a strong, and predominantly lower class, atheist opposition to Catholicism. These divisions are reflected in such conflicts as the Spanish Civil War and the 1968 student protests in Paris, while France and Italy also have sizeable communist parties.

Other countries like The Netherlands, West Germany and Switzerland are split between a Protestant majority and a large Catholic minority in a ratio of approximately 60/40. In these countries the Roman Catholic minority tends to be among the less affluent, so the ruling elite and Catholicism are not closely connected. Participation in religion is high because it provides a sense of identity for the two main subcultures. Religion plays an important role in such areas of social life as education, where separate Protestant and Catholic schools may be retained.

Religion in the third world

Martin has also drawn attention to the contrasting fate of religions in different third world countries. In some Latin American countries the Roman Catholic Church remains a key institution in society, and Protestantism has made few converts. In countries such as Mexico and Argentina, Protestants make up only about 2 per cent of the population. In Brazil, on the other hand, about 20 per cent of the population have become Protestant and by 1985 there were more Protestant than Catholic ministers. Most ministers represent strongly religious versions of Protestantism such as Pentecostalism and Seventh Day Adventism. Martin argues that Pentecostalism attracts the small shopkeepers and craft workers who have moved to the cities and whose means of earning a living fit in well with a religion that emphasizes self-discipline and thrift.

In Islamic societies religious change also varies from country to country. In Tunisia and Egypt the state has become somewhat secular: Islamic beliefs do not have a great influence on political decisions. In Iran the Islamic revolution of 1979 took the country in the opposite direction with religious leaders gaining most of the political power. In other countries there is a continuing conflict between the religious and the secular. In the Sudan, for example, there are strong advocates of religious pluralism and tolerance, but there are others who wish to see an Islamic state established. In Turkey attitudes towards religion are ambivalent. Some see religion as a cause of 'backwardness'. Others see it as the vital foundation on which the moral values of the society rest.

The future of religion

Far from predicting the demise of religion, Martin argues that it is likely to increase in importance. If anything the future is likely to see the forces of secularization in retreat. Impetus towards secularization originated in northwestern Europe, and here the factors which undermined religion have disappeared.

1 First, religion is no longer so closely associated with rich and powerful elites in society. It has therefore become more acceptable to people from lower classes.

2 Second, rationalism has lost some of its appeal. There is increasing interest in the mystical, the supernatural and the religious.

Outside Europe many countries retain strong religious influences on society. From Martin's viewpoint, 'There is no inevitable tilt to history down which every society is sociologically fated to fall.' Secularization is not an automatic and universal process.

Steve Bruce agrees with Martin that there is no inevitability about religious decline, and he accepts that the pattern of religious change varies from society to society. On the other hand he does believe that 'The modern western world is not a

religious place.' Low attendance rates, secularization within churches, the decline in the political significance of religion and religious pluralism all point to religion becoming no more than a 'leisure pursuit' of no great significance to society.

In parts of the world where religion still appears strong it is largely because it is a form of 'cultural defence'. It is used by ethnic or national groups to protect their identity from external threats. In Northern Ireland Protestants use it to maintain their identity in the face of a Catholic majority in Ireland as a whole. In Poland under communism the Catholic Church was a focus of nationalist opposition to Soviet domination.

In other circumstances religion remains resilient as a means of coping with **cultural transition**: it is a way of dealing with social changes. For example, religion remains important in the lives of Asian immigrants to Britain and their descendants since it provides for the 'reassertion of a sense of pride often denied them in their new surrounding society'.

In Bruce's view, though, special circumstances are required for secularization to be avoided, at least in the West. Culturally diverse societies cannot allow religion to have too much of a public role without creating intolerable conflict.

■ Secularization – conclusion

As the views of Martin and Bruce illustrate, the secularization thesis has not been definitively proved or disproved. This is partly because sociologists from Weber to Wilson have used the term 'secularization' in many different ways. This has led to considerable confusion since writers discussing the process of secularization are often arguing about different things.

Martin states that the concept of secularization includes 'a large number of discrete, separate elements loosely put together in an intellectual hold-all'. He maintains that there is no necessary connection between the various processes lumped together under the same heading. Because the range of meaning attached to the term 'secularization' has become so wide, Martin advocates its removal from the sociological vocabulary. Instead he supports a careful and detailed study of the ways in which the role of religion in society has changed at different times and in different places.

Glock argues that researchers have been unable to measure the significance of religion because 'they have not given adequate attention to conceptualizing religion or religiousness in a comprehensive way'. Until they have clearly thought out and stated exactly what they mean by religion and religiousness, Glock maintains that the secularization thesis cannot be adequately tested. In an attempt to solve this problem, Glock and Stark define five **core dimensions of religiousness.**

1 The **belief dimension** – the degree to which people hold religious beliefs.

2 **Religious practice** – the degree to which people engage in acts of worship and devotion.

3 The **experience dimension** – the degree to which people feel, and experience contact and communication with, the supernatural.

4 The **knowledge dimension** – the amount of knowledge people have of their religion.

5 The **consequences dimension** – the degree to which the previous dimensions affect people's day-to-day lives.

Glock and Stark argue that a clearly defined system in which to classify people in religious terms is necessary before any scientifically valid statement about religiousness can be made. Only with such a system can the extent of religiousness be measured. Only when different researchers use the same **conceptualization of religion** can their results be compared with any degree of validity.

Even if Glock and Stark's scheme were generally accepted it would still be dangerous to make sweeping statements about whether secularization had taken place or not. The national, regional, ethnic and social class differences in the role of religion discussed by Martin make it necessary to relate theories to specific countries and social groups.

■ Sociology, values and religion

Throughout this chapter it is evident that the ideological commitments of particular researchers have influenced their definition of religion and their view of its role in society. In terms of their value judgements, they have considered some aspects of religion as worthy of study and dismissed others as irrelevant.

The influence of ideology in the study of religion is clearly evident in Marxist perspectives. Marx believed that people's salvation lay in their own hands. People would find salvation when they fulfilled their true nature. Fulfilment could only be found in a truly socialist society, a society created by people. Marx's utopian vision left no room for religion. Since religion had no place in the ideal socialist society, it must be a response to the flaws of non-socialist societies. From this set of beliefs and values, the Marxist analysis of religion follows a predictable course: religion represents either a salve to the pain of exploitation or a justification for oppression. In either case, it is a distortion of reality which people can well do without.

The conservative tendencies of functionalism, with its preoccupation with social order, provide a similarly predictable analysis. The concern of the functionalist approach with discovering the basis of stability and order in society leads to an emphasis on particular aspects of religion. From this perspective religion is seen as reinforcing social norms and values and promoting social solidarity, all of which are required for a stable and smooth running social system. By its very nature, functionalist theory tends to discount the divisive and disruptive effects of religion and ignores the role of religion as an agency of social change.

The intrusion of value judgements into research is particularly clear in the secularization debate. Many of the arguments are based on particular researchers' judgements of the 'truly religious society' in terms of which they evaluate what they see in contemporary society. Thus Will Herberg sees the religion of American denominations as a poor substitute for true religion. Max Weber observes industrial society in the early twentieth century and pictures a rather pathetic and disenchanted populace without the support of the deep spirituality which religion provides. By contrast Talcott Parsons rather smugly observes American society in the middle years of the twentieth century, notes its high moral standards and assumes they must be based ultimately on Christian values.

Such divergent interpretations may say as much about the observers as the reality of their subject matter.

9

Power, politics and the state

■ Introduction

In this chapter we are mainly concerned with the nature and distribution of **power** in modern industrial societies.

Many sociologists argue that **political sociology** is the study of power in its broadest sense. Thus Dowse and Hughes state that 'politics is about "power", politics occurs when there are differentials in power'. In terms of this definition, any social relationship which involves **power differentials** is political. Political relationships would extend from parents assigning domestic chores to their children to teachers enforcing discipline in the classroom; from a manager organizing a workforce to a general ordering troops into battle.

However, the traditional study of politics has concentrated on the state and the various institutions of government such as Parliament and the judiciary. Sociologists have been particularly concerned with the state, but they have examined it in relation to society as a whole, rather than in isolation.

Sociologists often distinguish between two forms of power: authority and coercion.

1 **Authority** is that form of power which is accepted as legitimate, that is right and just, and therefore obeyed on that basis. Thus if members of British society accept that Parliament has the right to make certain decisions and they regard those decisions as lawful, Parliamentary power may be defined as legitimate authority.

2 **Coercion** is that form of power which is not regarded as legitimate by those subject to it. Thus from the point of view of the Republicans in Northern Ireland, the power of the British Government may be defined as coercion.

However, the distinction between authority and coercion is not as clearcut as the above definitions suggest. It has often been argued that both forms of power are based ultimately on physical force and those who enforce the law are able to resort to physical force whether their power is regarded as legitimate or not.

We will begin by looking at Max Weber's influential views on power and types of authority.

■ Max Weber – power and types of authority

Max Weber defined power as:

the chance of a man or a number of men to realize their own will in a communal action even against the resistance of others who are participating in the action.

In other words, power consists of the ability to get your own way even when others are opposed to your wishes.

Weber was particularly concerned to distinguish different types of **authority**. He suggested that there were three sources.

Charismatic authority

Charismatic authority derives from the devotion felt by subordinates for a leader who is believed to have exceptional qualities. These qualities are seen as supernatural, superhuman, or at least exceptional compared to lesser mortals.

Charismatic leaders are able to sway and control their followers by direct emotional appeals which excite devotion and strong loyalties. Historical examples which come close to charismatic authority might include Alexander the Great, Napoleon and Fidel Castro. More ordinary people, such as teachers or managers, may also use charisma to exercise power.

Traditional authority

Weber called the second type of authority **traditional authority**. In this case authority rests upon a belief in the 'rightness' of established customs and traditions. Those in authority command obedience on the basis of their traditional status which is usually inherited. Their subordinates are controlled by feelings of loyalty and obligation to long-established positions of power.

The feudal system of medieval Europe is an example of traditional authority: monarchs and nobles owed their position to inherited status and the personal loyalty of their subjects.

Rational–legal authority

The final type of authority distinguished by Weber was **rational–legal authority**. In this case, unlike charismatic and traditional authority, legitimacy and control stem neither from the perceived personal qualities of the leader and the devotion they excite, nor from a commitment to traditional wisdom. Rational–legal authority is based on the acceptance of a set of impersonal rules.

Those who possess authority are able to issue commands and have them obeyed because others accept the legal framework which supports their authority. Thus a judge, a tax inspector or a military commander are obeyed because others accept the legal framework which gives them their power. The rules on which their authority is based are **rational** in the sense that they are consciously constructed for the attainment of a particular goal and they specify the means by which that goal is to be attained. For example, laws governing the legal system are designed to achieve the goal of 'justice'.

Ideal types

Weber stressed that in reality authority would never conform perfectly to any of his three types. His three categories are **ideal types** each of which defines a 'pure' form of authority. In any particular example authority may stem from two or more sources. It is therefore possible to find examples of authority which approximate to one of these types, but it is unlikely that a *perfect* example of any could be found.

Weber's attempts to define power and authority have been highly influential. The pluralist view of power and the state has adopted Weber's definition as a basis for measuring who has power in modern industrial societies.

Pluralists concentrate on the **will** (or desires) of individuals or groups to achieve particular ends. The wishes that people have are then compared to actual decisions taken by a government. The group whose wishes appear to be carried out are held to possess greater power than those who oppose them. Therefore power is measured by comparing the stated wishes of individuals or groups who seek to influence government policy, with the actions taken by their government. (Pluralist views on power and the state are discussed fully below, see pp. 506–13.)

■ Steven Lukes – a radical view of power

Despite the acceptance of Weber's definition of power by many sociologists, some writers believe that it is too narrow. Steven Lukes has put forward a **radical view** of power as an alternative. He argues that power has three **dimensions** or **faces**, rather than just one.

Decision making

Like pluralists, Lukes sees the first face of power in terms of **decision making**, where different individuals or groups express different policy preferences and influence the making of decisions over various issues. Lukes would accept that if a government followed the policies advocated by the trades unions, this would represent evidence that the unions had power. However, he believes that it is misleading to concentrate entirely on decisions taken, for power can be exercised in less obvious ways.

Non-decision making

The second face of power does not concern decision making, but rather focuses on **non-decision making**. Power may be used to prevent certain issues being discussed, or decisions about them from being taken.

From this point of view individuals or groups exercising power do so by preventing those who take a decision from considering all the possible alternative sources of action, or by limiting the range of decisions they are allowed to take.

For example, a teacher might offer students the opportunity to decide whether to do a piece of homework that week or the following week. The class appears to have power, for they have been given the opportunity to reach a decision. In reality, however, most power still rests with the teacher who has limited the options open to the students. The students are not free to decide whether or not they do this particular piece of work, nor can they choose to reject doing homework altogether.

Shaping desires

The third face of power strays even further from an emphasis on decision making and the preferences expressed by members of society. Lukes claims that power can be exercised by **shaping desires**, manipulating the wishes and desires of social groups. A social group may be persuaded to accept, or even to desire, a situation which is harmful to them.

Some feminists would argue that men exercise power over women in contemporary Britain by persuading them that being a mother and housewife are the most desirable roles for women. In reality, feminists claim, women who occupy these roles are exploited by, and for the benefit of, men.

Lukes's definition of power

Having examined the nature of power Lukes is able to conclude that power can be defined by saying that 'A exercises power over B when A affects B in a manner contrary to B's interests.' In other words Lukes argues that power is exercised over those who are harmed by its use, whether they are aware they are being harmed or not.

Lukes has been responsible for refining the concept of power, and showing that it has more than one dimension. As he himself admits, though, it is ultimately a matter of opinion what is in a person's interests or what is good for them. A mother and housewife might deny that her role in society is any less desirable than that of her husband's. She might also deny that she is being exploited.

Despite this problem, the radical definition of power has become increasingly influential. Marxist sociologists in particular have used this definition to attack the evidence used by sociologists advocating other perspectives.

We will develop this issue of defining and measuring power as the various theories are examined in detail. Next, however, we will analyse the role of the state in relation to power.

■ The state

Definitions of the state

The definition of **the state** is probably less controversial than the definition of power. Weber provided a definition with which most sociologists are in broad agreement. He defined the state as 'a human community that (successfully) claims the monopoly of the legitimate use of physical force within a given territory'.

In modern Britain the state rules over a clearly defined geographical area which includes England, Northern Ireland, Wales and Scotland. Only the central authority is believed by most members of society to have the right to use force to achieve its ends. Other groups and individuals may resort to violence, but the actions of terrorists, football 'hooligans' and murderers are not seen as legitimate. The state alone can wage war or use the legal system to imprison people against their will.

On the basis of Weber's definition, the state can be said to consist of the government or legislature which passes laws, the bureaucracy or civil service which implements governmental decisions, the police who are responsible for law enforcement, and the armed forces whose job it is to protect the state from external threats.

Many sociologists see the state as consisting of a wider set of institutions and in Britain would include welfare services, and the education and health services. Some go even further and see nationalized industries as part of the state. However, in developing their theories of the state most sociologists have concentrated upon the more central institutions such as the government and the civil service.

The twentieth-century world has come to be dominated by **nation-states** which lay claim to territory in every corner of the globe. However, although states which conform to Weber's definition have existed for thousands of years, and include Ancient Greece, Rome and Egypt, and the Aztecs of Central America, the state is a comparatively new feature of many societies. Anthropologists have discovered a number of **stateless 'simple' societies**. These are sometimes called **acephalous** or **headless societies**.

Stateless societies

In the 1930s E.E. Evans-Pritchard carried out a study of the Nuer society in Africa. It consisted of some forty separate tribes, none of which had a headman or chief.

Only a few decisions had to be taken which affected the tribe as a whole, such as whether to mount a raid on a neighbouring tribe, or whether to initiate young men into adult status. Such decisions appear to have been reached informally through discussions between members of a tribe.

Each tribal grouping was based on a particular geographical area, but they did not claim exclusive rights to using that land. More than half the Nuer lived in tribal areas in which they were not born.

There was no legal system as such, and no particular individuals charged with special responsibility for policing the community. Instead men who believed they had been wronged were expected to challenge the offender to a duel to the death.

In this society there was no government or other institution which claimed a monopoly of the legitimate use of force, and it was not based upon a clearly defined territory. As such, Nuer society can be seen as **stateless**.

The feudal state

A number of commentators also believe that the modern centralized state is also a relatively new feature of many parts of Europe. They suggest that it did not develop until after the feudal period.

Under feudalism the legitimate use of force was not concentrated in the hands of a centralized authority. While in theory the monarch ruled at the centre, in practice military power and the control of particular territories was in the hands of feudal lords in each region. Gianfranco Poggi has described how, for example, in the Maconnâis in feudal France, the King was a 'dimly perceived, politically ineffective figure'. The Count of the Maconnâis had originally been granted land by the King in return for providing warriors, but by the twelfth century lesser feudal lords to whom the Count had granted territory effectively ruled their own territories and monopolized military power. Thus the state was not centralized in any one place, but located in many separate centres throughout the nation.

Only in the seventeenth century in France did the monarchy successfully establish its authority over the aristocracy in the regions. Furthermore, it was only in the nineteenth century that transport and communications had developed sufficiently for it to become possible for the centralized state to exercise close control over the far-flung corners of its territory.

The modern state

The **centralized state** developed comparatively recently in many areas of the world. However, its importance in industrialized societies has increased dramatically in the nineteenth and twentieth centuries.

In Britain, for instance, the state in this period greatly extended its involvement in, and control over economic affairs, and the provision of welfare, health care and education. These developments are reflected in the rising proportion of Gross National Product (the total amount of economic activity in a society that can be measured in monetary terms) spent by the Government. The economists C.V. Brown and P.M. Jackson have calculated that government spending as a proportion of GNP has risen in Britain from 8 per cent in 1890, to 29 per cent in 1932, 40.2 per cent in 1966 and 51.4 per cent in 1976. By 1991 it had gone back down to 40 per cent.

The increasing importance of the state in industrial societies has prompted sociologists to devote considerable attention to this institution. In particular they have debated which groups in society control the state and in whose interests the state is run. We will now examine the competing sociological perspectives on power and the state, beginning with a functionalist perspective.

■ Power – a functionalist perspective

Most sociological theories of power follow Weber's definition in two important respects.

1 Weber's definition implies that those who hold power do so at the expense of others. It suggests that there is a fixed amount of power, and therefore if some hold power, others do not. This view is sometimes known as a **constant-sum** concept of power. Since the amount of power is constant, power is held by an individual or group to the extent that it is not held by others.

2 The second important implication of Weber's definition is that powerholders will tend to use power to further their own interests. Power is used to further the sectional interests of the powerholders which are in conflict with the interests of those subject to that power.

However, neither of these assumptions is accepted by some functionalist writers.

■ Talcott Parsons – the variable-sum concept of power

Talcott Parsons rejects the constant-sum concept of power and the view that power is employed in the furtherance of sectional interests. Rather than seeing power as something which some hold at the expense of others, Parsons regards it as something possessed by society as a whole. As such, power is 'a generalized facility or resource in the society'. In particular, it is 'the capacity to mobilize the resources of the society for the attainment of goals for which a general "public" commitment has been made'.

In this sense, the amount of power in society is measured by the degree to which collective goals are realized. Thus, the greater the efficiency of a social system for achieving the goals defined by its members, the more power exists in society. This view is sometimes known as a **variable-sum** concept of power, since power in society is not seen as fixed or constant. Instead it is variable in the sense that it can increase or decrease.

Power and collective goals

Parsons's view of power is developed from his general theory of the nature of society. He begins from the assumption that **value consensus** is essential for the survival of social systems. From shared values derive **collective goals**, that is goals shared by members of society. For example, if materialism is a major value of Western industrial society, collective goals such as economic expansion and higher living standards can be seen to stem from this value. The more Western societies are able to realize these goals, the greater the power that resides in the social system. Steadily rising living standards and economic growth are therefore indications of an increase of power in society.

Parsons's view of power differentials within society also derives from his general theory. Since goals are shared by all members of society, power will generally be used in the furtherance of collective goals. As a result, both sides of the power relationship will benefit and everybody will gain by the arrangement. For instance, politicians in Western societies will promote policies for economic expansion which, if successful, will raise the living standards of the population as a whole.

Thus, from this viewpoint, the exercise of power usually means that everybody wins. This forms a basis for the cooperation and reciprocity which Parsons considers essential for the maintenance and well-being of society.

Authority and collective goals

As we saw in the last chapter, Parsons regards power differentials as necessary for the effective pursuit of collective goals. If members of society pool their efforts and resources, they are more likely to realize their shared goals than if they operate as individuals. Cooperation on a large scale requires organization and direction which necessitates positions of command. Some are therefore granted the power to direct others.

This power takes the form of **authority**. It is generally regarded as legitimate since it is seen to further collective goals. This means that some are granted authority for the benefit of all.

Parsons's views may be illustrated by the following example. One of the major goals of traditional Sioux Indian society was success in hunting. This activity involved cooperation and power relationships. During the summer months the buffalo, the main food supply of the tribe, were gathered in large herds on the northern plains of North America. The buffalo hunt was a large-scale enterprise under the authority and control of marshals who were appointed by the warrior societies. An effective hunt required considerable organization and direction and was strictly policed. In particular, the marshals were concerned to prevent excitable young warriors from jumping the gun and stampeding the herd, which might endanger the food supply of the entire tribe. Marshals had the authority to beat those who disobeyed the rules and destroy their clothes and the harness of their horses. Thus, by granting power to the marshals, by accepting it as legitimate, and obeying it on that basis, the whole tribe benefited from the exercise of their authority.

Power in Western democracies

Parsons's analysis of the basis of political power in Western democracies provides a typical illustration of his views on the nature of power. He argues:

Political support should be conceived of as a generalized grant of power which, if it leads to electional success, puts elected leadership in a position analogous to a banker. The 'deposits' of power made by constituents are revocable, if not at will, at the next election.

Just as money is deposited in a bank, members of society deposit power in political leaders. Just as depositors can withdraw their money from the bank, so the electorate can withdraw its grant of power from political leaders at the next election. In this sense power resides ultimately with members of society as a whole. Finally, just as money generates interest for the depositor, so grants of power generate benefits for the electorate since they are used primarily to further collective goals. In this way power in society can increase.

Many sociologists have argued that Parsons's views of the nature and application of power in society are naïve. They suggest that he has done little more than translate into sociological jargon the rationalizations promoted by the powerholders to justify their use of power. In particular, they argue that Parsons has failed to appreciate that power is frequently used to further sectional interests rather than to benefit society as a whole. We will analyse these criticisms in detail in the following sections.

■ Power and the state – a pluralist perspective

Pluralism is a theory which claims to explain the nature and distribution of power in Western democratic societies. **Classical pluralism** was the original form that this perspective took but it has been heavily criticized. Some supporters of this perspective have modified their position and have adopted an **elite pluralist** view which takes account of some of these criticisms.

We will first describe and evaluate classical pluralism, before considering elite pluralism at the end of this section.

■ Classical pluralism

This version of pluralism has important similarities with the Parsonian functionalist theory. Pluralists agree with Parsons that power ultimately derives from the population as a whole.

1 They accept that the government and state in a Western democracy act in the interests of that society and according to the wishes of its members.

2 They see the political systems of countries such as the USA, Britain and France as the most advanced systems of government yet devised, and regard them as the most effective way for a population to exercise power and govern a country.

3 They regard the exercise of power through the state to be legitimate rather than coercive, since it is held to be based upon the acceptance and cooperation of the population.

Pluralists, however, part company from Parsons in three important respects.

The nature of power

First, pluralists follow Weber in accepting a constant-sum concept of power. There is seen to be a fixed amount of power which is distributed among the population of a society. They do not accept Parsons's variable-sum concept of power that sees it as a resource held by society as a whole.

Sectional interests

Second, they deny that democratic societies have an all-embracing value consensus. They would agree with Parsons that members of such societies share some interests and wishes in common. For example, most citizens of the USA share a commitment to the constitution of the country and the political institutions such as the presidency, the Congress and the electoral system.

However, pluralists do not accept that members of society share common interests or values in relation to every issue. They believe that industrial society is increasingly differentiated into a variety of social groups and sectional interests, and with the increasingly specialized division of labour the number and diversity of occupational groups steadily grows. Groups such as doctors, teachers, business people and unskilled manual workers may have different interests. Each group

may be represented by its own union or professional association, and these groups may put forward conflicting requests to the government.

Pluralists do not deny the existence of class, or division based on age, gender, religion or ethnicity. However, they do deny that any single division dominates any individual's wishes or actions. According to their view, each individual has a large number of different interests. A male manual worker might not just be a member of the working class, he might also be a car owner, a mortgage payer, an avid reader of library books and a father of two children in higher education. Therefore, while he has certain interests as a manual worker, other interests stem from other aspects of his position in society. As a car owner he has an interest in road tax and petrol prices being kept low, as a mortgage payer in interest rates being reduced, as a library user in more government expenditure on this service, and as a father in higher student grants. Another range of interests could be outlined for a female professional.

To the founder of the pluralist perspective, the nineteenth-century French writer de Tocqueville, a democratic political system requires that individuals have a large number of specific interests. He believed that democracy would become unworkable if one division in society came to dominate all others. Such a situation could lead to a **tyranny of the majority**: one group in society would be in a permanent majority and the interests and wishes of the minority could be totally disregarded.

Northern Ireland could be seen as a contemporary example of this situation, where the population is split between a majority of Protestants and a minority of Catholics. Most individuals identify so strongly with their religious groupings that other interests are seen to be of secondary importance. The existence of a permanent majority of Protestants prevents a democratic system similar to that in the rest of the UK operating in such a way that each member of the Catholic minority has as much influence on government policy as each member of the Protestant majority.

The state

The third difference to the functionalist view follows from the pluralists' denial that a complete value consensus exists. Since individuals have different interests, political leaders and the state cannot reflect the interests of all members of society in taking any single decision.

To pluralists the state is seen as an 'honest broker' which takes account of all the conflicting demands made on it by different sections of society. The state mediates between different groups, ensuring that all of them have some influence on government policy, but that none gets its own way all the time. On one particular occasion the Government might take a decision which favours car owners, such as deciding to build a new motorway. On another it might decide against such a project in order to take account of the protests of environmentalists. On a third, the Government might reach a compromise, concluding that the road is necessary but changing the route in order to protect an area of particular environmental importance. Pluralists argue that every group over a period of time has its interests reflected in governmental decisions, but because of the divisions within society it is not possible for the state to satisfy everyone all of the time. In Raymond Aron's words 'government becomes a business of compromise'.

■ Classical pluralism – political parties and interest groups

Political parties

From a pluralist perspective, competition between two or more political parties is an essential feature of representative government. Using F.W. Riggs's definition, a **political party** is 'any organization which nominates candidates for election to a legislature'. Pluralists claim that competition for office between political parties provides the electorate with an opportunity to select its leaders and a means of influencing government policy.

This view forms the basis of Seymour M. Lipset's definition of democracy. According to Lipset:

Democracy in a complex society may be defined as a political system which supplies regular constitutional opportunities for changing the governing officials, and a social mechanism which permits the largest possible part of the population to influence major decisions by choosing among contenders for political office.

For efficient government, Lipset argues that competition between contenders for office must result in the granting of 'effective authority to one group' and the presence of an 'effective opposition' in the legislature as a check on the power of the governing party.

Pluralists claim that political parties in democratic societies are representative for the following reasons.

1 The public directly influences party policy, since, in order to be elected to govern, parties must reflect the wishes and interests of the electorate in their programmes.

2 If existing parties do not sufficiently represent sections of society, a new party will usually emerge, such as the Labour Party at the turn of the century in Britain or the SDP in 1981.

3 Parties are accountable to the electorate since they will not regain power if they disregard the opinions and interests of the public.

4 Parties cannot simply represent a sectional interest since, to be elected to power, they require the support of various interests in society.

However, as Robert McKenzie states, political parties must not be seen 'as the sole "transmission belts" on which political ideas and programmes are conveyed from the citizens to the legislature and the executive'. During their time in office and in opposition, parties 'mould and adapt their principles under innumerable pressures brought to bear by organized groups of citizens which operate for the most part outside the political system'. Such groups are known as **interest** or **pressure groups**.

Interest groups

Unlike political parties, interest groups do not aim to take power in the sense of forming a government. Rather they seek to influence political parties and the various departments of state. Nor do interest groups usually claim to represent a wide range of interests: instead their specified objective is to represent a particular interest in society.

Interest groups are often classified in terms of their aims as either protective or promotional groups.

1 **Protective groups** defend the interests of a particular section of society: trade unions such as the National Union of Mineworkers (NUM), professional associations such as the British Medical Association,

and employers' organizations such as the Confederation of British Industry are classified as protective groups.

2 Promotional groups support a particular cause rather than guard the interests of a particular social group. Organizations such as the RSPCA, Friends of the Earth and the Lord's Day Observance Society are classified as promotional groups.

3 Membership of promotional groups is potentially larger and usually more varied than that of protective groups since they require only a commitment to their cause as a qualification for joining.

4 By comparison, membership of protective groups is usually limited to individuals of a particular status, for example, miners for membership of the NUM.

In practice the distinction between protective and promotional groups is not clearcut since the defence of an interest also involves its promotion.

Interest groups can bring pressure to bear in a number of ways:

1 By contributions to the funds of political parties: such as trades union contributions to the Labour Party.

2 By illegal payments to elected representatives and state officials: in other words bribery. The Lockheed bribery scandal and the Poulson affair (although involving a particular company and individual rather than an interest group as such) provide an indication of how government officials can be corruptly influenced. The Johnson Matthey Bank affair is another example, while in 1994 it was revealed that at least one MP in Britain had received payments from Mohammed al-Fayed in return for asking questions on his behalf in the House of Commons.

3 By appealing to public opinion: an effective campaign by an interest group can mobilize extensive public support especially if it attracts widespread coverage by the mass media, and its arguments are seen to be valid. Certain conservation groups have successfully adopted this strategy, while in the mid-1990s protesters campaigning for rights for the disabled chained themselves to buses at the entrance to 10 Downing Street.

4 By various forms of civil disobedience: this approach has been used by a wide variety of interest groups from ratepayers' associations withholding rates to Women's Liberation groups disrupting beauty competitions to black organizations breaking segregation laws.

5 By the provision of expertise. It has often been argued that in modern industrial society, governments cannot

operate without the specialized knowledge of interest groups. By providing this expertise interest groups have an opportunity to directly influence government policy. In Britain, representatives of interest groups now have permanent places on some five hundred government advisory committees. Dowse and Hughes argue:

---

interest groups constitute a continuous mandate for the government and without them no government could conceivably be regarded as democratic. More to the point, no government could begin to operate without the assistance of interest groups.

Interest groups and democracy

Pluralists see interest groups as necessary elements in a democratic system for a number of reasons.

Voting in elections involves only minimal participation in politics for members of a democracy. Classical pluralists believe as many people as possible should participate as actively as possible in politics. They do not believe that in Britain, for instance, voting once every five years is an adequate level of participation. Interest groups provide the opportunity for many individuals to participate in politics who are not members of political parties. For example, many members of the Campaign for Nuclear Disarmament limit their active interest in politics to participation in the activities of this organization.

Interest groups are also necessary because even those who have voted for a government may not agree with all its policies. In a party-political system it is necessary to choose between the overall packages offered by the opposing parties. Interest groups make it possible to alter some parts of a governing party's policies while retaining those with which a majority of the population agree.

Clearly it is also vital that those who voted for a losing party have some opportunity to allow their voice to be heard. To the classical pluralist the large number and diversity of pressure groups allows all sections of society to have a say in politics.

Before an election a party seeking office outlines its proposed policies in a manifesto. The electorate can choose who to vote for on the basis of the alternative manifestos put forward. However, manifestos cannot be completely comprehensive: new issues not covered by them may arise: in the 1979 election in Britain no reference was made to the Falkland Islands in the manifestos of the major parties, since the Argentinian occupation of the islands had not been anticipated. Interest groups provide the means through which the public can make their views known to a governing party as circumstances change and new issues arise.

Furthermore, interest groups can mobilize public concern over issues which have been neglected or overlooked by the Government. The British interest group SHELTER draws the attention of the public and government alike to the plight of the homeless, while the Animal Liberation Front campaigns for the rights of voteless and voiceless animals.

According to classical pluralists then, all sections of society and all shades of political opinion are represented and reflected in a wide variety of groups in Western democracies. Anyone who feels they are being neglected by the Government can form a new pressure group in order to rectify the temporary flaw in the operation of the democratic system.

▋ Measuring power

Pluralists have provided empirical evidence to support their claim that Western societies are governed in accordance with democratic principles. The evidence they advance is based upon an attempt to show that a government's policies reflect a compromise between the wishes of the various sectional interests in society. They therefore concentrate upon the first face of power: decision making.

Pluralists compare the decisions taken by a government with the wishes of its general public, and the wishes expressed by different groups in the population. By examining evidence from opinion polls and the stated policy preferences of interest groups, pluralists reach the conclusion that countries such as Britain and the USA are genuinely democratic.

Robert A. Dahl – Who Governs?

One of the most famous studies supporting the pluralist view is *Who Governs?* by Robert A. Dahl.

Dahl investigates local politics in New Haven, Connecticut. He examines a series of decisions in three major **issue areas:**

1 urban renewal, which involved the redevelopment of the city centre;

2 political nominations, with particular emphasis on the post of mayor;

3 education, which concerned issues such as the siting of schools and teachers' salaries.

By selecting a range of different issues, Dahl claims that it should be possible to discover whether a single group monopolized decision making in community affairs.

Dahl finds no evidence of one group dominating decision making, but concludes that power was dispersed among various interest groups. He discovered that interest groups only became directly involved in local politics when the issues were seen as directly relevant to their particular concerns. Dahl claims that the evidence shows that local politics is a business of bargaining and compromise, with no one group dominating decision making.

For example, business interests, trades unions and the local university were involved in the issue of urban renewal. The mayor and his assistants made the major decisions in consultation with the various interest groups and produced a programme which was acceptable to all parties concerned.

Dahl rejects the view that economic interests dominate decision making. He concludes:

Economic notables, far from being a ruling group, are simply one of many groups out of which individuals sporadically emerge to influence the policies and acts of city officials. Almost anything one might say about the influence of economic notables could be said with equal justice about half a dozen other groups in New Haven.

Power in Britain

Similar studies on national politics have been conducted by pluralist researchers in Britain. In an important study using the decision-making approach, Christopher J. Hewitt examined twenty-four policy issues which arose in the British Parliament from 1944 to 1964. The issues covered four main policy areas:

1 foreign policy (e.g. the Suez crisis of 1956);

2 economic policy (e.g. the nationalization of road haulage);

3 welfare policy (e.g. the Rent Act of 1957);

4 social policy (e.g. the introduction of commercial television).

Hewitt compared the decisions reached by Parliament with the views of the interest groups involved and contemporary public opinion. In some cases the decisions favoured certain interest groups to the exclusion of others. In other cases government decisions favoured some groups but 'substantial concessions were made to the opposing interests'. However, Hewitt found that no one interest group consistently got its own way. He states that 'Neither the business group nor any other appears to be especially favoured by the government.'

Poll data on public opinion were available on eleven of the twenty-four issues included in the study. In only one case – the abolition of capital punishment in 1957 – did the decisions of Parliament oppose public opinion.

Hewitt's study suggests that both a variety of specialized interests and public opinion in general are represented in the British Parliament. He concludes:

> picture of national power that is revealed suggests a 'pluralist' interpretation since a diversity of conflicting interests are involved in many issues, without any one issue being consistently successful in realizing its goals.

The CBI

A study of the relationship between government and the Confederation of British Industry (CBI) by Wyn Grant and David Marsh reaches similar conclusions.

Created in 1965 from an amalgamation of three employers' federations, membership of the CBI includes 75 per cent of the top 200 manufacturing companies in Britain. It has direct channels of communication with government ministers and powerful civil servants, and is concerned with furthering the interests of private industry, particularly the manufacturing sector. In order to assess its influence on government, Grant and Marsh examined four pieces of legislation from 1967 to 1972.

1 The CBI fiercely opposed the Iron and Steel Act of 1967 which renationalized the iron and steel industry. Its views were rejected by the Labour Government and, according to Grant and Marsh, the CBI 'fought an almost entirely unsuccessful defensive action'.

2 The Clean Air Act of 1968 aimed to reduce air pollution. The two main interest groups involved were the CBI and the National Society for Clean Air. The CBI was successful in obtaining various modifications to the bill and the resulting act was a compromise between the views of the two interest groups.

3 The Deposit of Poisonous Wastes Act of 1972 was concerned with the disposal of solid and semi-solid toxic wastes. The Conservative Government was under strong pressure from conservation groups and in particular the Warwickshire Conservation Society which mobilized strong public support. Although the CBI obtained some important concessions, it by no means got all its own way. Grant and Marsh observed:

> It would seem, then, that a new interest group (The Warwickshire Conservation Society) with hardly any permanent staff can exert as much influence over a specific issue as the CBI.

4 The Industry Act of 1972 was directed at regional development. The CBI was particularly concerned to prevent the Government from having the right to buy shares in private industry. Its members were suspicious of any measures which might give the Government more control over private industry. The TUC, on the other hand, favoured direct government investment, particularly in labour-intensive service industries, to ease the problem of unemployment. In practice neither interest group appears to have had much influence though the TUC were happier than the CBI with the final act. The Government pursued a relatively independent policy which was a response to 'the immediate demands of economic and political situations' rather than to the pressures of either interest group.

Grant and Marsh conclude that 'the CBI has little consistent direct influence over the policies pursued by government'. Despite its powerful membership and its access to the highest levels of government, 'the CBI's ability to influence events is limited by the government's need to retain the support of the electorate and by the activities of other interest groups'.

▌ Pluralism – a critique

A large body of evidence from studies such as those of Dahl in the USA, and Hewitt and Grant and Marsh in Britain, appears to support the classical pluralist position. However, there are a number of serious criticisms of pluralism. These criticisms are concerned both with the methods pluralists use to measure power, and empirical evidence which seems to contradict their claim that power is dispersed in Western democracies.

Non-decisions and safe decisions

Marxists and other conflict theorists have suggested that pluralists ignore some aspects of power. In particular it is argued that they concentrate exclusively on the first face of power, decision making.

John Urry, for example, believes that pluralists ignore the possibility that some have the power to prevent certain issues from reaching the point of decision. As a result of this non-decision making, only **safe decisions** may be taken – decisions which do not fundamentally alter the basic structures of capitalist societies.

From this point of view, it is in the interests of the powerful to allow a variety of interest groups to influence safe decisions. This fosters the illusion of real participation and helps to create the myth that a society is democratic. It disguises the real basis of power and so protects the powerful.

Pluralists can also be criticized for ignoring what Steven Lukes has identified as the third face of power. They do not take account of the possibility that the preferences expressed in opinion polls or by pressure groups might themselves have been manipulated by those with real power. In Marxist terms the decisions might reflect the **false class consciousness** of members of society who do not realize where their own true interests lie. Real power might therefore rest with those who control institutions such as the media and the education system, which can play a part in shaping individuals' attitudes and opinions.

The consequences of decisions

Other writers have identified further ways in which power can be measured. Westergaard and Resler argue 'Power is visible only through its consequences.' Government legislation may fail to

have its intended effect. Despite an abundance of legislation aimed at improving the lot of the poor, Westergaard and Resler believe there has 'been little redistribution of wealth'.

1 Studies of actual decisions might give the impression that the interests of the poor are represented in government decisions.

2 Studies of the results of those decisions might provide a very different picture.

In any case, many sociologists deny that governments in Western democracies monopolize power. Governments might, for example, seek to reduce the level of unemployment in order to secure victory at the next election. However, it is not within their power to control all the actions of large corporations who can decide whether to close existing factories, making some of their workforce redundant, or invest their profits overseas.

Contradictory evidence

The above points pose fundamental questions about the pluralists' method of measuring power, but pluralism can also be criticized on its own terms. Some evidence suggests that different interest groups have more influence over government decisions than others. Decision making by governments does not always appear to support the view that power is equally distributed among all groups in society, or that the state acts impartially as an 'honest broker'.

In the USA, the NAACP (National Association for the Advancement of Colored People) is a case in point. Founded in 1910, the NAACP attempted to represent the interests of black Americans. Yet it made no important breakthroughs until 1954 when NAACP lawyers brought a case to the Supreme Court which resulted in a decision declaring racial segregation in education to be unconstitutional. Pluralists may point to this decision and the civil rights legislation of the 1960s and suggest that black interests are being represented. However, this ignores the fact that for over forty years, the NAACP could hardly dent the forces of racial prejudice and discrimination, and the fact that the black masses still tend to be concentrated at the base of the American stratification system.

In Britain a study by David Marsh and David Locksley contradicts the evidence supporting pluralism, for it suggests that the interest groups representing industry have more influence than other groups with respect to some issues. For example, in 1978 the CBI was successful in discouraging the then Labour Government from introducing legislation that would have resulted in workers sitting on the boards of companies. In a similar fashion in 1975 pressure from the CBI and the City of London played a major part in persuading the Labour Government to drop proposals to nationalize the twenty-five largest industrial companies in Britain.

Marsh and Locksley also claim that trades unions have had a considerable amount of influence over legislation relating to prices and wages policies, and industrial relations, although they have had much less impact on other areas of government policy. In recent years, though, the influence of unions has certainly declined.

In contrast to the influence of these important protective groups, promotional groups seem to possess much less influence. In a study of nuclear power policy, Hugh Ward found that 'the anti-nuclear movement in Britain has been very unsuccessful'. Interest groups such as Friends of the Earth have failed to persuade successive governments not to build more nuclear power stations. Ward claims that the Central Electricity Generating Board, the UK Atomic Energy Authority, and the GEC company carried much more influence with those governments than the promotional pressure groups opposing expansion.

Unrepresented interests

Classical pluralists assume not only that interest groups have equal power, but also that all major interests in society are represented by one group or another. This latter assumption is also questionable.

The fairly recent emergence in Britain of consumer associations and citizens' advice bureaus can be seen as representing the interests of consumers against big business and of citizens against government bureaucracies. It cannot be assumed that such interests were absent, unthreatened or adequately represented before the existence of such organizations. For instance, the unemployed are a group who, unlike employers and employees, still lack a powerful pressure group to represent them.

Reappraisals of classical pluralism

It is not surprising that given the strength and number of criticisms advanced against classical pluralism some of its supporters have modified their positions. David Marsh originally provided evidence to support classical pluralism, but in more recent times he has rejected the pluralist approach in favour of what he describes as the **fragmented elite model**.

Robert A. Dahl still supports the ideal of a pluralist democracy, but now accepts that it has certain **dilemmas**. He does not believe that the USA conforms perfectly to that ideal. The central dilemma is the unequal distribution of wealth and income: Dahl now argues this provides an unequal distribution of power. Wealthy individuals find it easier to take an active and effective part in political life. He also notes that the owners and controllers of large corporations exercise considerable power in making decisions. Dahl therefore calls for increasing democratic control over business, and a reduction in inequalities in wealth and income.

■ Elite pluralism

Some pluralists, however, have responded to criticisms by adapting the theory to take account of some of the weaknesses of classical pluralism.

David Marsh has described a number of recent attempts to explain the distribution of power and the operation of the state as **elite pluralist theories**. These theories share important similarities with classical pluralism:

1 they see Western societies as basically democratic;

2 they regard government as a process of compromise;

3 they agree that power is widely dispersed.

On the other hand:

1 they do not accept that all members of society have exactly the same amount of power;

2 they do not concentrate exclusively on the first face of power;

3 they see elites, the leaders of groups, as the main participants in decision making.

Representative elites –
J.J. Richardson and A.G. Jordan

J.J. Richardson and A.G. Jordan have analysed the British Government from an elite pluralist perspective. They argue that consultation among various groups has become the most important feature of British politics. Interest groups are not the only groups involved: government departments, and nationalized and private companies can also play an important part in the negotiations which determine policy. As far as possible the Government tries to minimize the conflict between the representatives of organized groups, and to secure the agreement of the different sides concerned with a particular issue.

In these circumstances the participation of the mass of the population is not required to make a country democratic. Members, and indeed non-members of organizations, have their sectional interests represented by the elites such as trades union leaders and the senior officials of promotional groups.

Unequal influence

Richardson and Jordan though, do not claim that all groups have equal power, or that all sections of society have groups to represent them. An important factor governing the degree of influence an interest group has is whether it is an insider or an outsider group.

1 **Insider groups** are accepted by the Government as the legitimate representatives of a particular interest in society, and are regularly consulted on issues deemed relevant to them.

2 **Outsider groups** lack this recognition and are not automatically consulted.

According to Richardson and Jordan, the wishes of insider groups, such as the National Farmers' Union and the CBI, carry more weight with the Government than those of outsider groups such as CND.

Richardson and Jordan also point out that some groups in society are in a better position to take action to force policy changes on the Government than others. In the 1970s the NUM exercised considerable power through the use and threatened use of strikes which posed serious problems for the Government by endangering energy supplies.

In contrast, Richardson and Jordan are also prepared to admit that some interests are not effectively represented at all. While teachers have well-organized unions to represent their views to the Government over educational issues, parents have no equivalent organizations.

Despite these apparent drawbacks to democracy in Britain, Richardson and Jordan believe that other factors ensure that the Government does not ignore the interests of significant sections of the population. This is because groups who are neglected by the Government tend to organize more to force the Government to take their views into account.

For example, until comparatively recently governments of most industrial societies showed little interest in environmental issues. When the problems of pollution and the destruction of the environment became more acute, new interest groups such as Greenpeace and Friends of the Earth sprang up to force these issues on to the political agenda. Situations where an interest in society is not represented will, therefore, be only temporary.

Measuring power

The elite pluralist position is also more sophisticated than classical pluralism in dealing with the problem of measuring power. Like classical pluralists Richardson and Jordan stress the importance of examining decisions to determine whose wishes are being carried out. But they also examine the second face of power: they discuss who has influence over what issues reach the point of decision. They are prepared to accept that it is possible for well-organized groups to keep issues off the political agenda for a time.

To illustrate their point they quote an American study by M. Crenson. This study compared two Indiana cities, East Chicago and Gary, which had similar levels of air pollution resulting from industrial activity. In East Chicago action was taken against this problem as early as 1949, whereas in Gary industrialists successfully prevented the problem emerging as an issue until the middle of the 1950s. Gary relied heavily on one industry – steel – and the importance of this industry to the city persuaded officials not to take action.

Once again though, Richardson and Jordan do not believe that non-decision making seriously undermines democracy. They claim that 'there is evidence that it is increasingly difficult to exercise this power'. They believe that in modern democracies it is possible for interest groups to force issues on to the political agenda even against the wishes of the Government and other organized interests. Among the British examples they cite are those of the Smoke Abatement Society persuading the Government to pass the Clean Air Act in 1956, and the Child Poverty Action Group reviving poverty as an issue in the early 1970s.

One reason why new issues can rapidly become important in the political arena is the existence of backbench MPs, who do not hold government office. They are keen to further their careers by showing their talents through advocating a new cause.

Elite pluralism – a critique

Clearly, elite pluralism does answer some of the criticisms advanced against classical pluralism. It allows for the possibilities that at least temporarily some interests may not be represented and some groups may have more power than others. It acknowledges that all individuals may not play an active part in politics, and it does not rely exclusively on measuring the first face of power, decision making. However, the analysis of elite pluralists may not be satisfactory in at least three ways.

1 In showing that democracies do not work perfectly their own evidence raises doubts about the basic pluralist view that power is widely dispersed in Western industrial societies.

2 While they note the existence of elite leaders, they fail to discuss the possibility that these elites monopolize power and use it in their own interests.

3 Elite pluralists take account of two faces of power, but ignore the third. They do not discuss the power of some members of society to influence the wishes of others.

▓ Elite theory

Elite theory differs from both pluralism and functionalism in that it sees power in society as being monopolized by a small minority. Elite theory sees society as divided into two main groups: a **ruling minority** who exercise power through the state, and the **ruled**.

There are, however, a number of ways in which elite theorists differ. They do not agree as to whether elite rule is desirable or beneficial for society. They differ in their conclusions about the inevitability of elite rule, and they do not agree about exactly who constitutes the elite or elites.

▓ Classical elite theory

Elite theory was first developed by two Italian sociologists, Vilfredo Pareto (1848–1923) and Gaetano Mosca (1858–1911). Both saw elite rule as inevitable and dismissed the possibility of a proletarian revolution leading to the establishment of a communist society. As such they were arguing against Marx's view of power and the state.

Because of the inevitability of elite rule neither saw it as desirable that any attempt should be made to end it. Pareto and Mosca agreed that the basis of elite rule was the superior personal qualities of those who made up the elites. Pareto believed that elites possessed more cunning or intelligence, while Mosca saw them as having more organizational ability. Since people were unequal, some would always have more ability than others, and would therefore occupy the elite positions in society.

According to both the classical elite theorists, apart from the personal qualities of its members, an elite owes its power to its internal organization. It forms a united and cohesive minority in the face of an unorganized and fragmented mass. In Mosca's words 'The power of the minority is irresistible as against each single individual in the majority.' Major decisions which affect society are taken by the elite. Even in so-called democratic societies, these decisions will usually reflect the concerns of the elite rather than the wishes of the people. Elite theorists picture the majority as apathetic and unconcerned with the major issues of the day. The mass of the population is largely controlled and manipulated by the elite, passively accepting the propaganda which justifies elite rule.

Although there are broad similarities between the work of these **classical elite** theorists, there are also some differences.

Vilfredo Pareto

Pareto placed particular emphasis on psychological characteristics as the basis of elite rule. He argued that there are two main types of governing elite, which, following his intellectual ancestor and countryman Machiavelli, he called lions and foxes.

1 **Lions** achieve power because of their ability to take direct and incisive action, and, as their name suggests, they tend to rule by force. Military dictatorships provide an example of this type of governing elite.

2 By comparison, **foxes** rule by cunning and guile, by diplomatic manipulation and wheeling and dealing. Pareto believed that European democracies provided an example of this type of elite.

Members of a governing elite owe their positions primarily to their personal qualities, either to their lion-like or fox-like characteristics.

Major change in society occurs when one elite replaces another, a process Pareto called the **circulation of elites**. All elites tend to become decadent. They 'decay in quality' and lose their 'vigour'. They may become soft and ineffective with the pleasures of easy living and the privileges of power, or set in their ways and too inflexible to respond to changing circumstances.

In addition, each type of elite lacks the qualities of its counterpart, qualities which in the long run are essential to maintain power. An elite of lions lacks the imagination and cunning necessary to maintain its rule and will have to admit foxes from the masses to make up for this deficiency. Gradually foxes infiltrate the entire elite and so transform its character. Foxes, however, lack the ability to take forceful and decisive action which at various times is essential to retain power. An organized minority of lions committed to the restoration of strong government develops and eventually overthrows the elite of foxes.

Whereas history to Marx ultimately leads to and ends with the communist utopia, history to Pareto is a never-ending circulation of elites. Nothing ever really changes and history is, and always will be, 'a graveyard of aristocracies'.

A critique of Pareto

Pareto's view of history is both simple and simplistic. He dismisses the differences between political systems such as Western democracies, communist single-party states, fascist dictatorships and feudal monarchies as merely variations on a basic theme. All are essentially examples of elite rule and by comparison with this fact, the differences between them are minor.

Pareto fails to provide a method of measuring and distinguishing between the supposedly superior qualities of elites. He simply assumes that the qualities of the elite are superior to those of the mass. His criterion for distinguishing between lions and foxes is merely his own interpretation of the style of elite rule.

Nor does Pareto provide a way of measuring the process of elite decadence. He does suggest, however, that if an elite is closed to recruitment from below it is likely to rapidly lose its vigour and vitality and have a short life. Yet as T.B. Bottomore notes, the Brahmins, the elite stratum in the Indian caste system, were a closed group which survived for many hundreds of years.

Gaetano Mosca

Like Pareto, Gaetano Mosca believed that rule by a minority is an inevitable feature of social life. He based this belief on the evidence of history claiming that in all societies:

> two classes of people appear – a class that rules and a class that is ruled. The first class, always the less numerous, performs all political functions, monopolizes power and enjoys the advantages that power brings, whereas the second, the more numerous class, is directed and controlled by the first.

Like Pareto, Mosca believed that the ruling minority are superior to the mass of the population. He claimed that they are 'distinguished from the mass of the governed by qualities that give them a certain material, intellectual or even moral superiority', and he provides a sociological explanation for this superiority seeing it as a product of the social background of the elite.

Unlike Pareto, who believed that the qualities required for elite rule were the same for all time, Mosca argued that they varied from society to society. For example, in some societies courage and bravery in battle provide access to the elite; in others the skills and capacities needed to acquire wealth.

Elite theory and democracy

Pareto saw modern democracies as merely another form of elite domination. He scornfully dismissed those who saw them as a more progressive and representative system of government. Mosca, however, particularly in his later writings, argued that there were important differences between democracies and other forms of elite rule. By comparison with closed systems such as caste and feudal societies, the ruling elite in democratic societies is open. There is therefore a greater possibility of an elite drawn from a wide range of social backgrounds. As a result, the interests of various social groups may be represented in the decisions taken by the elite. The majority may therefore have some control over the government of society.

As he became more favourably disposed towards democracy, Mosca argued that 'the modern representative state has made it possible for almost all political forces, almost all social values, to participate in the management of society'. But he stopped short of a literal acceptance of Abraham Lincoln's famous definition of democracy as 'government of the people, by the people, for the people'. To Mosca, democracy was government of the people, it might even be government for the people, but it could never be government by the people. Elite rule remained inevitable. Democracy could be no more than representative government with an elite representing the interests of the people.

Despite his leanings towards democracy, Mosca retained his dim view of the masses. They lacked the capacity for self-government and required the leadership and guidance of an elite. Indeed Mosca regretted the extension of the franchise to all members of society believing that it should be limited to the middle class. He thus remained 'elitist' to the last. (For a further perspective from early elite theory see the section on Michels, Chapter 5, pp. 290–1.)

Elite theory and the USA – C. Wright Mills

Whereas Pareto and Mosca attempted to provide a general theory to explain the nature and distribution of power in all societies, the American sociologist C. Wright Mills presents a less ambitious and wide-ranging version of elite theory. He limits his analysis to American society in the 1950s.

Unlike the early elite theorists, Mills does not believe that elite rule is inevitable: in fact he sees it as a fairly recent development in the USA. Unlike Pareto, who rather cynically accepts the domination of the masses by elites, Mills soundly condemns it. Since he sees elite rule as based upon the exploitation of the masses, he adopts a conflict version of elite theory. Because the elites and the masses have different interests, this creates the potential for conflict between the two groups.

The power elite

Writing in the 1950s, Mills explained elite rule in institutional rather than psychological terms. He rejected the view that members of the elite have superior qualities or psychological characteristics which distinguish them from the rest of the population. Instead he argued that the structure of institutions is such that those at the top of the institutional hierarchy largely monopolize power. Certain institutions occupy key **pivotal positions** in society and the elite comprise those who hold 'command posts' in those institutions.

Mills identified three key institutions:

1 the major corporations;

2 the military;

3 the federal government.

Those who occupy the command posts in these institutions form three elites. In practice, however, the interests and activities of the elites are sufficiently similar and interconnected to form a single ruling majority which Mills termed the **power elite**. Thus the power elite involves the 'coincidence of economic, military and political power'. For example, Mills claimed that 'American capitalism is now in considerable part military capitalism.' As tanks, guns and missiles pour from the factories, the interests of both the economic and military elites are served. In the same way Mills argued that business and government 'cannot now be seen as two distinct worlds'. He referred to political leaders as 'lieutenants' of the economic elite, and claims that their decisions systematically favoured the interests of the giant corporations.

The net result of the coincidence of economic, military and political power is a power elite which dominates American society and takes all decisions of major national and international importance.

Elite unity

However, things were not always so. The power elite owes its dominance to a change in the 'institutional landscape'.

In the nineteenth century economic power was fragmented among a multitude of small businesses. By the 1950s, it was concentrated in the hands of a few hundred giant corporations 'which together hold the keys to economic decision'.

Political power was similarly fragmented and localized and, in particular, state legislatures had considerable independence in the face of a weak central government. The federal government eroded the autonomy of the states and political power became increasingly centralized.

The growing threat of international conflict led to a vast increase in the size and power of the military. The local, state-controlled militia were replaced by a centrally directed military organization.

These developments led to a centralization of decision-making power. As a result, power was increasingly concentrated in the hands of those in the command posts of the key institutions.

According to Mills, the cohesiveness and unity of the power elite is strengthened by the similarity of the social background of its members and the interchange and overlapping of personnel between the three elites. Members are drawn largely from the upper strata of society; they are mainly Protestant, native-born Americans, from urban areas in the eastern USA. They share similar educational backgrounds and mix socially in the same high-prestige clubs. As a result they tend to share similar values and sympathies which provide a basis for mutual trust and cooperation.

Within the power elite there is frequent interchange of personnel between the three elites: a corporation director may become a politician and vice versa. At any one time, individuals may have footholds in more than one elite. Mills noted that

'on the boards of directors we find a heavy overlapping among the members of these several elites' – a general may sit on the board of a large corporation. Similarity of social origin and the interchange and overlapping of personnel strengthens the unity of the power elite.

Elite dominance

Mills argued that American society was dominated by a power elite of 'unprecedented power and unaccountability'. He claimed that momentous decisions such as the American entry into the Second World War and the dropping of the atomic bomb on Hiroshima were made by the power elite with little or no reference to the people.

Despite the fact that such decisions affect all members of society, the power elite is not accountable for its actions either directly to the public or to any body which represents the public interest. The rise of the power elite has led to 'the decline of politics as a genuine and public debate of alternative decisions'. Mills saw no real differences between the two major political parties, the Democrats and the Republicans, and therefore the public was not provided with a choice of alternative policies.

In Mills' analysis, the bulk of the population is pictured as a passive and quiescent mass controlled by the power elite which subjects it to 'instruments of psychic management and manipulation'. Excluded from the command posts of power the 'man in the mass' is told what to think, what to feel, what to do and what to hope for by a mass media directed by the elite. Unconcerned with the major issues of the day, 'he' is preoccupied with 'his' personal world of work, leisure, family and neighbourhood. Free from popular control, the power elite pursues its own concerns – power and self-aggrandizement.

■ Elite self-recruitment in Britain

C. Wright Mills's view of elites in the USA can also be applied to Britain. A number of researchers have found that the majority of those who occupy elite positions in Britain are recruited from the minority of the population with highly privileged backgrounds. This appears to apply to a wide range of British elites including politicians, judges, higher civil servants, senior military officers and the directors of large companies and major banks. There are high levels of **elite self-recruitment**: the children of elite members are particularly likely to be themselves recruited to elite positions.

There is also evidence that there may be some degree of cohesion within and between the various elites. Individuals may occupy positions within more than one elite: cabinet ministers and other MPs may hold directorships in large companies. Individuals may move between elites: the former Conservative minister James Prior decided to leave Parliament to take up the chair of the board of the giant company GEC. Directors may also sit on the boards of a number of different companies.

Elites are also likely to have a common educational background: many members of elites attended public schools and went to Oxford or Cambridge University. John Rex argues that this type of education serves to socialize future top decision makers into a belief in the legitimacy of the status quo. It creates the possibility that the elites will be able to act together to protect their own interests. Rex suggests:

---

the whole system of 'Establishment' education has been used to ensure a common mind on the legitimacy of the existing order of things among those who have to occupy positions of power and decision.

The following studies provide evidence for the existence of such elites in Britain.

'Top decision makers'

In a study conducted in the early 1970s Tom Lupton and Shirley Wilson traced the kinship and marital connections of six categories of 'top decision makers'. These categories were ministers, senior civil servants and directors of the Bank of England, the big five banks, city firms and insurance companies.

Lupton and Wilson constructed twenty-four kinship diagrams, usually covering three generations and indicating relationships by birth and marriage. Seventy-three of the top decision makers appeared on these diagrams, accounting for 18 per cent of the total number of people included in the twenty-four extended family groupings. Clearly there were close kinship and marital ties between the elites examined and certain families were disproportionately represented in the ranks of top decision makers.

Members of Parliament

Research on the social background of members of the British Parliament indicates a marked degree of elite self-recruitment. Studies by W.L. Guttsman showed that despite its claims to represent the nation, membership of the House of Commons has been far from representative in terms of social origin. Table 9.1 shows the 'social composition' of the House of Commons in 1951 and 1970. The figures refer to the percentage of the total membership which falls into each category

Table 9.1 shows the importance of public school and Oxbridge as a route to the Commons. In 1970 nearly 50 per cent of all MPs attended public schools and over 33 per cent went to Oxbridge.

Table 9.2 shows the result of research by George Borthwick *et al.* into the educational background of Conservative MPs. It compares the new MPs elected in the 1979, 1983 and 1987 elections with those first elected to Parliament before 1979 but who remained MPs after the 1979 election. It therefore highlights changes in background. It shows some decline in the numbers of public school educated MPs, but nevertheless over half of the 1987 entry had been to public schools and 44 per cent had been to Oxford or Cambridge University.

Table 9.1 The social composition of the House of Commons in 1951 and 1970

	1951	1970
Elementary school only	13.0	10.0
Public schools	48.7	47.5
Oxbridge (Oxford and Cambridge)	36.2	38.9
All universities	51.9	58.8
Army and navy	5.5	4.0
Lawyers	18.0	19.5
Other professions	13.0	21.0
Commerce and industry	22.0	22.5
Manual workers and clerks	21.0	13.0

(*Source*: adapted from Guttsman, 'The British Political Elite and the Class Structure', in P. Stanworth and A. Giddens (eds), *Elites and Power in British Society*, Cambridge University Press, 1974.)

Table 9.2 Educational background of Conservative MPs

	Number %	Public school %	Eton %	Oxford %	Cambridge %	Other universities %
Pre-1979	261	75	17	30	25	17
1979 entry	78	59	14	21	14	32
1983 entry	104	55	6	19	19	38
1987 entry	57	53	7	30	14	32

(*Source*: Borthwick, G., Ellingworth, D., Bell, C. and MacKenzie, D. (November 1991) 'The social background of British MPs', *Sociology*, p. 71.)

John Scott points out that cabinets, particularly Conservative ones, are even more educationally unrepresentative than the House of Commons as a whole. For example, four-fifths of Mrs Thatcher's 1983 cabinet were educated at public schools (no less than one-third of whom had been to Eton and Winchester alone).

Civil and public servants

The common educational background of political elites is paralleled by that of those in senior positions in public service. D. Boyd has shown that a majority of elites in all the categories he examined, except that of naval officers, attended public school.

This would not be so significant if public schools were not fee-paying (that is, they are therefore not open to all sections of society). Ron Hall's study of the social background of students who attended Eton, the most prestigious British public school, showed that the vast majority were drawn from the families of the aristocracy, landed gentry, the higher professions, high-ranking officers in the armed forces and directors and managers in industry and commerce.

Company directors

A study by Richard Whitley conducted in 1971 of directors of large British companies produced similar findings to those of Lupton and Wilson, and Guttsman. Whitley compiled a list of 261 directors from the top forty industrial firms, the major clearing banks and merchant banks, and the leading insurance companies. Sufficient information was available on some 50 per cent of the directors.

Once more the importance of public schools as a route to elite status is apparent. Some 66 per cent of the directors of industrial companies and 80 per cent of the directors of financial companies attended public schools. Oxbridge, the next stage on the road to the top, is again in evidence. Of those directors who went on to higher education, around 66 per cent from industrial companies and 87 per cent from financial firms went to Oxbridge.

As in the Lupton and Wilson study, Whitley discovered relationships of kinship and marriage between directors, particularly in the financial firms. Of the twenty-seven financial firms in the study, twenty-six were connected by kinship and marriage when relationships were traced back over three generations.

Company chairpersons

Elite self-recruitment is particularly evident when the social background of company chairpersons is investigated. From a study of 460 British company chairpersons conducted in 1971, Stanworth and Giddens found that only 1 per cent had working-class origins, 10 per cent had middle-class backgrounds and 66 per cent came from the upper class which is defined as 'industrialists, landowners (and) others who possess substantial property and wealth'. There were insufficient data to classify the remaining 23 per cent.

Again public schools and Oxbridge figure prominently: 65 per cent of the chairpersons attended public schools, 7 per cent were privately educated, 11 per cent went to other forms of secondary school, data on the remaining 17 per cent being unavailable. Despite the expansion of secondary education, there is little evidence of the supposed rise of the 'grammar school executive' from humbler origins. Stanworth and Giddens conclude that 'while this may take place at other levels of management, it is likely to stop short, as in previous generations, at the doors of the boardroom'.

Elite theory in the USA and Britain – an evaluation

The evidence provided by C. Wright Mills and by numerous researchers in Britain have shown that those occupying elite positions have tended to come from privileged backgrounds, and that there have been important connections between different elites. However, the significance of these findings is open to dispute.

Some Marxists claim that they provide evidence for a ruling class based upon economic power, rather than a ruling elite based upon the occupation of 'command posts'.

Furthermore it has been argued that these versions of elite theory fail to measure power adequately: they do not show that these elites actually have power, nor that they exercise power in their own interests against the interests of the majority of the population.

Robert A. Dahl has criticized Mills from a pluralist perspective. He has claimed that Mills has simply shown that the power elite has the 'potential for control'. By occupying the command posts of major institutions it would certainly appear that its members have this potential. But, as Dahl argues, the potential for control is not 'equivalent to actual control'. Dahl maintains that actual control can only be shown to exist '*by examination of a series of concrete cases where key decisions* are made: decisions on taxation and expenditures, subsidies, welfare programs, military policy and so on'. If it can then be shown that a minority has the power to decide such issues and to overrule opposition to its policies, then the existence of a power elite will have been established. Dahl claims that by omitting to investigate a range of key decisions, Mills has failed to establish where 'actual control' lies. As a result Dahl argues that the case for a power elite remains unproven.

Dahl's criticism of C. Wright Mills applies with equal force to British studies of elite self-recruitment. Furthermore, the British studies make no

attempt to measure the second and third faces of power (they make no reference to non-decision making nor do they discuss how the wishes of the population may be manipulated by elites). As such, studies of elite self-recruitment may reveal something about patterns of social mobility but they provide little direct evidence about who actually has power.

Both C. Wright Mills's work and most British studies of elite self-recruitment are rather dated. Most of the British studies were carried out in the 1970s and evidence about elite self-recruitment in the 1980s and 1990s is thin on the ground. The more recent research on political elites which we discussed earlier, and work by John Scott on the 'upper class' (see pp. 51–5) suggest that elite self-recruitment is still common in Britain but the evidence only covers a limited range of elites.

Elite theory and communist societies

As a general theory of power in society, elite theory has been strongly criticized. However, in a more limited application, it has found greater support. In particular a number of researchers have argued that a version of elite theory best described and explained the nature and distribution of power in communist societies, at least until the collapse of communism in Eastern Europe and the former USSR in the late 1980s and early 1990s. For example, T.B. Bottomore argued:

The political system of Communist countries seems to me to approach the pure type of 'power elite', that is, a group which, having come to power with the support or acquiescence of particular classes of the population, maintains itself in power chiefly by virtue of being an organized minority confronting an unorganized majority.

Raymond Aron also maintains that power in communist societies could be represented in terms of an elite model. He argued that in the USSR political, economic and military power were concentrated in the hands of a 'unified elite' which had 'absolute and unbounded power'. The ruling minority directed the economy, making decisions about investment and wage differentials. It commanded the military and controlled the media, education and public welfare. It made all important decisions on national and international issues.

Aron claimed that the unity of the ruling elite stemmed from the fact that 'Politicians, trade union leaders, public officials, generals and managers all belong to one party and are part of an authoritarian organization.' In a single-party state in which political parties other than the Communist Party were illegal and where all important organizations were under state control, Aron argued that the mass of the population was left 'without any means of defence against the elite'.

A number of researchers have also argued that the ruling minority in communist societies employed power primarily for self-enrichment rather than for the benefit of society as a whole. As we outlined in the previous chapter, this view was adopted by Milovan Djilas.

The view of the USSR as a totalitarian society dominated by a ruling elite with absolute power, concerned primarily with furthering its own interests at the expense of the mass of the population, has been criticized by David Lane. He claimed that the principal aim of the Soviet elite was the industrialization and economic development of the USSR. Centralized state control was a means to this end 'rather than simply being used to further the interests of the political elites'.

Elite rule was not predominantly exploitive. It was concerned with mobilizing a largely agrarian peasant population for industrial growth. Compared to pre-revolutionary days, there was greater economic and educational equality in the USSR. Lane rejected the view that there was a ruling elite with absolute power. For example, he showed how the military, leading scientists and industrial managers influenced the policies and decisions of political rulers during the Khrushchev era.

Since Bottomore, Aron, Djilas and Lane analysed communist societies, many of the latter have changed dramatically since Gorbachov's leadership of the USSR followed by the ending of the Communist Party's monopoly of power in nearly all Eastern European communist societies. In February 1990 a plenum of the Central Committee of the Communist Party decided to move towards a multi-party system. However much elites dominated these societies before the changes, events have demonstrated that their position was not unassailable.

Fragmented elites – government in Britain

A distinctive elite theory of power and the state is provided by Ian Budge, David McKay and David Marsh et al. Along with C. Wright Mills they accept that elite rule takes place in modern democracies, but they deny that the elite is a united group. Rather they believe that there are a large number of different **fragmented elites** which compete for power. They state 'The evidence points to a variety of groups, interests and organizations all exercising considerable influence over policies but divided internally and externally.'

Budge et al. deny that power is concentrated only in the hands of a state elite centred on the prime minister and the cabinet. They point out that political parties may be divided between different factions or groups: traditionally there have always been divisions between the 'left wing' and 'right wing' of the Labour Party over issues such as how many industries should be nationalized. Budge et al. claim there were similar divisions in Conservative cabinets in the 1980s and early 1990s between supporters of Thatcherite policies and the 'wets' urging a more cautious approach. Furthermore governments cannot always rely on the support of backbench MPs: in the 1974–9 Labour Government only 19 per cent of Labour MPs did not vote against government policy at some time. To complicate matters even further the House of Lords has the power to delay, and sometimes effectively kill, legislation.

For these reasons Budge et al. claim that elites within Parliament are too divided to be able to be the dominant force in British politics.

These divisions are further increased by the civil service. Ministers tend to rely on their civil servants for information and advice, to be guided by civil servants, and to develop departmental loyalties. Those representing spending ministries such as education and defence may as a result compete with each other to gain a larger share of the total government budget. Civil servants also have more direct methods of exercising power. Even when decisions have been reached, they have considerable room for manoeuvre in interpreting and implementing them.

Budge et al. use a very broad definition of the state. To them it includes not only central government, but also local government and a range of semi-independent institutions and organizations.

Local government, they argue, has both the ability and the will to challenge central authority. For example, Britain continues to have a considerable number of local education authorities which retain at least some grammar schools despite the attempts of successive Labour Governments to abolish them.

Further constraints on central government stem from the independence of the judiciary and the police. Judges have considerable discretion in interpreting the law, to the extent that they can have a major impact upon the effects of government legislation. To give just one example, judicial decisions have limited the scope of the Race Relations Act of 1971 so that it does not outlaw racial discrimination in private clubs. The police have almost as much independence. Budge *et al.* point out that the chief constables 'are wholly responsible for all decisions' in their force. If senior police officers do not effectively enforce a particular law, government decisions will have little impact.

Yet another important limitation on the Government is the existence of a large number of **quangos** (Quasi-Autonomous Non-Governmental Organizations). These range from organizations such as the Jockey Club, to the Trustees of National Museums, the BBC and nationalized industries. Although most of these organizations rely to some extent on government funding, they still have freedom to take an independent line. For example, at times the BBC has broadcast programmes against the wishes of, or critical of, the Government.

According to this view, then, there are a wide variety of elites within what can be broadly defined as the state, who limit the degree of power held by the Government. But Budge *et al.* do not see power as confined to the state. In common with elite pluralists they point out that some pressure groups have considerable power. In particular the unions have sometimes been able to thwart the Government through strikes, while the CBI and financiers have been able to veto some governmental decisions by using their financial power.

The Government also has to contend with the elites of international organizations such as NATO and the EC, and it is bound by the decisions of the Court of Justice of the EC. In 1976, for example, the British Government was forced by that court to introduce tachographs (which can read whether the drivers have broken EC regulations) into commercial vehicles.

Summary and critique

The fragmented elite theory sees power resting with a very wide variety of elites, government ministers, backbench MPs, senior civil servants, officials in local government, the chairpersons of nationalized industries, the leaders of other quangos, senior judges and police officers, top union officials, powerful business people and those occupying the senior positions in international organizations to which Britain belongs. Since the elite are fragmented and divided rather than cohesive and united, Budge *et al.* do not agree with C. Wright Mills that any single group in society monopolizes power. They would agree with pluralists that a wide variety of groups and interests are represented in society, but they would disagree that this adds up to a truly democratic government. As they put it, 'fragmentation does not guarantee effective popular control'.

Budge *et al.* may exaggerate the extent to which some elites act independently of political leaders. Since their study was published in 1983 the number of quangos in Britain has rapidly increased. For example, new funding councils for various parts of the welfare state have been introduced along with NHS trusts and some schools and all colleges have become formally independent of local authorities and the national government. Yet most such quangos still rely very heavily on government funding and in many the Government has a role in appointing officials.

The Further Education Funding Council is a case in point. This organization determines the funding of further education and sixth form colleges and in 1994 had an annual budget of £2.64 billion. Despite its control over such vast sums none of its members are elected, but are directly appointed by the Government. In 1994 two of its members were former Conservative politicians and four were businessmen, including Anthony Close from Forte, a business which contributed £80,500 to the Conservative Party in 1992. The Government not only determines the personnel involved, it also sets the overall budget and has directly intervened in the affairs of the FEFC by withholding funds from colleges unless they persuaded their staff to accept new contracts. Thus, while quangos might seem to produce independent elites which can come into conflict with the political elite, their autonomy can sometimes be illusory with the governmental elite remaining the dominant force.

The fragmented elite theory is also open to similar criticisms as the work of C. Wright Mills. It tends to assume that those in elite positions actually exercise power. Budge *et al.* back their analysis up with numerous examples, but do not provide systematic evidence on the basis of distinguishing the three faces of power.

Marxists and some other conflict theorists would claim that all elite theory fails to identify the underlying basis for power. In particular, Marxists argue that power derives from wealth in the form of owning the means of production, rather than from the occupation of senior positions in society. We will examine Marxist views on power and the state in the next section.

■ Power and the state – conflict perspectives

Conflict perspectives, like elite theory, see power as concentrated in the hands of a minority in society. Conflict theorists also agree with elite theorists who see power being used to further the interests of the powerful.

All conflict theories stress that the powerful and the powerless have different interests and that these differences may lead to conflict in society. Unlike elite theory, though, these approaches do not assume that power rests with those who occupy key positions in the state. They see the source of power lying elsewhere in society. In particular Marxists and neo-Marxists see power as being based upon economic resources.

A wide variety of Marxist-influenced conflict theories of power have been developed. We start this section by examining the work of Marx and his friend and collaborator Engels, before going on to consider the views of those who have developed less orthodox Marxist views.

■ Marx and Engels on power and the state

According to Marx, power is concentrated in the hands of those who have economic control within a society. From this perspective the source of power lies in the economic infrastructure.

1 In all **stratified societies** the means of production are owned and controlled by the ruling class. This relationship to the means of production provides the basis of its dominance. It therefore follows that the only way to return power to the people involves communal ownership of the means of production.

2 In a **communist society** power would be equally distributed amongst the whole of the population, since no person would have greater economic power than any other individual.

As we have seen in previous chapters, in capitalist society ruling-class power is used to exploit and oppress the subject class, and much of the wealth produced by the proletariat's labour power is appropriated in the form of profit or surplus value by the bourgeoisie. From a Marxist perspective the use of power to exploit others is defined as **coercion**. It is seen as an illegitimate use of power since it forces the subject class to submit to a situation which is against its interests. If ruling-class power is accepted as legitimate by the subject class, this is an indication of **false class consciousness**.

Ruling-class power extends beyond specifically economic relationships. In terms of Marxist theory, the relationships of domination and subordination in the infrastructure, will largely be reproduced in the superstructure (see p. 34 for a definition of these terms). The state (as part of the superstructure) reflects the distribution of power in society. The decisions and activities of the state will favour the interests of the ruling class rather than those of the population as a whole.

Marx himself did not write a detailed sociology of the state, but his associate, Engels, did try to spell out the origins and nature of the state.

The origins and evolution of the state

Engels claimed that in **primitive communist societies** the state did not exist. **Kinship** (or family relationships) formed the basis of social groupings. These societies were essentially agricultural, and no surplus was produced beyond what was necessary for subsistence. It was therefore impossible for large amounts of wealth to be accumulated and concentrated in the hands of a few. There was little division of labour, and the means of production were communally owned.

Only when societies began to produce a surplus did it become possible for a ruling class to emerge. Once one group in society became economically dominant, a **state** developed.

Engels believed that the state was necessary to 'hold class antagonisms in check'. In primitive communist societies all individuals shared the same interests; in **class societies**, a minority benefited from the existing social system at the expense of the majority. According to Engels the exploited majority had to be held down to prevent them from asserting their interests and threatening the position of the ruling class. Thus in ancient Athens the 90,000 Athenian citizens used the state as a method of repressing the 365,000 slaves.

The simplest way the state could control the subject class was through the use of force or coercion. Engels pointed to the police, the prisons and the army as state-run institutions used to repress the exploited members of society.

Engels believed that coercion was the main type of power used to control the population in early states. In ancient Athens and Rome, and the feudal states of the Middle Ages, ruling-class control of the state was clearly apparent. For example, the feudal state consisted exclusively of landowners; serfs possessed neither private property nor political rights. However, Engels believed that more advanced forms of the state were less obviously a coercive tool of the ruling class. Indeed, Engels described democracies as the 'highest form of state', for with such a state all members of society appear to have equal political power. Each individual in societies with universal suffrage can vote, and in theory therefore has as much influence over government policy as every other individual. According to Engels this would tend to mean that the existing social order would be perceived as fair, just and legitimate, since the state would be

seen to reflect the wishes of the population. As such the state would not need to rely so heavily on the use of force: in most cases the authority of the state would be accepted by the population.

In reality, however, Engels believed democracy was an illusion. Real power continued to rest with the owners of the means of production, and not with the population as a whole.

One way in which the ruling class could ensure that the state continued to act in its interest was through corruption. Troublesome officials who threatened to follow policies harmful to the bourgeoisie could be bribed. A second way to determine government policies was through the use of the financial power of capitalists. The state often relied upon borrowing money from the bourgeoisie in order to meet its debts. Loans could be withheld if the state refused to follow policies beneficial to the bourgeoisie.

The end of the state

Marx and Engels did not believe that the state would be a permanent feature of society. Since they believed its purpose was to protect the position of the ruling class and to control the subject class, they argued that it would become redundant once classes disappeared. In the immediate aftermath of the proletarian revolution, the proletariat would seize control of the state. They would use it to consolidate their position, establish communal ownership of the means of production, and destroy the power of the bourgeoisie. Once these objectives had been achieved class divisions would no longer exist, and the state would 'wither away'.

The views of Marx and Engels on the state are neatly summed up in the *Communist Manifesto* where they say 'The executive of the modern state is but a committee for managing the common affairs of the whole bourgeoisie.'

However, Engels did accept that in certain circumstances the state could play an independent role in society when its actions would not be completely controlled by a single class. Engels argued that at particular points in history two classes could have roughly equal power. He claimed that in some monarchies of seventeenth- and eighteenth-century Europe the landowning aristocracy and the rising bourgeoisie were in opposition to each other and both were equally powerful. In this situation the state could take an independent line since the warring classes effectively cancelled each other out.

Marx and Engels inspired many later Marxists to devote a great deal of attention to the study of power and the state, but their original work is sometimes vague, and has been interpreted in different ways. Furthermore the work of the founders of Marxism has not been entirely free from criticism from more contemporary sociologists adopting this perspective. Consequently a number of contrasting Marxist theories of the state have been developed. These differ over the precise way in which they see the bourgeoisie controlling the state, the extent to which they believe the state enjoys independence from ruling-class control, and the importance they attach to this institution for maintaining the predominance of the bourgeoisie in capitalist societies.

■ Ralph Miliband – an instrumentalist view of the capitalist state

The British sociologist Ralph Miliband, follows Marx and Engels in seeing power as being derived from wealth. He rejects the pluralist view that in 'democracies' equal political rights give each member of the population equal power. He refers to political equality as 'one of the great myths of the epoch', and claims that genuine political equality is 'impossible in the conditions of advanced capitalism' because of the power of those who own and control the means of production.

Miliband follows conventional definitions of the state, seeing it as consisting of the institutions of the police, the judiciary, the military, local government, central government, the administration or bureaucracy and parliamentary assemblies. He believes that it is through these institutions that 'power is wielded', and that this power is exercised in the interests of the ruling class.

Miliband sees the state as acting as the direct tool or **instrument** of those who possess economic power. They use it to preserve their economic dominance, maintain their political power and stabilize capitalist society by preventing threats to their position.

Elites and the ruling class

To Miliband the state is run by a number of elites who run the central institutions. These elites include cabinet ministers, MPs, senior police and military officers, and top judges. Together he sees them as acting to defend the ruling class or bourgeoisie: he believes all the elites share a basic interest in the preservation of capitalism and the defence of private property. In some ways Miliband's views are similar to those of the elite theorist C. Wright Mills, but Miliband sees elites acting in the interests of capitalists and not just in their own interests.

Miliband attempts to justify his claims by presenting a wide range of empirical evidence.

1 First, he tries to show that many of those who occupy elite positions are themselves members of the bourgeoisie. For example, he points out that in America from 1899 until 1949 60 per cent of cabinet members were businessmen, and this occupational group also made up about 33 per cent of British cabinets between 1886 and 1950.

2 Obviously the above figures do leave a considerable proportion of the state elite who are not from business backgrounds. To take account of this point Miliband advances his second type of evidence, which attempts to show that the non-business person in the state elite will, in any case, act in the interests of the bourgeoisie. He argues that groups such as politicians, senior civil servants and judges are 'united by ties of kinship, friendship, common outlook, and mutual interest'. The vast majority come from upper or middle-class families. Most share similar educational backgrounds since they have attended public schools and Oxford or Cambridge University. As such they have been socialized into identifying with the interests of the ruling class. Furthermore, even those few recruits to elite positions who come from working-class backgrounds will only have gained promotion by adopting the values of the ruling class. They will have undergone a process of **bourgeoisification**, and come to think and act as if they were members of the bourgeoisie.

3 Third, Miliband claims to be able to show that the actions of the state elites have, in practice, tended to benefit the ruling class. He points out that judges see one of their primary duties as the protection of private property. He suggests that Labour Governments have done little to challenge the dominance of the ruling class. Although the 1945 Labour Government nationalized a number of industries, it stopped far short of what many of its supporters would have wished. The existing owners were generously compensated, and the appointment of business people to run the industries

meant that they were operated in a capitalistic way which, if anything, assisted private industry.

Legitimation

Miliband also advances an explanation as to why the majority of the population should accept a state which acts against their interests. He examines various ways in which the subject class is persuaded to accept the status quo. In effect, he considers the third face of power, claiming that the economic power of the ruling class enables them to determine the beliefs and wishes of the remainder of the population. He believes this takes place through the **process of legitimation** which he regards as a system of 'massive indoctrination'. Miliband argues that the capitalist class seeks to:

---

persuade society not only to accept the policies it advocates but also the ethos, the values and the goals which are its own, the economic system of which it is the central part, the 'way of life' which is the core of its being.

Miliband illustrates his argument with an analysis of advertising by means of which capitalist enterprises promote both their products and the 'acceptable face' of capitalism. He argues that all advertising is political since it serves to further the power and privilege of the dominant class. Through advertisements, giant, privately owned corporations such as ICI, BICC, Unilever, ITT and the major banks and oil companies, promote the view that their major concern is public service and the welfare of the community. Profits are a secondary consideration and portrayed mainly as a means of providing an improved service.

The image of the corporation and its products is made even rosier by association in advertisements with 'socially approved values and norms'. Miliband argues that capitalism and its commodities are subtly linked via advertisements to 'integrity, reliability, security, parental love, child-like innocence, neighbourliness, sociability'. With these kinds of associations, the exploitive and oppressive nature of capitalism is effectively disguised.

Finally, advertising promotes the view that the way to happiness and fulfilment involves the accumulation of material possessions, in particular the acquisition of the products of capitalism. The individual is encouraged to 'be content to enjoy the blessings which are showered upon him' by the 'benevolent, public-spirited and socially responsible' capitalist enterprise.

Miliband argues that advertising provides one example of the ways in which capitalism is legitimated. He regards the process of legitimation as essential for the maintenance of capitalist power. If successful, it prevents serious challenge to the basis of that power: the private ownership of the means of production. In the following chapters, we will examine further aspects of the process of legitimation in detail.

■ Nicos Poulantzas – a structuralist view of the state

Nicos Poulantzas has criticized Miliband's view of the state and has provided an alternative interpretation from a Marxist perspective. A **structuralist** approach *emphasizes* the importance of social structure, and *minimizes* the importance of the actions of individuals in society. As such Poulantzas sees much of the evidence advanced by Miliband as irrelevant to a Marxist view of the state.

The state and the capitalist system

Poulantzas describes the state as 'the factor of cohesion of a social formation': in other words, the state is vital for maintaining the stability of the capitalist system. As part of the superstructure, it will automatically serve the interests of the ruling class. It is not necessary for members of the ruling class to occupy elite positions within the state: the existence of a capitalist system is itself sufficient to ensure that the state functions to benefit the ruling class. Similarly, the background of members of the state elite is of little importance: it is not their class origin but their class position which determines their behaviour. Since they occupy positions in a state which inevitably functions to benefit the bourgeoisie, their job will ensure they act in the interests of the bourgeoisie regardless of their background. They will not take actions harmful to capitalist interests.

Relative autonomy

Poulantzas takes this argument a stage further. He claims:

> the capitalist state best serves the interests of the capitalist class only when members of this class do not participate directly in the state apparatus, that is to say when the ruling class is not the politically governing class.

Poulantzas argues that the ruling class does not directly govern but rather its interests are served through the medium of the state. As such, the state is **relatively autonomous** from the ruling class. To some degree it is free from its direct influence, independent from its direct control. However, since the state is shaped by the infrastructure, it is forced to represent the interests of capital.

Poulantzas argues that the relative autonomy of the state is essential if it is to effectively represent capital. The state requires a certain amount of freedom and independence in order to serve ruling-class interests. If it were staffed by members of the bourgeoisie, it might lose this freedom of action. The following reasons have been given for the relative autonomy of the capitalist state.

1 As a group the bourgeoisie is not free from internal divisions and conflicts of interest. To represent its common interests the state must have the freedom to act on behalf of the class as a whole.

2 If the bourgeoisie ruled directly, its power might be weakened by internal wrangling and disagreement and it might fail to present a united front in conflicts with the proletariat. The relative autonomy of the state allows it to rise above sectional interests within the bourgeoisie and to represent that class as a whole. In particular, it provides the state with sufficient flexibility to deal with any threats from the subject class to ruling-class dominance.

3 To this end the state must have the freedom to make concessions to the subject class which might be opposed by the bourgeoisie. Such concessions serve to defuse radical working-class protest and contain the demands within the framework of a capitalist economy.

4 Finally, the relative autonomy of the state enables it to promote the myth that it represents society as a whole. The state presents itself as a representative of 'the people', of 'public interest' and 'national unity'. Thus in its ideological role, the state disguises the fact that essentially it represents ruling-class interests.

Repressive and ideological state apparatus

Poulantzas does not disagree with Miliband about the importance of legitimation. However, he goes much further in seeing this process as being directly related to the state. He uses a much broader definition of the state than Miliband. He divides it into the **repressive apparatus** – the army, government, police, tribunals and administration – which exercises coercive power, and the **ideological apparatus** – the church, political parties, the unions, schools, the mass media and the family – which is concerned with the manipulation of values and beliefs, rather than the use of force.

Most writers do not see institutions such as the family as constituting part of the state. Poulantzas argues they should be categorized in this way for the following reasons.

1 Like the repressive institutions of the state, they are necessary for the survival of capitalism. Without them the proletariat might develop class consciousness and challenge the capitalist system.

2 The ideological apparatus depends ultimately on the repressive apparatus to defend and maintain it. He gives the example of the defence of education through the French police and army intervening against the student revolts in Paris in 1968.

3 Poulantzas argues that changes in the repressive apparatus of the state lead to changes in the ideological apparatus. In fascist Germany, for instance, the state took direct control of much of the ideological apparatus.

4 He claims that the ultimate communist aim – the 'withering away' of the state – will only be achieved with the abolition of institutions such as the family.

Criticisms of Poulantzas

Miliband has tried to defend himself against the criticisms made by Poulantzas, and has put forward his own criticisms of the latter's work. In particular he accuses Poulantzas of **structural super-determinism**. In other words, Miliband does not believe that ultimately all aspects of the behaviour of the state are determined by the infrastructure. Such a theory, he claims, cannot account for the differences between fascist and 'democratic' states within capitalist systems.

Furthermore, Miliband argues that Poulantzas's theory is not backed up by empirical evidence. It is not sufficient to say that the state must act in the interests of capitalism, for such an assertion is only convincing to the extent that it is based upon evidence.

Miliband also questions the definition of the state proposed by Poulantzas. He expresses great scepticism about the claim that institutions such as the family can be seen as part of the state. He accepts that they might have an ideological role, but denies that they are in any sense directly controlled by the state. Although he agrees that they are part of the political system, he argues that they possess so much independence or autonomy that it is ridiculous to see them as part of the state.

Other writers have also attacked Poulantzas. Anthony Giddens argues that his theory of the relative autonomy of the state is 'vague and ambiguous'. Giddens suggests that Poulantzas does not explain satisfactorily how it is possible for the state both to have autonomy and to be certain to act in the long-term interests of the ruling class.

It can also be argued that the theory of the relative autonomy is impossible to prove or disprove. If the theory is accepted, any action the state takes can be interpreted one way or another as benefiting the bourgeoisie. If it does not appear to directly benefit them, it can be dismissed as a mere concession to the proletariat. Some neo-Marxists argue that concessions can be more than token gestures. To writers such as Gramsci, the working class do have some power and can influence the actions of the state. (We will analyse Neo-Marxist views later in this chapter.)

■ Evidence to support Marxism

Marxist writers have adopted more sophisticated methods of measuring power than either pluralists or elite theorists. They have examined all three faces of power identified by Steven Lukes, and have also extended the concept to include the effects of decisions.

The effects of decisions

As we saw earlier, the decision-making approach to measuring power used by pluralists has been heavily criticized. Marxists such as Westergaard and Resler argue that power can only be measured by its results: if scarce and valued resources are concentrated in the hands of a minority, that group largely monopolizes power in society. Westergaard and Resler maintain that 'power is visible only through its consequences; they are the first and final proof of the existence of power.' Put simply, the proof of the pudding is in the eating: whoever reaps the largest rewards at the end of the day holds the largest share of power.

Westergaard and Resler claim that the marked inequalities which characterize British society 'reflect, while they also demonstrate, the continuing power of capital'. The concentration of wealth and privilege in the hands of the capitalist class therefore provides visible proof of its power. Legislation on taxation which could lead to the redistribution of wealth is not usually enforced effectively. Furthermore, loopholes in the law often allow the wealthy to avoid paying much of their tax. Westergaard and Resler believe that the welfare state does little to redistribute income for it is largely financed out of the taxes paid by the working class.

Apart from information on the distribution of wealth and income, Westergaard and Resler use detailed examples to show that the activities of the state represent the interests of the ruling class.

Concessions to the working class

In Britain, as in other advanced capitalist societies, the state has implemented a wide range of reforms which appear to directly benefit either the subject class in particular or society as a whole. These include legislation to improve health and safety in the workplace, social security benefits such as old-age pensions and unemployment and sickness insurance, a national health service and free education for all.

However, these reforms have left the basic structure of inequality unchanged. They have been largely financed from the wages of those they were intended to benefit and have resulted in little redistribution of wealth. They can be seen as concessions which serve to defuse working-class protest and prevent it from developing in more radical directions which might threaten the basis of ruling-class dominance. In Westergaard and Resler's words, 'Their effects are to help contain working-class unrest by smoothing off the rougher edges of insecurity.'

Non-decision making

Marxists have also been concerned to examine the second face of power: non-decision making. John Urry, in criticizing Dahl, argues that he:

> ignores the process by which certain issues come to be defined as decisions and others do not. The study of decisions is the failure to study who has the power to determine what are decisions.

Many Marxists believe that the range of issues and alternatives considered by governments in capitalist societies are strictly limited. Only **safe decisions** are allowed, those which do not in any fundamental way challenge the dominant position of the bourgeoisie. The sanctity of private property is never questioned, the right of workers to keep the profits produced by their labour is never seriously proposed, and communism is never contemplated as a realistic alternative to capitalism.

Ideology

According to Marxists, the ability of the ruling class to suppress such questions is related to the third face of power. Numerous studies claim that the bourgeoisie are able to produce false class consciousness amongst the working class. Westergaard and Resler argue that ruling-class ideology promotes the view that private property, profit, the mechanisms of a market economy and the inequalities which result are reasonable, legitimate, normal and natural. If this view is accepted then the dominance of capital is ensured since 'no control could be firmer and more extensive than one which embraced the minds and wills of its subjects so successfully that opposition never reared its head.'

Westergaard and Resler claim that because of the pervasiveness of ruling-class ideology, the capitalist class rarely has to consciously and actively exercise its power. Capitalism and the inequalities it produces are largely taken for granted. A capitalist economy guarantees a disproportionate share of wealth to a minority and generates an ideology which prevents serious questioning of the established order. As a result, issues which might threaten the dominance of capital are usually prevented from reaching the point of actual decision. The capitalist class is therefore able to enjoy advantage and privilege 'merely because of "the way things work", and because those ways are not open to serious challenge'.

Criticisms of Marxism

Marxists provide a considerable amount of evidence to support their views. However, the Marxist theory of the state cannot explain why the state became stronger rather than 'withering away' in communist countries. Furthermore Marxists fail to take account of the possibility that there are sources of power other than wealth. Some conflict theorists deny that wealth is the only source of power, despite seeing economic power as important.

We will now consider the state from a Neo-Marxist viewpoint.

■ Neo-Marxist approaches to power and the state

A number of writers have put forward theories of the state and the distribution of power in society which are heavily influenced by Marxism, but which differ in some significant way from the original writings of Marx and Engels. This section examines the work of two such writers: the early twentieth-century sociologist Antonio Gramsci, and the contemporary British sociologist David Coates.

■ Antonio Gramsci – hegemony and the state

Antonio Gramsci (1891–1937) is among the most influential twentieth-century theorists who have themselves been influenced by Marx. Gramsci was an Italian sociologist and political activist. A leader of the Italian Communist Party, he is partly remembered for the part he played in the Turin Factory Council Movement in which industrial workers in that city unsuccessfully attempted to seize control of their workplaces. From 1926 until his death Gramsci was imprisoned by Mussolini's fascist government, and his main contributions to sociological theory are contained in his *Prison Notebooks* written during that time.

Gramsci parted company with conventional Marxists in arguing against **economic determinism**: he did not believe that the economic infrastructure determined to any great degree what occurred in the superstructure of society. He talked of a 'reciprocity between structure and superstructure': although the infrastructure could affect what took place in the superstructure, the reverse was also possible.

Gramsci did not deny that the economic infrastructure of society was important: it provided the general background against which events took place. An economic crisis might increase political awareness amongst the proletariat, for instance. However he felt that the actions of groups trying to maintain or change society were at least as important.

Political and civil society

Unlike traditional Marxists, Gramsci divided the superstructure of society into two parts: political society and civil society. **Political society** consisted of what is normally thought of as the state. This was primarily concerned with the use of force by the army, police and legal system to repress troublesome elements within the population. **Civil society** consisted of those institutions normally thought of as private, particularly the church, trades unions, the mass media and political parties.

In a novel way Gramsci claimed that 'the state = political society + civil society'. He used a very broad definition of the state, for he did not think of it in terms of particular institutions but rather in terms of the activities of a dominant class in society.

Hegemony

At one point in his work Gramsci described the state as:

the entire complex of practical and theoretical activities with which the ruling class not only justifies and maintains its dominance, but manages to maintain the active consent of those over whom it rules.

If the ruling class managed to maintain its control by gaining the approval and consent of members of society, then it had achieved what Gramsci called **hegemony**. Hegemony was largely achieved not through the use of force, but by persuading the population to accept the political and moral values of the ruling class. Here Gramsci stressed the importance of ideas in society: effective ruling-class control was only maintained to the extent that the ruling class could retain command of the beliefs of the population through civil society.

Gramsci's view on how hegemony could be maintained comes close to Marx's view of false class consciousness. However, unlike Marx, Gramsci did not see the ruling class as imposing entirely false beliefs and values on the population, nor did he see the state as a simple instrument or tool of ruling-class dominance. The state could only remain hegemonic if it was prepared to compromise and take account of the demands of exploited classes, and for three important reasons ruling-class hegemony could never be complete.

Historic blocs

In the first place, Gramsci saw both the ruling and subject classes as being divided. The ruling class was divided into groups such as financiers, small and large industrialists and landowners, while industrial workers and agricultural peasants were a major division within the subject class. No one group on its own could maintain dominance of society. Hegemony was only possible if there was some sort of alliance between two or more groups.

Gramsci called a successful alliance which achieved a high level of hegemony a **historic bloc**, but because of the different elements it contained it would always be something of a compromise between the groups involved.

Concessions

The second reason why the hegemony of one group would never be complete was that the state always had to make some **concessions** to the subject class. Gramsci said 'hegemony undoubtedly presupposes that the interests and tendencies of the groups over which hegemony is to be exercised are taken into account'. From this point of view the ruling class had to make concessions in order to be able to rule by consent instead of relying on the use of force. It had to adopt some policies which benefited the subject class.

Dual consciousness

If the ruling class were able to indoctrinate the population completely, then clearly it would not be necessary for them to make concessions. However, Gramsci maintained that this was never possible. He believed that individuals possessed **dual consciousness**. Some of their ideas derived from the ruling class's control over civil society and its ability to use institutions such as the church and schools to persuade people to accept that capitalism was natural and desirable. However in part individuals' beliefs were also the product of their activities and experiences. To a limited extent they would be able to see through the capitalist system, and realize that their interests lay in changing it. For example, their day-to-day experience of poor working conditions and low wages would encourage them to believe that at the very least some reforms of the system were necessary.

The overthrow of capitalism

According to Gramsci then, power derived only in part from economic control; it could also originate from control over peoples' ideas and beliefs. Since the ruling class was unable to completely control the ideas of the population, it could never completely monopolize power. Similarly the subject class would always have some influence over the activities of the state. The activities of political society would benefit them to the extent that they were able to realize where their interests lay and wrest concessions from the ruling class.

Like Marx, Gramsci looked forward with anticipation to a proletarian revolution, but he saw such a revolution arising in a rather different way. He did not accept that the contradictions of the capitalist economic system made a revolution a foregone conclusion.

The revolutionary seizure of power in Tsarist Russia by the Bolsheviks was only possible because of a complete absence of ruling-class hegemony in that country. The rulers lacked the consent of the subject classes and so those classes were able to overthrow them with a full frontal attack. Gramsci termed such a violent revolutionary seizure of power a **war of manoeuvre**, in which direct action was taken to secure victory.

In most advanced capitalist countries though, he saw the ruling class as having much more hegemony than they had possessed in Russia. Consequently countries such as Italy and Britain needed a good deal more preparation before they would have the potential for a proletarian revolution. Gramsci called such preparation a **war of position**, a kind of political trench warfare in which revolutionary elements in society attempted to win over the hearts and minds of the subject classes. It was only when individuals had been made to realize the extent to which they were being exploited, and had seen through the ideas and beliefs of the ruling class, that a revolution was possible. For this to happen, 'intellectuals' had to emerge within the subject classes to mould their ideas and form a new historic bloc of the exploited, capable of overcoming ruling-class hegemony.

■ David Coates – *The Context of British Politics*

Gramsci's views on the state are reflected in a number of more recent studies, including David Coates's book on British politics. Coates does place more emphasis on economic factors than Gramsci, but nevertheless eventually draws conclusions which are similar to Gramsci's. We will discuss his examination of the economic influences on the British state first, before considering those aspects of his work which can be seen as 'Gramscian'.

The state and multinationals

Coates starts his work by attempting to show the limitations on the state which are produced by the international capitalist system. He tries to demonstrate that each capitalist country cannot be analysed separately, for capitalism is not limited by national boundaries.

Multinational corporations with branches in a number of different countries form an increasingly important part of the modern capitalist system. The British Government's freedom of action is limited by these companies. The multinationals' decisions about where to invest money and where to open and close factories can have a tremendous impact on the British economy. The largest multi-nationals such as General Motors, wield massive economic power: General Motors has a greater turnover than the total wealth produced by the Danish economy.

Attempts to control multinationals are unlikely to be successful. If, for example, a government introduces exchange controls to prevent the companies moving profits abroad, then such controls can be bypassed through **transfer pricing**. This involves one part of a company selling commodities to a part of the same company in another country at unrealistically high or low prices. Through this technique multinationals effectively move resources from country to country whatever laws a particular government passes.

In any case, if the Government is not to risk jeopardising the high proportion of investment in Britain which comes from abroad, it cannot afford to pursue policies which would seriously threaten the interests of foreign capitalist companies operating in Britain.

The actions of the British Government are further restricted by the major international financial institutions and the World Bank. These organizations are intended to oversee the world's banking, financial and monetary systems. In the 1970s a British Labour Government was forced to seek a loan from the IMF (International Monetary Fund), but in order to secure it the Government had to comply with the IMF's instructions on how the British economy should be managed. (Global influences on states are discussed again later in the chapter, see pp. 541–3.)

The state and finance capital

Like the elite pluralists Richardson and Jordan, Coates stresses the international influences on the British Government. Unlike them, and in common with traditional Marxists, he emphasizes the economic limitations on governments. These constraints come not only from abroad but also from within British society.

Coates claims that **finance capital** (the banks, insurance companies and financial trusts in the City of London) have a particularly strong influence on the British Government. He calculates that in 1981 such institutions controlled assets worth some £562 billion, which represents about £10,000 for every member of the population. He suggests that all Governments rely to a considerable extent upon the support of these institutions. If, for example, the latter choose to sell sterling it can rapidly cause a currency crisis as the value of the pound falls.

If the Government takes measures which harm the City of London's position as a major financial centre in the world, it risks enormous damage to the British economy as a whole. This is because Britain imports more manufactured goods than it exports, and much of the difference in the balance of payments is made up by **invisible earnings** such as the income from the sale of insurance policies worldwide provided by Lloyds of London, and other financial services.

In comparison to financiers, Coates claims, **industrial capital** (in this case British-owned industry), has less influence over government policy. The CBI, for example, did not persuade the Government to reduce the value of the pound and reduce interest rates in the late 1980s. Both of these measures would have benefited industry. The first would have made British goods cheaper and easier to sell abroad; the second would have cut companies' costs by reducing the price of borrowing money. Both, however, would have made Britain less attractive as a financial centre for foreign investors.

Using such evidence Coates claims that finance capital has had more influence over the British Government than industrial capital, and the consequences have been the decline of British manufacturing industry and rising unemployment.

Divisions in the ruling class

These aspects of Coates's work have much in common with traditional Marxism, though they do place more emphasis on international constraints on the state. In other respects his work is much closer to that of Gramsci. He explicitly rejects the instrumentalist view of the state put forward by Miliband, and the structuralist relative autonomy approach advocated by Poulantzas.

In the first case, Coates argues that the state cannot be a simple instrument of the ruling class since the ruling class itself is divided in such a way that different 'fractions' of capital have different interests. Small and large industrialists, multinational and domestic concerns, finance and industrial capital, all place conflicting demands on the state. Often the state cannot serve one section of the ruling class without damaging another.

Coates rejects the structuralist view because he does not accept that the existence of a capitalist system ensures that ultimately the state will have to act in the interests of the ruling class as a whole. As he puts it, 'what capitalism generates around the state is not a set of unavoidable imperatives so much as a set of conflicting demands'. These conflicting demands stem not just from divisions within the ruling class, but also from divisions between classes.

Dual consciousness

Coates points out that capitalism produces not just an economic system but also a civil society. He follows Gramsci in seeing civil society as consisting of the **private** institutions such as the family, as well as the social relationships between a whole variety of groups. All these groups make demands on the Government, and they include workers and their unions, ethnic minorities and women, as well as capitalists.

Like Gramsci, Coates sees the exploited and oppressed groups as possessing dual consciousness. To some extent they are taken in by attempts to legitimate the capitalist system, but to some extent they also see through that system. According to Coates, individuals in Britain in exploited classes hold contradictory beliefs. They may accept the basic arrangements of capitalism such as wage labour, but nevertheless believe that the rich have too much power. They may be racist and sexist, but remain committed to human dignity and equal rights and opportunities for all. Many are loyal to parliamentary democracy, but strongly believe that ordinary people have little influence over government.

In this situation the state has to try to maintain its hegemony despite the existence of some degree of class consciousness among the population.

Hegemony

Coates follows Gramsci in seeing the state as the institution which attempts to cement an alliance or historic bloc of different sections of the population which is capable of maintaining hegemony. Again he agrees with Gramsci that this may involve making real concessions to exploited and oppressed groups. Coates argues that the ruling class do not monopolize power entirely. Trades unions, for example, can sometimes exercise a

genuine influence on government policy. He sees the nationalizations and improvements made in the welfare state under the 1945 Labour Government as representing real working-class gains, and not just token concessions.

According to Coates, most British Governments have been able to maintain a high degree of hegemony. They have achieved this by succeeding in getting the population to accept a 'national project'. Most people have been willing to go along with state policies which appear to offer some benefit to all sections of the population. Until the 1980s this was fairly easy in a rapidly expanding world capitalist economy: in the 1950s and 1960s full employment, rising wages and the provision of welfare services such as health and education produced a fairly stable society.

However, Coates is not convinced that ruling-class hegemony will remain easy to maintain in the future. He sees Mrs Thatcher's Conservative Party policies as an attempt to produce a new national project based upon an appeal to improve Britain's economic competitiveness by reducing public spending. Coates believes that the economic weakness of the British economy in the world capitalist system (which was in recession in the late 1980s) produced a crisis for the British state. Its legitimacy was increasingly questioned, and he doubted that Thatcherism would be successful in re-establishing ruling-class hegemony.

Coates's work provides a good example of how conflict theories of power and the state have become increasingly sophisticated. He identifies a wide range of groups, institutions and processes through which power is exercised and the activities of the state are influenced. The groups involved include members of the working class and trades unions as well as different fractions of capital at home and abroad. He denies that one group monopolizes power, or that all power stems from wealth, but agrees with other conflict theorists that power is very unequally distributed.

■ Abercrombie, Hill and Turner – *The Dominant Ideology Thesis*

Gramsci and Coates's most distinctive contribution to the study of power and the state lies in the emphasis they place upon ideas and beliefs as sources of power in addition to economic factors. However, some Marxists following a more traditional line reject this view. Abercrombie, Hill and Turner deny that there is a coherent **dominant ideology** in capitalist societies, and question the view that any such ideology is the main factor holding advanced capitalist societies together. In a rather similar way to Gramsci they suggest that members of the subject and ruling classes often hold contradictory views. For example, members of the subject class may support the welfare state, but believe in the importance of economic freedom and competition between individuals and companies; similarly they are often strongly nationalistic, but this does not square with the existence of multinational corporations.

Furthermore, Abercrombie *et al.* claim to have evidence that members of the subject class actually reject such elements of a dominant ideology that can be identified. They quote a number of studies

to support their point. Paul Willis's study of education, *Learning to Labour*, shows that working-class boys reject much of what schools teach them and attach greater value to manual labour rather than more highly rewarded non-manual jobs. Hugh Beynon's study of *Working for Ford* revealed that many factory floor workers are alienated from work and feel exploited.

Such evidence might be taken as support for Gramsci's theory of dual consciousness, but Abercrombie *et al.* see it in a very different light. They argue that it shows the importance of economic power, for if so many people reject ruling-class ideology, then it must be the ruling class's wealth rather than their ideological control that allows them to retain their dominance in society. Abercrombie *et al.* argue that it is factors such as the threat of unemployment, the risk of poverty and the possibility of being imprisoned which make the exploited conform in capitalist societies.

■ State-centred theories of power

The approaches we have considered so far have been **society-centred**: they see the state and its actions as shaped by external forces in society as a whole. We will now look at an alternative perspective which has a completely different viewpoint.

■ Eric A. Nordlinger – the autonomy of democratic states

Society-centred and state-centred approaches

According to Eric A. Nordlinger theories of power and the state are either society-centred or state-centred. To Nordlinger all the perspectives on the state and power examined so far are society-centred and society-centred approaches have 'a pervasive grip upon citizens, journalists and scholars alike'. Pluralism sees the state's actions as determined by the democratic will of the people; elite theory sees its actions as shaped by the wishes of a small group of powerful people;

Marxism sees the state as shaped by the interests of a ruling class. Although some Marxist and neo-Marxist theories concede that the state may have some autonomy from the ruling class, they do not go far enough because, in the final analysis, the state is portrayed as being unable to go against ruling-class interests.

Nordlinger criticizes all these approaches saying:

> the possibility that the state's preferences have at least as much impact on public policy as do society's is ignored; the state's having certain distinctive interests and divergent preferences is not considered; the state's many autonomous actions are not calculated; the state's numerous autonomy-enhancing capacities and opportunities are not examined.

Nordlinger argues that society-centred approaches have been so dominant that a very distorted and one-sided view of the state and power has been produced. Although society can and does influence the state, the reverse sometimes happens. This is what Nordlinger describes as the **state-centred approach** to the theory of power. The state acts independently or autonomously to change society.

This is true of democracies, as well as other types of state, even though they are supposed to be under the control of the electorate.

The autonomy of the democratic state takes three forms.

Type 1 state autonomy

Type 1 state autonomy occurs when the state has different wishes to those of major groups in society and implements its preferred policies despite pressure for it not to do so. For example, state policy in Sweden is often formulated by Royal Commissions. About 80 per cent of those who serve on the Commissions are civil servants and the recommendations are usually followed even when they are unpopular with the electorate or are opposed by elites outside the state. In Norway public–private committees which formulate public policy are often chaired by civil servants and again their recommendations are normally accepted whatever the opposition to them.

To Nordlinger there are many ways in which the state can enhance its autonomy from society. These include:

1 using secretive systems of decision making;

2 using honours, appointments or government contracts to persuade opponents to accept proposals;

3 using the state's resources to counter resources used by opponents (for example using the funds in the state bank to prop up a currency being undermined by speculators);

4 threatening to change a range of policies in such a way as to harm the interests of opponents of the state's policies;

5 taking actions or issuing statements which cause mistrust among different groups of opponents.

Because the state has considerable power of its own it is sometimes able to utilize it to prevent effective opposition.

Type 2 state autonomy

Type 2 state autonomy occurs when the state is able to persuade opponents of its policies to change their mind and support the Government. Nordlinger argues that this is quite common and examples of it can be found in classic pluralist studies such as Dahl's *Who Governs?*. Although

Dahl claimed that the authorities in New Haven were responsive to public opinion and the policies they adopted were shaped by interest groups, Nordlinger believes that the authorities played an active role in manipulating public opinion. For example, Dahl himself pointed out that there had been little or no interest in a programme of urban renewal until the mayor put the issue on the agenda and persuaded various interest groups to support him. None of the interest groups agreed with his proposals when they were first put forward. From this viewpoint then, Dahl's own evidence showed that the state could act autonomously in shaping public opinion rather than having its policies shaped by public opinion.

Type 3 state autonomy

Type 3 state autonomy occurs when the state follows policies which are supported, or at least not opposed, by the public or powerful interest groups in society. Very often significant groups in society may be unsure of what policies to support and leave it up to the state to decide. For example, between 1948 and 1971 the USA's grain farmers, industrial workers and exporters made little attempt to influence America's international monetary policy. Although the policy affected them a great deal they were unable to predict the effects of the state's policies and so were content to accept whatever policies the state adopted.

On many issues which are concerned with the state itself there is considerable apathy on the part of the public and the state has considerable freedom of manoeuvre even though the issues may be of great importance. Nordlinger suggests that such issues tend to include 'possible changes in the state units' formal powers relative to one another, policy implementation responsibilities, budgetary allotments, staffing, organization, and standard operating procedures'.

Nordlinger's views suggest that the state has considerable autonomy over many issues whether there is opposition from society or not. While he recognizes that the autonomy is only partial, he perhaps goes further in attributing independence to the state than other state-centred approaches. His theory is backed up by a limited number of empirical examples.

Other sociologists have conducted more detailed research in their attempts to show that the state acts as an independent source of power.

■ Theda Skocpol – *Bringing the State Back In*

The autonomy of states from society

Theda Skocpol is perhaps the most influential of the state-centred theorists. She has written extensively about the state as a source of power and is a strong supporter of what she calls *Bringing the State Back In*. She argues that pluralists, functionalists, Marxists and neo-Marxists have all tended to see the state as shaped by external pressures and have neglected the possibility that the state can shape society. Like Nordlinger she is critical of such approaches. For example, she says:

> virtually all neo-Marxist writers on the state have retained deeply embedded society-centred assumptions, not allowing themselves to doubt that, at base, states are inherently shaped by classes or class struggles and function to preserve and expand modes of production. Many possible forms of autonomous state action are thus ruled out by definitional fiat.

To Skocpol states can have considerable autonomy and as actors have the potential capacity to achieve their policy goals. These goals 'are not simply reflective of the demands or interests of social groups, classes or society' for states can have their own goals and pursue their own interests.

Skocpol believes that one of the main aims of states and parts of states is to increase their own power. She suggests that 'We can hypothesize that one (hidden or overt) feature of all autonomous state actions will be the reinforcement of the prerogatives of collectivities of state officials.' 'Policies different from those demanded by societal actors will be produced' as states 'attempt to reinforce the authority, political longevity, and social control of the state organizations.'

Skocpol gives a number of examples of states acting in pursuit of their own interests. In 1968 in Peru there was a coup organized by career military officers who used state power to plan economic growth, weaken opposition groups in society, and try to impose order. In Britain and Sweden, according to Skocpol, the civil services often oppose the policies of elected politicians and have

some success in ensuring that their policies are not implemented in such a way as to undermine the power of the state. In the USA both the White House and the State Department are fairly insulated from public opinion and democratic control and they often act autonomously. Skocpol's own research had found that in the USA after the First World War the Department of Agriculture was a powerful part of the state which acted independently in the pursuit of its own interests.

State capacities

Although all states have the potential to achieve their own goals, their capacity to do so will be affected by a number of factors.

1 Skocpol says that 'sheer sovereign integrity and the stable administrative control of a given territory are preconditions for any state's ability to implement policies'. Unless a state can largely command the territory for which it is responsible it will have no power base from which to achieve aims.

2 States which have a reliable and substantial source of income are more powerful than those which do not. For example, if a state relies heavily upon the export of a single commodity or product (as some third world states do) then it is vulnerable to a decline in demand for the product or a reduction in its value. On the other hand, economies which export a wide variety of products have a more reliable income.

3 States which govern a rich society obviously have more potential for raising domestic taxes than those which govern poor societies. This can strengthen their power base.

4 States which are forced to borrow large amounts of money can end up in a weaker position than those which have sufficient revenue to finance their activities.

5 States also tend to increase their power if they can recruit many of the most able and highly educated members of society into their ranks. Not only does this tend to improve the organization of the state, it also deprives non-state organizations and groups of the personnel who would be most likely to challenge and undermine the state's power.

Skocpol believes that whether a state becomes powerful or not partly depends upon how well organized groups in society are. She criticizes Marxists for claiming that states always reflect the interests of a dominant class, saying:

the political expression of class interests and conflicts is never automatic or economically determined. It depends on the capacities classes have for achieving consciousness, organization, and representation. Directly or indirectly, the structures and activities of states profoundly condition such class capacities.

To Skocpol, Marxist political sociology 'must be turned, if not on its head, then certainly on its side'. The state shapes the activity of classes as much as classes shape the activity of the state.

States' capacities are profoundly affected by their relationships with other states. Large and powerful armed forces increase the capacity of a state to defend its own territory or seize the territory of other states. Control over territory is the basis of the state's ability to raise revenue and finance its activities. States can be weakened by wars, especially if they incur crippling costs or they suffer military defeats. External threats can result in internal weakness and sometimes contribute to the state losing its autonomy from society.

States and social revolutions

In her most substantial empirical study Skocpol compared revolutions in France, China and Russia. She argues that in all these cases the activities of the states and the weak position that the states found themselves in played a vital role in causing revolutions. The Chinese, Russian and French states acted in ways which undermined their own power and produced a situation where the state was overthrown by particular classes. Although class conflict was important in all the revolutions, none of them could be understood without considering the role of the state as an autonomous actor. All three were *'imperial states –* that is, differentiated, centrally coordinated administrative and military hierarchies functioning under the aegis of the absolute monarchies'. Although there were differences in the circumstances which led to the revolutions Skocpol argues that in all of them 'The revolutionary crises developed when old-regime states became unable to meet the challenges of evolving international situations.'

In the following sections we will analyse these three revolutions in more detail.

France

France fought two wars in the middle years of the eighteenth century: the War of the Austrian Succession (1740–8) and the Seven Years War (1756–63). Both were expensive and France had little military success – in fact in the Seven Years War it lost a number of colonies to Britain. In eighteenth-century France around 85 per cent of the population were peasants but agriculture was not highly developed. France had a lower per capita income than Britain and other European competitors, restricting the wealth available for the state to tax. Furthermore, the tax system was inefficient with numerous exemptions and deductions for the elites who collected the taxes. Consequently the French state got into financial trouble. This was further exacerbated by French involvement in the American War of Independence when France sided with the American colonists against their British rulers.

In 1797 an Assembly of Notables was called and the finance minister proposed a new land tax to deal with the problem. The Notables rejected the proposal but advocated the establishment of a new body representing landowners, a body which would have to approve any new taxes. When the king refused there were demonstrations and protests in different parts of the country. The king then summoned the Estates General which consisted of various elites, but this body was unable to reach any agreement about what to do. While most members of the Estates General wanted to restrict the power of the king they could not agree how to do it. Consequently the French state was effectively paralysed and its weakness allowed popular protests to take place. Skocpol says:

By the summer of 1789, the result was the 'Municipal Revolution', a nation-wide wave of political revolutions in cities and towns throughout France, including of course the celebrated 'fall of the Bastille in Paris'. In the context of the simultaneous political crises of 1788–9, crowds of artisans, shopkeepers, journeymen, and labourers roamed the cities searching for arms and grain and demanding both bread and liberty.

The French monarchy was overthrown and replaced by revolutionary government.

China

In China the Ch'ing Dynasty ruled from 1644 to 1911. Some 80 per cent of the population were tenants or smallholders living off small plots of land which they rented or owned. Although markets had become commercialized, poor transportation meant that they tended to be localized. The Imperial Chinese state was a 'centralized, autocratic, and semi-bureaucratic administrative structure staffed (under the Ch'ing) by approximately forty-thousand officials'. The emperor was an absolute ruler but decisions were administered by officials who had to pass stringent exams or to buy official titles. The gentry was the dominant class and their position was based upon a combination of owning land and other types of wealth and on holding public offices.

In 1839–42 China fought and lost the Opium War with Britain and from that point onwards China began to be subject to increasing foreign influence and power. France, Russia, Japan and Britain gained their own spheres of influence within China, threatening the sovereignty of the Chinese state. At the same time as the state was becoming too weak to resist foreign intervention, Chinese agriculture was finding it difficult to feed a growing population. However, despite the greater numbers of people, government revenues failed to increase because they mainly depended upon a land tax which had not been raised since 1712.

Local magistrates demanded larger and larger fees for collecting taxes, causing resentment among the peasant population. There were major rebellions (such as the Taiping Rebellion of 1850–64) and the Imperial Government had to make concessions to the local gentry in return for their help in putting down such rebellions. The gentry won tax concessions which further weakened the finances of the state, and then China was defeated in the 1895–6 war with Japan.

At the start of the twentieth century the Government embarked on a series of radical reforms. The old exam system was replaced and new military academies were set up to train a modern army. However 'the new measures further undermined the already tenuous central power and exacerbated tensions between the gentry and the Manchu autocracy'. In 1910 the gentry demanded an end to parliamentary government and the state authorities refused. In 1911 the Government decided to buy all railway projects from the local

groups which had invested in them. This provoked the disturbances which led to the 1911 revolution. The army and the leaders of local assemblies seized power.

Initially China became a republic but a general subsequently took control and tried to make himself into a new emperor. Power then became concentrated in the hands of local military organizations. It was not until the communists seized power under Mao Tse Tung in 1949 that central authority was restored.

Russia

As in China the revolution in Russia led to the creation of a communist regime, although unlike in China it followed soon after the revolution. In France and China the revolutions took place in times of peace although earlier military crises had contributed to the revolutions. In Russia the revolution took place during the First World War. Russia's problems, though, were not just military.

The Russian landed nobility was economically weak and to a large extent was politically dependent on the tsars. Most nobles had relatively small estates and had little spare money to invest in agriculture or indeed in other enterprises. Although feudalism had come to an end with the emancipation of the serfs in the 1860s, economic development was slow and living standards remained well below those in much of Western Europe.

During the 1860s and 1870s Russia opened up to foreign investment and trade and during the 1890s significant industrialization began. However, this created new classes and new tensions. A small proletariat was created, working in the developing industries and concentrated in the larger cities. The proletariat worked under poor conditions and although unions were banned strikes soon became common. Despite the industrialization Russia lagged far behind many European countries in terms of economic development. This contributed to the economic and military weakness of the Russian tsars.

In 1905 Russia was at war with Japan and there was an unsuccessful attempt at a revolution involving a naval uprising and strikes. During the First World War Russia suffered crushing military defeats. Millions were killed and Russian military production could not keep up with supplying the troops. Some front-line troops had to enter battle without weapons. Much of the civilian population was also experiencing great hardship. The 1917 revolution started in Petrograd where severe food shortages provoked rebellion by the local population. Army units who were suffering similar deprivations refused to fire on the demonstrators and revolution soon spread throughout the country.

Conclusion

According to Skocpol in Russia, China and France it was the weakness of the state which ultimately caused revolutions. She comments:

> In all three cases...the ultimate effect of impediments to state-sponsored reforms was the downfall of monarchical autocracy and the disintegration of the centralized administrative and military organizations of the state.

In each case the state could have acted differently by introducing more effective reforms earlier to prevent the development of a revolutionary situation. Each regime was brought down by a combination of external pressures from other states and the way 'agrarian relations of production and landed dominant classes impinged upon state organizations'. While class relationships were important, none of the revolutions could be understood without reference to the actions taken by the states involved.

In all three countries the revolutions led to the collapse of the old state, but they were replaced sooner or later by states with even more centralized power and more autonomy than the old regimes. Napoleonic France and communist China and Russia were, to Skocpol, clear examples of states which could exercise power and which could sometimes act to pursue their own interests rather than the interests of groups within society.

■ Evaluation of state-centred theories

One of the problems with state-centred theories may be that they are often unclear about their precise theoretical position. Thus Bob Jessop argues:

> in their eagerness to criticize society-centred analysis, they have failed to distinguish three different sorts of claim about the state. It is not clear whether they are: (a) rejecting the so-called society-centred approach in its entirety and arguing that the state should be the independent variable; (b) bending the stick in the other direction for polemical purposes, one-sidedly emphasizing the importance of the state as a crucial causal factor; or (c) suggesting that a combination of society and state-centred perspectives will somehow provide a complete account of state-society relations.

Most critics are prepared to accept that the actions of the state should be taken into account in studies of power. However, many believe that Skocpol and similar writers exaggerate the importance of the state in an attempt to support their approach. Furthermore, Jessop argues that it is artificial and misleading to see the 'state' and 'society' as being quite separate institutions. He sees state and society as so intimately connected that it is not possible to completely separate them in accounts of power.

Both McLennan and Jessop argue that state-centred approaches offer misleading analyses of the so-called society-centred approaches which they are attacking. Jessop claims that they rest on a '"straw-man" account of the society-centred bias in other studies'. In reality, Jessop suggests, other theories do take account of the power of the state. McLennan argues in similar fashion that many Marxists, such as Poulantzas, recognize that the state has 'relative autonomy' and its actions are not entirely determined by society. McLennan concludes that 'Pragmatically it is always degrees of autonomy we are dealing with.'

This is true both of Skocpol's work and of many Marxist theories of power, and the theoretical difference between these approaches has been greatly exaggerated by many of the advocates of a state-centred approach.

Globalization and the power of the nation-state

A number of sociologists have begun to argue that the analysis of power cannot be confined to examining the distribution of power within particular nation-states. This is reflected in some of the theories we discussed earlier in this chapter. In his Gramscian discussion of British politics David Coates recognizes that the actions of the British state are limited by the operation of the international capitalist system (see pp. 532–4). Similarly the state-centred theories such as Skocpol's which we have just discussed acknowledge that state power is affected by the actions of other states.

State-centred theories do, however, tend to emphasize the autonomy of individual states and the significance of their actions. Approaches which emphasize the importance of **globalization** tend to see the power that exists outside nation-states as restricting their activities and limiting their power.

Kevin Bonnett – globalization, power and politics

Globalization

Kevin Bonnett argues that 'Power in Britain (or in any other advanced country) can no longer be understood as first and foremost existing *within* the society.' Nation-states are a comparatively recent historical creation: Italy and Germany did not become unified states until the late nineteenth century and many colonies did not become autonomous states until they achieved independence a few decades ago.

In some parts of the contemporary world, for example in the former Yugoslavia, nation-states have broken up and increasingly throughout the world, power is exercised *across* nation-states rather than *within* them. Bonnett says 'Many of the economic, political, military and ideological powers that shape our lives work across nations – and increasingly they operate on a global scale.'

Multinational corporations, international financial markets, trans-national communications systems (such as satellite TV) and trans-national organizations (such as the EC) all operate outside of the control of individual nation-states, yet have a profound influence on what goes on within them.

Bonnett acknowledges that international forces – such as colonial empires and international trade – have been significant for centuries but he believes that recently global forces have become more important. He claims 'What is new is the scale and intensity of . . . links and the fact that space and time are "shrunk" by the speed and relative cheapness of travel and electronic communications.'

Globalization and nationalism

While global forces seem to weaken the power of the nation-state from outside, they can also do so from within. Trans-national and global relationships may also strengthen 'localism or small-scale nationalism'. Ethnic and national groups seeking independence from large states can look to trans-national organizations or systems of security to assist them in asserting their independence and claiming nationhood. Thus 'The Baltic states and other parts of the former USSR have found it possible to proclaim independence – by virtue of links to wider economic and military networks' such as the EC and NATO. In Western Europe Scottish nationalists have stressed the practicality of becoming independent from England while remaining within the EC. Bonnett says:

> It has come to seem that almost any *people* with a shared culture or language now comes to define itself as a *nation*. And once they define themselves as a nation, the logical step in the contemporary world is to become a *nation-state* – claiming sovereign independence and national self-determination.

(We discuss nationalism in more detail on pp. 711–16.)

From this point of view the power of nation-states is under threat from two directions.

Internationalism threatens to reduce the power of states to exercise power independently, while small-scale nationalism and **localism** threaten to undermine the unity of existing states.

■ David Held – democracy and the cosmopolitan order

David Held is a British sociologist who has given detailed consideration to the implications of globalization for the state and democracy. He talks of the 'progressive enmeshment today of states and societies in regional and global networks' and discusses how democracy can be developed in a world in which the nation-state does not have all the power.

Examples of globalization

In terms of economics, governments find it hard to control their own economy. For instance, countries cannot determine their own interest rates without reference to those in other countries. If a government wants to cut interest rates to stimulate its economy, it may be unable to do so if other countries keep their rates high, thus attracting investment to them. World financial markets can undermine the value of a country's currency forcing its government to change policy to take account of the new circumstances. Furthermore, multinational companies use marketing and production systems which are global in scale. The same products are sold throughout the world and production can be moved from one country to another regardless of the wishes of national governments.

Ecological issues cut across national boundaries as well. The destruction of rain forests, air pollution and nuclear disasters can all lead to environmental damage in other parts of the world. With more people travelling, health issues such as AIDS become difficult to address in one country without taking account of the situation in others.

Like other writers on globalization, Held also points to the increased power of international and trans-national organizations. He notes that the 'European Community, the North Atlantic Treaty Organization or the International Monetary Fund diminish the range of decisions open to given

national "majorities".' Military issues also take on a global dimension with the existence of spy satellites for gathering intelligence and intercontinental missiles. With the ending of the Cold War as a result of the collapse of communism in Russia and Eastern Europe, there are closer contacts and more complex inter-connections between groups of nations which were formerly hostile to one another.

Held points out that some countries are in a particularly weak position when trying to maintain their independence and autonomy. Many Third World countries are heavily in debt to the First World and they rely upon them for aid and military protection. They are left 'vulnerable and dependent on economic forces and relations over which they have little, if any, control'.

Overall then, nations have become less and less isolated and at the same time less able to control their own affairs. This has serious implications for democracy.

Globalization and cosmopolitan democracy

Democracy is based upon the assumption that a group of people can exercise control over their own affairs. As it becomes more difficult to confine issues within national boundaries, it becomes harder to operate democracy along these lines. As well as bringing people together, globalism can create 'fragmentation' and 'disintegrative trends'. Closer global ties bring diverse cultures together and can increase the chances of conflict and war between people of different cultures and national identities. As the old power blocs of the Cold War become less dominant, people assert their local and regional ethnic or nationalist identities, threatening democracy. Globalization can 'weaken old political and economic structures without necessarily leading to the establishment of new systems of regulation'.

Held argues that these problems can only be tackled by producing a new democratic system which enables people in different nations and localities to decide together how they are going to tackle issues which cut across national boundaries

In fact, since the Second World War it has been recognized that some form of international law and global institutions might be necessary to create order in the world and deal with international issues. In the post-war period the World

Bank and the International Monetary Fund were introduced to try to regulate aspects of the world's monetary and economic systems, and the United Nations was established. Although the UN has tried to intervene in issues throughout the world Held argues:

> The image of international regulation projected by the Charter (and related documents) was one of 'states still jealously "sovereign"', but linked together in a 'myriad of relations'; under pressure to resolve disagreements by peaceful means and according to legal criteria.

Because of the emphasis on sovereignty of states though, the UN has not been able to act effectively in most of the situations it has tried to deal with. Members of the Security Council have been able to veto any policy they disapproved of and with China, the USA, Russia, the UK and France all as permanent members, there has rarely been agreement. Nevertheless, the UN has, according to Held, been useful. It has:

> provided a vision, in spite of all its limitations, of a new world order based upon the meeting of governments and, under appropriate circumstances, of a supranational presence in world affairs championing human rights.

Despite its having had some success, Held does not believe that the UN, or a similar body, can produce democracy in the new, globalized world. Instead he proposes a **cosmopolitan model of democracy** in which people can participate in decisions taken at different levels. Some decisions would be taken by new regional parliaments representing continents such as Africa and Latin America. The existing European Parliament could be strengthened. Some trans-national issues could be resolved by referenda held in those areas of the world affected by particular issues.

Individuals would be protected in the cosmopolitan model of democracy by the 'entrench-ment of a cluster of rights, including civil, political, economic and social rights, in order to provide shape and limits to democratic decision-making'. These rights would be incorporated into the constitutions of nation-states and international bodies. Such rights would be upheld by international courts which had strong powers to punish governments which refused to conform to them. Ultimately the world would need 'an authoritative assembly of all democratic states and societies – a re-formed UN, or a complement to it – would be an objective'.

Conclusion

Held admits that his proposals have many possible pitfalls. People might wish to ask questions about a new democratic international assembly, questions such as: 'Would it have any teeth to implement decisions? How would democratic international law be enforced' and 'Would there be a centralized police and military force?' However, Held believes that most concerns could be 'met and countered' and the establishment of the sort of international body he proposes is not beyond the bounds of possibility.

Held's views are perhaps somewhat idealistic. While many states are affected by global issues that does not necessarily mean that they have the same interests in relation to those issues. For example, poor Third World countries have an interest in changing aspects of the global economy from which the rich First World benefits and therefore have an interest in preserving. The disagreements among member states of the EC and the inability of the UN to take effective action in places such as Bosnia suggests that Held's vision of international democracy and cooperation will not easily become reality. Nevertheless, he may be right to point out that democracy must tackle the problem of globalization if power is not to become more distant from the citizens of nation-states. Identifying the problem is easier than finding the solution, but it could at least be seen as a step in the right direction.

▮ Michael Mann – the sources of social power

In recent work Michael Mann has started an ambitious project which aims to develop new theories of power and of sociological theory in general. However, far from simply entering current debates about power and sociological theory in an abstract way, he has tied his theory of social life to an account of the development of societies from 10,000 BC to the present day. In doing so, he has returned to a concern with the all-embracing questions about societal development with which the 'classical' sociologists Marx, Weber and Durkheim, were so concerned. Furthermore, Mann has a considerable advantage over these eminent sociologists since he has access to up-to-date historical and archaeological evidence which was unavailable to them.

Mann's work incorporates elements from the theories of power discussed in the two preceding sections of this chapter.

1 First, he agrees with writers such as Skocpol that the state can be an independent source of power arguing that 'political power' is as important as ideological, military and economic power.

2 Second, he follows theories of globalization in claiming that theories of power cannot be confined to examining how power is distributed within national boundaries. Like Held and others, Mann believes that networks of power can stretch across countries and across the globe. He does not, however see this as a particularly new phenomenon, claiming that networks of power have long extended across sizeable geographical areas.

In some ways Mann's work represents a more fundamental challenge to theories of power than state-centred approaches and the theory of globalization, for Mann starts his analysis by attacking perhaps the most basic concept of sociology, that of 'society'.

The non-existence of 'society'

Mann says 'if I could, I would abolish the concept of "society" altogether'. Although he continues to use the word 'society' for the sake of convenience, he is anxious to point out that 'societies are not unitary. They are not social systems (closed or open); they are not totalities.' Mann claims that it logically follows from this standpoint that non-existent societies cannot be divided into parts or sub-systems, as Parsons does, nor can they be analysed in terms of 'levels', as in the Marxist division between the infrastructure and the superstructure. Furthermore, he rejects the idea of societal evolution because of his belief that societies are not unitary.

How, then, is Mann able to justify his rejection of so many central concepts in sociological theory? His main argument is very simple: human behaviour is not, and has never been, exclusively related to, or caused by, a particular territory in which an individual lives. In the modern world, for example, the development of the mass media has led to many aspects of culture extending across national boundaries. Nor is the spread of cultural influences particularly new: for centuries major religions such as Islam and Christianity have had an influence which transcends national boundaries.

Like theorists of globalization, Mann claims that a society such as Britain is not a political unit which can be analysed independently. Britain is a member of the military alliance NATO, and of the economic grouping of nations, the EC. Many companies in Britain are owned by multinational corporations which are based abroad. Through trade, the British economy is affected by other countries, and cultural products from all parts of the world are imported. In order to understand the culture, politics, military activity and economics of Britain then, it is necessary to consider what happens in other parts of the world. Throughout history, according to Mann, trade, war and conquest have ensured that there has never been an isolated society.

Power networks and types of power

On the basis of such observations, Mann reaches the view that 'societies are constituted of multiple overlapping and intersecting sociospatial networks of power'. In order to understand social life, sociologists need to study the way that humans enter into social relationships which involve the exercise of power.

Since power is so central to his theory, Mann spends some time explaining what he means by the word and distinguishing different forms of power. He sees **power** as the ability to pursue and attain goals through mastery of the environment. Power, in this sense, can take two separate forms.

1 **Distributional power** is power over others. It is the ability of individuals to get others to help them pursue their own goals. Distributional power is held by individuals.

2 In contrast, **collective power** is exercised by social groups. Collective power may be exercised by one social group over another, for example when one nation is colonized by another. It may also be exercised through mastery over things, for example the ability to control part of nature through an irrigation scheme.

Having distinguished between different types of power, Mann goes on to explain the two main ways in which it can be exercised.

1 **Extensive power** is 'the ability to organise large numbers of people over far-flung territories in order to engage in minimally stable cooperation'. An example of extensive power would therefore be the influence over believers exercised by a major religion.

2 **Intensive power** on the other hand, is the ability 'to organise tightly and command a high level of mobilization or commitment from the participants'. Thus a religious sect might be seen as having intensive power in comparison to the more extensive power of a church.

In the final part of Mann's analysis of different types of power, he identifies a difference between authoritative and diffused power.

1 **Authoritative power** is exercised when conscious, deliberate commands are issued, and those to whom they are issued make a conscious decision to follow them. A football player following a referee's instructions to leave the field would be an example of authoritative power.

2 **Diffused power** spreads in a more spontaneous way. It involves power relationships, but ones which operate without commands being issued. Mann uses the example of market mechanisms: a company can go out of business not because someone commands that it does, but because it is unable to compete with other

Table 9.3   Michael Mann – examples of social power

	Authoritative	Diffused
Intensive	Army command structure	A general strike
Extensive	Militaristic empire	Market exchange

(*Source*: *Source of Social Power*, Volume 1, Cambridge University Press: Cambridge, 1986, p. 9.)

companies producing the same types of product. Often this type of power produces behaviour that appears as 'natural' or 'moral', or as resulting from 'self-evident common interests'.

By combining the distinctions between intensive and extensive, authoritative and diffused power, Mann is able to distinguish four principal types of power. Examples of the four types of power are given in Table 9.3.

The sources of power

So far this account of Mann's theory has explained the types of power that he believes exist, but not where that power comes from. Central to his approach is the simple idea that power can have four sources: these can be economic, ideological, political and military.

Mann follows Marx in thinking that **economic power** is important, but he does not attribute the primary role to it that Marx does, because of the importance of the three other sources. **Ideological power** involves power over ideas and beliefs; **political power** concerns the activities of states; and **military power** the use of physical coercion. In Marxist theory these sources of power are often seen as being united. From a Marxist point of view the group that has economic power – those who own the means of production – will also have ideological power through their ability to promote false class consciousness. Furthermore, the economically ruling class will exercise control over the state and will therefore have political power; through the state it will also monopolize military power.

Mann disagrees with the Marxist view, though, claiming that each source of power can be independent of the others. Ideological power can be wielded by churches or other religious organizations which may have little or no economic power.

The political power of a state does not ensure that it will have ideological power. In communist Poland, for example, much of the population appeared to attach more importance to the ideas of the Roman Catholic Church and the free trade union Solidarity than to those of the communist state. Even political and military power are not necessarily tied together. In feudal Europe, military power rested mainly in the hands of individual lords and not with the state. In modern societies in a *coup d'état* the army actually takes power from the political rulers. Thus in Chile, General Pinochet led a military coup in which power was seized from President Allende's elected government.

Of course Mann accepts that in a particular society at a particular time, two or more of the four sources of power might be monopolized by a social group, but all power never rests in one set of hands. Since no society is completely independent, networks of power will stretch across national boundaries, thus preventing a single group within a society having all the power.

An example of Mann's approach

In his explanation of social changes Mann explains how these various sources of power are related to each other. For example, he demonstrates how shortly after AD 1300 an innovation in military strategy led to a number of important social changes in Europe, and in particular a weakening in the influence of feudalism.

At the battle of Courtrai, Flemish infantrymen were faced by an attack from French mounted knights. At the time, semi-independent groups of armoured mounted knights were militarily dominant and the normal tactic for infantry who were attacked by them was to flee. On this occasion though, the Flemings were penned against a river and had no alternative but to fight. By adopting a close-knit formation the pike phalanx of the Flemings was able to unseat many of the knights and secure victory.

As a result, feudal mounted armies lost their dominance, and societies such as the Duchy of Burgundy, which did not adapt to the changed circumstances, declined. Furthermore, the change led to a centralization of state power and a reduction in the autonomy of feudal lords. It became recognized that mixed armies of cavalry, infantry and artillery were the answer to the pike phalanx, and states could more easily provide the resources to maintain this type of army than could individual lords. Thus, changes in the nature of military power led to an extension in the political power of the state.

On the surface, it might appear that this significant episode in history is an example of military technology determining the course of social change, but Mann believes ideological and military factors were also important. He suggests that pike phalanxes could not have succeeded unless the individuals in them were convinced that those on either side of them would stand firm. In societies such as Flanders and Switzerland, such trust was likely to develop because of the way of life of the burghers and free peasants there. Furthermore, the different types of army produced by the Flemings and the Swiss on one side, and feudal societies on the other, were related to their respective abilities to produce an economic surplus to finance their armies. Thus the four sources of social power were all linked: an extension of military power was related to the nature and distribution of ideological and economic power and led to an increase in the political power of the state. In this example military power was particularly important, but according to Mann, in other episodes in history, any of the other three sources of power can assume a more central role.

Conclusion

Other theories of power and the state tend to emphasize a particular source of power. Marxism stresses the importance of economic power, pluralism ideological power in democracies, and elite and state-centred theories emphasize political power. Mann's approach argues that any complete theory must embrace all of these, as well as including military power.

∎ Voting behaviour

We will now consider a rather different aspect of power – voting behaviour.

∎ Butler and Stokes – partisan alignment

Until the 1970s patterns of voting in post-war Britain followed a predictable pattern. Most **psephologists** (students of voting behaviour) agreed on the basic characteristics of British voting and on the explanation of these characteristics. David Butler and Donald Stokes were perhaps the most influential psephologists during the 1960s and early 1970s and their views became widely accepted.

There were two main features of the British political system at this time: partisan alignment and a two-party system. These were closely related to each other and together seemed to make it relatively easy to explain British voting.

Class and partisan alignment

The theory of **partisan alignment** (strong adherence to a particular party) explained voting in the following way.

1 It suggested that class, as measured by a person's occupation, was the most important influence on voting.

2 It claimed that most voters had a strongly partisan self-image: they thought of themselves as 'Labour' or 'Conservative'.

3 This sense of identity led to voters consistently casting their votes for the party with which they identified. Few people changed their votes between elections, there was little electoral volatility and there were few **floating voters** who were prepared to consider changing their allegiance.

Using the evidence from Butler and Stokes's research into the 1964 election, Ivor Crewe found that 62 per cent of non-manual workers voted Conservative, and 64 per cent of manual workers voted Labour.

Butler and Stokes themselves produced a range of figures which appeared to confirm that most voters had a strongly partisan self-image, and that

this self-image was closely related to voting. In 1964, for example, only 5 per cent of those they questioned did not claim to identify with a party. Of those who did identify with a party only 12 per cent said they identified 'not very strongly', while 41 per cent identified 'fairly strongly' and 47 per cent 'very strongly'. In the local elections in May 1963 85 per cent of those with a Conservative partisan self-image voted Conservative, and 95 per cent of those who identified with the Labour Party voted for it.

The strength of these political ties was reflected in the low **swings** (percentage changes in votes) between Conservative and Labour in successive elections. In the general elections of the 1950s the average swing was just 1.6 per cent. Few people changed the party they voted for because of the strength of their attachment to one or other of the major parties. As late as 1974 Butler and Stokes felt justified in saying 'class has supplied the dominant basis of party allegiance in the recent past'.

The two-party system

The second main feature of British voting patterns, the **two-party system**, was perhaps even more striking: together the Labour and Conservative parties dominated the political scene. In no election between 1945 and 1966 did their combined vote fall below 87.5 per cent of those cast, and the third most popular party, the Liberals, gained in excess of 10 per cent of the vote only once (in 1964).

The results did not surprise psephologists. If class determined voting, and there were two classes, then inevitably there would be two dominant parties to represent those classes. The Conservatives gained so many votes because middle-class non-manual voters identified with that party, while the Labour Party enjoyed similar levels of support among working-class manual voters. There was little room left for a third party. The Liberals were not believed to represent any particular class, and therefore could not rely on strongly partisan support from any particular section of the electorate. This was reflected in the very low vote they received in some elections: in 1951 the Liberals gained only 2.5 per cent of the votes cast.

Political socialization

So far we have examined the evidence for partisan alignment and the existence of a two-party system. However, this does not explain why there should be such a strong relationship between class and voting.

The explanation provided by Butler and Stokes was essentially very simple. To them, **political socialization** held the key to explaining voting. As children learned the culture of their society, they also learned the political views of parents and others with whom they came into contact. Butler and Stokes stated quite emphatically that 'A child is very likely indeed to share the parents' party preference.'

They saw the family as the most important agent of socialization, but by the time an individual was old enough to vote other socializing institutions would have had an effect as well. Butler and Stokes argued that schooling, residential area, occupation and whether they belonged to a union would all influence the way people voted. The Conservative Party could expect to get most support from those who:

1 attended grammar or public schools;

2 lived in middle-class areas where many people were homeowners;

3 were not members of unions.

Labour support would be most likely to come from those who:

1 attended secondary modern schools;

2 lived in working-class areas (and particularly on council estates);

3 were union members.

The most important factor, though, was whether voters had a manual or non-manual occupation.

All these factors were important because they influenced the extent to which voters came into contact with members of different classes and therefore whether they mixed with partisan Labour or Conservative supporters. Generally speaking, all these factors reinforced the effects of the voter's class background. For instance, children with parents who voted Labour were more likely to go to secondary modern schools and become trades union members.

In emphasizing the effects of socialization Butler and Stokes were denying that the **policy** preferences of an individual were important. Voters were not thought to pay much attention to the detailed policies outlined in party manifestos. They did not choose who to vote for on the basis of a rational assessment of which package of policies on offer would benefit them most. They voted emotionally, as an expression of their commitment to a particular party. To the extent that they had preferences for policies, these were largely shaped by the parties themselves: voters would trust their party to implement the best policies.

■ The 'problem' of deviant voters

The partisan alignment theory of voting was so widely accepted that in 1967 Peter Pulzer claimed that 'Class is the basis of British party politics; all else is embellishment and detail.' However, the partisan alignment theory could not explain the existence of **deviant voters**, those who did not conform to the general pattern.

Throughout the post-war period a significant number of the British electorate have been deviant voters. Deviant voters are normally defined as manual workers who do not vote Labour, and non-manual workers who do not vote Conservative. In other words deviant voters are those who do not vote for the party which is generally seen as representing their class.

The precise number of deviant voters fluctuated between elections, but generally there have been considerably more manual workers who did not vote Labour than non-manual workers who did not vote Conservative. According to Ivor Crewe, in the 1959 election 34 per cent of manual workers voted Conservative and 22 per cent of non-manual workers voted Labour.

The existence of deviant voters was important to psephologists both because of their political significance and the challenge they posed for the dominant partisan alignment theory.

1 They were politically important because they were central to determining the results of elections. (For most of the period since the war manual workers have formed a majority of the population; if there had been no deviant voters the Labour Party would have won every election.)

2 They were important for theories of voting because their existence seemed to directly contradict the claim that class was the basis of politics.

Consequently considerable attention was devoted to studying these voters and explaining their behaviour.

Deferential voters

One of the earliest explanations of working-class Conservative voting was given in the late nineteenth century by Walter Bagehot. He argued that the British are typically deferential to authority and prone to defer decision making to those 'born to rule' whom they believe 'know better'. Hence the attraction of the Conservative Party which, particularly in the nineteenth century, was largely staffed from the ranks of the landed gentry, the wealthy and the privileged. The Conservatives represented traditional authority and Bagehot argued that party image, rather than specific policies, was the major factor affecting voting behaviour. This led to the existence of the **deferential voter**.

In the early 1960s, Robert McKenzie and Alan Silver investigated the relationship between deferential attitudes and working-class support for the Conservative Party. They claimed that deference accounted for the voting behaviour of about half the working-class Tories in their sample. Deference was measured by giving respondents a choice between two 'candidates' for prime minister.

1 The first candidate had attended Eton, graduated from Oxford and served as an officer in the Guards. He was the son of a MP who was a banker by profession.

2 The second candidate was a lorry driver's son. He went to a grammar school, graduated from a provincial university and became an officer in the regular army.

Around half the working-class Tories chose the first candidate explaining their choice with statements like 'Breeding counts every time. I like to be set an example and have someone I can look up to.' By comparison only one-fifth of the working-class Labour voters selected this candidate.

Deferential Conservative voters tended to be older and to have lower incomes than the overall sample, and were more likely to be female. McKenzie and Silver suggested that deference was part of a more general traditional outlook. This would help to explain the high proportion of older deferential voters. Also many low-income workers had traditional rural backgrounds and women, with their attention centred on the home, were often insulated from change.

Secular voters

Those working-class Tories whose support for the Conservative Party could not be accounted for by deferential attitudes were termed **secular voters** by McKenzie and Silver. Seculars' attachment to the Conservative Party was based on pragmatic, practical considerations. They evaluated party policy and based their support on the tangible benefits, such as higher living standards, that they hoped to gain. They voted Conservative because of a belief in that party's superior executive and administrative ability.

McKenzie and Silver suggested that working-class support for the Conservatives had an increasingly secular rather than a deferential basis. They argued that this change helped to explain the increasing volatility of British voting patterns. Seculars were unlikely to vote simply on the basis of party loyalty. Almost all the deferentials but only half the seculars stated that they would definitely vote Conservative in the next election. The seculars were waiting to judge specific policies rather than basing their vote on traditional party loyalties.

The theory of the secular voter proved to be highly influential and is very similar to many later theories of voting. McKenzie and Silver believed that secular voters made up quite a small though increasing section of the electorate. However, despite their small numbers they represented a fundamental challenge to the partisan alignment theory since their motives for voting for a particular party were quite different from those of a partisan party supporter.

Contradictory socializing influences

Butler and Rose offered some explanations of deviant voting which were quite consistent with the theory of partisan alignment. They suggested that **contradictory socializing influences** on individuals would reduce their sense of loyalty to the party of their class. If, for example, one parent voted Labour and the other Conservative there would be a considerable chance of their children becoming deviant voters in later life. Social mobility could also lead to deviant voting if individuals ended up in a different class to that of their parents. For example individuals from a working-class background who experienced upward social mobility and gained middle-class jobs might vote according to their background rather than according to their current class position.

Embourgeoisement

Another explanation of deviant voting which was broadly consistent with the theory of partisan alignment suggested that a change was taking place within the working class. After the Labour Party was defeated in a third consecutive election in 1959, some psephologists began to consider the possibility that defeat had become inevitable for Labour in general elections.

Butler and Rose suggested that one section of the manual workforce was increasingly adopting middle-class attitudes and life styles. Affluent workers were enjoying living standards equal or even superior to those of the middle class and consequently were more likely to identify themselves as middle class and support the Conservative Party. (This argument is a version of the **embourgeoisement** theory which we discussed in the previous chapter.) In effect Butler and Rose were suggesting not that partisan alignment was less strong, but that the boundary between the middle and working classes had shifted so that some manual workers could now be considered middle class.

A study by Eric Nordlinger found no support for this explanation. The Labour voters in Nordlinger's sample earned on average slightly more than the working-class Tories although the factor which appeared to differentiate the two groups was not income as such, but the *degree of satisfaction* with income. Working-class Tories were found to be much more satisfied with their levels of income than their Labour counterparts. Satisfaction would lead to a desire to maintain the status quo, and hence support for the Conservative Party with its more traditional image. Dissatisfaction would lead to a desire for change, and hence support for Labour, with its image as the party of change.

The argument that working-class affluence leads to Conservative voting was further discredited by Goldthorpe and Lockwood's study of affluent workers in Luton. Goldthorpe and Lockwood found that affluence does not lead to middle-class identification nor to support for the Conservative Party. Of the affluent workers in Luton who voted in the 1955 and 1959 elections, nearly 80 per cent voted Labour which is a

significantly greater percentage than for the working class as a whole.

Goldthorpe and Lockwood found that the most common reason given for Labour support was 'a general "working-class" identification with Labour' and a feeling that the Labour Party more closely represented the interests of the 'working man'. However, there appeared to be little of the deep-seated party loyalty which is supposed to be characteristic of the traditional working class. Like their attitude to work, the Luton workers' support for Labour was largely instrumental. They were primarily concerned with the pay-off for themselves in terms of higher living standards.

Cross-class attachments

Goldthorpe and Lockwood argue that affluence as such reveals little about working-class political attitudes. They maintain:

> the understanding of contemporary working-class politics is found, first and foremost, in the structure of the worker's group attachments, and not, as many have suggested, in the extent of his income and possessions.

The importance of 'group attachments' is borne out by their research. Those affluent workers who voted Conservative usually had white-collar connections. Either their parents, siblings or wives had white-collar jobs or they themselves had previously been employed in a white-collar occupation. These 'bridges' to the middle class appeared to be the most important factor in accounting for working-class Conservatism in the Luton sample. Attachments with and exposure to members of another class seemed to have a strong influence on **cross-class voting**.

This idea was developed by Frank Parkin. He argues that through greater exposure to members of the middle class than their Labour counterparts, working-class Tories internalized the **dominant value system** which the Conservative Party represents.

Bob Jessop finds support for this view from a survey conducted in the early 1970s. He argues that members of the working class vote Conservative 'because they are relatively isolated from the structural conditions favourable to radicalism and Labour voting', conditions, that is, which serve to insulate manual workers from the middle class and the dominant value system. Such structural conditions are found in their most extreme form in the mining, shipbuilding and dock industries. Traditionally workers in these industries formed occupational communities in single industry towns. Insulation from members of the middle class both at work and in the community led to the development of a working-class subculture which provided an alternative to the dominant value system. In this setting strong loyalties to the Labour Party developed.

These views did nothing to alter the widespread acceptance of the partisan alignment theory of voting. In line with that theory writers such as Parkin tried to explain deviant voting in terms of political socialization. They added to the sophistication of the theory by examining situations in which individuals might experience contradictory socializing influences, but they did not change the basic framework within which voting was explained.

Middle-class radicals

Frank Parkin was one of the few writers who also analysed the reasons for deviant voting by middle-class Labour supporters. His explanation was quite different from that for working-class Conservatism. He found that these **middle-class radicals**

were likely to have occupations 'in which there is a primary emphasis upon either the notion of service to the community, human betterment or welfare and the like or upon self-expression and creativity.' Such occupations include teaching and social work. Since Labour is seen as the party mainly concerned with social welfare, voting Labour is a means of furthering the ideals which led people to select these occupations.

Middle-class Labour voters tend to be outside the mainstream of capitalism. Parkin states that their 'life chances rest primarily upon intellectual attainment and personal qualifications, not upon ownership of property or inherited wealth'. As such they have no vested interest in private industry which the Conservative Party is seen to represent.

In this case individuals were seen to be voting for the party which was most likely to serve their interests and beliefs. They were not voting according to political socialization: they themselves were actively evaluating what the competing parties had to offer.

Parkin's explanation for this group of deviant voters comes closer to the theories of voting that were to become popular in the 1970s and 1980s than to the theory of Butler and Stokes. In the next section we will look at various attempts to analyse the patterns of voting in Britain since 1974.

■ Patterns of voting since 1974

During the 1970s, and particularly from 1974 onwards, important changes started to take place in the pattern of British voting. In the following sections we will outline briefly the changes that took place and then examine possible explanations for these changes.

1 The first major change appeared to be the declining influence of class on voting behaviour. The distinction between manual and non-manual workers no longer appeared to account for the way most of the electorate voted. There seemed to be much more volatility than in early elections, with a substantial proportion of the electorate changing the party it voted for from election to election.

2 The second and closely related change was the rapid increase in the numbers of deviant voters. Studies

suggest that in the 1983 and 1987 elections a minority of manual workers voted Labour, while the Conservative share of the non-manual vote has been less than 60 per cent in every election since 1974.

3 The third change may help to explain the second: Britain might have changed from a two-party to a three-party system. In 1981 four leading members of the Labour Party broke away to form the new Social Democratic Party. They then joined with the Liberal Party to fight the 1983 election together. The resulting Alliance succeeded in gaining 26.1 per cent of the votes cast, only just over 2 per cent behind Labour's 28.3 per cent share. For the first time since the war the combined Labour and Conservative stranglehold over voting was seriously threatened. A third party (or in this case an alliance of two 'third' parties) seemed to have a

real chance of forming a government at some future date. The Alliance did less well in 1987 but still polled 22.6 per cent of the votes cast. After 1987 the Liberals and the SDP merged to form the Liberal Democrats. In 1992 their vote declined further to 18.3 per cent, but this was still much higher than their share of the vote in any election between 1945 and 1970.

4 The final change that appeared to be taking place was the decline of the Labour Party. Labour had done badly in 1979, only gaining 36.9 per cent of the votes cast, but the 1983 result was even more disastrous. At that election Labour received a lower share of the popular vote than at any time since 1918. It even seemed as if Labour could hardly be considered a national party any longer: it won only three non-London seats in the entire southeast of England. Labour's strength was increasingly confined to the traditional heartlands of its support in the depressed industrial regions of Wales, Scotland and the north of England.

A number of commentators speculated that Labour's decline might be permanent. If conventional explanations of voting behaviour were correct, then a number of social changes were threatening the basis of the Labour vote. By 1983 non-manual workers outnumbered manual workers. Employment in industry, and particularly 'heavy' industries such as mining and shipbuilding, was declining. This was precisely where Labour had traditionally enjoyed its most loyal support. As early as 1981 Peter Kellner claimed 'the sense of class solidarity which propelled Labour to victory in 1945 has all but evaporated'.

We will now consider a number of attempts to explain these changes. As psephologists took account of the alterations in voting behaviour, the emphasis placed upon political socialization by Butler and Stokes was increasingly rejected. It was replaced by an emphasis on the policy preferences of individual voters.

■ Bo Sarlvik and Ivor Crewe – partisan dealignment

Ivor Crewe was amongst the first commentators to criticize the approach of Butler and Stokes and to identify changing trends in British voting. In this section we will discuss his work with Bo Sarlvik, published in 1983. In later sections we will review Crewe's work on the 1987 and 1992 elections.

Sarlvik and Crewe argued that Butler and Stokes could not explain the reduction of class-based voting since 1974. Evidence suggested that embourgeoisement could not account for the decline in partisanship. Nor could Sarlvik and Crewe find any evidence that there had been a sudden and dramatic increase in voters whose parents had different party loyalties. They accepted that there had been more social mobility, but it was nothing like enough to account for the rise in deviant voting.

The decline in partisan voting

Tables 9.4 and 9.5 summarize some of the main findings of the *British Election Studies*, which have been conducted by a number of different researchers using survey techniques to collect standardized information about a large sample of voters. The findings appear to confirm Crewe's theory that partisan dealignment has taken place in Britain. (Sarlvik and Crewe originally defined **partisan dealignment** as a situation where:

---

none of the major occupational groups now provides the same degree of solid and consistent support for one of the two major parties as was the case in the earlier post-war period.

In later writings, however, Crewe distinguished between partisan dealignment and class dealignment. Partisan dealignment referred to a decline in the percentage of the electorate who had a strong sense of loyalty to a particular party; **class dealignment** referred to a decline in the relationship between the working class and Labour voting and the middle class and Conservative voting.)

Table 9.5 shows different measures of the strength of the relationship between class and voting including a measure of the amount of absolute class voting. This is the percentage of voters who were middle class and voted Conservative or who were working class and voted Labour. In other words it measures the percentage of non-deviant voters. In 1983 non-manual Conservative voters and manual Labour voters were in a minority of voters at 47 per cent.

The Alford Index is another measure of the degree to which class influences voting on a scale of 1 to 100. For Labour, if the score were 100, then all manual workers who voted would vote Labour. If the score were 0, Labour would gain the same proportion of votes in the middle class as in the working class. For the Conservatives, if the

Table 9.4 Occupational class and party choice, 1964–92 (%)

	1964		1966		1970	
	Non-manual	Manual	Non-manual	Manual	Non-manual	Manual
Conservative	62	28	60	25	64	33
Labour	22	64	26	69	25	58
Liberal	16	8	14	6	11	9

	February 1974		October 1974		1979	
	Non-manual	Manual	Non-manual	Manual	Non-manual	Manual
Conservative	53	24	51	24	60	35
Labour	22	57	25	57	23	50
Liberal	25	19	24	20	17	15

	1983		1987		1992	
	Non-manual	Manual	Non-manual	Manual	Non-manual	Manual
Conservative	55	35	54	35	56	36
Labour	17	42	20	45	24	51
Liberal etc.	28	22	27	21	21	14

Note: 'Liberal etc.' in the last row refers to the Liberal-SDP Alliance in 1983 and 1987 and to the Liberal
Democrats in 1992.

(*Source*: Denver, D. (1994) *Elections and Voting Behaviour in Britain*, Second Edition, Harvester
Wheatsheaf, London, p. 61.)

Table 9.5 Measures of class voting, 1964–92

	1964	1966	1970	Feb 1974	Oct 1974	1979	1983	1987	1992
Alford index (Labour)	42	43	33	35	32	27	25	25	27
Alford index (Conservative)	34	35	31	29	27	25	20	19	20
Absolute class voting	63	66	60	55	54	55	47	49	54

(*Source*: Denver, D. (1994) *Elections and Voting Behaviour in Britain*, Second Edition, Harvester
Wheatsheaf, London, p. 62.)

score were 100, then all non-manual workers who voted would vote Conservative. If the score were 0, the Conservatives would gain the same proportion of votes in the working class as in the middle class. By this measure the decline in partisan voting in the working class has been dramatic. It fell substantially between 1959 and 1983, dropping from 42 to 25.

From such evidence Sarlvik and Crewe concluded that most voters were no longer strongly loyal to a party on the basis of their class, and that there was much greater volatility in the electorate. In the four elections of the 1970s for example, less than half of the electorate (47 per cent) voted Labour or voted Conservative four times in a row.

The causes of partisan dealignment

First, they argued, factors other than class seemed to be increasingly related to voting. Such factors included whether voters rented or owned their housing, and whether they were members of trades unions. In 1979 the Conservatives were 51 per cent ahead of Labour among non-manual workers who were not in trades unions, but only 7 per cent ahead of those who were members. Labour was 33 per cent ahead of the Conservatives among manual trades union members, but actually 1 per cent behind among non-union manual workers.

Sarlvik and Crewe believed class boundaries were being blurred by factors such as these. There were fewer 'pure' members of the working class who had manual jobs, lived in council houses and belonged to trades unions; and fewer 'pure' members of the middle class who had non-manual jobs and were non-unionized. The increasing numbers of unionists in the middle class and the increasing numbers of homeowners in the working class had reduced the level of partisan alignment among individuals with the traditional party of their class and had resulted in class dealignment as well.

The second explanation of partisan dealignment put forward by Sarlvik and Crewe provided a more fundamental challenge to the theories of Butler and Stokes. They argued that it was misleading simply to see the voters as captives of their socialization, unable to make rational choices about which party to vote for. Instead, Sarlvik and Crewe claimed that voters' active decisions about which party's policies best suited them had to be included in any explanation of voting. From their analysis of the 1979 general election, Sarlvik and Crewe argued that 'voters' opinions on policies and on the parties' performances in office "explain" almost twice as much as all the social and economic characteristics taken together'.

According to Sarlvik and Crewe, the main reasons why the Conservatives won in 1979 were simply that the electorate was unimpressed with the performance of the previous Labour Government and supported most Conservative policies. Some issues were particularly important. Sarlvik and Crewe found that Conservative proposals designed to limit the power of trades unions and to privatize some state-run industries were the most important policies which persuaded Labour voters to switch to the Conservatives.

Despite the significance Sarlvik and Crewe attached to the policy preferences and active choices of the electorate, they did not claim that class was of no importance. They stated 'The relationships between individuals' social status and their choice of party have by no means vanished. But as determinants of voting they carry less weight than before.' Traditional theories could not be completely rejected: Sarlvik and Crewe still saw class as the most important aspect of a person's social status, but parties which wished to win elections could not just rely on the loyalty of their supporters – their policies had to appeal to voters as well.

■ Himmelweit, Humphreys and Jaeger – a consumer model of voting

Some psephologists went much further than Sarlvik and Crewe in rejecting the partisan alignment theory of voting. Himmelweit, Humphreys and Jaeger based their findings upon their own longitudinal study of voting, which followed a group of men who were 21 in 1959, through to the October election of 1974.

In their book *How Voters Decide* Himmelweit *et al.* argued that an understanding of voting should be based on analysing members of the electorate's deliberate selection of a party to vote for, and not on political socialization. They emphasized the rational choices made by voters. They believed that people decided how to vote by deciding what they wanted, and how far each party met their requirements.

To explain this theory Himmelweit *et al.* compared an elector's choice of party with a consumer making a purchase. For example, someone choosing a new car will take a number of factors into account such as price, comfort, performance, size, running costs and reliability. Some factors will be more important to a particular individual than others: one potential purchaser might put most emphasis on price and running costs, while another is primarily concerned with performance and size. Consumer choice is not always easy: you might want both cheapness and high quality, but if you cannot have both you will have to compromise.

Himmelweit *et al.* argue that choosing a party involves the same sort of process. Certain policies will be more important to you than others. One party will come closer to your views in their stated policy than another. No single party is likely to advocate all the single policies which you support. Consequently you will have to weigh up which party offers the most attractive package, taking into account the importance you attach to each issue.

Of course, a voter may not have 'perfect knowledge' of all the policies on offer, but there is more to buying products than examining the labels and listening to the claims of advertisers. Potential purchasers may have had some previous experience of the product and if it has proved satisfactory in the past they are more likely to buy it again, even if it is not exactly suited to their needs. In a similar way voters have experience of previous governments and they can judge the parties on the basis of past performance. One reason for the rise in 'deviant' voting, according to Himmelweit *et al.*, was the increasingly negative judgements made by voters on the parties they had previously chosen: they decided to opt for new brands because their old choices proved so unsatisfactory.

The image Himmelweit *et al.* provided of the voters, then, is of very calculating individuals trying to achieve their objectives as best they can. However, they did not dismiss more emotional factors in voting altogether. Two of these factors can be compared to brand loyalty, and advice from friends and relatives about products. You may identify with a particular product which you have used before and which you trust; you may also be influenced by what people you know tell you about products, and their recommendations. Similarly when voting you may have some loyalty to a party, and you may be influenced by the political preferences of others.

However these factors (which are similar to Butler and Stokes's concepts of party alignment and political socialization) were considered of little importance by Himmelweit *et al.* They argued that such factors were only important if

your policy preferences cancelled each other out. In other words only if two or more parties offered you equally attractive sets of policies would you be influenced by party loyalty or the opinion of others. By 1974 Himmelweit *et al.* thought party loyalty had a minimal impact on the electorate, though they accepted that it may have been more important bcforc then.

Himmelweit *et al.* provided statistical support for their consumer model of voting. They claimed that 80 per cent of voting in the October 1974 election could be predicted on the basis of their model.

If Himmelweit *et al.*'s theory is correct, it has important implications for the political parties. It suggests that all the parties have a chance of winning elections if they can tailor their policies to fit those preferred by a majority of the electorate. Regardless of how badly Labour did in 1983, such a **consumer model** does not suggest its decline is necessarily permanent or irreversible. The Conservative Party should not become complacent, and the Alliance (which was later succeeded by the Liberal Democrats) should not assume that it will retain high levels of support in the future.

According to this theory of voting, the parties are competing for the votes of the whole of the electorate, and not just for those of a small number of floating voters.

Criticisms

This radical new explanation of voting has been heavily criticized. Paul Whiteley describes the study as unreliable, since it was based on a small and unrepresentative section of the population. By 1974 Himmelweit *et al.*'s sample consisted of just 178 respondents, all of whom were male, aged about 37, and some 75 per cent of whom were non-manual workers. It cannot be assumed that the factors influencing the voting of this group will be typical of the factors influencing the voting of the rest of the population.

A more fundamental objection to explaining voting in terms of policy preference is raised by David Marsh. He points out that this type of explanation cannot fully account for voting unless it explains why people prefer certain policies in the first place. These types of theory deny the importance of class, but fail to suggest alternative influences on the choice of policy.

Table 9.6   Class voting in the 1983 election

Class	Conservative	Labour	Alliance	Others	
Petty bourgeoisie	71%	12%	17%	0%	100%
Salariat	54%	14%	31%	1%	100%
Foremen/Technicians	48%	26%	25%	1%	100%
Routine non-manual	46%	25%	27%	2%	100%
Working class	30%	49%	30%	1%	100%

(*Source*: Heath, Jowell and Curtice, *How Britain Votes*, 1985, p. 20.)

■ Heath, Jowell and Curtice – the continuing importance of class

Their conclusions contradict those of many other psephologists because Heath *et al.* use different and more sophisticated research methods.

Redefining class

The first, and perhaps most important, methodological change involves the definition and measurement of class. Heath *et al.* argue that defining the middle class as non-manual workers and the working class as manual workers is theoretically inadequate. They claim that classes can be more adequately defined in terms of **economic interests**, that is, according to their situation in the labour market. They therefore use a version of John Goldthorpe's neo-Weberian class scheme to distinguish five classes. (See pp. 116–17 for further details of Goldthorpe's class scheme.)

The five classes are:

1 The **salariat** which consists of managers, administrators, professionals and semi-professionals who have either considerable authority within the workplace or considerable autonomy within work.

2 **Routine non-manual workers** who lack authority in the workplace and often have low wages.

3 The **petty bourgeoisie** which consists of farmers, the owners of small businesses and self-employed manual workers. Their situation depends upon the market forces which relate to the goods and services they supply. They are not wage labourers and they are not affected in the same way as other workers by employment and promotion prospects. This group cuts across the usual division between manual and non-manual workers.

4 '**Foremen**' and **technicians** who either supervise other workers or who have more autonomy within work than the fifth class.

5 **Manual workers**. Heath *et al.* do not separate manual workers in terms of the degree of skill their job requires since they do not believe that skill levels have a significant impact on voting.

Apart from using new class categories, another important feature of Heath *et al.*'s work is the way they deal with the voting of women. Nearly all the previous studies classified women voters according to the occupation of their husband if they were married. Heath *et al.* argue that women's own experience of the workplace will have a greater impact on their voting than that of their husband.

Table 9.6 summarizes Heath *et al.*'s findings on class voting in the 1983 election.

The continued importance of class

These results suggest a stronger relationship between class and voting in 1983 than the results of studies using conventional definitions of class.

1 The working class remained a stronghold of Labour support.

2 'Foremen' and technicians (who would normally be categorized as part of the skilled working class) were strongly Conservative.

3 The petty bourgeoisie (some of whom would normally be defined as manual workers) were the strongest Conservative supporters.

Table 9.7 Odds ratio for working class voting Labour and salariat voting Conservative in general elections

				February	October		
Election	1964	1966	1970	1974	1974	1979	1983
Odds ratio	9.3	7.3	3.9	6.1	5.5	4.9	6.3

(*Source*: Adapted from Heath, Jowell and Curtice (1985) *How Britain Votes*, Pergamon, Oxford, p. 20.)

Table 9.8 Changes in party support 1964–83 and predicted share of the vote in 1983 if parties had retained the same level of support in each class from 1964

	Labour	Conservative	Liberal Alliance
% vote	44	43	11
% vote 1983	28	42	25
Predicted % vote in 1983 given changes in the class structure	37	48.5	12.5

(*Source*: Adapted from Heath, Jowell and Curtice (1985) *How Britain Votes*, Pergamon, Oxford, p. 20.)

4 The salariat and routine non-manual workers gave most of their support to the Conservatives, but it was also in these classes that the Alliance gained its greatest share of the votes.

Examining the results of one election does not reveal whether or not class-based voting has declined. Heath *et al.* therefore attempt to measure the strength of the relationship between class and voting since 1964. It is more difficult to measure this relationship using a fivefold division of the population into classes, so they decided to measure the strength of the relationship between class and voting by measuring the likelihood of the salariat voting Conservative and the working class voting Labour.

From their figures they calculated an **odds ratio** which determines the relative likelihood of a class voting for the party it could be expected to. The figures in Table 9.7 show how many times more likely it is for the working class to vote Labour and the salariat to vote Conservative than vice versa.

Table 9.7 produced some unexpected findings. There appear to have been wide variations in the relationship between class and voting, but no long-term dealignment. According to this measurement, 1983 was an average election and not a year in which the influence of class was at its lowest since the Second World War.

Changes in the class structure

Heath *et al.* claim that much of the change in levels of support for the different parties is the result of changes in the distribution of the population between classes. For example, the working class has shrunk as a proportion of the electorate while the salariat and routine non-manual groups have grown.

However, changes in the class structure alone cannot explain all the changes in levels of support for the parties in elections. Heath *et al.* calculated what percentage of the votes each party would have gained in 1983 if they had kept the same levels of support in each class that they had in 1964. The results are summarized in Table 9.8.

On these figures the Labour Party did even worse than expected, the Conservative Party failed to take advantage of changes in the social structure, while the increase in Liberal/Alliance support was far greater than would be anticipated. Consequently Heath *et al.* conclude that factors other than changes in the social structure must have affected patterns of voting.

Rejection of consumer theory

Heath *et al.* reject the view that it is detailed policy preferences which account for these changes. They measured people's views on various policies and asked them where they thought the major parties stood on these issues. They also asked voters which issues they thought were most important.

1 Unemployment and inflation came top of the list, and on both Labour had the most popular policies.

2 The Alliance proved most popular on the third most important issue (whether there should be more spending on welfare or tax cuts) while Labour and the Conservatives tied a little way behind.

3 Conservative and Alliance policies proved most popular on the fourth most important issue, defence.

On the basis of this evidence Labour should have won a handsome victory. If the six most important issues were taken into account, Labour and the Conservatives would have received the same share of the vote. Heath *et al.* therefore reject the consumer theory of voting; their evidence suggests that it cannot explain the Conservative victory in 1983.

Party images

Despite rejecting the consumer theory, Heath *et al.* do not deny that the actions taken by a political party affect the vote it obtains, but they believe that it is not the party's detailed policies that matter, but its overall political stance in the eyes of the electorate. They say 'It is not the small print of the manifesto but the overall perception of the party's character that counts.' If voters believe that a party has the same basic ideology as they have, they will be likely to vote for it. From this point of view Labour lost so badly in 1983 because many voters believed it had moved too far to the left, despite the extent to which they agreed with its policies.

Class, ideology and voting behaviour

Heath *et al.* use a more complex model of ideology than the simple left/right distinction that is usually employed. They argue that there are two main dimensions to ideological differences on issues.

1 **Class issues** are mainly economic: they concern such questions as whether industries should be nationalized or privatized, and whether income and wealth should be redistributed. The ideology which supports nationalization and redistribution can be called left wing, and the opposite right wing.

2 **Liberal issues** concern non-economic questions such as whether there should be a death penalty, whether Britain should retain or abandon nuclear weapons, and whether there should be a strong law and order policy or not. For the sake of convenience, the ideology which supports the death penalty, the retention of nuclear weapons and strong law and order policies will be called 'tough', while its opposite will be called 'tender'.

In terms of these differences the Labour Party supports left-wing and tender policies, the Conservative Party supports right-wing and tough policies, and (according to Heath *et al.*) the Alliance are perhaps slightly to the right of centre on class issues and more tender than tough on liberal issues. Liberal supporters have a distinctive ideological position and, according to these writers, it is one which is becoming increasingly popular with the electorate.

From their analysis of changes in voters' ideology Heath *et al.* find there have been distinct shifts. On average, voters increasingly support right-wing economic policies, but more tender social policies. These changes seem to have benefited the Alliance more than the other major parties, both of whom have experienced a significant move away from their ideology on one of the two dimensions. The study finds that the main reason for the high level of Alliance support in 1983 is the increasing proportion of voters whose ideological position roughly coincides with that party's.

Summary

The complex and highly sophisticated theory of voting devised by Heath *et al.* differs from both the partisan alignment and consumer theories. Class remains very important but it does not directly determine the party voted for. It is not specific policies that matter, but the class of the voters and how they perceive the ideological position of the parties. From this point of view the prospects for the parties in the future will be partly determined by changes in the class structure, but they can also affect their chances of success by the way they present themselves to the electorate.

Criticisms of Heath, Jowell and Curtice

Ivor Crewe has attacked the work of Heath *et al.* In particular he criticizes their use of an odds ratio table based upon the chances of the working class voting Labour and the salariat voting Conservative. Crewe says 'their odds ratio is a two-party measure applied to a three-party system.' It fails to take account of the growth of support for centre parties, the Liberals and the Alliance, in the elections of 1979 and 1983. Furthermore, Crewe points out that in 1983 the working class and the salariat combined made up a minority of the electorate (45 per cent).

The response to criticisms

Heath *et al.* have answered these criticisms. They argue that odds ratios are more appropriate for measuring the relationship between class and voting than the class index of voting used by Crewe. In Crewe's index all voters who do not vote Conservative or Labour are seen as a kind of deviant voter and are used as evidence that

classes have lost their 'social cohesion or political potential'.

Heath *et al.* point out that the centre parties can increase their share of the vote without any change in social classes. For example, if the Labour or Conservative Party change their policies and thereby appeal less to potential centre party voters, they can lose support without the electorate changing their views. Heath *et al.*'s odds ratio avoids this problem because the level of support for centre parties does not directly affect the ratio. It measures the strength of class-based voting in the class-based parties. It does not fall into the trap of assuming that a vote cast for somebody other than a Labour or Conservative Party candidate indicates a decline in the relationship between class and voting.

Heath *et al.* are happy to acknowledge that the odds ratio used in their original study measured the relationship between class and voting in a minority of the electorate. To counter this problem they calculated odds ratios for a number of other classes. They found the same 'trendless fluctuations' in the relationship between class and voting revealed in their original study. Once again they discovered no evidence that class was exerting less influence on voting behaviour than it had in the past.

■ The 1987 election

In the 1987 general election the overall Conservative majority in the House of Commons was reduced from 144 to 101. Compared to 1983 the Conservative share of the vote fell 0.3 per cent to 43.3 per cent, Labour gained 3.2 per cent achieving 31.5 per cent of the vote, and the Alliance vote fell 2.9 per cent to 23.1 per cent.

As we show in the following sections, some figures on this election suggest that class had more influence on voting patterns than it had had in 1983. The election therefore seemed to represent a slight reversal of some of the trends which had apparently been taking place since the 1970s. However, the result was interpreted differently by different psephologists. Although they amended their positions somewhat and developed their analysis, Ivor Crewe and Anthony Heath and collaborators continued to disagree about British voting. We will now examine their different interpretations of the 1987 election.

■ Ivor Crewe – the 1987 election and social divisions

According to Crewe's figures the percentage of people voting for the party representing their class increased marginally. Compared to 1983 the combined percentage of non-manual Conservative voters and manual Labour voters rose from 47 per cent to 48 per cent. Nevertheless deviant voters still made up a majority of the electorate (52 per cent). Crewe argues that the election largely confirms his analysis of trends in voting behaviour. He claims it shows that divisions continue to grow within both the middle and working classes.

Divisions in the middle class

Using data from a Gallup survey commissioned by the BBC, Crewe found that the Conservatives lost

Table 9.9   The new divisions in the middle class: voting in 1987

	University-educated		Public sector		Private sector	
	1987	1983–7	1987	1983–7	1987	1983–7
Conservative	34%	–9%	44%	–4%	65%	+1%
Labour	29%	+3%	24%	–	13%	–
Liberal/SDP	27%	+4%	32%	+4%	22%	–1%

(*Source*: I. Crewe, 'A New Class of Politics', *The Guardian*, 15 June 1987.)

support in the middle class. In both the 'core' middle class of professionals, administrators and managers, and the 'lower' middle class of office and clerical workers, the Conservative vote fell 3 per cent compared to 1983. These data would seem to suggest that the Conservative Party was losing support from all sections of the middle class. However, Crewe claimed to have discovered a major split in the class between university-educated and public sector non-manual workers on the one hand, and non-university-educated and private sector non-manual workers on the other. As Table 9.9 shows, the Conservatives lost 9 per cent of their vote amongst the university-educated middle class and 4 per cent amongst those working in the public sector.

Thus Crewe believes that 'new divisions' are opening up in the middle class. Education and the sector in which individuals work are both starting to exercise a strong influence on voting patterns resulting in an increasingly divided middle class.

Divisions in the working class

As we discovered in an earlier section (see pp. 552–4) Crewe has believed for some time that the working class is divided. Labour has been losing support in the 'new working class' who live in the south of the country, own their own homes, are non-union members and work in the private sector. Crewe found that these divisions continued to be very important in 1987. For example, the Conservatives led Labour by 46 per cent to 26 per cent amongst the working class in the South, and by 44 per cent to 32 per cent amongst working-class homeowners. Crewe claims that the Labour Party:

had come to represent a declining segment of the working class – the traditional working class of the

council estates, the public sector, industrial Scotland and the North . . . It was a party neither of one class nor one nation, it was a regional class party.

Policy preference and voting

Crewe also examined the influence of policies on voting in 1987. On the surface he found little support for his belief that policy preference was becoming more important in shaping voters' behaviour. When asked to name the two issues that concerned them most, respondents were most likely to mention unemployment, followed by defence, the NHS and education. On all these issues except defence, Labour policies enjoyed more support than Conservative policies. Crewe says 'Had electors voted solely on the main issues Labour would have won.'

Crewe therefore revised his earlier position that policy preference was crucially important in shaping voting. Instead Crewe argued that voters attach more importance to their own prosperity than they do to issues which they identify as problems for society as a whole. He said 'When answering a survey on the important issues respondents think of public problems; when entering the polling booth they think of family fortunes.'

The Gallup survey found that 55 per cent believed that the Conservatives were more likely to produce prosperity than other parties; only 27 per cent thought they were less likely to do so. Furthermore, respondents were more likely to say that opportunities to get ahead, the general economic situation and their household's financial situation had improved than they were to say the reverse. Thus Crewe believed that the main reason that the Conservatives won in 1987 was that people felt more prosperous and they trusted the Conservatives to deliver rising living standards.

Anthony Heath, John Curtice, Roger Jowell, Geoff Evans, Julia Field and Sharon Witherspoon – *Understanding Political Change 1964–87*

Heath *et al.* conducted the *British Election Study* into the 1987 election. Their findings were published in the book *Understanding Political Change*. In it they examined how voting and voters had changed between 1964 and 1987. They discussed a number of influential ideas on voting and political change by using data from successive election studies. In doing so they challenged many of the ideas put forward by other psephologists. In particular they raised doubts about whether the social psychology had changed much at all. Society and politics might have changed, but Heath *et al.*'s findings suggested that the reasons why people voted in particular ways had not altered much over more than two decades.

Volatility and party identification

First, Heath *et al.* examined the proposition that voters had become more volatile and less willing to identify with a party and remain loyal to it. In 1964 88 per cent of those questioned said they identified very or fairly strongly with a political party. By 1987 this had declined to 71 per cent. On the other hand there was no clear trend in the percentage of respondents who thought of voting for another party during the campaign and who could not therefore be considered party loyalists. In 1964 25 per cent of those asked thought of voting for another party; in 1983 the figure was the same, 25 per cent, and in 1987 it had increased only marginally to 28 per cent. Thus while some figures suggested a small but significant decline in partisan alignment, other figures were more ambiguous.

The research reached more clearcut conclusions on electoral volatility. Between the 1959 and 1964 elections 18 per cent of those who voted in both

elections changed who they voted for; between the 1983 and 1987 elections 19 per cent of those who voted in both changed their choice of party. Heath *et al.* used three different measures of volatility but obtained similar results for all of them. They said:

> All three measures show much the same changes over time, the differences being rather modest and showing no clear trend towards increasing volatility. Volatility was at its highest on all three measures between 1970 and 1974, but since then it has fluctuated.

Policy preference, parents and voting

In examining the extent to which party preference influences voting, Heath *et al.* note that the strength of the relationship will be influenced by the degree to which the policies of parties differ. If, for example, Labour and Conservative have very different manifestos at an election more people are likely to vote for a centre party such as the Liberals (now the Liberal Democrats) leaving Labour and Conservative supporters polarized in their views. If Labour and the Conservatives put forward less distinct sets of proposals at an election they are likely to pick up votes from centre parties and the voters for the two main parties are likely to have less distinctive views.

Heath *et al.* compared the 1964 and 1979 elections to examine changes in the relationship between policy preference and voting since the Liberals polled about the same proportion of the votes in those two elections and the perceived differences between Labour and the Conservatives were at a similar level in those two elections. They found that policies seemed to have a considerable amount of influence on voting in the 1979 election. This appeared to be in line with the theory that voters were becoming more rational and were increasingly influenced by their policy preferences. However, Heath *et al.* also found that 'issues were rather important in 1964'. The different policies of Labour and the Conservatives on nuclear weapons and on privatization versus nationalization both exercised a considerable influence on voting in that year. Heath *et al.* conclude that 'voters were rational and sophisticated in the 1960s just as they are today'. Thus Heath *et al.* accept the

Table 9.10 Absolute class voting 1964–87

	Middle-class Conservative plus working-class Labour as percentage of all voters	Middle-class Conservative or Liberal plus working-class Labour as percentage of all voters
1964	64.0	70.7
1966	64.4	69.9
1970	60.2	64.4
February 1974	55.5	66.5
October 1974	57.4	68.6
1979	56.7	64.3
1983	51.7	66.9
1987	51.6	66.3

(*Source*: Heath, A. *et al.* (1991) *Understanding Political Change*, Pergamon Press, Oxford, p. 65.)

importance of policy preference for voting but deny that this is anything new.

They also examined the influence of parents on voting and again found that there seemed to be relatively little change from the 1960s. While there had been a small decline in the likelihood of children voting the same way as parents, this could be explained by an increase in social mobility which meant that children ended up in a different class to that of their parents. Where children remained in the same class there was no evidence that political socialization in childhood had become less important.

The findings of Heath *et al.* on party identification, volatility, policy preference and the influence of parents on voting represent a challenge to the view of Crewe and others that a major change in the factors influencing voting took place in the 1970s. Heath *et al.* found that a similar mix of factors influenced voting in the 1970s and 1980s as it had done in the 1960s. The idea that a fundamental change had taken place was not supported by the evidence.

Class-based voting

As in their earlier study Heath and collaborators discussed the view that class was becoming less closely related to voting. They distinguished between absolute and relative class voting. **Absolute class voting** measures the proportion of people voting for the class their party is commonly held to represent, in other words the percentage of

voters who are not 'deviant voters'. Table 9.10 is based on the five-class model used by Heath *et al.* in their earlier study but with the working class and 'foremen' and technicians combined to form the working class, and the other three classes (petty bourgeoisie, routine non-manual workers and the salariat) combined to form the middle class.

Table 9.10 shows, and Heath *et al.* acknowledge, that absolute class voting has declined. However, it has declined rather less than it first appears if Liberals and other centre parties are regarded as class-based parties representing the middle class. Heath *et al.* argue that it is legitimate to see them in this way since they draw a comfortable majority of their votes from middle-class voters. Thus, to Heath *et al.* absolute class voting has declined, but not to the extent that psephologists such as Crewe have claimed.

On the other hand Heath *et al.* are unwilling to concede that **relative class voting** has declined, at least since 1970. Using an odds ratio which compares the chances of the salariat voting Conservative with the chances of the working class voting Labour (this statistical measure is explained further on p. 557), they found that there was little change between the 1983 and 1987 elections. They therefore confirmed their earlier claim that there had been 'trendless fluctuations' in relative class voting although this time they did say that these fluctuations had been typical only since 1970. They say 'Looking . . . at the Conservative:Labour log odds ratio, we see that this declined rapidly between 1964 and 1970. There is however no further decline after 1970.'

Heath *et al.* therefore modify their position from that expressed in the earlier work, *How Britain Votes*. They say that there has been a 'modest' decline in the relationship between class and voting, but much less than that claimed by many other commentators. However, one reason for this has simply been an increase in the number of candidates standing for centre parties. In 1964, 1966 and 1970 the Liberals contested only just over half the seats in the general elections. In later elections they, or other centre parties, have stood in nearly all constituencies. Simply by having a greater number of candidates they have attracted more votes away from the more clearly class-based parties and thus they have weakened the apparent relationship between class and voting. Any change in the relationship has more to do with political changes than any alteration in the psychology of the electorate.

Divisions within classes

Heath *et al.* examine Crewe's claims that there is a 'new working class' and that new divisions have opened up in the middle class. They concede that housing tenure has a relationship with voting, but deny that this is anything new. According to their figures, living in a council house influenced people to vote Labour as much in 1964 as it did in 1987. Similarly, being an owner-occupier was just as likely to influence somebody to be a Conservative voter in 1964 as it was in 1987. Union membership, or non-membership had some influence on voting, as did ethnicity (people from an ethnic minority were more likely to vote Labour), but there was no evidence that the strength of either of these relationships had increased. Indeed membership or non-membership of trades unions seemed to be becoming less of an influence on voting. However, region had become more important. In 1964 region had little effect on working-class voting patterns but in 1987 the working class living in the South were becoming proportionately more likely to vote Conservative, while those in the North, and in Wales and Scotland were becoming proportionately more inclined to vote Labour.

Heath *et al.* conclude that 'the working class is certainly fragmented' but with the exception of regional differences this fragmentation is nothing new.

Heath *et al.* found more evidence that there were new divisions in the middle class. In particular they found that 'welfare and creative professionals' were increasingly inclined to vote Labour while other members of the middle class were likely to remain loyal to the Conservatives. They also found that having had higher education was increasingly associated with non-Conservative voting in the middle class. Longer established divisions in the middle class were based on religion (with members of the Church of England being more likely than others to vote Conservative) and social background (with middle-class people from working-class backgrounds more likely than others to vote Labour).

Overall Heath *et al.* found that neither the middle class nor the working class were 'internally homogeneous' but this was nothing new and most of the divisions within the classes dated back at least as far as the 1960s.

'Pocket-book voting'

As we discussed earlier, another theory proposed by Crewe was that people voted according to their own economic interests: they voted for the party they thought would be best for their standard of living. Heath *et al.* examined this theory, calling it **pocket-book voting**. They did find that people who had voted Conservative in 1983 were less likely to vote Conservative again in 1987 if they felt that their own standards of living, or the standard of living in the country as a whole, had fallen. However, Heath *et al.* questioned the theory that voting was directly related to living standards. People were much more likely to mention the Government's general competence or incompetence as a reason for changing their vote than they were to mention standards of living. Furthermore those who did mention their own standard of living were also very likely to mention the interests of the social class to which they belonged. This suggested that they tended to see their own self-interest as tied to the interests of their class as a whole. Heath *et al.* claim 'pocket-book voting and class voting may not be rivals but rather may be different aspects of the same phenomenon'.

Conclusion

Heath *et al.* conclude that between 1964 and 1987 voting was affected by social changes (such as the contraction of the working class) but there had been little change in the factors shaping voting. Class, non-class social factors, policy preferences and party images all had an influence and no one factor could explain voting in either 1964 or 1987. Many of the apparent changes were due either to social change or to political change, and not due to changes in the motivation of voters. Many social factors had been working against the Labour Party, reducing the percentage of the population likely to vote for them. Other changes had benefited the Liberal Party and other centre parties. Politically, the success of the Liberals (and the SDP) had increased volatility and led to the apparent reduction in the importance of class. Part of this success, though was simply due to the increased number of candidates these parties had put up at elections.

As in their study of the 1983 election, Heath *et al.* calculated the effects of changes on Labour's electoral prospects. Comparing 1964 and 1987, the effects of social changes plus the increased number of Liberal candidates and the extension of the franchise to those aged over 18 could be expected to have disadvantaged the Labour Party by 8.4 per cent, advantaged the Liberal/Alliance by 8.9 per cent and made no overall difference to the Conservative vote. Obviously these changes made it difficult for Labour to win elections. Nevertheless, Labour did better in 1987 than it had done in 1983. We will discuss whether it has now become an impossible task for them to regain power in a later section.

Criticisms of Understanding Political Change

In a review of *Understanding Political Change* Ivor Crewe was rather less critical than he had been of Heath's earlier work in *How Britain Votes*. He even praised aspects of the book saying:

> The technical accuracy and theoretical interest of what Heath *et al.* have to say about volatility, tactical voting and other supposed consequences of partisan alignment are for the most part unchallengeable. Analysis and interpretation are authoritative, sophisticated and almost painfully cautious.

This more positive tone was hardly surprising since, as Crewe acknowledged, the conclusions of *Understanding Political Change* were rather closer to his own views than those of the earlier study.

Crewe said of the change in emphasis 'Earlier confidence has given way to caution: the missionary's impatience with the old primitives has mellowed into the old cleric's self-doubt and scepticism.'

Crewe notes that Heath and his collaborators gave less weight to the political values of parties and voters than they had done earlier and put more emphasis on social and political changes. Nevertheless, Crewe recognizes that there were still considerable differences between himself and Heath *et al.* and he identifies a number of weak spots in their analysis.

1 First, he argues that Heath *et al.* only take a very limited number of political changes into account. For example, while they analyse the extension of the vote to 18–20 year olds and the expansion in the number of Liberal candidates, they take no account of things such as changes in party leaders, or the impact of the press and other media. They give no good reason for excluding some possible influences on voting while paying close attention to others.

2 Second, they fail to consider the possibility that voting behaviour had shaped some of the factors they had analysed rather than the other way round. For example, the rise in the number of Liberal candidates could be seen as resulting from the great success enjoyed by Liberal candidates in by-elections between 1970 and 1974. Heath *et al.* may have got cause and effect the wrong way round. In other words, the rise in the number of candidates was caused by increased popularity and not vice versa.

3 Third, Crewe continues to insist that the relationship between class and voting had become much less strong. Crewe admits that measures of relative class voting give some indication of how ideologically distinctive classes are. Nevertheless, absolute measures are also important. For example, if Labour support fell to 25 per cent in the working class but to 0 per cent in the middle class this would show up as a strengthening of the class basis of voting in odds ratio tables. What this would fail to make clear was the fact that Labour could no longer be seen as the party of the working class since it was attracting just a quarter of their votes. To Crewe then, absolute measures of class voting are vital for measuring the 'political cohesion of a single class'. According to Heath *et al.*'s own figures Labour's share of the working-class vote fell from 68 per cent in 1964 to 48 per cent in 1984 and Crewe believes that such figures cannot but be taken to show that the working class lost some of its political solidarity.

The 1992 election and beyond

The 1992 results

The results of the 1992 election are given in Table 9.11.

They show that although the Conservatives won the election, their vote dropped by 0.4 per cent in the UK compared to the 1987 election. Labour's vote rose by 3.6 per cent and the Liberal Democrats lost 2.0 per cent of the vote compared to the Alliance's share in 1987. The Conservatives were returned to office with an overall majority for the fourth successive time having already held office for thirteen years. Nevertheless, their overall majority was cut from 101 to 21 and Crewe calculates that 'had a mere 1,702 people voted Labour rather than Conservative in the eleven most marginal Conservative seats, the government would have lost its overall majority'.

On the surface then, the decline of the Liberal Democrat vote seemed to firmly establish Labour as the only serious alternative to the Conservatives, and the small size of the Conservative's overall majority seemed to give Labour grounds for optimism. However, many commentators interpreted the result quite differently. What the result meant for Labour, and for the future of British politics generally, has been keenly debated.

Richard Rose – Labour's 'shattering' defeat

Labour's advantages

Richard Rose argues that the result of the 1992 election 'was shattering for Labour not only because it thought it was going to win but because, by all the old rules, it *should* have won'. From this point of view Labour fought the election under very favourable conditions yet it still ended up about 8 per cent behind the Conservatives. Rose identifies a number of factors which were working to increase the Labour vote in 1992.

1 Labour had been a relatively united party between 1987 and 1992, and the left wing which had lost Labour votes in previous elections no longer had much influence in the party.

2 The centre parties had been damaged by the arguments which surrounded the merger of the largest sections of the Liberal and Social Democratic Parties to form the Liberal Democrats. Labour therefore had a good opportunity to win votes from former Liberal and SDP voters.

3 The 1992 election was held because the Government had come to the end of its five-year term and was unable to put it off any longer. The conditions under which the Conservatives were forced to seek re-election were very far from ideal for them. In particular, 'The economy was in prolonged recession and unemployment had risen sharply in the South of England' which was the heartland of Tory support. If a sense of economic well-being helped governments win elections, then the poor economic situation seemed likely to seriously handicap the Conservatives.

4 The Conservative election campaign was widely seen as lacking in inspiration. It seemed 'at times even defeatist', suggesting that the Conservatives themselves were far from confident of success. This was hardly surprising since the opinion polls consistently indicated that Labour would win.

5 The Conservative Party had 'experienced two leadership contests, first to remove Margaret Thatcher and then to choose the relatively unknown John Major as her successor'. The elections had exposed divisions within the Conservative Party and resulted in their leader being much less experienced than the leader of the main opposition party, Neil Kinnock.

Taken together these factors meant that Labour expected to win. The question therefore was why they failed to do so.

A structural realignment in electoral competition

Rose observes that 'Election outcomes can be influenced both by short-term actions of party leaders and long-term structural change.' In 1992 the short-term factors were in Labour's favour. However, according to Rose, the long-term structural factors had so undermined Labour's vote that they outweighed any advantages which Labour enjoyed.

Table 9.11   The 1992 General Election

	Total number of votes	MPs elected	Share of UK vote (%)	Share of GB vote (%)
Conservative[a]	14,049,508	336	41.8	42.8
Change from 1987	+313,171	−39	−0.4	−0.4
Labour	11,557,134	271	34.4	35.2
Change from 1987	+1,527,190	+42	+3.6	+3.7
Liberal Democrat[b]	5,998,446	20	17.8	18.3
Change from 1987	−1,342,706	−2	−4.8	−4.8
Welsh/Scottish Nationalists[c]	786,348	7	2.3	2.4
Change from 1987	+245,886	+1	+0.6	+0.7
Others[d]	433,870	0	1.3	1.3
Change from 1987	+282,353	0	+0.8	+0.8
Northern Ireland parties[e]	785,093	17	2.3	–
Change from 1987	+54,941	0	+0.1	–
Total	33,610,399	651	United Kingdom turnout	77.7
Change from 1987	+1,080,835	+1	Change from 1987	+2.3

Notes

a   the figures for the Conservative party EXCLUDE 11 candidates in Northern Ireland who polled a total of 44,608 votes

b   the Liberal Democrats EXCLUDE 73 candidates standing for the 'Liberal party' who polled 64,744 votes: they are compared with the Liberal/SDP Alliance in 1987

c   the figures for the nationalists include 3 joint Plaid Cymru/Green candidates

d   the figures for 'others' EXCLUDE all candidates and votes in Northern Ireland: they include 253 Green candidates (170,047 votes), 73 Liberal party candidates (64,744 votes), 300 candidates for the Natural Law party (60,617 votes), and 220 'other' candidates who polled a total of 138,462 votes

e   the figures for Northern Ireland include ALL candidates and votes including Conservative (11 candidates), Natural Law (9), Workers (8) and 'others' (8), as well as the Ulster Unionists, the Democratic Unionists, the Popular Unionists, the SDLP, Sinn Fein and the Alliance.

(*Source*: Crewe, I. (September 1992) 'Why did Labour lose (yet again)?' *Politics Review*, p. 2.)

Figure 9.1   Share of vote by party since 1945

(*Source*: Rose, R. (October 1992) 'Long-term structural change or cyclical fluctuations? The 1992 Election in dynamic perspective', *Parliamentary Affairs*, p. 454.)

Figure 9.1 shows trends in votes for the three main parties since the war. To Rose this figure demonstrates that there has been a significant change since 1974. Before that date Conservative and Labour shares of the vote have been fairly similar. From 1974 onwards though, the Labour average declined while the Conservative vote stayed at about the same level. In the six general elections between February 1974 and 1992 the Conservative vote ranged between a low of 35.8 per cent in October 1974 and a high of 43.9 per cent in 1979. The Labour range was between a low of 27.6 per cent in 1983 and a high of 39.2 per cent in October 1974. Rose calculates that 'the mid point of the Conservative range is 6.4 per cent above that of Labour' and he notes that since 1979 the Conservative vote has usually been near the top of its range whilst the Labour vote has been near the bottom of its. From these figures he concludes that there has been a **structural realignment in electoral competition**. Labour's 'normal vote', ignoring short-term influences, has fallen to 33–4 per cent while the Conservative 'normal vote' has stayed as high as 40–1 per cent.

Structural changes

Rose identifies the following changes which have led to Labour's long-term electoral decline.

1 Cities, which used to be Labour strongholds, have declined as population centres leaving Labour with fewer urban constituencies where it can rely on winning.

2 In 1951 28 per cent of people were homeowners. By 1992 this figure had risen to almost 75 per cent. Since homeowners are more likely to vote Conservative than council tenants, this has reduced the normal level of Labour support.

3 Standards of living have risen sharply since 1951. Gross Domestic Product per capita has gone up 139 per cent even after allowing for inflation. Many more people own a range of consumer goods which were the prerogative of a rich minority in 1951. The number of poor, who are traditionally Labour supporters, has fallen substantially.

4 Educational standards have also risen fast. Between 1950 and 1992 the proportion of young people staying on to receive tertiary education nearly tripled. There are fewer voters with a very poor education, another group which has traditionally been prone to voting Labour.

5 Perhaps more controversially Rose also claims:

Structural changes in British society since 1951 have replaced an old system of class relations with new divisions of life style and taste. In 1951 the distinction between cloth caps and bowler hats, the civilian equivalent of officers and other ranks, was marked in many ways from manners and accents to voting.

Without the old class system Labour cannot rely on solid support from the working class. The working class is in any case shrinking from over two-thirds of the electorate in the 1950s to under a half by the 1990s.

6 Trades union membership has declined. It fell by a quarter in the 1980s alone and union members have always been more inclined to vote Labour than non-union members.

Together these changes have been steadily undermining Labour support making it increasingly difficult for it to win elections.

Political problems for Labour

Writing in 1992, Rose believes that Labour's long-term problems could well be compounded by shorter-term political problems by the time of the subsequent election.

1 The economy might well be in a better state than in 1992.

2 There was no guarantee that Labour would maintain party unity for a further five years, and any splits could have serious consequences in lost votes.

3 Labour could try for an electoral pact with the Liberal Democrats but to Rose political problems made such a pact 'impossible to conceive' at least until after the second general election of the 1990s. In any case, research suggested that voters who defected from the Liberals or Liberal Democrats were just as likely to change to voting Conservative as voting Labour.

4 In Scotland Labour was very successful in 1992 but at a future election a number of its seats could come under threat if there was any further revival of support for the Scottish Nationalist Party.

Rose also points out that despite Labour increasing its share of the vote in 1987 and again in 1992, it still had a mountain to climb. Even if Labour gained a further 3.4 per cent of the vote in the next election (its average increase in the previous two), it would still poll less votes than the Conservatives.

Rose does say that it is not inevitable that the Conservatives would win the next election, but he also says 'the hope for a Labour majority in Parliament in 1996 can be described as "Micawberism run mad", a passive hope that someday something will turn up'. He implies that if Labour could not win in 1992 when nearly all the short-term factors favoured the party, then its future prospects were dismal.

Conclusion

Rose's analysis is not particularly sophisticated and not backed up by his own detailed empirical research. Nevertheless, his case appears quite convincing and he was not alone in suggesting that Labour was in trouble. Most other psephologists though, have not gone quite as far as him in writing off Labour's future chances.

■ Ivor Crewe – the 1992 election

A devastating setback for Labour

Ivor Crewe reaches broadly similar conclusions to Rose about the performance of the parties in the 1992 election. According to Crewe the election was not a total success for the Conservatives even though they won their fourth consecutive election. It was the lowest share of the vote with which the Conservatives had won an election since 1922 and with a 2 per cent swing in its favour 'Labour came very close to toppling the Conservative government.' Nevertheless the election was 'a devastating setback for the Labour party'. It was its third worst percentage vote since the Second World War (with only the 1983 and 1987 elections being worse) and despite its gains, it still ended up 7.4 per cent behind the Conservatives.

Like Rose, Crewe argues that factors were working very much in Labour's favour. He identifies the following reasons why Labour might have been expected to win.

1 Unlike the previous two elections, the 1992 election was fought during a recession which harmed the electoral chances of the Government. Labour did not have the problem of being blamed for widespread strikes (as it had as a result of the 'Winter of Discontent' in 1978–9); it did not have the problem of 'left wing extremism and weak leadership' (as it did in 1983) and it did not have an unpopular unilateral nuclear disarmament policy (as it did in 1987). The Government had to contend with adverse publicity about 'unemployment, bankruptcies and house repossessions', all of which 'soared throughout 1992'.

2 In the early 1980s most Tory policies had been fairly popular, but by 1992 the Conservatives had implemented a number of very unpopular measures. The 'poll tax' became 'the worst policy disaster of any postwar government' and the Government was eventually forced into replacing it. The Government's economic policy 'was almost as great a shambles' and 'educational and health reforms were too long delayed for their claimed benefits to make an impact by election day'.

3 The Labour Party had transformed itself into a 'united disciplined, moderate and modern' party while its main competitor for anti-Conservative votes, the Liberal/SDP Alliance had lost support because of difficulties over merging to become the Liberal Democrats.

4 The Labour Party managed to get 'caring' issues such as health, education and unemployment to the top of the agenda during the election campaign and it was these issues on which it enjoyed the most favourable image with the electorate.

Like Rose, Crewe concludes that Labour should have won and he identifies the key question about the election as 'Why did Labour lose yet again?'

Class and voting

One possible reason for Labour losing could have been continuing class dealignment resulting in a further erosion of working-class support.

Table 9.12 shows the patterns of class voting in 1992 and the changes from the preceding two elections according to opinion poll evidence. Table 9.12 shows that Labour enjoyed the biggest swing in 1992 compared to 1987 amongst professional and managerial workers. But it also regained a considerable number of working-class votes with a 4.5 per cent swing compared to an overall swing of about 2 per cent. Crewe admits therefore that 'by conventional definitions class voting slightly increased'. The proportions voting for their traditional classes went up, 47 per cent of those voting

Table 9.12   Class voting in 1992

	Con	Lab	Lib Dem	Con lead over Lab	Swing to Lab
Professional/Managerial (ABs)					
Vote in 1992	55	23	22	+32	+5.5
Change from 1987	−1	+10	−9	−11	
Change from 1979	−9	+2	+6	−11	+5.5
Office/Clerical (C1s)					
Vote in 1992	50	29	21	+21	+1.0
Change from 1987	+2	+4	−6	−2	
Change from 1979	−4	−1	+5	−3	+1.5
Skilled Manual (C2s)					
Vote in 1992	41	40	19	+1	+3.0
Change from 1987	−2	+4	−2	−6	
Change from 1979	0	−4	+4	+2	−2.0
Semi-Skilled/Unskilled Manual (DEs)					
Vote in 1992	31	55	14	−24	+4.5
Change from 1987	−1	+8	−7	−9	
Change from 1979	−3	+2	+1	−5	+2.5
Unemployed					
Vote in 1992	27	56	17	−29	+0.5
Change from 1987	+1	+2	−4	−1	
Change from 1979	−13	+7	+6	−20	+10.0

(*Source*: Crewe, I. 'Why did Labour lose (yet again)?' *Politics Review*, September 1992, p. 5.)

being working-class Labour voters or middle-class Conservative voters compared to 44 per cent in 1987.

Furthermore the split between the 'traditional' and 'new' working class became less apparent. As Table 9.13 shows, the Conservative lead over Labour amongst the working class in the South was cut from 18 to 2 per cent: a 12 per cent Conservative lead amongst working-class owner-occupiers became a 1 per cent Labour lead, and amongst working-class non-union members Labour also regained the lead from the Conservatives.

Although Crewe argues that 'the rise in class voting should not be exaggerated' – for under half of those voting still cast their vote along class lines – the election provided little support for theories of class dealignment. Labour voting did increase in the middle class, weakening the relationship between class and voting in that class, but in the working class traditional patterns of voting returned to some extent. Labour's defeat could not

therefore be put down to a loss of support in the working class.

Issues and voting

Crewe's figures also suggest that issues may not have influenced the election result to the extent that would be expected by policy preference theories of voting. As in his analysis of the 1987 election, Crewe found that Labour policies tended to be more popular on the issues which people said were most important to them. When asked to select two issues, health, unemployment and education were the most frequently mentioned by opinion poll respondents. On all of them Labour enjoyed a healthy lead over the Conservatives.

Defence, which had been mentioned as one of the two most important issues by 35 per cent in 1987, was mentioned by only 3 per cent in 1992. Conservative policies on defence were much more popular than Labour's, and the decline in the

Table 9.13 Working-class voting in 1992

	The New Working Class				The Traditional Working Class			
	Lives in South	Owner occupier	Non-union member	Works in private sector	Lives in Scotland or North	Council tenant	Union member	Works in public sector
Conservative	40	40	37	32	26	22	29	36
Labour	38	41	46	50	59	64	55	48
Liberal Democrat	23	19	17	18	15	13	16	16
Con or Lab majority in 1992	Con +2	Lab +1	Lab +9	Lab +18	Lab +33	Lab +42	Lab +26	Lab +12
Con or Lab majority in 1987	Con +18	Con +12	Con +2	Lab +1	Lab +28	Lab +32	Lab +18	Lab +17
Swing to Labour 1987–92	+8.0	+6.5	+5.5	+8.5	+2.5	+5.0	+4.0	−2.5 (to Con)

(*Source*: Gallup/BBC survey (10–11 June 1987); Gallup post-election survey (10–11 April 1992).)

importance of defence to the electorate must have benefited Labour.

The economy and economic well-being

The economy did not appear to be a particularly important issue for most voters. Only 11 per cent mentioned prices as one of the two most important issues and 10 per cent mentioned taxation. However, as Crewe had observed about the 1987 election, what people say is important to them when asked by opinion pollsters may not be the same as what actually influences them when they come to vote. A feeling of economic well-being may be crucial to governments seeking re-election.

However, at first sight even this explanation does not seem to account for Labour's surprising failure: 30 per cent of respondents believed their living standards had fallen during the preceding year and only 25 per cent thought they had improved.

Nevertheless Crewe believes that voters' perceptions about the comparative abilities of the Labour and Conservatives to deliver economic prosperity played a crucial part in determining the result. If people did not feel that the Conservatives were making them better off (as they had in 1987), they did feel that they would be worse off under Labour. In general they blamed economic

problems on world recession or on Mrs Thatcher rather than John Major who had replaced her as Conservative leader. Many feared the economic effects of electing a Labour Government even though they thought Labour had better policies on most non-economic issues. In an exit poll (conducted on voters leaving the polling station), 53 per cent thought the Conservatives were the party most likely to take the right decisions on the economy whereas only 35 per cent saw Labour as the best party in this respect.

With one exception the opinion polls leading up to the election predicted that Labour would get a bigger share of the vote than the Conservatives. Even the exit polls considerably underestimated the margin of Conservative victory. In part these inaccuracies may have been due to the limitations of the opinion polls themselves, but there was also evidence of a late swing from Labour to the Conservatives. Amongst those who changed their mind at the last minute income tax, the economy, prices and interest rates were much more likely to be seen as important than they were by other voters. During the campaign the Conservatives attacked Labour claiming that if a Labour Government were elected it would result in a 'Double whammy' of more taxes and higher prices. The evidence suggests that this part of the Conservative campaign had some success in spreading fear of the financial consequences of a Labour Government, causing a last minute switch which contributed to Labour's defeat.

Other factors

As well as concern about Labour's competence to run the economy, Crewe identifies a number of other factors which may have contributed to the result.

1 Public perceptions of the leadership qualities of the Conservatives' John Major and Labour's Neil Kinnock may have been important. One poll found that 52 per cent thought Major would make the better leader compared to 23 per cent who named Kinnock. To Crewe 'Kinnock was a serious electoral liability'.

2 Despite the widespread view that Labour managed its campaign better than the Conservatives, it was the Conservatives who gained support during it. Across a whole range of issues Conservative policies gained in popularity as the campaign progressed. Crewe suggests that the electorate either developed a view that the Conservatives had more 'general governing competence than Labour' or that it feared that Labour might be incompetent.

3 A third factor which was cited by many as influencing the outcome was the coverage of the election by the press. Most papers supported the Conservatives and some were particularly strong in doing so. On election day the *Sun* published a front page picture of Neil Kinnock's head superimposed on a lightbulb with the headline 'If Kinnock wins today will the last person to leave Britain please turn out the lights.' Some people argued (including the *Sun* itself) that this was crucial in persuading a number of *Sun* readers in marginal constituencies to change their minds at the last minute, vote Conservative, and therefore allow the Conservatives to retain a slender overall majority.

Crewe finds some support for this view. Amongst *Sun* readers there was a big swing to the Conservatives of 7.5 per cent at the last minute. However, this was unlikely to have saved any more than six seats. Its effects should not be exaggerated because there was also a big swing amongst readers of the non-aligned *Independent* (7 per cent) and a rather small swing (2.5 per cent) amongst readers of the strongly pro-Tory *Daily Express*. Although the press did make a difference, it was not a decisive one.

Conclusion

Although Crewe saw the election as a 'devastating setback' for Labour since it had lost despite fighting the election 'in as ideal conditions as an opposition could hope to find' his findings are not quite as

pessimistic about Labour's prospects as Rose's. Crewe believes that the Conservatives might well have lost their overall majority if the opinion polls had not misleadingly shown Labour to be ahead. Fear of a Labour Government (rather than great enthusiasm for a Tory Government) 'galvanised Conservative support'. There was a high turnout amongst Conservative supporters, and waverers who were considering voting for the Liberal Democrats returned to the Conservative fold to avoid a Labour victory.

Nevertheless, Labour did not deprive the Conservatives of an overall majority despite the conditions under which the election was fought, a result which scarcely suggested that Labour could be confident of its future electoral prospects.

▋ Heath, Jowell and Curtice – *Can Labour Win?*

Heath, Jowell and Curtice were involved in conducting the *British Election Study* for the 1992 election as they had been in 1983 and 1987. They carried out two surveys about the 1992 election. One was a cross-section survey in which a sample of voters was interviewed in the week following the election. The second was a panel survey in which respondents interviewed in 1987 were re-interviewed in 1992. The second survey excluded voters who were too young to vote in 1987 but panel surveys provide a better indication than other types of surveys why people change their votes from election to election. (**Panel surveys** are a type of longitudinal study, which are discussed on pp. 848–9.)

The size of Labour's task

Like Richard Rose and Ivor Crewe, Heath, Jowell and Curtice start their analysis by noting that Labour lost despite factors operating in its favour such as the recession, the unpopularity of the poll tax, the weakness of the Liberal Democrats, the merits of the Labour campaign and the greater popularity of its policies compared to 1987. They say '1992 seemed to be Labour's best chance of victory since 1974. But the party still lost with nearly eight points less of the popular vote than the Conservatives.'

Nevertheless, Heath *et al.* believe that the election did offer some hope to Labour supporters.

They argue that in order to deprive the Conservatives of an outright victory in the election after 1992, Labour would need just a 0.5 per cent swing in its favour. On the other hand it would need a 4.1 per cent swing to win an overall majority. This would be a higher swing than Labour had achieved in any election since 1945.

In Labour's favour is the need to win a smaller share of the vote than the Conservatives to win an overall majority. Labour tends to be stronger in seats with a smaller electorate so it could win more seats than the Conservatives for the same number of votes. To win outright on the current constituencies Labour would need to be just over 0.5 per cent ahead of the Conservatives whereas the Conservatives would need to be more than 6.5 per cent ahead of Labour to gain an overall majority.

Heath *et al*. point out that one problem for Labour was that boundary changes were due to take place before the election following the 1992 election. If votes were cast as they had been in 1992, these would be likely to give the Conservatives around twelve extra seats while depriving Labour of five seats. On the other hand Labour stood to gain more than the Conservatives from any revival in Liberal Democrat fortunes since the latter were challenging the Conservatives in far more constituencies than they were challenging Labour.

Heath *et al*. therefore argue that there is 'a mountain Labour has to climb' to win an overall majority, but the 'lower slopes are rather gentler'. Depriving the Conservatives of an overall majority would be relatively easy for Labour if it could continue to progress from its 1992 position. However, as they noted earlier, Labour did fight the 1992 election under very favourable conditions making it seem unlikely that it could do even better in the future.

In order to explore future prospects in more depth Heath *et al*. go on to consider different theories of voting and their relevance for the different parties.

Volatility

Heath, Jowell and Curtice comment that the likelihood of a big swing to Labour would be greater if the electorate were becoming more volatile. However, they find little evidence that this is happening. According to their findings 22 per cent of people changed how they voted between 1987 and 1992, a slight increase on the 19 per cent who changed between 1983 and 1987. Nevertheless, this was still lower than the 24 per cent who changed the way they voted between the 1970 and February 1974 elections.

Social change and Labour's chances

Heath, Jowell and Curtice agree with commentators like Rose that Labour is handicapped by social changes which undermine Labour's electoral base. According to their figures the declining size of the working class could have been expected to cost Labour a 6 per cent share of the vote between 1964 and 1992.

As with volatility though, the theory of class dealignment could be seen as giving Labour some hope. If voters are becoming less and less influenced by class when deciding which party to support, then a decline in the size of the working class need not be a major disadvantage for Labour. As in their earlier work though, Heath *et al*. are generally critical of theories of class dealignment. Their figures suggest there was no change in the amount of relative class voting comparing the working class and salariat between the 1987 and 1992 elections. (For a definition of relative class voting see p. 562.). They therefore 'conclude that class remains important, and that the declining size of the working class is indeed an important long-term problem for Labour'.

There are some social changes which have benefited Labour including the increasing size of the ethnic minority electorate and an increase in those receiving higher education (both groups are more likely to vote Labour), and a decline in the number of regular churchgoers (who tend to vote Conservative). Overall though, Labour's prospects have certainly been harmed by social changes.

Social attitudes

Table 9.14 details the proportion of people agreeing with a number of statements about government policy. According to Heath, Jowell and Curtice it shows that 'on the face of it, the electorate was more left-of-centre on a number of key issues (though not all) at the time of the 1992 general election than they had been at the time of Labour's last election victory in 1974'. For example, more

Table 9.14   Long-term trends in attitudes

	October 1974	1979	1987	1992
Percentage agreeing that the government should ...				
Redistribute income and wealth to ordinary working people	54	52	50	48
Spend more money to get rid of poverty	84	80	86	93
Nationalise more companies	30	16	16	24
Privatise more companies	20	38	31	23
Not introduce stricter laws to regulate trade unions	—	16	33	40
Give workers more say in running places where they work	58	55	76	79
Put more money into the NHS	84	87	90	93
Percentage agreeing that ...				
Welfare benefits have not gone too far	22	17	34	46

(*Source*: Heath, Jowell and Curtice (1994) 'Labour's last chance?', in Heath *et al.* (eds) *Labour's Last Chance? The 1992 Election and Beyond*, Dartmouth Publishing, Aldershot, p. 285.)

people favoured redistribution of income and wealth, spending money to get rid of poverty, putting money into the NHS and giving workers more say at their places of work. Heath *et al.* thought that some of the apparent shift to the left may be illusory and result from 'people's perceptions that the *status quo* had shifted to the right'.

Nevertheless, to the extent that voting is influenced by attitudes to issues Labour could draw some comfort. There was little evidence that Labour's ideological position was becoming more unpopular or unacceptable to the electorate.

Party identification and political factors

If policies were not a major problem for Labour, trends in party identification were. Table 9.15 shows that identification with the Conservatives and Liberals was at a similar level in 1964 and 1992. On the other hand Labour appeared to lose the loyalty of many of its supporters in the late

1970s and early 1980s and it has failed to win them back. To Heath *et al.* the sudden change in Labour Party identification was so swift that it could not have resulted from long-term social trends. Rather it was a consequence of short-term political failure by the Labour Party. The 'winter of discontent', the formation of the SDP and disagreements over nuclear weapons within the party 'not only cost the party votes in the short-term but also broke the long-term bond that formerly linked them to the party'.

Labour's prospects

Although not denying the enormous task Labour faced in trying to gain an overall majority in a future election, Heath *et al.* see Labour as having more chance of success than either Richard Rose or Ivor Crewe. From their analysis it appears to be crucial that Labour should persuade more people to identify with the party.

Writing in 1994, Heath *et al.* found evidence that this might be happening.

Table 9.15 Trends in party identification

	Conservative %	Labour %	Liberal %	None %
1964	41	42	12	5
1966	39	45	10	5
1970	42	42	8	7
February 1974	38	39	14	6
October 1974	36	39	15	7
1979	39	38	12	9
1983	37	31	19	11
1987	39	32	17	11
1992	42	34	13	8

Notes: Liberal represents Liberal 1964–79; Liberal, SDP or Alliance 1983–87; Liberal Democrat 1992.
The figures are adjusted to take account of the sampling variation in the survey estimates. They do not sum to 100% because of 'other' parties.
Non voters excluded.

(*Source:* Heath, Jowell and Curtice (1994) 'Labour's last chance?' in Heath *et al.* (eds) *Labour's Last Chance? The 1992 Election and Beyond*, Dartmouth Publishing, Aldershot, p. 287.)

1 John Major's standing in the opinion polls had declined to make him the 'most unpopular Prime Minister for the longest period in opinion poll records' and Labour's then leader, John Smith, was much more popular than his predecessor Neil Kinnock had been.

2 The Conservatives had damaged their image as a result of splits within the party over Britain's relationship with the EC.

3 In September 1992 the actions of currency speculators had forced Britain to withdraw from the Exchange Rate Mechanism (which was supposed to protect the exchange rate of the pound).

4 A number of ministers were forced to resign or were dismissed between 1992 and 1994 as a consequence of 'either sexual scandals or failures in office'.

5 Perhaps most damaging of all, the Conservatives had their image as a low tax party undermined by raising a number of taxes and by imposing VAT on domestic fuel.

Opinion poll evidence suggested that the Conservatives were losing support. One poll in 1993 found that only 33 per cent of people believed the Government were competent and a succession of polls put Labour over 10 per cent ahead of the Conservatives. Furthermore, over four polls in 1993 Gallup found that on average only 30 per cent of the electorate identified with the Conservatives while 36 per cent identified with Labour.

Heath *et al.* remind the reader that Labour enjoyed a big lead in most opinion polls before the 1992 election, but it still lost. They also say that 'we would expect mid-term disaffection from a governing party to dissipate somewhat and be replaced by a 'homing tendency' at the following general election.' The Conservatives could expect to regain much of their support by the time voters actually got the chance to choose a new government. However, Heath *et al.* also raise the possibility that a major change could be taking place in British politics. They say:

It is at least plausible that the period since 1992 may have inflicted long term damage to the public's image of and affection for the Conservative Party of the kind inflicted on Labour some ten to fifteen years earlier.

If that were the case the Conservative and Labour Parties might return to being fairly evenly matched in their quests for election victories.

Politics in the mid-1990s

If anything political events in 1994 appeared to further undermine the Conservative's position and further strengthen Labour's. The Labour leader

John Smith died suddenly of a heart attack, and was replaced by Tony Blair. Many commentators saw Blair as having a special appeal to middle-class voters as being a moderate Labour leader who had the potential to win back former Labour voters who had deserted the party. In August 1994 one Gallup poll gave Labour an unprecedented 33.5 per cent lead over the Conservatives.

Although a lot could happen before Labour would have the chance to test its popularity at a general election, and mid-term opinion polls are not a reliable guide to the result of subsequent general elections, such figures suggested that social changes had not made Labour's prospects as gloomy as claimed by psephologists such as Richard Rose.

The democratic ideal

Abraham Lincoln defined **democracy** as 'government of the people, by the people, for the people'. Whether or not this definition describes the political process in so-called Western democracies is a matter of opinion. Democracy is an emotive term which to many implies the freedom of individuals to participate in those decisions which affect their lives. This suggests that the individuals should be directly and regularly involved in the political process. Only then will the ideal of government by the people become a reality.

However, from an elite pluralist perspective, there is no inconsistency between democracy and the exclusion of the majority from active participation in the political process. From this viewpoint, democracy is seen as a system of representative government whereby a plurality of elites represent the range of interests in society. The elite pluralists suggest that in a complex industrial society this is the only practical form that democracy can take. They imply that direct participation by the majority is not only unnecessary but undesirable. With mass participation, decision making would become so cumbersome and drawn out that the machinery of government would at best be inefficient, at worst grind to a halt. The elite pluralist perspective therefore implies that representative government is the only way the democratic ideal can be realized in contemporary society.

Social and industrial democracy

Elite pluralists have often been attacked for what many see as their narrow and restricted view of democracy. T.B. Bottomore argues that they tend 'to take representative government as the ideal instead of measuring it against the ideal of direct

participation by people in legislation and administration'. Bottomore regards the Western system of government as an 'imperfect realization of democracy in so far as it does permanently exclude many from any experience of government'. He sees this experience as essential for government by the people. Bottomore argues than only when the democratic ideal becomes an established feature of everyday life can a democratic system of national government be created. This would involve **social democracy** whereby people directly participate in the government of their local communities and **industrial democracy** whereby workers will directly participate in the management of their firms. Only this experience will provide 'the habits of responsible choice and self-government which political democracy calls for'. Bottomore argues that a truly democratic national government will only be possible when all the major institutions of society operate on democratic principles.

Democracy and social inequality

Democracy can be seen as a system in which every individual has an equal opportunity to participate in the political process and an equal say in the government of society. From this viewpoint Western societies cannot be considered truly democratic. The presence of widespread social inequality in all Western societies prevents this form of political equality. As Frank Parkin argues 'A political system which guarantees constitutional rights for groups to organize in defence of their interests is almost bound to favour the privileged at the expense of the disprivileged.' The combination of this kind of freedom and social inequality is very unlikely to result in political equality. Parkin therefore suggests that 'Only if the main contestants were to enjoy a roughly similar economic and social status could we say that pluralist democracy was a system of genuine political equality.'

One solution to the problem of political equality is to prevent powerful groups from organizing to defend and promote their interests. However this could hardly be called democratic since it denies the right of certain individuals to participate in the political process. A solution along these lines has been attempted in communist societies although, as Parkin argues, it is unlikely to result in political equality. He states:

> Egalitarianism seems to require a political system in which the state is able continually to hold in check those social and occupational groups which, by virtue of their skills or education or personal attributes, might otherwise attempt to stake claims to a disproportionate share of society's rewards.

In pursuit of political equality, communist societies have substituted the **dictatorship of the proletariat** for democracy. While there is little evidence that power is being returned to the people, the dictatorship of the proletariat may yet disappear. At least in theory Marxism offers a means of realizing the democratic ideal since only when all are equal can political equality become a reality. (We discuss the concept of democracy with reference to bureaucratic organizations in Chapter 5. See particularly pp. 289–94.)

■ Sociology, power, politics, the state and values

As in all areas of sociology, those who adopt a particular perspective on power and politics often claim objectivity and accuse their opponents of ideological bias. As Geraint Parry notes, the early elite theorists such as Pareto and Mosca believed they had established 'a neutral, "objective" political science, free from any ethical consideration'. From this standpoint, they dismissed Marxism as little more than ideology. Marxists have replied in a similar vein accusing elite theorists of merely translating ruling-class ideology into sociological jargon. However, it is doubtful whether any perspective has a monopoly on objective truth. It is possible to argue that all views on power, politics and the state owe something to the ideology and values of those who support them.

The ideological basis of Marxism is clearly visible. Marx was not only a sociologist but a political radical committed to the cause of the proletarian revolution. His writings reveal a vehement hatred of what he saw as the oppressive rule of the bourgeoisie. Marxists are committed to the idea of political equality believing that it can only be realized in an egalitarian society based on communist principles.

From this standpoint Marxists condemn the representative democracies of Western capitalist societies. Any reform in the political system which leaves the economic base of capitalism unchanged is seen as merely a concession to the proletariat which serves to maintain the status quo. Given their commitment to communism, it is noticeable that many Marxist writers were far more restrained in their criticisms of political inequality in the former USSR than they were in their criticisms of the West.

From the point of view of elite theory, Marxism is merely wishful thinking. Given the inevitability of elite rule, the egalitarian society is an illusion. However, the early elite theorists are just as vulnerable to the charge of ideological bias. Parry suggests that Pareto and Mosca began with a formula that was little more than a statement of conviction. They then scoured the history books selecting information which fitted their preconceived ideas. These ideas owed much to Pareto and Mosca's evaluation of the masses. They regarded the majority of people as generally incompetent and lacking the qualities required for self-government.

Elite theory has often been seen as an expression of conservative ideology. With its assertion of the inevitability of elite rule it can serve to justify the position of ruling minorities. Attempts to radically change the status quo, particularly those aimed at political equality, are dismissed as a waste of time. The removal of one elite will simply lead to its replacement by another.

Thus, as Parry observes, early elite theory 'offered a defence, in rationalistic or scientific terminology, of the political interests and status of the middle class'. In fact Mosca went as far as to suggest that members of the working class were unfit to vote.

Despite their claims to objectivity and neutrality, the early elite theorists were strongly opposed to socialism. T.B. Bottomore argues that 'Their original and main antagonist was, in fact, socialism, and especially Marxist socialism.' Thus the debate between Marxists and elite theorists can be seen, at least in part, as a battle between rival ideologies.

Like all members of society, sociologists are products of their time. C.J. Friedrich suggests that the early elite theorists, born in mid nineteenth-century Europe, were 'offspring of a society containing as yet many feudal remnants'. Elite theory, with its emphasis on rule by superior individuals, echoes feudal beliefs about the natural superiority of those born to rule. Lukács has suggested that elite theory was a product of those European societies in which democratic institutions were least developed. Italy is a case in point and therefore it may be no coincidence that both Pareto and Mosca were Italian.

Pluralism can be seen as an expression of either conservative or liberal ideology depending on the point of view of the observer. By implying that Western democracies are the best form of representative government that can be hoped for in complex industrial societies, elite pluralists can be seen to advocate the maintenance of the status quo. The inference from their argument is leave well alone. As Bottomore has stated, the elite pluralist conception of democracy as representative government is limited and restricted compared to the idea of direct participation.

A commitment to this idea might well result in a very different analysis of Western political systems. This is evident from Bottomore's own work. He regards the pluralist view of democracy as a poor substitute for the real thing. His belief, that direct participation in politics by all members of society is a realistic alternative to representative government, may well be influenced by a commitment to this ideal.

Frank Parkin has suggested that 'pluralism is

quite plausibly regarded as a philosophy which tends to reflect the perceptions and interests of a privileged class'. Pluralism claims that all major interests in society are represented. However, in an unequal society, the interests of the rich and powerful are likely to be better served than those of the underprivileged. With its emphasis on the representation of all interests, pluralism tends to disguise this situation. It is likely to divert attention from the inequalities which result from the operation of the political process. By doing so it may help to maintain the status quo and provide support for the privileged.

While it has often been seen as a reflection of conservative ideology, pluralism has also been interpreted as a liberal viewpoint. Liberalism is a philosophy which accepts the basic structure of Western society while advocating progressive reforms within that structure. These reforms are directed by a concern for individual liberty and a desire to improve the machinery of democratic government.

Many pluralists admit that Western democracies have their faults and are concerned to correct them. Thus Arnold Rose admits that the USA is not 'completely democratic' and looks forward to a number of reforms to make the existing system more representative. But he accepts that the basic framework of American society is sound and therefore does not advocate radical change.

Pluralism has found particularly strong support in the USA and many of the important pluralist writers, such as Dahl and Rose, are American. To some degree their writings can be seen as a reflection of American culture. Since the Declaration of Independence, American society has emphasized the liberty of the individual rather than social equality. In this respect, it is significant that the USA has no major socialist party unlike most of its West European counterparts.

This emphasis on liberty rather than equality is reflected in pluralist theory. From a pluralist perspective, democracy is a system of government which provides freedom for members of society to organize in the defence and promotion of their interests. Westergaard and Resler claim that pluralists 'value liberty more than equality' and see the free enterprise capitalist system as 'a bulwark of liberty'. The values of liberty and freedom of the individual are enshrined in the 'American Dream'. As a result, the writings of American pluralists may owe more than a little to the ethos of their society.

10
Sex and gender

10

Sex and gender

■ Introduction

Original sin in the Garden of Eden was woman's. She tasted the forbidden fruit, tempted Adam and has been paying for it ever since. In Genesis, the Lord said:

I will greatly multiply thy sorrow and thy conception; in sorrow thou shalt bring forth children; and thy desire shall be to thy husband, and he shall rule over thee.

Sociologists would regard the above quotation as a mythological justification for the position of women in society. Many women might see the summary it contains of their relationship with their spouses as an accurate description of their status through the ages, that is:

1 women produce children;

2 women are mothers and wives;

3 women do the cooking, mending, sewing and washing;

4 they take care of men and are subordinate to male authority;

5 they are largely excluded from high-status occupations and from positions of power.

These generalizations apply to practically every known human society. Some sociologists and anthropologists believe that there is not, and never has been a society in which women do not have an inferior status to that of men. In recent decades, particularly with the development of the Women's Liberation Movement, the explanation for such differences has been hotly debated.

Feminists have argued, with a good deal of justification, that until the 1970s nearly all sociology was written by men, about men and for men. There were relatively few female sociologists, nearly all sociological research used male samples, and aspects of society of particular relevance to women (such as housework and female crime)

were rarely studied. Sociology largely ignored women. Since the early 1970s, however, sociological studies by and about women have proliferated.

Nearly all the early research and theoretical debate specifically concerned with the **sociology of gender** focused on women and femininity. In recent years it has been recognized that a more complete understanding of gender can be developed by also studying men and masculinity, and research into masculinity has gradually become more common.

Sex and gender

Many writers use the distinction between **sex** and **gender** as the starting point for their analysis. The first person to make this distinction was the American psychoanalyst Dr Robert Stoller in 1968. Stoller made the common-sense observation that the vast majority of the population can clearly be categorized as male or female according to their physical characteristics: 'external genitalia, internal genitalia, gonads (the organs which produce sex cells), hormonal states and secondary sex characteristics'. Because of these differences women are capable of bearing and suckling children, whereas men are not. In addition there are differences in physique between men and women which usually mean that men are more muscular and stronger. Biological differences are widely believed to be responsible for the differences in both the behaviour of men and women and the roles that they play in society. Stoller cautioned, though, against such an assumption. He said:

Gender is a term that has psychological and cultural connotations, if the proper terms for sex are 'male' and 'female', the corresponding terms for gender are 'masculine' and 'feminine'; these latter might be quite independent of (biological) sex.

In other words, there is no necessary association between being a woman and being 'feminine', and between being a man and behaving in a 'masculine' way: girls are not necessarily caring and compassionate; boys do not have to be aggressive and competitive.

Sociologists such as Ann Oakley take this argument a stage further, claiming that feminine social roles, such as those of housewives and mothers who care for their children, are not an inevitable product of female biology. Nor does Oakley believe that being a man makes it inevitable that men will be breadwinners. To Stoller and Oakley it is the culture of a society which determines the behaviour of the sexes within it.

Most, though not all, sociologists of gender and feminists support this position. However, it is not immediately obvious how their claims can be justified. The belief that it is 'natural' for men and women to behave differently is widespread, and is supported by many scientists and some psychologists and sociologists.

We will now examine the relationship between sex and gender in detail. We will begin with those sociologists who believe that gender roles are **biologically determined**, and then consider those sociologists who argue that gender roles are **culturally determined**. NB

Sex and gender differences

Hormones and the brain

Some scientists believe that variations in the behaviour and social roles of men and women can be explained in terms of hormones and brain differences. Hormones are bodily secretions whose functions include the regulation of the development of male and female bodies so that they become capable of reproduction. The production and release of hormones is controlled by the hypothalamus in the brain. Both sexes produce a full range of sex hormones from a variety of glands (including the ovaries and testes). Normally women produce greater amounts of progesterone and oestrogen, while men produce more testosterone and other androgens. The higher levels of androgens in the male stop the hypothalamus from regulating hormonal production cyclically, which it does in the female menstruation and ovulation cycle. The activity of a wide range of hormones, is closely integrated with the activity of the nervous system, and so hormones can influence behaviour, personality and emotional disposition.

Animal experiments might seem to provide some evidence for a link between androgens and aggressive behaviour.

1 Castrated male rats tend to fight less, while female rats given extra androgens after birth are more aggressive in adult life than other female rats.

2 Goy and Phoenix claim that female rhesus monkeys given extra androgens display more 'rough and tumble play' than other females.

3 Some studies seem to show a direct link between testosterone levels in human males and aggression, using supposed measures of aggression such as being in jail.

4 Ehrhardt has studied the development and behaviour of girls exposed as foetuses to high levels of androgens. He claims that such girls are more likely to exhibit 'tomboy' characteristics than their sisters or other girls of the same age, IQ, and who had fathers of the same occupation. For example, they were likely to choose boys for playmates, enjoy outdoor play and athletics, but showed little interest in dolls and infant care. Ehrhardt explained these differences in behaviour as the product of the 'masculinization' of the girls' brains due to their exposure to high androgen levels.

Criticisms of hormonal explanations

All these studies are, however, suspect as methods of showing that male and female human behaviour is governed by hormones. Ruth Bleier points to a number of flaws in using animal behaviour to explain human behavioural differences. In general, she observes that it is dangerous to assume that the same hormonal changes would result in the same changes in behaviour in humans as they had in animals. She does not accept that such experiments are conclusive.

The experiments with rats defined aggression simply in terms of fighting behaviour, yet they have been used to explain the supposed dominance and aggression in human males in all spheres of social life. Furthermore, the experiments were carried out in unnatural laboratory conditions, and fighting might not have increased if the rats had been in their normal environment.

The rhesus monkey experiments failed to take account of the fact that the androgens produced masculinized genitalia in the female monkeys. Bleier refers to studies which show that rhesus mothers treat their offspring differently from an early age according to their sex. The behaviour of the monkeys could therefore have resulted from being treated as males because of their appearance. Oakley accepts that dominant males in monkey groups have higher testosterone levels than low dominance monkeys. However, she argues that social context affects hormone levels. Experiments show that when low dominance monkeys are caged only with females, their testosterone levels rise. Dominance, or lack of it, might affect testosterone levels, as well as vice versa.

In Ehrhardt's studies the baby girls were born with what appeared to be masculine genitalia, and in all but one case they were initially treated as boys. It is therefore possible that their 'tomboy' behaviour was entirely a product of their early socialization. Oakley refers to one case studied by Ehrhardt in which the child, who was originally treated as a boy, underwent an operation at seven months so that she took on the appearance of a girl. From 17 months old her name was changed from a boy's to a girl's, she was treated as a girl and dressed in girl's clothing. Later the mother commented on how 'feminine' the girl had become. This strongly suggests that it was environmental influences and not changes in the brain produced by hormones which led to the 'tomboy' behaviour.

■ Brain lateralization

There are claims that hormones have indirect effects on male and female brain development, as well as the direct effects discussed above. One area of research has concentrated on the issue of **brain**

lateralization. It is widely believed that the right and left hemispheres of the brain specialize in different tasks. The left hemisphere is supposed to specialize in language and analytic skills, while the right is held to be mainly responsible for visuo-spatial abilities, which relate to artistic, mathematical and engineering skills.

J.A. Gray and A.W.H. Buffery believe that the left hemisphere of the brain is more dominant in girls after the age of two, and that boys have greater abilities in those functions concentrated in the right hemisphere. According to Gray and Buffery this difference is due to hormonal influences on the brain, and accounts for the results of some tests which appear to show that girls have greater verbal ability than boys, but boys perform better in spatial and mathematical tests.

This explanation of sex differences is, however, as suspect as those which relate to hormones and aggression. Ruth Bleier has noted the contradictory findings of studies in this area. For example, some studies claim that girls' brains are less lateralized than boys; some claim the reverse to be true; and some find no difference between boys and girls.

Bleier also raises doubts about the results of verbal and visuo-spatial tests. On average girls do score slightly higher than boys in verbal tests and slightly lower in visuo-spatial tests. Nevertheless she says:

There are no clearcut sex differences in either verbal or visuo-spatial abilities. All females do not score better than all males in verbal tests, nor do all males score better than all females in visuo-spatial tests, nor do the majority of either sex perform better than the majority of the other . . . Comparable populations of males and females have the same range of test scores, the same range of abilities, and in some test situations the mean or average test scores may not differ at all, or, differ by only a few percentage points.

What small differences there are could well result from differences in socialization rather than from brain lateralization.

Genetics and evolution

In this section we consider the interaction of genetical and evolutionary factors, and how these have been used by some anthropologists and sociologists to account for human behavioural differences.

Lionel Tiger and Robin Fox – the human biogrammar

Anthropologists Lionel Tiger and Robin Fox argue that social scientists who assume that human beings behave simply in terms of the culture of their society are ignoring what they call the human **biogrammar**. The biogrammar is a genetically based programme which predisposes humanity to behave in certain ways. These predispositions are not the same as instincts since they can be considerably modified by culture, but they remain basic influences on human behaviour. In part they are inherited from our primate ancestors, in part they have developed during existence in hunting and gathering bands. Since 99.9 per cent of human existence has been spent as a hunter and gatherer, Tiger and Fox argue that it is reasonable to assume that, to some degree, people are genetically adapted to this way of life.

Although the biogrammars of men and women are similar in many respects, there are important differences between them. Tiger and Fox argue that compared to women, men are more aggressive and dominant. These characteristics are genetically based; in particular they result from differences between male and female hormones. These differences are due partly to genetic inheritance from humanity's primate ancestors, and partly to a genetic adaptation to a hunting way of life. Males hunt, which is an aggressive activity. They are responsible for the protection of the band and for alliances or wars with other bands. Thus men monopolize positions of power.

Since Tiger and Fox see dominance as a **sex-linked characteristic**, it comes as no surprise that politics is the province of men from the male elders in Australian Aborigine hunting and gathering bands to the House of Commons and House of Lords in present-day Britain.

By comparison, women are programmed by their biogrammars to reproduce and care for children. Tiger and Fox argue that the basic family unit consists of mother and child. In their words, 'Nature intended mother and child to be together.' It does not particularly matter how this basic unit is supported and protected. It can be by the addition of a single male, as in the case of the nuclear family, or by the impersonal services of a welfare state.

The close emotional bond between mother and child is a genetically based predisposition for both parties and it is particularly important for the welfare of the child. Tiger and Fox maintain that 'The mother is totally essential to the well-being of the child.' Unless this close emotional bond exists, the child will be unable to establish successful relationships in later life.

In short, Tiger and Fox argue that male and female biogrammars are adapted to a sexual division of labour in a hunting society. As they put it, 'We are wired for hunting.' Compared to cultural change, genetic change is slow. Thus the male and female biogrammars of a hunting existence continue in modern industrial society. From this it follows that attempts to abolish gender roles and replace them with unisex roles, however desirable this may be, will 'go against nature'.

Sociobiology – the evolution of human behaviour

Another attempt to link gender differences to genetics and evolution has been made by sociobiologists. Like Tiger and Fox they try to link human biological development and social behaviour.

Sociobiology was first developed by E.O. Wilson and has been applied to sex and gender by David Barash. It is based in part on Charles Darwin's theory of evolution, but it goes well beyond Darwin's original theory.

Like Darwin, sociobiologists believe that humans and other species develop and change through a process of natural selection. Individuals of a species vary in their physical characteristics, and from this point of view, those which are best adapted to their environment are most likely to survive and reproduce. Since offspring tend to have characteristics similar to those of their parents due to **genetic inheritance**, the characteristics of a species can change as the fittest survive.

Thus, to use a simple example, giraffes have gradually evolved long necks because members of the species with longer necks had better access to food supplies in the upper levels of trees than their shorter-necked counterparts. As longer-necked giraffes and their offspring survived more frequently, a long neck became encoded in the genetic make-up of the species.

Sociobiologists go beyond Darwin in two main ways.

1 First, they argue that it is not just physical characteristics that evolve, but also **behaviour**.

2 Second, they believe that behaviour in animals and humans is governed by a genetic instruction to maximize the chances of passing on their genes to future generations by breeding – that is, they try to ensure that they have offspring which survive. At the heart of sociobiology's attempt to explain sex differences in the behaviour of female and male humans is the claim that the two sexes employ different strategies to maximize their chances of passing on their genes.

Barash points out that human males produce millions of sperm during their lifetime, while women usually produce only one egg at a time, and about 400 in all during their lifetime. Furthermore, the female gestates the foetus in her body. The male therefore has an interest in making as many women as possible pregnant to produce the maximum number of offspring who will carry his genes. However, the woman invests so much time and energy in each offspring that she must go for quality in her mates, so that each offspring has a good chance of ultimate survival. She therefore selects only the most genetically suitable male partners.

Wilson and Barash go on to assert that different reproductive strategies produce different behaviour in males and females and also lead them to occupy different social roles. In terms of sexual behaviour, men are likely to be more promiscuous, while women will be more circumspect in their pursuit of the best possible genetic partner. Wilson says:

It pays males to be aggressive, hasty, fickle and undiscriminating. In theory it is more profitable for women to be coy, to hold back until they can identify males with the best possible genes.

Barash talks about there being advantages for men in 'playing fast and loose', and having a 'love 'em and leave 'em' attitude. Wilson claims that rape by males can be explained in this way.

Sociobiologists believe that women can tolerate infidelity by their partners more readily than men. Infidelity by men has little cost for women, but if the man's woman is unfaithful, the man may devote energy to raising someone else's child.

To Wilson and Barash, these differences have wider implications. Because a woman is always certain whether a child is genetically hers, she will be more willing to devote attention to childcare, and in a modern society may therefore be willing to become a housewife. In addition women's search for the best males to father their children leads to them seeking to marry males of a higher social status than themselves. Because women can produce so 'few' children, men must compete for access to the comparatively scarce reproductive capacities of females. The larger and more aggressive males will be more successful. Females do not need to compete for mates in this way, and ultimately this leads to the dominance of males over females.

In early societies one way in which men tried to attract females was through showing that they were the best providers by demonstrating they were successful hunters. To sociobiologists the roots of war and territoriality are to be found in the aggressive male's attempts to secure and retain access to his own females by preventing their access to other males.

Sociobiologists back up these sweeping claims largely with animal studies. They provide examples of ape species in which dominant males are more successful in mating, and of the male lions' domination of female prides. Wilson even claims there are examples of 'gang rape' by mallard ducks.

However, Barash denies that any of the views held by sociobiologists are sexist. He sees males and females as simply biologically different, each pursuing the maintenance of their genes in their own way.

Wilson admits that human males and females are not compelled to behave in the ways described above; they may choose different types of behaviour. But if they do, it goes against their biological predispositions and makes them less efficient at maintaining the species.

▮ Criticisms of evolutionary and genetic theories

There are numerous criticisms of the work of Tiger and Fox and the sociobiologists. Both these approaches assume a direct link between patterns of genetic inheritance and behaviour in humans. However, there is no scientific evidence that such a link exists.

In contrast to animals, human behaviour is shaped by environment rather than instinct. Steven Rose, Leon Kamin, and R.C. Lewontin note that, unlike most animals:

---

the human infant is born with relatively few of its neural pathways already committed. During its long infancy connections between nerve cells are formed not merely on the basis of specific epigenetic programming but in the light of experience.

Bleier raises questions about the importance attached to male hunting by Tiger and Fox. She claims that gathering vegetables and hunting small animals have been the principal means of subsistence throughout human history and both these activities are predominantly carried out by women. The earliest conclusive evidence of the systematic hunting of large animals (a predominantly male activity) dates from around 500,000 years ago. If Bleier is correct in assuming that hunting by males

is a comparatively recent activity, then it is difficult to see how it could have led to a biogrammar which produced male dominance.

Bleier is dismissive of sociobiology. She accuses it of being **ethnocentric**: of assuming that all human behaviour corresponds to that in the white capitalist world. For example, sociobiologists merely assert that females are 'coy' and males 'aggressive' without examining different societies. Oakley points out that there are many societies in which women are far from 'coy'. She says 'Amongst the Trobrianders, as also among the Lesu, Kurtatchi, Lepcha, Kwoma, and Mataco, women frequently take the initiative in sexual relationships.'

According to the critics then, sociobiology tries to explain 'universal' human behaviour which is not universal at all. Furthermore, the evidence they use from the animal world to support their case is selective. It ignores all the examples of animal species where males are not aggressive and dominant. Bleier notes that in some species of ape and monkey there are no dominance hierarchies at all. In others, such as Japanese macaques, the rank of a male within troop depends on the rank of his mother. Bleier points out that recent studies have revealed a wide variety of behaviour patterns in apes. There are examples of female apes who 'protect territory, fight for their own or other mothers' young, take food from males, and bond with other females to fight aggressive males'. In short, sociobiologists simply ignore the evidence which contradicts their view.

For this reason many feminists regard sociobiology as a spurious attempt to provide 'scientific' justification for male power.

▮ Biology and the sexual division of labour

Biologically based explanations of the behaviour of men and women have not been confined to those which have located these differences in the hormones, brains, or genes of the two sexes. Other writers, including anthropologists, have focused on more obvious physical differences between males and females, and related these to the allocation of social roles.

▮ George Peter Murdock – biology and practicality

Though an anthropologist like Tiger and Fox, George Peter Murdock operates from very different assumptions. He sees biological differences between men and women as the basis of the sexual division of labour in society. However, he does not suggest that men and women are directed by genetically based predispositions or characteristics to adopt their particular roles. Instead, he simply suggests that biological differences, such as the greater physical strength of men and the fact that women bear children, lead to gender roles out of sheer practicality. Given the biological differences between men and women, a sexual division of labour is the most efficient way of organizing society.

In a cross-cultural survey of 224 societies ranging from hunting and gathering bands to modern nation-states, Murdock examines the activities assigned to men and women. He finds tasks such as hunting, lumbering and mining to be predominantly male roles, and cooking, gathering wild vegetable products, water carrying and making and repairing clothes to be largely female roles. He states:

> Man with his superior physical strength can better undertake the more strenuous tasks, such as lumbering, mining, quarrying, land clearance and housebuilding. Not handicapped, as is woman by the physiological burdens of pregnancy and nursing, he can range farther afield to hunt, to fish, to herd and to trade. Woman is at no disadvantage, however, in lighter tasks which can be performed in or near the home, e.g. the gathering of vegetable products, the fetching of water, the preparation of food, and the manufacture of clothing and utensils.

Thus, because of her biological function of childbearing and nursing, woman is tied to the home base; because of her physique she is limited to less strenuous tasks.

Murdock finds that the sexual division of labour is present in all of the societies in his sample and concludes that 'The advantages inherent in a division of labour by sex presumably account for its universality.'

■ Talcott Parsons – biology and the 'expressive' female

Similar arguments are advanced to account for the role of women in industrial society. As we saw in Chapter 6 (pp. 322–3), Talcott Parsons sees the isolated nuclear family in modern industrial society specializing in two basic functions:

1 the socialization of the young;
2 the stabilization of adult personalities.

For socialization to be effective, a close, warm and supportive group is essential. The family meets this requirement and within the family, the woman is primarily responsible for socializing the young.

Parsons turns to biology for his explanation of this fact. He states:

> In our opinion the fundamental explanation of the allocation of roles between the biological sexes lies in the fact that the bearing and early nursing of children establish a strong presumptive primacy of the relation of mother to the small child.

Thus, because mothers bear and nurse children, they have a closer and stronger relationship with them. This is particularly so in modern industrial society since the isolation of the nuclear family:

> focuses the responsibility of the mother role more sharply on one adult woman. Furthermore the absence of the husband father from the home premises so much of the time means that she has to take the primary responsibility for the children.

Parsons characterizes the woman's role in the family as **expressive** which means she provides warmth, security and emotional support. This is essential for the effective socialization of the young.

It is only a short step from applying these expressive qualities to her children to applying them also to her husband. This is her major contribution to the second function of the isolated nuclear family: the stabilization of adult personalities. The male breadwinner spends his working day competing in an achievement-oriented society. This **instrumental** role leads to stress and anxiety. The expressive female relieves this tension by providing the weary breadwinner with love, consideration and understanding.

Parsons argues that for the family to operate efficiently as a social system, there must be a clearcut sexual division of labour. In this sense, the instrumental and expressive roles complement each other. Like a button and a buttonhole, they lock together to promote family solidarity.

Although Parsons moves a long way from biology, it forms his starting point. Biological differences between the sexes provide the foundation on which the sexual division of labour is based.

■ John Bowlby – the mother/child bond

John Bowlby examines the role of women, and in particular, their role as mothers, from a psychological perspective. Like Parsons, he argues that a mother's place is in the home, caring for her children especially during their early years.

Bowlby conducted a number of studies of juvenile delinquents and found that the most psychologically disturbed had experienced separation from their mothers at an early age. Many had been raised in orphanages and as a result had been deprived of maternal love. They appeared unable to give or receive love and seemed compelled to adopt a career of destructive and antisocial relationships.

Bowlby concludes that it is essential for mental health that 'the infant and young child should experience a warm, intimate and continuous relationship with his mother'. Bowlby's arguments imply that there is a genetically based psychological need for a close and intimate mother–child relationship. Thus the mother role is firmly attached to the female. (For further details of Bowlby's views and related research, see Chapter 7, p. 388.)

In this section we have examined some of the arguments which base the sexual division of labour on **biological differences** between the sexes. Although all the arguments allow some variation in the way gender roles are played, none holds out much hope for those who seek to abolish them. Apart from peripheral areas such as teenage clothes, they suggest that the day of unisex will never dawn.

■ Ann Oakley – the cultural division of labour

Ann Oakley rejects the views of Murdock, Parsons, and Bowlby. She does not accept that there is any natural or inevitable division of labour or allocation of social roles on the basis of sex. She says:

Not only is the division of labour by sex not universal, but there is no reason why it should be. Human cultures are diverse and endlessly variable.

They owe their creation to human inventiveness rather than invincible biological forces.

Oakley first takes George Peter Murdock to task, arguing that the sexual division of labour is not universal nor are certain tasks always performed by men, others by women. She maintains that Murdock's interpretation of his data is biased because he looks at other cultures through both Western and male eyes. In particular, she claims that he pre-judges the role of women in terms of the Western housewife–mother role.

Culture and gender roles

Oakley finds plenty of evidence from Murdock's own data to attack the assumption that biology largely determines the sexual division of labour. There are fourteen societies in Murdock's sample in which lumbering is done either exclusively by women or shared by both sexes, thirty-six societies in which women are solely responsible for land clearance, and thirty-eight in which cooking is a shared activity.

Oakley examines a number of societies in which biology appears to have little or no influence on women's roles.

1 The Mbuti Pygmies, a hunting and gathering society who live in the Congo rain forests, have no specific rules for the division of labour by sex. Men and women hunt together. The roles of father and mother are not sharply differentiated, both sexes sharing responsibility for the care of children.

2 Amongst the Australian Aborigines of Tasmania, women were responsible for seal hunting, fishing and catching opossums (tree-dwelling mammals).

3 Turning to present-day societies, Oakley notes that women form an important part of many armed forces, particularly those of China, the former USSR, Cuba and Israel.

4 In India, some 12 per cent of labourers on building sites are women.

5 In some Asian and Latin American countries, a quarter of the labour force in mines is female.

Oakley claims that the above examples show clearly that there are no exclusively female roles and that biological characteristics do not bar women from particular jobs. She regards as a myth the supposed 'biologically based incapacity of women to carry out heavy and demanding work'.

Culture and the mother–housewife role

Oakley also attacks the arguments of Parsons and Bowlby. Using the example of Alor, an island in Indonesia, Oakley shows how in this and other small-scale horticultural societies, women are not tied to their offspring, and this does not appear to have any harmful effects on the children.

In traditional Alorese society, women were largely responsible for the cultivation and collection of vegetable produce. This involved them spending considerable time away from the village. Within a fortnight of the birth of their child, women returned to the fields leaving the infant in the care of a sibling, the father or a grandparent.

Turning to Western society, Oakley dismisses Bowlby's claim that an 'intimate and continuous' relationship between mother and child is essential for the child's well-being. She notes that a large body of research shows that the employment of the mother has no detrimental effects on the child's development. Some studies indicate that the children of working mothers are less likely to be delinquent than those of mothers who stay at home. In fact Oakley claims that 'Working mothers enjoy their children more and are less irritable with them than full-time mothers.'

Oakley is particularly scathing in her attack on Parsons's view of the family and the role of the 'expressive' female within it. She accuses him of basing his analysis on the beliefs and values of his own culture and in particular on the myths of male superiority and of the sanctity of marriage and the family. Oakley argues that the expressive housewife–mother role is not necessary for the functioning of the family unit – it merely exists for the convenience of men. She claims that Parsons's explanation of gender roles is simply a validating myth for the 'domestic oppression of women'.

Oakley draws the following conclusions.

1 Gender roles are culturally rather than biologically determined.

2 Evidence from a number of different societies shows that there are no tasks (apart from childbearing) which are performed exclusively by females.

3 Biological characteristics do not bar women from particular occupations.

4 The mother role is a cultural construction. Evidence from several societies indicates that children do not require a close, intimate and continuous relationship with a female mother figure.

The social construction of gender roles

Oakley believes that gender roles are culturally rather than **biologically** produced. In other words humans learn the behaviour that is expected of males and females within their society. This behaviour is not produced by innate characteristics: studies of a number of societies show that gender roles can vary considerably. Whatever the biological differences between males and females, it is the culture of a society which exerts most influence in the creation of masculine and feminine behaviour. If there are biological tendencies for men and women to behave in different ways, these can be overridden by cultural factors.

Socialization and gender roles

Oakley outlines how socialization in modern industrial societies shapes the behaviour of girls and boys from an early age. Basing her work on the findings of Ruth Hartley, Oakley discusses four main ways in which socialization into gender roles takes place.

1 The child's self-concept is affected by **manipulation**. For example, mothers tend to pay more attention to girls' hair and to dress them in 'feminine' clothes.

2 Differences are achieved through **canalization** involving the direction of boys and girls towards different objects. This is particularly obvious in the provision of toys for girls which encourage them to rehearse their expected adult roles as mothers and housewives. Girls are given dolls, soft toys, and miniature domestic objects and appliances to play with. Boys, on the other hand, are given toys which encourage more practical, logical, and aggressive behaviour, for example bricks and guns.

3 The third aspect of socialization is the use of **verbal appellations**, such as 'You're a naughty boy', or 'That's a good girl.' This leads young children to identify with their gender and to imitate adults of the same gender.

4 Male and female children are exposed to **different activities**. For example, girls are particularly encouraged to become involved with domestic tasks. In addition numerous studies have documented how stereotypes of masculinity and femininity are further reinforced throughout childhood, and indeed adult life. The media have been particularly strongly attacked by feminists for tending to portray men and women in their traditional social roles.

■ Gender attribution

From the viewpoint described above gender is **socially constructed** in the sense that differences in the behaviour of males and females are learned rather than being the inevitable result of biology. The ethnomethodologists Suzanne J. Kessler and Wendy McKenna go a stage further. As **ethnomethodologists** they are interested in the ways that members of society categorize the world around them. From their perspective, **gender attribution** – the decision to regard another person as male or female – is socially produced in much the same way as gender roles.

For most people it seems obvious whether someone is male or female, and it is taken for granted that a decision about the sex of another will coincide with the biological 'facts'. Kessler and McKenna disagree; they deny that there is any clearcut way of differentiating between men and women.

Two or more sexes?

This startling claim is backed up by a range of arguments and evidence. Kessler and McKenna try to demonstrate that there are exceptions to every rule which is supposed to distinguish the sexes.

The full range of hormones are present in both men and women, thus hormones do not provide a clear dividing line between the sexes. Some women have high androgen levels, while some men have comparatively low levels of this hormone.

Some individuals have male chromosomes (XY), but are insensitive to the effects of androgen and thus appear to be physically female. Despite their male genetic make-up they are invariably identified as females.

Other individuals have a condition known as **Turner's Syndrome**. They have neither XY chromosomes, nor the normal female pairing of XX. Instead they have a single X chromosome, normally indicated by the figures XO. A small number of people with this condition do have a few XYY chromosomes as well as the predominant XO. They have a female appearance but can fail 'sex tests' for women's athletics competitions.

Kessler and McKenna argue that the main way of determining gender at birth is through an inspection of the genitals. However, even this may produce ambiguous evidence. Some babies and adults have both male and female genitals, a condition known as **hermaphroditism**.

Kessler and McKenna note that despite these anomalies both the public and scientists tend to see male and females as opposites, refusing to recognize the possibility of an **intermediate state**. However, this has not always been the case. Some societies have recognized a third gender role: the **berdache**. A number of North American Indian tribes contained berdache. They were usually 'men' who dressed and in some ways acted like women. In some societies they had a high status, in others a low one, but in all cases they were treated as a distinct gender. In Western industrial society hermaphrodites are almost always categorized as male or female. In tribes such as the Potock of East Africa they would be more likely to be allocated to a third category.

Allocation to sexes

Having questioned the most basic assumption (that there are just two sexes) Kessler and McKenna go on to discuss how individuals are allocated to sexes by others. This process was studied by interviewing **transsexuals**, people who seem biologically normal but who feel themselves to be members of the 'opposite' sex. Some, but not all, transsexuals undergo operations to alter their genitals, usually changing from male to female.

Normally gender and genitals are equated with each other: the connection between them is taken for granted. However, people are not expected to ask others whom they have just met to remove their clothes so that they can determine which sex they are. Various types of evidence are pieced together so that a gender attribution can be made by the observer. Someone with the appearance and behaviour of a female or male will simply be assumed to have the appropriate genitals. The existence of transsexuals means that this assumption is not always accurate. Biological males sometimes live as, and are accepted as females.

How then do people decide what gender another person is? According to Kessler and McKenna there are four main processes involved.

1 The **content and manner of the speech** of others is taken into account. Some male to female transsexuals have trained themselves to appear to be women by putting more inflection in their voice and by having more mobile facial movements when talking. Others introduce themselves as 'Miss' to settle any doubt there might be in an observer's mind.

2 The second important factor in gender attribution is **public physical appearance**. For example, female to male transsexuals may disguise their breasts by wearing baggy clothing or by using strapping.

3 The **information** people provide about their past life helps to determine gender attribution. Again transsexuals have to be careful to avoid suspicion. They may need a cover story. In one case a female to male transsexual attributed pierced ears to belonging to a tough street gang.

4 The final important factor is the **private body**. Usually there is little problem in keeping the body covered, but transsexuals may need to avoid certain situations (such as visiting beaches or sharing rooms with others) if they have not undergone the appropriate operations to change their sex physically.

Taking on the identity of a sex to which they do not belong biologically is difficult and demanding for the transsexual. For most people hormones, chromosomes, genitals and the gender attributed to them will all coincide. Nevertheless, the exceptions studied by Kessler and McKenna demonstrate that even the most basic division – that between male and female – can be seen as being at least in part a **social construct**.

■ Sex and gender differences – conclusion

Some sociologists have tried to move beyond the debate on whether sex or gender shapes the behaviour of men and women. Both David Morgan and Linda Birke argue that sex and gender interact. Sex differences influence gender differences and vice versa. Linda Birke argues that 'women's biology actually and materially affects their lives'. She suggests that feminists cannot ignore biological facts, for example that women menstruate and can give birth.

However, both Morgan and Birke also argue that the cultural interpretation placed on biological differences is very important. Thus David Morgan says:

if certain distinctions between men and women come to be seen as crucial, this itself is a cultural fact and has its consequences, although this is the outcome of a complex interaction between the biological and the cultural rather than the primary assertion of the former.

In the nineteenth century, for example, some people believed that men and women had fixed amounts of energy. Unlike men, women were believed to use up much of this energy in menstruation, pregnancy and the menopause. Today many people believe that hormonal differences play a major part in shaping the behaviour of men and women. Birke points out that this belief is held despite the fact that 'there simply is no one hormone or even class of hormone, that belongs uniquely to one gender or the other'. What matters most is the meaning attached to differences, real or imagined, in a society.

■ Gender inequality

So far in this chapter we have examined explanations for differences between men and women. These differences have sometimes been seen as the basis for inequalities between them, and we will now look at those inequalities in more detail.

The development of the Women's Liberation Movement has led to attention being focused on the subordinate position of women in many societies. Feminist sociologists have been mainly responsible for developing theories of gender inequality, yet there is little agreement about the causes of this inequality, nor about what actions should be taken to reduce or end it.

Three feminist approaches can be broadly distinguished:

1 radical feminism;
2 Marxist and socialist feminism;
3 liberal feminism.

There is considerable overlap between these approaches, and each contains feminists with a variety of views. Nevertheless, the distinction between these perspectives is important. It helps to clarify some of the major disputes within feminism, and feminists often attribute themselves to one of these categories. We will briefly outline each perspective before considering a more detailed examination of how they have been applied to particular aspects of gender inequality.

■ Radical feminism

Radical feminism blames the exploitation of women on men. To a radical feminist it is primarily men who have benefited from the subordination of women. Women are seen to be exploited because they undertake free labour for men by carrying out childcare and housework, and because they are denied access to positions of power.

Radical feminists see society as **patriarchal** – it is dominated and ruled by men. From this point of view men are the ruling class, and women the subject class. The family is often seen by radical feminists as the key institution producing women's oppression in modern societies. The family is certainly given more prominence than in Marxist sociology, where, as part of the superstructure, it is given only secondary importance.

Radical feminists tend to believe that women have always been exploited and that only revolutionary change can offer the possibility of their liberation. However, there are disagreements within this group about both the origins of women's oppression and the possible solutions to it. Some radical feminists, such as Shulamith Firestone, believe women's oppression originated in their biology, particularly in the fact that they give birth. Others do not see biology as so important; they see male rule as largely a product of culture. Some stress rape and male violence towards women as the methods through which men have secured and maintained their power.

Because men are seen as the enemies of women's liberation, many radical feminists reject any assistance from the male sex in their struggle to achieve the rights they seek. **Separatist feminists** argue that women should organize independently of men outside the male-dominated society. A few, like The Leeds Revolutionary Feminist Group, argue that only lesbians can be true feminists, since only they can be fully independent of men.

A particularly radical group, **female supremacists**, argue that women are not just equal but are actually morally superior to men. They wish to see patriarchy replaced by **matriarchy** (male rule replaced by female rule). From this perspective men are responsible not just for the exploitation of women, but also for conflict and war.

Most radical feminists broadly share the same aim as Marxists and liberal feminists – they seek equality between the sexes rather than dominance by either.

■ Marxist and socialist feminism

Marxist and socialist feminism do not attribute women's exploitation entirely to men. They see capitalism rather than patriarchy as being the principal source of women's oppression, and capitalists as the main beneficiaries. Like radical feminists they see women's unpaid work as housewives and mothers as one of the main ways in which women are exploited. Although men in general benefit, it is primarily capitalists who gain from women's unpaid work since new generations of workers are reproduced at no cost to the capitalist. (For a discussion of this issue see pp. 367–9.)

Thus Marxist and socialist feminists relate women's oppression to the production of wealth while radical feminists attribute greater importance to the reproduction of the species in the family. Marxist feminists also place much greater stress on the exploitation of women in paid employment. The disadvantaged position of women is held to be a consequence of the emergence of private property and subsequently their lack of ownership of the means of production, which in turn deprives them of power.

Although Marxist and socialist feminism agree with radical feminists that women as a group are exploited, particularly since the advent of capitalism, they are more sensitive to the differences between women who belong to the ruling class and proletarian families. In this respect women have interests in common with the working class, and Marxist and socialist feminists see greater scope for cooperation between women and working-class men than do radical feminists.

Marxist feminists share with radical feminists a desire for revolutionary change; however, they seek the establishment of a communist society. In such a society (where the means of production will be communally owned) they believe gender inequalities will disappear. This view is not shared by radical feminists who believe that women's oppression has different origins and causes, and therefore requires a different solution.

There is no clearcut division between Marxist and socialist feminists; they share much in common. Marxist feminists though, tend to seek more sweeping changes than socialist feminists. Socialist feminists tend to give more credence to the possibility of capitalist societies gradually moving towards female equality. They see more prospect for change within the democratic system.

◼ Liberal feminism

Liberal feminism does not have such clearly developed theories of gender inequalities as radical and Marxist and socialist feminism. Nevertheless, liberal feminism probably enjoys greater popular support than the other perspectives. This is largely because its aims are more moderate and its views pose less of a challenge to existing values. Liberal

feminists aim for gradual change in the political, economic and social systems of Western societies.

To the liberal feminist nobody benefits from existing gender inequalities; both men and women are harmed because the potential of females and males alike is suppressed. For example, many women with the potential to be successful and skilled members of the workforce, do not get the opportunity to develop their talents, while men are denied some of the pleasures of having a close relationship with their children. The explanation of this situation, according to liberal feminists, lies not so much in the structures and institutions of society, but in its culture and the attitudes of individuals.

Socialization into gender roles has the consequence of producing rigid, inflexible expectations of men and women. Discrimination prevents women from having equal opportunities.

The creation of equal opportunities, particularly in education and work, is the main aim of liberal feminists. They pursue this aim through the introduction of legislation and by attempting to change attitudes. In Britain they supported such measures as the Sex Discrimination Act and the Equal Pay Act in the hope that these laws would help to end discrimination. They try to eradicate sexism and stereotypical views of women and men from children's books and the mass media. They do not seek revolutionary changes in society: they want reforms that take place within the existing social structure, and they work through the democratic system. Since they believe that existing gender inequalities benefit nobody (although they are particularly harmful to women), liberal feminists are willing to work with any members of society who support their beliefs and aims.

Although the least radical of feminist perspectives, the liberal view could still lead to considerable social change. At the very least the changes it supports could lead to women having the same access as men to high-status jobs.

◼ Black feminism

Black feminism has developed out of dissatisfaction with other types of feminism. Black feminists such as Bell Hooks have argued that other feminists, as well as male anti-racists, have not addressed the particular problems faced by black women. Writing in 1982, Hooks claimed that black women in the USA had not joined:

together to fight for women's rights because we did not see 'womanhood' as an important aspect of our identity. Racist, sexist socialization had conditioned us to devalue our femaleness and to regard race as the only relevant label of identification.

Black women had joined in the fight for civil rights, but the organizations were dominated by men, and women's issues received no consideration.

Hooks argued that contemporary black women could learn a lot from some of their nineteenth-century counterparts who had pioneered a distinctive black feminism. Hooks describes the views of Sojourner Truth, a black American woman who had campaigned for black women to gain the right to vote along with black men. Truth had said that if black women failed in their campaign for voting rights, but black men succeeded, then 'the coloured men will be masters over the women, and it will be just as bad as it was before' (quoted in Hooks 1982, p. 4). At a convention of the women's rights movement in Ohio in 1852, white males argued that women should not have equal rights to men because they were physically inferior to men and were unsuited to heavy manual labour. Sojourner Truth countered this argument in a passionate speech saying:

Look at me! look at my arm! . . . I have plowed and planted, and gathered into barns, and no man could head me – and ain't I a woman? I could work as much as any man (when I could get it), and bear de lash as well – and ain't I a woman?

Truth's speech highlighted the differences in the experiences of black women and white women. For some black feminists these differences are the legacy of slavery. Patricia Hill Collins says that slavery 'shaped all subsequent relationships that Black women had within African-American families and communities, with employers, and among

each other, and created the political context for women's intellectual work'. To Collins, writing in 1990, most feminist theory has 'suppressed Black women's ideas' and has concentrated on the experiences and grievances of white and usually middle-class women. For example feminist critiques of family life tended to examine the situation of middle-class wives who were in a very different position from most black women. There was a 'masculinist bias in Black social and political thought' and a 'racist bias in feminist theory'.

Black feminism could correct that bias by drawing on black women's experiences. Many black women had been employed as domestic servants in white families. From this position they could see 'white power demystified'. They could see whites as they really were, yet they remained economically exploited outsiders. Thus black feminists could draw upon the 'outsider-within perspective generated by Black women's location in the labour market' and could develop a 'distinct view of the contradictions between the dominant groups' actions and ideologies'.

Like Hooks, Collins draws inspiration from the insights of Sojourner Truth to show how black women can attack patriarchal ideology. For example, they could attack the belief that women are fragile and weak by drawing on their own experience of physically demanding labour.

Rose M. Brewer sees the basis of black feminist theory as an 'understanding of race, class and gender as simultaneous forces'. Black women suffer from disadvantages because they are black, because they are women, and because they are working class, but their problems are more than the sum of these parts: each inequality reinforces and multiplies each of the other inequalities. Thus black women's problems can be represented as stemming from 'race × class × gender' rather than 'race + class + gender'. To Brewer the distinctive feature of black feminism is that it studies the 'interplay' of race, class and gender in shaping the lives and restricting the life chances of black women.

■ The origins of gender inequalities – feminist views

Although many feminists clearly align themselves to one of the perspectives that we have just outlined, others do not. Thus in the subsequent sections, not all the explanations for gender inequalities that we will discuss can be 'neatly' attributed to one perspective.

Feminists do not agree about the origins of inequality between men and women. Some believe that women have always had a subordinate position in all societies; others argue that the origins of gender inequalities can be traced back to particular historical events.

■ Shulamith Firestone – a radical feminist view

In her book *The Dialectics of Sex*, published in 1970, Firestone was the first to outline a radical feminist explanation of female inequality. To Firestone **sexual oppression** was the first and most fundamental form of oppression. Unlike Marxists, Firestone does not attach primary importance to economic differences in the explanation of inequality. Although she acknowledges the importance of the work of Marx and Engels, she criticizes them for confining their studies to economic production. To Firestone they ignored an important part of the material world: 'reproduction'.

Firestone believes that what she calls the **sexual class system** was the first form of stratification. It predated the class system and provided the basis from which other forms of stratification evolved. She provides a very clear explanation for its origins. She says 'men and women were created different and not equally privileged'. Inequalities and the division of labour between men and women arose directly from biology. Biological differences produced a form of social organization she calls the **biological family**. Although societies vary in the roles of men and women and the form the family takes, all societies share the biological family, which has four key characteristics.

The biological family

1 Women are handicapped by their biology. Menstruation, the menopause and childbirth are all physical burdens for women, but pregnancy and breastfeeding have the most serious social consequences. Because of the times when women are pregnant or looking after infants they are 'dependent on males (whether brother, father, husband, lover or clan, government, community-at-large) for physical survival'.

2 Women's dependence on men is increased by the long periods during which human infants are dependent, compared to the infants of other species.

3 The interdependence between mother and child and in turn their dependence on men has been found in every society, and it has influenced the psychology of every human being. Dependence on men produced unequal power relationships and **power psychology**.

4 The fourth characteristic of the biological family is that it provides the foundations for all types of inequality and stratification. Men derived pleasure from their power over women and wished to extend their power to the domination of men. The sexual class system provided the blueprint and prototype for the economic class system. The economic class system provided the means through which some men came to dominate other men. Because the sexual class system is the basis for other class systems, Firestone believes that it must be destroyed before any serious progress can be made towards equality. She says 'The sexual class system is the model for all other exploitative systems and thus the tapeworm that must be eliminated first by any true revolution.'

Biology and equality

Because sex class has a biological origin, **biological equality** is the only effective starting point for securing its elimination. Firestone believes that effective birth control techniques have helped to loosen the chains of women's slavery by giving them more control over whether they become pregnant. However, the pill and other contraceptives have not freed women from pregnancy altogether; this would only be possible when babies could be conceived and developed outside the womb. Once this occurred, women would no longer be forced into dependence on men for part of their lives.

However, even this would only be the first step towards a complete revolution. In addition to the biological changes, the economic class system and the cultural superstructure would also have to be destroyed. Economic equality would have to follow biological equality, and power psychology would need to be overcome.

The strength of Firestone's argument lies in its ability to explain all forms of stratification, but this radical feminist perspective on inequality has been subject to criticism. Firestone does not explain variations in women's status in different societies at different times. For example, in some societies women do not have primary responsibility for childcare and women's biology does not seem to make them dependent on men for long periods in all societies (as we saw in Oakley's discussion on the cultural division of labour, pp. 588–9). If this is the case, then it may not be biology alone that explains gender inequalities.

Sherry B. Ortner – culture and the devaluation of women

Sherry B. Ortner agrees with Firestone that women are universally oppressed and devalued but she claims that it is not biology as such that ascribes women to their status in society, but the way in which every culture defines and evaluates female biology. Thus, if this **universal evaluation** changed, then the basis for female subordination would be removed.

Ortner argues that in every society, a higher value is placed on culture than on nature. **Culture** is the means by which humanity controls and regulates nature. By inventing weapons and hunting techniques, humans can capture and kill animals; by inventing religion and rituals, humans can call upon supernatural forces to produce a successful hunt or a bountiful harvest. By the use of culture, humans do not have to passively submit to nature: they can regulate and control it. Thus humanity's ideas and technology (that is, its culture), have

power over nature and are therefore seen as superior to it.

Women and nature

This universal evaluation of culture as superior to nature is the basic reason for the devaluation of women. Women are seen as closer to nature than men, and therefore as inferior to men.

1 Ortner argues that women are universally defined as closer to nature because their bodies and physiological functions are more concerned with 'the natural processes surrounding the reproduction of the species'. These natural processes include menstruation, pregnancy, childbirth and lactation, processes for which the female body is 'naturally' equipped.

2 Women's social role as mothers is also seen as closer to nature. They are primarily responsible for the socialization of the young. Infants and young children are seen as 'barely human', as one step away from nature because their cultural repertoire is small compared to that of adults. Women's close relationships with young children further associate them with nature.

3 Since the mother role is linked to the family, the family itself is regarded as closer to nature compared to activities and institutions outside the family. Thus activities such as politics, warfare and religion are seen as more removed from nature, as superior to domestic tasks and therefore as the province of men.

4 Finally, Ortner argues that **woman's psyche**, her psychological make-up, is defined as closer to nature. Because women are concerned with childcare and primary socialization, they develop more personal, intimate and particular relationships with others, especially their children. By comparison, men, by engaging in politics, warfare and religion, have a wider range of contacts and less personal and particular relationships. Thus men are seen as being more objective and less emotional: their thought processes are defined as more abstract and general, and less personal and particular. Ortner argues that culture is, in one sense, 'the transcendence, by means of systems of thought and technology, of the natural givens of existence'. Thus men are seen as closer to culture since their thought processes are defined as more abstract and objective than those of women. Since culture is seen as superior to nature, woman's psyche is devalued and once again, men come out on top.

Ortner concludes that in terms of her biology, physiological processes, social roles and psychology, woman 'appears as something intermediate between culture and nature'.

Criticisms of Ortner

Ortner fails to show conclusively that in all societies culture is evaluated more highly than nature. Although many societies have rituals which attempt to control nature, it is not clear that nature is necessarily devalued in comparison to culture. Indeed it could be argued that the very existence of such rituals points to the superior power of nature.

Stephanie Coontz and Peta Henderson provide some examples which contradict Ortner. Among the Sherbo of West Africa children are seen as close to nature, but adults of both sexes are seen as close to culture. Coontz and Henderson also claim that not all societies devalue nature. The Haganers of Papua and New Guinea distinguish culture and nature, but do not rank one above the other.

■ Michelle Z. Rosaldo – the public and the domestic

The anthropologist Michelle Zimbalist Rosaldo was the first to argue that women's subordination was the consequence of a division between the public and the private (or domestic) world.

She argues that there are two distinctive areas of social life.

1 She defines the **domestic** as 'institutions and modes of activity that are organised immediately around one or more mothers and their children'. As her use of the word 'mother' implies, she believes that it is usually women who are associated with this sphere.

2 In contrast, the public sphere is seen as being primarily the province of men. She defines the **public** as, 'activities institutions and forms of association that link, rank, organise, or subsume particular mother child groups'.

Thus the domestic sphere includes the family and life in the place of residence of the family, while the public sphere includes the activities and institutions associated with rituals and religion, politics and the economy.

Like Firestone and Ortner, Rosaldo argues that women have been disadvantaged in every known society – 'women everywhere lack generally recognized and culturally valued authority'. Although she accepts that biology is the basis of women's oppression, she argues, like Ortner, that the link between the two is indirect. It is the *interpretation* given to women's biology that leads to their disadvantages, not the biology itself. This interpretation ties them to the rearing of children and the domestic sphere.

Men, on the other hand, are better able to keep their distance from domestic life. As a result, they do not need the same personal commitment to other humans as that required from mothers. Men are associated more with abstract authority, and with the political life of society as a whole. Men's separation from the domestic sphere sets them apart from the intimacy of the domestic world, and makes them more suitable for involvement in religious rituals. Rosaldo argues that as a consequence of men's involvement in religious and political life, they can exercise power over the domestic units which are the focus of women's lives.

Although Rosaldo argues that women have less power than men in all societies, she does believe that inequalities between the sexes are greater in some societies than in others. Even though she does not appear to accept that there is any prospect of a totally egalitarian society, she does believe that women can come closer to equality if men become more involved in domestic life.

Rosaldo justifies this claim with reference to societies in which men have an important domestic role. Thus the Mbuti Pygmies of Africa have a relatively egalitarian society because men and women cooperate in both domestic and economic life. Yet even here men retain some independence from the domestic sphere by having separate and secret flute cults.

Criticisms of Rosaldo

Undoubtedly the distinction between the domestic or private sphere and the public sphere provides a useful way of analysing and explaining the relative powerlessness of women in many societies. If women are largely excluded from the institutions which exercise power in society, then it is hardly surprising that men possess more power than women. Furthermore, this distinction also helps to explain how the position of men and women in society has changed (see for example the section on 'Gender and industrialization', pp. 600–2).

However, there are difficulties involved in Rosaldo's theory and in the use of the terms 'public' and 'domestic'. Janet Siltanen and Michelle Stanworth point out that there are many ways in which public and private lives overlap. For example, in modern industrial societies it is only women's labour in the home that makes it possible for men to devote themselves to work in the public sphere.

Linda Imray and Audrey Middleton argue that women's activities tend to be devalued even when they take place in the public sphere. When women take paid employment outside the home, the jobs they do are often regarded as being of less importance than those of men. From this point of view, the devaluation of women must have deeper roots than their association with domestic life. Certainly, as we will demonstrate in later sections, the increasing employment of women outside the private home has not produced equality for women within work.

Firestone, Ortner and Rosaldo agree that women's subordination to men is universal. They all to some extent agree that the ultimate source of inequality between the sexes is biology, or the interpretation placed on biology. However, these views are not accepted by some sociologists. Marxist and socialist feminists question the view that women's subordination has always been universal. They claim that it is necessary to examine history to find how and why inequality between the sexes came about. As Stephanie Coontz and Peta Henderson put it:

> a number of scholars have begun to address the issue of male dominance as a historical phenomenon, grounded in a particular set of circumstances rather than flowing from some universal aspect of human nature or culture.

We will study some of these viewpoints next.

■ The origins of gender inequality – Marxist and socialist perspectives

Marx's associate Engels devoted more attention to the sociology of gender than Marx himself. In *The Origins of the Family, Private Property and the State* Engels outlined his theory of how human societies developed.

■ Engels – inequality and private property

In the earliest phases of societal development (which Engels called **savagery** and **barbarism**) gender inequalities favoured women rather than men. There was a division of labour by sex, with men mainly responsible for procuring food and women mainly responsible for the domestic sphere, but women were not subordinate to men. Private property existed in only a rudimentary form and consisted mainly of simple tools, utensils and weapons. What private property there was passed down through the female, not the male, line. This was because monogamous marriage did not exist. Both men and women could have sex with as many partners as they chose. Consequently men could never be sure about who their children were. In contrast, as women give birth there is no such doubt about their offspring, and so the property was passed on to their children by the women.

According to Engels, it was during the period of barbarism that women suffered a 'world-historic' defeat. Men gained the upper hand when animals were domesticated and herded and became an important form of private property. Then meat and other animal products became crucial parts of the economy of early societies. Men gained responsibility for owning and controlling livestock, and were unwilling to allow this important property to be passed down the female line; through owning livestock men overthrew the dominance of women in the household. In Engels's words, 'the man seized the reins in the house also, the woman was degraded, enthralled, the slave of the man's lust, a mere instrument for breeding children'.

In order to ensure that they could identify their own children, men increasingly put restrictions on women's choice of sexual partners. Eventually, (during the period Engels calls **civilization**) monogamous marriage was established. By this stage men had gained control over what was now the patriarchal family.

Criticisms of Engels

Unfortunately Engels's theory was based upon unreliable anthropological evidence. His history of early societies no longer seems plausible in the light of more recent research into **simple societies** (which we discuss later in this chapter). Nevertheless, Engels's pioneering Marxist theory of the origins of gender inequalities laid the foundations upon which later Marxist and socialist feminists have built. Engels suggested that particular historical conditions led to the subordination of women, and he directed attention towards the material, economic reasons that could account for this.

■ Stephanie Coontz and Peta Henderson – women's work, men's property

Stephanie Coontz and Peta Henderson provide an example of an attempt to explain women's subordination from a Marxist/socialist perspective. They agree with Engels on a number of important points. Like him, they reject the view that women's subordination has always been a universal feature of human society, and they believe that the roots of women's oppression today are to be found in social causes. They emphasize that it was the difference between the roles of men and women in the production of goods that resulted in gender inequality, and not the difference between the contribution each makes to the reproduction of the species. In all these ways Coontz and Henderson reject the radical feminism of Firestone.

However they also disagree with Engels over some issues. For example, they deny that history started with a period of female dominance. On the basis of anthropological evidence, Coontz and Henderson argue that most early societies began with equality between the sexes. They accept that there was, from earliest times, a division of labour by sex, but this did not make inequality inevitable. In most (though not all) societies some women

were excluded from hunting and risky tasks such as trading and warfare which could involve travel over long distances. However, it was only pregnant women and nursing mothers who had these restrictions placed on them. It was a matter of social convenience rather than biological necessity which led to an early division of labour. For example, it was difficult for women nursing children to combine this activity with warfare as young infants could prove a considerable inconvenience in battle. Women did, nevertheless, become successful warriors in some societies, for example, Dahomey.

The existence of a sexual division of labour did not in itself lead to inequality. According to Coontz and Henderson the earliest societies were **communal**, the resources produced by men and women alike were shared by everyone. Meat from the hunt and gathered vegetables were given both to the kin and the non-kin of those who produced the food. Even strangers would usually be fed. In these circumstances it was not important to identify the father of a specific child since the offspring of particular individuals had no special rights to food.

Property and gender inequality

Like Engels, Coontz and Henderson believe that social inequalities developed as a result of changes in property ownership. They follow Engels in arguing that the introduction of herding and agriculture laid the foundations for gender inequalities. These new modes of production made it more likely that a surplus would be produced which could be accumulated or distributed. However, they suggest that some societies, including some North American Indian tribes, produced a surplus in favourable environmental conditions without developing herding or agriculture.

The most important factor in the transition to a **society with gender stratification** was the appearance of a form of communal property to which a group of kin had exclusive rights. **Kin corporate property**, as Coontz and Henderson describe it, meant that for the first time non-kin and strangers lost their right to share food and other resources. In these circumstances parenthood and kinship relationships became important, and senior members of kinship groups gained control over property. Age and seniority began to provide greater economic power, as well as higher status.

Patrilocality and gender inequality

So far Coontz and Henderson's theory has attempted to account for the origins of inequality, but it has not explained why it should be men who became the dominant group. According to Coontz and Henderson the key to this development lay in marriage arrangements. Some societies had a system of **patrilocality**, in other words wives went to live with their husband's kin. Women, as gatherers, continued to act as producers, but they lost control over the products of their labour. What they produced no longer belonged to their own kin corporate group but to that of their husband.

Not all societies had a system of patrilocality, some were **matrilocal**: husbands moved to live with their wife's kin group. Coontz and Henderson claim that such societies were more egalitarian; women retained greater power. Not only did the food they produced stay with their own kin group, but husbands had to share what they produced with their sister's household as well as their wife's. There was less opportunity for men to concentrate property in their own hands.

However, for a number of reasons matrilocal societies tended to be less successful. For example, patrilocal societies had more chance of producing a surplus. More successful kin groups could

expand by the practice of **polygyny** (men could marry a number of women) and in doing so increase the labour force. The extra wives could gather and process more food. Patrilocal societies therefore expanded at the expense of matrilocal ones so that societies in which women were subordinate became more common than those in which they enjoyed greater equality.

To Coontz and Henderson then, women's subordination arose out of a complex process in which kin corporate property made inequality possible, and patrilocal residence rules for those who married led to men's dominance. According to these sociologists, gender and class inequalities were closely linked: women lost power in the same process that led to some kin groups accumulating more property than others. Ultimately, property became largely owned by individuals rather than collective groups, and wealthy men came to dominate other men as well as women.

This theory of the development of gender inequalities is perhaps more sophisticated than Engels's, and it rests upon sounder anthropological evidence. Despite its claims to provide an entirely social explanation though, it still uses a biological starting-point. It assumes that women's capacities to give birth and suckle children tended to result in a division of labour in which women were largely responsible for cooking and gathering, and men for hunting.

■ Gender and industrialization

No blanket statements can be made about the position of women in industrializing societies. In different pre-industrial nations the position of women has varied, and has altered in several ways during industrialization. Nevertheless Britain, as the first nation to industrialize, gives some indication of the effects of industrialization on women in Western industrial societies.

■ Women and industrialization – a historical perspective

Ann Oakley has traced the changing status of women in British society from the eve of the Industrial Revolution to the 1970s. She claims that 'The

most important and enduring consequence of industrialization for women has been the emergence of the modern role of housewife as "the dominant mature feminine role".' In this section we summarize Oakley's view of the emergence of the housewife role.

The family as the unit of production

In pre-industrial Britain, the family was the basic unit of production. Marriage and the family were essential to individuals for economic reasons since all members of the family were involved in production. Agriculture and textiles were the main industries and women were indispensable to both. In the production of cloth, the husband did the weaving while his wife spun and dyed the yarn. On the farm women were in charge of dairy produce. Most of the housework – cooking, cleaning, washing, mending and childcare – was performed by unmarried children. The **housewife role** (which involved the domesticity of women and their economic dependence on men) had yet to arrive. Public life concerned with economic activity, and the private life of the family, were not as distinct as they are today.

The factory as the unit of production

During the early stages of industrialization (which Oakley dates from 1750 to 1841) the factory steadily replaced the family as the unit of production. Women were employed in factories where they often continued their traditional work in textiles.

The first major change which affected their status as wage earners was a series of factory acts, beginning in 1819, which gradually restricted child labour. Children became increasingly dependent upon their parents and this necessitated care and supervision, a role which fell to women. Oakley argues that 'The increased differentiation of child and adult roles, with the child's growing dependence, heralded the dependence of women in marriage and their restriction to the home.'

Restrictions on women's employment

From 1841 to the advent of the First World War in 1914, a combination of pressure from male workers and philanthropic reformers restricted female employment in industry. Women were seen by many male factory workers as a threat to their employment. As early as 1841, committees of male factory workers called for the 'gradual withdrawal of all female labour from the factory'. In 1842 the Mines Act banned the employment of women as miners. In 1851, one in four married women were employed; by 1911 this figure was reduced to one in ten.

Helen Hacker states that with the employment of women as wage earners:

Men were quick to perceive them as a rival group and make use of economic, legal and ideological weapons to eliminate or reduce their competition. They excluded women from the trade unions, made contracts with employers to prevent their hiring women, passed laws restricting the employment of married women, caricatured the working woman, and carried on ceaseless propaganda to return women to the home and keep them there.

Victorian ideology, particularly the versions of the upper and middle classes, stated that a woman's place was in the home. No less a figure than Queen Victoria announced 'Let woman be what God intended, a helpmate for man, but with totally different duties and vocations.' (Quoted in Hudson 1970, p. 46.) The following quotations from articles in the *Saturday Review* illustrate the ideal of womanhood in mid-Victorian times. In 1859:

Married life is a woman's profession, and to this life her training – that of dependence – is modelled.

And in 1865:

No woman can or ought to know very much of the mass of meanness and wickedness and misery that is loose in the wide world. She could not learn it without losing the bloom and freshness which it is her mission in life to preserve. (Quoted in Hudson 1970, pp. 53–4.)

Oakley claims that during the second half of the nineteenth century these attitudes began to filter down to the working class. Thus a combination of factors which included ideology, the banning of child labour, and restrictions on the employment of women, locked the majority of married women into the mother–housewife role.

The return to paid employment

Oakley states that from 1914 to 1950, there was a 'tendency towards the growing employment of women coupled with a retention of housewifery as the primary role expected of all women'. During these years women received many legal and political rights (for example the vote in 1928) but these had little effect on the central fact of their lives: the mother–housewife role.

Oakley concludes that industrialization has had the following effects on the role of women:

1 first, the 'separation of men from the daily routines of domestic life';

2 second, the 'economic dependence of women and children on men';

3 third, the 'isolation of housework and child care from other work'.

In twentieth-century British society, the house-wife–mother role has become institutionalized as 'the primary role for all women'.

Gender in contemporary societies – radical feminist perspectives

For radical feminists **patriarchy** is the most important concept for explaining gender inequalities. Although literally it means rule by the father, radical feminists have used it more broadly to refer to male dominance in society. From this point of view, patriarchy consists of the exercise of power by men over women. Kate Millett was one of the first radical feminists to use the term and to provide a detailed explanation of women's exploitation by men.

Kate Millett – radical feminism and sexual politics

In her book *Sexual Politics* Millett argues that politics is not just an activity confined to political parties and parliaments, but one which exists in any 'power-structured relationships, arrangements whereby one group of persons is controlled by another'. Such relationships of domination and subordination can exist at work where a man instructs his secretary to make a cup of tea, or in the family when a husband's meal is cooked by his wife. Political relationships between men and women exist in all aspects of everyday life.

According to Millett such relationships are organized on the basis of patriarchy, a system in which 'male shall dominate female'. She believes that patriarchy is 'the most pervasive ideology of our culture, its most fundamental concept of power'. It is 'more rigorous than class stratification, more uniform, certainly more enduring'.

Like other radical feminists Millett suggests that gender is the primary source of identity for individuals in modern societies. People react to others first and foremost as men and women, rather than in terms of their class membership. It is a rigid system of stratification: sex is ascribed and almost impossible to change.

The basis of patriarchy

Millett identifies no less than eight types of factors which explain the existence of patriarchy.

1 First, she considers the **role of biology**. Although she admits that it is difficult to be certain about the origins of patriarchy, she attributes some importance to superior male strength. She suggests that this on its own cannot explain female subordination, claiming that there may have been 'pre-patriarchal' societies in which men were not dominant. Furthermore, she points out that in contemporary, technologically advanced societies, strength is itself of little significance. Despite this she speculates that at some point in history strength may have assumed a degree of importance which accounts for the origins of patriarchy.

To Millett though, it is more significant that in early socialization males are encouraged to be aggressive and females to be passive. Males and females are taught to behave and think in ways which reinforce the biological differences which exist.

2 Millett points to **ideological factors** in her search for the roots of patriarchy. Again she attaches importance to socialization. Men are socialized to have a dominant temperament. This provides men with a higher social

status, which in turn leads to them filling social roles in which they can exercise mastery over women.

3 The third type of factors she considers important are **sociological** ones. She claims that the family is the main institution of patriarchy, although men also exercise power in the wider society and through the state. Within the family it is the need for children to be legitimate, to have a socially recognized father, that gives men a particularly dominant position. Mothers and children come to rely for their social status on the position of husbands and fathers in society.

The family therefore plays an important part in maintaining patriarchy across generations, socializing children into having different temperaments and leading them to expect and accept different roles in later life.

4 Millett discusses the **relationship between class and subordination**. She believes that women have a caste-like status that operates independently of social class. Even women from higher-class backgrounds are subordinate to men. She believes that the economic dependency of women on men almost places them outside the class system. Romantic love appears to place males and females on an equal footing but in truth it merely 'obscures the realities of female status, and the burden of economic dependency'. Women's inferior status is reinforced and underlined by the ability of men to gain psychological ascendancy through the use of physical or verbal bullying and obscene or hostile remarks.

5 In the fifth category Millett discusses the **educational factors** which handicap women and she expands upon the question of women's economic dependency. In traditional patriarchies women lacked legal standing and were not able to own property or to earn their own living. In today's society Millett accepts that women can and do take paid work, but believes that their work is usually menial, badly paid and lacking in status.

Furthermore, in societies in which women retain their roles as mothers and housewives much of that work is unpaid. She sees women as being essentially a reserve labour force who are made use of when they are needed (for example in wartime) but are discarded when not required.

Economic inequalities are reinforced by educational ones. Women tend to study the humanities which, according to Millett, have a lower status than sciences. As a result women lack knowledge and this restricts their power. For example, women often do not understand technology so they cannot compete on equal terms with men trying to earn a living.

6 The sixth way in which men retain patriarchal power is through **myth and religion**. Religion is used as a way of legitimating masculine dominance. As Millett puts it 'Patriarchy has God on its side.' To illustrate this point she notes that the Christian religion portrays Eve as an afterthought produced from Adam's spare rib, while the origins of human suffering are held to have their source in her actions.

7 The seventh source of men's power is **psychology**. Patriarchal ideology is 'interiorized' by women because of all the above factors. Women develop a passive temperament and a sense of inferiority. This is further reinforced by sexist European languages which use words such as 'mankind' to refer to humanity. Media images of women also play their part, but to Millett the greatest psychological weapon available to men is the length of time they have enjoyed worldwide dominance. Women have simply come to take men's dominance for granted.

8 Millett identifies **physical force** as the final source of male domination. Despite the extent of men's ideological power Millett believes that patriarchy is ultimately backed up by force. She points to many examples of the use of violence against women, such as the stoning to death of adulteresses in Muslim countries, and 'the crippling deformity of footbinding in China, the lifelong ignominy of the Veil in Islam'. In modern Western societies women are also the victims of violence. Millett does not admit that women are inevitably physically weaker, but 'physical and emotional training' make it very difficult for women to resist the force used against them by individual men. Rape and other forms of sexual violence are ever-present possibilities and ways in which all women are intimidated by all men.

Criticisms of Millett

Millett made an important contribution towards explaining the disadvantaged position of women within society. However, her work has been criticized by socialist and Marxist feminists. They have identified three main weaknesses in her theory of sexual politics.

1 First, Sheila Rowbotham argues that patriarchy is too sweeping a category. Because Millett regards all societies as patriarchal she fails to explain the particular circumstances which have produced male

domination in its current forms. According to Rowbotham, describing all societies as patriarchal implies that male domination has some universal cause which stems from the biology of women and the fact that they bear and rear children. In Rowbotham's words it 'ignores the multiplicity of ways in which societies have defined gender'.

2 Second, Rowbotham questions the assumption implied in the use of the term 'patriarchy' – that all men exploit all women. She says that 'patriarchy cannot explain why genuine feelings of love and friendship are possible between men and women, and boys and girls, or why people have acted together in popular movements.'

3 A third area of criticism of Millett and radical feminists in general is that they ignore the material basis of much of the oppression of women. Robert McDonough and Rachel Harrison criticize Millett for ignoring the possibility that women's lack of wealth and economic power is the most important factor determining their disadvantages. To Marxist and socialist feminists it is capitalism rather than patriarchy that explains women's oppression in modern societies.

■ Gender in contemporary societies – Marxist and socialist feminist perspectives

■ Marx and Engels and women under communism

Apart from explaining the origins of inequality between men and women, Engels also tried to foresee how women's position in society would change as capitalism developed. Engels believed that economic factors caused women's subservience to men, and only economic changes could lead to their liberation. He stated that 'The predominance of the man in marriage is simply a consequence of his economic predominance and will vanish with it automatically.' Men enjoyed greater power than women because it was men who owned the means of production, or who earned a wage outside the home.

However, Marx and Engels believed that capitalism would eventually lead to some reduction in inequalities between men and women. They argued that the demand for female wage labour would raise the status and power of proletarian women within the family.

Marx believed that despite its many evils, capitalist industry 'creates a new economic foundation for a higher form of the family and of relations between the sexes'. Female employment would largely free women from economic dependence upon their husbands and so from male dominance within the family.

Engels took a similar view maintaining that with female wage labour:

the last remnants of male domination in the proletarian home have lost all foundation – except, perhaps, for some of the brutality towards women which became firmly rooted with the establishment of monogamy.

However, the bourgeois wife in capitalist society was still required to produce heirs and so forced to submit to male control.

Although women have entered the labour force in increasing numbers in the twentieth century, many contemporary Marxist and socialist feminists deny that this has led to the changes anticipated by Marx and Engels. As we will indicate in a later section, women continue to be financially disadvantaged compared to men even when they take paid employment. They tend to get lower wages and lower status jobs than men (see pp. 614–18). Furthermore, they still seem to have less power than men within the family. (Further details can be found on pp. 365–6.)

Engels believed that true equality between men and women would arrive with the establishment of communism when the means of production would be communally owned. Engels predicted that the communal ownership of the means of production would be accompanied by the socialization of housework and childcare. Sexual inequality would end. Gender roles would disappear.

We will now examine his views in the light of evidence from communist societies.

Sex and gender in communist societies

The USSR

From a review of studies of the USSR, Nickie Charles found that women did make significant progress under communism. In 1991, just before the USSR broke up with the collapse of communism, women made up a majority of the Soviet workforce – 51 per cent. Under communism women were guaranteed the right to work and laws gave them the right to equal pay for equal work. Women also had right to paid maternity leave and breaks during working hours to feed their babies.

However, although Charles believes that women made significant gains under communism, she does not think that they achieved equality. In 1991 average wages for women were only about two-thirds of those for men. Laws made it easier for women to work and have children but this also meant that 'child care was viewed as a purely female concern'. As in Western capitalist societies, women continued to have most of the responsibility for childcare and housework even when they had full-time employment outside the home.

A study by David Lane showed that women continued to have less power than men under communism. For example, in 1973 women made up 47 per cent of the membership of the local soviets which carried out Communist Party policy and which were responsible for many services such as education, public health and welfare. In 1971 women accounted for 35 per cent of the elected members of the supreme soviets of the Union republics (the governing bodies of the various republics which made up the USSR). However the number of women on the powerful central governing bodies was small: in 1974 they made up only 1 per cent of the Council of Ministers of the USSR, only 4 per cent of the members of the Central Committee of the Communist Party were female,

and there were no women in the Politburo, the main policy-making body. Thus women were largely excluded from the higher levels of power.

If women's progress under communism in the USSR was limited, early evidence suggests that the move towards a market economy and a Western-style democracy have undermined some of the gains that were made. Charles found that in 1992 after the withdrawal of the right to employment, women had twice the redundancy rate of men. In the light of rising unemployment Charles thought it likely that women would 'be encouraged to return to the home either full or part-time' and state childcare services would be withdrawn.

Eastern Europe

Available evidence from East European communist societies suggested that despite official ideology endorsing sexual equality, women were lagging behind their counterparts in the USSR. Hilda Scott, who lived in Czechoslovakia from 1948 to 1973, surveyed the evidence on the position of women there and in Eastern Europe in general.

Scott stated that a labour shortage during the 1940s and 1950s resulted in women increasingly moving into areas traditionally defined as male employment. However, the sexual division within the labour market was largely re-established with the ending of the labour shortage.

Although there was less sexual inequality compared to the West, the evidence Scott presents is familiar. For example, in Czechoslovakia in 1968, the average wage of female workers was 27.9 per cent less than the average for men. Half the employees in the Czech food industry are female, yet in 1973, only five out of the 579 plant directors were women. As in the West, there was a clearly defined sector of the job market labelled 'women's work'.

Women's domestic responsibilities in Eastern Europe were similar to those in the USSR. A Czech survey conducted in 1966–7 of 500 female managers revealed that half of them did all the housework themselves.

Nickie Charles found that by the late 1980s women had high rates of participation in the East European labour market. Women made up 50 per cent of the workforce in East Germany and nearly 50 per cent in Czechoslovakia. In Poland and Hungary they made up about 44 per cent of the workforce. Charles argues that despite these figures women remained disadvantaged because of the persistence of a **familial ideology** 'which defined women primarily as wives and mothers'.

China

While Eastern Europe and the USSR have abandoned communism, China continues to be governed by a regime which calls itself communist although it has largely adopted a free-market, capitalist economy.

Nickie Charles believes that the early years of communist rule resulted in very considerable gains for women. Prior to the communists seizing power in 1949, women's lives were dominated by the male head of household. China was a largely peasant society and daughters were not valued as much as sons, women were expected to obey males, they were not expected to have their own jobs and they had little say in their choice of marriage partners. The communists introduced many new legal rights for women including a free choice of marriage partners, the right of widows to remarry and the right to seek divorce with the agreement of both partners. Women were granted formal equality under the law and despite resistance, their position improved.

In 1954 the 'Great Leap Forward' led to the setting up of communes and an attempt to take domestic work out of the home and away from being the exclusive preserve of women. Crèches, public dining rooms and sewing centres were all established. However, many of these policies were moderated or abandoned in the 1960s and while communes remained, 'the household regained its threatened status as a unit of production'. At the same time women regained their domestic responsibilities.

Since the death of Mao (China's first communist leader) in 1976, there has been no further attempt to undermine the family. With the liberalization of the economy there is evidence that women have become more likely to work in small family-owned businesses than for the state. Employment in small businesses 'is far more precarious than employment in state enterprises'. Charles finds that in contemporary China 'Women workers generally receive less pay and fewer benefits than do men and are concentrated in the less prestigious areas of the workforce.' Women's participation rates in the labour market are much higher than they were in pre-communist China, but have not risen to the 50 per cent level they have reached in some communist countries.

Cuba

Under the leadership of Fidel Castro, Cuba remains committed to communism. Castro took power in 1959 but it was not until 1975 that he introduced a Family Code which said that men and women were equal within the family and should share responsibility for domestic tasks. Charles comments that 'Cuba is alone in the world in writing an egalitarian domestic division of labour into law which is an enormous achievement in itself.' However, she claims that in practice 'the impact of this law seems not to have been very great'. Men remain dominant in the home partly because they continue to have considerably higher wages. They are also more likely than women to be in work. Female participation in work has risen from the very low level of 23 per cent in 1974, but it was still only 38 per cent in 1983.

Conclusion

All the examples examined above suggest that societies claiming to be communist have made inroads into reducing gender inequality, but none has succeeded in coming anywhere near to eradicating it. Nickie Charles argues that communist states have made much more effort than capitalist states to reduce the burden of childcare and housework on women but 'In both types of society women are to be found in the lowest paid and least skilled jobs.' Changes in the economic system with attempts to introduce a communist mode of production have made a difference but these have not fundamentally changed women's role within the family. Nor have they eradicated ideologies of gender difference. As a consequence communism has not achieved the gains for women promised by Engels.

■ Contemporary Marxist feminism

Some Marxist feminists have argued that women's position in society primarily benefits capitalism and capitalists rather than men. Margaret Benston argues that capitalism benefits from a large reserve labour force of women 'to keep wages down and profits up'. (For a discussion of the reserve army of labour theory see pp. 90–1, 621–2.) In their roles as **secondary breadwinners**, married women provide a source of cheap and easily exploitable labour. Because women have been socialized to comply and submit, they form a docile labour force that can be readily manipulated and easily fired when not required.

Compared to male workers, women are less likely to join unions, to go on strike or take other forms of militant action against employers. Even when women join unions, they often find themselves in male-dominated organizations where, according to Barron and Norris, men 'often do not share the interests or outlook of their fellow female unionists'. To some degree, sexist ideology splits the working class and in doing so serves the interests of capital. It divides workers along sex lines and thereby makes them easier to control.

Some Marxists also believe that women benefit capitalists and the capitalist system in their capacities as mothers and housewives by reproducing labour power at no cost to employers. (We discuss this in more detail on pp. 367–9.)

Criticisms of Marxist feminism

There are a number of difficulties with Marxist approaches which explain gender inequalities in terms of how they benefit capitalism. Some Marxist feminists claim that such explanations ignore many of the questions raised by feminists. In terms of the Marxist theory women appear insignificant: they sit on the sidelines of the grand struggle between capital and labour. Marxists may explain capitalism, but this does not explain patriarchy.

Heidi Hartmann compares the situation to a marriage in which the husband represents Marxism, the wife represents feminism, and it is the husband who has all the power. She says:

The 'marriage' of Marxism and feminism has been like the marriage of husband and wife depicted in English common law: Marxism and feminism are one, and that one is Marxism.

She does not believe that Marxism on its own can explain gender inequalities because it is 'sex-blind'.

In other words, Marxism can explain why capitalists exploit workers but not why men exploit women. For example, it might be possible to explain in Marxist terms how it benefits capitalism for housework and childcare to be carried out free of charge, but not why women in particular should be responsible for these tasks. Capitalism would benefit as much from househusbands as housewives.

Michelle Barrett also attacks Marxist theories which see capitalism alone benefitting from the exploitation of women. She points out that working-class men can benefit from the labour of their wives as well as capitalists. Furthermore, there may be cheaper alternative ways of reproducing labour power than the use of the nuclear family unit with unpaid housewives. It might be less expensive for capitalist countries to use migrant workers. They could be accommodated in cheap barracks and their early socialization is carried out in another country at no cost to capitalists.

Both Hartmann and Barrett accept that Marxism can play an important part in explaining gender inequalities; however, they believe that feminism must be fully incorporated into any adequate theory. Both these writers attempt to cement a 'marriage' between Marxist and feminist theory.

The 'marriage' of Marxism and feminism

In her article 'The unhappy marriage of Marxism and feminism' Heidi Hartmann claims that Marxism makes an important contribution to explaining Western industrial societies, including 'the structure of production, the generation of a particular occupational structure, and the nature of the dominant ideology'. It explains the creation of particular jobs, but to Hartmann it is 'indifferent' to who fills them. Thus it does not explain why women have lower-paid and lower-status employment outside the home, nor why they continue to carry the main burden of domestic responsibilities, even when they are working as well.

Following radical feminists, Hartmann argues that patriarchy provides the key to explaining the sexual division of labour. Unlike radical feminists though, she believes that patriarchy has a 'material' base which is not directly related to biological differences between men and women. Men maintain their material control over women by controlling women's labour power. They largely deny access for working women to jobs that pay a living wage. They force women into financial dependence on husbands and thereby control the labour of women in their capacities as housewives and mothers. Because of men's dominance within the family they also control women's bodies and sexuality. Women who are married become almost their husbands' property.

Hartmann believes that capitalism and patriarchy are very closely connected – she describes them as 'intertwined' – but she does not believe that the interests of men as a group and capitalists as a group are identical. For example, ruling-class men may benefit from increasing numbers of women entering the labour force, whereas working-class men may prefer their wives to stay at home to perform personal services for them.

Furthermore, Hartmann denies that capitalism is all-powerful: the capitalist system has to be flexible, and the need for social control may sometimes become more important than the need to produce the maximum possible profit. In this context Hartmann claims that historically there has been an accommodation between patriarchy and capitalism. They have learned to co-exist in a partnership that fundamentally damages neither partner.

Hartmann believes that in the nineteenth century capitalism gave way to pressure from men about female employment. Male-dominated trades unions in Britain persuaded the state to pass legislation limiting the degree to which women were permitted to participate in paid employment. Although capitalists may not have accepted this situation as ideal, it did have certain advantages for them. The **family wage**, paid to men and sufficiently large for them to be able to support their wives and children, led to some increase in the wage bill, but ensured that when women did work they could be paid very low wages. It also placated men since their power over women was maintained, and as such it reduced the likelihood of class conscious action by male workers.

Hartmann accepts that the increasing participation of women in work today has made them slightly less dependent on men. There are more opportunities for women to become independent. Nevertheless, she believes that the persistence of relatively low wage levels for women prevents patriarchy from becoming seriously undermined. She claims 'women's wages allow very few women to support themselves independently and adequately'.

In *Women's Oppression Today* Michelle Barrett adopts a similar approach. Although she considers herself a Marxist she believes that it is necessary to go beyond Marxism in order to explain women's oppression. Like Hartmann she sees the origins of women's oppression today as lying in the nineteenth century, and she argues that a coalition of men and capitalists led to women being excluded from work and being forced to take on a primarily domestic role.

In this process women's oppression became lodged in what she calls the **family-household system**: members of the household came to rely on the wages of a few adults (primarily men) while all family members relied on the unpaid housework mainly carried out by women. In the process an ideology was developed in which this division of labour in the family came to be accepted as normal and natural.

In the twentieth century the family-household system became an entrenched part of capitalism. Although there is no inevitable reason why capitalism needs women (as opposed to men, for example) to do the unpaid housework, the capitalist class do benefit politically from this division of labour. According to Barrett the working class is divided by the family-household system; husbands and wives, men and women, fight each other instead of uniting to fight capitalism.

Biology, capitalism and the oppression of women

Both Hartmann and Barrett move away from seeing gender inequalities as being an inevitable product of capitalism. Both accept that an extra dimension needs to be added to Marxist analysis since Marxism is sex-blind. However, according to some critics, neither has succeeded in unifying Marxism and feminism.

Johanna Brenner and Maria Ramas believe that Barrett has adopted a **dual-system approach**, in which class inequalities are explained in terms of capitalism, gender inequalities are explained in terms of patriarchal ideology, but the two approaches are not combined. They do not believe that Barrett has demonstrated a material need for men and women to have different roles within capitalism. According to Brenner and Ramas, there is a material basis for women's oppression under capitalism, and it is to be found in women's biology.

In pre-capitalist times women were able to combine the demands of childbirth, breastfeeding, and childcare with work, because work was largely based around the home. Furthermore, families could be flexible about when they carried out their work.

With the introduction of factory production though, work and home became separated, and it also became uneconomic to allow breaks from work to allow women to breastfeed their children. This would have entailed interruptions in production which meant that expensive machinery was not fully used. Furthermore, capitalists were unwilling to provide for expensive maternity leave or childcare facilities at work. With the long hours of work demanded in early factories, the high costs of any domestic help, and the lack of sterilization techniques which would have made bottle-feeding a viable proposition, there was little option but for mothers to withdraw from work.

Brenner and Ramas admit that many of the conditions that originally forced mothers into domestic roles have now changed. Bottlefeeding is now a safe option for babies; there is some provision for maternity leave; hours of work are shorter; it is easier to afford help with childcare; and in any case women are on average having fewer children. However, most women still get paid lower wages than most men, and for most working-class families there are likely to be real financial benefits if the woman rather than the man withdraws from work.

To Brenner and Ramas the sexual division of labour was at least in part produced by the rational choices taken by members of the working class. Because, however, the situation has now changed, there is considerable potential for greater gender equality. If that potential is to be realized though, it will require a political struggle in which more state nurseries are demanded. It is still cheaper for capitalism if the family rather than the state pays for childcare.

Michelle Barrett remains unconvinced by the arguments of Brenner and Ramas. She believes that ideology played a greater role in producing the family-household system than biology.

Marxist feminists continue to disagree amongst themselves as well as with other feminists, and they have yet to provide a conclusive explanation for gender inequalities. Marxism and feminism remain something of an unhappy marriage, but the writers in this section have begun to explore how best to avoid separation, or even divorce of the two perspectives.

■ Sylvia Walby – *Theorizing Patriarchy*

Sylvia Walby has developed an approach to understanding gender in contemporary societies which does not fit into any of the types of feminism described in earlier sections. Indeed she starts her 1990 book *Theorizing Patriarchy* by pointing out the main criticisms that have been made of other approaches.

Criticisms of existing perspectives

1 Radical feminism has been criticized for 'a false universalism which cannot understand historical change or take sufficient account of divisions between women based on ethnicity and class'.

2 Marxist feminism has been criticized for concentrating on gender inequalities under capitalism and therefore being unable to explain the exploitation of women in non-capitalist societies.

3 Liberal feminism has been seen as lacking 'an account of the overall social structuring of gender inequality'. Its approach can provide no more than partial explanations. For example it offers no explanation of how gender inequalities first developed.

4 Walby also identifies criticisms of what she calls **dual-systems theory**. By this she means approaches such as that of Hartmann (see pp. 607–8) which explain women's exploitation in terms of two separate systems of capitalism and patriarchy. Walby criticizes Hartmann for underestimating the amount of tension between capitalism and patriarchy and for failing to take account of aspects of patriarchy such as violence and sexuality.

Walby tries to improve other perspectives by incorporating their strengths into her own theory while avoiding their weaknesses.

Patriarchy

To Walby the concept of patriarchy must remain central to a feminist understanding of society. She says that '"patriarchy" is indispensable for an analysis of gender inequality'. However, her definition of patriarchy is distinctive from that of other feminists. She argues that there are six patriarchal structures which restrict women and help to maintain male domination. These consist of:

1 paid work;
2 patriarchal relations within the household;
3 patriarchal culture;
4 sexuality;
5 male violence towards women;
6 the state.

Each of these structures has some independence from the other structures but they can affect one another, reinforcing or weakening patriarchy in a different structure. Each structure is reproduced or changed by the actions of men and women but the existence of the structure also restricts the choices that humans, particularly women, can make.

Walby claims that patriarchy is not a fixed and unchanging feature of society (as some radical feminists seem to imply) but both its strength and its form change over time. For example, she believes that in Britain over the last two centuries patriarchy has become slightly less strong and has changed from **private patriarchy** to **public patriarchy**. (We will examine the idea of a shift from private to public patriarchy at the end of this section.)

Walby's concept of patriarchy does not see relations between males and females as the only source of inequality. She acknowledges that there are 'divisions between women based on ethnicity and class' and she discusses the ways that patriarchy racism and capitalism interact.

We will now examine in detail how Walby uses her concept of patriarchy to explain gender inequalities.

The structures of patriarchy

As we saw earlier, Walby identifies six structures of patriarchy. We will examine each of these in turn before looking at Walby's overall conclusions about changes in patriarchy.

Paid employment

Walby believes that **paid employment** has been and remains a key structure in creating disadvantages for women. In the nineteenth century in the UK regulations excluded women from whole areas of work altogether. Male-dominated trade unions and the state ensured that women's opportunities were severely restricted. In the twentieth century women, and particularly married women, were able to take employment, but not on equal terms with men. In recent years 'the degree of inequality between men and women in terms of pay, conditions, and access to well-rewarded occupations has declined only very slightly'. The gap between men's and women's wages has only declined a little and women continue to predominate in low-paid, part-time employment. In theory the state has supported greater equality between men and women in the labour market by passing the Equal Pay and Sex Discrimination Acts but in practice such policies are not 'pursued with vigour'.

Walby believes that the labour market has more influence than the family on women's decisions about whether to take paid employment. When women decide not to seek paid work they do so more because of the restricted opportunities open to them than because of cultural values which suggest that mothers and wives should stay at home. According to Walby when opportunities have been presented to women in the labour market, they have taken advantage of them. For example, the removal of the bar on married women working in some occupations during the Second World War led to a big increase in the numbers of married women in paid work. Feminist struggles and capitalism's demands for cheap labour have produced a big increase in women's employment but they have not prevented exploitation at work. Some women continue to stay at home because the wages they are likely to earn are too low for paid work to be worthwhile.

Household production

According to Walby, households sometimes involve distinctive **patriarchal relations of production**. Individual men directly exploit women by gaining benefits from women's unpaid labour, for example in the home. In the nineteenth century many women were forced into patriarchal relations of production through their exclusion from the labour market. In the twentieth century exploitation within this structure has been reduced, at least for some women. Women spend more time in paid work and the relaxation of divorce laws means that women 'are no longer necessarily bound to an individual husband who expropriates their labour till death does them part'.

For some groups of women, life within households may seem like an escape from exploitation. For example, Walby points out some black feminists believe that the family can be 'a site of resistance to racism' and life within the family may be less exploitive for black women than life in the labour market where they tend to get the least desirable jobs.

However, Walby does not see exploitation of women in the household as having disappeared. Women who are housewives spend as many hours on domestic labour as they did decades ago. Women with children who leave their husbands are disadvantaged in a 'patriarchally structured labour market'. They are unlikely to find a job with reasonable pay so that '"Liberation" from marriage is then usually a movement into poverty.' Some women continue to allow themselves to be exploited by their husbands because the alternatives are so unappealing. Marriage may offer personal survival and greater material comfort for many women when most women have such poorly paid work, but the short-term benefits of marriage for particular women undermine women's 'long-term interests in the eradication of the oppression which exists within the family'. This oppression is sometimes manifested in terms of violence and sexuality which we will examine shortly.

Culture

Walby believes that the **culture** of western societies has consistently distinguished between men and women and has expected different types of behaviour from them. She says that 'while variable across class, ethnicity and age in particular, femininity is consistently differentiated from masculinity over the last century and a half'. However, although the differentiation has remained strong, the characteristics which are seen as making a woman feminine have changed significantly.

In the nineteenth century women were thought more feminine if they confined their activities to the domestic sphere and did not take paid work. Walby claims that 'the key sign of femininity today . . . is sexual attractiveness to men'. Furthermore 'It is no longer merely the femininity of young single women that is defined in this way, but increasingly that of older women as well.' Sexual attractiveness was also important in Victorian times, but less important than today, and it was also 'relatively undercover' compared to contemporary culture.

Escaping from the confinement of domesticity has created greater freedom for women but the new emphasis on sexuality is not without its costs. In particular pornography increases the freedom of men while threatening the freedom of women. To Walby, 'The male gaze, not that of women, is the viewpoint of pornography' and pornography encourages the degradation of women by men and it sometimes promotes sexual violence.

Sexuality

Walby argues that 'heterosexuality constitutes a patriarchal structure'. However, she accepts that the nature of this patriarchal structure has undergone important changes.

In the nineteenth century women's **sexuality** was subject to strict control and was largely confined by a 'plethora of practices' to sex within marriage. Women's sexuality was therefore 'directed to one patriarchal agent for a lifetime', although the result was to reduce women's 'sexual interest in anything, including marriage'.

In the twentieth century it has become easier for women to be sexually active. Improved contraception has reduced the risk of unwanted pregnancy and the increasing availability of divorce has produced the possibility of exchanging 'an inadequate husband for a new one'. Walby refers to a study by Lawson and Sampson (quoted in Walby 1990, p. 125) conducted in 1988 which found that of women marrying in the 1960s, 75 per cent had remained faithful to their husbands during the first ten years of marriage whereas only 46 per cent of those who had married since the 1970s had done so. The study also found that for those married in the earlier period, men had been more likely to be unfaithful whereas for those married in the later period more women had had affairs.

Women themselves played an important part in fighting for greater sexual freedom in campaigning for birth control, abortion and easier divorce, but sexual liberalization has not worked to their advantage in every respect. For example, Walby says 'the sexual double standard is still alive and well'. Young women who are sexually active are condemned by males as 'slags'; those who are not are seen as 'drags'. On the other hand males who have many sexual conquests are admired for their supposed virility.

Today there is more pressure on women to be heterosexually active and to 'service' males by marrying or cohabiting with them. Thus heterosexuality remains patriarchal even though women have made some genuine gains.

Violence

Walby starts her discussion of **violence** by noting that 'Male violence against women includes rape, sexual assault, wife beating, workplace sexual harassment and child sexual abuse.' Like other feminists, she sees violence as a form of power over women. The use of violence or the threat of violence, helps to keep women in their place and discourages them from challenging patriarchy.

According to Walby, the lack of reliable evidence from the past makes it impossible to determine whether the amount of violence against women by men has increased or decreased. However, Walby does believe it is possible to determine that there have been changes in the response to male violence. The state, and in particular the police, have become more willing to take action against the worst offenders. Nevertheless, action against violent husbands is still infrequent and some women continue to be subject to male violence while other women continue to fear it.

The state

State policies relating to gender have changed considerably since the nineteenth century. For example there has been:

the cessation of legal backing to exclusionary practices in employment; the increased ease of divorce and financial provision for non-wage earners; the ending of state backing to exclusionary practices in education and the removal of most forms of censorship of pornography; the decriminalization of contraception and abortion under most circumstances; and minor changes in the law making it marginally easier for a women to leave a violent man.

Most of these changes have been gains for women but, to Walby, 'the state is still patriarchal as well as capitalist and racist'. State policies are no longer directed at confining women to the private sphere of the home but there has been little real attempt to improve women's position in the public sphere. Women still get paid lower wages than men and equal opportunities legislation is not often enforced. Women in one-parent families get little state benefit and women have been harmed by the greater availability of pornography. While the state itself is not so obviously as patriarchal as it used to be, it still does little to protect women from patriarchal power in society.

■ From private to public patriarchy

As we have seen in each of the preceding sections on the different structures of patriarchy, Walby recognizes that important changes have taken place in every aspect of gender relations. Liberal feminists tend to see these changes as progress. Radical feminists tend to argue that little has changed and patriarchal domination remains firmly intact. Marxists usually claim that industrialization and the advent of capitalism led to a deterioration in the position of women and since the Industrial Revolution little has improved.

Walby does not accept any of these general views, arguing instead that the nature of patriarchy has changed. To her, different aspects of patriarchy are interrelated and together they produce a system of patriarchy and it is this system which has changed.

In the nineteenth century patriarchy was predominantly private; in the twentieth century it became public. Table 10.1 summarizes how Walby characterizes this change.

Table 10.1   Private and public patriarchy

Form of patriarchy	Private	Public
Dominant structure	Household production	Employment/State
Wider patriarchal structures	Employment State Sexuality Violence Culture	Household production Sexuality Violence Culture
Period	Nineteenth century	Twentieth century
Mode of expropriation	Individual	Collective
Patriarchal strategy	Exclusionary	Segregationist

(*Source*: Walby, S. (1990) *Theorizing Patriarchy*, Blackwell, Oxford, p. 24.)

Private patriarchy

In **private patriarchy** an **individual patriarch**, the male head of household, controls women 'individually and directly in the relatively private sphere of the home'. It is 'the man in his position as husband or father who is the direct oppressor and beneficiary, individually and directly, of the subordination of women'. Women remain oppressed because they are prevented from entering the public sphere in areas such as employment and politics.

Although household production was the most important structure of private patriarchy, it was backed up by the other patriarchal structures which excluded women.

The shift away from private patriarchy

The shift away from private patriarchy was in part a consequence of **first wave feminism**. Between around 1850 and 1930 women in the USA and Britain campaigned for much more than just voting rights. They also sought:

---

the containment of predatory male sexual behaviour (Christabel Pankhurst's slogan was 'Votes for women, chastity for men'), access to employment, training and education, reform of the legal status of married women so they could own property, for divorce and legal separation at the woman's behest as well as that of the

---

husband. . . for the collective rather than private organization of meal preparation.

These campaigns took place 'against the background of an expanding capitalist economy' and capitalists required a larger workforce. There was pressure from male trades unionists to continue to exclude women from employment so that they could not compete for men's jobs.

The result was a series of compromises in which women gained more access to the public sphere, capitalists were able to employ more women in their enterprises, and male workers ensured that women were restricted in the employment opportunities open to them. (We will discuss Walby's ideas on male trades unionism and female employment later in the chapter. See p. 623 for further details.) These compromises led to the emergence of a new public form of patriarchy.

Public patriarchy 'is a form in which women have access to both public and private arenas. They are not barred from the public arenas, but are nonetheless subordinated within them.' In the public sphere women tend to be segregated into certain jobs which are lower paid and are given a lower status than men's jobs. The state and employment become the dominant structures of patriarchy but the other structures remain important. Women are no longer exploited so much by individual patriarchs but instead are exploited collectively by men in general through their subordination in public arenas. As Walby puts it 'Women are no longer restricted to the domestic hearth, but have the whole society in which to roam and be exploited.'

Variations in patriarchy

Walby does believe that there has been some reduction in patriarchal exploitation in certain areas as a consequence of the change from private to public patriarchy. The extent of any such reduction varies between groups of women, however, as does the balance between public and private elements of patriarchy. For example, Walby believes that Muslim women are more restricted by family structures than other women, and are therefore more subject to private patriarchy than other groups. Afro-Caribbean women, on the other hand, are more likely to have paid employment and to head their own families than other ethnic groups and are therefore more subject to public patriarchy.

Walby's arguments are largely confined to an examination of Britain and the USA but she does give some indications of how these compare to other countries. She suggests that the state has played a more important role in public patriarchy in some countries, whereas in others the labour market has been more important. In the former communist countries of Eastern Europe it was the state which was predominant. In the most capitalist and free market of western countries, the USA, employment has been of greatest importance. In Western Europe, with more developed welfare states, the state and employment have played a more equal role in public patriarchy.

■ Evaluation of Walby

Walby's theory of patriarchy incorporates the insights of many different feminists. Like Marxist

and socialist feminists she acknowledges the importance of economic inequality. Like many radical feminists she discusses how factors such as violence, sexuality and culture can maintain patriarchy. Like liberal feminists she attaches some importance to changes in the law and accepts that in some respects women's campaigns have won important citizenship rights. Walby recognizes that patriarchy has undergone significant changes and she attempts to explain and understand these changes through the use of the concepts of private and public patriarchy.

Nevertheless, her work has been criticized. Floya Anthias and Nira Yuval-Davis criticize her for using what they see as a **three systems approach**. According to them Walby treats gender, 'race' and class as separate systems which interact with one another. Anthias and Yuval-Davis believe that patriarchy, capitalism and racism are all part of one system which advantages some groups and disadvantages others.

Jackie Stacey praises Walby for 'an all-encompassing account of the systematic oppression of women in society' and for showing an awareness of historical changes in the position of women. However, she criticizes her for her use of the concept of structure. Stacey says that 'some structures are more clearly conceptualised than others (for example, paid employment and culture)'. In the case of some other structures, Walby does not make such a good case for the existence of relatively fixed relationships which contain women. Stacey believes that Walby neglects 'any consideration of identity and lived experience' by focusing on a structuralist analysis which 'fails to explain how people negotiate such a system'.

To Stacey, good feminist sociology pays more attention to the subjective states of women and to how women come to terms with or resist the oppression of which they are a victim.

■ Gender and paid employment

■ Gender inequalities at work

Most feminists believe that the position of women in the labour market is an important source of female disadvantage. (As we saw in a previous section, the radical feminist Firestone is an exception

since she sees women's oppression as biological in origin.) Some radical feminists (for example Kate Millett) see lack of employment opportunities as one – but only one – of many sources of gender inequalities. Marxist feminists, with their greater stress upon material, economic factors, generally attach rather more importance to employment opportunities. However, it is usually liberal feminists who have placed most emphasis on paid employment outside the home. They have sought the introduction of equal opportunities in the labour market through new legislation and through changing attitudes.

In terms of legislation, in the UK women have secured a number of important gains. In terms of attitudes, the election of the first British woman prime minister, Margaret Thatcher, might possibly have heralded an era in which women were accepted in any job in society.

Equal opportunity legislation

In 1970 the Equal Pay Act was passed. This specified that women were entitled to equal pay to men if they were doing the same or broadly similar work, or if their work was shown through a job evaluation scheme to be of the same value as that carried out by men. A five-year period was allowed for the implementation of the Act.

In 1982, however, the European Court decided that the Equal Pay Act was not consistent with EC legislation and it was strengthened. A 1984 amendment allowed women to claim equal pay for work of equal value if they could show that their job made demands as great as the work carried out by male employees in the same organizations in terms of factors such as skill, effort and decision making.

The 1975 Sex Discrimination Act barred discrimination on the grounds of sex in employment, education, and the provision of goods, services and premises. In employment, women were to be given equal access to jobs, and equal chances for promotion. Some types of job (for example toilet cleaning) were excluded from the provisions of the Act where there was considered to be 'a genuine occupational qualification by sex'.

Gender and the labour force

There have been considerable increases in the proportion of women who work. In Britain from 1961 to 1981 the number of employed females rose by 2.7 million, while the number of working men actually fell by about 200,000. In 1961 women made up 32.3 per cent of the labour force, and in 1981 39.5 per cent. According to the *Labour Force*

Survey women made up 44.43 per cent of those in employment in spring 1993.

Most of this rise has been due to the increasing numbers of married women who work. In the UK in 1993 two out of three married women were employed, compared to one in five in 1951. In 1993 46 per cent of women over 16 in Britain were in employment compared to 61 per cent of men over 16. However, it is overwhelmingly women who do part-time work: according to the Employment Department 886,000 men but 5,045,000 women worked part-time in 1993.

Gender and earnings

In 1970 women working as full-time employees earned about 63 per cent of the average male full-time employees' wage per hour. Table 10.2 shows that there was a considerable increase to 71 per cent in British women's pay as a proportion of men's in 1975. There was then little further rise

Table 10.2 Average gross hourly earnings, excluding the effects of overtime, full-time employees on adult rates

	Pence per hour		
	1975*	1983*	1993
Great Britain			
Females	98	288	668
Males	139	398	847
Differential	41	111	179
Female earnings as a percentage of male earnings	71	72	79
Scotland			
Females	93	276	631
Males	134	392	791
Differential	41	116	160
Female earnings as a percentage of male earnings	69	70	80
Wales			
Females	93	274	612
Males	135	374	728
Differential	42	100	116
Female earnings as a percentage of male earnings	69	73	84
* females aged 18 and over, males aged 21 and over			

(*Source:* Equal Opportunities Commission (1994) *Some Facts about Women*, based on *New Earnings Surveys*.)

Table 10.3 Employment in Great Britain by industry, 1993

Selected industries	Females (thousands) Full-time	Part-time	Males (thousands) Full-time	Part-time
Agriculture, forestry and fishing	10	40	143	12
Agriculture and horticulture	15	39	130	12
Energy and water supply	73	21	365	–
Other mineral and ore extraction	136	34	490	–
Metal goods, engineering, vehicles	402	112	1,734	18
Other manufacturing	490	202	1,106	35
Food, drink and tobacco	108	65	309	10
Paper products, printing and publishing	108	50	285	13
Construction	93	60	769	15
Distribution, hotels, catering, repairs	864	1,459	1,493	306
Retail distribution	520	963	677	188
Hotels and catering	181	404	206	93
Transport and communication	236	98	986	31
Inland transport (excl railways)	36	30	337	15
Banking, finance and insurance, etc	924	342	1,130	47
Business services	437	183	611	31
Other services	2,351	2,193	2,121	201
Sanitary	28	91	118	16
Education	603	589	430	53
Medical and other health services	589	603	239	22
All industries and services*	5,593	4,565	10,351	675

*Includes those not stating industry
–less than 10,000

Employees aged 16 and over

(*Source:* Labour Force Survey, Spring quarter.)

until the 1990s. In 1993 the figure stood at 79 per cent.

The legislation of the 1970s may have had some impact, but considerable differences remain between the average pay of men and women in Britain. In 1993, according to the *New Earnings Survey*, women working full-time in manual jobs still earned only 65 per cent of the average gross weekly earnings of men in such jobs. In non-manual occupations female full-time workers earned 64 per cent of the wage of male non-manual workers per week.

Again, although women make up an increasing proportion of the labour force, they are not equally represented throughout the occupational structure. There is both horizontal and vertical segregation in men's and women's jobs.

1 Horizontal segregation refers to the extent to which men and women do different jobs.

2 Vertical segregation refers to the extent to which men have higher-status and higher-paid jobs than women.

Table 10.3 gives an indication of the extent of horizontal segregation by industry. Agriculture, forestry and fishing; energy and water supply; mineral and ore extraction; construction; and transport and communication employees are predominantly male. Women are considerably more likely than men to work in distribution, hotels and catering; education and the health service. Employment in banking, finance and insurance is more evenly balanced between the sexes although, as in other types of employment, women are much more likely than men to work part-time.

Table 10.4 gives an indication of the extent of both horizontal and vertical segregation. Men dominate most areas of management and most higher-status professions such as medicine. When women have professional jobs they are more likely

Table 10.4 Employment in Great Britain by occupation, 1993

Occupation group	Females (thousands)	Percentage of group	Males (thousands)	Percentage of group	Total
Managers and administrators	1,265	33	2,566	67	3,770
Bank, building society and post office managers	22	23	72	77	94
Company secretaries	65	81	15	19	80
Professional	961	39	1,507	61	2,496
Medical practitioners	33	30	78	70	111
Primary and nursery school teachers	275	86	44	14	319
Associate professional and technical	1,094	49	1,148	51	2,208
Computer analysts/programmers	27	15	156	85	183
Nurses	416	90	45	10	461
Clerical and secretarial	2,828	76	890	24	3,883
Storekeepers and warehousepersons	47	16	250	84	297
Computer etc operators	120	72	48	28	168
Craft and related	349	11	2,843	89	3,482
Bakers, flour confectioners	11	28	28	72	39
Sewing machinists etc	134	92	11	8	145
Personal and protective services	1,610	66	827	34	2,412
Police officers (Sgt and below)	13	9	137	91	150
Care assistants and attendants	314	94	20	6	334
Sales	1,243	65	675	35	2,015
Technical and wholesale sales reps	36	17	183	83	219
Retail cash desk and check-out operators	180	90	20	10	200
Plant and machine operatives	484	21	1,827	79	2,377
Drivers of road goods vehicles	11	3	426	97	437
Assembliers/lineworkers of electrical and electronic goods	67	69	30	31	97
Other occupations	1,105	52	1,015	48	2,208
Postal workers, mail sorters	28	17	133	83	161
Counterhands, catering assistants	170	86	28	14	198
All occupations*	10,959	45	13,329	55	25,064

*includes those not stating occupation

(*Source:* Equal Opportunities Commission (1994) *Some Facts about Women,* based on *Labour Force Survey,* spring 1993.)

to be in lower-status and less well-paid professions such as primary and nursery school teaching, and nursing. Routine white-collar jobs such as clerical and secretarial work are overwhelmingly carried out by women. In retailing over 80 per cent of sales representatives are men but 90 per cent of cash desk and checkout operators are women. In manual jobs women are likely to have semi-skilled work such as assembling electrical goods whereas most skilled craft jobs are done by men.

Veronica Beechey claims that vertical segregation has actually increased this century in Britain.

Although women have made small gains in some areas (for example they have made some inroads into management) they now make up a much greater proportion of clerical workers than they used to.

Within particular occupations women are usually concentrated in the lowest reaches of the occupational structure. For example, civil service statistics shown in Table 10.5 reveal that in 1994 women occupied just 8.9 per cent of the top three grades in the civil service. They had been most successful in the Office of Public Service and Science,

Table 10.5 Women in top Whitehall jobs 1994

Department	Women as percentage of Senior staff
1 Office of Public Service and Science	23.5
2 Department of National Heritage	16.7
3 Home Office	15.6
4 Regulatory Bodies (e.g. OFTEL)	15.4
5 Department of the Environment	14.6
6= Customs and Excise	14.3
6= Department of Social Security	14.3
8 Department of Transport	13.8
9 Cabinet Office	13.3
10 Department of Health	10.5
11= Lord Chancellor's Department	9.1
11= Department of Employment	9.1
11= Department of Trade and Industry	9.1
14 Scottish Office	8.8
15 Welsh Office	6.7
16 Legal Departments and (including CPS)	6.4
17= HM Treasury	6.3
17= MAFF	6.3
19 Ministry of Defence	3.3
20 Central Statistical Office	0.0 (5)
21 GCHQ	0.0 (6)
22 Northern Ireland Office	0.0 (7)
23 Overseas Development	0.0 (11)
24 Department for Education	0.0 (15)
25 Inland Revenue	0.0 (24)
Others (Small Departments)	7.1
Total	**8.9**

(Figures in brackets indicate the number of top positions available)

(*Source*: Clement, B. (5 November 1994) 'Whitehall drive on equality "has ground to a halt"', *The Independent*, p. 6.)

where they held nearly a quarter of the top jobs, but in six departments (the Central Statistical Office, GCHQ, the Northern Ireland Office, Overseas Development, the Department for Education and the Inland Revenue) there were no women in the three most senior grades.

Few women occupy elite positions in society. According to the *Lloyds Bank Economic Bulletin* for July 1988, only 6 per cent of government ministers, 6 per cent of MPs, 13 per cent of life peers, 3 per cent of ambassadors and 6 per cent of army officers were women.

Even in occupations in which women predominate (such as primary school teaching) they tend to miss out on the senior jobs. In 1981 over 90 per cent of primary school teachers were women, but women held only 43 per cent of head teachers' jobs.

We will examine theories which attempt to explain such inequalities in a later section.

Women and employment – A Lifetime Perspective

Some of the most detailed information on women and employment has been provided by a study called *A Lifetime Perspective*, carried out in 1980 by Jean Martin and Ceridwen Roberts for the Department of Employment and the Office of Population Censuses and Surveys. The study used structured interviews and a sample of 5,888 women aged between 16 and 59. As the title of the study suggests, it adopted a lifetime perspective, and thus was able to provide data on patterns of employment during the course of women's lives.

At the time of the interviews 60 per cent of the women were working. The study confirmed the high percentage of women working part-time (26 per cent of the total sample) while 34 per cent were working full-time, 5 per cent were unemployed, 5 per cent were full-time students and 30 per cent were economically inactive. Despite the 30 per cent who appeared to be outside the labour force, there was evidence that paid employment took up at least part of the lives of the vast majority of adult women.

The researchers found no relationship between marriage and rates of employment. The key factor affecting whether women worked was whether they had children, and if so, the age of the youngest child. Childless women were most likely to work: 84 per cent had full or part-time jobs. This contrasted sharply with the figure for women with a child under 5: only 27 per cent worked. The likelihood of women working rose with the age of the youngest child: 64 per cent of women whose youngest child was aged 5–10 worked, and 76 per cent of those with a child aged 11–15.

As the above figures might suggest, the study found women were very likely to return to work after having children. Comparing different generations, there had been little increase in the proportions of women resuming work after having a family, but there had been a shortening of the period spent away from work. It was 9.6 years before one half of the women who had a first birth in 1950–3 had returned to paid employment, but the comparable figure was only 4 years for women who had a first birth in 1975–9. Furthermore, there was an increased likelihood that women would work between births. Martin and Roberts's survey indicates that paid employment was coming to occupy a greater proportion of the lifetime of women with children.

Another finding of the survey was that women themselves seemed to be attaching increasing importance to paid employment. Only 6 per cent of those working said that they would prefer not to be employed. The experience of marriage seemed to increase women's desire for work; young childless women had the least commitment to work.

Martin and Roberts found that women's attitudes were changing along with women's involvement in the labour force — the sample increasingly saw paid employment as a normal feature of the lives of married women. Most women, though, thought that other women should only go out to work if they did not have young children to look after: 60 per cent thought the mothers of preschool children should stay at home. For these women motherhood remained the prime responsibility for women, and work would have to be sacrificed if it interfered with their ability to care for young children. They still assumed that the mother, and not the father, should take on such responsibilities.

Martin and Roberts's survey provides some interesting data on women's involvement in, and attitudes to, paid work. Nevertheless, it has been criticized by Sarah Fildes for concentrating on the supply of women's labour, and not on the demand for it. The study implies that much of the increased participation of women in work is the result of women's increasing desire to work.

Some of the explanations for inequalities between working men and working women stress the limits placed on the types of employment opportunity which are normally offered to women. We will now look at these explanations.

■ Explanations for gender inequalities in employment

As we have seen in the previous sections, women face a number of disadvantages in paid work.

1 First, they tend to be paid less than men.

2 Second, they are more likely to be in part-time work.

3 Third, they tend to be concentrated in the lower reaches of the occupations in which they work.

4 Fourth, women tend to do particular types of jobs, usually those with a low status.

Some explanations for these inequalities concentrate on the characteristics of women and men. They generally see the inequalities in the labour market as stemming from women's role in the family. Other approaches concentrate on the labour market and the way in which it can restrict the opportunities open to women.

Functionalism and human capital theory

As we discussed earlier in the chapter (see p. 587), the functionalist Talcott Parsons argues that women are naturally suited to the 'expressive' role of childcare whereas men are more suited to the 'instrumental' role of competing in the labour market. This implies that women with children will give up or interrupt their careers in order to care for their children.

Human capital theory, which is advocated by some economists, argues that women's lack of commitment to paid employment is the cause of the disadvantages they suffer in the labour market. Because they are likely to abandon or interrupt their careers at an early age, women have less incentive to invest their time in undertaking lengthy programmes of training or education. They are therefore of less value to employers than their more highly trained and more skilled male counterparts.

Similarly, on average, women will have less experience of their jobs than men because they are less likely than men to be in continuous employment for many years. This makes it difficult for women to be promoted to higher-status and better-paid jobs. Once again women get paid less than men because they are worth less to the employer. Their lack of training, qualifications and experience which all result from the demands of childcare produce their disadvantages in the labour market.

Anne Witz is amongst the many critics of functionalist and human capital approaches. She argues that even when women do work continuously without taking career breaks they still tend to end up in the lower-paid and lower-status jobs. Teresa Rees points out that American research designed to test the theory has found that only about half the pay differentials between men and women can be explained in terms of human capital theory. Human capital theory also ignores causes of inequality between male and female employees located within the structure of the labour market.

Structural factors are the focus of the next theories we will look at.

The dual labour market theory

R.D. Barron and G.M. Norris were among the first British sociologists to apply **dual labour market theory** to gender inequalities. From this point of view there are two, not one, labour markets.

1 The **primary labour market** is characterized by high pay, job security, good working conditions and favourable promotion prospects.

2 The **secondary labour market** consists of lower-paid jobs with less job security, inferior working conditions and few opportunities for promotion.

Often primary and secondary labour markets exist side-by-side within a company, but transfer from the secondary to the primary is difficult, perhaps impossible.

Primary sector workers in a firm would include professional and managerial staff and highly skilled manual workers. Secondary sector workers include those doing unskilled or semi-skilled manual or non-manual jobs.

According to Barron and Norris, dual labour markets result from the tactics used by employers to obtain the types of labour they require. They are prepared to offer relatively high rewards to retain primary sector workers with the necessary skills and experience, but they regard secondary sector workers as more dispensable. Secondary sector workers can be easily replaced, and there is therefore little incentive to offer them high wages, job security or promotion prospects.

Both men and women can be found in the secondary sector, but Barron and Norris believe that women are more likely to get jobs in this sector. Employers tend to ascribe characteristics to women which make them particularly suited to these types of job: they are seen as easy to replace, as having less interest in gaining additional skills, and as less concerned than men with the size of their wage packets (since men are expected to be the main breadwinners within families).

The relatively low status of women in society and their tendency not to belong to unions

weakens their position further and makes it especially difficult for them to get a foothold in primary sector employment. Once recruited to the secondary sector, women are likely to remain captives within it for the rest of their working lives.

Dual labour market theory moves well away from looking at family life to explain the position of women in the labour market. It avoids concentrating on individual cases of discrimination and stresses the structures limiting women's employment opportunities. However, Veronica Beechey identifies a number of limitations to the theory.

1 First, some women in skilled manual jobs (for example in the textile industry) still receive low pay although their work is very similar to primary sector men's jobs.

2 Second, many women do have jobs in the primary sector, but not in industry, for example, nurses, teachers and social workers. The dual labour market theory is not particularly good at explaining the position of women outside manufacturing industry.

3 Third, the dual labour market theory cannot explain why women gain promotion less often than men even when they are doing the same jobs.

Deskilling and the labour process

Marxists and Marxist feminists tend to dismiss the approaches that have been discussed so far on the grounds that they fail to relate the position of women to the workings of the capitalist economy as a whole. The American Marxist Harry Braverman has devoted part of his analysis of the **labour process** in capitalism to the role of women. (For a full discussion of Braverman's theory see pp. 208–14.)

Braverman suggests that monopoly capitalism produced a progressive deskilling of work including clerical work, service sector work and retailing. According to Braverman, women have been drawn into these areas of work as the service sector has expanded, while the mainly male manufacturing sector has declined. He explains women's entry into such work in the following way.

1 Women are no longer needed to produce commodities such as food and clothing for their families since these items can now be more easily purchased.

2 Women were able to move quite easily from providing services for their family to providing them for other members of the community in return for a wage packet.

3 Women have had to become an increasingly important source of labour as the reserve supply of other types of labour (such as migrants from rural areas) has dried up.

4 Women are a particularly suitable source of labour in an economic system that increasingly wants to employ unskilled workers. Braverman believes that women have been used to replace skilled male workers and so helped employers to deskill their labour force.

As we discovered in an earlier section of the book (see pp. 210–14) a major problem with Braverman's views is his exclusive emphasis on deskilling. Not all jobs have been deskilled, nor for that matter do all women work in unskilled jobs. Furthermore, as Beechey points out, it is possible that some jobs attract low pay not because they require little skill, but simply because they are seen as women's jobs. Thus nurses get comparatively low wages despite the professional skills and training required in that occupation.

Women as a reserve army ✓ of labour

Veronica Beechey has developed a second strand of Marxist thought in order to explain the position of women in the labour market.

Marx argued that capitalism required a **reserve army of labour**, that is a spare pool of potential recruits to the labour force. According to Marx, because of their in-built contradictions, capitalist economies went through cycles of slump and boom, and it was essential to be able to hire workers during the booms, and fire them during the slumps. Furthermore, in their pursuit of surplus value capitalists tried constantly to improve the efficiency of their machinery. This reduced the workforce needed to produce existing products, but new products were constantly introduced. Again a reserve army provided the necessary flexibility to deal with these changes.

One of the main functions of the reserve army is to reduce the wages of all members of the labour force. A group of unemployed people looking for work creates competition in the workforce. This gives employers an advantage and allows them to reduce wages and increase the rate of exploitation.

Beechey identifies a number of ways in which women in modern Britain are particularly suited to form part of this reserve army.

1 They are less likely to be unionized and so are less able to resist redundancy than men.

2 Women's jobs are least likely to be covered by redundancy legislation, so it is cheaper to make them redundant rather than men.

3 Unemployed married women may not be eligible to receive state benefits if their husbands are working, and for this reason they might not appear in unemployment statistics. Beechey says 'Women who are made redundant are able to disappear virtually without trace back into the family.'

4 Because of their position within the family and the primary importance placed on their domestic role, women are likely to provide a particularly flexible reserve labour force. They are more likely to accept part-time work and variations in their hours of work.

5 Women are often prepared to work for less than men because they can rely on their husbands' wages as the main source of income for the family.

The reserve army of labour theory certainly seems to explain some of the changes that have taken place in the proportions of women working this century in Britain. For example, it would appear to account for the increased employment of women during the two world wars.

However, like the other theories examined in this section it has serious drawbacks. For example, Beechey herself admits that it cannot explain horizontal segregation in the labour market (why women are largely confined to certain types of job).

More seriously the theory has been challenged by Irene Bruegel who questions the assumption that it must serve the interests of capital if women are used as a reserve army of labour. She points out that women can also benefit capitalism by producing **use values** in the home since this reduces the amount that needs to be paid to male workers.

From a rather different point of view – the **substitution theory** – Gardiner claims that it benefits capital more if women are allowed to retain their jobs in a time of recession and rising unemployment since they can act as a comparatively cheap substitute for male workers.

Clearly the best way to test these theories is to examine what happens to women's employment when unemployment generally is rising. Veronica Beechey herself quotes figures which appear to support the theory of Gardiner that women are substituted for male workers rather than acting as a reserve army of labour. According to *The Equal Opportunities Commission Report* of 1983, in the period of recession from 1971–83 male employment declined from 13 million to 11.5 million, but female employment actually increased from 8.2 to 8.8 million. On the other hand, this increase was largely due to more women working part-time, so women do form a relatively flexible labour force.

This evidence does not therefore provide clearcut evidence for either the reserve army of labour theory or the substitution theory. More recently female part-time employment has continued to grow

Linda McDowell – gender and post-Fordism

Linda McDowell argues that fundamental changes have taken place in the labour market since the late 1960s and these have had important effects on gender and employment. McDowell uses the theory of post-Fordism to understand changes in the labour market. As we saw in Chapter 4 (see pp. 214–16), this theory argues that businesses have moved away from mass production towards the flexible production of small batches of specialized products. In doing so they employ a core of highly skilled workers who are capable of using their skills to produce a wide variety of products. Other work is carried out by part-time workers, workers on short-term contracts or is contracted out to other firms.

McDowell argues that these changes are reflected in the increased use of part-time female labour and the reduction in the employment of males in full-time permanent jobs. She points out that between 1971 and 1988 male employment fell by almost 1.8 million whereas female employment rose by about 1.7 million. Women have been used to fill the increasing proportion of jobs in parts of the growing service sector. These types of job have traditionally been done by women. Part-time workers are cheaper to employ because they do not have the same rights to unemployment and sick pay as full-time workers; their wages tend to be lower than those of full-time workers; and they are easier to dismiss because they do not have the same legal protections under employment legislation. Employers have been determined to cut costs and to have a more flexible labour force to cope with repeated recessions and increased competition in most areas of business.

Some women have benefited from these changes. A few have found secure and well-paid employment as core workers and have 'captured the labour market opportunities and rewards traditionally reserved for male workers'. Most, however, have not fared so well.

The majority of new jobs have been part-time. McDowell says:

> Part-time, 'flexible' work has not been created in response to 'demand' on the part of workers, whether men or women. Rather, many have had part-time or temporary jobs imposed on them or have taken them for want of alternatives while continuing to seek full-time and stable work.

McDowell points out that according to the *New Earnings Survey* pay per hour for female part-time workers fell from 81 per cent of that for female full-time workers in 1980 to 75 per cent in 1989. With the decline in the availability of well-paid and secure work for working-class men, this has left many working-class women considerably worse off.

McDowell has identified important changes in the position of women in the labour market. However, she bases most her arguments on the theory of post-Fordism which has been heavily criticized. Some sociologists have questioned the extent to which post-Fordist production has influenced industry and the extent to which employers have turned to 'flexible workers'. (See pp. 216–18 for detailed criticisms of post-Fordism.)

Men, trade unions and women in the labour market

Marxist feminist approaches to women and employment (such as the theory of the reserve army of labour) stress the relationship between the economic system and women's work. From a radical feminist perspective however, such approaches tend to ignore the role of men – and particularly male workers – in restricting women's employment opportunities.

Some feminists have tried to combine the insights of Marxist feminism with those of radical feminists to explain the disadvantages experienced by women in the labour market. They argue that these disadvantages are a consequence of both the operation of the capitalist economy and the attempts of men to maintain patriarchal control.

In an article critical of both dual labour market and Marxist theories, Jill Rubery has drawn attention to the activities of trades unions as a factor affecting gender divisions in employment. Like Braverman she notes that many areas of work have been deskilled, but she also points to reskilling in some occupations. Changes in technology and labour processes have been accompanied by struggles in which workers, through their unions, have tried to retain the definition of their work as skilled even when such a definition is no longer justified. For example, before the 1980s printing unions tried with some success to maintain the craft status of their work along with high wages, despite the threats posed by the introduction of new technology.

To male workers who wish to maintain a strong position in the labour market, women workers may pose as great a threat as new technology. Women may undercut male wages, depress wage levels generally, and increase unemployment. If there is an influx of women into a particular occupation it may make it easier for the employer to define that occupation as requiring little skill.

Rubery maintains that in response to these threats trades unions have played a crucial part in restricting opportunities for female employees.

Like Rubery, Sylvia Walby argues that unions have been an important factor producing female disadvantage in employment. From a study of engineering, clerical work and textiles in Britain she claims that two main strategies have been used by males in these industries – the exclusion of women altogether, or the confinement of women to the lower grades of work.

In many parts of the engineering industry exclusion was the main tactic used (at least until 1943), while in clerical and textile work male unionists used grading more effectively. In the weaving industry, for example, men were successful in allowing only a few women to be promoted to overlookers. In recent years male unionists have resorted mainly to tactics involving grading, as legislation has made it difficult to exclude women from whole areas of employment.

Although Walby follows Marxists in describing modern societies as capitalist, she puts particular stress on the concept of patriarchy in trying to explain gender inequalities in employment. She sees unions as patriarchal institutions. Her own research suggests that they are usually dominated by men, and they tend to act in the interests of

male employees even when women are a majority of the union's membership. Nevertheless, she accepts that women have made some gains in the union movement in recent years, and they have had some success in persuading unions to take gender equality more seriously.

Walby takes a different view to conventional sociological theories which see the origins of female disadvantage in the workplace stemming from the home. Walby believes that work is a major factor shaping domestic relationships. Women suffer such disadvantages in the labour market that they become only too willing to accept the main responsibility for domestic tasks. As she puts it, 'housework is as good as anything else a woman is likely to get'.

Heidi Hartmann takes a similar view to Walby. She too believes unions play a major role in disadvantaging women, and she also uses the concept of patriarchy. Hartmann is perhaps even more critical of the way patriarchal power has been used. She claims that men have deliberately used job segregation as a way of reinforcing their dominance over women in the domestic sphere. Women have come to rely on their husbands' wages for financial support. Men have managed to maintain a patriarchal society despite the increased use of female labour by capitalists. A vicious circle has been created for women in which low-paid work strengthens women's dependence on men in the home, and their domestic dependence makes it easy to recruit women to low-paid and low-status jobs.

Radical feminism and female employment

Radical feminists believe that women's disadvantages in the labour market stem from the exploitation of women by men and have little to do with the operations of capitalism. They concentrate in particular on how men exercise power over women at work and protect their own interests by intimidating women and excluding women from senior positions. Radical feminists claim that one way that men do this is through the use of sexual harassment.

Elizabeth A. Stanko defines **sexual harassment** as:

unwanted sexual attention. Its behavioural forms are many and include visual (leering); verbal (sexual teasing, jokes, comments or questions); unwanted pressures for sexual favours or dates; unwanted touching or pinching; unwanted pressures for sexual favours with implied threats of job-related consequences for non-co-operation; physical assault; sexual assault; rape.

Men back up these types of harassment with their power within organizations. They are usually in a position to hire or fire women and may take action against them if they complain. According to Stanko, sexual harassment is a common occurrence at work. She refers to a number of British studies which found that over half of the women questioned had experienced sexual harassment.

Stanko believes that men use sexual harassment to intimidate women who seek to enter areas of traditionally male employment. In such jobs 'men's working environments become part of men's territories'. The men talk about sport and about women. They may have pin-ups of nude females in the workplace and they resent any challenge to the assumption that they can maintain a working environment which is male dominated. Stanko says:

Sexual jokes, comments, teasing or touching of women are part of the building and sustaining of male solidarity ... Women, it is commonly assumed, by entering into men's territory, must expect and accept these displays of male heterosexuality.

In jobs predominantly done by women the situation is somewhat different. Here, 'sexualising women who work in traditional occupations serves to eroticise women's subordination'. Waitresses and barmaids, for example, are expected to be sexually attractive and to accept that during their work they may be the recipients of unwanted attention from males. Secretaries 'to some extent become office wives'. Some leave their jobs if their male boss seeks to start an affair.

Another radical feminist, Rosemary Pringle, argues that the work of secretaries is largely governed by patriarchal images of the job. It is difficult for secretaries to be taken seriously or to have their work valued because of those images. Secretaries rarely have a clear job description and instead their work is viewed largely in terms of ideas about femininity.

Pringle claims that 'If secretaries are represented as women, they are represented almost exclusively in familial or sexual terms: as wives, mothers, spinster aunts, mistresses and *femmes fatales*.' At every place of work where she conducted her study at least one person assumed that because Pringle was studying secretaries she must be investigating sexual scandals. Pringle argues that 'The emphasis on the sexual has made it easy to treat the work as trivial or invisible.' Secretaries are sometimes seen as doing little but sitting around and gossiping 'filing their nails or doing their knitting'. A secretary is often viewed as 'the extension of her boss, loyal, trustworthy and devoted'. The dominant images of secretaries make it very difficult for them to be regarded as skilled workers or considered as possible candidates for promotion into management.

Approaches such as those developed by Stanko and Pringle illustrate how men may use intimidation and ideological power to maintain their domination at work. These approaches add an extra dimension to an understanding of gender inequalities at work but like all the approaches examined so far, they are somewhat limited in scope. They emphasize the importance of some sources of gender inequality at work while neglecting others. For example, Stanko pays little attention to the operation of the labour market as a whole.

The next study we will examine attempts to overcome the limitations of previous approaches by trying to incorporate a wide range of factors into its explanations of gender differences in the labour market.

■ Rosemary Crompton and Kay Sanderson – *Gendered Jobs and Social Change*

Structuration

In their study of gender and work published in 1990, Rosemary Crompton and Kay Sanderson argue that gender inequalities in the labour market must be explained in different ways in different types of job. Structural features of the labour market interact with the actions taken by individuals making individual decisions about their working lives. They follow Anthony Giddens in using the concept of **structuration**. According to this view, 'what people do always presupposes some kind of structure (rules of behaviour, resources, etc.) but in what they do people simultaneously create the structure anew'. Thus, for example, men who choose to follow traditional masculine careers and women who choose to follow traditional feminine careers reinforce structural features of the labour market which produce gender differences. They help to make it difficult for other individuals to pursue careers which are not normally thought appropriate for their gender.

The structure of the labour market shapes people's choices but does not entirely determine them. Individuals can and do choose non-conventional career paths and employers sometimes choose to fill jobs with types of personnel who are not normally recruited to them. The actions of individuals may, then, help to transform the labour market over a period of time so that structural limitations on actions are weakened or the structure of the labour market changes. Thus Crompton and Sanderson believe:

---

the occupational structure is at the same time a social 'product' as it sets limits on, and creates opportunities for, the people with (and without) 'jobs' who are producing it.

(We discuss Giddens's concept of structuration in detail on pp. 904–7.)

A model of the occupational structure

In their analysis Crompton and Sanderson make use of a wide range of theories and concepts. Their overall model of the labour market is shown in Figure 10.1. The left axis (A/B) refers to the characteristics of employees and in particular how qualified they are. In line with human capital theory Crompton and Sanderson believe that the labour market and the position of individuals within it is partly shaped by the qualifications held by the members of the workforce. However, they are aware that the value of qualifications is not fixed. They note that occupational groups can try to increase the value of the qualifications they hold by restricting access to their profession so that a shortage of qualified workers can lead to the market value of their work increasing. (This is similar to the Weberian perspective on the professions, see pp. 60–1 for further details.)

The CD axis in Figure 10.1 refers to the characteristics of the labour market rather than those of the individual participants in it. Crompton and Sanderson see a division between occupational and organizational labour markets. **Occupational labour markets** have 'extensive (voluntary and involuntary) mobility' whereas **organizational labour markets** 'are restricted to and controlled by firms or organizations'. In this aspect of their theory Crompton and Sanderson make use of the dual labour market theory and indicate that workers with few skills in the occupational labour market tend to end up in **secondary labour market** jobs with few prospects.

Amongst more skilled workers those in the occupational labour market are able to 'move between jobs without incurring any employer penalty'. They may be self-employed or may be highly skilled professionals or craft workers whose skills are in demand. They are not tied to the internal labour market of a particular organization and therefore are not so restricted in their efforts to improve their pay or secure promotion.

Occupational internal labour markets often include workers similar to those in the occupational labour market but in this case the status and rewards of workers depend partly upon their skills and partly upon their position within the organization for which they work. Company lawyers and accountants are typical of workers in occupational internal labour markets.

People in **firm internal labour markets** depend much more on their position in a particular firm for their status and rewards. There may be some opportunity to move from one organization to another but only if the organizations are very similar. For example, senior workers in a local authority may be able to move to do a similar job in another local authority, but they are unlikely to find employment in any other type of organization. In firm internal labour markets an employee is typically a 'highly trained generalist rather than the mobile specialist' of occupational or occupational internal labour markets.

Gender and the labour market

The characteristics and actions of individuals workers and those seeking work interact with the characteristics of the labour market to give overall shape to patterns of employment. However, specific factors work within this overall framework to

Figure 10.1   A preliminary model of the occupational structure

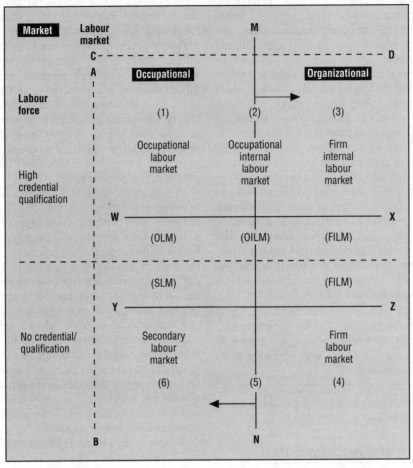

(*Source:* Crompton, R. and Sanderson, K. (1990) *Gendered Jobs and Social Change*, Unwin Hyman, London, p. 39.)

influence gender differences in employment. Crompton and Sanderson use the feminist concept of patriarchy although they see patriarchy as 'a particular aspect of gender relations' rather than as 'a universal system'. To them **gender segregation** is:

---

a product of the past sex-typing of occupations and conventional assumptions relating to the domestic roles of women, formal and informal exclusionary practices, and fluctuations in both the demand for labour and the nature of female labour available.

Conventional expectations and exclusionary practices can be overcome in some circumstances so that women can break into parts of the labour market to which they could not previously gain access. For example, they could use the 'qualifications lever' of high educational attainment to force their way into previously all-male domains. Whether this happens or not depends on the particular circumstances in different types of job.

Having outlined their theory Crompton and Sanderson go on to support and illustrate it by researching four areas of employment. We will now examine the findings of these case studies.

Pharmacy

The Pharmaceutical Society of Great Britain was founded in 1841 but the first woman was not admitted to the profession until 1879. By 1941 women still only made up about 10 per cent of pharmacists. Female membership of the profession increased by around 5 per cent per decade during the 1940s and 1950s, but at around twice that rate during the 1970s and 1980s. By 1983 a majority of undergraduates studying pharmacy were women.

Crompton and Sanderson argue that 'As an occupation, pharmacy has not been sex typed.' Although it involves high levels of scientific training, which are usually associated with mainly male professions, it also offers flexible patterns of employment and this is usually associated with predominantly female professions. Furthermore, men were unable to exclude females from the profession during the nineteenth century because, unlike accountancy, the constitution of the professional organization running the profession did not specify that the membership should be male. Women therefore became established in the profession relatively early in its development.

Regulations mean that a pharmacist has to be present if drugs are to be dispensed. This has led to the creation of considerable amounts of part-time work to cover for periods when full-time workers are not available. Women are attracted to such work because of the possibility of combining work with caring for their children.

Although women have come to be a high proportion of practising pharmacists, they tend to be concentrated towards the lower levels of the profession. Until the 1980s part-time pharmacists in the NHS could not achieve promotion. In companies such as Boots, pharmacists are required to be geographically mobile to gain promotion and women in the profession have been less geographically mobile than men. Thus although women have been able to enter the occupational labour market in pharmacy, they have had limited success in gaining promotion within it.

Accountancy

Women entered accountancy in large numbers much later than they entered pharmacy. The oldest professional association in accountancy, The Institute of Chartered Accountants of England and Wales, only started admitting women to its ranks in 1920. As late as the mid-1960s less than 1 per cent of accountants were women, although by 1986 women made up 36 per cent of people training to be accountants.

Unlike pharmacy there are a number of different recognized accountancy qualifications and the careers of some accountants are closely bound up with the firm internal labour market of particular organizations. Other accountants are self-employed or work in small independent accountancy practices. These accountants have occupational careers rather than ones based on organizations.

Crompton and Sanderson carried out in-depth interviews with six female qualified accountants. They found that those who worked in large organization were often subject to discrimination by their male bosses and this tended to block promotion prospects. One woman reported how her boss had openly stated that 'I just think that that's where women are most fulfilled, at home having a family.' There were also few opportunities for accountants in large organizations to work part-time. Women who had young children therefore faced a clear choice between their careers or being at home with their children.

Building societies

Unlike accountancy, the majority of building society workers are female. Crompton and Sanderson note that in the late 1980s over 70 per cent of building society workers were women. They attribute this partly to the very rapid expansion of employment in these organizations during the 1970s, a time when many married women were deciding to seek employment or to continue in work despite having children. Building societies recruited from this large pool of female labour.

Despite the predominance of women in this sector, they are concentrated towards the bottom of the hierarchies within building societies. Most of the clerical work is done by women but senior managers are almost exclusively male.

Crompton and Sanderson see building societies as examples of firm internal labour markets: prospects are largely tied to the chances of internal promotion. Men have been dominant in these labour markets and they have used their dominance to largely exclude women. Women tend to lack the formal qualifications, the willingness to do irregular overtime and the ability to be geographically mobile which are necessary to give an employee of a building society a good chance of promotion.

There are also unofficial practices which block women's promotions. Senior managers sometimes act as 'sponsors' or as 'mentors' for aspiring junior staff, helping them with their careers. The senior staff, who are almost always male, nearly always sponsor other males. Women also lack access to male-dominated informal networks and clubs which can be important ways of getting in with the right people to further their career.

In 1977 the Equal Opportunities Commission investigated alleged discrimination against women in the Leeds Building Society. It found that this building society tended to recruit men to its management training programmes even when women candidates were younger, better qualified and had more relevant work experience. The findings of the Equal Opportunities Commission persuaded a number of building societies to examine their recruitment policies.

Crompton and Sanderson themselves conducted studies at three building societies of different sizes, interviewing a total of eight managers and twenty-four clerical and supervisory workers. They found ample evidence of exclusionary practices by males. At one of the societies they studied (the 'Cloister Building Society') though, they did find that the majority of management trainees since 1980 were female. This suggested that male dominance was beginning to be challenged.

Cooking and serving

Work in catering and hotels has usually been considered 'women's work' because of its similarity to unpaid domestic work. It is generally low paid and low status although in some areas there are career prospects. Crompton and Sanderson conducted case study research on the school meals service in one education authority, and at two hotels.

Not surprisingly they found that school meal workers are almost all women. Since the school meals service is widely regarded as women's work and is seen as unskilled, there is little competition from men for the jobs. Women are attracted to the job because of the availability of part-time employment during school hours, making it relatively easy to combine work with looking after school-age children.

In hotels the situation is different. Although most employees are women, there are areas where men predominate. For example, most porters and many of the most senior and well-paid chefs are men. Management is fairly evenly split between males and females but 'women predominate in housekeeping and personnel, as managers within institutional catering and as proprietors of small establishments'. At lower levels in the hotel job hierarchy 'women are employed as counter and kitchen hands, waitresses, chambermaids, etc.'

Increasingly such workers are employed part-time and often on a casual basis. The hotel trade is highly competitive and employers are using more casual labour which can be laid off during slack times to cut costs. Male employees therefore tend to have more job security than female employees. Indeed this is a classic example of women at the lower levels in the profession being stuck in a secondary labour market with little security and few prospects.

Conclusion

Crompton and Sanderson believe that women continue to suffer considerable disadvantages within the labour market. However, the precise reasons for these disadvantages and the degree of inequality between men and women varies from industry to industry. Different factors are important in different parts of the labour market with diverse consequences. Overall though, Crompton and Sanderson do see some evidence of a reduction in gender divisions in employment. They say:

> The decline in manual occupations, and the intensification of competition between different types of disadvantaged labour at the lower levels of service employment, might be expected to result in a decline in sex-typed occupations in the structure as a whole.

At higher levels more women have been using their educational success and the 'qualifications lever' to force their way into male strongholds. However Crompton and Sanderson also note that women are increasingly employed in part-time work. Crompton and Sanderson conclude that while gender differences might become 'less oppressive and inegalitarian' they 'will be a persisting feature within work and employment' for the foreseeable future.

Evaluation

Dawn Burton has praised certain aspects of Crompton and Sanderson's study. She says:

> *Gendered Jobs and Social Change* provides a useful contribution to existing explanations of occupational segregation in Britain. The strength of Crompton and Sanderson's argument is that they point to a range of social, cultural and political processes which shape the division of labour between men and women in particular occupations.

Burton welcomes the lack of reliance upon a single theoretical framework to explain gender differences in all types of employment

However, she is less complimentary about the research methods. She points out that it is dangerous to generalize from case study research since the case studies selected may be unrepresentative of the phenomenon being studied. The findings of case study research become more reliable if a number of different case studies are examined, but Crompton and Sanderson only did this with building societies. Furthermore they were sometimes vague about the research methods used. Burton says:

> In some cases the reader does not know how many people were interviewed, how these individuals were selected, where they were interviewed, or whether they were representative of others working in the occupation concerned.

More fundamental objections to the study are raised by Lisa Adkins and Celia Lury. They see the reliance upon a wide range of factors for explaining gender inequalities as a weakness rather than a strength. They say:

> pluralistic conceptualization does little to move beyond previous understandings of the gendered dynamics of the labour market, and, indeed, in many ways, marks a regression in that such pluralism understates the significance of gender in the formation of occupations, occupational segregation, and forms of gendered inequality and exploitation.

In particular Adkins and Lury believe that Crompton and Sanderson see women as having more choices open to them than they really have. By applying Giddens's concept of structuration to men and women in the same way, the study fails to acknowledge that women's choices are strongly restricted by 'the actions of male workers'. Men shape the structure of the labour market much more than women.

■ Gender and stratification

In the previous section we have demonstrated that compared to men, women tend to get lower wages, have different types of job, and spend less years of their lives working in paid employment. Some women work exclusively as housewives, but increasingly women combine paid work outside the home with their domestic tasks.

These points raise serious problems for those who wish to identify the position of women in the stratification system of contemporary Western societies.

■ The problem of gender and class

Some approaches try to integrate women into theories of class alongside men; we analysed these approaches in Chapter 2 (see pp. 109–11). However, many feminist writers, and particularly radical feminists, argue that women should be seen as a distinct group in their own right and that gender differences are at least as important as those between different occupations.

As we indicated in an earlier section, the radical feminist Shulamith Firestone argued that women formed a **sex class** based upon their biological differences to men. Margaret Eichler criticizes this approach for being 'non- or pre-sociological, for it assumes a direct relationship between a biological and social difference'. Obviously men and women form fairly distinct biological groupings, but it may be difficult to see each as a different 'class', in the usual sense of the word. Some women are wealthy; a few have occupations of high status and which attract high rewards; there is therefore no clear economic dividing line between men and women.

Some writers have therefore turned to non-class forms of stratification for models with which to describe and explain gender inequalities.

Gender and caste

Kate Millett suggests in passing that women have a **caste-like status**, and Eichler notes some similarities between the position of castes and those of gender groupings.

1 Membership of a caste and of a gender are both ascribed at birth. This ascribed status provides the basis for the different groups having different cultures.

2 Social mobility between the groups is more or less impossible.

3 Different groups receive different levels of reward.

However, as Eichler points out, there are also important differences between caste and gender stratification.

1 In the caste system all members of the highest castes are clearly in an advantaged position over all members of lower castes: a Brahmin is always socially superior to an untouchable. Eichler suggests that the relationship between males and females in modern industrial societies is not so hierarchical. She says 'there are many women whose rank, by whatever criterion is higher than that of many men.'

2 Furthermore caste systems are based upon **endogamy**, that is individuals can only marry members of the same caste. Men and women on the other hand are expected to intermarry. Gender-based stratification is therefore **exogamous**: individuals must take a marriage partner from outside the group to which they belong.

Gender and minority groups

An alternative to defining women as a caste is to see them as a **minority group**. This approach is taken by Helen Mayer Hacker. She adopts Louis Wirth's definition of a minority group which reads:

A minority group is any group of people who because of their physical or cultural characteristics, are singled out from others in the society in which they live for differential and unequal treatment, and who therefore regard themselves as objects of collective discrimination.

By comparing the situations of American blacks and women, Hacker indicates some of the advantages of classifying women as a minority group.

1 Both groups have **high social visibility**: blacks in terms of their 'racial' characteristics and to some extent their styles of dress, women in terms of their sexual characteristics and feminine clothes.

2 Both groups have similar **ascribed attributes**, that is attributes which are assigned to them by the majority group simply on the grounds of their minority group membership. Blacks have been characterized as emotional, 'primitive' and childlike, women as irresponsible, inconsistent and emotionally unstable. Both groups, to some degree, have been or are regarded as having a low intelligence. Compared to whites, blacks have been labelled 'inferior'; compared to men, women have been labelled as 'weaker'.

3 The status of both blacks and women is **rationalized** in similar ways by the majority group. Their position is seen as a reflection of their ascribed characteristics: 'Blacks are all right in their place and contented with their lot.' The same applies to women: 'Their place is in the home and they find happiness and fulfilment in their roles as wives and mothers.'

4 Both groups adopt **accommodating behaviour** in adapting to their situation. Both are deferential and flattering to the majority group. Relative powerlessness forces both to adopt devious methods in their dealings with members of the majority group. Blacks have various strategies for outwitting whites; women use so-called 'feminine wiles' for getting their own way.

5 Both groups suffer from similar **discriminatory practices**: their education is limited to fit them for their ascribed status, and barriers are erected to prevent

them from entering the political arena. In the labour market, blacks are largely confined to 'black jobs', women to 'women's jobs'. These jobs have certain factors in common – low skill, low status and low pay.

Eichler criticizes minority group theory by saying:

as a stratification concept it is very limited: it focuses solely on the consequences of belonging to a minority group but does not tell us anything about the power relationship as such, its variations, limitations, different manifestations, etc.

■ Sex stratification

The most promising approaches to gender and stratification have tried to bridge the gap between the theories that see gender as unimportant compared to class stratification, and those which ignore class and emphasize the distinction between the position of men and women in society.

Eichler has sketched the outlines of how such a theory could be developed. She states 'Social stratification on bases other than sex is real, but so is sex stratification.' She argues that the basic problem is that much of the exploitation of women takes place outside the economy. It cannot therefore be discussed in terms of conventional Marxist notions of class, since it occurs within the context of the family.

If women are housewives and do not have paid employment they cannot be categorized according to their own occupation, yet Eichler does not accept that their position should simply be related to their husband's. Personal dependency of wives on husbands cuts across other class divisions: a working-class and a middle-class woman might both be refused credit unless they gained the agreement of their husband. Both might rely on their husband for any income they receive. Even in a family where husband and wife both work in paid employment, the wife might still be dependent if the husband makes most of the important decisions about family spending.

In conventional Marxist terms non-working wives cannot be considered part of the class system. They do not produce **exchange values** through producing commodities which are sold in the market; they do not produce a profit or **surplus value** for employers. The products of housewives' labour, are consumed by members of the family and are not sold.

Eichler argues that none of the above facts mean that women are not exploited. In effect what housewives do is no different from what many paid workers do. For example, a housewife might transform the raw materials – eggs, flour, milk and spices – into a cake. The cake is consumed in the family, and the husband probably eats part of it. A baker could perform exactly the same tasks which produce a commodity which is sold and creates surplus value for an employer. In effect the exchange value created by housewives is 'stolen': the services she provides and the commodities she produces are consumed but cannot be sold. She produces use values but not exchange values.

In a family in which both spouses work outside the home the wife can be seen as doubly or even triply exploited. Like other employees she is exploited by employers who extract surplus value from her labour. Within the family she may lose control over part of all the wages she has earned if the husband retains control over important financial decisions. Furthermore it is usual for the wife to continue to do most of the housework, and the husband will receive some of the benefits from the use values she creates in the home.

According to Eichler the reason a woman's position cannot be seen entirely in terms of the husband's social class is that the family is not a capitalist institution. The relationships within the family are not the same as purely economic relationships. A housewife might continue to produce use values, for example by cooking and cleaning, but be refused economic rewards for her efforts. Eichler uses the example of a housewife who continues to perform domestic duties conscientiously, but she is refused money by her husband because he knows she wishes to spend it on presents for her lover.

Eichler describes the family as a **quasi-feudal institution**. The husband provides money for food, shelter, clothing and protection in return for personal services. The situation of a wife has some similarities to that of a serf.

Eichler makes some interesting points about the situation of women, but fails to provide a clear analysis which can be applied to all women. She regards single working women as having a class position derived entirely from their work. From her point of view such a woman shares nothing in common with a housewife in terms of their positions in the stratification system. However, it can be argued that both might suffer the same types of discrimination, have a sense of common grievance, identify with each other as 'sisters' (if they are feminists), and have an inferior social status to men. Radical feminists would deny that it is only married women who form a distinctive grouping within society's stratification systems.

Eichler is also unclear about the causes of women's disadvantages. In part they seem to be based upon economic inequalities, but to some extent they are also based upon personal relationships between husbands and wives. Eichler tends to assume, without advancing any evidence, that husbands are dominant within marriage and that women still have primary responsibility for domestic tasks.

■ Romance and marriage

In Chapter 6 we examined the division of labour within marriage and the role of domestic labour in society, (see pp. 360–3 and 367–9). In this section we will therefore concentrate on the promise of marriage held out to women by the 'ideology of romance', the experience that women have of marriage, and the effects of marriage on wife and husband.

■ Angela McRobbie – the ideology of romance

In a study of fifty-six working-class girls aged 14–16 who attended a youth club in 1975, Angela McRobbie has examined what she calls the **ideology of romance**. McRobbie argues that these girls face what they themselves see as a very restricted future. They believe that it is normal and natural for women to get married and have children. For most of them marriage is, in any case, an economic necessity: few could hope to support themselves on the wages provided by a working-class woman's low-paid job.

Despite this limit on their future options and the apparent boredom of the lives led by their mothers, girls of this age are able to cope with their situation through their friendship with other girls. They are able to look forward to the future because of the ideology of romance.

McRobbie noticed a tendency amongst these girls to have a strong loyalty to a 'best friend'. This part of what McRobbie calls the **culture of femininity** might appear to exclude males, but in fact it is an important stepping-stone towards romance and marriage.

1 First, McRobbie suggests that many girls saw a pair as the most suitable unit to go out looking for boys.

2 Second, the culture of femininity developed between girls placed great emphasis on boyfriends, and fashion as a means of attracting them.

3 Third, many girls were united by a common admiration of male pop stars or other male media idols. McRobbie saw the idolization of such people essentially as a preparation for having real boyfriends. The posters on the wall provided substitute boyfriends for those who were too young to have the real thing.

The female best friends were very loyal to one another, but they realized that their relationship would not always be so strong. Eventually their primary loyalty would be transferred to their man.

According to McRobbie the culture of femininity is a major factor limiting the aspirations of these girls to romance and marriage. Among these girls anyone who put school work and a career first would be frowned on and subjected to ridicule.

The ideology of romance was also reinforced by boys. Girls who would have sex 'too readily' with different boys would be labelled as 'tarts' or 'whores' by boys and girls alike. Their marriage prospects would be damaged by their reputation. Without marriage the girls would have no standing in the community: there was no satisfactory place for single women in their working-class culture. One girl described the plight of her spinster aunt in these terms: 'Auntie Elsie, she's ever so nice but she never got married . . . I don't want to be like that.' Another girl expressed similar fears 'I worry a lot about not getting married. I mean, what if no one wanted me and I had to stay with me Mum and Dad?'

The girls were not entirely taken in by the ideology of romance. They realized from seeing their mothers and elder sisters that marriage might be less than perfect. They knew that romance might not last, and they were prepared to accept a less than blissful life with their husbands. 'Suzanne' said of her future husband, 'As long as he don't mind me having friends round while he's out I don't mind if he goes out every night.'

Despite their realism McRobbie found the girls were still fascinated with marriage, 'partly because of the status it would confer on them, and partly because it was the only possible means through which their sexuality could be expressed legitimately'. The girls were trapped both materially and ideologically: they would either move from one man's house to another's (from their father's house to their husband's), or they would end up being pitied like Auntie Elsie.

McRobbie's study provides an interesting analysis of the position and attitudes of some working-class girls. However, as McRobbie herself points out, it would not apply to the same extent to middle-class girls, whose options might be greater and horizons broader.

■ The experience and effects of marriage

Studies of married life suggest that the promise offered by the ideology of romance is rarely fulfilled in practice. This can be seen clearly from the day-to-day reality of the housewife role. Yet, Ann Oakley argues, it is still the primary role for married women in Britain and it takes precedence over other roles.

According to Oakley **housework** has the following characteristics.

1 It is exclusively allocated to women.

2 It is economically dependent on men.

3 It has the status of 'non-work' compared to 'real' or economically productive work.

4 It is unpaid, privatized and isolated.

The housewife works long hours – an average of 77 hours a week according to Oakley – and her work is accorded little prestige as reflected in the oft-heard statement, 'I'm only a housewife.' Housewives have little bargaining power compared to wage earners, for example they have no unions to represent their interests. They also lack many of the benefits available to wage earners. Glazer-Malbin and Waehrer state:

For while workers in the labour force receive such benefits as health insurance, pensions and paid

holidays and have access to retraining programs, the housewife receives benefits to a substantially lesser extent, if at all.

Housework is dull, tedious and unfulfilling. From a survey of forty housewives, Oakley concludes that they suffer from more monotony, social isolation and pressure of time than even assembly line workers, who are often seen as the most alienated workers in the labour force. The role of housewife is a dead-end job with no chance of promotion and little or no opportunity for job enrichment or personal development.

In a study of young working-class housewives with children, Dorothy Hobson argues that their isolation is a form of oppression. Many of these young wives miss working because of the lack of company they have as housewives. It is difficult for them to make friends; housework is repetitive and compulsive, an endless cycle of cleaning, washing up and tending to children. There is no physical or emotional separation of work and leisure. One woman found herself so bored by her life that she resorted to counting cars and talking to the cat to pass the time.

According to Hobson many women recognized their oppression but refused to challenge it. They came to accept their situation, despite being discontent. 'Anne', another woman in this study, said 'I'd love to go to work, you know, it's just a phase I go through for about five minutes and I forget it.'

Another view of marriage is provided by Mary Boulton's study of twenty-five middle-class and twenty-five working-class mothers in London. Many middle-class women thought that the demands of childcare involved a loss of their individuality, but it was only a minority who found childcare unfulfilling. Boulton stated 'Getting on for two-thirds of the women in this study experienced a strong sense of meaning, value, and significance in looking after their children.'

Women, men and marriage

Nevertheless other studies suggest that it is women who get the worse deal out of marriage. In *The Future of Marriage* (published in 1976) the American sociologist Jessie Bernard argues that any analysis of marriage must contain two parts: an examination of the husband's marriage and the wife's marriage. She maintains that the benefits each draws from the marriage are radically different.

Bernard examines a wide range of evidence dealing with the situation of married and unmarried men. It points overwhelmingly to the beneficial effects of marriage for men. Compared to single men, married men are more likely to have successful careers, high-income and high-status occupations; their mental and physical health is significantly better, and they are likely to live longer and happier lives. The evidence indicates that marriage itself produces these effects rather than suggesting that healthier, happier and successful men are more likely to get married. Bernard sums up the husband's marriage by claiming:

---

there is no greater guarantor of long life, health and happiness for men than a wife well socialized to perform the 'duties' of a wife , willing to devote her life to taking care of him, providing, even enforcing, the regularity and security of a well-ordered home.

The wife's marriage presents a very different picture. Survey after survey has shown that more wives than husbands express marital frustration and dissatisfaction, consider their marriages unhappy, and initiate divorce proceedings. Compared to their husbands, wives suffer considerably more stress, anxiety and depression.

A comparison of married women with unmarried women gives some indication of the gains and losses of the marriage transaction. Compared to single women, wives are more likely to suffer from depression, a range of neuroses and various other psychological problems. In terms of physical health, single women are significantly healthier than their married counterparts.

The most striking comparison is between unmarried men and unmarried women. A number of surveys reveal that compared to single women, single men are beset by various psychological maladies, and their level of earnings and job status are well below those of their female counterparts. Part, but not all of this difference is due to the **marriage gradient** which refers to the fact that men tend to marry below their status. Thus never-married women tend to be, in Bernard's words,

'the cream of the crop', never-married men, 'the bottom of the barrel'.

Finally, Bernard compares married men with unmarried women and finds few differences between them apart from the fact that 'women are spectacularly better off so far as psychological distress symptoms are concerned, suggesting that women start out with an initial advantage which marriage reverses'.

In terms of the gains and losses of marriage, it is difficult not to see the husband as the winner and the wife as the loser. Paradoxically, many if not most wives state that they are satisfied with and find fulfilment in marriage. Bernard argues that this is simply due to the fact that women have been socialized to believe that they ought to feel this way.

She singles out two main factors to account for the relative distress of the wife. They are the **Pygmalion effect** and the **housewife role**.

The Pygmalion effect is a phrase adopted from George Bernard Shaw's play *Pygmalion* (retitled *My Fair Lady* for the film version), which deals with the re-socializing of a working-class cockney girl into an upper-class lady. In terms of marriage, the Pygmalion effect refers to the wife's 'redefinition of the self and an active reshaping of the personality to conform to the wishes or needs of husbands'. Various studies have shown that, in marriage, the wife rather than the husband makes the adjustments, conforms to his wishes and increasingly comes to resemble him. To some degree she becomes his reflection and as such relatively passive, subordinate and helpless. Her self-image deteriorates as she accommodates to her husband rather than fulfilling herself as a person in her own right.

Bernard, however, does not think that it is marriage itself which is the main problem. According to her research it is primarily the housewife role that has harmful effects on women. She says 'In truth being a housewife makes women sick.' It is wives who do not work outside the home who suffer from the highest rates of physical and mental illness. Thus she believes that the 'housewife syndrome' can be viewed as 'Public Health Problem Number One'.

Women's liberation – proposals and prospects

From the 1960s onwards a vast literature in support of **women's liberation** has poured from the presses. Many suggestions have been made by feminist writers as to how women's position in society can be improved. There has, however, been no agreement about the ultimate aims of women's liberation, or how those aims are to be achieved.

David Bouchier distinguishes three objectives that have been advanced by feminists:

---

an integrated or egalitarian society where sex differences no longer count; an androgynous society where sex differences no longer exist; and a separatist society where men and women no longer share the same social world.

The first objective for an **egalitarian society** is generally supported by Marxist and socialist feminists. Liberal feminists also tend to have some sympathy with this aim, although they stop short of advocating a totally egalitarian society. Instead they support a society in which there is equality of opportunity. Many believe that since men and women have equal abilities this will lead to the gradual disappearance of significant inequalities between the sexes.

The second and third objectives for **androgyny** and **separatism** are generally supported by radical feminists. Shulamith Firestone expresses the strongest support for androgyny in her suggestion that babies should be conceived and developed outside the womb. Separatist feminists do not necessarily believe that women's liberation should lead to equality. Supremacists believe that women would be dominant in a future feminist paradise. Most feminists, however, do not regard a separatist society as either desirable or practicable.

We will now consider more specific proposals to improve the position of women in society.

The abolition of gender roles

Many feminist writers advocate the abolition of gender roles with the mother–housewife role being selected as the prime target. Ann Oakley argues

that the following steps must be taken to liberate women.

1 The housewife role must be abolished. Oakley rejects less radical solutions such as payment for housework, which, she argues, will simply reinforce the woman equals housewife equation.

2 The family as it now stands, must be abolished. This proposal follows from the first since the housewife and mother roles are part and parcel of the same thing. Abolishing the family will also serve to break the circle of the daughter learning her role from the mother, the son learning his role from the father.

3 The sexual division of labour must be eradicated in all areas of social life.

Oakley argues that 'We need an ideological revolution, a revolution in the ideology of gender roles current in our culture, a revolution in concepts of gender identity.' Thus, men and women must be seen as people, not as males and females.

Kate Millett, a radical feminist writer, argues that in a society without culturally defined gender roles, each individual will be free to 'develop an entire – rather than a partial, limited, and conformist – personality'. Thus females may develop so-called male traits, and vice versa. This would involve complete tolerance of homosexual and lesbian relationships, 'so that the sex act ceases to be arbitrarily polarized into male and female'. Thus, those who are biologically male and female may develop their personality and behaviour along lines best suited to themselves, rather than being cramped and confined by the culturally defined labels, male and female.

Modifications and alternatives to the family

The continuing debate on the role of women in society has produced a whole spectrum of modifications and alternatives to the housewife–mother role and the family. They range from Oakley's radical demands to abolish both, to more moderate suggestions which, in many cases, largely maintain the status quo with proposals to lighten the burdens of housework and motherhood. Ideas which fall into the latter category include payment for housework, the provision of crèches by employers, a free system of childcare provided as of right by the state for every mother who requires it, and maternity leave plus maternity benefits paid by employers or government, with the mother's job being held open should she wish to return to work.

Many radical feminists argue that such measures will not necessarily alter the position of women in the home. There, despite the fact that her burdens might be eased, she may still be relegated to the role of housewife and mother.

Shared roles

One of the simplest solutions to this problem has been put forward by Susan Brownmiller. She suggests that husband and wife should split their traditional roles down the middle. Each should work for half a day and spend the rest of the time taking care of the children. Jessie Bernard supports this idea, arguing that 'With one stroke, it alleviates one of the major responsibilities of men (sole responsibility for the provider role) and of women (exclusive responsibility for housework and child care).'

A variation of this shared role pattern was examined by R. and R. Rapoport in *Dual-Career Families*. They made a detailed study of five families in which each spouse followed his or her career. As things stand, this is not a viable alternative for most people because of the expense involved. The families studied by the Rapoports were fairly wealthy and all employed domestic help to perform many of the duties of the mother–housewife role.

Collective child-rearing

Systems of collective child-rearing provide an alternative to role sharing within the nuclear family. Suggestions range from re-creations of classic extended family networks to kibbutz-type collectives with specialized provision for child-rearing.

The Hungarian Marxist writers Vajda and Heller propose a **commune** or **collective family** which functions only as a family. All adults are responsible for the care of children within the commune. Relationships between adults can range from monogamy to promiscuity since 'the commune does not have value preferences concerning sexual relationships'. The **family commune** differs from the **kibbutz** since it deals only with domestic and childcare relationships and does not form a unit of production which involves the organization of occupational roles. However, the evidence of history shows that communes, especially those involving promiscuity, tend to be short-lived.

Other alternatives

A novel alternative to the present-day family is suggested by Alvin Toffler in *Future Shock*. He proposes a system of professional parents. These **pro-parents** would simulate family groups and adopt the roles of 'father', 'mother', 'uncle', 'aunt' and 'grandparent'. They would specialize in child-rearing as a paid occupation. This would end the amateur status of child-rearing and free many biological parents from their family roles: they would simply hand over their offspring to the professionals.

Many writers foresee a range of alternatives for the family's future. The socialist feminist Juliet Mitchell advocates various experiments in communal living to suit the personalities and circumstances of the individuals involved. She supports a 'range of institutions which match the free invention and variety of men and women'. Jessie Bernard takes a similar view. She looks forward to 'a future of marital options' hoping that 'people will be able to tailor their relationships to their circumstances and preferences'.

Two main themes dominate much of the writing on the future of the role of women in relation to the family. The first demands equality between the sexes; the second advocates freedom of choice with tolerance by all of the range of 'family life' that will emerge as a result.

■ Women and the labour market

Proposals to end discrimination against women in the labour market involve many of the suggested changes outlined above. Women must be freed from domestic burdens or share them equally with men if they are to compete for jobs on equal terms. An end to discrimination in the labour market would also involve the abolition of the sexual division of labour, the removal of distinctions between 'men's jobs' and 'women's jobs'.

The failure of women's entry into the labour market to end the sexual division of labour there has led some writers to suggest that women as a group must gain control over a significant part of the forces of production in order to remove discrimination. Juliet Mitchell argues on these lines when she states that 'Clearly then, their entry into the labour force is not enough: they must enter in their own right with their own independent economic interest.'

Many feminist writers reject **women's capitalism** as a goal in itself. They argue that it will simply result in equality of exploitation; most men and most women will be equally exploited. However, as Mitchell suggests, it could provide a power base from which to move towards socialism and equality for all people.

Raising consciousness and creating solidarity

D.H.J. Morgan has applied the Marxist concepts of ideology, class consciousness and class solidarity to the position of women in society. Just as the class system is justified and legitimated by ruling-class ideology, so the position of women is justified and legitimated by what may be termed **male ideology**. This ideology defines a woman's place, how she should act, think and feel as a woman, and so maintains her subordination and justifies her exploitation.

Just as ruling-class ideology creates false class consciousness, so male ideology produces what can be seen as **false gender consciousness**. From a Marxist perspective, class consciousness and class solidarity are essential before the subject class can overthrow its oppressors. In terms of the Marxist analogy, **gender consciousness** and **female solidarity** are necessary for women's liberation.

Arguably, it is in this area that the Women's Liberation Movement has had most success. Feminists of every variety agree that women must become aware of their exploitation by men before they will be willing or able to change their position in society. Without some degree of female

solidarity it seems unlikely that women will be able to achieve any of the aims of feminism. Most feminists also accept, though, that raising women's consciousness cannot on its own secure women's liberation. For this to occur either women will need to have greater power, or the ideology of **male supremacy** will have to be seriously challenged among men as well as among women.

The Women's Liberation Movement

Support for the **Women's Liberation Movement** is nothing new. As early as 1869 John Stuart Mill and Harriet Taylor said:

If the principle [of democracy] is true, we ought to act as if we believed it, and not to ordain that to be born a girl instead of a boy, any more than to be born black instead of white, or a commoner instead of a nobleman, shall decide the person's position throughout life.

In the early years of this century suffragettes mounted a campaign to secure the vote for women. As Sylvia Walby has pointed out, the 'first-wave' of feminism in the nineteenth and early twentieth centuries went well beyond a campaign for voting rights for women. There were also campaigns to make it easier for women to get divorced, for better education and training opportunities, and for married women to have the legal right to own property.

For most of this century feminists have been fighting for **civil rights**, that is legal equality for all adults regardless of sex. The battle for the legal emancipation of women has achieved some notable victories, for example the British Equal Pay and Sex Discrimination Acts. However, it was only in the 1960s that a women's movement with much broader aims emerged.

The USA

Juliet Mitchell argues that the Women's Liberation Movement in the USA was partly triggered by the radical movements of the middle and late 1960s. She points to the various civil rights organizations which campaigned for the rights of ethnic minority groups:

1 the Black Power Movement which spearheaded the demands of more militant blacks;

2 the Youth Movement represented by organizations such as Students for a Democratic Society;

3 the Peace Movement which coordinated protest against the war in Vietnam and later in Cambodia.

These movements preceded and paralleled the Women's Liberation Movement in the USA. They emphasized freedom, questioned established truths and attacked what they saw as oppression and exploitation.

Mitchell argues that such movements provided part of the impetus and philosophy for the Women's Liberation Movement. Women increasingly realized that they needed a movement of their own, since even as members of other radical movements, they were often treated in terms of their traditional stereotypes. For example when Stokely Carmichael, then leader of the SNCC (Student Nonviolent Coordinating Committee), a black civil rights organization of the mid-1960s, was asked about the role of women in the organization, he replied 'The only position for women in SNCC is prone.'

Barbara Deckard summarizes the results of women's participation in civil rights movements during the early and mid-1960s. She states:

Here many young women learned both the rhetoric and the organization of protest. Not surprisingly, as they become more sensitive to the blacks' second-class status, they became more aware of their own.

The result was the Women's Liberation Movement.

Britain and the USA compared

In Britain the Women's Liberation Movement was, according to David Bouchier, more influenced by the labour movement. In 1968 working-class women trades unionists went on strike at the Ford motor plant at Dagenham. This in turn prompted the union movement as a whole to take a more active interest in women's issues. The International Marxist Group was the first left-wing political organization to actively promote the Women's Liberation Movement. If in the USA radical oppression helped to stimulate the Women's Liberation Movement, in Britain class was more important. Women began to insist that their own disadvantages were at least as important as those suffered by the working class.

Because of these different origins the Women's Liberation Movement has tended to develop in different ways in Britain and the USA. In the USA the more moderate part of the movement has consisted of liberal feminists. The largest and most influential women's group in America is the liberal National Organization of Women with some 175,000 members. Alongside this liberal feminist tradition radical feminism has also had some support. It is significant that two of the USA's leading feminists (Kate Millett and Shulamith Firestone) are both radicals.

In Britain the Women's Liberation Movement has tended to be more socialist and Marxist in character, although there is some support for radical feminism. David Bouchier estimated that in 1983 that there were some 300 separate feminist organizations in Britain, but many feminists choose to work through existing left-wing political organizations. Many feminist groups are locally based: British feminists have been less successful than the Americans in creating their own independent national organizations.

There have, though, been attempts to develop organizations at a national level. Nickie Charles notes that between 1970 and 1978 the National Women's Coordinating Committee held national conferences for the women's movement. Between 1971 and 1978 the conference passed resolutions demanding seven rights for women.

In 1971 these were:

1 equal pay;
2 equal education and job opportunities;
3 abortion on demand and free contraception;
4 free nurseries 24 hours a day.

In 1975:

5 legal and financial independence for women;
6 the ending of discrimination against lesbians.

And in 1978:

7 freedom for women from the use or threat of physical or sexual violence by men.

The last issue caused a split in the national movement which resulted in the 1978 conference being the last. Radical feminists saw male violence as vital to understanding women's oppression whereas socialist feminists placed greater emphasis on economic factors.

However, the demise of the national movement did not prevent women's groups from making significant gains for women in Britain.

Nickie Charles suggests that one important feature of feminism in Britain has been the establishment of services run by women for the benefit of women. These have included refuges for women who have been the victims of domestic violence, women's advice centres and pregnancy testing services. Women have also had some success in running national campaigns over individual issues. For example, national campaigns have succeeded in persuading the Government to retain child allowances, and in protecting the facility for women to have abortions.

Despite the successes Charles believes that by the end of the 1970s the splits in the movement were beginning to weaken it. Radical, liberal and socialist feminists fought with each other to have their own analyses of and solutions to women's oppression accepted. There was also increasing recognition that women of different ages, classes and ethnic groups might have different interests. White, middle-class feminists had paid little attention to the way gender inequalities could be compounded by a 'racist and class-divided society', alienating many black and working-class women from the movement.

Charles believes that the Women's Liberation Movement in Britain has achieved some important reforms but has not succeeded in achieving a radical transformation for women. She argues that there has been 'restructuring' of the gender division of labour and:

> This restructuring has changed the distribution of women and men within the workforce and has made it more acceptable for men to be seen pushing prams and hanging out the washing; but it has not resulted in the elimination of women's subordination and it may have contributed to the fragmentation of the working class and the undermining of its resistance to capitalist exploitation.

Susan Faludi – Backlash

In her 1992 book – *Backlash: The Undeclared War Against Women* – Susan Faludi argues that the Women's Liberation Movement has run into increased opposition. Women have been told by

politicians, business leaders and advertisers, amongst others, that women have won the war for women's rights, and now enjoy equality with men. However, they are warned at the same time that the rights they have won have been at considerable cost. Faludi says:

> Behind this celebration of women's victory, behind the news cheerfully and endlessly repeated, that the struggle for women's rights is won, another message flashes. You may be free and equal now, it says to women, but you have never been more miserable.

In America, for example, magazines and newspapers have claimed that professional career women are prone to infertility and health problems such as alcoholism and hair loss, while women without children and women who do not get married are prone to depression or hysteria. Feminism is portrayed as the root cause of these problems.

Faludi denies that women have attained equality. For example, despite some newspaper reports that the pay differential between men and women was narrowing, in 1986 women working full-time still earned only 64 per cent of the male full-time worker's wage. The figures were exactly the same as they had been over three decades earlier in 1955. In Britain female workers had increased their earnings compared to men, but by 1991 female full-time workers still earned less than 80 per cent of male full-time workers.

Faludi is also critical of many of the claims about the supposedly harmful effects of women's liberation. She quotes numerous studies which have found that single women and women with careers tend to have more healthy and fulfilling lives than married housewives. Echoing the findings of Jessie Bernard's 1970s study (see pp. 633–4) Faludi found:

> The psychological indicators are numerous and they all point in the same direction. Married women in these studies report about 20 per cent more depression than single women and three times the rate of severe neurosis. Married women have more nervous breakdowns, nervousness, heart palpitations and inertia. Still other afflictions disproportionately plague married women: insomnia, trembling hands, dizzy spells, nightmares, hypochondria, passivity, agoraphobia and other phobias, unhappiness with

their physical appearance and overwhelming feelings of guilt and shame.

To Faludi then, the backlash is not a genuine attempt to improve the lives of women, but rather represents an attempt by men to reassert their dominance. However, Faludi is generally optimistic that this attempt will not succeed. She claims that there is 'no good reason, why the 1990s cannot be women's decade' and she concludes:

whatever new obstacles are mounted against the future march towards equality, whatever new myths invented, penalties levied, opportunities rescinded or degradations imposed, no one can ever take from women the justness of their cause.

Whether this optimism is justified remains to be seen.

■ Masculinity

In the earlier parts of this chapter we have seen that feminists have succeeded in putting the sociology of gender – and of women in particular – on the sociological map. Before 1970 few sociological studies were conducted about women and women's lives. Yet, paradoxically, some male sociologists have argued that men have also in some senses been 'invisible' in much sociology. While most studies have been conducted by men and the subjects of the research have been men, few have been about **masculinity**. Thus Jeff Hearn and David Morgan argue:

Studies which are routinely about men, in that men constitute the acknowledged or unacknowledged subjects, are not necessarily about men in a more complex, more problematized, sociological sense. They tend to be resource rather than topic. Studies of social mobility, for example, may be about men for methodological reasons or administrative convenience but they are rarely, if ever, about men in the sense that researchers believe that such studies might make any contribution to the sociology of gender or the critical understanding of men and masculinities.

Men are simply taken for granted in studies; they are assumed to be the norm and their behaviour is not explained in terms of gender or compared to that of women.

Similarly, Michael Kimmel argues that sociology 'was, in part, responsible for the reproduction of gender relations that kept masculinity invisible and rendered femininity problematic'. Women were seen as a deviation from the norm (men) and

their behaviour was therefore worthy of explanation in terms of their gender. Since the masculine gender was taken as the norm it did not need to be researched.

Kimmel argues that this situation could act in the interests of men. He says:

Men benefit from the inherited biological or sex-role definitions of masculinity, which imply activity, mastery, rationality, competence. If gender relations are encoded in our genes or culturally mandated, then the extent to which these definitions are based upon men's power over women is obscured.

It becomes unnecessary, for instance, to study how men use physical and sexual violence to control women or how men might help each other to exclude women from parts of society which they wish to reserve for themselves.

In this section we will examine some of the recent attempts that have been made to put right this 'neglect' of masculinity and to examine how masculinity shapes the lives of men and the social world in general.

■ David D. Gilmore – *Cultural Concepts of Masculinity*

Masculinity, sex and gender

In his 1990 book, *Manhood in the Making: Cultural Concepts of Masculinity*, the anthropologist

David D. Gilmore discusses the way masculinity is defined in a wide range of societies. Gilmore describes masculinity as 'the approved way of being an adult male in any given society' and his study is an attempt to discover the extent to which this varies from place to place. He uses both his own field data from ethnographic research and the findings of other anthropological studies. He includes examples from all continents and 'from warrior and pacifist societies, from egalitarian and stratified ones' and from 'hunting-gathering bands, horticultural and pastoral tribes, peasants and postindustrial civilizations'.

Gilmore does not see masculinity as a set of characteristics which are entirely determined by biology. He says that feminists 'have convincingly demonstrated that the conventional bipolar model based on biology is invalid and that sex (biological inheritance) and gender (cultural norms) are distinct categories'. He also says that 'the answer to the manhood puzzle must lie in culture' but nevertheless he does not believe that biology is unimportant. He claims that 'culture uses or exaggerates biological potential in specific ways'. Nearly always this involves making a very clear distinction between masculinity and femininity.

In the vast majority of societies masculinity is defined in fairly similar ways, suggesting that biological differences do play some part in influencing the cultural definitions which are adopted.

The typical features of masculinity

Gilmore suggests that there are three typical features of masculinity found in most societies. These are:

1 Man the impregnator. Men are expected to impregnate women. To do this they are normally required to take the initiative in courtship and sexual encounters. They are expected to compete with other men for access to women. For example in Sicily 'masculine honour is always bound up with aggression and potency. A real man in Sicily is "a man with big testicles".' In Italy it is particularly important that men are seen to be able to reproduce by making their wife pregnant.

Similarly in the Truk Islands in the South Pacific, 'the Trukese man must be the initiator, totally in command'. He must be 'potent, having many lovers, bringing his partners to orgasm time and again'. If he fails the woman laughs at him and the man is shamed.

Unlike the aggressive and war-like Trukese the Mehinaku Indians of the rain forests of central Brazil are a peaceful tribe and the men have never been warriors. Like the Trukese though, the men are very concerned about their manly image and sex is important in producing and maintaining that image. Gilmore says of Mehinaku men that 'a man who fails to bring his wife or lover to orgasm, fails to satisfy his partner, fails to beget children, is ridiculed and publicly shamed'. Knowledge of his failure soon spreads round the village and he can become an outcast. Not surprisingly then, the men have developed 'an elaborate system of magical therapy' to help men avoid this predicament.

2 Man the provider. Having impregnated women, in most societies men are then expected to protect them and their offspring.

According to Gilmore in the Mediterranean 'The emphasis on male honour as a domestic duty is widespread.' In the traditional Greek peasant village the honour of fathers rests upon their ability to provide their daughters with large dowries. In southern Italy the honour associated with being a good man partly rests upon a husband's ability to support his wife and children, while Spanish men pursue 'the breadwinning role as a measure of their manhood'.

Men of the Sambia in New Guinea have their manhood measured partly through their competence in hunting. Women are not allowed to hunt – it is an entirely male preserve. Although hunting produces only a small proportion of the food needed by the Sambia it has an important symbolic value. It provides the feathers and skins used in rituals. Men who fail in hunting are subject to ridicule and may have difficulty in finding a wife.

3 Man the protector. The third way in which most cultures define masculinity is in terms of men's role as protectors. Men must not simply impregnate women and provide for them and their children, they must also protect them from other men and any threats which might arise.

The Sikh Jats of the Punjab adhere strongly to the concept of *izzat* which is:

---

a philosophy of life which reflects their paramount concern for male power, in which 'a man's duty is to be stalwart in the defence of his family'. If anyone threatens a man's family he must, at the very least, threaten them back, and he must not be intimidated.

Gilmore says 'in this Sikh society, a man's first duty is to take risks in the service of his family'.

The Spanish in Andalusia use the concept of *hombria* to designate manliness. *Hombria* is 'physical and moral courage' in defending a man's own honour and that of his family. Men should always show courage and be stoical in the face of any threat.

In the East African Samburu tribe males have to demonstrate their bravery during *moranhood*. This starts at around the age of 14 or 15 and lasts about 12 years. The first test is a circumcision ritual which is performed without anaesthetic. The boy must not flinch, despite the pain as his foreskin is cut off, or 'he is forever shamed as a coward'. Later in *moranhood* the male proves himself by rustling cattle from other tribes. This runs the risk of being caught and beaten or even killed by the victims of the rustling. However, it confirms that the male has become manly, it makes him attractive to females, and shows that he will be able to take care of a family.

Masculinity and society

Gilmore argues that the roles of impregnator, protector and provider have some features in common. They are all dangerous or competitive and failure in any of the roles carries high costs. 'They place men at risk on the battlefield, in the hunt, or in confrontation with their fellows.' Men are expected to overcome the fear felt by all humans when they are placed at risk.

Gilmore suggests that this feature of masculinity may have benefits for society. Men are persuaded to do things which are necessary for society's survival which they would not otherwise do because of their desire for self-preservation. He says:

---

we may regard 'real manhood' as an inducement for high performance in the social struggle for scarce resources, a code of conduct that advances collective interests by overcoming inner inhibitions.

In putting forward these claims Gilmore uses a functionalist approach. He explains the existence of ideals of masculinity in terms of the functions they perform for society. However, Gilmore is critical of some aspects of functionalism. He does not see the type of masculinity described above as an inevitable feature of all societies. Rather, it is one of a number of **strategies of adaptation** which can reconcile 'individual and social needs' through

rewards and punishments. The societies described above all reward masculine men with high status and punish unmasculine men through ridicule and other negative sanctions, and in doing so persuade men to take physical and psychological risks they might otherwise avoid.

In a few societies though, masculinity has a very different meaning. Societies can work with a wide variety of definitions of masculinity.

Men in Tahiti and Semai

Tahiti, one of the Society Islands in Polynesia, have a much less marked differentiation between masculinity and femininity than most societies. Furthermore, the Tahitian concept of masculinity does not require men to act as providers and protectors. There is little need for men to take physical risks since there is no warfare, and there are few dangerous occupations. The lagoon offers a plentiful supply of fish so risky deep-sea fishing is not necessary. Families cooperate together in economic activities and there is no social pressure to be economically successful. Indeed traditional Tahitian culture encourages a 'laconic attitude towards work'. It also encourages men to be timid and passive. They are expected to ignore insults and they very rarely fight one another.

Tahitian men are neither protective of their women nor possessive towards them. When an English ship, the *Dolphin*, arrived at Tahiti in 1767 the ship's captain reported that the Tahitian women 'came down and stripped themselves naked and made all the alluring gestures they could to entice them onshore' (quoted in Gilmore 1990, pp. 204–5). The Tahitian men actually encouraged the women to do this and a later French explorer found that Tahitian men were extremely hospitable and even offered him their daughters.

The Semai people live in central Malaysia. Both men and women are strongly opposed to violence and aggression. Aggression is denoted by the word *punan* which also means taboo. The Semai try to avoid doing anything that frustrates another person and goes against their wishes. As a consequence both men and women are usually expected to agree to a request for sex, even if they are married and the person requesting sex is not their spouse. However, it is also considered *punan* if a person repeatedly pesters another person for sex. There is very little jealousy and Semai men and women tolerate the extra-marital affairs of their spouses as being no more than a loan.

The Semai do not engage in competitive sport and are not materialistic. Men do not have to compete with each other because farming is cooperative and if one man has too little land to get by, he simply asks another man for some of his. It is *punan* to refuse. Although the Semai do hunt, and hunting is reserved exclusively for males, the hunting is not dangerous or difficult. They hunt nothing larger or more dangerous than small pigs, they stop hunting before noon when it gets too hot, and 'If they encounter danger, they run away and hide without any shame or hesitation.'

There are some differences between men and women in both Tahitian and Semai society (although amongst the Semai they are not particularly pronounced), neither has a cultural image of 'the real man'. Gilmore suggests that the unusual characteristics of masculinity in these societies may result from the material circumstances in which the societies exist

Animals confronted with danger produce adrenalin which makes them more able to flee or to stay and fight the source of the danger. In humans the choice between fight or flight is shaped by cultural conditioning. Most cultures seem to have put more emphasis on men fighting than fleeing but the Tahitians and Semai are exceptions. This may be due to the plentiful supply of food and other resources in both societies and the lack of 'serious hazards' in their environments such as dangerous animals or aggressive neighbours .

Gilmore admits that it is impossible to show conclusively that the **ideology of passivity** was caused by the **material context**. It could be that the culture creates the situation where the people have little material ambition and are content with what they have. Therefore they have no need to be competitive. He suggests that there might be a 'feedback relationship in which the ideology, once formed, assists in and intensifies a matching adaptation to the environment'.

Whatever the factors giving rise to these cultures, it is clear that the ideology of 'Man-the-Impregnator-Protector-Provider' is not universal.

Evaluation

Gilmore's work can be criticized for using functionalist analysis, which has been the subject of

very strong criticism. Many feminists could criticize Gilmore for his apparent claims that men usually protect and provide for women. As we have seen in earlier sections of this chapter, it is often women who work harder than men and far from protecting their wives some men abuse and attack them. However, Gilmore's work does succeed in showing that culture has a very strong influence on ideologies of masculinity and that masculinity can therefore assume very different forms.

■ Victor J. Seidler – rationality and masculinity

Although Gilmore does use some examples from technologically advanced industrial or post-industrial societies he relies mainly on examples from more traditional agricultural societies. Victor J. Seidler concentrates instead on men in Western societies.

The Enlightenment

According to Seidler ideas of masculinity in Western societies are closely connected with the thinking and beliefs associated with the Enlightenment. **The Enlightenment** is the name given to a range of interconnected philosophical, scientific and social beliefs which developed in Western Europe in the seventeenth and eighteenth centuries. Enlightenment thinking rejected emotion, superstition and belief in the supernatural as ways of understanding the world. It argued that the natural world could only be understood through objective, detached, unemotional science. Knowledge could only come from reason and rationality. Reason was contrasted with nature. As Seidler puts it 'Nature is real but is bereft of consciousness and of value. It exists as separate and independent of the consciousness that is attempting to grasp it.' To understand the physical world humans had to detach themselves from it.

To Seidler and many other writers Enlightenment thinking is the foundation of modernity. **Modernity** is a phase in human history in which it is believed that humans can use scientific knowledge to ensure progress. Science allows nature to be conquered and controlled for the benefit of people. (We discuss these ideas in more detail on pp. 907–8.)

Masculinity, femininity and modernity

In modernity science came to be associated with masculinity. For example the sixteenth–seventeenth-century British philosopher Francis Bacon talked 'quite unashamedly about the new sciences as a masculinist philosophy'. In *The Protestant Ethic and the Spirit of Capitalism* Max Weber described how the rational pursuit of profit encouraged by certain forms of protestantism helped to produce the rationalization of the modern world (see pp. 459–62 for a discussion of Weber). However, not all humans were seen as capable of understanding and controlling nature through reason. That privilege was reserved for men.

Women were seen as being closer to nature than men. As such they were regarded as being more emotional, less able to be detached, impersonal and rational. Emotions were valued less than reason. Seidler says 'Emotions and feelings cannot be legitimated as sources of knowledge; rather, they reflect an interference or breakdown in the cool and autonomous logic of pure reason.' Men fear the consequences of being emotional. Emotions have no place, particularly in public arenas such as work, and so men suppress them. Seidler says 'It is as if we do not have emotional needs of our own as men, for needs are a sign of weakness.'

Seidler sees the association of men with reason and rationality, and of women with nature and emotion as harmful and destructive. It damages personal relationships, making it difficult for men to build strong relationships with women. He says:

self-sufficiency can make it difficult in relationships, for it creates its own forms of inequality as women are often left feeling that they alone have emotional needs and demands.

The association of men with reason contributes to the creation and maintenance of male, patriarchal power at every level. Men are liable to tell their female partners in arguments that they are being irrational and emotional and to refuse to discuss matters further until the woman 'calms down'. Indeed, Seidler believes that men have become so accustomed to expecting to be in control of nature and their own emotions, that they scarcely notice that they have power over women. Men are

'constantly talking for others, while presenting themselves as the neutral voice of reason'.

Evaluation

Seidler's argument provides some interesting insights into the nature of masculinity in Western societies. However, it is somewhat abstract and is not based upon detailed empirical evidence. He admits that it may not be possible to generalize his claims about masculinity saying 'I am talking from a particular experience of white, middle-class Jewish masculinity.' He also admits that it is not possible to identify one dominant form of masculinity in Western society.

Feminism and an increasing distrust of science have both contributed to the creation of a wider variety of masculinities in contemporary Western societies. We will examine some of these in the next section.

■ Jonathan Rutherford – 'Who's that man?'

Threats to traditional masculinity

Like Seidler, Rutherford links masculinity to ideas about reason. He says 'A history of masculinity is a struggle to tame and subdue the emotional and sexual self and to recognise the ascendant and superior nature of reason and thought.' However, Rutherford believes that traditional conceptions of masculinity are under increasing threat. Men's definitions of themselves and of masculinity have begun to change. They have become more ambiguous, uncertain and varied.

Rutherford believes that 'The reality of men's heterosexual identities is that their endurance is contingent upon an array of structures and institutions.' If these structures are threatened or weakened then masculine identities can be threatened or weakened. A number of changes have undermined male dominance of certain structures and institutions.

1 Working-class masculinities have been threatened by the decline of manual heavy industry. Throughout the

class structure male unemployment has risen while female employment, particularly in part-time jobs, has increased.

2 In the domestic sphere violent and sexual abuse of women and children by men has become better publicized.

3 The value of men's roles within the family have been questioned. Divorce laws 'far from being the Casanova's charter predicted by the popular press have been predominantly used by women leaving their husbands'.

4 The women's movement has brought masculinity into question. It has exposed patriarchal power and portrayed men as self-interested abusers of that power rather than as the heroic conquerors of nature.

5 Furthermore 'radical gay politics and black politics have produced new definitions of the world that are not attributed to the grand narrative of White Man.'

According to Rutherford, modern, white heterosexual men have long feared women, homosexuals and black men for the threats they can pose to their masculinity. The 'huge penis of the black man, the devouring female and the plague-like seduction of the homosexual' have in heterosexual white men's minds had the potential for challenging their masculine sexuality, their independence and their cool reason and calm rationality. As accounts of masculinity from the viewpoint of women, gay men and black men have gained in prominence, white heterosexual men have been forced to examine what masculinity means to them, and in some cases to change their beliefs.

Retributive man and new man

Rutherford recognizes that there have been numerous different responses to the changes outlined above. He says 'The marketplace has produced a plurality of masculine identities; different models of fatherhood, sexualised images of men and new sensibilities.' However, he argues that, at its simplest, the responses can be divided into two groups: those of 'retributive men' and those of 'new men'.

Retributive men try to reassert traditional images of masculinity. They attack those who would challenge their long-established and strongly held view of what it means to be a real man. They have the 'notion of traitors: cowardly

men who have abrogated their right to masculinity, and consequently to citizenship'.

The archetypal retributive man in contemporary popular culture is Rambo in films like *First Blood*. Rambo 'confronts a world gone soft, pacified by traitors and cowards, dishonourable feminised men'. Retributive man in the form of Rambo responds with violence, trying to destroy all that threatens his concept of masculine honour.

However, retributive man is less problematic on screen than in real life. Rutherford suggests that the image of retributive man is undermined by the example of people such as Michael Ryan who try to mirror screen images in their own behaviour. Ryan went on the rampage in Hungerford in England, indiscriminately shooting passers-by with his arsenal of firearms before shooting himself. The popular press portrayed Ryan in a less than flattering way as 'a lonely inadequate who employed a fantasy world to shore up his fragile masculinity'.

The alternative to the retributive man is the new man. The **new man:**

is an expression of the repressed body of masculinity. It is a fraught and uneven attempt to express masculine emotional and sexual life. It is a response to the structural changes of the past decade and specifically to the assertiveness and feminism of women.

For example, new men are liable to take fatherhood more seriously than traditional men. In films like *Kramer versus Kramer* (which is about the life of a lone father) men are portrayed as struggling with their new roles and trying to come to terms with having to acknowledge their own emotions. Mothercare have started featuring fathers in the photographs in their catalogues and there is a 'new liberalised image of men pushing buggies, attending births and cuddling babies in public without fear of shame and ridicule'.

Men's bodies have increasingly featured in adverts such as the advert for Levis 501s where a man undresses in a launderette. In such contexts men have now become sex objects in a way that was once the sole prerogative of women. Rutherford argues:

For men to put their bodies on display contradicts the code of who looks and who is looked at. It pacifies us. Men have held the power of the look, the symbolic owning of women's bodies. Reversing the gaze offers the symbol of men's bodies on offer to women.

The future of masculinity

Having described new men, Rutherford admits that they may be, at least partly, a media myth. He notes that research suggests that the division of labour between men and women in the home has not significantly changed. Women are still disadvantaged in the labour market to the extent that few families can afford to rely upon the wages of the woman while the man adopts the role of 'househusband'. Furthermore the 'men's movement' has scarcely developed. In the 1970s there was some attempt to establish such a movement. Rutherford says:

Its main form was the consciousness raising 'men's group', where men could explore areas of our lives such as sexuality and relationships, that had previously been taboo subjects in male company.

However most of the groups did not last long.

Most men have been left somewhat confused about what it means to be masculine. They can either try to defend the past by being retributive man, or embrace the future as new man. To Rutherford the choice is between 'change or violence'. He comes down firmly in favour of the former, arguing that men should 'learn to live our differences without resort to oppression'.

Evaluation

Rutherford's work is rather journalistic and relies on anecdotal rather than systematic evidence. However, it does illustrate that the concept of masculinity has become increasingly complex. It raises interesting questions about how masculinity is changing, questions which will no doubt be the subject of an increasing amount of research as this area of sociology develops.

■ Sociology, values and gender

Defining a situation as a problem involves a value judgement: it means that things are not as they ought to be. A large body of research in sociology has been directed by value judgements which state that particular social arrangements and circumstances are morally wrong. For example, alienating work, poverty and ruling elites are immoral. Such judgements draw attention to a subject, define it as worthy of study, commit sociologists to their research topic and give them the feeling that the questions they ask are of vital importance to the well-being of humanity.

Traditionally, men have defined problems in sociology. They have defined them in terms of male concerns and on the basis of male prejudice. As a result, sociology has, in many respects, been the sociology of men. For example, standard textbooks on the sociology of work have scarcely mentioned women. They could, with some justification, be retitled as 'the sociology of men's work'.

No sociologist wants to study something he or she considers insignificant. Given the prevailing definition of women in Western society and the fact that most sociologists used to be men, it was not surprising that there were so few serious studies of women before the 1970s. It took a woman, Ann Oakley, to produce the first detailed study of housework. In terms of cultural definitions of housework as relatively unimportant work – as somehow not 'real work' – it is not surprising that male sociologists avoided this area of research. In practice, the sociology of women has been largely an adjunct to the sociology of the family. Again this is not surprising given the traditional view that a woman's place is in the home. Sociologists study what they consider important. From the viewpoint of a male-dominated culture, women are not very important.

Two factors have been primarily responsible for the development of the sociology of women.

1 First, the definition of women's position in society as a social problem.

2 Second, the reassessment of women as people who are just as important as men.

In many areas of sociology, a subject and its treatment is influenced more by what happens in society than by developments within the discipline itself. In the case of women, changes in society, and in particular the Women's Liberation Movement, have led to the emergence of the sociology of gender as a subject area in its own right.

The sociology of gender has largely been developed by women, by feminists such as Shulamith Firestone and Kate Millett, and by female sociologists like Ann Oakley. They have opened up the discipline of sociology so that it no longer ignores half the human race. They and others like them were largely responsible for resurrecting Engels's writings on women. They have produced the most original and stimulating ideas in the area.

Beginning with different values, priorities and concerns, women often ask different questions from men. For example, when male sociologists talk about marriage and the family, they do so from a male viewpoint. The limitations of this approach are clearly revealed by Jessie Bernard's study of the 'wife's marriage'. But it is not simply a case of asking different questions. Male and female researchers often produce very different answers to the same questions.

Many early feminist writers argued that the views of male sociologists on the position of women in society were largely rationalizations and justifications for male dominance. The feminist critique of a sociology based on male ideology can be summarized as follows. Operating from a commitment to male dominance, male sociologists assume that the subordinate position of women is beneficial for society. However, the phrase 'beneficial for society' should read 'beneficial for men'. Male sociologists start from the value judgement that what's good for men is good for society.

Ann Oakley gave a number of examples of the intrusion of male ideology into scientific analysis.

1 Particularly in America, the 'mighty-hunter myth' was a part of the mythology of male dominance. This was simply translated by Tiger and Fox into the jargon of the male biogrammar. Thus a 'scientific myth' was created to justify male dominance.

2 George Peter Murdock, a Western male, looked at the role of women in non-Western societies in terms of the values of a male-dominated culture. He selected and interpreted the evidence in terms of his prejudices and found that the sexual division of labour was universal. His conclusions suggested that changes in the traditional roles of women would be dysfunctional for society.

3 Talcott Parsons, a product of American culture, argued that the 'expressive' female role is essential for the performance of the two 'irreducible functions' of the family. In Oakley's view this was simply a justification for the status quo. It relegated women to domestic roles and legitimized male dominance.

Feminist sociologists have succeeded in demolishing arguments such as those of Tiger and Fox, Murdock and Parsons. In doing so they have gone some way towards redressing the bias in mainstream (or as some feminists call it malestream) sociology. Yet, like their male counterparts feminist sociologists have not been able to prevent their own values from entering their work. Indeed feminists of different types have sometimes accused the work of their sisters as being value-laden. Liberal feminists have been accused of being over-optimistic and of ignoring the deep, structural causes of women's oppression; Marxist feminists have been accused of neglecting patriarchy, and radical feminists of neglecting the economic causes of gender inequality. Black feminists have accused all other feminists as having a white, middle-class bias and of ignoring the position of black women in society. In addition some feminists can be accused of making sweeping generalizations about the behaviour of men. In particular some radical feminists imply that all men oppress all women all the time.

However much the values of feminist sociologists have influenced their work, they have certainly succeeded in opening up the study of a previously neglected area of research, the sociology of gender. In doing so they have even persuaded some men to critically examine masculinity, rather than treating the behaviour of men as normal, natural and beneficial to society.

11

'Race', ethnicity and nationality

'Race', ethnicity and nationality

▊ Introduction

Racism and conflict between ethnic and national groups have long been a feature of human societies. We can illustrate this with a mumber of examples.

In 1601 Queen Elizabeth I issued a proclamation saying that 'Negroes and blackamoors' should be deported from England because they were 'infidels' and they were contributing to economic and social problems such as poverty and famine.

According to the historian Philip D. Curtin, in the eighteenth century some 9.5 million Africans were transported across the Atlantic to become slaves in North and South America and the Caribbean. John Taylor, a writer and traveller, described the black slaves in Jamaica as 'these ignorant pore souls' who differed 'from bruite beast, only by their shape and speech'. In 1884, long after the abolition of slavery, the *Encyclopaedia Britannica* continued to express similar views. It claimed that the African Negro occupied the lowest position in the evolutionary scale and this was supposedly demonstrated by abnormally long arms and a lightweight brain.

Another group who were widely seen as inferior in nineteenth-century Britain were the Irish. Frederick Engels, Karl Marx's friend and collaborator, described the Irish in *The Condition of the Working Class in England*. Writing in 1844–5 he said:

The southern facile character of the Irishman, his crudity, which places him but little above the savage, his contempt for all human enjoyments, in which his very crudeness makes him incapable of sharing, his filth and poverty, all favour drunkenness.

Over half a century later in 1901 the London writer Joseph Bannister was no less critical of a different group of people in his book *England Under the Jews*. He described Jews as 'Yiddish money pigs' who were unwilling to take baths and so were particularly prone to skin and blood diseases. Bannister believed that Britain was becoming dominated by Jews and in a private letter to a Jew he said 'It is a pity that some kind of vermin exterminator could not be invented by which your vile breed could be eliminated.'

Anti-Semitic feeling (hostile feelings towards the Jewish people) went beyond mere words in Hitler's Nazi Germany. In *Mein Kampf* (completed in 1927) Hitler outlined his view that the true Germans were a racial group called the Aryans. The Aryan race had been corrupted by contact with inferior races such as the Slavs and Jews, but Hitler aimed to put this right by creating an Aryan 'master race'. In 1935 the Nuremberg Laws withdrew the civil rights of Jews and forbade mixed marriages between Jews and Aryans. The 'Final Solution' to the Jewish 'problem' involved gassing millions of Jews (along with gypsies, homosexuals, and others) in concentration camps such as Auschwitz, Belsen and Dachau.

After the end of communist rule in Yugoslavia civil war broke out in the 1990s between the Muslims, the Croatians and the Serbs. In parts of Bosnia whole ethnic groups were driven out of an area so that it might be claimed by another group. This process became known as '**ethnic cleansing**'. Many thousands died as the Bosnian Serbs tried to seize territory from the Muslims and besieged towns and cities such as Gorazde, Srebrenica, and Sarajevo.

As the former Yugoslavia shows, examples of conflict and inequality between racial, ethnic or national groups are by no means confined to history. In Northern Ireland there is conflict between Catholics and Protestants, in Sri Lanka between Tamils and the Sinhalese, and in South Africa, despite the end of **apartheid** (a policy of racial segregation), conflict has continued between some Afrikaners, the Zulus and followers of the African National Congress. In Spain some Basques seek an independent state and in East Timor guerrilla leaders strive to regain independence from their Indonesian invaders. In Britain racially motivated attacks against British Asians and Afro-Caribbeans continue, and in Germany Turkish migrant workers are similarly victimized.

In Britain, France and other European countries extreme right-wing parties such as the British National Party, the National Front and Le Pen's Front National, which oppose immigration and blame problems on ethnic minorities, continue to attract support. In the USA evidence suggests that many years after the enactment of civil rights legislation American blacks and Hispanics are still seriously disadvantaged in areas such as employment and education.

In this chapter we will examine some of the reasons why conflict and inequality between racial, ethnic and national groups continues to occur. We start by considering the view that there is a biological basis for distinguishing '**races**' and explaining the conflicts and inequalities between them.

■ 'Race'

Biological theories of 'race' attempt to establish a relationship between **phenotype**, or physical characteristics such as hair and skin colour, and **genotype**, or the underlying genetic differences between groups of humans. As science has developed, the dominant thinking about this relationship has changed.

■ Michael Banton – theories of 'race'

Michael Banton has described the various attempts that have been made to divide human beings into different biological or racial groups. He distinguishes three main types of theory:

1 those which see 'race' as lineage;
2 those which see it as type;
3 and those which see it as subspecies.

Race as lineage

According to Banton the word 'race' was not used in English until 1508 when it appeared in a poem by the Scotsman William Dunbar. At that time 'the Bible was accepted as the authority on human affairs' and ideas on racial difference were therefore based on biblical teaching. This meant that it was generally accepted that all humans were ultimately descended from Adam and Eve. The idea of 'race' as lineage adopted a **monogenesist view**: humans belonged to a single species and had a common origin.

However, it was believed that there were different groups of humans who had become differentiated at some point in the past. Biblical events such as the Flood and the fall of the Tower of Babel had contributed to humans becoming dispersed around the globe. This had resulted in distinctive **lineages** or lines of descent which corresponded to differences in physical appearance and geographical origin between human groups. People had become different as the result of migration to different environments, but ultimately because 'God had guided the course of events.'

In some respects the idea of 'race' as lineage implied that all humans were basically equal, and, according to Banton this influenced ideas on slavery. Slave owners had 'mistrust and ethnocentric contempt' for their slaves but this did not stem 'from assumptions about racial superiority'. There was agreement among supporters and opponents of slavery alike that 'the Negro was no more amenable to the regimentation of slavery than any other man'. Nevertheless, the idea of 'race' as lineage did produce views which suggested the 'races' were unequal in some ways.

Some claimed that God had made people different in order to make them suited to particular areas of the earth. For example, many thought that only Africans could work effectively in the extreme heat of the tropics. Banton argues that 'The message was that each people was adapted to its own environment and therefore should stay where they were.'

In the seventeenth and eighteenth centuries British and American writers rarely used the word 'race' when writing about human groups, however a few were beginning to do so and were starting to suggest that certain 'races' were superior to others. In 1748 the English philosopher David Hume said that 'Negroes' were the only 'race' which had never developed a major civilization and this indicated that they were 'naturally inferior to the Whites'.

Such views were to become much more common in the nineteenth century as a new approach to classifying groups of humans gained in popularity.

'Race' as type

The idea of 'race' as **type** is based upon a belief that all humans do not share a common origin and that humanity is divided into distinctive groups. It is therefore a **polygenetic theory**, that is a theory that humanity has several origins rather than one.

Some versions of this theory suggested that humans from different 'races' could not interbreed and produce fertile children. Banton says 'It assumed that racial differences had existed from some very early period of prehistory when different stocks had been created either by God or by some natural catastrophe.' The idea of 'race' as type gained in popularity as people of European origin came into closer contact with other groups. Banton argues:

As the evidence about the diversity of human forms accumulated, more and more writers tended to refer to various kinds of type, and, indeed the construction of typologies of various kinds became a characteristic of nineteenth-century scholarship.

This new approach to 'race' developed in different countries at around the same time but some of the most influential views originated in America.

The Philadelphian doctor Samuel James Morton based his arguments upon the measurement of skull sizes. In 1839 Morton distinguished five 'races':

1 **Caucasian** (from Europe, India and parts of North Africa and the Middle East);

2 **Mongolian** (Chinese and Eskimos);

3 **Malay** (from Malaysia and the Polynesian Islands);

4 **American** (native Americans from North and South America);

5 **Ethiopian** (from sub-Saharan Africa).

From his measurements Morton claimed that 'Caucasians' had the largest cranial capacity and 'Ethiopians' the smallest. Morton equated cranial capacity with the size of the brain, and the size of the brain with intellectual development. He believed therefore that Europeans were more advanced than Sub-Saharan Africans.

Morton's ideas were developed further by J.C. Nott and G.R. Gliddon in their book *Types of Mankind* published in Philadelphia in 1854. Nott and Gliddon believed that there were distinctive groups of humans of a relatively permanent kind. These separate types gave rise to differences in behaviour between groups of humans. Furthermore, different types of human were naturally antagonistic to one another. According to Nott and Gliddon, prior to any biblical writings the Ancient Egyptians had already classified humans into four types. They also claimed that 'certain Types have existed (the same as now) in and around the valley of the Nile, from ages anterior to 3500 years BC.'. 'Types', or as Nott and Gliddon also called them 'races', were 'separated in physical organization' and those which were most different such as 'Blacks and Whites' did 'not amalgamate perfectly'.

Nott and Gliddon clearly believed in the superiority of white races. They claimed that Caucasians (who are supposed to originate from the Caucasus mountains) 'have in all ages been the rulers' and they had shown themselves to be the only humans capable of developing democracy. On the other hand dark-skinned 'races' were 'only fit for military governments'.

Nott and Gliddon's work was typical of that of many other writers in asserting that there were distinct biologically different 'races'; these races behaved in different ways: some races had remained 'pure' and untainted by interbreeding; and some of them were superior to others.

Banton comments that Nott and Gliddon's notions of racial purity and of racial inferiority and superiority were close to the racial thought of the Nazis.

An even bigger influence on Nazi thinking was the French writer Arthur de Gobineau. Writing in the 1850s he claimed that there was a distinctive Aryan race which migrated from a homeland in the East and which was superior to all other races. According to Gobineau, the Aryans had then spread out and were responsible for establishing most of the world's major civilizations. These included the civilizations of Egypt, Rome, China, Greece, Assyria and even Mexico and Peru.

'Race' as subspecies

The idea of 'race' as **subspecies** combines elements of the idea of 'race' as lineage and the idea of 'race' as type. The origins of this conception of 'race' are to be found in the work of the British biologist Charles Darwin and his **theory of evolution**.

According to Banton, Darwin saw a species as 'a class which was distinctive because its members inherited common characters but inherited them in different combinations which were subject to continual modification'. Members of the same species can breed with one another and produce fertile offspring. However, because species are constantly changing and evolving it is possible for different branches, subgroups or subspecies to develop. Where groups within a species become geographically separated and breed only within that group, they can develop their own distinctive characteristics.

Darwin observed in the Galapagos Islands that certain types of bird and turtle varied slightly from island to island: they were developing distinctive subspecies by breeding only with animals from the same island. When subspecies evolved in different ways they could eventually become so distinctive that the offspring of animals from different subspecies were infertile.

Darwin saw **evolution** as a slow process resulting from **natural selection**. Those members of a species which were best adapted to their environment were most likely to breed and therefore to pass on their genetic characteristics to future generations. There was also an element of **sexual selection** involved. Females would tend to select the most attractive males of their species with which to breed. Gradually the characteristics which made members of a species or subspecies more likely to breed and produce offspring became increasingly typical of the group as a whole.

Different human 'races' could develop in the same way as different subspecies of animal. Natural selection, sexual selection and chance variations in genes could result in distinct human groups with different physical appearances. Thus, although all humans had a common origin they could evolve to form different races.

■ Herbert Spencer – human subspecies and social evolution

The idea of 'race' as subspecies became increasingly popular in the latter part of the nineteenth century. The English functionalist sociologist Herbert Spencer developed his ideas about **social**

evolution at the same time as Darwin was developing his ideas about biological evolution. In applying evolutionary ideas to the study of society Spencer developed influential ideas about the relationship between 'race' and human social development.

The mixture of races

Spencer believed that societies could sometimes benefit from the mixing of races. He said 'Sundry instances point to the conclusion that a society formed from nearly-allied peoples of which the conquering eventually mingles with the conquered, is relatively well fitted for progress.' The fusion of different characteristics can make the society adaptable and able to make the most of the best characteristics of the various races of which its population is made up. Spencer gives the example of the Hebrews who:

---

not withstanding their boasted purity of blood, resulted from a mixing of many Semitic varieties in the country east of the Nile and who, both in their wanderings and after the conquest of Palestine, went on amalgamating kindred tribes.

The Romans, he claimed, gained strength from amalgamating with 'other Aryan tribes, Sabini, Sabelli and Samnites'. England too had benefited by the interbreeding of closely related groups including 'different divisions of the Aryan race' and 'varieties of Scandinavians'.

However, the outcome was rather different when societies were composed of mixed races which were less closely related. Following the principles of 'race' as subspecies, Spencer commented:

If instead of different species, remote varieties are united, the intermediate organism is not infertile; but many facts suggest the conclusion that infertility results in subsequent generations: the incongruous workings of the united structures, though longer in showing itself, comes out ultimately.

According to Spencer, the dangers of mixing very different human subspecies were not just biological: the societies which resulted were likely to be highly unstable. Mexico and other South American Republics were examples. Spain had an incongruous mixture of 'Basques, Celtic, Gothic, Moorish (and) Jewish' groups. Such societies required strong central government to keep the diverse 'racial groups from engaging in conflict with one another' and Spencer believed that too much government regulation hindered social evolution.

The evolutionary scale

According to Spencer then, societies could consist of one race, but often consisted of a mixture of several. The precise mixture helped determine whether or not a society became more evolved and civilized. Spencer developed a complex scheme for categorizing societies based on whether they had a complex or simple structure, and whether they were stable or unstable.

1 A **simple society** was 'a single working whole' which was not divided into different sections, groups or tribes.

2 A **compound society** is one where 'the simple groups have their respective chiefs under a supreme chief'.

3 **Doubly compound societies** were more complex still with a number of compound societies united under a single government.

Table 11.1 shows Spencer's classification system (though it omits **trebly compound societies** which Spencer discussed separately).

Spencer left the reader in no doubt that simple societies were less developed and therefore inferior to more complex ones. He described them as 'uncivilized' and referred to some as 'savage tribes'. More complex societies had evolved further, were more civilized and better adapted to their environment.

The degree to which different societies had evolved was, in Spencer's eyes, influenced by race. Weaker tribes tended to be conquered by stronger ones in a struggle for survival. Among **aboriginal tribes**, the lowest groups on his evolutionary scale, the combinations resulting from conquest constantly broke up. Among '**superior races**' complex societies were more stable. As a consequence they could evolve further. The most complex and therefore the most evolved societies of all were **trebly compound**. These were 'Ancient Mexico, the

Assyrian Empire, The Egyptian Empire, the Roman Empire, Great Britain, France, Germany, Italy, Russia'.

To Spencer social life and the evolutionary process involved the 'survival of the fittest'. Those individuals, groups and species which were not well adapted to their environment would die out. The historian Christopher Bolt notes that a number of nineteenth-century writers tried to justify the decline in numbers of native populations of New Zealand and the Americas. They argued that they were not well adapted and so could not survive. Bolt comments:

> With a large degree of wishful thinking, some Victorians maintained that if the survival-of-the-fittest principle operated as it should, the Negro population of North America and the West Indies might soon follow these tribes towards extinction.

The limitations of nineteenth-century ideas on 'race'

Although more sophisticated than theories of 'race' as type, the idea of 'race' as subspecies has also been used to suggest that certain 'races' are superior to others. All the approaches to 'race' examined so far have based their analysis on phenotypical differences in physical appearance between groups of humans. However, nineteenth-century scientists did not possess the scientific knowledge necessary to relate phenotypical differences to underlying genotype or genetic differences. Advances in genetics after the Second World War made this possible.

■ Steve Jones – genetics and evolution
Genetic differences

The geneticist Steve Jones has examined theories of 'race' in the light of increasing understanding of human genetics. There are 50,000 genes in each

Table 11.1 Herbert Spencer's Evolutionary Typology

SIMPLE SOCIETIES			
Headless	**Occasional headship**	**Vague and unstable headship**	**Stable headship**
Nomadic: (hunting) Fuegians, some Australians, Wood-Veddahs, Bushmen, Chépángs and Kusúndas of Nepal *Semi-settled*: most Esquimaux *Settled*: Arafuras, Land Dyaks of Upper Sarawak River	*Nomadic*: (hunting) some Australians, Tasmanians *Semi-settled*: some Caribs *Settled*: some Uaupés of the upper Rio Negro	*Nomadic*: (hunting) Andamanese, Abipones, Snakes, Chippewayans (pastoral) some Bedouins *Semi-settled*: some Esquimaux, Chinooks, Chippewas (at present), some Kamschadales, Village Veddahs, Bodo and Dhimáls *Settled*: Guiana tribes, Mandans, Corados, New Guinea people, Tannese, Vateans, Dyaks, Todas, Negas, Karens, Santals	*Nomadic*: *Semi-settled*: some Caribs, Patagonians, New Caledonians, Kaffirs *Settled*: Guaranis, Pueblos
COMPOUND SOCIETIES			
	Nomadic: (pastoral) some Bedouins *Semi-settled*: Tannese *Settled*:	*Nomadic*: (hunting) Dacotahs, (hunting and pastoral) Comanches, (pastoralal) Kalmucks *Semi-settled*: Ostayaks, Beluchis, Kookies, Bhils, Congo-people (passing into doubly compound), Teutons before fifth century *Settled*: Chippewas (in past times), Creeks, Mundrucus, Tupis, Khonds, some New Guinea people, Sumatrans, Malagasy (till recently), Coast Negroes, Inland Negroes, some Abyssinians, Homeric Greeks, Kingdoms of the Heptarchy, Teutons in fifth century, Fiefs of tenth century	*Nomadic*: (pastoral) Kirghiz *Semi-settled*: Bechuanas, Zulus *Settled*: Uaupés, Fijians (when first visited), New Zealanders, Sandwich Islanders (in Cook's time), Javans, Hottentots, Dahomans, Ashantees, some Abyssinians, Ancient Yucatanese, New Granada people, Honduras people, Chibehas, some town Arabs
DOUBLY COMPOUND SOCIETIES			
	Semi-settled: *Settled*: Samoans	*Semi-settled*: Tahitians, Tongans, Javans (occasionally), Fijians (since firearms), Malagasy (in recent times), Athenian Confederacy, Spartan Confederacy, Teutonic Kingdoms from sixth to ninth centuries, Greater Fiefs in France of the thirteenth century	*Semi-settled*: *Settled*: Iroquois, Araucanians, Sandwich Islanders (since Cook's time), Ancient Vera Paz and Bogota peoples, Guatemalans, Ancient Peruvians, Wahhábees (Arab), Omán (Arab), Ancient Egyptian Kingdom, England after the tenth century

(*Source*: Andreski, S. (ed.) (1971) *Herbert Spencer,* Thomas Nelson, London, pp. 150–2.)

human being and these genes determine the differences between humans. Genetic research has found some differences in groups of humans. For example, changes in fewer than ten genes determine skin colour. According to Jones, climatic variations have led to the evolution of differences in these genes amongst people from different climatic areas. Ultraviolet light from the sun allows humans to produce vitamin D in the skin. Vitamin D is essential to avoid rickets. Dark-skinned people do not manufacture vitamin D as easily as light-skinned people. In less sunny climates those with dark skins are less likely to survive into adulthood and are therefore unable to pass on their genes by having children.

There are genetic differences too between Europeans and the Japanese. Europeans are more tolerant of alcohol because their livers are more capable of breaking it down. In Japan a genetic variant of the liver enzyme is less effective at coping with alcohol. The Japanese drink less alcohol than the Europeans because when they do drink they tend to feel nauseous and their faces go red.

Genetic research also suggests that Africans:

are on a branch of the human family that split off from the others early on, and most of the rest of us are more closely related to each other than we are to the populations so far tested in Africa.

In the Pacific there seem to be two main genetic groups. One consists of the Australian aborigines and the people of New Guinea. Genetics suggest they have been settled in that area for a very long time. On the other hand, the peoples of other Pacific islands may have moved there more recently and they are more closely related to East Asians.

The absence of 'races'

Despite describing the existence of genetic differences between human groups, Jones does not believe that there is any genetic justification for distinguishing 'races'. He gives a number of reasons for this.

1 First, he suggests that to be able to show that there are different 'races' 'then the different peoples should be quite distinct from one another in a *large* sample of their genes, not just those for skin colour'. However, this is not the case. Geneticists have not found that the genes governing skin colour are related to other genetic patterns. Jones says 'The patterns of variation in each system are independent of each other. Our colour does not say much about what lies under the skin.'

2 Second, genetic diversity has relatively little to do with 'race'. About 85 per cent of the variations in human genes result from the differences between individuals from the same country. A further 5–10 per cent of genetic diversity comes from differences between countries in the same continent and populated by the same supposed 'race' (for instance, differences between the English and the Spanish, or between Nigerians and Kenyans). Jones concludes:

The overall genetic differences between 'races' – Africans and Europeans, say – is no greater than that between different countries within Europe or within Africa. Individuals – not nations and not races – are the main repository of human variation.

3 Third, overall, humans are much more homogeneous than other species. For example, one of Jones's areas of expertise is the genetic variations between snails. His research shows that variations between the snail populations in different Pyrenean valleys are greater than the variations between Australian Aborigines and English people. He says 'If you were a snail it would make good biological sense to be a racist: but you have to accept that humans are tediously uniform animals.'

Social definitions of 'race'

Steve Jones believes that many attitudes towards 'race' have no scientific basis. He argues:

Humanity can be divided into groups in many ways: by culture, by language and by race – which usually means by skin colour. Each division depends to some extent on prejudice and, because they do not overlap, can lead to confusion.

He gives the example of a secretary in Virginia USA. In 1987 she took her employers to court on the grounds that they had discriminated against her because she was black. The court ruled that she could not be black because she had red hair. She then got a job with a black employer and took him to court for discriminating against her because she was white. Again she lost the case. The court held that she could not be white because she had attended a black school.

Societies use different definitions of 'race'. Under apartheid in South Africa anyone who had just a single white ancestor was regarded as non-white or coloured, no matter what their actual skin colour was. In Haiti, on the other hand, the former ruler Papa Doc claimed that he lived in a white nation. Although most of the inhabitants had a dark skin colour nearly everyone could claim one or more white ancestors.

Some supposed 'races' are figments of the imagination. Genetic research suggests, for example, that there is no such thing as an 'Aryan race' and there is no evidence of a distinct Caucasian 'race' with its origins in the Caucasus mountains.

Attitudes to 'race'

Jones notes that thinking about 'race' has usually gone beyond classifying human groups. He says 'It is a tiny step from classifying people to judging them.' According to him the idea of 'distinct pure races which differed in quality had a disastrous impact'. Hitler's attempt to eradicate Jews was based upon 'scientific' claims that they were an inferior 'race'. In 1923 the US President Calvin Coolidge passed immigration laws establishing quotas ensuring that most immigrants were from western and northern Europe. This policy was based on the claim that there would be racial deterioration if 'Nordic' people inter-bred with those from other 'races'. Jones concludes that 'Much of the story of the genetics of race – a field promoted by some eminent scientists – turns out to have been prejudice dressed up as science.'

To Jones issues such as racism are moral issues rather than scientific ones, as modern science has shown that there can be no biological argument for racism. There are variations in human genotypes which affect physical characteristics (phenotypes). However, they are not sufficiently significant to allow different 'races' to be identified and they are not related to the culture, behaviour or morality of different groups of humans.

John Richardson and John Lambert – sociology and 'race'

Like Steve Jones, John Richardson and John Lambert criticize biological approaches to 'race'. They describe the idea of pure 'races' as 'misleading in the extreme' and deny that clearcut, biologically different 'races' can be distinguished. However, they do not deny that 'race' should be studied by sociologists.

Whatever the scientific limitations of the concept, it is widely believed that 'races' exist and this belief influences the behaviour of many members of particular societies. Richardson and Lambert refer to W.I. Thomas's dictum that 'if people define a situation as real, it is real in its social consequences'. Since people define 'race' as real it has social consequences. The study of these consequences form an important part of the sociology of 'race'.

The doctrine of racial superiority

As well as attacking some biological definitions of 'race', Richardson and Lambert also criticize the idea that some 'races' can be seen as superior to others. They outline three main problems with the doctrine of **racial superiority**.

1 There is no clear connection between biological differences and differences in behaviour and culture in groups of humans. Richardson and Lambert do not deny that biology has some bearing on social and cultural behaviour but claim that any links are 'remote and indirect'.

2 Social explanations of behavioural and cultural differences between human groups are far more convincing than biological ones. Biology is much less important in shaping human behaviour than animal behaviour. Richardson and Lambert say 'Unlike animals, human beings are not so rigidly bound to inbuilt instincts or innate biological triggers; on the contrary, human survival and progress is enhanced if cultural flexibility prevails.' The same 'race' can produce very different cultures in different parts of the world. (An example might be Afrikaners in South Africa who developed a different culture under the apartheid system to the more liberal culture of The Netherlands from which the Afrikaners' ancestors came.)

3 It is impossible to find any objective criteria to measure the 'superiority' or 'inferiority' of human groups. The Victorian Britons who argued for the superiority of white Europeans assumed that their urban, industrial societies were superior to other 'primitive' ones. However, as Richardson and Lambert comment:

> claims of 'progress' appear less convincing when we consider the subsequent problems of industrial pollution, personal alienation, and the possibility of nuclear warfare. The African pygmy or Mongolian herdsman is arguably in a more 'harmonious' relationship with his physical environment than is the urban inhabitant of London or New York.

In any case, if cultural achievements and technological developments are a measure of superiority and inferiority, history shows that different 'races' have been the most advanced at particular points in time. There were highly developed African civilizations such as the Ashanti and Zimbabwe when Europe was still in the 'Dark Ages'. Richardson and Lambert quote Goldthorpe who claims that in 1600 China was perhaps the most developed nation, followed by India and Arabia. The evidence does not therefore support the belief that Europeans are innately superior to people from other parts of the world.

The social construction of 'race'

To Richardson and Lambert, and to most other sociologists, 'race' is a **social construct**: it has no biological basis, rather it has to do with 'what people make of physical differences' and the 'everyday or commonsense notions' which influence them'. How people define 'races' and their attitudes to different 'races' are influenced by the dominant belief systems of the society in which they live. For example, stereotypes about particular groups vary from place to place and time to time. Furthermore:

> In some societies, at certain times, people are found to attach little weight to racial differences, while in other contexts we might find intense hostility and pronounced patterns of racial 'exclusion' and 'inclusion'.

In Richardson and Lambert's view though, people do not just passively accept definitions of 'race' in a particular society. Through their actions and interactions with others they may reinforce or challenge existing beliefs about 'race', or they may help to create new beliefs. At the same time their beliefs and actions 'take place within particular historical and cultural contexts which tend to limit human choices and make certain types of cultural response and behaviour more likely than others'.

In later sections of this chapter we will analyse in more detail how 'race' is socially constructed. In particular in the sections on racism we will examine the way that stereotypical beliefs about 'races' are created and sustained (see pp. 688–711).

Ethnicity is usually seen as defining groups in terms of their cultural characteristics rather than their supposed biological differences. In a later section we discuss the concept of ethnicity which many see as a more valid way of classifying human groups than 'race' (see pp. 673–88).

■ Migration and 'race' relations

Human groups which regard themselves as biologically or culturally different often live in close proximity to one another. Some sociologists have seen the process of **migration** and the social relationships and social changes which result from it as the key to understanding race relations. Patterns of migration will briefly be outlined before these theories are discussed.

Figure 11.1   Colonial migrations from the seventeenth to the nineteenth centuries

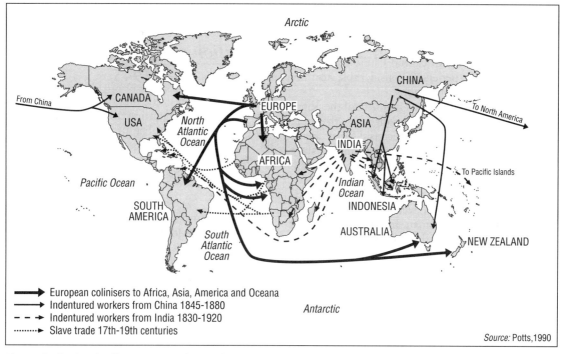

European colinisers to Africa, Asia, America and Oceana
Indentured workers from China 1845-1880
Indentured workers from India 1830-1920
Slave trade 17th-19th centuries

Source: Potts,1990

(*Source*: Castles, S. and Miller, M.J. (1993) *The Age of Migration: International Population Movements in the Modern World*, Macmillan, Basingstoke, p. 47.)

■ Stephen Castles and Mark J. Miller – international migration

Patterns of migration 1600–1945

Castles and Miller have described world migration patterns both before and after the Second World War. They note that 'population movements in response to demographic growth, climatic change and the development of production and trade have always been part of human history'. Nations have sometimes sought to encourage immigration as part of 'nation building'. Migration has also been caused by warfare and enforced migration has taken place as a result of deportation and enslavement.

From the sixteenth to the nineteenth century much migration was directly or indirectly related to **colonialism**. Colonial migrations are illustrated in Figure 11.1. Large numbers of people moved from the countries of the colonial powers in

Europe to the colonies. For example Spanish and Portuguese settlers moved to South America. The slave trade resulted in some fifteen million Africans being taken as slaves across the Atlantic, resulting in the black population of North and South America and the Caribbean. The slaves were either abducted by sailors or exchanged with African traders or chiefs for manufactured goods. They were made to work in plantations, mines and as servants. Products such as tobacco, coffee cotton and sugar were produced in the colonies and most of them were transported back to Europe.

In much of the Caribbean the native population of Caribs and Arawaks was completely wiped out. Slavery was abolished in 1834 in British Colonies, 1863 in Dutch colonies and not until 1865 in some states of the USA.

Following the abolition of slavery more use was made of **indentured servants** who contracted to work for their employers for a number of years. In the Indian sub-continent more than thirty million were recruited as indentured workers by the British and they were taken to work in areas as diverse as East Africa, Trinidad, Guyana and

Malaya. The Dutch also used indentured workers in the Dutch East Indies. As Castles and Miller point out, such movements of people during the colonial period has often left a legacy of ethnic division and conflict in former colonies. For example, Asians in Africa and Chinese in South-East Asia have experienced considerable hostility from the majority populations.

In North America the vast majority of the population are descended from immigrants; there are few surviving native Americans. Most black Americans are descended from the original slave population. In the nineteenth and early twentieth centuries there was also large-scale migration from Europe. Between 1800 and 1860 nearly two-thirds of migrants to the USA were from Britain, and over one-fifth were German. In the second half of the nineteenth century there were more migrants from Italy, Ireland, Spain and Eastern Europe.

Until 1880 anyone could migrate to the USA, but then restrictions were introduced. They were first placed on the entry of Chinese and Asians, and in 1920 they were extended to Europeans and Latin Americans.

Canada and Australia are also largely populated by the descendants of migrants. Most of the early emigrants to Canada came from northern Europe but there was some migration to Canada by Japanese, Indians, Chinese and blacks from the USA. British colonization of Australia started in 1788. In the second half of the nineteenth century some Indians, Chinese and South Pacific Islanders settled in Australia but from 1901 the parliament passed a 'White Australia Policy' which aimed to prevent non-whites emigrating to Australia.

In the nineteenth and early twentieth centuries there was considerable migration within Europe. For example, large numbers of workers moved to Germany from Poland, and Italy and France imported workers from a variety of countries including Belgium, Italy, Portugal and Spain. Between the First and Second World Wars there was less migration in Europe but in France there was immigration from Italy, Poland and Czechoslovakia.

Castles and Miller sum up saying:

> The period from about 1850 to 1914 was an era of mass migration. It was also a time of industrialisation and economic growth in Western Europe and the USA. Industrialisation was a cause of both emigration and immigration.

In the inter-war years 'xenophobia and economic stagnation' led to a decline in migration.

Migration to highly developed countries since 1945

Castles and Miller argue that there have been two main phases of migration to highly developed countries since 1945. The first phase lasted until the early 1970s, a period in which there was strong economic growth in developed countries. In this phase there were three main types of migration.

1 Some people migrated from the southern and eastern fringes of Europe to the more affluent countries of the north and west. The richer countries were facing a labour shortage and wanted to recruit cheap labour. Those who migrated were often denied citizenship rights. Belgium and Switzerland recruited workers from Italy, and France recruited from Spain. In Germany the **guestworker** system was established. The main sources of guestworkers were Italy, Greece, Turkey, Morocco, Portugal, Tunisia and Yugoslavia. By 1973 there were 2.6 million guestworkers who were allowed into Germany only on condition that they stayed for restricted periods and sometimes they were restricted to doing specific jobs. They had few civil rights, were not allowed to settle in Germany and could not bring their families with them.

2 The second type of migration involved emigration from colonies or former colonies to colonial powers. Again the motive was to recruit cheap labour to overcome a labour shortage in advanced industrial nations. France had large-scale immigration from Algeria, Morocco, Tunisia and West African colonies such as Mali and Senegal. The Netherlands had immigration from Indonesia and Surinam, and Britain from the Caribbean and the Indian subcontinent. (Britain is discussed separately on pp. 663–6.) This type of migration was usually permanent and the migrants were already or became citizens of the countries to which they moved.

3 The third type involved migration to North America and Australia. A 1965 amendment to the Immigration and Nationality Act in the USA was intended to remove racist bias in the law. It led to an increase in migration to the USA by the Asian and Latin American kin of US citizens. There was also considerable migration to Canada from Britain, Germany, Italy and The Netherlands, and to Australia from Britain, Italy, Greece and Malta.

The globalization of migration since the 1970s

Castles and Miller claim that there has been a major shift in migratory patterns since the early 1970s. In 1973 oil-producing countries increased the price of oil causing recessions in most rich capitalist countries. This resulted in a reduced demand for labour in Western Europe so recruitment of labour from former colonies slowed down. However, in Britain, France, The Netherlands and Germany ethnic minorities became more established as family members joined the original migrants and children were born in the countries to which their parents had migrated. Southern European countries such as Greece, Italy, Spain and Portugal started to have more immigrants than emigrants. Some of those who had emigrated in earlier years returned, and these countries also began to receive immigrants from Asia and Africa.

Outside Europe the USA, Canada and Australia continued to receive immigrants, although Australia restricted numbers quite severely. Oil-producing countries in the Middle East attracted workers from rich and poor countries alike. Throughout the world there was also an enormous increase in the number of asylum-seekers and refugees. In 1980 there were 8.2 million refugees; by 1992 this had risen to an estimated 20 million. Over this period people fled from many countries including Afghanistan, Lebanon, Uganda, Zaïre, Namibia, Argentina and Chile. The collapse of communism in the USSR and Eastern Europe also led to very large population movements. Over a quarter of a million people sought asylum in Germany in the first seven months of 1992, many from Romania and Yugoslavia.

According to Castles and Miller there has been a 'globalization of international migration'. By the 1980s and 1990s all regions of the world were experiencing substantial movements of people. Labour migration, especially in the Middle East and Asia, was often being accompanied by 'rigid control of foreign workers, the prohibition of settlement and family reunion, and the denial of basic rights'. However, the European experience suggested that pressures for longer stays to be allowed would grow and 'It therefore seems reasonable to predict that countries everywhere will become more ethnically diverse and cosmopolitan through migration.'

■ Migration to Britain
Immigration until 1945

Britain has long had an ethnically diverse population. John Richardson points out:

The early Roman invaders encountered a mixed population of Britons, Picts and Celts, and when the Romans finally withdrew from these shores in 410 AD. the succeeding centuries witnessed a series of forays and scattered settlements by varied groups of Angles, Saxons, Jutes, Danes and Vikings. This diversity was significantly enhanced by the arrival of the Normans.

Many other groups have migrated to Britain. Jews arrived in England with the Norman conquest, though they were expelled by Edward I in 1290. In 1440 Richard II decided to tax the 'alien' population. It was found that they consisted mainly of Scots, Irish, French and 'Doche' – people from north Germany and the Low Countries (now Belgium and The Netherlands). In the sixteenth, seventeenth and eighteenth centuries England accepted large numbers of Protestant refugees fleeing from religious persecution in Europe. Many were French and Dutch Protestants. From 1680 there was an influx of Huguenots (French Protestants) to England.

The next waves of migration mainly involved the Jews and the Irish. By 1660 a small Jewish community had re-established itself in London. The main period of Jewish immigration to Britain took place between 1870 and 1914. In that period 120,000 Jews fled persecution in Eastern Europe to settle in Britain. In the eighteenth century the Irish also had a small community in the capital. Between 1820 and 1910 there was a massive emigration from Ireland. Nearly half the population left Ireland to escape starvation and poverty in their native country. Although many went to the USA, others settled in British cities such as Liverpool, London, Glasgow and Manchester.

In the nineteenth century there were few restrictions on immigration to Britain but in 1905 the Aliens Act excluded immigrants 'without visible means of support'. However, the policy collapsed during the First World War when thousands of Europeans and members of the armed forces from

British Commonwealth countries were allowed temporary residence.

In 1920 a new Aliens Act introduced strict regulations banning 'aliens' from being admitted to Britain without the permission of a customs officer and excluding those who were considered unfit or who could not support themselves and their families. People with sufficient money or who were sponsored by a British citizen were allowed entry. In the late 1930s these laws prevented most Jews who wanted to flee to Britain to escape Nazi persecution from entering the country.

During the Second World War it again proved impossible to control the entry of refugees. Along with British troops, large numbers of Polish, Belgians and French were evacuated to Britain from Dunkirk. Refugees also came to Britain from Czechoslovakia, Norway, Greece and Denmark. The Polish made up the largest group of all: by the end of 1945 there were nearly 250,000 Poles in Britain.

The biggest groups of immigrants to Britain since the Second World War have come from the Asian subcontinent and the Caribbean. We deal with this period of migration in a later section (see pp. 663–6).

Stephen Small – Black People in Britain

Stephen Small points out that there have been black people (by which he means 'people of African-Caribbean and Asian origin') in Britain for many centuries. Some of the earliest blacks to come to Britain arrived with the armies of the Romans and some of them held senior positions. From the middle of the sixteenth century the numbers of blacks in Britain increased until 1601 when Elizabeth I decided to expel all blacks on the grounds they were causing economic problems.

Despite Elizabeth's policy, by 1715 there was a black community of some 15,000 in Britain. Many came to work as soldiers, servants and sailors. In the early nineteenth century there were usually over a thousand Lascars, Indian seamen employed by the British East India Company in London. Some blacks arrived in Britain as slaves with their white masters, although they were more likely to be employed as servants than as slaves. Some of those who were slaves 'continually fled their masters, seeking refuge in small but cohesive communities across England's ports'.

In 1772 a ruling by Lord High Chief Justice Mansfield held that nobody, including slaves, could be removed from Britain by force so the rights of slave owners were restricted. In Britain the slave trade was abolished in 1807 and slavery in 1838. Slavery was abolished later in the USA (in 1865), so in the intervening years some black American slaves fled to Britain to seek their freedom.

By no means all blacks in Britain in the nineteenth century came from low-status backgrounds. Some 'were the children of African dignitaries who were sent to England to be educated: others were the children of white masters in the Caribbean'. There were also politically active Asians who set up the London Indian Society which campaigned for Indian independence. In 1892 Dadabhai Naoroji, a mathematics professor at London University, became the first Asian MP.

At the end of the First and Second World Wars some blacks from Commonwealth countries or American-Africans who had fought in the British army or as allies of the British, settled in Britain.

Small points out that some writers and historians have emphasized the hostility and discrimination experienced by blacks in Britain. Apart from Elizabeth I expelling blacks in 1601, there were attempts to 'repatriate' blacks to Sierra Leone in the 1780s and in both 1823 and 1925 laws were passed prohibiting blacks from working on British ships. In 1919 there were anti-black riots in Liverpool and Cardiff, and again in Liverpool in 1948.

Other writers have claimed that despite such racism there has been considerable cooperation between working-class whites and blacks. Runaway slaves were often 'supported by the "London mob", and working-class whites helped them with food and shelter'. In the nineteenth century black British people were involved both in the Chartist movement (which campaigned for working-class political rights) and in the struggle to gain acceptance for trades unions.

Most black immigration to Britain has taken place since 1945 and we will examine this period in the next section. However, as Small says:

> It is important to recognize the long-standing multi-racial and multi-cultural nature of Britain, and the contribution of black people to the development of British society and culture.

New Commonwealth immigration to Britain 1945–61

The Nationality Acts of 1914 and 1948 imposed no restrictions on immigration to Britain from Commonwealth and Empire countries. Subjects of the British Empire had the right to enter Britain, vote, work and join the armed forces. Nevertheless there were relatively few people in Britain of Afro-Caribbean or Asian origin in the first few years after the Second World War. In 1953 the Civil Service estimated there to be 15,000 people of West African ethnic origin in Britain, 9,300 of Indian or Pakistani origin, and 8,600 of West Indian origin. Yet even in 1953 these ethnic minority groups were starting to increase quite rapidly.

In the aftermath of the Second World War, Britain was experiencing a serious labour shortage. The Government set up a working party to explore the possibility of employing more people from the Commonwealth in Britain. It suggested that female workers could be recruited for the health service.

In 1948 the first ships carrying groups of immigrants from Commonwealth countries arrived in Britain. The very first was the *Empire Windrush* which carried 492 Jamaicans to Britain to seek work. London Transport recruited thousands of workers from Barbados, Trinidad and Jamaica. In some cases it paid the fares to enable its new workers to get to Britain. The British Hotels and Restaurants' Association also ran a recruitment campaign in the West Indies. Some private companies set out to recruit New Commonwealth workers as well: textile companies in northern England advertised in the press in the Indian subcontinent. Woolf's rubber company in Southall recruited in the Punjab. Many, though by no means all, New Commonwealth immigrants were recruited to do relatively low-paid and unskilled jobs which employers could not fill with white British workers.

Table 11.2 shows estimated net immigration from New Commonwealth countries between 1953 and 1962. Although most of the earliest migrants in this period were from the West Indies, by the end of the period they were outnumbered by immigrants from Pakistan and India. Most of the first immigrants from South-East Asia were men, with their families being more likely to follow later. Early migration from the West Indies included a higher proportion of women than that from India and Pakistan, and a second generation, born in Britain, developed more quickly. There were also long-established Afro-Caribbean communities in cities such as Cardiff, Liverpool and London.

Politics and immigration control

In some areas there was tension between the recently arrived ethnic minorities and the white population. In 1958 there were 'race riots' involving clashes between the Afro-Caribbean population of Notting Hill in London and local whites. E. Ellis Cashmore argues that in Notting Hill and elsewhere 'From 1957 ethnic-minority groups became targets for sporadic unprovoked attacks.'

Table 11.2 Estimated net immigration from the New Commonwealth, 1953–62

	West Indies	India	Pakistan	Others	Total
1953	2,000				2,000
1954	11,000				11,000
1955	27,500	5,800	1,850	7,500	42,650
1956	29,800	5,600	2,050	9,350	46,800
1957	23,000	6,600	5,200	7,600	42,400
1958	15,000	6,200	4,700	3,950	29,850
1959	16,400	2,950	850	1,400	21,600
1960	49,650	5,900	2,500	−350	57,700
1961	66,300	23,750	25,100	21,250	136,400
1962[1]	31,800	19,050	25,080	18,970	94,900

[1] First six months up to introduction of controls.

(*Source*: Zig Layton-Henry (1992) *The Politics of Immigration*, Blackwell, Oxford, p. 13.)

Cashmore says 'It would be difficult to maintain that the violence of 1958 actually signified the beginning of racial conflict.' Even before then there had been considerable debate about the **'colour bar'**, the banning of 'coloured' people from jobs or places. (For example, landlords sometimes used notices saying 'Europeans Only' or 'No Coloureds' to exclude Asians and Afro-Caribbeans from renting their property.)

Such issues served to highlight immigration and race relations as subjects of political controversy. Even in the 1940s some politicians had raised the possibility of introducing immigration controls. In 1954 and 1955 the issue was raised again by both Conservative and Labour politicians, and a working party was set up to consider the issue. However, no action was taken at that time.

In the aftermath of the Notting Hill 'race riots' though, the campaign to introduce controls gained momentum. An opinion poll in May 1961 found 73 per cent in favour of the introduction of controls. In 1962 the Commonwealth Immigrants Act was introduced. Commonwealth citizens were denied the right of entry unless they met certain criteria. If they did they were issued with vouchers of one of three types.

1 **'A' vouchers** were given to those who could show that they had a job in Britain before they arrived.

2 **'B' vouchers** went to those who were held to have qualifications or skills which were in short supply in Britain, for example medical qualifications.

3 **'C' vouchers** were issued on the grounds of individual merit. Some went to people who had served in the British armed forces.

The 1962 Act was justified by many commentators on the grounds that the large number of immigrants was adding to Britain's economic problems. However, Cashmore points out that the Act 'did not cover migrants from the Irish Republic, so it would seem that economic considerations were not really paramount'. It was directed at black immigration rather than all immigration.

Cashmore also argues that the Act:

marked the start of the 'numbers game', as it was called, since the abiding concern of politicians, the media and the majority of the white population was with the actual numbers of New Commonwealth immigrants entering the country and not with the quality of the relations between settlers and native whites.

The 1962 Act was introduced by a Conservative Government, but the election of a Labour Government in 1964 made no difference to the overall direction of policy. In 1965 it tightened up on the issuing of work vouchers thus further restricting immigration. In 1967 large numbers of East African Asians entered Britain, particularly from Kenya. The Kenyan Government had introduced an 'Africanisation' policy and many Asians fled to Britain. East African Asians had not been covered by the 1962 Act so the Government rushed through new legislation. The 1968 Commonwealth Immigrants Act restricted entry to Britain for East African Asians who held British passports. Under the Act all Commonwealth citizens with British passports became subject to immigration controls unless they had at least one parent or grandparent who was born in the UK, or who was a citizen of the UK and its colonies. Andrew Pilkington comments:

The act proved to be racially discriminatory in nature. For its effects were to allow Kenyan whites to enter Britain but to prevent Kenyan Asians from doing so until they were lucky enough to be granted one of the limited number of vouchers issued each year.

In 1968 the Conservative shadow cabinet minister, Enoch Powell, made a famous speech in which he predicted that a multiracial Britain would prove to be disastrous. Powell claimed that Britain must be 'literally mad' to be allowing dependants of migrants to be entering Britain. He argued that it would eventually lead to racial conflict and serious violence. He said 'As I look ahead I am filled with foreboding. Like the Roman I seem to see "the River Tiber foaming with much blood".' (Quoted in Layton-Henry 1992, p. 81.) Powell was sacked from his job in the shadow cabinet, but the Conservative Party won the 1970 election and proceeded to restrict immigration even more.

The 1971 Immigration Act replaced employment vouchers with work permits for **non-patrials** (people without close family connections to the UK). Unlike the vouchers, the permits did not allow permanent residence or grant the right of settlement in Britain for dependants. **Patrials**, who had a parent or grandparent born in Britain, retained full citizenship rights. In practice New Commonwealth citizens from the Indian subcontinent and the West Indies were far less likely to be patrials than the predominantly white population of Old Commonwealth countries such as Australia and New Zealand.

Despite the new Act the British Government was forced to accept immigration by Ugandan Asians expelled from Uganda by its president, General Idi Amin, in 1972. Some 27,000 were accepted by Britain while others went to India and Canada.

Further changes were made to immigration laws under Margaret Thatcher's premiership in the 1980s. The 1981 British Nationality Act specified three categories of citizenship:

1 British;

2 British Dependent Territories;

3 British Overseas.

Once again those who were born in Britain, or who had parents or grandparents born in Britain, were granted British citizenship. Permanent settlers were also given British citizenship. British citizenship passed to children born overseas only if the parents were born in the UK. This excluded first-generation settlers from the Asian subcontinent and the West Indies. Someone who married a British citizen had to live in Britain for three years before they could apply for citizenship.

The Act was strongly criticized by the Labour Party. Roy Hattersley, its spokesperson on home affairs, condemned it as racist and sexist. Both the rules on children born outside the UK and on residence qualifications for prospective spouses were seen as discriminatory against Asians and Afro-Caribbeans.

In 1988 the Immigration Act made it more difficult for the families of immigrants to come to Britain. It repealed the automatic right of the families of men who had been settled in Britain before 1973 to join them in Britain. Dependants would only be allowed in if it could be shown that they could be provided with adequate housing and financial support and would not have to rely on state benefits.

Immigration to Britain since 1961

As a consequence of these changes, immigration from the New Commonwealth (including

Table 11.3 Acceptances for settlement in the UK: by category of acceptance

	Thousands			
	1981	**1986**	**1991**	**1992**
New Commonwealth[1]				
Own right	4.1	2.4	1.7	1.6
Husbands	3.2	3.2	6.3	6.0
Wives	10.0	7.4	9.7	9.6
Children	10.7	6.4	4.5	4.5
Others	3.4	3.3	5.8	6.1
Total New Commonwealth	31.4	22.7	28.0	27.7
Rest of the world				
Own right	11.6	8.6	3.7	4.0
Husbands	3.4	3.6	5.4	4.9
Wives	6.8	6.8	9.3	9.0
Children	3.7	3.9	4.5	3.9
Others	2.3	2.4	3.1	3.2
Total	27.7	25.2	25.9	24.9
Total acceptances	59.1	47.8	53.9	52.6

[1] Includes Pakistan

(*Source: Social Trends* (1994), HMSO, London, 1994, p. 59.)

Pakistan) declined from 136,000 in 1961 to 68,000 in 1972 and 22,800 in 1988. Table 11.3 shows that it had risen to 27,000 in 1992. The majority were allowed to come to Britain as the dependants of British citizens rather than as immigrants in their own right. Table 11.3 shows that acceptance for settlement from the New Commonwealth was almost matched by acceptances for settlement from the rest of the world.

There is little doubt that the immigration rules have been designed to limit the numbers of Asian and Afro-Caribbean migrants to Britain. As a result of the UK joining the EC, citizens of other member countries have an automatic right to work in Britain. Writing in 1992 Richard Skellington and Paulette Morris said:

> The word 'immigrant' is often wrongly used to refer only to black people. The majority of immigrants are white — from Eire or the Old Commonwealth (Australia, New Zealand and Canada) or from other European countries.

They point out that the 1981 census found that of 3.4 million people in Britain who were born elsewhere, 1.9 million were white. Furthermore they note that strict limitations on immigration to Britain from the New Commonwealth could not be justified in terms of Britain becoming 'overcrowded'. Emigration has generally exceeded immigration. Government figures show that between 1978 and 1992 there has been a net outflow of British citizens of over 120,000 (although overall, including non-British citizens, there has been a small net inflow of a mere 7,000).

Britain's ethnic minority population

It is only comparatively recently that the British Government has started collecting data specifically on ethnic minority groups. The *1991 Census* included a question asking people to assign themselves to an ethnic group from a list of options as shown in Table 11.4. There were a number of problems with this:

1 The options were by no means exhaustive: for example, no 'Irish' category was included and a considerable number of respondents described themselves as belonging to the category 'other' ethnic group.

2 The figures are based upon self-assigned ethnic groups, and are therefore shaped by the subjective views of the respondents.

3 The question mixed up nationality (e.g. Bangladeshi), and skin colour (e.g. Black other).

4 The figures do not distinguish between people from distinctive cultural groups but with the same national origin (e.g. Indian Sikhs and Hindus).

Nevertheless because the census is more comprehensive than any other survey, it provides perhaps the most reliable estimate of the size of the ethnic minority population in Britain.

Table 11.4 shows that in 1991 just over three million people, about 5.5 per cent of the population, described themselves as belonging to an ethnic minority group. Some 30 per cent of the ethnic minority population described themselves as Black Caribbean, Black African or Black other, and 28 per cent as Indian.

Britain's ethnic minority population is not evenly distributed throughout the country. The *1991 Census* found that more than 50 per cent live in the South East of England. Some 60 per cent of the black population and just over 30 per cent of

the Indian, Pakistani and Bangladeshi population live in London. Elsewhere the highest concentration of ethnic minorities is in the West Midlands (8 per cent). Lancashire, West Yorkshire and Greater Manchester also have sizeable ethnic minority populations.

In contrast, less than 1 per cent of the population claimed to belong to an ethnic minority in Scotland, Wales, the South West and the North. In rural areas less than 1 per cent of the population was found to be from ethnic minority backgrounds compared to over one-third of the population in the London boroughs of Tower Hamlets, Hackney and Brent.

■ Migration and assimilation

One influential approach to studying relationships between ethnic groups or **race relations** focuses on the process of migration by ethnic minority groups to a new society. It has sometimes been called the **immigrant-host model** because it tends to conceive of relationships between ethnic groups as between a dominant 'host' society and a smaller immigrant group.

The immigrant-host approach has usually adopted an optimistic view of race relations. Sociologists using this perspective have usually believed that eventually the immigrant group will adapt to the way of life of the host society and will be **assimilated** into it. Conflict based on 'race' and ethnicity will tend to decline or even disappear with the passage of time.

The immigrant-host model has sometimes been seen as similar to a functionalist view of society. Some sociologists who have used it see the host society as characterized by a basic consensus and a shared culture. The immigrant group is seen as temporarily disrupting the consensus and shared culture, before the society gradually adapts to the newcomers and the immigrants adapt to the society. The emphasis is usually on the second of these processes: the immigrants are expected to fit in with their new society more than their society is expected to adapt to them.

Thus, like functionalism the immigrant-host model emphasizes stability, shared moral values and slow evolutionary change involving a process of adaptation. Furthermore, one of the pioneers of this general approach, Robert E. Park, followed functionalists in using biological analogies in his work.

Table 11.4 Population: by ethnic group and age in Great Britain, 1991

	0–15	16–29	30–44	45–59	60 and over	All ages (= 100%) (thousands)
Ethnic group						
Ethnic minority group						
Black Caribbean	21.9	27.6	20.0	19.6	10.9	500
Black African	29.3	32.1	26.7	9.2	2.7	212
Black other	50.6	30.8	12.4	4.2	2.1	178
Indian	29.5	23.9	25.9	13.8	6.8	840
Pakistani	42.6	24.0	19.2	10.4	3.7	477
Bangladeshi	47.2	23.3	14.8	11.4	3.3	163
Chinese	23.3	29.7	29.4	12.0	5.7	157
Other Asian	24.4	25.2	33.0	13.3	4.1	198
Other	41.7	24.9	19.9	8.5	5.0	290
All ethnic minority groups	33.0	26.0	22.6	12.6	5.8	2,015
White	19.3	20.4	21.2	17.0	22.1	51,874
All ethnic groups	20.1	20.7	21.2	16.8	21.2	54,889

(*Source*: *Social Trends* (1994), London: HMSO, p. 26.)

Robert E. Park – race relations and migration

The nature of race relations

Robert E. Park was a leading member of the Chicago School of Sociology, based at Chicago University, which developed influential theories of social life during the 1920s and 1930s. At the time Chicago was a rapidly growing city and large numbers of people from diverse groups were migrating to Chicago both from within the USA and from other countries. The Chicago sociologists engaged in detailed empirical research in their city, and it was in this context that Park developed his theory of race relations.

Park describes race relations as:

the relations existing between peoples distinguished by marks of racial descent, particularly when these racial differences enter into the consciousness of the individuals and groups so distinguished, and by doing so determine in each case the individual's conception of himself as well as his status in the community.

'Race relations' only existed where people had a sense of belonging to different groups and there was some conflict between them. Thus there were, according to Park, no race relations in Brazil. Although Europeans and Africans lived together in Brazil, there was almost no 'race consciousness' and so little potential for conflict.

Park believed that different 'races' originated with the dispersal of a once concentrated population. The **great dispersion** was partly stimulated by the search for a more abundant food supply, and it was 'like the migration of plants and animals, centrifugal'. Each dispersed human group then 'developed, by natural selection and inbreeding, those special physical and cultural traits that characterize the different racial stocks'.

Eventually the **centrifugal dispersion** of humans was replaced by a **centripetal force** which brought people from the different 'racial stocks' together. European migration and conquest created race relations in many parts of the world and the mixing of different groups in cities had the same effect. Thus Park says, 'It is obvious that race relations and all that they imply are generally, and on the whole, the products of migration and conquest.'

Interracial adjustments

Park claimed that a complex process of **interracial adjustment** followed migration or conquests which brought different 'races' into contact. This process involved 'racial competition, conflict, accommodation and assimilation'.

Competition was a universal, biological phenomenon: the 'struggle for existence'. Just as plants might struggle for sunlight, humans struggled for scarce and prized goods and, in particular, land. Park says:

---

the invasion by one race or one people of the territories occupied and settled by another involves first of all a struggle for mere existence, that is to say a struggle to maintain a place on the land and in the habitat which has been invaded.

Failure in this struggle could lead to extinction both in plant species and in human 'races'. For example, the native population of Tasmania 'seem to have been hunted like wild animals by the European immigrants as were, at one time, the Indians in the USA'. Competition does not always take such an extreme form as this but it continues so long as there are different 'races' which have 'racial consciousness'.

Competition is a struggle by groups and individuals in the ecological order; **conflict** is a struggle between individuals in the social order. Park gives the example of conflict between 'negroes' and whites in the Southern states of the USA over 'jobs and places of relative security in the occupational organization of the community in which they live'.

If competition and conflict divide 'races', then accommodation and assimilation bring them together. Conflict ceases, at least temporarily, when the status and power of different 'races' has become fixed and is generally accepted.

Accommodation allows people 'to live and work on friendly terms' but it does not ensure that relations will remain harmonious. The groups with less power and status may eventually decide that their position is unsatisfactory and they may seek to improve it through engaging in competition.

On the other hand **assimilation** provides a permanent solution to the problems created by race relations. Assimilation can involve two processes:

1 first, 'a process that goes on in society by which individuals spontaneously acquire one another's language, characteristic attitudes, habits and modes of behaviour';

2 second, 'a process by which individuals and groups of individuals are taken over and incorporated into larger groups'.

Park claimed that Italians, French and Germans had resulted from the assimilation of a variety of racial groups and that the USA had been able to assimilate a variety of groups with 'ease and rapidity'.

Park was unclear about whether assimilation was inevitable or not. In one article he wrote 'The race relations cycle which takes the form, to state it abstractly, of contacts, competition, accommodation and eventual assimilation, is apparently progressive and irreversible.'

However, he recognized that, at the time he was writing, Japanese and 'negro' Americans had not assimilated into American society. He suggested that this was because both groups had 'a distinctive racial hallmark' in the form of physical differences from white Americans. The Irish, for example, could become 'indistinguishable in the cosmopolitan mass', but for other groups the situation was different. Park argues:

Where races are distinguished by certain external marks these furnish a permanent physical substratum upon which and around which the irritations and animosities, incidental to all human intercourse, tend to accumulate and so to gain strength.

An evaluation of Park

Although Park was generally optimistic about race relations in the long run, he seemed to believe that conflict would not necessarily disappear between all racial groups. Unlike some sociologists who have used the immigrant-host perspective, he did not believe that the migrants would necessarily adapt to the lifestyle of the hosts. For example, he was well aware that in some societies immigrants from Europe had become dominant, and in some cases had wiped out the indigenous population completely.

Nevertheless in several ways Park's work is open to criticisms which have been levelled at all immigrant-host theories. We will discuss these after the next section.

Sheila Patterson – *Dark Strangers*

The immigrant-host framework

In the 1950s Sheila Patterson conducted a study of first-generation immigrants from the West Indies in Brixton, London. She conducted interviews with 250 whites and 150 Afro-Caribbeans, and also did some observation and participant observation. She distinguished between a '**race situation**' and an '**immigrant situation**'. A 'race situation' involved clear divisions between racial groups, and was characteristic of South Africa where she had also carried out research. An '**immigrant situation**' is less clear cut. In Britain she found:

> The immigrant-host framework ... seemed to offer a far more satisfactory mode of interpreting the dynamics which were clearly taking place on both sides, the complex motivations of behaviour, the fluid, undefined, and uninstitutionalized relationships.

In Britain the relationship between the hosts and the immigrants was not fixed but was evolving all the time.

Unlike 'conquest societies', Britain was 'a homogeneous and peaceable society' in which she found that 'social relations are harmonious and voluntarily ordered among the great majority of the society's members'. In such a situation both the hosts and the immigrants had common aims. These were accommodation, integration and assimilation. The whole process involved adaptation whereby the hosts and immigrants adapted to living together.

However, to Patterson **adaptation** was rather different for the hosts and immigrants. The immigrants were expected to do rather more adapting than the hosts. For the immigrant group it involved considerable changes in lifestyle through **resocialization** and **acculturation**. For the hosts it was 'a more passive process of acceptance' which was 'largely unconscious'.

Accommodation, integration and assimilation

Patterson saw **accommodation** as the first stage of adaptation involving only 'minimal adaptation and acceptance'. She suggested some ways in which the West Indian immigrants in Brixton could accommodate themselves to the lifestyle of the host society.

1 In employment:

> One might hope to find West Indian workers settling into a job with one firm; generally conforming to British workers' customs and accepting their viewpoints; joining the union where this is customary.

On the employers' side, organizations could be expected to judge their West Indian workers on merit and to begin to give promotions to the most able and senior.

2 In housing, West Indian landlords might start to enforce 'certain standards of domestic hygiene and behaviour among their tenants' while white landlords could start to accept West Indian tenants.

3 In social life West Indians would need to adopt British habits such as 'queuing' and 'becoming regular and welcome clients in a local pub'.

4 Furthermore 'One might expect to find West Indian men marrying sooner, and taking a more permanent interest in their children's security and education.'

5 West Indians would have to become less sensitive so that they would start 'ceasing to regard ignorant but well-meaning remarks about their colour, country, or way of life as deliberate insults'.

Again the changes required of the host population were rather less demanding. Patterson says 'local people might be expected to be used to the presence of coloured people in public places, and not to stare at them or draw away from them in the streets, shops or pubs', and 'to offer new West Indian neighbours the customary welcome and cup of tea'. They should also begin to lose stereotypical views of West Indians and to judge individuals on their merits.

At the time of writing, West Indians had not been in Britain long enough to move beyond the accommodation stage, but longer established immigrant communities could reach a stage of **pluralistic integration**. In this stage:

> the incoming group as a whole through its organizations, adapts itself to permanent

membership of the receiving society in certain major spheres of association, notably in economic and civil life.

The host society accepts the immigrants as a permanently settled group and tolerates the group retaining a distinctive culture such as a different religion or pattern of family life. Patterson cites French-Canadians and Anglo-Canadians as examples of ethnic groups living in pluralistic integration.

The final stage of adaptation is **assimilation**. In this stage there is complete adaptation by the immigrants or minority group to the society and complete acceptance of them by the society. Assimilation may lead to **physical amalgamation** in which inter-breeding leads to a complete disappearance of the distinctive features of the immigrant group and their hosts. Patterson gives the example of the Huguenots in Britain.

Accommodation in Brixton |

Having set out the stages through which immigrant groups can pass on the road to assimilation, Patterson then examined how far West Indian migrants had progressed in Brixton in the 1950s.

In employment she found that the labour shortage had forced employers to accept West Indians as employees and they had not laid them off in large numbers when there was a small recession in 1956–8. Furthermore she found that, 'a minority of exceptional individual migrants have begun to move up from the bottom of the industrial ladder'. However, there was still considerable opposition to the employment of West Indians by white workers. For example, one white worker commented 'Look at those darkies at the exchange; they get sent out to jobs while local people are unemployed.'

There was also conflict resulting from the 'well-meant but rough humour' of some white workers. This was sometimes expressed in 'Nicknames such as "Sambo" and "Darkie", jocular references to "Jungle Jim", jokes about "pidgin English", and "doesn't it come off when you wash?".' Such observations did not prevent Patterson believing that 'the cockney's live-and-let-live attitude would eventually overcome the problems created by "nicknames" and "jocular references"'.

In housing the rising number of West Indian landlords and increasing acceptance of West Indian tenants by white landlords had reduced the problems faced by newly arrived immigrants. However, there were still problems, for example, notices on tobacconist's boards advertising rooms which said 'Sorry, no coloured' or 'English only'.

In social life Patterson found that 'Social relationships between migrants and the local population in Brixton are ... still mainly restricted to casual contacts in the streets, shops, buses, and public houses.' But there were real signs of progress. Local shops had accepted the West Indians as customers and in some cases had started stocking goods such as calypso records and West Indian food to supply their new customers. West Indians had adopted certain pubs as their locals and become 'welcome as regular customers'.

Some West Indians had adapted to what Patterson saw as the British way of life by establishing 'various forms of the elementary family unit' and the more prosperous were quite likely to be formally married. Patterson noted, though, that many family units had proved 'impermanent'. Few West Indians and whites had inter-married, so there was little short-term prospect of physical amalgamation. However, she did find that 'A minority of male migrants, ... have been associating with white 'misfits' and declassed women, usually drawn from the provinces or other parts of London.'

Conclusion

Overall Patterson found that West Indian migrants and the host community had not generally progressed beyond the accommodation stage. In some areas though, particularly employment, progress had been considerable and she generally felt optimistic about the future. It was possible that the white residents' feelings of 'strangeness and uncertainty' about the immigrants would result in 'a more rigid class-colour identification' but Patterson did not think it likely. According to her, the West Indian immigrant community was small, quite widely dispersed, individuals from it were starting to be upwardly mobile, and had in some respects a similar culture to white British. She could therefore 'hazard the guess that over the next decades in Britain the West Indian migrants and their children will follow in the steps of the Irish' and achieve almost complete assimilation into British society.

John Richardson and John Lambert – a critique of the immigrant-host model

Criticisms of the immigrant-host model

Richardson and Lambert identify four main flaws or limitations in the immigrant-host model.

1 First, they argue that it tends to be unclear about the status of the different stages that are usually outlined. Sometimes it is seen as inevitable that a society will inevitably move through these stages with a gradual movement towards assimilation; at other times the process seems less than inevitable. Both Patterson and Park recognized that there could be long delays before a society moved on to the next stage and sometimes reversals were possible. However, at times Park also suggested that the 'race relations cycle' was an inevitable process. Thus some of the theories contradict themselves. Richardson and Lambert argue that concepts like accommodation and assimilation 'are not really spelled out, and in practice it remains difficult to identify the exact stage of "adjustment" which has been reached'.

2 Second, Richardson and Lambert question the assumption built into these theories that assimilation is desirable. The theories tend to assume that migrant groups will or should want to give up their distinctive cultures to become fully integrated into the host society. They tend to neglect the possibility that both the immigrants and the hosts might value the cultural diversity of a multicultural society. The model also places most of the emphasis on the migrants changing and does not see the need for major changes in the host society. It can therefore be seen as ideologically biased in supporting the cultural domination of the majority ethnic group in a society.

3 Third, the immigrant-host model attaches little importance to the existence of racism as a cause of ethnic conflict and inequality. Many writers argue that in Britain and elsewhere, ethnic conflict results from the deeply and widely held racist views of the host society. The hosts are far more than suspicious or cautious about the newcomers: they have been brought up to have stereotypical views and hostile attitudes. In Brixton, for example, it could be argued that the 'nicknames' and 'jocular remarks' described by Patterson were evidence of outright racism by the white

Londoners and were scarcely indicative of a 'live-and-let-live' attitude. (Racism is discussed in detail on pp. 688–711.)

4 Fourth, the immigrant-host model has been criticized by conflict theorists for assuming that there is a consensus in the host society. It hides divisions between males and females and different classes as well as between ethnic groups. It tends to ignore the cultural diversity and the wide variations in values which may already be present amongst the hosts. For example, some groups may be very strongly opposed to immigration and hold entrenched racist views while other groups might welcome cultural diversity and be in favour of relaxing or removing immigration controls.

The strengths of the immigrant-host model

Despite noting such criticisms of this model Richardson and Lambert go on to point out some of its strong points. They believe that the process of migration can influence relationships between ethnic groups and it is therefore well worth studying. They argue:

The model effectively drew attention to the dislocation caused by migration, it bravely addressed the complexities of assimilation, and it demonstrated the dynamic processes of change, rather than settling for a misleadingly static view of black-white conflict.

It raised important issues, and although it 'failed to supply satisfactory answers to all the issues, at least it stimulated further development of the debates'.

Stephen Castles and Godula Kosack – a Marxist view of migration

In a 1973 study of migration to France, Germany, Britain and Switzerland, Castles and Kosack advanced a very different theory of migration to the immigrant-host model. Rather than seeing relations between immigrants and hosts in terms of cultural differences, they argued that migration had to be examined in the context of the international capitalist system.

They found that immigrants in the four countries studied had a number of similarities. These were a 'subordinate position on the labour market, concentration in run-down areas and poor housing, lack of educational opportunities, widespread prejudice, and discrimination from the subordinate populations and authorities'. Castles and Kosack argued that these similarities showed that the diverse immigrant groups 'had the same function and position in society, irrespective of their original backgrounds'.

Migration and the international economic system

Castles and Kosack regard migration as resulting from the development of the international economic system. According to them the richer European nations have exploited the poorer nations of the world causing their underdevelopment.

From colonial times onwards the Third World has been used as a source of cheap, easily exploited labour and cheap raw materials. The colonies were not allowed to develop, or in some cases even maintain, industries which competed with their European masters. Development has also been uneven in Europe leaving potential migrants in some of the more impoverished rural areas of southern Europe. The poor in the Third World have then been used as a reserve army of labour by successful capitalist nations during periods of economic prosperity and high employment.

Migration tends to increase the inequalities between richer and poorer nations. Those who migrate are a valuable resource: they are usually young and vigorous. The society where they were born has had to pay to maintain them during their childhood when they have not been able to contribute to the wealth of their nation. Castles and Kosack therefore see 'migration as a form of development aid for the migration countries' which are able to take advantage of the labour which has cost them little or nothing to produce.

In the countries experiencing immigration the process of migration tends to benefit certain groups and to harm others. Although immigration to Western Europe has not been great enough to actually reduce wages there, the extra supply of workers has helped to prevent wages rising as much as they might have done. The immigrants have increased competition for manual jobs. As a result:

> workers are likely to lose from the tendency for immigration to restrain increases in the general wage rate. By the same token, capitalists gain, as profit rates are kept high.

'Race prejudice' and the working class

As well as directly serving the interests of the ruling class by reducing its wage bills, immigration can also help to cement its power in capitalist societies. According to Castles and Kosack prejudice against immigrants has three main functions.

1 First, it serves to 'conceal and legitimate the exploitation' of immigrant workers 'by alleging that they are congenitally inferior'. Injustice and discrimination which would otherwise be unacceptable is tolerated if it is directed at a supposedly inferior group.

2 Second, immigrant workers are often used as scapegoats for the problems created by the capitalist system. They are a convenient explanation for problems such as unemployment and housing shortages. In reality though, such problems result from 'the deficiencies of capitalist society, which is unable to provide adequate living conditions and to guarantee security to the whole of the working population'.

3 Third, '**race prejudice**' serves to divide the working class. Workers are persuaded to accept discriminatory measures against immigrant workers and this means that there is little prospect of the working class uniting to oppose capitalist power. Castles and Kosack argue:

> The traditional class consciousness based on collective ideals and actions tends to be replaced by a sectional consciousness of the indigenous workers. Indeed, the change may go even further: the orientation towards collective action designed to improve the position of all workers may be replaced by aspirations for individual advancement, without any change in the non-egalitarian structure of society.

Castles and Kosack conclude that immigration benefits the ruling class by reducing its labour costs and by preventing the working class from seeking to change the status quo which works to the advantage of the richest and most powerful members of society. (We discuss Marxist views on 'race' and ethnicity further on pp. 706–8.)

■ Stephen Castles and Mark J. Miller – *The Age of Migration*

The increase in migration

In a more recent study written with Mark Miller and published in 1993, Castles has described the internationalization of migration since 1973. He has become rather more optimistic about the effects of migration than he was in 1973.

Castles and Miller argue that migration has increased as Third World countries have become more and more involved in the world capitalist system. In Third World countries which are developing, there is considerable migration from rural to urban areas and as this happens more people acquire 'the financial and cultural resources necessary for international migration'.

Rich capitalist countries have tried to restrict migration, but are unable to do so completely. There are considerable numbers of illegal immigrants to some richer countries, for example to the USA from Mexico. In any case most countries have now established ethnic minority populations so that 'even if migration were to stop tomorrow' cultural pluralism would affect the countries 'for generations'.

There are enormous pressures encouraging migration so that 'Most highly developed countries and many less-developed ones have become far more culturally diverse than they were even a generation ago.'

The consequences of cultural pluralism

Castles and Miller argue that many countries now have no choice but to come to terms with the existence of a variety of ethnic groups within their national boundaries. 'Marginalisation and isolation' of ethnic minority groups has served only to strengthen their ethnic identity and their culture has become 'a mechanism of resistance' for some minorities. Consequently, 'Even if serious attempts were made to end all forms of discrimination and racism, cultural and linguistic differences will persist for generations.'

Although the discrimination and exclusion of ethnic minority groups is undesirable in itself, the cultural pluralism it produces opens up new possibilities. A new **global culture** develops, encouraged by the mass media, international travel and migration. People become more familiar with the culture of different societies and ethnic groups. Therefore 'difference need no longer be a marker for strangeness and separation, but rather an opportunity for informed choice among a myriad of possibilities'. International migration might even, Castles and Miller suggest, 'give hope of increased unity in dealing with the pressing problems which beset our small planet'.

To Castles and Miller then, it is no longer possible for most countries to adopt the 'monocultural and assimilationist models' which were advocated by supporters of the immigrant-host theories.

However some countries have been relatively isolated from international migration for many years. With the break-up of the USSR and the Soviet bloc in Eastern Europe, a number of countries have suddenly been exposed to enormous social changes. In such a situation 'narrow traditional cultures seem to offer a measure of defence' for those subject to these pressures. Hence **exclusionary nationalism** has led to civil war in areas such as the former Yugoslavia.

■ Ethnicity

Like the immigrant-host model sociological approaches based on the idea of ethnicity place great emphasis on culture. They distinguish human groups primarily according to the distinctiveness of their lifestyles. They tend to attach little importance to 'race' as a biological difference between humans, although they do recognize that it is important when groups of humans *believe* they belong to a particular 'race'.

However, unlike the immigrant-host model, approaches based around the idea of ethnicity do not assume that in the long term immigrant groups will assimilate by adopting the culture of the host society. The approach implies that migrant groups will very often retain large elements of their original culture, although they may modify it in a new setting. In fact ethnicity studies are not just confined to migrant groups. Nation-states can contain distinctive ethnic groups without migration having taken place. These groups may or may not be thought of as 'races'.

In this section we will begin by discussing definitions of ethnicity and we will then examine a number of studies of ethnic groups in Britain. We will then evaluate the ethnicity approach.

■ Defining ethnicity
The origins of the term ethnicity

Thomas Hylland Eriksen points out that **ethnicity** derives from the Greek word *ethnos* which is itself derived from another Greek word *ethnikos*. This meant pagan or heathen. The term ethnic had this meaning in English until around the middle of the nineteenth century when it started being used as an alternative to 'race'. However, Eriksen argues that in modern anthropology and sociology an **ethnic group** is usually seen as being culturally rather than physically distinctive. This is certainly reflected in the views of the next writer who we will consider.

J. Milton Yinger – a definition of ethnicity

J. Milton Yinger argues that there is a difference between physically defined and socially defined 'races'. He argues that physically distinct 'races' may exist in theory but in practice the boundaries between physical 'races' have become so blurred that groups of humans with a distinct phenotype are difficult to distinguish.

Yinger says that **biological 'races'** are 'of relatively little interest to the social scientist' though

they may be of some interest to 'the biologist and physical anthropologist'. **Socially defined 'races'** consist of ethnic groups who are seen by themselves or others as having distinct biological characteristics, whether or not they really do form a distinct biological group.

To Yinger an ethnic group (or as he calls it, an **ethnie**) exists in the 'fullest sense' when:

> a segment of a larger society is seen by others to be different in some combination of the following characteristics – language, religion, race and ancestral homeland with its related culture; the members also perceive themselves in that way; and they participate in shared activities built around their (real or mythical) common origin or culture.

Yinger's definition is a fairly broad one and essentially any group which believes itself to be an ethnic group and which acts in terms of that belief to any extent is an ethnic group.

Yinger says that 'phenomena on many different levels of generality' can be called ethnic groups. These can be of three main types.

1 First, he claims that an immigrant population sharing 'a common former citizenship' can be the basis for an ethnie. In America Koreans, Filipinos and Vietnamese are examples of this type of ethnie.

2 Second, an ethnic group can also consist of 'a subsocietal group that clearly shares a common descent and cultural background'. He gives the examples of native American groups such as the Oneida Indians and the Iroquois and of Turkomans in Iran and Albanians in the former Yugoslavia.

3 Third, an ethnie can be composed of:

> pan-cultural groups of persons of widely different cultural and societal backgrounds who, however, can be identified as 'similar' on the basis of language, race or religion mixed with broadly similar statuses.

In America Hispanics from different Latin American countries are sometimes seen as forming one ethnic group. In Britain Asians are sometimes seen in the same way, despite linguistic and religious differences and despite originating from different countries.

John Richardson – ethnicity and other classification systems

Richardson identifies three main classification systems:

1 'race';
2 black/white;
3 ethnicity.

He argues that there are some advantages in using ethnicity rather than 'race' and black/white. Like most sociologists he disputes the existence of clearcut biological groups in the population. He also raises a number of problems with using the term black. It can be a confusing term since sometimes it is used to refer only to those of Afro-Caribbean origin, and sometimes in countries like Britain it is used more broadly to refer to disadvantaged minorities. However, when it is used in the second sense it is still not usually seen as appropriate to apply it to groups such as the Chinese, Cypriots and people from the Middle East, yet they are sometimes as disadvantaged in Western industrialized societies as groups who are commonly referred to as black.

Another problem is that many Asians do not regard themselves as 'black'.

In some ways then Richardson sees ethnic groups as a more acceptable term than the available alternatives. He sees ethnicity as based upon cultural differences between groups and says:

> This classificatory approach is attractive in so far as it highlights socio-cultural criteria (unlike the conventional 'race' systems) and it accommodates a potentially wide range of groups (unlike the two category black/white model).

Nevertheless, Richardson believes that there are serious problems with the idea of ethnicity as well. In particular it can be very difficult to distinguish clearly between ethnic groups. Many groups are themselves subdivided and they may overlap with other groups. Ethnic groups can be distinguished in different ways leading to different classifications. Thus, for example **territorial origin** could lead to distinctions between Bangladeshis, Pakistanis and Indians whereas **religious affiliation** would lead to a distinction between Hindus, Sikhs and Muslims. **Linguistic criteria** could produce a third system.

Conclusion

Whatever these problems it can be argued that the idea of ethnic groups is the least unsatisfactory ways of dealing with the problem of classification. It is more flexible and adaptable than other approaches, and can accommodate changes in peoples' perceptions about the groups to which they belong. Groups such as the Irish in England can be accommodated within the ethnicity framework whereas they cannot under the other alternatives.

This approach is not limited to describing immigrant groups and different facets of ethnicity (such as language, religion and territorial origin), and can be used as the basis of classification as appropriate to the sociological issue or issues under consideration. Above all it recognizes that social divisions between such groups are created, maintained, altered and challenged by humans and that they are not the inevitable product of supposed biological differences.

The idea of 'race' though, remains a useful term when ethnic groups are *thought* by themselves or by others to be distinguished by phenotype.

■ Studies of ethnicity

Studies of ethnicity often take the form of **ethnographic studies**, that is studies of the lifestyles of groups of people. Ethnographic studies of ethnic groups do not always focus on migrants and their descendants, but in Britain groups of migrants from the New Commonwealth have been the most common focus for such studies.

Migrants from the Caribbean and from South Asia were the subject of a number of early studies. These studies usually compared the lifestyles of Afro-Caribbeans or South Asians in Britain with their lifestyles in their native lands in order to evaluate the extent to which the British context has affected their cultures.

Later studies, which have taken place since a substantial second generation of British-born Afro-Caribbean and South Asians have become established, have tended to examine the extent to which traditional cultures have changed across the generations.

The studies we will look at are only a small sample of the numerous studies that have been undertaken, but they are fairly typical of the genre.

■ Roger and Catherine Ballard – Sikhs in the Punjab and in Leeds

Phases of development of South Asian communities

Between 1971 and 1974 the Ballards conducted research into the lifestyles of Sikhs in Leeds and in the Julundur Doab area of the Punjab. Although their research was confined to studying Sikhs, they claim to identify four phases of development which are common to most South Asian communities in Britain.

1 The **pioneer phase** took place before the Second World War and involved a small number of early migrants establishing the first South Asian communities in Britain.

2 The second phase involved **mass migration** mainly by males in the post-war era.

3 The third phase started around 1960 and during this phase increasing numbers of wives came to Britain, the communities became more established and some South Asians began to move into better housing. The Ballards call this the **phase of family reunions**.

4 The fourth stage involved a further consolidation and improvement in housing for some and the development of a substantial British-born **second generation**. For Sikhs in Leeds this stage started around 1970, but Pakistani and Bangladeshi groups there were only entering the third phase in the early 1970s.

Pioneers

Many of the very earliest Sikh migrants were pedlars and hawkers from the Bhatra caste who arrived in Britain in the early 1920s. By the 1930s there were small communities of Punjabis in most large British cities.

For example, Darshan Singh was an important early settler in Leeds. In 1938 he had accumulated enough money to buy a shop/warehouse. Like other successful pioneer settlers he then acted as a sponsor, encouraging relatives to come and settle and helping them once they arrived. Darshan Singh came from the Ramgarhia caste of craft workers and his influence resulted in most of Leeds' Sikhs belonging to the same caste.

Muslims and Gujeratis also became established in Leeds. Ex-sailors were the most important pioneers in these communities.

Mass migration

Mass migration started in the 1950s. The pioneers provided a foundation for new migrants, often offering them hospitality and accommodation while they looked for work. The Sikh migrants in this period did not think of themselves as permanent settlers. They tended to come from neither the poorest nor the most prosperous sections of Punjabi society. The poorest could not afford the fare to Britain, and the most prosperous had no reason to leave.

Living standards are relatively good in the Punjab but as families grow larger land is divided out and some people end up with holdings which are too small to sustain a family. Misfortune or a shortage of land could prompt one or more men to go abroad in search of earnings to help sustain their families in the Punjab.

The first post-war migrants were almost exclusively male. According to the Ballards they 'regarded their villages of origin as the only meaningful arena of social interaction and tended to view Britain as a social vacuum, a cultural no-man's land'. The migrants wanted to live as cheaply as possible in order to maximize the amount of the money they could send home.

This led to the formation of all-male households, usually with 'a single landlord who assumed a kind of patriarchal authority over its members'. The landlords bought their houses as a temporary investment with no intention of staying in Britain. Large, cheap houses which accommodated a considerable number of tenants could generate a substantial income, and when they were sold they could provide the ex-landlord with a large lump sum to take back to the Punjab.

Family reunions

The Ballards identify a number of reasons why South Asian immigrants were reluctant to bring their families to Britain.

The migrants' original intention had not been to settle in Britain and many were worried about the influence British culture would have on their families if they joined them in Britain: British culture was seen as 'morally degenerate'. In any case new immigration laws could make family reunions problematic.

Furthermore, separation of husbands and wives was not as traumatic as it might be for Westerners. Sikh families, and South Asian families generally, do not place as much emphasis on the bond between wives and husbands as Western families. The wives in Asia 'were still part of the joint household, under the care of the father or brother of the absent husband'. There has been a long tradition in the Punjab of men leaving their families for long periods, sometimes to work as soldiers.

However, 'male migrants were constantly homesick for their families and despite the quasi family ties of the all male household life for the settler was ascetic'. Sikhs put less emphasis on **purdah,** or the seclusion of women, than Muslims, so Sikhs tended to be less worried about their wives coming to Britain. By 1971 the vast majority of Sikh men in Leeds were living with their wives whereas Muslim and Hindu all-male households were still quite common.

Many of the earliest male migrants had made little attempt to preserve traditional Sikh culture and values. Few took part in religious rituals and many did not bother wearing turbans or growing long hair and beards. Seeing their stay as temporary and without having to worry about their family being corrupted by Western culture, they felt little need to try to protect themselves from Western influences. However, once they were joined by their families, Sikhs in Leeds became more concerned to ensure that their traditional family life and religion were preserved.

Far from encouraging assimilation, the establishment of a less impermanent Sikh community led to a more distinctive ethnic identity. The Ballards comment:

Throughout the 1960s, the Sikhs set about recreating as many of the institutions of Punjab society as possible. This was a strong contrast to the earlier period where they merely utilised those cultural values which eased their survival.

For examples, liaisons with white girls by Sikh men began to be condemned more strongly and regular attendance at Sikh Temples became the norm.

As the Sikh community became more established and less money was sent home to the villages, it also became more prosperous. Standards of housing improved and many Sikhs set up their own businesses. The Punjabi population created an 'elaborate infra-structure of services and businesses' including goldsmiths, travel agents, cinemas and grocers' shops'.

Although the Sikh community became increasingly entrenched and the likelihood of returning to Asia decreased, the belief in an eventual return (which has been called the **myth of return**) persisted. According to the Ballards, this provided a valuable justification for preserving Sikh culture. After all, the preservation of the culture would make the eventual return smoother. It also offered some psychological protection against racism since it was believed it would only have to be tolerated on a temporary basis pending the return to Asia. Thus the Ballards say that 'The importance of return as a real goal has gradually faded and instead it has become a central charter for the maintenance of Sikh ethnicity in Britain.'

The second generation

As a second generation born in Britain became a feature of more and more Sikh families, changes in lifestyle began to take place. Many moved out of the inner city and bought houses in suburban areas north of the city. Parents became increasingly concerned about their children's education and more eager for them to stay on at school and obtain high qualifications. More wives, including those with children, started taking paid employment.

Although the Sikhs adopted some aspects of Western materialism and came to value individual educational achievement, this did not undermine traditional values within the family. Nor did it prevent strong family networks extending across different households.

The second generation of British-born and British-educated children 'have been exposed to socialisation in two very different cultures at home and at school'. The Ballards suggest that many people believe that this leads to very strong tensions between parents and children and long-lasting conflict between the generations. Their research, however, found that the conflict was often only temporary. Children would start wearing British fashions and some would start to argue about the need to visit relatives and worship at the temples. A few would contemplate running away from their family.

However, these behaviours often represented little more than a temporary period of teenage rebellion. The research found that even in the case of the runaways:

---

almost all young Sikhs, as well as members of other South Asian groups, do eventually return to seek solutions within the context of their families. They have all been socialised into a deep-rooted loyalty to the family and they find the outside world alien and unsympathetic in comparison.

Generally the second generation have modified their parents' values to make them more applicable to a British context, but they have not abandoned them. Many young Sikhs become skilled at **multiple presentations of self**, changing their behaviour between the family and the outside world of work or education. The experience of racism makes Sikhs believe that 'however much they try to conform, they can never really be British because of the colour of their skins'. This encourages a strong sense of ethnic identity and leads many young Sikhs to be determined to bring up their own children with a strong 'sense of Punjabi identity'.

Conclusion

The Ballards claim that their account of Sikhs in Leeds is applicable to most groups of immigrants to Britain from rural areas of South-East Asia. They argue, though that well-qualified professionals from urban areas adopted Western values and tried to assimilate into British society. However, they suggest that faced with discrimination these groups too have developed a greater ethnic consciousness. The Ballards say 'peasants and professionals are coming closer together'.

Nevertheless, the Ballards are critical of approaches to the sociology of ethnicity which place too much emphasis on racism and other external constraints in explaining the behaviour of ethnic minorities. Such approaches ignore 'the culturally determined preferences of the group concerned'. Both **internal preferences** and **external constraints** are important in shaping the lifestyle of ethnic minorities and neither should be ignored.

For example, Sikhs and other Asian groups have not maintained a distinctive ethnic identity just because they have been the victims of racism. The first generation had no intention of adopting Western lifestyles and their intentions have had a strong bearing on the development of the communities.

While the first generation was more divided according to such factors as kinship, religion and caste, the second generation were somewhat different. Born in Britain and having experienced racism throughout their lives, they feel a greater sense of identity with other South Asians, whatever the differences between them. Thus, according to the Ballards the second generation was, in the 1970s, 'moving towards the establishment of an over-arching South Asian ethnic group'. This ethnic identity may have been prompted by external hostility but was still actively being created through the choices being made by young Asians in Britain.

■ Roger Ballard – Sikhs and Mirpuris Muslims

Divisions in the Asian community

In an article published in 1990 Roger Ballard updated his earlier work and described changes in Asian communities in the late 1970s and 1980s. In the earlier article Catherine Ballard and he had suggested that South Asians in Britain were being drawn closer together. In his later article Ballard stressed that there were strong divisions between South Asian groups in Britain. He argues:

As it becomes increasingly obvious that settlers of different backgrounds are following varied, and often sharply contrasting social trajectories, so it is becoming steadily more difficult, and increasingly inappropriate, to make generalisations which are valid for all 'Asians' in Britain.

He notes that there are divisions according to class, caste, region of origin, religion and different experiences of migration. In order to try to explain these divisions he compares the Sikhs who originated in Jullunder Doab in India, and who are discussed above, with Muslims from the Mirpur District in Kashmir, Pakistan.

Differences between the Sikhs and Muslims

Both the Jullunduris and Mirpuris migrated to Britain from predominantly rural areas and in both groups the main aim of the early migrants was to earn money to send back to Asia. However, after arrival in Britain they followed different paths.

The Sikhs were reunited with their families earlier than the Muslims and enjoyed more economic success. As described above, many Sikhs set up their own businesses and others aspired to and succeeded in gaining middle-class jobs and statuses. By 1990 most had moved away from inner cities and their children were enjoying educational success comparable with that of middle-class white children.

Most of the Mirpuri Muslims became 'international commuters' during their early years as migrants. They would work for a time in Britain before returning home to spend some time with their families. They would then return to Britain to earn more money. A few set up their own businesses, although they were not as numerous nor as successful as those of the Sikhs. However, most relied upon unskilled or semi-skilled work in industries such as textiles and engineering. Their wages were comparatively low and from the 1970s onwards they were more likely to be hit by unemployment.

Even after being joined by their families most were unable to afford to buy homes away from the inner-cities. Their children enjoyed less academic success than their Sikh counterparts.

Economic reasons for the differences

Having described the differences, Ballard then sets out to explain them. One important reason for the greater success of the Sikhs was the greater prosperity of their region of origin. Jullunder Joab is a relatively affluent agricultural area with fertile land and a good infrastructure. Mirpur also has fertile land but it has a higher population density so landholdings tend to be small, it is difficult to irrigate and the infrastructure is poor.

As a consequence of these differences migrants from Jullundur Doab tended to have more craft and business skills and higher educational qualifications than the Mirpuris. They also tended to be more literate.

Relying on unskilled and semi-skilled work in traditional manufacturing industries made the Mirpuris much more likely to lose their jobs once recession hit Britain. However, Ballard does not believe that such differences in economic situation can, on their own, account for the contrasting fortunes of the two groups. He argues that cultural differences may also be part of the explanation.

Cultural reasons for the differences

Ballard is very cautious about attributing too much importance to cultural factors. He expresses concern about the possibility of resorting to 'sweeping and inevitably stereotypical assertions about the allegedly "conservative" or "liberal" characteristics of the two religious traditions'. Nevertheless, he does believe that differences in religion and in community and family life could partly explain differences in the fortunes of South Asian groups. Ballard identifies three important cultural differences.

1 Muslims are allowed to marry close kin and often do so whereas as it is not permitted for Sikhs and Hindus. This means that kinship networks for Muslims tend to be more close-knit and geographically limited in scope.

2 The tradition of purdah is stronger in Islam than in Sikhism and it places greater restrictions on women in public places. As a result Muslim women in Pakistan are less likely to travel long distances or to take up paid employment outside the home than Sikh women in India.

3 Sikhs and Hindus cremate their dead whereas Muslims bury them. Consequently Muslims tend to develop stronger ties to a particular village or region where their ancestors are buried.

Together these factors make Muslim families less geographically mobile and more close-knit and even inward looking. As a result the male Mirpuris immigrants to Britain were rather more cautious about bringing their wives and children to Britain than the Sikh men. As international commuters, sometimes for up to 15 years, the Muslim men used up a lot of their money on travel. Furthermore, a higher proportion of their income was sent back to Asia to be spent or invested there. By the time the men decided that their families should settle in Britain the administrative obstacles had become greater, slowing down family reunions even more.

Muslim families have therefore had less time to become established in Britain and improve their living standards than some other groups of Asians. Once in Britain Muslim wives were less likely to take paid employment limiting the earning-power of the family. Thus, although the differences in the economic success of the two groups have been influenced by economic factors and the structural features of society, cultural factors such as religion and kinship patterns have had a part to play as well.

Conclusion

Ballard stresses at the end of his article that his account is rather oversimplified. He points out that 'Sikhs' and 'Mirpuris' are not homogeneous groups. For example, members of different Sikh castes such as the Jat (peasant-farmers) and the Ramgarhia (craft workers) have followed rather different paths. Furthermore, not all Jullunduris are Sikh and many British Pakistanis come from regions other than Mirpur.

Nevertheless, Ballard's work does show that it may only become possible to explain inequalities between ethnic groups if sociologists can develop a sophisticated understanding of cultural differences, as well as examining wider structural forces.

■ Ken Pryce – West Indians in Bristol

The study

Between 1969 and 1974 Ken Pryce conducted a study of West Indians in Bristol. He relied mainly upon participant observant to collect his data but supplemented them with other methods including interviewing. His study was based mainly on St Paul's, a poor inner-city area of Bristol with a large West Indian community. Most of the population studied were, like Pryce himself, of Jamaican origin.

Like Ballard, Pryce compared the ethnic minority in Britain with the lifestyle in the country of origin. Although most of his study is descriptive, he does make use of some Marxist concepts in explaining the behaviour of West Indians in Britain. Like most ethnographers of South Asians in Britain, Pryce found the ethnic group he studied to be far from homogeneous. However, he found that West Indians were not divided according to such factors as nationality, religion, language or region of origin, but were differentiated according to the subcultures they had adopted in Britain.

All West Indians in Britain faced a series of problems in adapting to life there. They tried to solve these problems in different ways by forming a number of distinctive subcultures which helped them cope in different ways with their situation.

Jamaican origins

Most of the original immigrants to Britain who settled in Bristol were poor, working-class Jamaicans. Modern Jamaica was originally established as a plantation society, ruled by Britain, where African slaves were put to work in the service of British economic interests. According to Pryce the culture of slaves was very much shaped by the experience of slavery and was influenced much more by Western culture than by African. He says:

Not only was the African culture of the slaves destroyed, but the plantation economies, being dependent parts of the larger metropolitan economy, had the effect of extending British capitalist modes and ways of thinking to the Caribbean.

African slaves lost both their religion and their patterns of family life: most were converted to Christianity, and under slavery it was impossible to maintain stable families. The slaves adopted the British language of their masters and, to Pryce, they internalized European values. He believes that Jamaican culture came to value all things European, particularly those which were British, while African culture was rejected and even despised. He says 'In Jamaica, the closer symbols, mannerisms, appearances and institutions approx-imate and conform to British standards, the higher their value and prestige.'

In modern Jamaica family life among the lower classes is characterized by instability and by the comparative rarity of formal marriage. Although the higher classes generally adopt the 'monoga-mous nuclear family and Christian marriage', the same is not true of the poor. When men and women become partners and decide to live together, they do not usually get married immedi-ately. Indeed many never get married because they tend to split up with the wife returning to her mother, taking any children with her. If the couple stay together long enough they may get married eventually, but this may be years after they have had their children.

To Pryce the instability of marriage in Jamaica stems 'directly from the institution of slavery'. Although Jamaica is very largely Protestant it has incorporated other elements into its religion. An important feature of Jamaican religion is 'its cultic diversity and the recrudescence of non-Christian features, typically confined to the masses'.

Thus **Pentecostalism**, which is popular in Jamaica, is based upon a literal interpretation of the *Bible* but it also emphasizes the importance of possession by the Holy Spirit.

Rastafarianism is based largely upon the *Old Testament*. Founded by Marcus Garvey in the early decades of the twentieth century, it preaches that black Africans living outside Africa will even-tually return to their continent of origin and will be freed from the oppression and exploitation they have suffered at the hands of whites.

When in the 1950s a considerable number of Jamaicans emigrated and settled in Bristol, they brought with them religious beliefs and patterns of family life which were to have a strong influence on their lives in Britain.

Orientations and subcultures

From his study of Bristol, Pryce found two main orientations to society within the West Indian community. These were the **expressive-disrep-utable orientation** and the **stable law-abiding ori-entation**. The main difference between them was that those adhering to the former were unwilling to earn a living through regular work, whereas those adhering to the latter did seek regular employment.

All West Indians in Britain faced difficulty in finding well-paid secure jobs and in affording comfortable accommodation. All faced problems of discrimination and rejection by white society, yet they responded in different ways:

1 Those who adopted the expressive-disreputable orientation rejected the society which rejected them.

2 Those who adopted the stable-law abiding orientation were more willing to accept or at least tolerate their situation and some adopted the values of white society wholeheartedly.

Within the expressive-disreputable orientation Pryce distinguished two subcultures:

1 the hustlers;
2 the teenyboppers.

Within the stable law-abiding orientation there were four subcultures:

1 in-betweeners;
2 mainliners;
3 proletarian respectables;
4 saints.

Each of these subcultures will now be discussed. Pryce's overall theory is illustrated in Figure 11.2.

Hustlers

Hustlers have conventional aspirations. They want to achieve material success. However, they have become disillusioned with trying to do so through conventional means. Many have experi-enced the 'humiliating effect of racial discrimina-tion' and have become demoralized by the experience. Originally many of those who become hustlers wanted to work hard to earn enough to return home, but they found it impossible to get jobs doing anything other than 'white man's shit work'. They earned too little to save up money and they became increasingly resentful of their situation.

Pryce argues that slavery produced a strong antipathy amongst black Jamaicans to taking orders from white bosses. Being dominated by whites threatened the West Indian male's sense of masculinity. In Britain the response to discrimina-tion has been to develop 'a dread of having to work as a menial' and 'abhorrence of having to take orders from a "cheeky white man" indifferent to him as an individual'.

Figure 11.2 Ken Pryce's theory of subcultural adaptations amongst West Indians in Bristol

(*Source*: Pryce, K. (1979) *Endless Pressure*, Penguin, Harmondsworth, p. 271.)

Rejecting what they see as 'slave labour', they turn to **hustles** to earn a living. Most hustles are illegal. They involve selling drugs, acting as prostitutes' pimps, or 'conning others'. Some hustlers sell fake marijuana. One earns a living by putting on dances but he may sell tickets by claiming a famous reggae star is to appear when there is no chance of this happening. The odd hustler resorts to less subtle tactics by carrying out an armed robbery. Earning a living through hustles, rather than through more conventional means, 'restores the hustler's sense of pride and his feeling of mastery

and autonomy'. He is reliant upon his own wits to make money and dependent on nobody.

Hustlers, and others of the expressive-disreputable orientation, believe it is very important to be strong and to be able to cope with pressure from difficult circumstances. Strength helps the hustler to avoid 'getting in a plight'. Pryce defines a **plight** as:

---

any form of misfortune or predicament involving loss of face – e.g. desertion by one's wife or husband, imprisonment, being crossed in a love affair, having the bailiff on one's front step, having to pawn one's clothes, going hungry, sexual impotence, losing a fight with one's friends watching.

The pressure of avoiding these plights means that people have to let off steam. This often takes place at a 'blues dance' where hustlers gather with teenyboppers and others to listen to loud reggae and soul, drink, dance and smoke marijuana.

Teenyboppers

According to Pryce a **teenybopper** is:

a West Indian youth in his teens or very early twenties, who is male, homeless, unemployed and who in the language of liberals and social workers, is 'at risk' in the community – that is, a young West Indian who is either already a delinquent or is in danger of becoming one.

Teenyboppers are often a product of the unstable family life characteristic of lower classes in the West Indies, and which is also found in some families in Britain. During the early stages of migration to Britain children were often left behind to be raised by relatives such as aunts or grandmothers, and this loosened attachments to parents. In Britain the frequent break-up of relationships, the absence of fathers in many homes, and the presence in some cases of their mother's new partner, combined with poverty 'militate against family cohesion'.

Conflict between children and parents breaks out over issues such as how late children can stay out and who they chose as friends. The teenyboppers end up leaving home early in their lives. They find the outside world hostile and experience racism when they try to find regular work. They suffer from drift and alienation and sooner or later come into conflict with the law.

Unlike hustlers, teenyboppers tend to be much more politically conscious. Some get involved with radical political organizations. The teenybopper has a 'schizoid orientation towards both his own Negro roots, which he despises, and the white bourgeois values which he had been indoctrinated to venerate as culturally and morally superior'.

However, he is rejected by white society and he 'responds to rejection with rejection'. Some teenyboppers turn to Rastafarianism with its promise of salvation through a return to Africa, while others are influenced more by Marxism and 'a hodge-podge of the ideas and doctrines of all left-wing revolutionary positions'.

In-betweeners

As their name suggests, although Pryce sees members of this group as stable and law-abiding, he also sees them as having characteristics in common with the expressive-disreputable groups. **In-betweeners** are described as being 18–35 and ambitious for material success. They have steady jobs and are usually quite well educated and qualified. They have, or would like, a stable and conventional family life.

However, they want to achieve these things without abandoning their black roots. They believe in the importance of 'black culture' and 'black pride'. They are against close integration with whites and many hope to return to the Caribbean to use their skills to improve society there. They mix with hustlers during their leisure time and may smoke marijuana, but generally they are not very involved in illegal activities.

Mainliners

Like in-betweeners, **mainliners** have conventional jobs, they aspire to material success and stable and conventional family lives. However, they have very different values. Mainliners are very law abiding, politically conservative and in favour of integration with whites. Many work in jobs such as race relations officers, youth workers, and health visitors. A few have their own businesses or work as supervisors. They are 'mostly, literate, middle-aged, well established West Indian residents'. They have no desire to return to the West Indies and adapt to life in Britain by adopting the lifestyle and culture of the British middle class.

Mainliners are seen as traitors to blacks by in-betweeners, and are regarded with thinly disguised contempt by Pryce. He criticizes them for claiming to represent the West Indian community and becoming self-appointed leaders. He claims that they are 'not necessarily accepted as social equals by their white colleagues, who are almost always of a higher social class and better educated than they'. Pryce is particularly scathing when he says 'There is no doubt that many mainliners are nothing more than pretentious pen-pushers who are less concerned with achieving results than with gaining recognition for themselves as individuals.'

Proletarian respectables and saints

The final two groups, **proletarian respectables** and **saints**, are both working class, hard working, law abiding and politically passive. Like other West Indians they suffer from discrimination but despite this they 'tenaciously pursue regular and stable employment'. The men usually have unskilled or semi-skilled manual jobs; the women routine low-paid service jobs in areas such as catering or the NHS. Many of the first generation came to Britain with families and their experience of work in the West Indies had led to them becoming accustomed to long hours, poor conditions and low pay. In Britain they may be slightly better off than they had been, so they struggle on despite hardship.

The saints are Pentecostalists. Their religion preaches that 'Sin is rebellion against the law of God' and that 'Salvation consists in deliverance from all sin and unrighteousness through faith and repentance, water baptisms, baptism of the spirit and continuance of a godly life.' These beliefs provide powerful sanctions against criminality and deviance, but the religion also offers comfort in a racist society. Saints devalue the significance of life in this world and look to salvation in life after death, making discrimination and hardship that much easier to bear.

Conclusion

Pryce concludes that all the subcultures are ways of dealing with the work situation that confronts West Indians in Britain. They are attempts to deal with or escape from 'pressures of poverty and race' which in turn have their origins in slavery and colonialism.

For centuries blacks have been exploited as a cheap 'reserve pool' of labour by British capitalism. In the West Indians political consciousness resulted from the anti-colonial struggle for independence. Immigration to Britain resulted not only in the importation of the Westernized values adopted by the slaves, but also in the introduction of anti-colonial attitudes. This is reflected not only

in the criminality of the hustlers, but also in the political consciousness of most teenyboppers and some in-betweeners.

Evaluation

Pryce's work demonstrates the value of ethnographic studies in revealing cultural differences within ethnic minority groups. However, like most studies it is geographically limited. Although Pryce claims that his findings are probably applicable to most British towns and cities with a sizeable West Indian population, his study was confined to Bristol and wider generalizations are therefore dangerous.

His study also concentrated very much on the men in the community. The cultures of West Indian women were discussed in much less detail and assumed much less significance in his overall theory.

Although Pryce tried to link his ethnographic study in Britain with a discussion of West Indian culture in the Caribbean, his attempt to do so has been criticized. Errol Lawrence argues that Pryce is quite wrong to claim that slavery destroyed African culture and that West Indians have almost completely adopted Western, European culture. Lawrence believes, for example, that African rituals and a belief in spirit possession had a strong influence on West Indian culture, and African languages influenced the way West Indians spoke English.

Furthermore, to Lawrence slaves did not simply passively accept slavery and the attempt to destroy their culture. As well as maintaining African elements in their lifestyle some slaves rebelled or ran away from their owners.

■ James McKay – primordial and mobilizationist explanations of ethnicity

So far in this section on ethnicity we have examined how ethnicity can be defined and have considered some ethnographic studies of ethnicity. However, we have not yet dealt with explanations of how ethnic groups come to be formed in the first place. James McKay and others have identified two main types of explanation of how ethnic groups form: primordial and mobilizationist.

Primordial approaches

McKay notes that the **primordial** approach was first proposed by the American sociologist Shils in 1957. Shils claimed that people often had a primordial attachment to the territory in which they lived or from which they originated, to their religion and to their kin. This attachment involved strong feelings of loyalty and, Shils said, 'a state of intense and comprehensive solidarity' (quoted in McKay 1982, p. 398).

Some writers see primordial attachments as a basic feature of social life and a natural and inevitable phenomenon in human groups. From this point of view humans always divide the world into groups of insiders and outsiders, 'us' and 'them', and have an emotional and intuitive bond with those who belong to their group. This comes either from socialization or from some basic psychocultural need for belonging.

Primordial ethnic attachments may persist for centuries or millennia, and be the basis for intense conflict between ethnic groups over long periods.

McKay suggests that a strength of the primordial approach is that it can account for 'the emotional strength of ethnic bonds', but he is also critical of it. He claims that this approach tends to be 'deterministic and static'.

1 It assumes that members of ethnic groups have little choice about their sense of attachment, whereas in reality ethnic attachments do vary in strength from individual to individual.

2 It tends to assume that all individuals will have an ethnic identity and thus offers no explanation of the existence of 'rootless cosmopolitans'.

3 The approach cannot easily deal with changes in ethnic identity amongst groups.

4 The primordial approach attaches so much importance to basic human emotions that it tends to 'talk as if ethnic and group identities existed in a political and economic vacuum'.

Mobilizationist perspectives

The **mobilizationist** approach suggests that there is nothing inevitable or natural about ethnicity. Ethnic identities are actively created, maintained and reinforced by individuals and groups 'in order to obtain access to social, political and material resources'. People use the symbols of ethnic identity to further their own ends and ethnic groups tend to be formed when people believe they can gain some advantage by forming them.

For example, South Asians or Afro-Caribbeans in Britain might develop an ethnic identity because they believe that membership of an ethnic group offers practical and emotional support in a hostile, racist society. By forming ethnic groups it might be possible to achieve changes in the law or other political changes which strengthen their position.

McKay is perhaps slightly more sympathetic to this approach than the primordial one, but still believes that it has its limitations. It tends to underestimate the emotional power of ethnic bonds and assumes that ethnicity is always related to some interests being pursued by the group. McKay argues that this is not always the case. He says 'the fact that *some* ethnic groups pursue political and economic interests does not mean that *all* ethnic groups have identical goals'.

Furthermore this approach sometimes confuses class and ethnic stratification, seeing the two as being little different. Ethnicity, though, involves more than class interests and can cut across class boundaries. In places such as Northern Ireland, South Africa and the Lebanon, ethnic conflicts have been stronger than conflict between classes and people have tended to identify with their ethnic group regardless of their social class.

Combining the approaches

McKay believes that the **affective, emotional ties** emphasized in the primordialist model and the **instrumental ties** stressed in the mobilizationist model tend to be interrelated and both are 'manifestations' of ethnicity. Rather than being irreconcilable opposites, the two theories can be combined. Ethnicity may be based primarily on mobilizationist, or primordialist interests in different sets of circumstances. By producing a matrix based on combining the two, McKay is able to distinguish five types of ethnicity. These are illustrated in Figure 11.3.

Ethnic traditionalists

Groups of **ethnic traditionalists** are held together primarily by emotional ties. They often have a long history and their children are socialized to internalize their culture. They are not particularly concerned with pursuing social and economic interests but are more interested in maintaining a culture. They identify strongly with the ethnic

Figure 11.3. **Five types of ethnicity**

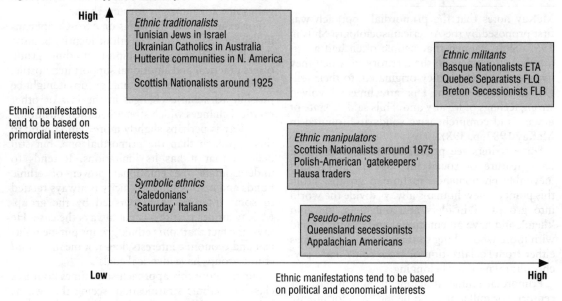

(*Source*: McKay, J. (1982) 'An exploratory synthesis of primordial and mobilizationist approaches to ethnic phenomena', *Ethnic and Racial Studies,* Vol. 5 no. 4, p. 404.)

group to which they belong. Examples include, 'the Hutterite colonies of North America, and beleaguered minorities in the Middle East such as Armenians, Assyrians, Copts, Kurds, Shiites and Lebanese Christians'. These groups may have material interests but they have not been mobilized to pursue them collectively.

Ethnic militants

Both primordial and political and economic interests are strong amongst **ethnic militants**. For example, the Basques in Spain have their own language and their own cultural symbols such as flags. However, they also have a political movement which tries to gain greater autonomy or even independence from Spain.

Symbolic ethnics

Symbolic ethnics have quite weak ethnic attachments in terms of both primordial and political and economic factors. They have only token involvement in or identification with their ethnic group. In the USA those of Scottish descent who

sometimes attend a clan festival and the Irish who occasionally join a St Patrick's Day parade are examples of symbolic ethnics.

Ethnic manipulators

This type of group tries to promote its political or economic interests but **ethnic manipulators** do not possess the same group solidarity and strong emotional ties as ethnic traditionalists and ethnic militants. Thus Scottish Nationalists in the 1970s were organized in a political party (the SNP), but its appeal was largely economic. It was not based upon an appeal to a very distinctive Scottish culture but upon the claim that Scotland would be better-off if it were ruled from Scotland rather than from Westminster.

Pseudo-ethnics

Pseudo-ethnics have the potential to become strong ethnic groups but that potential has not been realized. Leaders struggle to mobilize a sense of ethnic identity. Members of the group are more loyal to the state than to their ethnic group or potential ethnic group. For example, South Island secessionists in New Zealand want their part of the country to become independent, but they have a difficult task because those who live there do not have a strong sense of primordialist attachment to the island. McKay says:

It could be said that ethnic militants and manipulators possess an ethnic trait which they utilize in order to obtain access to societal resources, whereas pseudo-ethnics try to make their pursuit of political and economic goals more legitimate by finding an ethnic foundation on which they can be based.

Conclusion

McKay admits that his **matrix model approach** is not fully developed. It does not explain why ethnicity takes one form or another, but he believes that further research could help to develop causal theories based upon his matrix. He argues that the matrix can be used to examine how ethnic groups change over time and move from one part of the matrix to another. It can also be used to distinguish factions within ethnic groups. For example McKay says 'Orthodox Jews, members of Jewish "defence" organizations, and militant Zionists have different types and degrees of ethnic organization and identification.'

Whatever the merits or disadvantages of McKay's approach some critics have suggested that the whole ethnicity approach has limitations or is even inadequate. We will examine these criticisms in the next section.

■ Ethnicity – an evaluation

The ethnicity approach certainly has some advantages over biological theories of 'race' and the immigrant-host model. Unlike the former it does not base its arguments upon physical distinctions which modern genetics has found of little significance in themselves. Unlike the latter it does not assume that immigrant and other minority groups will assimilate by adopting the culture of the majority or of the hosts.

The ethnicity approach tends to be sympathetic to cultural diversity and to support **multiculturalism** – the belief that ethnic or cultural groups can

peacefully co-exist in a society showing respect for one-another's cultures. At least in theory, ethnographic studies allow the development of an insider's view of different cultures, and therefore facilitate a greater understanding of those cultures than is likely from other sociological approaches. Such studies also have the strength of recognizing the role that ethnic minorities have in shaping their own lives. They are not presented as the helpless captives of biology or the passive victims of racism. Ethnographic studies can reveal subtle variations and divisions within ethnic groups which are often lost in other approaches.

However, the ethnicity approach is far from perfect. Critics tend to argue that it places too much emphasis on the culture of ethnic minorities. While emphasizing how ethnic minorities shape their own lives, it sometimes neglects the wider forces which constrain members of ethnic minority groups. Both racism and structural features of society which may cause inequality tend to be neglected. Writers like Pryce do mention colonialism and refer to social classes, but their arguments still centre on the culture of the groups being studied.

Marxists and other conflict theorists believe that the analysis of racism and inequalities stemming from the structure of society should be the starting point for an understanding of ethnic difference and inequality, and not a subsidiary theme. The ethnicity approach is sometimes criticized for offering unconvincing explanations of why people form ethnic groups in the first place. The racism approach and conflict theories claim to have superior explanations. We will examine racism and conflict approaches in the next sections.

The ethnicity approach has theoretical links to symbolic interactionism. Both tend to use participant observation as a research method and both emphasize the importance of seeing the social world from the actor's point of view. It is not surprising then, that the ethnicity approach shares many of the limitations of symbolic interactionism. Not only does it tend to neglect social structure, it also relies upon research methods which can be seen as subjective. The findings of participant observation studies depend very much upon the observer's interpretations and they are liable to be questioned.

For example, some sociologists question the view of sociologists such as Pryce that West Indian family life is unstable and produces delinquency. Errol Lawrence attacks Pryce saying that he 'absolves the racist structures of the English education system by defining the Afro-Caribbean child's struggle against its racism as "maladjusted behaviour"'. Clearly Lawrence interprets the same behaviour very differently to Pryce.

Racism

Introduction

Many of the ethnicity approaches discussed in the preceding section recognize the existence of racism and accept that racism influences the behaviour of ethnic minority groups. However, they place more emphasis on the choices made by members of ethnic minority groups than on the constraints which can result from the hostility and discrimination of the ethnic majority.

Sociological approaches which attach particular importance to racism emphasize the limitations imposed on ethnic minorities by such hostility and discrimination. The focus of attention is not the ethnic minority itself, but the wider society in which it is a minority group. There is more concern with the inequalities between ethnic groups than with cultural differences, and racism is therefore a particularly important concept in conflict approaches to 'race' and ethnicity.

In this section of the chapter we will start by considering definitions of racism and related words, before discussing the extent of racism. We will then examine explanations for the existence of racism.

Definitions
Prejudice and discrimination

The terms prejudice and discrimination are general ones which can be applied to many issues other than those to do with 'race' and ethnicity. For example, people may be prejudiced against people who are very short or discriminate against other people because they are women.

In the *Dictionary of Race and Ethnic Relations* E.E. Cashmore defines **prejudice** as 'learned beliefs and values that lead an individual or group of individuals to be biased for or against members of particular groups'. Prejudice is therefore about what

Multiculturalism, with which the approach is often associated, is not accepted as politically desirable by all sociologists. We will discuss the values underpinning it in the final part of this chapter (see pp. 721–2).

people think and is not necessarily translated into actions.

Discrimination, on the other hand, is about actions. Cashmore defines it as 'the unfavourable treatment of all persons socially assigned to a particular category'.

Both prejudice and discrimination are often based on stereotypes about particular groups of people. **Stereotypes** are over-simplified or untrue generalizations about social groups. For example, short people might be stereotyped as being unusually aggressive, and women as being weak and passive. When stereotypes imply negative or positive evaluations of social groups, they become a form of prejudice, and when they are acted on they become discrimination.

Early sociologists of 'race' and ethnicity often use the terms **racial prejudice** and **racial discrimination** to describe prejudice or discrimination directed at groups by virtue of their membership of a supposed racial or ethnic group. However, the use of these terms has become less common and racism has largely replaced them as the most widely used term.

Racism

Racism is a controversial term with no single, generally accepted definition. Robert Miles has discussed the origins of the term and identified a number of different ways in which it has been used.

According to Miles **racism** is a relatively new word. There was no entry for it in the *Oxford English Dictionary* of 1910. Its first use in English seems to date from the 1930s. At that time it was used as a description of the nineteenth-century theories which claimed that there were distinct, biologically differentiated 'races'. As scientists began to reject this view some termed their nineteenth-century counterparts who advocated it

racists. Racism also came into use in the 1930s as a description of the beliefs of Hitler and the Nazi party in Germany.

This definition was an extremely narrow one. It meant that racism did not exist so long as it was not based upon a belief that there were biologically distinct races. The view that racism was a mistaken view about biological divisions between human groups was reflected in a definition used by UNESCO. During the 1950s and 1960s this organization arranged four conferences where experts from different countries came together to produce agreed statements about 'race' that could be issued by the UN. The fourth statement defined racism for the first time saying, 'Racism falsely claims that there is a scientific basis for arranging groups hierarchically in terms of psychological and cultural characteristics that are immutable and innate.' (Quoted in Miles 1989, p. 46.) While broadening the definition to include beliefs about psychological and cultural differences, this still retained the idea that racism had to be based upon supposedly scientific theories.

This view was rejected by the British Weberian sociologist John Rex. Rex specifically stated that racist theories did not have to be based upon a scientific justification. He defined racism as 'deterministic belief systems about the differences between the various ethnic groups, segments or strata'. Racist theories attributed characteristics to human groups which were determined by factors beyond their control and these characteristics could not be changed. Rex said:

It doesn't really matter whether this is because of men's genes, because of the history to which their ancestors have been exposed, because of the nature of their culture or because of divine decree. Whichever is the case it might be argued that this man is an X and that, being an X, he is bound to have particular undesirable qualities.

Rex's description of racism retains the idea that the word refers to theories about the differences between groups and the desirability or undesirability of these differences. Many contemporary definitions of racism do not limit the meaning of the term so that it refers only to theories and beliefs. Some also use racism to refer to behaviour which is based upon such theories and beliefs.

John Solomos, for example, defines it as 'those ideologies and social processes which discriminate against others on the basis of their putatively different racial membership'. It need not be based upon any specific theory about biological or cultural superiority because to Solomos 'racism is not a static phenomenon'. People may hold stereotypical views about people from different supposed racial groups and may discriminate against them without necessarily believing the group is inferior.

Some sociologists have described a **new racism** which does not involve clearly articulated beliefs about the superiority or inferiority of particular groups (see p. 708 for details).

A broad definition such as Solomos's perhaps comes closest to the meaning attached to racism in everyday language. People may be described as **racist** when they discriminate against members of other 'races' or express derogatory or stereotypical beliefs about them regardless of what sort of theory, if any, underlies their actions or beliefs.

Precise definitions of racism continue to vary between contemporary sociologists. We will examine these differences as this section of the chapter develops.

Cultural racism

Richardson defines **cultural racism** as 'a whole cluster of cultural ideas, beliefs and arguments which transmit mistaken notions about the attributes and capabilities of "racial groups"'. This definition is in line with many definitions of racism – for example it has much in common with Rex's definition. However, cultural racism always refers to the attributes of a society's culture rather than the beliefs held by individuals. An individual might hold racist beliefs, but it would only be an example of cultural racism where that belief was widely shared.

The idea of cultural racism is similar to some definitions of institutional racism which we discuss later.

Racialism

To add to the confusion, some sociologists distinguish between racism and racialism. John Rex, for example, describes **racialism** as 'unequal treatment of various racial groups' as opposed to racism which involves beliefs about racial groups. In other words racialism involves actions, whereas racism does not; it is only concerned with what people think.

This distinction is not usually made in everyday language and has not been adopted by all sociologists.

Institutional racism

The term institutional racism is perhaps even more controversial than racism. Not only is it used in widely varying ways, but some have questioned whether institutional racism actually exists.

According to Miles the idea of **institutional racism** originated in the work of American Black Power activists in the 1960s. In 1968 Carmichael and Hamilton defined racism as 'the predication of decisions and policies on considerations of race for the purpose of *subordinating* a racial group and maintaining control over that group'. Racism could be individual and overt, where people consciously and openly discriminated against blacks. However, it could also take the form of institutional racism. This was often covert or hidden. It did not require conscious discrimination since it took place as a result of 'the active and pervasive operation of anti-black attitudes' (quoted in Miles 1989, p. 51).

The idea of institutional racism was further developed by American sociologists such as Robert Blauner. Like Carmichael and Hamilton, Blauner argued that racism need not be conscious or based on individual prejudice. Blauner argued that racism was built into the way that major American institutions worked. Racism was 'located in the actual existence of domination and hierarchy' (quoted in Miles 1989, p. 52) and it ensured the continued domination of particular races by others.

Like Carmichael and Hamilton, some sociologists have defined institutional racism in terms of the domination of blacks by whites and have not used it to apply to any racial groups.

Wellman argues that racism is concerned with protecting an advantaged position in society. Since, in American society at least, whites tend to be advantaged and blacks disadvantaged, only whites can be racist.

Another American sociologist, Katz, argues that all white Americans are inevitably racist regardless of their individual beliefs because racism is 'perpetuated by Whites through their conscious and/or unconscious support of a culture and institutions that are founded on racist policies and practices' (quoted in Miles 1989, p. 56).

In Britain institutional racism has also been used in a variety of ways. David Mason identifies five of them.

1 The **conspiracy version** occurs when those in positions of power in public institutions deliberately set out to discriminate against racial groups. Mason cites the *Scarman Report*, which investigated the Brixton riots of 1981, in this context. Scarman denied that Britain was an institutionally racist society 'If by that what is meant is that it is a society which knowingly, as a matter of public policy, discriminates against black people.' (Quoted in Mason 1982, p. 38.)

2 The **structural Marxist** view of institutional racism does not depend upon the existence of conscious prejudice and discrimination. This argues that racism results from the consequences of state policy regardless of the intentions behind it. In other words if government policy results in inequality between racial groups, then this demonstrates that the state is racist whether or not individuals who hold positions in the state are racist as individuals.

The state acts to serve the interests of capitalists by trying to ensure profitability for their enterprises. In doing so it is bound to follow racist policies. For example, it might encourage the immigration of cheap easily exploited labour when it is needed, and then use that labour force as scapegoats for the failings of capitalism when unemployment rises and there is a shortage of adequate housing.

3 The **unintended consequences** approach to institutional racism has been particularly influential. This argues that institutions in society can lead to racial disadvantage and inequality as a consequence of following policies which were not designed to be racist. For example, in a 1960s study of housing in Birmingham Rex and Moore found that ethnic minority groups tended to end up in poor housing and had little success in obtaining council housing. This was partly because the council gave preference to those who had lived in the area longest. As fairly recent immigrants, most members of ethnic minorities were well down the list.

Similarly, Lord Scarman found that policing policies in Brixton, London, designed to reduce the number of 'street crimes' by stopping and searching suspects on the streets, resulted in discrimination against Afro-Caribbeans. Since they were most likely to be present on the streets when the police were looking for suspects, they were more likely to be stopped and arrested.

Neither of these policies may have been motivated by racial prejudice but both had the effect of discriminating against ethnic minorities. Sometimes it may be a question of what an organization does not do rather than the active policies it follows. For example, if job vacancies are not advertised in newspapers read by ethnic minority groups, then this can restrict their job opportunities even if the selection procedure adopted by an institution tries to provide equal opportunities.

4 The **colonialism version** of institutional racism suggests that the role in which racial or ethnic minority groups enter a society can result in institutional racism. John Rex argues that New Commonwealth immigrants to Britain were forced to take menial roles in keeping with their status as migrants from former colonies. Robert Blauner has developed a similar argument about the consequences of black Americans with the status of former slaves taking positions in society. In both cases the initial disadvantages created long-tern inequalities because the ethnic minority groups tend to be located at the bottom of their respective society's stratification systems and upward social mobility was very difficult.

5 The final type of institutional racism identified by Mason is **political opportunism**. This claims that institutional racism results not so much from prejudice but from the workings of the democratic process. Political groups will try to gain votes by taking advantage of 'race' like any other issue to increase their popularity since the primary aim of all politicians is to win elections. Thus all major political parties in Britain have sought to win over voters by supporting immigration controls and parties like the British National Party and National Front have sought electoral success by advocating openly racist views and policies.

Criticisms of the concept of institutional racism

In view of the wide variations in the way the term institutional racism has been used, it is not surprising that it has become a controversial concept. Even those who use it themselves tend to criticize sociologists who use the term in different ways.

Robert Miles, for instance, sees institutional racism as 'exclusionary practices' which disadvantage racial groups but are no longer justified in terms of racist beliefs. Using this fairly narrow definition he criticizes wider definitions. He argues that broad definitions of institutional racism that see it as stemming from the structure of society are 'inseparable from a theory of stratification that is simplistic and erroneous'. They assume that all members of ethnic minorities are equally disadvantaged by the structural factors. Consequently these approaches to the concept are not able to account for the differences in success between ethnic minority groups.

Miles is particularly critical of approaches which suggest that institutional racism is simply 'what "white" people do'. These rely too much on attributing racism to individual behaviour and ignore the possibility that there are some structural constraints limiting opportunities for the victims of institutional racism. Furthermore, they limit the application of the concept to one historical situation – the institutional racism of 'whites' against 'blacks' – when racism can and has appeared in other contexts.

The last point is also raised by John Richardson. He suggests that some views on racism:

run the risk of transforming race relations in Britain into a simple morality play in which white 'villains' persecute black 'victims' (although in the wings there are black 'heroes' and 'heroines' waiting to rescue the victims).

As Richardson points out, this denies the possibility of racism between ethnic minority groups or even that directed against whites.

Institutional racism – conclusion

Some sociologists take the existence of inequalities between ethnic minorities as evidence of institutional racism. If, for example, Afro-Caribbeans do less well in the British education system than other groups, this could be seen as a clear indication that British education suffers from institutional racism.

However, this is not necessarily the case. Other factors such as social class or family background *could* account for the differences and it cannot be automatically assumed that the education system is responsible.

Structuralist accounts of institutional racism though, tend to rely upon such evidence. If racism has nothing to do with the beliefs or actions of individuals and is simply the outcome of policies, whatever those policies were intended to achieve, then the only evidence that can be used to show that institutional racism exists is evidence of inequality.

The use of institutional racism in such a way tends to obscure the causes of inequalities between ethnic groups by attributing them to something which cannot be measured and is just assumed to be all-pervasive. For this reason, perhaps the term is most useful when it is used to refer to actual policies and practices in institutions which can be shown to have the effect of disadvantaging some groups.

This view is supported by John Richardson who says that 'institutional racism implies that racism is found in the chief policies of our dominant institutions'. While some sociologists do not use the term unless it can be shown that there was a deliberate intention to discriminate, Richardson believes that this usage is too restrictive. He argues:

---

regardless of the original intentions of the personnel involved, there is little doubt that their policies – or sometimes *lack* of policies – nevertheless have damaging social consequences for the less powerful ethnic and racial minorities.

■ Racism and the law

In the 1960s and 1970s the British Government passed laws making some forms of racial discrimination illegal. In this section we will outline that legislation and will briefly consider how effective it has been.

The 1965 Race Relations Act

The 1965 Race Relations Act banned discrimination on the grounds of 'race, colour, or ethnic or national origin' in 'places of public resort' such as restaurants and on public transport. It also made it illegal to incite racial hatred in speech or writing.

The Act was widely criticized for being too limited. It did not cover discrimination in housing or employment, both of crucial importance to people's life chances. Furthermore the **Race Relations Board** which enforced the legislation had little power. Zig Layton-Henry says that 'It quickly found that most of the complaints it received were outside its jurisdiction, and even

those it could deal with it had little power to enforce.'

The 1968 Race Relations Act

The 1968 Race Relations Act did extend the scope of the earlier act to include employment, housing and the provision of commercial and other services. Discriminatory advertising and notices were banned. The Race Relations Board was given the power to investigate complaints of racial discrimination, institute conciliation procedures, and, if those did not work, take legal proceedings.

The 1968 Act certainly strengthened race relations legislation but it still had important limitations. The Race Relations Board had to wait for complaints to be made to it and could not investigate discrimination where the victims might not be aware that they had been unfairly treated. It still excluded some important areas of 'social' life, particularly the police: complaints against them on the grounds of racial discrimination continued to be investigated by the police themselves.

Zig Layton-Henry suggests that the small number of cases which were effectively dealt with by the Board indicate that it still lacked teeth. From April 1969 to April 1970 982 complaints were investigated. In 734 cases it was decided that there was no discrimination, while 143 of the cases where it did find discrimination were related to advertising – Layton-Henry suggests that the legislation was effective in dealing with discrimination in that area. However, the Board was less effective in dealing with discrimination in employment and housing. It is much harder to prove that discrimination has taken place in these areas, and consequently few cases were brought to court. In fact of the 2,967 complaints investigated by the end of March 1972, only seven resulted in court cases. The penalties for those who were convicted usually involved the payment of very small sums in damages.

The 1976 Race Relations Act

The most recent act dealing with racial discrimination was the 1976 Race Relations Act. This introduced the idea of indirect discrimination which was seen as using unjustifiable requirements or conditions which had the effect of discriminating against an ethnic minority group, even if the criteria of exclusion were not directly ethnic or racial ones.

For example, if an employer stipulated that potential employees had to have been born in the UK or that they could not live in an inner-city area, then these policies could be seen as indirectly discriminatory since members of ethnic minorities are more likely to fall into these categories. The Act also established the **Commission for Racial Equality** which had the task of promoting racial harmony and could give legal assistance to those who believed they had been the victims of discrimination.

Layton-Henry says that the Commission for Racial Equality was 'a much more powerful body than its predecessors, with much greater scope and powers for strategic initiatives in enforcing the law'. In 1984 it got Parliament to accept a new code of practice in employment, and it has conducted a wide range of revealing investigations into many different organizations including Hackney Council, St George's Hospital Medical School and the National Bus Company. The Commission has exposed evidence of discrimination in the criminal justice system and has assisted local community relations councils.

However, like most other commentators Layton-Henry believes that the Commission for Racial Equality has not achieved as much as might have been possible with stronger powers and more resources. It has continued to be difficult to bring prosecutions and with limited resources the Commission has often had to make difficult decisions about which cases and investigations to pursue and which to drop. Furthermore, Layton-Henry comments:

The return of the Conservatives in 1979 created a less favourable environment for the Commission's work as the new government was generally hostile to what it called the 'race relations industry' and reluctant to allocate resources to it.

Legislation against any sort of discrimination is likely to have a limited impact. It is often difficult to prove that actions were motivated by prejudice, and changes in a society's culture, although slower to produce change, may have a greater effect in the longer term. In the next part of the chapter we will examine whether there is any evidence that legislation and/or cultural changes have led to any reduction in racism in Britain.

■ The extent of individual racism

The Institute of Race Relations 1969 Report

Some attempts have been made to discover how widespread racist beliefs are amongst individuals. In 1966–7 E.J. Rose and others carried out a study for the Institute of Race Relations which involved questionnaire research with a national sample of 2,500 people, and a more detailed study in five English urban areas which had large ethnic minority populations. The report was published in 1969.

The questionnaires included four key questions about racial prejudice. These were:

1 'If you had any choice would you particularly avoid having neighbours from any of these places – West Indies, India, Pakistan?'

2 'Do you think the majority of coloured people in Britain are superior, equal, or inferior to you?'

3 'Do you think the authorities should let or refuse to let a council house or flat to a family born in the West Indies, India or Pakistan?'

4 'Do you think a private landlord should let or refuse to let a house or flat to a family born in the West Indies, India or Pakistan?'

Respondents were then divided into categories.

1 Those who gave no hostile answers to these four questions were defined as **tolerant**;

2 those who gave one hostile answer as **tolerant-inclined**;

3 those who gave two hostile answers as **prejudiced-inclined**;

4 those who gave three or four hostile answers as **prejudiced**.

Rose and his fellow researchers found that in the five boroughs studied 35 per cent of the sample were tolerant, 38 per cent tolerant-inclined, 17 per cent prejudiced-inclined and 10 per cent prejudiced. They found that:

1 women were slightly more tolerant than men;

2 the most prejudiced were in the 45–54 age group and the least prejudiced were under 35 and over 65;

3 skilled manual workers and their wives and the lower middle class were more prejudiced than other classes;

4 those with post-compulsory education were less prejudiced than others;

5 Conservative voters were more prejudiced than Labour voters who in turn were more prejudiced than Liberal voters;

6 Tenants of private landlords were more prejudiced than owner-occupiers or council tenants.

Despite these differences overall, the study found that the most prejudiced in the population were not confined to specific social groups and could be found in all sections of society.

The biggest differences found between the 10 per cent of the population who were most prejudiced and the rest, were psychological. The most prejudiced people were 'much more prone than others to an authoritarian approach to life' and this approach to life involved 'an exaggerated need to submit to authority and acute hostility towards any outgroups'. These characteristics, the report suggested, stemmed from a hostility to ingroups and originally their parents. In trying to keep this hostility in check individuals overcompensated and became hostile to outgroups. For this 10 per cent of the population prejudice represented 'irrational "solutions" to personality inadequacies'.

The attitudes of those who were found to have less strong prejudice came from different causes. To Rose *et al.* it was the result either of misinformation about ethnic minority groups or of competition with ethnic minorities for scarce resources such as housing, hospital beds or school places.

Although little could be done about those with personality problems, the prejudice of others could be tackled through improved, more accurate information about ethnic minorities, and a reduction of competition through the provision of more houses, hospital beds and school places.

The British Social Attitudes Surveys

More recent data which give some indication of changes in the amount of individual racism have been produced by the *British Social Attitudes Surveys*. Since 1983 these annual surveys of a representative sample of the British population have included questions on racism. In general the results of the surveys offer some grounds for optimism.

Table 11.5 How would you describe yourself . . . as very prejudiced against people of other races, a little prejudiced or not prejudiced at all?

	1983 %	1987 %	1991 %
Very prejudiced	4	4	2
A little prejudiced	31	34	29
Not prejudiced at all	64	60	68

(*Source*: Jowell, R. *et al.* (1992) *British Social Attitudes Survey the 9th Report*, p. 183.)

Table 11.5 shows the percentage of respondents who described themselves as very prejudiced, a little prejudiced or not prejudiced. It shows that the percentage who described themselves as 'Not prejudiced at all' increased from 64 to 68 per cent between 1983 and 1991. Although this is a small increase, it does suggest some reduction in racism over that period.

Like the Institute for Race Relations study, the 1991 *British Social Attitudes Survey* found differences in prejudice according to party allegiance. Some 25 per cent of Labour supporters but 40 per cent of Conservative supporters admitted to being 'a little prejudiced' or 'very prejudiced'. Women were less likely than men to admit to being prejudiced.

The surveys also asked respondents whether they would be willing to have a boss or a member of their family from an ethnic minority background. The results are shown in Table 11.6. As the table shows, the proportions who would mind having a person of West Indian or Asian origin as their boss or as a member of their family have declined. However, respondents were much more likely to say they would accept a person from an ethnic minority background as a boss than as a member of their family.

The report did find that older age groups were considerably more likely to express an objection than those from younger age groups, providing further ground for supposing that racial prejudice was decreasing.

The report found very little support for increased Asian or West Indian immigration but it found that large majorities supported the anti-discrimination laws. Furthermore in 1991 73 per cent of respondents thought that racial prejudice had declined or remained as common as in the past. This compared to just 42 per cent in 1983. If these

Table 11.6 Objections by British whites to ethnic minority 'bosses' and family members

Percentage of respondents minding 'a little' or 'a lot'	1983	1984	1986	1989	1991
Person of West Indian origin					
– as boss	20	20	18	20	12
– in the family	57	51	46	52	44
Person of Asian origin					
– as boss	19	22	17	20	14
– in the family	51	53	50	49	43

(*Source*: Jowell, R. *et al.* (1992) *British Social Attitudes Survey the 9th Report*, p. 185.)

findings are to be believed, Britain is slowly becoming a less racist society, but the change has been slow and there is a very long way to go before individual racism will be eradicated.

Conclusion – studies of individual racism

These studies give some indication of how willing people are to say they are racist and they give an indication of changes over time. They also provide interesting data about the distribution of racist beliefs in different social groups. However, they do not measure how many people act in a racist or racialist way.

Furthermore the studies have methodological limitations. They rely upon measuring the strength of the racist beliefs held by individuals, beliefs which respondents in questionnaire or interview research may be unwilling to admit. They are based upon the idea that racism is a characteristic of individuals, and perhaps a minority of individuals, rather than a feature of a society's culture or structure. They therefore add little to sociological understanding of cultural racism or institutional racism. At the very least they need to be supplemented by studies of these types of racism.

Racism and the press

Many sociologists argue that racism is not just a matter of individual prejudice but is also a feature of many societies' cultures and institutions. As we saw earlier, such sociologists tend to use the terms cultural racism and institutional racism. We will analyse a number of the theories of racism later in this section when we deal with different aspects of

cultural racism (see for example pp. 702–11). In other chapters we will cover studies of the nature and extent of racism in the education system and criminal justice system (see pp. 780–4 and 421–5). In the next section of the chapter we will use the mass media as an example of how racism may be found in important social institutions.

The mass media may play a significant role in shaping attitudes to 'race' in society as a whole and in creating or sustaining cultural racism.

Paul Hartmann and Charles Husbands – racism and the press 1963–70

In a study of racism in the British press, Paul Hartmann and Charles Husbands examined a sample of copies of *The Times*, *Guardian*, *Daily Express* and *Daily Mirror* published between 1963 and 1970. They analysed the content of their sample in order to discover how the issue of 'race' was portrayed in the press. The articles which made reference to 'race' in Britain were most likely to be about immigration, race relations, crime, legislation and discrimination.

From an analysis of the headlines of these stories they found that many contained words indicating violence or conflict. Some 10 per cent of the headlines contained violent words like 'murder', 'kill', 'shoot' or 'burn' and 12 per cent contained words suggesting conflict such as 'hate', 'crisis', 'row', 'clash' and 'threat'. Some 6 per cent contained what Hartmann and Husbands called 'restrictive words' such as 'stop', 'curb', 'cut', 'ban' and 'bar'. In about 30 per cent of the headlines including the word 'race' or a word derived from it (such as racial), the headline also included a conflict or violent word.

Although many of the newspapers expressed opposition to racism in their editorials, the news coverage produced a negative image of ethnic minorities. Positive stories about 'race' relations were few and far between. Many stories associated ethnic minorities with conflict and violence or presented their presence in Britain as a problem. Hartmann and Husbands comment:

> coloured people have not on the whole been portrayed as an intimate part of British society. Instead the press has continued to project an image of Britain as a white society in which the coloured population is seen as some kind of aberration, a problem, or just an oddity, rather than as 'belonging' to society.

Teun A. van Dijk – racism and the press in the 1980s

Some years later Teun van Dijk carried out a similar study to that of Hartmann and Husbands. He examined all copies of *The Times*, the *Guardian*, the *Daily Telegraph*, the *Daily Mail* and the *Sun* published between 1 August 1985 and 31 January 1986, and all copies of the same papers plus the *Independent* published in the first six months of 1989. In the earlier period there were 2,700 articles which made reference to ethnic minorities but in the later period there were only 1,200.

In 1985–6 no less than 974 of the stories concerned inner-city disturbances in which members of ethnic minorities were involved. The most frequently occurring words in these stories were 'police', 'riot', 'black' and 'race'. The dramatic and rather negative term 'riot' was preferred to more neutral terms such as 'unrest' or 'disturbance'. Van Dijk argues:

> the prominent presence of the concept of 'black' in the headlines suggests that the disturbances are defined primarily in terms of ethnic background or colour. They are not defined as 'urban' or 'social' forms of protest or unrest, or as actions of 'youths', but specifically attributed to black people, usually

young males, despite the fact that about 30 per cent of the participants were white.

Words such as 'murder', 'attack', 'death' and 'terror' appeared frequently in the headlines. Thus a fairly typical headline was 'West Indian Gang Invaded Pub in Revenge Riot' (*Daily Telegraph*, 23 August 1985). Like Hartmann and Husbands, van Dijk found that ethnic minorities were frequently associated with violence or conflict in newspaper stories. Generally members of ethnic minorities were associated with negative actions and rarely portrayed as victims, for example in racially motivated attacks. Whites, on the other hand were quite often portrayed as victims and were less likely to be associated with negative actions.

Another story which received widespread coverage in 1985–6 was the Honeyford affair. Honeyford was a headmaster in a Bradford school who wrote a number of articles in which he claimed that white children were disadvantaged in schools where there was a majority of ethnic minority children. He attacked the idea of multicultural education, arguing that it could lead to the neglect of white culture. Honeyford was suspended but later reinstated. Van Dijk found that many headlines were sympathetic to Honeyford's position and critical of his opponents. For example, the *Daily Mail* on 17 October 1985 ran a story under the headline 'Rent-A-Rowdy Attack Forces Race Row Head out of College'. Van Dijk comments:

> These headlines first show that the tabloids tend to define as a 'mob' any group of people who engage in public actions which the tabloids do not like. In this case, this applies to a group of mostly Asian parents of the Bradford school, who picket the school, and demonstrate against Honeyford's return. For the tabloids, this legitimate protest is redefined as a violent battle, in which the opponents are implicitly qualified as irrational.

In the 1989 coverage there was less frequent mention of violence. Van Dijk found that 'ethnic reporting in 1989 has become less negative and aggressive'. However, he admitted that this could just be due to the types of stories that featured in the news at that particular time.

Furthermore, there were still many stories which portrayed ethnic minorities as a threat. A *Sun* headline on 2 February 1989 stated 'Britain Invaded by an Army of Illegals'. Some of the stories emphasized a supposed cultural threat from ethnic minorities. Van Dijk comments that 'Whereas in 1985 the major villains were young rioting blacks, now the "threat" to British society comes from fundamentalist Muslims.' Islamic fundamentalism featured so prominently in the news in that year because of the publication of Salman Rushdie's book *The Satanic Verses* which the Ayatollah Khomeini of Iran declared to be sacrilegious and consequently he issued a *fatwa* or death sentence against Rushdie. Rushdie, a British citizen was forced to go into hiding.

Although the findings for 1989 suggest there might have been some reduction in the amount of racism in the press, van Dijk's study indicates that the portrayal of ethnic minorities in at least some parts of the media continues to be predominantly negative.

■ Inequalities between ethnic groups in Britain

In this section we examine the statistical evidence about the extent of inequality between ethnic groups in Britain and evidence about whether this inequality is increasing or decreasing. The inequalities may be caused by individual racism, cultural racism or institutional racism, but may also be the result of other factors such as cultural differences or class inequality. (Details of some inequalities between ethnic groups are discussed elsewhere in the book. See pp. 777–8 for data on ethnic groups and educational achievement and p. 240 for information on ethnicity and unemployment.)

In 1991–2 Trevor Jones conducted research for the Policy Studies Institute (PSI) into inequality between ethnic minorities in Britain. He used data from the *Labour Force Survey* to determine the life chances of ethnic minorities compared to the rest of the British population. Figures were produced for 1984–6 and 1988–90. The study also incorporated some figures from earlier studies carried out by the PSI and its predecessor, Political and Economic Planning. These earlier studies were conducted in 1966–7, 1974–5 and 1982.

Employment

The most recent PSI study found that participation in employment was similar for white men and men from ethnic minorities. However, only 23 per cent of Pakistani and Bangladeshi women were in work in 1988–90, compared to 57 per cent of Indian women, 71 per cent of white women and 76 per cent of Afro-Caribbean women.

Tables 11.7 and 11.8 show the job levels of men and women from different ethnic groups. Indian, Chinese and Africa Asian males were found to have similar or better job levels than white males. It was found that members of these groups who were in the top category were very largely employed in professional rather than managerial jobs, whereas there was a much higher proportion of white men holding managerial jobs. As Jones says 'men from certain minority groups have penetrated to a remarkable extent into certain professions, but to a much lesser extent into the management of large organizations'. Afro-Caribbean, Pakistani and Bangladeshi men were all very under-represented in the highest category.

The differences amongst women were not as great. Chinese women were found to have been more successful than white women in becoming professionals, managers and employers, and African women had done as well as whites, but all other groups of ethnic minority women had done less well. There were high proportions of Pakistani and, to a lesser extent, Indian women in semi-skilled and unskilled manual jobs but more than 40 per cent of women from all groups had 'Other non-manual' jobs. Jones argues:

---

because of discrimination, and because of structural factors associated with the family, women of all ethnic groups are confined to a much narrower range of opportunities than are men. This means that the processes of racial disadvantage have much less room in which to operate.

Jones also looked at the extent to which the differences found were related to differences in educational qualifications. For example, he produced figures showing the proportion of people with qualifications at or above A-level standard who had professional or managerial jobs or who were employers. Amongst men, 37 per cent of whites with such qualifications had top jobs. Chinese, Indian and Africa Asian males all had higher proportions in this category (48 per cent, 45 per cent and 42 per cent respectively) but Pakistani men

Table 11.7   Job levels of male employees by ethnic group, 1988–90

	All origins	White	Total ethnic minority	Afro-Caribbean	African Asian	Indian	Pakistani	Bangla-dseshi	Chinese	African	Other/ Mixed
					Column percentages						
Professional Manager/Employer	27	27	21	12	27	25	12	12	30	21	30
Employees and Managers – large establishments	13	13	7	5	6	9	4	1	7	9	11
Employees and Managers – small establishments	7	7	5	3	10	5	4	5	10	3	7
Professional workers – employees	7	7	8	4	11	10	4	6	14	9	12
Other non-manual	20	20	22	19	30	18	16	14	19	34	31
Skilled manual and Foremen	32	33	28	39	26	29	34	5	10	20	18
Semi-skilled manual	15	15	23	23	13	24	31	65	36	18	16
Unskilled manual	4	4	5	6	3	4	6	5	4	4	2
Armed Services/inadequately described/not stated	1	1	1	1	0	0	1	0	1	3	3

(*Source*: Jones, T. (1993) *Britain's Ethnic Minorities*, Policy Studies Institute, London, p. 99.)

Table 11.8   Job levels of female employees by ethnic group, 1988–90

	All origins	White	Total ethnic minority	Afro-Caribbean	African Asian	Indian	Pakistani	Bangla-dseshi	Chinese	African	Other/ Mixed
					Column percentages						
Professional Manager/Employer	11	11	9	8	7	10	4	*	16	11	12
Employees and Managers – large establishments	6	6	4	5	3	4	1	*	4	5	4
Employees and Managers – small establishments	4	4	3	2	2	2	3	*	5	3	4
Professional workers – employees	2	2	2	1	2	4	0	*	7	2	3
Other non-manual	55	56	53	54	58	47	42	*	53	47	63
Skilled manual and Foremen	5	5	5	4	9	5	7	*	2	6	3
Semi-skilled manual	22	22	27	25	25	34	45	*	20	32	17
Unskilled manual	7	7	5	9	1	4	2	*	9	4	5
Armed Services/inadequately described/not stated	0	0	0	0	0	0	0	*	0	1	0

(*Source*: Jones, T. (1993) *Britain's Ethnic Minorities*, Policy Studies Institute, London, p. 100.)

did rather worse (30 per cent) and Afro-Caribbean men much worse (23 per cent). For men with no qualifications Bangladeshi and Afro-Caribbean men were more likely than other groups to be in one of the lowest job categories.

Amongst women the variations were again less great although women from all ethnic groups fared less well than men. Some 22 per cent of white women with A levels or above were in the top job category compared to 19 per cent for all ethnic minority groups, with Chinese women doing best (28 per cent) and Afro-Caribbean women worst (16 per cent).

Overall members of ethnic minorities do less well in the labour market than whites even when they have a similar level of qualifications. However there are wide variations between different ethnic groups and between men and women.

Table 11.9 Percentage of male employees in top SEG category (professional, manager or employer) during the 1980s

Ethnic origin	1982 PSI Survey	1984–6 LFS	1988–90 LFS
White	19	24	27
Afro-Caribbean	5	5	12
African Asian	22	22	27
Indian	11	23	25
Pakistani	10	11	12
Bangladeshi	10	13	12

(*Source*: Jones, T. (1993) *Britain's Ethnic Minorities,* Policy Studies Institute, London, p. 82.)

Using data from the earlier studies, Jones examined the extent to which the position of ethnic minorities in the labour market had changed. The results for men are shown in Table 11.9. The table shows that the proportions in the top category had increased for all groups. The increase had been greatest for Indian and Afro-Caribbean men, but the latter group had started from a very low base and were still less than half as likely as white men to get top jobs. The rate of upward mobility to these positions had been slower for Pakistani and Bangladeshi men than for whites, so the gap between these ethnic minorities and whites had been widening. In 1982 there was a higher proportion of African Asians than whites who were professionals, managers and employers, but by 1988–90 whites had caught up.

The most recent PSI study produced no figures on earnings differentials between ethnic groups. However the 1982 study did. It found that there was little difference in the earnings of women, but median earnings for white men were around £20 a week higher than for West Indian men, and £18 a week higher than for Asian men. Even at the same job level there were still substantial differences. For example, white professionals, employers and managers had a median income from employment of £129.00 per week compared to £110.20 for Asian and West Indian men.

Housing

Tenure patterns amongst ethnic minority groups have changed considerably since large-scale immigration from the New Commonwealth commenced in the 1950s. Early migrants found it difficult to obtain council housing because many councils had waiting lists based at least partly upon people's length of residence in an area. Newly arrived immigrants were likely to be towards the bottom of the lists. Some lacked the income or wealth necessary to become owner-occupiers and many relied upon finding accommodation in the private rented sector.

Immigrants from the West Indies tended to arrive in Britain before immigrants from South Asia and as time passed they were in a stronger position than most Asians to obtain council housing. These early patterns of tenure are reflected in the changes in the 1980s which are shown in. Tables 11.10 and 11.11.

Table 11.10 shows that there was a rise in owner-occupation for all groups except Indians and Pakistanis. Afro-Caribbeans and Bangladeshis increased their rate of owner-occupation during the 1980s but still had much lower rates than whites by 1988–90. In contrast African Asians, Indians and Pakistanis had higher rates than whites.

Quite surprisingly a 1974 study found that South Asians and Afro-Caribbeans with manual jobs were more likely to be owner-occupiers than those with non-manual jobs. Trevor Jones suggests that this 'could partly be seen as a response to the closure of other housing opportunities, particularly at the early stages of settlement'. Facing the problem of residence qualifications in getting council housing and discrimination from white landlords in private rented accommodation, some relatively low-paid members of ethnic minorities turned to owner-occupation as the best option. For some there may also have been 'a positive drive towards home ownership associated with the drive towards self improvement and capital accumulation that is typical of immigrant communities'.

Table 11.11 shows the small proportions of African Asians, Indians and Pakistanis living in council housing during the 1980s. However, there was still a high proportion of Afro-Caribbeans living in such housing and the same was true of Bangladeshis. Amongst all groups reliance upon council housing fell during the 1980s, partly because the number of council houses declined as many were sold to their tenants.

Patterns of housing tenure seem to suggest that different ethnic minorities have rather different positions in the housing market. Other types of

Table 11.10   Percentage of households owner-occupied by ethnic group during the 1980s

Ethnic group	1982 PSI Survey	1984–6 LFS	1988–90 LFS
White	59	60	65
Afro-Caribbean	41	38	46
African Asian	73	81	82
Indian	77	77	76
Pakistani	80	78	75
Bangladeshi	30	31	46

(*Source*: Jones, T. (1993) *Britain's Ethnic Minorities*, Policy Studies Institute, London, p. 140.)

Table 11.11   Percentage of households renting from local authority by ethnic group during the 1980s

Ethnic group	1982 PSI Survey	1984–6 LFS	1988–90 LFS
White	30	28	25
Afro-Caribbean	46	47	41
African Asian	19	8	9
Indian	16	12	11
Pakistani	13	13	11
Bangladeshi	53	49	36

(*Source*: Jones, T. (1993) *Britain's Ethnic Minorities*, Policy Studies Institute, London, p. 141.)

data on housing though, seem to suggest that all ethnic minority groups are disadvantaged in terms of housing.

The *1991 General Household Survey* found that 20 per cent of whites, but only 12 per cent of Indians, 9 per cent of Pakistanis/Bangladeshis, and 4 per cent of black Caribbeans lived in detached houses. All ethnic minority groups were more likely than whites to live in terraced houses.

There was also more overcrowding in ethnic minority households. Some 6 per cent of white households contained one person per room or more compared to 19 per cent of Indian households, 34 per cent of Pakistani/Bangladeshi households and 18 per cent of black Caribbean households.

Poverty

There have been no national studies of the incidence of poverty by ethnic groups but there have

been local studies which have produced revealing statistics. A study carried out by Islington Council (described in K. Amin and C. Oppenheim, 1992) found that in Islington 29 per cent of whites, 25 per cent of Asians, 35 per cent of Cypriots, 38 per cent of Irish and 39 per cent of Afro-Caribbeans had a net household annual income of less than £3,900.

Crime and justice

Members of ethnic minorities are more likely than whites both to end up in prison and to be the victims of crime. Home Office figures show that on 30 June 1992 prison population rates per 100,000 of the population were 9.6 for whites, 12.4 for Indians, Pakistanis and Bangladeshis, and 76.7 for West Indians, Guyanese and African.

Table 11.12 shows rates of victimization for different ethnic groups in 1991. For nearly all crimes ethnic minorities were more likely to be victims. Afro-Caribbeans were twice as likely as whites to be burgled and both Asians and Afro-Caribbeans suffered three times as many robberies/thefts from the person as whites.

Table 11.12   Victims of one or more crimes[1] in England and Wales: by ethnic origin and type of offence, 1991

Percentage who were victims of each offence	Ethnic origin of victim		
	White	Afro Caribbean	Asian
Assault	3	5	4
Threats	3	3	4
Robbery/theft from the person	1	3	3
Burglary	6	12	9
Other household theft[2]	7	6	4
Household vandalism	4	4	5
Vehicle (Owners)			
Vandalism	9	11	10
All thefts[3]	20	28	22
Bicycle (owners) theft	6	10	7

[1] Based on incidents occurring over the full recall period.
[2] Includes theft from a dwelling.
[3] Includes theft of, and from, vehicles and attempted theft.

(*Source*: *Social Trends* (1994) p. 155.)

Racially motivated attacks are a particular problem for ethnic minority groups. The PSI survey conducted in 1982 found that 1 per cent of whites, 2 per cent of West Indians and 7 per cent of Asians had been the victims of attacks which they specifically said had a racial motive or background. Some 2 per cent of whites, 10 per cent of West Indians and 16 per cent of Asians had been the victims of unprovoked attacks by a person or people from a different ethnic group to their own: attacks which may therefore have been racially motivated.

Although it is very difficult to produce reliable figures on racially motivated attacks because of the problems of determining the motives of assailants, a number of studies have shown that members of ethnic minorities are very much more likely than whites to be the victims of such attacks.

Inequalities between ethnic groups – conclusion

Data from this section and elsewhere in the book suggest that there has been some reduction in most types of inequality between whites and ethnic minority groups in Britain. Patterns of inequality vary by ethnic group with African Asians and Indians generally faring better than Afro-Caribbeans and Bangladeshis. Overall though, it is clear that ethnic minorities continue to have poorer life chances than the white population in Britain (with the possible exception of the Irish).

Many sociologists attribute much of the inequality to racism, theories of which we will now examine.

■ Theories of racism

■ Psychological theories of racism

The Frankfurt School

Some influential theories of racism have assumed that racism is a characteristic of an abnormal minority of the population and that the abnormality which causes racism is psychological. One such **psychological** theory was developed by The Frankfurt Institute for Social Research, often known as the **Frankfurt School**. This was a group of social scientists who were originally based at Frankfurt, though some fled to the USA during the 1930s around the time of the Second World War.

The rise of fascism in Germany in the 1930s with its the strong anti-Semitism, prompted the School to investigate the origins of prejudice and discrimination. Perhaps the most influential research in this area was conducted by Theodor Adorno who carried out a study to determine the causes of *The Authoritarian Personality*.

The Frankfurt School often adopted an interdisciplinary approach and much of its writing was influenced by the sociology of Marx and the psychoanalytic perspective of Sigmund Freud. Freud's work was particularly influential in developing theories of racism and prejudice.

Adorno's research was published in 1950 and it involved administering questionnaires to a sample of 2,000 Americans. Respondents were asked to agree or disagree with statements so that researchers could determine their attitudes towards religious and ethnic minorities, their views on politics and economics, and their moral values. About one-tenth of the total sample was interviewed in more depth. This sub-sample consisted of one group which had expressed the most prejudiced and authoritarian views and one group which had expressed the least prejudiced and authoritarian views. These groups were compared to determine what factors seemed to give rise to an authoritarian personality.

The Frankfurt School defined an **authoritarian personality** as one which involved 'stereotypic thinking, disguised sadism, the veneration of power' and 'the blind recognition accorded to anything that appeared forceful'. People with authoritarian personalities submitted to those in authority and were hostile to people who did not. They also tended to be hostile to any groups of people who were different from themselves, including members of ethnic minorities. They placed emphasis on 'traditional values ... externally correct behaviour, success, industry, competence, physical cleanliness, health, and uncritical conformist attitudes'. People with authoritarian personalities were seen as typical of those who were most likely to give uncritical support to Hitler in 1930s and 1940s Germany.

According to the research, such personalities had their origins in the way they had been brought up as children. The School argued:

Frequently the totalitarian characters are broken in their childhood, either by a strict father or by a general lack of love, and then repeat, for their part, that which had once been done to them, in order to be able to survive physically.

Their loveless and rigid upbringings had forced these authoritarian personalities to be emotionally cool towards others, especially those who were different from themselves, and to value conformity. They found it difficult to sympathize with others and to tolerate difference. They were therefore intolerant of members of ethnic minorities.

John Dollard – frustration-aggression as the cause of prejudice

Like the Frankfurt School Dollard was influenced by Freudian ideas and saw early upbringing as the key to explaining the development of racial prejudice. Writing in 1957 in an attempt to explain racism in the Deep South of the USA, Dollard argued that those who are frustrated become aggressive and need an outlet for their aggression.

In socializing children, parents force them to suppress basic drives (which in Freudian theory come from the id) and frustration arises. The children, however, cannot take their frustration out on the parents because they rely upon them for physical survival. The frustration is stored up and later in life is directed against an alternative, more

vulnerable target. In the Deep South black Americans fulfilled this function.

Criticisms of psychological theories

The theories of the Frankfurt School assume that racism and prejudice are confined to small numbers of abnormal individuals. However, many studies have found that some degree of racism is widespread in many societies and is not confined to an untypical minority. Many of the theories of racism which we will discuss next argue that racism is a product of a society's culture or its economic system, and is not therefore confined to a minority of individuals.

John Rex argues that Dollard's theory may be of some value in explaining why an individual 'should act competitively towards competitors'. He adds, though:

It is not easy to see, however, why we should apply it more to a ruling group, like the Whites of the Deep South rather than to those whom they ruled and oppressed and frustrated.

Since blacks in the Deep South suffered much more frustration than the whites, Dollard's theory would work better as an explanation of revolts by American blacks than as an explanation of discrimination by American whites.

■ E. Ellis Cashmore – *The Logic of Racism*

The study

In 1987 E. Ellis Cashmore published a study of racism in England in which he tried to understand *The Logic of Racism* from the viewpoint of English whites. It was based upon in-depth interviews with 800 people in the English Midlands. Although the main focus was on the views of ordinary working-class and middle-class whites, he also interviewed Afro-Caribbean and Asian British, and a number of local politicians and professionals such as teachers who had to deal with race relations issues in the course of their work.

Cashmore's main sample was based on four areas.

1 Newtown: an inner-city housing estate in Birmingham built during the 1960s. It had an overwhelmingly working-class population, nearly half of the population were under 30 and unemployment was high at 23.7 per cent. There was a large ethnic minority population of 13.4 per cent, most of whom were of Caribbean origin.

2 Chelmsley Wood: another working-class council estate but situated ten miles outside Birmingham and surrounded by suburban areas. Many people had been rehoused there from Birmingham and the biggest local employer was a nearby Rover factory. Like Newtown many of its residents were young with over 50 per cent being under 30. Its unemployment rate was lower than Newtown's at 16.3 per cent but was rising. Chelmsley Wood had a small ethnic minority population of 3.5 per cent.

3 Edgbaston: an area close to the centre of Birmingham but with an overwhelmingly middle-class population including many professionals and entrepreneurs. Unemployment was low at 4.2 per cent and there was a small but growing Asian population making up 6.1 per cent of all residents.

4 Solihull: a town ten miles west of Coventry with a very affluent population. Unemployment stood at just 4.2 per cent, less than 9 per cent of the houses were council houses and relatively few of the population were under 30 (38 per cent). Solihull had a very small ethnic minority population of around 1 per cent.

Cashmore examined the extent and nature of racism in different age groups in the white population in each of these four areas. The age groups were:

1 the middle aged (21–50);
2 the young (under 21);
3 older people (over 50).

Racism and the middle-age groups

In Newtown most whites aged 21–50 expressed considerable suspicion of ethnic minorities and sometimes demonstrated outright hostility.

1 Many believed that ethnic minorities received preferential treatment over housing. A number of individuals felt they personally had not been moved to a better council house or flat despite a long time on a waiting list because better residences had gone to ethnic minority groups.

2 A number of people also expressed resentment at the alleged nuisance caused by the noisiness of Afro-Caribbean neighbours who had parties or played music during the night.

3 Some residents feared street violence and held ethnic minorities responsible for its existence.

In Newtown the racism stemmed from competition over scarce resources, particularly housing, with some whites feeling they were missing out. Cashmore comments:

Given that life in Newtown is a struggle at the best of times for many, some residents are inflamed at the idea of blacks and Asians being allocated housing and awarded grants.

In Chelmsley Wood 'race' was a less pressing issue because of the smaller ethnic minority population. Whites saw them as less of an immediate threat because there were so few of them. Nevertheless, racism was still in evidence. In particular many whites criticized ethnic minorities for failing to assimilate by maintaining their own cultures and failing to mix with whites. Crude stereotypes of ethnic minority groups were common because the white residents of Chelmsley Wood had little direct contact with members of ethnic minorities. Cashmore describes the attitudes in the following way:

---

ethnics are *in* society but not *of* it. Asians, for instance, are popularly seen as having an instrumental attitude to British society, which offers them opportunities for making money. Blacks, being less entrepreneurial, settle for less in the eyes of many white council residents. They are content to amble along in a parasitic way, sponging off the state and augmenting their unearned income with the spoils of robberies.

The white middle-class in Edgbaston and Solihull tended to see people in terms of their own individualistic and competitive values. As in Chelmsley Wood, Afro-Caribbeans were likely to be seen as spongers, but Asians were accorded more respect.

Some at least were seen as hardworking and able to provide for themselves and their families.

Crude stereotypes were just as common in these areas as they were in Chelmsley Wood. There was 'an unquestioning acceptance of Asians as thrifty, hard working capitalists and West Indians as "lower-mentality" manual workers'. There was little direct competition for jobs or houses between ethnic minorities in the middle-class areas and most of their residents had little direct experience of Asians or Afro-Caribbeans.

Conflict between ethnic groups seemed a remote problem for them and many believed both conflict and racism were exaggerated. They accepted that there was some racism but believed that it was up to ethnic minorities to work hard and try to assimilate to overcome the racism. The white residents tended to disapprove of government legislation to ban discrimination seeing it as unwarranted state interference in the operation of the free market. By-and-large they did not see themselves as racist.

However, a number of the employers interviewed by Cashmore did say that they had decided not to employ an Afro-Caribbean or Asian person in the past. This was not, they said, because they had any objection to employing them themselves, but rather because their customers or their existing workforce would not be happy with such an employee.

Although the racism of the white middle-class seemed more restrained than that of some members of the working class, it is possible that it might affect the life chances of ethnic minorities more. Some of the middle-aged and middle-class residents of Edgbaston and Solihull were denying ethnic minorities opportunities and at the same time criticizing them for not making more attempt to succeed in British society.

Racism and the young

Perhaps the least racist white group of all were the young working class of Newtown. They had grown up alongside members of ethnic minorities and many felt that all youth in the area shared common grievances. Cashmore says that 'sheer familiarity and an apprehension of shared social conditions seems to foster a kind of mental assonance'. One of the Newtown youth, called 'John', saw 'no advantage in simply – and blindly – blaming his peers who have sat next to him at school and line up with him in dole queues'. The young had not experienced ethnic minorities as

newcomers or immigrants so it was hard to see them as outsiders who were taking their jobs.

Nevertheless, there were social divisions along ethnic lines. Most of the youth of Newtown stuck to friends from their own ethnic group from the time they left school and some of the young in Newtown did express racist views.

If racism and ethnic conflict were relatively muted in Newtown, the same was not found to be true of Chelmsley Wood. There, many white youths did blame ethnic minorities for unemployment and had highly stereotypical views of them. For example, one youth, 'Kevin', said 'They stink. Pakis really reek; you can tell one in a street a mile away. Blacks stink of sweat and a lot of them are pimps.'

Despite the small size of the ethnic minority population there was sometimes conflict between ethnic groups. In one reported incident a black woman was grabbed in a pub by a skinhead, a black man in the pub hit him and knocked him out, prompting disputes between groups of whites, blacks and Asians in the street outside the pub.

Although there was little actual violence on this occasion Cashmore describes conflicts of this kind as common. He argues that the lack of contact between whites and ethnic minorities leads to white youth relying largely upon the media for their beliefs about ethnic minorities. As a consequence they develop stereotypical views which rarely have a chance to be challenged through experience.

In the middle-class areas the youth often believed that the media exaggerated the amount of racism and discrimination. Most admitted that members of ethnic minorities suffered some problems but tended to argue that it was their own fault. The youth followed their parents in believing that individuals largely shaped their own lives and social conditions played little part in limiting people's opportunities. Thus if ethnic minorities were less successful than whites then it was mainly due to their lack of effort and their unwillingness to fit in with the culture of the host society.

However, not all the middle-class youth shared this view. In Solihull, for example, although living in an area remote from inner-city problems, a youth called 'Charles' suggested that the 'colour problem' was manufactured by the ruling class to divert attention from the problems of deprivation suffered by the poor. Another, called 'Kate', criticized older people for their unwillingness to tolerate different cultures.

However although the views of middle-class youths were varied, most shared their parents' version of racism based upon a belief in the personal inadequacy of most individuals in ethnic minority groups.

Racism and older people

In Newtown whites over 50 had experienced considerable changes during their lifetimes. They had seen slum clearance programmes and the introduction of tower blocks. They had also seen considerable numbers of people from ethnic minorities settle in the area. Many believed that the standard of living in their area had declined and they were willing to blame this on ethnic minorities.

Their complaints were similar to those of whites from the middle-age group living in Newtown.

1 They believed that ethnic minorities caused excessive noise, and deprived white people of jobs and houses.

2 Ethnic minorities were also accused of organizing prostitution, running various rackets and contributing to a general decline.

Many residents, like 'Mrs Dobbs', did not put all the blame on ethnic minority groups for failing to assimilate. She also blamed the Government and other authorities for allowing too much immigration and passing discrimination laws which, as she saw it, gave privileges to ethnic minorities which are not afforded to whites. People like Mrs Dobbs felt the area was being taken over by alien groups who were destroying the British way of life.

In Chelmsley Wood there was less fear of such a take-over. There were similar views to those in Newtown but they were expressed less strongly. Some residents thought that residential segregation was the answer to the problem: so long as ethnic minorities were kept at arm's length resentment could be minimized and problems limited. Here too the authorities were blamed for lax immigration control.

Whites over 50 in Edgbaston and Solihull followed those from the middle-age group in those areas in blaming ethnic minorities for any problems they faced. They believed that ethnic minority groups had made insufficient effort to integrate into white, English society and had been too keen on keeping their own distinctive cultures. Like the working class in the same age group, they did not approve of the Race Relations Acts. They did not believe that the Government should

intervene to regulate people's actions through such legislation, although they did support strong government action to restrict immigration. Cashmore comments:

> The middle class elderly share few of the worries that infect the working class. Their views are not motivated by insecurity over their houses or their personal safety . . . They are, however, anxious about changes that threaten to upset the equilibrium they value so much. Too much cultural diversity can lead to the destruction of the homogeneous and standardized world in which they have prospered.

Conclusion

Cashmore found that racism was present in all classes and in all age groups. He therefore rejects psychological theories of racism which see it as a characteristic of pathological individuals with abnormal personalities. Instead he seems to see racism as the product of a type of **natural conservatism**. He says that 'most people are conservative for no reason more mysterious than that they want stability and order'.

Many people in Britain have experienced major social changes since the end of the Second World War. These changes include immigration from the New Commonwealth and with it the introduction of 'unfamiliar beliefs, languages and lifestyles'. Cashmore goes on to say:

> If we accept that people are ordinarily conservative, then we can grasp a certain logic in their response to change . . . Racism in modern society typically arises in defence of the established order of things.

From Cashmore's point of view racism takes different forms in different sections of society but everywhere it has the same roots.

John Richardson praises Cashmore's work for trying to understand racism rather than just condemning it or counting the number of people who are racist. Richardson also says that the study produced 'illuminating' empirical data. However, he also describes it as 'modest in conceptual and theoretical terms'. Certainly it made no attempt to find wider structural or historical roots of racism beyond some innate conservatism.

Marxist theories of racism have usually taken a

much broader, theoretical approach while paying less attention to the 'logic of racism' from the viewpoint of ordinary people.

Oliver C. Cox – a Marxist theory of racism

Ethnicity, 'race' and racism

Oliver C. Cox developed an early theory of racism based on Marxist ideas. In 1948 he published his book *Class Caste and Race* in which he rejected approaches which saw racism as something which had always existed and was a product of natural human sentiments.

To Cox the idea of 'race' was itself a human creation. **Ethnic groups** were any socially distinct groups which 'lived competitively in a relationship of superordination or subordination with respect to some other people or peoples within one state, country or economic area'. Ethnic groups could be divided into those which were distinguished by culture and those which were distinguished by 'race'.

'Races' were identified according to physical characteristics but these characteristics did not have to reflect any real biological differences between groups. Cox said 'a race may be thought of as simply any group of people that is generally believed to be, and accepted as, a race in any given area of ethnic competition'. It was the belief in difference that was important, not any real differences that might exist.

To Cox racism was a comparatively recent phenomenon. It could not therefore have its origins in universal human sentiments which automatically made ethnic groups hostile to one another. He argued that 'one should miss the point entirely if one were to think of racial antagonism as having its genesis in some "social instinct" of antipathy between peoples'.

According to Cox there was no racism in ancient civilizations.

1 In Ancient Greece people were divided into Greeks and barbarians. The difference was not a racial one but was based on whether people were familiar with Greek language and culture. Those who were not familiar with it were barbarians.

2 In Ancient Rome citizenship was the key distinction. Freeborn people who possessed Roman citizenship

could come from any part of the Empire and were not limited by ethnic or racial group.

3 The Roman Catholic Church distinguished between Christians and heathens and heretics on the basis of religious belief and people from any racial group could convert to the religion and be accepted as equals. Even the early Portuguese explorers who were ruthless in their dealings with Africans did not see the latter as racially inferior; the Portuguese held to the Christian belief that all people were equal in the eyes of God.

However, towards the end of the fifteenth century things changed and racism began to develop.

Capitalism and racism

In 1493 as a result of Spanish pressure Pope Alexander VI issued a papal bull putting 'all the heathen peoples and their resources – that is to say, especially the coloured peoples of the world – at the disposal of Spain and Portugal'. At that point, according to Cox, racism was born.

To Cox racism is not 'an abstract, natural, immemorial feeling of mutual antipathy between groups, but rather a practical exploitative relationship with its socio-attitudinal facilitation'. In other words racism is a set of beliefs used to justify and therefore to sustain the exploitation of one group by another. It had its origins in the development of capitalism and its need to systematically exploit labour power.

The 'capitalist exploiter, being opportunistic and practical, will utilize any convenience to keep his labour and other resources freely exploitable'. It was hard to justify the use of slave labour in terms of religious beliefs which saw all humans as equal. It was therefore necessary to 'argue that the workers are innately degraded and degenerate, consequently they naturally merit their condition'.

Early capitalism went hand-in-hand with colonialism. As European nations conquered other areas of the world, they were able to exploit the workforce in the colonies and to justify their actions through racism. To Cox racism is always something developed by the exploiters against the exploited. He argues that 'race prejudice must be actually backed up by a show of racial excellence, secured finally by military might' and that 'the superior race controls the pattern of all dependent race prejudices'.

If racism is something developed to justify exploitation, it cannot be developed by those who are exploited. It is not only whites who are capable of racism but by chance it was whites who developed capitalism and therefore it was they who first developed it. According to Cox, if capitalism had not developed then 'the world might never have experienced race prejudice'.

Criticisms of Cox

Many writers since Cox have agreed with him that racism is related to capitalism and colonialism. However, many have also denied that racism can only exist within capitalism and that colonialism and capitalism are the only causes of racism. Social psychologists tend to disagree with Cox that only white people can be racist arguing that individuals from any ethnic group can be racist.

Cox's work has influenced some Marxists but most now reject his views as too simplistic. John Solomos says:

> the model of Marxism with which Cox was familiar was based on the conceptual baggage of 'base' and 'superstructure' and an instrumental view of the state as the agent of the capitalist class.

Cox saw racism as determined by the economic system. It existed because capitalism needed it to exist. The state acted in a racist way because the state was the instrument of the ruling class.

Many contemporary Marxists argue that such views are far too simplistic. The capitalist class is not all-powerful and the needs of the capitalist system do not in themselves determine everything that happens. An alternative approach has been developed at the Birmingham Centre for Contemporary Cultural Studies.

■ The Birmingham Centre for Contemporary Cultural Studies – a neo-Marxist theory of racism

A theoretical approach to racism

In a collection of articles called *The Empire Strikes Back* published in 1982, a group of sociologists at the Birmingham Centre for Contemporary Cultural Studies developed a neo-Marxist approach to

racism. In an introductory article John Solomos, Bob Findlay, Simon Jones and Paul Gilroy outlined the main features of this approach.

They agreed with Cox that racism was influenced by colonialism but argued that racism predated colonialism and was shaped by many other factors. According to them the nature of racism in Britain was not fixed but changed as history progressed. They agreed with other Marxist writers that racism was connected to the exploitation of migrant labour in capitalist societies, but again argued that this was not the only important factor. To them 'The construction of race as a "problem" has not come about by evolutionary means. It has emerged from a whole series of events: struggles, breaks, and discontinuities.' It was necessary to examine these complex events in order to understand racism.

Solomos *et al.* believed that it was necessary to examine the part played by ethnic minorities themselves in resisting and challenging racism and to consider how the working class came to accept racist beliefs. Racism was not something which was just imposed on exploited groups in society by an all-powerful ruling class. Although some exploited groups rejected racism, others accepted it and racist ideas were incorporated into their commonsense understanding of the world.

Like most Marxists Solomos *et al.* accept that economic factors are important in shaping social life. In Britain the 1970s' and early 1980s' issues to do with 'race' developed against a backdrop of economic crisis and rising unemployment. However, they said that 'There is no one-to-one correspondence between the "crisis of race" and the economic crisis' pointing out that 'Economic decline preceded popular acknowledgement of crisis, and the expulsion of blacks as a solution to national problems has a long history in British political thought.'

A variety of historical and political factors shaped the situation along with the development of the economy. The cultures of the working class and of ethnic minorities and the policies followed by the British state all interacted to produce a particular form of racism in the 1970s and early 1980s.

According to Solomos *et al.* this period saw the emergence of a **new racism** which stressed the cultural differences between ethnic groups rather than biological superiority and inferiority of particular 'races'. It drew upon long-established beliefs about British nationalism which went back centuries, and which appealed to some sections of the white working class. In a later chapter in the study Errol Lawrence tried to describe and explain the emergence of this new racism.

Errol Lawrence – the origins of racism in Britain

According to Lawrence racist ideas have a very long history. Even before colonialism 'white' was associated with goodness and purity whereas 'black' was associated with evil. Hence, for example, the distinction between black and white magic. The Christian religion had always characterized non-Christians as pagans. In early contacts between Europeans and other peoples, non-Europeans were usually portrayed as uncivilized.

With the advent of colonialism racist ideas were developed further. Members of the British working class fought both in the wars in which colonies were captured, and in the twentieth century they fought again in independence struggles in countries such as Kenya. Lawrence claims that by the time colonies were gaining independence colonial people had come to be seen as 'children needing protection or as the equally immature "brutal savage"'. Either way the newly independent states were seen as needing strong guidance from their former British 'masters'. Their success or failure was likely to be determined by the extent to which they adopted European culture and institutions.

According to Lawrence, in the 1970s in Britain the ruling class succeeded in 'reorganizing the common-sense racist ideologies of the white working class, around the themes of "the British nation", "the British people" and "British culture"'. The racist ideas that developed were not 'mere "relics" of a distant imperial past', but they did contain strong elements of ideologies developed during colonial times. These stressed the distinctive nature of British culture and the great traditions of British militarism which allowed Britain (and its working-class soldiers) to conquer large parts of the world.

Although the racist images 'are cross-cut by other contradictory images about the essential equality of all people . . . they nevertheless tend to pull popular opinion towards racist opinions and interpretations'. This meant that 'Black cultures are still likely to be viewed as "primitive" in comparison to British "civilization".'

The new racism

In the economic and political instability of the 1970s 'immigrants' came to be seen as a cause of the problems. The emphasis was no longer on outright inferiority but more on difference. British strength came from its way of life and the presence of 'aliens' with different cultures was sapping this strength and causing national decline. The British way of life was being undermined by 'foreigners' and it was unnatural for people with very different lifestyles to live together.

For example, the new racism attacked the family life of Afro-Caribbeans and Asians. Afro-Caribbeans were seen as incapable of maintaining stable families consisting of parents and children. Such families were viewed as the bedrock of British society. Asians, on the other hand had unnaturally large extended families which led to overcrowding and the isolation of Asians from the beneficial effects of British culture.

From this point of view, individuals could not be truly British simply by having a British passport or even by being born in Britain. Rather they had to think of themselves as British and have a British lifestyle and values.

Neither Afro-Caribbeans nor Asians were seen as measuring up to these criteria. They had different 'identities', 'loyalties' and 'anti-British attitudes'. Their presence was therefore bound to cause conflict between the 'immigrants' and the real 'British'. According to the logic of the new racism, the only solution to the problem was for the 'immigrants' to leave Britain and return to the countries where their culture was more acceptable.

To Lawrence the new racism was a response to the crisis in British society. Unemployment, rising crime and the apparent breakdown of family life were all causes of concern, and ethnic minorities were convenient scapegoats for these problems. However, the new racism was not an automatic and inevitable consequence of economic change. It had to be created using elements of old racist ideas, it had to be accepted by and make sense to the white working class, and it had to overcome opposition from antiracists.

■ Paul Gilroy – There Ain't No Black in the Union Jack

Paul Gilroy was one of the contributors to *The Empire Strikes Back*, a study by the Birmingham

Centre for Contemporary Cultural Studies. In 1987 his own book, *There Ain't No Black in the Union Jack* was published. This extended the earlier analysis to which he had contributed. Like Lawrence, Gilroy examined the new racism but he also discussed ethnic minority cultures. In doing so Gilroy was attempting to produce a more complete understanding of 'race' and ethnicity than studies which concentrated on racism or ethnicity alone. His study discusses a wide range of issues which overlap with the issues we consider in a number of sections in this chapter.

Race formation

Gilroy rejects both biological definitions of 'race' and studies of ethnicity which regard ethnic groups as having very strong and distinctive cultures which are slow to change. In his view **'race' formation** involves an ongoing process in which groups 'define themselves and organize around notions of "race"'. It is a 'continuous and contingent process' which varies from place to place and time to time. It is affected by racism but also by the conscious choices made by those who see themselves as belonging to racial groups.

Resistance to racism and political organization by 'races' play important roles in the process of 'race' formation. Gilroy says 'it is struggle that determines which definition of "race" will prevail and the conditions under which they will endure or wither away'. For example, in Britain the term 'black' had started to be used to refer both to Afro-Caribbeans and Asians. This implies the possibility of Afro-Asian unity in a struggle against racism. More recently, however, 'black' has become more commonly used to refer to Afro-Caribbeans alone. To Gilroy 'This development has its origins in an understanding of "race" which stresses the obstacles to political accommodation erected between culture and ethnicity.' It has resulted from struggles over the meaning of 'race', and Gilroy believes it reflects the increasing influence of the new racism which puts great emphasis on cultural differences.

Although influenced by Marxism, Gilroy moves further from Marxist orthodoxy than the Birmingham Centre for Contemporary Cultural Studies had done in *The Empire Strikes Back*. He accepts that struggles over 'race' have been influenced by the development of capitalism – for example in its use of slave and migrant labour – but he denies that the exploitation of 'races' is a form of class exploitation.

Nor does Gilroy believe that conflict between 'races' is simply a form of class conflict. He says 'The processes of "race" and class formation are not identical. The former is not reducible to the latter even where they become mutually entangled.' Racial divisions are separate and distinct from class divisions and Gilroy talks of 'The evident autonomy of racism from production relations.' Indeed, to Gilroy class conflict is becoming less important in modern capitalist societies. Instead, conflict has become much more based around new social movements which are concerned with non-economic issues. Examples include the 'women's movements, youth movements, anti-nuclear and peace movements, ecological movements, and various urban and citizen movements'.

Racism

Gilroy agrees with Lawrence there is a new form of racism in Britain and that it is based round cultural rather than biological distinctions. Gilroy sees this racism as intimately linked to 'discourses of patriotism, nationalism, xenophobia, Englishness, Britishness, militarism and gender difference'. The new racism involves specifying who may be regarded as a legitimate member of 'the Island Race' and who is considered an outsider. So-called 'immigrants', many of whom were actually born in Britain, are usually regarded as outsiders. They are portrayed as culturally different and therefore as threatening the British way of life. Their difference undermines a homogeneous British culture which is seen as having given Britain its strength.

This image of strength is stressed in celebrations of past military victories and was invoked during the 1982 war against Argentina over the Falklands. According to Gilroy during that war the white residents of the Falklands were seen as coming from the same cultural community as white British people. They were portrayed as being genuinely British even though they lived 8,000 miles from Britain itself.

Similar attitudes prevailed in relation to Zola Budd. In 1984 Budd, a talented white South African distance runner, was given British citizenship because her grandfather had been British. Her application for citizenship was processed rapidly and accepted enthusiastically by the Government. This contrasts with the much greater difficulties experienced by Asians and West Indians who try to secure British citizenship in order to emigrate to Britain. Indeed many Asians and Afro-Caribbeans who do have British citizenship and may have been born in Britain are sometimes treated as more alien than whites from New Commonwealth countries like the Falklands and South Africa. When black protestors demonstrated against Zola Budd because she refused to denounce apartheid in South Africa, the *Sun* newspaper said that they should be 'returned to their original homelands' because 'There is no place for them in Britain.'

Gilroy believes that 'the link between crime and blackness has become absolutely integral' to the new racism. Through much of the 1950s and 1960s Afro-Caribbeans were not portrayed as being particularly prone to criminality. Their presence in Britain was portrayed as creating housing problems and Afro-Caribbeans were certainly subject to much racial discrimination.

However, the turning point from which new racism developed was a speech by Enoch Powell. In 1968 he described the plight of an old white woman who had lived in a particular street all her life. Gradually, more and more blacks moved into her street. According to Powell, after she had refused a black neighbour's request to use her phone one night she began to suffer verbal abuse from blacks in her area. Gilroy comments that in Powell's speech:

> The anarchy represented by black settlement is counterposed to an image of England in which Britannia is portrayed as an old white woman, trapped and alone in the inner city.

She was surrounded by hostile aliens in her home – a corner of Britain had been taken over by outsiders. In Powell's view the aliens were liable to be criminals. In 1976 Powell argued that 'mugging' was a racial crime because it was predominantly carried out by blacks. This view of blacks as criminals was reinforced by media reporting of so called 'muggings' and various inner-city disturbances in the 1970s and 1980s.

(For details of a study of the 'panic' over mugging see pp. 422–5.)

Ethnic absolutism

As we saw earlier in the chapter (see p. 664), in his 1968 speech Powell had said 'As I look ahead, I am filled with foreboding. Like the Roman, I seem to see "the River Tiber foaming with much blood".' The blood would be the inevitable consequence of immigration which led to people from different cultures living side-by-side.

Gilroy calls the view that there are completely different cultures **ethnic absolutism**. He criticizes people like Powell for believing that cultures are fixed and unchanging. For Gilroy there are many overlaps between black and white cultures in Britain and indeed British culture, particularly youth culture, has become increasingly influenced by black culture. To him cultures are constantly changing and he attacks all those who analyse ethnic cultures as separate entities. This not only includes right-wing politicians who support the 'repatriation' of British blacks but also some left-wing thinkers and sociologists who study ethnicity. They too can be ethnic absolutists when they portray groups of Asians or Afro-Caribbeans as having quite distinct cultures from other British people.

Thus Gilroy is hostile to the sort of studies which we discussed in the 'Ethnicity' section of this chapter.

Black culture

In discussing black culture Gilroy concentrates on the music and youth culture of Afro-Caribbeans. He sees black culture as being formed partly as a response to racism and exploitation. For example, from slave songs to reggae, rap and hip-hop, black music and lyrics have expressed radical sentiments. However, black culture is much more than simply a reaction to racism: it is actively created in different contexts from diverse influences. Some of those influences are African and predate the large-scale exploitation of blacks by whites.

Black culture is an international culture which has been influenced by the **Diaspora**, or dispersal of African peoples throughout the world. In Britain there are strong Caribbean and Afro-American influences. Reggae music and the sound systems over which it is traditionally played have influenced black youth in Britain, as have North American traditions of soul and rap. Most styles of black music are based around African rhythms which were preserved in slave music and passed down to succeeding generations. Black music and culture not only has international origins, it is also influential throughout the world. Gilroy claims, for example, that 'Rastafari culture has been carried to locations as diverse as Poland and Polynesia, and hip-hop from Stockholm to Southall.'

Black culture has also influenced white youth. Gilroy attacks ethnic absolutists by suggesting how elements of black music have been adopted by whites. In the 1960s mods and others started using black American slang words such as 'dig'. The Beatles's early records contained cover versions of rhythm and blues and rock and roll songs originally recorded by black American artists. Later, reggae rhythms started to be incorporated into mainstream pop music.

In Britain Gilroy detects some evidence that racial divisions may be being weakened by music. In West London some Asians have become involved in hip-hop. White and black musicians worked together in the 1970s in groups like The Specials, who played ska music (a variation on reggae) and attacked racism in their lyrics. Gilroy quotes at length from David Emmanuel's 1984 hit 'Cockney Translation'. In this song cockney and black slang were translated. For example, some of the lyrics are:

Cockney say scarper we scatter
Cockney say rabbit we chatter
We say bleach Cockney knackered
Cockney say triffic we say wackard
Cockney say blokes we say guys
Cockney say alright we say Ites!
We say pants Cockney say strides
Sweet as a nut . . . just level vibes. Seen.

To Gilroy this suggested the increasing possibility of the black and white working classes working together to resist racism and class exploitation. Despite the differences between blacks and whites, their cultures were not completely separate and they influenced one another. Gilroy concludes on an optimistic note, suggesting that black and white cooperation offers an image of a better future. Eventually the different cultures may become so similar that people will no longer even think of each other as belonging to different 'races'.

Evaluation

Gilroy's work has been criticized by more conventional Marxists. They have criticized him for failing to define 'race' clearly and for continually referring to groups as 'races'. To Miles there is no biological basis for 'races'. 'Races' therefore do not exist and the term 'race' should not be used. He also criticizes Gilroy for arguing that class conflict has been replaced by 'race' conflict and other non-economic forms of conflict. To Miles and other Marxists class conflict is far from dead and economic exploitation continues to be an important factor in the exploitation of ethnic minorities and the production of racism.

Whatever its limitations, Gilroy's work represents an important advance over most earlier approaches to 'race' and ethnicity. It combines the study of ethnic minority cultures with an examination of racism and in doing so avoids the narrow focus of many of the other studies we have examined in this chapter. Gilroy also discusses the relationship between 'race', racism, ethnicity and nationality in suggesting that in Britain racism has become increasingly closely connected with a form of British nationalism.

We will now go on to discuss sociological approaches to nationalism and identity.

■ Nationalism and identity

■ Nationalism
The importance of nationalism

Stuart Hall has pointed out that 'the great discourses of modernity', liberalism and Marxism, both led people 'to expect not the revival but the gradual disappearance of the nationalist passion'. In Marxist theory classes, not nations, would become the great historical actors while liberalism saw national differences being eroded by a global market in which trade linked all parts of the world.

A number of contemporary sociologists also claim that a process of **globalization** has been taking place. In this process national boundaries become less significant in social life: communication systems such as satellite TV transcend them. The world's financial markets are linked by technology so that movements in share prices in one country can instantaneously affect prices on the other side of the world. International organizations such as the UN and the EC also reduce the importance of nations, while travel gives individuals a less localized view of the world.

However, many people have argued that there has been a great resurgence of **nationalism** in recent decades. Individuals usually seem to identify more with their nation than with any other grouping. Nationalism could be seen as being present in the 'new racism' described by Gilroy in the preceding section and in demands for independence by the Scottish and Welsh in Britain, Basques in Spain and Bretons in France. Nationalism was important in the collapse of the USSR with demands for independence coming from Lithuania, Estonia, the Ukraine and elsewhere contributing to the break-up of the country. In the former Yugoslavia violent civil war raged as Croatians, Serbs and Muslims fought for territory in future independent states. Benedict Anderson claims that 'since World War II every successful revolution has defined itself in nationalist terms' and argues:

the 'end of the era of nationalism' so long prophesied is not remotely in sight. Indeed, nationness is the most universally legitimate value in the political life of our time.

Whether or not Anderson is right to attach so much importance to nationalism, it has certainly been neglected in much social theory and it is clearly an important feature of social life and one which shows little sign of becoming less important.

The definition of nationalism

Benedict Anderson argues that a **nation** is 'an imagined political community – and imagined as both inherently limited and sovereign'.

1 It is **imagined** because most members of even a small

nation never meet one another or hear one another yet they feel they all belong to one community. Whatever inequalities divide members of a nation it is 'always conceived as a deep, horizontal comradeship'.

2 It is **limited** in the sense that nations include some people who are regarded as belonging, while excluding others as outsiders. No nation claims to include the whole of humanity.

3 It is **sovereign** because nationalism seeks or celebrates independence and self-government for a group of people.

Anderson claims that racism and nationalism are quite different concepts.

1 **Racism** is based on 'dreams of eternal contamination'. It sees groups of people as having fixed, biological characteristics. For example, Jews, 'the seed of Abraham' are 'forever Jews no matter what passport they carry or what languages they speak and read'.

2 **Nationalism**, on the other hand, does not condemn individuals to be seen as inevitably belonging to a particular group of people. It is possible to become a member of a nation while it is not possible to become part of a 'race' to which the individual did not originally belong.

Anderson's view that racism and nationalism are quite different have not been accepted by most sociologists. Robert Miles argues that 'ideologies of racism and nationalism have a common historical origin'. Racism was originally used to justify the exploitation of non-Europeans in various parts of the globe. With the end of colonialism, racism which saw distinct biological groupings in humanity, was to some extent replaced by nationalism, in which individuals see their nation as superior to other nations. To Miles racism and nationalism are similar because 'Both claim the existence of a natural division of the world's population into discrete groups which exist independently of class relations.' Both are used by people to justify beliefs that particular groups are superior to other groups.

However, Miles does acknowledge one important difference between nationalism and racism. He says 'the ideology of nationalism, unlike that of racism, specifies a particular political objective (national self-determination) and therefore a blueprint for political organisation on a world scale'. Thus, although Miles disagrees with Anderson about the relationship between nationalism and racism, he does agree that nationalism is based upon a belief that a group of people should have a sovereign state.

Thomas Hylland Eriksen examines the relationship between ethnicity and nationalism. To him 'Nationalism and ethnicity are kindred concepts.' Both are based upon the belief that a group of people is distinctive and has a shared culture. However, nationalism and ethnicity are different and the difference he identifies has a similar basis to the definitions of nationalism put forward by Anderson and Miles. Eriksen argues that a nationalist ideology 'is an ethnic ideology which demands a state on behalf of an ethnic group'.

Eriksen admits that this simple definition does pose certain problems when considering some examples of nationalism and ethnicity. Nationalism is sometimes used to try to unite diverse ethnic groups and it therefore 'stresses shared civil rights rather than shared cultural roots'. In Mauritius, for example, Mauritian nationalism is used to try to overcome the divisions between Hindus, Muslims, Chinese, French and Africans.

Another problem is that there are some marginal cases which could be seen as examples of nationalism or ethnicity. These may occur when some members of a group want full independence, while others want greater independence within an existing state. Scottish and Basque nationalism are both examples.

Although there is general agreement that nationalism is related to sovereignty, precise definitions vary and there is no agreement about the exact relationship between nationalism, 'race' and ethnicity.

■ Immanuel Wallerstein – the world system and peoplehood

Ambiguous identities

Wallerstein believes that in the modern world people have **ambiguous identities**. People from the same group will give varying answers when asked about their sense of identity. He gives some examples of this ambiguity by asking 'Are there Palestinians? Who is a Jew? Are Macedonians Bulgarians? Are Berbers Arabs? What is the correct label: Negro, Afro-American, Black (capitalized), black (uncapitalized)?' He points out that

'People shoot each other over the question of labels. And yet the very people who do so tend to deny that the issue is complex or puzzling or indeed anything but self-evident.' In an attempt to understand the ways in which labels come to be used Wallerstein sets out to examine how different types of label relate to the development of 'the world system'.

'Race', nationality and ethnicity

To begin his analysis Wallerstein distinguishes between three ways of describing what he calls **peoplehood**. These are 'race', nation and ethnic group. He suggests:

> a 'race' is supposed to be a genetic category, which has a visible physical form...' A 'nation' is supposed to be a sociopolitical category, linked somehow to the actual or potential boundaries of a state. An 'ethnic group' is supposed to be a cultural category, of which there are said to be certain continuing behaviours that are passed on from generation to generation and that are not normally linked in theory to state boundaries.

However, these terms are used very inconsistently and there are often arguments about whether a group of people is a racial, ethnic or national group. To Wallerstein all the terms are ideological: they are used to imply something about a group of people's past and to suggest how they should behave now. Thus a group which is persuaded that it is a national group may take action to secure its own state, whereas an ethnic group is more likely to defend its culture.

According to Wallerstein the use of different terms can be explained in terms of the world system, a concept which forms the basis of his whole theoretical approach.

The world system

Wallerstein argues that the development of capitalism led to the development of a **world system**. The capitalist economy gradually expanded so that every corner of the globe became part of an international economy. This international economy was and still is based upon the exploitation of some areas of the globe by other areas: the **core areas,** which have developed most, exploit the **peripheral areas** which are more distant from the centres of capitalist economic power. Core areas have traditionally been located in Europe, North America and Japan while the peripheral areas have been located in what is often called the Third World. However, the system is not fixed and countries can experience a change in their position. They may become more prosperous and powerful and move inwards towards the core, or they may decline and move outwards towards the periphery.

Peoplehood and the capitalist world economy

Wallerstein claims that 'race', nation and ethnicity each correspond to a different feature of the capitalist world economy.

1   Wallerstein argues that '"race" is related to the axial division of labour' in the world economy. Before capitalism spread over the globe there was more genetic homogeneity in particular regions than there is today. For example, before the advent of colonialism and slavery, few Europeans lived in Africa and few Africans lived in Europe or the Americas. Racial categories began to be used to distinguish the workforces in the core and peripheral areas. Those from the more powerful core countries were held to be from more superior 'races' than those from the weaker peripheral ones. This helped to justify the exploitation of the supposedly inferior 'races' by the supposedly superior ones.

Wallerstein cites South Africa as an example of how racial categories have continued to be constructed in line with distinctions between core and peripheral areas. When the country still had a system of apartheid, the Chinese population was designated as Asian and as non-white. However, visiting business people from the powerful core country of Japan were regarded as 'honorary whites', despite their apparent racial similarity to the Chinese South Africans.

2   Second, Wallerstein argues that 'nation' is related to the 'political superstructure' of the world system. Most

modern states came into existence as a result of the world system. In 1450, for example, political entities such as the Holy Roman Empire, the Mogul Empire and the Burgundian Netherlands covered areas which are now divided into several distinct states. Turkey, Syria, Germany and Italy were among the many modern states which did not exist then. It was colonialism that led to the division of Africa into sovereign states.

According to Wallerstein, nationalism only developed after sovereign states had been created as competitors in the world system. The states which compete often contain diverse groups of people and may be threatened by 'internal disintegration and external aggression'. Promoting nationalist sentiments helps the governments of states to prevent disintegration and to mobilize their populations to oppose external aggressors. Each state has a different position in the hierarchy of states which makes up the contemporary world system. Nationalist sentiments help to legitimate the position of the core nations in this hierarchy.

3   Third, ethnicity is related to 'the complex hierarchy within the labour segment'. Although all workers are exploited, some are exploited more than others. The most exploited often belong to ethnic minority groups. Different groups in the workforce have to behave differently to perform their tasks effectively in order to produce surplus value for their employers. Ethnicity involves cultural difference which leads to different types of socialization in households belonging to different ethnic groups. These differences in socialization help to prepare workers from different ethnic groups for their different roles in capitalist economies.

Evaluation

Wallerstein's view that nationalism is a comparatively recent development is widely accepted. His views on racism have much in common with a number of Marxists. It is his views on ethnicity, however, which are perhaps the most implausible. He advances no evidence to show that members of different ethnic groups are socialized in their families to do different jobs in capitalist economies.

As we show elsewhere in this chapter, ethnic minorities in Britain are by no means confined to the lower reaches of the occupational structure (see pp. 720–1). While Wallerstein may be right to see the 'peoplehoods' of 'race' 'ethnicity' and 'nationality' as social constructions, some of his explanations as to how they develop are open to question.

■ Stuart Hall – 'Our mongrel selves'

Capitalism and nationalism

Like Wallerstein, Hall examines the relationship between capitalism and the development of identity. Hall argues that capitalism has had contradictory effects: it created the nation-state and with it nationalism, but in recent times capitalism has also promoted forces which have undermined national cultures. On the one hand the global nature of the world has produced **transnational imperatives**. On the other hand 'globalization seems to have led to a strengthening of "local" allegiances and identities'.

In Western Europe a number of countries have seen the development of movements calling for greater degrees of regional autonomy or complete independence; in Eastern Europe and the former USSR there has been 'a revival of ethnic nationalisms among peoples submerged for decades within the supra-nationalism of the Soviet sphere of influence'. Political changes such as the collapse of Soviet communism and the process of globalization have weakened nation-states and their attempts to impose a single all-embracing culture on diverse ethnic groups within their boundaries. The ethnic groups have taken advantage of the situation to reassert their distinctive identities.

To Hall, attempts to promote nationalism in the modern world can be very dangerous. Most modern nation-states 'are inextricably multicultural – mixed ethnically, religiously, culturally and linguistically'. When groups within the boundaries of a state assert their rights and celebrate their differences, it can lead to violent conflict. In the former Yugoslavia this has led to 'ethnic cleansing', attempts to make whole areas 'ethnically pure' by killing or driving out members of other ethnic groups. In some states attempts to impose a single national culture on diverse groups lead to the development 'of an openly racist far right'. In France the Front National calls for the 'repatriation' of so-called 'immigrants', as do organizations such as the British National Party. In Germany, Turkish workers have been attacked and killed by right-wing nationalists.

However, Hall does not see nationalism as bad in itself. It has also been used by groups seeking independence from colonial powers which have oppressed them. Nationalism 'isn't necessarily either a reactionary or progressive force', it can be either.

Identity

According to Hall the forces outlined above are causing people to have a confused sense of identity: a mixed-up view of who they are. The ethnic and cultural diversity of most countries, different nationalisms and the process of globalization, all contribute to the confusion. Many people have a number of identities simultaneously and may act and think in terms of belonging to a whole variety of groups. Hall says:

Modern people of all sorts and conditions, it seems to me, have had, as a condition of survival, to be members, simultaneously, of several overlapping 'imagined communities'; and the negotiations across and between these complex borderlines are characteristic of modernity itself.

The novelist Salman Rushdie provides a good example of identity confusion. Born in Asia and brought up a Muslim, he is a British citizen who was condemned to death by the Ayatollah Khomeini of Iran for the allegedly anti-Islamic nature of his novel *The Satanic Verses*. Hall quotes Rushdie arguing that '*The Satanic Verses* celebrates hybridity, impurity, intermingling' and describing how mass migration has led to the creation of 'our mongrel selves'. Rushdie sees himself as representing a diverse mix of national, racial, religious, cultural and political identities.

Hall gives a graphic example of people's multiple identities illustrating how issues of gender, politics and class can add to the confusion created by racial ethnic and national differences. In 1991 the American president, George Bush, nominated a black conservative judge, Clarence Thomas, for the Supreme Court. A former colleague of Thomas, Anita Hill then accused him of sexually harassing and propositioning her. People took different sides in the ensuing arguments according to their sense of identity. Hall says:

Some blacks supported Thomas on racial grounds; others opposed him on sexual grounds. Black women were divided, depending on whether their 'identities' as blacks or as women prevailed. Black men were also divided depending on whether their sexism overrode their liberalism. White men were divided, depending not only on their politics, but on how they identified themselves with respect to racism and sexism. White conservative women supported Thomas, not only on political grounds, but because of their opposition to feminism. White feminists, often liberal on race, opposed Thomas on sexual grounds. And because judge Thomas is a member of the judicial elite and Anita Hall at the time of the alleged incident, was a junior employee, there were issues of social class position at work in these arguments too. (Quoted in Pilkington 1993, p. 63.)

Hall concludes that nationalism and ethnic absolutism are major threats to the modern world. With such pluralism in most parts of the world, tolerance of human diversity is essential if humans are to live together in anything approaching harmony. He says 'The capacity to live with difference is, in my view, the coming question of the 21st century.'

■ Ethnic minorities in the labour market and stratification system

There is considerable evidence that ethnic minorities are disadvantaged in the British labour market. As we have seen elsewhere in the book, ethnic minorities are more likely to suffer from unemployment (see p. 240). Furthermore, earlier in this chapter we saw that in general terms those from ethnic minorities tend to get paid lower wages and have lower-status jobs (see pp. 697–9). Although there are differences between ethnic groups, most groups continue to suffer from disadvantages even when factors such as fluency in English and educational qualifications are taken into account.

Discrimination in the labour market

The most straightforward explanation of disadvantages suffered by ethnic minorities in employment is that it results from the racism and prejudice of employers. From this point of view employers discriminate against ethnic minority groups by either refusing to employ them, employing them only in low-status and low-paid jobs, or refusing to promote them.

Evidence to support this point of view is provided by a study by Colin Brown and Pat Gay carried out in 1984–5. They conducted research in London, Birmingham and Manchester in which bogus applications were made for a variety of jobs by letter and by telephone. The supposed applicants were identified as being from ethnic minorities by the use of Hindu names for 'Asian' applicants and a Jamaican educational background for 'West Indian' applicants. In telephone applications ethnic accents were used to differentiate ethnic minority applicants from 'white' applicants.

Brown and Gay found that positive responses were significantly less common to applications by those who were identified as being from ethnic minorities. Some 90 per cent of white applicants but only 63 per cent of Asian and 63 per cent of West Indian applicants received positive responses.

Brown and Gay compared their results with those of similar studies carried out in 1973–4 and 1977–9. They found that the level of discrimination had remained about the same in all three studies. They concluded that 'there is no evidence here to suggest that racial discrimination in job recruitment has fallen over the period covered by these studies'.

In the *Third Policy Studies Institute Survey* Brown tried to measure the experience of racial discrimination by ethnic minorities. Of those who were currently in the job market or who had worked in the last 10 years, 26 per cent of West Indian men and 23 per cent of West Indian women claimed they had been refused a job for racial reasons. For Asians the corresponding figures were 10 per cent for men and 8 per cent for women.

There was less evidence of racism affecting promotion. Only 11 per cent of West Indian men and 3 per cent of women claimed they had been refused a better job because of their 'race' or colour.

These figures must be used with some caution. They rely upon the subjective beliefs of the respondents to the survey who might not be in a position to accurately assess whether they had been the victims of racial discrimination. Discrimination could be more common or less frequent than the figures indicate; however, they do suggest that at least some of the disadvantages experienced by ethnic minorities in the labour market could be the result of racism.

■ Ethnic minorities as an underclass

Some sociologists have tried to develop a more theoretical approach to explaining the position of ethnic minorities in the labour market and in society as a whole. Both British and American sociologists have suggested that ethnic minorities form an **underclass**. While some have defined an underclass in cultural terms others have seen the underclass as a structural feature of society. The idea of an underclass has already been discussed in detail in earlier chapters (see pp. 91–7 for a discussion of the underclass and stratification and pp. 154–60 for a discussion of the underclass and poverty). In this section we concentrate on the relationship between the concepts of underclass and ethnicity.

Charles Murray – Losing Ground

In his 1984 book *Losing Ground* Charles Murray argued that the USA had developed a black underclass. This underclass was distinguished by its behaviour. He claimed that increasing numbers of young blacks were withdrawing from the labour market: they were unwilling to work. At the same time there were increasing numbers of black single parents who had never been married.

Murray denied that such changes were the result of poverty and lack of opportunity. He argued that in the 1950s participation by blacks in the labour market was higher than in the 1960s, yet there was greater economic prosperity and lower unemployment in the 1960s than the 1950s.

To Murray the real reason for the changes in behaviour lay in welfare benefits. In his view Aid to Families with Dependent Children removed many of the incentives for men to work to support their families, and it enabled mothers to bring up their children on their own. The stigma of relying upon benefits had been reduced as more and more benefits were introduced for people with low incomes.

American critics of Murray have pointed out that the Aid to Families with Dependent Children was introduced some twenty years before the number of single-parent black families began to rise rapidly. Lydia Morris criticizes Murray for failing to explain the withdrawal of black youth from the labour market. The young unemployed have no automatic entitlement to benefit in the USA, so their behaviour cannot be explained in terms of the welfare system.

Some American sociologists have agreed with Murray that the USA has developed a black or ethnic minority underclass, but they have not agreed about the causes. They have attributed its development to structural forces rather than to the operation of the welfare system and the behaviour of welfare claimants. The most influential alternative view of the American underclass has been advanced by William Julius Wilson

William Julius Wilson – The Truly Disadvantaged

In his 1987 book *The Truly Disadvantaged* Wilson argues that blacks and Hispanics living in inner-city areas have come to form an underclass because of forces beyond their control. The disadvantages faced by urban blacks and Hispanics have historical roots and have created problems which continue to make it difficult to escape from the ghetto.

When poor blacks migrated from the rural south of the USA to the cities of the north, they faced the obstacle of racism when they tried to find work. The migrants had few skills and little prospect of career advancement. Their low levels of economic success encouraged whites to develop crude racial stereotypes which produced further problems for the ghetto poor. What work the blacks could find was largely unskilled and in manufacturing industry.

In the 1970s manufacturing industry began to decline and the industry which survived the recession moved away from city centres. Service sector work increased but much of it required qualifications which ethnic minorities in the inner cities did not possess. Some black and Hispanics had enjoyed success, gained qualifications and secured well-paid jobs. However, these individuals moved out of the city centres to the suburbs, leaving behind the most disadvantaged. The poor had become trapped in areas where there were few opportunities to improve their lot. Wilson says:

> the underclass exists mainly because of large scale and harmful changes in the labor market and its resulting spatial concentration as well as the isolation of such areas from the most affluent parts of the black community.

In 1990 in an address to the American Sociological Association Wilson abandoned the use of the term underclass. Although he stuck by his analysis of the problems faced by ethnic minorities in the inner cities of the USA, he argued that the term underclass had become a liability. It had been adopted by right-wing commentators who had used it to indicate that the problems of the poor were of their own making. To Wilson the problems resulted more from impersonal economic forces, and the connotations the term had taken on were unfortunate. He therefore suggested that the groups he was describing should be called the **ghetto poor** rather than the underclass.

Some American critics have argued that Wilson underestimates the effects produced by racism. From this point of view the black middle class is small and even those blacks with good jobs do less well than their white counterparts with similar qualifications. Problems for American blacks in the labour market are not confined to the poor.

The underclass in Britain

Some sociologists have argued that there is a British underclass composed mainly or exclusively of ethnic minorities. They have followed Wilson in arguing that the underclass has been created by structural forces and have tended to be critical of sociologists such as Murray who see the underclass in cultural terms.

One of the most influential views of this type was advanced by Anthony Giddens. Giddens argued that the underclass is composed of those

with a disadvantaged position in the labour market. As well as lacking skills and qualifications, they may also have to face prejudice and discrimination. Women and ethnic minorities are most likely to suffer from these problems and therefore are most likely to be found in the underclass. As we saw in Chapter 2 (see p. 94), Giddens believes that migrants are very likely to end up in the underclass.

To Giddens, when ethnic minorities such as Asians and West Indians in Britain and Algerians in France are heavily concentrated in the lowest-paid jobs or are unemployed, then an underclass exists. When members of the underclass do have jobs they are mainly in the secondary labour market. (We discuss the concept of a secondary labour market in the next section.)

John Rex and Sally Tomlinson – the underclass in Birmingham

Giddens's ideas were further developed in a study of the Handsworth area of Birmingham conducted by John Rex and Sally Tomlinson and published in 1979. They argued that New Commonwealth immigrants to Britain largely went to Britain 'to fill the gaps in the less skilled and the less attractive jobs in manufacturing industry as well as in the less skilled jobs in the service industries'. During the 1950s and 1960s Britain experienced a shortage of labour and immigration was encouraged to overcome the problem. The shortage was particularly acute in jobs requiring little skill, and immigrants were often employed in such jobs.

Rex and Tomlinson believe that there is not one but rather two distinctive labour markets in Britain. They support the **dual labour market theory**. This sees the **primary labour market** as consisting of jobs with high wages, good working conditions, job security and with opportunities for on-the-job training and promotion. In contrast the **secondary labour market** consists of jobs with low wages, poor working conditions, little job security and with few opportunities for on-the-job training and promotion. Highly skilled jobs are usually located in the primary sector of the labour market, and less skilled jobs in the secondary. Skilled workers are usually more crucial to a company's success than workers with few skills, and so their loyalty to their employer is encouraged with high wages and opportunities for promotion.

Asian and West Indian immigrants were usually recruited to jobs in the secondary labour market. Because such jobs offer few promotion prospects or opportunities for training, they have tended to remain in a disadvantaged position in the labour market. For this reason ethnic minorities form an underclass in Britain.

Rex and Tomlinson acknowledge that not all members of ethnic minorities work in the secondary labour market but they offer evidence to show that they are disproportionately represented in such jobs. For example, using data from the *1971 Census* they found that in the West Midlands only 1 in 8 West Indian men, 1 in 6 Pakistanis and 1 in 20 Indians were employed in vehicle manufacture, an industry which paid high wages. On the other hand, 33 per cent of West Indian men, more than 50 per cent of Indians, nearly 50 per cent of Pakistanis and 30 per cent of East African Asians worked in metal or metal goods manufacture; jobs in the metal industries tended to be poorly paid and offered few promotion prospects.

Rex and Tomlinson also found differences in the employment of women in the West Midlands in different ethnic groups. They say 'whereas the white woman typically becomes a secretary or a shopworker the immigrant woman works in a factory, or in a hospital and rather less frequently in service industries'.

In 1976 Rex and Tomlinson carried out a survey of Handsworth, Birmingham, in which structured interviews were conducted with a sample of 1,100 people. They found that 30 per cent of whites in Handsworth had white-collar jobs but only 9.5 per cent of West Indians and 5.1 per cent of Asians; 27.4 per cent of whites were in unskilled or semi-skilled manual work compared to 38.7 per cent of Asians and 44.1 per cent of West Indians. On the basis of their research Rex and Tomlinson argued that ethnic minority groups:

> were systematically at a disadvantage compared with working-class whites and that, instead of identifying with working-class culture, community and politics, they formed their own organisations and became in effect a separate underprivileged class.

In short, they formed an underclass which was perpetuated by the predominance of ethnic minorities in the secondary labour market.

Marxist approaches

Marxist sociologists agree with sociologists such as Giddens and Rex and Tomlinson (who use a Weberian approach) that ethnic minorities are disadvantaged in capitalist societies. However, they do not agree that they form an underclass in Britain. They reject the importance attached to status in underclass theories and place more emphasis on the workings of the economy and the role of ethnic minorities in the economic system.

Stephen Castles and Godula Kosack – a reserve army of labour

NB

In a study of immigrant workers in France, Germany, Switzerland and Britain, Stephen Castles and Godula Kosack found that the immigrants faced similar problems in the labour market to those identified in Handsworth by Rex and Tomlinson. In these four European countries immigrants were found to be concentrated in low-paid jobs or in jobs with poor working conditions. Most were manual workers in unskilled or semi-skilled work and they suffered high rates of unemployment. Castles and Kosack claim that in Britain this situation is mainly due to discrimination. In France, Germany and Switzerland the migrant workers are foreigners in the country in which they are working and restrictive laws and regulations prevent them from gaining employment in the more desirable jobs.

Discrimination and restrictive regulations are, however, only the immediate causes of the plight of immigrants. The poor treatment of immigrants ultimately derives from the need in capitalist societies for a **reserve army of labour**: it is necessary to have a surplus of labour in order to keep wage costs down since the greater the overall supply of labour, the weaker the bargaining position of workers. Furthermore, as Marxists, Castles and Kosack believe that capitalist economies are inherently unstable. They go through periods of boom and slump and a reserve army of labour needs to be available to be hired and fired as the fluctuating fortunes of the economy dictate. After the Second World War capitalist societies exhausted their indigenous reserve army of labour; women, for example, were increasingly taking paid employment. Capitalist countries in Europe therefore turned to migrant labour and immigration to provide a reserve pool of cheap labour which could be profitably exploited.

Castles and Kosack do not believe that such workers form an underclass outside and below the main class structure. They regard them as being part of the working class. Like other workers they do not own the means of production and so share with them an interest in changing society. However, Castles and Kosack believe that immigrant and migrant workers are the most disadvantaged groups within the working class and as such they form a distinctive strata. Thus Castles and Kosack believe that the working class is divided in two, with ethnic minorities constituting one working-class grouping and the indigenous white population the other.

This situation is beneficial to the ruling class in capitalist societies. Ethnic minorities are blamed for problems such as unemployment and housing shortages. Attention is diverted from the failings of the capitalist system. The working class is divided and cannot unite, develop class consciousness and challenge ruling-class dominance.

Annie Phizaklea and Robert Miles – class factions

Annie Phizaklea and Robert Miles have also advanced a Marxist analysis of the position of ethnic minorities in the labour market and class structure. On the basis of a study of South Brent, London, carried out in the mid-1970s, they agree with Castles and Kosack that migrant ethnic minority workers form a distinctive strata within the working class. However, they deny that immigration and migrant labour have actually created divisions within the working class. They point out that the working class can also be seen as divided by gender and level of skill. Working-class women sell their labour for a wage like working-class men, but unlike working-class men they have unpaid domestic responsibilities. Skilled manual workers have always tried to defend their own interests and ensure that they enjoy higher wages than other manual workers.

To Phizaklea and Miles the working class is not divided in two, but is split between a considerable number of class factions based upon gender, skill and ethnicity. Immigration did not divide a united working class; it added an extra dimension to existing divisions.

Andrew Pilkington – the underclass reconsidered

Despite the differences between the theories on ethnicity and employment examined so far, they share a good deal in common. Andrew Pilkington suggests:

> there is agreement that black workers are employed in predominantly nonskilled work, that they are locked into such work with few chances of escape and that this tends to segregate them from the indigenous workforce.

Pilkington believes that the underclass and Marxist theories are not supported by empirical evidence. Pilkington quotes figures from the *Labour Force Survey* for 1989—91. These showed that:

1 among West Indians and Guyanese 32 per cent of men and 63 per cent of women were in non-manual occupations;

2 among Indians the figures were 59 per cent for men and 62 per cent for women;

3 among Pakistanis/Bangladeshis they were 40 per cent for men and 64 per cent for women.

Thus for women there was little difference in the proportion of different ethnic groups in non-manual jobs. Amongst men, Indians were more likely than whites to have non-manual work and very substantial minorities of men in the other ethnic groups did not have working-class jobs. Pilkington therefore rejects the view that ethnic minorities are overwhelmingly trapped in jobs offering few prospects.

Pilkington also denies that ethnic minorities are segregated from the white workforce. He quotes a study of the labour market in Peterborough conducted by Blackburn and Mann in which it was found that 'the majority of immigrants are sharing jobs with the nativeborn', and that 'although immigrants receive less on average their conditions overlap very considerably with that of British workers' (quoted in Pilkington 1984, p. 90).

Pilkington fully accepts that ethnic minorities are disadvantaged in the labour market, but he does not agree that they are so disadvantaged that they constitute an underclass or subordinate stratum or faction of the working class. On the other hand he believes the situation is different for migrant workers in some other European countries. In France and Germany, for example, migrant workers can be seen to occupy a distinctive group at the bottom of the stratification system because 'they are predominantly located in nonskilled work with relatively few political rights'.

Sociology, values and 'race' and ethnicity

Sociologists, like other members of society, are a product of their time and place. While sociologists may try to study society without being influenced by the commonsense beliefs of other members of society, they may find it difficult or even impossible to be completely objective. This was certainly true in the nineteenth century. Sociologists generally accepted the view of scientists and others that humanity was divided into distinct biological 'races', some of which were superior to others. Not surprisingly they tended to see themselves and their own 'race' as being at the top of the hierarchy.

Thus to sociologists like Herbert Spencer white Europeans generally belonged to the most evolved 'races'. His beliefs did not stem from individual arrogance or ignorance. Colonialism undoubtedly contributed to persuading most Victorian English people that their 'race' was superior to the other 'races' which they and other European powers had conquered and ruled.

As large-scale migration between and within countries became more common, people from different 'races' increasingly lived close together. Sociologists supporting the immigrant-host model became less likely to claim that certain 'races' were superior to others. To them the problems of race relations were created by the difficulties encountered when immigrants or strangers settled in an established host society.

However, these views were still strongly influenced by the values of the sociologists who expressed them: it was always the 'immigrants' who were the problem, disrupting the harmony of the host society. The hosts were largely tolerant and some were even welcoming. Any fault lay with those who would not adapt to their new surroundings.

From this point of view the hosts were generally willing to accept the strangers; they were not filled with racism or hatred.

The views associated with the immigrant-host model seem to remain common amongst British whites today. For example, as we saw earlier, Ellis Cashmore found that some people in Birmingham and the Midlands criticized 'immigrants' for not fitting in with British ways. They resented it when 'immigrants' wanted to preserve their traditional cultures.

However, sociologists had begun to reject the idea that the culture of ethnic minorities was inferior to that of the white majority or to assume that 'immigrants' needed to change their cultures. Scientists had already discredited the ideas that distinct 'races' existed. The mood of the times was moving in favour of greater tolerance of diverse cultures. In the USA the civil rights and Black Power movements encouraged ethnic minorities to take pride in their distinctiveness. In Britain legislation outlawed discrimination and made open racism less respectable and acceptable. Rather than just expecting 'immigrants' to integrate, new approaches to issues of 'race' and ethnicity seemed necessary.

One approach was to emphasize the desirability of ethnic pluralism. This suggested that the cultures of ethnic minorities should not necessarily change to allow integration, but rather they should remain distinctive and separate. Studies of ethnicity were carried out to develop a greater understanding of the diverse ways of life of different ethnic groups.

This approach produced policies of multiculturalism. From this viewpoint, schools, for example, should accommodate all ethnic groups: the diet, religious practices, clothing, beliefs and values of different ethnic groups should be catered for in the education system.

Radical critics of this approach tended to dismiss it. James Donald and Ali Rattansi call it the 'saris, samosas and steel-bands syndrome'. It focused on the 'superficial manifestations of culture' and did not really address the underlying problems faced by ethnic minorities. Donald and Rattansi argue that multiculturalism ignores the 'continuing hierarchies of power and legitimacy'. If ethnic minorities are allowed or encouraged to wear saris, eat samosas and play in steel-bands, that does not necessarily mean that their cultures have the same power and legitimacy as white culture. Donald and Rattansi argue that the 'limits to this approach were cruelly exposed by intellectual as well as political responses to *The Satanic Verses* affair in the late 1980s'. Politicians and writers alike tended to side with Salman Rushdie against the British Muslim community who called for the book to be banned for blasphemy.

According to some sociologists the emphasis on culture in multiculturalism has its own dangers. The new racism identified by Solomos *et al.* (see pp. 707–8), and the ethnic absolutism described by Gilroy are based on the idea that ethnic groups are incompatible because their cultures are incompatible. Repatriation, which used to be justified on the grounds of biological difference, was supported by politicians like Enoch Powell on cultural grounds. Rivers of blood would flow simply because very different cultures could not mix.

Sociologists who stress the importance of racism suggest that the problems of 'race' and ethnicity cannot be solved by encouraging the tolerance of different cultures. To some, racism is deeply ingrained in the minds, culture and institutions of whites. Whites possess most of the power in the USA, Britain and similar countries, and racism ensures they keep their power. From this point of view ethnic minorities have to fight to gain power rather than relying on the tolerance of well-meaning liberals. The policies associated with this approach are often called **antiracism**. They involve seeking out, exposing and destroying the open or hidden racism present in society and its institutions.

Burnage High School in South Manchester became a notorious example of antiracism in 1986 when Ahmed Iqbal Ullah was murdered by a white boy in the school playground, despite the school's vigorous antiracist policy. Children in the school were taught about the evils of racism but that did not prevent the murder. The school banned white children from attending the funeral.

While nearly all sociologists today condemn racism, some disagree with some of the policies of antiracism. Paul Gilroy argues that antiracism has sometimes practised **moralistic excesses**. It has 'drifted towards a belief in the absolute nature of ethnic categories' and has therefore fallen into the trap of emphasizing 'race' to the exclusion of everything else. It sees the world in terms of black and white. Whites are the oppressors, blacks are the oppressed. All whites are racist, as are their institutions. Gilroy says:

> The antiracism I am criticizing trivializes the struggle against racism and isolates it from other political antagonisms – from the contradiction between capital and labour, from the battle between men and women. It suggests that racism can be eliminated on its own because it is readily extricable from everything else.

To Gilroy the views of some antiracists are no longer plausible. Not only are issues of 'race' and ethnicity bound up with other issues, racial and ethnic identities and cultures themselves cannot be separated into distinct and neat categories. Like Stuart Hall Gilroy believes that in the modern world there has been so much intermingling of different cultures it is no longer appropriate to treat different 'races' as discrete groups. He says:

> The outcomes of this cultural and political interaction reconstruct and rework tradition as they pursue their particular utopia. A vision of a world in which 'race' will no longer be a meaningful device for the categorization of human beings, where work will no longer be servitude and law will be disassociated from domination.

Gilroy's views are clearly very different from those of nineteenth-century sociologists. The same is true of multicultural and antiracist views. All three approaches would have been unthinkable in the nineteenth century, when the doctrine that some 'races' were superior to others dominated beliefs in sociology and society alike.

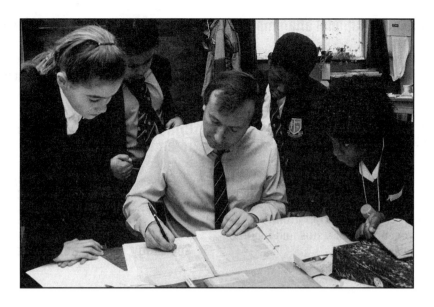

12
Education

12

Education

■ Introduction

In its broadest sense, **education** is simply one aspect of socialization: it involves the acquisition of knowledge and the learning of skills. Whether intentionally or unintentionally, education often also helps to shape beliefs and moral values.

In small-scale non-literate societies, such as hunting and gathering bands, education was hard to distinguish from other aspects of life. Young people learned their 'lessons' largely by joining in the social group. Knowledge and skills were usually learned informally by imitating examples provided by adults. Although adults sometimes instructed their young, they did so as part of their daily routine. Thus boys accompanied their fathers on hunting trips, while girls assisted their mothers with cooking and gathering vegetables.

In more complex pre-industrial societies, such as those of medieval Europe, specialized educational institutions slowly developed, along with the specialized role of teacher. However, such developments provided formal education only for a small minority of the population such as future members of the clergy and the sons of the wealthy. Formal education for the masses was only provided after industrialization was well under way.

British education

In Britain, free compulsory education conducted in formal institutions staffed by full-time professionals began in 1870. Although the state had contributed to the provision of education as early as 1833, only with **Forster's Education Act of 1870** did it assume full responsibility. In 1880 school attendance was made compulsory up to the age of 10. With the **Fisher Education Act of 1918** the state became responsible for secondary education and made attendance compulsory up to the age of 14. The school-leaving age was raised to 15 in 1947, and to 16 in 1972.

The raising of the school-leaving age was obviously accompanied by an expansion of schooling. For most of this century though, education has also expanded as a result of people continuing in education after the compulsory period of attendance, or returning to education later in life. In 1900 only 1.2 per cent of 18 year olds entered full-time further or higher education; by 1938 the figure had reached 5.8 per cent.

However, the real explosion of post-compulsory education came in the 1950s, 1960s and early 1970s. The *Robbins Report* of 1963 established the principle that all those capable of benefiting from higher education should be entitled to it. New universities were built, polytechnics were established and the Open University gave adults fresh educational opportunities. Children of school-leaving age were encouraged to stay on in school sixth forms, or to attend college. By 1990, 36 per cent of 16–18 year olds were in full-time education in Britain.

The growth in higher education slowed down in the late 1970s and early 1980s but rapid growth resumed in the late 1980s and early 1990s. Most existing universities expanded, as did the polytechnics which were given university status in 1993.

However, as Table 12.1 indicates, the proportion of the total wealth created by the country (**Gross Domestic Product** – GDP) which is devoted to education has fallen slightly from its peak in the 1980s. Nevertheless, in 1991–2 a vast sum of nearly £30 billion, more than a twentieth of the country's wealth, was spent on education.

In this chapter we are concerned with two main issues.

1 First, the role of education in society. A variety of viewpoints on the functions that education performs for society and the effects that it has will be examined.

2 Second, the question of why some social groups tend to enjoy more educational success than others will be considered.

■ Education – a functionalist perspective

Two related questions have guided functionalist research into education.

1 The first asks 'What are the functions of education for society as a whole?' Given the functionalist view of the needs of the social system, this question leads, for example, to an assessment of the contribution made by education to the maintenance of value consensus and social solidarity.

2 The second question asks 'What are the functional relationships between education and other parts of the social system?' This leads to an examination of the relationship between education and the economic system, and a consideration of how this relationship helps to integrate the society as a whole.

Table 12.1   Government expenditure on education in real terms: by type

UK	£ million at 1991–92 prices[1] and percentages		
	1970–1	1980–1	1991–2
Schools			
Nursery	58	114	
Primary	4,713	5,886	
Secondary	5,523	7,754	8,287
Special	442	917	1,280
Higher, further and adult education[2]	2,884	3,517	3,734
Polytechnics and Colleges Funding Council	.	.	993
Universities	2,325	2,698	2,668
Other education expenditure	706	1,027	1,394
Total	16,651	21,913	25,976
Related education expenditure	2,727	2,995	2,974
VAT on above expenditure	674	369	532
Total expenditure	20,051	25,277	29,482
Total expenditure as a percentage of GDP	**5.2**	**5.5**	**5.1**

[1] Adjusted to real terms using the GDP market prices deflator.
[2] Includes fees for polytechnics and colleges transferred to the Polytechnics and Colleges Funding Council in April 1989.

(*Source*: (1994) *Social Trends*, HMSO, London, p. 53.)

As with functionalist analysis in general, the functionalist view of education tends to focus on the positive contributions made by education to the maintenance of the social system.

■ Emile Durkheim – education and social solidarity

Writing at the turn of the century, the French sociologist Emile Durkheim saw the major function of education as the transmission of society's norms and values. He maintained:

> Society can survive only if there exists among its members a sufficient degree of homogeneity; education perpetuates and reinforces this homogeneity by fixing in the child from the beginning the essential similarities which collective life demands.

Without these 'essential similarities', cooperation, social solidarity and therefore social life itself would be impossible. A vital task for all societies is the welding of a mass of individuals into a united whole, in other words the creation of **social solidarity**. This involves a commitment to society, a sense of belonging and a feeling that the social unit is more important than the individual. Durkheim argued:

> To become attached to society, the child must feel in it something that is real, alive and powerful, which dominates the person and to which he also owes the best part of himself.

Education, and in particular the teaching of history, provides this link between the individual and society. If the history of their society is brought alive to children, they will come to see that they are part of something larger than themselves: they will develop a sense of commitment to the social group.

Durkheim's views can be illustrated by educational practices in the USA. There a common educational curriculum has helped to instil shared norms and values into a population with diverse backgrounds. It has provided a shared language and a common history for immigrants from every country in Europe. The American student learns about the Founding Fathers, the Constitution, about Abraham Lincoln who personifies the American values of equality of opportunity and achievement by his journey from the humble origins of a log cabin to the White House. By beginning their school day with an oath of allegiance to the Stars and Stripes, the symbol of American society, the students are socialized into a commitment to society as a whole.

Education and social rules

Durkheim argued that in complex industrial societies, the school serves a function which cannot be provided either by the family or peer group. Membership of the family is based on kinship relationships; membership of the peer group on personal choice. Membership of society as a whole is based on neither of these principles.

Individuals must learn to cooperate with those who are neither their kin nor their friends. The school provides a context where these skills can be learned. As such, it is society in miniature, a model of the social system. In school, the child must interact with other members of the school community in terms of a fixed set of rules. This experience prepares him or her for interacting with members of society as a whole in terms of society's rules.

Durkheim believed that school rules should be strictly enforced. Punishments should reflect the seriousness of the damage done to the social group by the offence, and it should be made clear to transgressors why they were being punished. In this way pupils would come to learn that it was wrong to act against the interests of the social group as a whole. They would learn to exercise self-discipline, not just because they wanted to avoid punishment, but also because they would come to see that misbehaviour damaged society as a whole. Science, and particularly social sciences like sociology, would help the child to understand the rational basis on which society was organized. Durkheim stated:

It is by respecting the school rules that the child learns to respect rules in general, that he develops the habit of self-control and restraint simply because he should control and restrain himself. It is a first initiation into the austerity of duty. Serious life has now begun.

Education and the division of labour

Finally, Durkheim argued that education teaches individuals specific skills necessary for their future occupations. This function is particularly important in industrial society with its increasingly complex and specialized division of labour.

The relatively unspecialized division of labour in pre-industrial society meant that occupational skills could usually be passed on from parents to children without the need for formal education. In industrial society, social solidarity is based largely on the **interdependence of specialized skills** – for example the manufacture of a single product requires the combination of a variety of specialists. This necessity for combination produces cooperation and social solidarity.

Thus schools transmit both general values which provide the 'necessary homogeneity for social survival' and specific skills which provide the 'necessary diversity for social cooperation'. Industrial society is thus united by value consensus and a specialized division of labour whereby specialists combine to produce goods and services.

David Hargreaves – Durkheim and the modern school

Durkheim's views have influenced some modern sociologists and educationalists. David Hargreaves has criticized the modern comprehensive school from a Durkheimian point of view. He claims that contemporary schools place far too much stress on developing the individual, and not enough on the duties and responsibilities that the individual should have towards group life in the school.

Furthermore, Hargreaves argues that many schools fail to produce a sense of dignity for working-class pupils. If pupils do not achieve individual success in competitive exams, they will tend to rebel and fail to develop a sense of belonging within the school. If the school fails them in not providing a sense of dignity and belonging, pupils may form subcultures which reject the values of the school, and therefore of the wider society. (See p. 766 for Hargreaves's work on subcultures.)

According to Hargreaves, these problems can be solved if greater stress is placed upon the social role of the individual pupil within school. Hargreaves says 'To acquire dignity a person must achieve a sense of competence, of making a contribution to, and of being valued by, the group to which he or she belongs.' Hargreaves proposes a number of changes to the curriculum in order to create a sense of competence and belonging.

1 He argues that pupils should have some freedom to pursue fields of study where they have a special interest or talent. In this way all pupils will develop a sense of their own worth.

2 In addition there should be compulsory parts of the curriculum: community studies would help pupils to have a clear view of their role in society.

3 Expressive arts, crafts and sports would also play a vital role. In putting on plays and taking part in team games like hockey and football, pupils would experience satisfaction by contributing to collective enterprises. They would develop a sense of loyalty to the school, and learn to respect one another for the contribution each could make to the school.

Criticisms of Durkheim

Durkheim's views on education are open to a number of criticisms. As Hargreaves's work suggests, it is far from clear that education in modern Britain succeeds in transmitting shared values, promoting self-discipline, or cementing social solidarity. Durkheim also assumes that the norms and values transmitted by the education system are those of society as a whole, rather than those of a ruling elite or ruling class.

Hargreaves shows more awareness of the existence of a variety of cultures and values in society, and points to some of the limitations of contemporary education. However, Hargreaves's proposals for changes in the curriculum are controversial. Many contemporary changes in education seem designed to encourage individual competition and to train pupils for particular vocations. It could be argued that sport and community studies are not the best subjects to study as the preparation of a future workforce.

Although Durkheim and Hargreaves both criticize education based upon individual competition in an exam system, other functionalists see competition as a vital aspect of modern education. We will now examine their views.

■ Talcott Parsons – education and universalistic values

The American sociologist Talcott Parsons outlined what has become the accepted functionalist view of education. Writing in the late 1950s, Parsons argues that after primary socialization within the family, the school takes over as the **focal socializing agency**: school acts as a bridge between the family and society as a whole, preparing children for their adult role.

Within the family, the child is judged and treated largely in terms of **particularistic** standards. Parents treat the child as their particular child rather than judging her or him in terms of standards or yardsticks which can be applied to every individual. Yet in the wider society the individual is treated and judged in terms of **universalistic** standards which are applied to all members, regardless of their kinship ties.

Within the family the child's status is **ascribed**: it is fixed by birth. However, in advanced industrial society, status in adult life is largely **achieved**: for example individuals achieve their occupational status.

Thus the child must move from the particularistic standards and ascribed status of the family to the universalistic standards and achieved status of adult society.

The school prepares young people for this transition. It establishes universalistic standards in terms of which all pupils achieve their status. Their conduct is assessed against the yardstick of the school rules; their achievement is measured by performance in examinations. The same standards are applied to all students regardless of ascribed characteristics such as sex, race, family background or class of origin. Schools operate on **meritocratic** principles: status is achieved on the basis of merit (or worth).

Like Durkheim, Parsons argues that the school represents society in miniature. Modern industrial society is increasingly based on achievement rather than ascription, on universalistic rather than particularistic standards, on meritocratic principles which apply to all its members. By reflecting the operation of society as a whole, the school prepares young people for their adult roles.

Education and value consensus

As part of this process, schools socialize young people into the basic values of society. Parsons, like many functionalists, maintains that value consensus is essential for society to operate effectively. In American society, schools instil two major values:

1 the value of achievement;
2 the value of equality of opportunity.

By encouraging students to strive for high levels of academic attainment and by rewarding those who do, schools foster the value of achievement itself. By placing individuals in the same situation in the classroom and so allowing them to compete on equal terms in examinations, schools foster the value of equality of opportunity.

These values have important functions in society as a whole. Advanced industrial society requires a highly motivated, achievement-oriented workforce. This necessitates **differential reward for differential achievement**, a principle which has been established in schools. Both the winners (the high achievers) and the losers (the low achievers) will see the system as just and fair since status is achieved in a situation where all have an equal chance. Again the principles which operate in the wider society are mirrored by those of the school.

Education and selection

Finally, Parsons sees the educational system as an important mechanism for the selection of individuals for their future role in society. In his words, it 'functions to allocate these human resources within the role-structure of adult society'. Thus schools, by testing and evaluating students, match their talents, skills and capacities to the jobs for which they are best suited. The school is therefore seen as the major mechanism for **role allocation**.

Criticisms of Parsons

Like Durkheim, Parsons fails to give adequate consideration to the possibility that the values transmitted by the educational system may be those of a ruling minority rather than of society as a whole. His view that schools operate on meritocratic principles is open to question, a point which we will examine in detail in later sections.

■ Kingsley Davis and Wilbert E. Moore – education and role allocation

Like Parsons, Davis and Moore see education as a means of role allocation, but they link the educational system more directly with the system of social stratification. As outlined in Chapter 2, Davis and Moore see **social stratification** as a mechanism for ensuring that the most talented and able members of society are allocated to those positions which are functionally most important for society. High rewards which act as incentives are attached to those positions; this means, in theory, that all will compete for them and the most talented will win through.

The education system is an important part of this process. In Davis's words, it is the 'proving ground for ability and hence the selective agency for placing people in different statuses according to their capacities'. Thus the educational system sifts, sorts and grades individuals in terms of their talents and abilities. It rewards the most talented with high qualifications, which in turn provide entry to those occupations which are functionally most important to society.

Criticisms of Davis and Moore

General criticisms of Davis and Moore's theory have been examined in Chapter 2. With respect to the relationship between education and social stratification, there are a number of more specific criticisms.

1 The relationship between academic credentials and occupational reward is not particularly close. In particular income is only weakly linked to educational attainment.

2 There is considerable doubt about the proposition that the educational system grades people in terms of ability. In particular, it has been argued that intelligence has little effect upon educational attainment.

3 There is considerable evidence which suggests that the influence of social stratification largely prevents the educational system from efficiently grading individuals in terms of ability.

We will consider these points in detail later.

■ Education – a liberal perspective

The liberal view of education is not a sociological perspective as such, rather it is a view adopted by many educationalists. Unlike functionalism it focuses on education in relation to the individual rather than to society. The main purpose of education from this viewpoint is held to be the promotion of the well-being of the individual, and only indirectly the improvement of society.

John Dewey – education and human potential

One of the most influential proponents of the liberal view of education was the American educationalist and philosopher John Dewey. Dewey argued that it was the job of education to encourage individuals to develop their full potential as human beings. He particularly stressed the development of intellectual potential. Schooling for all would help to foster the physical, emotional and spiritual talents of everyone, as well as their intellectual abilities.

Dewey was critical of the rote learning of facts in schools, and argued for progressive teaching methods. People should learn by experience: by doing things rather than being told. In this way they would not just gain knowledge but would also develop the skills, habits and attitudes necessary for them to solve a wide variety of problems. Furthermore, individuals would develop the ability and motivation to think critically about the world around them.

For Dewey, and similar educationalists, a progressive education system is a vital part of a successful democracy. Since in a democracy power rests with the people, it is necessary for the people to be able to think for themselves when exercising their power. Liberal education would be incompatible with a dictatorship, where free and critical thought could threaten the authority of the state. Dewey hoped that the education system he proposed would promote flexibility and tolerance, and individuals would be able to cooperate together as equals.

The liberal perspective and educational policies

Some liberals hope that education will help to reduce inequality. By developing the potential that exists within all human beings, the stratification system would become more open. Although liberals acknowledge that there is a need for reform, they believe that with relatively minor modifications education can come to play a full and successful role in industrial societies.

Liberal views have influenced a number of educational policies in both the USA and Britain. In the 1960s in the USA Lyndon B. Johnson stated 'The answer to all our national problems comes down to a single word: education.' (Quoted in Bowles and Gintis 1976, p. 19.) As a result, specially designed programmes of education for the underprivileged became the keynote of Johnson's war on poverty. However, as the chapter on poverty indicates, there is a wide gap between liberal ideals and what actually happens.

In the 1960s and 1970s Britain saw a movement towards progressive, child-centred education which was based largely upon liberal principles. Each child was held to be unique, and education was designed to foster equally the talents of each unique individual. In 1975 however, William Tyndale, a junior school in Islington, London, hit the headlines when teachers went on strike after the report of a government inspection of the school. Government enquiries and press reports criticized the school for its progressive education, arguing that lack of discipline had produced a situation in which children were failing to develop even basic skills in reading, writing and arithmetic.

This episode set the tone for the **new vocationalism** which developed in the 1980s and which can partly be seen as a reaction against liberal and progressive education. (For details of the new vocationalism see pp. 794–805.)

Liberal education has come under attack from Marxist sociologists as well as right-wing politicians. Marxists argue that the liberal view of education tends to ignore the inequalities in society which make liberal ideals impossible to achieve without major social changes.

■ Ivan Illich – *Deschooling Society*

Illich differs from the conventional liberal approach in that he advocates far more radical changes to the education system. In *Deschooling Society* he takes liberal views to their logical conclusion by arguing that formal schooling is unnecessary, and indeed harmful to society.

Though not a sociologist by training or profession – he studied theology and philosophy and spent several years as a Roman Catholic priest in New York – Illich's *Deschooling Society*, published in 1971, is an important contribution to the sociology of education.

The educational ideal

Illich begins with his views on what education should be. First there is the learning of specific skills such as typing, woodwork and speaking a foreign language. Next there is education as such which is not concerned with the acquisition of particular skills. Education should be a liberating experience in which individuals explore, create, use their initiative and judgement and freely develop their faculties and talents to the full.

Illich claims that schools are not particularly effective in teaching skills and in practice, diametrically opposed to the educational ideals in which he believes. He argues that the teaching of skills is best left to those who use those skills in daily life. He gives the example of Spanish-speaking teenagers in New York, many of whom were high school dropouts, who were employed to teach Spanish to school teachers, social workers and ministers. Within a week they had been trained to use a teaching manual designed for use by linguists with university qualifications, and within six months they had effectively accomplished their task. However, the employment of such 'skill teachers' is largely prevented by a system which demands professionals, that is, officially trained, specialized and certificated teachers.

The educational reality

Illich's main attack is on the failure of schools to match his educational ideals. He regards schools as repressive institutions which indoctrinate pupils, smother creativity and imagination, induce conformity and stultify students into accepting the interests of the powerful. He sees this **hidden curriculum** operating in the following way.

1 Pupils have little or no control over what they learn or how they learn it. They are simply instructed by an authoritarian teaching regime and, to be successful,

must conform to its rules. Real learning, however, is not the result of instruction, but of direct and free involvement by the individual in every part of the learning process. In sum, 'most learning requires no teacher'.

2 The power of the school to enforce conformity to its rules and to coerce its inmates into acceptance of instruction stems from its authority to grant credentials which are believed to bring rewards in the labour market. Those who conform to the rules are selected to go on to higher levels in the educational system. Illich states 'Schools select for each successive level those who have, at earlier stages of the game, proved themselves good risks for the established order.' Conformity and obedience therefore bring their own rewards.

3 Finally, students emerge from the educational system with a variety of qualifications which they and others believe have provided them with the training, skills and competence for particular occupations. Illich rejects this belief. He argues that, 'The pupil is "schooled" to confuse teaching with learning, grade advancement with education, a diploma with competence.'

Education and social problems

Illich sees the educational system as the root of the problems of modern industrial society. Schools are the first, most vital and important stage in the creation of the mindless, conforming and easily manipulated citizen. In schools individuals learn to defer to authority, to accept alienation, to consume and value the services of the institution and to forget how to think for themselves. They are taught to see education as a valuable commodity to be consumed in ever increasing quantities.

These lessons prepare pupils for their role as the mindless consumers to whom the passive consumption of the goods and services of industrial society becomes an end in itself. Responding to advertisements and the directives of the powerful, they invest time, money and energy in obtaining the products of industry. Deferring to the authority of professionals, individuals consume the services of doctors, social workers, lawyers. Trained to accept that those in authority know what's best for them, individuals become dependent on the directives of governments, bureaucratic organizations and professional bodies.

Illich maintains that modern industrial society cannot provide the framework for human happiness and fulfilment. Despite the fact that goods are pouring from the factories in ever increasing quantities, despite the fact that armies of professionals provide ever more comprehensive programmes to solve social ills, misery, dissatisfaction and social problems are multiplying. The establishment offers a solution which is at once simple and self-defeating: the consumption of even more goods and services. Illich concludes:

> As long as we are not aware of the ritual through which the school shapes the progressive consumer – the economy's major resource – we cannot break the spell of this economy and shape a new one.

Deschooling

Illich proposes a simple yet radical solution. As the title of his book *Deschooling Society* suggests, the answer lies in the abolition of the present system of education. Since schools provide the foundation for all that is to follow, **deschooling** lies 'at the root of any movement for human liberation'.

In place of schools Illich offers two main alternatives.

1 First, **skill exchanges** in which instructors teach the skills they use in daily life to others. Illich argues that

skills can best be learned by **drills** involving systematic instruction.

2 Second, and most important, Illich proposes **learning webs** which consist of individuals with similar interests who 'meet around a problem chosen and defined by their own initiative' and who proceed on a basis of 'creative and exploratory learning'.

Illich concludes that deschooling will destroy 'the reproductive organ of a consumer society' and lead to the creation of a society in which people can be truly liberated and fulfilled.

Although in sympathy with much of what Illich says, Marxists such as Bowles and Gintis argue that Illich has made a fundamental error. Rather than seeing schools as the basis of the problem and their removal as the solution, Bowles and Gintis argue that 'The social problems to which these reforms are addressed have their roots not primarily in the school system itself, but rather in the normal functioning of the economic system.' From their viewpoint, deschooling would only produce 'occupational misfits' and 'job blues' which are hardly sufficient to transform society as a whole. From a Marxist perspective liberation involves a revolutionary change in the economic infrastructure of society.

■ Social democratic perspectives on education

The social democratic view on education is not simply a sociological theory. According to the Centre for Contemporary Cultural Studies at Birmingham University, this perspective has been developed by a number of individual groups. In the Centre's opinion, social democratic thinking has been reflected in the work of sociologists such as A.H. Halsey, economists such as John Vaizey, Labour Party politicians, and the teaching profession. For most of the post-war period British educational policies have been dominated by this approach.

Equality of opportunity

Social democrats accept the basic institutions of parliamentary democracies such as Britain, but

argue that state intervention is necessary to reduce inequalities produced by the free market economy. They disagree with functionalists that education provides genuine equality of opportunity.

Halsey believes that education fails to offer the same opportunities to lower social classes as it does to higher classes. Halsey's work, which we will examine in detail later in the chapter (see p. 760), indicates that the children of parents with the least material resources tend to be found disproportionately among the 'failures' of the education system.

A.H. Halsey and Jean Floud were highly critical of the tripartite system of education introduced in 1944. Under this system children attended three types of school; grammar schools (for the academically able), technical schools (for those seen as having specifically technical abilities) and secondary moderns (for the less academically able). Selection procedures were partly based on an intelligence test, the eleven-plus. The majority of children went to secondary modern schools and Halsey and Floud claimed that in these schools children failed to develop their potential and this meant that Britain increasingly lacked the highly educated and trained workforce that a modern industrial society requires.

From this point of view, the education system was not just failing to provide equality of opportunity, it was failing to develop the potential of individuals. Social democratic perspectives suggest that the liberal ideal of individual development is compatible with the aim of social justice, but in the post-war period neither was being achieved.

Some social democratic theorists argued that education could actually create greater equality, as well as promoting equality of opportunity, if the system were run properly. In his book *The Future of Socialism* the Labour Party politician Anthony Crosland argued that a fairer education system would also, 'equalise the distribution of rewards and privileges so as to diminish the degree of class stratification'. If educational success or failure no longer depended upon class background, then the amount of social mobility would increase to the extent that class distinctions would become progressively blurred.

Economic growth

Social democratic perspectives also seemed to offer another advantage to parliamentary democracies. By making societies more meritocratic, and ensuring that everyone could develop their potential, each individual would be able to make the maximum possible contribution to society. In doing so they would encourage economic growth which would bring prosperity to all.

This point of view was most clearly stated by the American economist Theodore W. Shultz. He argued that skills and knowledge were forms of capital. Capital investment in humans could have the same effects as capital investments in machinery. If more were spent on education, the productivity and efficiency of the workforce would increase, and the extra money spent would soon be repaid by the extra contribution made to the economy. Shultz claimed that his theory could be illustrated by American agriculture, where farms

with a less educated workforce were not as productive as those with a more educated workforce.

Many of the policies of British governments since the Second World War appear to have followed the path outlined by social democratic theory. As we indicated in the introduction to this chapter, in the decades leading up to the 1980s expenditure on education rose substantially. The raising of the school-leaving age and the expansion of higher education were designed both to expand opportunities and ensure a more skilled workforce. The tripartite system of 1944 was originally intended to provide more opportunities for all social classes. However, social democratic critics argued that this system was wasting talent in secondary modern schools, and this was one of the reasons why Labour governments progressively introduced comprehensive schools. Other measures, such as compensatory education and Educational Priority Areas, were intended to assist working-class pupils who might be disadvantaged by their home background. (For further details see pp. 755–6.)

Functionalist theories of education suggested that education was already fulfilling the functions required of it. Social democratic theories acknowledged the limitations of education, but held up the vision of a much improved society that could result if the deficiencies of education were recognized and put right. It was claimed that education could help individuals achieve their potential, provide equality of opportunity, and produce a more egalitarian and prosperous society.

However, in the 1970s and 1980s, the hostility of some pupils to school, the continuing differences in educational achievement between classes, and economic recession, all raised serious doubts about the validity of the social democratic perspective. Numerous criticisms were advanced.

■ Criticisms and evaluation of social democratic theory
Equality of opportunity

First, even social democratic theorists themselves began to realize the limited inroads that had been made into reducing inequality of opportunity. In their book *Origins and Destinations* A.H. Halsey, A.F. Heath and J.M. Ridge find little evidence of increasing equality of opportunity (at least amongst males, to whom their study was confined) despite the changes that had been made to the education system (see pp. 785–7). As Marxist theories became more prominent in the sociology of education, it was argued that education could not possibly compensate for the inequalities in society as a whole.

Economic growth

A second type of criticism raised questions about the effectiveness of education in promoting economic growth.

In 1976 in a speech at Ruskin College the Labour prime minister James Callaghan initiated what became known as the 'Great Debate' on education. He claimed that education was failing to meet the needs of industry.

With the election in 1979 of Margaret Thatcher's Conservative Government, the political criticisms became stronger. New Right thinkers who influenced Conservative policies argued that the emphasis on equality of opportunity and on liberal ideals of developing individuals' potential were reducing educational standards. Comprehensives were believed to be holding back the most talented and contributing to the reduction in standards.

Furthermore, the New Right believed that the curriculum was not directed towards the skills required by employers. Far from promoting industrial growth, excessive expenditure on education was thought to be putting industry at a disadvantage. Profits from industry were not being reinvested in industry, but instead were wasted on an inefficient education system.

These views were reflected in a number of changes in education which we will examine later in the chapter (see pp. 794–805).

Workforce skills

A further area of criticism raises questions about the educational requirements of the workforce in advanced industrial societies. As Chapter 4 will show, sociologists over recent years have debated whether work has been reskilled or deskilled in advanced industrial societies (see pp. 208–9). If it has become **deskilled** (if the workforce requires less training) it is difficult to attribute the growth of education to the needs of the economy. Furthermore, there is doubt about the extent to which

formal education is necessary for training the workforce.

From an examination of studies analysing the relationship between education and the economy, Randall Collins concludes that only a minor part of the expansion of education in advanced industrial societies can be seen as directly serving the demands of industry for skills, training and knowledge. Writing in 1971 about American society, Collins claims that only 15 per cent of the increase in education of the US labour force during the twentieth century may be attributed to shifts in the occupational structure – a decrease in the proportion of jobs with low-skill requirements and an increase in the proportion of jobs with high-skill requirements.

However, it could be argued that the *same* jobs have greater skill and knowledge requirements as industrial society develops. For example, plumbers, clerks, doctors and managers today may require greater expertise and technical skills than they did at the turn of the century. Again Collins doubts that the rapid expansion of education is primarily a response to these requirements. He argues 'It appears that the educational level of the US labour force has changed in excess of that which is necessary to keep up with the skills requirements of jobs.' Collins concludes that the contribution of education to the economic system in advanced industrial societies has been exaggerated.

Collins reaches the following conclusions about the relationship between education and the economy.

1 Studies from various countries suggest that once mass literacy has been achieved, education does not significantly affect economic development.

2 Most occupational skills are learned 'on the job', and where specific training is required, firms provide their own apprenticeship and training schemes.

3 Higher education for particular professions such as medicine, engineering and law may be considered 'vocationally relevant and possibly essential'. However, much higher education, such as schools of business administration, represents an attempt to achieve 'professionalization'. As such, education serves to raise the status of the occupation, rather than to transmit the knowledge and skills necessary for its performance.

Collins's conclusions are controversial and some sociologists believe that education is becoming increasingly important in advanced industrial economies. Writing in 1988 M. White claimed that learning specific vocational skills was becoming less important for economic growth but high levels of general education were becoming more important. In a rapidly changing economy 'versatile and adaptable people capable of continuing to learn' were essential. Only with a good education would individuals be 'sufficiently flexible to respond to the opportunities, and cope with the hazards' of the future.

Whether Collins or White is right about the importance of education for economic growth, the existence of these debates does suggest that social democratic theorists cannot simply take it for granted that spending more money on education automatically benefits the economy.

Marxist criticisms

Birmingham University's Centre for Contemporary Cultural Studies has developed a comprehensive critique of social democratic policies from a Marxist point of view. According to its analysis, social democracy has contradictory aims: it is not possible to pursue equality of opportunity and equality at the same time. This is because equality of opportunity inevitably means that some will be more successful than others.

In the Centre's view even the Labour Party has done no more than pay lip-service to the idea of equality. Changes such as the introduction of comprehensives gave the impression of giving greater opportunities to the working class without really doing so. Labour governments were attempting to promote social cohesion rather than trying to transform society.

The writers from the Centre for Contemporary Cultural Studies claim that many of the changes in education in recent decades have been designed to benefit the capitalist economy at the expense of the working class. They would have much preferred the working class to have greater control over its own education. They argue that in the nineteenth and early twentieth centuries there was a close relationship between working-class education and radical political movements. Chartists and early feminists such as the suffragettes used education to promote the awareness of the working class and women of injustice in society. They encouraged political agitation and attempts to improve society. State education, on the other hand, has done as little to promote class or gender consciousness as it has done to promote equality.

Given the number and strength of criticisms levelled at social democratic perspectives, it was not surprising that new perspectives on education were developed. In terms of British politics the main challenge to social democracy came from the Conservative Party. In terms of sociology, conflict theorists (and particularly Marxists) argued that education played a very different role in society to that suggested by functionalists, liberals and social democrats.

■ Education – conflict perspectives

All the perspectives on education which we have examined so far have assumed that education either does – or could – function for the benefit of society as a whole. Liberal and social democratic views accept that there are limitations to the existing education system, but they specify the ways in which it could be altered and improved.

Conflict perspectives on education, in contrast, are based upon the view that groups within existing societies have fundamentally different interests. Thus, however education is organized in contemporary societies, some people will benefit from it more than others. This does not mean that conflict sociologists deny that education could be improved, but it does mean that many of them believe that significant improvements can only be achieved if they are accompanied by wider social changes.

■ Samuel Bowles and Herbert Gintis – schooling in capitalist America

The American economists and sociologists Bowles and Gintis argue that the major role of education in capitalist societies is the reproduction of labour power. In particular they maintain 'close "correspondence" between the social relationships which govern personal interaction in the work place and the social relationships of the education system'. According to Bowles and Gintis this **correspondence principle** provides the key to understanding the workings of the education system. Work casts a 'long shadow' over the education system: education is subservient to the needs of those who control the workforce, the owners of the means of production.

The hidden curriculum

The first major way in which education functions is to provide capitalists with a workforce which has the personality, attitudes and values which are most useful to them. Like Marx, Bowles and Gintis regard work in capitalist societies as both exploitive and alienating, yet if capitalism is to succeed it requires a hard-working, docile, obedient, and highly motivated workforce, which is too divided and fragmented to challenge the authority of management.

The education system helps to achieve these objectives largely through the **hidden curriculum**. It is not the content of lessons and the examinations which pupils take which are important, but the form that teaching and learning take and the way that schools are organized. The hidden curriculum consists of those things that pupils learn through the experience of attending school, rather than the stated educational objectives of such institutions. According to Bowles and Gintis the hidden curriculum shapes the future workforce in the following ways.

1 First, it helps to produce a **subservient workforce** of uncritical, passive and docile workers. In a study based upon 237 members of the senior year in a New York high school, Bowles and Gintis found that the grades awarded related more to personality traits than academic abilities. They found that low grades were related to creativity, aggressiveness and independence, while higher grades were related to perseverance, consistency, dependability and punctuality.

Far from living up to the liberal ideal of encouraging self-development, the American education system was creating an unimaginative and unquestioning workforce which could be easily manipulated by employers.

2 Second, Bowles and Gintis claim that the hidden curriculum encourages an **acceptance of hierarchy**. Schools are organized on a hierarchical principle of authority and control. Teachers give orders, pupils obey. Students have little control over the subjects they study or how they study them. This prepares them for relationships within the workplace where if workers are to stay out of trouble, they will need to defer to the authority of supervisors and managers.

3 Third, at school pupils learn to be **motivated by external rewards**, just as the workforce in a capitalist society is motivated by external rewards. Because students have so little control over, and a feeling of involvement in, their school work, they get little satisfaction from studying. Learning is based upon the **'jug and mug' principle**. The teachers possess knowledge which they pour into the 'empty mugs', the pupils. It is not therefore surprising that many pupils do not enjoy the process of schooling. Instead they are encouraged to take satisfaction from the external reward of a qualification at the end of their studies. The qualification offers the promise of employment, or better paid employment than would otherwise be the case.

The subsequent creation of a workforce motivated by external rewards is necessary, according to Bowles and Gintis, because work in capitalist societies is intrinsically unsatisfying. It is not organized according to the human need for fulfilling work, but according to the capitalist's desire to make the maximum possible profit. As a result the workers must be motivated by the external reward of the wage packet, just as the pupil is motivated by the external reward of the qualification.

4 Fourth, Bowles and Gintis claim that another important aspect of the hidden curriculum is the **fragmentation** of school subjects. The student during the course of the school day moves from one subject to another: from mathematics to history, to French to English. Little connection is made between the lessons: knowledge is fragmented and compartmentalized into academic subjects.

This aspect of education corresponds to the fragmentation of the workforce. Bowles and Gintis believe that most jobs in factories and offices have been broken down into very specific tasks carried out by separate individuals. In this way workers are denied knowledge of the overall productive process which makes it impossible for them to set up in competition with their employers. Furthermore, a fragmented and divided workforce is easier to control and this control can be maintained because of the principle of 'divide and conquer'. It becomes difficult for the workforce to unite in opposition to those in authority over them.

The benefits of the education system for capitalism

Bowles and Gintis believe then, that the hidden curriculum produces a passive and obedient workforce, which accepts authority without question, which is motivated by external rewards and is fragmented. They also argue that the formal parts of the curriculum correspond to the needs of capitalist employers.

Bowles and Gintis claim that capitalism requires a surplus of skilled labour. This maintains a high rate of unemployment and ensures that workers of all levels of skill have to compete with each other for jobs. Employers can pay low wages through being able to threaten dismissal and replacement by the reserve army of skilled workers. Since the mental requirements of most jobs are quite low, and most skills can be learned on the job, education tends to over-educate the workforce.

Apart from the direct benefits provided by the education system just outlined, Bowles and Gintis argue that education also has indirect benefits for capitalism through the **legitimation of inequality**. By making society appear fair and just, class consciousness does not develop and the stability of society is not threatened.

The illusion of equality of opportunity

From the functionalist perspective of Parsons, and Davis and Moore industrial societies are open and meritocratic: they provide genuine equality of opportunity. Social democratic theorists do not accept that this situation exists, but they do believe that changes to education could bring meritocracy closer to being a reality.

Bowles and Gintis reject the view that capitalist societies are meritocratic and deny that they can become so within a capitalist framework. They believe that class background is the most important factor influencing levels of attainment.

The idea that we all compete on equal terms is an illusion. Although education is free, and open to all, and despite the fact that individuals can apply for jobs at will, Bowles and Gintis claim that some have much greater opportunities than others. The children of the wealthy and powerful tend to obtain high qualifications and highly rewarded jobs, irrespective of their abilities. It is this the education system disguises with its **myth of meritocracy**. Those who are denied success blame themselves, and not the system which has condemned them to failure.

Intelligence, educational attainment and occupational reward

Bowles and Gintis base their argument on an analysis of the relationships between intelligence (measured in terms of an individual's **intelligence quotient** or **IQ**), educational attainment and occupational reward. They argue that IQ accounts for only a small part of educational attainment.

At first sight this claim appears incorrect. A large body of statistical evidence indicates a fairly close relationship between IQ and educational attainment. But is IQ the causal factor? Does a high IQ directly cause educational success? If it did, then people with the same IQ should have roughly the same level of educational attainment. Bowles and Gintis examine a sample of individuals with average IQs. Within this sample they find a wide range of variation in educational attainment which leads them to conclude that there is hardly any relationship between IQ and academic qualifications.

What then accounts for differences in attainment between people with similar IQs? Bowles and Gintis find a direct relationship between educational attainment and family background. The causal factor is not IQ, but the class position of the individual's parents. In general, the higher a person's class of origin, the longer he or she remains in the educational system and the higher his or her qualifications.

But why do students with high qualifications tend to have higher than average intelligence? Bowles and Gintis argue that this relationship is largely 'a spin-off, a by-product' of continued education. The longer an individual stays in the educational system, the more his/her IQ develops. Thus IQ is a *consequence* of length of stay, not the cause of it.

The above evidence leads Bowles and Gintis to

conclude that, at least in terms of IQ, the educational system does not function as a meritocracy.

They apply a similar argument to the statistical relationship between IQ and occupational reward. In general, individuals in highly paid occupations have above average IQs. However, Bowles and Gintis reject the view that IQ is directly related to occupational success. Within their sample of people with average IQs they find a wide range of income variation. If IQ were directly related to occupational reward, the incomes of those with the same IQ should be similar.

Again Bowles and Gintis find that family background is the major factor accounting for differences in income. They conclude that IQ itself has little direct effect on income variation. Thus, at least in terms of IQ, they reject the view that the placement of individuals in the occupational structure is based on meritocratic principles.

Finally, Bowles and Gintis examine the relationship between educational credentials and occupational reward. Again there is a large body of statistical evidence which indicates a close connection between the levels of qualification and occupational reward. Bowles and Gintis reject the view that this connection is a causal one. They argue, for example, that high qualifications, in and of themselves, do not lead directly to highly paid jobs. They find that the main factors accounting for occupational reward are the individual's class of origin, race and sex. There is considerable evidence to show that educational qualifications are far more valuable on the job market to the white male than the white female, to the white male than the black male, to the middle-class male than the working-class male.

The apparent connection between occupational reward and educational qualifications is simply due to the fact that in general white middle-class males obtain higher educational qualifications than other social groups and also obtain higher occupational rewards. Their IQ has little effect upon either their educational attainment or their occupational reward; their academic qualifications have little effect upon their future income. Thus Bowles and Gintis conclude:

the intellectual abilities developed or certified in school make little causal contribution to getting ahead economically. Only a minor portion of the substantial statistical association between schooling and economic success can be accounted for by the school's role in producing or screening cognitive skills.

The myths of education

If Bowles and Gintis's analysis is correct, then the educational system can be seen as a gigantic myth-making machine which serves to legitimate inequality. It creates and propagates the following myths:

1 educational attainment is based on merit;
2 occupational reward is based on merit;
3 education is the route to success in the world of work.

The illusion of meritocracy established in schools leads to the belief that the system of role allocation is fair, just and above-board. In particular, the 'emphasis on IQ as the basis for economic success serves to legitimate an authoritarian, hierarchical, stratified and unequal economic system'.

Education creates the myth that those at the top deserve their power and privilege, that they have achieved their status on merit and that those at the bottom have only themselves to blame. In this way the educational system reduces the discontent that a hierarchy of wealth, power and prestige tends to produce.

Thus Bowles and Gintis conclude that 'Education reproduces inequality by justifying privilege and attributing poverty to personal failure.' It efficiently disguises the fact that economic success runs in the family, that privilege breeds privilege. Bowles and Gintis therefore reject the functionalist view of the relationship between education and stratification put forward by Talcott Parsons and Davis and Moore.

Class conflict and education

Bowles and Gintis devote less attention to explaining how education and work correspond than they do to describing the similarities between them. Nevertheless, Bowles and Gintis do make some attempt to explain how such a close fit has come about. They admit that there has been conflict over the American educational system, and that in the past it has not always fitted neatly with the economy. They also admit that members of the working class have at certain times tried to shape the education system themselves.

However, Bowles and Gintis deny that the

conflict has produced any notable working-class victories. They claim that representatives of the ruling class have intervened at crucial times to ensure that their interests continue to be served. Any compromises that have taken place have come down heavily in favour of the ruling class, not the working class.

Bowles and Gintis also claim that working-class demands for changes in education have been of limited scope. They suggest that the working class is likely to be fairly content with the type of education system Bowles and Gintis have described because it does foster the attitudes and abilities that are appropriate for work in a capitalist society and as such it meets day-to-day needs. Furthermore, the role of the education system in legitimating inequality prevents members of the working class from seeing beyond their own life experiences. Exploited groups are not encouraged to see how the education system and the society it is part of could be transformed to serve working-class interests.

Education in communist societies

Bowles and Gintis provide a comprehensive Marxist view of education in a capitalist society, but their discussion of education in the former communist societies is more sketchy. However, they do express some criticisms of how education worked in the USSR and Eastern Europe under communist regimes.

They argue that there were similarities between the communist education systems and that of the USA. In particular, education in communist countries was also hierarchical and it encouraged some of the same personality traits as the American system. This was due to the failure of these societies to attain true communism. Bowles and Gintis state that 'These countries have abolished the private ownership of the means of production while replicating the relationships of economic control, dominance and subordination characteristic of capitalism.' The communist countries reduced inequalities, but a minority of state officials still controlled the means of production. Bowles and Gintis believe therefore, that only when there was genuine economic democracy, in which workers took control of the means of production, would a truly socialist education system develop.

■ Criticisms and evaluation of Bowles and Gintis

The work of Bowles and Gintis has been highly controversial. It has been criticized by Marxists and non-Marxists alike. The critics tend to agree that Bowles and Gintis have exaggerated the correspondence between work and education, and have failed to provide adequate evidence to support their case.

1 M.S.H. Hickox questions the view that there is a close correspondence between education and economic developments. He points out that in Britain compulsory education was introduced long after the onset of industrialization. Despite the fact that for a long time capitalists did not employ a workforce which had had its attitudes and values shaped by education, the development of capitalism did not appear to be affected.

2 Bowles and Gintis have been criticized for their claims about the way that schools shape personality. David Hogan questions the adequacy of their evidence saying 'the evidence is at the most only suggestive and requires considerable further research'. Bowles and Gintis did not carry out detailed research into life within schools. They tended to assume that the hidden curriculum was actually influencing pupils. There are, however, numerous studies which show that many pupils have scant regard for the rules of the school, and little respect for the authority of the teacher. Paul Willis (see pp. 741–4) showed that working-class 'lads' learned to behave at school in ways quite at odds with capitalism's supposed need for a docile workforce.

3 Bowles and Gintis have been criticized for ignoring the influence of the formal curriculum. David Reynolds claims that much of the curriculum in British schools does not promote the development of an ideal employee under capitalism. It does not seem designed to teach either the skills needed by employers, nor uncritical passive behaviour which makes workers easy to exploit. He says:

The survival in schools of a liberal, humanities-based curriculum, the emphasis upon the acquisition of knowledge for the purposes of intellectual self-betterment rather than . . . material gain, the limited swing to science within higher education, the continuing high status of 'pure disciplines' as against work-related applied knowledge, the decline in commercially important foreign languages at sixth form level . . . all suggests a lack of correspondence.

It might be added that the popularity of sociology as an 'A' level subject in Britain could hardly be seen as promoting unthinking workers! Even if the hidden curriculum could be shown to encourage docility, the presence of Bowles and Gintis themselves within the formal curriculum would undermine their claims about education.

4 A fourth area of criticism concerns the extent to which education legitimates inequality by creating the appearance that success and failure are based upon merit. M.S.H. Hickox refers to a study by Richard Scase in which only 2.5 per cent of a sample of English workers expressed the view that educational qualifications were an important factor in determining social class. Most of those interviewed placed a far greater emphasis on family background and economic factors. This would not suggest that education has succeeded in legitimating inequality in Britain.

5 Bowles and Gintis have been attacked for failing to adequately explain how the economy shapes the education system. David Reynolds suggests that it is simply not possible for British capitalists, or the 'capitalist state' to exercise detailed control over British schools. Local authorities have a considerable amount of freedom in the way they organize schools, and, once they 'shut the classroom door', teachers are not subject to close supervision. Reynolds claims that 'a large number of radicals have been attracted into teaching', and because of their independence they have not moulded education to suit the needs of capitalism.

Since Bowles and Gintis developed their theory of education in the 1970s, and early critics responded to it, the British education system has developed in such a way that their analysis may have become more relevant. For example, local authorities have lost some of their power over education because they no longer run colleges and some schools have opted out of local authority control. The freedom of teachers has been restricted by the introduction of a national curriculum and education has become more explicitly designed to meet the needs of employers. These changes will be discussed later in the chapter (see pp. 794–805).

Whatever the merits of Bowles and Gintis's work many sociologists sympathetic to Marxism have, however, felt the need to modify their approach. Some have denied that parts of the superstructure such as education, are exclusively shaped by the infrastructure; others have stressed that pupils and students are not simply the passive recipients of education.

■ Marxism, struggle, and the relative autonomy of education

In response to the criticisms of Bowles and Gintis, Marxists such as Henry Giroux have advocated a modified approach to the analysis of education within a broadly Marxist framework. Giroux makes the following general points.

1 He argues that working-class pupils are actively involved in shaping their own education. They do not accept everything they are taught, nor is their behaviour entirely determined by capitalism. Pupils draw upon their own cultures in finding ways to respond to schooling, and often these responses involve resistance to the school.

2 Giroux claims that schools can be seen as 'sites' of ideological struggle in which there can be clashes between cultures. Different classes, ethnic and religious groups all try to influence both the content and process of schooling. From this point of view the nature of education is not simply determined by the needs of capitalism, but is influenced by a continuing struggle between the groups involved.

3 The education system possesses **relative autonomy** from the economic infrastructure. Unlike Bowles and Gintis, Giroux argues that education has partial independence from the needs or requirements of capitalist industry. For example, he points out that in the USA in the early 1980s the education system produced more graduates than were required. Many became unemployed or had to take low-paid jobs which required little training. In this way the myth that education provided equal opportunity and the chance for upward mobility was undermined. Giroux stresses however, that the independence of education is only partial: in the final analysis, education cannot go against the fundamental interests of capitalism.

Criticisms of relative autonomy

Although in some respects Giroux's work is more subtle than that of Bowles and Gintis, Andy Hargreaves believes that it fails to solve the problems associated with Marxist theories of education. To Andy Hargreaves there is a massive contradiction built into the theory of resistance and relative autonomy: it claims that education is free to develop in its own way and is influenced by numerous social groups, yet it is still determined by the economy.

Hargreaves criticizes Giroux for failing to spell out in what circumstances education can develop independently, and how and when economic factors become paramount. He describes Giroux's theory as one in which 'anything goes'. Pupils might be indoctrinated with bourgeois ideology at school, or fight against the authority of the teachers. Both fit the theory of relative autonomy. It therefore becomes impossible to prove the theory wrong: any facts can be made to fit it. As Hargreaves says of such theories 'they appear to want to have it both ways, to assert both the dependence and independence of schooling; to have their cake and eat it'.

■ Paul Willis – *Learning to Labour*

In an important and much discussed study Paul Willis developed a distinctive, neo-Marxist approach to education. Like Giroux, Willis recognizes the existence of conflict within the education system, and he rejects the view that there is any simple, direct relationship between the economy and the way the education system operates. Like Bowles and Gintis, Willis focuses on the way that education prepares the workforce, but he denies that education is a particularly successful agency of socialization. Indeed, Willis argues that education can have unintended consequences on pupils, consequences which may not be completely beneficial to capitalism.

Despite some similarities with the work of Giroux, Willis's study is more sophisticated and it contains an extra dimension. As well as drawing upon Marxist sociology, Willis also adopted some of the research techniques associated with symbolic interactionism. Willis used a wide variety of research methods in his study of a Midlands school in England in the 1970s. He used 'observation and participant observation in class, around the school and during leisure activities, regular recorded group discussions, informal interviews and diaries'.

In the course of his research Willis did not just rely upon abstract analysis of the relationship between education and the economy, but tried to understand the experience of schooling from the perspective of the pupils. He soon found that schools were not as successful as Bowles and Gintis supposed in producing docile and conformist future workers.

The counter-school culture

The school Willis studied was situated in a working-class housing estate in a predominantly industrial small town. The main focus of his study was a group of twelve working-class boys whom he followed over their last eighteen months at school, and their first few months at work. The twelve pupils formed a friendship grouping with a distinctive attitude to school. The 'lads', as Willis refers to them, had their own **counter-school culture**, which was opposed to the values espoused by the school.

This counter-school culture had the following features. The lads felt superior both to teachers, and to conformist pupils who they referred to as 'ear 'oles'. The lads attached little or no value to the academic work of the school, and had no interest in gaining qualifications. During their time at school, their main objectives were to avoid going to lessons, or, when attendance was unavoidable, doing as little work as possible. They would boast about the weeks and months they could go without putting pen to paper. They resented the school trying to take control over their time – they constantly tried to win 'symbolic and physical space from the institution and its rules'.

While avoiding working, the lads kept themselves entertained with 'irreverent marauding misbehaviour'. 'Having a laff' was a particularly high priority. Willis described some of the behaviour that resulted:

During films in the hall they tie the projector leads into impossible knots, make animal figures or obscene shapes on the screen with their fingers, and gratuitously dig and jab the backs of the 'ear 'oles' in front of them.

In class:

---

there is a continuous scraping of chairs, a bad tempered 'tut-tutting' at the simplest request, and a continuous fidgeting which explores every permutation of sitting or lying on a chair.

Throughout the school the lads had an 'aimless air of insubordination ready with spurious justification and impossible to nail down'.

To the lads the school equalled boredom, while the outside world, particularly the adult world, offered more possibilities for excitement. Smoking cigarettes, consuming alcohol and avoiding wearing school uniform were all ways in which they tried to identify with the adult world. In the diaries kept by them, school warranted no more than a footnote in the description of the day. Going out at night was seen as far more important. Many of them also had part-time jobs which were more than just ways of earning cash: they were a means of gaining a sense of involvement in the male, adult world.

The lads' counter-culture was strongly sexist, emphasizing and valuing masculinity, and downgrading femininity. It is significant that the lads regarded the ear 'oles as cissies, lacking true masculine attributes. In addition the counter-culture was racist, seeing members of ethnic minorities as inferior.

According to Willis, the lads were anxious to leave school at the earliest possible moment, and they looked forward eagerly to their first full-time jobs. While the ear 'oles took notice of career lessons and were concerned about the types of job they would eventually get, the lads were content to go on to any work, so long as it was a male manual job. To them, all such jobs were pretty much the same and it made little difference whether they became tyre fitters, bricklayers' mates or factory workers. All these jobs were considered 'real work', in contrast to the 'pen pushers' jobs which the ear 'oles were destined for. Manual labour was seen by the lads as more worthy than mental labour. The sacrifices of working hard at school were simply not worth the effort. They saw little merit in years of extra study in which their freedom and independence were lost, and during which they would have little cash in their pockets.

Having described the counter-school culture, Willis observes that the education system seems to be failing to manipulate the personalities of pupils to produce ideal workers. They neither defer to authority nor are they obedient and docile. Education does not produce pupils who believe in individual achievement: instead they reject the beliefs that hard work and striving for individual success can bring worthwhile rewards. They have very little in common with the types of student that the work of Bowles and Gintis suggest the American education system produces.

Yet Willis believes, paradoxically, that the lads were well prepared for the work that they would do. It was their very rejection of the school which made them suitable for male, unskilled, or semi-skilled manual work.

Shop-floor culture and counter-school culture

When Willis followed the lads into their first jobs, he found important similarities between shop-floor culture and the counter-school culture. There was the same racism and sexism, the same lack of respect for authority, and the same emphasis on the worth of manual labour. Having a 'laff' was equally important in both cultures and on the shop-floor, as in the school, the maximum possible freedom was sought. The lads and their new workmates tried to control the pace at which they worked, and to win some time and space in which they were free from the tedium of work.

According to Willis both the counter-school culture and the shop-floor culture are ways of coping with tedium and oppression. Life is made more tolerable by having a 'laff' and winning a little space from the supervisor, the manager or the teacher. In both settings though, the challenges to authority never go too far. The lads and workers hope to gain a little freedom, but they don't challenge the institution head-on. They know that they must do a certain amount of work in the factory or risk dismissal, and they realize that the state can enforce school attendance if it is determined to do so.

Having described and compared the counter-school culture and the shop-floor culture, Willis analyses the significance of his findings for an understanding of the role of education in society.

Willis does not see the education system as simply being a successful agency of socialization that produces false class consciousness. He does believe that education reproduces the sort of labour force required by capitalism, but not directly or intentionally. He says that state schools, and the oppositional culture within them, are:

---

especially significant in showing a circle of unintended consequences which act finally to reproduce not only a regional culture but the class structure and also the structure of society itself.

The lads are not persuaded to act as they do by the school, nor are they forced to seek manual labour; rather they actively create their own subculture, and voluntarily choose to look for manual jobs. They learn about the culture of the shop-floor from fathers, elder brothers and others in the local community. They are attracted to this masculine, adult world and respond to schooling in their own way because of its lack of relevance to their chosen future work.

Capitalism and the counter-school culture

In the final part of his book Willis discusses the significance of the counter-school culture for capitalist society. Once again he does not simply argue that the lads' culture is entirely beneficial to capitalism, nor does he think it is entirely harmful. Willis claims that in some ways the lads see through the capitalist system, but in other ways they contribute to their own exploitation and subordination.

Willis identifies a number of insights into the workings of capitalism that the lads have which he calls **penetrations**. The lads see through at least part of the ideological smokescreen which tends to obscure the true nature of capitalism.

1 He says that they recognize that capitalist society is not meritocratic. They understand that they are unlikely to be upwardly socially mobile to any great extent.

2 The lads show an appreciation of the limitations of a strategy of pursuing individual achievement for improving their own lives. Willis claims that only collective action can dramatically change the position of the working class, and in their loyalty to their mates at school or on the shop-floor the lads recognize this. Willis states:

---

no conceivable number of certificates among the working class will make for a classless society, or

---

convince industrialists and employers – even if they were able – that they should create more jobs.

---

3 The lads can see through careers advice. They know that most of the jobs likely to be available in their area require little skill, and that their studies at school will not prepare them for their work. Even if they worked hard at school the qualifications they would get would be quite limited. They might be able to move into clerical work, or gain an apprenticeship, but the sacrifices would hardly be worth the small amount of extra pay.

4 They have come to understand the unique importance of manual labour power. In a sense they have followed in the footsteps of Karl Marx and found for themselves that it is labour power that creates wealth.

On the other hand, Willis does not believe that the lads have seen through all of the ideological justifications for capitalism. Given their antipathy to non-manual labour (the work of 'pen pushers') their critical understanding of capitalism is limited to what they can learn through their own experience. They have no overall picture of how capitalism works to exploit them.

Willis is particularly critical of their sexism and racism. Their attitudes to women and ethnic minorities merely serve to divide the working class, making it easier for it to be controlled. Furthermore, the lads' willing entry into the world of manual work ultimately traps them in an exploitive situation. At school they prepare themselves to cope with manual labour but in doing so they condemn themselves to 'a precise insertion into a system of exploitation and oppression for working-class people'.

In his wide-ranging research then, Willis tries to show that it is the rejection of school which prepares one section of the workforce (semi-skilled and unskilled manual labourers) for its future role. This is done through the actively created and chosen counter-school culture of some working-class pupils. The reproduction of labour power through education works in an indirect and unintentional way. The lads are not simply suffering from false class consciousness – in part they understand their own alienation and exploitation – yet in the end it is their own choices which help to trap them in some of the most exploitive jobs which capitalism has to offer. As Willis says, 'Social agents are not passive bearers of ideology, but active appropriators who reproduce existing structures only through struggle, contestation and a partial penetration of those structures.'

Paul Willis – criticism and evaluation

Undoubtedly Willis's study has been influential. Liz Gordon, for example, claims that it 'has provided the model on which most subsequent cultural studies investigation within education has been based'. Furthermore she believes that it has encouraged Marxists to pay more attention to the details of what actually happens within education and it has helped to overcome a tendency to provide oversimplified accounts of the role of education in society. Nevertheless Willis has his critics.

David Blackledge and Barry Hunt advance three main criticisms.

1 They suggest that Willis's sample is inadequate as a basis for generalizing about working-class education. Willis chose to concentrate on a mere twelve pupils, all of them male, who were by no means typical of the pupils at the school he studied, never mind of school children in the population as a whole.

2 In a related criticism they accuse Willis of largely ignoring the existence of a whole variety of subcultures within the school. Blackledge and Hunt point out that many pupils came somewhere in between the extremes of being totally conformist or being totally committed to the counter-school culture. They say:

Willis . . . seems to accept at face value the lads' view that the conformists in the school cannot, at the same time as being involved in their school work, also take an interest in some of the things that are at the centre of the world of the lads – music, clothes, the opposite sex, drink, etc.

As we will see in a later section, some interactionist studies have uncovered a wide variety of pupil subcultures and ways of reacting to school (see pp. 766–7).

3 Blackledge and Hunt suggest that Willis misinterpreted some evidence. For example, by examining Willis's own evidence they argue that there is little basis for claiming that the lads develop the same attitudes to work as previous generations of workers. They point to some differences between one of the lads, Joey, and his father. They say:

Joey's father obviously takes a pride in his work and derives considerable self-respect from it . . . He clearly enjoys the recognition by management that he is doing a demanding job well and has a good, friendly relationship with them . . . Joey . . . unlike his father . . . is not on good terms with other social groups and classes . . . (management for the father; conformists, teachers and ethnic minorities for the son); rather he displays a contempt for anyone who is not part of his own small world.

With such strong differences between the working father and the son at school, Blackledge and Hunt find it hard to understand how Willis believes that schooling becomes a preparation for the world of adult, male, manual work.

Willis might also be criticized for adopting some Marxist concepts uncritically. For example, Willis assumes that the workers he studies are exploited, and in claiming that the lads have 'penetrated' aspects of capitalism, he assumes that his highly critical stance towards modern British society is almost self-evidently true. Nevertheless, in trying to combine an ethnographic study of the school with an analysis of the role of education, Willis demonstrated how it is possible to move beyond the limited focus of most studies of education.

■ Differential educational achievement

Much of the research in the sociology of education has been directed towards explaining why some social groups tend to reach higher **levels of educational attainment** than others. Levels of attainment are usually measured in terms of qualifications. Attention has been directed particularly towards differences in achievement between social classes, between males and females, and between different ethnic groups. We will now examine explanations of these differences with reference to each type of social group, starting with social class.

Class and differential achievement

Research reveals that the higher the social class, the higher the levels of educational achievement are likely to be. The children of parents in higher social classes are more likely to stay on in post-compulsory education, more likely to achieve examination passes when at school, and more likely to gain university entrance.

In a study of 8,529 males born between 1913 and 1952 and educated in England and Wales, A.H. Halsey, A.F. Heath and J.M. Ridge found clear class differences. They divided their sample into three groups according to the father's occupation:

1 the **service class** who worked as professionals, administrators and managers;

2 the **intermediate class** who were clerical or sales workers, the self-employed and lower-grade technicians and foremen;

3 the **working class** including manual workers in industry and agriculture.

Halsey *et al.* found that a boy from the service class, compared to one from the working class, had four times as great a chance of being at school at 16, eight times the chance at 17, and ten times the chance at 18. Furthermore, they had an eleven times greater chance of going to university.

More recent figures from an official government survey, the *General Household Survey*, also show that there are big class differences in educational institutions attended. Table 12.2 shows that in 1990–1 a university or polytechnic was the last educational establishment attended full-time by 40 per cent of men and 24 per cent of women aged 25–59 who were not in full-time education and who had professional fathers. This compared with 3 per cent of men and just 1 per cent of women from unskilled manual backgrounds.

Table 12.3 shows the extent to which such differences in institutions attended lead to class differences in educational qualifications. The figures are again based on the *General Household Survey* of 1990–1.

The table reveals some large differences. For example, 51 per cent of the children of professional fathers had a degree or other higher education qualification compared to just 8 per cent of

the children of fathers with unskilled manual jobs. Some 60 per cent of the children of men with unskilled manual jobs had no qualifications, compared to 7 per cent of the children of professional fathers.

A variety of causes has been suggested for the relative educational 'failure' of the working class.

Intelligence, class and educational achievement

The most obvious explanation for differences in educational achievement is the intelligence of the individual. In Britain, the 1944 Education Act established the **tripartite system** of education. Children were allocated to one of three types of school – grammar, technical, or secondary modern – largely on the basis of their performance in an intelligence test, the 11+.

Educational psychologists (such as Sir Cyril Burt) were influential in the establishment of this system. Burt's research appeared to show that intelligence was largely inherited and could be measured by the use of a test. It therefore made sense to send children to the type of school best suited to their abilities. Grammar schools provided an academic education for those with a high measured intelligence, while secondary schools catered for those with a lower measured intelligence. In the 11+ exam there was a strong correlation between results and social class, with middle-class children getting higher average scores. Consequently more middle-class children gained places at grammar schools.

Burt's research into intelligence was later discredited – many of his results had simply been invented – and the tripartite system was gradually replaced by comprehensives which all children attended regardless of ability. In most areas the 11+ was phased out. Nevertheless, many studies continue to show that there is a correlation between measured intelligence and achievement in education. Working-class children continue to score less well in intelligence tests than middle-class children. This might lead to the conclusion that lower intelligence continues to explain class differences in achievement.

However, there are many reasons for not jumping to such a simplistic conclusion. As Bowles and Gintis have argued, simply because above

Table 12.2   Educational establishment last attended full time by sex and father's socio-economic group

Persons aged 25–59 not in full-time education   *Great Britain: 1990 and 1991 combined*

Educational establishment last attended full time[1]	Father's socio-economic group[2]							
	Professional	Employers and managers	Intermediate non-manual	Junior non-manual	Skilled manual and own account non-professional	Semi-skilled manual and personal service	Unskilled manual	Total
School								
Men	41	63	53	69	84	87	92	76
Women	35	56	51	67	81	87	91	73
Total	38	59	52	68	83	87	92	75
College of further education, other college[3]								
Men	18	16	20	15	9	8	5	11
Women	41	30	33	26	14	10	8	19
Total	30	23	27	20	12	9	6	15
Polytechnic								
Men	11	66	8	5	3	3	2	4
Women	6	5	6	3	2	1	1	3
Total	8	5	7	4	3	2	1	4
University								
Men	29	15	19	10	4	3	1	8
Women	18	9	9	5	2	1	0	5
Total	24	12	14	7	3	2	1	6
Bases = 100%								
Men	493	1983	536	468	4388	1485	594	9947
Women	498	2087	606	474	4473	1571	622	10331
Total	991	4070	1142	942	8861	3056	1216	20278

[1] Excludes those who never went to school.
[2] Excludes no answers, fathers who were members of the Armed Forces, or full-time students, and those fathers who had never worked.
[3] Colleges of further education include colleges of education in Scotland, Northern Ireland and outside the UK, as well as former colleges of education in England and Wales.

(*Source*: (1993) *General Household Survey 1990–91*, HMSO, London, p. 204.)

average intelligence is associated with high academic qualifications, it does not necessarily mean that one causes the other. Before reaching any conclusions, it is necessary to examine questions such as 'What is intelligence?', 'How is it measured?', 'Where does it come from?'

What is intelligence?

The American psychologist Arthur Jensen defines **intelligence** as 'abstract reasoning ability' and argues that it is 'a selection of just one portion of the total spectrum of human mental abilities'. It is the ability to discover the rules, patterns, and logical principles underlying objects and events, and the ability to apply these discoveries to solve problems.

Intelligence is measured by intelligence tests which give an individual's **intelligence quotient** or IQ. Such tests are designed to measure abstract reasoning ability, and so exclude questions such as 'Which is the highest mountain in the world?' which test knowledge and memory rather than the ability to reason. Thus a simple IQ test may ask for the next number in the following sequence: 2, 4, 6, 8. This question requires individuals to discover the pattern underlying the sequence of numbers and to apply their discovery to solve the problem.

Table 12.3 Highest qualification held[1] in Great Britain: by socio-economic group of father, 1990–1991

	Professional	Employers and managers	Intermediate and junior non-manual	Skilled manual and own account non-professional	Semi-skilled manual and personal service	Unskilled manual	All persons
Degree	32	17	17	6	4	3	10
Higher education	19	15	18	10	7	5	11
GCE 'A' level[2]	15	13	12	8	6	4	9
GCSE, grades A–C[2]	19	24	25	21	19	15	21
GCSE, grades D–G[2,3]	4	9	7	12	12	10	10
Foreign	4	4	4	3	2	2	3
No qualifications	7	19	18	40	50	60	35

[1] Persons aged 25–59 not in full-time education.
[2] Or equivalent.
[3] Includes commercial qualifications and apprenticeships.

(*Source*: (1994) *Social Trends,* London: HMSO, p. 52.)

Despite their widespread use, there is a large body of evidence to suggest that IQ tests are not a valid measure of intelligence, particularly when they are used to compare the intelligence of members of different social groups.

Culture and intelligence

Many researchers argue that IQ tests are biased in favour of the middle class since they are largely constructed by and standardized upon members of this group. If it is accepted that social classes and other social groups have distinctive subcultures and that this affects their performance in IQ tests, then comparisons between such groups in terms of measured intelligence are invalid.

This argument is best illustrated by the testing of non-Western populations with Western IQ tests. The Canadian psychologist Otto Klineberg gave a test to Yakima Indian children living in Washington State, USA. The test consisted of placing variously shaped wooden blocks into the appropriate holes in a wooden frame 'as quickly as possible'. The children had no problem with the test but produced low scores because they failed to finish within the required time. Klineberg argues that this does not indicate low intelligence but simply reflects the children's cultural background. Unlike Western culture the Yakima do not place a high priority on speed.

S.D. Porteus provides a similar example when administering IQ tests to Australian aborigines.

They were reluctant to perform the tests and found it difficult to understand Porteus's request that they take them as individuals. Aborigine culture states that problems should be solved not by the individual but by the group. Important problems are discussed by the tribal elders until a unanimous decision is reached.

These examples suggest that Western IQ tests are inappropriate for non-Western peoples. The same argument has been applied to the use of IQ tests within Western societies which contain different subcultural groups including social class subcultures. Thus, the British psychologist Philip Vernon states that 'There is no such thing as a culture-fair test, and never can be.' This suggests that conclusions based on comparisons of the average measured IQ of different social groups must be regarded at best with reservation.

Genes and intelligence

There is general agreement that intelligence is due to both **genetic** and **environmental factors**: it stems partly from the genes individuals inherit from their parents, and partly from the environment in which they grow up and live. Environmental influences include everything from diet to social class, from quality of housing to family size. Some psychologists, such as Arthur Jensen in America and Hans Eysenck in Britain, argue that IQ is largely inherited. They maintain that some 80 per cent of intelligence is genetically based.

Studies of identical twins raised in different environments show that they have different IQ scores. Since the twins are genetically identical, it can be argued that differences in their IQs are caused by environmental factors. But this does not allow an accurate measurement of how much of the IQ score of each twin is due to environmental factors, and prevents a reliable estimate of the genetic and environmental component of intelligence.

Despite objections to their views, Eysenck and Jensen maintain that genetically based intelligence accounts for a large part of the difference in educational attainment between social groups. Eysenck claims that 'What children take out of schools is proportional to what they bring into the schools in terms of IQ.' Jensen is more cautious when he suggests that 'genetic factors may play a part in this picture'. However, he does argue:

a largely genetic explanation of the evidence on racial and social group difference in educational performance is in a stronger position scientifically than those explanations which postulate the absence of any genetic differences in mental traits and ascribe all the behavioural variation between groups to cultural differences, social discrimination and inequalities of opportunity.

Environment and intelligence

Those who argue that differences in IQ between social groups are due largely to environmental factors make the following points. It is not possible to estimate the degree to which IQ is determined by genetic and environmental factors. Research has indicated that a wide range of environmental factors can affect performance in IQ tests. Otto Klineberg summarizes some of these factors:

The successful solution of the problems presented by the tests depends on many factors – the previous experience and education of the person tested, his degree of familiarity with the subject matter of the test, his motivation or desire to obtain a good score, his emotional state, his rapport with the experimenter, his knowledge of the language in which the test is administered and also his physical health and well-being, as well as on the native capacity of the person tested.

In the following sections we will examine evidence which indicates that the relatively low test scores of certain social groups are due, at least in part, to the factors outlined by Klineberg.

Many researchers now conclude that given the present state of knowledge, it is impossible to estimate the proportions of intelligence due to heredity and environment. Measurement of possible genetically based differences in IQ between social groups would involve the exposure of large numbers of individuals born into those groups to identical environments. Since this is neither morally acceptable nor practically possible, the debate will probably never be resolved.

In one sense the whole IQ debate can be seen as a storm in a teacup. It has been regarded as important because of the assumption that IQ directly affects educational attainment and level of income. If Bowles and Gintis are correct, this is not the case. They find that IQ is 'nearly irrelevant' to educational and economic success. Thus differences in IQ between social classes and ethnic groups, whether due mainly to environmental or genetic factors, may well have little real significance.

■ Class subcultures and educational attainment

Various studies have shown that even when IQ is held constant, there are significant differences in educational attainment between members of different social groups. Thus working-class students with the same measured IQ as their middle-class counterparts are less successful in the educational system.

It has therefore been suggested that class stratification is directly related to educational attainment. In particular, it has been argued that the subcultures and the distinctive norms and values of social classes influence performance in the educational system.

Values, class and educational attainment

This position was first spelt out in detail by the American sociologist Herbert H. Hyman in an article entitled 'The value systems of different classes' written in the 1960s. He argued that the **value system** of the lower classes creates 'a self-imposed barrier to an improved position'.

Using a wide range of data from opinion polls and surveys conducted by sociologists, Hyman outlined the following differences between working- and middle-class value systems.

1 Members of the working class place a lower value on education. They place less emphasis on formal education as a means to personal achievement, and they see less value in continuing school beyond the minimum leaving age.

2 Members of the working class place a lower value on achieving higher occupational status. In evaluating jobs, they emphasize 'stability, security and immediate economic benefits' and tend to reject the risks and investments involved in aiming for high-status occupations. Job horizons tend therefore to be limited to a 'good trade'.

3 Compared to their middle-class counterparts, members of the working class believe that there is less opportunity for personal advancement. This belief is probably the basis for the lower value placed on education and high occupational status. Hyman argues that although it is based on a realistic assessment of the situation – the working class does indeed have less opportunity – the belief itself reduces this opportunity still further.

The values Hyman outlined did not characterize all members of the working class – a sizeable minority did not share them. This minority included many manual workers with white-collar parents, a fact which influenced their choice of reference group. Such workers identified more with the middle class and as a result tended to have higher aspirations.

In general, however, Hyman concluded that 'the lower-class individual doesn't want as much success, knows he couldn't get it even if he wanted to, and doesn't want what might help him get success'. Thus, the motivation to achieve, whether in school or outside it, will generally be lower for members of the working class.

Jobs, attitudes and educational attainment

In 1970 Barry Sugarman, the British sociologist, related certain aspects of middle- and working-class subcultures more directly to differential educational attainment. He provided an explanation for differences in attitude and outlook between the two classes, arguing that the nature of manual and non-manual occupations largely accounted for these differences.

Sugarman claims that many middle-class occupations provide an opportunity for continuous advancement in income and status. This encourages planning for the future, for example the investment of time, energy and money in training to meet the requirements of higher-status jobs. Many white-collar jobs also provide sufficient income for financial investment in the future in the form of mortgages and insurance policies.

By comparison working-class jobs reach full earning capacity relatively quickly, but provide fewer promotion prospects and less income for investment. In addition they are less secure. Manual workers are more likely to be laid off or made redundant than white-collar workers. The absence of a career structure in many working-class jobs means that individual effort has less chance of producing improvements in income, status and working conditions. Collective action in the form of trades union pressure provides a more effective strategy.

Sugarman argues that differences in the nature of jobs tend to produce differences in attitude and outlook. Since they have less control over the future, less opportunity to improve their position, and less income to invest, manual workers tend to be fatalistic, concerned with immediate gratification and present-time oriented. Since they are more dependent on joint action to improve wages and working conditions, they tend to emphasize collectivism rather than individualism.

Sugarman argues that these attitudes and orientations are an established part of working-class subculture. Pupils from working-class origins will therefore be socialized in terms of them. This may account at least in part, for their low level of educational attainment.

1 **Fatalism** involves an acceptance of the situation rather than efforts to improve it: as such it will not encourage high achievement in the classroom.

2 **Immediate gratification** emphasizes the enjoyment of pleasures of the moment rather than sacrifice for future reward, and will tend to discourage sustained effort with its promise of examination success. It will also tend to encourage early leaving for the more immediate rewards of a wage packet, adult status and freedom from the disciplines of school.

3 Present-time orientation may further reduce the motivation for academic achievement whereas an emphasis on long-term goals and future planning can encourage pupils to remain longer in full-time education by providing a purpose for their stay.

4 Finally **collectivism** involves loyalty to the group rather than the emphasis on individual achievement which the school system demands. Sugarman therefore concluded that the subculture of pupils from working-class backgrounds places them at a disadvantage in the educational system.

Class subcultures – problems of methodology

Before continuing the theme of this section, it is important to make a number of criticisms of the concept of social class subculture and the methodology used to establish its existence.

1 First, the content of working-class subculture is sometimes derived from observation. In contrast to the behaviour of many members of the middle class, aspects of working-class behaviour appear to be directed by the attitudes, norms and values outlined above. However, this behaviour may simply be a response in terms of mainstream culture to the circumstances of working-class life. Thus, members of the working class may be realistic rather than fatalistic, they might defer gratification if they had the resources to defer, they might be future oriented if the opportunities for successful future planning were available.

From this point of view members of the working class share the same norms and values as any other members of society. Their behaviour is not directed by a distinctive subculture. It is simply their situation which prevents them from expressing society's norms and values in the same way as members of the middle class. (This view is examined in detail in Chapter 3 – see pp. 151–3.)

2 Second, the content of working-class subculture is sometimes derived from interviews and questionnaires. Hyman's data were largely obtained from these sources. Barry Sugarman gave a questionnaire to 540 fourth-year boys in four London secondary schools and his conclusions are largely based on data from this source.

However, what people say in response to interviews or questionnaires may not provide an accurate indication of how they behave in other situations. As Robert Colquhoun notes in his criticism of Sugarman, it cannot simply be assumed that 'a response elicited in a questionnaire situation holds in the context of everyday life situations'. Thus social class differences in response to interviews and questionnaires may not indicate subcultural differences which direct behaviour in a wide range of contexts.

3 Finally, in a criticism of American studies R.H. Turner notes that social class differences reported from interviews and questionnaire data are often slight. Sociologists tend to ignore similarities between classes and emphasize the differences (discussed in Colquhoun 1976, p. 112).

J.W.B. Douglas – The Home and the School

The warnings contained in the above criticism are applicable to an important **longitudinal** study (a study of the same group over time) by J.W.B. Douglas and his associates. The study was based partly on questionnaire data and utilized the concept of social class subculture. In *The Home and the School*, Douglas examined the educational career of 5,362 British children born in the first week of March, 1946 through primary school to the age of 11. In a second publication, *All Our Future*, he followed the progress of 4,720 members of his original sample through secondary school up to the age of 16 in 1962.

Douglas divided the students into groups in terms of their ability which was measured by a battery of tests including IQ tests. He also divided the students into four social class groupings and found significant variations in educational attainment between students of similar ability but from different social classes. Comparing the attainment of 'high ability' students, Douglas found that 77 per cent of upper middle class, 60 per cent of lower middle class, 53 per cent of upper working class and 37 per cent of lower working class students gained good certificates at GCE 'O' level. Comparing students of lower ability, he found even larger attainment differences related to social class.

Douglas also found that length of stay in the educational system was related to social class. Within the 'high ability' group, 50 per cent of the students from the lower working class left secondary school in their fifth year compared with 33 per cent from the upper working class, 22 per cent from the lower middle and 10 per cent from the upper middle class. Again social class differences were greater for lower ability students.

Parental interest in education

Douglas related educational attainment to a variety of factors including the student's health, the size of the family, and the quality of the school. The single most important factor appeared to be the degree of parents' interest in their children's education. In general, middle-class parents expressed a greater interest as indicated by more frequent visits to the school to discuss their children's progress. They were more likely to want their children to stay at school beyond the minimum leaving age and to encourage them to do so. Douglas found that parental interest and encouragement became increasingly important as a spur to high attainment as the children grew older.

Douglas also attached importance to the child's early years since, in many cases, performance during the first years of schooling is reflected throughout the secondary school. He suggested that during primary socialization, middle-class children receive greater attention and stimulus from their parents. This forms a basis for high achievement in the educational system. Douglas concluded 'We attribute many of the major differences in performance to environmental influences acting in the pre-school years.'

Pre-school socialization

Apart from this general observation, Douglas does not examine **pre-school socialization** in detail. A large amount of research, mainly conducted by psychologists, has explored the relationships between child-rearing practices, social class and educational attainment. Although the results of this research are far from conclusive, there is some measure of agreement on the following points.

1 Behaviour patterns laid down in childhood have important and lasting effects. In particular the child's personality is largely shaped during the years of primary socialization.

2 There are social class variations in child-rearing practices.

3 These variations have a significant effect upon attainment levels in the educational system.

Compared to working-class child-rearing practices, those of the middle class have been characterized as follows:

1 there is an emphasis on high achievement;

2 parents expect and demand more from their children;

3 they encourage their children to constantly improve their performance in a wide range of areas from childhood games to talking and table manners;

4 by rewarding success parents instil a pattern of high achievement motivation into their children.

By giving their children greater individual attention and setting higher standards for them to attain, parents provide a stimulating environment which fosters intellectual development. In this way, middle-class child-rearing practices lay the foundation for high attainment in the educational system.

Criticisms

The above views have been strongly criticized. A number of arguments have been advanced to suggest that working-class parents are not necessarily less interested in their children's education just because they go to their children's schools less frequently than their middle-class counterparts. Tessa Blackstone and Jo Mortimore make the following points.

1 Working-class parents may have less time to attend school because of the demands of their jobs. Blackstone and Mortimore say:

frequency of visits to their child's school may indicate more about the relatively flexible working hours of fathers in non-manual occupations than about their levels of interest in their child's education.

2 Working-class parents may be very interested in their children's education but they are put off going to school because of the way teachers interact with them. Blackstone and Mortimore argue that it is possible that:

working class parents feel ill at ease or the subject of criticism when they visit school. Teachers represent authority and parents who have had unhappy experiences at school or with authority figures may be reluctant to meet them.

---

3 Blackstone and Mortimore also quote evidence from the *National Child Development Study* which found that 89 per cent of middle-class but only 75 per cent of working-class children attended a school with a well-established system of parent–school contacts (quoted in Blackstone and Mortimore 1994, p. 80). Thus it was easier for the middle-class parents to keep in touch with the educational progress of their children.

Even if Douglas were right that big variations in child-rearing practices between social classes exist (which is far from established), the view that behaviour patterns laid down in childhood have a lasting effect has been challenged. In an important article entitled 'Personal change in adult life', Howard S. Becker shows that behaviour can change radically depending on the situation. He argues that changes in behaviour patterns in adult life show clearly that human action is not simply an expression of fixed patterns established during childhood. If Becker's view is correct, educational attainment is a reflection of what happens in the classroom rather than what happens in the cradle.

Basil Bernstein – speech patterns

In this section we have examined possible subcultural differences between social classes which may account for differential educational attainment. We conclude the section with a consideration of class differences in speech patterns and their relationship to educational attainment.

Since speech is an important medium of communication and learning, attainment levels in schools may be related to differences in speech patterns. Much of the early work in this area was conducted by the English sociologist Basil Bernstein. He distinguishes two forms of speech pattern which he terms the elaborated code and the restricted code. In general, members of the working class are limited to the use of restricted codes whereas members of the middle class use both codes.

Restricted codes are a kind of shorthand speech. Those conversing in terms of the code have so much in common that there is no need to make meanings explicit in speech. Married couples often use restricted codes since their shared experience and understandings make it unnecessary to spell out their meanings and intentions in detail.

Bernstein states that restricted codes are characterized by 'short, grammatically simple, often unfinished sentences'. There is limited use of adjectives and adjectival clauses, of adverbs and adverbial clauses. Meaning and intention are conveyed more by gesture, voice intonations and the context in which the communication takes place.

Restricted codes tend to operate in terms of **particularistic meanings** and as such they are tied to specific contexts. Since so much is taken for granted and relatively little is made explicit, restricted codes are largely limited to dealing with objects, events and relationships which are familiar to those communicating. Thus the meanings conveyed by the code are limited to a particular social group: they are bound to a particular social context and are not readily available to outsiders.

In contrast, an **elaborated code** explicitly verbalizes many of the meanings which are taken for granted in a restricted code. It fills in the detail, spells out the relationships and provides the explanations omitted by restricted codes. As such its meanings tend to be **universalistic**: they are not tied to a particular context. In Bernstein's words, the meanings 'are in principle available to all because the principles and operations have been made explicit and so public'. The listener need not be plugged in to the experience and understanding of the speaker since they are spelled out verbally.

To illustrate his points Bernstein gives the example of stories told by two 5 year olds, one with a working-class, the other with a middle-class background. The children were given four pictures on which to base their story. In the first, several boys are playing football. In the second the ball breaks a window. The third shows a woman looking out of the window and a man making a threatening gesture in the boys' direction. The fourth picture shows the boys retreating from the scene.

Using an elaborated code to spell out the detail in the pictures, the middle-class child describes and analyses the relationships between the objects, events and participants and his or her story can be understood by the listener without the aid of the pictures.

The working-class child using a restricted code, leaves many of his or her meanings unspoken, and the listener would require the pictures to make sense of the story. This story is therefore tied to a particular context whereas the first story is free from context and can be understood with no knowledge of the situation in which it was created.

Bernstein explains the origins of social class

speech codes in terms of family relationships and socialization practices and the nature of manual and non-manual occupations. He argues that working-class family life fosters the development of restricted codes. In the working-class family the positions of its members are clearcut and distinct: status is clearly defined in terms of age, sex and family relationship. This clarity of status therefore requires little discussion or elaboration in verbal communication. Father can simply say 'Shut up' to his offspring because his position of authority is unambiguous.

By comparison, members of middle-class families tend to relate more as individuals rather than in terms of their ascribed status as father, son, mother and daughter. Relationships tend to be less rigid and clearcut and based more on negotiation and discussion. As a result meaning has to be made more explicit, intentions spelled out, rules discussed, decisions negotiated. Middle-class family relationships therefore tend to encourage the use of an elaborate code.

Bernstein also sees a relationship between the nature of middle- and working-class occupations and speech codes. He argues that working-class jobs provide little variety, offer few opportunities to participate in decision making, and require manual rather than verbal skills. In a routine occupation in the company of others in a similar situation, the manual worker is discouraged from developing an elaborated code. By comparison, white-collar occupations offer greater variety, involve more discussion and negotiation in reaching decisions and therefore require more elaborated speech patterns.

Speech patterns and educational attainment

Bernstein uses class differences in speech codes to account in part for differences in educational attainment.

1 First, formal education is conducted in terms of an elaborated code. Bernstein states that 'the school is necessarily concerned with the transmission and development of universalistic orders of meaning'. This places working-class children at a disadvantage because they are limited to the restricted code.

2 Second, the restricted code, by its very nature, reduces the chances of working-class pupils to successfully acquire some of the skills demanded by the educational system.

Bernstein does not dismiss working-class speech patterns as inadequate or substandard: he describes them as having 'warmth and vitality', 'simplicity and directness'. However, particularly in his earlier writings, he does imply that in certain respects, they are inferior to an elaborated code. He suggests that an elaborated code is superior for explicitly differentiating and distinguishing objects and events, for analysing relationships between them, for logically and rationally developing an argument, for making generalizations and handling higher-level concepts. Since such skills and operations form an important part of formal education, the limitations of working-class pupils to a restricted code may provide a partial explanation for their relatively low attainment.

Educational psychology and speech patterns

Some educational psychologists have attached even more importance than Bernstein to speech patterns in explaining differences in educational achievement between classes. In particular American psychologists such as Martin Deutsch, Carl Bereiter and Siegfried Engelmann argue that the speech patterns of members of low-income groups are central to any explanation of their educational attainment. Where Bernstein is cautious, they state categorically that the speech patterns of low-income blacks and whites in America are inferior in practically every respect to those of members of higher-income groups.

Thus Bereiter states that the speech of many low-income children 'is not merely an underdeveloped version of standard English, but is a basically non-logical mode of expressive behaviour' (quoted in Labov 1973, p. 25). He argues that it is hopelessly inadequate to meet the requirements of the educational system, particularly with its failure to deal with higher-level concepts. Bereiter concludes that the speech patterns of the lower class retard intellectual development, impede progress in school, and directly contribute to educational failure.

Criticisms

Both Bernstein's ideas and the more extreme claims of psychologists such as Bereiter, have provoked strong criticism. In a detailed critique of

Bernstein's views, Harold Rosen attacks his arguments step by step. He states that Bernstein's view of social class is vague: at times he talks about the working class in general as having a restricted code; at others he specifies the lower working class. Bernstein lumps together all non-manual workers into a middle class whose members from top to bottom appear equally proficient in handling an elaborated code. He thus ignores possible variety within these classes.

Rosen also criticizes Bernstein's characterizations of working- and middle-class family life and work situations, demanding evidence for his assertions. Rosen notes a further lack of hard evidence for elaborated and restricted codes: Bernstein provides few examples to actually prove their existence. Finally, Rosen accuses Bernstein of creating the myth that the supposed middle-class elaborated code is superior in important respects to working-class speech patterns. Rosen concludes that 'It cannot be repeated too often that, for all Bernstein's work, we know little about working-class language.'

In this section we have examined possible subcultural differences between social classes which may account, in part, for the different attainment levels of members of these groups in the educational system. We will examine the implications and policies which stem from this view in the next section.

▌ Cultural deprivation and compensatory education

The picture of working-class subculture is not an attractive one. It is portrayed as a substandard version of mainstream middle-class culture. Its standard deteriorates towards the lower levels of the working class and at rock bottom it becomes the culture of poverty, which we outlined in Chapter 3.

From this portrayal, the **theory of cultural deprivation** was developed. This states that the subculture of low-income groups is deprived or deficient in certain important respects and this accounts for the low educational attainment of members of these groups. This theory places the blame for educational failure on the children and their family, their neighbourhood and the subculture of their social group.

The so-called **culturally deprived child** is deficient or lacking in important skills, attitudes and values which are essential to high educational attainment. His or her environment is not only poverty stricken in economic terms but also in cultural terms. The following quotation from Charlotte K. Brooks is typical of the picture of the culturally deprived child which emerged in Britain and the USA in the early 1960s:

---

he is essentially the child who has been isolated from those rich experiences that should be his. This isolation may be brought about by poverty, by meagreness of intellectual resources in his home and surroundings, by the incapacity, illiteracy, or indifference of his elders or of the entire community. He may have come to school without ever having had his mother sing him the traditional lullabies, and with no knowledge of nursery rhymes, fairy stories, or the folklore of his country. He may have taken few trips – perhaps the only one the cramped, uncomfortable trip from the lonely shack on the tenant farm to the teeming, filthy slum dwelling – and he probably knows nothing of poetry, music, painting, or even indoor plumbing. (Quoted in Friedman 1976, p. 121.)

The catalogue of deficiencies of the culturally deprived child includes linguistic deprivation, experiential, cognitive and personality deficiencies, and a wide range of 'substandard' attitudes, norms and values.

Cultural deprivation and equality of education

The theory of cultural deprivation poses problems for the liberal ideal of equality of opportunity in education. It had been argued that the provision of similar educational opportunities for all would give every student an equal opportunity to fulfil his or her talents. In the USA the high school provided a uniform system of secondary education. In Britain supporters of the comprehensive school argued that the replacement of the tripartite system of secondary education – the grammar, technical and secondary modern schools – with the comprehensive system would go a long way towards providing equality of educational opportunity. A single system of secondary schools should provide the same opportunity for all.

However it became increasingly apparent that a uniform state educational system would not provide everyone with an equal chance since many would enter and travel through the system with the millstone of cultural deprivation hanging round their necks.

This realization slowly changed the notion of equality of educational opportunity. Formerly it had been argued that equality of opportunity existed when access to all areas of education was freely available to all. Now it was argued that equality of opportunity only existed when the attainment levels of all social groups were similar. The emphasis had changed from equality of *access* to equality of *results*.

Compensatory education and positive discrimination

From the viewpoint of cultural deprivation theory, equality of opportunity could only become a reality by compensating for the deprivations and deficiencies of low-income groups. Only then would low-income pupils have an equal chance to seize the opportunities freely provided for all members of society.

From this kind of reasoning developed the idea of **positive discrimination** in favour of culturally deprived children: they must be given a helping hand to compete on equal terms with other children. This took the form of **compensatory education** – additional educational provision for the culturally deprived. Since, according to many educational psychologists, most of the damage was done during primary socialization when a substandard culture was internalized in an environment largely devoid of 'richness' and stimulation, compensatory education should concentrate on the pre-school years.

Operation Head Start

This thinking lay behind many of the programmes instituted by the Office of Economic Opportunity during President Johnson's war on poverty. Billions of dollars were poured into **Operation Head Start,** a massive programme of pre-school education beginning in Harlem and extended to low-income areas across America. This and similar programmes aimed to provide **planned enrichment,** a stimulating educational environment to instil achievement motivation and lay the foundation for effective learning in the school system.

The results were very disappointing. In a large-scale evaluation of Operation Head Start, the Westinghouse Corporation concluded that it produced no long-term beneficial results.

During the late 1960s and early 1970s the Office of Economic Opportunity tried a system of **performance contracting**. Experts were contracted to raise the educational standards of low-income pupils on a payment-by-results basis. Highly structured intensive learning programmes were often used, similar to those developed by Bereiter and Engelmann at the University of Illinois. (Bereiter and Engelmann devised a programme of pre-school language education which drilled young children in the use of standard English.)

Again the results were disappointing. Performance contracting sometimes produced short-term improvements but its effects were rarely lasting. From its evaluation of performance contracting, the Office of Economic Opportunity concluded that 'the evidence does not indicate that performance contracting will bring about any great improvement in the educational status of disadvantaged children' (quoted in Jensen 1973, p. 7).

Despite such gloomy conclusions, there is still support for compensatory education. Some argue that it has failed either because the programmes developed have been inappropriate or because the scale of the operation has been insufficient. Martin Deutsch maintains that only 'long-term enrichment with specially trained teachers, careful planning and supervision and adequate funding can produce positive effects'. B.M. Caldwell argues that programmes have failed to combat the influences of the home environment and suggests that children should be removed from their parents during the day and placed in institutions which provide 'educationally oriented day care for culturally deprived children between six months and three years of age' (quoted in Labov 1973, p. 56). This, she hopes, will break the cycle of culturally deprived parents producing culturally deprived children.

Educational Priority Areas

In Britain compensatory education began in the late 1960s with the Government allocating extra resources for school building in low-income areas and supplements to the salaries of teachers working in those areas.

Four areas – parts of Liverpool and Birmingham, Conisbrough and Denaby in the then West Riding of Yorkshire, and Deptford in southeast London – were designated **Educational Priority Areas** (EPAs). Programmes of compensatory education were introduced in the EPAs. These were based mainly on pre-school education and additional measures in primary schools to raise literacy standards. Though it is difficult to evaluate the results, reports from the EPAs were generally disappointing.

Eric Midwinter, who headed the Liverpool EPA, argues that compensatory education has concentrated too much on the child in the educational institution. He believes that 'No matter how much you do *inside* the school, you can make virtually no impact at all without the informed support of the home.' He advocates a community school with strong links between the school and the community as a whole. Parents must be educated to help their children; the community must be educated about education.

A.H. Halsey, who directed the EPA projects, argues that positive discrimination in England has yet to be given a fair trial. It has operated on a shoestring compared to American programmes – for example in 1973 only one-fifth of 1 per cent of the total education budget was spent on compensatory education. Writing in 1977, Halsey stated 'Positive discrimination is about resources. The principle stands and is most urgently in need of application.'

Criticisms of compensatory education

Despite continuing support for compensatory education, criticism of the idea and its theoretical basis has been strong. Compensatory education has not been favoured by Conservative Governments in Britain since 1979. Rather than trying to equalize outcomes in the education system, they have encouraged increased competition with the stated aim of raising standards throughout the education system rather than concentrating on improving the educational achievement of disadvantaged groups. Some critics of these policies have argued that Conservative reforms since 1979 have increased class inequality (see for example pp. 799–801).

The theory of cultural deprivation has also been strongly attacked by those who are in favour of reducing class inequalities in education. It has been seen as a smokescreen which disguises the real factors which prevent equality of educational opportunity. By placing the blame for failure on the child and his or her background, it diverts attention from the deficiencies of the educational system. William Labov argues that Operation Head Start is 'designed to repair the child rather than the school; to the extent it is based upon this inverted logic, it is bound to fail'. Basil Bernstein takes a similar view and criticizes the whole concept of compensatory education 'because it distracts attention from the deficiencies of the school itself'.

Others criticize the concept for diverting attention from the inequalities in society. D.C. Morton and D.R. Watson argue that patching-up operations such as programmes of compensatory education cannot remove inequality of educational opportunity which is rooted in social inequality in society as a whole. They claim that compensatory education serves as 'a diversion from the pursuit of a genuine egalitarian policy'. In their view equality of educational opportunity can only be possible in a society without social inequality. Compensatory education merely tinkers with a small part of the existing system; what is required is a radical change in the system as a whole.

■ Pierre Bourdieu – cultural capital and differential achievement

The cultural deprivation theory has been criticized for assuming or implying that higher-class cultures are superior to working-class culture. By implication, members of the working class are themselves to blame for the failure of their children in education.

In France Pierre Bourdieu and his colleagues at the Centre for European Sociology in Paris have developed their own distinctive cultural explanation for achievement, and of the role of education in society. Unlike cultural deprivation theory, this approach, **cultural capital theory**, is strongly influenced by Marxism. As such, it does not assume that the culture of higher social classes is in any sense superior to that of the working class.

Bourdieu argues that working-class failure is the fault of the education system and not working-class culture. The education system is systematically biased towards the culture of dominant social classes; it devalues the knowledge and skills of the working class.

Cultural reproduction

According to Bourdieu, the major role of the education system is **cultural reproduction**. This does not involve the transmission of the culture of society as a whole, as Durkheim argued, but instead, the reproduction of the culture of the 'dominant classes'. These groups have the power to 'impose meanings and to impose them as legitimate'. They are able to define their own culture as 'worthy of being sought and possessed' and to establish it as the basis for knowledge in the educational system.

However, this evaluation of dominant culture is 'arbitrary'. There is no objective way of showing that it is any better or worse than other subcultures in society. The high value placed on dominant culture in society as a whole simply stems from the ability of the powerful to impose their definition of reality on others.

Bourdieu refers to the dominant culture as **cultural capital** because, via the educational system, it can be translated into wealth and power. Cultural capital is not evenly distributed throughout the class structure and this largely accounts for class differences in educational attainment. Students with upper-class backgrounds have a built-in advantage because they have been socialized into the dominant culture. Bourdieu claims that 'The success of all school education depends fundamentally on the education previously accomplished in the earliest years of life.' Education in school merely builds on this basis: it does not start from scratch but assumes prior skills and prior knowledge. Children from the dominant classes have internalized these skills and knowledge during their pre-school years. They therefore possess the key to unlock the messages transmitted in the classroom; in Bourdieu's words, they 'possess the code of the message'.

The educational attainment of social groups is therefore directly related to the amount of cultural capital they possess. Thus middle-class students have higher success rates than working-class students because middle-class subculture is closer to the dominant culture.

Bourdieu is somewhat vague when he attempts to pinpoint the skills and knowledge required for educational success. He places particular emphasis on style, on form rather than content, and suggests that the way pupils present their work and themselves counts for more than the actual scholastic content of their work. He argues that in awarding grades, teachers are strongly influenced by 'the intangible nuances of *manners* and *style*'. The closer the student's style to that of the dominant classes, the more likely the student is to succeed. The emphasis on style discriminates against working-class pupils in two ways.

1 First, because their style departs from that of the dominant culture, their work is penalized.

2 Second, they are unable to grasp the range of meanings which are embedded in the 'grammar, accent, tone, delivery' of the teachers. Since teachers use 'bourgeois parlance' as opposed to 'common parlance', working-class pupils have an in-built barrier to learning in schools.

The social function of elimination

Bourdieu claims that a major role of the educational system is the **social function of elimination**. This involves the elimination of members of the working class from higher levels of education. It is accomplished in two ways:

1 by examination failure;
2 by self-elimination.

Due to their relative lack of dominant culture, working-class pupils are more likely to fail examinations which prevents them from entering higher education. However, their decision to vacate the system of their own free will accounts for a higher proportion of elimination. Bourdieu regards this decision as 'reasonable' and 'realistic'. Working-class students know what's in store for them. They know the dice are loaded against them. Their attitudes towards education are shaped by 'objective conditions' and these attitudes will continue 'as long as real chances of success are slim'.

These arguments lead Bourdieu to conclude that the major role of education in society is the contribution it makes to **social reproduction** – the reproduction of the relationships of power and privilege between social classes. Social inequality is reproduced in the educational system and as a result it is legitimated. The privileged position of the dominant classes is justified by educational success; the underprivileged position of the lower classes is legitimated by educational failure.

The educational system is particularly effective in maintaining the power of the dominant classes since it presents itself as a neutral body based on meritocratic principles providing equal opportunity for all. However, Bourdieu concludes that in practice education is essentially concerned with 'the reproduction of the established order'. This it does by ensuring working-class failure and the success of the higher class.

Raymond Boudon – class position and educational attainment

In *Education, Opportunity and Social Inequality* the French sociologist Raymond Boudon presents a fresh perspective on the relationship between social class and educational attainment. He argues that inequality of educational opportunity is produced by a **two-component process**.

The primary and secondary effects of stratification

We dealt with the first component, which he refers to as the **primary effects of stratification**, in the previous section. It involves subcultural differences between social classes which are produced by the stratification system.

However, although Boudon agrees that differences in values and attitudes between social classes produce inequality of educational opportunity, he argues that the **secondary effects of stratification** are probably more important. The secondary effects stem simply from a person's actual position in the class structure – hence Boudon uses the term **positional theory** to describe his explanation. He maintains that even if there were no subcultural differences between classes, the very fact that people start at different positions in the class system will produce inequality of educational opportunity.

For example, the costs involved and the benefits to be gained for a working-class boy and an upper middle-class boy in choosing the same educational course are very different simply because their starting positions in the class system are different. If the upper middle-class boy chose a vocational course such as catering or building, his choice would probably lead to **social demotion**: the job he would obtain as a result of the course would be of a lower status than that of his father. However, the situation would be very different for the working-class boy who selected a similar course. It may well lead to **social promotion** compared to the occupational status of his father. Thus there are greater pressures on the upper middle-class boy to select a higher level educational course, if only to maintain his present social position.

These pressures are compounded by the boys' parents. Boudon suggests that parents apply the same cost-benefit analysis as their children to the selection of courses. As a result there will probably be a greater pressure from upper middle-class parents for their son to take a course leading to professional status, whereas working-class parents would be more likely to settle for a lower-level course for their son.

The costs and benefits of education

Boudon also relates the costs and benefits of course selection to family and peer group solidarity.

If a working-class boy chose to become a barrister and followed the required courses, this would tend to weaken his attachment to his family and peer group. He would move in different circles, live a different life style and continue his education when most or all of his friends had started work.

The costs to family and peer group solidarity involved in this choice for the working-class student would result in benefits for the upper middle-class boy. His friends would probably be following similar courses and aiming for jobs at a similar level. His future occupation would be of a similar status to that of his father. Thus if the upper middle-class boy chose to become a barrister and selected the appropriate educational course, his choice would reinforce family and peer group solidarity. Again position in the class system directly affects the individual's educational career.

Boudon's positional theory argues that people

behave rationally: they assess the costs and benefits involved when choosing how long to stay in the educational system and what courses to take. For people in different positions in the stratification system, the costs and benefits involved in choosing the same course are different. As a result, Boudon argues 'even with other factors being equal, people will make different choices according to their position in the stratification system'.

In a complex and sophisticated analysis, Boudon attempts to assess the relative importance of the primary and secondary effects of stratification on educational attainment. He finds that when the influences of primary effects (subcultural differences) are removed, although class differences in educational attainment are 'noticeably reduced', they still remain 'very high'.

If Boudon's analysis is correct the secondary effects of stratification are more important in accounting for differential educational attainment. Thus even if all subcultural differences were removed, there would still be considerable differences in educational attainment between social classes and a high level of inequality of educational opportunity.

Boudon's work has important implications for practical solutions to the problem of inequality of educational opportunity. Even if positive discrimination worked and schools were able to compensate for the primary effects of stratification, considerable inequality of educational opportunity would remain. Boudon argues that there are two ways of removing the secondary effects of stratification.

A common curriculum and equality of opportunity

The first involves the educational system. If it provided a single compulsory curriculum for all students, the element of choice in the selection of course and duration of stay in the system would be removed. Individuals would no longer be influenced by their class position since all students would take exactly the same courses and remain in full-time education for the same period of time.

Boudon argues that the more **branching points** there are in the educational system – points at which students can leave or choose between alternative courses – the more likely working-class students are to leave or choose lower-level courses. Thus if there were not a branching point at the age

of 16 in British secondary education, inequality of educational opportunity would be reduced since a greater proportion of working-class students leave at 16 compared to middle-class students of similar ability.

Boudon supports this point with evidence from Europe and the USA. There are fewer branching points in the American educational system compared to those of Europe and statistics suggest that inequality of educational opportunity is lower in the USA. However, Boudon believes that the possibility of providing a common compulsory curriculum for all pupils up to school-leaving age is slim. The trend is in the opposite direction – more and more branching points and increasingly specialized and varied curricula.

Boudon argues that the gradual raising of the school-leaving age in all advanced industrial societies has reduced inequality of educational opportunity, but present trends indicate that this reduction will at best proceed at a much slower rate.

An egalitarian society and equality of opportunity

Boudon's second solution to the problem of inequality of educational opportunity is the abolition of social stratification. He sees moves in the direction of economic equality as the most effective way of reducing inequality of educational opportunity. As a result, he argues that 'the key to equality of opportunity lies outside rather than inside the schools' but since there is little evidence that economic inequality in Western industrial societies is decreasing, Boudon sees no real evidence to suggest that class differences in educational attainment will decrease significantly in the foreseeable future.

Boudon concludes that 'For inequality of educational opportunity to be eliminated, either a society must be unstratified or its school system must be completely undifferentiated.' Since there is little hope of either occurring in Western society, Boudon is pessimistic about prospects for eliminating inequality of educational opportunity.

■ Cultural or material factors?

Despite the differences between them, cultural deprivation and cultural capital theories both emphasize the importance of cultural factors. However, it is possible that **material factors**, such as family income, play a part in determining levels of attainment. Lower social classes may lack the money to provide their children with the same educational opportunities as middle- and upper-class parents.

Greater resources may allow parents to provide children with more educational toys, a greater range of books, a superior diet, more space in the home to do homework, greater opportunities for travel, private tuition and access to private fee-paying schools. In all these ways more affluent parents can provide their children with advantages before they attend school and during their school career.

Halsey, Heath and Ridge attempted to measure the importance of cultural and material factors. (For further details of the study see pp. 785–7.) They distinguished between family climate, which concerned cultural factors, and material circumstances. **Family climate** was measured in terms of levels of parental education, and attitudes to education; **material circumstances** were measured in terms of family income.

Halsey *et al.* found that both cultural and material factors had some effect on the educational attainment of children.

1 Family climate was important in determining what type of secondary school a child attended. Once a child was at school, however, family climate had little effect on the child's progress.

2 Material circumstances played a key role in determining how long children stayed at school. Halsey *et al.* stated 'on this analysis, class inequalities in school leaving had virtually nothing to do with family climate. Material disadvantage is far more important.'

As Table 12.4 shows, the decision as to whether to stay on in post-compulsory education is a key factor in children's educational careers. Once children chose to stay on after 16, most had some exam success: those from working-class backgrounds has almost as high a success rate as those from service-class backgrounds.

Halsey *et al.* suggest that a successful way of raising the educational achievement of the working class would be to offer grants to sixth-form students to encourage those from relatively poor backgrounds to stay on. The findings of this study tend to support the view that material circumstances affect the length of stay in education, which in turn has a crucial effect on the levels of achievement attained.

In later sections of this book we will examine how class inequalities in education have been affected by educational reforms in Britain since 1979.

Table 12.4   Social class, post-compulsory education and exam success

Father's social class	Percentage staying at school until 16 or older	Percentage of those staying on to 16 or later passing one or more 'O' levels	Percentage staying on to 18 or later	'A' level success rate: Percentage of those who stayed to 18 or later and passed one or more 'A' level
Service class	70	83.1	28.2	93
Intermediate	32.6	74	7.7	90
Working class	26.8	71	3	93

(*Source*: Halsey, A.H., Heath, A.F. and Ridge, J.M. (1980) *Origins and Destinations*, Clarendon Press, Oxford.)

■ Education – an interactionist perspective

The explanations of differential achievement that we have examined so far all suggest that pupils' progress in education is strongly influenced by factors over which individuals have little control. Intelligence and home background are presented as largely determining the performance of pupils within the education system.

Yet the most obvious place to look for an explanation of differential educational achievement is within the educational system itself. None of the previous approaches is based upon an examination of schooling, but it is widely assumed that schools play an important part in determining educational success and failure. Many parents (at least those who can afford it) spend considerable sums of money so that their children can attend fee-paying schools. It is highly unlikely that they would do so unless they believed that such schools would offer their children some advantage.

Before the establishment of comprehensives many parents were also anxious that their children gained a place at grammar schools, assuming that this would prove advantageous for their children. Supporters of the comprehensive system hoped that when all children in state education attended the same type of school, class inequalities in educational achievement would be greatly reduced. This did not happen. Despite comprehensives, class inequalities remain, and this has led to an emphasis on examining the differences in treatment that pupils receive even when they are attending the same school.

Interactionists have illuminated the processes within the education system that result in different levels of achievement. It is interactionists, far more than any other type of sociologist, who have researched into the details of day-to-day life in schools.

As we saw in previous sections, psychologists and sociologists have explained performance in the education system in terms of intelligence, cultural and material deprivation and social stratification. All these approaches are, from the interactionist point of view, **deterministic**; that is, they see human behaviour as directed and determined by forces beyond the control of the individual. Individuals are held to react in a predictable way to external stimuli such as the directives of subcultures or the pressures of stratification systems.

Self-concept and meanings

To interactionists, the explanation of human behaviour needs to take account of the subjective states of individuals, and the meanings that individuals attach to external stimuli. For example, a pupil who achieves a poor test result might interpret the result in different ways and attach different meanings to it.

1 They might attribute the result to their own lack of ability and resign themselves to continued failure in the education system.

2 They may believe the result has been caused by them failing to work sufficiently hard, and they might resolve to work with renewed effort.

3 On the other hand, they might attach little or no importance to the result, or they could deny the validity of the test and continue to believe that they have considerable ability despite the result.

Within education, as in society as a whole, other people are perhaps the most important source of external stimuli: their words and actions will constantly be interpreted and given meanings. To interactionists, your view of yourself, or **self-concept**, is produced in interaction with others. The self-concept of the pupil is influenced by the other pupils and the teachers with whom she or he interacts. The self-concept of a pupil may be modified if others constantly contradict it. For example, pupils who consider themselves to be a 'joker', may be forced to reconsider if nobody laughs at their jokes.

Interaction may be particularly important as the pupil develops the aspects of his or her self-concept concerned with academic ability.

Social roles

Another important interactionist concept is that of **social roles**. Within schools there are the obvious roles of pupils and teachers, but to interactionists these roles are not fixed and unchangeable.

Teachers may disagree with each other about the sort of person who makes the ideal teacher, and about the types of behaviour that are consistent with the pupil role.

Similarly, pupils may have different ideas about what makes the ideal teacher, or for that matter the ideal pupil. They may be unable to live up to the model of the ideal pupil held by their teachers. As a result, pupils may start to develop new patterns of behaviour. They may form subcultures in which the pupil role becomes modified and types of behaviour which are punished by their teachers are rewarded by their peers.

Cultural deprivation theories also use the idea of subculture, but in a very different way. To interactionists, subcultures emerge from interaction within school as pupils develop ways of coping with school life. Subcultures are actively produced by those who are members of them. In cultural deprivation theory, however, the subcultures which influence educational attainment exist prior to the child going to school, and those who fail in the education system are the passive victims of the limitations of their own upbringing.

These general concepts provide the framework for interactionist studies of education. We will now examine the findings of these studies.

■ Typing, labelling and the self-fulfilling prophecy

One of the most important aspects of the interactionist theory of education concerns the ways that teachers make sense of and respond to the behaviour of their pupils.

In their book *Deviance in Classrooms,* David H. Hargreaves, Stephen K. Hester and Frank J. Mellor analyse the ways that pupils come to be **typed** or classified. Their study is based upon interviews with teachers and classroom observation in two secondary schools. They examined the way that teachers 'got to know' new pupils entering their first year at the school.

Initially, teachers have limited knowledge about their new pupils as individuals. They may know about the types of catchment area from which pupils originate, and have a general image of first year pupils, but apart from this they can only start to build up a picture as the school year progresses. Hargreaves, Hester and Mellor distinguish three stages of typing or classification.

The first stage consists of **speculation**. The teachers make guesses about the types of pupils they are dealing with. The researchers noted seven main criteria on which initial typing was based. Teachers distinguished pupils according to:

1 their appearance;

2 how far they conformed to discipline;

3 their ability and enthusiasm for work:

4 how likeable they were;

5 their relationships with other children;

6 their personality;

7 whether they were deviant.

Hargreaves, Hester and Mellor stress that in the speculation phase teachers are only tentative in their evaluations, and they are willing to amend their views if initial impressions prove to be misleading. Nevertheless they do form a **working hypothesis**, a theory about what sort of child each pupil is.

Each hypothesis is then tested in the second phase, which Hargreaves *et al.* call **elaboration**. Gradually the hypotheses are either confirmed or contradicted, but either way the teachers become more confident in their judgements as their typing is refined.

When the third stage is reached, **stabilization** takes place. By this time the teacher feels that, 'He "knows" the pupil; he understands him; he finds little difficulty in making sense of his acts and is not puzzled or surprised by what he does or says.' By this time all the pupils' actions will be evaluated in terms of the type of pupil they are thought to be. Some pupils will be regarded as deviants, and for them it will be difficult for their behaviour to be seen in a positive light.

Typing and social class

Although Hargreaves *et al.* do emphasize that typing is a gradual process, other sociologists have suggested that it can be much more abrupt. In a study of an American kindergarten R.C. Rist found that as early as the eighth day of school the children were permanently seated at three separate tables. Furthermore, table 1 was reserved for 'fast learners', tables 2 and 3 for the less able. According to Rist though, it was not, in reality, ability which determined where each child sat, but the degree to which they conformed to the teacher's own middle-class standards. For example, the teacher seemed to take account of whether the children had neat and clean appearances, and whether they were known to come from an educated family which was in employment. In other words, the kindergarten teacher was evaluating and labelling pupils on the basis of their social class, not on the abilities they demonstrated in class.

Similar claims were made by Howard Becker. He interviewed sixty teachers from Chicago high schools and found that they tended to classify and evaluate students in terms of a standard of the 'ideal pupil'. This standard included the teachers' views of what constituted ideal work, conduct and appearance. Teachers perceived students from non-manual backgrounds as closest to this ideal; those from lower working-class origins as farthest from it. They interpreted the behaviour of lower-class students as indicating a lack of interest and motivation and saw them as unrestrained and difficult to control.

Becker argues that simply by perceiving certain students in this way, teachers experience problems in working with them. He concludes that the meanings in terms of which students are assessed and evaluated can have significant effects on interaction in the classroom and attainment levels in general.

The effects of typing

In itself the typing or **labelling** of pupils might not be that important, but many sociologists claim that it has important effects upon the progress of pupils. Teachers are in a position to affect their pupils' progress in a number of direct and indirect ways.

For example, Aaron V. Cicourel and John I. Kitsuse conducted a study of the decisions of counsellors in an American high school. The counsellors play an important part in students' educational careers since they largely decide which students should be placed on courses designed for preparation for college entry. Although the counsellors claimed to use grades and the results of IQ tests as the basis for classifying students in terms of achievement, Cicourel and Kitsuse found significant discrepancies between these measures and the ways in which students were classified. Like Becker, Cicourel and Kitsuse found that the student's social class was an important influence

on the way he or she was evaluated. Thus, even when students from different social backgrounds had similar academic records, counsellors were more likely to perceive those from middle- and upper-middle-class origins as natural 'college prospects' and place them on higher-level courses.

Cicourel and Kitsuse argue that counsellors' classifications of students' ability and potential are influenced by a whole range of non-academic factors such as the students' appearance, manner and demeanour, assessments of their parents, and reports from teachers on their conduct and adjustment. Cicourel and Kitsuse suggest that a counsellor's evaluation of an individual as a 'serious, personable, well-rounded student with leadership potential' may often have more effect than his or her grades upon his or her educational career. Cicourel and Kitsuse conclude that such procedures do not uphold the 'ideal of equal access to educational opportunities for those of equal ability'.

In an article based on the same research, Cicourel and Kitsuse examine the meanings employed by counsellors in the definition of students as 'conduct problems'. Again they found a range of factors which subtly combine to create the counsellors' picture of a conduct problem. These include 'the adolescent's posture, walk, cut of hair, clothes, use of slang, manner of speech'. Again social class is an important basis for classification since the characteristics used to type a conduct problem tend to be found in students from low-income backgrounds.

In British schools teachers often differentiate between pupils by making decisions about what exams to enter them for and what streams or bands to place them in. These decisions can influence the options open to pupils and the extent of their progress in similar ways to those discovered by Cicourel and Kitsuse. We will consider this particular question of banding and streaming in the next section.

Teachers can also affect pupil progress in other ways apart from determining what classes they are placed in and what courses they are placed on. Two closely related theories, the self-fulfilling prophecy and the labelling theory, both suggest that pupil behaviour can be changed by the way that teachers react to them.

The **labelling theory** suggests that typing leads to labels being attached to pupils.

The **self-fulfilling prophecy theory** argues that predictions made by teachers about the future success or failure of pupils will tend to come true because the prediction has been made. The teacher defines the pupil in a particular way, such as 'bright' or 'dull'. Based on this definition, the teacher makes predictions or prophecies about the behaviour of the pupil, for example, she or he will get high or low grades. The teachers' interaction with pupils will be influenced by their definition of the pupils. They may, for example, expect higher-quality work from and give greater encouragement to the 'bright' pupils. The pupils' self-concepts will tend to be shaped by the teacher's definition. Pupils will tend to see themselves as 'bright' or 'dull' and act accordingly. Their actions will, in part, be a reflection of what the teacher expects from them. In this way the prophecy is fulfilled: the predictions made by the teacher have come to pass. Thus the pupil's attainment level is to some degree a result of interaction between himself or herself and the teacher.

There have been a number of attempts to test the validity of the self-fulfilling prophecy. The most famous was conducted by Robert Rosenthal and Leonora Jacobson in an elementary school in California. They selected a random sample of 20 per cent of the student population and informed the teachers that these children could be expected to show rapid intellectual growth. They tested all pupils for IQ at the beginning of the experiment. After one year the children were re-tested and, in general, the sample population showed greater gains in IQ. In addition, report cards indicated that teachers believed that this group had made greater advances in reading skills.

Although Rosenthal and Jacobson did not observe interaction in the classroom, they claim that 'teachers' expectations can significantly affect their pupils' performance'. They suggest that teachers communicated their belief that the chosen 20 per cent had greater potential to the children who responded by improving their performance. Rosenthal and Jacobson speculate that the teachers' manner, facial expressions, posture, degree of friendliness and encouragement convey this impression, which produces a self-fulfilling prophecy.

Despite the plausibility of the self-fulfilling prophecy theory, it has been criticized. One area of criticism concerns the evidence. Rosenthal and Jacobson have been strongly attacked for the methodology they used in their study. In particular it has been suggested that the IQ tests they used were of dubious quality and were improperly administered. In a review of research in this area, C. Rogers summarizes the findings. He says:

> Some show effects only with younger children, some only with older ones. Some show effects with urban children, but not suburban. Some show quantitative but not qualitative effects on pupil-teacher interactions, while others show the exact opposite.

Notwithstanding these contradictions, Rogers claims that the overall evidence, on balance, suggests that the self-fulfilling prophecy is a real phenomenon. However, it can be argued that it is not the inevitable phenomenon that Rosenthal and Jacobson make it appear.

Some interactionists have come to realize that not all pupils will live up to their labels. In a study of a group of black girls in a London comprehensive school Margaret Fuller found that the girls resented the negative stereotypes associated with being both female and black. They felt that many people expected them to fail, but far from living up to their expectations they tried to prove them wrong. The girls devoted themselves to school work in order to try to ensure their success.

This interactionist then, recognizes that negative labels can have a variety of effects. However, this observation weakens the forcefulness of the labelling theory. It seems that labels will usually have an effect, but the type of effect they have is not predictable. Fuller's work avoids some of the pitfalls of the cruder versions of labelling theory which are rather deterministic in suggesting the inevitability of failure for those with negative labels attached to them. Her views are more in keeping with the non-deterministic interpretations of behaviour which are, for the most part, typical of interactionist research.

■ Banding and streaming

Labelling and the self-fulfilling prophecy theories suggest ways that teachers' reactions to individual pupils can affect their educational careers. It is also possible, though, that whole groups of pupils, not just individuals, can be treated in different ways. Despite the fact that under the comprehensive system all state-educated pupils attend the same type of school, this may not mean that they receive the same type of education. In many comprehensive schools pupils are placed, for at least part of the time, in different classes according to their supposed abilities.

Stephen J. Ball – banding at Beachside Comprehensive

In his book *Beachside Comprehensive* Stephen J. Ball examines the internal organization of a comprehensive school. At Beachside a system of **banding** was introduced for first year pupils. Pupils were placed in one of three bands on the basis of information supplied by their primary schools. The first band was supposed to contain the most able pupils, and the third band the least able. However, Ball found that factors other than academic criteria were influential in determining the bands in which the children were placed. In particular, for pupils of similar measured ability, those whose fathers were non-manual workers had the greatest chance of being placed in the top band.

Ball observed that most pupils were conformist and eager when they first entered the school, but gradually the behaviour of children began to diverge. He attributed this process to teachers having stereotypical views of the different bands. Band one was seen as likely to be hard working, dedicated and well behaved. Band three was not expected to be particularly troublesome either, but the pupils were expected to have considerable learning problems. Band two was expected to be the most difficult to teach and the least cooperative.

According to Ball, the effect of these views was a progressive deterioration in the behaviour of most band two pupils, which was reflected in higher levels of absence, more non-conformist behaviour and a lack of effort being put into homework.

As a result of teacher expectations different bands tended to be taught in different ways and encouraged to follow different educational routes. Band one pupils were 'warmed-up': they were encouraged to have high aspirations and to follow 'O' level courses in subjects with a high academic status. In contrast, band two children were 'cooled-out' and directed towards more practical subjects and towards CSE exams. The end result was that band two pupils were much less likely than their band one counterparts to take 'O' levels, to stay on at school after the age of 16, or take 'A' levels.

Ball admits that not all band two children failed. Some were able to overcome the difficulties that placement in this band produced. Nevertheless there was a strong relationship between banding and performance. Given that there was also a strong relationship between social class and banding, Ball claims that, 'working-class pupils tend to percolate downwards in the processes of academic and behavioural differentiation'.

Nell Keddie – streaming and classroom knowledge

While Ball examined the workings of a banding system, a study by Nell Keddie looked at the operation of **streaming** in a single subject in a large London comprehensive school. As well as looking at the classification and evaluation of students, Keddie also studied the ways that knowledge was evaluated and classified. She tried to work out the criteria used by teachers to categorize and evaluate classroom knowledge.

Keddie discovered that knowledge defined by teachers as appropriate to the particular course was considered worthwhile; knowledge from the student's experience which did not fit this definition was considered of little consequence. Knowledge presented in an abstract and general form was considered superior to particular pieces of concrete information. The knowledge made available to students depended on the teacher's assessment of their ability to handle it. Thus those students who were defined as bright were given greater access to highly evaluated knowledge.

Like other interactionists, Keddie found a relationship between perceived ability and social class. Pupils were streamed into three groups in terms of ability. There was a tendency for pupils from higher-status white-collar backgrounds to be placed in the 'A' stream, and for those from semi-skilled and unskilled manual backgrounds to be relegated to the 'C' stream.

Keddie observed the introduction of a new humanities course designed for all ability levels. Despite the fact that all streams were supposed to be taught the same material in the same way, Keddie found that teachers modified their methods and the information they transmitted depending on which stream they were teaching. There was a tendency to withhold 'higher grade' knowledge from 'C' stream pupils. Some teachers allowed the 'C' stream pupils to make more noise and do less work than those in the 'A' stream.

Keddie argued that teachers classified students in terms of a standard of the 'ideal pupil', similar to that described by Becker. The middle-class pupils in the 'A' stream were closest to this ideal and were therefore given greater access to highly evaluated knowledge. This results in 'the differentiation of an undifferentiated curriculum'.

Keddie then examined the students' definition of the situation and accounted for the 'success' of 'A' stream students in the following way. 'A' stream students were more willing to accept on trust the validity of the teacher's knowledge and to work within the framework imposed by the teacher. By comparison, 'C' stream pupils would not suspend their disbelief if the teacher made statements which did not match their own experience. For example, one pupil objected to a teacher's portrayal of the 'British family' because it did not fit his own experience.

From the teachers' viewpoint, such objections slowed down the transmission of the 'body of knowledge' they were concerned with getting across. Many of the questions asked by 'C' stream pupils were defined by teachers as irrelevant and inappropriate, as were their attempts to relate their personal experience to the course. In general 'C' stream pupils were less willing to work within the guidelines set by teachers. Keddie ironically commented, 'It would seem to be the failure of high-ability pupils to question what they are taught in schools that contributes in large measure to their educational achievement.'

Keddie concluded that classifications and evaluations of both pupils and knowledge are socially constructed in interaction situations. Appropriate knowledge is matched to appropriate pupils. This results in knowledge defined as high grade being made available to students perceived as having high ability. It results in pupils perceived as having low ability (in practice mainly working-class pupils) being actually denied knowledge which is essential for educational success.

■ Pupil subcultures and adaptations

From an interactionist point of view pupils experience school in different ways. They are treated differently by their teachers, given different labels, and often placed in different bands or streams.

The pupils attach different meanings to their education and find a variety of ways to relate to their experiences. Schools usually lay down a set of standards and indicate to their pupils how they are expected to behave.

However, not all pupils are able and willing to conform to the images of the ideal pupil held by teachers. If they fail to do so, pupils may well form their own subcultures which reject some of the values of the school.

David Hargreaves – streaming and pupil subcultures

In a study of a secondary modern school published in 1967, David Hargreaves related the emergence of subcultures to labelling and streaming. Pupils labelled as 'troublemakers' were placed in lower streams; those whose behaviour was more acceptable in higher streams. Those with negative labels attached to them had been defined as failures first, by being placed in a secondary modern which was seen as a second-rate institution, and second through the streaming system. Many teachers regarded them as no more than 'worthless louts'.

Faced with the problem of being unable to achieve high status within the school, such pupils attempted to protect their sense of worth and retain a positive self-concept. Students labelled as troublemakers tended to seek out each other's company, and within their group awarded high status to those who broke the school rules. Thus, disrupting lessons, giving cheek to teachers, failing to hand in homework, cheating and playing truant all brought prestige. According to Hargreaves then, two distinctive subcultures emerged within the school: the **conformists** and the **non-conformist delinquents**.

Peter Woods – pupil adaptations

Peter Woods argues, however, that schools are more complex than Hargreaves's work would suggest. Woods based his ideas upon a study of 'Lowfield', a secondary modern in a rural area of the Midlands.

Following Merton's **typology of adaptations** (see pp. 390–2) Woods suggests that pupils' ways of dealing with school life depend upon whether they accept or reject the aim of academic success and the institutional means which specify the appropriate forms of behaviour within the schools. Going beyond Merton, Woods points out that pupils may accept goals and means with a greater or lesser degree of enthusiasm, and for different reasons. In all, Woods identifies no less than eight different modes of adaptation to the school.

1 **Ingratiation** is the most positive adaptation. Pupils who try to ingratiate themselves identify completely with teachers, and try to earn their favour. Such pupils care little about other pupils' attitudes to them and they may be regarded by other pupils as 'creeps' or 'teacher's pets'.

2 **Compliance** is a less strong positive adaptation to the school; Woods regards this adaptation as typical of new pupils in secondary schools. It is also common among older pupils who are studying for external exams who comply for **instrumental** reasons, that is in order to achieve success in their exams.

3 **Opportunism** is an adaptation which often develops in the second year at school and may be a temporary phase before the pupil develops a stable attitude to the school. Opportunist pupils fluctuate between trying to gain the approval of their teachers and their peer group.

4 **Ritualists** are deviant to the extent that they reject the goals of education, but they are not difficult to control. They will 'go through the motions' of attending school, and will not break school rules, but they are not concerned either to achieve academic success, or to gain the approval of teachers.

5 Other pupils develop more deviant adaptations. **Retreatists** reject both the goals and the means laid down by the school, but without outright rebellion. They try to pass the time by daydreaming in lessons, 'mucking about' or 'having a laugh', but they are not consciously trying to oppose the values of the school.

6 According to Woods, a very common adaptation in later years at the school is **colonization**. This is characterized by 'indifference to goals with ambivalence about means'. Colonizers attach no great importance to academic success, but will try to get away with just enough to 'keep their noses clean'. They want to avoid trouble, but will copy or cheat if they think there is little chance of discovery.

7 **Intransigence** represents one of the most difficult adaptations for schools to cope with. Intransigent pupils are indifferent to academic success, and reject the accepted standards of behaviour. They are much less afraid than the colonizers to hide their deviance.

8 The final adaptation, **rebellion**, involves the rejection of both goals and means and their replacement with

alternatives. In this case school life is directed towards quite different objectives than those sanctioned by the school. For example, some girls might devote their school life to showing concern for their personal appearance, or discussing boys. Some boys might only be interested in escaping school to enter the world of unskilled manual work (see for example the description of Paul Willis's study, pp. 741–3).

Like many other interactionists, Woods relates his views in a very general way to social class, arguing that the more conformist adaptations tend to be typical of middle-class pupils, the less conformist of the working class. Middle-class pupils will, according to Woods, tend to find both the goals and means encouraged by the school, to be more in keeping with the cultural values of their families than will working-class pupils.

Criticisms of Peter Woods

Complicated though Woods's adaptational model is, some interactionists nevertheless feel that it fails to do justice to the complexities of interaction within schools. V.J. Furlong suggests that pupils do not consistently act in accordance with a subculture or a particular type of adaptation. He stresses that individual pupils will behave differently in different contexts. For example, teachers tend to be seen as 'strict' or 'soft', and even normally conformist pupils might resort to deviant activities when faced with a 'soft' teacher and encouraged to be disruptive by fellow pupils.

A further limitation of the adaptational and subcultural approaches is suggested by M. Hammersley and G. Turner. They point out that there may well be no single set of aims or values accepted by those in authority within a school. Not all teachers share a middle-class view of the world and middle-class values. Some may be in sympathy with at least some of the activities of 'deviant' pupils, and be less than enthusiastic about the most conformist among those they teach.

■ The interactionist perspective – an evaluation

The interactionist approach to the sociological study of education undoubtedly has advantages over some approaches. It is based upon far more detailed empirical evidence than, for example, functionalist and Marxist theories of the role of education in society. It has provided many insights into the day-to-day life of schools and other educational institutions. Furthermore, it is more sophisticated than some of the more deterministic theories of educational achievement. It shows that children's educational careers are not necessarily determined by such factors as IQ and home background.

Peter Woods claims that the interactionist perspective also has practical applications. He believes that it provides information which could lead to better teaching and a reduction in conflict and deviance within schools.

However, as in other areas of sociology, interactionist work has limitations. Some studies tend to be rather descriptive and do not always explain the phenomena they describe. For example, the description of different pupil adaptations advanced by Peter Woods does not fully explain why individuals adopt one particular adaptation rather than another.

Similarly it is difficult to support the interactionist contention that meanings and definitions of situations are simply constructed in classroom interaction. It is difficult to account for the apparent uniformity of meanings which result from a multitude of interactions. If meanings are negotiated in interaction situations, more variety would be expected. For example, is it simply coincidence that the sixty high school teachers interviewed by Becker all appear to hold the same concept of the 'ideal pupil'?

The relative uniformity of meanings which lie behind what counts as knowledge and ability, suggests that such meanings are not simply con-structed in the classroom but rather they have a wider and more fundamental basis. In addition many interactionists refer to the existence of class differences in education, but they fail to explain how those class differences originate. In these respects symbolic interactionism can be accused of having too narrow a focus, of failing to take account of factors external to the school which might constrain or limit what happens within education.

Some attempts have been made to combine ethnographic studies of schools with sociological perspectives which do take into account wider factors related to the overall structure of society. One such attempt was made by Willis (see pp. 741–3).

Another study by R. Sharp and A. Green highlights some of the limitations of interactionism. From their study of a number of classes in an infant school they found that a variety of constraints affected teachers' behaviour. The school favoured a progressive pupil-centred education which treated each individual as unique and dis-couraged the differentiation of pupils according to ability. However, even in the classrooms of teachers who were in full support of this philo-sophy, the teachers did start to stratify individuals and to treat groups of pupils differently. This was be-cause of the constraints under which the teachers worked, particularly the high pupil-teacher ratio (the large size of the classes).

Sharp and Green conclude that the meanings held by the individuals concerned do not, on their own, determine what happens within education, and that interactionism needs to broaden its con-cerns to take account of such factors as the educa-tional policies of the state which determine the conditions in which teachers and pupils work.

■ Gender and educational attainment

Although traditionally much of the research into educational achievement has focused on class, gender has attracted increased interest over recent years. Until recently statistics suggested that although girls often performed well in comparison to boys in the earlier years of their education, later in their educational careers they tended to fall behind. However, in the mid-1990s statistics showed that females had overtaken males in terms of the qualifications they achieved up to the age of 18.

Figure 12.1 shows that by 1990–1 25 per cent of boys but 29 per cent of girls had a highest qualification of one or more 'A' levels (or H grades in Scotland). Some fifteen years earlier male school leavers were more likely than female school leavers to obtain one or more 'A' levels or H grades: in 1975–6 18 per cent of boys and 16 per cent of girls had achieved this standard. Figure 12.1 also shows that girls have been consistently more likely than boys to have five or more GCSE

Figure 12.1 Highest qualification attained by school leavers: by sex

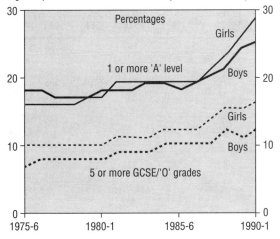

Highest qualification in the UK attained by school leavers: by sex

(*Source*: (1994) *Social Trends*, HMSO, London, p. 50.)

Table 12.5 Highest qualification held[1] in the UK: by sex, 1984 and 1992

	Males		Females	
	1984	1992	1984	1992
Degree or equivalent	9	12	4	7
Higher education below degree level	4	6	7	8
GCE 'A' level or equivalent[2]	31	36	12	17
GCSE, grades A-C or equivalent	12	14	20	24
Other qualification[3]	7	9	11	12
No qualification	34	23	45	32
Not known	2	–	2	–
All aged 16–59 (+100%) (millions)	15.9	16.9	15.8	16.8

1 Persons aged 16–59
2 Includes BTEC, City & Guilds and apprenticeships
3 Includes CSE below grade 1, YT certificate (YTS for 1984), RSA other qualifications

(*Source*: (1994) *Social Trends*, HMSO, London, p. 47.)

passes at grade C or above as their highest qualification. In 1990–1 12 per cent of boys and 16 per cent of girls had reached this level of educational achievement.

Although female school leavers may be doing better than male school leavers, there remains a substantial gap in educational qualifications between males and females in the population as a whole. Table 12.5 shows that in 1992 54 per cent of males but only 32 per cent of females had 'A' level qualifications or better in the UK.

Even though female school leavers tend to be better qualified than male ones, women are still less likely to enter higher education. Table 12.6 shows that in 1991–2 there were 695,000 male students in higher education compared to 602,000 females. However, it is clear that the gender gap in higher education has narrowed considerably since 1970–1 when less than a third of higher education students were female.

■ Explanations for gender differences in educational achievement

A variety of explanations have been advanced for gender differences in educational attainment and

we consider the most significant ones in the following sections. Most explanations are based upon the assumption that it is girls who are less successful.

Innate ability

One possible explanation for female under-achievement is that there are differences in **innate ability** between males and females. However, while researchers have looked for evidence that girls have lower levels of ability than boys, many test results suggest that if anything, girls have more innate ability than boys. Harvey Goldstein points out that on average girls performed better in the 11+. Some LEAs, in fact, adjusted girls' scores downwards in order to ensure that grammar schools were not predominantly occupied by girls.

When separate tests are carried out for different types of ability, girls also tend to perform better than boys overall. Goldstein summarizes the results for girls and boys aged 11 as follows:

broadly speaking, for achievement in mathematics and reading the average differences are small, while for both verbal and non-verbal reasoning tests the girls have higher average scores than boys.

Table 12.6   Full- and part-time students in higher education[1] in the UK: by sex and type of establishment

	Males (thousands)					Females (thousands)				
	1970–1971	1975–1976	1980–1981	1985–1986	1991–1992[2]	1970–1971	1975–1976	1980–1981	1985–1986	1991–1992[2]
Full-time and sandwich students										
Universities										
Ungergraduates	134	141	157	148	178	59	77	101	108	150
Postgraduates	33	37	34	37	46	10	13	15	17	28
Other[3]										
Undergraduates			120	146	207			95	129	211
Postgraduates			7	7	11			6	7	12
All full-time students	274	301	318	339	442	182	214	217	261	400
Part-time students										
Universities										
Ungergraduates	3	2	2	5	6	2	2	2	5	8
Postgraduates	15	17	20	22	31	3	5	8	11	23
Open University[4]	14	34	38	43	51	5	22	29	36	48
Other[3]										
Undergraduates			138	134	144			42	65	107
Postgraduates			9	12	21			3	5	17
All full-time students	142	168	207	215	253	23	50	86	122	202
All students	416	470	524	553	695	205	264	303	384	602

[1] Excludes students enrolled on nursing and paramedic courses at Department of Health establishments.
[2] Excludes 2.5 thousand non-university students in Scotland recorded as sex unknown.
[3] Polytechnics and other Higher Education establishments.
[4] Calendar years beginning in second year shown. Excludes short course students up to 1982/83.

(*Source*: (1994) *Social Trends*, HMSO, London, p. 47.)

Some researchers suggest that this is because girls mature earlier intellectually than boys. Certainly by the age of 16 boys have overtaken girls in their average scores for mathematics and reading, although girls continue to do better in reasoning tests.

As Goldstein points out though, the idea that such tests can measure innate ability is largely discredited (for a critique of IQ tests see pp. 747–8). Furthermore, there are many processes which might account for the comparative deterioration of girls in terms of mathematics and reading. Girls' experience of schooling may well explain the decline of their comparative performance in these areas.

The evidence for gender differences in attainment being the result of innate differences is very weak. Alternative explanations are much more plausible.

Early socialization

Early socialization may well account for any eventual relative failure of girls. Fiona Norman and her colleagues point out that before children start school, conditioning and sex stereotyping have already begun. From the types of play that girls and boys are encouraged to engage in and the types of toys they are given, different sets of aptitudes and attitudes can be developed.

Girls may have their educational aspirations affected through playing with dolls and other toys which reinforce the stereotype of women as 'carers'. Boys tend to be encouraged to be more active than girls, and this may be reflected in their attitudes in classrooms. Furthermore, boys are more likely to be given constructional toys which can help develop scientific and mathematical concepts. Stereotypes of men and women can be further reinforced by the media through comics, books, television and various types of advertising.

One possible consequence of early gender stereotyping is that girls may come to attach less value to education than boys. Research conducted by Sue Sharpe into a group of mainly working-class girls in London in the early 1970s found that the girls had a set of priorities which were unlikely to encourage them to attach great importance to education. She found that their concerns were 'love, marriage, husbands, children, jobs, and careers, more or less in that order'. Sharpe argued that if girls tended to see their future largely in terms of marriage rather than work, then they might have little incentive to try to achieve high educational standards.

In the 1990s Sharpe repeated her research and found that girls' priorities had changed. The changes may help to explain why the educational attainment of girls at school is now greater than that of boys (see p. 774 for more details).

Material factors

There is little doubt that the cultural factors involved in socialization play some part in explaining gender differences in educational attainment. It is less clear what part material factors might play as obviously both boys and girls come from families which are at every level of the stratification system.

However, J.W.B. Douglas and colleagues did suggest that in some families more resources are devoted to the education of sons than daughters. If parents believe that their son's future depends more upon his work than their daughter's, they may be less willing to finance post-compulsory education for daughters than sons.

Socialization in school

Most research into gender and education has focused on factors internal to schools. Many sociologists have claimed to detect bias against girls in the educational system.

Glenys Lobban claims that the early years of some educational reading schemes reinforce the gender stereotyping found in wider society. From a study of 179 stories in six reading schemes, Lobban found that only 35 stories had heroines compared to 71 which had heroes. Girls and women were almost exclusively portrayed in traditional domestic roles and it was nearly always men and boys who took the lead in non-domestic tasks. In at least three of the schemes females took the lead in only three activities in which both sexes were involved: hopping, shopping with parents, and skipping. Males took the lead in seven joint activities: exploring, climbing trees, building things, looking after pets, sailing boats, flying kites and washing cars. Summarizing the findings and the likely effects of the reading schemes Lobban says:

> The girls who read them have already been schooled to believe, as our society does, that males are superior to females and better at everything other than domestic work, and the stories in the schemes cannot but reinforce the damage that our society does to girls' self-esteem.

Lobban's research was conducted in the 1970s, but more recent research has also found evidence of gender stereotyping. In 1992 Lesley Best and her students examined a sample of 132 books for pre-school age children in an attempt to discover whether gender bias in children's books had decreased. They found that in these 132 books, 792 male and 356 female characters were portrayed. There were 94 male heroes but just 44 heroines. Some 75 per cent of the female characters featured in the book were portrayed in family situations compared to just 15 per cent of the male characters, and men were shown in 69 different occupations but women in only 18. Some characters were shown in non-traditional roles – there were two female sailors, a female jockey, and a male babysitter for example – but they were the exception rather than the rule. Lesley Best concludes that despite the existence of a few non-sexist books little had changed since Lobban's research. She says:

> it would seem that there is little attempt made in pre-school books to widen the horizons for either sex by presenting more women in a broad range of jobs or more men taking on a caring role.

Behaviour in the classroom – self-confidence and criticism

The active and dominant males in the reading schemes may be reflected in the behaviour of boys and girls in the classroom. From their own classroom observations and from the analysis of other studies, Barbara G. Licht and Carol S. Dweck reached some interesting conclusions about sex differences in the self-confidence of young children in education.

Licht and Dweck found that girls lack confidence in their ability to carry out intellectual tasks successfully. Despite the superior performance of young girls compared to boys in primary schools, it was the girls who generally expected to encounter most difficulty when learning new things. Boys are, according to Licht and Dweck, able to shrug off failures by attributing them to a lack of effort on their part, or unfair assessment by teachers. Girls, on the other hand, constantly underestimate their ability, fail to attach significance to their successes whilst losing confidence when they fail.

This is because girls blame failure on their own intellectual inadequacies while explaining success in terms of luck. In doing this, girls fail to convince themselves that they are capable of succeeding and they come to avoid challenging new situations in which they fear they will fail.

Licht and Dweck do not think that this situation is the result of conscious discrimination by teachers. Indeed, they found that in line with primary school teachers' own experiences, most of them expected greater success from their girl pupils. However, by examining fourth and fifth grade American classes Licht and Dweck found differences in the ways that boys and girls were evaluated. There was very little difference between the sexes in the amount of praise and criticism that girls and boys received for their academic achievements and failures. Boys, however, were criticized much more frequently for lacking neatness in their work, for failing to make sufficient effort and for misbehaviour in the classroom. Licht and Dweck concluded that girls begin to lose confidence because they get less criticism from teachers. The boys in their study were given ways of explaining away their failures in terms of behaviour which could be modified; the girls had no such excuses that they could make for themselves.

Michelle Stanworth – gender differences in further education

Michelle Stanworth examined the later stages of the education system in a study of 'A' level classes in a further education college. She interviewed teachers and pupils from seven different classes in the humanities department. Her findings suggested that in the sixth form a number of the attitudes displayed by teachers would impede the educational progress of girls. These attitudes were not confined to male teachers – they were also typical of their female colleagues.

Teachers found it much more difficult to remember the girls in their classes. Without exception, all the pupils whom teachers said it was difficult to name and recall were girls. Quiet boys were remembered, but quiet girls seemed to blend into the background and make little impression on their teachers.

Stanworth found that teachers held stereotypical views of what their female pupils would be doing in the future. Only one girl was seen as having the potential to enter a professional occupation. Interestingly, she was the most assertive of the girls in the classroom but her academic performance was not particularly good. The most academically successful girl was described by one teacher as being likely to become a 'personal assistant for someone rather important'. Even for this girl, marriage was suggested as one of the most significant aspects of her future life, and male teachers mentioned nothing other than marriage as the future for two-thirds of the female pupils.

When asked which students were given the most attention by teachers, the pupils themselves named boys two and a half times as often as girls, although girls outnumbered boys by nearly two to one in the classes studied. The pupils reported that boys were four times more likely to join in classroom discussions, twice as likely to seek help from the teacher, and twice as likely to be asked questions.

Furthermore, girls were consistently likely to underestimate their ability, while boys overestimated theirs. Pupils were asked to rank themselves in terms of ability in each class. In nineteen of the twenty-four cases in which teachers and pupils disagreed about the ranking, all the girls placed themselves lower than the teachers' estimates, and all but one boy placed themselves higher.

Stanworth found then, that interaction in the

classroom seemed to disadvantage girls considerably. They were encouraged to take less part in classes, and got less attention from teachers, and as a consequence lacked faith in their own ability. Teachers had an important role in these processes but pupils themselves contributed to the interaction which, according to Stanworth, 'Played an active part in the regeneration of a sexual hierarchy, in which boys are the indisputably dominant partners.'

Dale Spender – Invisible Women

Perhaps an even stronger attack on the education system is made by Dale Spender in her book *Invisible Women*. Spender claims that education is largely controlled by men who use their power to define men's knowledge and experiences as important, and women's knowledge and experiences as insignificant. Thus in economics, for example, the contribution of women's often unpaid work to the world's economy is usually ignored. Women who have made a notable contribution to human progress (such as Ada Lovelace who helped to develop computer software) are also ignored. Indeed, Spender sees the whole curriculum as being riddled with sexism which is bound to undermine girls' self-confidence and hinder their progress.

Quoting from a variety of studies, Spender goes on to argue that girls get less attention than boys in the classroom. She taped some of her own classes in which she consciously tried to divide her time equally between the sexes yet still found that only 38 per cent of her time was spent interacting with girls. Spender argues that girls have to wait longer than boys for what attention they do receive in the classroom, and that female contributions to discussion and debate are usually treated dismissively by the males present. Boys are often abusive and insulting to girls, yet teachers fail to rebuke them. Male pupils play an important part in damaging girls' education. Spender claims that 'boys do not like girls . . . they find them inferior and unworthy, and even despicable'. Boys communicate their low regard for the girls in the classroom, forcing them to retreat into keeping a low profile.

Although she concentrates on what happens in the education system, Spender does not hold the education system entirely responsible for the educational failure of girls. She points out that 'girls were just as familiar with the roles they were supposed to play, before they were allowed to attend schools', and today children learn to behave in masculine and feminine ways before they are old enough to start their formal education. Spender sees male dominance in society as a whole as the basic cause of girls' difficulties in education, but schools help to reinforce that dominance and ensure that it continues. Spender concludes:

> mixed-sex education is preparation for 'real life' . . . for in real life it is men who dominate and control; but this is not equality of educational opportunity; it is indoctrination and practice in the art of dominance and subordination.

Criticisms of Stanworth and Spender

These strong condemnations of the education system are not entirely accepted by some sociologists. Gay J. Randall points out that Stanworth's work was based upon interviews and not direct classroom observation. It therefore gives some indication of what pupils perceive to be happening in classrooms, but does not actually establish, for example, that teachers give more attention to girls. Randall also quotes Sara Delamont who accuses Spender of using inadequate data and failing to specify most of her research methods so that the findings could be checked in later research.

Randall's own research failed to find such clearcut bias as that of Stanworth and Spender. She observed classes which involved practical work in workshops and laboratories in an 11–18 comprehensive school. In a class of ten girls and nine boys she did find that the boys occupied the central position in the class more often than girls when teachers were giving an initial demonstration of the work they were to do. However, in the lessons she observed she found that girls had more contact with teachers than the boys. In one lesson girls averaged 49 seconds contact with the teacher to boys' 43 seconds; in another girls averaged 3 minutes 45 seconds, and boys just 56 seconds of individual attention.

Although the above study was only small scale, it does suggest that some caution should be exercised in considering claims that girls are always disadvantaged in classroom interaction. Randall suggests that perhaps in the laboratory, where pupils can talk to teachers on an individual level, girls are more forthcoming than they are when it would involve speaking in front of the whole class.

Reasons for improvements in female educational achievement

If education is really as biased against girls as Spender and Stanworth claim, then it is remarkable that girls have done so well up to the age of 18 in the past, and surprising that they are now doing better than males. A number of factors might account for the improved performance of females in education.

1 Changes in the labour market with the decline of heavy industry, the increase in service sector work, the increasing employment of 'flexible' part-time workers and workers on fixed-term contracts, have all increased employment opportunities for women. The rapid rise in the employment of married women, especially since the Second World War, has increased the incentives for women to gain educational qualifications.

2 These changes may be reflected in changing attitudes amongst females. When Sue Sharpe repeated her 1970s research on teenage girls in the 1990s (see p. 771) she found that their priorities had changed. They no longer attached primary importance to marriage and having children and instead 'almost unanimously endorsed the importance of having a job or career and, in this respect, emphasised being able to support themselves'. They therefore attached much more importance to education than their counterparts had in the 1970s.

3 The Women's Movement and female sociologists have drawn attention to gender inequalities in education. In doing so they have encouraged teachers to become more aware of the issue and have persuaded some to change their practices so that are less likely to disadvantage female pupils and students. Some schools and some Local Education Authorities (LEAs) have taken initiatives designed to improve educational opportunities for girls.

Despite the improvements in levels of educational attainment for females compared to males, impor-

tant differences remain. In particular, males and females still tend to chose different subjects to study and males enjoy greater levels of success in some subjects than females.

Gender and subject choice

Certainly there are pronounced differences in the subjects studied by males and females in the British education system. As Figure 12.2 shows, at GCSE level girls are more likely to gain a higher grade in French, history, English and biology, while in mathematics, geography and sciences other than biology, males are more successful.

The specialization of boys in technical and scientific subjects and girls in arts and humanities subjects is also evident at university. Table 12.7 shows that there are more males studying medicine and dentistry, agricultural subjects, physical sciences, mathematics, engineering and technology, architecture, building and planning, social studies and business and administration. There are

Figure 12.2 School leavers with grades A-C at GCSE[1]: by subject and sex, 1990–1

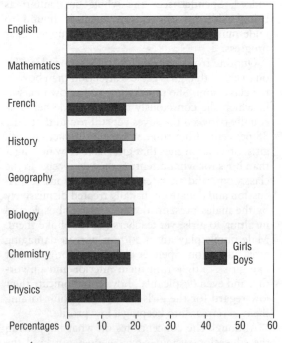

[1] includes GCSE/GCE 'O' Level/SCE grades A-C and CSE grade 1

(*Source*: (1994) *Social Trends*, HMSO, London, p. 51.)

Table 12.7 Universities[1]: full-time students analysed by subject group of study in the United Kingdom

	Academic years (students in thousands)							
	1984[2]–5	1985[3]–6	1986–7	1987–8	1988–9	1989–90	1990–1	1991–2
Medicine and dentistry								
Men	26.8	15.2	14.9	14.8	14.7	14.5	14.2	14.2
Women		11.5	11.5	11.5	11.8	12.0	12.2	12.6
Subjects allied to medicine								
Men	8.1	3.0	3.1	3.1	3.3	3.5	3.8	4.2
Women		5.7	5.8	5.9	6.1	6.7	7.6	8.9
Biological sciences								
Men	20.3	10.1	10.4	10.5	10.8	11.2	11.8	12.7
Women		10.5	10.9	11.3	11.9	13.2	14.4	15.8
Agriculture and related subjects								
Men	6.2	3.6	3.7	3.7	3.7	3.6	3.6	3.6
Women		2.6	2.7	2.6	2.7	2.7	2.8	3.0
Physical sciences								
Men	27.1	20.9	20.9	20.5	20.6	21.5	22.2	23.7
Women		6.3	6.4	6.7	6.9	7.6	8.4	9.5
Mathematical sciences								
Men	18.1	13.8	14.0	14.7	15.7	16.8	17.9	19.3
Women		4.7	4.6	4.6	5.0	5.5	6.1	6.4
Engineering and technology								
Men	39.4	36.7	37.3	37.4	37.1	37.9	39.2	41.8
Women		3.6	4.0	4.3	4.7	5.1	5.8	6.5
Architecture, building and planning								
Men	5.0	4.0	3.9	4.0	4.0	4.1	4.5	5.0
Women		1.3	1.4	1.5	1.6	1.8	1.8	1.9
Social studies								
Men	42.9	24.1	24.6	24.7	25.7	26.4	28.0	30.0
Women		19.6	20.6	21.3	22.7	23.4	25.2	27.3
Business and administrative studies								
Men	13.3	9.2	9.5	10.1	10.7	11.6	12.1	13.5
Women		5.3	5.9	6.5	7.0	7.7	7.9	8.9
Mass communications and documentation								
Men	0.9	0.4	0.4	0.4	0.5	0.6	0.7	0.9
Women		0.7	0.7	0.6	0.8	0.9	1.0	1.2
Languages and related disciplines								
Men	30.9	10.0	9.9	9.8	10.2	10.6	11.4	13.4
Women		21.2	21.2	21.5	22.4	23.7	25.2	27.4
Humanities								
Men	17.8	9.4	9.8	9.9	10.1	10.7	11.5	12.6
Women		7.9	8.0	8.2	8.5	9.2	10.1	11.3
Creative arts								
Men	4.1	1.9	1.9	2.0	2.3	2.3	2.3	2.5
Women		2.5	2.8	2.9	3.4	3.6	3.5	3.9
Education								
Men	11.0	4.7	5.0	4.4	4.4	4.4	4.4	5.3
Women		6.4	6.6	6.6	7.3	8.2	8.9	10.0
Multidisciplinary								
Men	33.3	17.8	18.2	18.4	19.2	20.0	20.8	22.3
Women		15.5	15.7	16.6	17.9	19.9	21.1	23.1

[1] Excludes the Open University and the former polytechnics and central institutions who obtained university status in 1992.
[2] Includes Ulster Polytechnic which merged with the University of Ulster in October 1984.
[3] A new subject classification was introduced in 1985 when certain subjects were reclassified and combinations of subjects were classified separately for the first time.

(*Source*: (1994) *Annual Abstract of Statistics*, HMSO, London.)

more females studying mass communications and documentation, languages, humanities, biological sciences, subjects allied to medicine, creative arts, education and multidisciplinary degrees.

There was a significant reduction in the gender differences in the numbers studying some subjects over the period from 1985–6 to 1991–2. For example, the number of female medicine and dentistry students increased by more than 1,000 while the number of male students studying these subjects declined by 1,000. However, such changes are not evident in all subjects: in some subjects gender differences have increased. As the number of females in higher education has gone up, in some traditional female subjects (such as subjects allied to medicine and education) the proportion of female students has risen even further. Thus although there have been important changes in higher education there is little sign of gender differences in subject choice disappearing.

Socialization and subject choice

Many of the factors which influence levels of attainment in education also influence the choice of subjects studied. Cultural factors, particularly early socialization, may encourage boys to develop more interest in and aptitude for technical and scientific subjects. When choosing which subjects to study, females and males may well be influenced by what they have learned about femininity and masculinity.

In her 1970s study, Sue Sharpe found that the girls she questioned were most inclined to choose office work as their preferred future employment, followed by a group of occupations which included teachers, nurses, bank clerks and shop assistants – all traditionally areas with high levels of female employment.

The girls interviewed rejected many jobs (such as mechanics, electricians, driving instructors and engineers) either because they defined them as 'men's' work, or because they felt that employers and society at large defined them as such. In these circumstances it was hardly surprising that most girls saw little point in studying subjects that are traditionally the province of men.

Schools and subject choice

Sue Sharpe also recognized, though, that the education system itself also plays a part in directing

girls towards 'feminine' subjects. Although she admitted that schools were improving in this respect, she believed that girls tended to be steered towards arts subjects and directed particularly to subjects such as cookery, needlework and typing.

Teresa Grafton and her colleagues carried out a study of a coeducational comprehensive school in south-west England. They found that in the first and second years nearly all girls took cookery and needlework from the craft options available, while nearly all boys took metalwork and woodwork. It was not compulsory for them to make these choices, but the school made it clear that there were only limited places available for members of either sex who wanted to study non-traditional subjects. In this way it was made clear what were regarded as the 'normal' choices.

In the fourth year subject choices could once more be made. The way the timetable was organized meant that the combinations pupils could opt for were limited. For example, in one set of choices, traditional girls' subjects (needlework and commercial skills) competed with traditional boys' subjects (woodwork and metalwork). Guidelines were issued to third year tutors which stressed that all subjects were open to both sexes but 'prior discussion' was necessary for boys who wanted to take the 'family and child option', while girls had to show a 'sincere desire' to take metalwork and woodwork.

Grafton and colleagues recognized that factors outside the school were important in influencing subject choice: pupils were guided by parents, siblings and friends. The researchers also describe the choices as being 'clearly closely related to sexual divisions in the home and in the labour market'. Nevertheless the organization of the school timetable and the sorts of advice that pupils received from teachers played a major part in directing the girls towards traditional and predictable subject areas.

Science and gender

Alison Kelly has attempted to explain why science tends to be seen as masculine and she identifies two main reasons.

First, Kelly argues that the way science subjects are packaged makes them appear boys' subjects. She claims that most science textbooks have very few women portrayed in them. From her observations of classes she found that teachers tended to use examples which were likely to be more in keeping with boys' experiences. For instance, cars were used as an example to illustrate acceleration when bicycles might have been more familiar to both sexes. In another lesson, a demonstration of eclipses was accomplished with the aid of a football. This was preceded by a conversation between the male teacher and the male pupils about the previous Saturday's football results. In such circumstances girls may feel less at home in science classrooms than boys.

However, Kelly argues that the second factor, the behaviour of pupils rather than teachers, makes the greatest contribution to turning sciences into boys' subjects. Boys tend to dominate science classrooms, grabbing apparatus before girls have a chance to use it, and shouting out answers to the questions directed at girls. In these respects science classrooms represent a small-scale version of society as a whole. Kelly argues:

> Boys act as if they have automatic priority over the resources of the laboratory, whether they be the apparatus, the teacher's attention, or just the physical space. One of the general principles of a patriarchal society – that males are more important than females – is acted out in the science classroom in a way which limits girls' opportunities to learn.

■ Ethnicity and educational attainment

Ethnicity and levels of attainment

In recent years there has been considerable interest in the educational performance of ethnic minorities. Numerous studies have been carried out including the government-sponsored Swann Committee report *Education for All*. Although the precise findings of studies have varied, most have found that, overall, ethnic minorities tend to do less well than other members of the population.

As Table 12.8 illustrates though, the *Swann Report* found important differences between ethnic minority groups. From a survey of five LEAs it was found that Asians did almost as well as the whites or 'others'. Asians were slightly less likely than 'others' to get five or more graded results in 'O' level or CSE examinations, but in other respects were just as successful. The *Swann Report* noted though that one Asian group (those of Bangladeshi origin) did particularly badly.

The average performance of West Indians was considerably worse than that of whites. Only 5 per cent of the West Indians in the *Swann Report* study passed an 'A' level, and only 1 per cent went to university.

However, such a gloomy picture of ethnic minority underachievement is not entirely supported by more recent research. Relying mainly on data from the *Labour Force Survey* Trevor Jones has found that members of all ethnic minorities are more likely to stay on in full-time education between the ages of 16 and 19 than are whites. In 1988–90 37 per cent of whites but 43 per cent of Afro-Caribbeans, 66 per cent of African Asians, 58 per cent of Indians, 55 per cent of Pakistanis, 46 per cent of Bangladeshis, 77 per cent of Chinese and 71 per cent of Africans in Britain aged 16–19 were in full-time education.

Jones suggests that the greater tendency for members of ethnic minorities to stay in education may be partly due to difficulties in finding jobs in a labour market in which racism is still common. However, it may also be partly due to 'a greater motivation towards self-improvement through educational achievement amongst ethnic minorities' and to 'strong family encouragement of young ethnic minority people to stay on in full-time education'.

Jones's analysis of the *Labour Force Survey* found that there were substantial ethnic differences in terms of the highest qualifications attained by individuals. Table 12.9 shows that there were wide variations between ethnic minority groups. For example, only 10 per cent of Bangladeshis of working age but 34 per cent of

Table 12.8   School leavers in 5 LEAs 1981–2 (percentages)

	Asians	West Indians	All others (5 LEAs)	All maintained school leavers in England
GSC and 'O' levels				
No graded results	19	19	19	11
At least 1 graded result (but less than 5)	64	75	62	66
5 or more graded results	17	6	19	23
'A' levels				
No 'A' level pass	87	95	87	86
At least 1 'A' level	13	5	13	14
Intended destination				
University	4	1	4	4
Other full-time further education	30	27	14	21
Employment	39	51	64	64
Not known	28	22	18	11

(*Source*: (1985) *Swann Report*.)

Table 12.9   Highest qualification by ethnic group, all persons of working age, 1988–90

	Column percentages										
	All origins	White	Total ethnic minority	Afro-Caribbean	African Asian	Indian	Pakistani	Bangla-deshi	Chinese	African	Other/Mixed
All Persons (16–59/64)											
GCE 'A' level/equivalent or higher	38	38	31	35	34	31	14	10	33	50	41
of which: Degree/equivalent	8	8	9	3	13	12	4	6	13	14	16
Higher education below degree level	6	6	6	8	4	4	1	1	10	13	7
GCE 'A' level/equivalent	24	24	16	24	17	14	9	4	11	24	18
of which: BTEC(general)/ONC/OND	2	2	2	3	3	2	1	0	1	6	3
City & Guilds	9	9	5	10	4	3	2	0	1	7	5
GCE 'A' level or equivalent	6	6	6	5	7	6	4	2	6	8	8
Trade apprenticeship	7	7	3	6	3	2	1	1	2	3	3
GCE 'O' level/equivalent	17	17	13	16	17	11	8	8	9	19	15
CSE (not grade 1)	5	5	5	9	5	4	3	4	1	2	4
Other	7	7	11	5	14	12	11	10	10	11	16
None	32	32	38	33	29	39	60	68	44	17	23
(Never received any education)	0	0	6	1	1	6	18	15	7	2	1
Not stated/not known	1	1	2	2	2	3	3	1	2	2	1

(*Source*: Jones, T. (1993) *Britain's Ethnic Minorities*, Policy Studies Institute, London.)

African Asians, 35 per cent of Afro-Caribbeans and 50 per cent of Africans had 'A' level/equivalent qualifications or higher. The gap between Afro-Caribbeans and whites was much smaller than that found in the *Swann Report* but Pakistanis and Bangladeshis were found to be much less well qualified than the white population.

We will now examine attempts to explain differences in educational attainment between ethnic groups.

■ Innate ability and attainment

As in the case of class and gender, some commentators have attributed differences in levels of achievement to IQ. Arthur Jensen and Hans Eysenck have both argued that blacks have genetically inherited levels of intelligence which are lower than those of whites. In America a large body of statistical evidence indicates that on average blacks score some 10 to 15 points below whites.

A strong case can be made for environmental factors accounting for this difference (for example, blacks are more likely to live in poverty than whites in America). However, Jensen and Eysenck point to evidence which suggests that differences in IQ remain when environments are equalized. When blacks and whites of similar income levels and occupational statuses are compared, blacks on average still have slightly lower test scores.

Jensen and Eysenck are mistaken in believing that this provides proof of blacks having inferior innate intelligence to whites. It is impossible to control all the possible environmental factors which could affect IQ scores. Bodmer suggests that over 200 years of prejudice and discrimination against blacks prevents an equalization of environment with whites.

Members of the Swann Committee examined the evidence in Britain. When they took into account environmental factors they found that differences in IQ scores between ethnic groups were sharply reduced. Indeed they argued that the differences were so insignificant that they could question the 'good sense or good will' of anyone who claimed that it mattered.

Cultural and material factors and attainment

A much more plausible explanation of ethnic differences in educational attainment is that they are due to various cultural factors which might influence educational attainment.

Language

One such factor is language. In some Asian households English is not the main language used. In some West Indian households 'creole' or 'patois' (variations upon conventional English) are spoken.

However, recent research evidence does not support the view that language is an important factor. A study by Geoffrey Driver and Roger Ballard found that by the age of 16, Asian children whose main home language was not English were at least as competent in English as their classmates. The *Swann Report* found that linguistic factors might hold back the progress of a few West Indian children, but for the vast majority they were of no significance.

Family life

A number of writers suggest that the nature of family life affects levels of attainment among ethnic minorities. From this point of view West Indians are held to have a family life which fails to encourage children to do well in education and in which there is an inadequate provision of toys, books and stimulation from parents. It has also been suggested that the West Indian population in Britain has a high proportion of one-parent families and large numbers of working women who leave their children without close parental supervision in the early years of their life.

In a study of West Indians in Bristol Ken Pryce described family life as 'turbulent', and he argued that 'West Indians lack a group identity and a tight, communal form of group life based on a sense of collective interdependence, and mutual obligation amongst kinsmen.'

In contrast to West Indian families, Asian families are widely believed to be more close-knit and supportive of their children's education. In a summary of his report, though with 'some caution', Lord Swann suggested that 'the Asian family structure, more tightly knit than either the white or the West Indian, may be responsible for their higher levels of achievement'.

Geoffrey Driver and Roger Ballard claim that the majority of the original South Asian immigrants to Britain came from rural areas and had little formal education. However, their research suggests that parents soon developed high aspirations for their children's education, and that parental attitudes may have contributed to their children's educational success. They say of Asian parents' attitudes to their children 'Not only have they encouraged them to work hard at school, but they have generally been prepared to give considerable support to their children's efforts to gain further qualifications.' Driver and Ballard conclude that membership of the Asian ethnic minority is a 'positive resource' which helps rather than hinders their education.

Despite the plausibility of the above arguments, some commentators are cautious about them. The

Swann Report was unable to comment in detail upon the effects of West Indian family life because, it argued, there was insufficient evidence to reach firm conclusions.

Furthermore, most researchers agree that the majority of West Indians are very concerned about their children's education. Ken Pryce found in Bristol that 'The majority of West Indian parents have great academic aspirations for their children.' In a study based upon a sample of the Handsworth area of Birmingham, John Rex and Sally Tomlinson did not find clear evidence that Asians were more interested in the education of their children than West Indians. From a sample of 400 white adults, 395 West Indians and 305 Asians, 89.1 per cent of the white parents, 79 per cent of the West Indians and 69.4 per cent of the Asians had made a recent visit to their child's or children's school.

Apart from the uncertainties over the precise nature of ethnic minority family life and its effects, the cultural arguments may also be criticized for ignoring other factors affecting educational attainment, particularly material factors and the workings of the education system itself.

Social class and attainment

As we saw in earlier sections, class appears to be related to educational achievement, with members of lower social classes gaining fewer qualifications and leaving the education system earlier than higher classes. Poor educational performances by ethnic minorities could be at least in part a result of their social class rather than their ethnicity.

The Swann Committee investigated this question and found that low average levels of achievement by West Indian children were influenced considerably by 'socio-economic factors'. The Committee claimed that when these factors were taken into account, the degree of underachievement by West Indian children was reduced by 'around 50 per cent and very possibly more'.

Some support for these conclusions is provided by Trevor Jones's analysis of the *Labour Force Survey*. He found that class makes a significant difference to the likelihood of staying on in education after 16. For example, 47 per cent of ethnic minority children from unskilled or semi-skilled manual backgrounds aged 16–19 were in full-time education in 1988–90 compared to 69 per cent of those from professional, managerial or employer backgrounds. The high concentrations of ethnic

minorities in low social classes could therefore affect their staying on rates.

Although class certainly accounts for some of the inequality in education between ethnic groups, it may not account for it all. The *Swann Report* and many other commentaries have suggested that racism may also be an important cause of the inequality.

■ Racism and the education system

The final area in which explanations for the differential levels of educational achievement between ethnic groups have been sought is the education system itself.

The Swann Report

The *Swann Report* certainly attached some importance to the role of the education system in explaining underachievement. It accepted that only a small minority of teachers were consciously racist, but thought there was a good deal of 'unintentional' racism. Teachers, and the books and other materials they used, sometimes supported a negative image of ethnic minorities.

Bernard Coard – racism and underachievement

Perhaps the strongest attack on the British education system's treatment of ethnic minorities has been advanced by Bernard Coard. He claims that the British education system actually makes black children become educationally subnormal by making them feel 'inferior in every way'. He says of the black child:

In addition to being told he is dirty and ugly and 'sexually unreliable' he is told by a variety of means that he is intellectually inferior. When he prepares to leave school, and even before, he is made to realize that he and 'his kind' are only fit for manual, menial jobs.

Coard goes on to explain some of the ways in which this takes place.

1 West Indian children are told that their way of speaking is second rate and unacceptable, the implication being that they themselves are second rate as human beings.

2 The word 'white' is associated with good; the word 'black' with evil. Coard gives an example of a children's book in which the 'white unicorn' and the 'white boys' are able to repel an attack by the violent and evil 'black pirates'.

3 The content of the education that children receive tends to ignore black people. Reading books often contain only white people, and when blacks do feature they are normally shown in subservient social roles such as servants. Coard claims that the people whose lives are studied and acclaimed (the heroes and figures from history and the present day) are white. Black culture, music and art are all conspicuous by their absence from the curriculum.

4 The attitudes to race conveyed in the classroom are reinforced by the pupils outside it. In playground arguments white children may describe West Indian children as 'black bastards'.

Coard believes that these experiences have important consequences for the child. He believes that black children develop an 'inferiority complex', a 'low self-image', and 'low expectations in life'. Teachers expect black children to fail and this produces a self-fulfilling prophecy in which they live 'up' to the expectations once they have been labelled. Not only are black children placed in lower streams and bands and in schools for the educationally subnormal, they themselves expect to fail, and as a result they do so. (For a full description of labelling and interactionist approaches to education see pp. 761–8.)

Coard's views on the British education system have caused considerable controversy. They have been both supported and criticized by other writers. Coard's analysis was based upon impressionistic evidence and personal experience, but his argument that teachers hold stereotypical views of ethnic minorities has been supported by the research of Elaine Brittan. Based upon a postal questionnaire using a sample of 510 teachers in primary and secondary schools in Britain, Brittan found that two-thirds of teachers perceived West Indian children as having low ability and being a disciplinary problem.

More direct evidence that teachers may consciously or unconsciously discriminate against ethnic minorities is provided by a detailed study of primary schools which we will now examine.

Cecile Wright – racism in multiracial primary schools

In 1988–9 Cecile Wright conducted an ethnographic study of four multiracial inner-city primary schools. The study involved classroom observation of a total of 970 pupils and 57 staff, observation outside the classroom, informal interviews with all the observed teachers some support staff and the four headteachers, interviews with the parent or parents of 38 children, and an examination of test results in three of the schools.

Wright found that 'the vast majority of the staff . . . seemed genuinely committed to ideals of equality of educational opportunity'. However, despite these ideals there was considerable discrimination in the classroom.

Asians in primary schools

In nursery units Asian children were largely excluded from group discussions because teachers assumed they would have a poor command of English. When they did involve the Asian pupils the teachers tended to speak to them in simplistic, childish language.

In general, in all classes 'Asian girls seemed invisible to the teachers.' They received less attention than other pupils and teachers sometimes expressed 'open disapproval of their customs and traditions'. For example, they disapproved when Asian girls tried to maintain some privacy when they had to get changed in the classroom for PE. Another example of insensitivity was when one teacher was handing out letters for pupils to take to their parents so they could give permission for their children to go on a school trip. The teacher said to the Asian girls 'I suppose we'll have problems with you girls. Is it worth me giving you a letter, because your parents don't allow you to be away from home overnight?'

Wright concluded that such comments from teachers made Asian pupils increasingly isolated from other pupils who picked up on teachers' comments and became hostile to the Asians. It led to the Asian pupils themselves being ambivalent towards the schools. For example, when Asian culture and celebrations were introduced into the school curriculum Asian pupils 'expressed some pride' in having their culture acknowledged but they were also 'concerned that this often exacerbated the teasing, ridicule and harassment which they felt they received daily, particularly from the white children'.

Afro-Caribbeans in primary schools

Despite the hostility of teachers towards Asian cultural traditions and their assumptions that Asians would have poor language skills, teachers did expect them to have some academic success. The same was not true of Afro-Caribbean children. For these children there were 'expectations of bad behaviour, along with disapproval, punishment and teacher insensitivity to the experience of racism'. In one class, for example, an Afro-Caribbean pupil called Marcus was frequently criticized for shouting out answers to questions whereas white pupils engaging in the same behaviour were not.

Generally, 'Afro-Caribbean boys received a disproportionate amount of teacher's negative attentions.' Compared to white boys whose behaviour was the same, they were more likely to be sent out of class, sent to see the headteacher or have privileges withdrawn. Afro-Caribbean Rastafarian children 'were seen by some teachers as a particular threat to classroom management' and were treated even more harshly.

Conclusion

All the schools made attempts to take account of the multicultural nature of their intake in what they taught. However they often failed to achieve their objectives in doing so. Teachers would mispronounce words or names relating to ethnic minorities, causing white children to laugh and black children to be embarrassed. Wright comments that 'This situation unintentionally served to make topics or areas of knowledge associated with ethnic minority values and culture appear exotic, novel, unimportant, esoteric or difficult.'

The problems of the ethnic minority children in the primary schools were further exacerbated by racism from other children. White children often refused to play with Asian children 'and frequently subjected them to threatening behaviour, name calling and hitting'. Both Asians and Afro-Caribbean children sometimes had to suffer 'intimidation, rejection and the occasional physical assault'.

Wright concludes that 'some black children are relatively disadvantaged' in primary schools. She argues that the earliest years of education provide 'the foundations of emotional, intellectual and social development' so that these early disadvantages might well hold back the children in later stages of their education.

Racism reconsidered

The emphasis upon the faults of the education system reflected in the above pieces of research should be treated with some caution.

1 First, teachers do not necessarily behave in the classroom in ways which reflect the negative stereotypes of ethnic minorities that they might hold. In a study of an inner-city secondary modern school Martin Hammersley found that racist comments in the staffroom did not lead to racism in the classroom. He found no evidence in the classes he observed of explicit discrimination, nor of 'covert' discrimination, though he accepted that covert discrimination was more difficult to identify.

2 Second, it certainly cannot be assumed that all teachers are racist. In a review of research into this area Monica J. Taylor admits that some teachers have negative views of West Indians, but she says 'it would also appear that many teachers are sensitively and actively concerned to evolve a consistent and fair policy towards the treatment of their black pupils'.

3 Third, it has been questioned whether black pupils have a low self-image which could contribute to their educational failure. Maureen Stone conducted a survey of a sample of 264 West Indian children aged 10–15 in Greater London. Using observation and interviews she found no evidence that West Indian children had a low self-concept or lacked self-esteem. Many of the pupils in her study were hostile to teachers and believed that teachers discriminated against them. However, since this did not appear to prevent the West Indian children from maintaining a positive image of themselves, it could not have produced a self-fulfilling prophecy that resulted in low levels of achievement. The *Swann*

Report also examined the evidence in this area and concluded that low self-esteem among ethnic minorities was not widespread.

As we saw in an earlier section (see p. 764), some sociologists believe that labelling theories of educational success or failure are too deterministic. Labelling theory seems to give those labelled little choice as to how they respond to labels: if they are defined as failures they will fail. The research of Stone and the findings of Lord Swann both indicate that labels might not be accepted by those who are labelled. Some sociologists therefore emphasize the positive and active part that pupils themselves play in determining how they react to the educational system.

The studies we will examine next place emphasis on the variety of ways in which ethnic minorities respond to racism in the education system.

Mairtin Mac an Ghaill – ethnic minorities in the sixth form

Mairtin Mac an Ghaill conducted an ethnographic study of twenty-five Afro-Caribbean and Asian students studying 'A' levels in a sixth form college in a Midlands city from 1986 to 1988. He used observation and carried out interviews with the students, their parents, their teachers and with representatives of the black community in the area.

To different degrees all the students 'spoke of the pervasiveness of white racism in relation to, *inter alia*, British immigration laws, the housing and labour markets, welfare institutions, policing and media presentation'. However, they disagreed over the extent of racism within education with some arguing that 'they experienced little personal racial antagonism' and others believing 'their schools, as part of the wider society, were seen as significant institutions in reproducing racial exclusiveness'.

Their beliefs about the extent of racism, though, did not directly determine their attitudes to education and their levels of academic success. Those who believed they were labelled as likely failures and who felt they were the victims of most racism were not necessarily those who had the most negative attitudes to education and nor those who put least effort into their academic work. The way that students 'perceived and responded to schooling' varied considerably and was influenced by the ethnic group to which they belonged, their gender,

and the class composition of their former secondary schools.

Schooling and class

Some of the students had been to predominantly working-class inner-city schools, some to more suburban schools and one to a private school. Eight females and four males went to single-sex schools. These varying experiences of schooling had affected the attitudes of individual students to the education system. The girl who went to a private school hated it and saw the other girls there as racist snobs. However, she reacted against this situation. She said 'The place could have made me fail but I was determined to prove them wrong about black people.'

Many of those who went to the inner-city schools identified an anti-academic culture at the schools and linked this with high rates of unemployment in the area. One Asian male, for example, said that teachers treated them as a problem but without realizing that 'they are one of the main causes of our problems'. Teachers did not expect them to do well but this student believed that 'It's just as bad for the white kids in many ways.'

Some of the girls thought they benefited from going to single-sex suburban schools. Although there was some racism, the environment was more academic and girls had greater chances of success in science subjects since there were no boys to dominate lessons.

Most pupils saw their parents as a major reason for their success in education. Mac an Ghaill says 'The students explicitly identified with their parents, seeing them as their main support and source of inspiration.' This contradicts the claims of some sociologists that parental culture holds some members of ethnic minorities back in the education system. However, a few of the girls did believe that their gender was a handicap at home. They were expected to do much more domestic work than their brothers, leaving them less time for their studies.

Gender and ethnicity

Gender also affected their experiences at school. Some of the students felt that Afro-Caribbean boys were treated particularly badly. Teachers saw them as a threat and disciplined them more than other groups. One Afro-Caribbean boy said:

The teachers treated black boys much worse than Asians and whites. Like, if we were standing together, they would break us up, saying gangs were bad. But they didn't seem to feel threatened in the same way with Asian and white boys.

Some students felt that teachers saw Asian girls as having more academic potential than Afro-Caribbean girls. An Afro-Caribbean student called 'Deborah' claimed 'There's no way that a black girl would be encouraged to do the good subjects. It was music and sport for us.'

Survival strategies

All the ethnic minority students experienced problems in the education system, but they experienced them differently depending on their gender and their ethnic group. Nevertheless, all of these students had enjoyed some success. They had done so through adopting a variety of survival strategies.

Some of the girls had banded together in their schools and used 'resistance within accommodation'. They would help each other out with academic work and would try to provide teachers with work which would get them good marks. However, they were less willing to conform to school rules relating to dress, appearance and behaviour in class.

Some of the other ethnic minority pupils were less hostile to their schools and tried to become friendly with specific teachers. They tried to avoid other teachers, who were racist, to prevent conflict. As one Asian student said 'You keep your head down. What choice have you? My mates knew who the racist teachers were and kept out of their way.'

Although only a small-scale study, Mac an Ghaill's research shows the importance of seeing how class, gender and ethnicity interact within the school system. He argues that 'we need to move beyond mono-causal explanations and direct our research to the multifaceted dimensions of a class-based school system that is racially and gender structured'.

This research also shows that negative labelling does not necessarily lead to academic failure amongst ethnic minority students. Although such labelling creates extra barriers, some students are able to overcome these barriers and 'In so doing, they are rejecting the model of white society presented by teachers and are resisting incorporation into white cultural identities.'

Conclusion

The variety of explanations examined above are not necessarily mutually exclusive. It is probable that a number of factors work together in producing the lower levels of achievement found in some ethnic minority groups. The *Swann Report* concluded that racial discrimination inside and outside school, along with social deprivation, were probably the main factors. Although the *Swann Report* attached little importance to cultural factors, it seems possible that they play some part in explaining differences in levels of achievement between ethnic minorities, as well as between ethnic minorities and the rest of the population.

Given the highly controversial nature of this issue it is not surprising that such varied explanations exist, and that a definitive answer to the question of why some ethnic minorities do poorly in education has not been reached.

■ The 'new' sociology of education – knowledge and power

In the previous sections on class, gender, ethnicity and educational attainment, we have advanced different explanations to account for variations in levels of achievement. Some of these explanations have been influenced by the **'new' sociology of education**, which is particularly concerned with what counts as valid and important knowledge.

Thus Pierre Bourdieu argued that the working class lacked the 'cultural capital' necessary to succeed in education; they lacked access to knowledge that was highly valued. In her study of a London school, Nell Keddie tried to establish that streaming led to those in lower streams being denied access to the high-status knowledge which could bring them exam success. Dale Spender argued that the curriculum of the British education system neglected issues which were of concern to women, and Bernard Coard advanced similar claims in relation to children of West Indian origin.

▉ Knowledge and power

In Britain, Michael F.D. Young and his associates have related **knowledge** to the overall distribution of power in society. They argue that those in positions of power will attempt to define what is taken as knowledge. They will tend to define their own knowledge as superior, to institutionalize it in educational establishments, and to measure educational attainment in terms of it. This is not because 'some occupations "need" recruits with knowledge defined and assessed in this way'. Rather it is to maintain the established order and to ensure that power and privilege remain within the same social groups.

Young has provided a promising framework but, as Karabel and Halsey note, he has yet to apply it to a detailed analysis of the relationship between knowledge and power.

Criticisms

Young and his associates have spent considerable time discussing the philosophical question of the nature of knowledge. They have implied that there is no objective way of evaluating knowledge, of assessing whether or not one form of knowledge is superior to another. If any knowledge is regarded as superior, it is simply because those with power have defined it as such and imposed their definition on others. It therefore follows that *all* knowledge is equally valid.

This view is known as **cultural relativism**. Carried to its extreme, it poses serious problems. As Gerald Bernbaum notes in his criticism of Young 'It is impossible to say what "being wrong" might constitute.' Thus from the standpoint of cultural relativism, Young's own views are no more valid than any other views.

Whatever the weaknesses of the views of Young and his associates, the content of the curriculum has become a central issue in education in contemporary Britain. In 1988 the British Government introduced a National Curriculum which allowed the Government to dictate much of the curriculum content of schooling. We will discuss the National Curriculum in detail later in this chapter (see p. 797 and 801–4).

▉ Education, opportunity and inequality

In this section we examine a number of questions that were raised earlier in the chapter but have yet to be considered in detail.

1 What, if any, changes have occurred in the degree of inequality of educational opportunity?

2 What is the relationship between educational attainment and occupational status and income?

3 What effect has the expansion of educational systems had on the degree of social inequality?

We will discuss these issues in terms of data from Britain and America.

▉ Inequality of educational opportunity

Many researchers in the field of education, particularly during the 1950s and 1960s, assumed that

inequality of educational opportunity was decreasing and would continue to decrease. In Britain the **1944 Education Act** established a tripartite system of secondary education for all. Since that date there has been a rapid expansion of higher education coupled with an increased availability of maintenance grants to provide support for those in need. It was assumed that this would provide greater opportunity of access to all levels of the educational system and as a result the level of attainment of working-class students would increase.

Halsey, Heath and Ridge – selection and opportunity

A study by A.H. Halsey, A.F. Heath and J.M. Ridge compared the educational careers of four generations of British pupils using data from the

Table 12.10 Percentages attending selective schools, i.e. grammar and technical schools

Class	Date of birth			
	1913–22	1923–32	1933–42	1943–52
Service class	69.7	76.7	79.3	66.4
Intermediate class	34.9	44.0	43.3	37.1
Working class	20.2	26.1	27.1	21.6
All	29.6	37.0	38.8	34.8

(*Source*: Halsey, A.H., Heath, A.F. and Ridge, J.M. (1980) *Origins and Destinations,* Clarendon Press, Oxford. p. 63)

Table 12.11 Percentage staying in education until the age of 16 or over

Class	Date of birth			
	1913–22	1923–32	1933–42	1943–52
Service class	52.4	61.0	77.3	78.6
Intermediate class	16.1	23.9	34.6	48.5
Working class	9.2	9.6	19.8	31.6

(*Source*: Halsey, A.H., Heath, A.F. and Ridge, J.M. (1980) *Origins and Destinations,* Clarendon Press, Oxford, p. 136.)

Oxford Mobility Study. (For more details of this study see pp. 100–2.) The results are shown in Table 12.10.

Halsey *et al.* found that all classes benefited from an expansion of grammar school places, and all classes suffered as the percentage of the population who attended declined for those who were born in the years 1943–52. However, the research found very little narrowing of the gap between the highest and lowest classes.

The authors concluded 'there are few grounds for supposing that the selection procedures became any more meritocratic in the post-war period'. They argued that class bias in the way that children were selected for secondary schools simply replaced the class bias that resulted from fee-paying before the 1944 Education Act which established the tripartite system.

Length of stay in selective schools

As well as examining class and changes in attendance at selective schools, Halsey *et al.* also looked at length of stay in education and access to university places. All their sample passed through the education system before the raising of the school-leaving age to 16, so they examined how many stayed on until that age. Here they did find some reduction in class inequalities, as Table 12.11 shows.

The rate of attendance for the working and intermediate classes more than trebled, while for the service class it increased by 50 per cent. However, Halsey *et al.* found no reduction in inequalities when examining who stayed on to 18 or over. As Table 12.12 shows, the rates more than doubled for all social classes, but it was the service and intermediate classes who gained most, and the working class least.

Halsey *et al.* suggest that **credentialization** has taken place whereby the basic levels of education required to improve the chances of getting a well-paid job have gradually increased. The working class caught up to some extent in terms of attendance rates at 16, but few stayed on long enough to gain sufficient qualifications to be upwardly socially mobile.

University entrance

The final area that Halsey *et al.* examined was class and university entrance. Once again they found evidence of increased opportunities for all classes because of the expansion of university places. Yet, as Table 12.13 shows, there was again little difference in the rates at which different classes were able to take advantage of these opportunities. Furthermore, as Halsey *et al.* point out, in absolute terms the service class gained much more than the working class. For both groups attendance at university more than trebled, but for the service class that represented an absolute increase of 19.2 per cent, for the working class a mere 2.2 per cent.

Overall then, Halsey *et al.* found only one area in which the relative chances of the highest and lowest classes were becoming more meritocratic (rates of attendance at 16 or over) and even that might have been rendered insignificant by credentialization. In other respects, there was no evidence of an increasingly meritocratic society.

Halsey *et al.*'s figures should, though, be viewed with some caution. They are based entirely on a male sample and the inclusion of female pupils might have made a significant difference to the findings. Furthermore, they are somewhat dated

Table 12.12   Percentage staying in education until 18 or over

Class	Date of birth			
	1913–22	1923–32	1933–42	1943–52
Service class	15.7	20.0	32.2	38.2
Intermediate class	6.1	6.2	5.9	14.4
Working class	3.1	2.3	3.8	6.4

(*Source*: Halsey, A.H., Heath, A.F. and Ridge, J.M. (1980) *Origins and Destinations,* Clarendon Press, Oxford, p. 140.)

Table 12.13   Attendance at university

Class	Date of birth			
	1913–22	1923–32	1933–42	1943–52
Service class	7.2	15.9	23.7	26.4
Intermediate class	1.9	4.0	4.1	8.0
Working class	0.9	1.2	2.3	3.1

(*Source*: Halsey, A.H., Heath, A.F. and Ridge, J.M. (1980) *Origins and Destinations,* Clarendon Press, Oxford, p. 188.)

and do not show the effects of more recent changes.

General Household Survey findings

Data from the British Government's *General Household Survey* can be used to examine recent changes in the relationship between education, class and inequality. Table 12.14 shows the highest qualification achieved by different age groups and by socio-economic group, the Government's way of defining class. By comparing age groups it is possible to identify general trends in the relationship between class and qualifications.

Table 12.14 suggests that amongst men there has not been any significant reduction in class inequalities in terms of gaining higher education qualifications.

1 The youngest group (25–29) was more likely to have higher education qualifications than the oldest age group (50–59) , but the sons of professional fathers had benefited from this increase more than the sons of unskilled manual fathers.

2 Amongst those from professional backgrounds the percentage obtaining degrees had increased from 51

per cent in the older age group to 61 per cent in the younger age group.

3 Amongst those from unskilled manual backgrounds the increase had been less rapid, rising from 9 per cent of the older members of the sample to 10 per cent of the younger members.

4 Younger men whose fathers had semi-skilled manual jobs or who were personal service workers were no more likely to have obtained higher education qualifications than older men from the same background.

5 The percentage of men getting some sort of qualification was greater in younger age groups than older ones in all social classes. For men from the lowest class, unskilled manual, it had increased from 35 to 70 per cent, whereas amongst men from professional backgrounds it had increased from 78 to 97 per cent. Thus the rate of increase was higher in the lowest social class.

Amongst men then, there may have been some reduction in class inequalities in achievement at lower levels in the education system, but if anything inequalities in higher education have increased.

Amongst women there is some evidence of reduced inequalities in educational attainment between classes both in terms of getting more advanced qualifications and in terms of getting any qualification at all. However, big differences remain. For example, even amongst the youngest age group, women from a professional background are still nearly six times more likely than those from an unskilled manual background to have obtained higher education qualifications.

Gender and opportunity

There are greater grounds for optimism when examining equality of opportunity in terms of gender and ethnicity. Government figures suggest that girls have caught up or even overtaken boys in many areas of schooling. For example, as Figure 12.1 showed, girls are now more likely than boys to pass one or more 'A' levels and have remained more likely than boys to have five or more GCSEs at grade C or above as their highest qualification when leaving school (see p. 769). Table 12.6 showed that the gap between males and females in terms of obtaining places in higher education

Table 12.14 Highest qualification level attained by age, sex and father's socio-economic group

Persons aged 25–59 not in full-time education   *Great Britain: 1990 and 1991 combined*

Age and highest qualification level attained[1]	Professional	Employers and managers	Intermediate non-manual	Junior non-manual	Skilled manual and own account non-professional	Semi-skilled manual and personal service	Unskilled manual	Total
				Father's socio-econimic group				
Men								
25–29 Higher education	61	35	42	32	18	12	10	26
Other qualifications	36	56	48	62	61	59	60	57
No qualifications	4	9	10	6	21	29	30	17
Base = 100%[2]	*109*	*341*	*111*	*79*	*689*	*180*	*70*	*1,579*
30–39 Higher education	54	38	44	32	22	14	7	27
Other qualifications	42	51	45	56	48	51	42	48
No qualifications	4	12	11	12	31	35	51	24
Base = 100%[2]	*188*	*613*	*181*	*118*	*1,172*	*405*	*151*	*2,828*
40–49 Higher education	57	40	48	38	23	16	14	28
Other qualifications	36	42	41	33	39	33	30	38
No qualifications	7	18	11	30	38	51	57	34
Base = 100%[2]	*111*	*535*	*146*	*138*	*1,256*	*420*	*155*	*2,761*
50–59 Higher education	51	31	41	41	15	12	9	20
Other qualifications	27	37	35	30	36	33	26	35
No qualifications	22	32	25	28	49	54	65	45
Base = 100%[2]	*59*	*412*	*81*	*102*	*1,069*	*377*	*176*	*2,276*
25–59 Higher education	56	36	44	36	20	145	10	25
Other qualifications	37	46	43	44	44	42	36	43
No qualifications	7	17	13	20	36	44	54	31
Base = 100%[2]	*467*	*1,901*	*519*	*437*	*4,186*	*1,382*	*552*	*9,444*
Women								
25–29 Higher education	47	26	32	18	13	6	8	18
Other qualifications	51	65	58	75	64	64	44	63
No qualifications	2	9	10	8	23	29	49	19
Base = 100%[2]	*107*	*381*	*121*	*79*	*710*	*217*	*78*	*1,693*
30–39 Higher education	53	29	36	22	14	11	7	20
Other qualifications	41	59	56	60	51	46	39	52
No qualifications	6	12	9	18	35	44	54	28
Base = 100%[2]	*170*	*661*	*198*	*136*	*1,375*	*428*	*177*	*3,145*
40–49 Higher education	41	28	32	27	10	10	6	17
Other qualifications	52	49	48	39	39	30	23	39
No qualifications	7	23	21	34	51	60	71	44
Base = 100%[2]	*124*	*582*	*189*	*152*	*1,284*	*491*	*184*	*3,006*
50–59 Higher education	42	24	32	22	8	5	5	13
Other qualifications	45	40	46	36	28	23	14	30
No qualifications	13	36	22	42	64	72	81	57
Base = 100%[2]	*93*	*438*	*93*	*104*	*1,063*	*413*	*177*	*2,381*
25–59 Higher education	47	27	33	23	11	8	6	17
Other qualifications	47	53	52	51	44	37	28	45
No qualifications	7	20	15	27	45	54	66	38
Base = 100%[2]	*494*	*2,062*	*601*	*471*	*4,432*	*1,549*	*616*	*10,225*

1 'Higher education' = qualifications above GCE 'A' level standard 'other qualifications' = qualifications at or below GCE 'A' level standard.

2 Excludes those who never went to school.

(*Source*: (1993) *General Household Survey 1990–91*, London: HMSO, p. 208.)

Table 12.15   Highest qualification by ethnic group, 45–59/64 age group, 1988–90

	All origins	White	Total ethnic minority	Afro-Caribbean	African Asian	Indian	Pakistani	Bangla-deshi	Chinese	African	Other/Mixed
All persons (45–59/64)											
GCE 'A' level/equivalent or higher	33	33	27	30	25	27	13	11	20	55	35
of which: Degree/equivalent	7	7	9	2	8	14	5	9	5	15	15
Higher education below degree level	6	6	6	10	3	4	1	1	5	16	6
GCE 'A' level/equivalent	20	20	13	18	15	9	6	2	10	24	14
of which: BTEC(general)/ONC/OND	1	1	1	0	0	1	0	0	2	4	1
City & Guilds	5	6	3	5	1	2	1	0	0	8	3
GCE 'A' level or equivalent	3	3	4	2	9	5	4	1	4	8	4
Trade apprenticeship	10	11	6	12	5	2	2	1	4	4	6
GCE 'O' level/equivalent	8	8	5	3	9	4	6	3	6	12	8
CSE (not grade 1)	0	0	0	0	0	1	1	0	0	0	0
Other	11	11	13	7	15	15	16	8	13	9	18
None	47	46	52	57	47	50	61	77	58	21	37
(Never received any education)	1	0	11	2	3	14	31	28	13	4	3
Not stated/not known	1	1	3	3	2	3	3	1	3	3	2

(*Source*: Jones, T. (1993) *Britain's Ethnic Minorities*, Policy Studies Institute, London.)

decreased considerably between 1970–1 and 1991–2, although males continued to have an advantage (see p. 770).

Ethnicity and opportunity

Changes in the relative success of ethnic groups have also taken place. In terms of higher-level qualifications there seems to have been little change in the relative performances of whites and ethnic minorities as a whole. Tables 12.15 and 12.16 are taken from Trevor Jones's study based on the *Labour Force Survey*. They show that amongst 45–59/64 year olds, 33 per cent of whites and 27 per cent of ethnic minorities had an 'A' level qualification, its equivalent or higher, in 1988–90. Amongst 24–44 year olds, 43 per cent of whites had this level of qualification and the proportion amongst ethnic minorities had also increased, reaching 34 per cent.

These overall figures disguise important variations between particular ethnic minority groups. The gap between whites and Afro-Caribbeans and whites and African Asians was found to be considerably smaller in the younger age group than the older one, but Bangladeshis and Pakistanis showed comparatively little progress.

Jones found more evidence of a decline in ethnic differences in attainment amongst those under 24. In this age group the higher proportions of ethnic minorities staying on in education compared to whites was leading to a narrowing of the difference between the qualifications of ethnic minorities and whites. Jones concludes:

young people are not only better qualified than their elders, but . . . the disparity between white and minority groups appears to be less in the younger age groups. This is particularly apparent in the case of women. It is also clear that a gap is opening up within the minority population, between relatively well-qualified African Asians and Indians, and poorly-qualified Pakistanis and Bangladeshis.

■ Education, occupational status and income

The functionalist view of the relationship between education and occupation argues that educational attainment in advanced industrial societies is increasingly linked to occupational status. There is a steady move from ascribed to achieved status and education plays an important part in this process. Educational qualifications increasingly form the basis for the allocation of individuals to occupational statuses. Thus, there is a 'tightening bond' between education and occupation.

Table 12.16   Highest qualification by ethnic group, 25–44 age group, 1988–90

	All origins	White	Total ethnic minority	Afro-Caribbean	African Asian	Indian	Pakistani	Bangla-deshi	Chinese	African	Other/Mixed
All persons 25-44											
GCE 'A' level/equivalent or higher	43	43	34	41	34	31	14	12	35	51	47
of which: Degree/equivalent	11	11	12	5	14	14	5	6	15	16	19
Higher education below degree level	7	7	7	10	5	5	2	1	11	14	8
GCE 'A' level/equivalent	25	26	16	26	15	12	7	5	9	21	20
of which: BTEC(general)/ONC/OND	2	2	2	3	2	1	1	0	1	4	2
City & Guilds	11	11	5	12	4	3	2	1	1	6	6
GCE 'A' level or equivalent	6	6	6	6	6	6	3	3	5	9	8
Trade apprenticeship	6	6	3	5	3	2	1	1	2	2	3
GCE 'O' level/equivalent	17	18	13	18	19	11	5	5	7	18	12
CSE (not grade 1)	5	5	4	10	3	4	2	1	2	1	3
Other	7	6	12	6	15	12	12	10	10	13	18
None	27	27	35	23	27	39	65	71	44	15	20
(Never received any education)	0	0	4	0	1	3	16	15	6	2	1
Not stated/not known	1	1	2	2	2	3	2	1	2	1	1

(*Source*: Jones, T. (1993) *Britain's Ethnic Minorities*, Policy Studies Institute, London.)

Education and occupation in Britain

Using data from the Oxford Mobility Study, A.H. Halsey found some support for this view. He divided the sample into two age groups: those aged from 40 to 59 and those aged from 25 to 39 in 1972. Comparing the two groups, Halsey found that the direct effect of education on an individual's first job is high and rising (the coefficient of correlation for the first group is 0.468, for the second 0.522), and the direct effect of education on the individual's present job is also rising (from 0.325 to 0.345).

Halsey concluded that occupational status was increasingly dependent on educational attainment but he also found that the effect of the father's occupational status upon the son's educational attainment was also rising. He wrote 'The direct effect of the class hierarchy of families on educational opportunity and certification has *risen* since the war.' Thus social background had a greater effect on education attainment at the very time when the bonds between education and occupation were tightening.

This led Halsey to conclude that 'education is increasingly the mediator of the transmission of status between generations'. Privilege was passed on more and more from father to son via the educational system. From this viewpoint education can be seen as a mechanism for the maintenance of

privilege rather than a means for role allocation based on meritocratic principles.

Education and social justice in Britain

Using data from the Essex Class Project (described on p. 68) which was conducted in the 1980s, Gordon Marshall and Adam Swift have examined the relationship between education, class and social justice in modern Britain. In particular they examined whether class had an effect on occupational status independent of educational achievement.

Marshall and Swift divided their sample into three groups according to educational attainment. These groups consisted of those with low qualifications (below GCSE grade C level), those with medium-level qualifications (GCSE grades C or above, or 'A' level or equivalent), and those with high-level qualifications (qualifications higher than 'A' level). (For a full definition see notes to Table 12.17.) They used a three class categorization system, based on John Goldthorpe's class scale, dividing the sample into service class (S on Table 12.17), intermediate class (I) and working class (W).

Table 12.17 shows that even when educational qualifications are taken into account, class background has a strong independent effect on the

Table 12.17 Intergenerational mobility and educational attainment

Educational			Male Destinations				Female Destinations				All Destinations		
			S	I	W		S	I	W		S	I	W
High	origins	S	92	3	5 100	(38)	78	22	0 100	(27)	86	11	3 100
		I	90	5	5 100	(40)	63	35	2 100	(49)	75	21	3 100
		W	91	9	0 100	(32)	57	39	4 100	(23)	76	22	2 100
Medium	origins	S	43	32	26 100	(47)	30	61	9 100	(23)	39	41	20 100
		I	31	41	29 100	(101)	22	63	16 100	(64)	27	49	24 100
		W	15	37	48 100	(110)	21	60	19 100	(78)	17	47	36 100
Low	origins	S	33	27	40 100	(15)	0	57	43 100	(7)	23	36	41 100
		I	13	33	54 100	(92)	13	37	50 100	(46)	13	34	53 100
		W	11	25	64 100	(157)	2	43	56 100	(108)	7	33	60 100

Key
S = Service class
I = Intermediate class
W = Working class

Low: holds no formal qualifications; CSE Grades 2–5; or job training (e.g. HGV driving licence) only.

Medium: holds CSE Grade 1; GCE 'O' or 'A' level or Scottish equivalents; Overseas School Leaving Certificate; ONC, OND, City & Guilds; HNC, HND, City & Guilds; RSA Clerical or commercial; or full apprenticeship qualification.

High: holds teacher training qualification; full nursing qualification; other technical or business qualification; professional qualification; degree or higher degree; or other vocational qualification equivalent to a degree.

(*Source*: Marshall, G. and Swift, A. (June 1993) 'Social class and social justice', *British Journal of Sociology*, p. 203.)

class destination of individuals. For example, 23 per cent of those from service-class backgrounds but with low levels of educational attainment still managed to end up in the service class despite their educational failure. Only 7 per cent of those with low educational qualifications from the working class ended up with service-class jobs. Marshall and Swift argue:

> If children from advantaged backgrounds suffer educational failure, their class position makes it likely that they will be able to call upon other resources, perhaps most importantly in the form of class-related social networks, which can protect them from the consequences.

British society cannot therefore be seen as meritocratic. While education influences the class position an individual may reach, class background is also very important. Marshall and Swift conclude that the only way to counteract class inequalities would be 'political intervention to ensure that the

procedures whereby individuals are allocated to occupations are strictly meritocratic'.

Education, occupation and income in the USA

In the USA, an important 1975 publication by Christopher Jencks and his associates entitled *Inequality: A Reassessment of the Effect of Family and Schooling in America*, attempted to assess, among other things, the relationship between educational attainment and occupational status and income.

Jencks re-analysed a large body of statistical data collected by sociologists and administrators. He found a fairly close relationship between occupational status and educational attainment claiming that 'education explains about 42 per cent of the variance in status'. However, he argued that to some degree this relationship is inevitable since education is a major determinant of occupational status. He writes 'Americans are impressed by people with a lot of schooling and they are deferential toward occupations that require extensive schooling.' However, Jencks did find what he regards as 'enormous status differences among people with the same amount of education'.

Jencks found a surprisingly weak relationship between educational attainment and income. He estimated that on average, the completion of high school adds between 10 to 12 per cent to an individual's income, and college education adds a further 4 to 7 per cent. However the rate of return is higher for white middle-class males and less for white working-class males, blacks and females. Jencks found that none of the expected factors were strongly related to income. He states:

> Neither family background, cognitive skill, educational attainment nor occupational status explains much of the variation in men's income. Indeed when we compare men who are identical in all respects, we find only 12 to 15 percent less inequality than among random individuals.

Jencks therefore concludes that educational attainment has relatively little effect on income.

Jencks's findings have produced a storm of protest, largely because they suggested that as an instrument of social change, education was relatively impotent. In particular, his methodology has been strongly criticized. Several critics have argued that Jencks's disillusionment with education as a means for producing greater equality strongly influenced his methods and the interpretation of his data. For example, James Coleman refers to his 'skilful but highly motivated use of statistics' (quoted in Karabel and Halsey 1977, p. 23). Thus, though Jencks's findings have not been disproved, they must be regarded with some caution.

■ Education and equality

If Jencks's findings are correct, they constitute a rejection of the social democratic view of the role and promise of education in society. Particularly during the 1960s, many social democrats believed that equalizing educational opportunity would reduce economic inequality. In particular, they argued, if the educational attainment of the poor and the working class in general improves relative to the rest of society, their bargaining

position in the market will show a corresponding improvement.

Education, productivity and equality

This view was supported by many economists. Lester C. Thurow summarizes their arguments as follows: increased educational attainment will increase an individual's skills, his or her productivity will therefore rise and with it income. It will also reduce the supply of low skill workers and increase the demand for their services, which will lead to an increase in their wages. The increased supply of highly skilled workers will tend to reduce their wages. The net result is that productivity rises, more money is made available for wages, and wage differentials decrease. Education at one and the same time increases output and reduces economic inequality in society.

In America, as Thurow shows clearly in an article entitled 'Education and economic equality', this has not happened. The rate of growth of productivity during the 1950s and 1960s was well behind the rate of growth in educational attainment. The rapid expansion of higher education and the flood of college graduates during these years appeared to have had little effect on economic growth.

Thurow also rejects the view that a reduction in inequality of educational opportunity will produce a reduction in economic inequality. Measured in terms of years of schooling, there has been a reduction in inequality of educational opportunity in the USA from 1950 to 1970. However from 1949 to 1969 inequality in the distribution of income increased. The statistics supporting Thurow's claim are shown in Table 12.18.

Thurow concludes that 'our reliance on education as the ultimate public policy for curing all problems, economic and social, is unwarranted at best and in all probability ineffective'.

Equality of opportunity and inequality

Jencks's disillusionment with the promise of education grew steadily during the 1960s as he observed the failure of the war on poverty which

Table 12.18   *a* Distribution of education among adult white males
           b Distribution of income among adult white males

a Percentage share of years of educational attainment		*b* Percentage share of total money income	
	1950	1970		1949	1969
Lowest fifth	8.6	10.7	Lowest fifth	3.2	2.6
Second fifth	16.4	16.4	Second fifth	10.9	9.4
Middle fifth	19.0	21.3	Middle fifth	17.5	16.7
Fourth fifth	24.9	22.3	Fourth fifth	23.7	25.0
Highest fifth	31.1	29.3	Highest fifth	44.8	46.3

(Source: Thurow, L.C. (1977), 'Education and economic inequality', in J. Karabel and A.H. Halsey (eds), *Power and Ideology in Education,* Oxford University Press, New York, p. 327.)

was spearheaded by a drive to improve the educational attainment of the poor. He rejected social democratic views on a number of counts. He argued that they put the cart before the horse: he echoed many of the views given in this chapter by maintaining that inequality of educational opportunity can only be reduced by first reducing inequality in society as a whole. He stated 'Equalizing opportunity is almost impossible without greatly reducing the absolute level of inequality.'

However Jencks's main contribution lies in his claim that educational attainment bears little relationship to income. If this is correct, then a reduction of inequality of educational opportunity will have little effect on income inequality. He argued that 'the evidence suggests that equalizing educational opportunity would do very little to make adults more equal'.

Jencks carried his argument one stage further by suggesting that even if everybody had the same educational qualifications, income, inequality would be little changed. He stated:

Giving everyone more credentials cannot provide everyone with access to the best paid occupations. It can only raise earnings if it makes people more productive within various occupations. There is little evidence that it will do this. If this argument is correct, equalizing everyone's educational attainment would have virtually no effect on income inequality.

Put simply, there are well-paid jobs and badly paid jobs. If everyone had the same educational qualifi-

cations, some would still end up in well-paid jobs and others in badly paid jobs.

Education as a marginal institution

Jencks thus rejected the view that reforms in the educational system could lead to significant changes in society as a whole. His main concern was inequality of income. He argued that a more equitable distribution of income required direct government intervention in the economic system rather than 'ingenious manipulations of marginal institutions like the schools'. Direct political action necessitated a commitment to the ideal of equality. Jencks concluded:

The first step towards redistributing income is not, then, devising ingenious machinery for taking money from the rich and giving it to the poor, but convincing large numbers of people that this is a desirable objective.

Thus Jencks saw changes in values rather than changes in the educational system as the route to the kind of society he wished to see.

By defining schools as 'marginal institutions' Jencks relegated them to the sidelines of any radical policy to change society. Karabel and Halsey reject this view arguing that Jencks ignored what actually goes on inside schools – how they legitimated success and failure, how they justified social stratification, how they legitimated inequality in society as a whole. Karabel and Halsey provide a timely warning in their criticism of Jencks:

Though it brilliantly demolished the peculiarly American myth that school reform can serve as a

---

substitute for more fundamental social change, 'Inequality' may unfortunately have replaced it with another equally destructive myth: that a viable strategy for social equality can afford to ignore the schools.

The new vocationalism – education in the 1980s and 1990s

The changing focus of educational policy

Equal opportunities in the 1980s and 1990s

In Britain from the middle of the 1970s governmental concern with equality and equality of opportunity was gradually replaced by other issues. Successive governments showed little interest in adopting policies that attempted to compensate for class inequalities. Interest in gender and ethnic inequalities remained strong and in many areas new policies were adopted to try to reduce these inequalities. However, these initiatives tended to be locally based: while many individual schools, colleges, higher education institutions and LEAs adopted equal opportunities policies which were particularly aimed at eliminating racism and sexism, governments paid less attention to developing policies concerned with these issues. Instead the main focus of national policy making shifted elsewhere and concentrated on the needs of industry and the economy.

The 'Great Debate'

Although Conservative Governments of the 1980s and 1990s introduced modifications to the education system which reflected the new priorities, the change in thinking began under the last Labour Government of the 1970s. In 1976 the Labour prime minister James Callaghan made a speech at Ruskin College calling for a 'Great Debate' on education. It was followed by a Green Paper (a government discussion document) on education. The paper argued:

It is vital to Britain's economic recovery and standard of living that the performance of the manufacturing industry is improved and that the whole range of government policies, including education, contribute as much as possible to improving industrial performance and thereby increasing the national wealth. (Quoted in Finn 1987, p. 106.)

In a period of rising unemployment and the apparent decline of Britain's economy, the concern was that education was failing to produce appropriately skilled and motivated young workers. Part of the social democratic view of education – that it should promote equality of opportunity – was deemed to be less important than the needs of industry. This emphasis, and the policies that followed from it, have become known as the **new vocationalism**.

Education and the New Right

Education and economic growth

Despite the fact that the 'Great Debate' was initiated by a Labour prime minister, it was in tune with some of the thinking of the New Right and the Conservative Governments after 1979. Although the latter rejected the **social engineering** implied in the idea that education could be used to make society more egalitarian, they did think that education could promote the social changes which they wanted to see. In particular the New Right argued that education should be largely concerned with promoting economic growth through concentrating on improving the skills of the workforce.

Some employers believed that education was failing to meet their needs, and the New Right believed that unemployment was rising partly because many school leavers were unemployable. However, the objectives were not to be achieved by 'throwing money at the problem', for, as Dan Finn puts it, the New Right saw a 'bloated public sector which was strangling the wealth-creating element of the economy'. Extra resources for education could only come from the profits of British industry and so reduce Britain's competitiveness.

In the first year of the Thatcher Government education expenditure was cut by 3.5 per cent and changes designed to overcome the supposed deficiencies of social democratic policies began to be made.

Competition, choice and standards

If the overall aim of New Right policies was to use education to promote economic growth, the mechanisms through which this was to be achieved were encouraging competition, increasing choice (particularly parental choice) and an emphasis on raising standards. At the same time the education system would be made more efficient, eliminating waste and saving the taxpayer money. These aims were made quite explicit in the handbook *Britain 1993*, published by HMSO. This described the aims of the Government's education reforms as:

– to raise standards at all levels of ability;
– to increase parental choice of schools and improve the partnership of parents and schools;
– to make further and higher education more widely accessible and more responsive to the needs of the economy;
and
– to achieve the best possible return from the resources invested in the education service. (Quoted in R.G. Burgess 'Education, an agenda for change' in Haralambos 1994, p. 71.)

An important part of the New Right's philosophy – and one which has exercised a strong influence on educational reforms – has been its hostility to state bureaucracies. New Right thinking generally holds that state-run institutions are inherently inefficient. They waste money because they do not

have to make a profit and they therefore have no interest in restricting their expenditure. The introduction of **market forces** through competition between institutions forces them to become more efficient.

For example, educational institutions have to compete to attract students or pupils. The ones that fail to attract the students lose funding. As a consequence they have to either raise their standards or they face the possibility of having to close. The greater the choice offered to parents as to which school their children attend, the greater the competition between schools. The greater the competition, the greater the incentive for schools to improve.

Stephen J. Ball quotes a New Right educationalist, Stuart Sexton, outlining these principles. Sexton was an adviser to the Conservative education ministers Mark Carlisle and Keith Joseph. Writing in his 1987 pamphlet *Our Schools – A Radical Policy* Sexton said:

To produce the quality and choice that we expect in education, to improve our schools, we need to change the way that we fund and manage them. Making the education service fully responsive to parental choice and student needs, with a direct financial relationship between provider and consumer, is the way to better standards, and a far better way than administrative tinkering and political exhortation. (Quoted in Ball 1990, p. 44.)

Testing and examining

One of the important mechanisms through which the New Right hoped to increase competition was through the increased use of testing and examining, and the publication of results. This was designed to provide information for parents to help them make informed choices about the school they chose for their children.

However, Conservative Governments of the 1980s and 1990s only supported the use of certain types of test. They generally opposed coursework and allowing pupils' teachers to assess their work. Instead they have favoured national, standardized tests and examinations. Conservative Governments supported the use of traditional unseen examination and test papers designed so that direct comparisons could be made between schools. To encourage greater competition Conservative Governments also introduced **league tables** detailing how successful a school had been in public examinations. This enabled the consumers of education (pupils, students and their parents) to take exam success rates into account when choosing schools or colleges.

Stephen Ball argues that in some respects the advocacy of standardized tests and examinations goes against New Right thinking. The New Right are generally 'against imposing uniformity on schools' and they 'value diversity'. However, in this case, most New Right educationalists thought that the advantages of being able to make direct comparisons between educational institutions outweighed the disadvantages of imposing a centralized state-run system of testing and examination.

Curriculum content, the New Right and traditionalism

Although the New Right and the Conservative Governments of the 1990s supported radical changes in the way education was organized and sought to introduce a more business-orientated curriculum, in other areas they supported the teaching of very traditional subjects. According to Stephen Ball they proposed the teaching of subjects such as Latin and Greek and opposed social science subjects, peace studies, and personal, social and health education. They were also hostile to multicultural education which encourages pupils to develop a knowledge of the culture of ethnic minorities. Similarly they were against the widespread teaching of ethnic minority languages (such as certain Asian languages) and instead emphasized the importance of European languages such as French, Italian, Spanish and German.

Again in this area there is some contradiction between New Right philosophy and the policies pursued. New Right thinking would suggest that there should be a free market in the choice of curriculum content by the consumers of education.

However, educational policies have also been influenced by philosophies other than those of the New Right, and by individuals who do not identify wholeheartedly with New Right thinking. In particular there has also been an emphasis on retaining the traditional values, organizations, and curriculum content of the British education system. The New Right has not been the only force

shaping educational policy under the Conservative Governments.

The New Right and the control of education

The New Right have probably been the most important single influence on educational changes in Britain since 1979, but there have been other significant influences. In a study of the introduction of the most important recent change in the education system, the **1988 Education Reform Act**, Richard Johnson argues that the legislation 'did not derive straightforwardly, from New Right theories'. Rather 'A multitude of practicalities intervened: political divisions, administrative dilemmas, strong opposition.' Opposition came, for example, from LEAs and from teachers and their unions. There were also divisions within Conservative ranks. For example, Mrs Thatcher's first education secretary, Keith Joseph, and more radical New Right thinkers favoured a voucher system. Under this system parents would be given a voucher by the state with a fixed value. It could be used to pay for education in either a privately owned or a publicly run school. However, this measure was never adopted because opposition to it was too strong.

In the next section we will briefly describe the main educational changes introduced in Britain between 1979 and 1994. As we have seen in this section, these changes were largely, but not completely, shaped by the New Right. After we have examined the nature of the changes made, we will evaluate some of the most important ones in detail.

■ Changes in education 1979–94

Schooling

Some steps were taken to prevent the ending of **selective schooling**. The Education Act of 1976, which compelled LEAs to draw up plans for comprehensive reorganization, was repealed. An **Assisted Places Scheme** was introduced which paid for state pupils to be educated at independent schools in the hope that this would encourage the most able to develop their talents.

The most far reaching package of changes was

introduced in the **1988 Education Reform Act.** The following measures were all introduced through this legislation.

1 **Testing and attainment targets** were introduced for children of 7, 11, 14 and 16 in the hope that standards would rise as schools competed with each other to succeed in reaching the targets.

2 For the first time the Government laid down a **National Curriculum** which required pupils to study mathematics, English, science, history, geography, technology, music, art and physical education, plus a foreign language for 11–16-year-old pupils. This was intended to ensure that pupils concentrated on what the Government saw as key subject areas. Since its introduction a number of changes have been made to the National Curriculum. We discuss these changes later.

3 The Act emphasized the idea of **parental choice** – in theory, at least, parents were given the right to send their children to the school of their choice to further encourage schools to compete and concentrate on improving their results. A policy of **open enrolment** compelled every school to recruit pupils up to the maximum which could be accommodated in its buildings.

4 The Act allowed the establishment of **City Technology Colleges** (CTCs). These would be inner-city educational institutions specializing in technology. They would be sponsored by private industry so that the state did not pay the full costs of building the colleges, and would be independent of LEAs. CTCs would cater for the 11–18 age groups and compete with existing state schools.

5 Existing schools were allowed to opt out of local authority control and be funded directly from central government. Opting out created a new category of **grant maintained schools** which were self-governing. Opting out had to be supported by parents in a ballot. By February 1994 814 out of 24,000 state schools had opted out and become grant maintained.

6 The 1988 Act also gave greater autonomy (independence) to schools in the way they spent their money. **Local management of schools** gave the responsibility for managing school budgets to headteachers and governors, thus reducing the power of LEAs.

7 Under the new system of **formula funding** the financing of schools was largely based upon the number of enrolments. This was intended to reward successful schools which attracted large numbers of pupils, while giving less successful schools the incentive to improve.

There were a number of other important changes in schooling which were not introduced in the 1988 Education Reform act.

1 The **Technical and Vocational Education Initiative** (TVEI) was started as a pilot scheme in 1983 in fourteen LEAs. It was a scheme for 14–18 year olds which ran alongside the conventional curriculum and included work experience. The TVEI became available to all secondary schools in 1986 and was later extended to include sixth form, further education and tertiary colleges. Roger Dale suggests that it was associated with the aim of producing pupils who could get jobs, carry them out successfully, and who had a better understanding of work and the economy.

2 The **Certificate for Pre-Vocational Education** (CPVE) was similar to TVEI in stressing preparation for work. CPVE, first taught in 1985–6, was for those over 16 who were uncertain of what work they wished to do. It offered work experience and was taught in schools and colleges. CPVE taught practical skills, but could be combined with taking exams in traditional subjects, though in practice it tended to be taken by pupils who were unsuccessful in the compulsory period of education. The CPVE was not a great success and was later replaced by other vocationally orientated qualifications such as GNVQs and NVQs.

3 In 1986 the **National Council for Vocational Qualifications** was set up with the aim of introducing standardized vocational qualifications related to working in particular occupations. By 1990 about 170 **NVQ**s (National Vocational Qualifications) had been established, with more being added to the list as time progressed. NVQs are intended to reward practical achievement with qualifications being gained by demonstrating 'competencies'. NVQs have four levels ranging from Level 1 (the equivalent of GCSEs) to Level 4 (the equivalent of postgraduate level study). After an initial 2-year pilot scheme, **GNVQ**s (General National Vocational Qualifications) were introduced nationally in 1994. These were intended to provide a vocationally orientated alternative to traditional academic exams such as 'A' levels.

4 One change which went against the general trends was the introduction of a new qualification for 16 year olds in 1988. The **General Certificates of Secondary Education** (GCSEs) replaced the two tier system of 'O' levels for more academic pupils and CSEs (Certificates of Secondary Education) for students judged to be less

able. These qualifications generally contrasted with Government policy in that they led to all students being entered for the same examination: GCSEs did not differentiate between academic and non-academic pupils. However, there were exceptions in some subjects (such as mathematics) where students could take different versions of GCSE exams with varying levels of difficulty.

GCSEs also went against the general thrust of Government policy by incorporating a considerable amount of coursework in the assessment methods. They therefore tended to encourage more student-centred teaching methods rather than the traditional 'chalk and talk' teaching which tends to be favoured by the New Right. Although, the Government later placed restrictions on the proportion of GCSE and 'A' level marks which could be awarded through coursework (restricting it to 20 per cent), a coursework component remained in the assessment of most subjects.

Further and higher education

As well as initiatives in schools, there were important changes in further and higher education during the same period.

1 The **1993 Education Act** compelled further education colleges to become independent, self-governing bodies, funded by the Further Education Funding Council rather than by LEAs. As in schools, funding was to be based largely on the recruitment of students, thus encouraging competition between further education colleges and other institutions such as schools with a sixth form.

2 The 1993 Education Act also allowed polytechnics to become universities.

3 Higher education was allowed to expand rapidly by the Government in the late 1980s and early 1990s but this expansion was financed partly through cutting back on grants to students. The value of student grants was gradually reduced from 1990 onwards. Instead of relying entirely on grants, students were given the opportunity to take out low-cost loans which had to be repaid once they had graduated and gained reasonably well-paid employment.

4 As in other areas of education, measures were introduced to make higher education more influenced by industry. The **1988 Education Reform Act** established a Polytechnic and Colleges Funding Council and a University Funding Council, both of which had strong representation from commerce and industry.

Training

A whole range of changes was introduced into training programmes. Some of these initiatives started even before the Conservatives took office in 1979. Many of them shifted power away from schools and colleges and towards the Department for Employment and new organizations which had closer links with employers than with educators.

1 Many of the early changes were associated with the extension of the activities of the **Manpower Services Commission** (MSC) (which later became the **Training Commission**). This organization was created in 1973 by the Employment and Training Act. It was made answerable to the Secretary of State for Employment, not the Minister of Education, and given responsibility for the selection and training of people for employment, and for ensuring that employers had a suitable supply of labour.

2 Its earliest measures were the **Job Creation Programme** of 1975, which provided temporary jobs for some of the unemployed, and the 1976 **Work Experience Programme**, which placed some of the young unemployed on 6-month work placements. As unemployment rose, the MSC both expanded its activities and became involved in educational areas which would previously have been the responsibility of the Department of Education and Science.

3 The **Youth Opportunities Programme** (YOP) of 1978 included both work experience and short training courses. Mrs Thatcher's Conservative Government was initially hostile to the MSC, but with unemployment rising rapidly it decided to extend YOP. Trainees on this scheme were entitled to one day a week off-the-job training, though not all received it. One area of training which the MSC started to develop was social and life skills, which aimed to develop positive attitudes to work, discipline, getting to work on time, and getting on with other trainees and employees at places of work.

4 In 1983 the **Youth Training Scheme** (YTS) replaced YOP. YTS was a 1-year training scheme, again combining work experience with education for school leavers.

5 In 1986 YTS was extended to a 2-year scheme. This scheme was designed to achieve the development of four 'outcomes'. Peter Raggat and Lorna Unwin describe these as 'competence in job skills; competence in a range of transferable core skills; ability to transfer skills and knowledge to new situations; personal effectiveness'. Raggat and Unwin argue that

2-year YTS schemes met hostility from employers who complained that 'its emphasis and the development, assessment and recording of the four outcomes was too time consuming and bureaucratic'.

6 Partly as a result of objections by employers, YTS was replaced in 1990 with **Youth Training**. The only requirement in this scheme was for employers to ensure that trainees followed some sort of training programme which led towards a Level 2 NVQ.

7 At the end of 1988 a White Paper (proposed government legislation) entitled *Employment for the 1990s* announced the Government's intention to set up a new type of organization to develop training. These were to be **Training and Enterprise Councils** or TECs. The first of them came into operation in 1990 and a network covering the whole of Britain was soon established. They are a national network of independent companies run by chief executives recruited from private industry. TECs are expected to deliver training and enterprise in their locality. They took over the running of Training Commission programmes such as Youth Training and Employment Training (a scheme for unemployed adults), but they were also given the job of evaluating the economic needs of their area and trying to stimulate economic development. Two-thirds of the board of each TEC has to consist of senior managers from major companies.

The above lists of educational and training initiatives since 1979 is by no means exhaustive. Nevertheless it does summarize most of the main changes. We will now look at some of these measures in more detail by examining sociological studies which have attempted to evaluate the effects of these changes, and in some cases to reveal the hidden agenda which may have encouraged their introduction.

■ Critical evaluations of the educational reforms

■ Stephen J. Ball, Richard Bowe and Sharon Gerwitz – competitive advantage and parental choice

The study

Between 1991 and 1994 Stephen Ball, Richard Bowe and Sharon Gerwitz conducted a study of fifteen schools in three neighbouring LEAs. The study included a mixture of LEA-controlled schools, grant maintained schools, two church schools and a CTC. The institutions served a variety of areas, some with mainly middle-class populations and some with a higher concentration of working-class residents. Some areas had substantial ethnic minority populations and others did not.

Ball *et al.* visited the schools, attended meetings, examined documents and interviewed a sample of teachers. They interviewed about 150 parents who had children in primary schools who were at the point of making the choice about the secondary schools their children should attend. They also interviewed some primary headteachers and examined LEA documents about changing patterns of choice. Ball *et al.*'s study attempted to discover the effects that parental choice and the encouragement of competition between schools was having on the education system, and particularly on opportunities for different social groups.

The effects on schools

The study found that the educational changes were having significant effects on secondary schools. This was particularly true of those schools which were undersubscribed: they had to try to do something to arrest their decline. More successful schools could afford to be fairly complacent but they too were starting to change some of their practices.

Most schools were 'paying a lot more attention to what parents want for their children's education. Or more precisely what schools *think* that parents want.' However, it was not the case that schools were equally keen to attract all students. The publication of league tables meant that schools were much more keen to attract academically able pupils who would boost the school's league table performance and thus improve its reputation. Thus according to Ball *et al.*:

In a sense there is a shift of emphasis from student needs to student performance: from what the school can do for the students to what the student can do for the school.

This emphasis has encouraged some schools to reintroduce streaming and setting and to direct more resources to children who are likely to be successful in examinations and tests.

As schools have concentrated on the more able pupils, they have paid less attention to those with Special Educational Needs (SENs). Indeed Ball *et al.* argue that 'some of the money and energy previously devoted to educational endeavours like SEN work are now focused on marketing activities'. In an effort to attract pupils, some schools have taken to publishing glossy brochures and some have brought in public relations firms. Staff are expected to devote more time and energy to marketing activities such as open evenings.

Ball *et al.* believe that these changes have led to 'a significant shift in the value framework of education'. Neighbouring schools have ceased to cooperate with each other and instead there is 'suspicion and hostility' between them as they compete for pupils. As competitive, market systems are introduced 'commercial rather than educational principles are increasingly dominant in making curriculum and organisation and resource allocation decisions'. In line with market values 'shrewdness rather than principles is rewarded'.

The education market and middle-class parents

As well as having profound effects on schools, the educational reforms have also altered the position of parents and pupils. With LEAs having less control over the allocation of pupils to schools, there is more opportunity for parents to manipulate the market. In particular, middle-class parents 'are exploiting the market in education and bringing their social and cultural advantages to bear'. They are in a better position than working-class parents to ensure that their children go to the school of their choice. There are a number of reasons for this.

First, middle-class parents possess more **cultural capital** than most working-class parents. (Cultural capital is a concept which was first developed by Pierre Bourdieu, see pp. 756–8 for details.) Middle-class parents are more likely to have the knowledge and contacts to 'play the system'. Ball *et al.* found from their interviews that strategies used by the middle class included:

---

attempting to make an impression with the headteacher at the open day, making a private appointment to visit the headteacher, knowing how to mount a successful appeal, and, most commonly, putting in multiple applications.

Second, gaining knowledge of the education system and manipulating it to your own advantage requires 'a great deal of stamina – to research, visit schools, make multiple applications and appeal'. Middle-class parents have their stamina 'sustained by knowledge, contacts, time and money'. Those with inside contacts in the education system, such as teachers and their relatives, are in a particularly good position.

Third, as well as making it easier to 'research' the education market, money confers all sorts of other advantages on middle-class parents and their children. These are:

1 Middle-class parents can afford to pay for the public transport necessary to send their children to more distant schools. They may also be able to pay for taxis and they are more likely to have cars to take their children to school.

2 They are more likely to be able to move house so that they live in the immediate catchment area of a successful school with a good reputation.

3 They are more able to afford extra help or coaching to get children into grammar schools. Of course, they are also much more likely to be able to pay to have their children educated privately.

4 Middle-class parents are more likely to be able to afford to pay for childcare. This gives them more time to take their children to more distant schools and to visit schools to make an informed choice about which school they want their children to attend.

Working-class and ethnic minority parents

Ball *et al.* did not find that working-class parents were any less interested in their children's education than their middle-class counterparts. However, they tended to lack the material resources and cultural capital which made it possible for many middle-class parents to influence the secondary school their children ended up at.

Many working-class parents preferred to send their children to the nearest school because of 'a complex pattern of family demands and structural limitations'. Not only was it more difficult for them to secure a place for their children in a distant but successful school, they actually placed considerable value on the advantages of obtaining a schooling close to home. Ball *et al.* say:

> They want their children to go to a school which is easily accessible and does not involve long and dangerous journeys; a school where friends', neighbours', and relatives' children also go; a school which is part of their social community, their locality.

Some, though by no means all, ethnic minority parents also suffer disadvantages in trying to manipulate the system to get their children into the best possible schools. If they were born abroad they may have limited experience of British education. Furthermore there are disadvantages for those:

> who do not feel confident enough about their English language skills to be able to negotiate the system or who do not have the necessary contacts to assist them in working it.

As Ball *et al.* put it, 'Their cultural capital is in the wrong currency and they are less able to accumulate the right sort.'

Conclusion

Ball *et al.* conclude that the encouragement of parental choice, the publication of exam results in league tables, open enrolments, formula funding

and other policies designed to make education more market orientated have all served to make education less egalitarian. Those whose children are already advantaged in the system seem to be gaining even more benefits while those who are already disadvantaged are losing further ground.

At the same time the ideology of educational institutions is changing in such a way that they are becoming more concerned with attracting the gifted and the advantaged than with helping the disadvantaged. According to Ball *et al.*'s research:

> we are likely to end up with a more socially differentiated and divisive system of education. In any market there are winners and losers. In this market we may all end up losing out!

■ The National Curriculum

The introduction and development of the National Curriculum

As we outlined earlier, the **National Curriculum** was introduced in 1988. It required 11–16-year-old pupils to study mathematics, English, science, history, geography, technology, music, art, physical education and a foreign language. Of these, English, mathematics and science were defined as **core subjects**. Schools were expected to spend about 10 per cent of teaching time on English, 10 per cent on mathematics and 10–20 per cent on science. The remaining subjects were defined as **foundation subjects** and each would take up around 10 per cent of school time with the exception of physical education, which would take up 5 per cent. All schools were expected to spend a minimum of 70 per cent of the teaching time on the National Curriculum, with any remaining time available being used for religious education and other subjects.

The National Curriculum also included **attainment targets** which would outline what children were expected to understand, know and do at four key stages at the ages of 7, 11, 14 and 16. These abilities would be regularly tested and there would be standardized tests for all pupils at each of these stages. The results of these tests would be published so that parents could compare the success of schools.

In fact these proposals were never implemented in full. Teachers' unions (particularly the National Union of Teachers) opposed some of the testing procedures and boycotted them. Partly as a consequence of such opposition, the Government ordered Sir Ron Dearing to examine the workings of the National Curriculum and propose reforms. In 1994 the findings of the *Dearing Report* were accepted. These greatly simplified the testing procedures and drastically slimmed down the National Curriculum itself. From 1994 it was decided that the National Curriculum should be confined to the three core subjects of English, mathematics and science.

Common criticisms of the National Curriculum

Denis Lawton identified a number of the most frequent criticisms made of the original National Curriculum. These were:

1 It was too bureaucratic. Many of the documents relating to the National Curriculum seemed more concerned with controlling the activities of teachers than improving the standard of what pupils learned.

2 It greatly centralized power in the hands of the Secretary of State for Education. It therefore undermined local democratic control of education and limited the choices open to parents. With one exception, they could no longer significantly affect the content of their children's education by choosing which school they attended since all schools had to teach a very similar curriculum.

3 The exception was private schools which were not subject to the National Curriculum. Thus the Government could be accused of only providing choice for those rich enough to afford private schooling.

4 The content of the National Curriculum was accused of being very traditional and unimaginative. Different groups objected to the exclusion of particular subjects. Lawton points out that it 'neglected important areas of learning such as political understanding, economic awareness, moral development, and many other cross-curricular themes'.

5 Many objected to the publication of test results. Schools that did badly risked losing pupils (and, with them, funding) and therefore entering a spiral of decline. This resulted in an unfair disadvantage to those left in the unsuccessful schools.

6 Some critics were worried that testing at 7 and 11 would lead to the labelling of some children as failures at an early age, damaging their future educational prospects.

The National Curriculum and power

The first two criticisms outlined above suggest that the National Curriculum was in conflict with the objectives of the New Right: it did not seem to be increasing choice and making education subject to market forces by freeing it from state bureaucracy. Geoff Whitty notes that some people have explained this apparent inconsistency by suggesting that the changes were:

> as much about increasing central government control at the expense of the teaching profession and local government, as they are about increasing the power of local communities, which are linked with parents in the government's rhetoric.

Whitty himself suggests that the Government's policies were not entirely inconsistent with the New Right's beliefs in the merits of the free market. From its point of view, it was sometimes necessary to use state power to get rid of state intervention in particular areas. In the short-term the state could be used to attack and weaken those who opposed New Right thinking. This included left-wing LEAs and teachers' unions. The Government could therefore ensure that:

> the pervasive collectivist and universalistic welfare ideology of the post-war era is restrained. In this way, support for the market, self-help, enterprise and the concept of the 'responsible' family and a common 'national identity' can be constructed.

In the long-term, then, the National Curriculum could free parents 'from dependency on professional experts' and persuade them to exercise choices in ways consistent with the Government's free market ideology.

From Whitty's point of view the National Curriculum is therefore designed to shift power in the short-term away from the opponents of the Government and towards the state. However, in the long term it can be used to reduce the need for state intervention since it ensures that parents will make the right curriculum choices when greater power is given to them.

The National Curriculum, class and cultural diversity

Long before the Government decided to introduce a National Curriculum sociologists were debating the merits of having different types of curriculum in schools. Some supported the use of a single curriculum for all pupils. For example, in 1975 Denis Lawton proposed a **common culture curriculum**. He accepted that there were important subcultural differences between social classes, but maintained there were sufficient similarities to form a school curriculum based on a common culture. He claimed that 'A heritage of knowledge and belief which includes mathematics, science, history, literature and, more recently, film and television is shared by all classes.'

However, it can be argued that no common curriculum can afford realistic solutions to the problem of inequality of educational opportunity in a stratified society. The very existence of stratification tends to prevent a common culture, since class subcultures largely arise from the position of social groups in stratification systems. Whatever the content of the curriculum it is bound to be more familiar to and therefore easier to understand for particular social groups.

Some critics have claimed that the National Curriculum favours higher social classes and disadvantages ethnic minorities in its choice of subject content and the way it is organized. We will now examine the National Curriculum in terms of how it affects ethnic minority groups.

The National Curriculum and ethnicity

Conrad McNeil discusses the National Curriculum from a 'black perspective'. Writing in 1988 he argued:

The culture reflected in it is no more than prevailing white Anglo-Saxon and totally excludes the significant input from the Caribbean, the African

---

and Indian continents and elsewhere. Furthermore, it reflects an imperialist and Eurocentric concept of a static Anglo-Saxon culture which no longer exists.

He gave a number of examples to support his claims.

1 In history the emphasis was on British history and carried the risk of having 'the same old diet of colonial domination' in which it is claimed that British colonialism benefited rather than harmed the peoples who were colonized. Asian, Afro-Caribbean and African history were neglected.

2 In terms of languages, McNeil noted that there were twelve languages in the UK spoken by over 100,000 people but less than half of them were European. However, the language component in the National Curriculum placed the emphasis on the teaching of European languages discouraging, for example, Asian pupils from studying Asian languages without studying a European language other than English as well.

3 Similarly in literature the culture of ethnic minorities would be neglected with the works of distinguished black writers largely forgotten, and the emphasis on traditional English writers such as Shakespeare, Milton, Hardy and Dickens.

Barry Troyna and Bruce Carrington identify another area in which the National Curriculum might disadvantage ethnic minorities. The 1988 Act specifically said that any new religious education syllabus had to reflect the dominance of Christian religious traditions and could not treat all major religions in the same way.

The National Curriculum and differentiation

As well as defining certain types of knowledge as worth acquiring while excluding other types, the National Curriculum also provided standards against which the performance of pupils could be measured. Richard Johnson argues that this is the main way in which the introduction of a National Curriculum will affect class differences in education. He says that the introduction of standardized testing at an early age 'means that individual children will be ranked and ordered as never before'. He describes the National Curriculum as 'a mechanism for differentiating children against fixed norms'.

Once differentiated, other reforms in education mean that children are likely to end up studying different courses, often in different institutions. Thus grammar schools, CTCs, private schools and grant maintained schools are likely to recruit successful, mainly middle-class children, while working-class children are more likely to end up in schools which have remained in local authority control. After the age of 16 pupils can be directed in different ways: academic, middle-class pupils towards traditional 'A' levels, and less academically successful, working-class pupils towards new vocational courses and training programmes.

To Johnson the National Curriculum did not encourage equality of opportunity despite the fact that it forced all children in the state sector to study the same subjects. Instead the renewed emphasis on testing and increased differentiation between types of school undermined the principles of comprehensive schooling and represented a move back towards the era of grammar schools and secondary moderns. He says 'As so often in the history of English education, institutional separations will become social segregations, especially on lines of class and race.'

■ Youth training schemes

Dan Finn – The hidden agenda of YTS

The new vocationalism involved in the various youth training schemes has been strongly attacked by some critics. Dan Finn refuses to accept that it is really designed to achieve its stated objectives. Finn claims that in 1983 confidential government papers leaked to the London magazine *Time Out* showed that the real purpose of the YTS was to restrict the number of workers joining trades unions, so reducing the bargaining power of the workforce. The YTS would also directly reduce the wage levels of young workers.

The Government paid employers for 'training' people on YTS, but in fact the trainees could be used as a source of cheap labour. Furthermore, the small allowances paid to people on the YTS would depress wage levels generally for young workers. The scheme would also reduce embarrassing unemployment statistics, since those participating were not classified as unemployed. In addition the Government hoped that it would help to reduce

crime and social unrest (for example, riots) by taking up the free time of young people.

Finn denies that there was any truth in the claim that school leavers were unemployable. He believes their unemployment was simply the result of a lack of jobs. He points out that many school pupils have experience of the world of work and prove themselves capable of holding down part-time jobs even before they leave school. In a survey of fifth form pupils in Rugby and Coventry, he found that 75 per cent had had some experience of working: they could hardly be totally ignorant of the world of work.

Finn regards the various youth training schemes as a way of coping with the surplus of labour in the 1970s and 1980s. Rather than being left to their own devices, swelling the unemployment statistics, school leavers would be taught the values and attitudes which would make them an easily exploited workforce. The schemes would help to lower the employment expectations of the working class so that they would 'know their place'.

John Clarke and Paul Willis – the transition from school to work

John Clarke and Paul Willis have reached similar conclusions. They argue that the new vocationalism is a way of producing people who want to work, but are kept in 'suspended animation' before work becomes available. They see the schemes as resulting from a 'crisis of profitability' in British industry. Trainees can be used as a substitute for full-time employees who would have to be paid more and would be eligible for redundancy payments.

Phillip Cohen – social and life skills

Phillip Cohen has produced an interesting analysis of the content of education received on training schemes, looking particularly at social and life skills training. Rather than 'reskilling' the population – training them in specific skills like bricklaying – Cohen sees these courses as deskilling the workforce. The schemes claim to teach 'transferable skills', but Cohen regards these as no more than a type of 'behavioural etiquette'. Trainees are taught that their chances of securing a job are determined by how well they can manage the impression of themselves given to others. The true nature of the labour market, and the fact that unemployment is a structural feature of society, are disguised. Individuals are persuaded that the 'personal' problem of unemployment results from their failure to 'market' themselves to employers.

Cohen uses an example from social and life skills literature to illustrate his point. In the example, a cartoon story, a white boy and a black girl ring up to enquire about a job. The girl does everything right. She is polite, explains exactly what information she requires, she takes a pen and paper with her to write down details, and has prepared a clear explanation of why she wants the job. She thanks the potential employer even though he shows no interest in employing her. The

boy does everything wrong, forgetting who he wants to speak to and running out of money for the phone box. He also admits that it is not really the sort of job he is looking for. Despite the contrasts both are equally unsuccessful: neither gets the job.

Cohen argues that the message of this story is that you should hide your feelings and if necessary be untruthful to secure work. Individuals must be in control of their own emotions and should not be 'uncool' by 'being yourself'. Encouraging this type of behaviour fosters an **inner detachment** so that there is no personal disappointment from failure. It allows the individual to cope with powerlessness without challenging the powerful. In short, it is intended to produce a workforce who will work anywhere, or who will accept unemployment, but in doing so must submerge their own personality.

Sociology, values and education

As members of society, sociologists, like everyone else, are committed to, or at least influenced by, political ideologies and values. To some degree, this will affect their choice of theoretical perspective, their methodology, and interpretation of data. Much of the criticism within the sociology of education has been levelled at the ideological assumptions and value judgements which are presumed to underlie the various viewpoints. We will now briefly examine this criticism.

Functionalist perspectives are often criticized for having a conservative bias: a prejudice in favour of maintaining things the way they are. The functions of education outlined by Durkheim, Parsons, and Davis and Moore are often similar to the 'official version' presented by Government departments. As such they are accused of uncritically accepting the establishment view, and, in doing so, supporting it. Their conservative viewpoint may prevent them from considering many of the possible dysfunctional aspects of education. A more radical political standpoint and less apparent commitment to the dominant values of their society might well produce a very different picture of the role of education in society.

Particularly during the 1950s and 1960s, sociologists were preoccupied with the question of inequality of educational opportunity. They felt it

was morally wrong, and also their views fitted Government policy which was concerned with getting the best return on investment in education. The 'wastage of talent' involved in unequal educational opportunity reduced the efficiency of the educational system in meeting the demands of the economy. It has been argued that a commitment to liberal and social democratic theories, with their emphasis on reform rather than radical change, influenced this type of research, directed the questions asked and the answers provided.

Both social democratic theory and liberalism are concerned with reform within the framework of existing social institutions. They do not advocate radical change. Thus theories such as cultural deprivation and solutions such as compensatory education suggest a reform of existing institutions rather than a revolutionary change in the structure of society. Many sociologists appeared to operate from the viewpoint that education was a good thing and that reforms in the educational system would lead to progressive social change in a society which, while far from perfect, was heading in the right direction.

Particularly during the late 1960s and 1970s, sociologists such as Michael Flude argued that reforms such as compensatory education can 'be seen as a part of a persuasive liberal ideology that diverts attention from the exploitive and alienating practices of dominant classes and the need for fundamental social change'.

The ideological basis of some reforms has also been attacked by interactionists. Supporters of compensatory education have been accused of basing their views on a commitment to middle-class values. Thus lower working-class subculture is judged to be deficient because it is evaluated in terms of middle-class standards. Nell Keddie suggests that the uncritical acceptance by many sociologists of teachers' definitions of knowledge and ability is based on the fact that both teachers and sociologists share the same middle-class prejudices. She maintains that the middle-class values of many sociologists limit their vision and therefore prevent them from asking important questions.

However, the interactionists themselves have been criticized for their value judgements, for their commitment to cultural relativism, and what Bill Williamson calls their 'romantic libertarian anarchism'. By this he means that the views of some interactionists seem to be coloured by an unrealistic commitment to a vision of society without government, in which everybody is free to express themselves in their own way, in which all knowledge and all views are equally valid. Williamson suggests that this view is a romantic dream with little or no chance of translation into practice. As such it diverts attention from a realistic consideration of the nature of power in society.

By comparison with the above viewpoints, the ideological bases of Marxist perspectives are clearcut. They begin from the value judgement that capitalist societies are exploitive, repressive and anti-democratic. This should not, however, detract from their usefulness. They lead to interpretations of the role of education in society which might not be possible if society as a whole were not examined from a critical stance. As Bowles and Gintis state, 'As long as one does not question the structure of the economy itself, the current structure of schools seems eminently reasonable.' Many of the questions that Marxists such as Bowles and Gintis ask derive directly from their commitment to socialism. At worst, their answers provide a fresh and stimulating view of the role of education in capitalist society.

The 1980s and 1990s have seen Government policies in Britain quite different from those of the 1960s. The Government has changed from being concerned with promoting equal opportunities, to being concerned with standards and the needs of industry. However, few sociologists have adopted the values of the New Right, and supported the thrust of Conservative Government policy. Most have criticized the philosophy behind educational reforms without necessarily dismissing all the changes that have taken place.

The majority of sociologists remain committed to the promotion of equality of opportunity within education. The rise of feminism has pushed the issue of gender and education towards the top of the sociological agenda. Similarly concern in society as a whole about racial conflict and the underachievement of some ethnic minorities, has led to a growing interest in the educational attainment of ethnic minority groups. Feminist and anti-racial values have increasingly come to influence the sociology of education. The abolition of class inequalities is no longer seen as sufficient to eradicate inequality of opportunity within education.

13
Methodology

13
Methodology

Introduction

Any academic subject requires a **methodology** to reach its conclusions: it must have ways of producing and analysing data so that theories can be tested, accepted or rejected. Without a systematic way of producing knowledge the findings of a subject can be dismissed as guesswork, or even as common sense made to sound complicated. Methodology is concerned with both the detailed research methods through which data are collected, and the more general philosophies upon which the collection and analysis of data are based.

As we have seen in this book, most areas of sociology are riven with controversy. Methodology is no exception to this general rule, although the divisions between those advocating different approaches have become less great than they were in the 1960s and 1970s. The main area of disagreement concerns – in the most general terms – whether sociology should adopt the same or similar methods to those employed in science.

Sociology first developed in Europe in the nineteenth century when industrialization resulted in massive social changes. Accompanying these social changes were intellectual changes during which science started to enjoy a higher reputation than ever before. Science appeared to be capable of producing objective knowledge that could be used to solve human problems and increase human productive capacity in an unprecedented way. It was not surprising, therefore, that many early sociologists chose to turn to science for a methodology on which to base their subject.

However, not all sociologists have agreed that it is appropriate to adopt the methodology of the natural sciences. For these sociologists, studying human behaviour is fundamentally different from studying the natural world. Unlike the subject matter of, for example, chemistry or physics, people possess consciousness which means (from the point of view of some sociologists) that sociology requires a different type of methodology from science.

It is possible, then, to identify two broad traditions within sociology.

1 Those who advocate the use of scientific and usually quantitative methods (numerical statistical methods).

2 Those who support the use of more humanistic and qualitative methods.

It should be stressed that not all sociologists fit neatly into these categories. Furthermore, as will become clear, there are divisions *within* these two broad camps as well as *between* them.

In recent years, some sociologists have questioned the need for such a rigid division between quantitative and qualitative methodology and have advocated combining the two approaches.

■ 'Scientific' quantitative methodology

As the introduction suggested, some sociologists have tried to adopt the methods of the natural sciences. In doing so they have tended to advocate the use of quantitative methods. The earliest attempt to use such methods in sociology is known as **positivism**.

■ Positivism, Durkheim and sociology

The French writer Auguste Comte (1798–1857) was the first person to use the word 'sociology', and he also coined the term 'positive philosophy'. Comte believed that there was a hierarchy of scientific subjects, with sociology at the pinnacle of that hierarchy. Comte was confident that scientific knowledge about society could be accumulated and used to improve human existence so that society could be run rationally without religion or superstition getting in the way of progress.

Emile Durkheim (1858–1917) advocated a similar methodology to that of Comte. He has been widely regarded as a positivist. Durkheim's classic study *Suicide* is often seen as a model of positivist research and it does indeed follow many of the methodological procedures of positivism. Certain aspects of Durkheim's work will be used to illustrate the positivist approach. However, strictly speaking Durkheim was not a positivist. As the discussion below will show he did not follow the positivist rule that states that sociological study should be confined to observable or directly measurable phenomena.

1 Social facts

First, as a positivist, Comte believed that the scientific study of society should be confined to collecting information about phenomena which can be objectively observed and classified. Comte argued that sociologists should not be concerned with the internal meanings, motives, feelings and emotions of individuals. Since these mental states exist only in the person's consciousness, they cannot be observed and so they cannot be measured in any objective way.

Durkheim agreed that sociologists should confine themselves to studying **social facts**. He argued that 'The first and most fundamental rule is: *Consider social facts as things.*' This means that the belief systems, customs and institutions of society – the facts of the social world – should be considered as things in the same way as the objects and events of the natural world. However, he did not believe that social facts consisted only of those things that could be directly observed or measured. To Durkheim, social facts included such phenomena as the belief systems, customs and institutions of society. Belief systems are not directly measurable or observable since they exist in the consciousness of humans. Nevertheless, Durkheim saw them as existing over and above individual consciousness. They were not chosen by individuals and they could not be changed at will. Social facts, such as

the customs of a particular profession, were external to each individual and constrained their behaviour. That is, each person had their options limited by the existence of customs and practices.

In Durkheim's view, society is not simply a collection of individuals, each acting independently in terms of his or her particular psychology or mental state. Instead members of society are directed by collective beliefs, values and laws, by social facts which have an existence of their own. In Durkheim's words, 'collective ways of acting or thinking have a reality outside the individuals'. Social facts therefore make individuals behave in particular ways. Durkheim's definition and use of the term 'social facts' distinguishes him from positivists such as Comte. In many other respects though he followed the logic and methods of positivism. (The differences between Durkheim's approach and positivism are further discussed on p. 820.)

2 Statistical data

The second aspect of positivism concerns its use of **statistical data**. Positivists believed it was possible to classify the social world in an objective way. Using these classifications it was then possible to count sets of observable social facts and so produce statistics. For example, Durkheim collected data on social facts such as the suicide rate and the membership of different religions.

3 Correlation

The third stage of positivist methodology entails looking for correlations between different social facts. A **correlation** is a tendency for two or more things to be found together and it may refer to the strength of the relationship between them. In his study of suicide Durkheim found an apparent correlation between a particular religion, Protestantism, and a high suicide rate.

4 Causation

The fourth stage of positivist methodology involves a search for **causal connections**. If there is a strong correlation between two or more types of social phenomena, then a positivist sociologist might suspect that one of these phenomena was causing the other to take place. However, this is not necessarily the case, and it is important to analyse the data carefully before any such conclusion can be reached.

The example of class and criminality can be used to illustrate this point. Many sociologists have noted a correlation between being working class and a relatively high chance of being convicted of a crime. This has led some (for instance, Robert Merton) to speculate that being working class was one factor which might cause people to commit criminal acts. This can be illustrated simply as:

BEING WORKING CLASS

↓

causes

↓

CRIME

However, there are other possibilities which might explain the correlation. It could be that a similar proportion of criminals come from all social classes but that conviction for crime causes criminals of middle-class origin to be downwardly socially mobile, and become working class; their criminal records might prevent them from obtaining non-manual work. In other words it is being criminal that causes a person to become working class, and not the other way round. This is illustrated as:

CRIME

↓

causes

↓

A PERSON TO BECOME WORKING CLASS

Furthermore, there is the even more serious possibility that an apparent connection between two social phenomena might be a spurious or indirect correlation. This occurs when two or more phenomena are found together but have no direct connection to each other: one does not therefore cause the other. It may be that some third factor has a causal relationship to both the phenomena or factors being examined. For example, it may be that gender is related both to social class and the likelihood of committing a crime, and that class and crime are not directly connected at all. Men may be more likely to commit crimes than women and may also be more likely to have manual jobs. Thus the original cor-

relation discovered could be a product of the concentration of men in the working class, as the diagram below illustrates:

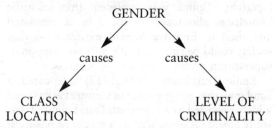

GENDER

causes   causes

CLASS   LEVEL OF
LOCATION   CRIMINALITY

A further possibility is that the police discriminate against the working class and arrest more members of that class than of the middle class even though the middle class are just as prone to crime.

Multivariate analysis

In order to overcome the problem of spurious correlation Durkheim devised a technique known as **multivariate analysis**. This involves trying to isolate the effect of a particular independent variable upon the dependent variables. The **dependent variable** is the thing that is caused (in the example used above, crime); the **independent variable/s** are the factor or factors that cause the dependent variable. In the diagram above gender is an example of an independent variable.

To assess the influence of a particular independent variable – that is to see if it is more or less important than another independent variable – it may be possible to produce comparisons where one variable is held constant, and the other is changed. For instance, the effect of gender on criminality could be isolated from the effect of class by comparing working-class men and women to see whether their crime rates were similar or different.

With the aid of computers and sophisticated statistical techniques quantitative researchers can analyse the relative importance of many different variables. Durkheim had to make do with less sophisticated research procedures, but he used the same logic in his study of suicide. For example, he checked whether or not Protestantism was associated with a high suicide rate regardless of nationality by examining suicide rates in a range of countries.

Laws of human behaviour

Positivists believe that multivariate analysis can establish causal connections between two or more variables. If these findings are checked in a variety of contexts (for example, in different societies at different times), then the researchers can be confident that they have attained the ultimate goal of positivism: a **law of human behaviour**.

A scientific law consists of a statement about the relationship between two or more phenomena which is true in all circumstances. Thus Newton's three Laws of Motion were supposed to describe the ways in which matter would always move. Similarly, Comte and Durkheim believed that real laws of human behaviour could be discovered. Durkheim claimed to have discovered laws of human behaviour that governed the suicide rate. According to Durkheim the suicide rate always rose during a time of economic boom or slump. Comte believed he had discovered a law that all human societies passed through three stages: the theological, the metaphysical, and the positive. In the first stage humans believed that events were caused by the actions of gods; in the second, events were held to be caused by abstract forces; but in the third scientific rationality triumphed so that scientific laws formed the basis of explanation.

Positivists and Durkheim then, believe that laws of human behaviour can be discovered by the collection of objective facts about the social world in a statistical form, by the careful analysis of these facts, and by repeated checking of the findings in a series of contexts. From this point of view humans have little or no choice about how they behave. What takes place in their consciousness is held to be irrelevant since external forces govern human behaviour: people react to stimuli in the environment in a predictable and consistent way. The implication is that humans react directly to a stimulus without attaching a meaning to it first. Thus a simple example would be if a motorist saw the stimulus of a red light, he or she would automatically react to it by stopping. It is this implication of the positivist approach that has attracted the strongest criticism, as will become clear as the chapter develops.

Positivism is based upon an understanding of science that sees science as using a mainly **inductive methodology**. An inductive methodology starts by collecting the data. The data are then analysed, and out of this analysis theories are developed. Once the theory has been developed it can then be tested against other sets of data to see if it is confirmed or not. If it is repeatedly confirmed then Durkheim and positivists such as Comte assume they have discovered a law of human behaviour.

■ Karl Popper – falsification and deduction

Despite the undoubted influence of positivist methodology within sociology the inductive method on which it is usually based has not, by any means, been accepted by all scientists. Indeed, many scientists now advocate and use an alternative, **deductive approach**. Although the logic of the deductive approach is similar in many ways to positivism, the differences have important implications.

This alternative methodology in both natural science and sociology is supported by Karl Popper in his book *The Logic of Scientific Discovery*. The deductive approach reverses the process of induction. It starts with a theory and tests it against the evidence, rather than developing a theory as a result of examining the data.

Popper argues that scientists should start with a 'hypothesis' or a statement that is to be tested. This statement should be very precise, and should state exactly what will happen in particular circumstances. On the basis of the hypothesis it should be possible to deduce predictions about the future. Thus, for example, Newton's Law of Gravity enables hypotheses about the movement of bodies of a given mass to be made, and these hypotheses can then be used to make predictions which can be tested against future events.

According to Popper it matters little how a scientific theory originates. It does not, as positivists suggest, have to come from prior observation and analysis of data. Scientists can develop theories however they wish – their theories might come to them in dreams or in moments of inspiration. What is important, and what makes them scientific, is their ability to be tested by making precise predictions on the basis of the theory.

Popper differs from positivists in that he denies that it is ever possible to produce laws that will necessarily be found to be true for all time. He argues that, logically, however many times a theory is apparently proved correct because predictions made on the basis of that theory come true, there is always the possibility that at some future date the theory will be proved wrong, or 'falsified'. For example, to Popper the hypothesis 'all swans are white' is a scientific statement because it makes a precise prediction about the colour of any swan that can be found. But, however many times the statement is confirmed – if five, five hundred or five thousand swans are examined and found to be white – the very next swan examined may prove to be black and the hypothesis will be falsified. Laws, whether of natural science or of human behaviour, do not, from this point of view, necessarily have the permanence attributed to them by positivists.

Popper suggests that scientists have a duty to be objective, and to test their theories as rigorously as possible. Therefore, once they have formulated hypotheses, and made predictions, it is necessary to try constantly to find evidence that disproves or falsifies their theories. In the natural sciences one method that has been developed in order to falsify theories is the laboratory experiment. This method, and its relevance to sociology, will now be examined. Popper's view of science will be evaluated later in the chapter (see pp. 856–61).

The laboratory experiment and sociology

The word 'science' conjures up an image of researchers in white coats carrying out experiments in laboratories. This image is not usually associated, however, with sociology. Indeed sociologists very rarely carry out laboratory experiments even if they support the use of 'scientific' methods in their research. The reasons for this will be examined later, but first, why does the laboratory experiment enjoy such popularity in natural science?

The main reason why scientists use the laboratory experiment is because it enables them to test precise predictions in exactly the way that Popper advocates. Laboratories are controlled environments in which the researcher can manipulate the various independent variables however they wish. They can calculate the effects of a single independent variable while removing the possibility that any other factors are affecting the dependent variable they are studying. This is achieved through the use of a **control** with which to compare the experiment.

For example, if an experimenter wished to determine the importance of the independent variable 'light' on the growth of plants, she or he could set up a laboratory experiment to isolate the effects of light from other independent variables. Thus the experimenter would set up an experiment and a control in which every variable other than the amount of light was held constant. Two sets of identical plants of the same species, age, condition and size would be kept at the same temperature, in an environment of the same humidity, planted in the same type and amount of soil, and given the same amount of water at the same time. The control group of plants would be exposed to a given intensity of light for a given period of time. The experiment group could be exposed to either more or less light than the control group. The results would be observed, measured and quantified. A single variable, light, would have been isolated to find the effects it had, independently of all the other variables.

The laboratory experiment allows researchers to be far more confident that they have isolated a particular variable than they would have been had they observed plants in the wild, where it would not be possible to regulate the various independent variables so tightly. Furthermore, the laboratory experiment facilitates replication: so long as the precise nature of the experiment is recorded, other scientists can reproduce identical conditions to see if the same results are obtained.

From Popper's point of view the experimental method is extremely useful because it allows the sort of precision in the making and repeated testing of predictions that he advocates. Laboratory experiments are quite frequently used in some 'social sciences', particularly psychology, but sociologists almost never make use of them. There are two main reasons for this.

1 Laboratories are unnatural situations. Members of society do not, in the normal course of events, spend their time under observation in laboratories. The knowledge that they are being studied, and the artificiality of the situation, might well affect the behaviour of those involved and distort the results so as to make them of little use.

2 It is impractical to carry out experiments in laboratories on many of the subjects of interest to sociologists. It is not possible to fit a community – let alone a whole society – into a laboratory. Nor is it possible to carry out a laboratory experiment over a sufficiently long time span to study social change.

Field experiments

As a consequence of the above difficulties, when sociologists do carry out experiments, they are normally outside a laboratory. Such experiments are known as **field experiments**. They involve intervening in the social world in such a way that hypotheses can be tested by isolating particular variables.

For example, Rosenthal and Jacobson tested the hypothesis that self-fulfilling prophecies could affect educational attainment by manipulating the independent variables of the pupils' IQ (intelligence quotient) scores known to teachers (see p. 764).

In an experiment into gender role socialization carried out at Sussex University, girl babies were dressed up in blue clothes, boy babies in pink, and the reactions of adults to their behaviour were recorded. Not only did the adults assume that the boys were girls, and vice versa, they interpreted their behaviour differently depending upon the sex they presumed them to be. Thus restless 'boys' (in reality the girls dressed in blue) were regarded as wanting to be active and to play, while restless 'girls' were regarded as being emotionally upset and in need of comfort.

In another experiment Sissons observed the reactions of members of the public when they were asked for directions by an actor. The location of the experiment was held constant (it took place outside Paddington Station), but the appearance of the actor varied. Halfway through the experiment the actor changed from being dressed as a businessman to being dressed as a labourer. Sissons found that the public were more helpful when the actor was dressed as a businessman rather than as a labourer.

Although field experiments overcome the problem of experiments taking place in an unnatural setting, these experiments do have other problems associated with them. First, it is not possible to control variables as closely as it is in the laboratory. Thus in Sissons's experiment, for example, it was not possible to carry out the two experiments at the same time and the same place, and since they took place at different times, factors such as the weather and the time of day might have affected the results.

Second, in some field experiments the fact that an experiment is taking place can affect the results. This is often known as the **Hawthorne Effect**, after a famous experiment conducted at the Hawthorne works of the Western Electricity Company in Chicago and analysed by Elton Mayo. The experiment was intended to test various hypotheses about worker productivity. Variables such as room temperature, the strength of the lighting and the

length of breaks were varied, but, irrespective of whether working conditions were improved or made worse, productivity usually increased. It appeared that the workers were responding to the knowledge that an experiment was taking place rather than to the variables being manipulated.

To avoid the Hawthorne Effect (which can render the results of experiments worthless), it is necessary that the subjects of experimental research are unaware that the experiment is taking place. This, however, raises a further problem: the morality of conducting experiments on people without their consent. Some sociologists strongly object to doing this. Some experiments, such as Sissons's, may not have great moral implications, but others do. In Rosenthal and Jacobson's experiment the researchers may have held back the educational careers of some children by lying to their teachers.

Although field experiments open up greater possibilities than laboratory experiments they are still likely to be confined to small-scale studies over short periods of time. Experimentation on society as a whole, or on large groups in society, is only likely to be possible with the consent of governments. Few governments are willing to surrender their authority to social researchers who are keen to test the theories and hypotheses they have developed! In any case it would cost a fortune and funds for research are limited. In these circumstances sociologists normally rely upon studying society as it is, rather than trying to manipulate it so that their theories can be tested directly.

■ The comparative method

The **comparative method**, as its name suggests, involves the use of comparisons. These may be comparisons of different societies, of groups within one or more society, and comparisons at the same or different points in time. Unlike the experiment, the comparative method is based upon an analysis of what has happened, or is happening in society, rather than upon the situations artificially created by a researcher. The data used in the comparative method may come from any of the primary or secondary sources discussed in detail later in this chapter.

The comparative method overcomes some of the problems involved with experimentation in 'social sciences'. Moral problems are not as acute as in experimentation, since the researcher is not intervening directly in shaping the social world. Furthermore, the researcher is less likely to affect artificially the behaviour of those being studied since the data, at least in theory, come from 'natural' situations.

The comparative method uses a similar 'scientific' logic to that employed by positivists, or to that used in the deductive approach supported by Popper. Systematic comparisons can be used either to establish correlations and ultimately causal connections and supposed 'laws', or rigorously to test hypotheses.

This method can be used to isolate variables to try to uncover the cause or causes of the social phenomenon being studied. It can be a far less convenient approach than laboratory or field experimentation. There is no guarantee that the available data will make it possible to isolate variables precisely when comparing, for example, the development of two different societies. There may be many ways in which they differ, and determining which independent variables caused the differences in the societies may not be straightforward. The comparative method is superior to the experiment, though, in that it allows the sociologist to study the causes of large-scale social change over long periods of time. The historical development of societies can be studied; this is not feasible using experiments.

The comparative method has been widely used in sociology particularly but by no means exclusively by those advocating a 'scientific' quantitative approach to the subject. The major founders of the discipline – Marx, Durkheim and Weber – all employed the comparative method.

Marx compared a wide variety of societies in order to develop his theory of social change and to support his claim that societies passed through different stages (see pp. 878–83 for further details).

Durkheim, too, used the comparative method in his study of the division of labour and the change from mechanical to organic solidarity (see pp. 184–6 for further details). Durkheim's study of suicide (which is considered later in this chapter) is a classic example of how detailed statistical analysis involving the comparison of different societies, different groups within society, and different time periods, can be used to try to isolate the variables that cause a social phenomenon (see pp. 817–20).

In *The Protestant Ethic and the Spirit of Capitalism* Weber systematically compared early capitalist countries in Western Europe and North America with countries such as China and India to try to show a correlation between early capitalism and Calvinism (see pp. 459–61).

Modern sociologists have followed in the footsteps of Marx, Durkheim and Weber. There are numerous examples of the use of this method throughout this book, including David Martin's comparison of secularization in different countries (pp. 494–6), Cicourel's comparison of juvenile justice in two Californian cities (pp. 412–13), and Goldthorpe and Lockwood's comparison of clerks and affluent manual workers (pp. 77–9).

■ Interpretive and qualitative methodology

Despite the considerable influence of the 'scientific' approaches to sociological methodology described above, an alternative series of approaches has long existed within sociology. These approaches claim either that 'scientific' approaches are inadequate on their own for collecting, analysing and explaining data or that they are totally inappropriate in a subject that deals with human behaviour. Thus some sociologists who advocate the use of interpretive and qualitative approaches suggest that they should be used to supplement 'scientific' quantitative methodology; others that they should replace 'scientific' approaches.

Qualitative data

Quantitative data are data in a numerical form, for example, official statistics on crime, suicide and divorce rates. By comparison, **qualitative data** are usually presented in words. These may be a description of a group of people living in poverty, providing a full and in-depth account of their way of life or a transcript of an interview in which people describe and explain their attitude towards and experience of religion.

Compared to quantitative data, qualitative data are usually seen as richer, more vital, as having greater depth and as more likely to present a true picture of a way of life, of people's experiences, attitudes and beliefs.

The interpretive approach

Sociologists who take an **interpretive approach** are usually the strongest advocates of qualitative data. They argue that the whole basis of sociology is the interpretation of social action. Social action can only be understood by interpreting the meanings and motives on which it is based. Many interpretive sociologists argue that there is little chance of discovering these meanings and motives from quantitative data. Only from qualitative data – with its greater richness and depth – can the sociologist hope to interpret the meanings that lie behind social action.

Interpretive sociologists usually reject the use of natural science methodology for the study of social action. They see the subject matter of the social and natural sciences as fundamentally different. The natural sciences deal with matter. Since matter has no consciousness, its behaviour can be explained simply as a reaction to external stimuli. It is compelled to react in this way because its behaviour is essentially meaningless. Unlike matter, people have consciousness. They see, interpret and experience the world in terms of meanings; they actively construct their own social reality. Meanings do not have an independent existence, a reality of their own which is somehow separate from social actors. They are not imposed by an external society that constrains members to act in certain ways. Instead they are constructed and reconstructed by actors in the course of social interaction.

People do not react automatically to external stimuli as positivists claim. Instead, they interpret the meaning of a stimulus before responding to it. Motorists who see a red light will not automatically stop in response to this stimulus. They will attach a meaning to the stimulus before acting. Motorists might conclude that the light is a decoration on a Christmas tree, and not a traffic signal, or alternatively that it indicates that a nearby building is a brothel. Having established the meaning of the stimulus to their own satisfaction, the motorists will then decide how they wish to respond. Motorists being pursued by the police might jump a red light rather than stop. If the stimulus is regarded as a decoration, motorists might stop to admire it, or continue on their way without giving

the light a second thought. Clearly, the motorist who concludes that the red light is advertising a brothel might respond in a variety of ways!

Whatever action is taken by an individual, advocates of interpretive sociology would argue that the causal explanation of human behaviour is impossible without some understanding of the subjective states of the individuals concerned. Thus a positivist might be content to discover what external factors led to a certain type of human behaviour while an advocate of a more qualitative approach would be interested in the meaning attached to the behaviour by those engaging in it.

It is at this point that opponents of positivist and 'scientific' methods begin to diverge. While some, like Weber, regard the understanding of meaning as necessary to making causal explanations possible, others, such as phenomenologists, regard understanding as the end product of sociological research and they reject the possibility of producing causal explanations at all.

The implications of three qualitative interpretive sociological approaches for methodology will now be briefly examined. They are dealt with in more detail in the next chapter.

■ 1 Max Weber

Weber defined sociology as the study of social action. Action is social when it takes account of other members of society. Weber believed that an explanation of social action necessitated an understanding of the meanings and motives which underlie human behaviour. The sociologist must interpret the meanings given to actions by the actors themselves. For instance, in order to explain why an individual was chopping wood the sociologist must discover the person's motives for doing so – whether they were doing it to earn money, to make a fire, to work off anger or for some other motive. According to Weber understanding motives could be achieved through *verstehen* – imagining yourself to be in the position of the person whose behaviour you were seeking to explain.

Weber's emphasis on meanings and motives is obvious throughout his work. For example, in *The Protestant Ethic and the Spirit of Capitalism* one of his main concerns was to interpret the beliefs and motives of the early Calvinists (see pp. 459–61). However, he was not simply concerned with understanding meanings and motives for their own sake. Weber wanted to explain social action and social change. He was interested in causality.

This can be seen clearly from *The Protestant Ethic and the Spirit of Capitalism*. Using the comparative method, Weber systematically compared the characteristics of early capitalist countries and technologically advanced oriental societies. By doing so he claimed to have isolated 'ascetic' Protestantism as a variable that contributed to the rise of capitalism. He saw the moral and religious beliefs and motives of the early Calvinists as one of the main factors accounting for the emergence of capitalism in the West. (For a fuller account of Weber's methodology, see pp. 889–90.)

■ 2 Symbolic interactionism

Symbolic interactionists do not reject the attempt to establish causal relationships within sociology, indeed they see this as an important part of the sociologist's work. However, they tend not to believe that statistical data provides any great insight into human behaviour. Interactionists see human behaviour as largely governed by the internal processes by which people interpret the world around them and give meaning to their own lives.

In particular, interactionists believe that individuals possess a 'self-concept', or image of themselves, that is built up, reinforced or modified in the process of interaction with other members of society. Thus human beings have an image of what sort of person they are, and they will tend to act in accordance with that image. They might see themselves as caring or tough, honest or dishonest, weak or strong and their behaviour reflects this sense of their own character.

The responses of others to an individual may make it impossible for him or her to sustain a particular self-concept; the self-concept will change, and in turn the behaviour of the individual will alter accordingly. Thus interactionists have tried to show how the labelling of people as deviant, or as educational successes or failures, can produce self-fulfilling prophecies in which their behaviour comes to live up (or down) to the expectations of others. (For details of these labelling theories see pp. 405–8 and 761–8.)

The implications of these views for sociological methodology have been developed by the American interactionist Herbert Blumer. He rejects what he regards as the simplistic attempts to establish causal relationships that characterize positivist methodology.

As an example, Blumer refers to the proposition that industrialization causes the replacement of extended families with nuclear families. He objects to the procedure of isolating variables and assuming one causes the other with little or no reference to the actor's view of the situation. He argues that data on the meanings and interpretations which actors give to the various facets of industrialization and family life are essential before a relationship can be established between the two factors. Blumer claims that many sociologists conduct their research with only a superficial familiarity with the area of life under investigation. This is often combined with a preoccupation for aping the research procedures of the natural sciences. The net result is the imposition of definitions on the social world with little regard for their relevance to that world. Rather than viewing social reality from the actor's perspective, many sociologists have attempted to force it into predefined categories and concepts. This provides little chance of capturing social reality, but a very good chance of distorting it.

In place of such procedures Blumer argues that sociologists must immerse themselves in the area of life that they seek to investigate. Rather than attempting to fit data into predefined categories, they must attempt to grasp the actor's view of social reality. This involves 'feeling one's way inside the experience of the actor'. Since action is directed by actors' meanings, the sociologist must 'catch the process of interpretation through which they construct their action'. This means the researcher 'must take the role of the acting unit whose behaviour he is studying'. Blumer offers no simple solutions as to how this type of research may be conducted. However, the flavour of the research procedures he advocates is captured in the following quotation: 'It is a tough job requiring a high order of careful and honest probing, creative yet disciplined imagination, resourcefulness and flexibility in study, pondering over what one is finding, and a constant readiness to test and recast one's views and images of the area.' (For a detailed discussion of symbolic interactionism see pp. 891–97.)

■ 3 Phenomenology
The nature of social reality

Phenomenology represents the most radical departure from the 'scientific' quantitative methodology examined at the start of the chapter. Phenomenologists go further than interactionists in that they reject the possibility of producing causal explanations of human behaviour. They do not believe that it is possible objectively to measure and classify the world. To phenomenologists, human beings make sense of the world by imposing meanings and classifications upon it. These meanings and classifications make up social reality. There is no objective reality beyond these subjective meanings.

Thus, for example, in Cicourel's study of juvenile justice (examined on pp. 412–13), police and juvenile officers had the problem of classifying the behaviour of juveniles into the categories: delinquent and non-delinquent. Cicourel did not find this process to be objective: it largely depended on the stereotypes held by the officials of the 'typical delinquent'. As such, the data on convictions for various delinquent acts were a social product based upon the common-sense assumptions of the authorities who created the statistics.

At first sight Cicourel's study might simply suggest that the statistics were invalid and that further research might well reveal the true rate of delinquency. However, phenomenologists reject this view. All statistics are social products that reflect the meanings of those who created them. The meanings are the reality which sociologists must examine. Crime statistics have no existence outside the meanings and interpretive procedures which produced them. To assume that there is a true crime rate that has an objective reality is to misunderstand the nature of the social world. From a phenomenological perspective, the job of the sociologist is simply to understand the meanings from which social reality is constructed.

Phenomenologists believe that the problem of classification is universal, and not unique to particular types of data. All people, all of the time, make decisions about how to classify things, and these decisions are the product of social processes. For example, on a simple level what one person might classify as a 'chair' might be classified by another person as a 'wooden object', and by a third person who was involved in a pub brawl as 'a missile'. From this point of view all data are the product of the classification systems used by those who produce them. If the classification system were different, the data would be different.

Furthermore, to phenomenologists there is no way of choosing between different systems of classification and seeing one as superior to another. It is therefore pointless to use data which rests upon the interpretations of individuals in order to try to establish correlations and causal relationships. Thus using official statistics to reach the conclusion that being working class causes a person to commit crimes would not be justified. The figures would only show how crime was defined and classified rather than what criminal actions had been carried out by particular groups within the population.

Phenomenologists believe that sociologists should limit themselves to understanding the meanings and classifications which people use to give order to and make sense of the world. With their exclusive emphasis upon meanings and the social construction of reality, phenomenologists concentrate almost entirely on the subjective aspects of social life which are internal to the individual's consciousness. They therefore tend to use rather different research methods from the more 'scientific' approaches.

The implications of the different approaches considered so far will now be discussed with reference to a particular area of social life: suicide.

The sociology of suicide

Arguably, the topic of suicide has received a disproportionate amount of attention from sociologists. A large number of books and articles have been written on the subject whereas other areas of social life that could be seen as equally important – for instance, murder – have not been the subject of so much interest. The main reason for this is the fact that Durkheim used this topic to illustrate his own methodological approach.

Durkheim – *Suicide: A Study in Sociology*

In 1897 Durkheim published his book *Suicide: A Study in Sociology*, and many studies of suicide have been, at least in part, a reaction to Durkheim's work. Some sociologists have tried to show how Durkheim's approach was successful in explaining suicide; others have tried to develop and improve his theory; others have rejected his whole approach. Suicide has become an area in which different methodological approaches have been tested and disputed.

Durkheim chose to study suicide for a number of reasons. In late nineteenth-century France sociology was gradually becoming established as an academic discipline and Durkheim wanted to reinforce this process and show how his particular approach to the subject was superior to others. He wished to use his study to show how there was a sociological level of analysis which was distinct from other disciplines and which made an important contribution to the explanation of social phenomena. Suicide was, and still is, widely regarded as a highly individual act. For example, it is often explained in terms of an individual's depression. It therefore appeared an unlikely candidate for sociological analysis with its emphasis on the social rather than the individual. There were established psychological theories of suicide. Durkheim attempted to show that suicide could not be fully explained by psychologists. Sociology could explain aspects of suicide which psychology could not.

Durkheim did not deny that particular circumstances would lead to a particular person taking his or her own life, but personal reasons could not account for the *suicide rate*. For example, he tried to show that there was no relationship between the incidence of insanity (which many psychologists associated with suicide) and the suicide rate. He found that Jews had higher rates of insanity than other religious groups, but they had lower rates of suicide.

Durkheim also chose to study suicide because of the availability of suicide statistics from a number of European countries. He regarded these statistics as social facts and so believed that they could be used to find the sociological causes of suicide rates. He could try to establish correlations, and using the comparative method could uncover the patterns that would reveal the causal relationships at work in the production of suicide rates. In this way he aimed to demonstrate that sociology was as rigorous a discipline as the natural sciences.

In order to achieve these objectives Durkheim first tried to show that suicide rates were relatively stable in a particular society over a period of time. As Table 13.1 shows, over the periods covered there was a remarkable consistency in the comparative suicide rates of the European societies in question. Durkheim felt able to claim: 'The suicide-rate is therefore a factual order, unified and definite, as is shown by both its permanence and its variability.' Furthermore, as will be discussed shortly, Durkheim found consistent variations in the suicide rate between different groups within the same society. He believed it was impossible to explain these patterns if suicide was seen solely as a personal and individual act.

Durkheim then went on to establish correlations between suicides and other sets of social facts. He found that suicide rates were higher in predominantly Protestant countries than Catholic ones. Jews had a low suicide rate, lower even than Roman Catholics. Generally married people were more prone to suicide than those who were single, although married women who remained childless for a number of years ended up with a high suicide rate. Durkheim also found that a low suicide rate was associated with political upheaval. The suicide rate in France fell after the *coup d'état* of Louis Bonaparte for example. War also reduced the suicide rate. After war broke out in 1866 between Austria and Italy the suicide rate fell 14 per cent in both countries.

Having established these correlations Durkheim used multivariate analysis to isolate the most important variables and to determine whether there was a genuine causal relationship between these factors and suicide. For example, Durkheim recognized the possibility that it might be the national culture rather than the main religion of particular countries that accounted for their suicide rate. In order to test whether this was the case he checked on differences within the population of particular countries to see whether these differences supported his views on the importance of religion. The evidence supported Durkheim. For example, Bavaria, the area of Germany with the highest number of Roman Catholics also had the lowest suicide rate. He also checked the relative importance of different factors: he found that high suicide rates were correlated with high levels of education. However, he established that religion was more important than level of education. Jews had a low suicide rate despite having a high level of education.

Types of suicide

From his analysis of the relationship between suicide rates and a range of social facts Durkheim

Table 13.1 **Rate of suicides per million inhabitants in the different European countries**

	Period 1866–70	Period 1871–75	1874–78	Numerical position in the 1 period	2 period	3 period
Italy	30	35	38	1	1	1
Belgium	66	69	78	2	3	4
England	67	66	69	3	2	2
Norway	76	73	71	4	4	3
Austria	78	94	130	5	7	7
Sweden	85	81	91	6	5	5
Bavaria	90	91	100	7	6	6
France	135	150	160	8	9	9
Prussia	142	134	152	9	8	8
Denmark	277	258	255	10	10	10
Saxony	293	267	334	11	11	11

(*Source*: Emile Durkheim, *Suicide: A Study in Sociology*, Routledge and Kegan Paul, London, 1970, p. 50)

began to distinguish types of suicide. He believed that the suicide rate was determined by the relationships between individuals and society. In particular, suicide rates were dependent upon the degree to which individuals were integrated into social groups and the degree to which society regulated individual behaviour. On this basis he distinguished four types of suicide: egoistic, altruistic, anomic and fatalistic, as illustrated in Figure 13.1

Egoistic suicide resulted from the individual being insufficiently integrated into the social groups and society in which he or she belonged. This, according to Durkheim, accounted for the discrepancy between the suicide rates of Protestants and Roman Catholics. He argued that the Catholic religion integrated its members more strongly into a religious community. The long-established beliefs and traditional rituals of the Catholic church provided a uniform system of religious belief and practice into which the lives of its members were closely intertwined. The Catholic faith was rarely questioned and the church had strong controls over the conscience and behaviour of its members. The result was a homogeneous religious community, unified and integrated by uniform belief and standardized ritual. By comparison, the Protestant church encouraged its members to develop their own interpretation of religion. Protestantism advocated 'free inquiry' rather than the imposition of traditional religious dogma. In Durkheim's view, 'The Protestant is far more the author of his faith.' As a result, Protestants were less likely to belong to a community that was unified by a commitment to common religious

beliefs and practices. Durkheim concluded that the higher rate of suicide associated with Protestantism 'results from its being a less strongly integrated church than the Catholic church'.

Durkheim also related egoistic suicide to 'domestic society' or family relationships. The unmarried and childless were less integrated into a family than the married and those with children. The former group had less responsibility for others and as a consequence was more prone to egoism and a high suicide rate.

Durkheim thought that **anomic suicide** was the other main type of suicide in industrial societies. Anomic suicides took place when society did not regulate the individual sufficiently. This occurred when traditional norms and values were disrupted by rapid social change that produced uncertainty in the minds of individuals as society's guidelines for behaviour became increasingly unclear. Not surprisingly, Durkheim found that suicide rates rose during periods of economic depression, such as the period following the crash of the Paris Bourse (stock exchange) in 1882. What was more surprising – and at first sight difficult to explain – was the rise in the suicide rate during a period of economic prosperity. The conquest of Rome by Victor-Emmanuel in 1870 formed the basis of Italian unity and led to an economic boom with rapidly rising salaries and living standards, but it also led to a rising suicide rate. Durkheim reasoned that both booms and slumps brought the uncertainty of anomie and so more suicides.

Durkheim thought egoism and anomie were problems that affected all industrial societies to a

Figure 13.1   Suicide types and the balance of society

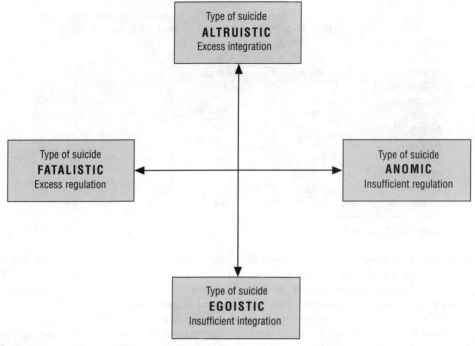

(*Source*: David Lee and Howard Newby, *The Problem of Sociology*, Hutchinson, London, 1983.)

greater or lesser extent. Because of the highly specialized division of labour in such societies they were less integrated than simple or 'primitive' societies.

Pre-industrial societies could suffer from the opposite types of suicide to egoistic and anomic: altruistic and fatalistic.

Altruistic suicide took place when the individual was so well integrated into society that they sacrificed their own life out of a sense of duty to others. In the past Hindu widows would kill themselves at their husband's funeral (suttee), and in traditional Ashanti society some of the king's followers were expected to commit suicide after the death of the monarch. Individuals were so strongly integrated into their society that they would make the ultimate sacrifice for the benefit of others.

The fourth and final type of suicide, distinguished by Durkheim as **fatalistic suicide**, occurred when society restricted the individual too much. It was the suicide 'of persons with futures pitilessly blocked and passions violently choked by oppressive discipline'. Durkheim thought this type of suicide was of little importance in modern societies, but it was of some historical interest, being the cause of high suicide rates among slaves.

Durkheim, suicide and methodology

Durkheim's study of suicide illustrates his views both on society and on methodology. He believed it was essential to get the right amount of integration and regulation in society: 'primitive' societies tended to have too much of both; industrial societies too little of either. He used quantitative 'scientific' methods, employing the comparative method in a highly systematic way. However, he did not simply follow the approach advocated by positivists. He used the supposedly objective statistics available on suicide to support the claim that unobservable forces shaped human behaviour. The total number of suicides was determined by such unobservable 'collective tendencies' which 'have an existence of their own' and are as 'real as cosmic forces'. According to some of today's sociologists, such as Steve Taylor, Durkheim adopted a realist rather than a positivist view of science (realism is discussed on pp. 860–1). However it is defined, it is nevertheless Durkheim's methodology in studying suicide that has attracted most attention from supporters and critics alike.

Positivist responses to Durkheim

Sociologists studying suicide who adopt positivist methods have generally praised most aspects of Durkheim's work. As early as 1930 Maurice Halbwachs carried out a review of his work. Halbwachs attempted to refine Durkheim's work and did not challenge the use of a 'scientific' approach in the study of suicide. Indeed he claimed that Durkheim had been able to provide 'a fully comprehensive treatment of the phenomenon of suicide, which could be modified and added to, but which in principle seems unassailable'. Halbwachs could add to and modify Durkheim's work by making use both of the more recent suicide statistics that had become available and new methods of statistical analysis such as the use of correlation coefficients. On the whole he confirmed what Durkheim had found. However, he did argue that Durkheim had overestimated the importance of religion in determining the suicide rate. Halbwachs claimed to have found that differences between living in urban and rural areas had more impact than differences between Catholics and Protestants.

Jack P. Gibbs and Walter T. Martin agreed with Durkheim and Halbwachs that suicide should be studied using scientific methods and statistical data. However, they believed that Durkheim himself had failed to use sufficiently rigorous methods. As noted earlier, Durkheim sometimes used concepts that could not be directly observed or measured and thus he did not entirely follow positivist methods. Gibbs and Martin picked up on this and attempted to rectify what they saw as a flaw in Durkheim's otherwise exemplary method. In particular they suggested that Durkheim failed to define the concept of 'integration' in a sufficiently precise and measurable way. They point out that 'one does not see individuals tied to society in any physical sense'. Consequently it was impossible to test the theory that lack of integration led to a high suicide rate.

Gibbs and Martin did not believe that integration itself could be measured directly. The type of data necessary to measure the durability and stability of social relationships was not available. They therefore proposed that 'status integration' could be used as an indicator of social integration. Status integration concerns the extent to which individuals occupy sets of social roles that are commonly found together. People with a high degree of status integration have job, family and other statuses that are commonly grouped together. Those

with a high degree of status incompatibility have unusual sets of statuses. Thus in their theory an occupation in which 75 per cent of its members are married is compatible with marriage, but if only 35 per cent are married it is not compatible. Individuals with compatible statuses are deemed to be highly integrated since it is assumed that they will have more and stronger social relationships than those with incompatible statuses. To Gibbs and Martin the greater the degree of status integration in a population the lower the suicide rate will be.

Gibbs and Martin's theory shows that some commentators criticized Durkheim for being insufficiently positivist and for making too little use of statistical data. The theory itself though does not bear close examination. They do not provide any evidence to show that status integration can be used to measure the strength of people's social relationships. Nor do they justify the use of statistics alone to identify compatible statuses. Hagedorn and Labowitz point out that male ballet dancers and male lion tamers are both uncommon but the former could be expected to have more incompatible statuses (quoted in Steve Taylor, 1982, p. 27).

■ Interpretive theories of suicide

Interpretive sociologists tend to make much stronger attacks on Durkheim's suicide than positivists. They tend to reject many of the basic principles of Durkheim's approach rather than quibbling about particular details. On the whole however, they do acknowledge the possibility of explaining the causes of suicide.

J.D. Douglas – The Social Meanings of Suicide

One of the best-known interpretive critics of Durkheim is J.D. Douglas. He particularly criticizes the use of official statistics in the study of suicide questioning their reliability. Douglas points out that the decision as to whether a sudden death is suicide is made by a coroner and is influenced by other people such as the family and friends of the deceased. Douglas suggests that systematic bias may enter the process of reaching a decision, and that this bias could explain Durkheim's findings.

For example, when a person is well integrated into a social group his or her family and friends might be more likely to deny the possibility of suicide both to themselves and to the coroner. They may feel a sense of personal responsibility that leads them to try to cover up the suicide. With less well-integrated members of society this is less likely to happen. While it might appear that the number of suicides is related to integration, in reality the degree of integration simply affects the chances of sudden death being recorded as suicide. Douglas sees suicide statistics as the result of negotiations between the different parties involved. However, he does suggest that the distortions in the statistics are systematic. By implication it might be possible to reduce or allow for these distortions to produce more reliable statistics that could be used to explain suicide.

Douglas's second main criticism of Durkheim is that it was ridiculous for Durkheim to treat all suicides as the same type of act without investigating the meaning attached to the act by those who took their own life. Douglas points out that in different cultures suicide can have very different meanings. For example, if a businessman in a modern industrial society kills himself because his business has collapsed it is a quite different act from the suicide of an elderly Innuit (Eskimo), who kills himself for the benefit of his society at a time of food shortage. Each act has a different motive behind it and a social meaning that is related to the society and context in which it took place.

In order to categorize suicides according to their social meanings Douglas suggests that it is necessary to carry out case studies to discover the meanings of particular suicides. These case studies could be based upon interviews with those who know the person well and the analysis of the suicide notes and diaries of the deceased. Although he did not carry out such research, Douglas nevertheless claims that the most common social meanings of suicide in Western industrial society are transformation of the soul (for example, suicide as a way of getting to heaven), transformation of the self (suicide as a means of getting others to think of you differently), suicide as a means of achieving fellow-feeling (or sympathy), and suicide as a means of getting revenge by making others feel guilty.

In other societies other meanings might be more common. For instance, religious beliefs might produce suicides with the social meaning 'transformation of the soul', that is, they were a method of getting to heaven.

■ Jean Baechler – suicide as problem solving

Douglas's approach has been developed further by the French sociologist Jean Baechler. He makes extensive use of case studies of suicide in existing literature and he classifies suicides according to their meanings. Baechler sees suicidal behaviour as a way of responding to and trying to solve a problem. Suicide is adopted when there seems to be no alternative solution. From this perspective it then becomes possible to classify suicides according to the type of solution they offer and the type of situation they are a response to; in other words according to the end pursued by the suicidal individual. On this basis Baechler divides suicides into four main types.

1 Escapist suicides take three forms. Some people take their own lives as a means of flight from an intolerable situation. For others, suicide is a response to grief about the loss of something in particular, perhaps a loved one or even a limb. Suicide may also be a means of self-punishment used by a person when they feel they have done wrong.

2 Aggressive suicides are a way of harming another person or people. There are four types of aggressive suicide. Vengeance suicides are intended to make another person feel guilty or to bring condemnation on them from society. For example, a wife might commit suicide to draw attention to her husband's cruelty. Crime suicides involve killing another person during the suicidal behaviour, for example when someone shoots a spouse and then turns the gun on themselves. Blackmail suicides are used to persuade someone else to change their behaviour and treat the suicide victim better. Appeal suicides are used to show others that the person concerned is in need of help. Blackmail and appeal are often the ends pursued by those who make suicide attempts that either fail or are not entirely serious.

3 Oblative suicides are ways of achieving something that is particularly valued by the suicide victim. Sacrifice involves giving up your own life to save another person. Transfiguration suicides are used by a person so that they can obtain a more desirable state, for example, to join a loved one in the afterlife.

4 Ludic suicides involve taking deliberate risks that might lead to death. There are two types, the ordeal and the game. Ordeals are ways by which an individual tries to prove themselves to others by showing their bravery.

Games involve taking risks 'for the hell of it', for example playing Russian roulette with nobody else present.

Baechler is more explicit than Douglas in suggesting that causes of suicide can be found. However, unlike Durkheim he does not believe that suicide can be explained wholly or even mainly in terms of external factors. As Baechler puts it, 'Whatever the external factor considered, it always happens that the number of those who do not commit suicide is infinitely greater than the number of those who do.' Not everyone whose business fails, spouse dies or who is a Protestant in an urban area kills themselves. Thus to Baechler suicide must always be at least partially explained through 'personal factors' that are particular to an individual. Baechler differs from the studies of suicide examined so far in that he includes attempted suicides under his general definition of 'suicidal behaviour'. Other sociologists have paid even more attention to the implications of attempted suicide (see pp. 824–6).

Criticisms of interpretive theories

Interpretive sociologists have been criticized in a number of ways. Steve Taylor criticizes both Douglas and Baechler for failing to recognize the value of Durkheim's work. He also questions the worth of schemes that are designed to categorize suicides according to their social meanings. Commenting on Baechler he points out that individual cases often fit a number of categories depending on the interpretation the researcher makes of the victim's motives. There is no reason to believe that these interpretations are any more reliable than suicide statistics. Taylor also criticizes Douglas for contradicting himself. At some points Douglas implies that suicide statistics can never be reliable since it is always a matter of judgement whether a death is a suicide. At other times he suggests that causes of suicide can be found. It is difficult to see how this can be if it is impossible to be certain whether an act is a suicide. Phenomenological sociologists have taken this type of criticism to its logical conclusion by denying there can be any objective data on which to base an explanation of suicide.

J. Maxwell Atkinson – *Discovering Suicide*

Scientific and quantitative methods are completely rejected by some phenomenologists. This can be seen clearly from J. Maxwell Atkinson's study of suicide. Atkinson does not accept that a 'real' rate of suicide exists as an objective reality waiting to be discovered. Sociologists who proceed with this assumption will end up producing 'facts' on suicide that have nothing to do with the social reality they seek to understand. By constructing a set of criteria to categorize and measure suicide – in scientific language by 'operationalizing' the concept of suicide – they will merely be imposing their reality on the social world. This will inevitably distort that world. As Michael Phillipson observes, the positivist methodology employed by Durkheim and other researchers 'rides roughshod over the very social reality they are trying to comprehend'. Suicide is a construct of social actors, an aspect of social reality. Official statistics on suicide are not therefore 'wrong', 'mistaken', 'inaccurate' or 'in error'. They are part of the social world. They are the interpretations made by officials of what is seen to be unnatural death. Since the object of sociology is to comprehend the social world, that world can only be understood in terms of the categories, perceptions and interpretations of its members. Thus, with reference to suicide, the appropriate question for sociologists to ask is, in Atkinson's words, 'How do deaths get categorized as suicide?'

Categorizing death

Atkinson's research focuses on the methods employed by coroners and their officers to categorize death. His data are drawn from discussions with coroners, attendance at inquests in three different towns, observation of a coroner's officer at work and a part of the records of one particular coroner.

Atkinson argues that coroners have a 'commonsense theory' of suicide. If information about the deceased fits the theory they are likely to categorize his or her death as suicide. In terms of this theory, coroners consider the following four types of evidence relevant for reaching a verdict.

1 They take into account whether or not suicide notes were left or threats of suicide preceded death.

2 Particular modes of dying are judged to be more or less likely to indicate suicide. Road deaths are rarely interpreted as an indicator for suicide whereas drowning, hanging, gassing and drug overdose are more likely to be seen as such.

3 The locations and circumstances of death are judged to be relevant. For example, death by gunshot is more likely to be defined as suicide if it occurred in a deserted lay-by than if it took place in the countryside during an organized shoot. In cases of gassing, a suicide verdict is more likely if windows, doors and ventilators have been blocked to prevent the escape of gas.

4 Coroners consider the biography of the deceased with particular reference to his or her mental state and social situation. A history of mental illness, a disturbed childhood and evidence of acute depression are often seen as reason for suicide. A recent divorce, the death of a loved one relative, a lack of friends, problems at work or serious financial difficulties are regarded as possible causes for suicide. This, as Atkinson points out, is remarkably similar to Durkheim's notion of social integration.

Referring to the case of an individual found gassed in his car, a coroner told Atkinson, 'There's a classic pattern for you – broken home, escape to the services, nervous breakdown, unsettled at work, no family ties – what could be clearer.' Thus coroners' views about why people commit suicide appear to influence their categorization of death.

Coroners' common-sense theories of suicide contain explanations of the causes of suicide. If information about the deceased's background fits these explanations, then a verdict of suicide is likely. Atkinson provides the following summary of the procedures used to categorize unnatural death. Coroners 'are engaged in analysing features of the deaths and of the biographies of the deceased according to a variety of taken-for-granted assumptions about what constitutes a "typical suicide", a "typical suicide biography"', and so on. Suicide can therefore be seen as an interpretation placed on an event, an interpretation which stems from a set of taken-for-granted assumptions.

This view has serious implications for research which treats official statistics on suicide as 'facts' and seeks to explain their cause. Researchers who look for explanations of suicide in the social background or mental state of the deceased may simply be uncovering and making explicit the taken-for-granted assumptions of coroners. Atkinson found that coroners' theories of suicide were remarkably similar to those of sociologists and psychologists. Since coroners use their theories of the cause of suicide as a means for categorizing suicide, this similarity might be expected. Thus social scientists who look for the causes of suicide in the social situation or mental condition of those officially classified as suicides may simply be revealing the common-sense theories of coroners.

Criticisms of phenomenology

Phenomenological views have themselves been subject to criticism. Barry Hindess points out that the criticisms of suicide statistics advanced by phenomenologists can be turned against the sociological theories of phenomenologists themselves. If suicide statistics can be criticized as being no more than the interpretations of coroners, then studies such as that done by Atkinson can be criticized as being no more than the interpretation of a particular sociologist. Just as there is no way of checking on the validity of the verdicts reached by coroners, there is no way of checking on the validity of the accounts of how coroners reach their decisions advanced by phenomenological sociologists. Hindess therefore dismisses the work of such sociologists as being 'theoretically worthless' and he says of their work 'A manuscript produced by a monkey at a typewriter would be no less valuable.' If phenomenological views were taken to their logical conclusion no sociology would be possible, and the attempt to understand and explain suicide would have to be abandoned.

■ Steve Taylor – beyond positivism and phenomenology
'Persons under trains'

In a more recent contribution to the study of suicide Steve Taylor has tried to move beyond all the approaches that have been examined so far. However, his own study starts by confirming the view of many critics of Durkheim that suicide statistics are unreliable. Taylor conducted a study of 'persons under trains', people who met their death when they were hit by tube trains on the London underground. Over a twelve-month period he found thirty-two cases where there were no strong clues as to the reason for the death. No suicide notes were left and no witnesses were able to state that the victim jumped deliberately. In effect, it was impossible to say with any certainty whether a suicide had taken place or not. Nevertheless, seventeen cases resulted in suicide verdicts, five were classified as accidental deaths and the remaining ten produced open verdicts. Taylor found a number of factors made suicide verdicts more likely. People with a history of mental illness and those who had suffered some form of social failure or social disgrace were more likely to have their deaths recorded as suicides. When a person who had died had no good reason to be at the tube station suicide verdicts were more likely. Taylor also found that the verdict was strongly influenced by the witnesses who testified to the dead person's state of mind. Where the witness was a close friend or family member they tended to deny the person had reason to kill themself and stress reasons why they might want to carry on living. Where the witnesses were less close to the person, for example in one case their landlady, they were less likely to deny suicidal motives.

Taylor's methodology

Taylor then found strong evidence to support the view that suicide statistics cannot be taken at face value. Specific factors seemed to have influenced the verdicts reached and distorted suicide figures in particular ways. However, Taylor does not follow phenomenologists in arguing that such problems make it impossible to explain suicide. Taylor's own theory is not based upon statistical evidence but upon attempts to discover 'underlying, unobservable structures and causal processes'. This type of approach is based upon a realist conception of science that is discussed later in this chapter. He develops his theory as an attempt to explain the key features of different types of suicide revealed in case studies.

Types of suicide

Taylor's theory is illustrated in Figure 13.2. He argues that suicides and suicide attempts are either 'ectopic' – they result from what a person thinks about themself, or 'symphysic' – they result from a person's relationship with others. Suicides and suicide attempts are also related either to certainty or uncertainty, people are sure or unsure about themselves or about others. Thus, like Durkheim, Taylor distinguishes four types of suicide connected

to diametrically opposed situations. In Taylor's theory however they are situations faced by particular individuals and are not related so closely to the wider functioning of society. We shall now look at the four types of suicide that Taylor identified.

The first two types are **ectopic** or **inner-directed suicides**.

1 Submissive suicide occurs when a person is certain about themselves and their life, they believe their life is effectively over and see themselves as already dead. Taylor says 'The world of the submissive is one of constricting horizons; of closing doors, blind alleys and cul-de-sacs'. The terminally ill may commit submissive suicide. In other cases a person may have decided that their life is valueless without a loved one that has died. In this type of suicide the suicide attempt is usually deadly serious, the person is sure they wish to die.

2 Thanatation is a type of suicide, or suicide attempt that occurs when a person is uncertain about themselves. The suicide attempt is a gamble that may or may not be survived according to fate or chance. If the attempt does not result in death the person learns that they are capable of facing death. In some cases the person may be exhilarated by the thrill of the risk taking and they may make several suicide attempts. Taylor quotes the novelist Graham Greene who periodically played Russian roulette with a revolver and the poet Sylvia Plath who deliberately risked death by driving her car off the road.

The other two are **symphysic** or **other-directed suicides**.

1 Sacrifice suicides occur when a person is certain that others have made their life unbearable. The person who takes their own life often attributes the blame for their death to others so that they will feel guilty or will suffer criticism from other members of society. For example, Taylor refers to a case in which a 22-year-old man killed himself because his wife was in love with his elder brother and she wanted a divorce. The man left letters making it clear that he felt that his wife and brother were responsible for his death.

2 Appeal suicides and suicide attempts result from the suicidal person feeling uncertainty over the attitudes of others towards them. The suicide attempts are a form of communication in which the victim tries to show how desperate they are to find out how others will respond. Suicide attempts may involve trying to persuade others to change their behaviour, or they may offer them chances to save the victim. Those who make the attempts

Figure 13.2 Steve Taylor's theory of suicide

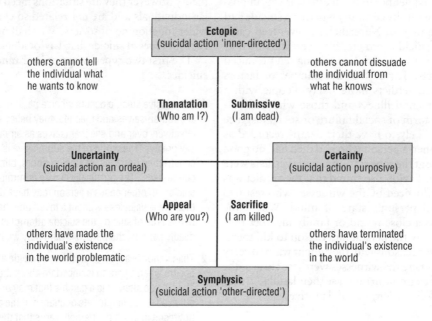

'combine the wish to die and the wish for change in others and improvement in the situation; they are acts both of despair and of hope'. For example, a woman slashed herself with a bread knife in front of her husband after he had discovered her having sex with a neighbour. Her husband took her to hospital and she survived. She later said that she was unsure whether she would bleed to death but wanted to show her husband how much she loved him and to appeal for forgiveness through her actions. In another case a man took an overdose of barbiturates in a car parked in front of his estranged wife's house. He left a note for his wife saying what he had done. However, a dense fog obscured the car so the wife did not see him when she returned to the house and therefore could not save him. Taylor also refers to Marilyn Monroe's death. She had rung her doctor before taking her fatal overdose and on previous occasions when she had rung him in an agitated state he had come round to calm her down. His failure to do so on this occasion removed any chance of discovery and rescue.

Evaluation of Taylor

Taylor's theory has some advantages over the other sociological theories examined so far. For example, it helps to explain why some suicide victims leave notes and others do not, why some suicide attempts seem more serious than others, and why some take place in isolation and others in more public places. However, his theory is hard to test. It rests upon the meanings given to suicidal actions by those who take part in them and these meanings can be interpreted in different ways. For those whose suicide attempts result in death the meanings can only be inferred from circumstantial evidence, they are no longer able to explain their motives. Individual suicides may result from a combination of motives with the result that they do not fit neatly into any one category.

■ Quantitative and qualitative methodology

The preceding sections of this chapter have outlined and illustrated the differences between these two broad approaches to methodology. Ray Pawson has described the impression that such descriptions tend to give to many students. He says that many students 'have their minds firmly fixed upon an image of a methodological brawl in which the beleaguered minority (the phenomenologists) have been for years trying to survive the onslaught of the wicked majority (the positivists)'. He claims that such a view is highly misleading.

Pawson is correct to point out that the distinction between positivism and phenomenology has sometimes been exaggerated, and some of his points will be examined shortly. However, the disputes are real. When Hindess compares phenomenologists' work to that which might be produced by monkeys, he illustrates the strength of some of the methodological battles that have taken place. Nevertheless, a number of points should be made to put these disputes into perspective.

1 Even those who have strongly advocated and are closely associated with either a quantitative or qualitative approach have not necessarily stuck rigidly to their own supposed methodological principles. Douglas points out how Durkheim in his study of suicide strayed away from basing his analysis entirely on 'social facts', and dealt with the subjective states of individuals. For example, he gave mental sketches of what it felt like to be a Roman Catholic or a Protestant in order to explain why their suicide rates should be so different. At the other extreme, even one of the most ardent critics of quantitative methods, Cicourel, has made extensive use of statistical data. In his study of juvenile justice in two Californian cities he collected statistics on law enforcement in the two cities, and he used a systematic comparison of the cities in order to explain their differing crime rates.

2 It can be argued that the 'methodological brawl' mentioned above has come to an end. Pawson says that the idea that 'positivists and phenomenologists are always at logger heads is a sixties' hangover; nowadays it is much more accurate to describe the relationship between those who do qualitative and those who do quantitative research as one of truce'. Many sociologists get on with actually doing research without worrying too much about the philosophical basis of that research. As the sections on primary sources will show, practical difficulties have at least as much influence on the choice of research methods as theoretical considerations. Furthermore, many sociologists now advocate methodological pluralism (see p. 856), where a mixture of quantitative and qualitative methods is used.

3 Finally, new philosophies of science have now made the disagreements of positivists and phenomenologists look somewhat outdated. The realist conception of science, which will be discussed in a later section (see p. 860–1), does not imply that science should be concerned only with that which can be observed directly. In this respect it does not exclude the use of qualitative methods in a 'social science' such as sociology.

The ways in which some of the methodological disputes examined at the start of the chapter have been superseded will become clearer as the chapter develops. Next, primary research methods will be examined. They will be evaluated both in terms of their practical usefulness and in terms of the theoretical problems associated with them.

■ The research process

This part of the chapter will deal with the major issues involved in actually carrying out research. It begins with a consideration of how researchers go about selecting topics for research, and goes on to examine the practical and theoretical issues involved in collecting and analysing data.

■ Choosing a topic for research

Before embarking upon research sociologists have to decide what they are going to study. This choice may be affected by a number of factors.

The value and beliefs of the researcher will obviously play some part. Sociologists are unlikely to devote considerable time and energy to issues that they think are unimportant or trivial. For example, Peter Townsend's values have led him to regard poverty as an important problem in contemporary industrial societies (see pp. 129–31) while Hall *et al.* believed the moral panic about 'mugging' was worthy of attention (see pp. 422–5). What a researcher believes is important may be influenced by developments within the discipline of sociology, or developments in the wider society. Sociology is a profession as well as a discipline, and many sociologists wish to advance their careers by criticizing or developing the work of fellow sociologists, or by trying to resolve some key sociological issue. This might explain why so many sociologists have followed Durkheim in studying suicide, while other areas of social life have been comparatively neglected. Similarly, routine clerical workers have been studied more than some other sections of the stratification system. This group is often seen as a crucial test of Marxist and Weberian theories of stratification whereas groups of less theoretical interest to sociologists, such as agricultural labourers, have not been studied so frequently.

When there are major changes in society, sociologists are likely to study them. Sociology was born in the nineteenth century, largely out of a concern with the changes wrought by the industrial revolution. In recent times sociologists have devoted more time to studying unemployment than they did in the 1950s and 1960s when rates of unemployment were very much lower and it seemed to be less serious as a social problem. Specific government policies can also stimulate research. Hence, for example, the concern with the 'new vocationalism' in the contemporary sociology of education (see pp. 794–805).

A very important factor affecting the choice of research topic is the availability or otherwise of grants to finance it. Research funds may come from charitable foundations, such as the Nuffield and Rowntree foundations, from industry, or from government – in Britain usually via the Economic and Social Research Council (or ESRC). The European Union sometimes provides funds for sociological research. Some small-scale research requires little funding, but major research projects can be very expensive, and the sort of research that gets done can be very strongly influenced by those who hold the purse strings. Payne *et al.* have suggested that the SSRC (the predecessor of the ESRC), 'had no pretensions to being anything other than a government organisation'. As an important source of funding for British sociology it tended to restrict the amount of sociological research that was critical of the government of the day. Industrial providers of research grants tend to want some practical benefits from the money they spend, so research into organizations and industrial sociology is most likely to receive funding from this source.

Other practical difficulties apart from money can affect the topics chosen by sociologists for their research. The availability of existing data on a topic or the practicality of collecting data will both have an influence. Durkheim chose to study suicide partly because statistics were available from many European countries. Some important groups in the population, for example, senior politicians and the directors of top companies, rarely form the basis of detailed studies. This is partly due to their unwillingness to reveal their activities to sociological scrutiny. Other relatively powerless groups, such as delinquent gangs, have been subject to detailed and frequent study.

▪ Primary sources

Primary sources of information consist of data collected by researchers themselves during the course of their work. **Secondary sources** consist of data that already exist. Primary sources would include data collected by researchers using questionnaires, conducting interviews or carrying out participant observation. Secondary sources include official statistics, mass media products, diaries, letters, government reports, other sociologists' work and historical and contemporary records. Secondary sources will be discussed later.

▪ Choosing a primary research method

Some of the factors that influence the choice of research topic can also influence the choice of research method used to study that topic. For example, the source of funding for a proposed project might well specify the type of method to be employed. Many funding bodies support the use of more quantitative methods. However, the most important factors influencing the choice of research method are the topic to be studied and the theoretical and practical considerations.

Some topics lend themselves more readily to the use of quantitative techniques such as questionnaires: research into voting in Great Britain tends to involve large-scale studies using quantitative statistical techniques because of the sheer numbers necessarily involved in the research if the data is to be of any use. Other topics, such as behaviour in classrooms, lend themselves more readily to qualitative methods.

As the earlier sections of this chapter have shown, those who support a particular theoretical approach tend to use either quantitative or qualitive methods. This commitment may well be the major influence on their choice of research method.

Reliability

Many of the debates about the merits of particular research methods focus on questions of reliability and validity. In the natural sciences data are seen to be 'reliable' if other researchers using the same methods of investigation on the same material produce the same results. By replicating an experiment it is possible to check for errors in observation and measurement. Once reliable data have been obtained, generalizations can then be made about the behaviour observed. No sociologist would claim that the social sciences can attain the standards of reliability employed in the natural sciences. Many would argue, however, that sociological data can attain a certain standard of reliability.

Generally speaking, quantitative methods are seen to provide greater reliability. They usually produce standardized data in a statistical form: the research can be repeated and the results checked. Questionnaires can be used to test precise hypotheses which the researcher has devised.

Qualitative methods are often criticized for failing to meet the same standards of reliability. Such methods may be seen as unreliable because the procedures used to collect data can be unsystematic, the results are rarely quantified and there is no way of replicating a qualitative study and checking the reliability of its findings.

Validity

Data are 'valid' if they provide a true picture of what is being studied. A valid statement gives a true measurement or description of what it claims to measure or describe. It is an accurate reflection of social reality. Data can be reliable without being valid. Studies can be replicated and produce the same results but those results may not be a valid measure of what the researcher intends to measure. For instance, statistics on church attendance may be reliable but they do not necessarily give a true picture of religious commitment.

Supporters of qualitative methods often argue that quantitative methods lack validity. Statistical research methods may be easy to replicate but they may not provide a true picture of social reality. They are seen to lack the depth to describe accurately the meanings and motives that form the basis of social action. They use categories imposed on the social world by sociologists, categories that may have little meaning or relevance to other members of society. To many interpretive sociologists only qualitative methods can overcome these problems and provide a valid picture of social reality.

Practicality

Researchers are sometimes attracted to quantitative methods because of their practicality. Quantitative methods are generally less time consuming and require less personal commitment. It is usually possible to study larger and more representative samples which can provide an overall picture of society. Qualitative research often has to be confined to the study of small numbers because of practical limitations. It is more suited to providing an in-depth insight into a smaller sample of people.

These points will be developed in the following sections.

■ Choosing a sample

Once a sociologist has chosen a topic for research and a method to carry out that research, she or he needs to decide upon a 'sample', that is the actual individuals to be studied.

A sample is a part of a larger population. It is usually selected to be representative of that population: those included in the sample are chosen as a cross-section of the larger group. The use of samples saves the researcher time and money since it reduces the number of individuals to be studied. If the sample is chosen carefully, it is possible to generalize from it, that is, to make statements about the whole relevant population on the basis of the sample.

The first stage in sampling involves identifying the 'relevant population'. A population in this sense includes all the relevant sampling units. The 'sampling unit' is the individual person or social group in that population. In a study of voting in Britain the relevant population would be all those entitled to vote, and the sampling unit would be the individual voter.

Having determined the sampling unit and the population the researcher might then try to obtain or to produce a 'sampling frame'. In a study of voting there is a ready-made sampling frame – the electoral register – since a sampling frame is simply a list of all the relevant sampling units in the population. It is important that the sampling frame is as comprehensive as possible: if it is not, the sample might be seriously distorted. Researchers have sometimes used telephone directories as a sampling frame for the population of a particular area, but the directory would not include those who have ex-directory numbers and those without a telephone. Since the latter would probably be people on low incomes, the results of a study on (for example) voting intentions based upon this sampling frame might be seriously misleading. Often, even apparently comprehensive sampling frames contain omissions. The electoral register does not include all adults living in Britain. Foreign nationals (except for some citizens of Eire), those who have failed to register as voters, and members of the House of Lords are among those who would be excluded. The introduction of the Poll Tax led to large numbers of people avoiding being placed on the electoral register in an attempt to get out of paying the tax.

Studies use imperfect sampling frames. The *British Crime Surveys* have used the electoral register (see pp. 399–401 for details of these surveys). Pat Mayhew, the Principal Research Officer responsible for the *Surveys*, admits that the most comprehensive sampling frame now available is not the electoral register, but the Post Office Address File. Mayhew notes that the electoral register does not include many people in institutions (such as mental hospitals and prisons) who may be particularly prone to being the victims of crime.

One government study, the Census, avoids the problems of sampling by studying all, or very nearly all, members of a large population. By law every household in Britain has to complete a Census form, although some individuals (including many of the homeless) may slip through the net.

Sociologists lack the resources to carry out such comprehensive studies as the Census and so they usually try to select a sample that contains the same proportions of people with relevant characteristics as are present in the population under consideration. If it contains 60 per cent women and 40 per cent men, then the sample should contain 60 per cent women and 40 per cent men. Other important characteristics such as age, occupation, ethnic origin and religion are often taken into account by researchers as they select their sample.

Other, more specialized factors may be taken into account depending upon the nature of the research. Opinion polls on voting intentions usually use a sample from a variety of constituencies chosen according to the share of the vote won by the major parties in those constituencies at the previous election. Thus a number of 'safe' Labour, 'safe' Conservative and more marginal seats would be included. Clearly the results would be distorted if the sample was chosen entirely from safe Labour seats. In a study of education the researcher might wish to select the sample to ensure that the types of schools attended by those in the sample reflect the proportions in the population as a whole.

If sampling has been carried out satisfactorily, researchers should be able to generalize on the basis of the results. This means that they should be able to make statements about the whole population without having conducted research into every member of that population. For example, opinion pollsters often claim to be able to predict the results of an election in Britain to within a couple of percentage points on the basis of a sample of perhaps one or two thousand people.

All research involves some sort of sampling, some selection of who or what to study. Those researchers who advocate 'scientific' quantitative methods tend to support the use of sophisticated sampling techniques and often claim to be able to generalize on the basis of their findings. Those who support interpretive qualitative methods tend to study smaller numbers of people so their studies are less likely to require complex sampling techniques. Different methods of producing a sample will now be examined.

■ Types of sampling
Random and systematic sampling

This is the simplest way to select a large sample. Using **random sampling** the researcher ensures that each sample unit has an equal chance of being chosen to take part in the research. This is often achieved by assigning numbers to each sample unit and selecting members of the sample by using a random number table. The nearest everyday equivalent to this is picking numbers out of a hat.

A less time consuming though slightly less random method, is to select, say, every tenth or twentieth number on a list. Since this method is not truly random it is known as **systematic sampling**.

Random sampling is not ideal. It relies on statistical probability to ensure the representativeness of the sample. In simple terms, it is based upon the so-called 'law of averages', and a relatively large sample is needed to be confident that the sample will be genuinely representative. Researchers therefore generally prefer to use the method to be discussed next, stratified random sampling.

Stratified random sampling

Stratified random sampling involves the division of the sampling frame into groups in order to ensure that the sample is representative. The researcher identifies the important variables which need to be controlled and allocates the sampling units to different groups according to these variables.

For example, the researcher might identify gender and class as important variables. In this case the population would be divided into working-class males, working-class females, middle-class males, middle-class females, upper-class males and upper-class females. The sample would then be selected at random from each of these groups ensuring that the proportions of the sample in each category were the same as the proportions in the population as a whole. If 20 per cent of the population were found to be working-class females, 20 per cent of the sample would be working-class females.

This is an effective method of choosing a representative sample because it allows the researcher to control the variables seen as important. It requires a smaller sample size to ensure representativeness than random sampling. However, stratified random sampling is often not practicable. Even if a sampling frame is available, it often does not contain the information necessary to divide the population into groups. Opinion pollsters can use the electoral register as a sampling frame but it does not provide information such as the occupation of the electorate. For this reason it cannot be used to produce a stratified random sample.

Quota sampling

Quota sampling allows researchers to control variables without having a sampling frame. When quota sampling is used the interviewers are told how many respondents with particular characteristics to question so that the overall sample reflects the characteristics of the population as a whole. For example, an interviewer might be required to administer a questionnaire to ten married females and ten married males aged between 20 and 35, five unmarried men and women of the same age group and so on. Once the quota for a particular category has been filled responses will not be collected from those in that category.

This is a particularly useful method of sampling when the overall proportions of different groups within a population are known. Government population statistics could be used to set the quota for a representative sample of different age groups in the British population.

Quota sampling can also be used when the study is based upon a simple comparison of two groups. For example, Hannah Gavron, in a study of mothers with young children, established a quota of thirty-eight working-class women with one or more children under five and born after 1930, and thirty middle-class women with the same characteristics. Although a rather crude form of quota sampling, this sort of approach can be useful when one variable is of particular interest. In Gavron's case social class was the key independent variable being isolated to compare the two groups.

Members of quota samples can be approached in various ways. Researchers often simply stop people on the street or knock on doors. Gavron contacted most of her sample by getting their names from doctors' lists of patients, getting the doctor to write to them, and then telephoning herself to arrange a visit.

Despite the simplicity of quota sampling it does have both theoretical and practical drawbacks in some circumstances. Quota sampling is not truly random because each person within the population does not have an equal chance of being chosen. For example, a researcher using a doctor's list can only contact patients on that list; a researcher stopping people on a particular street at a particular time can only question people who happen to be in that place at that time. The lack of genuine randomness may distort the results. A researcher for a political opinion poll who questions people at 11 o'clock on Tuesday morning in a city centre would be unlikely to gain much response from those who worked in the surrounding rural area.

Stopping people in the street may lead to a low response rate. Many people could refuse to cooperate, and those who do cooperate might be untypical of the population as a whole in a way that was not anticipated when the original quotas were set up.

Quota sampling usually requires the researcher to ask a number of personal questions to determine whether the respondent has the characteristics of a quota group on which information is required. Asking such questions at the start of an interview may put some interviewees off and others on their guard so that their responses are not as open and honest as they might otherwise have been.

Furthermore, practical problems can arise in filling quotas. In some circumstances people who have full-time jobs might prove more difficult to interview than people without jobs.

Despite these limitations quota sampling continues to be used because there are circumstances when random or stratified random sampling is not possible.

Multi-stage sampling

Multi-stage sampling can save the researcher time and money although it reduces the extent to which the sample is genuinely random. It simply involves selecting a sample from another sample. It is often used in opinion polls on voting intentions. In the first stage a few constituencies which, on the basis of previous research, appear to represent a cross-section of all constituencies, are selected. Some rural and some urban constituencies would be included and previous election results used to check that the constituencies selected are a reasonable mixture in terms of party support. In the second stage individual respondents are chosen from within these constituencies.

If multi-stage sampling was not used in this sort of research, opinion poll organizations would incur the prohibitive expense of sending researchers to every constituency in the country, to interview a mere three or four people in each to get an overall sample of two thousand. However, in multi-stage sampling the loss of randomness may be accompanied by an increase in sampling error.

Snowballing

Snowballing is a very specialized type of sampling and is usually only used when other methods are not practical. It involves using personal contacts to build up a sample of the group to be studied. For example, it was used by Laurie Taylor when he persuaded John McVicar, a former criminal, to obtain introductions to members of the London underworld of professional crime. Taylor then used these contacts to obtain introductions to more criminals. Clearly, such samples cannot be representative since to have any chance of being included those studies must be part of a network of personal contacts. But for groups such as professional criminals it is not easy to use other ways of obtaining a sample.

Non-representative sampling

Sociologists do not always try to obtain representative cross-sections of the population they wish to study. In terms of Popper's views of science (see pp. 811–12), researchers should try to disprove or falsify their theories. This means looking for untypical examples of a phenomenon which does not fit a particular theory. For example, in examining the view that differences in the behaviour of men and women are primarily shaped by biological rather than cultural differences, sociologists such as Ann Oakley have tried to find untypical examples of human behaviour. Feminist sociologists claim to have falsified the biological arguments about the behaviour of men and women by finding examples of societies in which women behave in ways more usually associated with men and vice versa. (See, for examples, p. 588.)

Goldthorpe and Lockwood's rejection of the embourgeoisement hypothesis (see pp. 77–9) provides an interesting example of the use of a non-representative sample. The embourgeoisement hypothesis stated that large numbers of affluent workers were becoming middle class as a result of their rising living standards. On the basis of available evidence, Goldthorpe and Lockwood doubted this claim. To test the embourgeoisement hypothesis they selected a sample from the most affluent manual workers. If any manual workers were becoming middle class, it would be members of this 'untypical' group. The research results showed little or no evidence of embourgeoisement. Having chosen the group most likely to confirm the hypothesis, Goldthorpe and Lockwood felt confident in rejecting the theory of embourgeoisement.

Case studies and life histories

Case studies

In general, **case studies** make no claims to be representative. A case study involves the detailed examination of a single example of something. Thus a case study could involve the study of a single institution, community or social group, an individual person, a particular historical event, or a single social action.

Howard Becker has described one aim of case studies as the attempt 'to arrive at a comprehensive understanding of the group under study'. Ken Pryce's participant observation study of a single West Indian community in the St Paul's area of Bristol attempted, at one level, simply to understand that particular community.

However, case studies can be used, as Becker claims, 'to develop more general theoretical statements about regularities in social structure and process'. As mentioned above, a case study of a particular society can be used to falsify a general theory about social life. Thus Gough's study of Nayar society showed that family structures based upon a marital bond are not universal (see pp. 318–19).

Case studies can also be used to produce **typologies**, or a set of categories defining types of a social phenomenon. Douglas suggests that case studies can be used to discover the different types of suicide by uncovering the different social meanings of suicide.

Case studies may be useful for generating new hypotheses which can then be tested against other data or in later studies. Paul Willis's study of a single school has produced a number of hypotheses about the relationship between education and capitalist societies which have proved to be a useful focus for research and the development of theories by other sociologists of education (see pp. 741–4).

A major drawback of case study research is that it is not possible to generalize on the basis of its findings. It is impossible to determine how far the findings of a study into one example of a social phenomenon can be applied to other examples. Alan Bryman suggests that one way to overcome

this problem is to carry out or use a number of case studies of the same type of phenomenon. However, as Bryman points out, it may be difficult to make direct comparisons of the results of studies carried out either by different people, or by the same person at different times. The data is likely to be more systematic if a single researcher, or group, collects data on a number of social groups at the same time. Yet if this is done the research ceases to be a case study as such.

Life histories

Life histories are a particular type of case study, one where the whole study concerns one individual's life. They can be carried out using a variety of methods but most frequently use extended, unstructured interviews. Some life histories make considerable use of personal documents. The following are some examples: a study of the life of a Polish peasant conducted by Thomas and Znaniecki; Gordon Allport's 'Letters from Jenny', a study of an ageing woman; and Robert Bogdan's study of Jane Fry, a transsexual. (All these examples are discussed in Plummer, 1983.) Like case studies, life histories, by their very nature, use an untypical sample. However, Ken Plummer argues that they have a number of uses and can be of considerable value in developing sociological theory.

Plummer suggests that life histories can be used as a 'sensitizing tool'. They can help the researcher develop an understanding of the meaning of concepts used by those she or he is studying. The 'rich detail' of life-history data can help cut through the 'dense jargon' that makes so much theoretical sociology difficult to comprehend. The life history allows the researcher to see the world from the social actor's point of view. This viewpoint is one that may challenge the assumptions and preconceptions of outsiders. For example, Plummer claims that Bogdan's study shows how transsexualism can seem a rational and reasonable choice from the actor's point of view, rather than as the sickness it appears to be to some psychiatrists. Like case studies in general, life histories can be used to falsify existing theories or to inspire new ones. A number of life histories can be used together to develop a theory, test it and refine it, and then test it again. Plummer refers to this theoretical approach as 'analytic induction'. The first life history allows the researcher to make preliminary hypotheses. These can be tested in subsequent life-history research. Where the hypotheses are found wanting they can be modified to fit the extra cases. As research proceeds the sociologist develops increasingly useful theories and generalizations. (This approach is similar to the 'grounded theory' advocated by Glasner and Strauss, see p. 848 for further details.)

■ Pilot studies

Having selected a research method and chosen a method of selecting a sample, some sociologists carry out a **pilot study** before embarking upon the main research project. A pilot study is a small-scale preliminary study conducted before the main research in order to check the feasibility or to improve the design of the research. Pilot studies are not usually appropriate for case studies, but they are frequently carried out before large-scale quantitative research in an attempt to avoid time and money being wasted on an inadequately designed project. A pilot study is usually carried out on members of the relevant population, but not on those who will form part of the final sample. This is because it might influence the later behaviour of research subjects if they had already been involved in the research.

Pilot studies can be useful for a number of reasons.

1 If interviews or questionnaires are to be used the questions may be tested to make sure that they make sense to respondents, i.e. they produce the sort of information required and they are unambiguous. Michael Young and Peter Willmott used a pilot study involving over a hundred interviews before carrying out their research into family life in Bethnal Green. They found the pilot interviews useful for developing questions that returned to particular themes so they could try to check the consistency of answers to reveal if any respondents were being untruthful.

2 Pilot studies may help researchers develop ways of getting the full cooperation of those they are studying. In a pilot study for her research into housebound mothers, Hannah Gavron found that it was necessary to establish a rapport with the respondent if she was to get full, open and honest answers. She therefore spent some time chatting to the respondent informally before starting the interview.

3 Pilot studies may be used to develop the research skills of those taking part. When Rex and Moore studied immigrants in Birmingham they used their pilot study to train the amateur interviewers they were using.

4 The pilot study may determine whether or not the research goes ahead. The researchers might discover insurmountable practical problems that lead to them dropping the project. In some cases a pilot study might be used to convince a funding organization of the usefulness of a particular project. If the pilot study is unsuccessful, the full study may be abandoned.

■ Social surveys

Social surveys can be defined as research projects which collect standardized data about large numbers of people. The data are usually in a statistical form and the most practical way of collecting such data is through the use of questionnaires. Other types of research method, such as unstructured interviewing or observation, would be less suitable for collecting standardized information about large groups because they would be both time consuming and difficult to translate into a statistical form.

Stephen Ackroyd and John A. Hughes have distinguished three main types of survey.

1 The first type, the factual survey, is used to collect descriptive information. The government Census can be seen as a type of factual survey, and the pioneering research done by Rowntree in his studies of poverty in York is a more sociological example. Rowntree's research was designed primarily to document the extent of poverty rather than to explain it, and this comment also applies to the more recent research on poverty by Mack and Lansley. (See pp. 126–8 and pp. 134–6 for further details of these studies.)

2 The second type, the attitude survey, is often carried out by opinion poll organizations. Instead of producing descriptive information about the social world, this type of survey attempts to discover the subjective states of individuals. Many polling organizations collect information about attitudes to political policies and personalities. Information on attitudes is often collected by sociologists interested in voting, for example Curtice, Heath and Jowell (see pp. 556–8). Sociologists who study stratification, such as Marshall, Newby, Rose and Vogler, sometimes collect data on attitudes in order to examine the issue of class consciousness (see pp. 88–9 for further details).

3 The third type of survey, the explanatory survey, is more ambitious than the other types for it goes beyond description and tries to test theories and hypotheses or to produce new theories. Most sociological surveys contain some explanatory element. Marshall *et al.*, for

example, tested the theory that routine white-collar workers had become proletarianized (see p. 68). Surveys such as that carried out by Townsend into poverty are designed to be both descriptive and explanatory. Townsend used survey data both to measure the extent of poverty and to develop theories to explain it.

Researchers usually want to be able to generalize from social surveys, and so surveys are usually based on carefully selected samples. The success of any survey depends ultimately on the quality of the data it produces. Most social surveys use questionnaires as a means of data collection. The advantages and disadvantages of this method and the reliability and validity of the data it produces will now be examined.

■ Questionnaires

A **questionnaire** consists simply of a list of pre-set questions. In questionnaire research the same questions are usually given to respondents in the same order so that the same information can be collected from every member of the sample.

Administering questionnaires

Questionnaires may be administered in a number of ways. Often they are given to individuals by interviewers, in which case they take the form of **structured interviews**. This method was used by Goldthorpe and Lockwood in the affluent worker study and by Willmott and Young in their survey of family life in London conducted in 1970. (See Chapter 6, pp. 340–2.) It has the advantage of having a trained interviewer on hand to make sure the questionnaire is completed according to instructions and to clarify any ambiguous questions. But questionnaires administered by interviewers involve the problem of **interviewer bias** this means that the responses given are influenced by the presence of the researcher. (See pp. 842–3 for a discussion of interviewer bias.) In addition, this method is expensive compared to the following alternatives.

The **postal questionnaire**, as its name suggests, is mailed to respondents with a stamped addressed envelope for return to the researcher. It provides an inexpensive way of gathering data, especially if respondents are dispersed over a wide

geographical area. The return rate, though, does not often exceed 50 per cent of the sample population and is sometimes below 25 per cent. This may seriously bias the results since there may be systematic differences between those who return questionnaires and those who do not. For example, the main response to a postal questionnaire on marital relationships might come from those experiencing marital problems and wishing to air their grievances. If most non-respondents were happily married, the researcher would be unjustified in making generalizations about married life on the basis of the returns.

A second way and one that obtains a far higher return rate is when questionnaires are administered to a group such as a class of students or workers at a union meeting. This method is less expensive than dealing with individual respondents while maintaining the advantages of the presence of an interviewer. However, the interviewer must ensure that respondents do not discuss questions within the group since this might affect their answers.

A third way of administering a questionnaire is to ask the questions over the telephone. This is often done by market research firms or marketing departments of companies, but it is not usually regarded as satisfactory by sociologists. Unless the researcher specifically wants a sample of people who have a telephone, the sample is unlikely to be representative of the population being studied.

Producing questionnaires and analysing the data

Questionnaires certainly tend to be used to produce quantitative data. Sometimes researchers may not have very clear hypotheses and will ask a wide range of questions on a topic. However, they must have some idea of what factors are important or interesting before they can start to construct a questionnaire.

In the process of choosing questions, researchers have to operationalize concepts. In other words abstract concepts have to be translated into concrete questions that make it possible to take measurements relating to those concepts. Sociologists classify the social world in terms of a variety of concepts. For instance, social class, power, family, religion, alienation and anomie are concepts used to identify and categorize social relationships, beliefs, attitudes and experiences that are seen to have certain characteristics in common. In order to transpose these rather vague concepts into measuring instruments, a number of steps are taken.

First, an **operational definition** is established. This involves breaking the concept down into various **components** or **dimensions** in order to specify exactly what is to be measured. Thus when Robert Blauner attempted to operationalize the concept of alienation, he divided it into four components – powerlessness, meaninglessness, isolation and self-estrangement. (See Chapter 4, pp. 188–92.) Similarly when Stark and Glock operationalized the concept of religion, they constructed five 'core dimensions of religiousness'. (See Chapter 8, pp. 496–7.)

Once the concept has been operationally defined in terms of a number of components, the second step involves the selection of **indicators** for each component. Thus an indicator of Blauner's component of powerlessness might be an absence of opportunities for workers to make decisions about the organization of work tasks. Indicators of 'religious practice' (one of Stark and Glock's 'dimensions of religiousness') might include attendance at a place of worship and acts of prayer.

Third, indicators of each dimension are put into the form of a series of questions that will provide quantifiable data for measuring each dimension. Thus indicators of 'religious practice' may be transposed into the following questions: 'How often do you attend church?' and 'How often do you pray?' Once questions have been constructed, the concept is operationalized.

Researchers have a number of choices to make during the process of operationalizing concepts in questionnaires. First they have to decide what form of question to ask.

Questions may be open-ended such as: 'What do you think of this firm's industrial relations record?' Open-ended questions allow the respondents to compose their own answers rather than choosing between a number of given answers. This may be more likely to provide valid data since respondents can say what they mean in their own words. However, this kind of response might be difficult to classify and quantify. Answers must be interpreted carefully before the researcher is able to say that a certain percentage of respondents attribute good industrial relations to effective management, an efficient union, high pay or whatever.

A second type of question, sometimes known as a **closed** or **fixed-choice** question, requires a choice between a number of given answers. For example, 'How about the idea of becoming a foreman? Would you like this very much/quite a lot/not much/or not at all?' Sometimes the respondent is asked to choose between two stated alternatives: 'Which would you prefer: a job where someone tells you exactly how to do the work or one where you are left to decide for yourself how to go about it?' A similar type of question requires the respondent to agree or disagree with a particular statement: 'Some people say that trade unions have too much power in the country: would you agree or disagree, on the whole?'

Compared to the open-ended type, fixed-choice questions provide responses which can be more easily classified and quantified. It requires relatively little time, effort and ingenuity to arrive at statements such as '46 per cent of affluent workers would very much like the idea of becoming a foreman' and, 'of those who are members of unions, 41 per cent agree that unions have too much power'. However, fixed-choice questions do not allow the respondent to qualify and develop their answers. It is therefore difficult for researchers to know exactly what they are measuring. Thus when respondents agree with the statement that trade unions have too much power, do they mean too much power over their members, over management, over the Labour Party or over the government? Other questions can be included to obtain further information – in fact in the affluent worker study Goldthorpe and Lockwood included a number of questions about workers' attitudes to trade unions. Yet many would agree that an unstructured interview would be required to examine as complex an area as trade union power.

If open-ended questions are used and the researcher wants the data to be in a statistical form it becomes necessary to code the answers. Coding involves identifying a number of categories into which answers can be placed. The researcher usually examines the answers given and establishes the principal types of answer that have been provided. Thus in the *British Crime Survey* of 1983 the answers to an open-ended question on the reasons why people had not reported crimes were classified as: 'Too trivial', 'Police could do nothing', 'Inappropriate for police, dealt with personally', 'Fear/dislike of police', 'Inconvenient', 'Police would not be interested', 'Fear of reprisals', 'Reported to other authorities' and 'Other answers/vague answers'.

Once the data have been collected and classified it is necessary to analyse them. In an explanatory survey this often involves using multivariate analysis to determine the relationships between the variables. For example, in his study of educational achievement A.H. Halsey tried to measure the relative importance of cultural and material factors in producing educational success or failure (see p. 759–60 for further details). Questionnaires are often designed to test a particular hypothesis: Goldthorpe and Lockwood used questionnaires to test the embourgeoisement thesis, while Marshall *et al.* used them to test various theories of stratification. In such cases the data is analysed in relation to the hypotheses which are being tested. The analysis of data from descriptive or attitude surveys is often more straightforward. Sometimes it involves little more than statements about the percentages of respondents who gave particular replies.

The advantages of questionnaires

Questionnaire research is certainly a practical way to collect data. Although designing the questionnaire and carrying out pilot studies may take some time, once in use questionnaires can be used to collect large quantities of data from considerable numbers of people over a relatively short period of time. Thus Mack and Lansley in their initial study of poverty used a sample of 1,174 people (see pp. 134–6 for further details), while the *British Crime Survey* of 1983 (discussed on pp. 399–401), used a sample of 16,000 households. Such large samples cannot be studied using more in-depth research methods without incurring prohibitive costs. Even when questionnaires are administered by interviewers this involves relatively little personal involvement, or danger or sacrifice by the researcher when compared with some participant observation studies. The results of questionnaire research can be relatively easily quantified, and with the assistance of computers the data can be analysed quickly and efficiently. Using computers the relationship between many different variables can be examined.

To some quantitative researchers, however, the theoretical advantages are more important than the practical ones. Although relatively few sociologists today claim to be positivists, a considerable number support the use of quantitative data on the grounds that it can be analysed more 'scientifically' and objectively than qualitative data. Quantitative data can be considered more reliable than qualitative data. Since each individual respondent answers precisely the same questions in the same order, they are all responding to the same stimuli. Any differences in response should, in theory, reflect real differences between respondents. Furthermore the figures produced can be checked by other researchers, and their reliability should therefore be high. Only when the data are quantified by means of reliable measuring instruments can the results of different studies be directly compared. Thus studies of British elections over several decades have produced data that can be used to determine changing patterns of voting and changing social attitudes within the British electorate. Heath *et al.* were able to use data from their own and other election studies to reveal ideological shifts in the electorate, and to check the claim that class was becoming less important in determining voting behaviour. (See pp. 556–8 for details.)

From a positivist point of view, statistical data from questionnaires can be analysed so that new theories can be produced. More typically, however, such data are used to test existing hypotheses, since the researcher must have a reasonably clear idea of the sort of information that is important before they set the questions. Whether questionnaires are used inductively (as in the former case) or deductively (as in the latter), they can be used to try to establish causal relationships through multivariate analysis. Ivor Crewe used statistical data to check his theory that housing tenure, among other factors, had an influence on voting behaviour independent of social class (see pp. 552–4). Many sociologists regard questionnaires as a suitable method for testing precise hypotheses in a rigorous manner: Marshall *et al.* used questionnaire data to back up their claim that they had falsified the proletarianization thesis (see p. 68).

As has already been mentioned, questionnaire research can generally use larger samples than qualitative methods. For this reason, sociologists who have carried out a social survey tend to feel more justified in generalizing about a wider population than those who have carried out an in-depth study of a smaller number of people. This is particularly likely where a questionnaire is used in conjunction with sophisticated sampling techniques so that the researcher can be confident that the sample is representative. Researchers into such areas of social life as poverty, voting, crime and stratification who have carried out social surveys using questionnaires have not hesitated to make claims about the British population as a whole, not just those questioned during the research.

Despite the importance of the theoretical points discussed above, questionnaires are not only used by positivists or those who strongly believe in the advantages of quantitative data. In many circumstances they are used when resources are limited and data are needed on large numbers of people. They are particularly useful when straightforward descriptive data are required. However, the validity of the statistical data, produced for explanatory surveys in particular, has been questioned by some sociologists who advocate a more interpretive, qualitative approach. These criticisms will now be examined.

The disadvantages of questionnaires

Interpretive sociologists vary in their views on survey research and the data it produces. Weber's methodological position implies that such data can be one – but only one – of the types of data required in sociological research. Interactionists often see statistical data as inadequate for producing sociological explanations of human behaviour. Phenomenologists go further, for they see the data produced as an artificial creation of the researcher. Above all, critics argue that despite the reliability of questionnaire data it lacks validity. To phenomenologists in particular, the methodological assumptions on which questionnaires are based are entirely false. They put forward six main objections.

1 It cannot be assumed that different answers to the same question reflect real differences between respondents. However much care is taken with the wording of questions, respondents may interpret them differently. People who choose the same response may not mean the same thing. People who choose different responses may not mean different things. This may result from the wording of questions. For example, the word 'uptight' in low-income black American areas usually refers to a close relationship between friends, but when it entered the vocabulary of mainstream America it changed its meaning to anxious and tense. Even common words and phrases carry different

associations for different groups. As Irwin Deutscher observes, 'Within a society, as well as between societies, the sociologist seeks information from and about people who operate verbally with different vocabularies, different grammars and different kinds of sounds.' Thus a questionnaire, which provides little opportunity to qualify meaning, might not provide comparable data when administered to members of different social groups.

2 In designing the questionnaire researchers assume that they know what is important. Respondents cannot provide information which is not requested, they cannot answer questions that are not asked. For this reason, it is difficult to develop hypotheses during the course of the research and researchers are limited to testing those theories which they have already thought of.

3 Questionnaire research involves the operationalization of concepts and some interpretive sociologists argue that such procedures produce a distorted picture of the social world. The process of breaking down a concept so that it can be quantified imposes sociological constructs, categories and logic on the social world. Thus when Blauner sought to measure alienation (see pp. 188–91) he employed a concept which might have had no reality in the social world he sought to understand. Indeed Blauner admits that 'It is difficult to interpret a finding that 70 per cent of factory workers report satisfaction with their jobs because we do not know how valid or reliable our measuring instrument is.' The workers were not allowed to reveal their attitudes to their work in their own way. As the phenomenologist Michael Phillipson observes, 'the instruments of the observer create the very order they are supposedly designed to reveal'.

4 The validity of the data may be reduced by the unwillingness or inability of respondents to give full and accurate replies to questions. Quite simply, respondents may lie. Attempts to check the accuracy of self-report studies on crime (see p. 401) have found that some 20 per cent of respondents do not tell the truth. Even if respondents want to tell the truth they may be unable to do so because of faulty memory or because they lack the relevant information. Thus the *British Crime Surveys* may have underestimated the amount of unreported crime because victims may have been unaware or may have forgotten that they had been the victims of crime. Furthermore, even when respondents are honest, and not hampered by ignorance or forgetfulness, there are some types of

questions where the validity of the answers can still be queried. This is particularly true of questions about attitudes. It cannot be assumed that stated attitudes will be translated into actual behaviour. For instance, in the 1930s La Piere travelled to 251 establishments such as restaurants, hotels and campsites in the USA with two Chinese people. They were refused service or accommodation at only one of these places, yet when the same establishments were sent a questionnaire a few months later, only one said that they would accept Chinese customers. When observation or participant observation is used the researcher relies less on respondents' accounts and may therefore have more chance of producing valid data.

5 A fifth reason for doubting the validity of questionnaire data is the distance maintained between the researcher and the subject of the research, particularly in the case of postal questionnaires. As Alan Bryman puts it,

---

The quantitative researcher adopts the posture of an outsider looking in on the social world. He or she applies a preordained framework on the subjects being investigated and is involved as little as possible in that world. This posture is the analogue of a detached scientific observer.

To a positivist this approach encourages objectivity, but to an interpretive sociologist it precludes the possibility of understanding the meanings and motives of the subjects of the research. Unlike participant observation the researcher does not undergo similar experiences to the subjects of the research, and so cannot draw so easily on experience to understand the behaviour of those being studied. Using questionnaires it is not possible to see how people act and react towards each other, nor is it possible to examine the way that self-concepts change during the course of interaction. Interactionists in particular do not believe that the researcher can gain genuine insights into the subjective states underlying the behaviour of those being studied unless the researcher gets close to those they are studying.

---

6 Finally, when open-ended questions are used, and the researcher requires quantitative data the coding of answers will take place. As in the operationalization of concepts this involves researchers imposing their own order on the data. The differences in the precise answers given to questions are glossed over as a number of answers which are not identical are placed together in a single category. This process obscures the differences that do exist between the answers.

Despite the strength of these criticisms it is increasingly accepted by most sociologists that there is a place for survey research in sociology. After all, there would be little point, for example, in carrying out participant observation or in-depth interviewing to discover the percentages of males and females living in a large town! It is usually when statistical data from questionnaires is used to try to establish causal relationships that opponents of quantitative research become most concerned about the validity of the data being used.

Interviews
Types of interview

Interviews take a number of forms depending upon how structured they are. A completely **structured interview** is simply a questionnaire administered by an interviewer who is not allowed to deviate in any way from the questions provided. The interviewer simply reads out the questions to the respondent. At the other extreme, a totally **unstructured interview** takes the form of a conversation where the interviewer has no predetermined questions. Most interviews fall somewhere between these two extremes.

Interviews of a more structured variety may allow the interviewer to probe the respondents' answers so that they can, if necessary, be clarified. The interviewer may also be allowed to prompt the interviewee, that is, give them extra guidance to help them answer the question. For example, Goldthorpe and Lockwood's team of researchers was able to prompt interviewees who could not decide how to answer a question about whether they had actively done anything to find a different job by suggesting that they might have read job adverts in local newspapers.

In unstructured interviews the conversation develops naturally, unless the respondent fails to cover an area in which the researcher is interested. Eventually the interviewer will direct the conversation back to the areas he or she wishes to cover. Hannah Gavron, for example, in her study *The Captive Wife*, interviewed 76 housewives. She had a schedule of areas she wished to cover in each interview, but she did not direct the wives to these areas unless it became essential. In this way she hoped to avoid directing the interview too much, and so to avoid influencing the responses. At the same time, however, she achieved some standard-ization of the data collected, and direct compar-isons between the women became possible.

As highly structured interviews are very similar to questionnaires, the rest of the discussion of interviews will concentrate on interviews of a less structured variety.

Conducting interviews

Having a conversation with somebody is extremely common in human interaction, and it might be thought that interviewing requires no special preparation. However, the sociological researcher needs to overcome the problems of making contact, and gaining the cooperation of respon-dents. Having made contact with and persuaded a person to take part in the interview, the researcher then needs to try and ensure that the respondent gives full, honest and open answers.

Interviewers have used a variety of methods to make contact with respondents. They have tele-phoned in advance, written letters and turned up at interviewees' houses. At the initial point of contact it is important that the interviewers establish why they wish to carry out the interview and what the information is to be used for. They may also need to explain how the interviewee was selected and why they are suitable for research. Gavron used letters of introduction from the interviewee's doctor in order to establish contact. When she met them she explained the nature and purpose of her research.

The most common way of conducting inter-views is to be **non-directive**: to refrain from offer-ing opinions, to avoid expressions of approval and disapproval. Often an interviewer will spend some time trying to establish rapport or understanding between themselves and the interviewee. They may do this simply by talking informally before the interview proper starts. Once the interviewee feels that he or she is not going to be criticized or judged, that they can talk freely and can rely upon a sympa-thetic audience, it is hoped that they will talk with the honesty and openness the researcher is seeking. Since the respondent does not have to answer the questions (since they may be asked about private or personal aspects of their lives which they would not usually discuss with a stranger) it is often argued that non-directive interviewing is the most effective type of interviewing.

In contrast, Howard Becker suggests that inter-viewers may be inhibited by adopting this rela-tively passive approach and a 'bland, polite style of conversation'. He suggests that on certain occa-sions a more active and aggressive approach can provide much fuller data. This involves the inter-viewer taking 'positions on some issues' and using 'more aggressive conversational tactics'. Becker adopted these tactics in his interviews with Chicago schoolteachers (discussed in Chapter 12, p. 763). He claims that American schoolteachers believe they have a lot to hide from what they regard as a 'prying, misunderstanding, and poten-tially dangerous public'. They are therefore unlikely to volunteer certain information. By adopting an aggressive stance, being sceptical and at times even pretending to be stupid, Becker managed to prize out much of this information. In particular he claimed to have uncovered the ways in which teachers categorized and evaluated stu-dents in terms of their class and ethnic back-grounds, information they would prefer to keep hidden for fear of being accused of prejudice and discrimination. Becker states: 'I coerced many interviewees into being considerably more frank than they had originally intended.' He suggests that this approach is particularly useful for one-off interviews. Similar information can be picked up more subtly over a series of interviews without running the risk of antagonizing respondents. The apparent success of Becker's rather unorthodox tactics suggests that there is no one best way of interviewing.

It is normal for a single interviewer to inter-view a single respondent. This has a number of advantages. It may be easier to establish rapport, confidentiality can be ensured, and the respondent is not distracted or influenced by the presence of other interviewees. In some circumstances though, sociologists have carried out group interviews. For example, Paul Willis in his study of education interviewed several of the 'lads' together. (See pp. 741–3 for further details.) It can be argued that this might be more likely to produce valid data than a one-to-one interview. The lads' activities usually took place in a group context, and a group interview would reflect this. In group interviews Willis was able to observe interaction between the 'lads' and they felt more at ease than when talking alone to an older and middle-class interviewer.

Interviews are not natural social situations. However, sociologists have found ways to min-imize the extent to which respondents may see them as artificial or unnatural. This is essential for valid data to be obtained.

The advantages of interviews

Interviews are not seen as the ideal research method by any particular group of sociologists. They represent a compromise between more structured research methods like questionnaires and the more in-depth methods such as participant observation. As such, those who support the use of more quantitative methods tend to prefer interviews to participant observation.

Compared to participant observation, interviews can utilize larger samples so generalizations are more justified. With some coding of responses it is possible to produce statistical data from interviews, and it is easier to replicate the research and check results. Because there is usually some degree of structure in an interview it is easier to make direct comparisons than it is by using data from participant observation.

To sociologists who prefer more qualitative methods, interviews have clear advantages over questionnaires. The concepts and words used by interviewer and interviewee alike can be clarified, the researchers' concepts are less likely to be imposed on the social world, issues can be explored in greater depth and the researcher does not limit the responses to fixed choices. For these reasons interviews can be useful for generating new hypotheses and theories which the researcher would not otherwise have thought of. For example, when Elizabeth Bott started her interviews with twenty families in her investigation into conjugal roles she had not considered the possibility that friendship networks might affect the type of conjugal relationship that developed. Had she been using questionnaires she would not have included the questions that would have been necessary to discover the information which she needed to formulate her theory. (See pp. 359–60 for further details of Bott's study.)

The above arguments, though, do not explain why sociologists should sometimes choose to use interviews in preference to all other research methods. They are not as reliable as questionnaires and they are not as likely to produce valid data as participant observation. A major reason for the widespread use of interviews is their sheer practicality. There is no other method which allows access to so many different groups of people and

different types of information. As Ackroyd and Hughes put it,

Using as data what the respondent says about himself or herself potentially offers the social researcher access to vast storehouses of information. The social researcher is not limited to what he or she can immediately perceive or experience, but is able to cover as many dimensions and as many people as resources permit.

In short, interviews are more flexible than any other research method. They can be used to extract simple factual information from people. They can be used to ask people about their attitudes, their past, present or future behaviour, their motives, feelings and other emotions that cannot be observed directly. Interviewers can explore each question or issue in as much depth or superficiality as they wish. The range of information available from interviews can be demonstrated from the following examples.

In his study of schizophrenia R.D. Laing used in-depth interviews to study the past behaviour and emotional states of people with schizophrenia and their families (see pp. 325–6). The family is such a small and closed social grouping that participant observation is almost impossible without changing the family's behaviour.

Howard Becker used interviews to study fifty marijuana smokers. Via interviews he was able to try to explore the whole of the 'deviant career' of the drug users from the time they first tried the drug to when they became regular users involved with a subculture of marijuana smokers. Interviewing allowed him to discuss the motives and circumstances that led to them trying the drug and continuing to use it.

Interviews are often used to carry out research into groups who might not otherwise consent to being the subject of research. Laurie Taylor could only produce data about professional crime in Britain because he was able to gain the trust of the criminals he interviewed. Clearly participant observation would have been out of the question, and he would have been unlikely to have obtained a satisfactory response rate using postal questionnaires. Furthermore, because of Taylor's lack of familiarity with professional criminals he might have had difficulty deciding what questions to ask them. Once again, the flexibility and practicality of interviews is evident.

The disadvantages of interviews

Stephen Ackroyd and John A. Hughes have observed that

The foundations of interviewing are to be found in the mundane observation that people can report on what they feel, tell others about aspects of their lives, disclose what their hopes and fears are, offer their opinions, state their beliefs, answer questions about who they see regularly, what they did last week, how much they spend on food, and so on, to put it simply they can impart masses of information about themselves.

The problem is that these masses of information may be neither valid nor reliable. Interviews have many of the same drawbacks as questionnaires: the responses given may not be accurate and may not reflect real behaviour. Respondents may lie, may forget, they may lack the information required.

To give a simple example, some of the criminals interviewed by Laurie Taylor later claimed that they had made up fanciful stories about their escapades in order to see how gullible Taylor was. However, even if respondents are not handicapped by forgetfulness or ignorance, and have no wish to deceive, they may still not give valid answers. As critics of questionnaire data have pointed out, interviewees may not act in accordance with their stated beliefs. When reflecting on past events, they may alter their interpretation in the light of subsequent experience. Because interviews are artificial, Cicourel has asked whether they 'capture the daily life, conditions, opinions, values, attitudes, and knowledge base of those we study as expressed in their natural habitat' (quoted in A. Bryman, 1988, p. 114).

David Matza's work on delinquents in the USA can illustrate the sort of problem that arises with interview data (see pp. 396–8 for further details). Matza interviewed 100 delinquents in training school and found that a surprisingly large number of them disapproved of most crimes. Matza concluded that delinquents did not, on the whole, strongly reject society's values. Critics, however, have pointed out, that apart from the question of how truthful the delinquents were, Matza failed to take account of the possibility that they had modified their views as a result of their punishment. At the time of their offences they may have regarded the laws they were breaking contemptuously and only later did they change their minds.

Interviewees may also be influenced by the presence of the researcher. The answers given may be influenced by the way the interviewees define the situation. William Labov, for instance, found that young black American children responded differently when interviewed in different contexts. Interviewed by a white interviewer in a formal setting the children said little when asked to describe a toy jet plane. This type of evidence had led some psychologists to conclude that these children were linguistically deprived and that this deprivation contributed to their failure in education. However, Labov produced evidence to show the apparent linguistic deprivation was the result of interviewing techniques and not a genuine reflection of the children's linguistic ability. When the children were interviewed by a black interviewer in a formal setting they were more forthcoming. When the children sat on the floor with the interviewer and they were able to bring their best friend with them the children opened up and became fluent and articulate. Labov argued that when children defined the situation as hostile they were unable to demonstrate their real abilities. When they defined the situation as friendly they were able to give a much better account for themselves. Clearly such factors as the age, skin colour, sex, clothing and accent of the interviewer may affect the interviewees' definition of the interview, and so affect their behaviour.

A further problem with unstructured interviews is that there is more opportunity for the interviewer (usually without realizing it) to direct the interviewee towards giving certain types of response. Consciously or unconsciously, respondents might give the sort of answers they believe that the interviewer wants to hear rather than saying what they truly believe. This problem is known as **interviewer bias**. It can never be totally eliminated from interview research simply because interviews are interaction situations. Interviewer bias is demonstrated in a study conducted by Stuart A. Rice in 1914 (discussed in Deming, 1971, p. 347). Two thousand destitute men were asked, among other things, to explain their situation. There was a strong tendency for those interviewed by a supporter of prohibition to blame their demise on alcohol, but those interviewed by a committed socialist were much more likely to explain their plight in terms of the industrial situation. The interviewers apparently had their own views on the reasons for destitution which they communicated to the respondents.

In order to conduct an interview successfully and interpret the responses correctly the interviewer must also be aware of the social conventions of those being interviewed. For example, certain activities may be regarded as more 'socially desirable' by members of one group than by members of another. As a result there may be differences between social groups in terms of their members' willingness to admit to particular activities.

The importance of this can be seen from a study conducted by Bruce Dohrenwend in New York to investigate the relationship between mental health and ethnicity (discussed in Phillips, 1971, pp. 41–4). Respondents were asked whether or not they had experienced a list of symptoms associated with mental illness. Compared with Jews, Irish and blacks, Puerto Ricans reported experiencing more of the symptoms and therefore appeared to have a higher rate of mental illness. Yet Dohrenwend found that the symptoms were regarded as less undesirable by Puerto Ricans than by members of the other ethnic groups. As a result they were more ready to admit to them.

A study by Derek Phillips and Kevin Clancy produced similar findings with reference to social class. It indicated that members of the lower class were more willing to report a range of symptoms associated with mental illness than members of other social classes. This reflects class differences in judgements of the social desirability of the items in question.

Such findings cast serious doubt on the validity of interview data and therefore on the use to which those data are put. Thus there may be few, if any, grounds for arguing, on the basis of such data, that mental illness is a lower-class 'problem' resulting from the assumed strains and stresses of lower-class life. As Derek Phillips suggests, the frequently discovered relationship between social class and mental health may well be due 'to a greater willingness of lower-class persons to admit to or report certain behaviours and experiences which middle and upper-class persons regard as highly undesirable'.

Despite the problems associated with interviews, they are unlikely to be abandoned as sources of data by sociological researchers. As David Silverman points out, conversations are an integral part of social life, and as one of the main ways in which people communicate they are invaluable as

a way of trying to understand society. Silverman says

They offer a rich source of data which provides access to how people account for their troubles and good fortunes. Human beings can never fully see the world through the eyes of another person, but talking to other people can certainly provide insights into their perspectives on social life. Perhaps only through participant observation can researchers develop greater insights.

Observation and participant observation

Observation

All sociological research involves observation of some sort. The use of observation is not confined to researchers advocating any particular methodological approach. Thus positivists believe that the social world can be objectively observed, classified and measured. Observation has also been frequently used by qualitative social researchers: numerous interactionist sociologists have observed interaction in the classroom when studying education. Similarly in studying suicide the ethnomethodologist J. Maxwell Atkinson observed the process of decision making in coroners' courts. However, there are limits to the situations in which social life can be observed in 'natural' settings without affecting the validity of the data produced.

There are a considerable number of social situations in which the presence of an observer is prohibited, or is unlikely to be allowed. Sociologists who study politics are not allowed to observe the deliberations of the British Cabinet, nor can they observe private conversations between members of the government and their senior officials. Sociologists interested in family life are unlikely to be allowed to observe interaction between married couples in the bedroom, nor is it probable that sociologists who study work will be able to observe the board meetings of large companies.

Even when observation is allowed, the researcher's presence might alter the behaviour of those being observed to such an extent that the data is of little use. In small, closely knit social units such as families the observed can hardly be expected to act naturally with an observer present. Despite this, in certain situations sociologists might judge that some useful and valid data can still be produced. For example, in his study of secondary schooling, David Hargreaves found that some teachers he observed altered their behaviour considerably. Some refused to talk to the class as a whole when he was present. But others appeared to carry on as normal, and Hargreaves believed that some of his data were therefore valid (see p. 766 for further details of Hargreaves's study). In such situations the longer the researcher observes, the more likely those being studied are to forget about his or her presence and the more likely they are to act naturally.

Given the danger that the researcher will influence those being studied, valid data can most reasonably be expected to result when the presence of passive outsiders is quite normal. Thus in courtrooms, the Visitor's Gallery of the House of Commons, or on terraces at a football match a sociological researcher is able to blend into the background without any great difficulty. In other circumstances it may be necessary for the observer to get involved in the activities of those being studied. To be accepted, she or he will have to become a **participant observer**.

Ethnography and participant observation

Ethnography is the study of a way of life. It was first introduced into the social sciences by anthropologists who studied small-scale, pre-industrial societies. Bronislaw Malinowski's study of the Trobriand Islands (p. 448) is an example of an ethnographic study. Anthropologists increasingly recognized the need to get as close as possible to the societies they were investigating. More recently, the same approach has been applied to the study of groups within industrial society.

As a means for gathering data, **participant observation** has a long history in sociology. It has been used by researchers with widely differing theoretical perspectives. As such it is a research technique that has been adapted to meet the requirements of sociologists with various views on the nature of social reality. However, it has been particularly associated with the work of symbolic interactionists such as Herbert Blumer, Howard Becker and Erving Goffman. This method became widely employed in the USA in the 1960s and

since then has been regarded by many sociologists as the most appropriate way of obtaining qualitative data.

Joining the group, collecting and recording the data

One of the most important decisions that participant observers have to make is how to approach the social group they wish to join. Researchers may decide to be an **overt** participant observer, where they declare their true identity and purpose, or a **covert** participant observer where the fact that they are a researcher is not revealed. Sometimes researchers choose to be partially open but do not provide those being studied with the full story.

Some researchers strongly advocate being open from the start, arguing that it is both morally and practically the best way to carry out participant observation. The American sociologist Ned Polsky in his study of *Hustler Beats and Others* suggests that it is morally correct to be truthful, and the research can easily be ruined if the covert participant observer is uncovered. Another advantage is that the open researcher may be able to avoid participation in distasteful, immoral, or illegal behaviour. (Howard Parker, when studying Liverpool delinquents, could refuse to take part in the theft of car radios without damaging his relationship with the people he was studying.) Furthermore, the researcher is free to ask questions without arousing suspicion.

Sometimes researchers are less open without actually lying to those they are studying. William Foote Whyte in a study of an Italian American slum simply described himself as a writer without elaborating further. Ken Pryce in his study of the West Indian community in Bristol found that he could be quite open with some of the groups, but among others (such as those engaged in illegal activities) he had to be more guarded.

The main disadvantage of being open is that it may affect the behaviour of those being studied. 'Doc', one of the key members of the street-corner gang studied by Whyte, said to him, 'You've slowed me up plenty since you've been down here. Now, when I do something, I would have to think that Bill Whyte would want to know about it and how to explain it. Before I used to do things by instinct.' The knowledge that they are being observed can influence people's behaviour as they become more self-conscious and think about their actions.

An obvious advantage of covert participant observation is that the members of the group being studied are not likely to change their behaviour as a result of being studied since they are kept in ignorance of the fact that they are being observed for research purposes. Some studies may not be possible without participant observation being covert either because the group would change its behaviour too much, or the researcher would not be allowed to join in the first place. For example, Jason Ditton wanted to study thefts by bread van salesmen during the course of their work. Clearly the salesmen might have become much more cautious if they knew that they were being observed, indeed they might have stopped stealing altogether. Another researcher, who called himself 'James Patrick', had to keep even his name secret as he feared for his personal safety when studying violent Glasgow gangs. Similarly, William Chambliss needed to maintain secrecy when conducting a study of organized crime in Seattle (see pp. 417–18). Researchers have also had to keep their work secret when studying such groups as the Masons and certain religious sects.

If secrecy is maintained, then the researcher has little choice but to become a full participant in the group. However, if the researcher is open, there is an element of choice in the degree of involvement. Some researchers remain fairly detached. Others become much more involved. Ken Pryce found himself going to clubs and blues dances, drinking with and talking to local residents well past midnight during his study of West Indian life in Bristol.

Becoming too much of a participant can cause difficulties. In particular the researcher may have the problem of 'going native'. They may become so much a part of the group that they are unable to stand back and analyse the situation objectively. On the other hand, those who experience this problem have at least achieved complete acceptance by the group and they may well have a true insider's view. Perhaps the most complete insider's view can be provided by those who become sociological researchers, and use their own experiences as a source of data. Simon Holdaway was a police officer for a number of years before becoming a sociologist and could genuinely claim to provide a view from *Inside the British Police*. The more detached participant observer can perhaps be more objective, but may not understand the behaviour of those being studied quite as well. Very often the researcher cannot predict how involved they will become. It depends to some extent upon how much rapport they build up with the subjects of their research.

To be successful, the participant observer must gain the trust of those observed. In his study of black 'street corner' men in Washington DC (pp. 151–3), Elliot Liebow had to win over Tally, the leader of the group. Only when Liebow had gained Tally's trust did Tally admit that he had lied to him at the start of their acquaintance. The close and relatively long-lasting relationships established through participant observation provide greater opportunities for developing trust than are provided by other research techniques. Interviews and questionnaire surveys usually involve one-off, short-lived encounters. Particularly with groups such as low-income blacks and teenage gangs, a relationship of trust is necessary to secure cooperation. As Lewis Yablonsky notes from his research on teenage gangs, 'Their characteristic response to questionnaires investigating the gang's organization or personal activities is one of suspicion and distrust. To the gang boy every researcher could be a "cop".' In this type of situation participant observation is more likely to provide valid data than other research techniques.

Once the researcher has entered the group and gained its trust, he or she must then go about collecting the data and recording it. Much of this involves watching and waiting, and taking part where necessary, but some participant observers have supplemented the data gained in this way with some interviewing. This has the advantage of allowing the researcher to request the precise information required, without waiting for it to crop up in normal conversation. It is obviously only possible where the research is overt. Whyte used interviews with a 'key informant', 'Doc', to gain most of the background information required. Pryce made extensive use of formal and informal interviews.

Recording the data from interviews can be relatively straightforward: Pryce used a tape recorder. Recording data from participant observation is more difficult. Tape recorders would probably inhibit the natural behaviour of those being studied, taking notes could have a similar effect, and may in any case be impracticable. Most researchers have to opt for the best means available: committing what has taken place to memory, and writing it down as soon as possible. Ditton used to retire to the lavatory to take notes in private. Pryce had to wait until he got home. He said

---

I had to rely heavily on memory, my method was to write down these observations as soon as possible after hearing or observing them. The rule of thumb I constantly exercised was to record them while they were still fresh in my mind, generally the same day...I believe most of the information I recorded in this way was fairly accurate, if not accurate word for word, accurate in tone, flavour and in the emotions expressed.

Not all sociologists, though, would accept Pryce's claim.

The advantages of participant observation

Supporters of participant observation have argued that, compared to other research techniques, it is least likely to lead to sociologists imposing their reality on the social world they seek to understand. It therefore provides the best means of obtaining a valid picture of social reality. With a structured interview (a predetermined set of questions which the interviewee is requested to answer) or a questionnaire (a set of printed questions to which the respondent is asked to provide written answers) sociologists have already decided what is important. With preset questions they impose their framework and priorities on those they wish to study. By assuming the questions are relevant to the respondents they have already made many assumptions about their social world. Although participant observers begin the work with some preconceived ideas (for example, they will usually have studied the existing literature on the topic to be investigated) at least they have the opportunity to directly observe the social world.

The value of this opportunity is clear from Whyte's observations: 'As I sat and listened, I learned the answers to questions I would not have had the sense to ask if I had been getting my information solely on an interviewing basis.' Intensive observation over a period of years provided Whyte with a picture of what was important in the lives of the Italian Americans he studied. Without this exposure to their daily routine he would have remained ignorant of many of their priorities. Had he relied solely on interviews, this ignorance would have prevented him from asking important and relevant questions.

Liebow was particularly concerned about the danger of distorting the reality he wished to observe. He states that from the outset of his research, 'there were by design, no firm presumptions of what was or was not relevant'. He did his best simply to look and listen and to avoid any preconceptions of what was or was not important. Liebow chose participant observation because he believed that the method would provide a 'clear, firsthand picture' of the 'life of ordinary people, on their grounds and on their terms'. By observing what was said and done, where, when and by whom, he hoped to discover how a group of black street-corner men saw and organized their lives. Liebow claims that, 'Taking this inside view makes it easier to avoid structuring the material in ways that might be alien to the material itself.'

In participant observation, it is also more difficult for the people being studied to lie or mislead the researcher than it is in other research methods. The researcher is on the spot and witnesses actual behaviour rather than relying upon people's accounts of their lives.

Participant observation is a particularly appropriate method for symbolic interactionists because it allows an understanding of the world from the subjective point of view of the subjects of the research. Because researchers experience many of the same events as the observed, they are better able to put themselves in their position and to understand why they interact with others in particular ways. Pryce felt that participant observation allowed him to understand and explain the subjective views of some West Indians in Bristol. He said 'There is a tendency to either ignore or disregard the subjective feelings of members of the West Indian minority.' One of those subjective feelings was the belief of some that there was no point in trying to earn a living through ordinary employment which was dismissed as 'slave labour' and 'shit work'. Howard Parker also believed he could see the world through the eyes of those he studied – he felt justified in calling his book *View from the Boys*.

Interactionists believe that behaviour is largely governed by the self-concept held by an individual. Self-concepts are not fixed and static, but change during the course of interaction. Similarly, the meanings people attach to their own behaviour change as the context in which that behaviour takes place alters. Participant observation studies are often carried out over an extended period of time and it is therefore possible to study the process through which such changes happen.

This can be illustrated by Jock Young's study of marijuana smokers in Notting Hill. He found that the behaviour, the meaning attached to that behaviour, and the self-concepts of those involved altered in response to police attempts to discourage marijuana smoking. The drug users in the area became more secretive, attached more importance to taking the drug, and in response to what they saw as persecution they saw themselves as being in opposition to some of society's values. (For further details see pp. 406–7.) Such changes and the way they came about would have been difficult to identify and explain on the basis of interview or questionnaire data.

Many interactionists see observation or participant observation as the best means of studying interaction. Much interaction takes place almost instinctively, and those involved cannot be expected to recall precise details if asked in an interview. Furthermore, it is difficult for complete participants to be detached and objective when discussing their relationships with others. It is easier, for example, for an outsider to comment on group relationships. Parker was able to describe in detail the relationships between members of delinquent gangs he studied. In St Paul's, Pryce was able to distinguish a number of different subcultures which a resident of the area might not have been fully aware of.

Critics of participant observation argue (as will be discussed later) that the findings of such studies lack objectivity, that they are unreliable and depend too much upon the interpretations of the observer. Defenders of this research method generally believe that these objections can be overcome, and that participant observation can be made sufficiently systematic to be regarded as being a reliable as well as valid research method.

Finally, participant observation provides in-depth studies that can serve a number of useful purposes. In particular it is useful for generating new hypotheses. Rather like unstructured interviews, participant observation can go in unexpected directions and so can provide sociologists with novel insights and ideas. Although less useful for testing hypotheses because the type of data produced is not entirely under the control of the researcher, it may be useful for falsifying theories.

Thus Parker's study of British delinquents could be used to test how far Albert Cohen's explanation of American delinquency (see pp. 393–4) is applicable to Britain.

The limitations and disadvantages of participant observation

Participant observation has many practical disadvantages. It is often very time consuming: Cicourel spent four years studying juvenile justice in California. The researcher can usually only study a very small group of people and has to be physically present for the research to proceed. In personal terms such research may be highly inconvenient and demanding. The researcher may be required to move house, to live in an area they would not otherwise choose and to mix with people they would rather avoid. They may find it necessary to engage in activities they dislike to fit in with the group and they may even face personal danger. 'James Patrick' left Glasgow in a hurry when the gang violence began to sicken him and he felt concerned for his own safety. There are also limits on who can be studied using this method. Higher class and more powerful groups in society in particular may exclude participant observers. Individual researchers may lack the skills, knowledge or personality to be accepted by a particular group.

More serious, though, are the theoretical objections that have been raised. First, to quantitative researchers the samples used in participant observation are too small and untypical for generalizations to be made on the basis of the findings. Any conclusions can only apply to the specific group studied. Thus Pryce would not have been justified in making generalizations about all West Indians in Britain on the basis of a study of Bristol.

Second, such studies cannot be replicated so the results cannot be checked. It is therefore difficult to compare the results with the findings of other studies. The data from participant observation rely upon the particular interpretations of a single individual, and is specific to a particular place and time. Cicourel admits that his participant observation study relied heavily upon his own observational and interpretive skills. If the reader has little faith in Cicourel's skills then he or she will have little reason to accept his findings. It is quite possible that a different researcher would have reached quite different conclusions. As Whyte admits 'To some extent my approach must be unique to myself, to the particular situation, and to the state of knowledge existing when I began research.' Moreover the account of social life produced by participant observation is the result of a highly selective method of data collection. The participant observer usually records only a small fraction of all possible data he or she could have used. The observer selects what to record and what to omit and imposes a framework upon the data in the process of interpreting them.

A third theoretical objection is that the validity of the data is bound to be affected by the presence of the researcher, since the group being studied will not act naturally. This point is rejected by many participant observers. Whyte, for example, felt that eventually he was able to blend into the background so that social life carried on as normal around him.

To critics, and particularly those who support the use of positivist methods, participant observation is simply 'unscientific'. It is not systematic or rigorous, its findings cannot be checked, the research cannot be replicated, it is a subjective rather than objective research method. However, some interactionist sociologists have suggested that this sort of qualitative research need not lack rigour.

Glaser and Strauss claim that qualitative research can be used to generate and refine what they called 'grounded theory'. The whole process of collecting and analysing qualitative data can be systematic. Theories can be produced which are grounded in the data and in the real social world. In the early stages the researcher starts to develop categories and then further data are collected to see if they fit with these categories. Hypotheses begin to emerge as the initial hunches of the researcher are backed up or refuted by the data that is being produced. Causal explanations can be produced, and may be tested in follow-up studies.

Becker has shown how this sort of approach can be used when he was studying the behaviour of medical students. From observing the behaviour and listening to the comments of medical students he began to distinguish between 'cynical' and 'idealistic' attitudes to medicine. In the former case patients tended to be regarded as little more than animated visual teaching aids; in the latter as human beings whose pain and suffering the students felt a duty to relieve. Having found that these categories seemed to work, Becker went

on to how often and in what circumstances the students were cynical or idealistic. Noting that students tended to be idealistic when talking to other students, Becker advanced the hypothesis that 'Students have "idealist" sentiments' but 'group norms may not sanction their expression'. Becker says that it is perfectly possible to check the hypotheses produced by participant observation, and that this research method need not be unsystematic. He says of participant observation that 'the technique consists of something more than merely immersing oneself in data and having "insights"'.

■ Longitudinal research

In most sociological studies researchers study a group of people for a relatively short period of time. They analyse their data, produce a report on their research and move on to new endeavours. However, some researchers study a group over an extended period, collecting data on them at intervals. Such studies are known as **longitudinal** or **panel studies**.

Longitudinal studies were first used by researchers in the USA in the 1940s to measure changes in public attitudes. It was seen as more reliable to follow a particular sample over a period of time when measuring changing attitudes, than to select a new sample from time to time. By using a 'panel' the researcher could be sure that changes in the attitudes measured would not result from changes in the composition of the sample.

Longitudinal studies originated as extended attitude surveys. Since then they have usually been used to collect quantitative data in social surveys, though not necessarily about attitudes. Sometimes a particular age group or cohort is followed over a number of years. The Child Health and Education Survey has tried to follow the development of every child born in Britain between 3 and 9 March 1958. Another longitudinal study was carried out by J.W.B. Douglas. *In All Our Future* he followed the educational progress of a sample of children through their school careers (see pp. 750–1). Another example is provided by D.J. West and D.P. Farrington's *Who Becomes Delinquent*. This study was concerned with 411 London schoolboys. It followed their development from age 8 to 18 in order to determine what factors were associated with delinquency.

Longitudinal studies are usually large-scale quantitative studies but some qualitative studies also extend over considerable periods of time. Alan Bryman commented.

> There is an implicit longitudinal element built into much qualitative research, which is both a symptom and a cause of an undertaking to view social life in processual, rather than static terms.

In other words, methods such as participant observation are based upon the assumption that social life should be explained in terms of an unfolding story. Parker's study of Liverpool delinquents provides a good example of this. Parker showed how the type of delinquency engaged in by 'the boys' changed as the research developed and the boys grew older. A major advantage of any longitudinal study is its ability to pick up such changes: a study extending over a shorter time span cannot, and so the results can be misleading.

Supporters of longitudinal studies also see them as more likely to provide valid data than other types of research. As W.D. Wall and H.L. Williams point out, retrospective studies which ask people to report on past events in their lives rely upon fallible human memories. Wall and Williams also say 'Human beings naturally seek for causes and may unconsciously fabricate or exaggerate something to account for the present state of affairs.' Longitudinal studies help to overcome this problem because recent events are less likely to have been reinterpreted in the light of subsequent consequences.

Quantitative longitudinal studies often examine a large number of variables because the researchers are unsure what data may prove to be important or required later in the research. For example, West and Farrington collected information relating to no less than 151 variables in their study of delinquency. Although the researcher still has to decide what variables to study, examination of so many limits the extent to which they impose their own theories upon the research.

Longitudinal studies do, of course, have disadvantages. It may be necessary to select people who are accessible and willing to cooperate over an extended period. Furthermore, the size of the sample is liable to fall as some individuals become unwilling to continue to take part, or prove impossible to trace. Douglas's original sample of 5,362 children in 1957 was reduced to 4,720 by 1962. Since those who were lost may not have been representative of the sample as a whole, the results may have been distorted.

More serious criticisms question the overall validity of the data. Quantitative longitudinal studies collect data using such research methods as questionnaires and interviews. As earlier sections have shown, some sociologists question the validity of data collected in this way. A particular problem with longitudinal studies is that the subjects of the research are conscious of the fact that their behaviour is being studied. This may influence them and change their behaviour because they think more carefully about their actions.

■ Secondary sources

Secondary sources consist of data which have already been produced, often by people other than sociologists. Secondary data produced by the government are often used by sociologists. Organizations such as trade unions, companies and charities are a useful source of data, as are documents such as letters, diaries and autobiographies produced by individuals. The secondary sources used by sociologists may be contemporary or historical, and the data available from them may be primarily qualitative or quantitative. When sociologists refer to existing sociological studies by other writers in their own research, these become secondary sources.

Sociologists usually use secondary sources for

practical reasons. They can save time and money and they may provide access to historical data that cannot be produced using primary research because the events concerned took place before current members of society were born.

Secondary sources are invaluable to sociologists but have to be used with great caution. Their reliability and validity is open to question and often they do not provide the exact information required by a sociologist.

Specific types of secondary sources will now be examined. At the end of the section there will be a general discussion on how to evaluate all types of secondary sources.

■ Official statistics

A vast range of statistics are produced by the government. In recent years the Government Statistical Service (which was set up in 1941) has coordinated the production of government statistics, but the production of large-scale statistical data goes back at least to 1801, when the first Census was conducted. Sociologists interested in demography have used statistical data from the Census and elsewhere to examine a wide range of topics which include birth and death rates, marriage and fertility patterns, and divorce. Sociologists who study deviance have used official crime and suicide statistics. The many official economic statistics are of interest to sociologists concerned with work. Figures on inflation, unemployment and employment, strikes and productivity have also been used. Indeed, almost every area of sociological research has found some use for official statistics.

Some statistics, such as unemployment figures, are published monthly; others, such as crime statistics, annually. Information from the Census is produced once every decade. Other statistical surveys are carried out on an irregular basis, for example the *British Crime Surveys*. One of the reference books that is most frequently consulted by sociologists in Britain is *Social Trends*, which has been produced annually since 1970 and summarizes statistical data on society.

Much of the statistical information made available by the government would not exist if it were left to sociologists. They lack the resources and power to carry out the work that goes into producing these data. For example, each household is compelled by law to return a census form, and has a legal duty to provide accurate information; it would be impossible for sociologists to obtain this information independently. Official statistics are easily accessible and cost sociologists nothing to produce. Sociologists generally acknowledge that such statistics are useful, but they do not necessarily agree about what use can be made of them. Some sociologists do not accept the reliability and validity of official statistical data, while others are prepared to place more trust in them.

In the past, some positivists tended to accept official statistics uncritically. Durkheim believed suicide statistics were sufficiently reliable and valid to measure the extent and social distribution of suicide (see pp. 817–20). Using official statistics, he tried to establish correlations between suicide

and other 'social facts' and ultimately to discover causal relationships and laws of human behaviour. Similarly, many of the early structural and subcultural theories of crime were based upon the assumption that the official crime statistics accurately identified the working class as the group most prone to criminal activity.

Today sociologists are more cautious about the use of official statistics on areas of social life such as suicide and crime, but most would accept the reliability and validity of statistics from the Census. (Earlier parts of this book have shown how inaccurate some official statistics can be, for instance many crimes remain unreported and as such cannot be recorded in official data.)

Victimization and self-report studies

Despite this, many researchers believe that problems like these can be overcome. For example, **victimization** or **self-report** studies use questionnaires administered to members of the population in order to determine the extent of reported and unreported crime. The *British Crime Surveys* provide examples of victimization studies (see pp. 399–401 for further details). D.J. West and D.P. Farrington's longitudinal study of delinquency in London (discussed on p. 848) included a self-report study in which members of the sample were asked thirty-eight questions about delinquent acts they might have carried out. It is sometimes argued that on the basis of such studies it is possible to estimate the real amount of crime in society as a whole, and to calculate the extent of criminality in social groups. The figures can be used to determine the accuracy of official figures, and appropriate adjustments can then be made to them. Even so, as Peter Eglin points out, 'The question remains, however, whether an error estimate calculated for some set of, say, national statistics in some given year will be generalizable to other times or other places.'

An even more serious problem concerns the question of the validity of the answers given by respondents in surveys. Stephen Box has noted that in self-report studies respondents may exaggerate their criminality, or alternatively they might be unwilling to admit to their crimes. In effect self-report studies measure how many crimes people say they have committed, rather than the actual number. Furthermore, in measuring the criminality or delinquency of an individual the researcher has to decide what offences or actions to include in the list of questions. Among West and Farrington's thirty-eight questions, for instance, respondents were asked about stealing school property worth more than 5p, and annoying, insulting or fighting other people (strangers) in the street. The precise wording and number of questions included in the questionnaire ultimately determine the amount of crime or delinquency uncovered, and in any case respondents may interpret the questions in different ways. Whether or not an offence is included in the statistics depends upon the choices made by the researcher. In the *British Crime Surveys* the researchers discounted certain events because they did not believe that they constituted crimes. The statistics produced by such studies are therefore of dubious validity. However, several sociologists believe that self-report and victimization studies provide some indication of the real extent of crime, and help to correct the misleading impression (provided by the official figures) that crime is an overwhelmingly working-class phenomenon.

A phenomenological view

Ethnomethodologists and phenomenologists reject the use of statistics for measuring or determining the causes of the social facts to which they claim to refer. As earlier parts of this book show, sociologists such as Cicourel and Atkinson believe that statistics are the product of the meanings and taken-for-granted assumptions of those who construct them. Thus Cicourel claims that the stereotypes held by the police and juvenile officers lead to youths from lower social classes being more likely to be seen as delinquent. Justice is negotiable and statistics produced by official agencies are socially created (see pp. 412–13). Similarly, Atkinson has described how the common-sense theories held by coroners influence the way they categorize sudden deaths (see pp. 823–4). Both Cicourel and Atkinson regard official statistics as social creations.

This does not mean that official statistics are of no sociological interest. Indeed phenomenological sociologists believe they are important: they can be studied in order to discover how they are produced. This helps the sociologist to understand the common-sense theories, taken-for-granted assumptions, stereotypes and categorization procedures of officials involved in the production of

the statistics. To writers such as Cicourel, this is the only use that can be made of official statistics, including those such as census statistics, which appear to be based upon far more objective categories. To Cicourel, all statistics involve classifying things as 'this' or 'that', and such decisions are subjective.

Cicourel's views may become less convincing though when applied to such data as the age and sex distribution of a population. There may be considerable room for interpretation when considering whether an act is criminal or a sudden death is a suicide. There is less room for interpretation when deciding whether somebody is male or female.

A conflict view

In response to both positivist and phenomenological views a number of conflict sociologists have developed alternative perspectives on official statistics. They argue that official statistics are neither hard facts, nor subjective meanings. Instead they consist of information which is systematically distorted by power structures in society. Ian Miles and John Irvine argue that official statistics are 'developed in support of the system of power and domination that is modern capitalism — a system in which the state plays a particularly important role'.

Miles and Irvine do not believe that statistics produced by the government are complete fabrications because, as they point out, such a viewpoint would be unable to explain why the state frequently publishes figures that are embarrassing to the government. For instance, figures on inflation, crime and unemployment often seem to suggest that government policies are not working. The statistics are not complete distortions but they are manipulated through the definitions and collection procedures used so that they tend to favour the interests of the powerful. Miles and Irvine say that official statistics are produced according to the needs of the various state agencies for information to coordinate their activities and justify their programmes. They are related to a single ideological framework underpinning the concepts and categories employed. A number of examples can be used to illustrate these points.

Theo Nichols argues from a Marxist point of view that the categories used in the Census and other official statistics disguise the true nature of class in capitalism. They were until recently based on the Registrar General's scale, which used status as an indicator of social class. To Nichols (as a Marxist) class is based upon the relationship to the means of production. Thus the official statistics gave the impression of a status hierarchy and disguised the existence of classes that are in opposition to each other as exploiters and exploited.

Ann and Robin Oakley have argued from a feminist perspective that official statistics are sexist. They point out that in 80 per cent of cases a man is defined as the head of household, and women engaged in housework, or unpaid domestic labour, are defined as economically inactive despite the contribution that housework makes to the economy. They also claim that the criminal law uses sexist categories. Only women can be convicted of infanticide, while the law discriminates against women who are prostitutes by exonerating their male clients.

Unemployment statistics received particular attention in the 1980s from those who were critical of the Thatcher government's record. The definition of unemployment has been recast many times, and almost always in ways that reduce the figures (see pp. 237–9).

Like phenomenologists, conflict sociologists tend to believe that official statistics are invalid for measuring the things they refer to, but they do reveal something about those who produce them. However, rather than seeing them as based merely upon subjective meanings, conflict sociologists see them as reflecting the ideological frameworks which are produced by capitalist or patriarchical society. Official statistics can therefore be analysed to uncover those frameworks and the power structures that produce them.

■ Historical sources

Historical documents are of vital importance to sociologists who wish to study social change which takes place over an extended period of time. There are limits to the period over which a sociological study using primary sources can extend and past events may be important in understanding how contemporary patterns of social life came about.

One area in which historical statistical sources have been of considerable importance is the study of family life. Chapter 6 showed how the development of family life since before the industrial revo-

lution has been a major topic of sociological inquiry. Peter Laslett made extensive use of parish records in order to discover how common nuclear and extended families were in pre-industrial England. Such data have been most useful in correcting the assumption that extended family households were the norm in pre-industrial Britain (see p. 338). However, findings based upon such secondary sources need to be used with caution. Many parish records have not survived and the documents which Laslett used relate only to particular villages which happened to have complete records. It may therefore be dangerous to accept generalizations based upon such findings.

Michael Anderson's research on the family (see p. 339) is based upon early Census statistics which are more readily available. Nevertheless, Anderson chose to concentrate on one town, Preston, so the patterns of family life described are again not necessarily representative. Anderson also points out that Census statistics do not provide an in-depth picture of family relationships. He lists the sort of descriptive, qualitative data that can be used to supplement statistical data in the historical study of the family as

---

tracts, reports of missionary and charitable societies, descriptions of crimes, newspaper investigations into the condition of the people, parliamentary investigations and the evidence of some witnesses to them, speeches in parliamentary debates and some aspects of novels.

Like qualitative data from primary research, qualitative secondary sources may be unreliable and are open to a number of interpretations. Many of the secondary sources mentioned above are highly subjective and are likely to reflect the ideologies of those who produced them. Nevertheless, they do reveal something of the perspectives of their producers.

Whatever the problems of historical research, without using historical documents sociologists would be confined to producing a rather static view of social life. Without them Max Weber would have been unable to consider the influence of religion on the development of capitalism (see pp. 459–61) and Michael Mann would not have had the opportunity to discuss the relationship between different sources of social power throughout history (see pp. 544–6).

■ Government reports

Government reports are designed to provide the government of the day with information on contemporary events and issues. They usually provide a mixture of quantitative and qualitative data and the research is often very expensive to conduct. They may provide access to data on a scale that sociologists cannot afford to collect themselves. Examples of important reports are the *Swann Report* which examined education and ethnic minorities, the *Black Report* into inequalities in health, and the *Scarman Report* which examined inner-city riots, particularly in Brixton. Although undoubtedly useful, reports like these do not necessarily provide the data that sociologists need to test their hypotheses.

In addition, the findings of the reports may reflect the views of those responsible for producing them. For example, the *Scarman Report* was seen to reflect the 'liberal' view of Lord Scarman. He attributed the riots primarily to deprivation and policing methods. The findings of the *Black Report* appeared to reflect the views of at least one member of the team which produced it: Peter Townsend. The report concluded that inequalities in health were largely due to material inequalities in society as a whole, a view Townsend has supported for many years.

■ Life documents

Life documents are created by individuals and record details of that person's experiences and social actions. They are predominantly qualitative and may offer insights into peoples' subjective states. They can be historical or contemporary and can take a wide variety of forms. Ken Plummer illustrates this diversity when he says,

---

People keep diaries, send letters, take photos, write memos, tell biographies, scrawl graffiti, publish memoirs, write letters to the papers, leave suicide notes, inscribe memorials on tombstones, shoot films, paint pictures, make music and try to record their personal dreams.

All these sources, along with many others, have the potential to be useful to sociologists.

The use of life documents has a long history in sociology. Their use was popularized by W.I. Thomas and F. Znaniecki in their study *The Polish Peasant in Europe and America*, which was published between 1918 and 1920. Thomas and Znaniecki made use of 764 letters, a lengthy statement by one Polish peasant about his life, reports from social work agencies, court reports and articles from Polish newspapers. From such sources they tried to understand and explain the experience of migration for the hundreds of thousands of Polish people who moved to America in the early years of the twentieth century.

The study was widely regarded as a classic at the time, but according to Plummer it is now rarely mentioned and infrequently read. This is partly because life documents themselves have fallen out of favour as a source for sociologists. Those who favour more quantitative methods tend to regard life documents as an inadequate source of data. They are difficult to obtain and the ones that exist are likely to cover an unrepresentative sample of the population. Like all data, personal documents are open to interpretation. They may say more about the subjective states of individuals than the events they are describing. It is unlikely that the husband, wife, or political opponent of a diary writer would describe events in quite the same way. Personal documents which are meant to be read by others (such as letters and autobiographies) may be written with an audience in mind. As Ponsonby once commented, 'letters may be said to have two parents, the writer and the recipient' (quoted in Plummer, 1983, p. 23). Such documents may be designed more to justify actions than to make a real attempt to explain the writer's feelings or motives. Diaries, when they are available, may have greater validity if they are not intended for public consumption. One way of overcoming the scarcity of diaries and the unrepresentative nature of examples that exist, is for the researcher to prompt those being studied to keep diaries. Young and Willmott asked the subjects of their research into family life in London to keep diaries, recording how much time they spent on different activities and how they felt about them. Oscar Lewis, studying poverty in Mexico, persuaded a number of families to keep detailed diaries recording the events of a single day. Such diaries may be more systematic than those obtained by chance; however, they may be less valid. The awareness that they will be used for research might influence the details included by their writers.

Despite these limitations, Plummer believes that personal documents should play a crucial role in sociology. Using them as a source avoids a preoccupation with abstract theories 'which can kill off any concern for the joy and suffering of active human beings'. Compared to other secondary sources personal documents allow much greater insight into the subjective states of individuals, which in turn shape their behaviour. Plummer supports symbolic interactionist approaches to studying social life. From this point of view some sort of participant observation may be the ideal method for studying social life. Where this type of research is not possible life documents are the best alternative since they offer insights into the 'ordinary ambiguous personal meanings' that shape people's actions in their everyday lives. (More details of Plummer's theoretical standpoint are included in the section on case studies and life histories, see pp. 833–4).

■ The mass media and content analysis

Many parts of the mass media are notoriously inaccurate. Sociologists would, for example, be unlikely to turn solely to a national newspaper for an objective account of social life in Britain. Although some parts of the mass media may provide sociologists with useful data, their main importance is as objects of study. Rather like the official statistics, mass media reports can be used to analyse the ideologies of those who produce them. Some sociologists have been highly critical of parts of the mass media for producing distorted images of society which might mislead the public or adversely affect the socialization of children.

Sociologists carrying out content analysis of the mass media may use quantitative methods, qualitative methods, or a combination of the two. Quantitative methods appear to provide reliable data which can be checked by other researchers. They do not depend upon the arbitrary interpretations of the person carrying out the study. For example, G. Lobban conducted a study of the portrayal of gender roles in children's reading schemes. She listed and counted the toys and pets that children had, the activities they engaged in, the skills they

learned and the roles that adults were shown in (see p. 771). In a somewhat similar study Tuchman studied the portrayal of women from 1952 to 1974 on American television using quantitative techniques. She found that men predominated in all types of programme and that women were rarely shown in occupational roles.

The simplicity and reliability of quantitative content analysis makes it appealing, however it is not without its problems. Simply counting the number of items tells you nothing about their significance and the meanings of the texts or images being studied can only be implied. An alternative is to use qualitative methods borrowed from the analysis of literature. Such methods often derive from semiotics, or the science of signs. They stress that the meaning of part of a book can only be understood if the researcher places it in the context of the work as a whole. The reader, viewer or researcher has to try to understand the perspective of the writer, discover the rules governing that person's writing, to interpret the meanings of the work being studied. As John Scott points out though, different researchers might produce very different interpretations of a particular text or other product of the mass media. There may be no clear way of determining which of the various possible interpretations is superior. Mass media researchers have therefore tried to find ways of making interpretations more reliable. This often involves combining quantitative and qualitative methods.

The work of the Glasgow University Media Group illustrates some of the benefits of combining methods. In their first study they examined British television news coverage of industrial relations, particularly strikes. They used quantitative methods, for example counting the frequency with which different verbs were used to describe the actions of management and workers. Management was usually described as 'offering' or 'proposing', while workers were more often described as making 'claims' or 'demands'. They also used qualitative methods, trying to interpret the meaning that the different stories conveyed to viewers. To evaluate the reliability of these interpretations they cross-checked them with a number of different researchers. By using different techniques of content analysis together they added credibility to their claims that television coverage of industrial relations tended to favour government and management viewpoints and to neglect the viewpoint of workers.

John Scott – assessing secondary sources

John Scott has provided some useful guidelines for evaluating secondary sources (or as he calls them, documents). The criteria can be applied to all secondary sources, including existing sociological research. They offer systematic ways of trying to ensure that researchers use them with as much care as they employ in producing primary data.

Scott identifies four criteria:

1 Authenticity – this refers to the question of how genuine a document is. There are two aspects of authenticity, soundness and authorship. Scott says, 'A sound document is one which is complete and reliable. It should have no missing pages or misprints and, if it is a copy of an original it should be a reliable copy without errors of transcription.' When the document is not sound, the researcher needs to consider carefully how far the omissions detract from its reliability and validity. The question of authorship concerns who it was written by. Many documents are not actually produced by those to whom they are attributed. For example, many letters signed by the Prime Minister may have been written by civil servants and might reveal little about the Prime Minister's own views. The most extreme problem of authenticity occurs when documents are faked, as in the case of the so-called 'Hitler Diaries' which were originally authenticated as the work of the former German leader but which later proved not to be genuine.

2 Credibility – this issue relates to the amount of distortion in a document. Any distortion may be related to sincerity or accuracy. In a sincere document the author genuinely believes what they write. This is not always the case, the author may hope to gain advantage from deceiving readers. For example, politicians may distort accounts of their actions or motives in their diaries or memoirs to justify what they have done. Inaccuracy might result from unintended distortions, such as when an account is written some time after the events described and faulty memory makes absolute accuracy impossible.

3 Representativeness – Scott points out that 'Sampling of documents must be handled as carefully and as systematically as the sampling of respondents in a survey.' A researcher must be aware of how typical or untypical the documents being used are 'in order to be able to assign limits to any conclusions drawn'. Two factors which may limit the possibility of using representative documents are survival and availability. Many documents do not survive because they are not stored, and others deteriorate with age and become unusable. This is obviously a particular problem when doing historical research in sociology. Other documents are deliberately withheld from researchers and the public gaze, and thus do not become available. For example, many official documents are not made available for thirty years, others which are classified as secret may never be made public. Individuals and private organisations may also be unwilling to make many of their documents available to researchers.

4 Meaning – this concerns the ability of a researcher to understand the document. At one level the researcher may have difficulty with its literal understanding. It may be in a foreign language, old-fashioned handwriting or it could use archaic vocabulary which is difficult to comprehend. Interpretative understanding is even more difficult to achieve, it involves 'understanding of what the document actually signifies'. For example, there has been a long-standing debate about whether suicide statistics signify more about suicides or about the officials who define certain acts as suicides (see pp. 817–26). Some of the problems involved in deciphering meaning are discussed in the section on the mass media (see pp. 854–5). Whether quantitative content analysis or qualitative semiotic analysis is chosen interpretative understanding is always open to debate.

Scott shows that all secondary sources need to be evaluated and used with great care. Research using them needs to be as systematic and rigorous as research which produces primary data. The same care should be employed when reading and using existing sociology books and studies. In particular, as Scott points out 'readers must always be aware of the interests and commitments of authors' since these may influence the way that secondary and other sources are interpreted and used.

■ Triangulation or methodological

As an earlier section indicated (p. 808), it is difficult to see quantitative and qualitative methods as mutually exclusive. Increasingly sociologists are combining both approaches in single studies. As Bryman puts it, 'The rather partisan, either/or tenor of debate about quantitative and qualitative research may appear somewhat bizarre to an outsider, for whom the obvious way forward is likely to be a fusion of the two approaches so that their respective strengths might be reaped.' In reality, the degree to which quantitative and qualitative approaches are different has been exaggerated. Bryman points out that 'Most researchers rely primarily on a method associated with one of the two research traditions, but buttress their findings with a method associated with the other tradition.' The practice of combining quantitative and qualitative research has a long history, and is evident in the approach advocated by Weber (see p. 889–90).

Bryman has suggested a number of ways in which using a plurality of methods – a practice known as **triangulation** – can be useful.

1 Qualitative and quantitative data can be used to check on the accuracy of the conclusion reached on the basis of each.

2 Qualitative research can be used to produce hypotheses which can then be checked using quantitative methods.

3 The two approaches can be used together so that a more complete picture of the social group being studied is produced.

4 Qualitative research may be used to illuminate why certain variables are statistically correlated.

The following examples illustrate the advantages of combining research methods. In her study of the Unification Church, or Moonies, Eileen Barker used participant observation, questionnaires and in-depth interviewing. She claimed that this combination of methods allowed her to 'see how the movement as a whole was organized and how it influenced the day-to-day actions and interactions of its members'. She tried to test hypotheses formulated from qualitative data using questionnaires.

Quantitative techniques have been used to analyse data systematically from observation or participant observation. For example, Delamont used the Flanders Interaction Analysis Categories in her studies of classroom interaction. These allowed her to categorize the different types of interaction and to time them in order to determine differences in the educational experience of boys and girls. She used qualitative data to explain the reasons for the quantitative relationships she found.

The combination of method is not just confined to the use of primary data. In a study of secondary schooling Paul Corrigan used interviews, observation and historical and contemporary documents. These enabled him to place his analysis of school life within the context of the historical development of the education system in Britain.

Bryman believes that both qualitative and quantitative research have their own advantages. Neither can produce totally valid and completely reliable data, but both can provide useful insights into social life. He argues that each has its own place, and they can be most usefully combined. Generally quantitative data tends to produce rather static pictures, but it can allow researchers to examine and discover overall patterns and structures in society as a whole. Qualitative data is less useful for discovering overall patterns and structures, but it does allow a richer and deeper understanding of the process of change in social life. Bryman says 'A division of labour is suggested here in that quantitative research may be conceived of as a means of establishing the structural element in social life, qualitative research the processual.' As the next section will show, the view that sociology should use both qualitative and quantitative methods, does not necessarily preclude the possibility that it can be scientific.

■ Sociology and science

■ Scientific methodology

The early parts of this chapter showed how sociologists have adopted varying views on the relationship between sociology and science. Positivists claim that science uses established methods and procedures, and that these methods and procedures can be applied to the social sciences. They believe that social facts can be observed objectively, measured and quantified. Analysis of statistics can reveal correlations, causes and ultimately laws of human behaviour. From this point of view, sociological studies using such methods can be considered to be scientific. Positivists see the use of scientific methods as highly desirable, and they tend to be critical of those sociologists who study subjective and unobservable mental states.

Popper also sees it as highly desirable that sociology should be scientific, but argues that science is a deductive rather than inductive methodology. Scientists should make precise predictions on the basis of their theories so that they can strive conscientiously to falsify or disprove them. Popper rejects many sociological theories as being unscientific because they are not sufficiently precise to generate hypotheses that can be falsified. He is particularly critical of Marxism for failing to make precise predictions: for example, for failing to specify exactly when and under what circumstances a proletarian revolution would take place in capitalist societies. Marxism cannot be falsified since the day of the proletarian revolution and the dawning of the truly communist society is pushed further into the future. Marxism is an article of faith rather than a scientific theory.

Like positivists then, Popper believes that it is possible for 'social sciences' in general, and sociology in particular, to become scientific by following a particular set of methodological procedures. He parts company with positivists in denying that science can deliver the final, incontrovertible truth, since the possibility of falsification always exists. Instead he believes that the longer a theory has stood the test of time, the more often researchers have failed to falsify it, the closer it is likely to be to the truth.

Phenomenologists reject the view that natural science methodology is appropriate to sociology. To phenomenologists, objective observation and measurement of the social world is not possible. The social world is classified by members of society in terms of their own stereotypes and taken-for-granted assumptions. In these circumstances the social world cannot be measured objectively; statistics are simply the product of the categorization procedures used. The best that sociologists can hope to do is study the way that members of society categorize the world around them. They cannot collect meaningful statistical data and establish correlations, causal connections and laws. Indeed, phenomenologists reject the whole possibility of finding laws of human behaviour.

■ The social context of science

All the views discussed so far are based upon the assumption that there are established methods and procedures that characterize science. However, as Kaplan has pointed out, it is necessary to distinguish between reconstructed logics and logics in use. **Reconstructed logics** consist of the methods and procedures scientists claim to use. Both positivism and Popper's methodological approach represent reconstructed logics. There is no guarantee that scientists actually do follow such guidelines. **Logics in use** refer to what scientists actually do during their research, and this may depart considerably from their reconstructed logics.

Michael Lynch has conducted research in a psycho-biological laboratory which illustrates how scientists may be less objective than they claim. The scientists studied brain functioning by examining thin slices of rats' brains under microscopes. Photographs and slides of the brain slices were examined to see how useful they were in developing theories of brain functioning. Sometimes unexplained features were found in the photographs. Very often these were put down to some error in the production of the photograph or slide: they were seen as artefacts, rather than being a real feature of the rat's brain. (An artefact is something produced by the research process which does not exist in the phenomenon being studied.) Some of these features were held to be an error in staining, others were believed to be the result of scratching of the specimen when it was being sliced.

There was much discussion in the laboratory about whether these features were artefacts or not. In reaching their conclusions, the scientists were influenced by their existing theories, the types of features they were looking for and expected to find. If the visible marks on the slide or photograph did not fit their theories of how rats' brains functioned they were much more likely to dismiss the marks as errors. Their interpretations of the data were guided by their theories. Far from following Popper's methodology and striving to falsify their theories, the researchers tried to use the evidence to confirm them. Many scientists may be reluctant to dismiss perhaps years of intellectual effort and research because a single piece of evidence does not support the theory that they have developed.

The social context of Darwin's theory of evolution

It may also be the case that the sort of theories that are developed in the first place – and which scientists try to confirm rather than falsify – are influenced by social factors rather than the detached pursuit of objective knowledge. Roger Gomm has used Darwin's theory of evolution as an example to illustrate this. Darwin claimed that species developed and evolved by a process of natural selection. Most followers of Darwin believed that this process took place gradually. Natural selection occurred through adaptation to the environment. Genetic differences between members of a species make some better suited to survival in a particular environment. Those that have a better chance of survival are more likely to produce offspring and so shift the species towards their genetic characteristics. For example, giraffes with longer necks may have been more likely to survive and produce offspring than those with shorter necks because they were able to feed off leaves which other species and certain members of their own species could not reach.

Gomm points out that both the ideas of natural selection and gradual evolution are not supported by all the evidence. According to Gomm, Darwin himself did not believe that evolution was a gradual process, but that it was initiated by sudden genetic changes or mutations. Fossil records do not support the gradualist theory of evolutionary change; instead there appear to be rapid periods of genetic change and eras of mass extinction. Gomm claims that the popularity of 'gradualism' was not the result of careful interpretation of the evidence but 'because it lined up with a preference for gradual social and political change among the dominant social groups of the time'. Darwin's theories were often misused, for example by the English functionalist sociologist Herbert Spencer, to indicate how societies should be run. Those in power did not want it to appear that revolutionary change was the answer to society's problems because it could undermine their dominance.

The idea of natural selection suggests, as Herbert Spencer put it, 'survival of the fittest'. The weak – those unsuited to survival in a particular environment – must perish to ensure the healthy genetic development of a species. In this theory competition is the key to genetic and evolutionary progress.

However, as Gomm points out, 'the idea of natural selection as a red in tooth and claw struggle for survival is only a half truth at best. It leaves out of account the extent to which individuals within a species cooperate with each other.' In his book *Mutual Aid* the Russian anarchist Prince Peter Kropotkin amassed a wealth of evidence to show that cooperation rather than conflict allowed animals to survive in flocks, herds or other groups. Many animals are best able to resist predators, or at least ensure that casualties are minimized, in such groupings.

Why then was Darwin's competitive vision of the natural world preferred to Kropotkin's equally carefully argued cooperative vision? Gomm argues that it was because Darwin's views fitted more closely with the ideologies of dominant social groups in Victorian Britain.

1 It justified the free market capitalist system and did not support socialist ideas which argued for state intervention in the economy.

2 It legitimated harsh social policies which saw the poor as 'unfit' and therefore as not worthy of much assistance. (See pp. 146–7 for details of Herbert Spencer's Darwinist views on poverty.)

3 Since evolution allowed species to be seen as superior or inferior, it allowed groups within the species to be placed on an evolutionary scale. Gomm argues that the idea of evolution as progress, 'allowed the Victorians to lay out the peoples of the world on an evolutionary ladder, with Australian Aboriginals at the bottom (least evolved) and Victorian intellectual males at the top'. It therefore justified the colonization of non-Western people on the grounds that the British Empire would civilize them. A similar use of a scientific theory to legitimate the domination of one group by another (that is women by men) is provided by sociobiology (see pp. 584–6).

■ Thomas Kuhn – paradigms and scientific revolutions

The preceding section argues that the interpretation of evidence is governed by the theories that scientists hold, and that these theories themselves may be influenced by social and ideological factors. This suggests that in practice scientists operate in very different ways from those advocated by Popper or positivists.

Thomas Kuhn has developed an analysis of science which also sees it as being far from the objective pursuit of knowledge. In *The Structure of Scientific Revolutions*, Kuhn argues that science is characterized by a commitment to a scientific paradigm. A **paradigm** consists of a set of beliefs shared by a group of scientists about what the natural world is composed of, what counts as true and valid knowledge, what sort of questions should be asked and what sort of procedures should be followed to answer those questions. A paradigm is a complete theory and framework within which scientists operate. It guides what evidence is collected, how that evidence is collected, and how it should be analysed and explained. When scientists work within a paradigm, they tend to look for data that supports and refines that paradigm. The way that scientists perceive the world around them is also governed by the paradigm – they see the world in ways that are consistent with the paradigm.

Kuhn does not believe that the same methods and procedures are found throughout scientific history, rather they are specific to particular sciences at particular times. Nor does Kuhn believe that scientists are entirely objective – paradigms are not accepted or rejected on the basis of evidence alone. Each paradigm has a social base in that it is grounded in a community of scientists committed to a particular view of the world or some part of it. Older scientists trained to think within the framework provided by an established paradigm find it difficult to see the world in any other way. Furthermore, they have a vested interest in maintaining it for their academic reputations and careers rest upon the work they have done within that paradigm. Consequently, scientists may ignore evidence which does not fit 'their' paradigm.

Scientific revolutions

Scientific beliefs do change, but, according to Kuhn, rather than changing gradually they are changed by scientific revolutions. In a scientific revolution one scientific paradigm is replaced by another, for instance, when Newton's paradigm in physics was replaced by Einstein's. Change in science is not a gradual process of accumulating new knowledge, but a sudden move from one paradigm to another. This occurs when an accepted paradigm is confronted by so many 'anomalies' or things it cannot explain, that a new paradigm is developed which does not suffer from the same anomalies. A community of scientists may resist the change, but once a new generation of scientists who have been trained within the new paradigm start practising, the new paradigm is accepted. A science then returns to its 'normal' state in which the paradigm is elaborated and developed, but the framework which it lays down is largely unquestioned.

Kuhn's work raises serious questions about the other views of science. To Kuhn a scientific subject is one in which there is, most of the time at least, an agreed paradigm. There is no guarantee, however, that the accepted paradigm is correct: it may well be replaced by a new paradigm in the future. Scientific training has more to do with learning to see the physical world in a particular way than it has to do with a commitment to discovering the truth through objective research.

If Kuhn's view of science is accepted, it is doubtful if sociology can be seen as a science. The sociological community has not accepted one paradigm, or in sociological vocabulary one 'perspective'. Marxists, functionalists, interactionists and ethnomethodologists all see the social world in different ways: they ask different questions and get different answers. Even within a perspective there is a lack of consensus. There are many variations within Marxism while within functionalism Durkheim and Parsons reached different conclusions on many issues, and they did not analyse societies in the same ways. In this situation sociology can be regarded as 'pre-paradigmatic': a single paradigm has not yet been accepted, and as such sociology is pre-scientific. It could, of course, become scientific if sociologists were to agree upon a perspective that all practitioners of the subject could accept. Given the present state of the subject such an outcome seems highly unlikely.

Whether it is desirable for sociology to become like a science is questionable. Sociology seems to exist almost in a permanent state of revolution, but the constant conflict may help to push the subject forward at a rapid pace.

Criticisms of Kuhn

Although influential, Kuhn's work has been criticized. It has been seen as having little relevance to social science and as being based upon inadequate evidence. Anderson, Hughes and Sharrock argue that Kuhn is doing no more than describing natural science and his views have little relevance to sociology. Furthermore, they believe that he has underestimated the degree to which there is conflict and disagreement in natural science. Most of the time alternative paradigms are debated. Anderson *et al.* claim that a careful examination of the history of science shows that 'The periods of revolution grow in size while those of settled "normality" contract.'

The realist view of science

So far, this part of the chapter appears to suggest that it is either impossible or undesirable for sociology to be a science. Despite the claims of positivists and Popper, it seems inappropriate for a subject which deals with human behaviour to confine itself to studying the observable, to ignore the subjective, to try to falsify theories or to make precise predictions. However, in recent years the realist theory of science – which stresses the similarities between social and natural science – has been developed. Realists such as Roy Bhaskar, Russell Keat, John Urry and Andrew Sayer argue that none of the above points disqualifies sociology from being a science. They believe that positivists, Popper and indeed Kuhn, are mistaken about the nature of science.

'Closed' and 'open' systems

Sayer argues that there is a difference between **closed** and **open** systems as objects of scientific study. Within closed systems all the relevant variables can be controlled and measured. In scientific laboratory experiments closed systems may be produced, and certain branches of science such as physics and chemistry have much more scope for the study of closed systems than others.

There are many areas of science in which all the relevant variables cannot be controlled or measured. As a result it is not possible to make the precise predictions advocated by Popper. For example, doctors cannot predict with certainty who will become ill, seismologists cannot predict exactly when an earthquake will occur and meteorologists cannot predict the weather with anything like absolute precision. In all these cases the reasons for the lack of precision are similar – some of the variables cannot be measured or the processes involved are too complex for accurate predictions to be made.

Sociology has similar problems. Within society as a whole or within a social group innumerable variables may influence what happens. Thus sociologists cannot be expected to predict exactly what the divorce rate will be in five years' time, or whether a revolution will occur within a given period of time.

Human consciousness

However, even if it is accepted that a science does not need to make predictions, this still leaves the problem of human consciousness to be dealt with. As outlined earlier, positivists believe that a science should confine itself to the study of the observable, whereas interpretive sociologists believe that reference must be made to internal and unobservable meanings and motives in explaining human behaviour. Realists point out though that science itself does not confine itself to studying observable phenomena. As Keat and Urry say, scientists may 'postulate the existence of entities which have not been observed, and may not be open to any available method of detection'. Viruses, sub-atomic particles and magnetic fields all form part of scientific theories despite the impossibility (at present) of directly observing them. Scientists cannot easily observe continental drift, because it takes place too slowly, nor can they see the mechanisms which produce it because they are below the earth's surface. Darwin could not observe evolution, because it took place too slowly.

Causality

To realists then, both Popper and positivists have failed to define science accurately and so the objections raised by interpretive sociologists to seeing sociology as a science become irrelevant. Realists see science as the attempt to explain the causes of events in the natural or social world in terms of underlying and often unobservable structures, mechanisms and processes. Realists produce causal explanations and explain them in terms of such structures, mechanisms and processes. An example of a mechanism or process in science would be Darwin's idea of natural selection. In sociology examples include ideas on the concentration of capital and the pauperization of the proletariat.

To realists, explaining the mechanisms through which events take place is a vital part of causal explanation. This requires the researcher to specify which factors or variables determine whether these mechanisms operate. For example, in different conditions the concentration of capital might be slowed down, speeded up or halted. Similarly, in Darwin's theory of evolution the actual consequences of the operation of natural selection depend upon the precise and changing environmental conditions in which species evolve.

According to realists, events take place and mechanisms operate within the context of structures. Keat and Urry argue that a structure is a 'system of relationships which underlie and account for the sets of observable social relationships and those of social consciousness'. Similarly, Sayer defines structures as 'sets of internally related objects or practices'. He uses the example of the relationship between landlords and tenants to illustrate a structure in society. The existence of a landlord depends upon the existence of tenants, and 'The landlord tenant relation itself presupposes the existence of private property, rent, the production of an economic surplus and so on; together they form a structure.'

Structures impose limitations or constraints upon what happens, but mechanisms and the variables which affect them determine the actual course of events. For example, the structure of relationships between landlords and tenants does not determine which individual occupies the property being rented, but it does determine that the tenant pays rent and the landlord does not. Structures are often unobservable, but a natural or social scientist can work out that they are there by observing their effects. Social classes cannot be seen, nor can the infrastructure and superstructure of society, but to a Marxist they are real.

Science and sociology

According to the realist view of science much of sociology is scientific. To realist sociologists such as Keat and Urry, Marxist sociology is scientific because it develops models of the underlying structures and processes in society which are evaluated and modified in the light of empirical evidence. Unlike positivists, realists do not automatically reject interpretive sociology as unscientific because they believe that studying unobservable meanings and motives are perfectly compatible with a scientific subject.

From this point of view there is relatively little difference between social and natural sciences. Some branches of natural science which have the luxury of studying 'closed' systems can be more precise than sociology, but others face the same difficulty as sociology in trying to deal with highly complex open systems. Both natural sciences and sociology have common aims: they try to develop models and theories that explain the world as objectively as possible on the basis of the available evidence. Whether sociology can be completely objective is the subject of the next section.

■ Sociology, methodology and values

One of the reasons that sociologists have been so concerned with the question of whether sociology is a science is the widespread assumption that science is objective, or value free. Robert Bierstedt has stated 'Objectivity means that the conclusions arrived at as the result of inquiry and investigation are independent of the race, colour, creed, occupation, nationality, religion, moral preference, and political predisposition of the investigator. If his research is truly objective, it is independent of any subjective elements, any personal desires, that he may have.'

Many of the founders of sociology believed that sociology could and should be value free. Early positivists such as Comte and Durkheim argued that objectivity was attainable by adopting a 'scientific' methodology. Marx also believed that his sociology was objective and 'scientific', although he saw society very differently. Weber did not think complete value freedom was possible, but he did believe that once a topic for research had been chosen the researcher could be objective. He argued that sociologists should not make value judgements, that is, they should not state what aspects of society they found desirable or undesirable.

Despite the claims of these important sociologists, it is doubtful whether their own work met the criteria necessary for complete value freedom. The concluding sections of Chapters 2–12 have shown that the values of sociologists have influenced their work whatever area of social life they have studied.

Functionalists in general have been accused of holding politically conservative views for assuming that existing social institutions serve a useful purpose. This implies that anything other than slow evolutionary change is harmful to society.

Durkheim accepted the need for certain changes in society, but his personal values are evident in his belief that the inheritance of wealth should be abolished and professional associations established (see p. 184–6).

Few would claim that Marx's sociology was free from his political and moral beliefs. Marx's desire for proletarian revolution influenced most aspects of his work.

Weber's work often appears more value free than that of functionalists or Marxists, but there is little doubt that his personal values influenced his research. Weber's writings on bureaucracy (see pp. 271–5) are strongly influenced by his fear that bureaucratic organizations would stifle human freedom. In his words, 'What can we oppose to this machinery in order to keep a portion of mankind free from this parcelling-out of the soul, from this supreme mastery of the bureaucratic way of life' (quoted in Nisbet, 1967, p. 299).

Even if it is true that such eminent sociologists allowed their values to influence their research, it does not necessarily follow that it is impossible to achieve value freedom in sociology. To many contemporary sociologists there is, however, no prospect of a completely value-free sociology. According to this view, total objectivity is impossible because values inevitably enter every stage of the production of sociological knowledge.

Weber recognized that values would influence the choice of topics for study. He argued that the sociologist had to have some way of choosing from the almost infinite number of possible areas of social life which could be studied. Weber believed that 'value relevance' would influence the choice. Researchers would choose to research topics which they thought were important, and more significantly which they thought were of central importance to society. Weber himself chose to study the advent of capitalism and the nature of bureaucracy, because he saw them as the most important developments in Western societies. The values of other sociologists have also been evident in their choice of topics for research. Peter Townsend had demonstrated his belief that poverty is a serious problem by devoting years of his life to its study

(see pp. 129–34). Marxists have shown the importance they attach to inequality in their studies of wealth, income and stratification. Simply by selecting an issue to study, sociologists reveal what aspects of society they believe are significant.

Having selected a topic, sociologists then choose what aspects of that topic to study, and what approach they are going to adopt. According to Alvin Gouldner this involves making 'domain assumptions'. These are the basic assumptions that sociologists make about the nature of social life and human behaviour. Gouldner says 'Domain assumptions about man and society might include, for example, dispositions to believe that men are rational or irrational; that society is precarious or fundamentally stable; that social problems will correct themselves without planned intervention; that human behaviour is unpredictable; that man's true humanity resides in his feelings and sentiments.'

Gouldner believes that in practice all sociologists tend to commit themselves to a particular set of domain assumptions, and these direct the way that research is conducted and conclusions are reached. Without some starting point research cannot proceed and sociological knowledge cannot be created. Domain assumptions about human behaviour – such as whether it is governed by external or internal stimuli and whether it is rational or irrational – will tend to determine whether quantitative or qualitative methods are adopted.

In designing and carrying out research all researchers have to be selective. When producing a questionnaire or planning an interview some questions have to be chosen and others excluded. The choice will be influenced by the theories and hypotheses to which a particular researcher attaches credibility. Once the data has been collected researchers need to interpret the results, and very often the results do not speak for themselves.

For example, it could be argued that the study of Goldthorpe and Lockwood into 'affluent workers' was guided to some extent by the desire to disprove a particular hypothesis (in this case the embourgeoisement thesis) and this influenced the range of questions included in the questionnaires. The data produced was interpreted in different ways by different sociologists (for further details of the study see pp. 77–9).

Similarly, the proletarianization thesis has guided much of the research into routine non-manual workers, and Marxists and non-Marxists have tended to produce different types of data which they have interpreted in different ways, and which has led them to very different conclusions (see pp. 65–9).

Interpretive sociologists have tended to be very critical of those using quantitative methods. They have argued that many sociologists simply impose their own views of reality on the social world. As a result they distort and misrepresent the very reality they seek to understand. Research techniques such as interviews, questionnaires and social surveys are a part of this process of distortion. They come between the sociologist and the social world and so remove any opportunity he or she might have of discovering social reality.

From this point of view direct observation of everyday activity provides the most likely if not the only means of obtaining valid knowledge of the social world. This at least allows researchers to come face to face with the reality they seek to understand. Since the social world is seen to be a construction of its members, that world can only be understood in terms of members' categories and constructs. Thus Jack Douglas argues that sociologists must 'study the phenomena of everyday life on their own terms', they must 'preserve the integrity of that phenomena'. While phenomenologists might be looking in the right direction, the problem of validity remains unsolved. Though face to face with social reality, the observer can only see the social world through his or her own eyes. No two sociologists will see that world in exactly the same way. A participant observer cannot note and record everything that happens in her or his presence and, like the sociologist devising a questionnaire, has to be selective. In these circumstances the researcher's values will influence what events they believe to be important.

Because of these sorts of considerations, Derek Phillips argues 'An investigator's values influence not only the problems he selects for study but also his methods for studying them and the sources of data he uses.' In *Anti-Minotaur: The Myth of a Value Free Sociology*, Gouldner makes a similar

point. He argues that just as the bull and the man in the mythical creature the Minotaur cannot be separated, so facts and values cannot be separated in sociological research. Weber argued that sociologists' values should be kept out of their research, and they should not make value judgements – judgements about right or wrong. Gouldner regards this as dishonest. Since sociologists must have values they should be open about them so that others can decide for themselves to what degree values have influenced the research. Gouldner says:

> If sociologists ought not to express their personal values in the academic setting, how then are students to be safeguarded against the unwitting influence of these values which shape the sociologists selection of problems, his preferences for certain hypotheses or conceptual schemes, and his neglect of others. For these are unavoidable and, in this sense, there is and can be no value-free sociology. The only choice is between an expression of one's values, as open and honest as it can be, . . . and a vain ritual of moral neutrality which, because it invites men to ignore the vulnerability of reason to bias, leaves it at the mercy of irrationality.

Given these problems sociology might appear to consist of little more than personal opinions. If this were the case there would seem little point in the subject existing. However, although sociologists cannot free themselves of their values, arguably this is not possible in any subject including the natural sciences. By adopting rigorous methods sociologists can try to minimize the extent to which their values affect their sociological conclusions, even if they cannot eradicate that influence. As Peter Berger puts it,

> there is peculiar human value in the sociologist's responsibility for evaluating his findings, as far as he is psychologically able, without regard to his own prejudices, likes, or dislikes, hopes or fears . . . It is evident that this goal is not always achieved, but in the very effort lies a moral significance not to be taken lightly.

14

Sociological theory

14

Sociological theory

■ Introduction

A theory is a set of ideas that provides an explanation for something. A sociological theory is a set of ideas that provides an explanation for human society. Critics of sociology sometimes object to the emphasis that sociologists place on theory, and suggest it might be better to let 'the facts' speak for themselves. But there are no facts without theory. For example, in Western society, the generally accepted facts that the world is round and orbits the sun are inseparable from theories that explain the nature and movement of heavenly bodies. However, in some non-Western societies whose members employ different theories, the view that the world is flat and the solar system revolves around it is accepted as a statement of fact. Clearly the facts do not speak for themselves.

Like all theory, sociological theory is selective. No amount of theory can hope to explain everything, account for the infinite amount of data that exist or encompass the endless ways of viewing reality. Theories are therefore selective in terms of their priorities and perspectives and the data they define as significant. As a result, they provide a particular and partial view of reality.

Structural versus social action theories

Sociological theories can be characterized as falling into two main categories: structural perspectives and social action perspectives. They differ in the way that they approach the analysis of society. Structural or macro perspectives analyse the way society as a whole fits together. Thus, despite their differences, both functionalism and Marxism use a model of how society as a whole works. Many functionalists base their model of society around the assumption of functional prerequisites or basic needs, and go on to explain how different parts of society help to meet

those needs. Marxists, on the other hand, see society as resting upon an economic base or infrastructure, with a superstructure rising above it. They see society as divided into social classes which have the potential to be in conflict with each other. The main differences between functionalist and Marxist perspectives, then, concern the ways they characterize the social structure. Functionalists stress the extent to which the different elements of the social structure fit together harmoniously. Marxists stress the lack of fit between the different parts, particularly social classes, and so emphasize the potential for social conflict.

Marxism is one example of a conflict perspective. There are a variety of interpretations and adaptations of Marx's work, and some neo-Marxists question some of the concepts used by Marx while accepting his overall approach. Other conflict theorists agree with Marx and neo-Marxists that there is conflict in society, but disagree about the causes and types of conflict. They draw upon the work of Max Weber, who argued that many groups, apart from classes, can be in conflict for the scarce resources in society (see pp. 36–9).

Not all sociological perspectives base their analysis upon an examination of the structure of society as a whole. Rather than seeing human behaviour as being largely determined by society, they see society as being the product of human activity. They stress the meaningfulness of human behaviour, denying that it is primarily determined by the structure of society.

These approaches are variously called social action approaches, interpretive sociology, or micro sociology. Max Weber was the first sociologist to advocate a social action approach. In modern sociology there are two main varieties of this type of sociology.

Symbolic interactionists try to explain human behaviour and human society by examining the ways that people interpret the actions of others, develop a self-concept or self-image, and act in terms of meanings. They do not deny the existence of some elements of a social structure; for example, they acknowledge the presence of social roles, and some interactionists also use the concept of social class. However, they believe the social structure is fluid and constantly changing in response to interaction.

Ethnomethodology moves even further from a structural approach by denying the existence of a social structure as such. To ethnomethodologists, the social world consists of the definitions and categorizations of members of society. These subjective meanings are social reality. The job of the sociologist, in their view, is to interpret, describe and above all to understand this subjective reality.

It is not possible to provide clear dividing lines between sociological perspectives. There are many approaches that do not fit neatly even into such broad categories as structural or social action perspectives. For example, the description of Marx's social theories later in this section will show that elements of a social action approach can be found within his work. Nevertheless, it is reasonable to divide much sociology into these two categories because the emphasis within perspectives like functionalism and Marxism is so different from that found within interactionism and ethnomethodology.

Some sociologists have made a self-conscious attempt to bridge the apparent gulf between social action and structural perspectives: Max Weber was arguably the first sociologist to try to combine an analysis of the structures of society with individual social actions; more recently, the sociologist Paul Willis has tried to combine Marxist analysis with an interactionist approach to social action; and Anthony Giddens, another sociologist, has also tried to bridge the gap that seems to separate structural and social action approaches.

This brief summary cannot do justice to the subtleties and complexities of sociological theory. Some of these complexities will be examined later in this chapter, but it is important to note that the chapter is far from comprehensive. There are a number of other perspectives that have not been included.

Figure 14.1 provides a simplified summary of the main theories that will be examined.

▌ Functionalism

Functionalist analysis has a long history in sociology. It is prominent in the work of Auguste Comte (1798–1857) and Herbert Spencer (1820–1903), two of the founding fathers of the discipline. It was developed by Emile Durkheim (1858–1917) and refined by Talcott Parsons (1902–79). During the 1940s and 1950s functionalism was the dominant social theory in American sociology. Since that time it has steadily dropped from favour, partly because of damaging criticism, partly because other approaches are seen to answer certain questions more successfully, and partly because it simply went out of fashion.

Society as a system

Functionalism views society as a system, that is, as a set of interconnected parts which together form a whole. The basic unit of analysis is society, and its various parts are understood primarily in terms of their relationship to the whole. The early functionalists often drew an analogy between society and an organism such as the human body. They argued that an understanding of any organ in the body, such as the heart or lungs, involves an understanding of its relationship to other organs and, in particular, of its contribution towards the maintenance of the organism. In the same way, an understanding of any part of society requires an analysis of its relationship to other parts, and most importantly, of its contribution to the maintenance of society. Continuing this analogy, they argued that just as an organism has certain basic needs which must be satisfied if it is to survive, so society has basic needs which must be met if it is to continue to exist. Thus social institutions such as the family and religion are analysed as a part of the social system rather than as isolated units. In particular, they are understood with reference to the contribution they make to the system as a whole.

Figure 14.1   Sociological perspectives

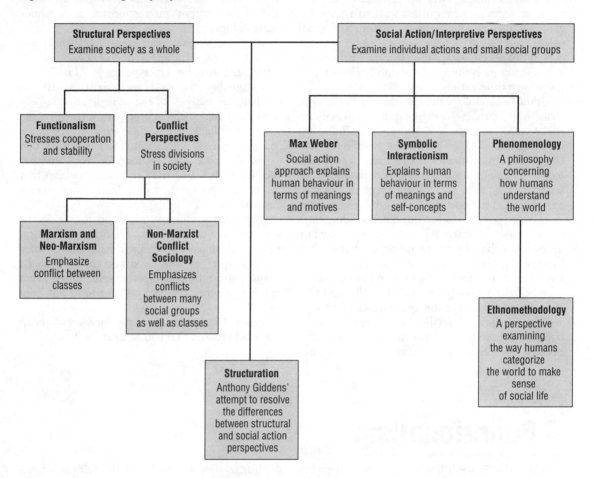

Functional prerequisites

These basic needs or necessary conditions of existence are sometimes known as the **functional
prerequisites** of society. Various approaches have
been used to identify functional prerequisites.
Some sociologists have examined a range of
societies in an attempt to discover what factors
they have in common. For example, Davis and
Moore claimed that all societies have some form
of social stratification, and George Peter Murdock
maintains that the family exists in every known
human society. From these observations it is
assumed that institutional arrangements, such as
social stratification and the family, meet needs
that are common to all societies. Thus from the
universal presence of social stratification it is
argued that all societies require some mechanism
to ensure that social positions are adequately

filled by motivated persons. From the universality
of the family it is assumed that some mechanism
for the reproduction and socialization of new
members is a functional prerequisite of society.

However, the problem with this approach is its
assumption that the presence of the same institution in every society indicates that it meets the
same need. Simply because a form of stratification
exists in all societies does not necessarily mean it
reflects 'the universal necessity which calls forth
stratification in any social system', as Davis and
Moore claim. Put another way, it cannot be
assumed that stratification systems perform the
same function in all societies. (Davis and Moore's
theory of stratification is outlined in Chapter 2,
pp. 26–7.)

An alternative approach to the identification of
functional prerequisites involves an analysis of
those factors which would lead to the breakdown

or termination of society. Thus Marion J. Levy argues that a society would cease to exist if its members became extinct, if they became totally apathetic, if they were involved in a war of all against all, or if they were absorbed into another society. Therefore, in order for a society to survive, it must have some means of preventing these events from occurring. These means are the functional prerequisites of society.

To ensure that members of society do not become extinct, for example, a system for reproducing new members and maintaining the health of existing members is essential. This involves role differentiation and role assignment. Individuals must be assigned to produce food and to reproduce and care for new members of society. In order for these essential services to be maintained, individuals must be sufficiently motivated to perform their roles. If they were totally apathetic, the social system would collapse through lack of effort. A system of goals and rewards is necessary to motivate members of society to want to do what they have to do in order to maintain the system. By specifying the factors that would lead to the termination of society, Levy claims to have identified the basic requirements that must be met if society is to survive.

The problem with this approach to the specification of functional prerequisites is its reliance on common sense and ingenuity. In the case of a biological organism it is possible to identify basic needs, since it can be shown that if these needs are not met, the organism dies. However, societies change rather than die. As a result, it is not possible to identify unequivocally those aspects of a social system which are indispensable to its existence. Functionalists using Levy's approach have drawn up lists of functional prerequisites that are often similar in content but never quite the same.

A related approach involves the deduction of functional prerequisites from an abstract model of the social system. For example, if society is viewed as a system, certain survival needs can be deduced from an abstract model of a system. Any system is made up of interconnected parts. If a system is to survive, there must be a minimum amount of integration between its parts. There must be some degree of fit, which requires an element of mutual compatibility of the parts. From this type of analysis, the functional prerequisites of society may be inferred. Thus any social system requires a minimum amount of integration between its parts.

From this assumption, functional analysis turns to an examination of the parts of society, to investigate how they contribute to the integration of the social system. In this respect religion has often been seen as a powerful mechanism for social integration. Religion is seen to reinforce the basic values of society. Social norms which derive from these values structure and direct behaviour in the various institutions of society. The parts of the social system are integrated in that they are largely infused with the same basic values. Were the various institutions founded on conflicting values, the system would tend to disintegrate. Since religion promotes and reinforces social values, it can be seen as an integrating mechanism. But the problem of deducing functional prerequisites such as integration from an abstract model of the social system is that they are inferred rather than unequivocally identified.

The concept of function

The concept of 'function' in functionalist analysis refers to the contribution of the part to the whole. More specifically, the function of any part of society is the contribution it makes to meeting the functional prerequisites of the social system. Parts of society are functional in so far as they maintain the system and contribute to its survival. Thus a function of the family is to ensure the continuity of society by reproducing and socializing new members. A function of religion is to integrate the social system by reinforcing common values. Functionalists also employ the concept of 'dysfunction' to refer to the effects of any social institution which detract from the maintenance of society. However, in practice they have been primarily concerned with the search for functions, and relatively little use has been made of the concept of dysfunction.

The ideology of functionalism

Functionalist analysis has focused on the question of how social systems are maintained. This focus has tended to result in a positive evaluation of the parts of society. With their concern for investigating how functional prerequisites are met, functionalists have concentrated on functions rather than dysfunctions. This emphasis has resulted in many institutions being seen as beneficial and useful to society. Indeed some institutions, such as the family, religion and social stratification, have been seen as not only beneficial but indispensable. This view has led critics to argue that functionalism has a built in conservative bias which supports the status quo. The argument that certain social arrangements are beneficial or indispensable provides support for their retention and rejects proposals for radical change. Response to this criticism will be examined in a later section (see p. 876). (For various views on the ideological basis of functionalism, see the concluding sections of Chapters 2 to 12.)

This section has presented a brief outline of some of the main features of functionalist analysis. The sections that follow will consider the views of some of the major functionalist theorists.

■ Emile Durkheim
Social facts as constraints

Critics of functionalism have often argued that it pictures the individual as having little or no control over his or her own actions. Rather than constructing their own social world, members of society appear to be directed by the system. For example, they are organized into families and systems of stratification because society requires these social arrangements in order to survive. Many have questioned the logic of treating society as if it were something separate from its members, as if it shaped their actions rather than being constructed by them.

Durkheim rejects this criticism. He argues that society has a reality of its own over and above the individuals who comprise it. Members of society are constrained by 'social facts', by 'ways of acting, thinking and feeling, external to the individual, and endowed with a power of coercion, by reason of which they control him'. Beliefs and moral codes are passed on from one generation to the next and shared by the individuals who make up a society. From this point of view it is not the consciousness of the individual that directs behaviour, but common beliefs and sentiments that transcend the individual and shape his or her consciousness. Having established to his own satisfaction that social facts can, at least for purposes of analysis, be treated separately from social actors, Durkheim is free to treat society as a system which obeys its own laws. He is now in a position to 'seek the explanation of social life in the nature of society itself'.

The causes and functions of social facts

Durkheim argues that there are two ways of explaining social facts. In both cases the explanation lies in society. The first method involves determining the cause of a social fact, of seeking to explain its origin. In Durkheim's view, 'The determining cause of a social fact should be sought among the social facts preceding it and not among the states of individual consciousness.' As was discussed in Chapter 13 (see pp. 817–20), the causes of variations in suicide rates are to be found in social facts, in society rather than in the individual. However, the explanation of a social fact also involves an analysis of its function in society, of its contribution to 'the general needs of the social organism', of its 'function in the establishment of social order'. Durkheim assumes that the explanation for the continuing existence of a social fact lies in its function, that is, in its usefulness for society.

Durkheim is at pains to point out the distinction between cause and function. Thus the cause of the Christian religion lies in the specific circumstances of its origin among a group of Jews under Roman rule. Yet its functions, the reasons for its retention over a period of nearly 2,000 years, require a different form of explanation. Durkheim argues that 'if the usefulness of a fact is not the cause of its existence, it is generally necessary that it be useful in order that it might maintain itself'. Social facts therefore continue in existence because they contribute in some way to the maintenance of society, because they serve 'some social end'.

Social order and human nature

Much of Durkheim's work is concerned with functional analysis, with seeking to understand the functions of social facts. He assumes that society has certain functional prerequisites, the most important of which is the need for **social order**. This is necessary because of human nature. Durkheim has a 'homo duplex' model of human nature: that is, he believes humans have two sides to their nature. One side is selfish or egotistical. Humans are partly driven by selfish biological needs, such as the need to satisfy hunger. Inevitably this means that they tend to look after their own interests which makes it difficult for individuals to be integrated into society. However, there is another side to human nature: the ability to believe in moral values. Society has to make use of this side of human nature if social life is to be possible. But how is social life to be achieved? This question still needs to be answered.

The collective conscience and social stability

Durkheim sees the answer in consensus, in a 'collective conscience' consisting of common beliefs and sentiments. Without this consensus or agreement on fundamental moral issues, social solidarity would be impossible and individuals could not be bound together to form an integrated social unit. Without social obligations backed by moral force, the cooperation and reciprocity that social life requires would be absent. If narrow self-interest rather than mutual obligation were the guiding force, conflict and disorder would result. In Durkheim's words, 'For where interest is the only ruling force each individual finds himself in a state of war with every other.' The collective conscience constrains individuals to act in terms of the requirements of society. Since the collective conscience is a social fact and therefore external to the individual, it is essential that it be impressed upon him or her. Thus Durkheim argues that, 'society has to be present in the individual'.

Religion and social order

Durkheim's functionalism is set in the framework of the above argument. It may be illustrated by his analysis of the functions of religion. Social order requires that individuals experience society within themselves, realize their dependence upon it and recognize their obligations, which are fundamentally social. By symbolizing society and so making it sacred, religion meets these requirements. It makes social life possible by expressing, maintaining and reinforcing the sentiments or values that form the collective conscience. Social obligations are represented in sacred terms and so transformed into religious duties. Thus Peter Berger, commenting on Durkheim's views notes, 'To marry becomes a sacrament, to work becomes a duty pleasing to the gods, and to die in war, perhaps, becomes a passport to a happier after-

life.' In symbolizing society, religion awakens in the individual an appreciation of his or her reliance on society. By recognizing their dependence on supernatural power, people recognize their dependence on society. Religion integrates the social group, since those who share religious beliefs 'feel themselves united to each other by the simple fact that they have a common faith'. The highly charged atmosphere of religious rituals serves to dramatize this unity and so promotes social solidarity. In this way religion functions to meet the essential requirements of social life. It ensures that society is 'present within the individual'. (To read further on Durkheim's work on religion see pp. 446–7.)

Threats to social solidarity

Durkheim was aware of the possibility that societies might not function smoothly. This is evident in his work on the division of labour (see pp. 184–6), which suggests that industrial societies based on organic solidarity might break down. They could be undermined if egoism or anomie started to reduce the control that society had over the individual. Although Durkheim saw the possibility of conflict within industrial society he believed that it could be kept within manageable limits through the existence of professional associations, the teaching of moral values in the education system, and through society functioning in a way which treated all its members fairly.

■ Talcott Parsons
The problem of social order

Today the name of Talcott Parsons is synonymous with functionalism. Over a period of some 50 years, Parsons published numerous articles and books and during the 1940s and 1950s he became the dominant theorist in American sociology. This section will briefly examine aspects of his work.

Like Durkheim, Parsons begins with the question of how social order is possible. He observes that social life is characterized by 'mutual advantage and peaceful cooperation rather than mutual hostility and destruction'. A large part of Parsons's sociology is concerned with explaining how this state of affairs is accomplished. He starts with a consideration of the views of the seventeenth-century English philosopher Thomas Hobbes, who claimed to have discovered the basis of social order.

According to Hobbes, humanity is directed by passion and reason. Its passions are the primary driving force, reason being employed to devise ways and means of providing for their satisfaction. If people's passions were allowed free reign, they would use any means at their disposal, including force and fraud, to satisfy them. The net result would be 'the war of all against all'. However, fear of this outcome is generated by the most basic of human passions, that of self-preservation. Guided by the desire for self-preservation, people agree to restrain their passions, give up their liberty and enter into a social contract with their fellows. They submit to the authority of a ruler or governing body in return for protection against the aggression, force and fraud of others. Only because of this sovereign power is the war of all against all prevented, and security and order established in society.

Hobbes presents a picture of humans as rational, self-interested and calculating. They form an ordered society with their fellows through fear of the consequences if they do not. This is very different from Durkheim's view of people acting in response to moral commitments and obeying social rules because they believe them to be right. Parsons shares Durkheim's views. He argues that Hobbes's picture of people pursuing personal ends, restrained only by sovereign power, fails to provide an adequate explanation for social order. Parsons believes that only a commitment to common values provides a basis for order in society.

Parsons illustrates this point by reference to social relationships, which at first sight would appear to exemplify Hobbes's view of people as self-interested and calculating. He examines transactions in the market place. In a business transaction, the parties concerned form a contract. In order for the conduct of business to be orderly, it is essential that contracts be bound by a 'system of regulatory, normative rules'. In Parsons's view, fear of the consequences is insufficient to motivate people to obey the rules. A moral commitment is essential. Thus, rules governing business transactions must ultimately derive from shared values which state what is just, right and proper. Order in the economic system is therefore based on a general agreement concerning business morality. From this agreement stem rules which define a

contract as valid or invalid. For example, a contract obtained by force or fraud is not binding. Parsons argues that the world of business, like any other part of society, is, by necessity, a moral world.

Value consensus

Value consensus forms the fundamental integrating principle in society. If members of society are committed to the same values, they will tend to share a common identity, which provides a basis for unity and cooperation. From shared values derive common **goals**. Values provide a general conception of what is desirable and worthwhile. Goals provide direction in specific situations. For example, in Western society, members of a particular workforce will share the goal of efficient production in their factory, a goal which stems from the general view of economic productivity. A common goal provides an incentive for cooperation. Roles provide the means whereby values and goals are translated into action. A social institution consists of a combination of roles. For instance, a business firm is made up of a number of specialized roles that combine to further the goals of the organization. The content of roles is structured in terms of norms, which define the rights and obligations applicable to each particular role. Norms can be seen as specific expressions of values. Thus the norms that structure the roles of manager, accountant, engineer and shop-floor worker owe their content partly to the value of economic productivity. Norms tend to ensure that role behaviour is standardized, predictable and therefore orderly. This means that from the most general level – the central value system – to the most specific – normative conduct – the social system is infused with common values. This provides the basis for social order.

Social equilibrium

The importance Parsons places on value consensus has led him to state that the main task of sociology is to analyse the 'institutionalization of patterns of value orientation in the social system'. When values are institutionalized and behaviour structured in terms of them, the result is a stable system. A state of 'social equilibrium' is attained, the various parts of the system being in a state of balance. There are two main ways in which social equilibrium is maintained. The first involves socialization, by means of which society's values are transmitted from one generation to the next and internalized to form an integral part of individual personalities. In Western society, the family and the education system are the major institutions concerned with this function. (See Chapter 12, pp. 728–9, for Parsons's views on the functions of education; Chapter 6, pp. 322–3, for his views on the functions of the family.) Social equilibrium is also maintained by the various mechanisms of social control which discourage deviance and so maintain order in the system. The processes of socialization and social control are fundamental to the equilibrium of the social system and therefore to order in society.

Functional prerequisites

Parsons views society as a system. He argues that any social system has four basic functional prerequisites – adaptation, goal attainment, integration and pattern maintenance. These can be seen as problems that society must solve if it is to survive. The function of any part of the social system is understood as its contribution to meeting the functional prerequisites. Solutions to the four survival problems must be institutionalized if society is to continue in existence. In other words, solutions must be organized in the form of ordered, stable social institutions which persist through time.

The first functional prerequisite, **adaptation**, refers to the relationship between the system and its environment. In order to survive, social systems must have some degree of control over their environment. At a minimum, food and shelter must be provided to meet the physical needs of their members. The economy is the institution primarily concerned with this function.

Goal attainment refers to the need for all societies to set goals towards which social activity is directed. Procedures for establishing goals and deciding on priorities between goals are institutionalized in the form of political systems. Governments not only set goals but allocate resources to achieve them. Even in a so-called free enterprise system, the economy is regulated and directed by laws passed by governments.

Integration refers primarily to the 'adjustment of conflict'. It is concerned with the coordination and mutual adjustment of the parts of the social system. The law is the main institution which meets this need. Legal norms define and standardize relations between individuals and between institutions, and so reduce the potential for conflict. When conflict does arise it is settled by the judicial system and does not therefore lead to the disintegration of the social system.

Pattern maintenance refers to 'the maintenance of the basic pattern of values, institutionalized in the society'. Institutions that perform this function include the family, the educational system and religion. In Parsons's view, 'the values of society are rooted in religion'. Religious beliefs provide the ultimate justification for the values of the social system. (See Chapter 11, pp. 449–50 for Parsons's analysis of the functions of religion.) Parsons maintains that any social system can be analysed in terms of the functional prerequisites he identifies. Thus, all parts of society can be understood with reference to the functions they perform in the adaptation, goal attainment, integration and pattern maintenance systems.

Social change

Functionalism has often been criticized for failing to provide an adequate explanation for social change. If the system is in equilibrium, with its various parts contributing towards order and stability, it is difficult to see how it changes. Parsons approaches this problem by arguing that in practice, no social system is in a perfect state of equilibrium, although a certain degree of equilibrium is essential for the survival of societies. The process of social change can therefore be pictured as a 'moving equilibrium'. This may be illustrated in the following way: the adaptation, goal attainment, integration and pattern maintenance systems are interrelated; a change in one will therefore produce responses in the others. For example, a change in the adaptation system will result in a disturbance in the social system as a whole. The other parts of the system will operate to return it to a state of equilibrium. In Parsons's words, 'Once a disturbance has been introduced into an equilibrated system there will tend to be a reaction to this disturbance, which tends to restore the system to equilibrium.' This reaction will lead to some degree of change, however small, in the system as a whole. Though social systems never attain complete equilibrium, they tend towards this state. Social change can therefore be seen as a 'moving equilibrium'.

Social evolution and pattern variables

Parsons views social change as a process of 'social evolution' from simple to more complex forms of society. He regards changes in adaptation as a major driving force of social evolution. The history of human society from the simple hunting and gathering band to the complex nation-state represents an increase in the 'general adaptive capacity' of society. As societies evolve into more complex forms, control over the environment increases. While economic changes might provide an initial stimulus, Parsons believes that in the long run, cultural changes, that is changes in values, determine the *broadest* patterns of change'. For example, he argues that the structure of modern societies owes much to values inherited from ancient Israel and classical Greece.

Parsons identifies two sets of cultural values which he calls pattern variables A and B. These pattern variables consist of the ways that society answers basic questions such as: 'How should rewards be allocated to individuals?' and 'Should members of society look after their own interests or those of the social groups to which they belong?'

The two sets of pattern variables are summarized in Table 14.1.

According to Parsons, with the exception of family life, pattern variables A are typical of simple societies; pattern variables B are typical of advanced industrial societies. Social change therefore requires a movement towards the adoption of pattern variables B. If a society fails to do this it will stagnate, for pattern variables A stop a society developing. For example, in the traditional Hindu caste system a person's role in society was ascribed at birth. This prevented the most able individuals from filling the most important social roles. The caste system therefore meant that society was not run efficiently and social progress was held back. Parsons accepts that pattern variables A will not disappear completely even in the most advanced societies. They are retained within the family, because they provide the emotional security that is necessary for the successful socialization of children (see pp. 322–3).

Social differentiation

Social evolution involves a process of **social differentiation**. The institutions and roles which form the social system become increasingly differentiated and specialized in terms of their function. Thus religious institutions become separated from the state, the family and the economy become increasingly differentiated, each specializing in fewer functions. This produces a problem of integration. As parts of society become more and more specialized and distinct, it becomes increasingly difficult to integrate them in terms of common values. This problem is solved by the generalizing of values, a process discussed in Chapter 8 with reference to religion (p. 491). Values become more general and diffuse, less specific and particular. In Western society, for example, the highly generalized values of universalism and achievement can be applied to all members of society despite the wide variation in their roles. Universal standards of achievement are generally accepted and provide the basis for differential reward and role allocation. Thus despite increasing social differentiation, social integration and order are maintained by the generalizing of values. Parsons admits that his views on social evolution represent little more than a beginning. However, they do offer a possible solution to the problem of explaining social change from a functionalist perspective.

■ Robert K. Merton

In a closely reasoned essay, originally published in 1949, the American sociologist Robert K. Merton attempts to refine and develop functionalist analysis. He singles out three related assumptions which have been employed by many functionalists and questions their utility.

The problem of functional unity

The first assumption he terms the 'postulate of the functional unity of society'. This assumption states that any part of the social system is functional for the entire system. All parts of society are seen to work together for the maintenance and integration of society as a whole. Merton argues that particularly in complex, highly differentiated societies, this **functional unity** is doubtful. He pro-

Table 14.1 Talcott Parsons's concept of pattern variables

Pattern variables A	Pattern variables B
Ascription Status is ascribed; it is determined by the type of family into which a person is born.	**Achievement** Status is achieved through a person's own efforts; for example, through hard work.
Diffuseness People enter into relationships with others to satisfy a large range of needs; for example, the relationship between mother and child.	**Specificity** People enter relationships with others to satisfy particular needs; for example, the relationships between a customer and shopkeeper.
Particularism Individuals act differently towards particular people; for example, they are loyal to their family but not to strangers.	**Universalism** Individuals act according to universal principles; for example, everyone is equal before the law, so a policewoman would arrest her husband if necessary.
Affectivity Gratification is immediate. People act to gratify their desires as soon as possible.	**Universalism** Gratification is deferred; for example, saving money to put a deposit on a house in the future.
Collective orientation People put the interests of the social groups to which they belong before their own interests.	**Self-orientation** People pursue their own interests first, rather than those of the social group to which they belong.

vides the example of religious pluralism to illustrate this point.

In a society with a variety of faiths, religion may tend to divide rather than unite. Merton argues that functional unity is a matter of degree. Its extent must be determined by investigation rather than simply beginning with the assumption that it exists. The idea of functional unity implies that a change in one part of the system will automatically result in a change in other parts. Again Merton argues that this is a matter for investigation. It should not simply be assumed at the outset. He suggests that in highly differentiated societies, institutions may well have a high degree of 'functional autonomy'. Thus a change in a particular institution may have little or no effect on others.

Functions, dysfunctions and non-functions

Merton refers to the second assumption as the 'postulate of universal functionalism'. This assumption states that 'all standardized social or cultural forms have positive functions'. Merton argues that the assumption that every aspect of the social system performs a positive function is not only premature, it may well be incorrect. He

suggests that functionalist analysis should proceed from the assumption that any part of society may be functional, dysfunctional or non-functional. In addition, the units for which a particular part is functional, dysfunctional or non-functional must be clearly specified. These units may be individuals, groups or society as a whole. Thus poverty may be seen as dysfunctional for the poor but functional for the non-poor and for society as a whole. (This view forms the basis of Herbert Gans's analysis of poverty outlined in Chapter 3, pp. 167–8.) Merton suggests that the postulate of universal functionalism should be replaced by 'the provisional assumption that persisting cultural forms have a *net balance of functional consequences* either for the society considered as a unit or for subgroups sufficiently powerful to retain these forms intact, by means of direct coercion or indirect persuasion'.

The problem of indispensability

Merton's third criticism is directed towards the 'postulate of indispensability'. This assumption states that certain institutions or social arrangements are indispensable to society. Functionalists have often seen religion in this light. For example, Davis and Moore claim that religion 'plays a unique and indispensable part in society'. Merton questions the assumption of indispensability, arguing that the same functional prerequisites may be met by a range of alternative institutions. Thus there is no justification for assuming that institutions such as the family, religion and social stratification are a necessary part of all human societies. To replace the idea of indispensability, Merton suggests the concept of 'functional equivalents' or 'functional alternatives'. From this point of view, a political ideology such as communism can provide a functional alternative to religion. It can meet the same functional prerequisites as religion. However, Merton is still left with the problem of actually identifying functional prerequisites.

Merton argues that the postulates of the functional unity of society, universal functionalism and indispensability are little more than articles of faith. They are matters for investigation and should not form prior assumptions. Merton claims that his framework for functionalist analysis removes the charge that functionalism is ideologically based. He argues that the parts of society should be analysed in terms of their 'effects' or 'consequences' on society as a whole and on individuals and groups within society. Since these effects can be functional, dysfunctional or nonfunctional, Merton claims that the value judgement present in the assumption that all parts of the system are functional is therefore removed.

■ Functionalism – a critique
Teleology

Functionalism has been subjected to considerable criticism. Part of this criticism is directed to the logic of functionalist inquiry. In particular, it is argued that the type of explanation employed is **teleological**. A teleological explanation states that the parts of a system exist because of their beneficial consequences for the system as a whole. The main objection to this type of reasoning is that it treats an effect as a cause. Thus Davis and Moore's theory of stratification outlines the positive effects or functions of social stratification and then proceeds to argue that these effects explain its origin. But an effect cannot explain a cause since causes must always precede effects. Therefore the effects of stratification cannot occur until a system of social stratification has already been established. It may be argued that members of society unconsciously respond to social needs, and so create the institutions necessary for the maintenance of society. However, there is no evidence of the existence of such unconscious motivations.

Assessing effects

Functionalism is on stronger logical ground when it argues that the continued existence of an institution may be explained in terms of its effects. Thus, once an institution has originated, it continues to exist if, on balance, it has beneficial effects on the system. But there are problems with this type of explanation. It is extremely difficult to establish that the net effect of any institution is beneficial to society. A knowledge of all its effects would be required in order to weigh the balance of functions and dysfunctions. As the debate on the functional merits and demerits of stratification indicates, there is little evidence that such knowledge is forthcoming (see Chapter 2, pp. 26–8).

The problems involved in assessing the effects of a social institution may be illustrated in terms of the analogy between society and a physical organism. Biologists are able to show that certain parts of an organism make positive contributions to its maintenance, since if those parts stopped functioning life would cease. Since societies change rather than die, sociologists are unable to apply similar criteria. In addition, standards exist in biology for assessing the health of an organism. In terms of these standards, the contribution of the various parts can be judged. There are no comparable standards for assessing the 'health' of a society. For these reasons there are problems with the argument that a social institution continues to exist because, on balance, its effects are beneficial to society.

Value consensus and social order

Functionalists such as Parsons, who see the solution to the problem of social order in terms of value consensus, have been strongly criticized. First, their critics argue that consensus is assumed rather than shown to exist. Research has failed to reveal unequivocally a widespread commitment to the various sets of values that are seen to characterize Western society.

Second, the stability of society may owe more to the absence, rather than the presence, of value consensus. For example, a lack of commitment to the value of achievement by those at the bottom of stratification systems may serve to stabilize society. Thus Michael Mann argues that in a society where members compete for unequal rewards, 'cohesion results precisely because there is no common commitment to core values' (quoted in Mennell, 1974, p. 126). If all members of society were strongly committed to the value of achievement, the failure in terms of this value of those at the base of the stratification system might well produce disorder.

Third, consensus in and of itself will not necessarily result in social order. In fact it may produce the opposite result. As Pierre van den Berghe notes, 'consensus on norms such as extreme competition and individualistic *laissez-faire*, or suspicion and treachery . . . , or malevolence and resort to witchcraft is hardly conducive to social solidarity and integration' (quoted in Mennell, 1974, p. 127). Therefore the content of values rather than value consensus as such can be seen as the crucial factor with respect to social order.

Determinism

Functionalism has been criticized for what many see as its deterministic view of human action. Its critics have argued that in terms of functionalist theory, human behaviour is portrayed as determined by the system. In particular, the social system has needs, and the behaviour of its members is shaped to meet these needs. Rather than creating the social world in which they live, people are seen as creations of the system. Thus David Walsh argues that Parsons treats human action 'as determined by the characteristics of the system *per se*': by means of socialization, humanity is programmed in terms of the norms and values of the social system; it is kept on the straight and narrow by mechanisms of social control which exist to fulfil the requirements of the system; its actions are structured in terms of social roles which are designed to meet the functional prerequisites of society. Humanity is pictured as an automaton, programmed, directed and controlled by the system.

Walsh rejects this view of humanity. Arguing from a phenomenological perspective he claims that humanity actively constructs its own social world rather than being shaped by a social system which is somehow external to its being. Walsh maintains that the concept of a social system represents a 'reification' of the social world. Functionalists have converted social reality into a natural system external to social actors. In doing so, they have translated the social world into something that it is not. They have tended to portray the social system as the active agent whereas, in reality, only human beings act.

Coercion and conflict

Critics of functionalism have argued that it tends to ignore coercion and conflict. For example, Alvin Gouldner states, 'While stressing the importance of the ends and values that men pursue, Parsons never asks *whose* ends and values these are. Are they pursuing their own ends or those imposed upon them by others?' Few functionalists give serious consideration to the possibility that some groups in society, acting in terms of their own particular interests, dominate others. From this point of view, social order is imposed by the powerful, and value consensus is merely a legitimation of the position of the dominant group. In his criticism of one of Parsons's major works, *The Social System*, David Lockwood argues that Parsons's approach is 'highly selective in its focus on the role of the normative order in the stabilization of social systems'. In focusing on the contribution of norms and values to social order, Parsons largely fails to recognize the conflicts of interest that tend to produce instability and disorder. Lockwood argues that, since all social systems involve competition for scarce resources, conflicts of interest are built into society. Conflict is not simply a minor strain in the system that is contained by value consensus. Instead it is a central and integral part of the system itself.

Functionalism reconsidered

Despite the widespread criticism of functionalism, it should not be rejected out of hand. Durkheim's work, for example, has provided insights which have helped modern sociologists to understand contemporary societies. Jonathon H. Turner and Alexandra Maryanski argue that although functionalism has many flaws it remains useful. Many of its basic assumptions still guide much sociological research: society should be seen as an integral whole; its parts are interdependent; social institutions exist and they do have effects; society is structured and the social structure directs human behaviour.

■ Conflict perspectives

There are many varieties of conflict perspectives within sociology. This section will deal with some of the more influential ones. Despite their differences, all have a model of society as a whole, and all adopt a structural approach. Furthermore, all conflict perspectives use, in one form or another, the notion that there are groups in society that have different interests. In this respect they believe that social arrangements will tend to benefit some groups at the expense of others. Because of the existence of different interests, the potential for, and likelihood of, conflict is always present. Different groups pursuing their separate interests are likely to clash and produce some degree of instability in society. Conflict theorists tend to agree that the existence of groups with different interests does not mean they will be in conflict all the time: there may be periods of truce, or it may be that some social groups are persuaded that their interests are not different from those of other groups. Nevertheless, periods of harmony do not last forever, and eventually conflict will return.

Conflict theories differ from functionalism in stressing the existence of competing groups, while functionalists stress cooperation between social groups. (Most functionalists believe that all members of society share the same interests and that there is a consensus over society's values.)

Conflict theories also differ from each other in important respects. Some theories stress conflict between particular social groups. For example, feminism, which takes a number of forms, sees conflict between men and women as a very important feature of society. (Feminism was discussed in detail in Chapter 10.) The racism approach to explaining ethnic disadvantage focuses on conflict between ethnic groups (see pp. 688–711).

Many conflict theories take their inspiration from the work of Karl Marx or Max Weber. Marxist and Weberian conflict theories tend to disagree over the precise basis on which society is divided into different groups, and the exact nature of the conflict that results from these divisions.

■ Marxism

This section will focus on certain major themes in the work of Karl Marx (1818–83). Marx's views on various aspects of society have been examined in other chapters of the book. This section will seek to combine them in an overall perspective. The volume of Marx's writings over a period of about 40 years was enormous. Many of his major projects remained unfinished, and part of the material published after his death was drawn from rough notes outlining future projects. Marx's writings contain inconsistencies, ambiguities and changes in emphasis. For these reasons there are many and varied interpretations of his work. This section, therefore, represents a particular interpretation of his ideas.

The historical perspective

Marx regards people as both the producers and the products of society. They make society and themselves by their own actions. History is there-

fore the process of human self-creation. Yet people are also a product of society: humans are shaped by the social relationships and systems of thought that they create. An understanding of society therefore involves a historical perspective which examines the process whereby humanity both produces, and is produced by, social reality. A society forms a totality and can only be understood as such. The various parts of society are interconnected and influence each other. Thus economic, political, legal and religious institutions can only be understood in terms of their mutual effect. Economic factors, however, exert the primary influence and largely shape other aspects of society. The history of human society is a process of tension and conflict. Social change is not a smooth, orderly progression which gradually unfolds in harmonious evolution. Instead it proceeds from contradictions built into society which are a source of tension and ultimately the source of open conflict and radical change.

Dialectical materialism

It is often argued that Marx's view of history is based on the idea of the **dialectic**. Dialectical movement represents a struggle of opposites, a conflict of contradictions. Conflict provides the dynamic principle, the source of change. From this viewpoint, any process of change involves tension between incompatible forces. The struggle between incompatible forces grows in intensity until there is a final collision. The result is a sudden leap forward, which creates a new set of forces on a higher level of development. The dialectical process then begins again as the contradictions between this new set of forces interact and conflict, and propel change.

The idea of dialectical change was developed by the German philosopher Hegel. He applied it to the history of human society, and in particular to the realm of ideas. Hegel saw historical change as a dialectical movement of human ideas and thoughts. He believed that society is essentially an expression of these thoughts. Thus in terms of the dialectic, conflict between incompatible ideas produces new concepts that provide the basis for social change. Marx rejects the priority Hegel gives to thoughts and ideas. He argues that the source of change lies in contradictions in the economic system in particular and in society in general. As a result of the priority he gives to economic factors, to 'material life', Marx's view of history is often referred to as **dialectical materialism**. Since people's ideas are primarily a reflection of the social relationships of economic production, they do not provide the main source of change. It is in contradictions and conflict in the economic system that the major dynamic for social change lies. Since all parts of society are interconnected, however, it is only through a process of interplay between these parts that change occurs.

The material basis of social life

History begins when humans actually produce their means of subsistence, when they begin to control nature. At a minimum this involves the production of food and shelter. Marx argues that, 'The first historical act is, therefore, the production of material life.' Production is a social enterprise since it requires cooperation. People must work together to produce the goods and services necessary for life. From the social relationships involved in production develops a 'mode of life' which can be seen as an expression of these relationships. This mode of life shapes human nature. In Marx's words, 'As individuals express their life so they are. What they are, therefore, coincides with their production, with what they produce and how they produce it.' Thus the nature of humanity, and the nature of society as a whole, derive primarily from the production of material life.

The emergence of contradictions

The major contradictions that propel change are found in the economic infrastructure of society. At the dawn of human history, when humans supposedly lived in a state of primitive communism, those contradictions did not exist. The means of production and the products of labour were communally owned. Since each member of society produced both for themselves and for society as a whole, there were no conflicts of interest between individuals and groups. However, with the emergence of private property, and in particular, private ownership of the means of production, the fundamental contradiction of human society was created. Through its ownership of the means of production, a minority is able to control, command and enjoy the fruits of the labour of the majority. Since one group gains at the expense of the other, a conflict of interest exists between the minority who owns the means of production and the majority who perform productive labour. The tension and conflict generated by this contradiction is the major dynamic of social change.

For long periods of history, people are largely unaware of the contradictions that beset their societies. This is because their consciousness – their view of reality – is largely shaped by the social relationships involved in the process of production. Marx maintains that, 'It is not the consciousness of men that determines their being, but, on the contrary, their social being determines their consciousness.' The primary aspect of an individual's social being is the social relationships they enter into for the production of material life. Since these relationships are largely reproduced in terms of ideas, concepts, laws and religious beliefs, they are seen as normal and natural. Thus when the law legitimizes the rights of private property, when religious beliefs justify economic arrangements, and the dominant concepts of the age define them as natural and inevitable, members of society will be largely unaware of the contradictions they contain. In this way the contradictions within the economic infrastructure are compounded by the contradiction between human consciousness and objective reality. This consciousness is false. It presents a distorted picture of reality since it fails to reveal the basic conflicts of interest that exist in the world humanity has created. For long periods of time humanity is, at most, vaguely aware of these contradictions, yet even a vague awareness produces tension. This tension will ultimately find full expression and be resolved in the process of dialectical change.

▊ Alienation

The course of human history involves a progressive development of the means of production – a steady increase in human control over nature. This is paralleled by a corresponding increase in human alienation, an increase that reaches its height in capitalist society. Alienation is a situation in which the creations of humanity appear to humans as alien objects. Such creations are seen as independent from their creators and invested with the power to control them. People create their own society but will remain alienated until they recognize themselves within their own creation. Until that time humans will assign an independent existence to objects, ideas and institutions and be controlled by them. In the process they lose themselves, become strangers in the world they created; they become alienated.

Religion provides an example of human alienation. In Marx's view, 'Man makes religion, religion does not make man.' However, members of society fail to recognize that religion is of their own making. They assign to the gods an independent power, a power to direct their actions and shape their destiny. The more people invest in religion, the more they lose themselves. In Marx's words, 'The more man puts into God, the less he retains of himself.' In assigning their own powers to supernatural beings, people become alienated from themselves. Religion appears as an external force controlling human destiny whereas, in reality, it is human-made. Religion, though, is a reflection of a more fundamental source of alienation. It is essentially a projection of the social relationships involved in the process of production. If people are to find themselves and abolish illusions of religion, they must 'abandon a condi-

tion which requires illusions'. Humanity must therefore eradicate the source of alienation in the economic infrastructure. (Marxist views on religion are examined in Chapter 8, pp. 450–1.)

In Marx's view, productive labour is the primary, most vital human activity. In the production of objects people 'objectify' themselves; they express and externalize their being, then they lose themselves in the object. The act of production then results in human alienation. This occurs when people regard the products of their labour as commodities, as articles for sale in the market place. The objects of their creation are then seen to control their existence. They are seen to be subject to impersonal forces, such as the law of supply and demand, over which they have little or no control. In Marx's words, 'the object that labour produces, its product, confronts it as an alien being, as a power independent of the producer'. In this way people are estranged from the object they produce, they become alienated from the most vital human activity – productive labour.

Alienation and capitalism

Alienation reaches its height in capitalist society where labour is dominated by the requirements of capital, the most important of which is the demand for profit. These requirements determine levels of employment and wages, the nature and quantity of goods produced and their method of manufacture. Workers see themselves as prisoners of market forces over which they have no control. They are subject to the impersonal mechanisms of the law of supply and demand. They are at the mercy of the periodic booms and slumps which characterize capitalist economies. The workers therefore lose control over the objects they produce and become alienated from their product and the act of production. Their work becomes a means to an end, a means of obtaining money to buy the goods and services necessary for their existence. Unable to fulfil their being in the products of their labour, the workers become alienated from themselves in the act of production. Therefore the more the workers produce, the more they lose themselves. In Marx's words, 'the greater this product the less he is himself'. (Alienation and labour in capitalist society are examined in Chapter 4, pp. 179–81.)

In Marx's view, the market forces which are seen to control production are not impersonal mechanisms beyond the control of humanity, they are human-made. Alienation is therefore the result of human activity rather than external forces with an existence independent of humanity. If the products of labour are alien to the worker, they must therefore belong to somebody. Thus Marx argues that 'The alien being to whom the labour and the product of the labour belong, whom the labour serves and who enjoys its product, can only be man himself. If the product of labour does not belong to the worker but stands over against him as an alien power, this is only possible in that it belongs to another man apart from the worker.' This person is the capitalist who owns and controls the means of production and the products of labour, who appropriates the wealth that labour produces. Alienation therefore springs not from impersonal market forces but from relationships. This will come when the contradiction between human consciousness and objective reality is resolved. Then people will realize that the situation in which they find themselves is human-made and therefore subject to change by human action.

Communism

Given the priority Marx assigns to economic factors, an end to alienation involves a radical change in the economic infrastructure. In particular, it requires the abolition of private property and its replacement by communal ownership of the means of production, that is the replacement of capitalism by communism. Marx saw communism as 'the positive abolition of private property and thus of human self-alienation and therefore the real reappropriation of the human essence by and for man. This is communism as the complete and conscious return of man himself as a social, that is human being.' In communist society conflicts of interest will disappear and antagonistic groups such as capitalists and workers will be a thing of the past. The products of labour will no longer be appropriated by some at the expense of others. With divisions in society eradicated, humans will be at one with their fellows, truly social beings. As such they will not lose themselves in the products of their labour. They will produce both for themselves and others at one and the same time. In this situation 'each of us would have doubly affirmed himself and his fellow man'. Since individuals are at one with their fellows, the products of their labour, in which they objectify themselves, will not result in

the loss of self. In productive labour each member of society contributes to the well-being of all and so expresses both their individual and social being. The objects which they produce are owned and controlled at once by themselves and their fellow humans.

■ Class

In Marx's view humans are essentially social beings. He writes that 'society does not consist of individuals, but expresses the sum of inter-relations, the relations within which these individuals stand'. An understanding of human history therefore involves an examination of these relationships, the most important of which are the relations of production. Apart from the communities based on primitive communism at the dawn of history, all societies are divided into social groups known as classes. The relationship between classes is one of antagonism and conflict. Throughout history opposing classes have stood in 'constant opposition to one another, carried on an uninterrupted, now hidden, now open fight that each time ended either in a revolutionary reconstruction of society at large, or in the common ruin of contending classes'. Class conflict forms the basis of the dialectic of social change. In Marx's view, 'The history of all hitherto existing society is the history of the class struggle.'

The two class model

Class divisions result from the differing relationships of members of society to the means of production. The structure of all societies may be represented in terms of a simplified two-class model consisting of a ruling and subject class. The ruling class owes its dominance and power to its ownership and control of the means of production. The subjection and relative powerlessness of the subject class is due to its lack of ownership and therefore lack of control of the means of production. The conflict of interest between the two classes stems from the fact that productive labour is performed by the subject class, yet a large part of the wealth so produced is appropriated by the ruling class. Since one class gains at the expense of another, the interests of their members are incompatible. The classes stand opposed as exploiter and exploited, oppressor and oppressed.

The labour of the subject class takes on the character of 'forced labour'. Since its members lack the necessary means to produce for themselves they are forced to work for others. Thus during the feudal era, landless serfs were forced to work for the landowning nobility in order to gain a livelihood. In the capitalist era, the means necessary to produce goods – tools, machinery, raw materials and so on – are owned by the capitalist class. In order to exist, members of the proletariat are forced to sell their labour power in return for wages. Ownership of the means of production therefore provides the basis for ruling class dominance and control of labour.

Class and consciousness

Members of both social classes are largely unaware of the true nature of their situation, of the reality of the relationship between ruling and subject classes. Members of the ruling class assume that their particular interests are those of society as a whole; members of the subject class accept this view of reality and regard their situation as part of the natural order of things. This false consciousness is due to the fact that the relationships of dominance and subordination in the economic infrastructure are largely reproduced in the superstructure of society. In Marx's words, the relations of production constitute 'the real foundation on which rise legal and political superstructures and to which correspond definite forms of social consciousness. The mode of production in material life determines the general character of the social, political and spiritual processes of life.' Ruling class dominance is confirmed and legitimated in legal statutes, religious proscriptions and political legislation. The consciousness of all members of society is infused with ruling class ideology which proclaims the essential rightness, normality and inevitability of the status quo.

While the superstructure may stabilize society and contain its contradictions over long periods of time, this situation cannot be permanent. The fundamental contradictions of class societies will eventually find expression and will finally be resolved by the dialectic of historical change. A radical change in the structure of society occurs when a class is transformed from a 'class in itself' to a 'class for itself'. A class in itself refers to members of society who share the same objective relationships to the means of production. Thus, as wage labourers, members of the proletariat form

a class in itself. However, a class only becomes a class for itself when its members are fully conscious of the true nature of their situation; when they are fully aware of their common interests and common enemy; when they realize that only by concerted action can they overthrow their oppressors; and when they unite and take positive, practical steps to do so. When a class becomes a class for itself, the contradiction between the consciousness of its members and the reality of their situation is ended.

■ Social change
The transition from feudalism to capitalism

A class becomes a class for itself when the forces of production have developed to the point where they cannot be contained within the existing relations of production. In Marx's words, 'For an oppressed class to be able to emancipate itself, it is essential that the existing forces of production and the existing social relations should be incapable of standing side by side.' Revolutionary change requires that the forces of production on which the new order will be based have developed in the old society. Therefore the 'new higher relations of production never appear before the material conditions of their existence have matured in the womb of the old society'.

This process may be illustrated by the transition from feudal to capitalist society. Industrial capitalism gradually developed within the framework of feudal society. In order to develop fully, it required 'the free wage labourer who sells his labour-power to capital'. This provides a mobile labour force which can be hired and fired at will, and so efficiently utilized as a commodity in the service of capital. However, the feudal relations of production, which involved 'landed property with serf labour chained to it', tended to prevent the development of wage labourers. Eventually the forces of production of capitalism gained sufficient strength and impetus to lead to the destruction of the feudal system. At this point the rising class, the bourgeoisie, became a class for itself, and its members united to overthrow the feudal relations of production. When they succeeded, the contradiction between the new forces of production and the old relations of production was resolved.

Once a new economic order is established, the superstructure of the previous era is rapidly transformed. The contradiction between the new infrastructure and the old superstructure is now ended. Thus the political dominance of the feudal aristocracy was replaced by the power of the newly enfranchised bourgeoisie. The dominant concepts of feudalism, such as loyalty and honour, were replaced by the new concepts of freedom and equality. In terms of the new ideology the wage labourer of capitalist society is free to sell his or her labour power to the highest bidder. The relationship between employer and employee is defined as a relationship between equals; the exchange of labour for wages as an exchange of equivalents. But the resolution of old contradictions does not necessarily mean an end to contradictions in society. As in previous eras, the transition from feudalism to capitalism merely results in the replacement of an old set of contradictions by a new.

The transition from capitalism to communism

The predicted rise of the proletariat is not strictly analogous with the rise of the bourgeoisie. The bourgeoisie formed a privileged minority of industrialists, merchants and financiers who forged new forces of production within feudal society. The proletariat forms an unprivileged majority which does not create new forces of production within capitalist society. Marx believed, however, that the contradictions of capitalism were sufficient to transform the proletariat into a class for itself and bring about the downfall of the bourgeoisie. He saw the magnitude of these contradictions and the intensity of class conflict steadily increasing as capitalism developed. Thus there is a steady polarization of the two major classes as the intermediate strata are submerged into the proletariat. As capital accumulates, it is concentrated more and more into fewer hands, a process accompanied by the relative pauperization of the proletariat. Production assumes an increasingly social and cooperative character as larger and larger groups of workers are concentrated in factories. At the same time the wealth produced by labour is appropriated by fewer and fewer individuals, as greater competition drives all but the larger companies out of business. Such processes magnify and illuminate the contradictions of capi-

talism and increase the intensity of conflict. It is only a matter of time before members of the proletariat recognize that the reality of their situation is the alienation of labour. This awareness will lead the proletariat to 'a revolt to which it is forced by the contradiction between its humanity and its situation, which is an open, clear and absolute negation of its humanity'. (Marxist views on class and class conflict are outlined in Chapter 2, pp. 32–6.)

The communist society that Marx predicted would arise from the ruins of capitalism will begin with a transitional phase, 'the dictatorship of the proletariat'. Once the communist system has been fully established, the reason for being of the dictatorship (and therefore its existence) will end. Bourgeois society represents 'the closing chapter of the prehistoric stage of human society'. The communist society of the new era is without classes, without contradictions. The dialectical principle now ceases to operate. The contradictions of human history have now been negated in a final harmonious synthesis.

■ Marxism – a critique

Judging from the constant reinterpretations, impassioned defences and vehement criticisms of Marx's work, his ideas are as alive and relevant today as they ever were. Specific criticisms of Marx's views on society have been examined in previous chapters and will not therefore be covered in detail in this section. Many of his critics have argued that history has failed to substantiate Marx's views on the direction of social change. Thus they claim that class conflict, far from growing in intensity, has become institutionalized in advanced capitalist society. They see little indication of the proletariat becoming a class for itself. Rather than a polarization of classes, they argue that the class structure of capitalist society has become increasingly complex and differentiated. In particular, a steadily growing middle class has emerged between the proletariat and bourgeoisie. Turning to communist society, critics have argued that history has not borne out the promise of communism contained in Marx's writings. Significant social inequalities are present in communist regimes and there are few, if any, signs of a movement towards equality. Events in Eastern Europe and the Soviet Union in the late 1980s and early 1990s suggest that the promise of communism has been replaced by the desire for Western-style democracies.

Particular criticism has been directed towards the priority that Marx assigns to economic factors in his explanation of social structure and social change. Max Weber's study of ascetic Protestantism argued that religious beliefs provided the ethics, attitudes and motivations for the development of capitalism. Since ascetic Protestantism preceded the advent of capitalism, Weber maintained that, at certain times and places, aspects of the superstructure can play a primary role in directing change (see Chapter 8, pp. 459–61). The priority given to economic factors has also been criticized by elite theorists who have argued that control of the machinery of government rather than ownership of the means of production provides the basis of power. They point to the example of communist societies where, despite the fact that the means of production are communally owned, power is largely monopolized by a political and bureaucratic elite (see Chapter 9, pp. 521–2.) However, as previous chapters have indicated, Marxism is sufficiently flexible to counter these criticisms, and to provide explanations for historical changes which have occurred since Marx's death.

Economic determinism

The section closes with a brief examination of what many see as the central issue of Marxism, the question of 'economic determinism'. Critics have often rejected Marxism on this basis though they admit that the charge of economic determinism is more applicable to certain of Marx's followers than to Marx himself. It is possible to select numerous quotations from Marx's writings which support the views of his critics. In terms of these quotations, history can be presented as a mechanical process directed by economic forces which follow 'iron laws'. Humans are compelled to act in terms of the constraints imposed by the economy and passively respond to impersonal forces rather than actively construct their own history. Thus the proletariat is 'compelled' by its economic situation to overthrow the bourgeoisie. The contradictions in the capitalist infrastructure will inevitably result in its destruction. The superstructure is 'determined' by the infrastructure and human consciousness is shaped by economic forces independent of human will and beyond

humanity's control. In this way Marx can be presented as a crude positivist who sees causation solely in terms of economic forces.

A defence of Marx

On closer examination, however, Marx's writings prove more subtle and less dogmatic than many of his critics have suggested. Marx rejects a simplistic, one-directional view of causation. Although he gives priority to economic factors, they form only one aspect of the dialectic of history. From this perspective the economy is the primary but not the sole determinant of social change. The idea of the dialectic involves an interplay between the various parts of society. It rejects the view of unidirectional causation proceeding solely from economic factors. Instead it argues that the the various parts of society are interrelated in terms of their mutual effect. Marx described the economic infrastructure as the 'ultimately determinant element in history'. Yet he added that 'if somebody twists this into saying that the economic element is the only determining one, he transforms that proposition into a meaningless, abstract and senseless phrase. The economic situation is the basis, but the various elements of the superstructure . . . also exert their influence upon the course of the historical struggle and in many cases preponderate in determining their *form*.' Thus the various aspects of the superstructure have a certain degree of autonomy and a part to play in influencing the course of history. They are not automatically and mechanically determined by the infrastructure.

Marx consistently argued that 'man makes his own history'. The history of human society is not the product of impersonal forces, it is the result of people's purposive activity. In Marx's view, 'It is not "history" which uses men as a means of achieving – as if it were an individual person – *its* own ends. History is *nothing* but the activity of men in pursuit of their ends.' Since people make society, only people can change society. Radical change results from a combination of consciousness of reality and direct action. Thus members of the proletariat must be fully aware of their situation and take active steps in order to change it. Although a successful revolution depends ultimately on the economic situation, it requires human initiative. People must make their own utopia.

■ Neo-Marxism

Neo-Marxists are sociologists whose work has been inspired by Marx's theories, but who nevertheless have developed a distinctive approach of their own. In one way or another they have broken with conventional Marxist theory in order, as they see it, to understand society more adequately. There is no clear dividing line between Marxists and neo-Marxists. As the last section indicated, there are various interpretations of Marx's work, and it is possible for Marxists to disagree without rejecting Marx's overall approach. Nevertheless, some sociological theories that might be described as Marxist are sufficiently different from Marx's own work to merit the description of 'neo-Marxist'.

■ Antonio Gramsci

Most neo-Marxist perspectives are characterized by the use of some concepts that are different from those that Marx used. Generally they reject the extent to which Marx concentrated upon economic, material factors in determining the historical development of societies. An example of neo-Marxism, the work of Antonio Gramsci, was examined in Chapter 9 (see pp. 530–2). Gramsci suggested that ownership of the means of production was not sufficient to guarantee that a ruling class would monopolize power in a society. In order to maintain its leadership and dominance, or, as he called it, 'hegemony', a ruling class had to actively try to win support from other members of society. He did not believe that the ruling class could ever rely upon false class consciousness to guarantee its position, since all members of the subject classes had some awareness of their exploitation. The ruling class needed to make some real concessions to other groups in society to win their support. Thus the state could not always act exclusively in the interests of the owners of the means of production. Gramsci also differed from Marx in placing greater emphasis on the importance of divisions within classes as well as between classes. Thus, for example, agricultural and industrial workers might to some extent have different interests, and the state might exploit the existence of these divisions in order to maintain ruling class hegemony.

Like many neo-Marxists, Gramsci attaches rather more importance than Marx to the culture of a society, and to the institutions of the superstructure, such as the church, the mass media, and the education system. He also placed more stress upon the role of ideas in maintaining political stability.

Marxism and other perspectives

Some neo-Marxists have tried to develop Marxism by drawing upon other sociological perspectives. For example, Paul Willis in his study of the transition from school to work (see pp. 741–3), combined a Marxist analysis of society with a study of small-scale interaction that owes much to an interactionist perspective. Similarly, Ian Taylor, Paul Walton and Jock Young in *The New Criminology* argued that the insights of various sociological perspectives were necessary in order to produce a 'fully social theory' of crime. Taylor, Walton and Young nevertheless claimed that their theory would only make sense if the insights of other perspectives were related to an overall Marxist framework for the analysis of society.

Before examining the strengths and weaknesses of neo-Marxism, a particular example will be examined in more detail.

■ The Frankfurt School and Jürgen Habermas

The 'Frankfurt School' refers to a group of sociologists who have been connected to the Institute of Social Research at Frankfurt University, founded in 1923. Much of their work has been devoted to developing the work of Karl Marx to take account of social changes since his death. However, the Frankfurt School has at times departed quite significantly from more orthodox Marxism, and has been influenced at times by non-Marxist thinkers such as the psychoanalyst Sigmund Freud.

Jürgen Habermas - legitimation crises

The most recent important sociologist to emerge from this school is Jürgen Habermas. In his book

Legitimation Crisis Habermas analyses what he calls 'late capitalism' in a way that is influenced by Marx, but that also diverges from conventional Marxism. Marx predicted that an economic crisis that brought capitalism to an end was inevitable. Habermas disagrees, arguing that the state may be able to intervene in the economy in late capitalist countries in ways that delay the collapse of the economic system indefinitely. Marx argued that the state was part of the superstructure of capitalism. Habermas believes that the state is now so involved in economic life that it is itself part of the economic base of society. Marx believed that the potential for class conflict would increase as capitalism developed and the poor became poorer. Habermas, on the other hand, argues that 'class compromise . . . has become part of the structure of advanced capitalist countries'. The working class has, at least for the moment, largely been bought off, and there is little class consciousness.

Habermas does follow Marx, though, in arguing that advanced capitalist societies tend to be subject to crises. Unlike Marx, he sees the tendency towards crisis as being largely within the realm of ideas rather than within the economy. As the state solves economic problems, it creates problems of legitimation and motivation. The increased state involvement in the economy demonstrates to the population that the state is capable of shaping life in society. In 'bourgeois democracy' the state also claims to follow the principles of justice, equality and freedom. This leads to problems of legitimation for the state. Habermas claims that the state cannot prop up the economy at the same time as successfully persuading the population that it is acting in the interests of everyone. If the state fails to show that it is willing to promote justice and equality using the power it has demonstrated in controlling the economy, the population will cease to believe that the state reflects the interests of all members of society. Habermas believes that the state will always, in the end, act in the interests of the bourgeoisie and will choose to opt for ensuring the stability of the economy on which bourgeois power rests. In doing so, though, it exposes itself as the representative of ruling class interests, and so threatens social stability. An economic crisis is diverted, but a legitimation crisis is created.

Habermas's analysis of advanced capitalism reflects his general belief that non-material factors are as important as material factors. For example he believes that language is as important in distinguishing humans from animals as is the fact that humans work.

Marx thought that human liberation could only be achieved once the means of production were communally owned, and material equality for members of society was achieved. Habermas suggests that more than this is required. He claims that true knowledge, and with it the impossibility of human indoctrination and subordination, can only be achieved in the sphere of communication. Thus, for example, when two or more people are communicating, truth can only emerge if they have the same opportunity to speak, and they have equal opportunities to contradict each other.

■ Neo-Marxism – a critique

Much of the appeal of Marx as a sociologist lies with the simplicity of his basic theory. This simplicity is both its principal strength and its main weakness. On the one hand, it provides the basis for a study of society that has a clear starting point. From this starting point it is possible to develop logically connected arguments and to make predictions about the development of societies. On the other hand, it leaves Marx open to the criticism that he has ignored important factors that influence social life.

Neo-Marxism has developed as a response both to the criticisms levelled at Marx, and to developments in societies since his death which seem to undermine his theory. Neo-Marxists have been able to overcome some criticisms of Marx, but in doing so have left themselves open to the claim that they have developed no clear alternative approach to understanding society. Neo-Marxists reduce the role of the economy in their theories, and attach more importance to cultural and ideological aspects of society. But they are generally unable to specify when, and in what circumstances, cultural or economic factors are more important in shaping society. Some Neo-Marxists move so far away from Marx that their views seem little different to some of the theories that will now be examined.

■ Conflict theory

Conflict theory has its origins in the work of Max Weber. As Chapter 2 indicated (see pp. 36–9), Weber rejected the view that the division between the owners and non-owners of property was the only significant division between groups in society. He argued that there could be numerous divisions within the two basic classes, depending upon the 'market situation' of individuals. Furthermore, he suggested that people could be divided by their status situation and political interests as well as by their economic position. 'Parties' could be formed on the basis of status groupings or classes, but it was also possible for them to cut across class or status groups. Weber's views on classes, status groups and parties reflect the main themes of conflict theory. Conflict theorists argue that the social structure is much more complex than Marx's work suggests. It consists of many different groups, not just two classes. Furthermore, although conflict theorists accept that these groups have different interests, these interests are not just economic. For example, a particular group might strive for greater prestige or status rather than greater economic power.

In a neat summary of conflict theory, Ian Craib describes it in the following way: 'Society is like a more or less confused battle ground. If we watch from on high, we can see a variety of groups fighting each other, constantly forming and reforming, making and breaking alliances.'

Conflict theory has strongly influenced the work of John Goldthorpe on stratification (see pp. 115–16), and Anthony Giddens's sociological theory, which will be examined later (see pp. 904–7). However, in order to illustrate and evaluate conflict theory, the work of another sociologist, Ralph Dahrendorf, will now be examined.

■ Ralph Dahrendorf – Authority and Conflict

Post-capitalism

Dahrendorf's conflict theory arises out of a critical evaluation of the work of Karl Marx. Dahrendorf accepts that Marx's description of capitalism was generally accurate in the nineteenth century when Marx was writing, but he argues that in the twentieth century it has become outdated as a basis for explaining conflict. Dahrendorf argues that important changes have taken place in countries such as Britain and the USA. They are now 'post-capitalist' societies. He claims that far from the two main classes becoming polarized, as Marx predicted, the opposite has happened. The proportion of skilled and semi-skilled workers has grown, as has the size of the 'new middle class' of white-collar workers such as clerks, nurses and teachers. Inequalities in income and wealth have been reduced, partly because of changes in the social structure, and partly because of measures taken by the state. Social mobility has become more common, and, crucially, the link between ownership and control in industry has been broken. Managers, rather than owners, now exercise day-to-day control over the means of production. In these circumstances, Marx's claim that conflict was based upon the ownership or non-ownership of wealth is no longer valid. This is because there is no longer a close association between wealth and power. Shareholders, for example, might own the wealth of a company, but in practice they do not exercise close control over the management.

In view of these changes, Dahrendorf argues that conflicts are no longer based upon the existence of the two classes identified by Marx, nor are they based upon economic divisions. Instead, Dahrendorf sees conflict as being concerned with authority.

Authority

To Dahrendorf, authority is legitimate power attached to the occupation of a particular social role within an organization. Thus, for example, a manager in a company, or a teacher in a classroom, has the right to take certain decisions regardless of the wishes of the workforce or pupils. A manager has the authority to instruct workers to arrive on time and a teacher has the authority to instruct pupils to do homework. All organizations, or associations as Dahrendorf calls them, have positions of domination and subjection. Some are able to take decisions legitimately and issue commands, and others are not. It is this situation which Dahrendorf sees as the basis for conflict in 'post-capitalist' societies.

Authority and quasi-groups

Dahrendorf believes that the existence of dominant and subordinate positions produces a situation in which individuals have different interests. Those occupying dominant positions have an interest in maintaining a social structure that gives them more authority than others. Those in subordinate positions have, on the other hand, an interest in changing a social structure which deprives them of authority. This conflict of interests is present in a much wider range of social relationships than the economic conflict of interests between the ruling class and the subject class that Marx identified as the basis for conflict in society.

As a consequence, there are many different 'quasi-groups' or potential groups that could be in conflict with each other. Some of these quasi-groups will join together and act to pursue their interests. Individuals may belong to a whole variety of different groups, and they are not necessarily confined in all areas of social life to subordinate or dominant groups. Dahrendorf says, 'Since domination in industry does not necessarily involve domination in the state, or a church, or other associations, total societies can present the picture of a plurality of competing dominant (and, conversely, subjected) aggregates.' Thus, a person who is a manager and has a position of authority in a company will tend to act to maintain that authority, but if, for example, the same person has a subordinate position in a religious organization, they may try to change the organization to increase their own authority.

Dahrendorf and conflict theory - a critique

Not surprisingly, Marxists do not accept Dahrendorf's view that Marx's theory is no longer applicable to contemporary societies. For example, the British Marxists John Westergaard and Henrietta Resler believe that Britain is still fundamentally divided between two classes, and they deny that inequality has been dramatically reduced. More importantly though, some sociologists question whether Dahrendorf's approach can actually explain conflict. Ian Craib points out that Dahrendorf admits that subordinate groups may defer to the authority of dominant groups as well as challenging it. Thus members of a workforce may work conscientiously or they may strike, but Dahrendorf fails to explain adequately why they will follow one course rather than another. Craib suggests that Dahrendorf's only answer is to suggest that it is a matter of individual choice, but this does not actually explain why on some occasions there is conflict, for example a strike, and on others there is none.

More generally, conflict theory, whether Dahrendorf's or that of other writers, produces a rather confused picture of the social structure. Society is portrayed as consisting of so many different groups, all of which may be in conflict with each other, that it is difficult to get a clear picture of how society works. It is not clear what the end result of the conflict will be, who will win and who will lose. Nor does conflict theory provide an adequate explanation of why one group will be successful and another will not. Marxism and neo-Marxism give more coherent answers to these types of question. On the other hand, conflict theory is able to encompass conflict between such groups as men and women, which does not fit neatly into a Marxist framework for understanding society.

■ Social action and interpretive perspectives

Sociologists who adopt social action or interpretive perspectives usually reject the view that society has a clear structure that directs individu-

als to behave in certain ways. Some social action theorists do not deny the existence of a social structure, but see this structure as rising out of the action of individuals. Thus Weber, who to some extent spans the gap between structural and social action perspectives, acknowledges the existence of classes, status groups and parties, but he challenges the view of Durkheim that society exists independently of the individuals who make it up. Symbolic interactionists accept the existence of social roles, but deny that these roles are fixed and inflexible, or determined by the supposed 'needs' of the social system. Phenomenology and ethnomethodology represent a much more radical rejection of structural perspectives. They deny the existence of any sort of social structure. All of these perspectives argue that sociologists need to understand and interpret human behaviour and discover the meanings that lie behind it. Phenomenology and ethnomethodology claim that sociology can go no further than reaching an understanding of the meanings individuals attach to the world around them. These perspectives will now be examined in detail.

◼ Max Weber

The German sociologist Max Weber (1864–1920) is widely regarded as one of the three great founders of sociology, with Marx and Durkheim. Although Weber identified aspects of the social structure such as class, parties, status groups and bureaucracies, all these groupings were made up of individuals carrying out social actions. Furthermore, it was social actions which, accord ing to Weber, should be the focus of study in sociology.

Social action

In one of his most important works, *Economy and Society*, Weber said, 'Sociology (in the sense in which this highly ambiguous word is used here) is a science concerning itself with the interpretive understanding of social action and thereby with a causal explanation of its course and consequences.' By making this statement Weber was trying to spell out the precise limits of what could and could not be explained in sociological terms. To Weber, a social action was an action carried out by an individual to which a person attached a meaning; an action which, in his words, 'takes account of the behaviour of others and is thereby oriented in its course'. Thus, an action that a

person does not think about cannot be a social action. For example, an accidental collision of bicycles or an involuntary cry of pain are not social actions because they are not the result of any conscious thought process. Furthermore, if an action does not take account of the existence and possible reactions of others, it is not social. If a person prays in private, in secrecy, it cannot be a social action – nobody knows about it and the actor could not be taking account of the possible reactions of others.

Social action and Verstehen

Having identified the subject matter of sociology, Weber went on to suggest how social action could be explained. Before the cause of a social action could be found, it was necessary to understand the meaning attached to it by the actor. He distinguished two types of understanding.

First, he referred to *aktuelles Verstehen*, which can roughly be translated as direct observational understanding. For example, it is possible to understand that someone is angry by observing their facial expression. Similarly, it is possible to understand what is happening when a woodcutter hits a piece of wood with an axe, that is, the woodcutter is chopping wood. However, this is not, to Weber, a sufficient level of understanding to begin to explain social action.

The second type of understanding is *erklärendes Verstehen*, or explanatory understanding. In this case the sociologist must try to understand the meaning of an act in terms of the motives that give rise to it. Thus *erklärendes Verstehen* would require an understanding of why the woodcutter was chopping wood. Was it in order to earn a wage, to make a fire, or work off anger? To achieve this type of understanding it is necessary to put yourself in the shoes of the person whose behaviour you are explaining. You should imagine yourself in their situation to try to get at the motives behind their actions.

Causal explanations

Even this level of understanding is not sufficient to explain a series of actions or events. For a full causal explanation it is necessary to determine what has given rise to the motives which led to the actions. Here Weber advocated the use of methods closer to a positivist approach. He attempted to discover connections between events and to establish causal relationships. This can be seen from his study, *The Protestant Ethic and the Spirit of Capitalism* (see pp. 459–61). Weber tried to show that there was a relationship between ascetic Protestantism and capitalism. He claimed that ascetic Protestantism preceded capitalism and was found almost exclusively in those countries that became capitalist. Nevertheless, this was not sufficient to convince Weber that there was a causal connection between the two, because it did not establish how or why ascetic Protestantism contributed to the rise of capitalism. In order to establish this link, Weber tried to understand the motives of ascetic Protestants for adopting capitalist behaviour. He believed that their main motive was to convince themselves that they were predestined to go to heaven.

Weber's work on the rise of capitalism illustrates his belief that social actions, particularly those involving large numbers of people behaving in similar ways, could lead to large-scale social changes such as the advent of capitalism. Furthermore, even when Weber sounds rather like a structuralist sociologist, he usually insists that he is really describing a type of social action. Thus, while society might contain institutions and social groups, these institutions and social groups are composed of individuals engaged in social action. Weber said, 'when reference is made in a sociological context to a state, a nation, a corporation, a family or an army corps, or to similar collectivities, what is meant is . . . only a certain kind of development of actual or possible social actions of individual persons'.

This point of view can be seen in Weber's work on bureaucracy. Bureaucracies might be perceived as institutions that closely control and direct human behaviour or social actions. Although Weber was aware of, and indeed concerned about, the power of bureaucracies in restricting human freedom, he nevertheless saw them as composed of individuals carrying out social actions. Thus he believed that bureaucracies consisted of individuals carrying out 'rational' social actions designed to achieve the goals of bureaucracies. Significantly, Weber saw the whole development of industrial societies in terms of a move towards rational social action. Thus, to Weber, modern societies were undergoing a process of rationalization, as affective or emotional action, and action directed by custom and tradition (traditional action), became less important.

Materialism and idealism

Given the importance that Weber attached to social action, it is not surprising that he also attached considerable importance to the role of ideas in shaping social life. Weber was very much opposed to what he saw as the one-sided materialism of Marxism. He denied that human beliefs were entirely shaped by material or economic forces; indeed, his work on Protestantism suggested that religious beliefs could transform an economic system. However, Weber was equally concerned to reject a one-sided idealism that saw human history as directed by the ideas and beliefs held by people. Instead, Weber maintained that both material factors and beliefs were important. He believed that religious beliefs could develop quite independently of material factors, for example through theological arguments within a church. On the other hand, new beliefs would only be taken up if circumstances made them likely to thrive. Thus, material circumstances might affect whether or not ideas became widely accepted, but they did not determine what ideas were produced in the first place.

Weber adopted a similar type of argument to explain the role of religion in the advent of capitalism. To Weber, before capitalism could fully develop it was necessary to have both the appropriate beliefs, and the appropriate material circumstances. In a simple tribal society neither would be present. According to Weber, many oriental societies had the economic conditions which could have led to capitalism, but they lacked a religion which encouraged rational activity. Countries such as Britain and the USA had both the material conditions and the beliefs of ascetic Protestantism, which were necessary preconditions for the development of capitalism.

Weber – a critique

Weber has undoubtedly made a great contribution to the development of modern sociology, although like the other classical sociologists his work has been hotly debated. Criticisms and evaluations of specific parts of Weber's work can be found in earlier chapters (see pp. 275–81, 461–2).

For the purposes of this chapter, a central weakness of Weber's sociology can be identified. He has been accused of 'methodological individualism', a criticism summed up by David Lee and

Howard Newby in the following way: 'Weber was willing to treat all social forces and pressures as if they could be explained (or reduced) to the actions and purposes of seemingly isolated individuals'. The structural approaches examined earlier, particularly those of Durkheim and Marx, were strongly opposed to any such view. Furthermore, in Weber's own work, his social action approach exists rather uneasily alongside his views on particular types of social institution. Thus it is hard to reconcile his view that bureaucracies could severely restrict human freedom, or that society was divided into social classes, with his claim that society simply consisted of individuals choosing courses of action according to their motives.

Symbolic interactionism

Symbolic interactionism, usually referred to as interactionism in the main part of the text, is a distinctly American branch of sociology. It developed from the work of a group of American philosophers who included John Dewey, William I. Thomas and George Herbert Mead. Like Max Weber, symbolic interactionists are concerned with explaining social actions in terms of the meanings that individuals give to them. However, they tend to focus on small-scale interaction situations rather than large-scale social change.

George Herbert Mead (1863–1931) is generally regarded as the founder of symbolic interactionism. His views will now be examined.

George Herbert Mead

Symbols

In Mead's view, human thought, experience and conduct are essentially social. They owe their nature to the fact that human beings interact in terms of symbols, the most important of which are contained in language. A symbol does not simply stand for an object or event: it defines them in a particular way and indicates a response to them. Thus the symbol 'chair' not only represents a class of objects and defines them as similar, it also indicates a line of action, that is, the action of sitting. Symbols impose particular meanings on objects and events and in doing so largely exclude other possible meanings. For example, chairs may be made out of metal, cane or wood, and on this basis be defined as very different objects. However, such differences are rendered insignificant by the fact that they are all categorized in terms of the symbol 'chair'. Similarly, chairs can be stood on, used as a source of fuel or as a means for assaulting another, but the range of possible activities that could be associated with chairs is largely excluded by the course of action indicated by the symbol 'chair'. Symbols provide the means whereby humans can interact meaningfully with their natural and social environment. They are human-made and refer not to the intrinsic nature of objects and events but to the ways in which people perceive them.

Without symbols there would be no human interaction and no human society. Symbolic interaction is necessary since humans have no instincts to direct their behaviour. Humans are not genetically programmed to react automatically to particular stimuli. In order to survive they must therefore construct and live within a world of meaning. For example, they must classify the natural environment into categories of food and non-food in order to meet basic nutritional requirements. In this way humans both define stimuli and their response to them. Thus when hunters on the African savannah categorize antelope as a source of food, they define what is significant in the natural environment and their response to it. Via symbols, meaning is imposed on the world of nature and human interaction with that world is thereby made possible.

Role-taking

Social life can only proceed if the meanings of symbols are largely shared by members of society. If this were not the case, meaningful communication would be impossible. However, common symbols provide only the means by which human interaction can be accomplished. In order for interaction to proceed each person involved must interpret the meanings and intentions of others.

This is made possible by the existence of common symbols, but actually accomplished by means of a process that Mead terms 'role-taking'.

The process of role-taking involves one person taking on the role of another by imaginatively placing themselves in the position of the person with whom they are interacting. For example, if a person observes another smiling, crying, waving a hand or shaking a fist, they will put themselves in that person's position in order to interpret the intention and meaning. On the basis of this interpretation they will make their response to the action of the other. Thus if individuals observe someone shaking a fist, they may interpret this gesture as an indication of aggression but their interpretation will not automatically lead to a particular response. They may ignore the gesture, respond in kind, attempt to defuse the situation with a joke, and so on. The person with whom they are interacting will then take their role, interpret their response and either continue or close the interaction on the basis of this interpretation. In this respect human interaction can be seen as a continuous process of interpretation with each taking the role of the other.

The self

Mead argues that through the process of role-taking individuals develop a concept of 'self'. By placing themselves in the position of others they are able to look back upon themselves. Mead claims that the idea of a self can only develop if the individual can 'get outside himself (experientially) in such a way as to become an object to himself'. To do this they must observe themselves from the standpoint of others. Therefore the origin and development of a concept of self lies in the ability to take the role of another.

Mead distinguishes two aspects of the self. The 'me' is your definition of yourself in a specific social role. For example, you might see yourself as a 'good parent' or a 'loyal friend'. The 'I' is your opinion of yourself as a whole. The 'I', which can also be called your 'self-concept', is built up from the reactions of others to you, and the way you interpret those reactions. It can exercise considerable influence over your behaviour. For example, if you see yourself as cowardly on the basis of the self-concept you have built up, you are unlikely to act bravely in dangerous situations.

The notion of self is not inborn, it is learned during childhood. Mead sees two main stages in its development. The first, known as the **play stage**, involves children playing roles that are not their own. For example, children may play at being a parent, a doctor or a nurse. In doing so they become aware that there is a difference between themselves and the role they are playing. Thus the idea of a self is developed as the child takes the role of a make-believe other. The second stage in the development of self is known as the **game stage**. In playing a game, children come to see themselves from the perspective of the various participants. In order to play a game such as football or cricket, children must become aware of their relationship to the other players. They must place themselves in the roles of the others in order to appreciate their own particular role in the game. In doing so, they see themselves in terms of the collective viewpoint of the other players. In Mead's terminology they see themselves from the perspective of 'the generalized other'.

In Mead's view, the development of a consciousness of self is an essential part of the process of becoming a human being. It provides the basis for thought and action, and the foundation for human society. Without an awareness of self, the individual could not direct action or respond to the actions of others. Only by acquiring a concept of self can the individual take the role of self. In this way thought is possible, since in Mead's view the process of thinking is simply an 'inner conversation'. Thus, unless individuals are aware of the self, they will be unable to converse with themselves and thought will be impossible.

By becoming 'self-conscious', people can direct their own action by thought and deliberation. They can set goals for themselves, plan future action and consider the consequences of alternative courses of action. With an awareness of self, individuals are able to see themselves as others see them. When they take the role of others, they observe themselves from that standpoint and become aware of the views of themselves that others hold.

This provides the basis for cooperative action in society. Individuals will become aware of what is expected of them and will tend to modify their actions accordingly. They will be conscious of the general attitudes of the community, and judge and evaluate themselves in terms of this generalized other. From this perspective, thought becomes 'an inner conversation going on between this generalized other and the individual'. Thus people are constantly asking what other people will think and expect when they reflect upon themselves. In this way conduct is regulated in terms of the expectations and attitudes of others. Mead argues that, 'It is in the form of the generalized other that the social process influences the behaviour of the individuals involved in it. . . that the community exercises control over the conduct of its individual members.'

Culture, social roles and institutions

Mead accepts that a society has a culture, and that this culture suggests appropriate types of behaviour for particular social roles. For example, a culture might specify that the role of doctor should not involve anything that might harm patients. People will tend to act in ways that are consistent both with the expected behaviour in a particular role, and with that person's concept of self. From Mead's point of view, social institutions such as the family or the state have an existence, in the sense that particular social roles are attached to them. Thus the institution 'the family' consists of the social roles of mother, father, daughter, son, sister, brother and so on.

Although the existence of a culture and social roles do shape human behaviour to some extent, humans still have considerable choice as to how they behave. Mead gives a number of reasons why this is so.

1 Many cultural expectations are not specific. Society may, for example, demand that people wear clothes, but there is usually considerable freedom as to which clothes to wear.

2 Individuals have considerable choice as to which roles they enter, for example they have an element of choice in what job they do.

3 Some social roles encourage a diversity of behaviour, for example fashion designers are encouraged to develop novel designs.

4 Society does not have an all-embracing culture. Subcultures exist and people can choose which of them to join.

5 Many cultural meanings indicate possibilities rather than requirements. Thus the symbol 'chair' suggests

the possibility that people can sit on the object, but they are not compelled to do so.

6 At times it may be impossible to act in accordance with a social role: for example, parents may find themselves unable to care adequately for their children. In such circumstances new and innovative behaviour is necessary.

Social roles are not therefore fixed or unchanging; in reality they are constantly being modified in the course of interaction.

The individual and society

Mead's view of human interaction sees humans as both actively creating the social environment and being shaped by it. Individuals initiate and direct their own action while at the same time being influenced by the attitudes and expectations of others in the form of the generalized other. The individual and society are regarded as inseparable, for the individual can only become a human being in a social context. In this context individuals develop a sense of self, which is a prerequisite for thought. They learn to take the roles of others, which is essential both for the development of self and for cooperative action. Without communication in terms of symbols whose meanings are shared, these processes would not be possible. Humanity therefore lives in a world of symbols that give meaning and significance to life and provide the basis for human interaction.

■ Herbert Blumer
The basic premises of symbolic interactionism

Blumer, a student of George Herbert Mead, has systematically developed the ideas of his mentor. In Blumer's view, symbolic interactionism rests on three basic premises.

1 Human beings act on the basis of meanings that they give to objects and events, rather than simply reacting either to external stimuli such as social forces or to internal stimuli such as organic drives. Symbolic interactionism therefore rejects both societal and biological determinism.

2 Meanings arise from the process of interaction rather than simply being present at the outset and shaping future action. To some degree meanings are created, modified, developed and changed within interaction situations rather than being fixed and preformed. In the process of interaction actors do not slavishly follow preset norms or mechanically act out established roles.

3 Meanings are the result of interpretive procedures employed by actors within interaction contexts. By taking the role of the other, actors interpret the meanings and intentions of others. By means of 'the mechanism of self-interaction', individuals modify or change their definition of the situation, rehearse alternative courses of action and consider their possible consequences. Thus the meanings that guide action arise in the context of interaction via a series of complex interpretive procedures.

Blumer argues that the interactionist perspective contrasts sharply with the view of social action presented by mainstream sociology. He maintains that society must be seen as an ongoing process of interaction, involving actors who are constantly adjusting to one another and continuously interpreting the situation. By contrast, mainstream sociology, and functionalism in particular, have tended to portray action as a mechanical response to the constraints of social systems. This view fails to see 'the social actions of individuals in human society as being constructed by them through a process of interpretation. Instead action is treated as a product of factors which play on and through individuals.' Rather than actively creating their own social world, humans are pictured as passively responding to external constraints. Their actions are shaped by the needs of social systems and the values, roles and norms which form a part of those systems. Blumer rejects this view, arguing that 'the likening of human group life to the operation of a mechanical structure, or to the functioning of a system seeking equilibrium, seems to me to face grave difficulties in view of the formative and explorative character of interaction as the participants judge each other and guide their own acts by that judgement'.

Social action and social systems

Although he is critical of those who see action as a predictable and standardized response to external constraints, Blumer accepts that action is to some degree structured and routinized. He states that 'In most situations in which people act towards one another they have in advance a firm understanding of how to act and how other people will act.' However, such knowledge offers only general guidelines for conduct. It does not provide a precise and detailed recipe for action that is mechanically followed in every situation. Within these guidelines there is considerable room for manoeuvre, negotiation, mutual adjustment and interpretation.

Similarly, Blumer recognizes the existence of social institutions and admits that they place limits on human conduct, but even in situations where strict rules prevail, there is still considerable room for human initiative and creativity. Evidence in support of this view is presented in the chapter on organizations and bureaucracy (see Blau's research on 'unofficial practices', pp. 276–8). Even when action appears particularly standardized and structured, this should not be taken as an indication that actors are merely responding to external forces. Blumer argues that, 'The common repetitive behaviour of people in such situations should not mislead the student into believing that no process of interpretation is in play; on the contrary, even though fixed, the actions of the participating people are constructed by them through a process of interpretation.' Thus standardized action is constructed by social actors, not by social systems.

Much of Blumer's work has been concerned with developing an appropriate methodology for his view of human interaction. This aspect of his work is discussed in Chapter 13 (see p. 816).

■ Fred Davis
Physical disability and social interaction

This section examines a typical piece of research conducted from an interactionist perspective. It provides specific illustrations for many of the general points made in the preceding sections. (For further applications of the interactionist approach see Chapter 12, pp. 761–7; Chapter 5, pp. 304–9; and Chapter 7, pp. 405–12.)

In an article entitled *Deviance Disavowal: The Management of Strained Interaction by the*

Visibly Handicapped, Fred Davis examines inter-action situations involving people with physical disabilities and able-bodied people. Davis obtained his data from lengthy interviews with people who were blind, facially disfigured wheel-chair users. He was concerned with interaction situations that lasted longer than a passing exchange but not long enough for close familiar-ity to develop. Such situations would include a conversation with a fellow passenger, getting to know someone at work and socializing at a party. The person with a physical disability wishes to present themselves as 'someone who is merely dif-ferent physically but not socially deviant'. Such people seek to achieve ease and naturalness in their interaction with others, since this will sym-bolize the fact that they have accepted their pre-ferred definition of self, but their disability poses a number of threats to the type of sociability they desire. This stems from the fact that they are defined as 'different', 'odd' and something other than normal by those who do not share their dis-ability.

Threats to sociability

The first threat to sociability involves the possibil-ity that others will become preoccupied with the disability. The norms of everyday, casual sociabil-ity require an individual to act as if the other were a whole person rather than expressing concern or interest in a particular aspect of their person. However, there is a danger that the visible disabil-ity will become the focal point of the interaction. Davis's respondents stated that the able-bodied person was unlikely to make explicit references to the disability but it appeared to be 'uppermost in his awareness'. They sensed the able-bodied person's discomfort and felt it placed a strain on the interaction. In particular they noted 'confused and halting speech, the fixed stare elsewhere, the artificial levity, the compulsive loquaciousness, the awkward solemnity'. Such responses dis-rupted the smooth flow of interaction.

A second threat to sociability arises from the possibility that the disability will lead to displays of emotion which exceed acceptable limits. Thus able-bodied people may be openly shocked, dis-gusted, pitying or fearful. Such emotional displays overstep what is usually considered appropriate and so place a strain on the interaction. Even if able-bodied people manage to contain their emotion, sociability may be further threatened by what Davis terms the 'contradiction of attributes'. This involves an apparent contradiction between the normal attributes of people with physical dis-abilities – such as their job, interests and other aspects of their appearance – and their disability. This contrast often appears discordant to others and can result in remarks such as, 'How strange that someone so pretty should be in a wheelchair.' According to Davis's respondents, such remarks 'almost invariably cast a pall on the interaction and embarrass the recovery of smooth social posture'.

Finally, sociability may be threatened by uncer-tainty concerning the ability of people with physi-cal disabilities to participate in particular activities. For example, a sighted person might be unsure whether person with a visual disability should be invited to the theatre or whether a wheel-chair user should be asked to play a game of bowls. This uncertainty can place a strain on the interaction when people are invited to partici-pate in such activities. If the person with the phys-ical disability refuses, the able-bodied person might wonder if it is because they are simply being polite or if it is because their disability actually prevents participation. Similarly, the person with the physical disability might wonder whether the able-bodied person genuinely wants their company or if they are merely acting out of pity. Such uncertainties threaten to mar the ease and smoothness of the interaction process.

Deviance disavowal and normalization

Having examined the threats that a visible disabil-ity poses to the 'framework of rules and assump-tions that guide sociability', Davis then looks at the way people with physical disabilities cope with these threats. He argues that they attempt to 'disavow deviance', to present themselves as 'normal' people who happen to have a disability. Davis identifies three stages in the process of 'deviance disavowal and normalization'.

The first stage, 'fictional acceptance', follows the standard pattern of interaction when two people meet. There is a surface acceptance of the other, which involves polite conversation and no apparent recognition of important differences between them. In the case of people with physical disability however, 'the interaction is kept starved at a bare subsistence level of sociability'. The person with the physical disability is treated like the poor relative at a wedding reception. Yet, they must maintain this polite fiction, no matter how 'transparent and confining it is', in order to move to the next stage which involves 'something more genuinely sociable'. If they exposed the polite fiction, the interaction might cease and the next stage would not be reached.

In order to move beyond 'fictional acceptance', people with physical disabilities must redefine themselves in the eyes of the able bodied. They must project 'images, attitudes and concepts of self' which encourage others to accept them as 'normal' people. Davis's respondents used a number of strategies to disavow deviance and project their desired self-image. For example, they talked about their involvement in normal, every-day activities, joked about their disability to imply it was relatively insignificant, and tried to give the impression that they were not offended by the unease of others. In this way they attempted to symbolize their normality.

Once others have accepted the person with the physical disability as 'normal', the relationship can then move to a third stage, which Davis terms the 'institutionalization of the normalized relationship'. This can take two forms. In the first, the disabled person is fully accepted into the world of able-bodied persons who largely forget the disability. This can cause problems, however, since at certain times special consideration is needed for the disability. Thus the person with the disability must achieve a delicate balance between 'special arrangements and understandings' and normal relationships. A second form of institutionalization involves a process whereby the able-bodied person becomes rather like an adopted or honorary member of the 'disabled' group. In this way the person vicariously shares the experiences and outlook of the people with physical disabilities and gains a 'strictly in-group license to lampoon and mock the disability in a way that would be regarded as highly offensive were it to come from an uninitiated' able-bodied person. Once a normalized relationship is institutionalized the strains which previously beset the interaction process are largely removed.

Davis's study provides a classic example of the type of research that typifies symbolic interactionism. It focuses on small-scale face-to-face interaction. It portrays the complex process of role-taking and shows how interaction develops via a series of interpretive procedures. It emphasizes the importance of symbols and reveals how a phrase or a gesture can symbolize a set of attitudes. It illustrates the priority that interactionists assign to the concept of self. People with physical disabilities are shown interacting with self, projecting images of self and managing the impressions of self that others receive. Davis's study subtly portrays the flexibility, creativity and mutual adjustment that interactionists see as the essence of human interaction.

■ Symbolic interactionism – a critique

Interaction in a vacuum

Interactionists have often been accused of examining human interaction in a vacuum. They have tended to focus on small-scale face-to-face interaction with little concern for its historical or social setting. They have concentrated on particular situations and encounters with little reference to the historical events leading up to them or the wider social framework in which they occur. Since these factors influence the particular interaction situation, the scant attention they have received has been regarded as a serious omission. Thus in a criticism of Mead, Ropers argues that 'The activities that he sees men engaged in are not historically determined relationships of social and historical continuity; they are merely episodes, interactions, encounters, and situations.' (Quoted in Meltzer, Petras and Reynolds, 1975, p. 97.)

The origin of norms

While symbolic interactionism provides a corrective to the excesses of societal determinism, many critics have argued that it has gone too far in this direction. Though they claim that action is not determined by structural norms, interactionists do admit the presence of such norms. However, they tend to take them as given rather than explaining their origin. Thus Fred Davis refers to the 'framework of rules and assumptions that guide sociability', in other words the norms of sociability.

Yet he simply assumes their existence rather than attempting to explain their source. As William Skidmore comments, the interactionists largely fail to explain 'why people consistently choose to act in given ways in certain situations, instead of in all the other ways they might possibly have acted'. In stressing the flexibility and freedom of human action the interactionists tend to downplay the constraints on action. In Skidmore's view this is due to the fact that 'interactionism consistently fails to give an account of social structure'. In other words it fails to adequately explain how standardized normative behaviour comes about and why members of society are motivated to act in terms of social norms.

The source of meanings

Similar criticisms have been made with reference to what many see as the failure of interactionists to explain the source of the meanings to which they attach such importance. As the chapters on education and deviance have shown, interactionism provides little indication of the origins of the meanings in terms of which individuals are labelled by teachers, police and probation officers (see Chapter 12, p. 768 and Chapter 7, p. 411). Critics argue that such meanings are not spontaneously created in interaction situations. Instead they are systematically generated by the social structure. Thus Marxists have argued that the meanings that operate in face-to-face interaction situations are largely the product of class relationships. From this viewpoint, interactionists have failed to explain the most significant thing about meanings: their origin.

Interactionism and American culture

Symbolic interactionism is a distinctly American branch of sociology and to some this partly explains its shortcomings. Thus Leon Shaskolsky has argued that interactionism is largely a reflection of the cultural ideals of American society. He claims that 'Symbolic interactionism has its roots deeply imbedded in the cultural environment of American life, and its interpretation of society is, in a sense, a "looking glass" image of what that society purports to be.' Thus the emphasis on liberty, freedom and individuality in interactionism can be seen in part as a reflection of America's view of itself. Shaskolsky argues that this helps to explain why the interactionist perspective finds less support in Europe, since there is a greater awareness in European societies of the constraints of power and class domination. By reflecting American ideals, Shaskolsky argues that interactionism has failed to face up to, and take account of, the harsher realities of social life. Whatever its shortcomings, however, many would agree with William Skidmore that, 'On the positive side, it is clearly true that some of the most fascinating sociology is in the symbolic interactionist tradition.'

◼ Phenomenology

Phenomenology is a branch of European philosophy which was first developed by Edmund Husserl (1859–1938), and was developed along more sociological lines by Alfred Schutz (1899–1959), a pupil of Husserl's who moved to the USA with the rise of fascism in Europe. It differs from the social action approaches that have been examined so far in that it denies the possibility of explaining social action as such. Its emphasis is upon the internal workings of the human mind and the way that humans classify and make sense of the world around them. It is not concerned with the causal explanation of human behaviour in the same way as other perspectives. Phenomenologists try to understand the meaning of phenomena or things, rather than explaining how they came into existence.

◼ Making sense of sensory experience

According to phenomenologists, individuals only come into contact with the outside world through their senses: touch, smell, hearing, sight and taste.

It is not possible to know about the outside world except through these senses. Simply possessing senses, though, is not enough for a person to be able to make any sense out of the world. If humans took their sense experiences at face value, they would be confronted by an unintelligible mass of impressions, of colours, lights, sounds, smells, feelings and tastes that were meaningless. In order to overcome this problem, humans begin to organize the world around them into phenomena; they classify their sense experiences into things that appear to have common characteristics. For example, a distinction may be made between animate and inanimate objects. This distinction may be refined by dividing animate objects into mammals and non-mammals. Mammals may be divided into different species and species subdivided into different breeds. Thus humans have a series of shorthand ways of classifying and understanding the world external to their own consciousness. For example, a small white animal making a barking noise may be identified as a poodle.

Husserl did not believe that this process was in any sense objective; the classification of phenomena was entirely a product of the human mind, and could not be evaluated in terms of whether it was true or false. He did not deny the existence of physical objects beyond and outside the human mind, but he argued that since people could only come into contact with them through their senses, they could never be sure about their true nature. Thus, in trying to secure knowledge, humans had to 'bracket' reality and common-sense beliefs: to put them inside brackets and forget about whether they were true or false.

Once they had done this, they could turn their attention to a phenomenological understanding of the world. In order to understand social life, he argued, phenomenologists should study the way that humans placed the external world into categories by distinguishing particular phenomena. In doing so it would be possible to understand the meaning of a phenomenon by discovering its essence. What Husserl meant by this was that the researcher could find the distinguishing features (the essence), of a group of things (or phenomena), which humans classed together. Thus, for example, it might be found that a distinguishing feature – part of the essence of – a boat, was that it could float. In Chapter 13 the description of Atkinson's work on suicide (see pp. 823–4) shows how he tried to understand the nature of the phenomenon of suicide by investigating how coroners distinguished it from other types of death.

Alfred Schutz – the phenomenology of the social world

The general approach adopted by phenomenology is a type of philosophy of knowledge, rather than a sociological perspective. Alfred Schutz was the first to try to explain how phenomenology could be applied to develop insights into the social world. Schutz's main contribution was to insist that the way that humans classified and attached meaning to the outside world was not a purely individual process. Humans developed what he called 'typifications', the concepts attached to classes of things that are experienced. Thus a 'bank manager', a 'football match', 'dusting' and 'a tree', are examples of typifications. These typifications are not unique to each person, but are shared by members of a society. They are passed on to children through learning a language, reading books or speaking to other people.

By the use of typifications people are able to communicate with others on the basis of the assumption that they see the world in the same way. Gradually, a member of society builds up a stock of what Schutz calls 'common-sense knowledge', which is shared with other members of society and allows humans to live and communicate together. Schutz believes that such knowledge is essential to accomplish practical tasks in everyday life. For example, he describes the way in which a simple act such as posting a letter rests upon common-sense knowledge and the existence of shared typifications. The person posting the letter assumes that another person (a postman whom they may never have met) will be able to recognize the piece of paper with writing on it as a letter, and, along with other postmen, will deliver it to the address on the envelope. People also assume that the recipient of the letter, again someone they might not have met, will have common-sense knowledge similar to their own, and will therefore be able to understand the message, and react in an appropriate way.

Although Schutz stresses that knowledge is shared, he does not think that it is fixed and unchanging. Indeed, common-sense knowledge is constantly modified in the course of human interaction. Schutz acknowledges that each individual has a unique biography, and interprets and experiences the world in slightly different ways, but the existence of a stock of common-sense knowledge allows humans to understand, at least partly, each other's actions. In doing so, they convince themselves that there are regular and ordered patterns in the world, and to social life. From this point of view, humans create between themselves the illusion that there is stability and order in society, when in reality there is simply a jumble of individual experiences that have no clear shape or form.

▆ Ethnomethodology

Ethnomethodology is a comparatively recent sociological perspective. Many of the concerns of ethnomethodology have reflected the type of approach developed by Schutz. Schutz, however, did not carry out detailed research into social life, he merely speculated about the nature of society. Ethnomethodologists have applied phenomenological ideas in carrying out research.

In 1967 Harold Garfinkel first coined the term 'ethnomethodology'. Roughly translated, ethnomethodology means a study of the methods used by people. It is concerned with the methods used by people (or 'members' as ethnomethodologists refer to them) to construct, account for and give meaning to their social world.

Social order as a fiction

Ethnomethodologists follow Schutz in believing that there is no real social order, as other sociological perspectives assume. Social life appears orderly to members of society only because members actively engage in making sense of social life. Societies have regular and ordered patterns only because members perceive them in this way. Social order therefore becomes a convenient fiction; an appearance of order constructed by members of society. This appearance allows the social world to be described and explained, and so made knowable, reasonable, understandable and accountable to its members. It is made accountable in the sense that members of society become able to provide descriptions and explanations of their own actions and of the society around them that are reasonable and acceptable to themselves and others. Thus in Atkinson's study, coroners were able to justify and explain their actions to themselves and to others in terms of the common-sense ways they went about reaching a verdict.

The point of ethnomethodology according to Zimmerman and Weider is to explain 'how members of society go about the task of seeing, describing, and explaining order in the world in which they live'. Ethnomethodologists have therefore conducted investigations into the techniques that are used by members to achieve the appearance of order. Two studies will now be examined in detail to illustrate the above points.

▆ Harold Garfinkel
The documentary method

Garfinkel argues that members employ the 'documentary method' to make sense and account for the social world, and to give it an appearance of order. This method consists of selecting certain aspects of the infinite number of features contained in any situation or context, defining them in a particular way, and seeing them as evidence of an underlying pattern. The process is then reversed and particular instances of the underlying pattern used as evidence for the existence of the pattern. In Garfinkel's words, the documentary method 'consists of treating an actual appearance as "the document of", as "pointing to", as "standing on behalf of" a presupposed underlying pattern. Not only is the underlying pattern derived from its individual documentary evidences, but the individual documentary evidences, in their turn, are interpreted on the basis of "what is known" about the underlying pattern. Each is used to elaborate the other.' For example, in the case of Atkinson's study of coroners, those deaths defined as suicide were seen as such by reference to an underlying pattern. This pattern is the coroner's common-sense theory of suicide. However, at the same time, those deaths defined as suicide were seen as evidence for the existence of the underlying pattern. In this way particular instances of the pattern and the pattern itself are mutually reinforcing and are used to elaborate each other. Thus the documentary method can be seen as 'reflexive'. The particular instance is seen as a reflection of the underlying pattern and vice versa.

Garfinkel argues that social life is 'essentially reflexive'. Members of society constantly look at particular activities and situations in terms of presumed underlying patterns, and in turn confirm the existence of those patterns by referring to particular expressions of them in activities and situations. In this way members produce accounts of the social world that not only make sense of and explain, but actually constitute that world. Thus in providing accounts of suicide, coroners are actually producing suicide. Their accounts of suicide constitute suicide in the social world. In this respect, accounts are a part of the things they describe and explain. The social world is therefore constituted by the methods and accounting procedures in terms of which it is identified, described and explained. Thus the social world is constructed by its members by the use of the documentary method. This is what Garfinkel means when he describes social reality as 'essentially reflexive'.

An experiment in counselling

Garfinkel claims to have demonstrated the documentary method and its reflexive nature by an experiment conducted in a university department of psychiatry. Students were invited to take part in what was described as a new form of psychotherapy. They were asked to summarize a personal problem on which they required advice and then ask a counsellor a series of questions. The counsellor sat in a room adjoining the student; they could not see each other and communicated via an intercom. The counsellor was limited to responses of either 'yes' or 'no'. Unknown to the student, the adviser was not a counsellor and the answers received were evenly divided between 'yes' and 'no', their sequence being predetermined in accordance with a table of random numbers.

In one case a student was worried about his relationship with his girlfriend. He was Jewish and she was a Gentile. He was worried about his parents' reaction to the relationship and the problems that might result from marriage and chil-

dren. His questions related to these concerns. Despite the fact that the answers he received were random, given without reference to the content of questions and they sometimes contradicted previous answers, the student found them helpful, reasonable and sensible. Similar assessments of the counselling sessions were made by the other students in the experiment.

From comments made by students on each of the answers they received, Garfinkel draws the following conclusions. Students *made* sense of the answers where no sense existed; they imposed an order on the answers where no order was present. When answers appeared contradictory or surprising, the students assumed that the counsellor was unaware of the full facts of their case. The students constructed an appearance of order by using the documentary method. From the first answer they perceived an underlying pattern in the counsellor's advice. The sense of each following answer was interpreted in terms of the pattern, and at the same time each answer was seen as evidence for the existence of the pattern. Thus the students' method of interpretation was reflexive. Not only did they produce an account of the counselling session, but the account became a part of, and so constituted, the session. In this way the accounting procedure described and explained, and also constructed and constituted social reality at one and the same time. Garfinkel claims that the counselling experiment highlights and captures the procedures that members are constantly using to construct the social world in their everyday lives.

Indexicality

This experiment can also be used to illustrate the idea of 'indexicality', a central concept employed by Garfinkel and other ethnomethodologists. Indexicality means that the sense of any object or activity is derived from its context; it is 'indexed' in a particular situation. As a result any interpretation, explanation or account made by members in their everyday lives is made with reference to particular circumstances and situations. Thus the students' sense of the counsellor's answers was derived from the context of the interaction. From the setting – a psychiatry department – and the information they were given, the students believed that the counsellor was what he claimed to be and that he was doing his best to give honest and sound advice. His answers were interpreted within the framework of this context. If identical answers were received to the same set of questions from fellow students in a coffee bar, the change of context would probably result in a very different interpretation. Such responses from fellow students may be seen as evidence that they had temporarily taken leave of their senses or were having a joke at their friend's expense or were under the influence of alcohol and so on. Garfinkel argues that the sense of any action is achieved by reference to its context. Members' sense of what is happening depends on the way they interpret the context of the activity concerned. In this respect their understandings and accounts are indexical: they make sense in terms of particular settings.

Disrupting the social world

Garfinkel encouraged his students actually to disrupt the social world in order to reveal the way that members made sense of it and reached understandings. For example, he suggested they go into supermarkets and haggle over the price of goods, or go back to their own homes and act as if they were lodgers. In such ways they would demonstrate the fragile nature of social order. The victims of these experiments found it difficult or impossible to index them in the situation in which they took place. Thus parents, faced with a child acting as a lodger in their own home, became perplexed or angry, and desperately tried to make sense of their child's actions by, for example, believing that the child must be ill.

■ Don H. Zimmerman – *The Practicalities of Rule Use*

Studies of bureaucracies, as Chapter 5 indicated, have often been concerned with the nature of rules in bureaucratic organizations. The bureaucrat is usually seen as strictly conforming to formal rules or else acting in terms of a system of informal rules. In either case the behaviour is seen to be governed by rules. Zimmerman's study suggests an alternative perspective. Rather than seeing behaviour as governed by rules, he suggests that members employ rules to describe and

account for their activity. Part of this activity may be in direct violation of a stated rule yet it is still justified with reference to the rule. This paradox will be explained shortly.

Rules and rule violations

Zimmerman studied behaviour in a US Bureau of Public Assistance. Clients applying for assistance were assigned to caseworkers by receptionists. Officially, the assignment procedure was conducted in terms of a simple rule. If there were four caseworkers, the first four clients who arrived were assigned one to each caseworker. The next four clients were assigned in a similar manner, providing the second interview of the day for each caseworker, and so on. However, from time to time the rule was broken. For example, a particular caseworker may have had a difficult case and the interview may have lasted far longer than usual. In this situation a receptionist may have reorganized the assignment list and switched the next client to another caseworker.

Justifying rule violations

Such rule violations were justified and explained by the receptionists in terms of the rule. In their eyes, by breaking the rule they were conforming to the rule. This paradox can be explained by the receptionists' view of the intention of the rule. From their viewpoint, the rule was meant to keep clients moving with a minimum of delay, so that all had been attended to at the end of the day. Thus, violating the rule to ensure this outcome can be explained as following the rule. This was the way the receptionists justified and explained their conduct to themselves and to their fellow workers. By seeing their activity as conforming to a rule, they created an appearance of order.

However, rather than simply being directed by rules, Zimmerman argues that the receptionists were constantly monitoring and assessing the situation and improvising and adapting their conduct in terms of what they saw as the requirements of the situation. Zimmerman claims that his research indicates that 'the actual practices of using rules do not permit an analyst to account for regular patterns of behaviour by invoking the notion that these practices occur because members of society are following rules'. He argues that the use of rules by members to describe and account for their conduct 'makes social settings appear orderly for the participants and it is this *sense and appearance* of order that rules in use, in fact, provide and what the ethnomethodologists in fact study'.

Zimmerman's research highlights some of the main concerns of ethnomethodology. It provides an example of the documentary method and illustrates the reflexive nature of the procedures used by members to construct an appearance of order. Receptionists interpret their activity as evidence of an underlying pattern – the intent of the rule – and they see particular actions, even when they violate the rules, as evidence of the underlying pattern.

▮ Ethnomethodology and mainstream sociology

Garfinkel argues that mainstream sociology has typically portrayed man as a 'cultural dope' who simply acts out the standardized directives provided by the culture of his society. Garfinkel states that, 'By "cultural dope" I refer to the man-in-the-sociologist's society who produces the stable features of society by acting in compliance with preestablished and legitimate alternatives of action that the common culture provides.' In place of the 'cultural dope', the ethnomethodologist pictures the skilled member who is constantly attending to the particular, indexical qualities of situations, giving them meaning, making them knowable, communicating this knowledge to others and constructing a sense and appearance of order. From this perspective, members construct and accomplish their own social world rather than being shaped by it.

The nature of social reality

Ethnomethodologists are highly critical of other branches of sociology. They argue that 'conventional' sociologists have misunderstood the nature of social reality. They have treated the social world as if it has an objective reality which is independent of members' accounts and interpretations. Thus they have regarded aspects of the social world such as suicide and crime as facts with an existence of their own. They have then attempted to provide explanations for these

'facts'. By contrast, ethnomethodologists argue that the social world consists of nothing more than the constructs, interpretations and accounts of its members. The job of the sociologist is therefore to explain the methods and accounting procedures that members employ to construct their social world. According to ethnomethodologists, this is the very job that mainstream sociology has failed to do.

The documentary method and mainstream sociology

Ethnomethodologists see little difference between conventional sociologists and the person in the street. They argue that the methods employed by sociologists in their research are basically similar to those used by members of society in their everyday lives. Members employing the documentary method are constantly theorizing, drawing relationships between activities and making the social world appear orderly and systematic. They then treat the social world as if it had an objectivity separate from themselves. Ethnomethodologists argue that the procedures of conventional sociologists are essentially similar. They employ the documentary method, theorize and draw relationships, and construct a picture of an orderly and systematic social system. They operate reflexively like any other member of society. Thus when functionalists see behaviour as an expression of an underlying pattern of shared values, they also use instances of that behaviour as evidence for the existence of the pattern. By means of their accounting procedures, members construct a picture of society. In this sense the person in the street is their own sociologist. Ethnomethodologists see little to choose between the pictures of society that people create and those provided by conventional sociologists.

▮ Ethnomethodology – a critique

Alvin Gouldner pours scorn upon ethnomethodology for dealing with trivial aspects of social life, and revealing things that everybody knows already. He gives an example of the type of experiment advocated by Garfinkel. An ethnomethodologist might release chickens in a town centre during the rush hour, and stand back and observe as traffic was held up and crowds gathered to watch and laugh at policemen chasing the chickens. Gouldner goes on to explain that Garfinkel might say that the community has now learned the importance of one hitherto unnoticed rule at the basis of everyday life: chickens must not be dropped in the streets in the midst of the lunch rush hour.

More seriously, critics have argued that the members who populate the kind of society portrayed by ethnomethodologists appear to lack any motives and goals. As Anthony Giddens remarks, there is little reference to 'the pursuance of practical goals or interests'. What, for example, motivated the students in Garfinkel's counselling experiment or the receptionists in Zimmerman's study? There is little indication in the writings of ethnomethodologists as to why people want to behave or are made to behave in particular ways. Nor is there much consideration of the nature of power in the social world and the possible effects of differences in power on members' behaviour. As Gouldner notes, 'The process by which social reality becomes defined and established is not viewed by Garfinkel as entailing a process of struggle among competing groups' definitions of reality, and the outcome, the common-sense conception of the world, is not seen as having been shaped by institutionally protected power differences.'

Critics have argued that ethnomethodologists have failed to give due consideration to the fact that members' accounting procedures are conducted within a system of social relationships involving differences in power. Many ethnomethodologists appear to dismiss everything which is not recognized and accounted for by members of society. They imply that if members do not recognize the existence of objects and events, they are unaffected by them. But as John H. Goldthorpe pointedly remarks in his criticism of ethnomethodology, 'if for instance, it is bombs and napalm that are zooming down, members do not have to be oriented towards them in any particular way, or at all, in order to be killed by them'. Clearly members do not have to recognize certain constraints in order for their behaviour to be affected by them. As Goldthorpe notes, with reference to the above example, death 'limits interaction in a fairly decisive way'.

Finally, the ethnomethodologists' criticism of mainstream sociology can be redirected to themselves. As Giddens remarks, 'any ethnomethodological account must display the same characteristics as it claims to discern in the accounts of lay actors'. Ethnomethodologists' accounting procedures therefore become a topic of study like those of conventional sociologists or any other member of society. In theory the process of accounting for accounts is never ending. Carried to its extreme, the ethnomethodological position implies that nothing is ever knowable. Whatever its shortcomings, however, ethnomethodology asks interesting questions.

■ Uniting structural and social action approaches

The earlier parts of this chapter have shown how sociology can be divided into two types of approach. Structural approaches, such as functionalism and some versions of Marxism, emphasize the way that the structure of society directs human behaviour. Social action or interpretive approaches, such as those advocated by Weber, symbolic interactionists and ethnomethodologists, argue that humans create society through their own actions. This distinction is not neat and clear-cut; most perspectives in sociology show some concern with both social structure, and social action, but most perspectives emphasize one aspect of social life at the expense of another.

However, many sociologists have argued that it would be desirable to produce a sociological theory that combined an understanding of social structure and social action. C. Wright Mills, for example, claimed that 'The sociological imagination enables its possessor to understand the larger historical scene in terms of its meaning for the inner life and external career of a variety of individuals.' It has often seemed as though sociologists could only understand one of these elements at a time. They might try to understand the 'larger historical scene' using a structural perspective; or alternatively they might try to understand the life of individuals using a social action approach. Generally they do not attempt to understand both simultaneously.

Anthony Giddens – the theory of structuration

The duality of structure

Over recent years the British sociologist Anthony Giddens has attempted to overcome the division between structure and action. Although the details of his argument are complex, his basic point is simple. Giddens claims that structure and action are two sides of the same coin. Neither structure nor action can exist independently; both are intimately related. Social actions create structures, and it is through social actions that structures are produced and reproduced, so that they survive over time. Indeed he uses a single word, 'structuration', to describe the way that structures relate to social actions, so that certain sets of social relationships survive over space and time. Giddens talks about the 'duality of structure' to suggest both that structures make social action possible, and at the same time that social action creates those very structures. He says that 'structure has no existence independent of the knowledge that agents have about what they do in their day-to-day activity'. In other words, it is you, I, and every other individual that creates structures.

The clearest way that Giddens explains this is using the examples of language and speech. The English language is to Giddens a structure; it is a set of rules about how to communicate, which seems independent of any individual. The grammar and vocabulary of English cannot simply be changed at will by members of society. Yet if that language is to be reproduced, if it is to survive, it must be spoken or written by individuals in ways that follow its existing rules. Thus, Giddens says, 'when I utter a grammatical English sentence I contribute to the reproduction of the English language as a whole'. The structure of the language ultimately depends upon the people who use it. For the most part, competent English speakers will follow the rules of English and

reproduction will take place. However, this is not inevitable. Languages change, new words are invented and accepted by being used, some old words are forgotten and fall into disuse. Human agents, by their actions, can therefore transform as well as reproduce structures.

Rules and resources

In social life in general Giddens identifies two aspects of structure: 'rules' and 'resources'. **Rules** are procedures that individuals may follow in their social life. Sometimes interpretations of these rules are written down, for example in the form of laws or bureaucratic rules. Such written expressions are not the rules themselves. Thus a rule might state how to go shopping by paying a shop assistant, while the written interpretation of a rule of this sort might be the law of theft. Such structural rules can either be reproduced by members of society or they can be changed through the development of new patterns of interaction.

The second aspect of structure, resources, also come into being through human actions and can be changed or maintained by them. **Resources** take two forms, allocative and authoritative. 'Allocative resources' include raw materials, land, technology, instruments of production and goods. For Giddens such resources are never just there, given by nature; they only become resources through human actions. Thus land is not a resource until someone farms it or puts it to some other use. 'Authoritative resources' are non-material resources that result from some individuals being able to dominate others. In other words, they involve the ability to get others to carry out a person's wishes, and in this way humans become a resource that other individuals may be able to use. As in other parts of his theory, Giddens insists that authoritative resources only exist in so far as they are produced by human interaction. Authority is not something a person has unless they are actually using it.

Social systems

Having discussed what he means by structure, Giddens goes on to explain what he sees as the nature of social systems and institutions. A social system, he argues, is simply a pattern of social relations that exists over a period of time and space. Thus, for example, nineteenth-century

Britain is a social system because it was a geographically defined space, over a particular period of time, where there were certain reproduced sets of social relationships and social practices. Of course Giddens would not believe that Britain was the same 'system' in 1899 as it was in 1801; social relationships and practices would have changed continuously as patterns of interaction changed. Similarly, institutions such as the state or bureaucracies are seen by Giddens as patterns of behaviour that display some continuity over time, but which may also change as time passes.

Agency and reproduction

Giddens's views on structures, systems and institutions are closely tied in with his idea of human action (or 'agency' as he usually refers to it) since they are all part of the 'duality of structure'. According to Giddens, human agents are constantly intervening in the world by their actions, and in doing so they have the capacity to transform it. He would not, though, accept the view that individuals just create society, any more than he would accept that society determines individual behaviour. Structure affects human behaviour because of the knowledge that agents have about their own society. There is a large stock of 'mutual knowledge' of 'how to go on', or how to get things done. Agents know from what they have learnt how to go about their everyday lives and accomplish objectives. For example, 'competent' members of society know how to go to a bar and order a round of drinks, just as other competent members know how to serve the customer ordering the drinks. Routine, mundane behaviour like this is constantly carried out and much of it requires little thought. This is so because the agents involved are drawing upon their knowledge of the rules of society, which exist in the structure of society. At the same time they are making use of resources that are also part of the structure of society. They make use of material commodities, like money, drinks and glasses, and of authoritative resources, such as the right of the bar staff to demand payment; a right which is recognized by the customers.

Giddens seems to think that humans have a basic desire for some degree of predictability in social life. They have a need for what he calls 'ontological security' or 'confidence and trust that the natural and social worlds are as they appear to be'. He suggests tentatively that this may be connected to the human 'basic security system', essentially a natural concern with the physical survival of the body. Thus it would be unsettling if people did not know whether they were expected to have to give money to, or take money from, bar staff, and even more unsettling if they were to worry that the bar staff were not what they seemed, and were a group of mass murderers intent upon poisoning their customers.

Agency and transformation

According to Giddens the existence of mutual knowledge, and a need for ontological security tend to produce regulations in social life. Patterns of behaviour are repeated, and in this way the structure of society, the social system and the institutions are all reproduced. However, this whole process also involves the ever-present possibility that society can be changed. Agents do not have to behave as others do, nor do they necessarily act in accordance with their habits forever. Giddens describes 'the reflexive monitoring of actions' in which humans are constantly able to think about what they are doing and to consider whether their objectives are being achieved. If they are not being achieved, then agents may start to behave in new ways, patterns of interaction may change, and with them the social structure.

For Giddens the very concepts of 'agent' and 'agency' involve people having the ability to transform the world around them through their actions, as well as being able to reproduce it. That does not mean that agents necessarily transform society, or for that matter reproduce it in ways which they intend. Human actions may well have consequences that were not anticipated by the agents involved. He gives the example of going home and switching on a light in order to illuminate a room. An unintended consequence of this might be that a burglar is alerted and flees the house, in doing so is apprehended by the police, and ultimately ends up spending several years in prison. Such unintended consequences can also result in patterns of social life that were not necessarily intended to be produced by any individual. Thus, for example, decisions by individuals in society about where to live might produce a situation, which nobody had actually intended, in which some inner-city areas start to decay and develop a concentration of social problems.

Determinism and voluntarism

In his theory of the duality of structure, Giddens tries to show how the traditional distinction between social structure and social action does not necessitate seeing society in terms of one or the other: structure and agency are locked together in the processes through which social life is reproduced and transformed. In a similar fashion, he tries to resolve the dispute between determinists, who believe that human behaviour is entirely determined by outside forces, and voluntarists, who believe that humans possess free will, and can act as they wish. Giddens believes neither theory to be true, but he sees both as having some element of truth. He believes that only in very exceptional circumstances are humans completely constrained. Complete constraint only occurs where physical force is used, for example where a person is unwillingly knocked to the ground by someone else. In all other circumstances, even where people claim to 'have no choice', there are options open to them. Thus if a person holds a gun to someone's head and threatens to shoot them if they do not hand over some money, the option of refusing is still open, even though there is a risk of death by making that choice. In other words it is nearly always possible to 'do otherwise', to do something different. Constraints according to Giddens do not therefore determine actions, but operate 'by placing limits upon the range of options open to an actor'.

In society humans are constrained by the existence of power relationships. Giddens sees all social action as involving power relationships. He sees power as the ability to make a difference, to change things from what they would otherwise have been, or, as he puts it 'transformative capacity'. For him, the idea of human agency involves the idea of transformation capacity, and this capacity of power may be used to change things, or the actions of other people. It can therefore be used to exercise power over other people, and so constrain people and reduce their freedom. At the same time though, power also increases the freedom of action of the agents who possess it. What restricts one person, enables another to do more.

Most of Giddens's work is highly abstract, and he offers few examples of how his theory of structuration could be applied to the study of society. However, he does praise Paul Willis's book *Learning to Labour*. (For details of the study see

pp. 741–3). Giddens claims that Willis's work shows how structures can be actively reproduced by the action of agents as an unintended consequence of the actions. Thus by their rejection of school and their determination to do manual jobs, 'the lads' reproduce some general features of capitalist-industrial labour. Furthermore, constraints are not simply experienced as external forces of which they are passive recipients. Instead 'the lads' are actively involved in making the decisions that come to constrain them. Because they choose not to work hard at school, they end up with very limited options in later life when they are choosing what work to do. Giddens claims that if sociology is to progress beyond the division between action and structure, it requires more studies like Willis's, which show how structures are reproduced by purposeful human agents.

Criticisms of Giddens

Although Giddens's ideas are still developing, they have been the subject of some criticism. Margaret S. Archer criticizes Giddens for locking agency and structure too tightly together. She suggests that the concepts have different implications. The idea of structure tends to stress the limits on human action, the idea of agency stresses the existence of free will, and the two are never reconciled. In her view, Giddens puts too much emphasis on the ability of agents to transform structures simply by changing their behaviour. Giddens's work implies that if people were to start acting differently tomorrow, then all of society's structures would immediately be changed.

According to Archer this is not the case. The possibilities for changing social structures, and the extent to which humans have the ability to transform the social world, depend upon the nature of the social structures. She uses the example of Fidel Castro's policy on illiteracy when he took power in Cuba. He wanted to conquer illiteracy by getting each literate person to teach an illiterate to read. Archer points out that literacy could not be achieved overnight, and, furthermore, how quickly it could be achieved depended upon a structural feature of Cuban society: the percentage of the population who were literate. Thus if 1 per cent of the population were literate, a much more lengthy period would be involved than if 50 per cent of the population were literate. This demonstrates to Archer that structural features of society cannot just be changed at will, at least not on a time scale that the actors involved might wish.

Archer similarly takes Giddens to task for suggesting that 'material resources' only enter social life and exercise a constraining influence on social actions when humans choose to make use of them. For example, a flood or volcanic eruption, or a shortage of land, is not the product of human will, but exercises a real, material constraint on options, regardless of human actions. To give another example, once all the coal in the ground has been burned, it cannot be burned again.

In short, Archer suggests people cannot just change or reproduce society as they wish. Some structural features of society are beyond their control and constrain behaviour. She accepts that humans have both some degree of freedom, and some limits on how they act, but a theory that does not move beyond this generalization says little. Giddens notes both the possibility of freedom of action and social change, and the constraints and the reproduction of social institutions. What Giddens does not do, though, is explain which of these will happen in particular circumstances. Archer says 'The theory of structuration remains incomplete because it provides an insufficient account of the mechanisms of stable replication versus the genesis of new social forms.'

■ Postmodernism

Postmodernism has recently become an increasingly fashionable subject of debate in academic and intellectual circles. This does not just apply to sociology. The term was first used in architecture to describe the reaction against the post-war concrete tower blocks. Later it began to be used in discussions of the arts and culture, more recently it has become influential in areas of study such as politics, economics and sociology.

There are several theories of postmodernism which differ in important respects. However, sociological theories of postmodernism do have certain things in common. They all agree that changes, and perhaps fundamental ones, are starting or have taken place in some contemporary societies. They all, at least by implication, see societies as having been through various phases and have some conception of modernity, the phase that logically precedes postmodernity.

Pre-modern and modern

Many of the classic nineteenth-century sociologists, such as Comte, Durkheim, Weber and Marx, shared a common intellectual interest in the social changes associated with industrialization. They all saw these changes as having shaped the modern world. Comte and Weber in particular saw them as involving the progressive triumph of scientific rationality. Comte believed that modern society would be dominated by science.

The influence of religion, superstition and philosophy would be replaced by 'positivist' science (see p. 479). Weber believed that the modern age would be increasingly shaped by rationalization and bureaucracy as affective and traditional actions became less important (see pp. 271–4). Marx and Durkheim put less emphasis on scientific and rational thinking, but both had strong beliefs that society was developing progressively, in Marx's case towards a communist utopia (see p. 881), in Durkheim's towards a complex society based upon organic solidarity (see pp. 184–5). All of them believed that they had used scientific analysis to uncover the big story (called 'metanarrative' by some postmodern theorists) of human development. All thought they could outline the future direction of social change.

The belief in progress and the faith placed in science can both be seen as characteristic of modern thinking. Many sociologists would suggest that in pre-modern societies, such as simple tribal societies, religion, superstition and tradition formed the basis of social life. There was little conception of social change as progressive. Instead, following the seasons, it was seen as circular.

The Enlightenment

Modern ways of thinking are usually seen as having their origins in the eighteenth-century Enlightenment. This was a broad European intellectual movement that sought to sweep away the prejudices of previous generations, and replace them with a more rational basis for social life. David Harvey, a contemporary commentator on postmodernism, describes the Enlightenment in the following way: 'The idea was to use the accumulation of knowledge generated by many individuals working freely and creatively for the pursuit of human emancipation and the enrichment of daily life. The scientific domination of nature promised freedom from scarcity, want, and the arbitrariness of natural calamity. The development of rational forms of social organization and rational modes of thought promised liberation from the irrationalities of myth, religion, superstition, release from the arbitrary use of power as well as from the dark side of our own human natures.' The hopes of Enlightenment thinkers were reflected in the French Revolution, and inherited by the nineteenth-century sociologists mentioned above.

Postmodernism and the Enlightenment

Postmodern theorists tend to argue that the Enlightenment 'project' (the aims of Enlightenment thinkers) has been abandoned in contemporary societies. People no longer believe in the inevitability of progress, the power of science to solve all problems, the perfectibility of humanity or the possibility of running societies in a rational way. People are more pessimistic about the future and much less willing to believe that the truth can be found in grand theories or ideologies such as Marxism. There is now a much wider variety of beliefs and most people are unwilling to accept that one set of ideas gives the absolute truth and all others are false. They see no simple recipe for solving the world's problems.

Postmodernism and architecture

These changes are reflected in architecture where the term postmodernism was first adopted. Modern architecture was characterized by the use of new, cheap and efficient materials to mass produce housing or offices for urban populations. The application of scientific knowledge using such materials as steel, concrete and glass would enable problems of accommodating people to be solved. The Swiss-born modern architect Le Corbusier saw architecture as producing 'machines for

modern living'. He advocated the building of the type of functional highrise tower block that was to become a common feature of towns and cities throughout the world. However, by the 1970s tower blocks were beginning to fall out of favour. Charles Jencks (quoted in D. Harvey, 1990, p. 39) dates the end of modernism in architecture from the destruction of the Pruitt-Igoe housing development, in St Louis in 1972.

The development of highrise blocks was based on Le Corbusier's ideas. According to some theorists, modern architecture has given way to postmodern architecture. This distrusts the scientific and idealistic approach of modern architecture and, instead of looking to a high-tech future, borrows from the past. According to Harvey examples of postmodern architecture include 'imitation medieval squares and fishing villages, custom-designed or vernacular housing, renovated factories and warehouses, and rehabilitated landscapes of all kinds'. Prince Charles's denunciations of modern architecture for defacing cities such as London can be seen as a typical postmodern attitude.

According to the theory of postmodernism we have lost faith in all grand plans for the future of humanity, not just in architecture but in all areas of social life. Diversity is the order of the day. We have entered an era in which anything goes, all styles and fashions are permissible so long as none is taken too seriously. If this is true then it seems to challenge the assumptions on which the foundations of sociology were laid. The next sections will outline the claims of some postmodern theorists in more detail, starting with those who give strongest support to the concept and its implications.

■ Jean-Francois Lyotard – postmodernism and knowledge

Language-games

The French theorist Lyotard argues that post-industrial society and postmodern culture began to develop at the end of the 1950s, although the rate of development and the stage reached varies between and within countries. Lyotard sees these developments as related to technology, science and some social developments, but most importantly to changes in language. The key concept he uses is that of 'language-games'. Lyotard seems to see social life as being organized around these language-games. Language-games serve to justify or legitimate peoples' behaviour in society. They are games in which the participants can try to assert certain things to be true or right. Each statement or utterance is a 'move' that may aid the participant in trying to win the game, to get their version of what is true or right accepted.

Narrative

In simple or pre-industrial societies such as the South American tribe Cashinahua, narrative – the telling of stories, myths, legends and tales – is the principle language-game. The narrator establishes his right to speak and the legitimacy of what he is saying according to who he is. He starts the story by giving his Cashinahua name to show that he is an authentic member of the tribe who has had the story passed down to him. It is therefore an example of self-legitimation: what he says should be accepted because of who he is. Narratives help to convey the rules on which social order is based, they play a key role in socialization.

Science and metanarratives

With the Enlightenment narrative, language-games were largely replaced by scientific 'denotative' games. The scientist sees narrative as 'belonging to a different mentality: savage, primitive, underdeveloped, backward, alienated, composed of opinions, custom, authority, prejudice, ignorance, ideology.' In denotative language-games it is irrelevant who is speaking, statements are judged as to whether they are true or false. Scientific statements are scrutinized and are 'subject to argumentation or proof' by other participants in the game. Evidence and rational argument are employed to establish whether a statement should be accepted or rejected.

However, probing deeper, Lyotard argues that science is unable to rid itself entirely of narrative knowledge. Science tries to maintain distance between itself and social conventions so that it can remain objective. But this raises the question of the purpose of science. How can the vast expenditure on science be justified if it is kept separate from social life? In the end science rests upon 'metanarratives', narratives that give meaning to other narratives. They give a sense of

purpose to scientific endeavour and a sense of direction to social life. These metanarratives suggest that humans can progress through science towards defeating ignorance and oppression. Science can help humans conquer nature and become more self-conscious. These metanarratives have had a major influence on Western thought from the French Revolution to twentieth-century Marxism. Knowledge is also justified as being good in itself for human beings, enabling them to fulfil their potential. (This is reflected in the Liberal ideal of education examined on pp. 730–2).

■ Postmodernism

According to Lyotard, metanarratives of human emancipation, self-fulfilment and social progress are undermined by the advent of postmodernism. An 'incredulity towards metanarratives' develops. People no longer believe that reason can conquer superstition, that humans can be perfected or that communism can produce a perfect society.

The postmodern era has two main characteristics. First, the search for truth is abandoned as denotative language-games fall into disrepute. Knowledge fragments into a multiplicity of different language-games that are specific to particular areas of science or social life. Diversity is the order of the day as people lose faith in the search for one great truth that unites and justifies all knowledge.

Second, denotative language-games are replaced by technical language-games. Here, statements are judged not by whether they are true, but by whether they are useful and efficient or not. Emphasis shifts from the ultimate ends of human activity, towards the technical means through which things can be achieved. In universities, for example, researchers ask what use something is rather than whether it is true. Research becomes geared to producing knowledge that is saleable.

Knowledge and computer technology

Lyotard does not devote much attention to explaining how these changes have come about.

However, he seems to attribute most importance to technology. He says that postmodernism rests upon the 'miniaturization and commercialization' of machines. Computer technology has become the principal 'force of production'. Most postmodern scientific developments are concerned with communication, language and information storage. Knowledge that cannot be translated into a form useable by computers tends to get lost or disregarded. Increasingly economic activity centres around information technology. Social life is monitored and controlled more and more by computerized machines, and control over knowledge becomes the major source of power. Knowledge is no longer an end in itself but something to be bought and sold, perhaps even fought over. He speculates that future wars will not be about territorial disputes, but about disputes over the control of knowledge.

To Lyotard, postmodern society is based on the production and exchange of knowledge that can be sold. Grand theories of truth, justice and progress have fallen out of fashion. Language-games concern whether things are efficient and saleable rather than whether they serve some ultimate human purpose or goal. Lyotard's analysis sometimes sounds like a Marxist attack on capitalism. In fact, though, he praises the consequences of postmodernism. The search for truth in modern thinking led only to 'as much terror as we can take' (for example, repression under Stalin in Communist USSR). Postmodernism offers the possibility of tolerance and creative diversity in which humans are not corrupted by some doctrinaire metanarrative.

Lyotard – a critique

Like most advocates of postmodernism, Lyotard indulges in a number of paradoxes. While attacking 'metanarratives', Lyotard himself makes the most sweeping generalizations about the direction of human development, as well as making moral judgements about its desirability. While dismissing the possibility of objective knowledge, he claims to have identified and accurately described the development of key features of human societies. The evidence he uses to support his claims is sparse, leaving the reader with little reason to prefer Lyotard's 'language-game' to that of other social theorists. While rejoicing in diversity Leotard ends up celebrating language-games con-

ducted according to one set of rules, those of the technical language-game. Terry Eagleton, a Marxist critic of Lyotard, sees this as nothing more than a justification for capitalism and the pursuit of profit regardless of the human consequences (quoted in Steven Connor, 1989, p. 41).

■ Jean Baudrillard – *Simulations*

Baudrillard does not explicitly discuss the concept of postmodernism in his most influential book, *Simulations*. Nevertheless he is widely seen as a postmodern theorist. Like Lyotard, he sees societies as having entered a new and distinctive phase, and he relates this change to language and knowledge. Unlike Lyotard, he is rather pessimistic about the consequences of this change, seeing it as a kind of trap from which escape is impossible.

Signs and the economy

Baudrillard argues in contradiction of Marxists that society has moved away from being based upon production and being shaped by the economic forces involved in exchanging material goods. The central importance of the buying and selling of material goods has now been replaced by the buying and selling of signs and images, which have little if any relationship to material reality. Baudrillard is not explicit about what he means in this context, but examples might include the way cars, cigarettes, pop stars and political parties have become more associated with images than any substance that might lie behind them (engines, nicotine content, music and policies respectively). The images are everything, the reality nothing.

The development of signs

Baudrillard argues that signs in human culture have passed through four main stages.

1 In the first stage, signs (words, images, etc.) are a 'reflection of a basic reality'.

2 In the next stage, the sign 'masks and perverts some basic reality'. Images become a distortion of the truth but they have not lost all connection with things that really exist.

3 In the third stage, the sign 'masks the absence of some basic reality'. For example, icons may disguise the fact that God does not exist.

4 Finally, the sign 'bears no relation to any reality whatsoever: it is its own pure simulacrum'.

A simulacrum is an image of something that does not exist and has never existed. To Baudrillard modern society is based upon the production and exchange of free-floating images. Signifiers (words and images) have no connection with anything real that is signified (the things that words and images refer to).

Examples of simulacra

Baudrillard provides a number of examples to illustrate this rather sweeping claim. Disneyland is described as 'a perfect model' of a simulacrum. It is a copy of imaginary worlds such as 'Pirates, the Frontier, Future World'. Simulacra are not confined to theme parks. According to Baudrillard the whole of Los Angeles is a kind of make-believe world founded upon stories and images that have no grounding in reality, it is 'nothing more than an immense script and a perpetual motion picture'.

In contemporary society the predominance of signifiers tends to destroy any basic reality to which they might refer. He gives the example of a Phillipino tribe called the Tasaday, the mummy of Ramses II, and a family called the Louds who were the subject of a fly-on-the-wall TV documentary in the USA. The Tasaday Indians were discovered in a remote area of the Phillines and began to be studied by anthropologists. However, the government believed that the traditional culture of the Tasaday was being destroyed by this process and they decided to return them to the jungle and isolate them from contemporary civilization. Thus they were turned into a simulation of a primitive society. They were no longer in their original and natural state, but they had come to represent all primitive peoples to Western scientists.

Science and technology also destroyed the originality of the mummy of the Egyptian Pharaoh Ramses II. Once it was removed from its original sight and placed in a museum it began to deteriorate and scientific techniques had to be used to try to preserve it. At the same time, though, they altered it and destroyed its authenticity. The Louds family was similarly destroyed. Chosen as a 'typical' Californian family, 300 hours of film of their life were broadcast. During the process the cohesion of the family fell apart and they went their separate ways. Whether this was due to television or not, the reality of the family was inevitably changed by the fact that they had become the object of a public spectacle. Attempts to capture reality unavoidably lead to its destruction, so that science and TV culture capture nothing but images of things which never existed or have already been destroyed.

Power and politics

Baudrillard is consistently gloomy about the consequences of all this. If it has become impossible to grasp reality, it is also impossible to change it. Society has 'imploded' and become like a black hole in which nothing can escape the exchange of signs with no real meaning. For example, the meaning of a terrorist outrage becomes arbitrary. It can equally easily be interpreted as the work of left-wingers or right-wingers or political moderates who want to discredit extremists of both sides. In Baudrillard's view power is no longer unequally distributed, it has just disappeared. Nobody can exercise power to change things. He compares the situation to nuclear deterrence where the two sides cancel each other out and make action impossible. While President Kennedy was assassinated because he might have real power, Johnson, Nixon, Ford and Reagan were merely puppets without any genuine chance of changing America or the outside world. With the end of the real and its substitution by simulacra, and the end of effective power, we are all trapped in a kind of prison, deprived of our freedom to change things and condemned to the interminable exchange of meaningless signs.

Television

Baudrillard, then, differs from Lyotard in that he sees humans as trapped into a type of powerless uniformity, and not liberated by plurality and diversity. If anything, Baudrillard is even more vague than Lyotard in explaining how the postmodern era came about. However, he does seem to attach special importance to the mass media and to TV in particular. He talks about 'the dissolution of life into TV' and says 'TV watches us, TV alienates us, TV manipulates us, TV informs us'. It seems that it is TV that is primarily responsible for ushering in a situation where image and reality can no longer be distinguished.

Baudrillard – a critique

Baudrillard's writing is highly abstract. It relies upon the use of examples to illustrate arguments and consequently offers no systematic evidence to justify his case. For example, Baudrillard makes no attempt to show that individuals are immersed in the world of TV, that Disneyland is seen as anything more than fantasy by its customers, or that the residents of Los Angeles have lost their grip on reality. His analysis of politics degenerates into totally unsubstantiated assertions. For example, he describes Reagan as a 'puppet' who, in common with other 'postmodern' politicians, has no power. David Harvey accepts that Reagan's election might have owed a good deal to his TV image, but the reality of his policies and their very real effects on the lives of many Americans cannot be denied. He says: 'A rising tide of social inequality engulfed the United States in the Reagan years, reaching a post-war high in 1986. . . . Between 1979 and 1986, the number of poor families with children increased by 35 per cent. . . . In spite of surging unemployment (cresting at over 10 per cent by official figures in 1982) the percentage of unemployed receiving any federal benefit fell to only 32 per cent, the lowest level in the history of social insurance.' In addition nearly 40 million were left with no medical insurance. Perhaps, then, it is Baudrillard who has lost his grasp of reality rather than the 'postmodern' world.

■ David Harvey – Marxism and postmodernism

David Harvey himself offers a very different view of postmodernism from that of either Lyotard or Baudrillard. Indeed, Harvey is sceptical about the use of the word postmodernism. He accepts that important changes have taken place in society but he does not regard them as absolutely fundamental. He rejects the claim that metanarratives have outlived their usefulness, since he uses Marxism as the basis of his analysis. He makes a greater effort to explain the changes in contemporary societies than most other theorists of postmodernism, and he puts particular emphasis on economic factors in influencing change. He can be described as a neo-Marxist who has been influenced by theories of postmodernism. His work is much more explicitly sociological than that of Lyotard and Baudrillard.

Continuities and changes in capitalism

Harvey argues that a capitalist economic system remains at the heart of contemporary western societies. This economic system retains three basic characteristics which have not disappeared with the postmodern era.

1 Capitalism is based upon economic growth and is defined as being in crisis when there is no growth.

2 Capitalism is based upon workers being paid less than the value of the commodities they produce so profits can be made. The 'dynamics of class struggle' are therefore inevitably involved in capitalist economies and societies.

3 Capitalism is dynamic. It is always producing new ways of organizing work and technological innovation as businesses seek to get ahead of their competitors.

These basic characteristics mean that capitalism is always likely to change. As it develops, new ways of controlling labour and trying to ensure profitability become necessary. According to Harvey, and to Marxist theory in general, periods of crisis are unavoidable. These crises lead to changes in the economy which may have important consequences for society and culture.

Harvey sees postmodernism as a response to one such crisis and dates its arrival at 1973. From the end of World War II until 1973 capitalism was fairly stable. There was steady growth in most countries, rising living standards and relative harmony between social classes. From 1973 a series of economic problems struck the world capitalist economy. Oil producers increased the price of oil, unemployment began to rise, profits fell and many countries experienced stagflation, i.e. high inflation without economic growth. These problems led to, in Harvey's words, a different 'regime of accumulation', different ways of trying to ensure growth and profitability. This in turn helped to produce some of the cultural changes that have been termed postmodern, and produced a new 'mode of social and political regulation'.

Harvey stresses that many aspects of the postmodern era are not entirely new. Capitalism has always contained contradictory tendencies which can be found throughout its history. He says 'there is never one fixed configuration, but a swaying back and forth between centralization and decentralization, between authority and deconstruction, between hierarchy and anarchy, between permanence and flexibility'. Nevertheless he believes that capitalism has now swayed more towards the latter, postmodern, set of characteristics, and away from the former, modern, ones.

Economic change and postmodernism

The shift from modernism to postmodernism is characterized by a change to 'flexible accumulation'. Harvey is among those who claim that flexibility in business (often termed post-Fordism) has begun to replace Fordism (see pp. 214–18 for the debate on post-Fordism). He sees flexible accumulation as involving rapid changes in labour markets, products and patterns of consumption; more rapid technological change; increasing employment in the service sector; the reduction of trade union power; high unemployment; and reduced security for workers who are expected to be flexible enough to accommodate the ever-changing demands of their employers. Businesses can no longer rely upon regular and long-term profits and so have to constantly adapt to succeed. In terms of consumption new products such as computer games and new services in the leisure industry have led to cultural changes. Capitalists have succeeded in encouraging rapid shifts in fashion (for example, in clothes and music) which allow profits to be continually renewed.

Cultural and social changes

These economic changes underlie the cultural, political and social changes that have been the focus of attention for some other writers. In particular, the penetration of capitalism into so many areas of leisure to encourage consumption has resulted in 'the ferment, instability, and fleeting qualities of a postmodern aesthetic that celebrates difference, ephemerality, spectacle, fashion and the commodification of cultural forms'. As mass production has become less profitable, flexible accumulation has led to capitalism exploiting

smaller markets with more specialized tastes, thus encouraging cultural diversity.

Increasing geographical mobility and the development of large-scale tourism have led to an increased intermingling of the world's cultures. Faster and cheaper travel and the pervasiveness of mass communications, have, according to Harvey, affected the way people perceive space and time. Both have been compressed and he associates this with the speeding up of production and the use of techniques such as 'just in time' (see p. 215).

A sense of time and place has been weakened in the postmodern era. For example, in major cities you can eat food from around the world, French croissants, Japanese sushi, American doughnuts, Chinese crispy fried duck, listen to world music from every continent, buy 'Kenyan haricot beans, Californian celery and advocados, North African potatoes, Canadian apples and Chilean grapes' in supermarkets. Furthermore, 'the world's geographical complexity is nightly reduced to a series of images on a static television screen'.

Time gets confused as people can visit the 'Old World' at Disneyworld or dress up to attend a medieval weekend at a castle. Times, places and cultures get mixed together in close proximity. This becomes reflected in art, philosophy and social thought and is typified by 'ephemerality, collage, fragmentation'. Firm foundations for knowledge or beliefs seem undermined by this diversity and confusion, but to Harvey such foundations need not and should not be lost.

Time and space have also been compressed in the world financial system. Trading in stocks, shares, currencies and commodities continues twenty-four hours a day and with computer technology takes place almost instantaneously. What happens in Tokyo affects the markets in London, New York and elsewhere. All countries of the world are affected by the enormous debts owed by the Third World to the First. According to Harvey the world financial system has become so complex it is almost impossible for national governments to understand, never mind control. (The relative powerlessness of national governments can be illustrated by the stock market crash in October 1987, and the turmoil in the money markets in 1992 which forced the British government to take the pound out of the European Exchange Rate Mechanism).

These developments, combined with a shift to

flexible accumulation, have encouraged political changes. They can be related to the increasing importance of image in politics. Despite the problems experienced by America under President Reagan, he was able to get re-elected as a 'tough but warm, avuncular and well-meaning person who had an abiding faith in the greatness and goodness of America'. Both Reagan and Thatcher caught the economic mood of the times by encouraging entrepreneurship, necessary in a period of flexible accumulation. Both stressed the limitations of government power and the need to trust the markets, though both were forced to intervene in the economy to deal with problems such as Third World debt. Both weakened trade union power, making it easier for capitalists to make a profit under the new conditions.

According to David Harvey postmodernism has not just affected governments, it has also influenced the development of political and social movements. Class issues and workers' movements have become less important as sources of opposition to capitalism. Political opposition has become more fragmented into diverse movements representing particular groups or issues. There are 'religious, mystical, social, communitarian, humanitarian' movements which 'define themselves directly in terms of an antagonism to the power of money and of rationalized conceptions of space and time over daily life'. Issues relating to Women's Liberation, ethnic inequalities and poverty in the Third World have become increasingly important.

But Harvey also detects some evidence that these diverse social movements may be starting to come together. Some political leaders such as Jesse Jackson in the USA have urged the development of a 'Rainbow Coalition' of oppressed minorities. Harvey claims to have found signs of 'a new internationalism in the ecological sphere . . . and in the fight against racism, apart- heid, world hunger, uneven geographical development'. He cites Live Aid as one example, though admitting that it confined itself largely to image-making rather than political organization. Nevertheless he sees a possibility of launching a 'counterattack' against some of the worst consequences of post-modernism.

Harvey rejects the belief of many postmodern theorists that the Enlightenment project should be abandoned. Modern societies can be systematically studied and understood, ways of improving them and the lives of those who live in them can be found. Society is real and consists of more than language-games or simulacra. If he is right, the study of sociology is still worthwhile, indeed essential.

Bibliography

Abbott, P. and Payne, G. 'Women's social mobility: the conventional wisdom reconsidered' in G. Payne and P. Abbott *The Social Mobility of Women* (Falmer Press, Basingstoke, 1990)

Abbott, P. and Wallace, C. *The Family and the New Right* (Pluto Press, London, 1992)

Abel-Smith, B. and Townsend, P. *The Poor and the Poorest* (G. Bell & Sons, London, 1965)

Abercrombie, N., Hill, N. and Turner, B.S. *The Dominant Ideology Thesis* (Allen & Unwin, London, 1980)

Abercrombie, N. and Urry, J. *Capital Labour and the Middle Classes* (Allen & Unwin, London, 1983)

Abercrombie, A. and Warde, A. (eds) *Social Change in Contemporary Britain* (Polity Press, Cambridge, 1992)

Aberle, D. 'A note on relative deprivation theory as applied to millenarian movements and other cult movements' in Lessa and Vogt (1965)

Abrams, M. and Rose, R. *Must Labour Lose?* (Penguin, Harmondsworth, 1960)

Ackroyd, S. and Hughes, J. *A Data Collection in Context* (Longman, London, 1981)

Adkins, L. and Lury, C. 'Gender and the labour market: old theory for new?' in H. Hinds, A. Phoenix and J. Stacey (eds) *Working Out: New Directions for Women's Studies* (Falmer Press, London, 1992)

Adler, F. *Sisters in Crime* (McGraw Hill, New York, 1975)

Adorno, T.W. *et al. The Authoritarian Personality* (Harper, New York, 1950)

Aginsky, B.W. 'A Pomo's soliloquy' in A. Dundes (ed.) *Every Man His Way: Readings in Cultural Anthropology* (Prentice-Hall, Englewood Cliffs, 1968)

Ahrne, G. 'Class and society: a critique of John Goldthorpe's model of social classes' in J. Clark *et al.* (1990)

Albrow, M. *Bureaucracy* (Pall Mall Press, London, 1970)

Alexandrov, G.F. *et al.* 'The urban strata of contemporary capitalist society' in P. Hollander (ed.) *American and Soviet Society* (Prentice-Hall, Englewood Cliffs, London, 1971)

Allan, G. *Family Life: Domestic Roles and Social Organization* (Blackwell, London, 1985)

Allen, H. 'Fines for women: paradoxes and paradigms' in Carlen and Cook (1989)

Allen, S. and Watson, A. 'The effects of unemployment: experience and response' in S. Allen, A. Watson, K. Purcell and S. Wood (eds) (1986)

Allen, S., Watson, A., Purcell, K. and Wood, S. (eds) *The Experience of Unemployment* (Macmillan, London, 1986)

Allen, V.L. *The Sociology of Industrial Relations* (Longman, London, 1971)

Amin, K. and Oppenheim, C. *Poverty in Black and White* (CPAG, London, 1992)

Anderson, B. *Imagined Communities* (Verso, London, 1983)

Anderson, M. *Approaches to the History of the Western Family 1500–1914* (Macmillan, London, 1980). 'The historical study of family structure' in M. Bulmer (1977). 'Family, household and the Industrial Revolution' in M. Anderson (ed.) *Sociology of the Family* (Penguin, Harmondsworth, 1971)

Anderson, R.J., Hughes, J.A. and Sharrock, W.W. *Philosophy and the Human Sciences* (Croom Helm, London, 1986). *Classic Disputes in Sociology* (eds) (Allen & Unwin, London, 1987)

Andreski, S. (ed.) *Herbert Spencer* (Nelson, London, 1971)

Anthias, F. and Yuval-Davis, N. *Race, Nation, Gender, Colour and Class and the Anti-racist Struggle* (Routledge, London, 1992)

Arber, S., Dale, A. and Gilbert, N. 'The limitations of existing social class classifications of women' in A. Jacoby (ed.) *The Measurement of Social Class* (Social Research Association, Guildford, 1986)

Archer, M.S. 'Morphogenesis versus structure and action' *British Journal of Sociology* vol. 33, no. 4 (1982)

Arensberg, C.M. and Kimball, S.T. *Family and Community in Ireland* 2nd edn (Harvard University Press, Cambridge, USA, 1968)

Armstrong, P. 'Competition between the organizational professions and the evolution of management control strategies' in K. Thompson (1984)

Arnot, M. and Weiner, G. *Gender Under Scrutiny* (Hutchinson, London, 1987)

Aron, R. 'Social class, political class, ruling class' in Bendix and Lipset (1967). *Main Currents in Sociological Thought* vols 1 and 2 (Penguin, Harmondsworth, 1968 and 1970)

Ashton, D.N. *Unemployment under Capitalism* (Wheatsheaf, London, 1986)

Atkinson, A.B. *The Economics of Inequality* (Oxford University Press, Oxford, 1983)

Atkinson, J. 'The changing corporation' in David Clutterbuck (ed.) *New Patterns of Work* (Gower, Aldershot, 1985). 'Societal reactions to suicide' in *Cohen Discovering Suicide* (Macmillan, London, 1978)

Austin, R. 'Liberation and female criminality in England and Wales' *British Journal of Criminology* vol. 21 (1981)

Baechler, J. *Suicides* (Blackwell, Oxford, 1979)

Bainbridge, W.S. and Stark, R. 'Cult formation: three compatible models' *Sociological Analysis* no. 40 (1979)

Ball, S.J. *Beachside Comprehensive. A Case-study of Secondary Schooling* (Cambridge University Press, Cambridge, 1981). *Politics and Policy Making in Education* (Routledge, London, 1990)

Ball, S.J., Bowe, R. and Gerwitz, S. 'Market forces and parental choice' in S. Tomlinson (ed.) *Educational Reform and its Consequences* (IPPR/Rivers Oram Press, London, 1994)

Ballard, R. 'South Asian families' in R.N. Rapoport *et al.* (eds) (1982). 'Marriage and kinship' in C. Clarke, C. Peach and S. Vertovec (eds) *South Asians Overseas* (Cambridge University Press, Cambridge, 1990)

Ballard, R. and Ballard, C. 'The Sikhs' in J.L. Watson (ed.) *Between Two Cultures* (Basil Blackwell, Oxford, 1977)

Banton, M. *Racial Theories* (Cambridge University Press, Cambridge, 1987)

Barash, D. *The Whisperings Within* (Harper & Row, New York, 1979)

Barber, B. 'Some problems in the sociology of professions' *Daedalus* vol. 92, no. 4 (1963). 'Acculturation and Messianic Movements' in Lessa and Vogt (1965)

Barker, D.L. and Allen, S. (eds) *Dependence and Exploitation in Work and Marriage* (Longman, London, 1976)

Barker, E. *The Making of a Moonie* (Blackwell, Oxford, 1984).'New religious movements: yet another great awakening?' in P.E. Hammond (ed.) *The Sacred in a Secular Age* (University of California Press, Berkeley, 1985)

Barrett, M. 'Rethinking women's oppression: a reply to Brenner and Ramas' *New Left Review* (August, 1984). *Women's Oppression Today* (Verso, London, 1980)

Barrett, M. and McIntosh, M. *The Anti-social Family* (Verso, London, 1982)

Barron, R.D. and Norris, G.M. 'Sexual divisions and the dual labour market' in Barker and Allen (1976)

Barrow, J. 'West Indian families: an insider's perspective' in R.N. Rapoport *et al.* (eds) (1982)

Barton, L. and Walker, S. (eds) *Social Crisis and Educational Research* (Croom Helm, London, 1984)

Bates, I., Clarke, J., Cohen, P., Finn, D., Moore, R. and Willis, P. *Schooling for the Dole?* (Macmillan, London, 1984)

Beck, J., Jenks, C., Keddie, N. and Young, M.F.D. (eds) *Worlds Apart: Readings for a Sociology of Education* (Collier-Macmillan, London, 1976)

Becker, H.S. *Outsiders* (The Free Press, New York, 1963). *Sociological Work* (Transaction Books, New Brunswick, 1970). 'Social-class variations in the teacher-pupil relationship' and 'Personal change in adult life' in Cosin, Dale, Esland and Swift (1971). 'Labelling theory reconsidered' in P. Rock and M. McIntosh (eds) *Deviance and Social Control* (Tavistock, London, 1974)

Beckford, J.A. *Cult Controversies* (Tavistock, London, 1985)

Beechey, V. 'The sexual division of labour and the labour process: a critical assessment of Braverman' in S. Wood (ed.) (1983). 'Women and production: a critical analysis of some sociological theories of women's work' in A. Kuhn and A.M. Wolpe (eds) *Feminism and Materialism* (Routledge & Kegan Paul, London, 1978). 'Women and employment in contemporary Britain' in V. Beechey and E. Whitelegg (eds) *Women in Britain Today* (Open University Press, Milton Keynes, 1986).

Bell, C.R. *Middle Class Families* (Routledge & Kegan Paul, London, 1968)

Bell, N.W. and Vogel, E.F. (eds) *A Modern Introduction to the Family* rev. edn (The Free Press, New York, 1968)

Bellah, R.N. 'Religious evolution' in Lessa and Vogt (1965). 'New religious consciousness and the crisis in modernity' in Glock and Bellah (1976)

Bendix, R. and Lipset, S.M. (eds) *Class, Status, and Power* 2nd edn (Routledge & Kegan Paul, London, 1967)

Benet, M.K. *Secretary: An Enquiry into the Female Ghetto* (Sidgwick & Jackson, London, 1972)

Benson, J.K. 'Organisations: a dialectical view' *Administrative Science Quarterly* no. 22 (1977)

Benston, M. 'The political economy of women's liberation' in Glazer-Malbin and Waehrer (1972)

Benyon, J. 'Politics: the Thatcher phenomenon' in M. Haralambos (ed.) *Developments in Sociology* vol. 5 (Causeway Press, Ormskirk, 1989)

Berger, B. and Berger, P.L. *The War Over the Family* (Hutchinson, London, 1983)

Berger, P.L. *Invitation to Sociology* (Penguin, Harmondsworth, 1966). 'Religious institutions' in N.J. Smelser (ed.) *Sociology: An Introduction* (John Wiley & Sons, New York, 1967). *The Sacred Canopy: Elements of a Sociological Theory of Religion* (Doubleday, New York, 1967). *A Rumour of Angels: Modern Society and the Rediscovery of the Supernatural* (Allen Lane, London, 1970)

Berger, P.L. and Luckmann, T. *Sociology of Religion and Sociology of Knowledge* in Robertson (1969)

Berger, P.L., Berger, B. and Kellner, H. *The Homeless*

Mind: Modernization and Consciousness (Penguin, Harmondsworth, 1974)

Berlin, I. *Karl Marx* 4th edn (Oxford University Press, Oxford, 1978)

Bernard, J. *The Future of Marriage* (Penguin, Harmondsworth, 1976)

Bernbaum, G. *Knowledge and Ideology in the Sociology of Education* (Macmillan, London, 1977)

Bernstein, B. 'Social class and linguistic development: a theory of social learning' in Halsey, Floud and Anderson (1961). 'A socio-linguistic approach to social learning' in Worsley (1970). 'Education cannot compensate for society' in Cosin, Dale, Esland and Swift (1971). 'Language and social context' in Giglioli (1972)

Best, L. '"Dragons, dinner ladies and ferrets": sex roles in children's books' *Sociology Review* (February 1993)

Béteille, A. *Inequality Among Men* (Blackwell, Oxford, 1977)

Béteille, A. (ed.) *Social Inequality* (Penguin, Harmondsworth, 1969)

Bettelheim, B. *The Children of the Dream* (Thames & Hudson, London, 1969)

Beynon, H, *Working for Ford* (Allen Lane, Harmondsworth, 1973). 'The end of the industrial worker?' in N. Abercrombie and A. Warde (eds) *Social Change in Contemporary Britain* (Polity Press, Cambridge, 1992)

Bhaskar, R. *The Possibility of Naturalism* (Harvester Press, Brighton, 1979)

Bierstedt, R. *The Social Order* (McGraw-Hill, New York, 1963)

Birke, L. *Women, Feminism and Biology* (Wheatsheaf, Brighton, 1986)

Birnbaum, N. and Lenzer, G. (eds) *Sociology and Religion: A Book of Readings* (Prentice-Hall, Englewood Cliffs, 1969)

Blackburn, R.M. and Mann, M. 'Ideology in the non-skilled working class' in Bulmer (1975)

Blackburn, R.M. and Stewart, A. 'Women, work and the class structure' *New Society* (1 September 1977)

Blackledge, D. and Hunt, B. *Sociological Interpretations of Education* (Croom Helm, London, 1985)

Blackstone, T. and Mortimore, J. 'Cultural factors in child-rearing and attitudes to education' in B. Moon and A. S. Mayes (eds) *Teaching and Learning in the Secondary School* (Routledge, London, 1994)

Blau, P.M. *The Dynamics of Bureaucracy* 2nd edn (University of Chicago Press, Chicago, 1963). *On the Nature of Organizations* (John Wiley & Sons, New York, 1974)

Blau, P.M. and Meyer, M.W. *Bureaucracy in Modern Society* 2nd edn (Random House, New York, 1971)

Blau, P.M. and Schoenherr, R.A. *The Structure of Organizations* (Basic Books, New York, 1971)

Blauner, R. *Alienation and Freedom* (University of Chicago Press, Chicago, 1964). 'Work satisfaction and industrial trends in modern society' in Worsley (1972)

Bleier, R. *Science and Gender* (Pergamon Press, New York, 1984)

Blumer, H. 'Society as symbolic interaction' in Rose (1962). *Symbolic Interactionism* (Prentice-Hall, Englewood Cliffs, 1969)

Bodmer, W.F. 'Race and IQ: the genetic background' in K. Richardson and D. Spears (eds) *Race, Culture and Intelligence* (Penguin, Harmondsworth, 1972)

Boh, K. 'European family life patterns – a reappraisal' in K. Boh *et al.* (eds) (1989)

Boh, K., Bak, M., Clason, C., Pankratova, M., Qvortrup, J., Sgritta, G.B. and Waerness, K. *Changing Patterns of European Family Life* (Routledge, London, 1989)

Bolt, C. *Victorian Attitudes to Race* (Routledge & Kegan Paul, London, 1971)

Bonnett, K. 'Power and politics' in M. Haralambos (ed.) *Developments in Sociology* vol. 10 (Causeway Press, Ormskirk, 1994)

Bordua, D. 'A critique of sociological interpretations of gang delinquency' in Wolfgang, Savitz and Johnston (1962)

Borthwick, G., Ellingworth, D., Bell, C. and MacKenzie, D. 'The social background of British MPs' *Sociology* (November 1991)

Bott, E. *Family and Social Network* 2nd edn (Tavistock, London, 1971)

Bottomore, T.B. *Classes in Modern Society* (Allen & Unwin, London, 1965). *Elites and Society* (Penguin, Harmondsworth, 1966)

Bottomore, T.B. and Rubel, M. (eds) *Karl Marx: Selected Writings in Sociology and Social Philosophy* (Penguin, Harmondsworth, 1963)

Bouchier, D. *The Feminist Challenge* (Macmillan, London, 1983)

Boudon, R. *Education, Opportunity and Social Inequality* (John Wiley & Sons, New York, 1974)

Boulton, M.G. *On Being a Mother* (Tavistock, London, 1983)

Bourdieu, P. 'Intellectual field and creative project' and 'Systems of education and systems of thought' in Young (1971). 'Cultural reproduction and social reproduction' in Brown (1973). 'The school as a conservative force: scholastic and cultural inequalities' in Eggleston (1974)

Bourdieu, P. and de Saint-Martin, M. 'Scholastic excellence and the values of the educational system' in Eggleston (1974)

Bourdieu, P. and Passeron, J. *Reproduction in Education, Society and Culture* (Sage Publications, London, 1977)

Bourne, R. 'The snakes and ladders of the British class system' *New Society* (8 February 1979)

Bowlby, J. *Forty-four Juvenile Thieves* (Tindall & Cox, London, 1946). *Child Care and the Growth of Love* (Penguin, Harmondsworth, 1953)

Bowles, S. and Gintis, H. *Schooling in Capitalist America* (Routledge & Kegan Paul, London, 1976)

Box, S. *Deviancy, Reality and Society* (Holt, Rinehart & Winston, London, 1981). *Crime, Power and Mystification* (Tavistock, London, 1983). *Recession, Crime and Punishment* (Macmillan, London, 1987)

Box, S. and Hale, C. 'Liberation and female criminality in England and Wales' *British Journal of Criminology* vol. 23, no 1 (1983)

Bradshaw, J., Mitchell, D. and Morgan, J. 'Evaluating adequacy: the potential of budget standards' *Journal of Social Policy* (1987)

Braithwaite, J. *Corporate Crime in the Pharmaceutical Industry* (Routledge, London, 1984)

Braudillard, J. *Simulations* (Semiotext, 1983)

Braverman, H. *Labor and Monopoly Capitalism* (Monthly Review Press, New York, 1974)

Brenner, J. and Ramas, M. 'Rethinking women's oppression' *New Left Review* (April 1984)

Brewer, R.M. 'Theorizing race, class and gender: the new scholarship of Black feminist intellectuals and Black women's labor' in S.M. James and A.P.A. Busia (eds) *Theorizing Black Feminisms* (Routledge, London, 1993)

Bridgewood, A. and Savage, D. *1991 General Household Survey* (HMSO, London, 1993)

Brierley, P. *'Christian' England* (MARC Europe, London, 1991)

Brierley, P. and Longley, D. (eds) *UK Christian Handbook 1992/93 edition* (MARC Europe, London, 1991)

Brittain, E. 'Multiracial education. Teacher opinions on aspects of school life' *Educational Research* vol. 18, no. 2 (1976)

Britten, N. and Heath, A. 'Women, men and social class' in E. Gamarnikow, D. Morgan, J. Purvis and D. Taylorson *Gender, Class and Work* (Heinemann, London, 1983)

Brown, C. *Black and White in Britain: The Third PSI Survey* (Heinemann, London, 1984)

Brown, C. and Gay, P. *Racial Discrimination 17 Years after the Act* (Policy Studies Institute, London, 1985)

Brown, C.V. and Jackson, P.M. *Public Sector Economics* (Martin Robertson, Oxford, 1982)

Brown, J.C. 'The focus on single mothers' in C. Murray *The Emerging British Underclass* (The Institute of Economic Affairs, London, 1990)

Brown, M. and Madge, N. *Despite the Welfare State* (Heinemann, London, 1982)

Brown, R. (ed.) *Knowledge, Education and Cultural Change* (Tavistock, London, 1973)

Bruce, S. *Rise and Fall of the New Christian Right in America* (Clarendon Press, Oxford, 1988). 'Religion in the modern world' in M. Haralambos (ed.) *Developments in Sociology* vol. 8 (Causeway Press, Ormskirk, 1992)

Bruegel, I. 'Women as a reserve army of labour: a note on recent British experience' *Feminist Review* no. 3 (1979)

Bryman, A. *Quantity and Quality in Social Research* (Unwin Hyman, London, 1988)

Bryson, V. *Feminist Political Theory. An Introduction* (Macmillan, London, 1992)

Buckle, A. and Farrington, D.P. 'An observational study of shoplifting', *British Journal of Criminology* vol. 24, no. 1 (1984)

Budge, L., McKay, D. and Marsh, D. *The New British Political System* (Longman, London, 1983)

Bulmer, M. (ed.) 'Sociological research methods. An introduction' in *The Historical Study of Family Structure* (Macmillan, London, 1977). *Working-Class Images of Society* (Routledge & Kegan Paul, London, 1975)

Burawoy, M. *Manufacturing Consent* (University of Chicago Press, Chicago, 1979)

Burgess, R.G. 'Education: an agenda for change' in M. Haralambos (ed.) *Developments in Sociology* vol. 10 (Causeway Press, Ormskirk, 1994)

Burgoyne, J. and Clark, D. 'Reconstituted families' in R.N. Rapoport *et al.* (eds) (1982)

Burgoyne, J. and Clark, D. *Making a Go of It: A Study of Stepfamilies in Sheffield* (Routledge & Kegan Paul, London, 1984)

Burnham, J. *The Managerial Revolution* (Putman & Co, London, 1943)

Burns, T. 'Leisure in industrial society' in Smith, Parker and Smith (1973)

Burns, T. (ed.) *Industrial Man* (Penguin, Harmondsworth, 1969)

Burns, T. and Stalker, G.M. *The Management of Innovation* 2nd edn (Tavistock, London, 1966)

Burton, D. 'Gender relations at work in Britain' in A. Warde and N. Abercrombie (eds) *Stratification and Social Inequality: Studies in British Society* (Framework Press, Lancaster, 1994)

Butler, D.E. and Rose, R. *The British General Election of 1959* (Frank Cass, London, 1960)

Butler, D. and Stokes, D. *Political Change in Britain* (Macmillan, London, 1974)

Butterworth, E. and Weir, D. (eds) *The Sociology of Modern Britain* rev. edn (Fontana, Glasgow, 1975)

Campbell, A. *Delinquent Girls* (Basil Blackwell, Oxford, 1981)

Caplan, L. (ed.) *Studies in Religious Fundamentalism* (Macmillan, London, 1987)

Caplovitz, D. *The Poor Pay More* (The Free Press, New York, 1963)

Caplow, T. *The Sociology of Work* (McGraw-Hill, New York, 1954)

Carlen, P. *Women, Crime and Poverty* (Open University Press, Milton Keynes, 1988)

Carlen, P. and Cook, D. (eds) *Paying for Crime* (Open University Press, Milton Keynes, 1989)

Carson, W.G. 'White-collar crime and the enforcement of factory legislation' in Carson and Wiles (1971)

Carson, W.G. and Wiles, P. (eds) *Crime and Delinquency in Britain* (Martin Robertson, London, 1971)

Cashmore, E.E. 'Rewriting the script' *New Society* (December 1985). *United Kingdom?* (Unwin Hyman, London, 1989). *The Logic of Racism* (Allen & Unwin, London, 1987)

Castles, S. and Kosack, G.C. *Immigrant Workers and Class Structure in Western Europe* (Oxford University Press, Oxford, 1973)

Castles, S. and Miller, M.J. *The Age of Migration* (Macmillan, London, 1993)

Centre for Contemporary Cultural Studies (eds) *Women Take Issue* (Hutchinson, London, 1978). *The Empire Strikes Back* (Hutchinson, London, 1983). *Unpopular Education* (Hutchinson, London, 1981)

Chambliss, W. *On the Take: From Petty Crooks to Presidents* (Indiana University Press, Bloomington, 1978)

Chambliss, W.J. 'Functional and conflict theories of crime' and 'The state and criminal law' and 'Vice, corruption, bureaucracy and power' in Chambliss and Mankoff (1976)

Chambliss, W.J. and Mankoff, M. *Whose Law? What Order?* (John Wiley & Sons, New York, 1976)

Chandler. J. *Women Without Husbands. An Exploration of the Margins of Marriage* (Macmillan, London, 1991). 'Women outside marriage' *Sociology Review* (April 1993)

Charles, N. *Gender Divisions and Social Change* (Harvester Wheatsheaf, Hemel Hempstead, 1993)

Chester, R. 'Divorce' in Butterworth and Weir (1975)

Chester, R. 'The rise of the neo-conventional family' *New Society* (9 May 1985)

Child, J. and Macmillan, B. 'Managers and their leisure' in Smith, Parker and Smith (1973)

Cicourel, A.V. *The Social Organization of Juvenile Justice* (Heinemann, London, 1976)

Cicourel, A.V. and Kitsuse, J.I. *The Educational Decision-Makers* (Bobbs-Merrill, Indianapolis, 1963). 'The social organization of the high school and deviant adolescent careers' in Cosin, Dale, Esland and Swift (1971)

Clark, J., McLoughlin, I., Rose, H. and King, R. *The Process of Technological Change* (Cambridge University Press, Cambridge, 1988)

Clark, J., Modgil, C. and Modgil, S. (eds) *John H. Goldthorpe: Consensus and Controversy* (Falmer Press, Basingstoke, 1990)

Clarke, J. and Willis, P. 'Introduction' in Inge Bates *et al.* (1984)

Clarke, J. and Critcher, C. *The Devil Makes Work: Leisure in Capitalist Britain* (Macmillan, London, 1985)

Clayre, A. *Work and Play* (Weidenfeld & Nicolson, London, 1974)

Clegg, S.R. *Modern Organizations* (Sage, London, 1990). 'Modern and postmodern organizations' *Sociology Review* vol. 1, no. 4 (1992)

Clegg, S.R. and Dunkerley, D. *Organization, Class and Control* (Routledge & Kegan Paul, London, 1980)

Clement, B. 'Whitehall drive on equality "has ground to a halt"' *The Independent* (5 November 1994)

Clinard, M.B. *Sociology of Deviant Behavior* 4th edn (Holt, Rinehart & Winston, New York, 1974)

Cloward, R.A. and Ohlin, L.E. *Delinquency and Opportunity* (The Free Press, Glencoe, 1961)

Coard, B. *How the West Indian Child is Made Educationally Sub-normal in the British School System* (New Beacon Books, London, 1971)

Coates, D. *The Context of British Politics* (Hutchinson, London, 1984)

Coates, K. and Silburn, R. *Poverty: The Forgotten Englishmen* (Penguin, Harmondsworth, 1970)

Cohen, A.K. *Delinquent Boys* (The Free Press, Glencoe, 1955). *Deviance and Control* (Prentice-Hall, Englewood Cliffs, 1966)

Cohen, P. 'Against the new vocationalism' in I. Bates *et al.* (1984)

Cohen, S. (ed.) *Images of Deviance* (Penguin, Harmondsworth, 1971)

Cohen, S. and Taylor, L. *Psychological Survival: The Experience of Long-Term Imprisonment* (Penguin, Harmondsworth, 1971)

Cohn, N. *The Pursuit of the Millennium* (Secker & Warburg, London, 1957)

Collins, P. H. *Black Feminist Thought* (Unwin Hyman, London, 1990)

Collins, R. 'Functional and conflict theories of educational stratification' in Cosin (1972)

Colquhoun, R. 'Values, socialization and achievement' in Beck, Jenks, Keddie and Young (1976)

Comte, A. *The Positive Philosophy* (Bell & Sons, London, 1986)

Connor, S. *Postmodernist Culture* (Blackwell 1989)

Coon, C.S. *The Hunting Peoples* (Jonathan Cape, London, 1972)

Coontz, S. and Henderson, P. (eds) *Women's Work. Men's Property* (Verso, London, 1986)

Cooper, D. *The Death of the Family* (Penguin, Harmondsworth, 1972)

Corrigan, P. *Schooling the Smash Street Kids* (Macmillan, London, 1981)

Coser, L.A. *Masters of Sociological Thought* 2nd edn (Harcourt Brace Jovanovich, New York, 1977)

Coser, L.A. and Rosenberg, B. (eds) *Sociological Theory: A Book of Readings* 4th edn (Macmillan, New York, 1976)

Cosin, B.R. (ed.) *Education: Structure and Society* (Penguin, Harmondsworth, 1972)

Cosin, B.R., Dale, I.R., Esland, G.M. and Swift, D.F. (eds) *School and Society* (Routledge & Kegan Paul, London, 1971)

Cox, O.C. *Caste, Class and Race* (Monthly Review Press, New York, 1970)

Coyle, A. *Redundant Women* (The Women's Press, London, 1984)

Craft, M. (ed.) *Family, Class and Education* (Longman, London, 1970)

Craib, I. *Modern Social Theory* (Wheatsheaf Books, Brighton, 1984)

Crewe, I. 'The disturbing truth behind Labour's rout' *Guardian* (13 June 1983). 'The grim challenge of the ballot box' *Guardian* (1 October 1988). 'A new class of politics' *Guardian* (16 June 1987). 'Tories prosper from a paradox' *Guardian* (15 June 1987). 'On the death and resurrection of class voting: some comments on how Britain votes' *Political Studies* (1986).'Why did Labour lose (yet again)? *Politics Review* (September 1992) 'Changing votes and unchanging voters' *Electoral Studies* (December 1992)

Criddle, B. 'Candidates' in David Butler and Dennis Kavanagh (eds) *The British General Election of 1987* (Macmillan, London, 1988)

Critcher, C., Dicks, B. and Waddington, D. 'Portrait of despair' *New Statesman and Society* (23 October 1992)

Crompton, R. *Class and Stratification: An Introduction to Current Debates* (Blackwell, Oxford, 1993)

Crompton, R. and Jones, G. *White-Collar Proletariat. Deskilling and Gender in Clerical Work* (Macmillan, London, 1984)

Crompton, R. and Sanderson, K. *Gendered Jobs and Social Change* (Unwin Hyman, London, 1990)

Cross, M. 'Generating the "new" poverty: a European comparison' in R. Simpson and R. Walker (eds) *Europe: For Richer or Poorer?* (Child Poverty Action Group, London, 1993)

Crossland, A. *Future of Socialism* (Cape, London, 1981)

Curtin, P.D. *The Image of Africa* (Macmillan, London, 1965)

Dahl, R.A. *Who Governs?* (Yale University Press, New Haven, 1961). *Modern Political Analysis* 4th edn (Prentice-Hall, New Jersey, 1984). 'A critique of the ruling elite model' in Urry and Wakeford (1973)

Dahrendorf, R. *Class and Class Conflict in an Industrial Society* (Routledge & Kegan Paul, London, 1959). 'The erosion of citizenship and its consequences for us all' *New Statesman* (12 June 1987). 'Footnotes to the discussion' in D.J. Smith (ed.) *Understanding the Underclass* (Policy Studies Institute, London, 1992)

Dale, R. 'Examining the gift-horse's teeth: a tentative analysis of TVEI' in Stephen Walker and Jen Barton *Youth, Unemployment and Schooling* (Open University Press, Milton Keynes, 1986)

Dalla Costa, M. and James, S. *The Power of Women and the Subversion of the Communists* (Falling Wall Press, Bristol, 1973)

Daniel, W.W. and Millward, N. *Workplace Industrial Relations in Britain, The DE/PS1/SSRC Survey* (Heinemann, London, 1983)

Darwin, C. *On the Origin of Species* (Penguin, Harmondsworth, 1968, first published 1859)

Davie, G. 'Religion' in M. Haralambos (ed.) *Developments in Sociology* vol. 5 (Causeway Press, Ormskirk, 1989)

Davis, F. 'Deviance disavowal' in Lindesmith, Strauss and Denzin (1975)

Davis, K. *Human Society* (Macmillan, New York, 1948)

Davis, K. and Moore, W.E. 'Some principles of stratification' in Bendix and Lipset (1967)

Deakin, N. 'Mr Murray's Ark' in C. Murray, *The Emerging British Underclass* (The Institute of Economic Affairs, London, 1990)

Deal, T. and Kennedy, A. *Corporate Cultures* (Penguin, London, 1982)

Dean, H. 'In search of the underclass' in P. Brown and R. Scase (eds) *Poor Work: Disadvantage and the Division of Labour* (Open University Press, Milton Keynes, 1991)

Dean, H. and Taylor-Gooby, P. *Dependency Culture: The Explosion of a Myth* (Harvester Wheatsheaf, Hemel Hempstead, 1992)

Deckard, B.S. *The Women's Movement* (Harper & Row, New York, 1975)

Delamont, S. 'Beyond Flanders' fields: the relationship of subject matter and individuality to classroom style' in M. Stubbs and S. Delamont (eds) *Explorations in Classroom Observation* (Wiley, Chichester, 1976)

Delphy, C. *Close to Home* (Hutchinson, London, 1984)

Delphy, C. and Leonard, D. *Familiar Exploitation* (Polity Press, Cambridge, 1992)

Deming, W.E. 'On errors in surveys' in Franklin and Osborne (1971)

Dennis, N. 'Relationships' in Butterworth and Weir (1975)

Dennis, N., Henriques, F. and Slaughter, C. *Coal is our Life* (Eyre & Spottiswoode, London, 1956)

Desai, M. 'Drawing the line: on defining the poverty threshold' in P. Golding (ed.) *Excluding the Poor* (Child Poverty Action Group, London, 1986)

Deutscher, I. 'Asking questions (and listening to answers)' in Bulmer (1977)

Devine, F. *Affluent Workers Revisited* (Edinburgh University Press, Edinburgh, 1992). '"Affluent workers" revisited' *Sociology Review* vol. 3 (February 1994)

Dewey, J. *Democracy and Education: An Introduction to the Philosophy of Education* (Macmillan, New York, 1953)

Dhondy, F. 'The Black explosion in schools' *Race Today* (February 1974)

DHSS *Inequalities in Health: Report of a Research Working Group* (1981)

van Dijk, T.A. *Racism and the Press* (Routledge, London, 1991)

Ditton, J. *Part-time Crime* (Macmillan, London, 1977)

Djilas, M. *The New Class* (Thames & Hudson, London, 1957)

Dollard, J. *Caste and Class in a Southern Town* (Doubleday, New York, 1957)

Dollard, J. et al. *Frustration and Aggression* (Yale University Press, New Haven, 1939)

Donald, J. and Rattansi, A. (eds) *'Race' Culture and Difference* (Sage, London, 1992)

Douglas, J.D. (ed.) *Understanding Everyday Life* (Routledge & Kegan Paul, London, 1971). *The Social Meanings of Suicide* (Princeton, 1967)

Douglas, J.W.B. *The Home and the School* (MacGibbon & Kee, London, 1964)

Douglas, J.W.B., Ross, J.M. and Simpson, H.R. *Natural Symbols* (Barrie & Jenkins, London, 1970)

Downes, D. *The Delinquent Solution* (Routledge & Kegan Paul, London, 1966)

Downes, D. and Rock, P. *Understanding Deviance* 2nd edn (Clarendon Press, Oxford, 1988)

Dowse, R.E. and Hughes, J.A. *Political Sociology* (John Wiley & Sons, London, 1972)

Driver, G. 'West Indian families: an anthropological perspective' in R.N. Rapoport *et al.* (eds) (1982)

Driver, G. and Ballard, R. 'Contemporary performance in multiracial schools: South Asian pupils at 16 plus' in A. James and R. Jeffcoats (eds) (1981)

Dumazedier, J. *Towards a Society of Leisure* (Collier-Macmillan, London, 1967)

Duncan, J.G. and Rodgers, W. 'Lone-parent families and their economic problems: transitory or persistent?' in Organisation For Economic Co-operation and Development *Lone-Parent Families: The Economic Challenge* (OCDE, Paris, 1990)

Durcan, J., McCarthy, W.E.J. and Redman, G.P. *Strikes in Post-War Britain* (Allen & Unwin, London, 1983)

Durkheim, E. *The Rules of Sociological Method* (The Free Press, New York, 1938). *The Division of Labour in Society* (The Free Press, New York, 1947). *Professional Ethics and Civic Morals* (Routledge & Kegan Paul, London, 1957). *Moral Education* (The Free Press, Glencoe, 1961). *The Elementary Forms of the Religious Life* (Collier Books, New York, 1961). *Suicide: A Study in Sociology* (Routledge & Kegan Paul, London, 1970)

Dye, T.R. and Zeigler, L.H. *The Irony of Democracy* 3rd edn (Duxbury Press, North Scituate, 1975)

Edgell, S. *Middle-class Couples* (Allen & Unwin, London, 1980). *Class* (Routledge, London, 1993)

Edwards, P.K. and Scullion, H. *The Social Organization of Industrial Conflict. Control and Resistance in the Workplace* (Blackwell, Oxford, 1982)

Edwards, R. *Contested Terrain, the Transformation of the Workplace in the Twentieth Century* (Heinemann, London, 1979)

Eglin, P. 'The meaning and use of official statistics' in Anderson, Hughes and Sharrock (1987)

Ehrenreich, B. and J. 'The professional-managerial class' in Pat Walker (ed.) *Between Labour and Capital* (Harvester Press, Sussex, 1979)

Ehrhardt, D.A. 'Early androgen stimulation and aggressive behaviour in male and female mice' in *Physiology and Behaviour* no. 4 (1969)

Eichler, M. *The Double Standard. A Feminist Critique of Feminist Social Science* (Croom Helm, London, 1980)

Eisenstadt, S.N. 'The Protestant ethic thesis' in Robertson (1969)

Eggleston, J. (ed.) *Contemporary Research in the Sociology of Education* (Methuen, London, 1974)

Elliott, J.E. 'Demographic trends in domestic life, 1945–87' in D. Clark (ed.) *Marriage, Domestic Life and Social Change* (Routledge, London, 1991)

Engels, F. *The Origin of the Family, Private Property and the State* (Lawrence & Wishart, London, 1972). 'On the history of early christianity' in Birnbaum and Lenzer (1969).*The Condition of the Working Class in England in 1844* (Progress Publishers, Moscow, 1973)

Eriksen, T.H. *Ethnicity and Nationalism* (Pluto Press, London, 1993)

Esland, G. 'Professions and professionalism' in G. Esland and G. Salamon (eds) *The Politics of Work and Occupations* (Open University Press, Milton Keynes, 1980)

Etzioni, A. *Modern Organizations* (Prentice-Hall, Englewood Cliffs, 1964)

Etzioni, A. (ed.) *A Sociological Reader on Complex Organizations* 2nd edn (Holt, Rinehart & Winston, New York, 1969)

Evans, M. (ed.) *The Woman Question* (Fontana, London, 1982)

Evans Pritchard, E.E. *Social Anthropology* (Cohen & West, London, 1951)

Eversley, D. and Bonnerjea, L. 'Social change and indications of diversity' in R.N. Rapoport *et al.* (eds) (1982)

Eysenck, H. *Crime and Personality* (Routledge & Kegan Paul, London, 1964). *Race, Intelligence and Education* (Temple Smith, London, 1971)

Fagin, L. and Little, M. *The Forsaken Families* (Penguin, Harmondsworth, 1984)

Faludi, S. *Backlash: The Undeclared War Against Women* (Chatto & Windus, London, 1992)

Farrington, D.P. and Morris, A.M. 'Sex, sentencing and reconviction' *British Journal of Criminology* vol. 23, no 3 (1983)

Feeley, D. 'The family' in L. Jenness (ed.) *Feminism and Socialism* (Pathfinder Press, New York, 1972)

Field, F. 'What is poverty?' *New Society* (25 September 1975). *Poverty Politics* (Heinemann, London, 1982). 'No thought for human indignity' *The Independent* (3 February 1993). *Losing Out: The Emergence of Britain's Underclass* (Blackwell, Oxford, 1989)

Field, M.G. 'Workers (and mothers): Soviet women today' in D.R. Brown (ed.) *Women in the Soviet*

Union (Teachers College Press, New York, 1968)

Fildes, S. 'Gender' in M. Haralambos (ed.) *Developments in Sociology* vol. 4 (Causeway Press, Ormskirk, 1988)

Filmer, P., Phillipson, M., Silverman, D. and Walsh, D. *New Directions in Sociological Theory* (Collier Macmillan, London, 1972)

Finch, J. *Family Obligations and Social Change* (Polity Press, Cambridge, 1989)

Finn, D. *Training Without Jobs* (Macmillan, London, 1987). 'Leaving school and growing up' in I. Bates *et al.* (1984)

Firestone, S. *The Dialectic of Sex* (Paladin, London, 1972)

Fletcher, R. *The Family and Marriage in Britain* (Penguin, Harmondsworth, 1966)

Fletcher, R. *The Shaking of the Foundations. Family and Society* (Routledge, London, 1988)

Flude, M. 'Sociological accounts of differential educational attainment' in Flude and Ahier (1974)

Flude, M. and Ahier, J. (eds) *Educability, Schools and Ideology* (Croom Helm, London, 1974)

The Frankfurt Institute for Social Research *Aspects of Sociology* (Heinemann, London, 1973)

Friedman, A. *Industry and Labour: Class Struggle at Work and Monopoly Capitalism* (Macmillan, London, 1977)

Friedman, N.L. 'Cultural deprivation: a commentary on the sociology of knowledge' in Beck, Jenks, Keddie and Young (1976)

Fuller, M. 'Black girls in a London comprehensive school' in M. Hammersley and P. Woods (eds) (1984)

Furlong, V.J. 'Interaction sets in the classroom: towards a study of pupil knowledge' in M. Hammersley and P. Woods (eds) (1984)

Gallie, D. *In Search of the New Working Class* (Cambridge University Press, Cambridge, 1978). 'Employment, unemployment and social stratification' in D. Gallie (ed.) *Employment in Britain* (Blackwell, Oxford, 1988)

Gans, H.J. 'The Negro family: reflections on the Moynihan Report' in Rainwater and Yancey (1967). 'Culture and class in the study of poverty: an approach to anti-poverty research' in Moynihan (1968). 'Poverty and culture: some basic questions about methods of studying life-styles of the poor' in Townsend (1970). *More Equality* (Pantheon, New York, 1973)

Garfinkel, H. *Studies in Ethnomethodology* (Prentice-Hall, Englewood Cliffs, 1967)

Gavron, H. *The Captive Wife* (Routledge & Kegan Paul, London, 1966)

Gershuny, J. 'Changes in the domestic division of labour in the UK 1975–87: dependent labour versus adaptive partnership' in N. Abercrombie and A. Warde (eds) (1992)

Gerth, H.H. and Mills, C.W. *Character and Social Structure* (Harcourt Brace, New York, 1953)

Gerth, H.H. and Mills, C.W. (eds) *From Max Weber, Essays in Sociology* (Routledge & Kegan Paul, London, 1948)

Ghaill, M.M. 'Coming of age in 1980s England: reconceptualizing black students' schooling experience' in D. Gill, B. Mayor and M. Blair (eds) *Racism and Education: Structures and Strategies* (Sage, London, 1992)

Gibbons, D.C. and Jones, J.F. *The Study of Deviance* (Prentice-Hall, Englewood Cliffs, 1975)

Gibbs, J. 'Issues in defining deviant behaviour' in R.A. Scott and J.D. Douglas (eds) *Theoretical Perspectives on Deviance* (Basic Books, New York, 1972)

Gibbs, J. and Martin, W. *Status Integration and Suicide* (University of Oregon Press, Oregon, 1964)

Giddens, A. '"Power" in the recent writings of Talcott Parsons' in Worsley (1970). *The Class Structure of the Advanced Societies* (Hutchinson, London, 1973). *New Rules of Sociological Method* (Hutchinson, London, 1976).*Studies in Social and Political Theory* (Hutchinson, London, 1977). *Central Problems in Social Theory* (Macmillan, London, 1979). *The Constitution of Society* (Polity Press, Cambridge, 1984)

Giddens, A. and Turner, J.H. (eds) *Social Theory Today* (Polity Press, Cambridge, 1987)

Giglioli, P.P. (ed.) *Language and Social Context* (Penguin, Harmondsworth, 1972)

Giles, C., and Johnson, P. *Taxes Down, Taxes Up: The Effects of a Decade of Tax Changes* (The Institute for Fiscal Studies, London, 1994)

Giles, C. and Webb, S. *Poverty Statistics: A Guide for the Perplexed* (The Institute for Fiscal Studies, London, 1993)

Gill, C. *Work, Unemployment and the New Technology* (Polity Press, Cambridge, 1985)

Gill, D., Mayor, B. and Blair, M. (eds) *Racism and Education: Structures and Strategies* (Sage, London, 1992)

Gilmore, D.D. *Manhood in the Making: Cultural Concepts of Masculinity* (Yale University Press, New Haven, 1990)

Gilroy, P. 'Police and thieves' in Centre for Contemporary Cultural Studies *The Empire Strikes Back*, (Hutchinson, London, 1983). 'The myth of black criminality' in *Socialist Register* (Marlin Press, London). *There Ain't No Black in the Union Jack* (Hutchinson, London, 1987). 'The end of antiracism' in J. Donald and A. Rattansi (1992)

Giroux, H. 'Ideology, agency and the process of schooling' in L. Barton and S. Walker (eds) (1984)

Gitlins, D. *The Family in Question* (Macmillan, London, 1985)

Gladwin, T. *Poverty USA* (Little Brown, Boston, 1967)

Glaser, B. and Strauss, A. *The Discovery of Grounded Theory* (Adline, Chicago, 1967)

Glasgow University Media Group, *Bad News* (Routledge & Kegan Paul, London, 1980)

Glasner, P. *The Sociology of Secularisation* (Routledge & Kegan Paul, London, 1977)

Glass, D.V. (ed.) *Social Mobility in Britain* (Routledge & Kegan Paul, London, 1954)

Glass, D.V. and Hall, J.R. 'Social mobility in Britain: a study of intergenerational changes in status' in Glass (1954)

Glazer-Malbin, N. and Waehrer, H.Y. (eds) *Woman in a Man-Made World* (Rand McNally, Chicago, 1972)

Glock, C.Y. *Religion and the Face of America* (University of California Press, Berkeley, 1958)

Glock, C.Y. and Bellah, R.N. (eds) *The New Religious Consciousness* (University of California Press, Berkeley, 1976)

Glock, C.Y. and Stark, R. *Religion and Society in Tension* (Rand McNally, Chicago, 1965). 'Dimensions of religious commitment' in Robertson (1969)

Glover, D. and Strawbridge, S. 'The sociology of knowledge' in M. Haralambos (ed.) *Sociology New Directions* (Causeway Press, Ormskirk, 1985)

Gluckman, M. 'Preface' in Bott (1971)

Glyn, A. and Harrison, J. *The British Economic Disaster* (Pluto Press, London, 1980)

Goffman, E. *Asylums* (Penguin, Harmondsworth, 1968)

Golding, P. and Middleton, S. 'Why is the press so obsessed with welfare scroungers?' *New Society* (26 October 1978)

Goldstein, H. 'Gender bias and test norms in educational selection' in M. Arnot and G. Weiner (1987)

Goldthorpe, J.H. 'Social stratification in industrial society' in Bendix and Lipset (1967). Review article 'A revolution in sociology?' *Sociology* (September 1973). Correspondence 'A rejoinder to Benson' *Sociology* (January 1974). 'The current inflation: towards a sociological account' in J.H. Goldthorpe and F. Hirsch (eds) *The Political Economy of Inflation* (Martin Robertson, London, 1978). *Social Mobility and Class Structure in Modern Britain* (Clarendon Press, Oxford, 1980). 'Women and class analysis: in defence of the conventional view' *Sociology* no. 14 (1983)

Goldthorpe, J.H. and Llewellyn, C. 'Class mobility in modern Britain: three theses examined' *Sociology* (May 1977). 'Class mobility' *British Journal of Sociology* (September 1977)

Goldthorpe, J.H., Llewellyn, C. and Payne, C. *Social Mobility and Class Structure in Modern Britain* 2nd edition (Clarendon, Oxford, 1987)

Goldthorpe, J.H., Lockwood, D., Bechhofer, F. and Platt, J. *The Affluent Worker: Industrial Attitudes and Behaviour* and *The Affluent Worker: Political Attitudes and Behaviour* and *The Affluent Worker in the Class Structure* (Cambridge University Press, Cambridge, 1968 and 1969)

Goldthorpe, J.H. and Payne, C. 'On the class mobility of women' *Sociology* vol. 20 (1986). 'Trends in integenerational mobility in England and Wales, 1979–83' *Sociology* vol. 20 (1986)

Gomm, R. 'Science and values' in R. Gomm and P. McNeill *Handbook for Sociology Teachers* (Heinemann, London, 1982)

González, N.L. 'Toward a definition of matrifocality' in N.W. Whitten and J.F. Szwed (eds) *Afro-American Anthropology* (The Free Press, New York, 1970)

Goode, W.J. *World Revolution and Family Patterns* (The Free Press, New York, 1963). 'A sociological perspective on marital dissolution' in Anderson (1971)

Goodman, A. and Webb, S. *For Richer, For Poorer* (Institute for Fiscal Studies, London, 1994)

Gordon, D.M. 'Class and the economics of crime' in Chambliss and Mankoff (1976)

Gordon, L. 'Paul Willis – education, cultural production and social reproduction' *British Journal of Sociology of Education* vol. 5, no. 2 (1984)

Gorz, A. 'Work and consumption' in P. Anderson and R. Blackburn (eds) *Towards Socialism* (Collins, London, 1965)

Goss, M.E.W. 'Influence and authority among physicians in an outpatient clinic' in Etzioni (1969)

Gough, E. 'Is the family universal? The Nayor case' in N.W. Bell and E.F. Vogel (eds) *A Modern Introduction to the Family* (Collier-Macmillan, London, 1959)

Gough, K. 'An anthropologist looks at Engels' in Glazer-Malbin and Waehrer (1972)

Gouldner, A.W. *Patterns of Industrial Bureaucracy* (The Free Press, Glencoe, 1954). *Wildcat Strike* (Routledge & Kegan Paul, London, 1957). *The Coming Crisis of Western Sociology* (Heinemann, London, 1971). 'Bureaucracy is not inevitable' in Worsley (1972). *For Sociology* (Penguin, Harmondsworth, 1975)

Goy, R. and Phoenix, C.H. 'The effects of testosterone propionate administered before birth on the development of behaviour in genetic female rhesus monkeys' in C.H. Sawyer and R.A. Gorski (eds) *Steroid Hormones and Brain Function* (University of California Press, Berkeley, 1971)

Grafton, T., Miller, H., Smith, L., Vegoda, M. and Whitfield, R. 'Gender and curriculum choice' in M. Arnot and G. Weiner (1987)

Graham, E. 'The politics of poverty' in Roach and Roach (1972)

Graham, J.M. 'Amphetamine politics on Capitol Hill' in Chambliss and Mankoff (1976)

Gramsci, A. *Selections from the Prison Notebooks* (Lawrence & Wishart, London, 1971)

Grant, W. and Marsh, D. *The Confederation of British Industry* (Hodder & Stoughton, London, 1977)

Gray, J.A. and Buffery, A.W.H. 'Sex differences in emotional and cognitive behaviour in mammals including man: adaptive and neural bases' *Acta Psychologia* no. 35 (1971)

Greeley, A. *Unsecular Man: The Persistence of Religion* (Shocken Books, New York, 1972)

Green, E., Hebron, S. and Woodward, D. *Women's Leisure, What Leisure?* (Macmillan, London, 1990)

Grint, K. *The Sociology of Work: An Introduction* (Polity Press, Cambridge, 1991). 'The sociology of work' in M. Haralambos (ed.) *Developments in Sociology* vol. 8 (Causeway Press, Ormskirk, 1992)

Grint, K. and Woolgar, S. 'Computers, guns, and roses: what's social about being shot?' *Science, Technology and Human Values* vol. 17, no. 3 (1992)

Guttsman, W.L. *The British Political Elite* rev. edn (MacGibbon & Kee, London, 1968). 'The British political elite and the class structure' in Stanworth and Giddens (1974)

Habermas, J. *The Theory of Communicative Action* vol. 1 (Heinemann, London, 1984)

Habermas, J. *Legitimation Crisis* (Heinemann, London, 1976)

Hacker, A. 'The social and economic power of corporations' in Wrong and Gracey (1967). 'Power to do what?' in Lopreato and Lewis (1974)

Hacker, H.M. 'Women as a minority group' in Glazer-Malbin and Waehrer (1972)

Halbwachs, M. *Les Causes de Suicide* (Alcan, Paris, 1930)

Hall, E.T. *The Hidden Dimension* (Doubleday, New York, 1966). *The Silent Language* (Doubleday, New York, 1973)

Hall, S. 'Our mongrel selves' *New Statesman and Society* (19 June 1992)

Hall, S., Critcher, C., Jefferson, T., Clarke, J. and Roberts, B. *Policing the Crisis* (Macmillan, London, 1979)

Halmos, P. *The Personal Service Society* (Constable, London, 1970)

Halsey, A.H. 'Government against poverty in school and community' in Wedderburn (1974). 'The EPAs and their schools' in Eggleston (1974). 'Towards meritocracy? The case of Britain' in Karabel and Halsey (1977). 'Whatever happened to positive discrimination' *The Times Educational Supplement* (21 January 1977)

Halsey, A.H., Floud, J. and Anderson, C.A. *Education, Economy and Society* (The Free Press, New York, 1961)

Halsey, A.H., Heath, A. and Ridge, J.M. *Origins and Destinations* (Clarendon Press, Oxford, 1980)

Hammersley, M. 'Staffroom racism' (unpublished manuscript)

Hammersley, M. and Turner, G. 'Conformist pupils' in M. Hammersley and P. Woods (eds) (1984)

Hammersley, M. and Woods, P. (eds) *Life in School, the Sociology of Pupil Culture* (Open University Press, Milton Keynes, 1984)

Hammersley, M. and Woods, P. (eds) *The Process of Schooling* (Routledge & Kegan Paul, London, 1976)

Hannerz, U. *Soulside: Inquiries into Ghetto Culture and Community* (Columbia University Press, New York, 1969)

Haralambos, M. *Right On: From Blues to Soul in Black America* (Eddison Press, London, 1974)

Haralambos, M. (ed.) *Developments in Sociology* vol. 5 (Causeway Press, Ormskirk, 1989)

Hargreaves, A. 'Resistance and relative autonomy theories: problems of distortion and incoherence in recent Marxist analyses of education' *British Journal of Sociology of Education* vol. 3, no. 2 (1982)

Hargreaves, D.H. *Social Relations in a Secondary School* (Routledge & Kegan Paul, London, 1967). 'Reactions to labelling' in Hammersley and Woods (1976). *The Challenge for the Comprehensive School* (Routledge & Kegan Paul, London, 1982)

Hargreaves, D., Hestar, S. and Mellor, F. *Deviance in Classrooms* (Routledge & Kegan Paul, London, 1975)

Harrington, M. *The Other America: Poverty in the United States* (Penguin, Harmondsworth, 1963)

Harris, C.C. *The Family* and *The Family and Industrial Society* (Allen & Unwin, London, 1969 and 1983)

Harris, N. *Beliefs in Society* (Penguin, Harmondsworth, 1971)

Hart, N. *When Marriage Ends: A Study in Status Passage* (Tavistock, London, 1976)

Hartmann, H. 'The unhappy marriage of Marxism and feminism: toward a more progressive union' in Lydia Sargent (ed.) *The Unhappy Marriage of Marxism and Feminism: A Debate on Class and Patriarchy* (Pluto Press, London, 1981). 'Capitalism, patriarchy, and job segregation by sex' in M. Blaxall and B. Reagan *Women and the Workplace* (University of Chicago Press, Chicago, 1976)

Hartmann, P. and Husband, C. *Racism and the Mass Media* (Davis-Poynter, London, 1974)

Harvey, D. *The Condition of Postmodernity* (Blackwell, 1990)

Hawkins, K. *Unemployment* 2nd edn (Penguin, Harmondsworth, 1984)

Hazelrigg, L.E. 'Cross-national comparisons of father-to-son occupational mobility' in Lopreato and Lewis (1974)

Hearn, J. and Morgan, D.H.J. 'Men, masculinities and social theory' in J. Hearn and D.H.J Morgan (eds) *Men, Masculinities and Social Theory* (Unwin Hyman, London, 1990)

Heath, A. *Social Mobility* (Fontana, Glasgow, 1981). 'The attitudes of the underclass' in D.J. Smith (ed.) *Understanding the Underclass* (Policy Studies Institute, London, 1992)

Heath, A., Curtice, J., Evans, G., Jowell, R., Field, J. and Witherspoon, S. *Understanding Political Change* (Pergamon Press, Oxford, 1991)

Heath, A., Jowell, R. and Curtice, J. *How Britain Votes* (Pergamon, Oxford, 1985). 'Trendless fluctuation: a reply to Crewe' *Political Studies* (1987). 'Can Labour win?' in A. Heath, R. Jowell, J. Curtice with B.

Taylor (eds) *Labour's Last Chance?* (Dartmouth Publishing, Aldershot, 1994)

Heath, A. and MacDonald, S. 'Social change and the future of the Left' *Political Quarterly* (October–December 1987)

Heelas, P. 'Sacralization of self and New Age capitalism' in Abercrombie and Warde (1992)

Heidensohn, F. *Women and Crime* (Macmillan, London, 1985)

Heider, K.G. *The Dugum Dani: A Papuan Culture in the Highlands of West New Guinea* (Wenner-Gren Foundation for Anthropological Research, New York, 1970)

Held, D. 'Democracy: from city states to a cosmopolitan order' in D. Held (ed.) *Prospects for Democracy* (Polity Press, Cambridge, 1993)

Henwood, F. and Miles, I. 'Unemployment and the sexual division of labour' in David Fryer and Philip Ullah *Unemployed People* (Open University Press, Milton Keynes, 1987)

Herberg, W. *Protestant – Catholic – Jew* rev. edn (Anchor Books, New York, 1960)

Herskovits, M.J. *The Myth of the Negro Past* (Beacon Press, Boston, 1958)

Hewitt, C.J. 'Elites and the distribution of power in British society' in Stanworth and Giddens (1974)

Hickox, M.S.H. 'The Marxist sociology of education: a critique' *British Journal of Sociology* (December 1982)

Higgins, J. 'Poverty' in M. Haralambos (ed.) *Developments in Sociology* vol. 1 (Causeway Press, Ormskirk, 1985)

Hill, S. *The Dockers* (Heinemann, London, 1976)

Hills, J. *Changing Tax: How the System Works and How to Change It* (Child Poverty Action Group, London, 1984)

Himmelweit, H.T. *et al. How Voters Decide* (Open University Press, Milton Keynes, 1985)

Himmelweit, S. 'Production rules OK? Waged work and the family' in L. Segal (ed.) *What is to be Done About the Family?* (Penguin, Harmondsworth, 1983)

Hite, S. *Hite Report* (Dell Publishing, New York, 1977)

HMSO *Social Trends* (HMSO, London, annually)

Hobsbawm, E.S. *Industry and Empire* (Penguin, Harmondsworth, 1970)

Hobson, D. 'Housewives: isolation as oppression' in Centre for Contemporary Cultural Studies (1978)

Holdaway, S. *Inside the British Police* (Blackwell, Oxford, 1983)

Hood, R. *Race and Sentencing* (Clarendon Press, Oxford, 1992)

Hooks, B. *Ain't I a Woman: Black Women and Feminism* (South End Press, Boston, 1981)

Hosking, G. 'Religion and the atheist state' *The Listener* (8 December 1988)

Hough, M. and Mayhew, P. *Taking Account of Crime: Findings from the Second British Crime Survey* (HMSO, London, 1985). *The British Crime Survey:*

First Report (HMSO, London, 1983)

Howard, J.R. 'The making of a Black Muslim' in R.W. Mack (ed.) *Class and Power* 2nd edn (American Book Company, New York, 1963)

Hudson, K. *The Place of Women in Society* (Ginn, London, 1970)

Hughes, G. 'Taking crime seriously? A critical analysis of New Left realism' *Sociology Review* vol. 1, no 2 (1991)

Hughes, J. 'Bureaucracy' in R.J. Anderson and W.W. Sharrock *Applied Sociological Perspectives* (Allen & Unwin, London, 1984)

Humpheries, J. 'Protective registration, the capitalist state and working class men' *Feminist Review* (Spring 1981). 'Class struggle and the persistence of the working-class family' *Cambridge Journal of Economics* vol. 3 (1977)

Hunter, J.D. *Evangelism: The Coming Generation* (University of Chicago Press, Chicago, 1987)

Husserl, E. *Ideas* (Allen & Unwin, London, 1931)

Hyman, H.H. 'The value systems of different classes' in Bendix and Lipset (1967)

Hyman, R. *Strikes* 3rd edn (Fontana, Aylesbury, 1984)

Illich, I. *Deschooling Society* (Penguin, Harmondsworth, 1973). *Medical Nemesis* (Calder & Boyars, London, 1975)

Imray, L. and Middleton, A. 'Public and private: marking the boundaries' in E. Gamarnikow, D. Morgan *et al.* (eds) *The Public and the Private* (Heinemann, London, 1983)

Irvine, E. *The Family in the Kibbutz* (Study Commission on the Family, London, 1980)

Irvine, J., Miles, I. and Evans, J. (eds) *Demystifying Social Statistics* (Pluto Press, London, 1979)

Irwin, J. *The Felon* (Prentice-Hall, Englewood Cliffs, 1970)

James, A. and Jeffcoate, R. (eds) *The School in the Multicultural Society* (Harper & Row, London, 1981)

James, E. *America Against Poverty* (Routledge & Kegan Paul, London, 1970)

Jencks, C. *Inequality: A Reassessment of the Effect of Family and Schooling in America* (Penguin, Harmondsworth, 1975)

Jenkins, C. and Sherman, B. *The Collapse of Work* (Eyre Methuen, London, 1979)

Jensen, A.R. *Educational Differences* (Methuen, London, 1973)

Jessop, B. *Traditionalism, Conservatism and British Political Culture* (Allen & Unwin, London, 1974). *State Theory* (Pennsylvania State University Press, Pennsylvania, 1990)

Johnson, D. 'Families and educational institutions' in R.N. Rapoport *et al.* (eds) (1982)

Johnson, R. 'A new road to serfdom? A critical history of the 1988 Act' in Department of Cultural Studies, University of Birmingham, *Education Limited: Schooling and Training and the New Right since 1979* (Unwin Hyman, London, 1991)

Johnson, T.J. *Professions and Power* (Macmillan, London, 1972)

Jones, S. 'We are all cousins under the skin' *The Independent* (12 December 1991)

Jones, T. *Britain's Ethnic Minorities* (Policy Studies Institute, London, 1993)

Jones, T., MacLean B. and Young, J. *The Islington Crime Survey* (Gower, Aldershot,1986)

Jordan, B. 'Universal welfare provision creates a dependent population. The case against' *Social Studies Review* (November 1989)

Jowell, R., Brook, L., Prior, G. and Taylor, B. (eds) *British Social Attitudes Survey 9th Annual Report* (Dartmouth Publishing, Aldershot, 1992)

Kaplan, A. *The Conduct of Inquiry* (Chandler Publishing, New York, 1964)

Karabel, J. and Halsey, A.H. (eds) *Power and Ideology in Education* (Oxford University Press, New York, 1977)

Kautsky, K. *Foundations of Christianity* (Russell, New York, 1953)

Kay, T. 'Unemployment' in M. Haralambos (ed.) *Developments in Sociology* vol. 5 (Causeway Press, Ormskirk, 1989)

Kaysen, C. *The Corporation in Modern Society* (Harvard University Press, Cambridge, USA, 1959)

Keat, R. and Urry, J. *Social Theory as Science* 2nd edn (Routledge & Kegan Paul, London, 1982)

Keddie, N. 'Classroom knowledge' in Young *Tinker, Tailor – The Myth of Cultural Deprivation* (Penguin, Harmondsworth, 1973)

Kelley, M.R. 'Alternative forms of work automation under programmable automation' in Stephen Wood (ed.) (1989)

Kellner, P. 'Labour's wilderness year' *New Statesman* (30 October 1981)

Kellner, P. and Wilby, P. 'The 1: 2: 4 rule of class in Britain' *Sunday Times* (13 January 1980)

Kelly, A. *Science for Girls* (Open University Press, Milton Keynes, 1987)

Kelly, H.E. 'Biosociology and crime' in C.R. Jeffery (ed.) *Biology and Crime* (Sage, London)

Kelly, R., Holborn, M. and Makin, J. 'Unit 2: positivistic theories' in Open College of the North West *Criminology Distance Learning Course* (Preston Polytechnic, Preston, 1983)

Kelsall, R.K. 'Recruitment to the higher civil service' in Stanworth and Giddens (1974)

Kelvin, P. and Jarrett, J.E. *Unemployment. Its Social Psychological Effects* (Cambridge University Press, Cambridge, 1985)

Kerr, C., Dunlop, J.T., Harbison, F.H. and Mayers, C.A. *Industrialism and Industrial Man* (Heinemann, London, 1962)

Kerr, C. and Siegel, A. 'The inter-industry propensity to strike' in A. Kornhauser, R. Dubin and A.M. Ross (eds) *Industrial Conflict* (McGraw-Hill, New York, 1954)

Kessler, S.J. and McKenna, W. *Gender: An Ethnomethodological Approach* (John Wiley & Sons, New York, 1978)

Keynes, J.M. *The General Theory of Employment, Interest and Money* (Macmillan, London, 1936)

Kiernan, K. 'Men and women at work and at home' in R.Jowell, L. Brook, G. Prior and B. Taylor (eds) *The British Social Attitudes Survey, the 9th Report* (Dartmouth Publishing, London, 1992)

Kiernan, K. and Wicks, M. *Family Change and Future Policy* (Joseph Rowntree Foundation, York, 1990)

Kimmel, M. 'After fifteen years: the impact of the sociology of masculinity on the masculinity of sociology' in J. Hearn and D.H.J. Morgan (eds) *Men, Masculinities and Social Theory* (Unwin Hyman, London, 1990)

Kincaid, J. 'Poverty and the Welfare State' in Irvine, Miles and Evans (1979)

Kincaid, J.C. *Poverty and Equality in Britain: A Study of Social Security and Taxation* (Penguin, Harmondsworth, 1973)

Kinsey, R., Lea, J. and Young, J. *Losing the Fight Against Crime* (Blackwell, Oxford, 1986)

Klineberg, O. 'Race and IQ' *Courier* (November 1971)

Kling, R. 'Audiences, narratives and human values in social studies of technology' *Science, Technology and Human Values* vol. 17, no. 3 (1992). 'Computerization and social transformations' *Science, Technology and Human Values* vol. 16, no. 3 (1991)

Kluckhohn, C. 'The concept of culture' in D. Lerner and H.D. Lasswell (eds) *The Policy Sciences* (Stanford University Press, Stanford, 1951)

Knutssen, J. *Labelling Theory: A Critical Examination Scientific Reference Group* (National Swedish Council for Crime Prevention, Stockholm, 1977)

Kolko, G. *The Triumph of Conservatism* (The Free Press, New York, 1963). *Railroads and Regulations* (Princeton University Press, Princeton, 1965)

Kuhn, T.S. *The Structure of Scientific Revolutions* (University of Chicago Press, Chicago and London, 1962)

Kumar, K. *Prophecy and Progress: The Sociology of Industrial and Post-Industrial Society* (Penguin, Harmondsworth, 1978)

Labov, W. 'The logic of nonstandard English' in Keddie (1973)

Laing, R.D. *Self and Others* (Penguin, Harmondsworth, 1971). 'Series and nexus in the family' in Worsley *The Politics of the Family* (Penguin, Harmondsworth, 1976)

Laing, R.D. and Esterson, A. *Sanity, Madness and the Family* (Penguin, Harmondsworth, 1970)

Land, H. 'Women: supporters or supported?' in Barker and Allen *Sexual Divisions and Society: Process and Change* (Tavistock, London, 1976)

Lander, B. 'An ecological analysis of Baltimore' in Wolfgang, Savitz and Johnston (1962)

Lane, D. *Politics and Society in the USSR* (Weidenfeld & Nicolson, London, 1970). *The Socialist Industrial State* (Allen & Unwin, London, 1976)

Lane, J.K. *Soviet Economy and Society* (Blackwell, Oxford, 1985)

Lane, T. and Roberts, K. *Strike at Pilkingtons* (Fontana, London, 1971)

La Pierre, R.T. 'Attitudes versus actions' *Social Forces* vol. 13 (1934)

Laslett, P. 'Mean household size in England since the sixteenth century' in Laslett (1972). *Household and Family in Past Time* (ed.) (Cambridge University Press, Cambridge, 1972). *Family Life and Illicit Love in Earlier Generations* (Cambridge University Press, Cambridge, 1977)

Laurance, J. 'Unemployment: health hazards' *New Society* (21 March 1986)

Lawrence, E. 'Just plain common sense: the "roots" of racism' in Centre for Contemporary Cultural Studies (1982). 'In the abundance of water the fool is thirsty: sociology and black pathology' in Centre for Contemporary Cultural Studies (1982)

Lawton, D. *Class, Culture and the Curriculum* (Routledge & Kegan Paul, London, 1975). *Education, Culture and the National Curriculum* (Hodder & Stoughton, London, 1989)

Layton-Henry, Z. *The Politics of Immigration* (Blackwell, Oxford, 1992)

Lea, J. 'The analysis of crime' in Young and Matthews (1992)

Lea, J. and Young, J. *What is to be Done About Law and Order?* (Penguin, Harmondsworth, 1984)

Leach, E.R. *A Runaway World?* (BBC Publications, London, 1967)

Lee, D. and Newby, H. *The Problem of Sociology* (Hutchinson, London, 1983)

Leeds Revolutionary Feminist Group, The 'Political lesbianism: the case against heterosexuality' in M. Evans (ed.) (1982)

Le Grand, J. *Strategy of Equality: Redistribution and the Social Services* (Allen & Unwin, London, 1982). 'The middle-class use of the British social services' in R.E. Goodin and J. Le Grand *Not Only the Poor* (Allen & Unwin, London, 1987)

Lemert, E.M. *Human Deviance, Social Problems, and Social Control* 2nd edn (Prentice-Hall, Englewood Cliffs, 1972)

Lenin, V.I. *Selected Works* (Lawrence & Wishart, London, 1969)

Lessa, W.A. and Vogt, E.Z. *Reader in Comparative Religion: An Anthropological Approach* 2nd edn (Harper & Row, New York, 1965)

Levy, M.J. *The Structure of Society* (Princeton University Press, Princeton, 1952)

Lewis, O. *Five Families* (Basic Books, New York, 1959). *The Children of Sanchez* (Random House, New York, 1961). *La Vida* (Random House, New York, 1966)

Licht, B.G. and Dweck, C.S. 'Some differences in achievement orientations' in M. Arnot and G. Weiner (1987)

Lichtheim, G. *Marxism* 2nd edn (Routledge & Kegan Paul, London, 1964)

Liebow, E. *Tally's Corner* (Little Brown, Boston, 1967)

Lindesmith, A.R., Strauss, A.L. and Denzin, N.K. (eds) *Readings in Social Psychology* 2nd edn (Dryden, Hinsdale, 1975)

Linton, R. 'Present world conditions in cultural perspective' in R. Linton (ed.) *The Science of Man in World Crisis* (Columbia University Press, New York, 1945)

Lipset, S.M. *Agrarian Socialism* (University of California Press, Berkeley, 1950). 'Political sociology' in R.K. Merton *et al.* (eds) *Sociology Today* (Basic Books, New York, 1959). *Political Man* (Mercury Books, London, 1963)

Lipset, S.M., Trow, M. and Coleman, J. *Union Democracy* (The Free Press, Glencoe, 1956)

Lipset, S.M. and Zetterburg, H.L. 'Social mobility in industrial societies' in S.M. Lipset and R. Bendix (eds) *Social Mobility in Industrial Society* (University of California Press, Berkeley, 1959)

Little, K. *West African Urbanization* (Cambridge University Press, Cambridge, 1965)

Littler, C. 'Deskilling and changing structures of control' in S. Wood (1983)

Littler, C.R. and Salaman, G. *Class at Work* (Batsford, London, 1984)

Lobban, G. 'Data report on British reading schemes' *Times Educational Supplement* (1 March 1974)

Lockwood, D. *The Blackcoated Worker* (Allen & Unwin, London, 1958). 'Some remarks on "The social system"' in Worsley (1970). 'Sources of variation in working class images of society' in Bulmer (1975)

Lombroso, C. and Ferrero, W. *The Female Offender* (Philosophical Library, New York, 1958)

Lopreato, J. and Lewis, L.S. *Social Stratification: A Reader* (Harper & Row, New York, 1974)

Luckmann, T. *The Invisible Religion: The Transformation of Symbols in Industrial Society* (Macmillan, New York, 1967)

Lukes, S. *Emile Durkheim: His Life and Work* (Allen Lane, London, 1973). *Power: A Radical View* (Macmillan, London, 1974)

Lupton, T. and Wilson, C.S. 'The social background and connections of "top decision makers"' in Urry and Wakeford (1973)

Lynch, M. *Art and Artefact in Laboratory Science* (Routledge & Kegan Paul, London, 1983)

Lyotard, J.F. *The Postmodern Condition* (Manchester University Press, Manchester, 1984)

McClosky, H. 'Political participation' in *International Encyclopedia of the Social Sciences* (Collier-Macmillan, New York, 1968)

McCulloch, A. 'Alternative households' in R.N. Rapoport *et al.* (eds) (1982)

McDonough, R. and Harrison, R. 'Patriarchy relations of production' in A. Kuhn and A.M. Wolpe (eds) *Feminism and Materialism* (Routledge & Kegan Paul, London, 1978)

McDowell, L. 'Gender divisions in a post-Fordist era: new contradictions or the same old story?' in M. McDowell and R. Pringle (eds) *Defining Women: Social Institutions and Gender Divisions* (Polity Press, Cambridge, 1992)

McGuire, M.B. *Religion, the Social Context* (Wadsworth Publishing, California, 1981)

MacInnes, J. *Thatcherism at Work* (Open University Press, Milton Keynes, 1987)

Mack, J. and Lansley, S. *Poor Britain* (Allen & Unwin, London, 1985). *Breadline Britain 1990s, the Findings of the Television Series* (London Weekend Television, London, 1992)

McKay, J. 'Primordial and mobilisationist approaches to ethnic phenomena' *Ethnic and Racial Studies* (1982)

McKenzie, R.T. 'Parties, pressure groups and the British political process' in R. Rose (1969)

McKenzie, R.T. and Silver, A. 'The working class Tory in England' in Worsley (1972). *Angels in Marble* (Heinemann, London, 1968)

MacKenzie, W.J.M. 'Pressure groups in British Government' in R. Rose (1969)

McLanahan, S. and Booth, K. 'Mother-only families' in A. Booth (ed.) *Contemporary Families* (National Council on Family Relations, Minneapolis, 1991)

McLellan, D. (ed.) *Karl Marx: Selected Writings* (Oxford University Press, Oxford, 1977)

McLennan, G. *Marxism, Pluralism and Beyond* (Polity Press, Cambridge, 1989)

MacNeil, C. 'The National Curriculum: a Black perspective' in B. Moon (ed.) *New Curriculum – National Curriculum* (Hodder & Stoughton, London, 1990)

McNeill, P.A. 'Chronicle of crime: an interview with Pat Mayhew' *New Statesman and Society* (9 December 1988). *Research Methods* (Tavistock, London, 1985)

McRobbie, A. 'Working class girls and the culture of femininity' in Centre for Contemporary Cultural Studies (1978)

Maduro, O. *Religion and Social Conflicts* (Orbis Books, New York, 1982)

Maguire, M. and Pointing, J. (eds) *Victims of Crime: A New Deal?* (Open University Press, Milton Keynes, 1988)

Maguire, R., Morgan, R. and Reiner, R. (eds) *The Oxford Handbook of Criminology* (Oxford University Press, Oxford, 1993)

Malinowski, B. *Magic, Science and Religion and Other Essays* (Anchor Books, New York, 1954)

Mangin, W. 'Poverty and politics in cities of Latin America' in W. Bloomberg and H.J. Schmandt *Urban Poverty: its Social and Political Dimensions* (Sage Publications, Beverly Hills, 1968)

Mankoff, M. 'Introduction to perspectives on the problem of crime' in Chambliss and Mankoff (1976)

Manis, J.G. and Meltzer, B.N. (eds) *Symbolic Interaction* 2nd edn (Allyn & Bacon, Boston, 1972)

Mann, K. *The Making of an English Underclass* (Open University Press, Milton Keynes, 1992)

Mann, M. *Consciousness and Action among the Western Working Class* (Macmillan, London, 1973). *The Sources of Social Power* vol. 1 (Cambridge University Press, Cambridge, 1986). *The Sources of Social Power* vol. 2 (Cambridge University Press, Cambridge, 1993)

Mannheim, H. *Comparative Criminology* (Routledge & Kegan Paul, London, 1960)

Mannheim, K. *Ideology and Utopia* (Routledge & Kegan Paul, London, 1948)

Marcuse, H. *One Dimensional Man* (Abacus, London, 1972)

Marsh, D. (ed.) *Pressure Politics* (Junction Books, London, 1983)

Marsh, D. and Locksley, G. 'Labour: the dominant force in British politics?' in D. Marsh (ed.) (1983)

Marshall, G. *In Search of the Spirit of Capitalism: Max Weber and the Protestant Ethic Thesis* (Hutchinson, London, 1982). 'John Goldthorpe and class analysis' in J. Clark *et al.* (1990)

Marshall, G., Newby, H., Rose, D. and Vogler, C. *Social Class in Modern Britain* (Hutchinson, London, 1988)

Marshall, G. and Swift, A. 'Social class and social justice' *British Journal of Sociology* (June 1993)

Marsland, D. 'Universal welfare provision creates a dependent population. the case for' *Social Studies Review* (November 1989)

Martin, D. *A General Theory of Secularisation* (Blackwell, Oxford, 1978). *A Sociology of English Religion* (Heinemann, London, 1967). *The Religious and the Secular* (Routledge & Kegan Paul, London, 1969). *Tongues of Fire: The Explosion of Protestantism in Latin America* (Blackwell, Oxford, 1991). 'The secularisation issue: prospect and retrospect' *British Journal of Sociology* vol. 42, no. 3 (1991)

Martin, J. and Roberts, C. *Women and Employment: a Lifetime Perspective* (HMSO, London, 1980)

Marx, K. *Capital* vol. 1 (Penguin, Harmondsworth, Middlesex, 1970, first published 1867). *Capital* vol. 3 (Lawrence & Wishart, London, 1974). See also under Bottomore and Rubel, and McLellan

Mason, D. 'After Scarman, a note on the concept of institutional racism' *New Community* (Summer 1982)

Matthews, M. *Privilege in the Soviet Union* (Allen & Unwin, London, 1978)

Matthews, R. 'Squaring up to crime' *Sociology Review* vol. 2, no 3 (1993)

Matthews, R. and Young, J. (eds) *Issues in Realist Criminology* (Sage, London, 1992)

Matthews, R. and Young, J. 'Reflections on realism' in Young and Matthews (1992)

Matza, D. *Delinquency and Drift* (John Wiley & Sons, New York, 1964)

Matza, D. and Sykes, G. 'Juvenile delinquency and subterranean values' *American Sociological Review* (October 1961)

Mayhew, P. and Aye Maung, N. *Surveying Crime, Findings from the 1992 British Crime Survey* (Home Office Research and Statistics Department, London, 1992)

Mayhew, P., Elliot, D. and Dowds, L. *The 1988 British Crime Survey* (HMSO, London, 1989)

Mayo, E. *The Human Problems of an Industrial Civilization* (Macmillan, New York, 1933)

Mead, G.H. *Mind, Self and Society* edited by C. Morris (University of Chicago Press, Chicago, 1934)

Meltzer, B.N., Petras, J.W. and Reynolds, L.T. *Symbolic Interactionism* (Routledge & Kegan Paul, London, 1975)

Mencher, S. 'The problem of measuring poverty' in Roach and Roach (1972)

Mennell, S. *Sociological Theory* (Nelson, London, 1974)

Merton, R.K. *Social Theory and Social Structure* enlarged edn (The Free Press, New York, 1968)

Meyer, A.G. *The Soviet Political System* (Random House, New York, 1965)

Michels, R. *Political Parties* (The Free Press, Glencoe, 1949)

Midwinter, E. 'The community school' in J. Rushton and J.D. Turner (eds) *Education and Deprivation* (Manchester University Press, Manchester, 1975)

Milbrath, L. *Political Participation* (Rand McNally, Chicago, 1965)

Miles, I. and Irvine, J. 'The critique of official statistics' in Irvine, Miles and Evans (1979)

Miles, R. *Racism* (Routledge, London, 1989). *Racism after Race Relations* (Routledge, London, 1993)

Miliband, R. *The State in Capitalist Society* (Weidenfeld & Nicolson, London, 1969). 'Politics and poverty' in Wedderburn (1974). *Marxism and Politics* (Oxford University Press, Oxford, 1977)

Mill, J.S. *The Subjection of Women* (Oxford University Press, Oxford, 1974)

Millar, J. and Glendinning, C. '"It all really starts in the family": gender divisions and poverty' in C. Glendinning and J. Millar (eds) *Women and Poverty in Britain: the 1990s* (Harvester Wheatsheaf, Hemel Hempstead, 1992)

Miller, S.M. and Roby, P. 'Poverty: changing social stratification' in Townsend (1970)

Miller, W.B. 'Lower class culture as a generating milieu of gang delinquency' in Wolfgang, Savitz and Johnston (1962). 'The elimination of the American lower class as national policy: a critique of the ideology of the poverty movement of the 1960s' in Moynihan (1968)

Millett, K. *Sexual Politics* (Doubleday, New York, 1970)

Mills, C.W. *White Collar: The American Middle Classes* (Oxford University Press, New York, 1951). *The Power Elite* (Oxford University Press, New York, 1956). *The Sociological Imagination* (Oxford University Press, New York, 1959)

Milward, N. and Stevens, M. *British Workplace Industrial Relations 1980–84* (Gower, Aldershot, 1986)

Mintzberg, H. *The Structuring Of Organizations* (Prentice-Hall, New Jersey, 1979). *Structure in Fives: Designing Effective Organizations* (Prentice-Hall, New Jersey, 1983)

Mitchell, J.J. *Woman's Estate* (Penguin, Harmondsworth, 1971)

Mogey, J.M. *Family and Neighbourhood* (Oxford University Press, Oxford, 1956)

Mooney, J. *The Ghost-Dance Religion and the Sioux Outbreak of 1890* (Phoenix Books, Chicago, 1965)

Morgan, D.J.H. *Social Theory and the Family* (Routledge & Kegan Paul, London, 1975). 'The family' in M. Haralambos (ed.) *Developments in Sociology* vol. 10 (Causeway Press, Ormskirk, 1994)

Morgan, D. 'Gender' in R. Burgess (ed.) *Key Variables in Social Investigation* (Routledge & Kegan Paul, London, 1986)

Morris, L. *Dangerous Classes: The Underclass and Social Citizenship* (Routledge, London, 1994)

Morris, T. *The Criminal Area* (Routledge & Kegan Paul, London, 1957)

Morton, D.C. and Watson, D.R. 'Compensatory education and contemporary liberalism in the US: a sociological view' in J. Raynor and J. Harden (eds) *Equality and City Schools* vol. 2 (Routledge & Kegan Paul, London, 1973)

Mosca, G. *The Ruling Class* (McGraw-Hill, New York, 1939)

Mouzelis, N.P. *Organisation and Bureaucracy* 2nd edn (Routledge & Kegan Paul, London, 1975)

Moynihan, D.P. 'The Negro family: the case for national action' in Rainwater and Yancy (1967). (ed.) *On Understanding Poverty* (Basic Books, New York, 1968)

Murdock, G.P. *Social Structure* (Macmillan, New York, 1949)

Murray, C. *Losing Ground* (Basic Books, New York, 1984). 'Underclass' *Sunday Times Magazine* (26 November 1989)

Nash, R. *Teacher Expectations and Pupil Learning* (Routledge & Kegan Paul, London, 1976)

National Advisory Commission *Report of the National Advisory Commission on Civil Disorders* (Bantam Books, New York, 1968)

Neibuhr, H.R. *The Social Sources of Denominationalism* (The World Publishing Company, New York, 1929)

Nelson, G.K. 'Religion' in M. Haralambos (ed.)

Developments in Sociology vol. 2 (Causeway Press, Ormskirk, 1986)

Nichols, T. and Beynon, H. *Living with Capitalism* (Routledge & Kegan Paul, London, 1977). 'Social class: official, sociological and Marxist' in Irvine, Miles and Evans (1979)

Nicolson, C. *Strangers to England* (Wayland Publishers, London, 1974)

Nisbet, R.A. *The Sociological Tradition* (Heinemann, London, 1967)

Nordlinger, E.A. 'The working-class Tory' *New Society* (13 October 1966). *Working-Class Tories* (MacGibbon & Kee, London, 1967). *On the Autonomy of the Democratic State* (Harvard University Press, Massachusetts, 1981)

Norman, F., Turner, S., Granados, J., Schwarez, H., Green, H. and Harris, J. 'Look, Jane, look: anti-sexist initiatives in primary schools' in G. Weiner (ed.) *Just a Bunch of Girls* (Open University Press, Milton Keynes, 1988)

Oakley, A. *Housewife* (Allen Lane, London, 1974). *The Sociology of Housework* (Martin Robertson, Oxford, 1974). *Subject Women* (Martin Robertson, Oxford, 1981). 'Conventional families' in R.N. Rapoport *et al.* (eds) (1982)

Oakley, A. and Oakley, R. 'Sexism in official statistics' in Irvine, Miles and Evans (1979)

Oakley, R. 'Cypriot families' in R.N. Rapoport *et al.* (eds) (1982)

OPCS Monitor *General Household Survey Preliminary Results for 1988* (Government Statistical Service, London, 1989)

Oppenheim, C. *Poverty the Facts* (Child Poverty Action Group, London, 1993)

Oppenheimer, M. 'The proletarianization of the professional' in P. Halmos (ed.) *Professionalization and Social Change* (University of Keele, Monograph 20, Keele, 1973)

Ortner, S.B. 'Is female to male as nature is to culture?' in M.Z. Rosaldo and L. Lamphere (eds) *Woman, Culture and Society* (Stanford University Press, Stanford, 1974)

O'Toole, R. *Religion: Classic Sociological Approaches* (McGraw Hill Ryerson, Toronto, 1984)

Pahl, R. *Divisions of Labour* (Blackwell, Oxford, 1984)

Pareto, V. *A Treatise on General Sociology* edited by A. Livingstone (Dover Publications, New York, 1963)

Park, R.E. *Race and Culture* (The Free Press, Glencoe, 1950)

Parker, H.J. *View From the Boys* (David & Charles, Newton Abbot, 1974)

Parker, R. 'Families and social policy: an overview' in R.N. Rapoport *et al.* (eds) (1982)

Parker, S. 'Work and leisure' in Butterworth and Weir *The Sociology of Leisure* (Allen & Unwin, London, 1976)

Parkin, F. *Middle-Class Radicalism* (Manchester University Press, Manchester, 1968). *Class Inequality and Political Order* (Paladin, St Albans, 1972). Review of 'Class in a capitalist society' by J. Westergaard and H. Resler *British Journal of Sociology* (March 1977)

Parry, G. *Political Elites* (Allen & Unwin, London, 1969)

Parry, N. and Parry, J. *The Rise of the Medical Profession* (Croom Helm, London, 1976). 'Social closure and collective social mobility' in Scase (1977)

Parsons, T. *The Structure of Social Action* (McGraw-Hill, New York, 1937). *The Social System* (The Free Press, New York, 1951). 'The social structure of the family' in R.N. Anshen (ed.) *The Family: Its Functions and Destiny* (Harper & Row, New York, 1959). *Structure and Process in Modern Societies* (The Free Press, Chicago, 1960). 'The school class as a social system' in Halsey, Floud and Anderson (1961). *Essays in Sociological Theory* (The Free Press, New York, 1964). 'Religious perspectives in sociology and social psychology' in Lessa and Vogt (1965). 'The normal American family' in S.M. Farber (ed.) *Man and Civilization: The Family's Search for Survival* (McGraw-Hill, New York, 1965). 'Family and church as "boundary" structures' in Birnbaum and Lenzer (1969). *Politics and Social Structure* (The Free Press, New York, 1969). *The Evolution of Societies* edited by J. Toby (Prentice-Hall, Englewood Cliffs, 1977)

Parsons, T. and Bales, R.F. *Family, Socialization and Interaction Process* (The Free Press, New York, 1955)

Patrick, J. *A Glasgow Gang Observed* (Eyre Methuen, London, 1973)

Patterson, S. *Dark Strangers* (Penguin, Harmondsworth, 1965)

Pawson R. 'Methodology' in M. Haralambos (ed.) *Developments in Sociology* vol. 5 (Causeway Press, Ormskirk, 1989)

Payne, G., Ford, G. and Robertson, C. 'A reappraisal of social mobility in Britain' *Sociology* (May 1977)

Pearce, F. *Crimes of the Powerful* (Pluto Press, London, 1976)

Pearce, F. and Tombs, S. 'US capital versus the Third World: Union Carbide and Bhopal' in Pearce and Woodiwiss (1993)

Pearce, F. and Woodiwiss, M. *Global Crime Connections* (Macmillan, Basingstoke, 1993)

Penn, R. 'Skilled manual workers in the labour process' in Stephen Wood (ed.) (1983). *Skilled Workers in the Class Structure* (Cambridge University Press, Cambridge, 1984). 'The Nuffield Class Categorization' *Sociology* vol. 36 (1981)

Peters, B.G. *The Politics of Bureaucracy* (Longman, New York, 1978)

Phillips, D.L. *Knowledge From What?* (Rand McNally, Chicago, 1971). *Abandoning Method* (Jossey-Bass, San Francisco, 1973)

Phillips, M. 'The new road to Wigan Pier' *Guardian* (21 November 1992)

Phillipson, M. 'Theory, methodology and conceptualization' in Filmer, Phillipson, Silverman and Walsh (1972)

Phizaklea, A. and Miles, R. *Labour and Racism* (Routledge & Kegan Paul, London, 1980)

Piachaud, D. 'Peter Townsend and the Holy Grail' *New Society* (10 September 1981). 'Problems in the definition and measurement of poverty' *Journal of Social Policy* (1987)

Pilkington, A. *Race Relations in Britain* (UTP, Slough, 1984). 'Race and ethnicity' in M. Haralambos (ed.) *Developments in Sociology* vol. 9 (Causeway Press, Ormskirk, 1993)

Piore, M. 'Perspectives on labour market flexibility' *Industrial Relations* vol. 45, no. 2 (1986)

Platt, J. 'Variations in answers to different questions on perceptions of class' *Sociological Review* (August 1971)

Plummer, K. 'Misunderstanding labelling perspectives' in D. Downes and P. Rock (eds) *Deviant Interpretations* (Martin Robertson, London, 1979). *Documents of Life: Introductions to the Problems and Literature of a Humanist Method* (Allen & Unwin, London, 1982)

Poggi, G. *Development of the Modern State* (Hutchinson, London, 1978)

Pollak, O. *The Criminality of Women* (University of Philadelphia Press, Philadelphia, 1950)

Pollert, A. 'Dismantling flexibility' *Capital and Class* no. 34 (1988)

Polsky, N. *Hustlers, Beats and Others* (Adline, New York, 1967)

Popper, K.R. *The Logic of Scientific Discovery* (Hutchinson, London, 1959)

Poulantzas, N. 'The problem of the capitalist state' in Urry and Wakeford (1973). 'The capitalist state: a reply to Miliband and Laclau' *New Left Review* (January-February 1976)

President's Commission on Law Enforcement and the Administration of Justice in D.R. Cressey and D.A. Ward (eds) *Delinquency Crime and Social Process* (Harper & Row, New York, 1989)

President's Commission on Income Maintenance Programs *Poverty Amid Plenty* (US Government Printing Office, Washington DC, 1969)

Pringle, R. 'What is a secretary?' in M. McDowell and R. Pringle (eds) *Defining Women: Social Institutions and Gender Divisions* (Polity Press, Cambridge, 1992)

Pryce, J. *Endless Pressure* (Penguin, Harmondsworth, 1979)

Raggatt, P. and Unwin, L. 'Introduction: a collection of papers' in P. Raggatt and L. Unwin (eds) *Change and Intervention: Vocational Education and Training* (Falmer Press, London, 1991)

Rainwater, L. 'The problem of lower-class culture and poverty-war strategy' in Moynihan (1968). *Behind Ghetto Walls* (Adline, Chicago, 1970)

Rainwater, L. and Yancey, W.L. (eds) *The Moynihan Report and the Politics of Controversy* (MIT Press, Cambridge, 1967)

Randall, G.J. 'Gender differences in pupil-teacher interaction in workshops and laboratories' in G. Weiner and M. Arnot (eds) (1987)

Rapoport, R. 'Ideologies about family forms – towards diversity' in K. Boh *et al.* (eds) (1989)

Rapoport, R. and Rapoport, R.N. *Leisure and the Family Life-Cycle* (Routledge, London, 1975). *Dual-Career Families* (Penguin, Harmondsworth, 1971). 'British families in transition' in R.N. Rapoport *et al.* (eds) (1982)

Rapoport, R.N., Fogarty, M.P. and Rapoport, R. (eds) *Families in Britain* (Routledge & Kegan Paul, London, 1982)

Rees, T. *Women and the Labour Market* (Routledge, London, 1992)

Rein, M. 'Problems in the definition and measurement of poverty' in Townsend (1970)

Reiner, R. and Cross, M. *Beyond Law and Order. Criminal Justice Policy and Politics into the 1990s* (Macmillan, Basingstoke, 1991)

Rex, J. *Race Relations in Sociological Theory* (Weidenfeld & Nicholson, London, 1970). 'Capitalism, elites and the ruling class' in Stanworth and Giddens (1974). *Race and Ethnicity* (Open University Press, Milton Keynes, 1986)

Rex, J. and Moore, R. *Race, Community and Conflict* (Institute of Race Relations/Oxford University Press, London, 1967)

Rex, J. and Tomlinson, S. *Colonial Immigrants in a British City* (Routledge & Kegan Paul, London, 1979)

Reynolds, D. 'Relative autonomy reconstructed' in L. Barton and S. Walker (eds) (1984)

Richardson, J. 'Race' in M. Haralambos (ed.) *Developments in Sociology* vol. 3 (Causeway Press, Ormskirk, 1987). 'Race' in M. Haralambos (ed.) *Developments in Sociology* vol. 6 (Causeway Press, Ormskirk, 1990)

Richardson, J. and Lambert, J. *The Sociology of Race* (Causeway Press, Ormskirk, 1985)

Richardson, J.J. and Jordon, G. *Governing Under Pressure* (Martin Robertson, Oxford, 1979)

Rist, R. 'Student social class and teacher expectations: the self-fulfilling prophecy in ghetto education' *Harvard Educational Review* vol. 40 (1970)

Roach, J.L. and Roach, J.K. (eds) *Poverty: Selected Readings* (Penguin, Harmondsworth, 1972)

Robbins, T. and Robertson, R. *Church-state Relations: Tensions and Transitions* (Transaction Books, New Brunswick, 1987)

Roberts, E. *A Woman's Place: An Oral History of Working Class Women 1890–1940* (Basil Blackwell, Oxford, 1984)

Roberts, K. *Contemporary Society and the Growth of Leisure* (Longman, New York, 1978). 'Leisure' in M. Haralambos (ed.) (1986)

Roberts, K., Cook, F.G., Clark, S.C. and Semeonoff, E. *The Fragmentary Class Structure* (Heinemann, London, 1977)

Roberts, K., Noble, M. and Duggan, J. 'Youth unemployment: an old problem or a new life-style?' in Kenneth Thompson (ed.) *Work, Employment and Unemployment* (Open University Press, Milton Keynes, 1984)

Robertson, R. *The Sociological Interpretation of Religion* (Blackwell, Oxford, 1970)

Robertson, R. (ed.) *Sociology of Religion* (Penguin, Harmondsworth, 1969). 'Church-state relations and the world system' in Robbins and Robertson (1987)

Robinson, L.W. 'When will revolutionary movements use religion?' in Robbins and Robertson (1987)

Roethlisberger, F.J. and Dickson, W.J. *Management and the Worker* (Harvard University Press, Cambridge, 1939)

Rogers, C. *The Social Psychology of Schooling* (Routledge & Kegan Paul, London, 1982)

Roof, W.C. and McKinney, W. *American Mainline Religion* (Rutgers University Press, New Brunswick, 1987)

Ropers, R.H. *Persistent Poverty: The American Dream Turned Nightmare* (Plenum Press, New York, 1991)

Rosaldo, M.Z. 'Women, culture and society: a theoretical overview' in M. Rosaldo and L. Lamphere (eds) *Women, Culture and Society* (Stanford University Press, Stanford, 1974)

Rose, A.M. *The Power Structure: Political Process in American Society* (Oxford University Press, New York, 1967). (ed.) *Human Behaviour and Social Processes* (Routledge & Kegan Paul, London, 1962)

Rose, D. and Marshal, G. 'Developments' in M. Haralambos (ed.) *Sociology* vol. 4 (Causeway Press, Ormskirk, 1988)

Rose, E. *et al. Colour and Citizenship* (Oxford University Press, Oxford, 1969)

Rose, R. 'Long-term structural change or cyclical fluctuations? The 1992 Election in dynamic perspective' *Parliamentary Affairs* (October 1992)

Rose, R. (ed.) *Studies in British Politics* 2nd edn (Macmillan, London, 1969)

Rose, S., Kamin, L.J. and Lewontin, R.C. *Not in Our Genes. Biology, Ideology and Human Nature* (Penguin, Harmondsworth, 1984)

Rosen, H. *Language and Class* 3rd edn (Falling Wall Press, Bristol, 1974)

Rosenfeld, E. 'Social stratification in a "classless" society' in Lopreato and Lewis (1974)

Rosenthal, R. and Jacobson, L. *Pygmalion in the Classroom* (Holt, Rinehart & Winston, New York, 1968)

Ross, A.M. and Hartman, P.T. *Changing Patterns of Industrial Conflict* (John Wiley & Sons, New York, 1960)

Rosser, R. and Harris, C. *The Family and Social Change* (Routledge & Kegan Paul, London, 1965)

Routh, R. *Occupation and Pay in Great Britain 1906–79* (Macmillan, London, 1980)

Rowbotham, S. *Woman's Consciousness, Man's World* (Penguin, Harmondsworth, 1973). 'The trouble with patriarchy' in M. Evans (ed.) (1982)

Rubery, J. 'Structured labour markets, worker organisation and low pay' in A.H. Amsden (ed.) *The Economics of Women and Work* (Penguin, Harmondsworth, 1980)

Rubington, E. and Weinberg, M.S. (eds) *Deviance: The Interactionist Perspective* 2nd edn (Macmillan, New York, 1973)

Ruggiero, V. 'Realist criminology: a critique' in Young and Matthews (1992)

Rutherford, J. 'Who's that man?' in R. Chapman and J. Rutherford (eds) *Male Order: Unwrapping Masculinity* (Lawrence & Wishart, London, 1988)

Ryan, W. *Blaming the Victim* (Orbach & Chambers, London 1971)

Sabel, C. *Work and Politics: the Division of Labour in Industry* (Cambridge University Press, Cambridge, 1982)

Salaman, G. *Work Organizations: Resistance and Control* (Longman, London, 1979)

Sarlvick, B. and Crewe, I. *Decade of Dealignment* (Cambridge University Press, Cambridge, 1983)

Saunders, P. *Social Class and Stratification* (Routledge, London, 1990)

Savage, M., Barlow, J., Dickens, P. and Fielding, T. *Property, Bureaucracy and Culture: Middle Class Formation in Contemporary Britain* (Routledge, London, 1992)

Sayer, A. *Method in Social Science* (Hutchinson, London, 1984)

Scase, R. (ed.) *Industrial Society: Class, Cleavage and Control* (Allen & Unwin, London, 1977)

Schultz, T.W. 'Investment in human capital' *American Economic Review* (March 1961)

Schutz, A. *The Phenomenology of the Social World* (Heinemann, London, 1972, first published 1932)

Schwartz, A.J. 'A further look at the "culture of poverty": ten Caracas barrios' *Sociology and Social Research* (July 1975)

Scott, H. *Women and Socialism* (Allison & Busby, London, 1976)

Scott, J. *The Upper Classes. Property and Privilege in Britain* (Macmillan, London, 1982). 'The British upper class' in D. Coates, G. Johnston and R. Bush (eds) *A Socialist Anatomy of Britain* (Polity Press, Cambridge, 1985). 'Documents in social research' *Social Studies Review* (September 1990). *Who Rules Britain?* (Polity Press, Cambridge, 1991). *Matter of Record: Documentary Sources in Social Research* (Polity Press, Cambridge, 1990)

Scraton, S. 'Leisure' in M. Haralambos (ed.) *Developments in Sociology* vol. 8 (Causeway Press, Ormskirk, 1992)

Secombe, W. 'Domestic labour: reply to critics' *New Left Review* (November-December 1975)

Seidler, V.J. *Unreasonable Men: Masculinity and Social Theory* (Routledge, London, 1994).*Rediscovering Masculinity: Reason, Language and Sexuality* (Routledge, London, 1989)

Selznick, P. *TVA and the Grass Roots* (Harper Torchbooks, New York, 1966)

Sen, A.K. *Poverty and Famines: An Essay on Entitlement and Deprivation* (Clarendon Press, Oxford, 1981). 'Poor relatively speaking' *Oxford Economic Papers* (1985)

Sharp, R. and Green, A. *Education and Social Control* (Routledge & Kegan Paul, London, 1975)

Sharpe, S. *Just Like a Girl: How Girls Learn to be Women* (Penguin, Harmondsworth, 1976). *Just Like a Girl* (2nd edition) (Penguin, Harmondsworth, 1994)

Shaskolsky, L. 'The development of sociological theory – a sociology of knowledge interpretation' in L.T. and J.M. Reynolds (eds) *The Sociology of Sociology* (McKay, New York, 1970)

Shiner, L. 'The concept of secularization in empirical research' in K. Thompson and J. Tunstall (eds) *Sociological Perspectives* (Penguin Books, Harmondsworth, 1971)

Siltanen, J. and Stanworth, M. (eds) *Women and the Public Sphere* (Hutchinson, London, 1984)

Silverman, D. *Qualitative Method and Sociology* (Gower, Aldershot, 1985). *The Theory of Organisations* (Heinemann, London, 1970)

Sinfield, A. *What Unemployment Means* (Martin Robertson, Oxford, 1981)

Sissons, M. *The Psychology of Social Class* (Open University Press, Milton Keynes, 1970)

Skellington, R. and Morris, P. '*Race' in Britain Today* (Sage, London, 1992)

Skidmore, W. *Theoretical Thinking in Sociology* (Cambridge University Press, Cambridge, 1975)

Skocpol, T. *States and Social Revolutions* (Cambridge University Press, Cambridge, 1979). 'Bringing the state back in: strategies of analysis in current research' in P. Evans, D. Rueschemeyer and T. Skocpol (eds) *Bringing the State Back In* (Cambridge University Press, Cambridge, 1985)

Small, S. 'Black people in Britain' *Sociology Review* (April 1994)

Smart, C. *Women, Crime and Criminology* (Routledge & Kegan Paul, London, 1976). 'The new female criminal: reality or myth' *British Journal of Criminology* vol. 19 (1979). *Feminism and the Power of Law* (Routledge, London, 1989)

Smith, D.J. (ed.) *Understanding the Underclass* (Policy Studies Institute, London, 1992)

Smith, M.G. *West Indian Family Structure* (University of Washington Press, Seattle, 1962)

Smith, M., Parker, S. and Smith, C. *Leisure and Society in Britain* (Allen Lane, London, 1973)

Smith, P. and Morton, G. 'Union exclusion and the decollectivization of industrial relations in contemporary Britain' *British Journal of Industrial Relations* vol. 31, no. 1 (1993)

Snider, L. 'The politics of corporate crime control' in Pearce and Woodiwiss (1993)

Solomos, J. 'Varieties of Marxist conceptions of "race", class and the state: a critical analysis' in J. Rex (ed) *Theories of Race and Ethnic Relations* (Cambridge University Press, Cambridge, 1986). *Race and Racism in Britain* 2nd edn (Macmillan, London, 1993)

Solomos, J., Findlay, B., Jones, S. and Gilroy, P. 'The organic crisis of British capitalism and race: the experience of the seventies' in Centre for Contemporary Cultural Studies (1982)

Sombart, W. *Luxury and Capitalism* (University of Michigan Press, Ann Arbor, 1907)

Spencer, H. *Structure, Function and Evolution* (Nelson, London, 1971)

Spender, D. *Invisible Women: Schooling Scandal* (Women's Press, London, 1983)

Spicker, P. *Poverty and Social Security* (Routledge, London, 1993)

Spiro, M.E. 'Is the family universal? – The Israeli case' in Bell and Vogel (1968)

Stacey, J. 'Untangling feminist theory' in D. Richardson and V. Robinson (eds) *Introducing Women's Studies* (Macmillan, London, 1993)

Stacey, M. *Tradition and Change: a Study of Banbury* (Oxford University Press, Oxford, 1960)

Stanko, E.A. 'Keeping women in and out of line: sexual harassment and occupational segregation' in S. Walby (ed.) *Gender Segregation at Work* (Open University Press, Milton Keynes, 1988)

Stanworth, M. *Gender and Schooling* (Hutchinson, London, 1983). 'Women and class analysis: a reply to John Goldthorpe' *Sociology* vol. 18, no. 2 (1984)

Stanworth, P. and Giddens, A. (eds) *Elites and Power in British Society* (Cambridge University Press, Cambridge, 1974)

Stark, R. and Glock, C.Y. *American Piety: The Nature of Religious Commitment* (University of California Press, Berkeley, 1968)

Stark, W.S. and Bainbridge, W.A. *The Future of Religion* (University of California Press, Berkeley, 1985)

Stevenson, K. and Brearley, N. 'Left realism in criminology and the return to consensus theory' in Reiner and Cross (1991)

Stewart, A., Prandy, K. and Blackburn, R.M. *Social Stratification and Occupations* (Macmillan, London, 1980)

Stoller, R. *Sex and Gender: On the Development of Masculinity and Femininity* (Science House, New York, 1968)

Stone, M. *The Education of the Black Child in Britain* (Fontana, Glasgow, 1981)

Strauss, A., Erlich, D., Bucher, R., Sabschin, M. and Schatzman, L. 'The hospital and its negotiated order' in P. Worsley *et al.* (eds) *Modern Sociology* (Penguin, Harmondsworth, 1978)

Sugarman, B. 'Social class, values and behaviour in schools' in Craft (1970)

Sussman, M.B. and Burchinal, L.G. 'The kin family network in urban-industrial America' in Anderson (1971)

Sutherland, E.H. 'Is "white collar crime" crime?' in Wolfgang, Savitz and Johnston (1962). *White Collar Crime* (Holt, Rinehart & Winston, New York, 1960)

Swann, Lord *Education for All: a Brief Guide* (HMSO, London, 1985). *Education for All* Commd. No. 9453 (HMSO, London, 1985)

Sykes, G.M. and Matza, D. 'Techniques of neutralization: a theory of delinquency' in Wolfgang, Savitz and Johnston (1962)

Tausky, C. *Work Organizations* (F.E. Peacock, Itasca, 1970)

Taylor, D. 'Incipient fundamentalism: religion and politics among Sri Lankan Hindus in Britain' in L. Caplan (1987)

Taylor, F.W. *Scientific Management* (Harper & Row, New York, 1947)

Taylor, I. 'Left realist criminology and the free market experiment in Britain' in Young and Matthews (1992)

Taylor, I., Walton, P. and Young, J. *The New Criminology* (Routledge & Kegan Paul, London, 1973)

Taylor, L. *Deviance and Society* (Michael Joseph, London, 1971). *In the Underworld* (Unwin Paperbacks, London, 1984)

Taylor, L. and Walton, P. 'Industrial sabotage: motives and meanings' in Cohen (1971)

Taylor, M.J. *Caught Between. A Review of Research into the Education of Pupils of West Indian Origin* (NFER, Nelson, Windsor, 1981)

Taylor, S. *Durkheim and the Study of Suicide* (Macmillan, London, 1982). *Suicide* (Longman, London, 1989). 'Beyond Durkheim: sociology and suicide' *Social Studies Review* (November 1990)

Thomas, W.I. and Znaniecki, F. *The Polish Peasant in Europe and America* (University of Chicago Press, Chicago, 1919)

Thompson, E.P. 'Time, work discipline and industrial capitalism' *Past and Present* no. 38 (1967)

Thompson, P. 'The end of bureaucracy?' in Haralambos (ed.) 1989. 'The labour process: changing theory changing practice' *Sociology Review* vol. 3, no. 2 (1993). *The Nature of Work, an Introduction to Debates on the Labour Process* (Macmillan, London, 1983)

Thompson, P. and McHugh, D. *Work Organisations* (Macmillan, London, 1990)

Thurow, L.C. 'Education and economic equality' in Karabel and Halsey (1977)

Tiger, L. and Fox, R. *The Imperial Animal* (Secker & Warburg, London, 1972)

de Tocqueville, A. *Democracy in America* vol. 1 (Vintage, New York, 1945, first published 1835)

Toffler, A. *Future Shock* (Pan, London, 1971)

Tomlinson, S. *Ethnic Minorities in British Schools* (Heinemann, London, 1983). 'Home, school and community' in M. Craft *Education and Cultural Pluralism* (Falmer Press, London, 1984)

Torrey, J. 'Illiteracy in the ghetto' in Keddie (1973)

Towler, R. *Homo Religiosus: Sociological Problems in the Study of Religion* (Constable, London, 1974)

Townsend, P. (ed.) *The Concept of Poverty* (Heinemann, London, 1970). 'Measures and explanations of poverty in high and low income countries' in Townsend (1970). 'Poverty as relative deprivation' in Wedderburn (1974). *Poverty in the United Kingdom* (Penguin, Harmondsworth, 1979). *The International Analysis of Poverty* (Harvester Wheatsheaf, Hemel Hempstead, 1993)

Townsend, P., Corrigan, P. and Kowarzik, U. *Poverty and Labour in London* (The Low Pay Unit, London, 1985)

Troeltsch, E. *The Social Teachings of the Christian Churches* vols 1 and 2 (University of Chicago Press, Chicago, 1981)

Troyna, B. and Carrington, B. *Education, Racism and Reform* (Routledge, London, 1990)

Tumin, M.M. 'Some principles of stratification: a critical analysis' in Bendix and Lipset (1967). *Social Stratification: The Forms and Functions of Social Inequality* (Prentice-Hall, Englewood Cliffs, 1967)

Tunstall, J. *The Fishermen* (MacGibbon & Kee, London, 1962)

Turner, B.S. *Religion and Social Theory: a Materialistic Perspective* (Humanities Press, Atlantic Highlands, 1983)

Turner, J.H. and Maryanski, A. *Functionalism* (Benjamin/Cummings Publishing, California, 1979)

Tylor, E.B. *Religion in Primitive Culture* (Peter Smith, Gloucester, 1970)

Urry, J. and Wakeford, J. (eds) *Power in Britain* (Heinemann, London, 1973)

Vajda, M. and Heller, A. 'Family structure and communism' in Glazer, Malbin and Waehrer (1972)

Valentine, C.A. *Culture and Poverty* (University of Chicago Press, Chicago, 1968)

Valentine, C.A. and Valentine, B.L. 'Making the scene, digging the action, and telling it like it is: anthropologists at work in a dark ghetto' in N.E. Whitten Jr and J.F. Szwed (eds) *Afro-American Anthropology* (The Free Press, New York, 1970)

Veness, T. *School Leavers* (Methuen, London, 1962)

Vernon, P.E. *Intelligence and Cultural Environment* (Methuen, London, 1969)

Vogel, E.F. and Bell, N.W. 'The emotionally disturbed child as the family scapegoat' in Bell and Vogel (1968)

Walby, S. *Patriarchy at Work* (Polity Press, Cambridge, 1986). *Theorizing Patriarchy* (Blackwell, Oxford, 1990)

Walker, A. 'Blaming the victims' in C. Murray, *The Emerging British Underclass* (The Institute of Economic Affairs, London, 1990)

Walker, C. and Walker, A. 'Poverty and the poor' in M. Haralambos (ed.) *Developments in Sociology* vol. 11 (Causeway Press, Ormskirk, 1994)

Walker, R. 'Consensual approaches to the definition of poverty' *Journal of Social Policy* (1987)

Wall, W.D. and Williams, H.L. *Longitudinal Studies and the Social Sciences* (Heinemann, London, 1970)

Wallerstein, I. 'The construction of peoplehood: racism, nationalism, ethnicity' in E. Balibar and I. Wallerstein (eds) *'Race', Nation, Class* (Verso, London, 1991)

Wallis, R. *The Elementary Forms of the New Religious Life* (Routledge & Kegan Paul, London, 1984)

Wallis, R. and Bruce, S. *Sociological Theory, Religion and Collective Action* (The Queen's University, Belfast, 1986)

Walsh, D. 'Functionalism and systems theory' in Filmer, Phillipson, Silverman and Walsh (1972)

Ward, H. 'The anti-nuclear lobby: an unequal struggle' in D. Marsh (ed.) (1983)

Warde, A. 'Domestic divisions of labour' *Sociology Studies Review* (September 1990)

Warde, A., Hetherington, K. and Soothill, K. *Divisions of Labour Re-Visited: Greater Manchester, 1990* (Lancaster Regionalism Group, Lancaster, 1991)

Warr, P., Banks, M. and Ullah, P. 'The experience of unemployment among black and white urban teenagers' *British Journal of Psychology* vol. 76 (1985)

Warwick, D. *Bureaucracy* (Longman, London, 1974)

Warwick, D. and Littlejohn, G. *Coal, Capital and Culture* (Routledge, London, 1992)

Watts, A.G. *Education, Unemployment and the Future of Work* (Oxford University Press, Oxford, 1983)

Weber, M. *The Protestant Ethic and the Spirit of Capitalism* (Charles Scribner's Sons, New York, 1958). *The Sociology of Religion* (Beacon Press, Boston, 1963). See also under Gerth and Mills

Wedderburn, D. 'Workplace inequality' *New Society* (9 April 1970). (ed.) *Poverty, Inequality and Class Structure* (Cambridge University Press, Cambridge, 1974). 'Review symposium' *British Journal of Sociology* (XXXII)

Wedderburn, D. and Craig, C. 'Relative deprivation in work' in Wedderburn (1974)

Wedderburn, D. and Crompton, R. *Workers' Attitudes and Technology* (Cambridge University Press, Cambridge, 1972)

Weiner, G. and Arnot, M. *Gender and the Politics of Schooling* (Hutchinson, London, 1987)

Wesolowski, W. 'Some notes on the functional theory of stratification' in Bendix and Lipset (1967). 'The notion of strata and class in socialist society' in Béteille (1969)

West, D.J. and Farrington, D.P. *Who Becomes Delinquent?* (Heinemann, London, 1973)

Westergaard, J. 'Radical class consciousness: a comment' in Bulmer (1975)

Westergaard, J. and Little, A. 'Educational opportunity and social selection in England and Wales: trends and policy implications' in Craft (1970)

Westergaard, J. and Resler, H. *Class in a Capitalist Society* (Penguin, Harmondsworth, 1976)

White, M. 'Education policy and economic goals' in G. Esland (ed.) *Education, Training and Employment* vol. 2. *The Educational Response* (Addison Wesley, Wokingham, 1990)

Whiteley, P. *The Labour Party in Crisis* (Methuen, London, 1983)

Whyte, W.F. *Street Corner Society* 2nd edn (University of Chicago Press, Chicago, 1955)

Wilensky, H.L. 'Work, careers and social integration' in Burns (1969)

Wilensky, H.L. and Edwards, H. 'The skidder: ideological adjustments of downward mobile workers' in Lopreato and Lewis (1974)

Wiles, P.N.P. 'Criminal statistics and sociological explanations of crime' in Carson and Wiles (1971)

Williams, J.A. Jr 'Interview-respondent interaction' in Franklin and Osborne (1971)

Williams, M. *Society Today* (Macmillan, London, 1986)

Williamson, B. 'Continuities and discontinuities in the sociology of education' in Flude and Ahier (1974)

Willis, P. *Learning to Labour* (Saxon House, Farnborough, 1977). 'Youth unemployment, a new social state' in *New Society* (29 March 1984)

Willmott, P. 'Urban kinship past and present' *Social Studies Review* (November 1988)

Willmott, P. and Young, M. *Family and Class in a London Suburb* (Routledge & Kegan Paul, London, 1960)

Wilson, A. *Family* (Tavistock, London, 1985)

Wilson, B.R. *Religion in a Secular Society* (C.A. Watts, London, 1966). *Religious Sects* (Weidenfeld & Nicolson, London, 1970). *Contemporary Transformations of Religion* (Oxford University Press, London, 1976). *Religion in Sociological Perspective* (Oxford University Press, Oxford, 1982)

Wilson, E.O. *Sociobiology: The New Synthesis* (Harvard University Press, Cambridge, Massachusetts, 1975)

Wilson, R. *Difficult Housing Estates* (Tavistock, London, 1963)

Wilson, W.J. *The Truly Disadvantaged* (University of Chicago Press, Chicago, 1987). 'Studying inner-city dislocations' *American Sociological Review* (1991)

Witty, G. 'The New Right and the National Curriculum: state control or market forces?' in B. Moon (ed.) *New Curriculum – National Curriculum* (Hodder & Stoughton, London, 1990)

Witz, A. 'Women at work' in D. Richardson and V.

Robinson (eds) *Introducing Women's Studies* (Macmillan, London, 1993)

Wolfgang, M.E., Savitz, L. and Johnston, N. (eds) *The Sociology of Crime and Delinquency* (John Wiley & Sons, New York, 1962)

Wood, S. 'The transformation of work?' in Stephen Wood (ed.) *The Transformation of Work?* (Unwin Hyman, London, 1989). *The Degradation of Work, Skill, Deskilling and the Labour Process* (Hutchinson, London, 1982)

Woodiwiss, M. 'Crime's global reach' in Pearce and Woodiwiss (1993)

Woods, P. *The Divided School* (Routledge & Kegan Paul, London, 1979). *Sociology and the School. An Interactionist Viewpoint* (Routledge & Kegan Paul, London, 1983)

Woolgar, S. and Grint, K. 'Computers and the transformation of social analysis' *Science, Technology and Human Values* vol. 16, no 3 (1991)

Worsley, P. *The Trumpet Shall Sound* 2nd edn (MacGibbon & Kee, London, 1968)

Worsley, P. (ed.) *Modern Sociology: Introductory Readings* (Penguin, Harmondsworth, 1970). *Problems of Modern Society* (Penguin, Harmondsworth, 1972). *Introducing Sociology* 2nd edn (Penguin, Harmondsworth, 1977)

Wright, C. 'Early education: multiracial primary school classrooms' in D. Gill, B. Mayor and M. Blair (eds) *Racism and Education: Structures and Strategies* (Sage, London, 1992)

Wright, E.O. *Class, Crisis and the State* (New Left Books, London, 1978). *Classes* (Verso, London, 1985). 'Rethinking, once again, the concept of class structure' in E.O. Wright (ed.) *The Debate on Classes* (Verso, London, 1989)

Wrong, D.H. and Gracey, H.L. (eds) *Readings in Introductory Sociology* (Macmillan, New York, 1967)

Yeo-chi King, A. 'A voluntarist model of organization' *The British Journal of Sociology* (September 1977)

Yinger, J.M. 'Towards a theory of assimilation and dissimilation' *Ethnic and Racial Studies* (1981)

Young, J. 'The role of the police as amplifiers of deviancy, negotiators of reality and translators of fantasy' in Cohen (1971). 'Foreword' in Pearce (1976). 'Risk of crime and fear of crime: a realist critique of survey-based assumptions' in Maguire and Pointing (1988). 'Ten points of realism' in Young and Matthews (1992). 'Incessant chatter: recent paradigms in criminology' in Maguire, Morgan and Reiner (1993)

Young, J. and Matthews, R. (eds) *Rethinking Criminology: the Realist Debate* (Sage, London, 1992)

Young, J. and Matthews, R. 'Questioning left realism' in Matthews and Young (1992)

Young, K. 'Class, race, and opportunity' in R. Jowell *et al.* (eds) (1992)

Young, M. and Willmott, P. *Family and Kinship in East London* (Penguin, Harmondsworth, 1961). *The Symmetrical Family* (Penguin, Harmondsworth, 1961)

Young, M.F.D. 'An approach to the study of curricula as socially organized knowledge' in Young (1971)

Young, M.F.D. (ed.) *Knowledge and Control* (Collier-Macmillan, London, 1971)

Zaretsky, E. *Capitalism, the Family and Personal Life* (Pluto Press, London, 1976)

Zimbalist, A. (ed.) *Case Studies on the Labor Process* (Monthly Review Press, London, 1979)

Zimmerman, D.H. 'The practicalities of rule use' in Douglas (1971)

Zimmerman, D.H. and Wieder, D.L. 'Ethnomethodology and the problem of order' in Douglas (1971)

Zuboff, S. *In the Age of the Smart Machine* (Basic Books, New York, 1988)

Index

opportunity structures, *394*
oppression, *10–11, 451*
  of women in capitalism, *608–9*
organizational assets, *71*
organizational structure
  and charismatic authority, *272*
  and rational-legal authority, *272–3*
  and traditional authority, *272*
organizations, *270–313*
  and accountability, *311*
  definition, *270*
  democracy in, *291–2*
  a dialectical view, *310*
  and the division of labour, *270–1*
  interactionist perspective, *304–9*
  Marxist perspectives, *299–301*
  mechanistic, *279*
  Mintzberg's types, *282*
  modern and postmodern, *284–7*
  as negotiated order, *308–9*
  organic, *279–81*
  postmodern, *286–7*
  power and conflict in, *299–304*
  the problem of, *311–12*
  and professionals, *301–4*
  rules in, *288*
  status and power in, *280–1*
  and values, *312–13*
organized crime, *433*
  US, *417*
orientations
  future-time, *74*
  instrumental, *193–4*
  present-time, *750*
  to work, *78, 81*
  working class, *750*
Ormrod, R., *375*
Ortner, Sherry B., *596–7*
O'Toole, Roger, *453*
ownership
  and class model, *96, 118*
  individual, *36*
  wealth and the capitalist class, *50*
Oxford Mobility Study, *100–4*

Pahl, R.E., *238, 369*
paid employment
  gender and, *614–29*
  women and marital conflict, *374–5, 589*
panel studies, *848–9*
panel surveys, *571*
panopticon, *201*
paradigms, and scientific revolutions, *858–61*
parental choice, in education, *797, 799–801*
parental interest, in education, *751*
parenthood, single, *349–51*
parents
  marital status of, *376*
  professional, *636*
Pareto, Vilfredo, *312, 515, 516, 517, 576, 577*
Park, Robert E., *666–8, 671*

Parker, Howard, *844, 846, 847, 849*
Parker, Roy, *378*
Parker, Stanley, *252–4, 256*
Parkin, Frank, *73, 108, 110, 550–1, 575–6, 577*
Parry, Geraint, *576, 577*
Parry, Jos, *60–1*
Parry, Noel, *60–1*
Parsons, Talcott, *7, 9, 12, 219, 805, 867, 871–4, 876, 877*
  on education, *728–9*
  on 'expressive' role of women, *587, 619, 647*
  on the family, *322–3, 327, 329, 335–7, 345, 357, 381, 587, 589*
  on marriage, *373*
  on power, *505–6, 507*
  on religion, *449–50, 458, 485–6, 491, 497*
  on social mobility, *98*
  on stratification, *24–6*
participant observation, *687, 843–8, 863*
  and ethnography, *844–8*
particularistic values, *728*
parties, *38–9*
partisan alignment, and class, *547*
partisan dealignment, *552–4*
party identification
  and political factors in voting, *573–4*
  volatility and, *561*
party images, *558*
paternalism, *198*
patrials, *664–5*
patriarchal ideology, *441*
patriarchy, *260, 262, 331, 592, 602–3, 777*
  and capitalism, *367*
  concept of, *610*
  private, *610, 612–14*
  public, *610, 612–14*
  structures of, *610–12*
  theorizing, *609–14*
  variations in, *614*
'Patrick', 'James', *845, 847*
patrilocality, and gender inequality, *600*
pattern maintenance, *873*
Patterson, Sheila, *669–70, 671*
pauperism, *91*
pauperization, *36*
Pawson, Ray, *826–7*
Payne, C., *103–4*
Payne, Geoff, *100, 104, 105, 828*
Pearce, Frank, *414, 415, 416–17, 444*
pecuniary model of society, *79, 81, 85*
peer group, *4*
penetrations, of capitalism, *743, 744*
Penn, Roger, *83, 117, 213–14*
Pentecostalism, *681, 684*

peoplehood, and world system, *713–15*
performance contracting, *755*
performance-related pay, *229*
Perry, John, *349–50*
personal service ethic, *186–7*
personality
  stabilization of adult, *322–3*
  structuring of the, *322*
personality market, *183*
Peters, B. Guy, *294, 311*
Peterson, D.W., *475*
Petras, J.W., *897*
petty bourgeoisie, *36, 58, 112, 556*
pharmacy, and gender, *627*
phenomenological psychiatry, *325*
phenomenology, *16, 816–17, 863, 889, 897–9*
  criticisms of, *824*
  deviance and, *412–13*
  and religion, *456–7*
  and scientific methodology, *857*
phenotype, *651*
Phillips, Derek, *843, 863*
Phillipson, Michael, *823, 838*
Phizaklea, Annie, *720*
Phoenix, C., *582*
physical amalgamation, *670*
physical disability, and social interaction, *894–5*
Piachaud, David, *131, 132, 134, 137*
picketing, secondary, *227*
Pilkington, Andrew, *664, 716, 720–1*
pilot studies, *834*
Piore, Michael J., *214–15*
place, sense of, *913*
Platt, J., *77–9*
plight, *682–3*
Plummer, Ken, *411–12, 833, 853, 854*
pluralism, *56, 577*
  classical, *506–10*
  critique, *512–13*
  elite, *513–15*
  and leisure, *255–7*
  methodological, *827, 856*
  and power, *502*
  power and the state, *506–15*
  unions and industrial conflict, *219–21*
Poggi, Gianfranco, *504*
policing, *422–5, 429–31*
  and female crime, *439*
  military, *429*
  minimal, *430*
policy preferences, *548, 560–2*
political attitudes, *79, 81–2*
political parties
  classical pluralist view, *508*
  definition, *508*
political power, *545, 546*
political socialization, *548*
  contradictory influences, *549–50*
political society, *531*

UK (*contd*)
  poverty and the expansion of welfare, *170–2*
  poverty in, *126–8, 130–7*
  poverty statistics, *137–41*
  power in, *510–11*
  South Asians in, *352–3, 676–80*
  strike statistics, *225*
  underclass in, *92, 154–60, 718–19*
  unemployment statistics, *237–9*
  voting patterns since 1974, *551–9*
  West Indians in, *354, 669–70, 680–4*
  workers' attitudes to automation, *197–9*
Ullah, Philip, *250, 251*
underachievement
  ethnic minority, *780–4*
  female, *769–74*
underclass, *85, 91–7*
  attitudes of the, *157*
  causes of the, *158*
  as claimants, *96–7*
  and class conflict, *94*
  composition of, *94, 158*
  culture of the, *92*
  and the dual labour market, *94–5*
  and the erosion of citizenship, *92–3*
  ethnicity and the, *717–19, 720–1*
  heterogeneity of the, *95–6*
  and poverty, *154–60*
  and single parenthood, *350*
  in UK, *91–2, 154–60, 718–19*
  in USA, *91–2*
  use of term, *97*
  and the working class, *96*
understanding *see Verstehen*
unemployment, *237–46*
  by age, *240, 241*
  by class, *239*
  by ethnicity, *240–1*
  by gender, *239–40, 241*
  by region, *241*
  causes of, *241–3*
  cyclical, *242*
  the effects of, *246–52*
  and employment, *158–9*
  frictional, *241*
  gender and the effects of, *250–1*
  health and, *249*
  ILO definition, *239*
  leisure and, *248*
  long-term, *96, 247, 158*
  market liberal theory of, *243–5*
  Marxist theories of, *245–6*
  natural rate of, *243*
  the personal effects of, *247–51*
  psychological reactions to, *248–9*
  regional, *242*
  sectoral, *242*
  social distribution of, *239–41*

statistics in UK, *237–9*
  structural, *241–2*
  and underclass, *155*
unemployment statistics
  official, *238–9*
  seasonally adjusted, *238*
  underlying trends, *238*
unintended consequences, *690, 741–4*
union consciousness, *223*
union democracy, *291–2*
unionism, and poverty, *164*
unions, *80, 85*
  attitudes to, *193–4*
  competition between, *223–4*
  derecognition of, *229*
  exclusion in the 1980s and 1990s, *229–30*
  of ideological mobilization, *199*
  inclusion, *229*
  and Marxism, *223*
  pluralism and industrial conflict, *219–21*
  and the power of labour, *223–4*
  under Thatcherism, *226–9*
  and women in the labour market, *622–3*
universal evaluation, of women's position, *596*
universalistic values, education and, *728–9*
university entrance, *786–7*
unskilled workers, *119, 299–300*
Unwin, Lorna, *798–9*
upper class, *49–56*
Urry, John, *64, 70–1, 512, 530, 860, 861*
USA
  education, *755*
  elite theory in, *517–18, 521*
  interactionism and culture, *897*
  organized crime, *417*
  poverty index, *143*
  schooling in, *735–40*
  secularization of religious institutions in, *488–90*
  the underclass in, *91–2*
  war on poverty, *168–70*
use values, *367, 369, 621, 631*
USSR
  bureaucracy in the former, *289–90*
  sex and gender in, *605*
  see also Russia
utopian ideology, radical, *266*

Vaizey, John, *732*
Vajda, M., *636*
Valentine, Betty Lou, *151*
Valentine, Charles A., *151, 168*
validity, *829*
value consensus, *8, 24–5, 390, 449, 505, 872*
  education and, *728–9*
  and social order, *876–7*

values, *5–6*
  class and educational attainment, *748–9*
  and deviance, *443–4*
  dominant, *550–1*
  and education, *805–6*
  and the family, *381–2*
  formal, *397*
  and gender, *646–7*
  leisure and work, *266–7*
  and organizations in sociology, *312–13*
  particularistic, *336*
  poverty and, *168–73*
  power and the state, *576–7*
  race and ethnicity, *721–2*
  and religion, *497*
  and social stratification, *24–6, 120–2*
  and sociology, *16–17*
  subterranean, *388, 397*
  universalistic, *336*
  or value freedom, *861–3*
van den Berghe, Pierre, *877*
van Dijk, Teun A., *696–7*
variables
  dependent, *810*
  independent, *810*
Vernon, Philip, *747*
Verstehen, *815*
  and social action, *889*
victimization, *850–1*
  ethnic minorities in UK, *700–1*
  studies, *399–401, 426–7*
Victoria, Queen, *601*
violence, *424, 638*
  domestic, *437*
  and patriarchy, *612*
vocationalism, new, *730, 794–9, 804*
Vogel, E.F., *318*
Vogler, Carolyn, *32, 68–9, 82, 84, 88–9, 104–7, 834*
volatility, *572*
voluntarism, and determinism, *906*
de Vos, Klaas, *142*
voting
  class-based, *562–3, 568–9*
  consumer model of, *554–5, 558*
  cross-class, *550–1*
  issues and, *569–70*
  patterns since 1974, *551–9*
  'pocket-book', *563*
voting behaviour, *547–59*
  and class, *556–9*
  see also deferential voters; deviant voters; floating voters; secular voters
voucher system, for education, *796*

Waddington, Dave, *251–2*
Waehrer, H.Y., *633*
wage labour, *181*
  and domestic labour, *367*